A Century in The Sun

FRONT PAGES OF THE 20TH CENTURY

THE BALTIMORE SUN

A Century in The Sun

FRONT PAGES OF THE 20TH CENTURY

Design and Research Editor : Jennifer Halbert

Production Assistant : Walt Driver

Research Assistants : Dee Lyon, Paul McCardell *and* Eugene Balk

Special thanks to : Bill Marimow, John Carroll, Sandy Levy, Francis Przybylek, Carol Dreyfuss *and* Ed Hewitt

Also available:

A Century in The Sun : Photographs of Maryland

A Century in The Sun : Postcards of Maryland's Past

Marylanders of the Century

Published by *The Baltimore Sun*,
501 North Calvert Street,
Baltimore, Maryland 21278.

Library of Congress
Cataloging-in-Publication Data applied for.

ISBN 1-893116-07-7

Contents

Introduction

By Frederick N. Rasmussen

The front page.

I'm not talking about that much beloved and roisterous play by Ben Hecht and Charles MacArthur of the same name, that chronicled the city room exploits of the fictional but now legendary Hildy Johnson and Walter Burns in 1920s Chicago, but rather the first thing a reader scans after picking up the morning newspaper.

It is the front page, after all, with its imposing dignity and inherent drama that reports the major stories that happened the previous day or developed while we safely slept the night away.

With dramatic color photographs set against dark and imposing headlines and sub-headlines, it is something that is not easily put down or ignored. It conveys a certain importance, dignity, a stateliness, if you will.

Also, the front page just happens to be the front door to the rest of the paper through which all readers must pass.

The saying that today's newspaper is wrapping up tomorrow's fish or lining bird cages is probably, alas, all too true.

However, like something frozen in amber, front pages preserve and record the drama of great events as well as the triumphs, tragedy and foibles of humankind.

They are the record, raw history in the making.

Their dramatic impact is still capable of stirring human emotions and delivering a punch despite the passage of time.

Who cannot help but feel a tinge of emotion when reading a sampling of headlines from the 20th century:

GIANT TITANIC GOES DOWN;
1,500 PERISH; 675 ARE SAVED

LINDBERGH IS IN PARIS

WOMAN'S SUFFRAGE AMENDMENT IS
FINALLY RATIFIED; TENNESSEE HOUSE
VOTES 49 TO 47 IN FAVOR OF IT

GERMANY INVADES AUSTRIA,
HITLER SENDS ULTIMATUM

ALLIES INVADING FRANCE,
TROOPS LAND IN NORMANDY

ROOSEVELT DIES AT GEORGIA HOME;
TRUMAN SWORN IN AS PRESIDENT

2,300 CARS CROSS BAY BRIDGE IN SIX HOURS

KENNEDY MURDERED BY DALLAS SNIPER;
JOHNSON SWORN IN AS 36th PRESIDENT

DR. KING KILLED BY SNIPER IN MEMPHIS

GUARDSMEN KILL 4 KENT STATE STUDENTS

COLTS TOP COWBOYS, 16-13, IN SUPER BOWL

AGNEW RESIGNS

FORD PARDONS NIXON

BALTIMORE'S COLTS ARE GONE

SHUTTLE EXPLODES AFTER LIFTOFF, KILLING 7

IMMORTAL CAL

It wasn't until the early 1920s, that the front pages of *The Sun* and *Evening Sun* took on their present look.

Up until that time, advertisements crawled down the left side of the page and across the bottom advertising a variety of products and services ranging from clothing, theater listings, railroad tickets, hats to ads touting highly doubtful medical remedies.

An example of this indignity is the front page for January 23, 1901, that announced Queen Victoria's death. Two columns over from the news story about the queen who reigned over Great Britain and Ireland for 63 years, seven months and two days, is an advertisement that reads: "When you catch cold. Take Jayne's Expectorant."

As the 20th century draws to a close — all 36,525 days of it — The Baltimore Sun presents a collection of front pages from *The Sun* and *The Evening Sun* that chronicles the major worldwide, national and local events that have influenced and continue to shape our lives.

THE SUN

VOLUME CXXVIII—NO. 58. BALTIMORE, WEDNESDAY MORNING, JANUARY 23, 1901. TWELVE CENTS A WEEK

THE SUN

SUMMARY OF THE NEWS

Government Weather Report.

Washington, Jan. 22—Forecast for Wednesday and Thursday: The United States Weather Bureau tonight issued the following forecast:

Maryland, the District of Columbia, Delaware and Virginia, fair Wednesday; northeasterly winds, becoming southerly; fresh to brisk on the coast. Thursday, probably fair.

West Virginia, fair Wednesday; southerly winds. Thursday, occasional rains probable.

North Carolina, fair Wednesday; northerly winds, becoming variable, fresh to brisk on the coast. Thursday, probably fair.

Generally fair weather is indicated for the Atlantic Coast States, with slightly higher temperature in New England and no marked changes in temperature in the Middle and South Atlantic States.

N.Y. And New England Forecast.
[Special Dispatch to the Baltimore Sun.]

New York, Jan. 22—The forecast for the Middle States and New England tomorrow is that far weather will prevail, with some cloudiness and haziness on the coasts; fresh northeasterly and easterly winds and slightly lower, followed in the interior of this section by slowly rising temperature. On Thursday fair to partly cloudy, warmer weather will prevail, with haze or fog on the coasts, and fresh easterly to southeasterly winds, and on Friday partly cloudy, slightly warmer weather and fresh southerly winds, followed by rain or snow near the lakes.

European steamers now sailing will have mostly hazy weather and fresh northeasterly and easterly breezes to the Banks.

The Weather In Europe.
[Copyrighted by New York Herald Company, 1901.]
[Special to the Baltimore Sun.]

London, Jan. 22—Dull, gloomy weather conditions prevailed in this city today, with temperatures between 47 and 51 degrees. A moderate west wind was blowing. The barometer recorded 39.27 inches in the evening.

Paris, Jan. 22.—Dull, but mild weather prevailed in Paris today. Thermometer ranged between 46 and 48 Fahr. The barometer was steady, with a light breeze blowing from west-southwest.

Berlin, Jan. 22.—Clouds overhung this city today and the barometer is falling. It registered 30.38 inches in the morning, when a southeast wind was blowing. the temperature then was 41

Baltimore Local Report

United States Weather Bureau, Observer's Office, Johns Hopkins University. Oliver L. Fassig, Section Director, Jan. 22.

Time	Barometer reduced to sea level	Thermometer	Relative humidity	Direction of wind	Velocity of wind	Force	Rainfall	State of weather
8 A.M.	30.16	41	84	N.	5	Light	T.	Cloudy
8 P.M.	30.32	38	75	N.	6	Light	.00	Clear

Mean barometer......30.23 | Max. temperature......46
Mean temperature......44 | Min. temperature......41

The maximum velocity of the wind was 14 miles an hour, from the north.

Thermometer Record.

The table below gives the minimum temperature of the day and the state of the weather at 8 P.M. yesterday at the stations named:

Portland......18	Clear	Mont'ery.....46	Clear
Boston.........34	Clear	New Or.......54	Cloudy
New York....40	Clear	Galveston....66	Clear
Phila...........40	Clear	Memphis.....40	Clear
Atlan. Cy.....36	Cloudy	Cincinnati...32	Cloudy
Wash...........36	Clear	Pittsburg.....34	Cloudy
Norfolk........46	Cloudy	Cleveland....28	Clear
Hatteras......46	Cloudy	Detroit.........22	Clear
Charlotte.....42	Clear	Chicago........32	Cloudy
Wilming.......50	Cloudy	St.Paul.........10	Cloudy
Savannah....52	Clear	St. Louis......32	Clear
Jack'ville.....50	Clear	Omaha.........22	Clear
Key West....60	Cloudy	Salt L. Cy....34	Cloudy
Atlanta........46	Clear	Denver.........28	Cloudy

Forecast For Baltimore And Vicinity

The United States Weather Bureau forecast for Baltimore, Washington and vicinity is for fair weather.

Foreign Affairs

Queen Victoria died at Osborne House, Isle of Wight, at 6.30 P.M. yesterday. London time. Edward VII is now King of Great Britain.

The reply of the envoys to the Chinese Government will say that evidence of good intentions must be shown before troops are withdrawn.

The Bulgarian Cabinet has resigned on account of internal differences.

The commission sent to South Africa to investigate alleged wrongs in military hospitals reports that it finds no evidence of neglect of patients.

Dr. Meyers, a British physician who was studying yellow fever in Brazil, has died from the disease.

City and Suburban

Mayor Hayes admits that he has an offer for the Western Maryland railroad. The reports concerning the sale of the road bring out the fact that it has increased in value 25 times over since 1873 and is now valued at $16,750,000, independent of its tidewater franchises.

Mayor Hayes called the three city engineers in conference on the sewer question and proposes to put down improved pavements on streets torn up for sewers— Governor Smith has not decided whether he will call an extra session of the Legislature — The School Board adopted a new sched-ule of salaries and completely reorganized the school system.

Receiver J. Frank Aldrich, of the Ameri can National Bank, stated to a meeting that the bank had total assets of $711,767, of which he could classify as "good" only about $394,000, which includes the capital stock of $200,000—The ninth annual conference of the field workers' department of the International Sunday-school Convention was begun at First Reformed Church— A committee from the Woman's Christian Temperance Union called on Mayor Hayes to endeavor to enlist his support in the movement for a curfew law.

Dr. George C. Worthington was surrendered by his bondsmen and was sent to the penitentiary to begin a 10-year term for manslaughter—The Hamburg-American steamer Aclila has been libeled for $80,000 for the damage done the British steamer Crafhorne in the collision between the two vessels near Fort Carroll on January 16—John Young, 73 years old, was convicted of murder in the second degree for shooting and killig his wife, Ellen Young, sentence being suspended under a motion for a new trial.

The Baltimore county Farmers' Institute continued its sessions at Towson.

Financial.

At the Baltimore Stock Exchange trade was dull, with continued softness in some issues. In Wall street stock opened firm, reacted later, but finally advanced under good buying and active support, closing at net gains for most of the railroad shares. An exception was Missouri Pacific, which broke sharply from an early advance. Gold engagements of $1,400,000 were announced for export.

Maryland.

The frequency of robberies in Cumberland is causing alarm in that city.

Mr. William C. Somervell died at Solomon's Island, aged 39 years.

Mr. Charles A. Eyler, of Eyler's Valley, Frederick county, died January 21, aged 82 years.

Numerous fires are reported from various parts of the State.

Peace has been established between the warring factions of the Havre de Grace City council.

says the finances of the association are in better shape now than ever before.

Congress.

The Senate ratified the Spanish treaties by a vote of 38 to 19=Resolutions of regret upon the death of Queen Victoria were adopted=The Legislative, Executive and Judicial Appropriation bill was completed so far as the committee amendments were concerned.

The House also adopted a resolution expressing regret upon the death of Queen Victoria, and then adjourned out of respect to her memory=The claim of the Cramps for about $1,300,000 against the Government was sent to the Court of Claims.

National Affairs.

The House Committee on Coinage has asked Hon. W. J. Bryan for his views, expressed orally or in writing, on the currency question.

The internal revenue collections for December, 1900, were $25,212,543.

The National Board of Trade began its thirty-first annual meeting in Washington yesterday.

District Of Columbia.

An exploding lamp set fire to the house of Wilson Hallstock, Seventeenth street and Massachusetts avenue southeast, destroying it and burning his grandson, Raymond Creek, to death.

Mrs. L. Z. Leiter reported to the police the loss of a dismaond pendant from a necklace.

A verdict for the defendant was returned in the case of Aames Stiff against the Capital Traction Company for $10,475 damages.

Mr. S. H. Kauffmann was elected president of the board of trustees of the Corcoran Gallery of Art.

Mary Allen, a hotel chambermaid, is under ball charged with the theft of a sunburst valued at $400 from Mrs. Grace C. Reel.

Virginia And West Virgina.

A strike is on among the coal handlers at the docks of the Chesapeake and Ohio Road at Newport News.

The Virginia Legislature will meet in extra session at Richmond today.

Three deaths in Stafford county are attributed to the drinking of "schapps."

At Princeton, W. Va., Dr. W. W. Dickey was acquitted of the murder of Miss Maggie Calfree.

Miscellaneous.

United States Senators elected yesterday were: S. B. Elkins in West Virginia; F. M. Simmons, North Carolina: W. J. Sewell, New Jersey; J. W. Bailey, Texas; James H. Berry, Akansas; R. J. Gamble, South Dakota; Knute Nelson and N. E. Clagys, Minnesota; J. R. Burton, Kansas, and Shelby McCullom, Illinois. No choice was made in Delaware.

Creek Indians are reported to be on the warpah near Muskegee, I. T.

Fire in the Grand Opera House at Cincinnati endangered many lives.

All the city officials of Hamilton, Ohio, were arrested for disregarding an injunction not to interfere with a gas company that competed with the municipal plant.

Heavy sales of pig iron at advanced prices were made in Pittsburg.

Where To Find Today's News.

The classification of THE SUN'S news today is as follows:

	Pages.		Pages.
Foreign	1, 2, 8	Local	6, 7, 12
Gen. Telegraph	2, 8, 9	Sporting	6
Washington	9	Maryland	10
N.Y. Topics	6	Virginia	8, 10
Shipping	11	Financial	11

QUEEN WAS HARD WORKER

Saw Every Important Dispatch From Foreign Office.

London, Jan. 22.—The papers devote columns of space to historical and personal reminiscences and the scenes and incidents of the Queen's life.

It is generally recognized that until a few ago there was no harder worker in the Kingdom. Roughly estimated, she signed 50,000 documents yearly. No dispatch of any gravity was ever issued from the Foreign Office until seen by the Queen. Some idea of the work thus entailed is gatherable from the fact that the Foreign Office handles considerably over a thousands dispatches weekly.

After every sitting of the House of Commons the Government leader in the House was in the habit of forwarding to the Queen an abstract of the business done. She personally attended to these abstracts and frequently returned them with marginal notes asking for explanations.

BOYHOOD OF FUTURE RULERS

How The Duke Of York And The Czar Played Together.

Some interesting personal reminiscences of the royal families of England and Russia are given by Mr. A.T. Worm. Mr. Worm is in Baltimore as advance agent for Mr. James O'Neill, who will appear here next week at Ford's Opera House in "The Count of Monte Cristo."

Mr. Worm is a Dane and came from the neighborhood of the Castle of Fredensborg, which is about 25 miles from Copenhagen. His father's farm adjoined the castle property and he was a playmate of the young royalties when they or their parents visited the present King Christian IX, now 88 years old, and his wife, Queen Louise, who died last year. One of the Danish Princesses, as is well known, is the new Queen of England and another became Czarina of Russia, being the mother of the present Czar. Mr. Worm knew the present Czar and the Duke of York about 15 years ago when they were lads and thought more about playing than rulling empires. He gave the following account yesterday of his experiences with these future rulers:

"The royal boys were democratic in their tastes and were allowed when they visited the castle with their parents to play with the boys of the neighborhood. In all we were a party of from 10 to 20 in number and we had big times. Several soldiers were sent along to see that no harm happened to the coming kings and that they did not get entirely too familiar with the rest of us, but as the soldiers always had flirtations on hand with the nursegirls who were around they paid little attention to their mission and we all did pretty much as we pleased.

"Our favorite game was that of robbers and soldiers. When these came together there was hot work. For some reason the Duke of York always took the part of the leaeer of the soldiers. He was a strong, athletic, manly boy, a good fencer and a good fellow. The present Czar always took the part of the robber leader. He was never very strong physically or mentally as I knew him and was not in any way the equal of the English Prince. Whether or not their preferences in regard to the sides they chose to lead in our mimic warfare were any indication of their future policies as crowned heads will have to be decided by historians.

"At that time railroads were just being built in Denmark on an extensive scale. One of our favorite games was that in which one side took the part of soldiers guarding the train and the other that of bold robbers who issued from the wood and tried to carry off the treasure. Each side acted with earnestness and the fur flew.

"Once our party of soldiers was unusually hard pressed and it looked as if Nicholas and his gang of outlaws were going to win the day, but the Duke of York got warmed up to his work, polished off three youngsters who were trying to take him prisoner and saved the day. I was always among the followers of the Duke and found him a brave and resourceful leader.

"The Czar Alexander and the then Prince of Wales came out sometimes to see their sons at play and appeared to be much interested in the outcome of our struggles. An incident which particularly impressed itself on my mind was when the two made a bet one day on the strength of their respective sons. The Duke of York knew, and so did all of us, that he was the stronger, but rather than shame the Russian before his father he allowed himself to be overcome, which you will understand was a noble piece of self-sacrifice for a youngster proud of his strength.

"Somehow or other Czar Alexander heard the truth and he was loud in his praises of the English boy's considerate action. Czar Alexander was a man of wonderful strength and some of his performances were truly remarkable. When he heard how his son could have been overcome by a boy of the same age he remarked that while his son was weak he was not. To prove it he lifted up his sister-in-law, the Princess of Wales, by a strong leather belt which she wore, and while she held herself rigidly upright he held her out at arm's length over the edge of a balcony of the castle on which the royal couples were enjoying their after dinner coffee.

"When all the boys were there together they spoke Danish, which they naturally learned from their mothers"

VICTORIA IS DEAD; EDWARD VII IS KING

Life Of Aged Sovereign Goes Out At Osborne As The English Night Comes On.

A RALLY SHORTLY BEFORE THE END

She Recognizes Members Of Royal Family, Also The Kaiser. Her People Mourn For Her As If From Personal Loss. Messages Of Sympathy From All Over World.

Queen Victoria's long reign is at last ended. She died at Osborne House, Isle of Wight, at 6.30 P.M. yesterday, London time, which is 1.30 P.M. Baltimore time. Edward VII is now King.

Victoria's fatal illness began with a paralytic stroke, suffered on Wednesday of last week. It was her first serious illness in all her long life and she did not submit to prompt precautions. Her condition rapidly grew worse, and in the last few days all hope of saving her life had been abandoned.

About 10 o'clock yesterday morning the royal sufferer had a slight rally, recognizing her eldest son and others about her bedside. She soon sank into a fitful sleep and remained unconscious to the end.

The new King will be proclaimed today and Parliament will also meet. The formal coronation will take place in about six months.

Complete sketches of Victoria and her reign and of the new King and Queen were given in THE SUN last Monday. The leading facts of their lives are summarized elsewhere in this issue.

LAST HOURS OF VICTORIA

Rallied, Recognized Her Family And Then The Sands Ebbed Out.

[Special Cablegram to the Baltimore Sun.]

London, Jan. 22—The last moments of Queen Victoria are described by a special correspondent, who acquired the facts from an official source. He says:

"The monarch passed away peacefully, without pain. It was feared she was dying about 9 o'clock in the morning. Carria were sent to Osborne cottage and rectory to bring all the Princes and Princesses and the Bishop of Winchester to her bedside.

"It seemed very near the end, so near it was feared they could not arrive in time; but when things seemed at the worst the Queen in one of the rallies due to her wonderful constitution opened her eyes, recognized the Prince and Princess of Wales and the Kaiser and asked to see one of her faithful servants, a member of the household. He hastened to the room, but before he got there the Queen had passed into a fitful sleep.

"In her momentary rally the Queen spoke a few words of great moment to the Prince of Wales. All those in the bedroom were in tears.

"The physicians could give no hope. Nobody left the house. The sands were slowly ebbing. Nobody could say at what moment they would be exhausted; but 4 o'clock marked the beginning of the end. Again the family was summoned. This time the relapse had no following rally. The end was calm and peaceful, at 6.30 P.M. the Queen died like the setting sun."

Almost Superhuman Vitality.

The Westminster Gazette says: "Our special correspondent is informed on good authority that her Majesty completely astonished those around her by her almost superhuman vitality. 'Wonderful' is the verdict of one who can speak with a certain measure of authority."

Those who profess to know about it say the real cause of death was a clot of blood on the brain and that the Queen died in absolute repose. It was told in the bulletins that she she slept a large part of this afternoon, almost to the time of her death.

In the morning about 10 o'clock as previously stated, there was an attempt to introduce her relatives, but even then the Queen was not in a condition to say more than a few words. The Kaiser went in just for half a minute, touched her hand and went out deeply affected. Whether the Queen recognized him or not is regarded here as open to doubt. The doctors, whether for diplomacy's sake or not, gave the opinion that she had done so. The Kaiser's grief is especially great at present, because this death is almost sure to be followed by another; for it is understood that bad news has arrived concerning the condition of the Empress Frederick, his mother.

The Prince of Wales telegraphed to Lord Clarendon, the Lord Chamberlain, to go to Osborne. Lord Pembroke has not been sent for. On the death of the sovereign these officials do not naturally go out of office, but of course the new sovereign invariably chooses his own gentlemen in waiting.

Body To Lie In State

The probabilities are that the body will lie in state in St. Paul's, while the burial, which may not take place perhaps for 10 days, will be at Frogmore, where the Queen will be placed next to the late Prince Consort.

The coronation of the new King, who will assume the title of Edward VII, will not take place before six months.

Nobody seems to know anything definitely as to the length of the period of mournng that will be ordered, but it is stated that in all probability it will be three months quite black and three months black and white for the general public, though it will rest with the King as to that.

The Queen was particular about mourning. Even today the royal household is still in mourning for the late Prince Consort. Eleven months after the death of the Duchess of Teck the Duchess of York was wearing a mauve gown when dining with the Queen, who looked at her severely for a few minutes and said: "I do not call that mourning."

NEW KING NOW REIGNS

Kaiser Wilhelm Was The First To Salute Him As Such

Cowes, Isle of Wight, Jan. 23—Queen Victoria is dead and Edward VII reigns, This great change in existing conditions has taken place quietly, almost gently, upon the anniversary of the death of Queen Victoria's father, the Duke of Kent.

The end of her career, seldom equaled by any women in the world's history, came in a simply furnished room in Osborne House, She lay in a great four-posted bed and was a shrunken atom, whose aged face and figure were a cruel mockery of the fair girl who, in 1837, began to reign over England.

Around her were gathered almost every descendent of her line. Well, within view of her dying eyes there hung a portrait of the Prince Consort. It was he who designed the room and every part of the castle.

Bishop Prayed As She Died.

In scarcely audible words the white-haired Bishop of Winchester prayed beside her as he had often prayed with his sovereign, for he was her chaplain at Windsor. With bowed heads the imperious ruler of the German Empire and the man who is now King of England, the woman who has succeeded to the title of Queen, the Princes and Princesses and those of less than royal designation listened to the Bishop's ceaseless prayer.

Six o'clock passed and night was coming on. The Bishop continued his intercession. One of the younger children asked a question in shrill, childish voice and was immediately silenced. The women of the royal family sobbed faintly and the men moved uneasily.

At exactly half-past 6 Sir James Reid, one of the Queen's physicians, held up his hand and the people in the room knew that England had lost its sovereign. The Bishop pronounced the benediction.

The End Was Painless.

The Queen passed away peacefully. She suffered no pain. The wheels of the world were jarred when the announcement came, but in the palace at Osborne everything pursued the usual course.

The body was embalmed and will probably be taken to Windsor Saturday. The coffin has arrived from London.

Sir Arthur John Rigge, private secretary to the Queen, makes an official statement of her last illness. For several weeks she had been failing. On Monday week she summoned Lord Roberts and asked him some very searching questions regarding the war in South Africa. She went for a drive Tuesday, but was visibly affected.

On Wednesday she suffered a paralytic stroke, accompanied by intense phsycial weakness. It was her first illness in all her life, and she would not admit it. Then her condition grew so serious that, against her wishes, the family were summoned. When they arrived her reason had practically succumbed to paralysis and weakness.

The events of the last few days, described in the bulletins, are too fresh to need repetition.

An incident characteristic of the Queen's solicitude for others occurred two days ago when, in one of the intervals of consciousness, she summoned strength to suggest to her dressers, who had been acting as nurses, to take the opportunity of getting some fresh air. Monday afternoon she asked that her little Pomeranian spaniel be brought to her bedside.

Kaiser Comforts New King

The Prince of Wales was greatly affected when the doctors informed him that his mother had breathed her last. Emperor William, himself deeply affected, did his best to minister comfort to his sorrow-stricken uncle, whose new dignity he was the first to acknowledge.

News of the Queen's death was given promptly to the outside world.

When the 4 P.M. bulleting announced that she was sinking all the watchers at the gates of Osborne House made up their minds to remain to the end. The cold was intense, and a few favored ones sought shelter in the royal lodge, just inside, where they waited in silence. The telephone bell rang at 7.04 P.M., but before a royal servant had time to take the message the chief of the Queen's police emerged from the darkness and, with bared head, said:

"Gentlemen, the Queen passed away at 6.30."

From all parts of the world messages of condolence are pouring in. They came from crowned heads, millionaires and paupers, and are variously addressed to the Prince of Wales and the King of England.

Emperor Williams's arrangements are not settled. His yacht will arrive here Wednesday, but it is believed that he will not depart until the funeral. Several other royal personages are likely to be present at this ceremony, wich may be the most imposing one of the kind ever seen.

TO PROCLAIM NEW RULER

Ceremony Will Take Place Today. Parliament Will Meet.

London, Jan. 23.—A telegram to the Lord Mayor, timed at Osborne 6.45 P.M. Tuesday, said:

My beloved mother has just passed away, surrounded by her children and grandchildren.

EDWARD.

The Lord Mayor replied as follows:

Your Royal Highness' telegram announcing the nation's great loss I have received with profound distress and grief, and have communicated this most sad intimation to my fellow-citizens. Her Majesty's name and memory will forever live in the hearts of her people.

To Proclaim New King Today.

The Privy Council will meet in London today and the proclamation of the King will occure thereafter at all places required by custom. The King will come to London to preside over the councl.

Shortly before midnight an official announcement was issued calling Parliament to assemble at 4 o'clock this afternoon to enable members of the House of Lords and House of Commons to take the oath of allegiance to Edward VII.

At the offices of the Lord Chamberlain at St. James' Palace, of the City Remembrancer, at the Guild Hall, and at the College of Heralds, the officials were busy even before the death of the Queen was announced, preparing for the formalities which will attend the proclaiming of the new ruler of the United Kingdom. All the ancient gazettes, court circulars and other papers which describe the ceremonial of 1837 have been taken from the libraries, that the officials may familiarize themselves with the forms of pageantry by which a sovereign is proclaimed.

Some Ancient Customs.

The City Remembrancer said:

"It will depend on the pleasure of the new monarch to decide how far the ancient customs will be modified to suit modern methods: but in a country where precedents are so firmly adhered to as England it may be anticipated that we shall follow closely the acts which prevailed when the late Queen ascended the throne.

"The Privy Council, which is a large body, will meet at St. James' Palace, where the form of proclamation declaring that 'we,' etc., 'with one voice and consent of tongue ang heart declare and proclaim the high mighty Prince Albert Edward,' etc., 'who, by the death of the monarch, has become our only lawful and rightful liege,' etc.

"This proclamation will give the new title the King may assume; but this is not yet announced to us. The proclamation will then be sent to the Heralds College, and the following day the Earl Marshal, the Garter King-at-Arms, the heralds and other officials, the college members and the household troops will proceed from the palace, clad in their splendid surcoats, and proceed to Trafalgar Square. There the King-at-Arms will halt, command silence and read the proclamation.

"Proceeding down the Strand to Temple Bar, a halt will again be made to demand an entrance into the city to proclaim the King. There the Lord Mayor's sheriffs, in their state carriages, will form a great procession. When the Earl Marshal's party comes just within the city boundary the proclamation will be read again and the procession will pass down Ludgate Hill and Cheapside to the Royal Exchange, where similar ceremonies will close the spectacle."

Looking To Edward's Reign.

Everywhere the topic of conversation is what will happen under the new reign. Much interest is shown in the way in which the enormous fortune of the dead Queen will be distributed, the general notion being that Osborne House will go to Princess Beatrice and that she and Princess Christian will come into a considerable portion of Victoria's wealth.

The probability that King Edward will take up a practically permanent residence in Buckingham Palace is much canvassed. This is a question that comes home to Londoners. Queen Victoria's prefeence for Balmoral Castle and Osborne House had been a complaint of long standing in the Metropolis, and it is hoped that the new reign will see a change in this respect. The presence of the court in London would give a brightness and gayety which have long been absent.

There was a remarkable scene outside of the Mansion House early Tuesday afternoon. On the receipt of alarming reports something resembling a groan was uttered by the hundreds of people assembled and then some one started to sing the national anthem. All heads were bared, and in a moment the crowds were singng "God Save the Queen" with a fervor proving how earnestly they wished for her recovery. The passengers in carriages, cabs and omnibuses joined in the singing, the drivers reverently doffing their bats.

THE DEAD QUEEN.

Ascended throne of Great Britain and Ireland June 20, 1837.
Died January 22, 1901, at Osborne House, Isle of Wight.
Length of Reign—63 years, 7 months and 2 days.
Length of Longest Previous Reign in Enlish History (George III's)—59 years 3 months 4 days.
Length of Reign Exceeded in Europan History Only By Louis XIV of France—72 years 3 months 18 days, and By Sancho II of Navarre and Castile, 65 years.
Born May 24, 1819, at Kensington Palace, London.
Age at Death—81 years 8 months 29 days.
Most aged sovereign in English history, 1 month and 4 days older than George III.
Married February 10, 1840, to Prince Abert of Saxe-Coburg, who died December 14, 1861.
Had 4 sons and 5 daughters, 40 grandchildren and 36 great-grandchildren; 2 sons and 4 daughters survive.
Had 20 Premiers at the head of Government during her long reign, from Viscount Melbourne to the Marquis of Salisbury. The Parliament recently elected was the fourteenth of her reign.
Leaves private fortune estimated at $20,000,000.
Formally crowned in Westminster Abbey June 28, 1838. Proclaimed Empress of India January 1, 1877.

"BEST ENGLISH RULER"

Premier Of Canada Bestows This Praise On Victoria.

Ottawa, Quebec, Jan. 22—Sir Wilfrid Laurier, the first French-Canadian Premier of the Dominion upon whom the Queen conferred signal honors, was deeply affected by the news of her death. His tribute to her was uttered under the stress of strong emotion. He said:

"We British subjects of all races and origins in all parts of the world were inspired by sentiments of exalted and chivalrous devotion of the person of her most gracious Majesty. This devotion was not the result of any mauldin sentimentality, but it sprang from the fact that the Queen, the sovereign of the many lands which constitute the British Empire, was one of the noblest women that ever lived, certainly the best English ruler and the best that probably ever ruled in any land.

"We know that the present war in South Africa was particularly painful to her Majesty. She had hoped that the closing years of her long and properous reign would not be saddened by such a spectacle, but it was not in the decrees of Providence that this hope and wish should be gratified. We had hoped that when the end of this long and glorious reign came it would close upon a united empire wherin peace and good will should prevail among all men. Let us still hope that this happy consummation may not be long delayed."

When the news of the Queen's death reached Ottawa the Secretary of State issued a proclamation continuing in office all who held positions under the Crown. This is merely formal. All public buildings in the Dominion placed the Union Jack at half-mast and it will so remain until sundown on the day of the Queen's funeral.

St. Johns, N.F., Jan. 22—The announcement of Queen Victoria's death has called forth expressions of the keenest regret in Newfoundland, the oldest colony of the British Empire. The Colonial Cabinet adopted resolutions of condolence, which were cabled to London. Tomorrow will be observed as a day of mourning throughout the colony.

Halifax, N.S., Jan. 22.—At this fountain head of British naval and military power in the Western Hemisphere, symbols of mourning for the death of Queen Victoria are everywhere displayed. Flags fly at half-mast on ships and from frowning fortresses, and the royal standard for the first time in long years is at half-mast at the citadel. The general officer commanding the garrison will order all the forces to wear mourning.

THE NEW KING.

Born November 9, 1841, at Buckingham Palace, London.
Age at Accession to Throne—59 years 2 months and 13 days.
Older at accession than any monarch of England, except William IV, who was aged 64 years 10 months and 5 days when his brother, George IV died, in 1830.
Married to Princess Alexandra, eldest daughter of King of Denmark, on March 10, 1863, at Windsor Castle.
Had 3 sons and 3 daughters, of whom 1 son and 3 daughters are living. Has had 6 grandchildren.
Thirty-ninth ruler of England since William the Norman conquered the land in 1066.
Fifty-fifth ruler of England since Alfred the Great, who died just one thousand years ago.
First Edward on the throne for 348 years.
Seventh sovereign of the House of Hanover, which began In 1714, with George I.
Created Prince of Wales and Earl of Chester by patent under the Great Seal on December 4, 1841, twenty-five days after his birth.
Has sat in the House of Lords since 1862 as Duke of Cornwall.
Takes lively interest in the sports of England and has won most of the famous turf events, including the Derby in 1896, with his horse Persimmons, and in 1900, with Diamond Jubilee.
Sovereign of the Order of the Garter and the Order of St. Andrew and member of most of the continental orders of knighthood.
Has had an annual income of $500,000 since his marriage and will exchange this by becoming King for Parliamentary grants of more than $2,000,000 annually.
Is a thirty-third degree Mason, Grand Master of the Grand Lodges of England, Ireland, Scotland and Wales, Grand Prior of the Knights Templar in England, and Grand Patron of the Scottish Rite Masons of the United Kingdom.

A SHOCK IN LONDON

'Though Victoria's Death Had Been Expected, It Came Like A Surprise.

NATION FEELS ITS LOSS

A Sense Of Personal Sorrow Overhangs The People.

THE SITUATION IS A NOVELTY

Few Now Living Remember When The Last Change In The Sovereignty Of England Took Place—Looking To The Future With A Feeling Of Uncertainty.

[Special Cablegram to the Baltimore Sun.]

London, Jan. 22.—"Dead" was the word which echoed from thousands of voices in London at 7 o'clock this evening. The Queen had died at 6.30 and the news soon spread.

Between 7 and 8 o'clock the scene on the Strand beggared description. At that time Londoners were driving down in shoals to the theatres. Greater and greater grew their numbers until the Strand was blocked by carriages. Most of the theatres closed their gates, placing heavy blackboarded notices outside to the effect that owing to the death of the Queen the performance was postponed until further notice.

Not only those who came to see the performances stood in blank amazement, but also those who were to have given the performances. In a little time the Strand was crowded with actors having paint still on their faces, with make-up scarcely off, musicians with their instruments, carpenters and scene shifters in shit sleves, all seeming not quite to know what to do or where to go, all contributing to make up the vast crowd which soon overflowed the pavements and filled the street.

A Vast Crowd In The Strand.

Those living in the East End came in vast cowds to see what was going on in the western part of the town. Persons who lived in the West End made tracks eastward to see what was taking place there. These two vast waves of humanity met in the narrow Strand and added themselves to the already large floating masses.

Amid such surroundings cabs and omnibuses were blocked up in one great inextricable mass. Men and boys were yelling, as if bedlam were let loose, "Death of the Queen! Extra, special, evening paper!"

At the same time people rushed into the telegraph offices and fired off telegrams all over the country. There was a general rush to telephones, all telling the same oft-repeated tale, "The Queen is dead." All this remember, happened little more than an hour after the Queen had breathed her last at Osborne.

The shops on the Strand promptly began to shut up, but before they did several clothiers had dressed their windows with black ties and mourning gloves, upon which forthwith there was a run, causing these shops to remain open later than they would have done otherwise.

The notices put up in front of the theatres telling of the postponement of the plays were ready last evening, and the evening before, for that matter. Most of those who came to see the plays decided to get out of their carriages and walk about to see the other kind of show—that of the streets—which, indeed, was more striking than anything they could have seen in a playhouse. They will never forget the human drama upon the Strand.

Great Bells Toll The News.

Meanwhile, as if to impress the solemnity of the occasion more deeply, the sonorous notes of "Big Tom" from the top of St. Paul's began to ring out from the east, and hose of "Big Ben" from the tower house of the Commons were borne over the night air like the booming of heavy-caliber guns. Clang, clang, clang, came from all the intervening churches, each tolling the knell of the dead, tolling slowly and solemnly with a minute between each one.

Down Fleet street the way to the offices of the evening papers was besieged by leather-lunged newspaper venders, who cought each other in anxiety to be first served and rush off to the West End. Bicycle boys weighted down with newspapers picked their way, goodness knows how, with infinite skill through the dense crowds, and the presses of the papers were insufficient to supply the first demand.

The impression left of all this was of a wild sort of fury and tangle, discordant sounds dominated or punctuated by the great boom of the two mammoth bells and the discordant jangle of the rest.

Around St. Paul's the people rallied by thousands. They had come to hear "Big Tom" ring out. And toll it did, impressively resounding with the full force of 16 tons of hollow metal and with just one minute between each cavernous-sounding rumble, which filled out into volumes of sound.

At the Mansion House there was yet another great scene. Crowds were surging and swaying and special police were everywhere trying to restrain the people, who all at the same time wanted to read the bulletn sent by the Prince of Wales 15 minutes after the Queen's death.

On the way to Trafalgar Square busts of the Queen were already being decorated with crepe. In the square from all quarters could be heard the constant ringing of bells. 'Buses were crowded to overflowing by persons who had made up their minds to see the town from their tops. Rain began falling and the crowd began to hurry down off the 'bus tops.

People Felt Personal Sorrow.

It is difficult to define the general sentiment, but it was as if a cord which held something had all at once broken. Few who have not been in London during the last few days can realize in the least the terrible tension which has been among the people. These last three days have seemed almost like months, so general, so acute, has anxiety been. Time has been leaden-footed.

To a foreigner there might have seemed, perhaps, a lack of display of sentiment. It was not so at all, it was merely a depth of feeling which extinguished all thought of expression. Every rally of the Queen had quickened the pulsations of the people. When she slept they had sighed with relief and hoped it might do her good. And when the bulletins showed her weak, they, too, felt weakness. It was as if they were suffering illness the same as the Queen.

WRITING HER EPITAPH

London Papers Give Victoria A Great Place In History.

[Special Cablegram to the Baltimore Sun.]

LONDON, Jan. 23.—The London papers pay devoted tributes to Queen Victoia's worth. Following are extracts:

The Times: "The confidence inspired by her Majesty's personal character enabled her on many occasions to use her intimate knowledge with effect in smoothing the rugged places of international relations or in modifying a policy which, through sheer inadequacy of information, would have led to undesirable friction. We have also to thank the Queen for influence of the most potent kind consistently and vigorously used to enforce high ideals of social and personal virtue, of religious faith and of Christian life."

Daily News: "We may be thankful her Majesty was spared the infliction of senile decay; that her subjects will always be able to think of her as one summoned from incessant labor to eternal peace."

Daily Graphic: "The glorious Victorian epoch has come to an end, the story of which will live forever as one of the most fragrant and most splendid pages of human history. Pride, honor, country throbbed through all her strain; and shall we praise? God's praise was hers before, and on our futile laurels she looks down."

Chronicle: "The end has come to a noble life, a brilliant reign, an epoch of our national history. Victoria's monument is already built, more costly than marble, it has sprung up in a night, more enduring than granite or bronze, sacred to her memory forever. High and low, rich and poor, one with another, the subjects of Victoria have built her monument in their hearts."

Express: "We will leave her greatness to the unerring judgment of time, and treasure her goodness as a precious recollection of our own. The future will analyze her policy as a ruler and compare her critically with Elizabeth. By her subjects of today her memory will be cherished more nearly as that of a gentle lady who loved them. And so, goodby, dear Queen."

Daily Mail: "She passes from life beloved and honored. We who must one day follow her can but pace up and down the shore yet a while, and, looking toward the unknown ocean, think of the traveler who sailed yesterday. So in faith and hope, and in the firm belief that death cannot conquer all, we bid farewell to the mighty dead, and pray that the wisdom which under Providence guided her, may descend upon her son, our sovereign lord, the King."

St. James Gazette: "It is often true of individuals that they do not recognize the depth of their affection for some loved one until they are brought face to face with the probable loss. Similarly, although there never has been any question that the Queen held a place in the hearts of her subjects such as no sovereign ever held before, we probably never quite realized until the last day or two how nearly she touched the personal affections of each of us."

The same paper goes on echoing faithfully the general tone: "We rejoice to see," it says, "that the great qualities of our sovereign are acknowledged with appreciation by the press of the whole world. We do not refer to our own colonies, for happily it now goes without saying our sentiments are theirs also.

"It is especially gratifying to see how genuine and deep is the admiration for the Queen expressed throughout the length and breadth of the United States. When it is remembered that her Majesty is only one generation removed from the King whose short-sighted folly goaded America into the assetion and vindication of her independence it is touchingly interesting to note a leader of thought in the United States pay the highest tribute to Queen Victoria possible from any American citizen, by comparing her character with that of George Washington."

On the subject of the German Emperor, whose conduct is keenly appreciated here, the St. James Gazette says:

"We shall not readily forget the promptitude with which the head of a powerful foreign nation brushed aside the splendid ceremonial commenerating the greatness of his own royal dynasty in order to put himself among us and give proof of his respect for and devotion to our dying Queen. We do not, of course, mean that any political significance attaches to the prescence of the Kaiser, nor even that we look for any change in public opinion in Germany, but we on our side should certainly find it easier than before to avoid feelings of irritation or offense at the actions of that great kindred nation ruled by the warm-hearted grandson of our Queen. If these two results, the mollifying of domestic differences and the promotion of a kindred feeling for Germany, should in any degree be the outcome of these days through which we are passing, who can doubt that the Queen herself would exceedingly rejoice that such should be her last legacy to her people?"

The Times publishes a two-column article under the caption "Loyal Appreciation of the New King," in which it says:

"If anything can in some measure console the nation for the irreparable loss it has sustained, it is the well-founded conviction that the Queen has left behind her a worthy successor, who may be trusted to walk in her footsteps. In the whole range of English social and political life no position is more difficult to fill satisfactorily and without reproach than that of the heir apparent; and it may be justly said that the way this position has been filled has contributed to the remarkable increase in the devotion to the Throne and the dynasty which has been one of the most striking characteristics of Victoria's reign. As Albert Edward has been a scrupulously constitutional Prince, we may confidently predict that he will be a scrupulously constitutional King."

LABOUCHERE EXALTS HER

Noted Radical Says Victoria Was A Factor For Peace.

LONDON, Jan. 23—Henry Labouchere, in Truth, will have a remarkable tribute to Queen Victoria, a tribute all the more remarkable because of his democratic ideas and frank criticisms of royalty.

"Among all her millions of subjects," he says, "there are but few who will not mourn for her loss as for one of their own household. Nor will the mourners be found among her own subjects alone. It is not too much to say that never in the history of the world has a single death caused such universal grief.

"Alike in happiness and sorrow she lived a life beyond reproach, without thought of self and unreservedly devoted to the duties of the hour. Although occupying perhaps the proudest position everfilled by a woman, and never wanting in a certain queenly dignity, her tastes, habits, demeanor and even her dress were marked by the rarest simplicity.

"She has been indeed the mother of her people and as a mother she will be mourned. In all the affairs of state she manifested the same wisdom that inspired her private life, nor did her own country alone enjoy the fruits of her experience and segacity.

"Through her kindred and descendants abroad her influence for many years has been felt in Continental politics, always on the side of peace; and in at least one crisis she is known to have rendered service to the whole of Europe.

"Her sudden and lamentable breakdown was due entirely to worry and overwork. She had been greatly distressed by events in South Africa and by domestic griefs."

THE SUN

VOLUME CXXIX—NO. 104. BALTIMORE, SATURDAY MORNING, SEPTEMBER 14, 1901. TWELVE CENTS A WEEK

THE SUN

SUMMARY OF NEWS

Government Weather Report.

WASHINGTON, Sept. 13.—The United States Weather Bureau tonight issued the following forecast for Saturday and Sunday:

Maryland, Delaware, District of Columbia, Virginia, New England, Eastern New York, New Jersey and Eastern Pennsylvania, fair Saturday; light to fresh winds, mostly westerly. Sunday fair.

N. Y. And New England Forecast.

[Special Dispatch to the Baltimore Sun.]

NEW YORK, Sept. 13.—The forecast for the Middle States and New England tomorrow is that fair weather will prevail, with nearly stationary temperature and slight to fresh northwesterly and southwesterly winds. On Sunday fair weather, slowly rising temperature and fresh southeasterly winds will prevail, and on Monday fair to partly cloudy weather, with moderate temperature, followed by rain in the northern district.

Baltimore Local Report.

United States Weather Bureau, Observer's Office, Johns Hopkins University, R. C. Easton, Observer, September 13.

Time	Barometer reduced to sea level	Thermometer	Relative humidity	Direction of wind	Velocity of wind	Force	Rainfall	State of weather
8 A.M.	29.80	74	63	NW	12	Fresh	.00	Cloudy
8 P.M.	29.85	70	77	W	7	Light	.00	Clear

Mean barometer......29.77	Max. temperature......[illegible]
Mean temperature......74	Min. temperature......[illegible]

The maximum velocity of the wind was 19 miles an hour, from the west.

Thermometrical Record.

The table below gives the maximum temperature of the day and the state of the weather at 8 P. M yesterday at the stations named:

Boston	80	Cloudy	Eastport	66	Cloudy
New York	80	Cloudy	Galveston	86	Cloudy
Philadelphia	80	Cloudy	Memphis	78	Cloudy
Atlantic Cy.	80	Cloudy	Cincinnati	72	Cloudy
Cape May	78	Cloudy	Pittsburg	70	Clear
Washington	78	Clear	Buffalo	70	Clear
Norfolk	86	Clear	Cleveland	68	Clear
Hatteras	84	Clear	Detroit	72	Clear
Charlotte	86	Cloudy	Chicago	72	Clear
Wilmington	92	Clear	Duluth	74	Cloudy
Savannah	94	Clear	St. Paul	74	Cloudy
Jacksonville	92	Clear	St. Louis	80	Cloudy
Key West	88	Clear	Omaha	86	Cloudy
Atlanta	82	Rain'g	Huron	70	Cloudy
Montgomery	90	Cloudy	Helena	58	Cloudy
New Orleans	88	Cloudy	Salt Lake Cy.	72	Clear
Palestine	80	Cloudy	Denver	80	Cloudy

Forecast For Baltimore And Vicinity

The United States Weather Bureau forecast for Baltimore, Washington and vicinity is for fair weather.

City And Suburban.

Members of the City Council tell in interviews published on the last page the measures they will introduce at the approaching session.

The Police Board decided that Captain Ward was illegally in office, and declared the captaincy which he has held to be vacant.

All immigrants entering the port of Baltimore will be put through a severe course of questioning to find out whether they are anarchists.

The Hebrew new year began at sunset with solemn services in the synagogues, during which prayers for the President were offered.

Mr. Harry E. Garner, of Baltimore, has received an interesting letter from his father, Prof. R. L. Garner, "the man who makes monkeys talk," who is in the interior of Africa. The letter appears on the last page.

Mr. Clifford M. Lewis, proprietor of the Logan, an apartment house in Washington, and Miss Mayme Burke, also of Washington, came to Baltimore and were married at the Cardinal's residence.

Miss Josephine Hankey, for 35 years a public school teacher, died at her home, 808 East Preston street.

The grand jury for the September term of the United States Court was drawn and summoned for next Wednesday—Receivers were appointed by consent for the clothing manufacturing firm of Cooper & Blum, composed of Manil Cooper and Harry G. Blum—The wills of Michael Bersick and William H. Mullikin were admitted to probate—Arthur F. Bell filed a caveat to the will of his father, William H. Bell—Victor C. Washington, colored, pleaded guilty of embezzling $138 in postal funds and was sentenced to one year in the penitentiary.

Miss Ida M. R. Riley was appointed vice-principal of the Reisterstown High School to succeed the late Miss Elizabeth H. Davis.

Financial.

At the Baltimore Stock Exchange all speculative issues were depressed and declined under pressure to sell. In Wall street stocks had a sharp break early, but closed steady, though net declines were general through the list. Money was firm. It was thought that gold imports would be made next week

Maryland.

One house was destroyed by fire in Crisfield and four others were badly damaged.

Michael J. McPartland, a Democratic nominee for the Legislature in Allegany county, was killed in a coal mine, where he was at work.

National Affairs.

Rear-Admiral Francis M. Ramsay has been appointed to fill the vacancy on the Schley Court of Inquiry created by the retirement of Admiral Henry L. Howison.

Secretary Gage announces that the Treasury Department will continue the purchase of bonds.

Where To Find Today's News.

The classification of The Sun's news today is as follows:

	Pages		Pages
Foreign	3	Local	7, 12
Gen. Telegraph	1, 2, 6, 9	Sporting	8
Washington	2, 9	Maryland	7
N. Y. Topics	8	Virginia	8
Shipping	11	Financial	11

WASHINGTON HEARS IT

Secretary Hay Will Notify The New President Early This Morning.

WASHINGTON, Sept. 14.—The official announcement of President McKinley's death was received at the White House at 2.35 A. M. as follows:

BUFFALO, N. Y., Sept. 14.

Col. B. S. Montgomery, Executive Mansion, Washington:

The President died at a quarter past 2 o'clock this morning.

GEORGE B. CORTELYOU.

Immediately upon receipt of the official dispatch, the following was sent to Secretary Cortelyou:

Members of the executive staff in Washington are deeply affected and beg to tender their profound sympathy to Mrs. McKinley.

O. F. PRUDEN, Assistant Secretary.

Secretary Hay said that the official notification to Mr. Roosevelt of the death of President McKinley would not be sent until morning, when Mr. Roosevelt can be reached by telegraph. The Secretary, as the premier of the Cabinet, will wire this notification.

Secretary Gage, upon being informed of the death of President McKinley said:

"It seems like mockery to attempt to eulogize him. No words can carry from one mind to another a proper understanding of that unique personality. He himself must be his best interpreter. His acts, his utterances, with their indescribable charm, have made him known to the American people. Through these they understand and appreciate him. In their hearts can be found the love and the gratitude which his unselfish, untiring and affectionate devotion to his country justly inspire.

"If I speak of him it must be simply and without exaggeration. In an active life extending now over a long period I have met many men of superior powers and manifold graces, but after nearly five years of close association with this man and a constant study of his mental and moral characteristics I have come to regard in him the combined qualities which make a man truly great as the superior of all the men I have ever known. In his death our people are indeed stricken with the most grievous loss."

FRIDAY AN UNLUCKY DAY.

[Special Dispatch to the Baltimore Sun.]

BUFFALO, Sept. 13.—Superstitious persons are commenting upon the fatality of signs. President McKinley was shot Friday, September 6; his relapse occurred Friday, September 13. It has also been noted that a flock of blackbirds appeared at the Milburn house this morning and have been [illegible] about the lawn ever since.

PRESIDENT EXPIRES AFTER A HARD FIGHT FOR LIFE

Death Of The Nation's Chief Takes Place At 2.15 This Morning At Buffalo.

FOR HOURS ON VERGE OF DISSOLUTION

He Takes Farewell Of His Wife, And His Last Words, As Reported By Dr. Mann, Are "Good-By, All, Good-By. It Is God's Way. His Will Be Done, Not Ours."

A LONG STRUGGLE AGAINST DEATH, WITH HOPE ABANDONED

President William McKinley died at 2.15 o'clock this morning.

From 5 P. M. on his death had been momentarily expected. His sinking spell early Friday morning had been attended by the gravest results and his heart developed weakness which the physicians said would be fatal.

Late in the afternoon they announced that the President was dying. Oxygen, digitalis and a saline solution were administered, but the President continued to sink. His extremities became cold, and the pulse almost ceased, but still the spark of life was there.

Relatives, close friends and Cabinet Ministers were called and bade the last farewell. Mrs. McKinley entered the room, kneeled at the bedside and sobbed.

Dr. Mann states that the President's last words were: "Good-by, all; good-by. It is God's way. His will be done, not ours." He also chanted part of the hymn: "Nearer, My God, to Thee."

Vice-President Roosevelt, who was hunting in the Adirondacks when summoned, is speeding to Buffalo, and is expected to arrive early this morning.

END OF LONG STRUGGLE

Tearful Farewells And Then A Wait Until Death Came To The President.

BUFFALO, N. Y., Sept. 14.—The President died at 2.15 A. M.

From authoritative officials the following details of the final scenes in and about the death chamber were secured:

The President had continued in an unconscious state since 8.30 P. M. Dr. Rixey remained with him at all times until death came. The other doctors were in the room at times, and then repaired to the front room, where their consultation had been held.

"About 2 o'clock Dr. Rixey noted the unmistakable signs of dissolution and the immediate members of the family were summoned to the bedside. Mrs. McKinley was asleep and it was deemed desirable not to awaken her for the last moments of anguish.

RELATIVES AT BEDSIDE.

"Silently and sadly the members of the family entered the room. They stood about the foot and sides of the bed where the President's life was ebbing away. Those in the circle were: Abner McKinley, the President's brother; Mrs. Abner McKinley, Miss Helen, the President's sister; Mrs. Sarah Duncan, another sister; Miss Mary Barber, a niece; Miss Sarah Duncan, Lieut. J. F. McKinley, a nephew; William M. Duncan, a nephew; Charles G. Dawes, Comptroller of the Currency; F. M. Osborne, a cousin; Col. Webb C. Hayes, John Barber, a nephew; Secretary George B. Cortelyou, Col. W. C. Brown, business partner of Abner McKinley; Dr. Rixey, the family physician, and six nurses and attendants.

In an adjoining room sat Drs. McBurney, Wasdin, Parke, Stockton and Mynter.

It was now 2.05 o'clock and the minutes were slipping away. Only the sobs of those in the circle about the President's bedside broke the silence. Five minutes passed, then six, seven, eight.

"THE PRESIDENT IS DEAD!"

Now Dr. Rixey bent forward and then one of his hands was raised as if in warning. The fluttering heart was just going to rest. A moment more and Dr. Rixey straightened up. With choking voice he said:

"The President is dead!"

Secretary Cortelyou was the first to turn from the stricken circle. He stepped from the chamber to the outer hall and then down the stairway to the large room where the members of the Cabinet, Senators and distinguished officials were assembled. As his tense, white face appeared at the doorway a hush fell upon the assemblage.

"Gentlemen, the President has passed away," he said.

STATESMEN WEEP.

For a moment not a word came in reply. Even though the end had been expected the actual announcement that William McKinley was dead fairly stunned these men who had been his closest confidants and advisers. Then a groan of anguish went up from the assembled officials. They cried outright like children. All the pent-up emotions of the last few days were let loose. They turned from the room and emerged from the house with streaming eyes for the fate of the dead President.

HIS LAST WORDS.

He died unattended by a minister of the Gospel, but his last words were an humble submission to the will of God, in whom he believed. The Chief Magistrate was reconciled to the cruel fate to which an assassin's bullet had condemned him and faced death in the same spirit of calmness and poise which had marked his long career. His last conscious words, reduced to writing by Dr. Mann, who stood at his bedside when they were uttered, were as follows:

"Good-by all! Good-by! It is God's way. His will be done; not ours."

Friends came to the door of the sick room, took a longing glance and turned tearfully away. The President was unconscious during this time.

Members of the Cabinet, one by one, saw the President momentarily, and there was a hushed exchange. Then the President softly chanted part of the hymn "Nearer, My God, to Thee." Just before he lapsed into unconsciousness he begged the doctors to let him die.

DID HE DIE AT 2 O'CLOCK?

It is said that President McKinley really died at 2 o'clock, and that after he had been pronounced dead efforts were made to revive the spark of life. When this was found impossible Mr. Cortelyou made the reluctant announcement.

Senator Burrows, of Michigan, and Representative Alexander left the house soon after the announcement of the President's death.

"It took place at 2 o'clock," said Mr. Alexander. "I went up stairs and met Col. Webb Hayes. 'How is the President?' I asked. 'He passed away at 2 o'clock,' replied Colonel Hayes. 'He died peacefully and without pain, like a man sinking to sleep. For three hours or more he had been practically dead and his extremities had been wholly dead. Only a faint flicker at intervals told that he still lived. Occasionally he uttered a faint exclamation 'Oh!' and before he quite lost consciousness Dr. Stockton, bending over him, heard him repeating the words of the hymn 'Nearer, My God, to Thee.'

"Secretaries Root, Wilson, Long and Hitchcock, Attorney-General Knox, Senators Hanna, Fairbanks and Burrows and Representatives Ryan and myself filed through the President's room about 11 o'clock and saw him for the last time alive. So quietly did he pass away that the members of the Cabinet who were gathered in the dining room did not know when he died."

TO MOVE THE BODY.

No definite arrangements for the funeral have been made, but the President's body will be removed to Washington Sunday at the latest and will lie in state there.

Senator Burrows, who left the house with his handkerchief pressed to his eyes, could hardly speak so great was his emotion.

"The President's death seemed painless," said he. "He seemed to fall into calm and peaceful repose."

HIS WIFE AT BEDSIDE

"I Cannot Let Him Go," She Said, "The Country Cannot Spare Him."

[Special Dispatch to the Baltimore Sun.]

BUFFALO, Sept. 13.—Dr. McBurney arrived at the Milburn house a little before 8 P. M., having been driven from the railroad station in 12 minutes.

Shortly after his arrival oxygen was administered to the President, and under its influence the sufferer aroused. He was fully conscious and whispered to Dr. Rixey that he knew the end was at hand. The President asked to see his wife, and Mrs. McKinley was sent for.

She entered his room, and it was apparent to those present that of the two principal figures in this intense drama President McKinley the more fully realized the significance of the awful moment. There was no show of fear in the attitude of the nation's Executive. Mrs. McKinley did not seem to realize fully that she was probably seeing her husband for the last time alive, and the President made it plain that his great solicitude was for the wife over whom he had watched with such care and love.

Mrs. McKinley sank to her knees at the side of the bed, her husband's hands were clasped in hers. Her head was bowed and buried in the bed covering. Sobs shook her for a moment. Then she looked up at Dr. Rixey, and with almost a smile on her face said:

"I know that you will save him. I cannot let him go; the country cannot spare him."

The President was soon lapsing into insensibility. The physicians assisted Mrs. McKinley to her feet and led her from the room. On the outside Mr. Milburn told her that the President was dying and that he could live until morning only in the event of a direct interposition of Providence. She then came to a full realization of the loss that was upon her and showed symptoms of a collapse.

Herbert P. Bissell rushed to the assistance of the sorrowing wife, who was being literally supported by Mr. Milburn. Word was sent to Dr. Wasdin, who came from the President's chamber and administered a restorative.

Little by little Mrs. McKinley came back to her normal condition, and at 8.30 o'clock was clear-minded and in full possession of her strength. Several ladies were with her, and in their sympathy she found surcease. To one she whispered:

"I will be strong for his sake."

An attempt was made to persuade Mrs. McKinley to retire and get rest. She refused. She said her duty was there and she would remain within call of those who were with her husband. She hoped that the President would arouse and she might then have the comfort of a last word with him.

Mrs. McKinley was bearing up bravely and in a manner which surprised her friends. It is feared that she cannot hold her strength under the strain. She will be closely watched, and at the first show of a return of the malady that has made her an invalid for years, she will be treated by Dr. [illegible], who fully understands her case.

STORY OF LAST HOURS

A Long And Hard Fight Which Ended In The Final Fate Of All Men.

[Special Dispatch to the Baltimore Sun.]

BUFFALO, N. Y., Sept. 14.—Hope and fear alternated all of Friday among the watchers in and around the Milburn house.

Every fragment of information was eagerly sought in the hope that it might be construed to mean that reasonable hope of the President's recovery might be entertained. Members of the President's family, the physicians, officials of the Government and all who passed in and out of the house during the day were questioned as to the President's condition, but little of an encouraging nature could be learned.

The truth was too evident to be passed over. The President's life was hanging in the balance. The watchers felt that at any moment might come the announcement of a change which would foreshadow the end.

When the slight improvement noted in the early bulletins seemed to be maintained in the afternoon and it was learned that the President was taking small quantities of nourishment hope rose that he would pass the crisis in safety. Everybody knew, and no attempt was made to conceal it, that the coming night would in all human probability decide whether the President was to live or die. It was known that he was being kept alive by heart stimulants and that the physicians had obtained a supply of oxygen to be administered if the worst came.

A FEW FEEBLE WORDS.

During most of the day the President was conscious when he was not sleeping. Early in the morning when he awoke he looked out of the window and saw that the sky was overcast with heavy clouds.

"It is not so bright as it was," said he.

His eyes then caught the waving branches of the trees glistening with rain, and their bright green evidently made an agreeable impression upon him.

"It is pleasant to see them," said he feebly.

As fast as steam could bring them the President's Cabinet, members of his family and the physicians, who had left convinced that the President would recover, were whirled back to this city. They went at once to the house in which he was, and the information which they obtained there was of a nature to heighten rather than to relieve their fears.

MRS. McKINLEY NOT AWAKENED.

Secretary Cortelyou and Mr. Milburn had announced at half-past 4 o'clock that the efforts of the doctors had produced a rally. Mrs. McKinley was then sleeping, and great care was taken to prevent her from being awakened.

Dr. Wasdin returned to the house at 8.15 o'clock and hurried in. Abner McKinley, the President's brother, came out a few minutes later to tell his coachman, who had been waiting for him more than an hour, that he did not intend to go to his hotel for breakfast. The guard was changed and the sentinels were posted under command of Lieut. Charles N. Murphy.

After the wounds had been dressed and the morning consultation had been held the President's physicians issued a 9 o'clock bulletin, which read as follows:

"The President's condition has somewhat improved during the last few hours. There is a better response to stimulation. He is conscious and free from pain. Pulse, 128; temperature, 99.8°."

The apparent improvement in the President's condition was due to the action of digitalis, strychnine and other medicines that had been given to sustain the heart action.

SENATOR HANNA RETURNS.

Senator Hanna, who went to Cleveland day before yesterday jubilant in the belief that the President was going to get well, reached the Milburn house at 2 minutes before 10 o'clock. He was one of the first to be notified of the alarming symptoms which had made their appearance. It was noticed that he limped painfully, showing that his rheumatism was troubling him more than usual.

Mr. Hanna, in his anxiety to reach the President's bedside, had come from Cleveland, a distance of 183 miles, at the rate of 63 miles an hour, by a special train. With him came Mrs. Hanna, Judge William R. Day, of Canton, Ohio; Col. Myron P. Herrick, of Cleveland; Senator Fairbanks, of Indiana; Mrs. Duncan and Miss McKinley sisters of the President; Miss Duncan and Mrs. Herrick. They joined Secretaries Wilson and Hitchcock, Mr. and Mrs. Herman Baer, Abner McKinley, Mrs. Lafayette McWilliams, John I. Milburn, Wilson S. Bissell, John N. Scatcherd and Representative Alexander, who were in the house. The new arrivals were informed of the critical condition of the President.

Early in the morning, on the advice of the physicians, Dr. [illegible]

EXTRA

5 O'CLOCK A. M.

of Washington, had been summoned. Dr. Janeway was at St. Hubert's Inn, in the Adirondacks. He started for Buffalo as soon as he had been notified by Mr. Cortelyou that his presence here was desired. Dr. Johnston was at Jamaica Island, off Portsmouth, N. H. He is regarded as an authority on troubles of the heart.

Senator Hanna left the house at 12.25 o'clock looking very grave.

"From all that I can gather," said he "I believe there is a fighting chance."

"Are you hopeful?" was asked.

"I am always hopeful," replied Senator Hanna. "That is my nature. When I drove up this morning I saw a rainbow in the sky and I took it for a good omen. I wish I could give you better news."

Gen. Harrison Gray Otis came in soon afterward. Senator Depew also called at the house.

WATCHING THE PULSE.

The President was still asleep at 1.30 o'clock. Injections of saline solution and digitalis in light doses had been used. One of the physicians sat constantly at the bedside with his fingers on the President's pulse, ready at any alarming change in the action of the heart to apply the remedies which were in readiness to be used as a last resort. Tanks of oxygen were at hand to be drawn upon and other appliances that medical skill and science could provide were within reach. The beating of the pulse was sufficiently strong to enable the physicians to permit the President to have his sleep out.

A bulletin dated at 2.30 o'clock was issued at 3 o'clock. It read as follows: "The President has more than held his own since morning and his condition justifies the expectation of further improvement. Pulse, 128; temperature, 99.4°.

Secretary Cortelyou at 4.45 o'clock issued the following bulletin, dated at 4 o'clock:

The President's physicians report he is only slightly improved since the last bulletin. The pulse and temperature are the same at this hour

Secretary Root arrived at 5.10 o'clock, and hastened into the house.

A SERIES OF BULLETINS.

The bulletins that follow tell the subsequent tale:

9.20 P. M.—Governor Yates, of Illinois, just came from Milburn house. He says that though the President is still breathing, it is almost a stretch of the truth to say that life remains in him.

9.27 P. M.—The pulse has left the President's extremities and he may live until midnight. Consciousness seems to have finally left. In his most recent lucid moment the President comforted Mrs. McKinley.

9.30 P. M.—The President is conscious only when he is given oxygen. Mrs. McKinley is not with him. She saw him for 10 minutes half an hour ago, and under the circumstances bore up well. Nobody but Secretary Cortelyou and the physicians is with him.

9.35 P. M.—Dr. Mynter, who has just left the house, says the President is slowly dying. The approach of death is already evident, as the body is getting cold. Dr. Mynter says, however, the President may last until 2 o'clock in the morning. There is hardly any pulse to be felt.

9.38 P. M.—Secretary Cortelyou sent word by Harry Hamlin from the President's room: "The President is a dying man, and you might as well know it." Attorney-General Knox has arrived.

10 P. M.—The doctors have suspended all medical treatment.

10.45 P. M.—President McKinley is barely breathing. Physicians expect each breath to be his last. Mrs. McKinley is being cared for in another room. She is in a pitiable state, approaching prostration. These are the President's last words: "Good-by, all; good-by. It is God's way. Let His will, not ours, be done." This is from Dr. Mann, who says the President still breathes:

11 P. M.—Senator Hanna, Abner McKinley and his wife, Mrs. Baer and Miss McKinley, Lieut. James McKinley, Mrs. Barber and the Misses Barber have just left the President's room. Senator Hanna and Abner McKinley will return.

MARVELOUS VITALITY.

11.05 P. M.—A messenger from the house announces that the President's vitality is marvelous. Conditions remain unchanged and death may come in one minute or not for an hour or more.

11.12 P. M.—Dr. Mann has just said: "The President is pulseless and is dying. He may live an hour."

12 Midnight.—Secretary of the Navy John D. Long has just arrived in time to see the President alive though unconscious.

12.30 A. M.—Coroner Wilson reached the house a few minutes ago. This led to startling reports of death, which are not confirmed.

12.30 A. M.—Frank Baird announced from Secretary Cortelyou that the President is still alive and his condition practically as it had been for an hour.

1 A. M.—President still alive.

1.30 A. M.—No change reported.

2 A. M.—It is again announced that the President is alive.

2.15 A. M.—The President is dead.

AN AUTOPSY LIKELY

Physicians Anxious To Learn Cause Of President's Heart Weakness.

BUFFALO, Sept. 14.—It is almost certain that an autopsy on the President's body will be held to determine the exact cause of death.

This is the wish of all the surgeons and physicians who were in attendance. The peculiar action of the President's heart was more or less of a puzzle to them all, and Dr. McBurney expressed the opinion that in the interest of science, as well as in the interest of the Government and the world, it was desirable that the exact cause of death be discovered.

The President's heart gave trouble from the beginning, but its erratic action was at first thought to be due to the shock of the wound. When the wound had begun to progress favorably the heart gave more trouble and anxiety than ever.

The President's death was due to heart exhaustion, but some of the physicians do not believe there was organic heart trouble. The theory of at least one of the physicians is that the original shock of the first bullet over the heart had much to do with the trouble which caused death.

"DREADFUL NEWS"

Ex-President Cleveland On The Strange Spectacle In Free America.

PRINCETON, N. J., Sept. 14.—When interviewed by a correspondent who conveyed to him the first news of President McKinley's death ex-President Cleveland made the following statement:

"This is dreadful news, and the more cruel because it strikes down the confident and comforting expectation which all our people were encouraged to entertain that their President would be saved from death. In the gloom surrounding this third Presidential murder within the memory of men not yet old we can scarcely keep out of mind a feeling of stunning amazement that in free America, blessed with a government [illegible]

THE SUN

VOLUME CXXIX—NO. 123. BALTIMORE, SUNDAY MORNING, OCTOBER 6, 1901. PRICE 2 CENTS

Holliday Street Theatre.

THE WHITE SLAVE

CHASE'S THEATRE

PERCY HASWELL STOCK COMPANY

CATHERINE

BECAUSE SHE LOVED HIM SO

AUDITORIUM THIS WEEK

AMERICA'S GREATEST VAUDEVILLE COMPANY.

HYDE'S COMEDIANS

FORD'S "Here's to You, Tom Moore."

ANDREW MACK

TOM MOORE

Coming to Ford's Next Week

PRIMROSE AND DOCKSTADER'S

GREAT AMERICAN MINSTRELS

ACADEMY TOMORROW NIGHT

"SURE TO CREATE A SENSATION"

Sadie Martinot

THE Marriage Game

BY CLYDE FITCH

LULU GLASER OPERA CO.

DOLLY VARDEN

ACADEMY

The Brigadiers

THE VANISHING BRIGADIERS

THE FETE OF THE GONDOLIERS

1851 ARION 1901

ANNOUNCEMENT

Lucas Brothers

STATIONERS

PRINTERS

LITHOGRAPHERS

BLANK BOOK MAKERS

Low Prices

BEST GRADE STATIONERY

HIGH CLASS BLANK BOOKS

10c. per 100 Pages Up

MIMEOGRAPHS

TYPEWRITER SUPPLIES

FINE WRITING PAPERS

ENGRAVING AND EMBOSSING

Lucas Brothers

116 E. BALTIMORE ST.

ESTABLISHED IN 1804

York and Frederick Fairs

Goldsmith Bros.

206 East Baltimore street

35 West Lexington street

Experimenting Unnecessary

Great Scott's

Great Scott's

GOMPRECHT & BENESCH

Eutaw Furniture Co.

316-318-320 N. EUTAW ST.

OPEN EVENINGS

GOMPRECHT & BENESCH

Eutaw Furniture Co.

316-318-320 N. EUTAW ST.

MacDonald

J. S. MacDONALD

Mercantile Laundry Co.

A MODERN LAUNDRY

ARCHER'S Laundry 6 Offices

W. J. CHAPMAN

COAL AND COKE

"TO BURN"

SHARP & LOMBARD STS

HAT BOX HATS

$2

THE HAT BOX

The Hub

GENTLEMEN'S EXPERTLY TAILORED FALL AND WINTER SUITS AND OVERCOATS

$15.00

$10 and $12.50 Overcoats, $7.50

THE HUB

MARYLAND TELEPHONES!

In Your Home for $24 a Year

CALVERT BANK

To the White Voters of Baltimore City:

It has been charged that the Democratic Party has raised the race issue in the present Campaign. We ask you to read the appeal printed below, sent to the negro voter throughout the city by a Republican committee.

Tuesday, October 1

Tuesday, October 8

Wednesday, October 9

Wednesday, October 2

MARYLAND SAVINGS BANK

THE SUN

SUMMARY OF NEWS

HAWKES CRIED "YOU LIE"

THE LETTER TO SCHLEY

Judge-Advocate Lemly Defends Sampson's Instructions.

ORDERS SEEMED CONFLICTING

WHAT DID SAMPSON MEAN?

THE SUN

VOLUME CXXXI—NO. 5. BALTIMORE, WEDNESDAY MORNING, MAY 21, 1902. PRICE ONE CENT

FREE CUBA IS BORN A NEW REPUBLIC

Tomas Estrada Palma Inaugurated As The First President Of The Island.

AMERICAN FLAG AT LAST HAULED DOWN

Outburst Of Popular Enthusiasm Marks The Culmination Of The Hopes Cherished In Years Of Blood And Fiery Trial.

GENERAL WOOD GIVES UP THE TRUST HE HAS HELD

WASHINGTON, May 20.—The following dispatch was received at the White House tonight from General Wood at Havana:

"To the President of the United States, Washington:

"I have the honor to report to you that in compliance with instructions received I have this day, at 12 o'clock sharp, transferred to the President and Congress of the Republic of Cuba the government and control of the island, to be held and exercised by them under the provisions of the Constitution of the Republic of Cuba. Documents sent to me were read, and Mr. Palma in accepting the responsibilities on behalf of the island expressed himself in kind and endearing words, and thanked the Republic of the United States and its officials for all that has been done for Cuba and for the fulfillment of promises made. The ceremony was most impressive, and I embark on the Brooklyn with my staff for the United States.

WOOD."

CHANGE QUICKLY MADE

Transfer Of Cuba's Government Occupied But Ten Minutes At The Palace.

[Copyrighted by New York Herald Company, 1902.]
[Special to the Baltimore Sun.]

HAVANA, May 20.—With ceremonies which occupied 10 minutes Cuba today came into ...

VOLCANO IN FURY

One Of The Most Awful Sights Ever Witnessed By Man.

AMERICAN TARS HEROES

They Refuse To Quail Even Before Great Pelee's Wrath.

FRENCHMEN BURST INTO TEARS

New Eruption Spreads Wild Alarm At Fort de France—People Sleep At Water's Edge Ready To Swim For Escape If The Dreaded Upheaval Comes To Destroy The City.

[Copyrighted by New York Herald Company, 1902.]
[Special to the Baltimore Sun.]

FORT DE FRANCE, MARTINIQUE, May 20.—Destruction is again being done by Mount Pelee, the volcano having resumed an activity even greater than that exhibited just before St. Pierre was wiped out of existence.

For 24 hours the volcano has been in con...

Great Scott

Great Scott

THE SUN

SUMMARY OF NEWS

EXTRA THE SUN EXTRA

VOLUME CXXXIV—NO. 84. BALTIMORE, MONDAY MORNING, FEBRUARY 8, 1904. PRICE ONE CENT

TWENTY-FOUR BLOCKS BURNED IN HEART OF BALTIMORE

CITY'S MOST VALUABLE BUILDINGS IN RUINS

LOSS VARIOUSLY ESTIMATED AT FROM $50,000,000 TO $80,000,000

BLAZE STILL SPREADING EASTWARD AND SOUTHWARD AT 3.30 A. M.

Starting In John E. Hurst Building The Fire Sweeps South To Lombard, East To Holliday And North To Lexington, Destroying Wholesale Business Houses, Banks, Continental, Equitable, Calvert, B. And O. Central, The Sun And Other Large Buildings.

THE SUN TODAY.

This edition of The Sun is printed from the presses of the Washington Star, through the courtesy of that paper. When the great fire was close to The Sun Building, in Baltimore, a force of editors, reporters, compositors and stereotypers was sent to Washington and duplicate news facilities were installed in the Star office.

SUMMARY OF THE NEWS.

Government Weather Report.

Washington, Feb. 7.—The Government Weather Bureau issued the following forecast for Monday and Tuesday.

Maryland, District of Columbia, Virginia, Deleware and Eastern Pennsylvania, fair, much colder Monday; cold wave at night; brisk to high northwest winds; Tuesday fair and cold.

West Virginia, fair Monday, except snow in the mountain districts, cold wave; Tuesday fair and cold.

North Carolina, fair and colder Monday, cold wave at night in the interior; Tuesday fair and cold; diminishing northwest winds.

Forecast For Baltimore And Vicinity.

The Government forecast for Baltimore and vicinity is for fair and much colder weather, with cold wave at night.

$20,000 IN MONEY SAVED

Officers Of Federal Savings Bank Find Vault Empty.

Early in the afternoon $20,000 in coin and bills was taken out of the vaults of the Federal Savings Bank, on the northeast corner of Hanover and Lombard streets. The money, it was said, was secured by Mr. James H. L. Foote and placed in the vault of the National Enameling and Stamping Company, two squares down Hanover street and out of t e track of the fire.

Later some of the officers of the bank came around and, not knowing that the money had already been saved, with the aid of Deputy Marshal Manning, Sergeant Armiger, Sergeant Hughes and Patrolmen Scheib and Bagnell, effected an entrance into the bank and opened the safe, which they found empty.

Although for three hours nearly everything around the bank building was blazing, it did not catch fire until 7 o'clock and was only partially destroyed.

RINGS IN BANK SAFE

Treasurer Rabbe Has To Be Identified To Get Them.

While the fire was blazing a red furnace half a square away and the building of the Federal Savings bank, at the southwest corner of Lombard and Hanover streets, was beginning to smoke, Mr. Conrad C. Rabbe, the treasurer of the bank, entered the building in company with Patrolman Scheib, of the Northwestern district, and Patrolman Johnson, of the Western, and got from the safe in the bank two handsome diamond rings belonging to him.

Patrolman Scheib took possession of the rings and refused to relinquish them until Mr. Rabbe had appeared before Deputy Marshall Manning and been identified.

PHONE SERVICE CRIPPLED

Trolley Cars Switched Over Different Routes.

The underground conduits proved the salvation of the telephone and telegraph systems in the heart of the city. They both worked with a reasonable degree of satisfaction until the telephone operators in the Exchange Building, on St. Paul street, and the Western Union and Postal Telegraph operators in the Equitable and Continental buildings had to abandon their posts. The telephone operators had to move about 7 o'clock, but the telegraph operators remained for a considerable time later. In the outlying disricts, where the telephone service was controlled by branch exchanges there was not much trouble.

The trolley service, thanks to the system of switches and curves laid within the last few years, was in good shape in nearly all parts of the city, except where the fire was blazing. The cars were crowded all day.

STEAMERS READY TO MOVE

Vessels At Lgiht Street Wharf On The Alert.

Along Light street wharves all the steamers had steam up and crews standing by ready to leave at any moment. The Tivoli moved from her wharf to one farther down the stream.

Captain Fowler had the steamer Anthony Groves, Jr., loaded and ready to leave for Philadelphia. The fruit steamer Salvatore Di Giorgio, at Bowley's wharves, was ready to start.

The city fireboat Cataract took up a position at Pratt and Light streets at 7 o'clock P.M. and forced water through 2,000 feet of hose, which it was supposed would reach to German street. The hose was cut by wagons running over it and the attempt was abandoned.

ENGINE AND TRUCK LOST

Walls Of Hurst Building Fall On And Wreck Them.

The city Fire Department lost two fine pieces of apparatus. They were N. 15 engine and No. 2 truck. Arriving first on the scene of action, they took up their stations at Hopkins Place and German street.

It was but a very short while before the heat became so intense as to drive the firemen away, and the falling walls from the Hurst Building fell on the apparatus, wrecking it. The horses, which were not far away, had their hair singed, but were not seriously burned.

CHIEF HORTON HURT

Stunned By Stepping On A Live Wire And Rendered Unconscious.

Chief Horton was badly shocked by stepping on a live wire early in the afternoon, and was taken in a patrol wagon up to his headquarters at No. 23 Engine House, Saratoga street, near Howard, where he was attended by Dr. Geer.

The Chief showed no burns, but was badly stunned, and was in a semi-conscious condition until late in the afternoon. He suffered acute pain in the head and was given opiates to relieve him. His driver, Clarence Kirby, was given the post of nurse and Dr. Geer paid several visits during the course of the afternoon.

Fire, which started at 10.50 o'clock yesterday morning, devastated practically the entire central business district of Baltimore and at midnight the flames were still raging with as much fury as at the beginning.

To all appearances Baltimore's business section is doomed. Many of the principal banking institutions, all the leading trust companies, all the largest wholesale houses, all the newspaper offices, many of the principal retail stores and thousands of smaller establishments went up in flame, and in most cases the contents were completely destroyed.

What the loss will be in dollars no man can even estimate, but the sum will be so gigantic that it is hard for the average mind to grasp its magnitude. In addition to the pecuniary loss, will be the immense amount of business lost by the necessary interruption to business while the many firms whose places are destroyed are making arrangements for resuming business.

There is little doubt that many men, formerly prosperous, will be ruined by the events of the last 24 hours. Many of them carry little or no insurance, and it is doubtful if many of the insurance companies will be able to pay their losses dollar for dollar, and those that do will probably require time in which to arrange for the payment.

APPALLED INTO SILENCE

All day and all night throngs crowded the streets, blocking every avenue to the fire district and moving back out of danger only when forced to do so by the police on duty. Many of the spectators saw their all go up in flame before their eyes, and there were men with hopeless faces and despairing expressions seen on every hand. In fact, the throng seemed stunned with the magnitude of the disaster and scarcely seemed to realize the extent of it.

They stood around usually in dazed silence, and only occasionally would a word of despair be heard. That they were almost disheartened was apparent to the casual observer, and there is litle wonder, for the crushing stroke fell with the suddenness of lightning from a cloudless sky.

STARTS IN HURST BUILDING

At 10.50 o'clock in the morning the automatic fire-alarm box, No. 854, in the basement of the wholesale dry goods house of John E. Hurst & Co., German street and Hopkins place, sounded an alarm. Almost before the alarm had reached the various engine houses the entire building was a roaring mass of flames from top to bottom.

GASOLINE EXPLODES

After burning fiercely for perhaps 10 minutes there was a loud explosion from the interior of the building as the gasoline tank used for the engine in the building let go. Instantly the immense structure collapsed and the flying, flaming debris causee the flames to be communicated to the adjacent buildings on all four corners.

By this time the first of the fire apparatus hae reached the scene and was quickly put to work, but the fire had already gone beyond control and swept with irresistible force and incredulous swiftness on its devastating way. It was known that the conflagration would prove vastly destructive, but not one of those who witnessed it at this time imagined for an instant the terrible results that would ensue.

CHIEF HORTON DISABLED

Chief Engineer Horton, of the Fire Department, was quickly on the ground, but scarcely had he begun to direct the force of firemen when a live trolley wire fell on him at the corner of Liberty and Baltimore streets, knocking him senseless, and he had to be carried to his home and placed in bed. By this accident the city was deprived of the services of its most experienced and trusted firefighter, and, although District Chief Emerich, who succeeded Chief Horton in command on the ground, did apparently all that was possible, those present could not but regret that Chief Horton was not there.

Mayor McLane came down and was on the ground until a late hour in the night. He walked around the burning district and conferred with various officials as to the steps necessary to be taken at various stages of the fire.

It is thought the loss will be over $50,000,000.

AID FROM WASHINGTON.

Four general alarms were speedily sent in and within half an hour after the first alarm every piece of fire apparatus in Baltimore was on the ground and at work. Realizing the gravity of the peril a telegram was sent to Washington for aid and two engines from that city were placed on a special train and hurried to the city over the Baltimore and Ohio railroad in record-breaking time. It was said that the trip was made in 37 minutes.

It was an awe-inspiring sight to witness the progress of the flames. A building eight or ten stories in height would suddenly break into flames from top to bottom almost in an instant and would burn fiercely until with a crash that could be heard for blocks the walls would collapse and the spot be marked only by a heap of blazing ruins. The crash of falling walls was almost incessant and now and then could be heard the muffled roar of an explosion as some gasoline tank or chemical substances became ignited by the heat and let go with terrific force.

MANY FIREMEN INJURED.

Every minute almost the lives of the firemen were in imminent danger from falling walls or leaping flames, and more than 50 of them were carried from the ground more or less severely burned. Undismayed by the danger or the hopelessness of the task, however, they continued the unequal struggle, and took the hose into narrow alleys, where the flames roared menacingly overhead on both sides of them, and directed streams of water where it was thought someeffect could be produced.

Long ladders were placed against the walls of fiercely burning buildings and brave firemen climbed up and broke in windows and turned streams of water into the doomed buildings until the walls swayed and rocked and the crowd of onlookers shouted to them to come down, and many turned away their eyes in momentary apprehension of a fatal calamity.

Apparently every person in Baltimore was in the vicinity of the fire, and the various streets leading to the fire district were packed during the entire day. The entire police force, in charge of Marshal Farnan and Deputy Marshal Manning, was on the ground and with ropes succeeded in keeping the crowd back from the dangerous points. As the fire spread farther and farther the ropes were shifted and the crowd moved back one block at the time.

GREAT BUILDINGS GONE.

The section devastated contains the largest and most modern buildings in the city and this renders the calamity the more appalling. Immense office buildings, 10 and 12 stories high, large modern wholesale houses made of brick and steel, all disappeared as if built of the flimsiest material.

The exact origin of the fire is not known, but the explosion which started the spread of the flames to other buildings is said to have been caused by a gasoline engine in the Hurst Building. Mr. S. F. Ball of West Fayette street who was standing on the corner of Sharp and Baltimore street when the fire first broke out, said that in less than 10 minutes the entire Hurst Building was a roaring mass of flames from top to bottom. When the explosion occurred Mr. Ball was cut on both hands and a hole was cut through his hat by flying fragments of glass.

TO LOMBARD STREET

From German street the fire spread rapidly to Lombard street, leaping from building to building, and sometimes skipping two or three buildings, and in this way a block would become ignied in a remarkably short space of time. At Lombard street the fire paused for some time and the large building of Guggenheimer, Well & Co. stood for a time apparently undamaged. It was evidently doomed however, and all arrangements were made for dynamiting it in order to save the Lord L. Jackson building, just across Lombard street. The Guggenheimer, Well & Co. building suddenly burst into flame and in a very short time the floor began falling in with a crash, the heavy lithographing machinery, weighing many tons, causing a detonation that made many think the place had really been dynamited. The walls quickly followed the floor and the Jackson building was saved after a hard struggle. A number of the other buildings on the south side of Lombard street became ignited, however, and both sides of that street from Liberty to Charles were practically ruined, the houses on the north side being completely destroyed and those on the south side, with the exception of the Jaikson building, badly damaged.

ACROSS SHARP STREET

Meantime the flames had swept through the block to the east and quickly began the destruction of the buildings on the west side of Sharp street. With scarcely a pause they jumped over to the east side of Sharp and the large row of buildings on that side of the street began to crackle and burn. Hardly had a portion of the fire apparatus been shifted to meet the new point threatened when the fire was sweeping madly across to the west side of Hanover street, and here the scene was repeated. Almost before the firemen realized the fact the buildings on the east side of Hanover street were blazing.

TO BALTIMORE STREET

At this time the scene in this portion of the burning district was magnificent in its spectacular grandeur. Looking up Hanover street to Baltimore nothing but a seething, roaring mass of flames, mingled with dense smoke, could be seen. Baltimore street was iself a roaring furnace, and on every side were flying cinders. The roar of the flames was broken at frequent intervals by the crash of falling walls, and now and again the detonation of some explosion sounded above the other noises.

DYNAMITE USED

After crossing Hanover street there was little to oppose the onrushing flames and the blaze continued its destructive course without a check to Charles street. Prior to this time there had been much talk of dynamiting, the material was on the ground and Mr. Roy C. Lafferts, the Government expert, who had comes from Washington especially to take charge of the work of dynamiting the buildings, was on the ground with his apparatus in readiness.

By this time it was thoroughly realized that the flames were completely beyond control and only desperate measures could be expected to relieve the situation. In this strait of City Engineer-Fendall and Mr.Lafferty laid a charge in the building adjoining Armstrong, Cator & Co.'s on the west and set it off. The building fell with a crash, but the blazing ruins ignited the Armstrong building and the situation was, if anything, made worse.

Armstrong, Cator & Co.'s building burned rapidly. A large charge of dynamite was let off in it, but the structure failed to collapse and the idea of destroying it with dynamite was abandoned.

The flames by this time were raging fiercely and all along German street to Charles and it was then that Mr. Lafferty set off six charges of dynamite, each charge containing 100 pounds, in the building at the southwest corner of Charles and German streets. The tremendous force of the explosions tore the massive granite columns that supported the building and left it with apparently almost no support, but the walls failed to collapse and stood until the flames had crossed Charles street and were eating into the block between Charles and Light street.

THE CARROLLTON GOES.

The fire had meantime been communicated to the row of streets, and all those places, occupied principally by wholesale produce and grain dealers, were in flames.

Shortly before midnight the Carrollton Hotel was in flames and the fire was sweeping toward Calvert street with irresistible fury.

The fireman working on the south side had succeeded in checking the flames at Lombard street, and as the wind was blowing from the northwest there was no danger of it spreading farther in that direction. The western limit had also been reached at Howard street, and the danger was now to the east and north.

The progress of the flames toward the north had in the meantime been so rapid as to be simply appalling. From structure to structure they flew, licking up the massive buildings as if they were composed of paper. In the block between German and Baltimore streets they flew along, and almost before it could be realized the buildings along Baltimore street were blazing from roof to basement.

MULLIN'S IN RUINS.

For a time it was hoped the fire could be kept from crossing to the north side of Baltimore street and the fireman made a desperate effort to prevent it. The effort was useless, however, and soon the tall, narrow building of Mullin's Hotel began to dart out tongues of flame from several stories and in a few minutes the entire building was an immense flaming torch. At almost the same instant the remainder of the buildings between Sharp and Liberty streets were ablaze and the fire began its march to the north. The small two and three story buildings on Little Sharp street burned comparatively slowly and in this narrow space the two Washington companies fought a plucky battle with the devouring element. They were hemmed in on both sides by fire and directed the streams at the buildings from which smoke and flame were pouring, at a distance of only two or three yards.

ACROSS CHARLES STREET.

It was utterly, heartbreakingly useless. The flames darted rapidly from place to place, and soon the entire south side of Fayette street was in the grasp of the flames. Down Fayette to Charles they swept, and in a space of time that seemed incredibly short the building occupied by J. W. Putts & Co. was evidently doomed.

Seeing that nothing could save it Mr. Fendall, acting under instructions from Chief Emerich, decided to destroy the building with dynamite, in the hope of preventing the fire from crossing Charles street. The explosion was successful in accomplishing the object, and the entire corner collapsed instantly, but this had, apparently, no effect upon the progress of the sire, for almost before the sound of the falling walls had died away the building on the east side of Charles street began to blaze, and it was evident that the block between Charles and St. Paul streets was doomed.

CALVERT AND EQUITABLE GO.

In a desperate, but futile, effort to prevent the fire going further to the east, building after building was dynamited in this block, but it was all of no avail and the fire proceeded steadily onward. The Daily Record Building was soon in flames, and not many minutes later the fire had leaped over St. Paul street and the lofty, massive Calvert Building began to emit smoke and flame. The Equitable Building, just over a narrow alley, quickly followed, and these two immense buildings gave forth a glare that lighted the city for miles around.

It was thought that the fire could be prevented from crossing to the north side of Fayette street and here again a desperate stand was made by the firemen. Again it was useless and soon the large building of Hall, Headington & Co., on the northwest corner of Charles and Fayette streets, was blazing brightly. With scarcely a pause the fire darted across the east side of Charles street and began to lap up the handsome building of the Union Trust Company, while at the same time the large buildings of the west of Hall, Headingon & Co., occupied by Wise Brothers and Oppenheim, Oberndorf & Co., were aflame throughout.

MILLIONS IN A FEW BLOCKS

A detailed Estimate of Loss In The Wholesale District.

A careful and conservative estimate, of the loss in the wholesale business district in which the fire originated, places it at something over $16,007,000. This district is bounded by Baltimore, Liberty, Charles and Lombard streets and contained many of the largest dry goods, clothing and shoe houses in the city, besides two prominent banks—the National Exchange and Hopkins Place Savings Bank. The estimate was made for The Sun last nigt by Mr. George E. Taylor, of the insurance firm of Jenniss & Taylor, Holliday and Water streets. Mr. Taylor sat in his office dictating to a reporter of The Sun until it was stated that the fire was only a few doors away, when he found it necessary to remove the valuables and papers from his office.

The estimate is for each building in this section, the loss given representing the building with its contents. According to this the heaviest losers were John E. Hurst & Co., R. M. Sutton & Co., and the Daniel Miller Company, all of which were heavily stocked with dry goods, and in each of which cases the loss in building and contents was placed at $1,500,000. The Armstrong, Cator & Co.'s. loss is estimated at half a million, and the great majority were $100,000 or more apiece. This district contained about 125 buildings, among them some of the finest business structures in town, which were occupied by more than 150 firms. The list follows:

HOPKINS PLACE.

12 to 20—John E. Hurst, dry goods, $1,500,000; over $1,000,000 insurance.

22—Vacant building. $50,000.

24—Wiliam Koch Importing Company, toys, $150,000.

26—Samuel D. Goldberg, pants; F. & Chas. Burger & Co., clothing; $75,000.

28 to 32—The Daniel Miller Company, dry goods; $1,500,000; carry more than $1,000,000 insurance on contents.

34—Dixon-Bartlett Company, shoes; $175,000.

36—Joyner, Witz & Co., hats and caps; $100,000.

38—Spragins, Buck & Co., shoes; $125,000.

40—Cohen-Adler Shoe Company; $125,000.

LIBERTY STREET

35 and 37—L. S. Fiteman, ladies' wrappers; Jacob R. Seligman, paper, and Nathan Rosen, ladies; cloaks; $100,000.

39—Morton, Samuels & Co., boots and shoes, and Strauss Bros., storage; $100,000.

41—Baltimore Rubber Company, $135,000.

43—Guggenheimer, Well & Co., lithographers and printers, $125,000.

WEST BALTIMORE STREET

127—M. Friedman & Sons, clothing, and F. Schleunes, cloths; $150,000.

129—Schwartzkopf Toy Company, $100,000.

131—A. Federleicht & Sons, cloths, $75,000.

SOUTH LIBERTY STREET.

5—Whitaker's saloon, $15,000.

7—C. J. Stewart & Sons, hardware, $25,000.

9—O'Connell & Bannan, saloon, $25,000.

11 and 13—National Exchange Bank; building, $75,000; contents $50,000.

AT 3:30 THIS MCRNING.

At 3:30 o'clock this morning the fire had not crossed Jones falls on the east, although a number of lumber yards on the east side of the falls were ablaze. The wind was still from the north. West of Charles and north of Lombard the fire had practically burned out. East of Charles and south of Lombard the flames are still spreading. It was expected to reach Pratt street before daylight. The fire probably will reach the water front west of Jones falls.

The Lutheran Church at Broadway and Canton avenue caught fire at 3 o'clock.

SIGNS OF ABATING

Mayor McLane and Doctor Geer have just returned from a circuit of the fire. The Mayor said:

"I feel the conflagration shows some signs of abating. I have received a telegram from New York stating that the Fire Department of that city has sent over six engines, six hose carriages, six trucks and horses. These will probably reach Baltimore between 6 and 7 o'clock A.M."

Police Marshal Farnan said:

"I think the fire is practically under control."

HOPKINS PLACE

21—S. Lowman & Co., clothing, $125,000.

23—John E. Hurst & Co., storage, $150,000.

25—Findlay, Roberts & Co., hardware, $75,000.

27—Lawrence & Gould Shoe Company and Bates Hat Company, $125,000.

29—S. Ginsberg & Co., clothing, $125,000.

31—Winkelmann & Brown Drug Co., $125,000.

33 and 35—R. M. Sutton & Co. dry goods, $1,500,000.

37—Chesapeake Shoe Company, $100,000.

39—S. F. and A. F. Miller, clothing manufacturers $150,000.

41—S. Halle Sons, boots and shoes, $100,000.

43 and 45—Strauss Bros., dry goods, $250,000.

Rear of 37 and 89—A. C. Meyer & Co. patent medicines, $150,000.

WEST LOMBARD STREET

108 and 110—Matthews Bros., paper-box manufacturers, $75,000.

112 and 114—Strauss, Eiseman & Co., shirt manufacturers, $150,000.

116 and 118—North Bros. & Strauss, have been moving to new building formerly occupied by Heywood Bros.-Wakefield Company, northeast corner Pratt and Greene streets; building $75,000; stock may be about $75,000.

WEST GERMAN STREET.

103—Standard Suspender Company and Daniel A. Boone & Co., liquors, $60,000.

105—Bradley, Kirkman, Reese Company, paper, $75,000.

107—George A. Eitel, neckwear manufacturer; Charles L. Linville and J. J. Murphy, sewing silks, $75,000.

109—MCDonald & Fisher, wholesale paper, $100,000.

111—Wiley, Bruster & Co., dry goods, and F. W. & E. Dammann, cloth, $125,000.

113—Henry Oppenheimer & OO., CLOTH•
ING, AND Vansant, Jacobs & Co., shirts, $175,000.

16—Joseph R. Stonebraker & Co., liquors, $75,000.

18—Lewis Lauer & Co., shirts, $100,000.

20—Champion Shoe Manufacturing Company and Diggs, Currin & Co., shoes, $100,000.

22-Mendels Bros., ladies' wrappers, $125,000.

24—Blankenberg, Gehrmann & Co., notions, $125,000.

26—Leo Keene & Co., ladies' cloaks, and Henry Pretzfelder & Co., boots and shoes, $125,000.

28—Peter Rose & Sons harness manufacturers, $125,000.

30—James Robertson Manufacturing Company, plumbers' supplies, $100,000.

32—R. Jandorf & Co., boots and shoes, and James Robertson Manufacturing Company, storage, $100,000.

34—Rasch & Gaynor, window shades, $75,000.

36—Fusselbaugh-Balke Company, wall paper, $65,000.

BALTIMORE STREET.

101—Ades Bros., umbrella manufacturers, and Ferdinand Hahn & Sons, cloth, $75000.

103—Ades Bros. and A. Hoff, clothing; $75,000.

105—Douglas, Henry & Co., hosiery and underwear, $75,000.

107—L. Greif & Bros., clothing, $150,000. laces; $125,000.

111—Florence W. MacCarthy Company, notions and laces; $150,000.

113—Thalheimer Bros., clothing; $150,000.

115—Fisher Bros., liquors, wholesale, and Silberman and Todes, notions, dry goods, etc.; $150,000.

117—Silberman & Todes, $150,000.

119 and 121—New building, not occupied; $75,000.

123—M. Moses & Son, merchant tailors; $75,000.

125—J. Goldsmith & Son, clothing, and Sugar & Shear, clothing; $100,000.

HOPKINS PLACE.

7 and 11—Hopkins Place Savings Bank, $75,000.

13—Cohen & Samuels, hats and caps; $75,000.

15—F. Arnold & Sons, surgical instruments; $60,000.

17 and 19—Michael Ambach & Sons, clothing; $250,000.

HANOVER STREET.

2 and 4—Marburg Bros., tobacco; $100,000.

6—United Shirt and Collar Company, $50,000.

8—Mack Bros. & Mack, clothing, and John A. Griffith & Co., tailors' trimmings; $60,000.

10—Standard Cap Manufacturing Company and Elias Coplan, neckwear manufacturer, $75,000.

12—Reliable Pants Manufacturing Company, clothing, and L. M. Levering, druggists' supplies, $75,000.

14—Simon Neuberger & Bro., dry goods, $100,000.

HANOVER STREET.

1—S. M. Fleischer, ladies' and gents' furnishings, $75,000.

3—D. S. Wallerstein, millinery, $50,000.

5—The Brainerd-Armstrong Company, silks, and Carter, Webster & Co., storage of notions, $75,000.

7—Vogts, Quast & Co., tailors' trimmings, $75,000.

9 and 11—Woodward, Baldwin & Co., dry goods, $15,000.

13 and 15—Bouldin Bros., notions, $150,000.

17 and 19—Carter, Webster & Co., white goods, $150,000.

21—Edward Jenkins & Sons, coach and harness makers' supplies, $150,000.

23—Johnson, Boyd & Co., notions, $$00,000.

25—Linthicum Rubber Company, boots and shoes, $125,000.

27—M. I. Blum & Bro., clothing, $100,000.

29—S. Kirson & Bro., clothing, $75,000.

31—Edward Jenkins & Sons, storage, and Lapsley & Brom Company, storage, window shades, $75,000.

33 and 35—Philip F. Gehrman & Co., laces and embroideries, and Phillips Bros.' Company, dry goods, $200,000.

WEST GERMAN STREET.

5 and 7, Amon, Green & Co., cotton, and other offices; $75,000.

9, Sadler, Rowe & Co., books and stationery; $50,000.

11, George Mayo, manufacturer and proprietary medicines, $50,000.

13, Van Zandt, Jacobs & Co., shirts, $50,000.

15, Caplan & Greenbaum, clothing, and Crucible Steel Company, $50,000.

17, Carey, Bain & Smith, dry goods, and F. R. Kent, spool cotton and thread, $50,000.

WEST BALTIMORE STREET.

1—Oehm's Acme Hall, $150,000.

5 and 7—Consolidated Gas Company, $100,000.

9 and 11 and back to 4 and 10 West German—Armstrong, Cator & Co., notions and millinery, $500,000.

13 and 15—Wiegert & Co., shoes; Steiger Bros., trunks; Dowell, Helm & Co., storage, and M. and J. Oppenheimer & Sons, jewelry, $100,000.

17 and 19—Dowell, Helm & Co., millinery, $150,000.

THE SUN

LIGHT FOR ALL

VOLUME CXXXVIII—NO. 154. BALTIMORE, THURSDAY MORNING, APRIL 19, 1906. 14 PAGES PRICE ONE CENT

THE SUN
SUMMARY OF THE NEWS

Government Weather Report.

Washington, April 18.—The Government Weather Bureau tonight issued the following forecast for Thursday and Friday:

Maryland, District of Columbia and Virginia, fair Thursday and Friday; variable winds.

Delaware, fair Thursday and Friday; light to fresh south winds.

West Virginia, fair Thursday; Friday, rain and cooler.

North Carolina, fair Thursday and Friday; light to fresh east to southeast winds.

The Mississippi river continues to rise [bel]ow Helena, Ark., and dangerous stages may be expected.

There has been no change in the weather conditions east of the Mississippi river, except a general rise in temperature.

In the Lower Lake region, the Upper Ohio Valley and the Middle Atlantic States the weather will be fair Thursday and Friday.

The winds along the Middle Atlantic coast will be light to fresh south; on the South Atlantic coast, light to fresh east to southeast.

Steamers departing Thursday for European ports will have light to fresh south winds, with fair weather to the Grand Banks.

Baltimore Local Report.

United States Weather Bureau, Observer's Office, Johns Hopkins University, C. F. von Herrmann, section director, April 18.

Time	Therm'ter	Relative humidity	Direction of wind	Velocity of wind	Rainfall	State of weather
8 A. M.	[illegible]	37	N	12	.00	Clear
8 P. M.	[illegible]	31	NW	3	.00	Clear

Normal temperature.... [illegible] Max. temperature.... [illegible]
Mean temperature.... [illegible] Min. temperature.... [illegible]

Maximum velocity of the wind, 13 miles an hour, from the north. [illegible]

Hourly Temperature.

[illegible]

Thermometrical Record.

The following table shows the minimum [illegible]

...state of the weather at 8 o'clock last night at the stations named:

Station	Temp.	Weather	Station	Temp.	Weather
Eastport	38	Clear	Cincinnati	48	Clear
Boston	46	Clear	Detroit	46	Clear
New York	50	Clear	Chicago	52	Clear
Phil'delphia	54	Clear	St. Paul	56	Cloudy
Atlantic Cy.	46	Clear	St. Louis	50	Cloudy
Washington	50	Clear	Kansas City	52	Clear
Hatteras	50	Clear	Omaha	56	Cloudy
Charlotte	46	Clear	Williston	42	Clear
Charleston	54	Clear	Bismarck	50	Cloudy
Savannah	52	Cloudy	Helena	38	Clear
Jacksonville	56	Cloudy	Salt Lake Cy	44	Clear
Montgomery	54	Clear	Denver	40	Rain'g
New Orleans	62	Clear	Amarillo	48	Cloudy
Galveston	60	Cloudy	Los Angeles	50	....
Memphis	52	Clear			

The Weather In Europe.

[Copyright by New York Herald Company, 1906.]
[Special to the Baltimore Sun.]

London, April 18.—Clouds overcast the sky today, the temperature ranging from 40° to 50° Fahr. The barometer registered 20.68 inches at 6 o'clock in the evening, and the wind was blowing fresh from the northeast.

Paris, April 18.—The weather was rainy today in Paris and thunder was heard. The maximum temperature was 51° and the minimum 42° Fahr. A fresh northeast wind is blowing at midnight and the barometer is falling.

Forecast For Baltimore And Vicinity

The official forecast for Baltimore and vicinity is for fair weather today and tomorrow.

Foreign Affairs.

Father Gapon, the labor leader, is missing from St. Petersburg, and it is thought he has been kidnapped.

Abramoff, the Cossack officer who maltreated Maria Spiridonovo, a girl revolutionist, in prison, has been assassinated.

The seismograph at Laibach, Austria, more than 7,000 miles from San Francisco, recorded the first shock.

The wounded of the Kearsarge are on the way to New York.

City And Suburban.

The Paint and Powder Club achieved a triumph in its opening production of "The Brigand's Trust."

A banquet in celebration of the passage of the Haman Oyster Culture bill was held at the Merchants' Club.

The police census just completed for the Health Department gives the city's population as 543,034.

Permits to build 68 two and three story dwellings have been applied for by local contractors.

The proposed independent sugar refinery for Baltimore now seems assured, the promoters having obtained an option on the "Sea Wall" property, Anne Arundel county, as a favorable site.

City Engineer Fendall will be sent abroad to study the well-paved streets of Europe.

The body found in the harbor Tuesday was identified as that of Capt. Francis Mack, of Roxbury, Mass.

Mr. and Mrs. James Jung observed their golden wedding at St. Michael's Catholic Church, where a nuptial mass was celebrated by their three sons, who are priests.

The Interstate Commerce Commission's investigation of the affairs of the Baltimore and Ohio was again marked by acrimonious feeling between the attorneys.

Congress.

Brief sessions of both houses were held yesterday. The House passed a resolution providing for the immediate relief of San Francisco through the War and Navy Departments.

Representative Gill, of Maryland, offered in the House the resolution of sympathy for San Francisco, which was adopted.

The Senate, after a brief session, adjourned in order to allow the Democratic Senators to hold a caucus on the Railway Rate bill.

National Affairs.

President Roosevelt sent a special message to Congress scoring Judge Humphreys for his immunity decision in the Beef Trust cases, and calling upon Congress to prevent such an attempt to "make the law a farce."

Democratic Senators held a long conference on the Railroad Rate bill, but were unable to reach an agreement.

The Daughters of the American Revolution contributed about $40,000 to complete their Continental Hall.

District Of Columbia.

Referee McCalmont decides that Richard A. Johnson, son-in-law of Senator Gorman, is entitled to the benefit of the bankruptcy act.

Dr. Louis MacCall, a prominent Georgetown physician, is dead.

John Richard Garner and James Henry Gaskins, both colored, were sentenced each to 15 years in the penitentiary for killing John Patterson.

Virginia And West Virginia.

Stockholders of the Southern Railway Company authorized an issue of $200,000,000 50-year 4 per cent. bonds.

Mr. J. A. Reagan, a prominent resident of Danville, accidentally killed himself.

Edwin Howell, colored, accused of the murder of George Fauver, committed suicide by hanging himself in his cell.

The original commission of Lord Fairfax was found among a lot of old papers in Winchester.

Miscellaneous.

Half of San Francisco was destroyed by earthquake and fire, 200 lives being lost more than 1,000 persons injured and enormous property loss caused.

John Alexander Dowie secured a temporary injunction preventing Voliva and his followers from interfering with his going to Zion City and permitting him to hold services in Zion City.

Prominent scientists gathered in Philadelphia to celebrate the anniversary of Benjamin's Franklin's birth.

Father Louis Martin, General of the Jesuits, died of cancer of the throat, in Rome.

The statue erected in Paris to the memory of Benjamin Franklin will be unveiled today.

The drydock Dewey was sighted near Port Said, and should have reached there last night.

Strikers in and around Lens, France, had combats with troops and wounded many, only dispersing when the riot act was read.

Where To Find Today's News.

The classification of THE SUN'S news today is as follows:

	Pages		Pages
Gen. Telegraph	1, 2, 10, 11, 12	Local	6, 7, 9, 14
Foreign	12	Sporting	8, 12
Washington	2, 5	N. Y. Topics	12
Maryland	10	Markets	13
Virginia	10	Shipping	12, 13

ESTIMATES DEAD AT 500

New York American Says Asylum Fell, Killing Many Orphans.

[Special Dispatch to the Baltimore Sun.]

New York, April 18.—The New York American tomorrow will say:

"The great conflagration which followed the disastrous earthquake shocks at San Francisco today has wiped out virtually all the wholesale district and cut a wide path through the shopping and hotel sections, and there is no means of checking the flames.

"Latest estimates places the number of dead at 500 and the property loss probably exceeds $40,000,000. United States troops form a cordon around San Francisco, and while the populace is fleeing in panic no one is allowed to enter the city.

"A report from Oakland says an orphan asylum fell this afternoon, killing scores of children.

"Two ships at anchor in San Francisco bay have been sunk.

"The Palace Hotel, one of the finest on the Coast, is in flames, and the California and the Berkley Hotels have been demolished by dynamite. Flames are spreading and there is no water with which to fight them.

"There was another earthquake shock at 1.30 o'clock this afternoon, the extent of which has not been learned. As soon as the Postal Telegraph Company's building was vacated it was blown up with dynamite in the hope of checking the spread of the flames.

"General Funston, acting in co-operation with Mayor Schmitz, has ordered out the regulars and the streets of the city are being patrolled by armed troops, with orders to shoot down anyone caught robbing the dead and wounded or trying to break into buildings."

Santa Fe Bridge Settles.

Stockton, Cal., April 18.—A sharp earthquake shock was felt here at 5.13 o'clock this morning. The Santa Fe bridge over the San Joaquin river settled several inches. [illegible]

EARTHQUAKE AND FIRE RAVAGE SAN FRANCISCO

Two Hundred Persons Killed And Over One Thousand Wounded In The Greatest Catastrophe On Pacific Coast.

PROPERTY LOSS MAY EXCEED $200,000,000

Collapse Of Structure Started Flames Which Swept Over The Business Section—Many Handsome Buildings In Ruins—Flames Are Still Sweeping On Tnreatening The Whole City.

SUMMARY OF THE GREAT DISASTER

There were three shocks, the first at 5.13 A. M.

A large part of San Francisco destroyed by the earthquake and fire.

At least 200 persons have been killed.

It is estimated that over 1,000 persons were injured.

The property loss is placed at over $100,000,000.

Eight square miles of the city were reduced to ruins last night and the fire was still spreading.

Earthquake shocks broke the water mains, so that there were no means of combating the flames.

Dynamite was used to blow down structures, in the hope of checking the flames.

The entire business section along Market street, from Ninth to the water, was laid waste by the flames. Many of the finest buildings in the city were wrecked.

Only one building of the Leland Stanford University, at Palo Alto, withstood the shock, and two persons were killed.

Many buildings were destroyed in San Jose, 50 miles south of San Francisco, and from 15 to 20 persons were killed.

The State Insane Asylum at Agnew was reported wrecked and a number of the patients killed or injured.

The effect of the disturbance was felt all the way across the continent and was also noted in Austria.

Messages of sympathy soon began to pour in on Mayor Schmitz, with offers of aid from many cities, including Baltimore, Boston wiring $25,000.

The President ordered troops to the city for patrol duty, and tents for the homeless.

ENTIRE CITY IN DANGER

Flames Were Still Spreading At 10 O'Clock Last Night, Carrying Destruction.

San Francisco, April 18.—Earthquakes and fire today have put nearly half of San Francisco in ruins. At least 200 persons have been killed, 1,000 injured and the property loss will exceed $100,000,000.

At 10 P. M. tonight it looks as if the entire city would be burned. The Associated Press men are trying to get matter to Oakland by boat, but they are very uncertain. The Government is furnishing tugs, but the confusion is so great that they cannot be relied upon. It will be impossible to send full details for several days.

Thousands of people were fleeing to the hills tonight and clamoring for places on the ferryboats to cross the bay.

The damage was believed at 10 P. M. to have reached $200,000,000 and 50,000 persons are thought to be homeless.

OUTBREAK OF THE DISASTER.

Night added to the horror, and as darkness fell the sky was illuminated in all directions. As the flames spread into the residence districts people left their homes and fled to the parks and squares.

A series of rather severe earth shocks at 7 o'clock further increased the terror and many left homes that were not in danger.

Thousands are homeless and destitute and all day long streams of people have been fleeing from the stricken districts to places of safety.

It was 5.13 this morning when a terrific earthquake shock shook the whole city and surrounding country. One shock apparently lasted two minutes, and there was almost immediate collapse of flimsy structures all over the city. The water supply was cut off and when fires broke out in various sections there was nothing to do but let the buildings burn.

Telegraph and telephone communication was shut off for a time. The Western Union was put completely out of business and the Postal Company was the only company that managed to get a wire out of the city. About 10 o'clock even the Postal was forced to suspend. Electric power was stopped and street cars did not run. Railroads and ferryboats also ceased operations.

FIRES RAGING ALL DAY.

Fires have been raging all day and the Fire Department has been powerless to do anything except dynamite buildings threatened. All day long explosions have shaken the city and added to the terror of the inhabitants.

Following the first shock there was another within five minutes, but not nearly so severe. Three hours later there was another slight quake.

TOWNS AROUND BAY DAMAGED.

Santa Rosa, to the north, Napa, Vallejo and all towns around the bay are damaged. These reports, alarming as they were, created little interest in San Francisco, where the people were in a frantic state.

Today's experience has been a testimonial to the modern steel building. A score of these structures were in course of construction, and not one suffered from the earthquake shock. The completed modern buildings were also immune from harm from the seismic movements. The buildings that collapsed were all flimsy wooden and old brick structures. The damage by earthquake does not begin to compare with the loss by fire. The heart of the business quarter of San Francisco has been destroyed by fire.

EIGHT SQUARE MILES OF RUINS.

Fire has done the great damage. An area of thickly-covered ground of eight square miles has been burned over, and there is no telling when the fire will be under control.

Mayor Schmitz was about early and took measures for the relief and protection of the city. General Funston was quickly communicated with, and by 9 o'clock Federal soldiers were guarding the streets and assisting the firemen in dynamiting buildings.

FOUR LOOTERS SHOT.

General Funston realized that stern measures were necessary and gave orders that looters were to be shot at sight. Four men were summarily executed before 8 o'clock this afternoon. At a meeting of 50 citizens, called by the Mayor, it was announced that 1,400 tents would be pitched in Golden Gate Park and that arrangements had been made to feed the destitute in the public squares.

A finance committee, with James D. Phelan at the head, was appointed, and Mayor Schmitz was instructed to issue drafts for all funds needed by this committee.

A general meeting of the citizens' committee has been called for tomorrow morning.

The burnt district extends from the water front south of Market street to Market street and west to Eleventh street, north of Market. The fire extends out Hayes and McAllister streets, nearly to Fillmore, and from the water front along Market to Montgomery, and north from the water front to Montgomery street. Manufactories, hotels, wholesale houses and residences, comprising the principal part of the business quarter, have been destroyed.

HANDSOME BUILDINGS GONE.

The City Hall, a structure costing $7,000,000, was first wrecked by the earthquake and then destroyed by fire. The Palace Hotel, value estimated at $3,000,000, also burned.

The beautiful Claus Spreckels building, at Third and Market streets, was gutted. The Rialto building and dozens of other costly structures were also destroyed. The Hall of Justice is threatened and will undoubtedly go. The Examiner and the Call buildings are gone and the Crocker building, across the street from the Palace Hotel, is on fire.

No afternoon papers were issued and it is doubtful if the morning papers will appear. The Southern Pacific tracks are in such condition that only a crippled train service has been possible.

The Chronicle building and its new annex are still standing.

The dreadful earthquake shock came without warning at precisely 5.13 o'clock this morning, its motion apparently being from east to west. At first the upheaval of the earth was gradual, but in a few seconds it increased in intensity. Chimneys began to fall and buildings to crack, tottering on their foundations.

The people became panic-stricken and rushed into the streets, most of them in their night attire. They were met by showers of falling buildings, bricks, cornices and walls. Many were instantly crushed to death, while others were dreadfully mangled. Those who remained indoors generally escaped with their lives, though scores were hit by detached plaster, pictures and articles thrown to the floor by the shock. It is believed that more or less loss was sustained by nearly every family in the city.

The tall steel-frame structures stood the strain better than brick buildings, few of them being badly damaged. The big 11-story Monadnock office building, in course of construction, adjoining the Palace Hotel, was an exception, however, its rear wall collapsing and many cracks being made across its front. Some of the docks and freight sheds along the water front slid into the bay. Deep fissures opened in the filled-in ground near the shore and the Union Ferry Depot is injured. Its high tower still stands, but will have to be torn down.

PART OF CITY HALL DOWN.

A portion of the new City Hall, which cost over $7,000,000, collapsed, the roof sliding into the courtyard and smaller towers tumbling down. The great dome was moved, but did not fall.

The new postoffice, one of the finest in the United States, was badly shattered.

The Valencia Hotel, a four-story wooden building, sank into the basement, a pile of splintered timbers, under which were pinned many dead and dying occupants of the house. The basement was full of water and some of the helpless victims were drowned.

FIRE ADDS TO HORROR.

Scarcely had the earth ceased to shake when fires broke out simultaneously in many places. The fire department promptly responded to the first calls for aid, but it was found that the watermains had been rendered useless by the underground movement. Fanned by a light breeze, the flames quickly spread and soon many blocks were seen to be doomed. Then dynamite was resorted to and the sound of frequent explosions added to the terror of the people.

All efforts to stay the progress of the fire, however, proved futile. The south side of Market street, from Ninth street to the bay, was soon ablaze, the fire covering a belt two blocks wide. On this, the main thoroughfare of the city, are located many of the finest edifices in the city, including the Grant, Parrott, Flood, Call, Examiner and Monadnock buildings, the Palace and Grand Hotels and numerous wholesale houses.

At the same time the commercial establishments and banks north of Market street were burning. The business district in this section of the city extended from Sansome [illegible]

street to the water front and from Market street to Broadway. Fires also broke out in the Mission and the entire city seemed to be in flames.

1,000 MEN PATROL STREETS.

At 9 o'clock this morning 1,000 men from 1,000 strong, arrived from Angel Island a the Presidio arrived down town to patrol the city streets. The Thirteenth Infantry, little later and went on patrol duty. The soldiers have been ordered to shoot down thieves caught in the act of robbing the dead and to guard with their lives the millions of dollars' worth of property which has been placed in the streets that it may escape the ravages of the flames.

The First California Artillery, 200 strong, two companiees, has been detailed to patrol duty on Ellis street. Two more companies are patroling Broadway in the Italian section. The Ellis street contingent of guardsmen are under the command of Capt. G. A. Grattan. Capt. William A. Miller is commanding the forces on Broadway.

Mayor Schmitz, who has established his office at police headquarters, has named a committee of safety, comprising many prominent citizens.

Mayor Schmitz sent out word to the bakeries and milk stations throughout the city that their food supplies must be harbored for the homeless. Tents have been placed in every park in the city and those who have lost their homes will be given food and shelter.

The prisoners confined in the city prison on the fifth floor of the Hall of Justice were transferred in irons to the basement of the structure. Later they were removed to the Broadway Jail, and if necessity arises they will be taken to a branch county jail on the Mission road.

TO PAY INSURANCE.

Commissioner E. Myron Wolf announced at noon that the 80 odd fire insurance companies interested had decided to pay dollar for dollar to every one insured with them. The companies will not discriminate between fire and earthquake, and every one insured will be paid to the extent of the loss. Only two of the companies affected are Pacific Coast concerns, the others having principal offices in the East or in Europe, and all will stand the loss without danger of failure.

One of the first orders issued by Chief of Police Dinan was the closing every saloon in the city. This step was taken to prevent drink-crazed men from rioting in the city streets.

HELPED VICTIM TO DIE?

A. W. Hussey came to the station at the Hall of Justice this morning and told how, at the direction of a policeman whom he did not know, but whose star number he gave as 615, he had cut the arteries in the wrists of a man pinioned under timbers at the St. Katherine Hotel.

According to the statement made by Hussey, the man was begging to be killed and the policeman shot at him, but his aim was defective and the bullet went wide of the mark. The officer then handed Hussey a knife with instructions to cut the veins in the suffering man's wrists, and Hussey obeyed orders.

Chief of Police Dinan directed that Hussey be locked up. There has been no opportunity to investigate his story, but the police believe that the awful calamity rendered him insane and that the incident reported to them had no existence excepting in the imagination of the man who made the report.

COAL BUNKERS COLLAPSE.

The sheds over the Southern Pacific long wharf on San Francisco bay have completely collapsed. Many of the bunkers fell into the bay, carrying with them thousands of tons of coal. The long wharf was one of the most important shipping points about the bay, and freight traffic will be interrupted greatly.

As a result of the breaking of the mains of the Spring Valley Water Company the town of San Mateo was flooded. It was owing to the broken mains that the fire gained such headway in San Francisco. The town of San Rafael, despite its own troubles, dispatched fire-fighting apparatus to San Francisco.

The Metropolitan Opera Company, from New York, had just opened its season there and all the scenery and costumes were soon reduced to ashes. From the opera house the fire leaped from building to building, leveling them to the ground in quick succession. The Call editorial and mechanical departments were totally destroyed in a few minutes and the flames leaped across Stevenson street toward the 15-story stone-and-iron Claus Spreckels Building, which, with its lofty dome, is the most notable edifice in San Francisco. Two small wooden buildings furnished fuel to ignite the splendid pile. Thousands of people watched the flames licking the stone walls.

At first no impression was made, but suddenly there was a cracking of glass and an entrance was effected. The inner furnishings of the fourth floor were the first to go. Then, as if by magic, smoke issued from the top of the dome. This was followed by a most spectacular illumination. The round windows of the dome shone like so many full moons; then long, waving streamers of flames burst forth. Women wrung their hands and wept, saying: "It is so terrible."

The tall and slender structure, which had withstood the forces of the earth, appeared doomed to fall before the fire. But after a time the light grew less intense, and the flames, finding nothing to consume, deid out, leaving the building standing, but completely gutted.

PALACE HOTEL THREATENED.

The Palace Hotel, the rear of which was constantly threatened, was the scene of much excitement, the guests leaving in haste, many with only the clothing they wore. Finding that the hotel was not in present danger, many returned and made arragements for the removal of their belogings, though little could be taken away owing to the utter absence of transportation facilities.

The Parrott Building, in which were located the chambers of the State Supreme Court, the lower floors being devoted to an immense department store, was ruined, though its massive walls were not all destroyed. A little farther down Market street the Academy of Sciences, the Jennie Flood Building and the History Building kindled and burned like so much tinder. Sparks carried across the wide street ignited the Phelan Building, and the army headquarters of California, General Funston commanding, were burned.

Nearing the bay, the waters of which did the firemen good service along the docks, the fire took the Rialto Building, a handsome skyscraper, and converted scores of solid business blocks into smoldering piles of bricks.

Banks and commercial houses supposed to be fireproof, though not of modern build, burned quickly, and the roar of the flames could be heard even on the hills which were out of the danger zone. Here many thousands of persons congregated and viewed the awful scene. Great sheets of flames rose high in the heavens or rushed down some narrow street, joining midway between the sidewalks.

HOTELS AND THEATRES.

All efforts to prevent the fire from reaching the Palace and Grand Hotels were unsuccessful, and both were completely destroyed, together with all their contents.

All of San Francisco's best playhouses, including the Majestic, Columbia, Orpheum and Grand Opera House, are masses of ruins. The earthquake demolished them for all practical purposes and the fire completed the work of demolition. The handsome Rialto and Casserly buildings were burned to the ground, as was everything in that district.

The scene at the Mechanics Pavilion during the early hours of the morning and until noon, when all the injured and dead were removed because of the threatened destruction of the building by fire, was one of indescribable sadness. Sisters, brothers, wives and sweethearts searched eagerly for some missing dear one. Thousands of persons hurriedly went through the buildings inspecting the cots on which the sufferers lay, in the hope that they would find some loved one that was missing.

FIRE DROVE OUT INJURED.

The dead were placed in one portion of the building and the remainder was devoted to hospital purposes. After the fire forced the nurses and physicians to desert the building the eager crowds followed them to the Presidio and the Children's Hospital, where they renewed their search for missing relatives.

Up to a late hour this afternoon more than 750 persons who were seriously injured by the earthquake and the fire had been treated at the various hospitals throughout the city.

The front of the Bailey and La Coste Building, on Clay street, near Montgomery, fell in and three men and seven horses were killed.

Captain Gleason, of the Police Department, was severely injured at noon today by falling tiling.

The stereotypers and the pressmen of the Examiner and the Call, as soon as the shock was felt, rushed out of their buildings and found that the coffee house at Stevenson and Third streets had collapsed. They immediately set to work with axes and other implements to rescue those inside.

From the Cliff House comes word that the great pleasure resort and show place of the city, which stood upon a foundation of solid rock, has been swept into the sea. Not a thing stands to tell where the monster stone building once stood. It has been leveled to the foundation, and only the rock lining the seacoast remains intact.

One of the big losses of the day was the destruction of St. Ignatius' Church and College, at Van Ness avenue and Hayes street. This was the greatest Jesuitical institution in the West and was built at a cost of a couple of millions.

At 7 tonight the fire had swept from the south side of the town across Market street into the Western addition and was burning houses at Golden Gate avenue and Octavia street. This result was reached after almost the entire southern district from Ninth street to the eastern water front had been converted into a blackened waste. In this quarter were hundreds of factories, wholesale houses and many business firms, in addition to thousands of homes.

On the North Side the fire tonight was not making such rapid headway as in the Western addition.

The firemen are making desperate efforts to prevent the enlargement of the devastation. Temporary headquarters were established in tents in Portsmouth Square this evening for Mayor Schmitz, Chief of Police Dinan and General Funston, but this site became too dangerous about 6 o'clock and was abandoned. Later the flames swept the square.

AGNEW ASYLUM WRECKED.

Supervisor Fred Horner, of Oakland, who returned from San Jose this afternoon, states that the Agnew Asylum, near that city, is a total wreck; that many of the inmates were killed and that the remainder are running around loose, terrorizing the community.

The superintendent of the institution and his wife were both killed.

In Oakland five persons were killed by the collapse of the Empire Building. The Gore block, at the junction of Market and Pine streets, is in flames and probably will be a total loss.

The Santa Fe roundhouse and machine shops at Point Richmond, across the bay, have collapsed.

The greatest destruction occurred in that part of the city which was reclaimed from San Francisco bay. Much of the devastated district was at one time low, marshy ground, covered by water at high tide. As the city grew it became necessary to fill in many places of this low ground in order to reach deep water. The Merchants' Exchange building, a 14-story steel structure, was situated on the edge of this reclaimed ground. It had just been completed and the executive offices of the Southern Pacific Company occupied the greater part of the building.

NOB HILL SLIGHTLY HIT.

The damage by the earthquake to the residence portion of the city, the finest part of which is on Nob Hill and Pacific Heights, seems to have been slight. On Nob Hill are the residences of many of the millionaires who in the early seventies became wealthy through mining investments or the construction of the Central Pacific Railroad. They include the Stanfords, Huntingtons, Hopkins, Crockers, Floods and others.

The magnificent Fairmount Hotel, not yet completed, stands on the brink of Nob Hill, overlooking the bay. The hotel was not seriously damaged. The construction of the hotel was started by Mrs. Herman Oelrichs, of New York, as a monument to her father, United States Senator James Fair, but she recently sold it for $3,000,000.

To the westward of Nob Hill, on Pacific Heights, are many fine new residences, but little injury was done to any of them.

SOME NOTABLE BUILDINGS.

The Palace Hotel was a seven-story building, about 300 feet square. It was built 30 years ago by the late Senator Sharon, whose estate was in the courts for many years. At the time it was erected the Palace Hotel was the best-equipped hotel in the West.

The offices of three morning papers, the [illegible]

(Continued on Page [illegible])

Fair Tomorrow

THE EVENING SUN

Last Edition

VOLUME II—NO. 18. 12 PAGES BALTIMORE, MONDAY, NOVEMBER 7, 1910. PRICE ONE CENT

LATHAM'S ALL-OVER-BALTIMORE FLIGHT THE MOST SPECTACULAR IN THE HISTORY OF AVIATION—FULL PARTICULARS ON 12TH PAGE

ADVERTISING TALKS

WRITTEN BY
WILLIAM C. FREEMAN

I get many good suggestions from readers of these Advertising Talks, most of whom are not engaged in any branch of the advertising business.

W. B. WINSTOCK, of the advertising department of the Evening Bulletin, of Philadelphia, wrote to me the other day as follows:

"One thought that I have always had in mind regarding advertising is that millions of dollars each year are absolutely thrown to the winds because of lack of sound and HONEST ADVICE TO THE PROSPECTIVE ADVERTISER.

"For instance, a prospect comes along and wants to come into a campaign of advertising—we'll say general advertising. The first thing I ask him is:

"'Is your business ripe for advertising at this time? Have you the proper DISTRIBUTION? CAN YOU BACK UP YOUR ADVERTISING? Can you afford to go into a STEADY, PERSISTENT CAMPAIGN? Is your organization right? ARE YOU READY TO SPEND MONEY AND GET RESULTS ON THE SLOW PROCESS?'

"Eight out of every ten are not ready — not organized right — distribution poor — and when I find these conditions I very strongly discourage the advertiser from entering a campaign until he is ready in every detail.

"I strongly impress upon him the importance of this and by this method save him from wasting his money and also save publicity from being damned forever. In many cases the prospect becomes a future advertiser and prospers.

"I have been working along these lines for fifteen years. THIS POLICY HAS WON OUT BIG FOR THE ADVERTISER and has been the source of great satisfacton to me.

"If this idea were to be followed by publishers, solicitors, agents and those who handle appropriations, the advertising world would be the better for it."

I do not know Mr. Winstock, but I'll wager he is a good advertising man — A CREATOR OF BUSINESS.

Men of his type are needed in the advertising end of publications as well as in all other branches of advertising. These men are not solicitor's, they are advertising creators.

There seems to be a new era in the relationship of the buyer, the seller, the planner and the writer of advertisements, which is good for the business and which is making it such a GREAT FORCE today.

(To be continued.)

This Is The Day!

DR. CRIPPEN GETS 15-DAY RESPITE

Hanging Postponed Until November 23 By Home Office.

SUBSTITUTE OFFERS TO DIE

Crippen Thinks Something May Yet Save His Life—Belle Elmore Reward Not Responsible.

London, Nov. 7.—The date for the execution by hanging of Dr. H. H. Crippen, murderer of his wife, Belle Elmore, the music-hall singer, was today postponed for two weeks or more. Though no definite date has been set, it is probable Crippen will die on Wednesday, November 23. The date originally fixed was tomorrow.

Crippen Happy.

Crippen was overjoyed when the High Sheriff informed him of the postponement.

"I believe that something will yet intervene to prove my innocence," he declared.

The condemned man was cautioned against letting his hopes mount too high.

Offers His Life For Crippen.

After the news of Crippen's stay of execution became public an elderly, unidentified man appeared at the Cambridge Police Court and requested that he be allowed to hang in place of Dr. Crippen, urging that the professional skill of the latter would prove a blessing to humanity, whereas he himself was of no value to the world. The man displayed eccentricities and his sanity will probably be investigated.

The postponement was ordered officially by the Home Office, which is taken by many to indicate that Home Secretary Winston Churchill will at least give the case a thorough hearing before he allows Crippen to go to the gallows.

Later in the day it was semi-officially announced that the execution would take place on Wednesday, November 23, unless the Home Secretary shall decide to grant a commutation or pardon to the wife-murderer.

Philadelphia Rumor Not Responsible.

At Scotland Yard it was said that the postponement of the execution had nothing to do with the Philadelphia report that Mrs. Crippen is alive and hiding as the result of a fiendish plot to send her husband to death. The authorities declared that they had not heard of the rumor, nor had they heard of the offer of Dr. Munyon, the Philadelphia patent-medicine manufacturer, to pay $50,000 for information leading to the discovery of Belle Elmore alive.

Churchill Not Likely To Interfere.

Solicitor Newton, who has represented Crippen ever since the latter was arrested at Feather Point, Quebec, is busily engaged with the other lawyers in drafting a petition to Home Secretary Winston Churchill asking either that he grant an unconditional pardon to Crippen or that he commute the sentence to life imprisonment. Acting in the King's name, the Home Secretary is now the only official who has the power to save Crippen from the gallows. While it is believed Secretary Churchill will investigate the case thoroughly, it is hardly likely he will interfere to save the prisoner. It is against precedent in England for the Home Secretary to intervene when a jury has found a prisoner It is against precedent in England for the Home Secretary to intervene when a jury has found a prisoner guilty and the Court of Criminal Appeal has sustained the verdict. Unless, therefore, Crippen's lawyers can bring to light a great deal of hitherto unrevealed evidence it is believed the American will die on November 23.

Crippen was allowed two Sundays between his original trial and the date first fixed.

United States Will Not Interfere.

Washington, Nov. 7.—Relieved of the necessity of immediate action by the postponement of the hanging of Dr. H. H. Crippen for two weeks, the State Department will probably suggest that any evidence that Belle Elmore Crippen, his supposed victim, is still alive, as reported by Francis Tracy Tobin, a Philadelphia lawyer, be laid before the British Consul at Philadelphia. The department does not consider it necessary to interfere. It is regarded solely as a mater for the consideration of the British authorities. If the evidence that she is alive is sufficient it is for them to make a search for her, or to determine, through persons who, as Mr. Tobin asserts, have communicated with her since the hunt for Crippen began, whether the woman is still alive.

Bonfires On Election Nights
PROHIBITED.
OFFICE OF THE
BOARD OF POLICE COMMISSIONERS.
BALTIMORE, MD., Oct. 21, 1910.

Heretofore from time to time fires have been built in the streets on election nights, and prior to elections boys have been in the habit of collecting boxes, barrels, etc., and resorting on the night of election to tearing down fences as well as other depredations to secure material for these fires, all of which is not only against the law, but dangerous and reprehensible. The police will exercise the strictest vigilance to prevent these practices and arrest all offenders, but the Board feels that the citizens can and ought to co-operate with the police to stop them by exercising their authority in their homes and their influence generally against such infractions of the law.

The Board therefore takes this means of bringing the matter to the attention of citizens, and asks their aid in the enforcement of the law.

JOHN B. A. WHELTLE,
C. BAKER CLOTWORTHY,
PETER E. TOME,
Police Commissioners.

NOTICE!
AS TO SELLING OR FURNISHING INTOXICATING LIQUORS ON ELECTION DAY.
OFFICE OF THE
BOARD OF POLICE COMMISSIONERS.
BALTIMORE, MD., Oct. 21, 1910.

In connection with the election to be held in Baltimore city on Tuesday, November 8, 1910, the Board of Police Commissioners directs the attention of all keepers of places where intoxicating liquors are sold to the provisions of Sections 682 and 685 of Article 4, Public Local Laws (Charter), which forbid the selling or furnishing of intoxicating liquor to any person on any days upon which elections are required by law to be held, under penalty of fine from $100 to $500 for first offense, revocation of license and fine of $500 to $1,000 or imprisonment in jail or House of Correction three to twelve months, or both, for second offense.

Note—"Election Day" means from midnight of the previous day to midnight of the day on which election is held.

JOHN B. A. WHELTLE,
C. BAKER CLOTWORTHY,
PETER E. TOME,
Police Commissioners.

TWO DEATHS IN HAGERSTOWN

Former Justice Garver, 66, And William Bakers, 67 Years Old.

[Special Dispatch to The Evening Sun.]

Hagerstown, Md., Nov. 7.—Former Justice of the Peace Daniel H. Garver, aged 66 years, died suddenly of Bright's disease last night at his home, South Mulberry street. He taught school in Cavetown and Hagerstown for about 30 years. He was a member of the Lutheran Church and a staunch Democrat. Born, near Smithsburg, he married Miss Jennie Beard, daughter of the late Nicholas Beard, of Chewsville.

Surviving are his widow and six children, including Edward S. Garver, of the auditor's department of the Pennsylvania Railroad at Philadelphia. He was a step-brother of Rev. Edward Smith, pastor of the Smithsburg Methodist Church.

William H. Baker, aged 67 years, died yesterday evening at his home, West Church street, of internal injuries sustained in a fall received at the Hagerstown Woodenware Factory last Tuesday. He formerly resided at Sharpsburg and was a member of the Lutheran Church His widow and two children survive.

THIRTY MEN ARE LASHED TO MAST

Rescuers Lining Dover Coast Unable To Reach Them.

LARGEST SAILING SHIP BUILT

Steering Gear Disabled In Collision, Schooner Preussen Drifts On The Rocks.

Dover, England, Nov. 7.—Within a stone's throw of safety, 30 members of the crew of the five-masted steel schooner Preussen, the largest sailing vessel in the world, are lashed to the rigging of the ship today, while great waves wash over them and threaten any moment to drown them.

Lifeboats and staunch sea-going tugs, braving the gale, are hovering nearby, but would be dashed to pieces if they attempted to go alongside. The storm shows no signs of abating. It is not believed the men can hold on much longer. Along the shore thousands of persons have gathered to watch the dramatic scene, and though every man is willing to risk his life to save the imperiled mariners not one can turn a hand.

The Preussen, a German-owned vessel, early Sunday collided in the channel with the steamship Brighton. Neither ship seemed seriously damage, the Brighton making port under her own steam.

Life Lines Failed To Catch.

Nothing further was heard of the Preussen, until she was dashed on the rocks at South Foreland, and it is surmised that her steering gear was disabled by the collision. For hours tugs and tiny lifeboats braved the storm in an effort to take off the crew. Lifelines were fired from the shore, but for some unaccountable reason the crew failed to make them fast.

Exposed For Thirty Hours.

From the shore the sailors can be seen clinging to the rigging, with waves breaking over them. They have been in this exposed position for 30 hours and it is not believed they can stick much longer.

The Preussen was built in 1902 and was the largest and fastest sailing ship afloat.

NO MOOSE, BUT THREE DEER

Two Oakland Men Return From A Trip To Maine Woods.

[Special Dispatch to The Evening Sun.]

Oakland, Md., Nov. 7.—Paul Naylor and Ralph Weber, who spent upward of a month in the Maine woods on a hunting trip, have returned to Oakland. They failed to land a moose, but they did bag three good-sized deer, two of which were shipped to Oakland by express.

E. Ford Bechtol, of Berkeley Springs, W. Va., killed a fine, three-pronged buck while hunting in Persley mountain, in Morgan county, W. Va.

R. D. Fisher and William Hovermale each bagged a fine young turkey while on hunting trips. Hovermale's weighed 10 pounds.

J. C. Barton, Harry Kellar, Roy Witter and Harvey Carmack each bagged a wild turkey while hunting in the mountains of Fulton county, north of Hancock.

FISH FOR ANTIETAM CREEK

Fifteen Cans Emptied Into Stream Near Waynesboro.

[Special Dispatch to The Evening Sun.]

Waynesboro, Pa., Nov. 7.—Fifteen cans of brook trout were received Saturday from the Government hatcheries at Washington, for stocking the streams in the vicinity of Waynesboro.

The fish are of good size and were placed in the Antietam creek near Welty's mill.

FIRST FREIGHT BY AEROPLANE

Consignment Of Silk Carried From Dayton To Columbus.

PARMALEE MAKES 52 MILES

Leaves At 10.40 And Arrives With Cargo At 11.50—Average Height, 1,000 Feet.

Columbus, Ohio, Nov. 7.—Aviator Parmalee landed here at the Driving Park at 11.50 today, after a 52-mile cross-country flight from Dayton in a Wright biplane, carrying a consignment of silk from a Dayton firm to the Morehouse-Martens Company, of this city. He maintained an altitude of 1,000 feet during the flight. He left Dayton at 10.40.

$2,000,000 INHERITANCE TAX

Queer Fight Started In Supreme Court By Mr. Wickersham.

Washington, Nov. 7.—A queer tangle is involved in proceedings urged by Attorney-General Wickersham in the Supreme Court of the United States today to prevent persons who paid over $2,000,000 as inheritance taxes from recovering the money from the United States Treasury.

Eight claimants have judgments to the amount of $350,000 rendered in their favor by United States Circuit Courts, and one of the questions now at issue is whether an expired time limit will bar the Government from getting a Supreme Court review of the judgments. The Department of Justice years ago tried hard enough to obtain such a review, but was balked by a deadlock among the justices of the Supreme Court.

In 1906 a motion was filed to have the Supreme Court review a Circuit Court judgment in favor of a tax claimant. The judges split evenly, and so were obliged to affirm the judgment of the lower court. In two similar cases occurring afterward the Government attempted to get into the Supreme Court, but failed because of the continued deadlock.

This prevented a decision by the highest court, and so the Government refused to pay the judgments declared by the Circuit Courts. The money remained in the treasury and the attorneys-general watched for a chance to get a test case into the Supreme Court.

One Case Slips Through.

Attorney-General Wickersham finally accomplished the feat, and just before the close of the last term of the Supreme Court a decision was announced favorable to the Government.

Thus that single case was safely disposed of, but there were eight claimants who still held their judgments for $350,000 against the Government. They will argue in court that motions to get such cases as these tax suits into the Supreme Court must be made within a year after the judgment is entered in the lower court. More than 12 months have passed since six of the eight cases were decided.

Time Limit Denied.

Mr. Wickersham, in a new brief, quoted authorities to show that the Supreme Court was not bound by a one-year limit. He said also that unless those judgments were reversed the Government would lose $2,600,000, the amount due in similar cases that were not taken into court, but would be governed by action on those that were contested.

WOMAN IMPALED ON FENCE

Invalid Falls From House Top, Where She Sought Fresh Air.

New York, Nov. 7.—Mrs. Helen M. Post, 78 years old, fell from the roof of the Corona, a four-story apartment building at 159 and 161 Willoughby avenue, Brooklyn, yesterday, and was killed. Her body was impaled on a picket fence in the front of the building.

1,000 MORE MEN JOIN THE STRIKERS

Decisive Action To Be Taken At Mass-Meeting Today.

ONE UNION LEADER MAY DIE

Valentine Hoffman, Stricken With Paralysis From Overwork, In Critical Condition.

New York, Nov. 7.—The joint executive council of the local unions affiliated with the International Brotherhood of Teamsters went into session today determined to force peace with the big express companies or tie up every wheel in the greater city and surrounding towns.

One Thousand More Go Out.

As an earnest of what may be expected, 1,000 drivers of taxicabs and more than half of the delivery wagon drivers employed by Park and Tilford did not report for work this morning. Other drivers were ordered to hold themselves in readiness for the word to quit. The fight of the men is being directed by Samuel Gompers, head of the American Federation of Labor, who has established headquarters in the Hotel Victoria.

Situation Very Dangerous.

Not in years has this city faced a situation so fraught with danger as at present. If a general strike is ordered, the first place to be tied up will be the big coal-delivery yards. These supply the coal which keeps the big downtown skyscrapers with the fuel for running elevators and heating purposes. Incidentally the coal-wagon drivers are a hardy bunch that can be depended on to pull strike-breakers from wagons. The delivery-wagon drivers, drivers of mail and city garbage and ash collecting wagons are all well organized and can be ordered out on signal.

The strike of the taxicab chauffeurs was decided on to enforce closed-shops conditions. There are 3,000 union chauffeurs in the city, but those called out were only the ones employed by concerns that do not recognize the union. Police guards have been sent to all of the garages to prevent disorder.

Dodging Gaynor's Orders.

The express wagons of the big companies were moving through the city today with inscriptions tacked on them reading:

"This wagon is engaged in Interstate Commerce only." Through this this sign the companies planned to get around the decision of the city authorities that every driver must have a city license. Incidentally it was said that the express companies expected in case of violence to call on the Federal Government for protection.

Daniel J. Tobin, president of the International Brotherhood of Teamsters, said just before he entered the conference of the leaders that he considered the situation serious. He said that he had done all in his power to arrange an amicable settlement, but that the officers of the express companies did not seem inclined to make any concession whatever to the men. While refusing to admit that the outcome of the conference will be a general strike, Tobin's attitude indicated that he expects nothing else.

Hoffman May Die.

The condition of Valentine Hoffman, leader of the local strike, who was stricken with paralysis, was reported to be serious today. The attending physician said that his attack was due to overwork in connection with the strike.

INFANTILE PARALYSIS FATAL

Judge's Daughter Fourth Victim Within Ten Days.

Logansport, Ind., Nov. 7.—Marie Rosana Myers, youngest daughter of Supreme Court Judge Quincy Myers, is dead today, the fourth victim of infantile paralysis to die here within the last ten days. She had been sick only since last Tuesday. There are ten other cases of infantile paralysis in this city.

DR. COOK READY TO PROVE CLAIMS

Letter Sent From London Says Data Has Been Completed.

WAS THE POLE DISCOVERED?

Eskimos Claim Neither Peary Nor Cook Came Within 100 Miles Of Earth Top.

New York, Nov. 7.—That Dr. Frederick A. Cook has finally decided to emerge from his "retreat" and press his claims as the real discoverer of the North Pole was learned today when Capt. B. S. Osbon, one of his closest friends, received a letter from him stating that he is finally about ready to "prove his case."

The letter was dater London, England, October 16, and in it Dr. Cook said that he has almost completed his letters and original data for submission to the scientific societies.

In discussing the Knud Rasmussen report from Greenland, that Rasmussen has interviewed the Cook and Peary Eskimos and has concluded that neither Cook nor Peary reached a point within 199 miles of the pole, Captain Osbon said today:

Eskimos' Testimony Reliable.

"Of course, there can be no question that those hardy natives of the North are capable of making astronomical observations and did make them, and thus can positively say how far north both Cook and Peary went. In Dr. Cook's letter to me he says: 'My case will eventually rest on its own merits without reference to rival interests.

"When the data and maps of Dr. Cook are compiled and published, as they will be very soon, they will convince the world that Dr. Frederick A. Cook is not in the least disturbed by the yarns handed out from time to time for the purpose of discrediting claims which he will give to the world at large in the very near future."

FIGHT MARYLAND LEATHER

Eight Concerns Make Complaint Against "Discrimintaion."

Washington, Nov. 7.—Led by the United States Leather Company, seven other big leather concerns today joined in a complaint against the raise in freight rates before the Interstate Commerce Commission today.

The complaint is against several hundred railroads and water lines. It is charged that these carriers, by joint and concerted action improperly to increase their revenue, raised the rates on leather from 2 to 5 cents a hundred pounds in September. The commission is asked to suspend this raise and by investigation to ascertain what would be a reasonable rate.

One plea of the big leather concerns is that while the rates were raised on them no change was made in rates on the product of their competitors in Virginia, West Virginia, Maryland and Pennsylvania.

OPERATOR BADLY BURNED

Coal-Oil Lamp Explodes In His Office.

[Special Dispatch to The Evening Sun.]

Hagerstown, Md., Nov. 7.—Edwin Biershing, of Hagerstown, telegraph operator at Mason and Dixon, was seriously injured by the explosion of a kerosene lamp. In a few minutes the interior of the room was on fire. In his efforts to extinguish the blaze Biershing's clothes caught fire and he was badly burned about the hands and arms.

He finally succeeded in extinguishing the fire with chemical extinguishers.

LAST CALL FOR BATTLE OF BALLOTS

Tennessee The One Dark Cloud On Democratic Horizon.

EXPECT EIGHT NEW SENATORS

Time Of First Election Returns, Congress Uncertain Till Next Day—Money Is Scarce.

[From a Staff Correspondent.]

Washington, Nov. 7.—According to Democratic hopes and beliefs Tennessee is the only dark spot on the political map for the party.

In the claims for the elections tomorrow the Democrats do not concede, however, that the Republicans will win the Governorship in that State, but owing to the unfortunate and unavoidable conditions down there it is feared the result may show that the Republicans and Indepedents who have fused on the head of the ticket will pull Captain Hooper through.

Should this happen it will be the first defeat for Senator Taylor at the polls in Tennessee.

The embarrassing situation is generally charged, of course, to the record and acts of Governor Patterson, and on account of the stand he took earlier in the year it may be that no power can now elect even so universally popular a man as Senator "Bob" Taylor.

If he fails to connect on the Governorship, it is believed this will not cause the loss of the State to the Democrats so far as the other offices are concerned, and the usual number of Democratic Congressmen are confidently counted on.

May Oust Eight Republican Senators.

A private letter has been received here from a Democratic Senator who is regarded as one of the best-posted men in the party. From information he has been getting he predicts that the Democrats at large will in all probability control sufficient Legislatures to be elected tomorrow to enable them to retire no fewer than eight Republican Senators. They are the Legislatures of Missouri, Nevada, Montana, Indiana, Ohio, Delaware, New York and New Jersey.

The Senator also thinks there is an even chance that the Republicans will lose Nebraska, and if this proves true Gilbert M. Hitchcock will succeed E. J. Burkett, the present Senator from that State.

Not Sure Of Landslide.

Should there be a landslide tomorrow in favor of the Democrats that anywhere approaches that of 20 years ago it will be pretty safe to reckon early in the evening when the returns come rolling in that possibly a few more of the States have gone Democratic and are apt to elect Democratic Senators. But really with the information at hand in advance of the rain of ballots the Democrats have not felt warranted in claiming they are likely to retire more than eight or nine Republican Senators.

"Slaughter Of Governors."

Some of the Democratic prophets look for a slaughter of Republican candidates for Governors of States tomorrow that will equal the reverses in this respect that the Republicans had in the landslide of 1882, when the country went Democratic from one end of the Union to the other, and when even the late Ben Butler on a Democratic ticket swept Massachusetts.

"Bill Nye's" Lament.

Bill Nye, the humorist, was then living and was editor of the Laramie Boomerang out in Wyoming. Bill was an ardent Republican, but his party's defeat did not knock the sense of humor out of him, for his leading editorial the next day started off about like this:

"We have met the enemy and we are 'his'n.' With a plug hat bet on Wyoming, a pair of boots on Colorado, an overcoat on New York and a suit of clothes on Massachusetts it begins to look as if we, during the coming winter, will be wrapped in deep meditation and a bed quilt."

Ohio Somewhat Improved.

Latest advices are that the situation has improved some for the Republicans in Ohio, due to the earnest appeals made to the votes to save President Taft's State in order to prevent the Administration from getting a black eye, but all the signs still point to a Democratic victory in Ohio.

Champ Clark To Win.

The Republicans appear to believe there is a slight hope that Champ Clark may be beaten in his district for Congress. They have been crowding the House minority leader, but if Clark should be left in the race it would be about the greatest surprise of the campaign. It is believed that Clark's prospect of being Speaker of the House will pull him through, although on account of things that have been sprung on him and the amount of political trickery going on, it is probable that his majority will be cut down.

BOLD BANK ROBBERY

Safe Blown Open, $4,000 Stolen; Sheriff 100 Feet Away.

Toledo, Ohio, Nov. 7.—The vault of the Home Savings Bank at Metamora, 22 miles west of here, was blown open early today by four yeggs, who escaped with $4,000 in currency.

The robbery was executed under the eyes of Deputy Sheriff Wheeler, who, with a companion, stood 100 feet from the bank while the yeggs blew off the vault door. Wheeler could get only one man to come to his assistance, and made no attempt to attack the robbers until they came out of the building with their loot. A score of shots were fired, but no one was hit.

THE EVENING SUN

Last Edition
Showers--Warmer

VOLUME IV—NO. 154. | PRESS RUN SATURDAY, M'n'g...90,563 Ev'g...37,414 (127,977 | SAME DAY 1911, M'n'g...84,862 Ev'g...33,329 | BALTIMORE, MONDAY, APRIL 15, 1912. | 14 PAGES | PRICE ONE CENT

ALL TITANIC PASSENGERS ARE SAFE; TRANSFERRED IN LIFEBOATS AT SEA

PARISIAN AND CARPATHIA TAKE HUMAN CARGO

Steamship Virginian Now Towing Great Disabled Liner Into Halifax

ALL DOUBT AS TO STEAMER REACHING PORT SET AT REST

Wireless Messages State That No Lives Have Been Lost On The Damaged Vessel.

Canso, N. S., April 15.—The White Star liner Titanic, having transferred her passengers to the Parisian and Carpathia, was at 2 o'clock this afternoon being towed to Halifax by the Virginian, of the Allan Line.

The Virginian passed a line to the Titanic as soon as the passengers had been transferred, and the latest word received by wireless was that there was no doubt that the new White Star liner would reach port.

Agents of the White Star Line at Halifax have been ordered to have wrecking tugs sent out to aid the Virginian with her tow into port.

Montreal, April 15.—A message to the Montreal Star, from its correspondent at St. Johns, N. B., at 1.15, says that the Titanic is being towed toward port by the Allan liner Virginian. This followed a report that the Titanic had sunk, and it was explained that the wireless operator misread a message saying the Titanic was being towed, interpreting it to mean that she had sunk.

New York, April 15.—Wireless dispatches from Capt. H. J. Haddock, of the White Star liner Olympic, say that 20 boatloads of passengers have been taken from the sinking Titanic by the Carpatha, of the Cunard line, and that others have been taken off by the Allen liner Parisian.

The Parisian and Carpathia are standing by the Titanic, and the Baltic was reported as approaching by the Olympic's captain.

A second dispatch said the Virginian had passed a line to the Titanic and will tow her to Halifax.

This information came direct to the local office of the White Star Line, and Vice-President Franklin in making it public declared that he personally had no doubt that the Titanic would be safely towed to port. He declared that she has plenty of watertight compartments and that, while she may sink several feet because of weight of water in the forward compartments and the necessity of trimming ship, she will not go down.

Conflicting statements regarding the final disposal of the passengers of the Titanic are made in different dispatches. One statement is that they will be brought to New York on special trains and another that they will be retransferred to the Baltic.

First News Of Accident.

The position of the Titanic when she was last heard from was 41.46 north; 50.14 west. The first news of the accident was received by wireless operator at Cape Race. It said:

"Have struck an iceberg; we are badly damaged. Rush aid."

Within half an hour the Virginian, of the Allan Line, had been communicated with, and her captain was headed directly to the scene. Shortly afterward the Virginian sent the following to her local agents:

"Titantic says she is badly damaged as result of striking an iceberg. She demands immediate assistance, and we are rushing to her help."

From time to time other wireless advices was received. In each it was stated that the Titanic was still in touch and it was not until 12.37 o'clock that the Virginian reported she had lost the Titanic.

Throughout this morning the White Star offices here were besieged by friends of passengers on the big liner who wanted definite information. The telephones were kept busy with inquiries. To all the White Star officials extended assurances that the vessel was afloat and that the passengers were not in danger.

The Titanic was scheduled to sail from New York on her return trip on next Saturday, and so great was the desire to travel on the new vessel that 600 bookings had been made in the first cabin.

CAPT. E.J. SMITH

400 FT. ICEBERG

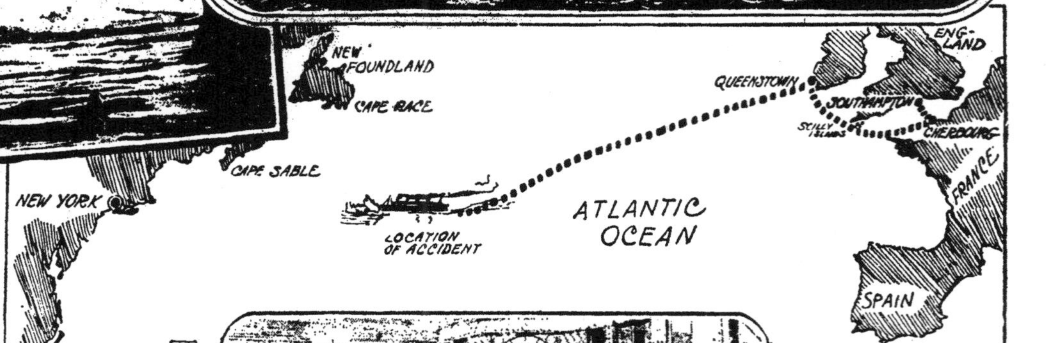

WRECK OF TITANIC IS UNPARALLELED

Halifax, N. S., April 15.—Held afloat only by her watertight compartments, the great White Star liner Titanic is slowly crawling toward this harbor.

Her passengers have been taken off to other vessels. They are to be again transferred to the Baltic, of the White Star Line this afternoon.

The Baltic will take them to their journey's end in New York, where they are due next Thursday.

The disaster to the Titanic was unparalleled in the history of navigation. The largest, most luxurious and best-appointed vessel ever laid down, she seemed proof against any disaster, and it is to the very fact that she was a new steamer that the passengers on board—noted financiers and society leaders—owe their lives.

Hardly Any Other Vessel Could Have Stood Shock.

Hardly another craft afloat could have withstood the terrific shock when the Titanic, driving along at better than half speed, although in the midst of ice fields, crashed bow on, into a great submerged mountain of ice which tore away her steel plates.

Only meagre advices regarding the wreck have been received here by the wireless, and these fail to clear up how the accident took place, or whether there was a panic among the passengers.

That Captain Smith, admiral of the White Star's fleet, and in command of this latest ocean creation, realized the danger was shown by an immediate appeal for aid. The wireless of the Titanic picked up the Cape Race station and immediate aid was demanded. The Allan Liner Virginian was the first to be reached, but almost before she had turned her prow toward the wounded leviathan other craft had started on the same errand.

Waiting And Great Alarm.

Then came a cruel waiting time, punctuated with brief wireless messages that caused the utmost alarm.

"Hurry! Hurry!" was the burden of every word that came flashing through the air, but it was plain from the start that the badly needed aid must come from the steamers that were in the immediate vicinity.

Finally word came that the situation on board the Titanic was so serious that the women and children had been placed in the lifeboats and that they were ready to be transshipped, as the steamer was certain to sink. Captain Smith told the steamers that were headed toward him that he was working his pumps to capacity and believed he could keep afloat, although the danger was very grave.

Wireless Suddenly Ceases.

After this word all communication with the Titanic and the Virginian was cut off. This was due to the atmospheric conditions, although for a time it was feared the liner might have sunk so low her motors had been crippled. It developed, however, that there were reserve motors and storage batteries for the wireless, and when this became known some apprehension was relieved. Finally at 8.30 a brief wireless stating that the Titanic was still afloat and proceeding slowly under her own steam was picked up. Then came word that the Cunard liner Carpathia, the Allan liners Parisian and the Virginian were "standing by" and that the Baltic was coming up fast.

Another brief and fragmentary wireless followed telling that the transhipment of the Titanic's passengers had been begun. The first boatloads were rowed to the Carpathia. The boats of the Titanic are the very latest in the lifeboat line, wide and non-sinkable.

They are capable of accommodating 50 passengers in addition to the crew. However, there was no necessity of overcrowding and only 35 passengers were loaded in each of the boats. The work of transfer, dangerous at any time, was less hazardous than usual because there was no wind and the sea was calm.

Valuables Removed.

Many passengers carried their most valuable belongings with them, but there was no attempt, so far as could be made out from the meagre advices that have reached here, to move hand baggage. The women and children were the first to leave the ship. They had a trying time, but all were safely landed on the Carpathia and Parisian.

One report said that some of the passengers were also placed on board the Virginian; still another that the Virginian had taken the Titanic in tow.

In relaying many messages were mutilated.

PARISIAN CAFE ON TITANIC

WOMEN AND CHILDREN IN LIFEBOATS

Cape Race, N. F., April 15.—Wireless advices from the Allan liner Virginian, which was rushing to the aid of the disabled White Star liner Titanic, stated that the last word received from the wireless operator on the Titanic was at 3.05 o'clock this morning.

In that message he reported the women and children had been placed in lifeboats ready to be taken off at a moment's notice. This message, however, was questioned, but the Virginian's operaor insisted it was as he received it.

The message, he said, was interrupted in the middle, which is believed here to mean either that the engines had been put out of commission or that the Titanic's wireless had failed from some local cause.

Soon afterward the Virginian quit responding to messages from the shore station.

Seven Great Ships Rush To Rescue.

In addition to the Virginian there were in the vicinity of the Titanic racing toward her today the White Star liners Olympic and Baltic, the Hemburg-American liner Cincinnati, the Cunarder Mauretania, the Prinz Adelbert, Amerika, Frederick Wilhelm and half a dozen freighters.

SPECIAL TRAINS FOR WRECK VICTIMS

New York, April 15. John I. Waterbury, a director of the International Mercantile Marine Company, said at 2.25 this afternoon, that instructions would be sent to the captains of the various ships on which the Titanic's passengers have taken refuge to take them to Halifax as quickly as possible. He said that the company has made arrangements with the New Haven road to have a number of special trains made up to bring the passengers to this city at once.

The New Haven road has started 20 cars, including all equipment needed, to Halifax, where they will await the shipwrecked party. The special trains will start for this city as soon as possible after the Titanic's passengers reach Halifax.

Narrowly Missed Collision Leaving Port

New York, April 15. The Titanic, the greatest of modern leviathans, exceeds even the monster Olympic in size. In addition she is the most luxuriously fitted and finished vessel ever sent to sea. Capt. E. J. Smith, a veteran shipmaster of the White Star

[Continued on Page 2.]

Bulletins

Washington, April 15.—Following an interchange of wireless messages with revenue cutters off the New England coast, the service headquarters here today announced that it would not send aid to the disabled liner Titanic.

"The only revenue cutters now anywhere near the Titanic are at least three days' run away from the disabled liner," an official said. "Manifestly it would be too late to do any good."

St. John's, N. F., April 15.—An unsigned wireless dispatch picked up here read:

"All Titanic's passengers safe."

Washington, April 15.—Up to 12 o'clock neither the Navy Department nor the revenue cutter service had received any wireless messages regarding the Titanic. The revenue cutter service is expecting word from the Government radiograph stations at Cape Elizabeth and Fort Leavitt, Maine, both of which have a range of about 900 nautical miles.

Halifax, N. S., April 15.—Wireless messages received by the nearest wireless station at 4.30 said:

"Most passengers of Titanic in lifeboats. Sea quiet."

It was unsigned.

It is thought to have come from one of the boats hurrying to the stricken liner.

London, April 15.—Lloyd agents here today were reinsuring the cargo of the disabled Titanic, but in doing so, indicated their belief in the gravity of the situation by demanding and receiving a premium of 50 per cent.

London, April 15.—According to information here the Titanic carried about $5,000,000 in bonds and diamonds.

FORMER MISS POLK IS A PASSENGER

Mrs. W. E. Carter, Of Philadelphia, Was A Baltimore Belle.

Mrs. William E. Carter, now of Philadelphia, was Miss Lucile Polk, of Baltimore, the only daughter of Mr. and Mrs. W. Stewart Polk, 2902 St. Paul street. Mr. and Mrs. Carter are on board the Titanic with their two children, Lucile, 14 years old, and William, 9 years old, accompanied by a French governess and valet.

She is a woman of unusual attractiveness, daintiness and refinement. In family and fortune she is well equipped for the society in which she had become a favorite. On her paternal side she is a descendant of the Scotch-Irish family that gave the United States its eleventh President. One ancestor was Robert Bruce Polk, who married Magdalene Tasker, of France, and settled on the Eastern Shore of Maryland in 1680 on a grant of land received from Lord Baltimore. A nearer ancestor was Capt. Robert Polk, who married Elizabeth Digby Peale, celebrated as an artist and founder of Peale's Museum in Baltimore. Her mother, Mrs. W. Stewart Polk, was a famous Kentucky belle.

Rated As One Of City's Most Attractive Debutantes.

When Mrs. Carter, as Miss Polk, made her debut at the Monday german, she was considered one of the most attractive debutantes the city has ever known. She was a great beauty, with light hair and sparkling eyes, and was largely entertained. She was married to William E. Carter, a wealthy Philadelphian, about 15 years ago, when quite young. After her marriage she made her home with her husband in Philadelphia.

Of late years Mr. and Mrs. Carter have spent a great deal of their time in England, where their two children were at school.

A year ago they took a beautiful old house, Rotherby Manor, in Leicestershire where they have been living, and where Mr. Carter has been hunting with several packs of hounds. Their young daughter has been at school at Wycomb Abbey, and their young son has been at a preparatory school at Rugby.

On their return to America, it is their intention to open Gwedna, their handsome country home at Bryn Mawr. They also have a villa at Newport, which they will occupy in July.

THE SUN

VOLUME CL—NO. 152. PRESS RUN YESTERDAY, M'n'g..90,190 Ev'g...38,934 129,124 || SAME DAY 1911, M'ng..85,113 Ev'g...34,002 BALTIMORE, TUESDAY MORNING, APRIL 16, 1912. 16 PAGES PRICE ONE CENT

GIANT TITANIC GOES DOWN; 1,500 PERISH; 675 ARE SAVED

Carpathia En Route For New York With The Rescued, Who Are Mostly Women And Children.

GREATEST OF SEA DISASTERS

Huge Ship Struck Iceberg At 10.25 Sunday Night, She Sank At 2.20 o'Clock Monday Morning, Long Before The Vessels Hurrying To Her Rescue Reached The Spot.

The Titanic, of the White Star Line, bound from Liverpool to New York on her maiden trip, was sunk about 1,100 miles east of New York in collision with an iceberg.

Fifteen hundred to 1,800 persons were reported drowned and 675 to 866 were reported saved.

The Titanic, after sending out the wireless signal of distress, transferred the women and children to the life boats.

The steamer Olympic reported that the steamer Carpathia reached the Titanic's position at daybreak, but found only the boats and wreckage.

The Carpathia is returning to New York with the survivors.

Col. John Jacob Astor and his bride were returning from their honeymoon, and it is believed Colonel Astor was among those drowned.

Col. Archibald Butt, Francis D. Millet, Bruce Ismay and other well-known men it is feared are also lost,

Capt. Isaac E. Emerson received a cablegram saying that Mr. and Mrs. Alfred G. Vanderbilt, reported among the passengers, were not on board.

Mrs. William C. Carter, the only person on board from Baltimore, is believed to have deen saved.

The dispatches indicate that besides the crews of the lifeboats practically none but women and children was saved. On board the ship were many men and women of great wealth and distinction, the passenger list being the most notable ever borne across the Atlantic on one vessel.

NEWS OF APPALLING AFFAIR HELD BACK

(Special Dispatch to the Baltimore Sun.)

New York, April 15.—In the darkness of night and in water two miles deep the Titanic, newest of the White Star fleet and greatest of all ocean steamships, sank to the bottom of the sea at 2.20 o'clock this morning.

Dispatches received late tonight from the Cape Race wireless station in Newfoundland and admissions reluctantly made at the same time by the New York officials of the White Star Company warrant the fear that of the 2,170 persons who were aboard the great vessel when she received her mortal wound in collision with an iceberg more than 1,500 have gone to their death in her shattered hulk, while 675, most of whom are women and children, have been saved.

MAY BE WORST IN HISTORY

Should these grim figures be verified the loss of the Titanic—costliest, most powerful, greatest of all the ocean fleet—while speeding westward on her maiden voyage will take rank in maritime history as the most terrible of all recorded disasters of the sea.

There is as yet no information as to those who are among the saved and the greater number of the unfortunates who must be numbered with the lost. The officers of the White Star company themselves, at the hour of going to press, had been able to learn no details of the horror that will carry grief into 1,000 American homes, some of them among the proudest in the metropolis.

WOMEN AND CHILDREN FIRST

One point is known from which may be derived a sad satisfaction. In a desperate situation, where the salvation of all was not possible, the women and children were cared for first. These were sent away in the first of the boats launched from the sinking ship, the only boats apparently which did not share the fate of the mammoth vessel.

America and Britain are spared the horrors that attended the sinking of the French liner La Bourgogne in 1898, when the women and children were trampled under foot and cut down with knives amid the mad rush of the panic-stricken crew for first places in the ship's boats.

COLONEL ASTOR AND BRIDE ABOARD

Among the most noted passengers on the Titanic were Col. John Jacob Astor and his bride, formerly Miss Madeline Force, whose marriage to the New York multimillionaire last year created no end of gossip and encountered some obstacles. Several clergymen requested to perform the ceremony declined to do so, even though a great fee was offered. Colonel and Mrs. Astor were returning from their honeymoon spent abroad. According to one report Mrs. Astor was among those rescued and aboard the Carpathia, while Colonel Astor was supposed to have been lost. The report could not be confirmed.

SURVIVED BLOW FOUR HOURS

The first reports of disaster received early this morning indicated that the Titanic had been in collision with an iceberg not long after 10 o'clock Sunday night. It appears, therefore, that this most splendid of modern steam-power creations, equipped with every device for the safeguarding of life at sea, remained afloat only a little more than four hours after she sustained the mortal thrust that sent this $10,000,000 creation to the bottom of the sea with her precious freight of human lives, ere ever she had completed her first trans-Atlantic trip.

FEW DETAILS KNOWN

Of the conditions which made the disaster possible, as little definite information is available as is accurate knowledge of its terrible results. It is a natural assumption that such a collision could not happen except in a dense fog.

The weather service station at Cape Race, N. F., however, reported that at noon today the weather was fair and that a fresh wind was blowing from the west. The temperature was slightly above the freezing point. The barometer at that time registered 30.20 inches, indicating an absence of fog.

NEWS APPARENTLY WITHHELD

For nearly 14 hours news of the stupendous and stunning nature of the disaster was apparently withheld, all the wireless and other messages sent out and given to the public up to 7 o'clock this evening making it appear that the Titanic had been kept afloat by her water-tight compartments after striking the iceberg, and that all of the passengers and the members of the crew had been taken off by other steamers which had hurried to the rescue.

The first information that the liner had gone down when the nearest of the steamers rushing to save the flyer and her human freight was still far away and that only the lifeboats filled almost to the point of sinking, and some wreckage were found afloat when help finally reached the scene, was contained in a flash stating that the Titanic had sunk and that many persons had been lost.

Even after that the White Star Line office here continued to insist that the Titanic was being towed to Halifax by the Carpathia and the Virginian.

FIRST NEWS OF DISASTER

The first information of the loss of the vessel and the deplorable loss of life was contained in a flash which read:

"Titanic reported sunk. Many lives lost."

STILL HEDGING.

Not until an hour and a half later did the White Star Line officials admit that lives had been lost. Even at 7.30 o'clock the following statement was given out at the offices here:

"Captain Haddock, of the Olympic, sends a wireless message to the White Star offices here that the steamer Titanic sank at 2.20 A.M. after all passengers and crew had been lowered to lifeboats and transferred to the Virginian. The steamship Carpathia, with several hundred passengers of the Titanic, is now en route to New York."

Vice-President Franklin positively refused to give out the full text of the message received from Captain Haddock. This attitude led to the belief that the message intimated a loss of life, which the company desired to confirm before spreading alarm.

SURVIVORS FIRST CLASS.

Mr. Franklin said Captain Haddock's message was very brief and "neglected to say that all the crew had been saved."It is said that the Carpathia had six or seven hundred of the Titanic's passengers aboard, including all of the first cabin, and that the vessel should reach New York Friday morning.

No information had been received from the Virginian or Parisian at the White Star Line offices, although it was said "to be known"that many of the Titanic passengers were in these vessels.

Vice-President Franklin said he had canceled arrangements for the special trains which they had planned to send to Halifax to bring the rescued passengers to this city by rail, as it was believed that the boats which had the Titanic passengers aboard would steam direct for New York.

AWFUL TRUTH OUT

Vice-President Franklin, at 8.40 o'clock, conceded that there had been "a horrible loss of life" in the Titanic disaster. He said that he had no information to disprove The Associated Press report from Cape Race to the effect that only 675 of the passengers and crew had been rescued. He said that the monetary loss could not be estimated that it would run into the millions. "We can replace the money," he added, "but not the lives."

News of the probable terrible loss of life in the sinking of the Titanic was limited in its circulation in the early evening, but by 9 o'clock it had brought a great crowd of persons to the White Star Line offices, near the foot of Broadway. Women were in tears and men were frantic after their plea for assuring news was met with frank admission that very little was known of the fate of passengers who were not in the first or second cabin.

All of the White Star Line officials and subordinates available were on duty at the offices and planned to make a night of it under siege by reporters, relatives of passengers and others.

News of the sinking of the liner and the terrible loss of life in consequence come with all the greater shock because

Continued on Page 2

DISASTER EPITOMIZED IN OLYMPIC'S DISPATCH

New York, April 15.—The text of the message from the steamer Olympic reporting the sinking of the Titanic and the rescue of 675 survivors, which reached here late tonight, also expressed the opinion that 1,800 lives were lost.

"Loss likely totals 1,800 souls,"the dispatch said in its concluding sentence.

It is hoped and believed here that this is an error unless the Titanic had more passengers on board than was reported. The list as given out showed 1,310 passengers and crew of 860, or 2,170 persons in all. Deducting 675, the known saved would indicate a loss of 1,495 persons.

A later wireless message coming from the Olympic read that 866 of the Titanic's passengers, mostly women and children, were being brought to port by the Carpathia. Other messages tended to confirm this information, which, if true, would reduce the number of persons probably lost by 200, and leave only 450 passengers unaccounted or if, as seems probable, all those saved were passengers.

The Olympic's first dispatch follows:

"Carpathia reached Titanic position at daybreak. Found boats and wreckage only. Titanic sank about 2.20 A. M. in 41.16 N.; 50.14 W. All her boats accounted for containing about 675 souls saved, crew and passengers included. Nearly all saved women and children. Leyland liner California remained and searching exact position of disaster. Loss likely totals 1,800 souls."

PARTIAL LIST OF SURVIVORS

Cape Race, N. F., April 15.—Following is a partial list of the first-class passengers who were rescued from the Titanic, according to a wireless from the Carpathia tonight. There are many errors and discrepancies in the report as received by the operators:

MISS LUCILLE CARTER.
MR. WILLIAM CARTER.
MR. AND MRS. J. B. THAYER,
MRS. JOHN JACOB ASTOR AND MAID.
MRS. EDWARD D. APPLETON.
MRS. ROSE ABBOTT.
MISS G. M. BURNS.
MISS D. D. CASSEBORO.
MRS. WILLIAM M. CLARKE.
MRS. B. CHIBINACE.
MRS. E. G. CROSBYE.
MRS. H. E. CROSBYE.
MISS JEAN HIPPACH.
MRS. HENRY B. HARRIS.
MRS. ALEX C. HOLVERSON.
MISS MARGARET HAYS.
MRS. BRUCE ISMAY.
MR. AND MRS.ED N. KIMBALL.
MR. F. R. KENYON.
MISS EMILIE KENCHEN.
MISS G. F. LONGLEY.
MRS. A. F. LEADER.
MISS BERTHA LAVORY.
MRS. ERNEST LINES.
MR. JOHN ROGERSON (probably Ryerson),
MRS. SUSAN P. ROGERSON.
MISS EMILY B. ROGERSON.
MRS. ARTHUR ROGERSON.
MASTER ALLISON and nurse, Miss K. T. Andrews.
MISS NINETTE PANHART.
MISS E. W. ALLEN.
MR. AND MRS. D. BISHOP.
MRS. JAMES BAXTER.
MR. GEORGE A. BAYTON.
MISS C. BONNELL.
MRS. J. M. BROWN,
MISS G. C. BOWEN,
MR. AND MRS. R. L. BECKWITH,
COUNTESS OF ROTHES,
MR. C. ROLMANE,
MISS MARY CLINES,
MRS. SINGRID LINDSTROM,
GUSTAV J. LESUEUR,
MRS. TUCKER AND MAID,
MRS. J. B. THAYER,
MR. J. B. THAYER, JR.,
MR. H. WOOLMER,
MISS ANNA WARD,
MR. RICH M. WILLIAM,
MRS. THOMAS POTTER, JR,
MRS. EDNA S. ROBERTS.
MR. AND MRS. L. HENRY.
MRS. W. A. HOOPER.
MR. MILE.
MR. J. FLYNN.
MISS ALICE FORTUNE.
MRS. ROBERT DOUGLAS.
MISS HILDA SLAYTER.
MRS. P. SMITH.
MRS. BRAHAM.
MISS ROBERTS.
MISS CUMMINS.
MRS. FLORENCE MARE.
MISS ALICE PHILLIPS.
MRS. PAULA MUNGO.
MRS. CARL H. BEHR,
MISS DESSETTE,
MRS. WILLIAM BUCKNELL,
MR. A. H. BARKWORTH,
MR. H.B. STEFFASEN,
MRS. ELSIE E. BOWERMAN,
MRS.D. W. MARVIN,
MR. PHILIP EMOCK,
MR. JAMES GEOGHT,
MISS RUBERTA MAIMY,
MR. PIERRE MARSHALL, JR.
MRS. W. E. MINAHAN,
MISS APPIE RANELT,
MAJOR ARTHUR PELICHEN,
MISS RUTH TAUSSIG,
MISS ELLA THOR,
MR. AND MRS. E. Z. TAYLOR,
GILBERT M. TUCKER,
MRS. M. ROTHSCHILD,
MISS MADELINE NEWELL,
MRS. MARJORIE NEWELL,
MRS. HELEN W. NEWSON,
MR. E. C. OSTBY,
MISS. HELEN R. OSTOYL,
MRS. PAUL SCHABERT,
MR. AND MRS. J. O. SWIFT,
COL. ALFONSO SIMONIUS,
MRS. LUCIEN T. SLOPER,
MRS. WALTER P. SPEDDEN,
MRS. WILLIAM B. SILVEY,
MR. AND MRS. C. E. STENGEL,
MRS. W. A. SPENCER,
ROBERT DOUGLAS SMITH,
MR. AND MRS. JOHN SMART,
MR. ADOLPH SAALFELD,
R. S. SILVERTHORN, JR.
MISS AUGUSTA SERF,
MRS. MARK FORTUNE,
MISS MABEL FORTUNE,
MR. AND MRS. FRAYENTHAL,
MISS EDITH ROSENBAUM,
MRS. GEORGE RHEIMS,
MRS. GEORGE STONE,
MAX STEHLI,
MR. FREDERICK SEWARD,
MISS E. W. SCHUTES,
WILLIAM SLOPER.

OPENED WITH AXES

Clash Between Militia And Police Precedes Cook County Democratic Convention.

TWO MEETINGS IS RESULT

State Body Must Decide Between Rival Delegations.

BOTH SIDES WERE ENJOINED

County Juge Owens Personally Orders Police To Better Down Armory Doors When Soldiers Refuse Him Admittance — Then The Hearst-Harrison Delegates, Wearing "Harmony" Badges, March Through Breach — Sullivan Forces Meet Elsewhere.

Chicago, April 15—Conflict of court orders and the battering of sledges and axes on barred doors preceded the Cook County Democratic Convention today, which split and chose two sets of delegates to the State convention in Peoria April 19.

For more than three hours 25 militiamen. unarmed and under the command of a captain of the Seventh Regiment, Illinois National Guard, held possession of the Seventh Regiment Armory, while two rival forces—the Hearst-Harrison faction and the followers of Roger C. Sullivan, Democratic national committeeman — disputed the right of each other to enter the armory.

The Sullivan men insisted that the coun-

[Continued on Page 11.]

GROUND RENTS.

Mrs. Anne Bresee West has purchased a ground rent on No. 1707 Riggs avenue.

Mrs. S. Emma Rowe has purchased a ground rent on No. 1905 E. North avenue.

Mrs. Virginia C. Bolte has purchased ground rents on Nos. 914, 916 and 940 N. Gilmor street.

The Title Guarantee and Trust Company examined and guaranteed the titles.

ADVERTISING DIRECTORY.

"Sun Want Ads" will be received at your nearest drug store at regular office rates.

Washington—SUN Bureau, 716 Fourteenth street northwest.

New York—New York Herald and all of its branch offices.

THE SUN will receive "Wat Ads" for the New York Herald at regular office rates.

THE SUN

VOLUME CLII—NO. 112. PRESS RUN YESTERDAY, M'n'g...92,706 Ev'g...41,704 134,410 || SAME DAY 1912, M'n'g...80,246 Ev'g...37,818 BALTIMORE, SATURDAY MORNING, MARCH 8, 1913. 16 PAGES PRICE ONE CENT

26 DEAD, 20 MISSING, 60 HURT WHEN DYNAMITE SHIP EXPLODES

Disaster Off Curtis Bay Causes Loss Estimated At $150,000, And Shock Is Felt In Four States.

STEAMER IS SMASHED; TUG BURNED

New Collier Jason Riddled—Captain Vandyke And Mate Diggs, Of The Atlantic, Give Their Lives For Others—James Goodhues And Companions Save 25 With Launch—Quarantine Suffers—Shock Felt 100 Miles Away.

At least 26 persons were killed, 20 are missing, and more than 60 were injured in an explosion of 350 tons of dynamite, followng a fire on board the British tramp steamer Alum Chine, in the harbor off Fort Carroll, about 10.30 o'clock yesterday morning.

The 20 missing are thought to have gone down with the Alum Chine. Many of the stevedores were known only by numbers, and it is feared their names will never be known.

There were also a number of negroes who were believed to have been around the Alum Chine and barges looking for work who are believed to have been caught by the hail of death.

The crew of the revenue cutter Guthrie will search for bodies today.

The disaster caused a damage which is estimated at $150,000.

NEW COLLIER JASON RIDDLED BY DEBRIS

The brand new collier Jason, which had but recently been completed by the Maryland Steel Company and which was to have been turned over to the United States Government in a few days, was riddled by huge fragments of steel and iron catapulted from the steamer Alum Chine, bringing death to several members of the crew of the collier and working terrible havoc to the ship itself.

The Jason is valued at $1,000,000, but it is not thought that the loss to her will amount to more than $10,000. Work of restoration will take some months, however, necessitating a long delay before the vessel is turned over to the Government. Secretary of the Navy Josephus Daniels has notified the company that the builders must be responsible for the loss. The company sent a letter to the Secretary regretting the loss of life. The head of the navy promises to make a full investigation.

STEAMER RENT INTO A THOUSAND PIECES

The Alum Chine was itself rent into a thousand pieces by her death-dealing cargo. The ship leaped into the air. Then there came a crash and a flare, fragments of iron, steel, woodwork and cases that had contained the explosive were hurled hundreds of feet into the air and the ship—or what was left of her—sank beneath the waters.

The Atlantic Transport tug Atlantic, the crew of which heroically attempted to save the men on the steamer and the stevedores who were at work on the barge beside it, was caught in the path of destruction and burned to the water's edge, her captain, William Vandyke, and her mate, Henry M. Diggs, paying for their bravery with their death. The loss of the Alum Chine is placed at $50,000 and that of her cargo at $7,000. The Atlantic was valued at $5,000. A car float, which was near the steamer, turned turtle and disappeared from view. Its loss is placed at $1,000.

QUARANTINE HOSPITAL SUFFERS HEAVILY

The Quarantine Hospital at Wagner's Point suffered heavily from the shock and the explosion. Every window in the building was shattered and doors were torn from their fastenings. Patients at the hospital were hurt by falling glass.

Those who were witnesses of the scene describe the explosion simply as a roar and a flash—a roar, they say, such as has never been heard before and a flash that mounted seemingly hundreds of feet in the sky. The fragments of steel and iron fell like meteors into the harbor, bringing death and injury and terror to all who were within range.

FACED DEATH WITHOUT A MOMENT'S WARNING

Many of the men who were on the Alum Chine and on the barge from which the vessel was being loaded were caught face to face with the selection of instant death through the flames or explosion or a fight for life in the swirling waters.

TRIED TO SAVE THE LAST ON BOARD.

The heroism of Captain Vandyke and Mate Diggs, of the Atlantic, stands out as a gripping picture of men who were willing to risk their lives to save others—though they were fully cognizant of the danger they were facing in their attempts at rescue.

The tug, which was near the Alum Chine when the fire broke out, had already saved a number of men of the crew and was putting off, when two others on board the steamer sent out a cry for help. The Atlantic put back, placed the men on board and was backing away when caught in the explosion and sent recoiling away, a veritable pyre. The act of heroism on the part of the two men probably cost the lives of others on board the tug, who had been taken from the Alum Chine a few minutes before.

James T. Goodhues, his brother Jerome and several companions who were in a launch near the scene of the explosion, saved nearly 30 members of the crew of the Alum Chine and the stevedores on the barge.

TUGS DO VALIANT SERVICE.

The tugs Britannia, the Curtis Bay and the Mary P. Riehl and the revenue cutter Guthrie all did yeoman service. These vessels were in the neighborhood of the ill-fated steamer and immediately put on full steam to her assistance. The Guthrie went to the Quarantine Hospital for a physician to attend the injured and dying on board the Collier Jason, and then hurried to shore to send for ambulances and physicians. Collector of the Port William F. Stone hastened to do all in his power to render assistance and sent the cutter back to cruise about the spot where the accident occurred for the purpose of picking up bodies of the dead.

HOUSES SHAKEN IN MANY PLACES.

The rumble following the explosion shook the houses all along the eastern section of Baltimore county and in the northeastern and southern parts of the city. Windows were broken and houses trembled as if there had been an earthquake. Sparrows Point and Curtis Bay, especially, felt the shock, while the heavy iron doors in the barracks at Fort Howard and Fort Carroll shook on their hinges.

Persons in Northwest Baltimore, however, knew nothing of the explosion, although the tremors of the earth resultant from the shock was felt in Philadelphia, Atlantic City and a number of towns in Maryland, Pennsylvania, New Jersey and Delaware. In Dover, Del., the sessions of the Legislature were interrupted and the Speaker of the House paused to remark that "there must have been an earthquake somewhere."

NO WRECKAGE FOUND AFTERWARD.

In evidence of the terrible character of the explosives there was not a particle of wreckage to be found about the place where the Alum Chine, the Atlantic and the barge went down save a few oars thought to be from the Alum Chine and a few blackened boards from the burned tug.

As soon as the crews of the tugs which hastened to the assistance of the victims got near enough to render assistance they were kept busy dragging the survivors from the waters or in snatching them from the flames of the burning Atlantic. One man was picked up naked swimming

[Continued On Page 7.]

At The Moment Of The Explosion

PHOTOGRAPH TAKEN TWO MILES AWAY

The above photograph, taken immediately after the explosion, was made by Alfred Waldeck while two miles away. He was on a gasoline launch going from the Baltimore Yacht Club to Wagner's Point, when his attention was called to a column of smoke from the Alum Chine.

As he watched, flames poured from the hatch. This was followed almost immediately by the boom of the explosion. Seizing his camera, Mr. Waldeck snapped the column of water, smoke and vapor that rolled hundreds of feet into the air.

The photograph was taken while the launch was at full speed.

Mr. Waldeck said:

"Immediately after the explosion the Alum Chine appeared to be lifted into the air and then dissolve into smoke and vapor. The dense cloud looked as though it was lifted thousands of feet into the air.

"I saw no wreckage from the vessel, but when the cloud broke it looked as if it were raining."

Mr. Waldeck, who is the official photographer for the Sewerage Commission, was on his way to take a picture of the water front at the Elliott shops, when he had the opportunity to take this remarkable view.

THE SUN WILL RECEIVE CONTRIBUTIONS

The Sun will be glad to receive contributions for the relief of the families of the men killed or maimed by the terrible dynamite explosion. All moneys received by The Sun will be turned over to the Federated Charities, which also will receive contributions.

Most of the victims of the explosion, who lived in Baltimore, are men with families—large ones in many instances—and their earning capacity has been limited to supplying the needs of their wives, children and of themselves from day to day.

Large and small contributions alike will be welcomed and accounted for in the columns of The Sun.

Makeup Of The Sun Today

ADVERTISING DIRECTORY.

"SUN Want Ads" will be received at your nearest drug store at regular office rates.

Washington — SUN Bureau, 716 Fourteenth street northwest.

New York—New York Herald and all of its branch offices.

THE SUN will receive "Want Ads" for the New York Herald at regular office rates.

ALL WANT ADS ARE INSERTED IN BOTH MORNING and EVENING EDITIONS OF THE SUN AT THE ONE RATE.

THE SUN

VOLUME CLIII—NO. 151. PRESS RUN YESTERDAY (MORNING, 93,941) (Extras Not Included) (EVENING, 44,511) 138,452 BALTIMORE, TUESDAY MORNING, OCTOBER 14, 1913. 16 PAGES PRICE ONE CENT

SUMMARY OF THE NEWS

LOCAL FORECAST FOR TODAY.

Fair.

Government Weather Report.

Maryland, Delaware, District of Columbia and Virginia, fair Tuesday; Wednesday fair and warmer; light to moderate northwest winds, becoming variable.

North Carolina, fair Tuesday; Wednesday fair and warmer; light to moderate north winds.

West Virginia, fair and warmer Tuesday and Wednesday.

Winds for Tuesday and Wednesday: North Atlantic, moderate to brisk northwesterly; Middle Atlantic, moderate northwesterly; South Atlantic, light to moderate northerly.

Baltimore Weather Report.

United States Weather Bureau, Observer's Office, Baltimore Custom House. October 13.

Time.	Temperature.	Relative humidity.	Direction of wind.	Velocity of wind.*	Precipitation.	State of weather.
8 A. M.	54	68	NW	3	.00	Clear
8 P. M.	54	60	N	4	.00	Clear

Normal temperature....59 | Highest temperature..60
Mean temperature......56 | Lowest temperature...53

Maximum velocity of the wind, 26 miles an hour, from the north. *In miles per hour.

Hourly Temperatures.

6 A. M.	53°	1 P. M.	59°
7 A. M.	53°	2 P. M.	60°
8 A. M.	54°	3 P. M.	60°
9 A. M.	56°	4 P. M.	60°
10 A. M.	58°	5 P. M.	59°
11 A. M.	58°	6 P. M.	57°
Noon	59°	7 P. M.	56°
		8 P. M.	54°

Today's Almanac For Baltimore.

Sun rises.......6.15 A.M. | Moon south...11.46 P.M.
Sun sets........5.30 P.M. |

Street lights lit Tuesday..........5.00 P.M.
Street lights out Wednesday..........5.10 A.M.

High water..........6.41 A.M., 6.26 P.M.

[Calculations expressed in Eastern standard time.]

PHASES OF THE MOON FOR OCTOBER.

First quarter.........6th | Last quarter..........22d
Full moon............15th | New moon.............29th

Weather By Telegraph.

State of the weather at 8 o'clock last night and the highest temperature for the day at the places named:

Atlantic City, clear	60	Louisville, clear	72
Boston, cloudy	64	Memphis, clear	80
Buffalo, clear	52	Montreal, clear	50
Charleston, clear	76	New Orleans, clear	76
Chicago, clear	66	New York, clear	58
Cleveland, clear	54	Pittsburgh, clear	56
Denver, clear	78	Philadelphia, clear	60
Detroit, clear	58	Portland, Me., clear	62
Duluth, cloudy	60	Salt Lake City, clear	76
Eastport, cloudy	52	San Francisco, clear	64
Galveston, clear	74	St. Louis, clear	78
Hatteras, clear	68	St. Paul, clear	78
Helena, cloudy	66	Tampa, clear	82
Jacksonville, clear	70	Washington, clear	60
Kansas City, cloudy	78	Winnipeg, clear	70

City And Suburban.

George Porsch, of Putty Hill, shot himself in the roof of the mouth and in the temple, but his attempt at suicide failed.

Great opportunities are anticipated for the Maryland Steel Company when the Pennsylvania Railroad disposes of its steel interests.

Henry Clay Frick and Henry Phipps came to Baltimore to attend the wedding of Miss Frances Shoemaker Dixon and Childs Frick.

Thousands of Italians joined in a great celebration of Columbus Day.

Four persons were hurt by automobiles in the western section of the city.

The steering committee of the Baltimore Wanderlust will meet this evening to pass upon "rules of the road."

Judge Robert S. Lovett, chairman of the Union Pacific Railroad board, went with President Daniel Willard as far as Chicago over the Baltimore and Ohio railroad.

The Young Women's Christian Association will make an effort in February to raise between $300,000 and $400,000 for a new home.

The funeral of George William Kerner, formerly vault custodian of the Baltimore Trust Company and a Union veteran, was largely attended.

Domestic And State.

Arkansas will be "dry" after January 1, 1914.

Adolphus Busch, of St. Louis, left an estate valued at $75,000,000.

Three girls and eight boys were arrested at South Bend, Ind., on charges of ribbery.

William S. Luckey won the aeroplane race around Manhattan Island.

The proposal to change the name of the church provoked spirited debate in the House of Deputies of the Protestant Episcopal General Convention in New York.

The Sulzer Court of Impeachment will hear argument today upon questions raised affecting the testimony of certain witnesses.

A residence and store in Crisfield were robbed.

Ex-Congressman William H. Jackson celebrated the seventy-fifth anniversary of his birthday at Salisbury, Md., with a reception at church.

Circuit Court of Caroline County held that the consolidation of three schools with the Ridgely school was illegal.

National Affairs.

President Wilson probably will sign the Urgent Deficiency bill.

A personal debate between Representatives Underwood and Hobson, of Alabama, occurred on the floor of the House.

The President nominated an attorney for Hawaii.

Country bankers testified before the Senate Currency Committee.

The Clapp bill to prohibit inter-State transportation of campaign funds was discussed in the Senate.

Charles A. Prouty will retire as a member of the inter-State Commerce Commission to become director of the physical valuation of railways.

Foreign.

The German Foreign Office decided that the Mexican situation was such as to necessitate the presence of a German warship in Mexican waters.

Yellow fever appeared at Carmen and Campeche, Mexico.

The United States called upon General Huerta to protect the lives of the deputies arrested in Mexico City.

Baron Alverstone resigned the British Lord Chief Justiceship.

The discovery of new land by Russia in the Far North was confirmed.

Miss Sylvia Pankhurst was rescued from the London police by suffragettes, who made a violent assault upon the uniformed men.

SUES RICH WIDOW FOR $20,000

Coachman's Wife Charges Alienation Of Husband's Affections.

Plainfield, N. J., Oct. 13.—Claiming $20,000 damages for the alleged alienation of her husband's affections, Mrs. Abby K. Schneider, of this place, has brought a suit in the Supreme Court against Mrs. Katharine Coman, a prepossessing widow of Plainfield. The papers were served today.

Mrs. Schneider is past 50, while her husband, John A. Schneider, is about half her age. The couple were married two years ago, but separated in less than 12 months. Schneider was engaged as a coachman by Joseph H. Coman, who, with his wife, lived at Fanwood. The couple were reputed to be quite wealthy and to have prominent relatives in New York. They made no friends. Coman died last spring.

Mrs. Coman, who is a blonde, 35 years old, laughed heartily and said it was true that papers had been served. "Schneider was my husband's coachman and after his death I retained his services," she said.

She denied that there was any ground for the suit.

DIED.

[Received Too Late for Classification.]

WARFIELD.—On October 13, 1913, at her home, No. 3117 Abell avenue, SARAH J., widow of the late Joshua A. Warfield. Due notice of the funeral will be given.

NEW IDEAS IN CHARTER

Cleveland Attempting To Wipe Out Partisan Elections.

HAS "PREFERENTIAL VOTING"

All Party Nominations, Primaries And Designations Abolished—Responsibility Is Concentrated.

[From a Staff Correspondent.]

Cleveland, Oct. 13.—Clevelanders had traveled some distance on the road to reform, as shown in a former dispatch, when came the home-rule amendment to the State Constitution. This gave them an opportunity to move faster and farther in the direction they wished to go, and they promptly embraced it.

The home-rule amendments read, in part, as follows:

"Municipalities shall have authority to exercise all powers of local self-government * * * not in conflict with general laws.

"Any municipality may frame and adopt or amend a charter for its government, etc.

"The legislative authority of any city or village by a two-thirds vote of its members and upon petition of 10 per cent. of its electors shall forthwith provide by ordinance for the submission to the electors of the question, 'Shall a commission be chosen to frame a charter?' * * * The ballot containing such question shall bear no party designation and provision shall be made thereon for the election from the municipality at large of 15 electors who shall constitute a commission to frame a charter; provided that a majority of the electors * * * shall have voted in the affirmative. Any charter so framed shall be submitted to the electors of the municipality at an election to be held at a time fixed by the charter commission and within one year from the date of its election, etc." Other amendments gave the cities wide latitude in the buying and owning of public utilities.

It was these amendments that set the cities of Ohio to studying municipal government and devising new charters. Cleveland began work at once. A charter commission headed by Mayor Baker promptly submitted a new charter. By a great majority it was adopted on July 1, 1913. The provisions for electing officers went into effect at once and the administrative provisions will go into effect January 1, 1914.

City And County Governments Overlap.

Before considering the very interesting and novel provisions of this new charter it must be understood that the government of Cleveland, like that of other Ohio cities, is mixed up with the county in which it is situated and with the State. Thus the Legislature has divided the State into school districts, which do not necessarily follow city boundaries. Each district has its school board, to which must be paid a certain proportion of the taxes, and which spends the money as it sees fit. The city, as such, has nothing to do with the schools.

Again, the county levies and collects the taxes. The taxes are apportioned by a board consisting of the Mayor, City Solicitor and one county official, if the city is larger than the balance of the county, or by the Mayor and two county officials if the county is the larger. These boards first take out the State's proportion of the taxes, for all taxes for general purposes are in a lump and must not exceed 1 per cent. on the assessment; then the school tax is deducted, and the remainder is apportioned between the county and city.

Extra Taxes For Special Purposes.

It should be explained also that while the 1 per cent. limit includes all taxation for general purposes, the counties may levy and collect special taxes for sinking funds and interest on bonded indebtedness incurred for special purposes, such as building a city hall, or a sewerage system, or buying a street railway or the like.

Cleveland has a total indebtedness of about $40,000,000, and about requires $1,500,000 to support it. This increases its tax rate to $1.36, but that includes State taxes.

Wealth Doubled In Ten Years.

The increase in Cleveland's taxable basis given above is correct, but misleading. In the old days of pull and politics, much of the property of influential citizens escaped taxation or was assessed too low. It is estimated that the taxable basis was not much more than half what it should have been. Admitting this, however, Cleveland's wealth more than doubled from 1902 to 1912.

The figures for the past few years are under a new system of assessment, made under a scientific set of tables, by unprejudiced experts. This new system is being adopted in many cities and counties.

Cleveland's new charter follows generally what is known out here as the "Federal plan." Perhaps the most notable difference between this and the "commission form" is that it provides for a fairly large City Council.

Even the advocates of a legislative body, however, smile at the absurdity of dividing a Council into two branches.

Finds City Council Desirable.

Mayor Baker, in discussing the Council feature, said:

"There are some sound reasons for retaining a City Council, at least here. A charter should fit the city for which it is made, as a suit of clothes should fit the man for which it is intended. No one form of charter will fit every city, as no one suit will fit every man.

"Here in Cleveland the members of the Council are the medium through which the people generally come in touch with their government. We have a large foreign population. In some sections of the city a man might stay a week and never hear an English word, and in one ward 39 languages and dialects are spoken. These people especially need somebody they can go to and who will look after them when they have any transactions with the city.

"I am not in any way reflecting on these new citizens. Quite the contrary. In fact, I have found them more intelligently progressive than many of the well-to-do. I have found that if I make a proposition to a meeting in one of the richer wards I am very apt to hear the objection, 'But it has never been done before'—therefore impossible. But if I explain it in a ward of foreigners they do not ask, 'Is it new?' but 'Is it true?' and they nearly always get the correct answer."

Powers Of Council Set Forth.

The Cleveland Council consists of 26 members, one from each ward. The Mayor and heads of departments have seats in the Council, but no votes. It makes all appropriations, including those for the budget, which is prepared by the Mayor, and it may change the items in the budget, but must give reasons therefor publicly. It may not make an appropriation unless the money therefor is actually in the treasury, to the credit of the fund to be drawn from. Nor can any contract for more than $1,000 be let without the consent of the Board of Control, consisting of the Mayor and his heads of departments. The Council is also granted the very novel power of fixing the salaries of the succeeding Council. It likewise fixes the salaries of the Mayor and his heads of departments, but salaries cannot be changed during their term of office. The Board of Control fixes the salaries of minor officials.

If a Councilman, is absent from a regular meeting, he forfeits 2 per cent. of his annual salary, unless his absence is authorized by a two-thirds vote.

Free Hand For Mayor.

The Mayor is the executive head of the city and has almost a free hand. Except the Councilman from each ward, the Mayor is the only city charter official chosen by the people. He appoints the directors of the six departments—of Law, Public Serv-

[Continued On Page 7.]

CHESTNUTS KILL TWO BOYS

Ptomaine Poisoning Results From Eating Diseased Nuts.

Forestville, Conn., Oct. 13.—Ptomaine poisoning from eating chestnuts is the cause given by the physician for the death of Edward Roberts, 6 years old, and his 3-year-old brother, Raymond.

The physician believes the nuts were affected by chestnut blight. The lads gathered them in a field near their home.

A double funeral for the boys was held today.

AT 106 SHE CHOPPED WOOD

"Aunt Kate" Casto Dies At Reedy, W. Va., Aged 106.

Parkersburg, W. Va., Oct. 13.—Mrs. Katherine Casto, aged 106 years, died today at her home near Reedy, in Jackson county.

"Aunt Kate," as she was familiarly known, had enjoyed perfect health until a week ago, when she suffered a stroke of paralysis. Before that time it was no uncommon occurrence for her to chop wood, milk cows and do other chores about the farm, where she had resided nearly a century.

AVIATOR JEWEL LOST

Participant In Aerial Derby May Have Been Caught In Gale And Blown Out To Sea.

New York, Oct. 13.—Albert J. Jewel, a young aviator, who was to have flown a Moisant monoplane as No. 14 in the aerial derby this afternoon, started to fly from the Hempstead Plans aviation field on Long Island to the Oakwood Heights field, Staten Island, this morning, but did not reach his destination, and tonight all trace of him is lost.

Some of the aviators are of the opinion that Jewell, caught in the gale that was blowing, may have been carried out to sea and lost, while others express the belief that he landed at some out of the way point on Long Island and has simply neglected to report his whereabouts.

Jewell is 27 years old and has a wife and family living on Staten Island. It is said that he came here from California. He received his license from the Aero Club six months ago, assuming the name Sidney Jordan. The longest flight he ever took is said to have been something over an hour's duration. He had never done any cross-country flying nor made any trips across water.

Last night he told friends that he had tested the motor and that it was running well. He promised to make an early start today and was very confident that he would reach Staten Island in safety. He even boasted that he would win the Times derby, or at least finish close to the winner. He was jubilant over the prospects of the race and the condition of his machine. The fact that he had never been up in the air with his new motor did not seem to worry him.

Jewel left his house in Hempstead at 6 o'clock this morning and went to the Hempstead Plains aviation field, where he met Alfred Heinrichs, another aviator, who was to start him. Before he left Heinrichs cautioned him about the new motor, but the young aviator expressed perfect confidence, saying that both his engine and monoplane were reliable, and that should any mishap occur he could glide with no blades turning for two miles and a half, a distance sufficient to enable him to land in safety.

With his friends, other aviators, and a group of soldiers at the Hempstead Plains encampment watching, Jewel rose about 500 feet in the air and turned southwest. He sailed along without any appearance of difficulty and in a short time faded out of sight over the Belmont Park race track, which was in the direction he intended to take. That was the last seen or heard of him.

He said before he left that he would fly over Jamaica and Jamaica Bay, across Brooklyn and Coney Island, and then over the Narrows to Staten Island, where he would land at Oakwood Heights. Points along this route and for miles on either side of it were telephoned to and visited this afternoon and tonight by searchers without success.

Mrs. Jewel, the aviator's young wife, was distracted tonight. She left Hempstead Plains Sunday with her 3-year-old daughter Dorothy and Mrs. G. H. La Pointe and went to her mother's home on Staten Island, thinking that her husband would fly from Hempstead to Oakwood Heights the same day, and that she would see him start in the race today.

ARMY AVIATOR KILLED

Two Other German Officers Injured When Aeroplanes Fall.

Berlin, Germany, Oct. 13.—Lieutenant Koenig, a military aviator, fell and was killed today at the Neuendorf aerodrome near Berlin. The wings of his machine collapsed at an altitude of 500 feet.

Lieutenants Seron and Bohnstedt, while making an aeroplane flight between Berlin and Stuttgart today, fell and were badly injured. A sudden gust of wind capsized the machine. Both officers were taken to a hospital.

TRACED BY MOVING PICTURES

Ex-Clergyman Who Abducted His Daughter Arrested In Japan.

Tokio, Oct. 13.—John Eills, the business manager of the Japan Advertiser, wanted in Boston for the abduction of his daughter and for contempt of court, was arrested today on an ambassadorial requisition on a charge of perjury, as abduction is not extraditable in Japan.

Formerly A Clergyman.

Eills was formerly a clergyman, a telegraph operator and a broker. He is wanted by the Boston authorities for the abduction of his daughter, who was awarded by the courts to his wife after their separation.

Mrs. Eills resorted to moving pictures to trace the couple, and by this means they were located.

APPOINTED AUXILIARY BISHOP

Mgr. Edward Kozlowski To Succeed Bishop Koudelka.

Rome, Oct. 13.—Mgr. Edward Kozlowski, of Bay City, Mich., was today appointed by the Pope to be Auxiliary Bishop of Milwaukee on the recommendation of Cardinal de Lai, secretary of the Consistorial Congregation.

Rt. Rev. Joseph M. Koudelka, the present Auxiliary Bishop of Milwaukee, was appointed Bishop of the Diocese of Superior.

WOULD RECALL WALTER PAGE

Imprudent And Sacrificed Truth, Says Mayor Fitzgerald.

Boston, Oct. 13.—The recall from England of Ambassador Page was urged by Mayor Fitzgerald in a Faneuil Hall address yesterday on the ground that the Ambassador was imprudent and had "sacrificed truth in order to cater to English nobility."

The Mayor characterized as "arrant nonsense" a statement credited to Mr. Page at Southampton to the effect that the United States is still English and English-ruled.

"No particular blood can lay claim to leadership in this country at the present time," said Mayor Fitzgerald.

GUATEMALA FOR FEDERATION

Minister Mendez Negotiating With Bankers For $25,000,000 Loan.

Washington, Oct. 13.—Guatemalan Minister Mendez issued a statement today outlining the position of President Cabrera, of Guatemala, toward the proposed federation of the five Central American Republics.

He said the President was an earnest advocate of the plan and hoped to see such a union, "not through force, but through public opinion arising as the logical result of the proximity and the progress of the republics."

OYSTER WAR BREAKS OUT ON TANGIER SOUND

Armed Dredgers Invade Private Beds, Remove Boundary Stakes And Wreck Watch Houses.

WOMEN TAKE PART IN RAID

Resolution Denouncing Joshua W. Miles And Benjamin K. Green, And Declaring Their Intention Of Wiping Out Oyster Culture By Force, Was Passed At Massmeeting Of Oystermen.

Westover, Md., Oct. 13.—Ninety men, armed with guns and accompanied by 38 women, their wives and daughters, marched from their homes in Fairmount, Somerset county, today to the leased oyster beds in Tangier Sound and removed the stakes marking the boundary of the private grounds.

The raiders were members of the oyster dredging forces, and their avowed purpose was to make war on the oyster planters, who, they declare, "had invaded the sacred territories of Fairmount's possessions and leased oyster grounds for the purpose of private planting."

Somerset county has been stirred for several days because of the threatened outbreak of oystermen against the planters of the county, and the affair came to a climax today.

The first raid was made upon Porpoise Point, where Mr. Crockett, of Crisfield, has taken up between 150 and 200 acres of bottom. The stakes of the Crockett grounds were pulled up and the watchhouse, erected by the proprietor, demolished. The following notice was posted on the spot:

Threats For Planter.

"This job has been completed by a body of men large enough and strong enough to repeat it. The man who dares to again take up this ground for planting purposes and to hold it as such, will meet with a fate similar to the watch house."

The party then went to "Harris Rock," where the Cox firm has secured more than 1,500 acres of bottom, and pulled up all of the stakes in sight. Everything in the way of oyster planting paraphernalia within several miles of Fairmount was demolished and a warning sent to all oyster planters in this section that other planting interests would be served in a similar manner.

While the women kept guard with their guns, the men pitched into the work before them and soon cleared away the marks of private ownership placed on the grounds by oyster planters. As soon as this work was over, the populace of Fairmount declared the day a holiday, and held a large gathering to arrange a further program against the oyster planters of the county.

A meeting was held tonight by the oystermen of the district, at which the following resolutions were passed:

Warlike Resolution Passed.

"Gathered tonight in the interests of our God-given rights, we, the oystermen of middle Somerset county, feel it our duty to enter our solemn and sincere protests against the crime which is being practiced against us by the oyster planters of Tangier Sound. Although law-abiding in our tendencies and desiring to preserve the peace and harmony of our State and county, we are determined to save to the great masses of our county and State the natural oyster rocks, bars and beds which have been appropriated, and are being appropriated, by private planters for personal interests.

"We fully intend to protect our rights by every lawful means at our command, and if lawful means do not secure the proper results, then we propose to resort to the primitive means of early pioneers and with the strength of man hold that which is ours.

"We gladly take this opportunity to denounce Joshua W. Miles, the boss of Somerset's Democratic party, as a man who has played both sides of this question, as a man who has claimed to be the friend of the oysterman while his secret acts have proved him to be one of their most treacherous enemies.

"Likewise do we denounce Benjamin K. Green, a resident of this community and a member of the Board of Shellfish Commissioners of Maryland, as a tool of Miles and the selfish interests which seek to betray the trusts of the oystermen and secure control of the natural bars and rocks of Tangier Sound and the Chesapeake Bay. As long as life remains in our beings we shall remain true to the teachings of our fathers, that the privileges given us by God shall not be filtered by the selfishness of man. First with the laws, next with the acts of our Legislature, but last with the might of arm and ammunition will we protect that which is threatened by the encroachment of the few who scheme against the many."

Miles Burned In Effigy.

Following the meeting it was announced that the oystermen of the district, supported and reinforced by the oystermen of the county, would begin action on Crane's Point, a large section of bottom now leased by the A. E. Tull Oyster Company. According to the expressed plans of the oystermen, they will advance against Crane's Point and destroy every mark of oyster culture in those waters.

After the meeting tonight Joshua W. Miles and Benjamin K. Green were burned in effigy. It seems to be the belief of the oystermen that the county leader of the Democratic party and the Somerset member of the Shellfish Commission have betrayed them. Mr. Green's home is in Fairmount, the scene of today's outbreaks.

SHINBONE GRAFTED ON SPINE

New Haven Man Cured Of Spinal Injury By Operation.

New Haven, Conn., Oct. 13.—Ralph M. Armstrong, a prominent clubman of this city, is recovering at a local hospital from an unusual operation—that of the grafting of a piece of his shinbone into his spine.

He injured his spine a year ago by falling in a bathtub at his home. He apparently recovered, but some months later again suffered spinal injuries while playing baseball. An operation was decided upon and Armstrong was declared today to be cured.

WARD MINSTREL, KILLED

Denver Man Fatally Hurt When Train Strikes Auto.

Lawrence, Kan., Oct. 13.—Arthur Dudley, of Leavenworth, Kan., known on the minstrel stage as Harry Ward, was killed and C. C. Clark, of Denver, was fatally injured when their automobile was struck by a Chicago, Rock Island and Pacific passenger train near here today. Clark died this afternoon.

The men were motoring from Denver to Kansas City.

Dudley was 40 years old. A brother, Bide Dudley, is a newspaper man in New York.

LORD CHIEF JUSTICE RESIGNS

Sir Rufus Isaacs Expected To Succeed Lord Alverstone.

London, Oct. 13.—Confirmation of the resignation by Baron Alverstone of the Lord Chief Justiceship was given today.

The choice of his successor appears to lie between Sir Rufus Isaacs, the Attorney-General, and Sir Samuel Evans, president of the probate, divorce and admiralty court.

The opinion prevails in official circles that Sir Rufus will be appointed.

ALL MOTHER-TEACHERS TO GO

Three More Suspensions And Other Cases Under Investigation.

New York, Oct. 13.—Three more teachers who have become mothers were suspended today by the Board of Education, which holds maternity among instructors a cause for dismissal.

Dr. William H. Maxwell, Superintendent of Schools, is preparing a list of all teachers who have borne babies since January 1 last, and action will be taken on them as well as on the three now under suspension at a meeting to be held October 22.

Abraham Stern, chairman of the committee on elementary schools, said there would be no delay in acting upon the cases of all teachers reported by Dr. Maxwell.

Dr. Ira S. Wile, the champion of teacher-mothers, says there will be about 15 on Dr. Maxwell's list, and that all will be dismissed by the School Board. He thinks they will gain reinstatement if they carry their fight into the courts.

MARBURY SEES PRESIDENT

Has Long Conference On Political Conditions In Maryland.

Washington, Oct. 13.—William L. Marbury, who withdrew on Saturday from the long-term fight for the United States Senate, called on President Wilson at the White House today and had a conference lasting some time.

At its conclusion neither the President nor Mr. Marbury would discuss what had transpired. Mr. Marbury was in excellent humor and willing to talk of everything but the conference. It is understood, however, that he talked with the President on political conditions in Maryland and took advantage of the opportunity to say a good word for some of the men in the State in whom he is interested and whom he believes to be deserving of consideration by the Administration.

Mr. Marbury said he had gotten off his shoulders the political burden that had rested upon them for some months and now felt free to advocate the Democratic cause wherever it would do good and without fear that any would suspect his motives to be selfish.

"While I was a candidate," said he, "some might have misunderstood my motives when I stood upon a platform and advocated Democratic candidates. Now no one can do so."

TO MAKE DRY LAWS EFFECTIVE

Tennessee Legislature Again In Extraordinary Session.

Nashville, Tenn., Oct. 13.—Adjournment of both houses of the Tennessee Legislature convened, each with a quorum, to pass measures designed to make Tennessee's prohibition laws effective, was taken immediately today out of respect to the memory of the late Senator Nathaniel Butler, whose death occurred since the last session.

After adjournment the regular and independent Democrats of both houses met and named a committee which recommended three measures such as Governor Hooper favors and such as a successful filibuster blocked at the last special session. Supporters of the measures, which most of the regular Democrats opposed last time, say they have safe majorities in both houses.

PROHIBITION BILL UPHELD

Arkansas Will Be "Dry" After January 1, 1914.

Little Rock, Ark., Oct. 13.—The State Supreme Court sustained the validity of the Going Prohibition bill today and Arkansas will become "dry" after January 1 next.

The law requires a petition, containing the names of a majority of white adults of any community after the entire county has been voted wet under local option, before the county judge may grant a liquor license.

MANY LOST IN NOME STORM

Siberian And Alaskan Coasts Strewn With Wrecks.

Nome, Alaska, Oct. 13.—The steamship Victoria, after discharging cargo, sailed last night for Solomon, a placer mining camp of 300 inhabitants, 40 miles southeast of here, which is reported to have been entirely destroyed by the recent tidal storm. The Victoria is expected to bring away those who wish to leave.

More than a score of lives are believed to have been lost in the storm. Besides the eight persons drowned at Nome more than a dozen are reported to have perished from small vessels at sea. Nearly all the gasoline boats in Northern Bering Sea were demolished.

Most of the Eskimos on Seward Peninsula have been rendered destitute. Only one native house at the village of Sinuk, near Cape Rodney, is left standing. The missionary building, two schoolhouses and the winter supply of coal were destroyed.

The gasoline schooner Nera, which sailed from St. Michael a few days before the big storm of last Sunday with Herbert Guisler, his native wife and three boys and several unknown persons, was wrecked on the beach at Simrock, and all were lost. Four bodies have been found.

The gasoline schooner Princess, which sailed from St. Michael with the Nera, was wrecked on the beach at Cape Prince of Wales. She was manned by Charles Green and Martin Bramble, who were drowned.

The gasoline schooner Sea Wolf, which has just returned from Siberia, reports that the gasoline schooner El Sueno is a total wreck at Kalooch Bay, Siberia. On board were Capt. Alex. Allen, E. T. McIntyre, Martin Morrison and a moving-picture man, name unknown. It is believed all were drowned. The Eskimos say the El Sueno was abandoned before she struck.

The Sea Wolf sighted the wrecked schooner Marie at Cape Prince of Wales. She reports many other schooners, with launches, dories and other small boats, strewn along the Siberian and Alaskan coasts.

PRESIDENT BUYS NEW BIKE

Messenger Boy Hit By Wilson Automobile Made Happy.

Washington, Oct. 13.—Spick and span and glistening with newness, a bicycle was sent this afternoon to Robert Crawford, 2202 Railroad avenue southeast, who was run down and injured October 4 by President Wilson's automobile while the President was returning to the White House from an afternoon spin.

The new bicycle is a gift of the President and was purchased by Dr. Cary T. Grayson, the President's physician, to take the place of the one destroyed in the accident.

Robert is employed as a messenger boy by one of the telegraph companies and had been at work but one day when the accident occurred. The bicycle he was riding he had just purchased, and he was paying for it on the installment plan.

The loss of the machine was the greatest concern of the boy when lifted from the street by the President, who at once assured him that he would have a new one.

Robert left Providence Hospital yesterday, and the bicycle was sent to his home this afternoon.

WOMEN KIDNAP MINERS WIVES

Party From Strikers' Tent Colony Hold Them Prisoners.

Trinidad, Col., Oct. 13.—Mrs. John Ludwig and Mrs. Matt Beiger, wives of miners working at Delagu, were kidnapped today by a party of women from the strikers' tent colony at Ludlow and are held prisoners, according to a report issued by the Victor American Fuel Company officials this afternoon.

Deputy sheriffs left for Ludlow to investigate.

DISASTER DUE TO EXPLOSION

Flash And Attempts To Launch Volturno's Boats Caused Nearly All Loss Of Life.

MEN ON LINERS HEROES

Defied Death To Save Those On Burning Ship.

OIL AIDED WORK OF RESCUE

Eye-Witnesses Send Thrilling Accounts Of Catastrophe — Little Boats Tossed About For Hours On Roaring Billows To Pick Up Possible Survivors — Sailor Jumps Into Sea To Help Swimmer Too Exhausted To Grasp Life Belt.

Fishguard, England, Oct. 13.—Though the report of Captain Barr, of the Cunarder Carmania, the first of the vessels to reach the burning Volturno in answer to her wireless distress signals last Thursday, will not be obtainable until after that vessel docks at Liverpool and the commander's account of the catastrophe is in the hands of the company's officials, enough additional details were obtained through other sources today to make a most thrilling narrative of the bravery of the "men who go down to the sea in ships" and of the many hours of appalling terror through which those aboard the doomed vessel passed, some of them, alas! to be claimed by death when rescue seemed so near, with hundreds willing to hazard their own lives, but forced to stand idle with an agonizing sense of their own helplessness in the face of the elements.

REPORT TO COMPANY FIRST.

Captain Barr met the newspaper correspondents with a positive refusal to say a word about the Volturno until the Carmania reached Liverpool and he had delivered his report to the Cunard Company.

He referred his would-be interviewers to the ship's bulletin for an accurate account of the tragedy. The greater part of the contents of this had already become history.

The fire on the Volturno appears to have originated in her cargo hold. When it became evident that the flames had gained the mastery, Capt. Francis Inch devoted all his energy to the salvation of his passengers.

The Carmania's bulletin says that six small boats were launched from the Volturno, that two of them with 35 persons each on board got away and that the other four were smashed against the ship's side and all their occupants perished.

SHOUTED ENCOURAGEMENT.

After the failure of the lifeboats from the Carmania to reach the burning ship, and when Captain Barr maneuvered his vessel close to the Volturno, the passengers on board the Cunarder did everything in their power to encourage the terrified crowd huddled together in the after part of the Volturno. They waved handkerchiefs and shouted through megaphones, to which they received answering signals from the emigrants on the Volturno.

Frustrated in his attempts to establish communication between the Carmania and the Volturno, Captain Barr sent out broadcast wireless signals which brought to the vicinity an international fleet to the succor of the doomed ship.

Late on Thursday afternoon Captain Barr made another attempt to reach the Volturno by throwing overboard life rafts, which he hoped might be secured by those on board, but this attempt also proved futile.

In the meantime the despairing messages from Captain Inch, of the Volturno, calling for succor grew more insistent as the flames ate their way through. Great clouds of smoke enveloped the ship.

ATTEMPT TO REACH GERMAN SHIP FAILS.

At about 7 o'clock in the evening Captain Inch succeeded in lowering a boat in charge of the second officer of the Volturno and a crew of four men, with the intention of taking a line to the Grosser Kurfuerst.

The small boat, after a desperate struggle, reached the German liner's side only to be dashed to pieces. Its occupants managed to seize lines thrown out by the German sailors and were thus saved.

About 9.30 o'clock at night the sky was suddenly illuminated with a lurid glare as the flames burst through another part of the Volturno.

A LAST DESPAIRING APPEAL.

Captain Inch then sent a last despairing appeal and 20 minutes later there occurred a terrific explosion, which to the helpless thousands of spectators on board the surrounding vessels seemed to seal the doom of those on the stricken ship.

This last message read:

Cannot something be done to help us? We must abandon the ship. Her plates are buckling. Stand close as I may have to jump for it.

Captain Francis Inch handed this to the wireless operator of the Volturno just before he was driven out of his room by the flames. Shortly afterward the Volturno was a raging furnace from funnel to forecastle.

The rescue of the only passenger taken on board the Carmania, Walter Trintpohl, a German, was affected by a gallant seaman of the Carmania's crew.

His name is Highway. When he saw that the efforts of those who were trying to reach the man struggling in the water from ladders hanging down the ship's side were useless, he dived from the upper deck of the Carmania and attached a life line to the exhausted swimmer.

SUBSIDENCE OF STORM FORTUNATE.

After describing the rescue of Trintpohl, the bulletin proceeds that the hope of saving more of those on board the Volturno had been almost abandoned when the sea suddenly moderated and the deed of rescuing ships was able to get away a number of lifeboats and take off the survivors.

Captain Inch left his vessel at 8 o'clock on Friday morning, carrying with him all the ship's papers.

The first intimation received by the passengers of the Carmania that anything unusual had happened was while they were at breakfast on Thursday, when the continuous breaking of green seas on the decks above them and the plunging of the vessel indicated that the Carmania's course had been changed and that she was speeding in the face of the gale.

DOUBLE CREWS FOR STOKEHOLDS.

Immediately on receipt of the "S. O. S." signal Captain Barr double-manned the

[Continued on Page 2.]

EXTRA THE EVENING SUN 3.45 P.M.

VOLUME V—NO. 65. Press Run Yesterday {M'n'g...105,195 Ev'g...75,319} 180,514 | Same Day 1911 {M'n'g...84,439 Ev'g...33,922} BALTIMORE, TUESDAY, JULY 2, 1912. 14 PAGES PRICE ONE CENT

GOV. WILSON IS NOMINATED

UNDERWOOD AND FOSS WITHDRAWN---CLARK MEN GET RELEASE

On the forty-sixth ballot, and after all the other candidates opposing him had been eliminated, Woodrow Wilson, Governor of the State of New Jersey, was nominated for the Presidency of the United States by the Democratic National Convention.

Missouri insisted upon voting for "old Champ Clark," as one enthusiast endearingly called him, and there were some other scattering votes.

The name of Underwood, of Alabama, was withdrawn from the contest at 2.25 this afternoon.

Woodrow Wilson's nomination came upon the fourth ballot of today's session, but from the moment almost that the convention assembled it was certain that he would be the speedy choice of the delegates.

The speech of withdrawal was made by Senator Bankhead, who had placed Mr. Underwood in nomination.

In his address to the convention Senator Bankhead urged that no one would suggest Mr. Underwood for the Vice-Presidency and explained that Mr. Underwood felt he could be of more service to the country in his position on the floor of the House.

At 2.28 Senator Stone released all Clark men from their obligations to Clark. That opened the way for Wilson's nomination.

Right on the heels of Stone's action Governor Foss of Massachusetts was withdrawn.

As soon as Foss' name had been withdrawn Congressman Fitzgerald, of Brooklyn, said: "And I move that we nominate by acclamation that distinguished representative of Democracy of New Jersey, Gov. Woodrow Wilson."

The match was in and the powder was set off. There was a wild outburst of cheers from every section of the hall. Every delegation, with the exception of Missouri, was on its feet yelling and cheering.

Over in the Nebraska delegation Bryan sat with a broad smile on his face.

Senator Reed, of Missouri, blocked motion to make Wilson's nomination unanimous, claiming that Missouri wanted to be registered as voting for Clark to the last.

James was vainly pounding for order. Governor Francis, Stone and Reed went back to the platform. Reed was recognized.

"Without the slightest desire to indicate any feeling of resentment against this motion," he said, "we must object to it. We want a rollcall so that Missouri's vote can be recorded on this ballot for old Champ Clark."

Delegate J. J. McClelland, of West Point, Mo., demanded the right to make a statement. As a delegate from Missouri, he said.

"I want to say that no people ever loved a man as the Democrats of Missouri have loved old Champ Clark.

"No one deplores the conditions that have arisen more than I. We are for Clark first, last and all the time, but if any man in Missouri stands for harmony and unity he should vote Wilson here."

United States Senator Clarence W. Watson, of West Virginia, played a prominent part in the closing scenes of the most spectacular national convention of the Democracy in many years. Convinced that the whole people wanted the New Jersey man and believing that a long deadlock would be fatal to the party, he announced that he would swing the West Virginia delegation to Wilson. The break followed.

Illinois swung her solid delegation with the tide. Other delegations which had been solid for Clark disintegrated. Each of the succeeding ballots showed that the end was at hand.

And finally, when the venerable Senator Stone released the Clark delegates and whn Underwood and Foss withdrew, the final ballot was taken.

Nominee of the Democratic party for President of the United States, chosen today in Baltimore.

LOCAL YOUTHS TO FLY AT TOLCHESTER

Made Their Own Machine, Which Was Taken To Resort Yesterday.

After six months of hard labor three young Baltimoreans have completed the erection of a flying machine, and today they are engaged in assembling the machine at Tolchester, where they expect to make several flights tomorrow afternoon and Thursday.

The amateur aviators are Henry Ellason, son of Captain Ellason, president of the Tolchester Steamboat Company; Robert Stewart and Olern Snyder. The young men took the machine to the resort yesterday. It measures 18 feet from tip to tip and is on the Wright model. It cost a considerable sum to build, as all the timber used is spliced oak.

HE FORGOT THE "FOURTH"

Hopeful Mr. Woodson Must Have Overlooked National Holiday.

The paramount question in Baltimore last week was: "Well, who is going to get it?" The paramount question today was: "Well, when'll we get away?" To this there are a variety of answers. Some delegates merely look pained and say nothing. Others show unmistakable signs of rabies. But there is one person who still keeps his composure.

An alternate seized Urey Woodson, secretary of the National Committee, by the arm and whispered the question in a pleading, confidential way. Urey whispered in reply, and the alternate, coming back to his friends, reported, "Thank Heaven there is one man who has not lost hope! He says we ought to get away by Saturday."

JOKERS AT LARGE

Letter Addressed In Freak Way To Underwood.

The comic man always gets in his work in such times as these. For instance, a letter received at the Belvedere and forwarded to Washington was addressed:

WOOD
OSCAR
Hotel Belvedere,
Baltimore, Md.

Which, being interpreted by the astute Billy Farrell, was discovered to mean Oscar-under-Wood.

"But," said Dorsch, the village cut-up, "where is the gentleman's middle initial?"

"That's easy," replied Farrell. "When you see the joke it will double-you!"

WOMEN ATTENDING LAWYERS' MEETING

Reception To Them Likely To Be Annual Feature Of Sessions.

[From a Staff Correspondent.]

Cape May, N. J., July 2.—The presence of an unusually large number of judges and women is a noticeable feature of the seventeenth annual meeting of the Maryland Bar Association, now being held in Cape May Hotel.

"Shop talk" is the rule at the session, and it may be that because of relationship to members of the bench or bar the female contingent is attracted. A reception to the women last night in the hotel ballroom was the first that has been held at any of the association's meetings, and was so enjoyable that it will probably be a feature of future gatherings.

This afternoon will also be devoted to their entertainment. In their honor will be a bridge whist party. For those who do not care to remain indoors a yachting trip has been arranged to Lewes, Del., and to the fishing grounds 10 miles out in the ocean.

Judge Burke Morning Speaker.

The hotel ballroom was well filled this morning to hear Judge Burke, of the Court of Appeals, talk on "Progressive Democracy." The Judge caught his audience at once by a humorous introduction.

When invited to address the association he began by saying "he felt like the delegate to the Baltimore convention who, when dead broke, was asked by a stranger to change a $100 bill. The delegate replied that he could not change the bill, but he thanked the stranger for the compliment." When Judge Burke concluded the bathing time had arrived, and the majority of those present hastened off for a dip in the ocean, further business being postponed until tonight.

The annual banquet will be held this evening.

IT WASN'T A "FLASK"

"Jim Ham" Lewis, Beau Brummel of the visiting delegates, was called to the chair to preside last night. Immediately "Jim Ham" delivered himself of a flowery appeal for order. A moment later he caused a burst of applause when, looking down from his chair, he shouted:

"Will the gentleman in the Alabama delegation kindly put that flask away?"

"It's not a flask," replied the delegate addressed, rising to protest; "it's whisky."

And the galleries howled with delight.

THE SUN

VOLUME CLV—NO. 44. Press Run Saturday (Extras Not Included) Morning, 95,678 Evening, 47,104 || 142,782 BALTIMORE, MONDAY MORNING, JUNE 29, 1914. 12 PAGES PRICE ONE CENT

AUSTRIAN HEIR AND WIFE SLAIN

Archduke Francis Ferdinand With Duchess Of Hohenberg Murdered In Bosnia.

HAD JUST ESCAPED BOMB

Two Assassins Nearly Lynched By Angry Populace.

BOTH GLORY IN EXPLOITS

Double Homicide Gavrio Prinzip, Youthful Servian Student—Says He Had Long Intended To Kill Some Eminent Person Fellow-Conspirator, A Young Compositor Named Gabrinovics, Asserts He Got Bomb From Anarchist.

Sarayevo Bosnia, June 28 Archduke Francis Ferdinand, heir to the Austria Hungarian throne, and the Duchess of Hohenberg, his morganatic wife, were shot dead today by a student in the main street of the Bosnian capital a short time after they had escaped death from a bomb hurled at the royal automobile

They were slain while passing through the city on their annual visit to the annexed provinces of Bosnia and Herzegovin

The Archduke was struck full in the face and the Duchess was shot through the abdomen and throat They died a few minutes after reaching the palace, to which they were hurried with all speed

TWO ATTACKS MADE

Those responsible for the assassination took care that it should prove effective, as there were two assaults, the first with a bomb and the second with a revolver The bomb was thrown at the royal automobile as it was proceeding to the Town Hall, where a reception was to be held

The Archduke saw the deadly missile hurtling through the air and warded it off with his arm It fell outside the car and exploded, slightly wounding two aide de camps in a second car and half a dozen spectators

FUSILLADE DEADLY.

It was on the return of the procession that the tragedy was added to the long list of those that have darkened the pages of the recent history of the Hapsburgs

As the royal automobile reached a prominent point in the route to the palace, Gavrio Prinzip, a youthful Servian student, sprang out of the crowd and poured a deadly fusillade of bullets from an automatic pistol at the Archduke and Princess

Prinzip and a fellow conspirator, a compositor from Trebinje named Gabrinovics, barely escaped lynching by the infuriated spectators They were finally seized by the police, who afforded them protection Both are natives of the annexed province of Herzegovina

BOMB WARDED OFF

The first attempt against the Archduke occurred just outside the Girls' High School His car had started again after a brief pause for an inspection of the building when Gabrinovics hurled the bomb This was so successfully warded off by the Archduke that it fell directly beneath the following car, the occupants of which, Count von Boos Waldeck and Colonel Meizzo, were struck by slivers of iron

Archduke Francis Ferdinand stopped his car and, after making inquiries as to their injuries and lending what aid he could, continued his journey to the Town Hall There the burgomaster began the customary address, but the Archduke sharply interrupted and snapped out:

"Herr Burgomaster, we have come here to pay you a visit and bombs have been thrown at us This is altogether an amazing indignity."

After a pause, the Archduke said "Now you may speak

ON ERRAND OF MERCY

On leaving the hall the Archduke and his wife announced their intention of visiting the wounded members of their suite at the hospital on their way back to the palace They were actually bound on their mission of mercy, when, at the corner of Rudolf and Franz Josef streets Prinzip opened fire

A bullet struck the Archduke in the face The Duchess was wounded in the abdomen and another bullet struck her in the throat, severing an artery She fell unconscious across her husband's knee At the same moment the Archduke sank to the floor of the car

With them at the time was the Governor of the city, who escaped injury The bodies of his murdered companions collapsed across him and protected him from stray bullets

DEAD BEFORE REACHING PALACE.

The Governor shouted to the chauffeur to rush to the palace at top speed Physicians were in prompt attendance, but their services were useless, as the Archduke and his wife were dead before the palace was reached

The murders occurred with such rapidity that many persons near the scene did not even hear the shots The street is very narrow and the assassin was able to fire at close range

The assassins were interrogated by the police and both seemed to glory in their exploit Prinzip said he had studied for a time at Belgrade He declared he had long intended to kill some eminent person from nationalist motives He was awaiting the Archduke at a point where he knew the automobile would slacken speed, turning into Franz Josef strasse The presence of the Duchess in the car caused him to hesitate, but only for a moment Then his

SUMMARY OF THE NEWS

AMERICANS SAVE TOWN

Gunboat Machias Stops Dominican Bombardment.

ONLY A FEW SHOTS NEEDED

GIRL UNCONSCIOUS A WEEK

$1,200 FOR THEIR FIREWORKS

CONGRESS TO KEEP AT IT

RECEIVERS FOR WOOLEN MILLS

CUMBERLAND STORM SWEPT

HIS ARM BROKEN FOURTH TIME

LEE AND LEWIS CLASH

Both Name Man For Reservation Superintendent At Sharpsburg

MAY TAKE FIGHT TO WILSON

RAILROAD WORK RESUMED

DIDN'T CARE FOR ALIMONY

SALISBURY BANKS TO MERGE

ARISTOCRATS FOR SUFFRAGE

ANCHOR LINER ON ROCKS

WOMEN FARMERS INJURED

WINS FORTUNE WITH "DIVINER"

$10 MINIMUM WAGE FOR WOMEN

EXISTENCE OF TOWN AT STAKE

MISSING CHILD FOUND DEAD

YALE LOSES FOUR FROM CREW

STORM BATTERS "AMERICA"

RAIN FOLLOWS THEIR PRAYER

HOT WEATHER TO CONTINUE

WOULD OUST CONSTABULARY

The Net Paid Circulation of The Evening Sun for the month of April was **50,749**

THE EVENING SUN

Last Edition
CLOSING FINANCIAL AND MARKET QUOTATIONS.
3 P. M.

VOLUME XI—NO. 18. | Press Run Yesterday (Extras Not Included) {Morning, 98,981 / Evening, 58,259} 157,240 | BALTIMORE, SATURDAY, MAY 8, 1915. | 16 PAGES | PRICE ONE CENT

1,457 PERISHED ON LUSITANIA; U. S. ASKS BERLIN TO EXPLAIN

America's Request To Kaiser's Foreign Office In Effect Asks If Germany Is Responsible.

SEEKING ALL FACTS, SAYS BRYAN; WHITE HOUSE KEEPS SILENCE

"No Time To Lose Our Heads," Declares Senator Stone---Seriousness Of The Situation Is Not Denied---Officials Stay At Posts.

New York, May 8.—Germany will attempt to prove that the Lusitania was a cruiser and that her destruction by German torpedoes was strictly legal. This line of defense against the charges of "wholesale murder" made by English and American papers was set forth today by Dr. Ehrich Hassenfelder, acting German Consul-General in New York.

"If the Lusitania mounted a gun, she was an armed cruiser of war," he said, "and laid herself open to all the perils of warfare. Whether she was an armed cruiser remains to be established."

Count von Bernsorff, the German Ambassador, locked himself into a suite at the Ritz-Carlton today and refused to receive anyone.

Washington, May 8.—The State Department today asked Berlin for a report on the Lusitania disaster.

It expressed a desire that it be based on the statement of the submarine commander who made the attack—assuming that the liner was sunk by a submarine.

In effect the Kaiser's Foreign Office was asked if Germany was responsible for the Lusitania's loss, with that of Americans on board. If so, full details were wanted.

The request was directed to Ambassador Gerard, in Berlin, to be presented to the German Foreign Office.

Aside from this announcement, Secretary of State Bryan said:

"All we need to tell the public is that we are arriving at the facts as fast as possible and doing everything possible for the injured."

Pressed for details, the Secretary admitted he had heard that some one on the Lusitania saw a submarine's periscope, seemingly bearing out the theory that the vessel was torpedoed.

He would not particularize further.

The desirability of making a statement concerning the international legal aspects of the case was urged on him, but, for the time, he refused it.

Senator Stone, Chairman of the Foreign Relations Committee of the upper house of Congress, issued the following statement at noon concerning the Lusitania's destruction:

"The tragedy is, of course, to be profoundly regretted. If the reports as to the loss of life are true, the sympathies of the civilized world will be deeply stirred. But for us, it seems to me that good sense dictates that we keep our heads until we get our bearings. It is a bad time to get rattled and act impulsively. Don't 'rock the boat.' "

"Without expressing an opinion as to our relations to this event or as to our duty in the premises, there are some facts we cannot overlook and are bound to consider. We cannot overlook the fact that the Lusitania was a British ship flying the British flag and subject at any time to be put into the actual naval service of the Government. Indeed, it is stated that at the time she was attacked she was carrying military reservists to England for service in the British Army.

"True, there were American citizens aboard, but it must not be forgotten that they went aboard a belligerent ship with full knowledge of the risk and after official warning by the German Government. When on board a British vessel they were on British soil. Was not their position substantially equivalent to being within the walls of a fortified city? If American citizens stay within a city besieged or threatened and the enemy attacks, what should our Government do if our citizens should be injured?

"I express no opinion at this time. I am merely suggesting reasons why we should maintain our equilibrium and not 'rock the boat' until we know what we are about.

"Aside from the possible loss of American lives let us ask ourselves just where we come in.

"At the present moment and with the lights now before me, I confess that it appears to me that from our standpoint as a neutral nation the Gulflight case presents a more delicate and serious complication than the case of the Lusitania."

Doing Everything Possible.

Ambassador Page, of London, advised the State Department that he had called on the Queenstown Consulate for a full report and instructed that everything possible be done to aid American survivors from the Lusitania. He said he had sent Capts. W. A. Castle and A. M. Miller, military attaches at the Embassy, to help.

A kind of strained calm prevailed in official circles. The White House and executive department were silent.

Nobody pretended, however, to have anything but the liner's destruction and its possible effect in this country on his mind.

Garrison Gives Up Trip.

Owing to the Lusitania disaster Secretary of War Garrison has abandoned the trip on which to was to leave tonight to inspect Tennessee and Alabama river and harbor improvement work. All arrangements for his accommodations were canceled.

He said nobody suggested to him that the trip be given up, but he did not want to be away when such "interesting" things were happening. He could not say when he would go.

Just how soon a Cabinet meeting would be called to consider the situation could not be learned. Secretary Bryan canceled an engagement to attend a dinner with other notables this afternoon at Bryan's Point, near Mount Vernon.

Officials all said they thought it a bad time to be away from their posts.

Course Not Decided On.

It was tacitly understood that the Administration had not definitely decided on a course and would not do so until all facts were at hand.

There seemed to be an undercurrent of feeling, however, that there was not much the United States could do.

Chairman Flood of the Foreign Relations Committee of the Lower House, was heard from at his home at Appomattox, but would say no more than that the situation was serious—he must know more details before commenting further. To secure these details every effort was being made.

Besides the State Department's request for information from Germany, Ambasador Page, at London, and Consul Frost, at Queenstown, had been instructed to furnish all obtainable particulars by cable as speedily as they could.

Confidentially, high officials admitted that what they feared most was the effect of the Lusitania incident on American public opinion. They were apprehensive so much feeling might be created as to add greatly to the Government's difficulties in adhering to a strictly neutral policy.

REVISED LIST SHOWS 1,457 PERSONS ON LUSITANIA PERISHED

New York, May 8.—The Cunard Line at 11 o'clock today issued a revised statement which showed that the total on board the Lusitania when she sailed from this city was 2,049. They were divided as follows:

Passengers---
First cabin, 286.
Second cabin, 625.
Third cabin, 288.
Total passengers, 1,199.
Officers and crew, 850.
Total on board, 2,049.

Previous figures had said that there were 2,160 on the liner.

According to the latest revised figures, the number of lost is 1,457.

AMERICAN LINER NEW YORK SUNK, IT IS REPORTED

New York, May 8.—American Line officials this afternoon scouted a rumor which they admitted was in circulation locally that the steamer New York, of their line, due in Liverpool tomorrow, had been torpedoed. The line officials declared they had had absolutely no word from their London office and were not worried by the rumor, which they attributed to nervousness incidental to the Lusitania disaster.

The Philadelphia, of the American Line, passed out the Narrows shortly after noon.

David Lindsay, of the American Line, was emphatic in his declaration that the company had not received a line from any point which would substantiate the rumor in even the slightest degree.

ITALY STIRRED BY TORPEDOING OF LUSITANIA

Rome, May 8.—The sinking of the Lusitania has caused a most unfavorable impression here. The Giornale d'Italie declared that the destruction of the ship bearing peaceful innocents, such as women and children, was a "premeditated crime."

It is reported that Italy has decided to proclaim the annexation of Turkish islands in the Ægean. This would amount to a declaration of war against Turkey, causing Austria and Germany to intervene.

Market Licenses

Notice is hereby given that the Assistant Market Masters of all the City's markets will distribute at once certificates for market stalls for the 1915 market year, which began May 1st, 1915.

Certificates are exchangeable for licenses upon payment of the proper charges at the office of the undersigned, Room 404, City Hall.

All 1915 licenses must be taken out not later than June 1st, 1915.

No licenses for stalls for the 1915 market year will be issued to stallholders who are in arrears.

Stallholders in arrears are hereby notified that unless all arrearages are paid before June 1st, 1915, the City will be compelled to take legal action against them for nonpayment.

JAMES F. THRIFT,
Comptroller.

Prominent Americans Believed Lost

ALL BALTIMOREANS WHO WERE ABOARD THE LUSITANIA NOW THOUGHT TO HAVE PERISHED

All of the Baltimoreans who sailed aboard the Lusitania are believed to be dead.

No names of persons from this city have appeared as yet in any of the lists of survivors of the disaster.

Among the ill-fated steamer's passengers were at least two Baltimoreans—C. Harwood Knight and his sister, Miss Elaine Knight, who recently occupied apartments at the Walbert—and two former Baltimoreans—Henry B. Sonneborn, of Paris, whose mother, Mrs. Wilhelmina Sonneborn, lives at 2209 Brookfield avenue, and Leo M. Schwabecker, also now of Paris.

Another passenger, David W. Thomas, a Welsh coal operator, visited this city frequently and was well known here.

Mr. Stone's Wife Here.

Herbert S. Stone, son of Melville E. Stone, general manager of the Associated Press, was aboard the ship. His wife is at the Stafford Hotel, where she has been all winter. She is the daughter of Mrs. William G. McCormick, 504 Cathedral street.

The fact that the ship on which her son sailed was torpedoed could not be kept from Mrs. Sonneborn, who is nearly 80 years old and has been in failing health for some time, but details of the disaster are being kept from her. Mr. Sonneborn had been visiting his folks here since last October. He left his apartment in Paris, where he has been living for three years, in order to escape the discomforts of war. Two weeks ago he left Baltimore with his friend Mr. Schwabecker, with whom he lives in the French capital, for a visit to New York prior to his return to Paris. Neither is married.

Mr. Knight Insisted On Going.

Mr. and Miss Knight, who are natives of this city, left Baltimore two weeks ago to visit their niece, Mrs. J. P. Hartt, 591 Bridge street, Denham, Mass., which is near Boston. They were cautioned by friends not to attempt the oversea voyage at this time, but Mr. Knight was anxious to get back to Paris to pursue his studies in music and would not consent to any delay.

SURVIVORS GIVE THRILLING ACCOUNT OF SCENE AS BIG LINER WAS HIT, AND OF RESCUES

Queenstown, May 8.—Latest advices from the Lusitania tragedy say that the crew was orderly during the final moments of the tragedy and did their best to launch their boats. Most of the survivors agree that two torpedoes struck the Lusitania, one completely shattering her engine room.

The first torpedo struck absolutely without warning in the stokehold. Splinters of steel flew high in the air and the great boat shook from stem to stern. Almost immediately afterward another explosion followed. The second torpedo completed the tragedy. Fumes from the explosive permeated every section of the smashed steamer. Many of the passengers fell to the deck unconscious. Others staggered to the boats and were helped on board.

Many Boats Were Useless.

The steamer was listing badly and many of her boats were useless.

David A. Thomas, millionaire coal operator of Cardiff, Wales, who, with his daughter, Lady Mackworth, were passengers on the Lusitania, told a thrilling story of the escape of his daughter and of Captain W. T. Turner, of the lost liner.

"Lady Mackworth went down with the ship and was picked up unconscious after being in the water for three and a half hours," said Mr. Thomas. "Her life was saved by her forethought in putting on a life belt. She was taken to Queenstown suffering from the shock and exposure, but is glad to be alive.

"The Lusitania was torpedoed without notice. At the time she was about 15 miles off the Irish coast. The explosions tore great holes in the hull beneath the water line and the liner went down in about 12 or 15 minutes.

Calls It Dastardy Outrage.

"It was a most dastardly outrage and it deserve the condemnation of the whole civilized world. Had the disaster occurred at night or during rough weather probably not a soul on board would have been saved. I question whether any boats on the port side were successfully launched. This was the side that was torpedoed and the ship immediately listed.

"We were at luncheon when suddenly the vessel was stopped and shook from stem to stern with the force of an explosion well forward that seemed to throw her on her beam ends. We had not believed it possible that an attack would be made upon us, but there was not a passenger who did not realise that the unexpected had happened.

Crew Rushed To Places.

"Officers and men rushed for their stations almost without orders and the work of clearing the boats was begun. Many of the passengers ran here and there about the decks, although Captain Turner and his officers tried their best to pacify them. Many of the women, however, were hysterical and some of them, with infants in their arms, caught at the fastenings of the boats and hampered the launching.

"As soon as the explosions occurred and the officers learned what had happened the ship's course was directed toward the shore, with the idea of beaching her. There is a difference of opinion as to the number of torpedoes fired. Some say there were two, but my belief is that only one was launched.

Captain Goes Down With Ship.

"Captain Turner is a brave man. He remained upon the bridge until the ship went down and he was swallowed up in the maelstrom which followed. He wore a life belt which kept him afloat when he arose to the surface, and he remained in the water for three hours before he was picked up by a lifeboat.

"During the last few minutes of the life of the Lusitania she was a ship of panic and tumult. Excited men and terrified women ran shouting and screaming about the decks. Lost children cried shrilly. Officers and seamen rushed among the panic-stricken passengers, shouting orders and helping the women and children into lifeboats. Women clung desperately to their husbands or knelt upon the decks. Piles of life preservers were distributed among the passengers, who hastily donned them and flung themselves into the water.

"In their haste and excitement the seamen overloaded one lifeboat and the davit ropes broke while it was being lowered, the occupants being thrown into the water. The screams of these terri-

[Continued on Page 2]

Scores Of Lost, Including Vanderbilt, Hubbard, Frohman and Others.

BRITISH ADMIRALTY ABANDONS HOPE MORE WILL BE RESCUED

703 Survivors Landed At Queenstown English Naval Authorities Accused Of Not Taking Proper Precautions.

Washington, May 8.—The State Department at 1.45 this afternoon announced that 132 Americans are thought to have perished on the Lusitania.

Queenstown, May 8. — The body of Charles Frohman, the New York theatrical manager, one of the victims of the Lusitania, has been recovered, according to a statement issued by the Cunard officials.

New York, May 8.–Hope for Alfred G. Vanderbilt, Charles Klein and Elbert Hubbard has been abandoned.

Copenhagen, May 8.—The Berlin newspapers today proclaim in headlines of colossal type the torpedoing of the Lusitania and declare that Germany has registered a new triumph for her naval policy. The editorial comment generally declares that England received what she deserved.

New York, May 8.—Basing their estimates on the British Admiralty's announcement that only 703 passengers and sailors of the Lusitania had been saved, local officials of the Cunard Line stated this afternoon that the death list would total 1,364.

The revised lists, they stated, showed 1,251 passengers on the liner, while the crew numbered 816, a total of 2,067. The local officials said the announcement in London that the Lusitania carried 2,168 persons was undoubtedly an error, due to incorrect passenger lists.

The statement of the local office explains the discrepancy between the New York figures on the number lost and those of London, the latter being 1,457.

London, May 8.—Men, women and children to the number of 1,457—scores of them Americans—perished when the Cunard liner Lusitania was torpedoed by a German submarine off the south coast of Ireland yesterday afternoon. The full extent of the greatest sea horror of the war was fixed this afternoon when the British Admiralty abandoned hope that any more survivors might be landed.

Up to the time the Admiralty abandoned hope 703 survivors had been landed at Queenstown or other points on the Irish coast. Six hundred and fifty-eight were picked up and landed last night, while 45 more were landed today.

While the wrath of England against Germany has been raised to a pitch of mad passion that demands terrific reprisals, there is also anger directed against the British Admiralty. The naval authorities are accused of neglecting to furnish proper safeguards for the Lusitania and her precious cargo of human lives. Inquiry will be made in Parliament as to why more precautions had not been taken to prevent the torpedoing of the liner.

Reports received here today asserted that the first rescue ships reached the point where the Lusitania sank three hours after she had gone to the bottom. Admiralty officials refused to comment on the reports, but the critics of First Lord of the Admiralty Churchill accept that as wholly true.

The announcement of the Admiralty that hope of saving more than those already landed was as follows:

"No more reports regarding the Lusitania have been received. The number of survivors given may be regarded as approximately correct.

THE SUN

VOLUME CLVIII—NO. 99. PRESS RUN YESTERDAY (MORNING, 108,331 | EVENING, 66,029) (Extras Not Included) | 174,360 BALTIMORE, FRIDAY MORNING, MARCH 10, 1916. 16 PAGES PRICE ONE CENT.

VILLA, VOWING DEATH TO AMERICANS, MAKES RAID OVER BORDER AND SLAYS 16; U. S. TROOPS IN MEXICO AFTER BANDITS

SENATE FOLLOWS LEAD OF HOUSE ON PROHIBITION

Adopts McIntosh Amendment For Separate Votes In Baltimore And Wet Counties.

GOES EVEN ONE STEP FURTHER

Additional Provision Put In Bill To Permit Manufacture Of Liquors In Dry Territory If If They Are Sold Outside.

[From THE SUN Bureau.]

Annapolis, March 9.—The Prohibition bill, with the McIntosh amendment, passed both branches of the Legislature in today's session. The Senate also amended the bill by providing that liquor may be manufactured in "dry" territory for sale in "wet." The House has made the bill the special order for tomorrow at noon to consider the amendment.

If, as is expected, the House concurs in the amendment, the two branches will be in agreement and the bill will go to Governor Harrington for his signature. He will sign it.

The bill, with only the McIntosh amendment inserted, passed the House this afternoon by the staggering vote of 92 to 4. After that branch had acted upon it, the Senators on both sides went into conference and the great majority of them agreed to accept the bill with that amendment.

A stand was made on the Senate side, however, for an amendment permitting the manufacture of liquor in "dry" territory for sale in "wet." This was largely in the interest of the distilleries in Baltimore county in the event the county goes "dry."

WAS OVERLOOKED IN THE HOUSE

It was contended that such an amendment would have been adopted in the House, but that in the confusion Tuesday night, after the adoption of the McIntosh amendment, the amendment was overlooked and the bill was ordered printed for its third reading. A number of the "drys" objected to such an amendment on the Senate side, however, and the matter was fought out on the floor. The amendment was carried there by a vote of 16 to 11.

Then the Senate suspended the rules and by a vote of 20 to 6 passed the bill with the McIntosh amendment and the ...

... Temperance Committee, had reported the House bill favorably.

NORRIS OFFERS HIS AMENDMENT

Senator Norris then offered an amendment that liquor could be manufactured in "dry" territory for sale in "wet." Senator Williams, of Cecil, one of the "dry" leaders, opposed this. He said that a feeling of good will had been developed regarding the bill; that it could be passed without difficulty with only the McIntosh amendment inserted, although he did not think so much of the amendment himself, and thought a good many others agreed with him, and that the wise thing to do was to handle the Norris amendment as a separate piece of legislation. He said that he was afraid entanglements would follow when the Norris amendment was sent to the House for concurrence, assuming that the Senate adopted it. He closed by asking the Senate to vote the amendment down.

[Continued on Page 8.]

KANSAS IS SATISFIED WITH PROHIBITION LAW

One Reason Is That Drinkers Can Get Their Liquor Without Much Trouble.

BIG QUANTITIES ARE CONSUMED

Prohibitionists Themselves Figure That More Than 6,000,000 Gallons Are Drunk Annually, But This Doesn't Begin To Represent The Total Amount.

ARTICLE XII.

[From a Staff Correspondent.]

Topeka, Kan., March 8.—There can be little doubt that a big majority of the people of Kansas are favorable to the Prohibition law and that public sentiment in its favor has been increasing in recent years. When the act was submitted to the people in 1880 it was approved by a majority of 8,000 votes only, in an election in which 30,000 votes or so were thrown out for improper marking and in which many thousands of citizens did not vote at all. It is doubtful if a majority of all the voters were then in favor of the law. Today, if the question were resubmitted, it would carry by an enormous majority.

"I am in favor of resubmission, although I am a prohibitionist," said a prominent lawyer of Topeka to me, "because I should like to have the rest of the country know just what the people here think of prohibition."

Most of the prohibitionists, however, do not think that way. A measure providing for the initiative and referendum was defeated by the Kansas Legislature because it was thought it might be utilized to bring about another vote on prohibition.

Resubmission Candidate Badly Beaten.

A year or two ago, in the Gubernatorial election in which Governor Capper was the successful candidate, the question of prohibition was passed upon in a way. One of the candidates was Mr. J. B. Billard, of Topeka, who ran on a resubmission platform. He got only 47,000 votes out of a total of about 500,000. Some of the prohibitionists say that Billard's 47,000 represents the total strength of the "wet" vote in the State. That, however, I do not believe to be the case. Mr. Billard's own statement regarding the facts sounded plausible.

"I had no complete organization," he told me, "and could not cover the State thoroughly. It became evident early in the campaign that I could not win and ...

[Continued on Page 8.]

GERMANS FAIL AT VAUX

Paris Reports All Attacks On Village Repulsed.

NEW GAINS IN CORBEAUX WOOD

Berlin Claims Capture Of Armored Fort Of Vaux And Adjoining Positions In Night Assault.

Paris, March 9.—The Germans have been repulsed between Douaumont and the village of Vaux after several heavy attacks accompanied by intense artillery fire and violent infantry assaults, according to the French official statement issued tonight, which says the attackers were completely defeated after having penetrated the village of Vaux. Further progress for the French in the Corbeaux wood also is reported.

The French official statement follows:

"In the Argonne our artillery has continued its bombardment of the enemy's routes of communication, notably in the eastern Argonne and in the region of Montfaucon and Nantillois.

"To the west of the Meuse, the enemy attempted several counter-attacks during the night to regain ground lost by him yesterday. Two abortive attacks were preceded by an intense artillery preparation directed against the village of Bethincourt. The attacks were stopped by our batteries, which prevented the enemy from debouching from the Corbeaux wood. The renewed efforts of the enemy have not been able to dislodge us from the large stretch of territory which we have reconquered and consolidated. Our troops continued to make progress during the course of the day in the Bois des Corbeaux, almost the whole of which we hold.

Hurled Back From Vaux.

"To the east of the Meuse the Germans directed several attacks against our front from Douaumont as far as Vaux. At the outskirts of the village of Douaumont an attack was broken by our infantry and artillery fire. Furious assaults against the village of Vaux likewise were repulsed with heavy losses for the enemy.

"Finally the Germans launched against our trenches bordering the foot of the slopes of the ridge dominating Fort Vaux violent attacks in solid formations, which were driven back, the Germans suffering enormous losses from our curtain of fire. Some detachments of German infantry which had penetrated the village of Vaux were driven out immediately at the point of the bayonet by a counter-attack.

"In Belgium our artillery has displayed activity against the enemy positions to the south of Lombaertzyde.

"In Champagne we effectively bombarded the defensive organizations of the enemy to the west of Navarin, to the east of the Butte du Mesnil and in the region of Massiges."

Claim Victory In Night Assault.

Berlin, March 9.—The village and armored fort of Vaux, northeast of Verdun, has been captured by the Germans, the War Office announced today.

The announcement says that in addition, numerous fortified positions were captured. The assault was made in the night by Posen reserve regiments. The official statement says:

"The artillery activity on both sides frequently increased to great violence.

"The French recaptured the western part of a trench near the farm of Maisons de Champagne, where hand grenade fighting occurred yesterday.

"To the east of the river, to shorten the connections between our positions to the south of Douaumont and our lines in the Woevre district, the village and armored fort of Vaux with numerous adjoining fortified positions ...

U. S. TO COMPARE ORDERS

Britain Asked For Copy Of Instructions On Armed Ships—Challenges German Memo.

[Continued on Page 8.]

Detail Of 250 Men From 13th U. S. Cavalry Engaged In Battle 15 Miles Below Border.

MORE TROOPS ASSEMBLED

U. S. Gives Notice Of Intention To Hunt Outlaw Down—Many Bandits, Including Pablo Lopez, Killed In Raid On Columbus, N. M.

MEXICO ASKS: "BE PATIENT"

Mexico City, March 9.—"My Government sincerely regrets this affair, and asks the American people to be patient," said Marcelino Davalos, who is acting as Foreign Minister of the Carranza Cabinet, in a statement to the Associated Press today.

"The Government asks the American people to remember that Villa is a common enemy," he continued, "and an outlaw to be hunted down by all men. The Mexican Government will use the most vigorous means to run this man to earth and avenge his horrible acts."

It is stated unofficially that General Trevino, with a large force, already is in pursuit of Villa.

Senor Davalos said he had communicated by telegraph with General Carranza, and that the General later would make a full statement to the American people.

FREE REIN FOR PURSUIT

Colonel Slocum's Action In Sending Troopers After Bandits Upheld At Washington.

Washington, March 9.—Washington stands squarely behind Colonel Slocum in sending his cavalrymen into Mexico in pursuit of Francisco Villa and his band of outlaws who raided Columbus, N. M., today, murdering American soldiers and citizens and firing the town.

Secretary Lansing tonight informed the de facto government of Mexico through Eliseo Arredondo, the Ambassador designate here, that he trusted no objection would be made to the action of the American troops, they having followed what is known in military circles as a "hot trail."

No orders have been issued for the return of the soldiers and it is not probable any will be issued for the present.

WRATHFUL OVER RAID.

Shocked indignation occasioned by news of Villa's outrage was quickly succeeded by undisguised satisfaction in official and Congressional circles over the knowledge that after three years patient forbearance United States troops actually were on Mexican soil to avenge the death of their comrades and bring ...

[Continued on Page 2.]

VILLA REPORTED HURT

Pursuing Americans Said To Have Killed 100 Bandits In Fighting In Deep Ravine.

Columbus, N. M., March 9.—Francisco Villa, outlawed Mexican bandit, raided United States territory today. With 500 men he attacked Columbus, killed at least 16 Americans—soldiers and civilians—and fired many buildings before he was driven back across the international border.

Not less than 250 troopers of the Thirteenth United States Cavalry followed the Villa band into Mexico. Reports to Col. H. J. Slocum, commanding United States troops at this point, late today stated that the pursuit extended 15 miles south and ended at 2 P. M. In this engagement a corporal, Capt. George Williams, adjutant of the Thirteenth Cavalry, was wounded.

VILLA SEEN WOUNDED.

In the fighting Villa is reported to have been wounded. One report was that 100 of the Villistas were killed in the fight, which occurred in a deep ravine.

The report of the wounding of Villa was circumstantially confirmed by one of the Mexican bandits who was taken prisoner. He said he was riding close to Villa when he was shot and that Villa ...

16 AMERICANS KILLED.

WEATHER AND SUMMARY

LOCAL FORECAST FOR TODAY. Partly cloudy, warmer.

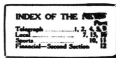

WEATHER FOR TODAY

Fair and warmer: fresh west winds.

Detailed Weather Report on Page 8.

THE SUN

INDEX OF THE NEWS

	Page
Telegraph	1, 2, 4, 5, 6
Local	7, 15, 16
Sports	10, 11
Financial—Second Section	12

VOLUME XVII—NO. 5. PRESS RUN SUNDAY, January 28, 1917. } 97,705 BALTIMORE, SUNDAY MORNING, FEBRUARY 4, 1917. * 56 PAGES PRICE FIVE CENTS.

U. S. SEIZES INTERNED GERMAN WARSHIPS AT PHILADELPHIA AND LINERS AT PANAMA; DANIELS ASKS CONTROL OF MUNITIONS PLANTS

Crews Of Kronprinz Wilhelm And Prinz Eitel Friedrich Are Imprisoned In The Isolation Barracks.

RESERVATION CLOSELY GUARDED

Attempt Is Made To Scuttle The United States Torpedo Boat Jacob Jones.

Washington, Feb. 3.—Convoying of American merchantmen through European waters with warships is being considered by the Government.

The sailing of American vessels for Europe is now considered by the State Department as a military measure. No general order has yet gone out.

Philadelphia, Feb. 3.—Early tonight the interned German auxiliary cruisers Kronprinz Wilhelm and Prinz Eitel Friedrich were seized by order of the Navy Department and their crews imprisoned in an isolation barracks. The seizure was followed by the placing of an armed guard at the yard entrance, while marines were assigned to patrol the landside limits of the Government preserve.

Motorboats and other light craft with machine guns aboard patrolled the river and prevented vessels from coming within a prescribed area. Commandant Russell issued orders recalling shore leave of all marines and sailors. Visitors to the yard were strictly forbidden.

TRIED TO SCUTTLE TORPEDO BOAT

An attempt was made today to scuttle the United States torpedo-boat destroyer Jacob Jones by opening several of her seacocks at the Philadelphia Navy Yard, according to unofficial but reliable reports. Officials at the yard refused either to confirm or deny the reports, pointing out that upon instructions from Washington a strict censorship had been placed upon all activities at the navy yards throughout the country.

An officer of the Jacob Jones, it was said, found that the ship was listing heavily to port as she was being towed from her anchorage in the Delaware river to a dock and all persons aboard were detained and questioned. The chief machinist's mate, whose identity was not disclosed, was arrested and placed in irons in the brig of one of the battleships. Whether the prisoner is a German sympathizer or a fanatic is not known.

More than two feet of water was in the hold of the Jacob Jones when it was discovered that her seacocks had been opened. They were quickly closed and two Government tugs assisted in warping the destroyer in her dock.

The local navy yard virtually was placed upon a war basis today.

MUNITION SHIPS SAIL.

Disregarding the new sea peril announced by Germany, four steamers, one flying the American flag, laden with munitions and other rich cargoes destined for war zone, sailed from here today. They are the British ships Menapp Range, for Leith, and Saxoleine, for Havre; the Italian liner Italia for Genoa, and the Norwegian ship Admiralen, for Liverpool.

Among the half dozen steamers that cleared for foreign ports was the American tanker Gold Shell for Bordeaux and Rouen, France.

LINERS AT PANAMA SEIZED

Panama, Feb. 3.—Four Hamburg-American line steamships which have been in Cristobal harbor were seized this afternoon by the Canal Zone authorities. Night harbor traffic at Cristobal has been stopped, and strict protective measures have been taken throughout the Canal Zone.

The steamers seized are the Savoia, of 2,614 gross tons, the Grunewald, of 4,707 gross tons, the Sachsenwald, of 3,559 gross tons, and the Prinz Sigismund, of 4,689 gross tons. The vessels have been in the harbor since the beginning of the war.

THE KRONPRINZESSIN SEIZED.

Boston, Feb. 3.—United States Marshal Mitchell tonight took physical possession of the North German Lloyd liner Kronprinzessin Cecelie, which has been nominally in his custody since the litigation instituted against the owners by the National City Bank of New York.

Capt. Charles A. Polack and the skeleton crew of 112 men who have made the ship their home for more than two years were put ashore and housed for the time being at the Immigration Bureau. They made no resistance. The German engineers, firemen and others were replaced by American citizens and 50 men of the city police force were put on board to protect the vessel from any willful damage.

This action followed notice to the Marshal by attorneys for the National City Bank and the Guarantee Trust Company of New York that they would hold him liable for any damage to the ship to the extent of their claims, which amount to $2,500,000.

United States District Attorney Anderson said he wished to make it plain that the seizure was purely a civil proceeding.

LINER DISABLED BY INTENT.

New York, Feb. 3.—Word reached the police today that coincident with the publication of the news of the rupture with Germany the Austrian freighter Himalaya, which has been lying in Newark Bay, an estuary of New York harbor, has been put out of commission. The report had it that the piston-heads and other parts of her engines had been smashed by crowbars and axes.

Confirmation of the report that the Himalaya had been put out of commission was contained later from an authoritative source.

MOVE TO SAFEGUARD SHIPS.

Washington, Feb. 3.—Removal of the crews of the German auxiliary cruisers Kronprinz Wilhelm and Prinz Eitel Friedrich was ordered by the commandant of the Philadelphia Navy Yard, on instructions from Secretary Daniels to take whatever steps he deemed necessary to safeguard the interned ships in the existing situation.

Having voluntarily submitted to internment, these vessels actually are in custody of the United States Government, subject to such disposition of ships and crews as the Government sees fit to make.

The Kronprinzessin Cecilie at Boston and the prize ship Appam, at Newport News, taken over by United States marshals, already technically were in the custody of the courts pending the outcome of litigation over their possession. The crews merely had been permitted to live aboard and continue in physical possession under bonds given by the German Government.

DIED.

[Received too late for classification.]

KNAPP.—On February 3, 1917, at 11.15 at his residence, No. 847 Hollins WILLIAM A. KNAPP. [illegible] of funeral will be given.

AMERICAN SHIP SUNK BY U-BOAT

Housatonic, With Contraband, Sent Down Near Scilly Islands.

ALL ON BOARD SAVED BY BRITISH STEAMER

Submarined Vessel Formerly Hamburg-American Liner Georgia.

London, Feb. 3.—The American steamer Housatonic has been sunk by a German submarine. It is believed the Housatonic was sunk near the Scilly Islands. The rumor is current that she was attacked without warning.

The Housatonic was submarined at noon. All the officers and crew were saved by a British armed steamer.

SENSATION IN WASHINGTON.

Washington, Feb. 3.—News of the sinking of the Housatonic created a sensation here, but State Department officials pointed out that it would depend entirely upon the circumstances whether the incident would affect the present situation.

The ship was carrying contraband, and if she was destroyed with proper warning and provision for the safety of her crew or in an attempt to escape, the United States merely would have a claim for damages as in the Frye case.

The first effect of the incident in official quarters was to direct attention anew to the President's declaration in his address to Congress today that if American ships and lives were sacrificed "in needless contravention of the just and reasonable understandings of international law" he would again go before Congress for authority to "use any means that may be necessary for the protection of our seamen and our people."

FORMERLY GERMAN LINER.

The Housatonic sailed from Galveston on January 6 and from Newport News on January 16 for London. The Housatonic formerly was the Hamburg-American Line steamer Georgia, and American registry was granted to her in April, 1915. Prior to that time she had been laid up at New Orleans since the beginning of the war.

UNDER CONTRACT TO LONDON FIRM.

New York, Feb. 3.—The steamship Housatonic, sunk by a German submarine, was under charter to Brown, Jenkinson & Co., of London, it was asserted tonight by Edward F. Geer, president of the Housatonic Steamship Company. On her last trip to Europe, which was in August, she carried a cargo of supplies to Rotterdam for the Belgian Relief Commission.

APPAM IN U. S. HANDS

German Prize Crew Of Liner Held Under Bond Taken Off By Coast Guard Crews.

Washington, Feb. 3.—Lieut. Hans Berg and his German prize crew were removed from the liner Appam at Newport News, Va., today by Coast Guard cutters under direction of a United States marshal. The ship is in the custody of the Federal Court pending appeal to the Supreme Court from a decision awarding her to her English owners.

Lieutenant Berg notified the embassy here by long distance telephone. He had been allowed to retain possession of the vessel under bond given by the German Government.

QUEBEC HITS A MINE

French Liner Running To The West Indies Goes Down.

New York, Feb. 3.—The Quebec, a passenger ship which plied between France and the West Indies, has been sunk after striking a mine, the French Line, owners of the vessel, announced here today. The news came in a cablegram from the French Line offices in France and gave no details.

DEUTSCHLAND PIER AFIRE

Blaze Does Slight Damage To Tool Shop At New London.

New London, Conn., Feb. 3.—A tool shop on the State pier, a portion of which is leased by the Eastern Forwarding Company for storage and handling of cargo for the German submarine merchantman Deutschland, was burned today.

The loss was small. In the shop was metal used in the pier construction work.

WHAT WILL DEUTSCHLAND DO?

Capt. Hinsch Says She Would Have 24 Hours To Get Out.

New Haven, Conn., Feb. 3.—Severance of diplomatic relations with Germany quickly brought about augmentation of the protective forces at many of the munition plants in Connecticut today.

Capt. Frederick Hinsch, manager of the Eastern Forwarding Company at New London, when asked what effect the present situation would have on the submarine merchantman Deutschland, if it arrived there, replied:

"In any event it would have 24 hours in which it could leave port again," he stated. Asked if it could unload cargo his answer was: "That would be up to Washington."

Only A Step To War.

GUARD NAVAL ACADEMY

Captain Eberle Bars All Visitors From Government Reservation. Cancels Basketball Game.

Annapolis, Md., Feb. 3.—Immediately upon the receipt of information from the Navy Department at Washington of the break in diplomatic relations between the United States and Germany, Capt. Edward W. Eberle, superintendent of the Naval Academy, issued an order barring all visitors from the grounds of the Government reservation. This also caused the cancellation of the basketball game between teams of the midshipmen and West Virginia University, scheduled for this afternoon, and also the dance tonight at which the regiment of midshipmen was to be the hosts.

In accordance with the order of Superintendent Eberle, a cordon of guards was thrown about every entrance to the Government grounds, and strict vigilance will be maintained in every respect. The order also affects the naval experiment station and the marine barracks.

Absolutely no one outside of the midshipmen, residents of the academy, or employes about the Government reservation is admitted.

MORE GUARDS FOR WHITE HOUSE

Gates To Grounds Closed And Extra Police Bars Entrance.

Washington, Feb. 3.—Additional guards were thrown about the White House today soon after the President delivered his speech to Congress. The gates to the White House grounds were promptly closed and extra police were stationed to keep anyone from entering. Newspaper men and others with business at the Executive offices were passed through a special gate, after they had satisfied the policemen of their identity.

In spite of the unusual situation the Congressional Union for Woman Suffrage, announced that its "picketing" outside of the White House grounds would be continued to show that the women thought they should have a part in reaching momentous decisions possibly involving the nation in war.

NEW YORK GUARD CALLED OUT

Every Arsenal, Armory, Water Shed And Bridge Will Be Protected.

New York, Feb. 3.—The entire National Guard of New York State and the naval militia were ordered out tonight by Governor Whitman after a conference with Maj. Gen. John F. O'Ryan.

General O'Ryan was directed to have every arsenal, armory and water shed adequately guarded by the militia men, and Commodore Forshew, of the naval militia, was ordered to protect all bridges.

The Governor's order was issued at the direct request of Mayor John P. Mitchel of this city soon after Mr. Whitman arrived here tonight from Albany. Governor Whitman said he would remain in New York tomorrow to keep in close touch with the situation.

"Of course, all of our people will support the President loyally," he declared.

A strict military censorship was established at National Guard headquarters immediately after the Governor's order was issued. "I think it is the patriotic duty of newspapers not to seek or publish any information concerning the use of troops at this time," said General O'Ryan.

BIG SHIP DELAYS SAILING TIME

American Liner St. Louis, Due To Sail Today, Will Not Leave Before Monday.

MAY BE CONVOYED ACROSS ATLANTIC

Twelve U. S. Steamships Are Now In Or Approaching New War Zone.

New York, Feb. 3.—An indication of the tension felt in shipping circles here was shown tonight by the announcement that the American Line steamship St. Louis, which had obtained clearance papers to sail tomorrow for Liverpool, would not leave before noon Monday at the earliest. The following statement was issued from the offices of the company:

"The officials of the American Line are in consultation with the Department of State at Washington and have decided not to sail the St. Louis before 12 o'clock noon Monday, February 5."

ST. PAUL DUE IN TODAY.

The St. Louis was to have departed today, but it was said that inability to obtain coal had necessitated a postponement of her sailing until tomorrow. Tonight the announcement that another postponement had been ordered was made.

The American Line steamship St. Paul, which left Liverpool last Saturday and ordinarily would be due here tomorrow, may be delayed, it was said tonight, by the heavy northwest gales of the last three days. No wireless messages have been received from her.

Reports that the St. Louis would be convoyed by a warship of the United States or of the Entente Powers could not be confirmed at the office of the line. Several persons who had booked passage

[Continued on Page 2.]

OUTLINES NEUTRAL WAY

President Wilson Calls Upon Other Nations To Follow Course Of United States.

Washington, Feb. 3.—It was reported tonight in diplomatic quarters, but unconfirmed in any American official source, that President Wilson in advising neutrals of his action in severing diplomatic relations with Germany has invited other neutrals to follow his course.

President Wilson's address to Congress today said he would expect neutrals to follow his course if he found it necessary to take further steps to protect American rights.

Officials tonight did not make clear whether the President expected the neutrals to follow his example in the steps already taken, or whether he expected them to follow the steps the United States would take in the next eventuality.

Some officials who were asked to explain the uncertainty declined to discuss the subject, and others were inclined to the belief that the President hoped other neutrals, by severing diplomatic relations, would make a combined protest with the United States against the latest war zone decree. The effect of a united neutral protest, some officials hoped, would have the effect of modifying Germany's announced intentions.

MAY ABANDON INAUGURATION

Sentiment Growing For Doing Away With Public Ceremonies.

Washington, Feb. 3.—While no decision has been reached officially, there is a very decided sentiment in all official quarters to abandon the public ceremonies of inauguration on March 5 and simply have the President take the oath of office in the White House on Sunday, March 4. The army and navy reception at the White House probably will be abandoned.

Those officials who favor abandoning the public ceremonies feel that with the President facing such critical international affairs the good of the country demands that he shall not be called upon to participate in public functions.

TROOPS RUSHED BACK

Order At El Paso To Hurry Departure Of Sixth Pennsylvania Infantry To East.

El Paso, Texas, Feb. 3.—An order received at the military headquarters today speeding up the departure of the Sixth Pennsylvania Infantry by 10 days is taken here by military officers to mean the state troops will be used at Eastern military depots because of the crisis with Germany.

This regiment will leave the sixth instead of the sixteenth of this month.

A Deming, N. M., dispatch states it is reported that the First Arkansas Infantry which left for the state camp yesterday will be diverted to San Antonio.

One Liner Gets Back Safely.

Amsterdam (Via London), Feb. 3.—The Handelsblad says that the Holland-America liner Nieuw Amsterdam, which was on her way to America and had been recalled by wireless, arrived off the Hook of Holland yesterday.

American Ship Sunk By Submarine Just After Wilson Broke Off Diplomatic Relations And Handed Passports To Von Bernstorff.

ANY OVERT ACT MEANS WAR

Nation Going Ahead With Plans In Case Of Hostilities--Senate To Rush Neutrality Act. Demand Made For Release of Americans Taken Prisoner By Raider.

With lightning like rapidity on the part of United States officials events moved within the last few hours toward warlike plans.

Following the breaking of diplomatic relations with Germany and the sinking of an American ship by a submarine, although without loss of life, Federal authorities seized the two interned German warships at Philadelphia. Four Hamburg-American steamers in the harbor of Cristobal, Panama, were also taken in charge. Plans were made to safeguard the canal and its night use forbidden.

President Wilson announced that an overt act by Germany would be followed by action.

Secretary Daniels asked the right to commandeer all private shipbuilding and munitions plants with Government contracts and to operate them.

The Senate, at the request of President Wilson, tried to hasten the passage of the neutrality bills prepared by the Department of Justice.

President Wilson himself was put under a stronger guard at the White House.

In Baltimore an order was issued to collect all the equipment of the Naval Militia and prepare it for shipment. This includes the guns on the Montgomery and the field pieces in the armory. Railroads have established guards around the grain elevators and terminals.

Word to seize the three German steamers interned in the Baltimore harbor is expected at any hour by the port authorities.

Washington, Feb. 3.—President Wilson has broken off diplomatic relations with Germany and warned the Kaiser that ruthless sacrifice of American lives and rights means war.

Similar action is waiting for Austria when she notifies this Government that she joins in the campaign of unrestricted submarine warfare.

The President made formal announcement of his action to the country and to the world today at a joint session of Congress.

BREAK TO BE COMPLETE.

Passports have been handed to Count von Bernstorff; Ambassador Gerard with all his staff and all American consuls have been ordered out of Germany. All German consuls in the United States are expected to withdraw, that the severance of relations may be complete. American diplomatic interests in Berlin have been turned over to Spain; German diplomatic interests in the United States have been taken over by Switzerland. Foreign diplomatic interests which the United States had in charge in Germany have been turned over to various neutrals.

Two years of diplomatic negotiation, marked with frequent crises, and attended with the loss of more than 200 American lives on the high seas, have culminated with an act which in all the history of all the world has always led to war. Every agency of the American Government has been set in motion to protect the country against acts of German sympathizers. These moves are of necessity being kept secret.

RELEASE OF AMERICANS DEMANDED.

With the notice of severance of relations the United States sent to Berlin a demand for the immediate release of 64 Americans taken from ships captured by German raiders in the South Atlantic.

At the request of the President, Congress immediately after hearing his address began work on new laws [illegible]

WEATHER--*Fair*
The Evening Sun Has Over
69,000
Net Paid Circulation.

THE EVENING SUN

3.45

VOL. XIV—NO. 146. PRESS RUN: MORNING [illegible] YESTERDAY EVENING [illegible] 179,811 SUNDAY 104,336 BALTIMORE, FRIDAY, APRIL 6, 1917. 20 PAGES. PRICE ONE CENT.

PRESIDENT PROCLAIMS WAR

EVERY TEUTON SHIP IN PORTS OF U. S. SEIZED

VOLUNTEER CALL ISSUED; ALIENS WARNED

U. S. Customs Officials And Armed Forces Take Over Interned Liners

Three Vessels Seized Here; Machinery Found Damaged.

STARS AND STRIPES RAISED TO MASTHEADS; POWDER ON BOARD

Germany's vast mercantile fleet, interned in United States ports, was seized today by United States armed forces.

It was America's first act of war. Ninety-one German vessels, representing a total tonnage of 594,696, are in the United States Government hands.

Three liners—the Bulgaria, Neckar and Rhein—were taken over in the Baltimore harbor by United States officials. Eighty-one officers and men were detained. The Stars and Stripes are now floating over the ships.

The Government code word that the House had passed the "war resolution," flashed from coast to coast before daybreak, set thousands of Government men in action.

In New York alone the ships seized are worth $51,600,000. The three vessels in the Baltimore waters are worth approximately $2,000,000.

Coincident with the seizures, it was announced from Washington, that crews taken off the merchantmen will be treated as "enemy aliens," not as prisoners of war.

Extraordinary precautions are being taken all over the country to avoid possible trouble from crews of the ships. Warships have been guarding the vessels since it became certain a declaration of war would be forthcoming. Two destroyers have been constantly on duty in the Hudson river in New York. They moved in closer early today and were accompanied by five naval cutters.

$51,600,000 IN SHIPPING SEIZED IN N. Y. HARBORS

27 Passenger Liners, Sailing Vessels And Freighters Taken Over.

New York, April 6.—Germany's $51,600,000 mercantile fleet, which had been interned here since the outbreak of the war, was seized by the United States today.

There were 27 passenger liners, freighters and sailing ships in the fleet, among them the Vaterland, one of the biggest and finest passenger liners in the world.

The German officers and crews, numbering more than 3,000 men, were taken to Ellis Island for internment.

This was the first decisive war measure against Germany in the metropolis

[Continued on Page 2]

THREE INTERNED GERMAN LINERS ARE SEIZED HERE

Rhein, Neckar And Bulgaria Taken Over—Cylinders Are Wrecked.

War history, in the making, began for Baltimore this morning.

While the city slept the Bulgaria, the Neckar and the Rhein, war-bound merchant vessels, were seized by the United States Government; the Black Eagle of Germany disappeared from the Patapsco for some time to come, and property valued at approximately $2,000,000 came into the possession of this country.

A deputy United States marshal raised the Stars and Stripes over the ships at 10.30 o'clock.

The seizure was accomplished peacefully and without the slightest disorder

[Continued on Page 2]

President's Proclamation And Call For Volunteers

Washington, April 6. — President Wilson this afternoon issued a proclamation to the American people, declaring that a state of war exists between the United States and the Imperial German Government.

Strong warnings to aliens that acts of violence or intrigue against the United States will be met with drastic action was contained in the President's proclamation.

The text of the proclamation follows:

By the President of the United States:

A Proclamation.

Whereas, the Congress of the United States in the exercise of the constitutional authority vested in them have resolved, by joint resolution of the Senate and House of Representatives bearing date this day "that the state of war between the United States and the Imperial German Government which has been thrust upon the United States is hereby formally declared";

Whereas, it is provided by Section 4067 of the Revised Statutes, as follows:

Aliens Liable To Detention.

Whenever there is declared a war between the United States and any foreign nation or government, or any invasion or predatory incursion is perpetrated, attempted or threatened against the territory of the United States by any foreign nation or government, and the President makes public proclamation of the event, all natives, citizens, denizens or subjects of the hostile nation or government, being males of the age of 14 and upwards, who shall be within the United States and not actually naturalized, shall be liable to be apprehended, restrained, secured and removed, as alien enemies.

The President is authorized in any such event by his proclamation thereof, or other public act, to direct the conduct to be observed on the part of the United States toward the aliens who become so liable; the manner and degree of the restraint to which they shall be subject, and in what cases, and upon what security their residence shall be permitted, and to provide for the removal of those who not being permitted to reside within the United States refuse or neglect to depart therefrom; and to establish any other regulations which are found necessary in the premises and for the public safety.

Whereas, by Sections 4068, 4069 and 4070, of the revised statutes, further provision is made relative to alien enemies:

Proclaims State Of War.

Now, therefore, I, Woodrow Wilson, President of the United States of America, do hereby proclaim to all whom it may concern that a state of war exists between the United States and the Imperial German Government; and I do specially direct all officers, civil and military, of the United States that they exercise vigilance and zeal in the discharge of the duties incident to such a state of war; and I do, moreover, earnestly appeal to all American citizens that they in loyal devotion to their country dedicated from its foundation to the principles of liberty and justice, uphold the laws of the land and give undivided and willing support to those measures which may be adopted by the constitutional authorities in prosecuting the war to a successful issue and in obtaining a secure and just peace;

Directs Conduct Toward Aliens.

And, acting under and by virtue of the authority vested in me by the Constitution of the United States and the said sections of the Revised Statutes, I do hereby further proclaim and direct that the conduct to be observed on the part of the United States toward all natives, citizens, denizens or subjects of Germany, being males of the age of 14 years and upward, who shall be within the United States and not actually naturalized, who for the purpose of this proclamation and under such sections of the Revised Statutes are termed alien enemies, shall be as follows:

Must Preserve The Peace.

All alien enemies are enjoined to preserve the peace toward the United States and to refrain from crime against the public safety and from violating the laws of the United States and of the states and territories thereof, and to refrain from actual hostility or giving information, aid or comfort to the enemies of the United States, and to comply strictly with the regulations which are hereby or which may be from time to time promulgated by the President: and so long as they shall conduct themselves in connection with law they shall be undisturbed in the peaceful pursuit of their lives and occupations and be accorded the consideration due to peaceful and law-abiding persons, except so far as restrictions may be necessary for their own protection and for the safety of the United States, and towards such alien enemies as conduct themselves in accordance with law all citizens of the United States are enjoined to preserve the peace and to treat them with all such friendliness as may be compatible with loyalty and allegiance to the United States.

And all alien enemies who fail to conduct themselves as so enjoined, in addition to all other penalties prescribed by law, shall be liable to restraint, or to give security, or to remove and depart from the United States in the manner prescribed by Sections 4069 and 4070 of the Revised Statutes and as prescribed in the regulations duly promulgated by the President.

Regulations Decreed.

And pursuant to the authority vested in me I hereby declare and establish the following regulations, which I find necessary in the premises and for the public safety:

(1) An alien enemy shall not have in his possession at any time or place any firearm, weapon or implement of war, or component part thereof, ammunition, Maxim or other silencer, bomb or explosive or material used in the manufacture of explosives;

(2) An alien enemy shall not have in his possession at any time or place, or use or operate any aircraft or wireless apparatus, or any form of signaling device, or any form of cipher code, or any paper, document or book written or printed in cipher or in which there may be invisible writing.

(3) All property found in the possession of an alien enemy in violation of the foreign relations shall be subject to seizure by the United States.

(4) An alien enemy shall not approach or be found within one-half mile of any Federal or state fort, camp, arsenal, aircraft station, Government or naval vessel, navy yard, factory or workshop for the manufacture of munitions of war or of any products for the use of the army or navy.

Bars All Criticism.

(5) An alien enemy shall not write, print or publish any attack or threats against the Government or Congress of the United States, or either branch thereof, or against the measures or policies of the United States, or against the person or property of any person in the military, naval or civil service of the United States, or of the states or territories or of the District of Columbia, or of the municipal governments therein;

(6) An alien enemy shall not commit or abet any hostile act against the United States or give information, aid or comfort to its enemies;

(7) An alien enemy shall not reside in or continue to reside in, to remain in, or enter any locality which the President may from time to time designate by Executive order as a prohibited area in which residence by an alien enemy shall be found by him to constitute a danger to the public peace and safety of the United States, except by permit from the President, and except under such limitations or restrictions as the President may prescribe;

(8) An alien enemy whom the President shall have reasonable cause to believe to be aiding or about to aid the enemy, or to be at large to the danger of the public peace or safety of the United States; or to have violated or to be about to violate any of these regulations shall remove to any location designated by the President by Executive order, and shall not remove therefrom without a permit, or shall depart from the United States if so required by the President;

(9) No alien enemy shall depart from the United States until he shall have received such permit as the President shall prescribe, or except under orders of a court, judge or justice, under Sections 4069 and 4070 of the Revised Statutes.

(10) No alien enemy shall land in or enter the United States, except under such restrictions and at such places as the President may prescribe.

Registration May Come.

(11) If necessary to prevent violations of these regulations, all alien enemies will be obliged to register.

(12 An alien enemy whom there may be reasonable cause to believe to be aiding or about to aid the enemy, or who may be at large to the danger of the public peace or safety, or who violates or attempts to violate or of whom there is reasonable ground to believe that he is about to violate any regulation duly promulgated by the President, or any criminal law of the United States, or the states or territories thereof, will be subject to summary arrest by the United States marshal, or his deputy, or such other officer as the President shall designate, and to confinement in such penitentiary, prison, jail, military camp or other place of detention as may be directed by the President.

Applies To All U. S. Possessions.

This proclamation and the regulations herein contained shall extend and apply to all land and water, continental or insular in any way within the jurisdiction of the United States.

In witness whereof I have hereunto set my hand and caused the Seal of the United States to be affixed.

Done at the city of Washington, this 6th day of April, in the year of Our Lord, One Thousand Nine Hundred and Seventeen, and of the Independence of the United States the One Hundred and Forty-first.

WOODROW WILSON.

By the President.

ROBERT LANSING.
Secretary of State.

Washington, April 6.—President Wilson this afternoon issued a call for volunteers to bring the army and navy up to war strength and gave his indorsement to the General Staff bill, designed to obtain men by selective conscription.

"The necessary men," said the President, in a statement, "will be secured for the regular army and the National Guard by volunteering, as at present, until, in the judgment of the President, a resort to selective draft is advisable."

The following statement was issued at the White House:

The principles embodied in the legislation presented by the War Department to the Military Committees of the Senate and House have my entire approval and its specific recommendations embody the best judgment of the officers of the War Department. It proposes to raise the forces necessary to meet the present emergency by bringing the regular army and the National Guard to war strength and by adding the additional forces which will now be needed so that the national army will comprise three elements—the regular army, the National Guard and the so-called additional forces, of which a first 500,000 are to be authorized immediately and later increments of the same size as they may be needed.

Enlistment For War Period.

In order that all these forces may comprise a single army, the term of enlistment in the three is equalized and will be for the period of the emergency. The necessary men will be secured for the regular army and the National Guard by volunteering, as at present, until, in the judgment of the President, a resort to a selective draft is desirable. The additional forces, however, are to be raised by selective draft from men ranging in age from 19 to 25 years.

The quotas of the several states in all of these forces will be in proportion to their population.

No Permanent Policy.

This legislation makes no attempt to solve the question of a permanent military policy for the country, chiefly for the reason that in these anxious and disordered times a clear view cannot be had either of our permanent military necessities or of the best mode of organizing a proper military peace establishment.

The hope of the world is that when the European war is over arrangements will have been made composing many of the questions which have hitherto seemed to require the arming of the nations, and that in some ordered and just way the peace of the world may be maintained by such co-operations of force among the great nations as may be necessary to maintain peace and freedom throughout the world.

When these arrangements for a permanent peace are made we can determine our military needs and adapt our course of military preparation to the genius of a world organized for justice and democracy. The present bill, therefore, is adapted to the present situation, but it is drawn upon such lines as will enable us to continue its policy, or so much of it as may be determined to be wise, when the present crisis has passed.

ENGLAND HAILS U. S.

Lloyd George, For Cabinet, Sends Stirring Message.

London, April 6. — Stating that he spoke at the instance of the Imperial War Cabinet, Premier Lloyd George this afternoon sent a stirring message to America recognizing her entrance into the war.

COAST GUARD ON DUTY

Twenty Fast Cutters Automatically Become Part Of Navy.

Washington, April 6.—Automatically with the beginning of war with Germany today, the coast guard fleet of 20 fast seagoing cutters became a part of the navy. They will still be under Capt. B. P. Bertholf, but subject to naval orders. It is expected they will be very valuable as submarine hunters and in general patrol work.

Naval Militia Gets Word To Prepare

Order For Actual Mobilization Expected By Men At Any Minute.

The Maryland Naval Militia received word this afternoon that they will likely be called at any minute to mobilize for Federal service. Everything is in readiness for the sailors to enter the service, all their equipment having been ready for several days.

Commander Charles F. Macklin was in Washington today conferring with the Navy Department in reference to the calling of the local Naval Militia.

TEXAS FEARS U-BOATS

Reported Presence In Gulf Causes Rush For Insurance.

Galveston, Texas, April 6. Reports that the Government has evidence of the presence in the Gulf of Mexico of German submarines caused many people here today to apply for insurance against bombardment, riots and civil disturbances.

Negro Is Seized In German Plot

U. S. Government Agents Arrest Him In Conspiracy To Incite Blacks To Rebel.

Birmingham, Ala., April 6. The third arrest in connection with German plots to incite negroes to rebellion was made here today when a negro, addressing members of his race at a local depot, declared they should join the German Army. Good pay, social equality and unrestricted franchise were offered.

Government agents made the arrest.

U-Boats Nearby Says Wireless

Warnings To Shipping Tell Of Submarines Between Porto Rico And Bermuda.

New York, April 6.—Wireless warnings today flashed to the Allied shipping that German submarines were sighted last night between Porto Rico and Bermuda. This locality is close to the Great Circle trade route between New York, the West Indies and South America. The warning read:

"Submarines reported 9 P. M., April 5, latitude 26 north, longitude 56.42 west. Take all precautions."

TO ENLARGE NAVY STATIONS

Washington, April 6. Enlargement of all naval training stations is to be effected at once, the Navy Department announced today. The station at Chicago will be one of the first to be enlarged.

President Signs Resolution And Issues Proclamation To The People; Orders Flashed To Fleet And All Naval Stations.

CALL FOR NAVAL MILITIA IS EXPECTED TO COME BY NIGHT

Washington, April 6.—After being in session just two hours and fifteen minutes the Senate adjourned until noon Monday.

Washington, April 6. The United States is at war with Germany. Formal entrance into the conflict came at 1.13 o'clock today.

At that hour President Wilson attached his signature to the Flood-Martin resolution, declaring that a state of war exists between this nation and the Imperial German Government, and pledging all the vast man and material resources of the country to bringing that war to a successful close. The resolution had been signed at the Capitol by Vice-President Marshall just one hour before.

Five minutes after the President had signed the resolution he addressed a proclamation to the American people and issued a call for volunteers for the army and navy.

ORDERS TO ALL ARMED FORCES

Simultaneously from a window in the White House executive offices Lieutenant-Commander Byron McCandless signaled across the street to the Navy Department that war was formally on and orders were flashed out from the Government wireless to the ships at sea and to the forts of the United States.

The following message was sent from the Arlington wireless on its way around the world, addressed to every United States war vessel and naval station:

"The President has signed an act of Congress which declares that a state of war exists between the United States and Germany."

This notice, the Navy said, is not an order to mobilize.

There were prospects that such an order would go through shortly, however.

NOTICE GIVEN TO THE WORLD.

Simultaneously every steam whistle in Washington and on the Potomac river nearby was opened wide, and their screeches could be heard in every nook and cranny of the nation's capital.

While the ink was still wet on the historic war resolution passed by the House and Senate, messages to all the countries of the earth were sent notifying them of this Government's action.

The State Department informed the Swiss Minister here, representing German interests in the United States, of this country's action. The Minister will communicate the word formally to Berne by cable and thence to Berlin.

United States representatives in every foreign and South American capital should have the news within the next 24 hours.

The President signed the resolution in the presence of Mrs. Wilson and his niece, Miss Helen Woodrow Bones.

It had been brought to him there by a messenger after Vice-President Marshall had affixed his signature in open session of the Senate at 12.13 o'clock.

SENT TO STATE DEPARTMENT

From the White House the engrossed document was sent to the State Department, there to rest as probably the most momentous paper filed away in the Government records.

It bears no outward mark of difference from hundreds of thousands of other state papers in the department files. But it marks the beginning of a new war of civilization, according to President Wilson—a war, the end of which must determine whether democracy or imperialism shall rule the world.

Immediately after signing the joint resolution for war the President issued a proclamation to the people of the country declaring a state of war exists between the United States and the Imperial German Government.

HOUSE VOTE ON BILL 373 TO 50.

Amid scenes that long will be remembered, the House this morning passed the Flood-Martin resolution, declaring that a state of war exists.

Three hundred and seventy-three votes were cast for the measure; 50 were cast against it; nine members were absent—and Speaker Champ Clark did not vote.

Immediately upon the Senate convening at noon Vice-Presi-

WEATHER FOR TODAY
Probably thunder showers; winds moderate and variable.
Detailed Weather Report on Page 6.

THE SUN

INDEX OF THE NEWS.
Telegraph ... 1, 2, 3
Maryland-Virginia ... 3
Local ... 3, 4, 5, 7, 14
Sports ... 8
Financial ... 9

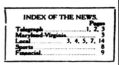

VOL. CLXI—NO. 37. PRESS RUN YESTERDAY {MORNING. 99,770 / EVENING. 68,196} 167,966 || SUNDAY. 102,442 BALTIMORE, THURSDAY MORNING, JUNE 28, 1917. 14 PAGES. ONE CENT IN BALTIMORE AND SUBURBS | ELSEWHERE TWO CENTS.

U. S. TROOPS PITCH CAMP IN FRANCE READY TO JOIN ALLIES ON FIRING LINE; LEGISLATURE ENDS: VOTE BILL DIES

TIES HUSBAND TO BED; SHOOTS HIM TO DEATH

Mrs. Minnie Carter, Frostburg, Driven To Desperation By His Brutality.

RAN TWO MILES TO NEIGHBORS

Woman Says Drunken Man Had Beaten And Thrown Her Unconconscious From House And Destroyed Her Kitchen Garden.

Cumberland, Md., June 27.—Mrs. Minnie Carter, 28 years old, shot to death her husband, Hugh Enoch Carter, 30 years old, while he slept in their home at Hoffman, a mining village not far from Frostburg, about 3 o'clock this morning.

It is alleged the woman was driven almost insane by ill-treatment from her husband. Before she fired the fatal shots she tied her husband to the bed with a clothes line. The first bullet went through the brain, lodging under the skin on the other side of the head, while the other two shots were fired into the heart. Any one of the three shots would have been fatal.

Fled After Shooting.

After firing the shots Mrs. Carter secured a long butcher knife and, cutting the cords that bound the body to the bed, she rushed from the house, shouting to neighbors. She found her way over the mountain to the home of Frank Klosterman, a distance of three miles, where she aroused the inmates and told the story of her tragic deed. Mr. Klosterman, at her request, telephoned for the authorities. County Detective Walter W. Clay placed her under arrest. She said she was glad to be taken to jail.

When the officers told Mrs. Carter they were going to her home, she asked that she might accompany them and point out the house, but she wanted protection from a sister of her husband who, she said, might be there. She was assured that she would be kept from harm. When the party reached Hoffman she pointed out the house, saying: "Go around to the back door and go into the bedroom and you will find him lying on the bed, dead."

Kissed Lifeless Body.

She led the way and when they reached the bed the woman threw herself on the lifeless form of her husband. Catching him around the neck, she pulled his face to hers and kissed him most affectionately. She wept bitterly. When she was lifted up by the officers her hands were covered with blood that had oozed from the wounds on the head and heart. Mrs. Carter then told Detective Clay the full story of the affair.

She said: "My husband came home last night in company with a friend, Joe Brode, and both were very drunk. I told Brode to leave my home. My husband refused to let him go and began to quarrel with me. I became frightened and, hoping to avert a scene in the presence of Brode, I left the house and went to the home of a neighbor, Katie Seifarth, whom I told of the trouble. She begged me to stay all night with her, but I returned home.

Thrown Over Porch.

"When I got back, Enoch began to quarrel and ordered me from the house. I did not go and he pushed me to the door and threw me over the porch. I fell to the ground and was unable to get up, so he came with a bucket of cold water and threw it on me. He then picked me up and carried me back into the house and laid me on the floor. I must have been made senseless by the fall from the porch, for when I got up my husband was sitting at the table. I struggled to my feet and sat down near the table. He got a can of corn and with a large butcher knife opened it. He began to eat and when he had finished, he asked me to go to bed. I told him I was not going to bed and he went into the room. Thinking that I might prevent further trouble, I got up and undressed and went to bed with him. He began quarreling again. We talked and argued for some time. He became quiet and fell asleep.

Says "He Made Me Do It."

"When I thought he was sound asleep I crept out of bed and went to the kitchen and secured the clothesline. I came back into the bedroom and went over to see if he was still asleep, and finding that he was, tied one end of the rope around his wrist and threw the other part of the rope under the bed. Going to the other side, I took his other hand and tied it tight, so that he could not move. I then went to the buffet drawer, secured the pistol and box of cartridges and loaded the gun. I carried it to the bedroom and put it under my pillow and lay down again to give him time to get sound asleep. When I thought he was sound asleep I got up, took the pistol and went to the side where he was lying. I put the pistol close to his head and fired. I fired two more shots at his heart. Believing that I had killed him, I took the butcher knife that he had opened the can of corn with and cut the ropes. I ran from the house after calling several times for the neighbors. He made me do it."

"Good Man When Sober."

Upon reaching the Klosterman home, after her flight over the mountain, Mrs. Carter told Mrs. Klosterman:

"I am frail and weak. My husband is a good man when he is sober, but when he is drunk he makes my life a living hell. I got out of the hospital but two months ago and his abuse has nearly killed me many nights. I just couldn't stand it. Sunday night he came home in one of his drunken fits. He beat me and threw me from the house. I was unconscious. A neighbor picked me up and I stayed at their home that night."

Mrs. Carter was brought to jail here. She expressed sorrow for her act tonight, saying:

"I did not kill him because I hated him, for I loved him when he was sober, but he made me do it. I am sorry now that he is dead."

She said they had been married three years and lived happily the first two until Carter began to drink. She told of his having thrown her off the porch last Sunday, of his having wrecked her garden with pick and shovel while drunk Monday night and of bespattering with dirty water the walls of the kitchen which she had freshly papered with her own hands.

Arrested For Beating Wife.

She had taken great pride in the garden and his vandalism added to her desperation. She showed her sunburned arm which came from work. Mrs. Carter accused relatives of her husband with giving him whisky. He was to have had a hearing tonight before Justice Gatehouse, Frostburg, for wife-beating, having been arrested yesterday.

Mrs. Carter said: "After I had tied his hands and prepared the gun with which to shoot him, I was so nervous that I could hardly hold the revolver and when I took first aim and heard

[Continued on Page 3.]

FOOD CONTROL BILL MADE MORE DRASTIC

President Given Authority Only To Allow The Manufacture Of Wine During The War.

CAN COMMANDEER FACTORIES

Wide Powers To Operate Oil Wells And Mines And To Seize Any Supplies Needed For Defense Conferred.

Washington, June 27.—Food control legislation assumed new and more drastic form today when the Senate Agriculture Committee virtually redrafted many of the principal features of the House measure and reported it with material extensions of Government power and a new "bone-dry" prohibition provision to stop manufacture of intoxicating beverages during the war. The President would be authorized to permit wine making and to commandeer existing distilled spirits.

The amended bill was presented to the Senate by Senator Chamberlain, who will move tomorrow to have it substituted for the draft the Senate has been debating and proceed with all expedition toward final action.

The new prohibition plan, all leaders admitted tonight, greatly complicates the situation and precludes enactment of the legislation by July 1.

In extending the scope of the legislation and the President's powers, the committee adopted amendments which would provide for government control, in addition to food, feeds and fuel, of iron, steel, copper, lead and their products, farm implements and machinery, fertilizers and binding twine materials.

Gives Best Powers To Government.

Other important amendments approved would authorize the government to take over and operate factories, packing houses, oil wells and mines, regulating wages of their employes, and to commandeer supplies of any and every kind when needed for the army and navy "or other public use connected with the public defense."

Another would empower the government to buy and sell, for general civilian purposes, food, feeds and fuel, with limitation upon the general legislation, making it apply to agencies and products only in interstate or foreign commerce.

The amendments are declared by Senators who have been opposing as well as those supporting the legislation to improve the bill and remove almost all opposition except upon prohibition.

The prohibition section was written into the bill by a vote of 9 to 7.

The committee rejected by 8 to 7 its subcommittee's recommendation that the President be given authority to permit continuance of manufacture of malt and fermented beverages.

While the committee was revising the House or Lever measure the Senate debate on the original Chamberlain draft was suspended. The discussion on the redraft was postponed until tomorrow.

Filibuster Considered.

The possibility of a filibuster because of the drastic prohibition proposal is being considered. Senate leaders agree that the prohibition fight will probably be long and one of the most strenuous

[Continued on Page 2.]

House Combine, Loth To Drop Political Sandbag, Finally Quits.

REPUBLICANS PLAY A WINNING GAME

Soldier Vote More Valuable To Democrats Than To Them.

[From THE SUN Bureau.]

Annapolis, June 27.—Common sense finally prevailed in the State House today, to the extent that the Legislature adjourned sine die. It did not prevail to the extent of compelling the passage of the Soldiers and Sailors' Vote bill; that measure, designed to give Marylanders who are going forth to offer their lives for their country, the simple privilege of participating in the Government they are protecting, was defeated through the stubborn and selfish partisanship and factionalism of the Mahon-Preston-Jackson-Weller combination.

Of course, the Wilson ballot law, which the combination demanded as its pound of flesh before the Soldiers' Vote bill could be passed was beaten. It was killed Tuesday night, when the Senate rejected the House separate repealer bill by a decisive vote and then put the "clincher" on the rejection. The combination had put the repealer through the House overwhelmingly.

PUBLIC DISGUST OVER FARCE.

Today's adjournment sine die was a belated submission to public opinion,

[Continued on Page 7.]

AN APPEAL BY THE PRESIDENT.

To the Officers, Teachers and Scholars of the Sunday Schools of the United States of America:

The present insistent call of our beloved country must be heard and answered by every citizen of the United States in proportion to his or her ability to maintain the national power and honor. Many citizens will render their aid by force of arms on the battle field, while others will make the nation strong by their patriotic gifts and support to the common cause. It is, therefore, highly fitting that the Sunday schools of the nation should observe a special patriotic day, and on this occasion should make a special contribution to the American Red Cross for the alleviation of the suffering entailed by the prosecution of the present war. It is my earnest hope that your generosity may be unstinted in this the hour of the nation's need, and that this special day may mean much to you in the understanding of the cause for which our beloved land now contends.

WOODROW WILSON.

NOTE.—Next Sunday, July 1, has been designated as Patriotic Sunday, to be observed as recommended by the President in the above letter.

28 BRITISH SHIPS SUNK BY U-BOATS LAST WEEK

American Sailing Ship Galena Sent Down Off French Coast; All Hands Safe.

MANY LIVES LOST WITH 3 CRAFT

Only Six Of Norwegian Steamer's Crew Rescued—22 On Greek And Six On Danish Vessel Perish—British Liner Mongales Sunk By Mine.

London, June 27.—Twenty-one British vessels of more than 1,600 tons each and seven under 1,600 tons were sunk by mines or submarines last week, according to the weekly statement of losses issued by the Admiralty this evening.

No fishing vessels met with disaster.

The American sailing ship Galena 1,048 tons, was sunk by a bomb on June 25, off Ushant Island (off the coast of France, 26 miles northwest of Brest). There were no casualties. Fifteen survivors were taken to Brest.

A Central News despatch from Copenhagen says the Norwegian steamship Kong Haakon has been sunk by a German submarine, and that only six of the crew were saved. (There are two Norwegian ships King Haakon of 2,231 and 874 tons gross.)

The Norwegian steamship Maggie (1,118 tons gross) has been sunk in the Atlantic. The crew were saved.

Eight Americans On Galena.

New York, June 27.—The Galena was formerly the barkentine Foohng Suey. She left here March 22 with cargo for Rouen, France. She carried a crew of 18 men commanded by Capt. P. V. Marshall, among whom, according to the records of the United States Commissioner of Shipping here, were eight American citizens.

Under the name of Foohng Suey the vessel was built in 1888 at Glasgow, Scotland, and when launched Queen Victoria is said to have pressed the button that released her from the stocks. She was built for the sugar carrying trade out of the Hawaiian Islands and was named by a Chinese merchant of Honolulu, the name signifying "Fair Wind—Good Water."

In 1913 the vessel was badly wrecked by a hurricane off the Virginia capes, after which she was sold for a barge. The European war and the demand for ocean tonnage resulted in her again being restored to her status as a sailing ship. Her masts were replaced and under the new name of Galena, early in the present year, she was put back into service on the high seas.

22 Lost With Greek Steamer.

New York, June 27.—The Greek steamship N. Hadzikyriakos was torpedoed and sunk by a German submarine

[Continued on Page 2.]

FRENCH GREET TROOPS WITH FRANTIC CHEERS

Enthusiasm Rises To Fever Pitch When Second Contingent Arrives Safely.

SOLDIERS EAGER FOR ACTION

Transferred To Camp Near Landing Port, Where General Sibert Has Command — Soon To Be Moved Close To Front.

A French Seaport, June 27.—The second contingent of American troops arrived and disembarked this morning.

The troops landed amid the frantic cheers of the people, who had gathered for hours before in anticipation of duplicating yesterday's surprise.

Enthusiasm rose to fever pitch when it was learned that the transports and convoys had successfully passed the submarine zone. The port was speedily beflagged in honor of the occasion.

All the troops now arrived were transferred today to a camp not distant from this point, where Major-General Wm. L. Sibert is installed. Thence they probably will go soon to a point near the front. All the troops are in excellent shape, enthusiastic over the successful trip and their reception and eager for action.

Major-General Pershing, the American commander, is expected tomorrow when additional troops are expected.

The harbor is dotted with convoys. The streets are filled with soldiers in khaki and with bluejackets. Great numbers of truck, are transporting immense supplies to the camp in which the troops are concentrating.

2,700 Marines Slipped Away.

New York, June 27.—So quietly did a regiment of marines included in that part of the Pershing expedition which already has landed in France slip away from the League Island Navy Yard that a sailor baseball team at practice on the parade ground did not know 2,700 men under command of Col. Charles A. Doyen were on their way to the batlle front. No drums or bugles sounded and the only ceremony which attended the leave-taking was a brief speech to the officers by Major-Gen. George Barnett, command of the corps. The story of their quiet march from barracks was released here tonight.

At 2.30 o'clock on the afternoon of the departure the baseball players had the parade ground all to themselves, and no one was in sight on the street in front of the home of the post commander. A few seconds later the head of a column of soldiers of the sea in khaki and in heavy marching order swung into the brick-paved street in front of the commander's house. Major-General Barnett and a little group of other officers from headquarters took up posts on the turf of the parkway beside the curb.

Barnett Bade Them Good-By.

The company officers of the battalion stepped out in front of Major-General Barnett and saluted. For half a minute the corps commandant addressed them. He spoke in an every-day conversational tone which could not be heard a dozen yards away, and the message was simply that he trusted that the marines who were setting out that day to fight under General Pershing would stanchly uphold the high traditions of the corps.

The officers saluted and marched back to their places. The battalion stood at rigid attention for a moment. Then, with a snap, rifles jumped to shoulders, squads swung into column formation, and the line passed swiftly on down the street to the gate of the navy yard.

No cheering crowd greeted the men as

[Continued on Page 2.]

Advance Guard Of Army Lands 40 Days After Getting Orders.

RECORDS BROKEN BY SWIFT ACTION

Force, Many Thousands Strong, Fully Equipped For Service.

U. S. AIRCRAFT EXPERTS LAND IN ENGLAND.

Washington, June 27.—Safe arrival at a British port of a party of about 125 aircraft experts sent from this country to investigate European methods of aircraft designing and manufacture was announced late today by the Aircraft Production Board.

Included in the delegation are men representing legal, manufacturing, designing, engineering, military and naval experience and training.

Washington, June 27.—The advance guard of the mighty army the United States is preparing to send against Germany is on French soil tonight.

In defiance of the German submarines, thousands of seasoned regulars and marines, trained fighting men with the tan of long service on the Mexican border, or in Haiti, or Santo Domingo, still on their faces, have been hastened overseas to fight beside the French, the British, the Belgian, the Russian, the Portuguese and the Italian troops on the western front.

NEWS THRILLS WASHINGTON.

News of the safe arrival of the troops sent a new thrill through Washington.

No formal announcement came from the War Department. None will come, probably, until Maj.-Gen. Pershing's official report has been received. Then there may be a statement as to the numbers and composition of the advance guard.

Press dispatches from France, presumably sent forward with the approval of [redacted]rshing's staff, show that M[redacted] Sibert, one of the new maj[redacted]s of the army, has been given command of the first force sent abroad, under General Pershing as commander-in-chief of the expedition.

MOVEMENT UNRIVALED.

One thing stands out sharply, despite the fact that the size of the task that has been accomplished is not fully revealed as yet. This is that American enterprise has set a new record for the transportation of troops.

Considering the distance to be covered and the fact that all preparations had to be made after the order came from the White House the night of May 18, it is practically certain that never before has a military expedition of this size been assembled, conveyed and landed without mishap in so short a time by any nation. It is a good augury of future achievements. The only rival in magnitude is the movement of British troops to South Africa in the Boer War, and that was made over seas that were unhampered by submarines, mines or other obstacles.

NET GAIN TO ALLIES.

The American forces will be a net gain to the Allies. It will throw no single burden of supply or equipment upon them. The troops will be fed, clothed, armed and equipped by the United States. Around them at the camp on French soil tonight are being stored supplies that will keep them going for months, and more will follow.

General Pershing and his staff have been busy for days preparing for the arrival of the men. Despite the enormous difficulties of unpreparedness and submarine dangers that faced them, the plans of the Army General Staff have gone through with clocklike precision.

When the order came to prepare immediately an expeditionary force to go to France, virtually all of the men now across the seas were on the Mexican border. General Pershing himself was at his headquarters in San Antonio. There were no army transports available in the Atlantic. The vessels that carried the troops were scattered on their usual routes. Army reserve stores were still depleted from the border mobilization. Regiments were below war strength.

WHEELS QUICKLY IN MOTION.

That was the condition when President Wilson decided that the plea of the French High Commission should be answered and a force of regulars sent at once to France. At his word the War Department began to move. General Pershing was summoned quietly to Washington. His arrival created some speculation in the press, but at the request of Secretary Baker the newspapers generally refrained from discussing this point.

There were a thousand other activities afoot in the department at the time. All the business of preparing for the military registration of ten million men, of providing quarters and instructors for nearly 50,000 prospective officers, of finding arms and equipment for millions of troops yet to be organized, of expanding the regular army to full war strength, of preparing and recruiting the National Guard for war, was at hand.

PUBLICITY AVOIDED.

General Pershing dropped quietly into the Department and set up the first headquarters of the American expeditionary forces in a little office hardly large enough to hold himself and his personal staff. There, with the aid of the General Staff, of Secretary Baker and of the chiefs of the War Department Bureaus, the plans were worked out.

Announcement of the sending of the force under General Pershing was made May 18. The press gave the news to the country and there were daily stories. There came a day when General Pershing was no longer in the department. Officers of the General Staff suddenly were missing from their desks. No word of this was reported. Then came word from England that Pershing and his officers were there. All was carried through without publicity.

Other matters relating to the expe

[Continued on Page 2.]

Baltimore Men At The Battle Front

American Troops Landed In France Today

The Baltimore Red Cross Hospital Unit--doctors, nurses, ambulance drivers--landed with the troops for active service today.

What Service Are YOU Giving To The Nation?

YOU would be driving an ambulance over shell-scarred roads in France—if you could.

YOU would be at the operating table in a war hospital, bringing wounded boys back to life—if you could.

YOU would be a nurse, helping fathers of families to grope their way out of the shadow of death—if you could.

YOU would check the whole ghastly torrent of pain and anguish—if you could.

YOU CAN

You can have a share in it all—in all the splendid work of building up again what war beats down. You can give to the American Red Cross, knowing that thus you are multiplying your own capacity to help, for your money will be used to give skilled, scientifically trained, efficient workers more power in succoring wounded men and destitute women and children.

Ten million young men are registered here for military service—your own young men. Think of the multitude of mothers and fathers and wives and children whose happiness and welfare is bound up with those ten million.

Seven million men have died in Europe in the war. Ten million more have been gravely wounded or crippled for life. Do you grasp the misery which lies behind those facts?

One hundred million dollars is a little sum for one hundred million people to give to such sufferings as that.

This is your Red Cross Week—when you can make your own eagerness to help effective. Will you do it?

Send your check or money order to Mr. R. Brent Keyser, Chairman, 17 South Street.

Executive Committee, Baltimore Red Cross Chapter.

This advertisement is paid for by a special contribution, and not one cent comes out of the Red Cross War Fund.

WEATHER FOR TODAY.
Fair; moderate northwest to north winds.
Detailed Weather Report on Page 6.

THE SUN

VOL. CLXI—NO. 152 PRESS RUN YESTERDAY MORNING } 101,596 || SUNDAY 106,890 BALTIMORE, FRIDAY MORNING, NOVEMBER 9, 1917. 14 PAGES. ONE CENT IN BALTIMORE; ELSEWHERE TWO CENTS

REVOLUTIONISTS SEIZE PETROGRAD; IMMEDIATE PEACE IS DECLARED FOR AND ARREST OF KERENSKY ORDERED

LATEST DEVELOPMENTS OF THE WAR

Petrograd again is in turmoil.

The Provisional Government has been thrown out of power by the Extreme Radicals headed by Nickolai Lenine; Premier Kerensky has fled the capital; several of his ministers have been placed under arrest, and the Winter Palace, the seat of the Government, has been bombarded by the guns of the cruiser Aurora and of the St. Peter and St. Paul fortress and forced to capitulate to the revolutionists.

A congress of the Workmen and Soldiers' Delegates of all Russia has convened in Petrograd and will discuss the questions of organization of power, peace and war and the formation of a constituent assembly. A delegation has been named by the congress to confer with other revolutionary and democratic organizations with a view to initiating peace negotiations for the purpose of "taking steps to stop the bloodshed."

As yet the details of the disorders which followed the assumption of power by the Radical element are meagre, but it is known that from its moorings in the Neva, the cruiser Aurora fired shrapnel and solid shot against the Winter Palace for four hours, with the guns of the great fortress and machine guns stationed in front of the Palace keeping in accord with the salvos from the warship. Desultory fighting also took place at various points inside the city, the revolutionaries capturing vantage points along the Nevsky Prospekt and various bridges over the Neva. It is possible that the casualties among the citizenry were slight, as the Workmen's and Soldiers' Delegates took precautions to warn the people to seek refuge in their homes.

Reports as to the whereabouts of Kerensky are various. Some of them say that he has sought safety in Moscow, while others assert that he has gone to the front in an endeavor to obtain the backing of the troops to forestall a debacle of his Government. Cossack regiments are declared already to have announced their readiness wholeheartedly to support the Government on condition that no compromise with the revolutionists is made, but on the other hand it is asserted that delegates from the Black and Baltic Sea fleets have declared themselves in favor of the Radicals.

There has been no cessation in the retreat of the Italians across the Venetian plains toward the new line of defense on which it is purposed to stand and face the invading Germans and Austro-Hungarians. The larger units of the Italians are falling back without molestation, according to the Rome official communication, but considerable fighting has taken place in the hills of Vittorio and at other points in the north.

Along the line in France and Belgium only artillery duels and raiding operations by the French and British forces are taking place.

Additional ground has been gained by the British troops against the Turks in Palestine and along the Tigris river.

Dictatorship Believed Essential To Save Land From Chaos.

TRYING TO COMMIT NATIONAL SUICIDE

Fighting Spirit Seems Dissipated In Impotent Struggles.

[*From The Sun Bureau.*]

Washington, Nov. 8.—If Russia is to be a military factor again in this war a military dictator must rise up and take command of her, restoring the rule of iron. Only immediate and smashing moves in this direction will save that benighted country from chaos, surrender or civil war. This is the conviction which Washington has yielded to, following the receipt of incomplete reports from Petrograd of the "bloodless" triumph of Maximalist forces, the banishment of Kerensky from power, the dissolution of the Provisional Government and the frank announcement that a separate peace would be negotiated at once.

GERMANY'S GOLDEN CHANCE.

To say that such an overthrow was expected is not to minimize its gravity. To add that this seems as fair a time as any for the two elements in Russia to settle their differences, by force of arms, does not relieve the situation of its depressing influence. An uprising against Kerensky may have been expected in official circles, and this may be an acceptable time for Russians to fight it out among themselves, but meantime the Central Powers will be permitted to withdraw even greater bodies of men from the Western front and to hurl them with renewed energy against the Allies in Italy and France.

Meantime Russia is further debilitating herself, consuming whatever is left of fighting power in trying to make her national suicide more complete. She will be yielding more and more to the Prussian propagandists, to the "softheads" among her own people and to the clamor for confiscation and division of Russian wealth among the long-haired and the shirt-tailed proletariat.

NOT YET FIT FOR DEMOCRACY.

The real truth seems to be that Russia in no sense is fit for democracy, any more than the average Mexican is fit for it. Certainly Russia has shown no evidence of ability to govern herself within the five or six months that she has been floundering around in shallow water. Regime after regime has arisen and fallen. Personality after personality has loomed above the horizon for a brief period, only to sink back in the face of the first flurry and remain innocuous.

And all this has taken place without bloodshed, without a great deal of fuss and with no convulsive struggle at all. If this means anything, it means that there is not much, if any, real fight left in Russia. There was not enough to organize a skirmish when Czar Nicholas was overthrown; there was not enough when Milinkoff was summarily kicked out; there was not enough when Kerensky was elevated to the premiership: when Korniloff mutined or when the provisionals were booted overboard.

If there is any marrow in the bones of the men who are now running Russia or seeking to run it, no evidence of the fact is patent. If there is any red blood in the veins of the Russian people they have concealed the fact for so long a time that the rest of the world has forgotten that it ever existed.

MAY BE A STRONG MAN.

There may be a strong man somewhere in Russia. If there is such a person, whether he be royalist, militarist or peasant, the allied world is prepared to welcome him to power and to support him with all the resources that can be given him. For some few weeks Kerensky seemed to be that person, notwithstanding his feeble health. He had fire; he had a degree of courage; he was young and picturesque and persuasive.

But Kerensky has muddled. He has sought to lead one element while dickering with the other. He has played politics instead of fighting a war. And though he may not be submerged by the developments of the past 24 hours, what of prestige he may have had has been neutralized. In some quarters today it is hoped that Kerensky will come out of this business on top and that he will be stronger than ever for having overcome the most pernicious of his enemies. If this happens he may be forgiven some of the weaknesses he has displayed, but it remains to be seen if he can come back.

DICTATOR VS. CIVIL WAR.

If there is not a military dictatorship such as was promised Russia for a few brief hours when Korniloff headed toward Petrograd with his legions, then the chances are that the country will be plunged into some sort of civil war. It may not be another French revolution, for there does not seem to be enough manhood and spirit left in Russia to organize even a mob versus mob fight, but it will be enough of a frenzy and furor to make the country totally passive in so far as Germany and Austria are concerned.

There is a degree of relief felt in Washington today over the turn of affairs in Russia, little as is actually known about it. Many leading men who have felt for months that no genuine support might ever again be expected from the Russians are now reconciled to the situation. They take the position that the remainder of the Allies would have had to crush Germany anyway and that they might as well learn soon or late exactly how big a job they have before them.

ITALIAN DRIVE A TEST.

Already some sense of this is determined by the strength of the drive against Italy. There is not a doubt that the bulk of the German and Austrian armies which have been operating on the Russian front are now concentrated against Italy. If they are held in the Venetian plains, then the Allies will understand that the aggressive power of their enemies has been fathomed for the first time. Such a revelation will be of great military value to the conference about to begin in London. J. F. E.

Winter Palace Bombarded And Women Defenders Forced To Capitulate.

WORKMEN'S CONGRESS BEGINS ITS SESSIONS

Lenine Welcomed Back And Chosen As An Officer Of The Body.

Petrograd, Nov. 8.—Government forces holding the Winter Palace were compelled to capitulate early this morning under the fire of the cruiser Aurora and the cannon of the Sts. Peter and Paul Fortress across the Neva river. At 2 o'clock this morning the Woman's Battalion, which had been defending the Winter Palace, surrendered. The Workmen and Soldiers' delegates are in complete control of the city.

Premier Kerensky was reported last night at Luga, 85 miles southwest of Petrograd.

GUNS OPEN FIRE.

Late yesterday evening, after the Government forces had been driven into the Winter Palace, the palace was besieged and a lively fire of machine guns and rifles began. The cruiser Aurora, which was moored at the Nicolai bridge, moved up within range, firing shrapnel. Meanwhile the guns of the St. Peter and St. Paul fortress opened fire.

The palace stood out under the glare of the searchlights of the cruiser and offered a good target. The defenders held out for four hours, replying as best they could with machine guns and rifles. There was spasmodic firing in other parts of the city, but the Workmen and Soldiers' troops took every means to protect citizens, who were ordered to their quarters. The bridges and the Nevsky Prospekt, which early in the afternoon were in the hands of the Government forces, were captured and held during the night by the Workmen and Soldiers' troops.

BATTLE IS SPECTACULAR.

The battle at the palace, which began shortly after 6 o'clock, was a spectacular one, armed cars of the revolutionaries swinging into action in front of the palace gates while flashes from the Neva were followed by the explosion of shells from the guns of the Aurora, a cruiser of 6,730 tons, with a complement of 573 men.

At noon the city presented a normal aspect. Even the noonday band accompanying the guard of relief under the previous administration continued its function.

There were the customary lines in front of the provision stores and children played in the parks and gardens. There was even a notable lessening of the patrols, only a few armed soldiers and sailors moving about the streets.

WORKMEN'S CONGRESS MEETS.

The General Congress of Workmen and Soldiers' Delegates of all Russia was convened here last night with 560 delegates in attendance. The chairman declared that the time was not propitious for political speeches and the order of business of the congress approved was as follows:

First. Organization of power.
Second. Peace and war.
Third. A constituent assembly.

The officers elected comprise 14 Maximilasts, including Nikolai Lenine, the Radical Socialist leader; M. Zinovieff, an associate of Lenine, and Leon Trotzky, president of the central executive committee of the Petrograd Council of Workmen and Soldiers' Delegates. In addition, seven Revolutionary Socialists were appointed.

A delegation was named to initiate peace negotiations with the other revolutionary and democratic organizations, "with a view to taking steps to stop bloodshed."

ASSUMES FULL POWER.

The official news agency today made public the following statement:

"The Congress of the Councils of Workmen and Soldiers' Delegates of all Russia, which opened last evening, issued this morning the three following proclamations:

"'To all provincial councils of workmen and soldiers' and peasants' delegates: All power lies in the Workmen and Soldiers' Delegates. Government commissaries are relieved of their functions. Presidents of the Workmen and Soldiers' Delegates are to communicate direct with the revolutionary government. All members of agricultural committees who have been arrested are to be set at liberty immediately, and the commissioners who arrested them are in turn to be arrested.'

KERENSKY DECLARED FUGITIVE

"The second proclamation reads:

"'The death penalty re-established at the front by Premier Kerensky is abolished, and complete freedom for political propaganda has been established at the front. All revolutionary soldiers and officers who have been arrested for complicity in so-called political crimes are to be set at liberty immediately.'

"The third proclamation says:

"'Former Minister Konovaloff, Kishkin, Terestchenko, Maiantovitch, Nikitin and others have been arrested by the revolutionary committee.

"'M. Kerensky has taken flight and all military bodies have been empowered to take all possible measures to arrest Kerensky and bring him back to Petrograd. All complicity with Kerensky will be dealt with as high treason.'"

Nikolai Lenine was introduced by Trotzky as "an old, old comrade, whom we welcome back."

Lenine said: "Now we have a revolution. The peasants and workmen control the government. This is only a preliminary step toward a similar revolution everywhere."

FOR A DEMOCRATIC PEACE.

The text of the proclamation of the military revolutionary committee reads:

"To the army committees of the active army and to all councils of Soldiers and Workmen's delegates and to the garrison and proletariat of Petrograd:

"We have deposed the government of Kerensky which rose against the revolution and the people. The change which resulted in the deposition of the provisional government was accomplished without bloodshed.

"The Petrograd Council of Soldiers and Workmen's delegates solemnly welcomes the accomplished change and proclaims the authority of the military revolutionary committee until the creation of a government by the Soldiers and Workmen's delegates.

"The Petrograd Council of Workmen

Dr. Birckhead Takes Air Ride In British Seaplane And Goes Down In Submarine

As A Guest Of British Admiralty He Sees Every Part Of The Armada That Guards The Empire—Goes Aboard Battleships, Visits Docks And From H. M. S. Ganges He Wrote Of All He Saw.

The Sun prints today a letter from Dr. Hugh Birckhead written on board the English battleship Ganges and mailed on October 13 from Harwich. On that day Dr. Birckhead had returned from a tour arranged for him by the British Admiralty to let him see the activities of the British Navy.

In the course of this tour Dr. Birckhead went up in the air in a British seaplane and down under the water in a British submarine. He describes graphically these thrilling experiences. Two more letters from Dr. Birckhead, written to The Sun before he sailed for home, will follow. One of these will be printed in The Evening Sun this afternoon and the other one, mailed the day before he sailed for home, in The Sunday Sun. Dr. Birckhead arrived in Baltimore yesterday.

By HUGH BIRCKHEAD.

H. M. S. Ganges, Harwich, October 13.—I am just completing an inspection tour, arranged for me by the Admiralty, of the activities of the British Navy.

I felt London for Edinburgh on Monday night, accompanied by Commander Colthorpe. On our arrival at the Capital of Scotland on Tuesday morning we were taken in charge by Captain Fitzclarance, who met us in an official motor car, and went at once out of the city, through the beautiful suburbs, past the great buildings of the University, down to the Firth of Forth. This broad expanse of water was filled with every kind of craft which represents the British Navy. They stretched endlessly into the distance, and gave one the impression of incalculable strength. We were told, as we stepped into the launch that had been sent for us, that they had orders to proceed to sea on one-half hour's notice.

MAKES TOUR OF FLEET.

We first took a tour of the fleet, passing battleships, battle-cruisers, destroyers, large submarines of the "K" class and the extraordinary new craft called seaplane carriers. These last were quite new to my unaccustomed eyes, consisting principally of a great storage area for the planes, and a long stretch of deck over which these aircraft may make a running start. The smokestack has been transferred to the stern.

It is one of the great questions before modern naval authorities how these huge planes may be swiftly carried from place to place, as they are the natural and most effective enemy of the submarine.

We then went aboard the Renown, a battle-cruiser of the newest type, and were conducted at once to the captain's cabin, where we were cordially welcomed by that officer, who took us in charge and personally conducted us over the great vessel. There is a crew of 1,300 men on the Renown, 500 of them being stokers, 116 boys under 18 years of age, and 100 marines. This is an oil-burning ship of the latest type, having been in commission one year. We marveled at its spaciousness, cleanliness and perfect ventilation. There were not anywhere the usual nautical odors which one associates even with an ocean liner. The quickness, attention and evident keenness of the crew were remarkable, as the ship had just returned from a long and tedious night of duty out at sea and many of the officers had had no sleep. Having inspected the ample quarters of the officers and crew, kitchens, bakery (where 15,000 pounds of bread are baked per day) dryrooms, and so forth, we went up on the decks to look over the armament.

We were particularly interested in the anti-aircraft guns, also the arrangement of the forward guns (no longer in turrets, but placed behind shields in groups of three), and the six largest guns which can send a projectile for many miles across the sea. We were also particularly struck by the planning of the direction of the ship while in action and the method by which the surface of the water forward is divided mathematically by little observation holes through which a man gazes fixedly at his particular area without the distraction of being able to see all about him. Of course, a great deal that we saw cannot be written down, but the general impression was of an alertness and efficiency beyond anything which a landsman has imagined.

LUNCHEON IN "KING'S CABIN."

Captain Hodges conducted us to the side of his ship and we descended to our launch again and crossed the water to the great dockyard at Rosyth. Here we were the guests at luncheon of Captain Warleigh on board the Crescent. This ship was the first important charge given to the present King of England when he was a naval officer, and luncheon was served in "the King's cabin." Captain Warleigh's simplicity and courtesy made it hard to believe that he was responsible for the activities of 4,000 men stationed at Rosyth, and was then facing some most difficult problems. In spite of the entrance of orderlies with telegrams and messages, which he quickly disposed of, he gave us the impression that his time was absolutely ours.

After luncheon a special officer was called to conduct us over the great dock yard. Rosyth is one of the largest achievements of the British Navy since the war began. It is the newest and is soon to be the most important base of the fleet, even overshadowing Portsmouth. In 1914 it was impossible to dock a ship here, but by June, 1916, great drydocks, workshops, cranes and the huge interior basin for floating the largest ships were all complete. At present a city is being built upon the sloping hills back of the harbor, and already its rows of bungalows suggest its eventual size.

We passed a crane which could lift with ease 250 tons and then came upon drydocks 900 feet long and 40 feet across. In one of them the Tiger, a cruiser of 2,300 tons, was being repaired. It fitted easily into its vast concrete inclosure, leaving ample room for the activities of workmen engaged ceaselessly in thier task of reparation. The dockyard employs 6,000 men and 3,000 women, working night and day.

We were told that by two weeks after the battle of Jutland all the vessels that had been injured in this famous sea fight were completely repaired and ready for another encounter. It was daz-

[Continued on Page 13.]

FOUR ARE LOST ON ROCHESTER

Steamer From Baltimore Torpedoed and Sunk On November 2.

CAPTAIN AND 31 MEN REACH SHORE SAFELY

One Boat With Second Mate And 13 Of Crew Is Still Missing.

London, Nov. 8.—The American steamship Rochester was torpedoed and sunk at dusk on November 2.

Four sailors are known to have lost their lives in the sinking of the steamer. One boat with the second mate and 13 men is missing.

CAPTAIN AND 31 MEN SAVED.

The captain and 22 men have been landed at Buncrana. One lifeboat with nine survivors reached Ross Port, in the county of Mayo, yesterday.

RAN TO BALTIMORE.

New York, Nov. 8.—The American steamship Rochester plied between Baltimore and British ports. She was in command of Capt. Erik Kokeritz and carried a crew of about 50 men.

The Rochester was formerly the steamship Yaguez, built at Ecorse, Mich., in 1912. She registered 2,551 tons gross and was 247 feet long.

ONE OF FIRST TO BRAVE "SUBS."

The Rochester, one of the four American steamships to run successfully the German submarine blockade following the declaration of unrestricted submarine warfare, was owned by Furness, Withy & Co., a British firm, and was in the British Admiralty service. She was formerly owned by the Kerr Steamship Company. When last heard from the ship was on her way to this port, according to her owners.

The Rochester left New York for Bordeaux on her first blockade running trip on February 10 in company with the American steamship Orleans. Their voyage was watched with keen interest both in America and France. The Orleans arrived at Bordeaux a week ahead of the Rochester, but both ships were given an enthusiastic reception by the people of the city.

LEFT HERE SEPTEMBER 25.

The Rochester sailed from this port about September 25 for Manchester, England to go through the canal to Liverpool.

On board were a crew of about 34 persons, one of which was C. F. Berman, first assistant engineer, whose wife lives at 120 South Broadway.

All the crew were signed on here by Shipping Commissioner Kirwan, and they represented the United States, Russia, Sweden, Norway, Denmark, Chili and Spain. Several shipped from Maryland and the Marconi operator put down his residence as the United States.

CLEVELAND DOCTOR MURDERED

Found In Downtown Hotel With A Wound On Head.

Cleveland, Ohio, Nov. 8.—Dr. Harry L. Chapin, a prominent Cleveland physician, was found dying in a room in a downtown hotel early this evening under circumstances pointing to murder.

Lying in blood, conscious, but unable to speak or rise, Dr. Chapin was discovered by a maid. He had a large wound on the right side of his head which Coroner Byrne said was caused by an exceptionally heavy blow by a piece of pipe or a weight. No motive for the crime is known.

Dr. Chapin, who had been leading a semi-retired life in a hotel for five years, received a call on a telephone to go to a room on the third floor of another hotel. Some time before that a maid of the latter said she saw two men in the room arguing vigorously about some business matter.

The dead physician was known as an author and a writer of photoplay scenarios. A recent work on mythology has lately been placed in the hands of reviewers. Dr. Chapin's wife was formerly Mrs. Valentine Fries, widow of a millionaire lumberman and yacht owner, of Sandusky, Ohio.

LIVENZA CROSSED; 17,000 ARE CUT OFF

Germans Announce Fresh Success Against Retiring Italians.

REAR GUARD HINDERS ADVANCE

Defending Airplanes Also Bomb Hostile Forces And Bring Down Five Enemy Machines — Larger Units Fall Back Unmolested.

Berlin, Nov. 8 (Via London).—Austro-German forces in Northern Italy have crossed the Livenza river, army headquarters announced today.

Italian troops to the number of 17,000 were cut off from the Tagliamento and captured, the official statement adds. The total number of prisoners taken by the Austro-German forces is now more than 250,000, it is asserted.

The text of the communication follows:

"Italian Front—Our detachments, advancing on the mountain roads, have broken the resistance of the enemy rear guard. By an outflanking movement our attacking columns cut off the retreat of the enemy troops still holding out on the middle Tagliamento between Tolmezzo and Gemona and on permanent fortified works at Monte Saint Simeone.

"Up to the present 17,000 Italians, among them a general, with 80 guns have had to surrender.

"In the plain fighting has developed along the Livenza river. By a vigorous advance German and Austro-Hungarian division, in spite of destroyed bridges, have forced the crossing and have thrown the enemy back westward.

"The total number of prisoners captured now has been increased to more than 250,000 and the booty in guns to more than 2,300."

Rear Guard Delays Advance.

Rome, Nov. 8.—Withdrawal of the Italian line was continued yesterday, the War Office announced today. The larger units retired unmolested.

Italian troops fought numerous rear-guard actions, in the course of which they succeeded in holding up the Austro-German advance temporarily.

Italian aeroplanes continued bombarding hostile forces along the Tagliamento and brought down five enemy aeroplanes.

The text of the statement reads:

"During yesterday we continued the withdrawal of our line. The larger units have retired without being molested by the enemy.

"Numerous engagements took place between the hills of Vittorio and the confluence of the Monticana and the Livenza, in the course of which our brave covering troops succeeded in detaining the enemy's advance.

"In spite of strong resistance on the part of hostile machines our aviators renewed their bombardments of enemy troops along the Tagliamento. Five enemy aeroplanes were brought down."

Reinforcements Badly Needed.

[*By the Associated Press.*]

Italian Headquarters, Nov. 8.—The bulk of the Austro-German invading forces today presents a main frontage of about 35 miles back of and along the Tagliamento river, with reconnaissance parties thrust forward eight or ten miles west of the river for the purpose of feeling for the points of least resistance. This is producing detached engagements, but no battle in force has yet occurred.

The Italian Army still has in reserve large bodies of troops, which, however, naturally feel the effects produced by the recent retirement of their main body. Large reinforcements at this moment therefore would render invaluable assistance, in the opinion of the military authorities.

RACE RIOT AVERTED

Negro Troops At Montgomery Start Out To Rescue Fellow-Soldier, But Are Rounded Up.

Montgomery, Ala., Nov. 8.—Quick work by the military police early tonight, coupled with the determination of Maj. John C. Fulton, commander of the Tenth Training Battalion (negroes), prevented probable serious trouble when some of the negro soldiers became excited over the report that one of their comrades had been captured by a mob. For a time it appeared there was danger of a race riot, but the military police took the situation in hand and at midnight everything was quiet, with most of the soldiers in quarters and a cordon of sentries out with orders to arrest and hold all stragglers.

The trouble started when Jim Long, a negro chauffeur, was arrested after running into a white woman. Long was taken to the police station and released on bond, but the negro soldiers heard that "a soldier is being taken out to be lynched," and started out to rescue their comrade. As the soldiers started through the streets they were joined by several hundred others, with a large number of white persons.

Military police went to the centre of the disturbance and sent about 70 of the soldiers to headquarters for interrogation. They were later sent to camp under guard.

E. C. Ramage, living in the southern part of the city, reported to the police that negro troops had searched his automobile while he was driving near the city with his wife and son, and that the "soldiers roundly cursed" him.

Colonel Stansbury, of the One Hundred and Twelfth military police, ordered all soldiers to their quarters and called an extra military police service to keep everything moving smoothly. All roads were patrolled by the policemen and all automobiles stopped and their numbers taken.

Baker Lower Age Limit.

Washington, Nov. 8. — Secretary Baker today reduced from 21 years to 20 years and nine months the minimum age for students in the third officers' training camp which is to be opened in January for enlisted men.

The purpose is to open the camp to men who will be 21 at the end of their three months' training.

Notice of Dissolution

Notice is hereby given that the partnership heretofore existing between Thomas M. Nelson, of Chambersburg, Pa., and Walter J. Satterfield, of Baltimore, Md., under the firm name of Nelson Shoe Co., was dissolved the first day of October, 1917, by mutual consent.

Thomas M. Nelson.
Walter J. Satterfield.

The business will be continued under the firm name—Nelson Shoe Co.—by Walter J. Satterfield, who is authorized to settle the affairs of the firm. Baltimore, Nov., 1917

WEATHER FOR TODAY.

Light rain in morning, fair and cooler in afternoon; fresh south winds.

Detailed Weather Report on Page 10.

THE SUN

INDEX OF THE NEWS

	Pages.
Telegraph	1, 2, 3, 4, 6, 12
Local	11, 13, 14, 15, 16
Financial (Second Section)	8
Sports (Second Section)	13

VOLUME XVIII—NO. 45 PRESS RUN SUNDAY, October 27, 1918 } 127,853 BALTIMORE, SUNDAY MORNING, NOVEMBER 10, 1918.*** [illegible] 68 PAGES PRICE FIVE CENTS.

KAISER HAS ABDICATED; GERMAN PEOPLE TO FORM THEIR OWN GOVERNMENT

SHIP HITS MINE OFF THE COAST

Nineteen Are Missing, 65 Landed At Ocean City, Md.

SHE GOES DOWN WITHIN 20 MINUTES

Cutters Stand By As The Saetia, Big American Freighter, Sinks.

[Special Dispatch to The Sun.]

Ocean City, Md., Nov. 9.—Twenty minutes after striking what is believed to have been a mine, the American steamer Saetia, a 5,000-ton freighter, sank 25 miles off shore here at 9.05 o'clock this morning.

Nineteen members of the crew are missing, and 47 men were landed at this city shortly after 4 o'clock this afternoon. The chief engineer, Charles Turner, of Hartford, Conn, was injured

Shortly after 9 o'clock tonight a raft with 18 survivors was picked up by a patrol boat. Other rafts are said to have been sighted.

EXPLOSION PRECEDES.

The sinking of the ship was preceded by an explosion a few minutes after 8 o'clock. A few minutes later two more violent explosions followed. Although the ship was light, having just left an American convoy off the Delaware Capes, she went down within 20 minutes, according to her master, Capt. W. S. Lynch, of Pleasantville, N. J., who landed at this place.

Coast guards and a number of destroyers rushed to the aid of the steamship, which submerged before any could come alongside. However, a number of the crew were picked up in the water, but at a late hour today 18 sailors were missing.

BOILERS BLOW UP.

Although a vigil was kept by the score of destroyers and fishing boats, no more survivors were picked up. Little hope is held out for those who were among the "black watch" in the engine room at the time the mine was struck. The explosions which followed the first, it is believed, were the boilers. Despite a crushed left leg, the chief engineer was able to talk after he was given stimulants at a hospital in Salisbury, Md. He held very little hope for the "black watch" on duty at the time the boilers exploded.

JUST LEFT CONVOY.

The Saetia left its convoy returning from France three days ago and was heading in for Philadelphia. Just 25 miles off this place she ran into a mine, which sent her quivering from bow to stern. The first explosion threw half of the crew into the sea.

Captain Lynch immediately ordered "all hands on deck," but before lifeboats could be lowered the cold salt water pouring in upon the boilers caused the additional explosions. The ship careened violently, settling heavily at the stern. With the water pouring in through the shaft alley, in the stern, only the bow remained on the surface within 15 minutes. A few minutes later the ship had settled entirely in about 300 feet of water.

Due to the excitement and the short time to "put off" in the lifeboats, none of the crew could give a coherent account of the sinking. It is believed, however, that a number of the sailors were taken down by the suction of the freighter as she made her final plunge.

U. S. LAUNCH CAPSIZES.

The first rescue ship, a United States Coast Guard powerboat, to return capsized in the heavy sea which was running all day. All the men were picked up within a few miles of the shore, while hundreds of persons crowded the shore. The last survivors of the ship were landed here at 4 o'clock. A heavy sea has been running and it is probable that a number of the missing men of the Saetia went down. It was only with the greatest skill that the larger powerboats could ride out the rough seas, and no persons could hope to fight long against it. The destroyers and revenue cutters, however, spent the night patrolling the adjacent waters for any survivors.

SIX HOURS IN HEAVY SEA.

Those who were landed here were scantily clad and fatigued after several hours in the water. Their weakened condition was aggravated by the six hours' ride in the small boats which were like a cork in the heavy seas.

The Seaside Hotel has been turned over to the local chapter of the Red Cross by Daniel Trimpers. Here the

(Continued on Page 2.)

PRINCE MAXIMILIAN SOUNDS DEATH KNELL OF GERMANY'S MILITARY MIGHT.

London, Nov. 9.---Just before Prince Maximilian of Baden offered his resignation as Imperial Chancellor he issued an appeal "to Germans abroad" in which he said:

"In these difficult days the hearts of many among you, my fellow-countrymen, who outside the frontier of the German fatherland are surrounded by manifestations of malicious joy and hatred, will be heavy. Do not despair, German people.

"Our soldiers have fought to the last moment as heroically as any army has ever done. The homeland has shown unprecedented strength in suffering and endurance.

"In the fifth year, abandoned by its Allies, the German people could no longer wage war against the increasingly superior forces.

"The victory for which many had hoped has not been granted to us. But the German people has won this still greater victory over itself and its belief in the right of might.

"From this victory we shall draw new strength for the hard time which faces us and on which you also can build."

WHOLE LINE FORGES AHEAD

Yanks Fight Their Way On Against Spirited Resistance.

BRITISH TROOPS TAKE MAUBEUGE

French Armies Also Push On Over The Belgian Border.

[By the Associated Press.]

With the American Army on the Sedan Front, Nov. 9 (6 P. M.). The American troops fought their way forward today along virtually the entire line despite the fact that the weather was about as bad as could be. The Americans started in today with the knowledge that with Germany's action on the armistice conditions imminent, an early cessation of hostilities was among the possibilities. This fact, however, only appeared to make the men more anxious to accomplish as much as possible against the enemy while he was deciding what response to make.

HARD GROUND COVERED.

The resistance encountered was spirited on the whole, though consisting largely of machine-gun activity. The terrain crossed and captured was on par with the most difficult ground the Americans have taken thus far. It gives them the most advantageous positions possible for a further advance.

The principal obstacle in the path of the Americans as they work northeast is a series of hills behind Chaumont-Devant-Damvillers, close to which place they already have pushed their line. The Americans have a half circle around the heights preparatory to encircling and outpinching them, as they have so frequently done in the last offensive.

Five American ambulances drove by mistake into the German lines northeast of Lion-Devant-Dun and were captured. This incident was witnessed by some comrades who organized a rescue party and returned with the ambulances, four prisoners and three guns.

This evening the Americans were in complete control of both sides of the Meuse, and had in addition, occupied Remoiville wood. They also crossed the river at Mouzon, thus making their line on both sides complete from Villers-Devant-Mouzon southward.

DIVISION REACHES MOUSAY.

One division reached Mousay in its forward march, despite machine-gun resistance and a particularly heavy fire from mine throwers. There was a violent enemy reaction toward the northern point of the line, especially at Villers-Devant-Mouzon. The enemy shelled Montigny and Saulmory and the Saulmory-Sassey road and the new American positions at Lion and St. Germain intermittently today and there were occasional bursts of machine-gun fire from Stenay. The American artillery replied and the German cannonade moderated.

Fires are burning in Stenay and the towns to the northeast. There was considerable enemy activity today in a retiring movement to the northward and eastward. A new German unit had been identified on this sector.

The Americans have begun work on a

(Continued on Page 2.)

ARMISTICE WILL BE SIGNED AT SENLIS

By WALTER DURANTY

[Special Cable to the Baltimore Sun and the New York Times.]

Copyrighted.

Paris, Nov. 9.—Le Temps says tonight:

"If the German answer is in the affirmative, the armistice will be signed at Senlis, the headquarters of the Allied generalissimo."

It must be a strange experience for the inhabitants of a little French town whose main street was gutted by boche incendiaries in 1914 to see French military automobiles containing travel-worn German envoys flash by on their errand of humiliation. Doubtless they will remember the tragic day of September, when their Mayor and fellow-townsmen had been shot and nights far more recent when the earth shook, as often experienced in that very spot, to the crash of bursting air bombs and the thunder of big batteries. With such memories in the hearts of the people, Senlis salutes the day of retribution.

300 BOLSHEVIKI KILLED

Attempt To Start Counter-Revolution At Tomsk Easily Suppressed By Czechs.

By Carl W. Ackerman.

[Special Cable to the Baltimore Sun and the New York Times.]

[Copyrighted.]

Irkutsk, Nov. 4 (Delayed).—During the Bolsheviki uprising at Tomsk, on November 1, 300 Bolsheviki were killed and wounded and six Russians were killed, according to a telegraphic report to Czech headquarters. Following a counter-revolution attempt, martial law was proclaimed under the Czechs' local Siberian government.

At 2 o'clock in the morning a Bolshevik band, assisted by disloyal Siberians, proceeded to the penitentiary and armed the convicts, whom they let out. The two bands, one at the railway station and the other at the factories, attempted to seize and destroy everything of value. The battle which ensued between the loyal Siberians and the Bolsheviki lasted till morning.

This was the first serious clash with the Bolsheviki since the Czechs marched across the country, establishing their Volgda front.

Irkutsk is patrolled by armed guards.

ELECTION RESULT NOT VITAL

Westminster Gazette Says Wilson Is Not Weakened.

Special Cable to The Baltimore Sun and The New York Times.

[Copyrighted.]

London, Nov. 9.—"The American election returns in ordinary circumstances," says the Westminster Gazette, "would mean a weakening of the position of the President, who can no longer command a majority in both houses, but the position of America in the war will not be weakened by the untoward event, for the Republicans are as zealous as the Democrats in the determination to pursue the issue with Germany to a definite conclusion and on the platform have been, if anything, more aggressive in their war speeches than the Democrats."

25 KILLED BY GAS

Nearly Twoscore Other Workmen Overcome In Pittsburgh Steel Mill.

Pittsburgh, Nov. 9.—Twenty-five men are dead, several others are in a critical condition and nearly twoscore were overcome as a result of inhaling gas fumes at the Eliza furnaces of the Jones & Laughlin Steel Co. here late today. The victims were at work relining a furnace when the accident occurred. In some unknown manner the carbon monoxide gas, which comes from molten metal, escaped from adjoining furnaces into the one in which the workers were engaged.

As soon as word of the accident spread through the plant other workmen dropped their tasks and formed rescue squads. In this manner many lives were saved. Coroner Samuel Jamison announced tonight that he will conduct a thorough investigation into the cause of the accident.

WAR NEWS CENSORSHIP EASED

American Press Dispatches Released After Passing Field Officers.

Washington, Nov. 9.—All American press dispatches from the western front hereafter will come through direct when passed by the field censor without being diverted for further censorship. Heretofore, whenever such dispatches referred to troops other than American, they had to pass through the Press Bureau at London, often occasioning hours of delay.

Secretary Daniels announced today that, through the efforts of Vice-Admiral Sims and Lieut.-Com. George Barr Baker, the London censor has just ordered that messages "without exception" from American correspondents in France bearing the password of the field censor shall be transmitted without further censoring or diversion.

This follows a modifying order issued October 2, under which the correspondents have been permitted to write about American troops brigaded with the British and French. Until then only dispatches relating to separate American forces were permitted to come through direct.

Accused Aircraft Men Named.

Chicago, Nov. 9.—The names of three men, recently indicted in the Federal District Court on charges of conspiracy in connection with the aircraft inspection service, were made public today. The defendants are Lucian M. Simpson, Vincennes, Ind.; Clarence L. Hogue, who was formerly in charge of the Chicago office of the service, and E. J. Coner, formerly of Oak Park, Ill., but now in Washington, D. C.

SURRENDER IS NOW AWAITED

Abdication Will Cause No Easing Up Of Armistice Conditions.

DELEGATES LEARN THEIR FULL DEFEAT

Marshal Foch Reads Terms Of Armistice To Them At Headquarters.

Washington, Nov. 9.—The tremendous news from Germany that the Kaiser had decided to abdicate was heard in Washington with scarcely more than a ripple of interest. Everywhere the question was asked: "Has the armistice been signed?" So far as the American Government knew late tonight it had not been, and the prevailing belief was that the German answer to Marshal Foch could not be expected before tomorrow.

HAD BEEN EXPECTED.

To members of the Government and diplomats who a few short weeks ago would have been amazed and gratified beyond belief the announcement that William II had bowed before the will of the world was accepted as a thing to be expected. It was accepted as one of the acts in the great tragedy surprising now only, perhaps, because it was enacted before instead of after, the capitulation of the war machine about to be broken to pieces on the western front.

There was no statement from the White House or from other Government sources. President Wilson, whose demand, "Autocracy must go," has been blazoned upon every response to the German pleas for peace, was waiting. He wanted to know who follows the Kaiser and wanted something more than a decree by Prince Maximilian sent broadcast by wireless to prove that the Kaiser and his power actually have gone.

NO LET-UP IN TERMS.

The one thing that officials emphasized was that whatever might happen within Germany at this late date could make no difference in the military program of the Allied and American Governments. There will be no modification of the surrender armistice terms which Marshal Foch has given the Germans until 11 o'clock Monday morning to accept or reject and unless the acceptance is forthcoming the uninterrupted advance of the victorious armies will continue until the white flag of surrender appears.

Military men as well as civilian officials and diplomatic observers regard acceptance of the armistice terms, harsh as the Germans may deem them, as inevitable. Knowledge that the army is beaten and soon must be in retreat across its own borders, probably to join in the revolution at home, is regarded as certain to force the most obstinate among the enemy to yield within the time allowed.

MAY SEEK DELAY.

As to the effect of the Kaiser's decision upon the speed with which the German reply might be sent to Marshal Foch, no one was prepared to speak with confidence. The first thought was that with the promulgation of the Chancellor's decree the courier probably had been started back with instructions that the armistice envoys waiting within the Allied lines accept at once and bring hostilities to an end. But it was recog-

(Continued on Page 2.)

Crown Prince To Renounce Imperial and Prussian Thrones and Regency To Be Set Up With Prince Max, Present Chancellor, as Regent

REVOLUTION REPORTED TO COVER WESTERN GERMANY

Paris, Nov. 9.---The abdication of Emperor William is officially announced from Berlin, according to a Havas dispatch from Basel. The Havas agency is the semi-official French news agency.

Amsterdam, Nov. 9.--Prince Max of Baden has been appointed Regent of the Empire, the Berlin newspapers semi-officially announce.

London, Nov. 9.---A German wireless message received in London this afternoon states:

"The German Imperial Chancellor, Prince Max of Baden, has issued the following decree:

" 'The Kaiser and King has decided to renounce the throne.

" 'The Imperial Chancellor will remain in office until the questions connected with the abdication of the Kaiser, the renouncing by the Crown Prince of the throne of the German Empire and of Prussia and the setting up of a regency have been settled.

" 'For the regency he intends to appoint Deputy Ebert as Imperial Chancellor and he proposes that a bill shall be brought in for the establishment of a law providing for the immediate promulgation of general suffrage and for a constitutional German national assembly, which will settle finally the future form of government of the German nation and of those peoples which might be desirous of coming within the empire.

" 'The Imperial Chancellor.

" 'Berlin, Nov. 9, 1918.' "

The resignation of the German Ministers of the Interior, Instruction, Agriculture and Finance are reported in a telegram received from Berlin. The Prussian food controller again has requested to be relieved from office and the resignation of the Prussian Minister of Public Works has been in the hands of the Cabinet for for some time.

EBERT LEADER OF SOCIAL DEMOCRATS

Deputy Ebert who, according to the German wireless message, is to be appointed Imperial Chancellor, is Friedrich Ebert, vice-president of the Social Democratic party and president of the Main Committee of the Reichstag.

Ebert's election to the latter office in June of this year was taken to mean at the time that the Socialist minority in the Reichstag had either been reclaimed by the military government or that the Socialists had gained ascendancy. Later events have proved that the Socialists were in the saddle.

Ebert quite recently declared in the Reichstag that the German people would no longer permit themselves to be without the right to decide their fate. It was he who informed the Reichstag of the release of Dr. Liebknecht.

REIGNING HOUSE OF BRUNSWICK ALSO ABDICATES

London, Nov. 9.—A telegram received from Copenhagen from Brunswick by way of Berlin asserts that Emperor William's son-in-law, the Duke of Brunswick, and his successor have abdicated. The reigning Duke of Brunswick, whose abdication is announced in a telegram from Brunswick by way of Berlin, is Ernest Augustus, a son of the Duke of Cumberland. On May 24, 1913, he married Princess Victoria Louisa, the only daughter of Emperor William. They have three sons, the eldest, Ernest Augustus, whose right to the throne also has been renounced, being born March 18, 1914.

ELECTORAL REFORM TO BE AN IMMEDIATE STEP

Berne, Switzerland, Nov. 9.—The groups forming the majority of the German Reichstag, says a Berlin message, have agreed to present at the approaching session of that body a plan for elections to the Reichstag and to the lower houses of the confederated German States by equal, direct, secret ballot, following the principles of proportionate representation and all without distinction of sex. The voting age is to be set at 24 years.

Proportionate representation in the Reichstag would give the Social Democratic Party, on the basis of the last

EXTRA | THE EVENING SUN | FINANCIAL EDITION GIVING CLOSING QUOTATIONS

VOL. XVIII—NO. 21. PRESS RUN SATURDAY (MORNING, 101,501 / EVENING, 89,855) 191,356 BALTIMORE, MONDAY, NOVEMBER 11, 1918. Published every week-day by The A. S. Abell Co. Entered at second-class matter at Baltimore postoffice. 20 PAGES. PRICE TWO CENTS

VICTORY!

TERMS OF SURRENDER REQUIRE HUNS TO MOVE ARMIES BACK OF THE RHINE; ARMISTICE LIMITED TO THIRTY DAYS

FOCH HALTS ARMIES PROMPTLY AT 11 A. M.

Armistice Proclaimed By Commander-In-Chief In Order To Generals.

The Hague, Nov. 11.—A perplexing question was precipitated by the arrival of the former Kaiser and his party in Holland. They were all heavily armed and their internment, therefore, is suggested.

The Dutch officials are silent on the question of internment.

When the former Kaiser's train arrived at Eysden station 7.30 yesterday morning it was seen that all the attendants on the 10 cars were heavily armed.

Wilhelm, who walked up and down the station platform calmly smoking a cigarette, was attended by the former Crown Prince and an old man in uniform, supposed to be Field Marshal von Hindenburg.

London, Nov. 11 (11.10 A. M.).—Marshal Foch issued the following order to all Allied army commanders today:

"Hostilities will cease November 11 at 11 A. M. at the whole front French line.

"The Allied troops wlil not, until further orders, go beyond the line reached at that hour."

It is officially announced here that the armistice with Germany was signed at 5 A. M. today. Prime Minister Lloyd George announced that the cessation of hostilities was effective at 11 o'clock on all fronts in Europe.

Premier Lloyd George plans to have members of the House of Commons attend a thanksgiving service at St. Margaret's this afternoon.

"The empire and its Allies have won the greatest victory in history," declared Lloyd George in an address from the steps of his residence.

"You are well entitled to rejoice. It is you, and your sons and daughters, who have done it. Let's thank God."

DOXOLOGY CHANTED BY CROWD

Special constables were called out today to assist the police in handling the crowds celebrating the signing of the armistice.

At the Mansion House the Lord Mayor came out on the steps and made a speech. He then led the crowd in chanting the Doxology.

At the Stock Exchange there was excitement when two special policemen shouted "All clear!"

AMERICANS GET GLAD NEWS

The American Young Men's Christian Association Eagle hut in the Strand was quickly emptied of shouting soldiers, who eagerly read the extras.

"Fine; but we are ready to return to the front, if necessary," declared Private A. Bredoziky, of Chicago, who was wounded in Flanders.

"Glorious!" said Private August Horn, of Brooklyn, who also was wounded in Flanders. "I made a date with the Statue of Liberty to return in November."

"Hurray! Tell the folks at home as soon as possible," shouted Private W. A. Lewis, of St. Paul, Minn.

KAISER'S WHEREABOUTS IN DOUBT

Reports of the former Kaiser's present whereabouts are contradictory.

The latest information received here stated he had motored to Count Bentinck's castle at Middachem, Holland, with two officers. He has but little baggage with him, and was said to look worried.

All reports tended to show that in addition to the Emperor all the kings, princes, grand dukes and other royalty of the empire had renounced their "divine right" to rule over a people which already had abrogated that right by revolution.

William Hohenzollern, the former Kaiser, with his wife and son, the former Crown Prince, were believed to have reached the castle of Count von Bentinck, at De Steeg, near Utrecht, Holland. With them were said to be Field Marshal von Hindenburg and suite of ten.

Germany was still dominated by the revolutionists, but reports indicated that the Socialists were rapidly assuming control of the governmental functions.

EBERT NOW BIGGEST FIGURE

The biggest figure in Germany was Frederick Ebert, Socialist and saddlemaker, who had assumed the Chancellorship. Prince Maximilian of Baden, former Chancellor, was a mere lay figure as self-appointed "regent."

Republics have been set up in Saxony, Baden, Wurttemberg, Bavaria and Schleswig-Holstein. Other German states were in temporary control of Workmen

[Continued On Page 2]

America Has Won Everything She Fought For, Says Wilson

Washington, Nov. 11.—"America's great work now is to assist in the establishment of "just democracy throughout the world," said President Wilson in a proclamation announcing the signing of the armistice today. He said:

My Fellow-Countrymen: The armistice was signed this morning. Everything for which America fought has been accomplished. It will now be our fortunate duty to assist by example, by sober, friendly counsel and by material aid in the establishment of just democracy through the world.

WOODROW WILSON.

The President then ordered that all Government departments be given a holiday.

DRAFT CALLS OFF; MEN NOT IN CAMPS TO BE DISCHARGED

Provost-Marshal Crowder Issues Order Stopping Further Inductions Into Army And Entrainments.

London, Nov. 11.—All recruiting has been ordered suspended and all notices calling men to the colors have been canceled.

Washington, Nov. 11.—President Wilson today authorized Provost Marshal-General Crowder to notify all draft boards that calls now outstanding for military service be canceled.

Pending further instructions no more inductions will be made into the army nor entrainment permitted under these calls, according to an official announcement today.

CROWDER SENDS INSTRUCTIONS TO BOARDS

The following instructions have been sent by the Provost Marshal-General to all local boards:

"Pending developments in the situation which arises because of the fact that Germany has signed an armistice providing for the cessation of hostilities the President directs that all general and voluntary special calls now outstanding for the induction and mobilization of registrants of whatever color or qualifications for the army be hereby canceled. Pending further instructions no more inductions shall be made into the army nor entrainment permitted or undertaken under such calls.

Discharges Ordered.

"The President further directs that all registrants who are already inducted into the army under these calls because of the fact that the day and hour specified in their classification lists have arrived, but who have not been actually entrained for a mobilization camp, shall be hereby discharged from the army. The local board shall so notify each such registrant."

YANKS GO WILD AS PEACE NEWS REACHES LINE

By WEBB MILLER.

With the American Armies in France, Nov 11 (2.10 P. M.).—Motorcycle couriers tore along the roads today, shouting:

"It's over, boys!"

Marching columns, tired and mud-spattered, were galvanized into new life. They shouted, laughed and sang.

I saw several doughboys under full packs fox trotting in the middle of the road. The cheers rang from column to column.

Grim Men Become Laughing Boys.

In the race back to the nearest cable office, I passed many detachments who had not heard of the armistice. It was easy to tell by their appearance who had heard the news, and who had not. Two words—"Its over" changed the grim men into laughing boys.

Shortly before 11 o'clock the American gunners stood with watch in hand as the seconds ticked away. They fired right up to the last, saving the shell cases of the final rounds as souvenirs. Several 14-inch naval guns sent their final shells hurtling far into the German lines.

Little is now available regarding news from the extreme front lines, where the men are dug in in little fox holes.

Just as a unit commander started to phone his forward lines that the war was over, he was interrupted by the announcement that another town and wood had been captured.

I sat in a dugout northeast of Verdun when Marshal Foch's order arrived at ..40. A captain began telephoning feverishly to all the batteries in his sector. Immediately the fire began to quicken until the fog was pierced by a veritable sheet of flame, the gun flashes melting into one.

Crazy, Plumb Crazy."

As the captain finished reading the order to each battery faint cheers came over the wire.

"What do the boys think of it?" I asked.

"They're crazy; plumb crazy," was the response.

Owing to the difficulty of communication probably many of the advance units received the news after 11 though the officers worked like h... to reach all detachments.

Bells Peal In Verdun

Within one minute after the fire ceased the bells in war-shattered ... began pealing.

Only a few minutes before ... boches spitefully fired a few ... into Verdun. As silence again ... on the streets after the explosion ... in gand shouting doughboys ... of the buildings.

American flags were flung ... windows of the ruined buildings ... motive whistles screeched. A real American celebration began and was going strong when I left.

Germans Given Only Fourteen Days To Get Out Of Occupied Territories.

REQUIRED TO PAY IN FULL OR ALL DAMAGE DONE

Washington, Nov. 11.—President Wilson this afternoon told Congress and the world the terms accepted when she signed the armistice today.

The terms follow:

Cessation of hostilities.

Evacuation of invaded territories, including Alsac-Lorraine and Luxemburg.

Surrender of vast amounts of guns and equipment.

Evacuation of left bank of Rhine.

Surrender of vast amounts of rolling stock in occupied territory.

Abandonment of Bucharest and Brest treaties.

Unconditional surrender all German forces in East Africa.

Reparation for damage done.

Surrender of scores of submarines and large war craft.

Concentration of aircraft at stipulated points.

Evacuation of all Black Sea ports.

Restoration of all Allied and United States merchant vessels.

Duration of the armistice is to be 30 days.

THE PRESIDENT'S SPEECH

The President's address follows:

Gentlemen of the Congress:

In these anxious times of rapid and stupendous change it will in some degree lighten my sense of responsibility to perform in person the duty of communicating to you some of the larger circumstances of the situation with which it is necessary to deal.

The German authorities, who have, at the invitation of the supreme war council. been in communication with Marshal Foch have accepted and signed the terms of armistice which he was authorized and instructed to communicate to them. These terms are as follows:

MILITARY CLAUSES ON WESTERN FRONT.

One—Cessation of operations by land and in the air six hours after the sognature of the armistice.

Two—Immediate evacuation of invaded countries: Belgium, France, Alsace-Lorraine, Luxemburg, so ordered as to be completed within 14 days from the signature of the armistice. German troops which have not left the above-mentioned territories within the period fixed will become prisoners of war. Occupation by the Allied and United States forces jointly will keep pace with evacuation in these areas. All movements of evacuation and occupation will be regulated in accordance with a note annexed to the stated terms.

Three—Repatriation, beginning at once and to be completed within 14 days, of all inhabitants of the countries above mentioned, including hostages and persons under trial or convicted.

Four—Surrender in good condition by the German armies of the following equipment: Five thousand guns (2,500 heavy, 2,500 field), 30,000 machine guns. Three thousand minenwerfer; 2,000 airplanes (fighting bombers — firstly D., seventy-threes and night bombing machines). The above to be delivered in situ to th Allied and United States troops in accordance with the detailed conditions laid down in the annexed note.

ALLIES TO HOLD RHINE CROSSINGS

Five—Evacuation by the German armies of the countries on

[Continued On Page 2]

TODAY. ... change in temperature; ... southeast winds. Weather Report on Page 10.

THE SUN

VOLUME XIX—NO. 4 PRESS RUN SUNDAY, January 19, 1919 123,620 BALTIMORE, SUNDAY MORNING, JANUARY 26, 1919. ** Published every Sunday by The A. S. Abell Co. Entered as second-class matter at Baltimore Postoffice. 68 PAGES PRICE FIVE CENTS.

INDEX OF THE NEWS

Peace Conference Unanimously Adopts League Of Nations As Integral Part Of Treaty—To Be Open To All Powers

PRESIDENT DEMANDS THAT LEAGUE BE MADE VITAL THING

Tells Peace Conference, In Opening Discussion, That It Is Keynote Of Whole Fabric of Future Peace Of World—First In Thought Of All Peoples.

Paris, Jan. 25.—Following is President Wilson's address before the Peace Conference today:

Mr. Chairman—I consider it a distinguished privilege to be permitted to open the discussion in this conference on the league of nations. We have assembled for two purposes—to make the present settlements which have been rendered necessary by this war and also to secure the peace of the world, not only by the present settlements, but by the arrangements we shall make at this conference for its maintenance.

The league of nations seems to me to be necessary for both of these purposes. There are many complicated questions connected with the present settlements which perhaps cannot be successfully worked out to an ultimate issue by the decisions we shall arrive at here. I can easily conceive that many of these settlements will need subsequent consideration; that many of the decisions we make shall need subsequent alteration in some degree, for if I may judge by my own study of some of these questions they are not susceptible of confident judgments at present.

It is, therefore, necessary that we should set up some machinery by which the work of this conference should be rendered complete.

We have assembled here for the purpose of doing very much more than making the present settlements that are necessary. We are assembled under very peculiar conditions of world opinion. I may say, without straining the point, that we are not the representatives of governments, but representatives of the peoples.

Must Satisfy People.

It will not suffice to satisfy governmental circles anywhere. It is necessary that we should satisfy the opinion of mankind.

The burdens of this war have fallen in an unusual degree upon the whole population of the countries involved. I do not need to draw for you the picture of how the burden has been thrown back from the front upon the older men, upon the women, upon the children, upon the homes of the civilized world, and how the real strain of the war has come where the eye of the Government could not reach, but where the heart of humanity beats.

We are bidden by these people to make a peace which will make them secure. We are bidden by these people to see to it that this strain does not come upon them again. And I venture to say that it has been possible for them to bear this strain because they hoped that those who represented them could get together after this war and make such another sacrifice unnecessary.

It is a solemn obligation on our part, therefore, to make permanent arrangements that justice shall be rendered and peace maintained.

For Permanent Processes.

This is the central object of our meeting. Settlements may be temporary, but the action of the nations in the interest of peace and justice must be permanent. We can set up permanent processes. We may not be able to set up a mermanent decision.

Therefore, it seems to me that we must take as far as we can a picture of the world into our minds. Is it not a startling circumstance, for one thing, that the great discoveries of science, that the quiet studies of men in laboratories, that the thoughtful developments which have taken place in quiet lecture rooms have now been turned to the destruction of civilization? The powers of destruction have not so much multiplied as they have gained facilities.

The enemy, whom we have just overcome, had at his seats of learning some of the principal centers of scientific study and discovery, and he used them in order to make destruction sudden and complete. And only the watchful and continuous co-operation of men can see to it that science, as well as armed men, is kept within the harness of civilization.

U. S. Ardor Genuine.

In a sense, the United States is less interested in this subject than the other nations here assembled. With her great territory and her extensive sea borders, it is less likely that the United States should suffer from the attack of enemies than that

(Continued on Page 3.

President And Col. House American Members Of Commission To Draft Constitution.

WILSON OPENS DEBATE

Lloyd George, Bourgeois, Orlando And Others Pledge Their Countries — Small Nations Protest Against Decision Of Supreme Council To Restrict Committees, But Resolutions Are Adopted.

Paris, Jan. 25.—The Peace Conference unanimously adopted today the league of nations project and appointed a committee representing the associated governments to elaborate a constitution for the league, including its prerogatives.

President Wilson opened the discussion at the request of the permanent chairman, Premier Clemenceau. He was followed by Premier Lloyd George for Great Britain, Leon Bourgeois for France, Premier Orlando for Italy and representatives of China and Poland.

WILSON AND HOUSE ON COMMISSION

President Wilson and Col. E. M. House were named as the American members of the commission.

Representatives of the other great powers will be: For Great Britain, Lord Robert Cecil and Gen. Jan Christian Smuts; for France, Leon Bourgeois and Ferdinand Larnaude, dean of the faculty of law of the University of Paris; for Italy, Premier Orlando and Viterio Scialoia; for Japan, Viscount Chinda and K. Ochiai. The delegates of the small nations will be announced later.

CLEMENCEAU PRESENTS RESOLUTION

The session of the Peace Conference opened at 3 o'clock this afternoon in the Salle de la Paix of the Foreign Office with the same imposing setting as the first session, but with little ceremony and the manifest purpose of business.

M. Clemenceau was again in the chair, with President Wilson and the full American delegation at his right, and Premier Lloyd George and the British delegation at his left.

M. Clemenceau read a resolution on the league of nations to the effect that such a league was to be organized by international co-operation for the purpose of making secure international obligations and safeguarding the nations against war. The league would be an integral part of the peace treaty and would be opened to all civilized nations favoring its aims.

In opening the discussion President Wilson declared the conference had solemn obligations to make a permanent settlement. The present conference, the President added, could not complete its work until some further machinery of settlement should be set up.

LEAGUE EYE OF NATIONS.

"We are not here alone," he said, "as representatives of governments, but as representatives of peoples, and in the settlements we make we need to satisfy, not the opinions of governments, but the opinion of manknid."

President Wilson contended that a league of nations must be a vital thing and not casual or occasional. It must have continuity.

"It should be the eye of nations, an eye which never slumbers," he declared.

On his travels, the President said, people everywhere had greeted the league, as the first thing in their interest.

PLAIN PEOPLE RULE.

"Select classes of men no longer direct the affairs of the world," said the President, "but the fortunes of the world are now in the hands of the plain people.

"The wish of the people, therefore, must be heard. The war had swept away those old foundations by which small coteries had "used mankind as pawns in a game." Nothing but emancipation from the old system, he contended, would accomplish real pace.

The President saw American soldiers in the streets—soldiers who had come, not alone for war, but as "crusaders in a great cause," and he added, "and I, like them, must be a crusader, whatever it costs to accomplish that end."

TO MAKE PEACE SECURE.

After declaring that the conference was for the purpose of a settlement arising out of the war and to make peace for the world, President Wilson said:

"A league of nations seems necessary for both purposes. There are many questions which we feel cannot ultimately be worked out here, that may require subsequent consideration, subsequent alterations even to some degree."

He described how the war burden was borne by the people as well as by the armies and said:

"We are bidden by these sufferers to make peace secure for them and see to it that the strain need never to borne again."

LLOYD GEORGE BACKS PLAN.

At the conclusion of the reading of a translation of President Wilson's speech, Premier Lloyd George said:

"I should not have intervened at all, but it was necessary for me to state how emphatically the people of the British Empire are behind this proposal, and if the leaders of the British Empire have not been able to devote as much time during the last five years as they would have liked to this question, the reason is that they were entirely occupied with other questions that were more urgent for the moment.

"Had I the slightest doubt as to the wisdom of this league or nations it would have vanished before the spectacle as I saw it last Sunday when I visited a region which but a few years ago was one of the fairest in this very fair land.

"We drove for hours through what was a wilderness of desolation. It did not look like a country where there were habitations of men, but it was torn and shattered and rent beyond all recognition. We visited one city which had been very beautiful, but where we saw scenes which no indemnity can ever make good.

"One of these cruelest features was the knowledge that Frenchmen, who love their land almost more than any other people, had had to assist the enemy in demolishing their own homes. I said to myself that it is surely time we set up some other methods to settle quarrels than this organized slaughter.

"I do not know if we shall succeed in our enterprise, but it is already a success that we have undertaken it."

The Italian Premier, Vittorio Orlando, followed Mr. Lloyd George. He declared that no people were readier to accept the league of nations in its entirety than the Italian people.

Leon Bourgeois, the veteran French supporter of the league of nations, spoke next, pledging the French "to do everything that can help to put us on the road which has been pointed out by President Wilson."

The Chinese and Polish delegates declared that they supported the plan.

FIRST SIGN OF DIVISION.

The first signs of a division in the conference was when it proceeded to consider the four resolutions framed by the Council of the Great Powers, providing for committees on labor, responsibility for the war, reparation for damages and ports, railways and waterways.

Camille Huysmans, in behalf of Belgium, asked for two members on the committees of labor, reparation and the league of nations, and one each on the others. Serbia made a similar request.

Brazil was more emphatic, declaring against "a cut-and-dried program" and saying that the conference should be master of its own decisions.

M. Venizelos said that Greece was entitled to membership on the committees of reparation and ports. M. Bratiano, for Roumania, and Dr. Benes, for Czecho-Slovakia, as well as the delegations representing Portugal, China, Siam and Poland, also asked for places on the committees.

It looked for a time as though the small nations had formed a bloc and would contest the decisions of the great powers to restrict the committees.

CZECHS DEMAND VOICE.

"We will have something to say," declared Dr. Benes, "in winding up the Austro-Hungarian Empire, and it is difficult to understand how any committee can act without information that the Czecho-Slovaks alone can give."

M. Bratiano added: "The smaller nations have greater interests at stake than the great powers on many of these questions."

M. Clemenceau finally, in a good tempered speech, said that the council had not imposed its decisions, but had simply convoked the conference to consider the plan.

"After 48 years of public life," he said, "I am satisfied that the larger the committee is, the less it accomplishes. I beg the delegates not to waste time on questions of procedure when millions of men are waiting to be demobilized. Let us organize the committees at once and so get to work. We have no desire to be unjust to anyone, but wish to devise a procedure leading to rapid results."

The resolutions were adopted by the conference without change.

PART OF TREATY.

The resolution for the creation of the league follows:

"The conference, having considered the proposals for the creation of a league of nations, resolved that:

"It is essential to the maintenance of the world settlement which the associated nations now are met to establish that a league of nations be created to promote international obligations and to provide safeguards against war. This league should be created as an integral part of the general treaty of peace and should be open to every civilized nation which can be relied on to promote its objects.

"The members of the league should periodically meet in international conference and should have a permanent organization and secretaries to carry on the business of the league in the intervals between the conferences.

COMMITTEE OF 15 NAMED.

"The conference therefore appoints a committee representative of the associated Governments to work out the details of the constitution and the functions of the League and the draft of resolutions in regard to breaches of the law of war for presentation to the Peace Conference.

"That a commission composed of two representatives apiece from the five great powers and five representatives to be elected by the other powers be appointed to inquire and report upon the following:

"First, the responsibility of the authors of the war; second, the facts as to breaches of the laws and customs of war committed by the forces of the German Empire and their allies on land, on sea and in the air during the present war; third, the degree of responsibility for these offenses attaching to particular members of the enemy's forces, including individuals, however highly placed; fourth, the constitution and procedure of a tribunal appropriate to the trial of these offenses; fifth, any other matters cognate or ancillary to the above which may arise in the course of the inquiry and which the commission finds it useful and relevant to take into consideration."

LABOR RESOLUTION.

The resolution in regard to international legislation on industrial and labor questions reads:

"That a commission composed of two representatives apiece from the five great powers and five representatives to be elected by the other powers represented at the Peace Conference be appointed to inquire into the conditions of employment from the international aspect and to consider the international means necessary to secure common action on matters [illegible]

(Continued on Page 2.)

"HEY, THERE, STOP A MINUTE, CAN'T YOU? THAT'S MY WIFE."

Maryland Soldiers Sing Out As "Miles Of Smiles" Are Shown In France To Homesick Boys—Figures Quickly Recognized And Given Tumultuous Greeting—Story Of What It Meant To Them Written By One Of Them.

By J. M. Cain.

The moving pictures of Maryland men and women taken by The Sun last November were sent to France in December. Marguerite F. Harrison, of The Sun Staff, is now with the One Hundred and Fifteenth Regiment for the purpose of showing the films. The following letter tells of their reception in the Seventy-ninth Division:

I thought I would write you and tell how the "Miles of Smiles" went when they were shown us. I judge the people back home were aware of the fact that The Sun was going to send a lot of moving pictures showing how the people took the armistice and a thousand other things we wanted to see, but we didn't know anything about it over here. The first inkling I had of it was when a mob came running into my billet and yelled, "Heh, you Bawlamer Sun, do you know anybody by the name of Mrs. Harrison on the paper?"

Now, it is a long, long trail from Headquarters Troop barracks to "M. E. H.'s" erudite reviews, so you may know I was puzzled. "Yeah," I said, "I think I do, anyway. Maybe she's forgotten who I am, though. What about it?"

Breaking The News.

"Why, hell, you poor nut, she's here."

"Where?" I gasped.

"Over there in the theatre. She's got a lot of moving pitchers she's going to show this afternoon."

Well, you should have seen an old and decrepit soldier crawl out of his bunk, grab his hat and streak it out of the door. The rest followed on the double. "There he goes," they said, and were left behind, for I tell you I was in a hurry, with no time for silly, boyish chatter.

She was there, and so was a mob, pushing and shoving for standing room. She hadn't forgotten who I was, either, and I camped right down beside her and let a lot of lieutenants and captains do some work for once in their life, winding and assorting the collection. I had other things to attend to—business of being told how things were back home generally, how the old shop looked, who was doing what and how the office managed to get along without me, anyhow.

Football Training Proves Handy.

But I mean to say I had to use muscle in the process and resurrect a lot of football technique I had nearly forgotten. The stiff arm, the elbow dig, the shoulder buck and the profane remark had all to be utilized. For there was a crowd around that would make the annual fight after the City-Poly game look like a birthday party, and everybody had something to ask or something to tell her, and generally both, and she had to reply to them all.

It went something like this: "Yes, we hope to have Bill Conway back soon; they are sending the wounded back. Yes, we've got a reel of Easton pictures and the whole town is in it—have you heard just how badly he was wounded? Your wife is in the Clifton Park picture? Then you'll see her—because we're afraid he's making light over it and is worse off than he says. Your mother was on Charles street? You'll see her then—and we've all had to do things we never did before. I've even done police court reporting. Something you want me to put in the paper? Certainly."

So you see why I needed the football tactics. I used them, too, and stayed put.

Well, in about a half hour they got the machine going and the show was on. And if you have any doubt on the subject, let me tell you they made the biggest hit that has ever been made in this neck of the woods. There are a good many around the P[illegible] are not from Baltimore, but it made no difference. It was real United States, and those who had no mothers to look at relieved their feelings by letting out yells when the close-up of Baltimore girls came on the scene. Tell The Sun telephone operators they just about split even with the Green Spring Valley bunch of beauties. A pleasant time was had, you may be sure. Everyone was unanimous on that point.

[illegible] the hollers that greeted the per-formance at Division Headquarters were as naught compared to what took place that night when she took the pictures over to the town where the Three Hundred and Thirteenth Infantry is billeted. They stormed and yelled and laughed and some of them cried. Mrs. Harrison introduced the pictures with a little speech, and she can make a rattling good five-minute talk if you don't know it. A big howl greeted her as she closed, with calls of "Come on—shoot; speed it up. Wonder if ole Abe Ullman's s'loon is in it. Wisht I had some of his beer and free lunch right now."

"That's My Wife!"

They started. Mrs. Harrison had told them if they wanted to gaze on any part of the film to call out and the camera man would hold a while. The reel hadn't much more than gotten under way when there came in a yell, "Hey you, Baltimer Sun girl, that's me wife."

From then on the calls were frequent. Once a cultivated voice floated out, "Do you mind holding that one a few seconds?" There was a yell and a rude person said, "Listen at the Duke, he's seen 'is best girl."

After it was over a mob gathered. They wanted to be told, and even more they wanted to tell. It was a grand and glorious opportunity to make known unto the Sunpaper reporter "The Things."

A large, slow-talking, carefully shaved and "policed-up" man in O. D. would come up, stand around for 10 minutes and when he finally got a chance with elaborate politeness would become articulate in about this fashion:

"Are you from the Sunpaper?"

"Yes."

"Do you write things for the paper?"

"Yes."

"Well, if you ever get a chance you might mention dis here."

"Dis here," laboriously, soberly and courteously drawled out, was usually a gem of beautiful cut and rare vintage. As he talked the large one could bask in the May morning smile and become more at ease, and when he got through had the satisfaction of seeing a brief memorandum made. There were many pages in the notebook filled with memoranda after awhile, and you might be interested to know that your special correspondent, moving-picture expert, shipyard worker and music critic will come back with the goods. She will have something to say. Several thousand gentlemen who grabbed the golden opportunity saw to that. One soldat said she "got an earfull"—and I think he put it conservatively.

Mrs. Harrison Voted All Right.

Anyway, as the session prolonged itself after the show, Mrs. Harrison took a notion she was going to stay in town overnight, just to look around and see what everything was like, so as to have a little more first-hand knowledge. An officer gave up his room, and when it became known that she was going to stay in Issencourt, instead of the more palatial town of Somilly, where the division headquarters is, the Three Hundred and Thirteenth to a man decided she was all right—dam if she ain't—and that the thing to do was to wait and see what the Sunpaper was going to say after awhile.

Well, it's all over now—here, anyhow. You have sent over a smile to thousands, you have let them see their home folk, and I don't think anybody on your side of the water can quite know what that means. And you needn't be afraid that the boys over here don't appreciate that and the things you have done for them. In fact, I think many of them have got to the point where they think the Sunpaper is their only friend on earth, and certainly their only hope of salvation from this land of rain and [illegible]

CONGRESS "UP IN AIR" ON BIG PROBLEMS

Most Of Session Wasted In Endless Talk Over Unimportant Matters.

ONLY FIVE WEEKS REMAIN

Senate's Debate Over Relief Bill As Foolish As It Was Futile—Revenue Bill Held Up—Nothing Done On Railroads Or Reconstruction.

[*From The Sun Bureau.*]

Washington, Jan. 25.—There remain five weeks before the expiration of the present Congress on March 4. In that period Congress must settle more matters than it has settled in as many months just past, unless it adjourns with much of the business of the country "up in the air." Which is what it probably will do, and, it may be, what it had best do, for it has various questions before it which, conceivably, had better be delayed than be settled by this Congress in the way in which this Congress inclines to settle things. It is possible that delay will offer opportunity for public opinion to formulate wise policies which even the very unpromising next Congress may adopt.

Congress has been jogging along for a good many weeks now, fooling with all sorts of relatively unimportant matters. In the House they have been having lengthy debates lately about such matters as the Rivers and Harbors bill, the Legislative, Executive and Judicial Appropriation bill, and the like. In the Senate they have had many speeches upon the league of nations, most of them designed to convince the statesmen of Europe that President Wilson is a "dub" who should not be taken seriously. When the Senators were not discussing the league of nations and the President, they pulled newspaper clippings out of their waistcoat pockets, and, upon the strength of brief and usually vague dispatches from Timbuctoo and other such places, grew red in the face about Russia, or Japan, or the Czecho-Slovaks, or some other nation or group.

Most of this week the Senators have devoted to debate over the $100,000,000 appropriation for the hungry in Europe, which debate unquestionably was one of the most ludicrous performances in matter and in consequence which ever happened outside of the Maryland House of Delegates. If there is any doubt about the jackassicality of the matter of the debate, read the Congressional Record; if there is any about the consequence of it, look at the overwhelming vote by which the bill was passed, after Senator Borah and the 17 or 18 other Senators who stood with him had talked their heads off in opposition. That debate, it may be remarked in passing, was so much like those in the House of Delegates that one found himself looking over the right-hand side of the chamber to see whether George Lewis was buzzing around the plastered-hair statesmen of the city delegation.

Revenue Bill Delayed.

Meantime, of course, the Revenue bill, beyond a doubt the most essential measure before Congress, not only so far as the proper conduct of the financial affairs of the Government are at stake, but the most essential so far as there is to be a real speeding of the work of reconstructing trade and industry is of value—meantime, the Revenue bill has been kicked around in conference between the House and the Senate. Work was begun upon that bill last June, which was late enough in all conscience. But nearly nine months have passed since it was then belatedly started, and the end is not yet in sight.

The kicking around of the bill in conference began about a month ago, and, as this is written, the kicking is more furious than at any time previous. The Senators and the Representatives on the conference committee are said to be in grave division over excess profits, inheritance taxes and estate taxes. Of course, they will settle the questions at issue soon or late. The bill must be passed. But the settling probably will be done by the "vowing she would ne'er consent, consented" route, with the consequent waste of about all the time that can be wasted.

As to "reconstruction legislation," that program without form or substance, of which all the statesmen, and chambers of commerce, and merchants and manufacturers' associations and the like talked so volubly in the weeks immediately preceding and following the capitulation of Germany, Congress has not done a single, solitary thing. As a matter of fact, there never was any probability that it would or could do much toward reconstruction, other than to hasten the passage of the Revenue bill and to make a start upon the railroad problem. All the talk, Congressional and otherwise, about "readjusting labor and social conditions" and that sort of thing was merely the chasing of verbal butterflies. Legislative action upon social reforms and such will mainly follow, it will not lead, the actual readjustments.

"Balled Up" On Railroads.

In its real tasks of reconstruction Congress has fallen down miserably on the Revenue Bill, as has just been pointed out and as everyone knew without it being pointed out; and on railroad legislation Congress is more balled up at this minute than it has been at any time since the Administration took over the roads last year. It is vastly more balled up than it was when the railroad question came acutely to the fore, just after the signing of the armistice. Then the majority of Congress seemed to be rather clear in its mind that it wanted a system of regional unification and regional control of the roads—that conclusion having been reached by the very simple method of saying: "We won't go back to the old order of private ownership; we are scared of Government ownership; here is a nice proposition, 50-50 as between one, unified national system and the old separate company scheme; 50-50 as between private control and Government control." But since it so easily

(Continued on Page 2.)

URGE RHINE LINE ON WILSON

Four Frenchmen Of Letters Explain Need Of Safeguards.

[Special Cable to the Baltimore Sun and the New York Times. Copyrighted.]

Paris, Jan. 25.—A sample of the things that the French insist upon in their talks with President Wilson, as he receives one small group after another, is afforded by the conversation that four members of the Society of Men of Letters had with him on Wednesday. The four were: Georges LeComte, president of the society; General Malleterre, the Abbe Wetterle, who represented Alsace-Lorraine for many years in the German Reichstag, and Firmin Roz.

Like so many others who have seen him, they told him the Germans must be pushed back beyond the Rhine, not only in Alsace-Lorraine and the Starre valley immediately north, but from the entire left bank region. They told him they needed peace for their efforts as thinkers and their tasks as writers.

The believed his league of nations was one safeguard of peace, but France, which had been involved four times in a century, needed other security for its future, which could be afforded only by ridding the whole left bank in perpetuity of all German soldiers and fortifications. Mr. Wilson made no comment.

TO SERVE AS JOINT TRUSTEES

Balfour Outlines Service Before United States And Britain.

[Special Cable to the Baltimore Sun and the New York Times. Copyrighted.]

London, Jan. 25. — A. J. Balfour makes a striking pronouncement on the services which the United States and the British Empire can render to small and oppressed nations as joint trustees of civilization in the foreword which he contributes to the first number of the Landmark, the new organ of the English-speaking unions. He says:

"That we shall always be friendly countries I do not doubt, but that does not content me in the least. I want something much more than that. I want every member, every citizen of the British Empire, whether he lives in this small island or whether he belongs to the great British dominions overseas, and every citizen of the great American republic to feel that they are joint trustees for civilization and the world of those principles of peace and of liberty for which we are all struggling at this moment. And I believe that that is what will happen, and I believe that the time will come when all small and oppressed nations will instinctively look, and not look in vain, to the all-powerful protection of international arrangements of which the heart, the very heart and core, will be a union of soul, a union of sentiment and a union of belief of the great free English-speaking community now scattered over the whole world."

ACCUSED OF KILLING HUSBAND

New Yorker Shot While Walking At Florida Resort.

Orlando, Fla., Jan. 25.—Mrs. Margaret Simmons Darling is under arrest here charged with killing her husband, Lloyd E. Darling, who died last night four hours after being shot. The shooting is alleged to have occurred while the couple were out walking. Darling was the son of Mr. and Mrs. Hiram Darling, of Gloversville, N. Y., who are stopping here.

YANKS' EYES IN GOOD SHAPE

Many Men's Sight Saved By Magnets, Says Col. Greenwood.

New York, Jan. 25.—Eye trouble in the American Army abroad has not increased, but, on the contrary, is below the average, Lieut.-Col. Allen Greenwood, of Boston, who has been senior consulting oculist with the American Expeditionary Force, said upon his arrival here today on the steamship Rochambeau.

"Many men's sight has been saved by magnets in extracting metals from the eye," Colonel Greenwood said. "We have 70 workers at Paris making glasses for the soldiers. At Savenay we have a hospital, which is also a school, and a New York teacher named Baker, who I understand, has been blind since he was six years old, was brought to France, and, with other teachers, has been doing wonderful work."

Colonel Greenwood denied reports which he said he had heard that "the American blind are coming into Paris for treatment by thousands."

There had been only 110 cases, he said, and 70 of these had been returned to the United States.

STOPS PASSENGER SERVICE

Clyde Line Couldn't Compete With The Government.

Norfolk, Va., Jan 25.—Discontinuance by the Clyde Line Steamship Company of passenger service on the Philadelphia-Norfolk Line, beginning Monday, was announced today by William A. Marable, Norfolk agent of the line.

Inability to compete with Government controlled lines and the railroads was given by Mr. Marable as the reason for the discontinuance. He said that the Government in turning back the line to its owners retained power to enforce the scale of wages and overhead charges and that this forced the operation of the company's steamers at a loss.

ON TRIAL, KILLS SELF, FREED

Defendant Slashes Throat In Cell While Awaiting Verdict.

New Albany, Ind., Jan. 25.—Just a few minutes before a Circuit Court jury trying the case of Charles Schneider, 43 years old, charged with murder, returned a verdict of not guilty today Schneider cut his throat with a razor, and was found dead in his cell when a court attache went to summon him to the courtroom to hear the verdict. He was accused of the murder of Stephen Miller, town marshal of Port Fulton, Ind., last July.

The jury's verdict of not guilty was based on the decision that Schneider was of unsound mind at the time of the killing.

$134,512 FOR SACK OF FLOUR

Resold Many Times, Proceeds To Go To Red Cross.

San Francisco, Jan. 25.—The Shriners' Red Cross has sold a sack of flour for $134,512.84, John D. McGilvray, potentate of Islam Temple, San Francisco, announced today, making public advices from North Carolina, where Shriners collected $370 at Sudan Temple, New Bern, in the twenty-sixth sale of the sack of flour. All proceeds of the sale go to the American Red Cross.

Started from San Francisco by Clarence F. Pratt, historian of the temple, the sack has been sold in Honolulu and 15 States since May, 1917.

It will be sold again at a large "Victory ceremonial" to be held by Islam Temple.

DIED.

Received Too Late For Classification.

CRAIG.—Suddenly, at Wilmington, Del., on January 25, 1919, HAZEL, aged 23 years, beloved wife of Harry M. Craig and daughter of Mr. and Mrs. Charles L. Hawthorne.

Funeral will take place from the residence of her father, 345 Rosebank avenue, Govans, of which due notice will be given.

SYKES.—On January 25, 1919, THERESA C., aged 21 years, beloved wife of George A. Sykes and daughter of Julia and the late Jacob Meriek. Rest in peace.

Funeral will take place from her late residence, [illegible] of which due notice will be given.

WEATHER—Fair.

"Mr. Bingley Retrenches," a short story by Elizabeth Jordan, starts tomorrow in THE EVENING SUN.

THE EVENING SUN

FINANCIAL EDITION
GIVING CLOSING QUOTATIONS.

VOL. XXI—NO. 104. PRESS RUN YESTERDAY {MORNING, 109,574 / EVENING, 81,408} 190,982 ‖ SUNDAY 138,275 BALTIMORE, WEDNESDAY, AUGUST 18, 1920. Published every week-day by The A. S. Abell Co. Entered as second-class matter at Baltimore Postoffice. 22 PAGES. * PRICE TWO CENTS.

Woman's Suffrage Amendment Is Finally Ratified; Tennessee House Votes 49 To 47 In Favor Of It

POLISH FORCES DRIVING REDS FROM WARSAW

Danzig Corridor Freed Of Bolsheviki—Graudenz Saved.

REPULSE OF RUSSIANS RESEMBLES A ROUT

Morale Of Poles Excellent, Says Premier After Visiting Front.

London, Aug. 18.—Russo-Polish armistice negotiations opened in Minsk at 7 o'clock last night, according to an official wireless received from Moscow today. After the delegates had exchanged credentials adjournment was taken until today.

Paris, Aug. 18.—The Polish counter-offensive has freed the Danzig corridor and completely disengaged Graudenz (60 miles south of Danzig, on the Vistula), it was officially announced by the French Foreign Office today.

Bolsheviki Driven Far Back.

London, Aug. 18.—The Bolshevik recoil from Polish counter-attacks in several sectors had begun to assume proportions of a rout, according to latest advices from various sources today. Only stubborn resistance at critical points had enabled the Russian forces to prevent annihilation of many of their retreating divisions.

The Bolshevik withdrawal measured more than 10 miles at some points, and in the vicinity of Ciechanof (50 miles north and west of Warsaw, on the river Lidynia) the Poles advanced 15 miles on a 20-mile front.

All unofficial advices from Warsaw declare the "Red danger" is temporarily over and that the city's imperiled defenses have been restored.

The attack on Novog was stopped at the outer forts. A shrapnel barrage tore great gaps in the ranks of the advancing Reds. They came doggedly on until within machine-gun range, when a hailstorm of bullets mowed them down in great windrows. As they crumpled and began to give way, the Polish infantry charged, bayoneting the retreating Russians. The withdrawal became a rout and Polish cavalry, taking up the pursuit, drove the soviet forces back 10 miles before they could re-form their ranks.

North of Lublin (100 miles southeast of Warsaw) the Bolsheviki were reported to have been completely routed by a surprise attack.

Moscow Claims Success.

The latest communique from Moscow, however, declared the Poles had been flung back "at the point of the bayonet" northeast of Novo-Georgievsk (an important fortress at the junction of the rivers Vistula and Bug, 15 miles northwest of Warsaw) following "fierce fighting." According to the communique several villages were occupied by the Bolsheviki on the west bank of the Vryka (a river flowing southeastward from the old Russian-German frontier and joining the Vistula just east of Novo-Georgievsk, passing 12 miles west of Ciechanof, which the Poles claimed to have recaptured).

A dispatch to the Times from Danzig said the British Commissioner there was reported to have ruled that munitions ships en route to Poland would not be allowed to enter the harbor. Several were said to be approaching at the time the ruling was made.

Another dispatch to the Times from Brussels said the Belgian Cabinet had definitely decided not to aid Poland pending the outcome of the peace negotiations at Minsk. At the same time, the Belgians ordered back two munitions trains which attempted to cross the frontier, en route from France to Poland.

Poles' Morale Excellent.

Warsaw, Aug. 17 (Delayed).—Premier Witos and Ministers Skulski, Daszynski, Grabinski and Slivinski completed a tour of the various fighting sectors today. They reported finding the Polish morale "excellent."

Russian soviet authorities have forwarded authorization for foreign journalists to visit Minsk.

Lines Broken, Russians Admit.

Moscow, Aug. 18 (By Wireless Via London).—"The enemy has broken through our lines to the northward," the Russian official communique said today. (This evidently refers to the Polish claim that the Russians have been ejected from the Danzig corridor).

"Our renewed offensive has resulted in recapture of Ciechanof (50 miles northwest of Warsaw).

"To the southeast we occupied Hrublesof (80 miles north of Lemberg) and other villages.

FLOWING SLEEVES AID IN RELIEVING DROUGHT

Eighteenth Amendment Finds New Foe In Feminine Wrist Flask, Hidden Under Puffs.

[*Special Dispatch to The Evening Sun.*]

Chicago, Aug. 18.—Returning vacationists from many summer resorts bring back word that the "flowing" sleeve will be the rage this winter. This style will be used as a means to circumvent the Eighteenth Amendment. According to the returning vacationists, there have been many merry parties at the resorts, where the supply of "hooch" was plentiful. It has been too hot for the men to wear coats and without the masking coat tail, where is a gentleman to carry his flask?

The women at the resorts have adopted long sleeves, with capacious puffs around the wrist. These puffs will easily accommodate a pint bottle. Clothing manufacturers have already adopted the new style. A South Market street merchant has started his cutters on a new blouse, intended for outing use. The sleeves are to be fashioned like the bottom of a sailor's trousers.

The jewelry novelty trade has conceived the idea of fashioning a dainty flask curved to fit the forearm.

'GOOD EVENING

THE BROKEN WING.

A robin's blithely singing in the tree,
But he's not singing, singing now for me;
For he who said that I was passing fair
No more shall quaff the dewy morning air.

The daffodils are dancing in the sun,
And over grasses little zephyrs run;
Ah, once I danced and once I ran as they,
Now I'm a silent shadow all the day.

And when the purple deepens into night,
And stars forget their offerings of light,
I seem the soul of some too-hopeful Spring
That through Oblivion trails a broken wing.

—Laura Blackburn.

HURRAH! WRITE AGAIN.

Dear Editor:

Saw this in your own dear paper:

"Returning to Baltimore for the first time in 47 years, Mrs. James F. Brandin was very much pleased u2F Brandin was very much impressed with the growth of the city and natural beauty of Druid Hill Park."

What does she think she is—a submarine?

Some more freaks: "He took her in his arms and kissed her eyes, one after the other!" Say, how many has she? You're only allowed two guesses!

Lamped this in front of an "intelligent" office on Franklin street:

"Wanted: towe whitie cookes; $12 peas a weak."

And this in a lunch-room window, corner Druid Hill avenue and McMechen street:

"Beacon and eggs."

Yours in fun,

FROM A. TO Z.

"Glamis Hath Murdered Sleep."

IN MEMORIAM.
GREEN.—In ever-loving and thankful memory of Dorothy Leader Green, who fell on sleep 8th July, 1915.

—Head And All Snooped From "C. T. S's" Joyous Col. In Detroit News.

SEIZE HER, GRAND OP. SCOUTS!

Our little Eva, protege of Mme. Lagemarcine Grupe, has Galli-Curci looking like a scrubwoman and is coming into her own, entertaining them from the mezzanine floor of the Hotel Julien Dubuque, which, among other things, is America's most beautiful hotel.—*Cascade (Ia.) Pioneer.*

SAYINGS OF A FLAPPER.

A waiter measures you from tip to tip.

When a woman says "in a minute" her words carry "wait."

A woman loves for you to tell her three things—flattery, gossip and style.

It doesn't cost much to entertain hopes.

Egotists are usually good flatterers.

The little things that count—adding machines.

Every girl loves to hear her enemies' faults.

A summer vacation consists in flirtations, hotels and menus.

A house is painted for improvement. So is a woman's face. —Selma Wertheimer.

THE MORE URGENT NEED.

An indignant subscriber writes the Weekly: What this country needs is not a phonographic record to preserve a candidate's voice but something to preserve what's left of the voice of the people.—*Capper's Weekly.*

A Swedish Rose Tells The World.

Personal—Oscar Rose (Swede) is not in politics whatever and strongly objects to working where politics are used for influence. Is not matrimonially inclined.

—Ad In The Morning Alberton.

IN RE ROASTING EARS.

We learned this in the year of our Lord, 1920: Roasting ears that are sweet when cooked and eaten on the day they are picked lose their sweetness if held until tomorrow. Our veteran linotype operator, Jack Williams, to whom we alluded the other day as being stoutly opposed to the prohibition policy of this paper, says it is because the alcohol evaporates from the corn.—*Fort Scott (Kan.) Tribune.*

HER MODESTY.

The self-made man proclaims the fact,
Repeats it ev'ry day.
The self-made woman tries to act
As if she grew that way.
—Cartoons Magazine.

The prayer of faith shall save the sick, and the Lord shall raise him up; and if he have committed sins they shall be forgiven him.—James, v, 15.

NEGROES ANNOUNCE "BLACK HOUSE" PLANS

Balloting To Elect "President Of Africa" Will Begin This Evening.

New York, Aug. 18.—Napoleon Bonaparte Francis, of Hayti, and Paisley Herford, of Liberia, were favored candidates today for the office of provisional president of Africa, with headquarters in a presidential "Black House" to be located at Washington, according to Marcus Garvey, chairman of the Universal Negro Improvement Association here.

Balloting will begin at Liberty Hall here tomorrow and thousands of votes have been received by mail from all parts of the country, Garvey said. An American negro leader will also be elected. Among those seeking the latter office are B. R. Gordon, of Los Angeles; W. C. Mathews, of Boston, and C. John Bruce, of New York.

The "Black House" will be erected as near the White House in Washington as possible, Garvey declared, adding that negotiations were already under way to get a site for this purpose.

"There are 15,000,000 negroes in this country, and we are unable to elect a leader to the White House. We will elect a provisional president, who will direct African affairs from a Black House in Washington, and also a leader of the black race in the United States. Both men will serve terms of four years."

A meeting will be held here tonight at which candidates for both offices were to outline their policies.

McAdoo To Campaign After Labor Day

Calls At White House, But Does Not See President—Thinks Cox Is Gaining.

Washington, Aug. 18.—W. G. McAdoo will take the stump in the Democratic national campaign shortly after Labor Day, he said here today. Mr. McAdoo called at the White House, but did not see President Wilson.

"Governor Cox is going stronger every day, in my opinion," said Mr. McAdoo. "This is one campaign which the dodgers can't win. Cox's straightforward attitude on big questions of the day is winning him much support."

PUBLIC KEPT IN DARK ON AFFAIRS OF STATE

Washington Government's Policy Of Secretiveness Made Target For Adverse Criticism And Attacks.

SUBJECT RENDERED ACUTE BY RUSSO-POLISH EVENTS

Attitude Taken By Administration Contrasts Strongly With That Pursued In Great Britain.

By Stanley M. Reynolds,
Staff Correspondent of The Evening Sun.

Washington, Aug. 18.—No phase of the present Administration's conduct of foreign affairs offers a basis for more frequent attacks on the part of its critics than its alleged shortcomings in the matter of taking the public into its confidence.

Time and again before, during and since the European war, Republicans in and out of the Senate have charged the President and the State Department with concealing important information relative to our dealings with other nations until such rare intervals when the Administration presents the results of these dealings to the country as accomplished facts. There is frequent reference in the criticisms to the pledge of "pitiless publicity" upon which the present Administration entered office 7½ years ago, and, for campaign purposes, its opponents note with derision, in speaking of the Government's foreign affairs, the President's insistence, in his 14 peace points, on establishing a world policy of "open covenants, openly arrived at."

Right now there is going on in Washington a series of interchanges between the corps of newpsaper correspondents here and the officials of the State Department, in which the newspaper men are earnestly urging the adoption of a policy whereby the public can be assured of greater publicity in these matters.

Fight An Old One.

The fight is not a new one. It has been made before with the present Administration and with previous administrations, resulting now and then, and for a while, in some improvement, but never for long. The subject is at the moment acute, because of the attitude of the State Department in withholding authoritative information concerning the further development of its Russian-Polish policy, and its continued refusal to disclose the important features of its recent correspondence with Japan on the Saghalien incident and the California anti-Japanese legislation.

The complaint is made that important announcements are seldom preceded by any effort on the part of responsbile officials of the department, through the newspapers, to prepare the public in advance for the step taken, nor subsequently is any effort made to explain in detail the reasons for the action taken. The result is frequently a hiatus of official utterances between important steps that come with the suddenness of bolts from a clear sky.

Also, the complaint is made that, as in the case of the Japanese correspondence, the first official disclosure comes from the foreign capital concerned, tinged with the kind of comment which the foreign government most desires to convey. In this case, although the first note was written by this Government, it was the Japanese Foreign Office which gave out the fact not only of its receipt but as to certain of its contents. Moreover, in sending its reply, the Japanese Government took the Japanese press, and through it the Japanese people, into its confidence, and, again, through Japanese press dispatches, the American public got its first and only information of an authoritative kind. Although the Japanese reply has been in the hands of the State Department for more than a week, the department has refused to make public either its note or the reply, or to discuss the correspondence in any way.

England In Striking Contrast.

By way of contrast, it is noted that invariably in England, when a question of foreign negotiations is up, the British Premier is not only questioned publicly in Parliament on the subject, but, in replying, goes into the minutest detail in explaining publicly before the Commons what has transpired, what will or will not be done, and the reasons for the decisions arrived at. It was so in the Russian-Polish matter. Whereas the State Department confined itself to the bare publication of the Colby note, after it had been sent, Lloyd George, on the same day, in Parliament, discussed publicly to the extent of eight newspaper columns every detail of the British-French-Russian negotiations, and as publicly answered inquiries directed at him from the floor.

The benefit of such a system of taking

[Continued On Page 2, Column 4]

CHAPMAN'S BODY AT HOME

Fans At Cleveland Plan Erection Of Monument.

Cleveland, Aug. 18.—A large number of baseball fans were at the station here when the body of Ray Chapman, former shortstop of the Cleveland Indians, arrived at 10 o'clock from New York. Mrs. Chapman and Tris Speaker, manager of the Indians, accompanied the body.

Mrs. Chapman left the train a short distance from the station to avoid newspaper men and photographers.

Speaker refused to discuss the death with newspaper men, and attempts were made to block the taking of photographs of the casket. Announcement of the funeral arrangements was expected today.

Hundreds of dimes for a "flower from a fan" fund were received today. The money will be used for a huge floral piece. Plans were rapidly taking shape for a memorial fund for Chapman. Tentative plans call for the erection of a shaft to the player's memory in the American League ball park here.

DAVIS LEAVES FOR AMERICA

London, Aug. 18.—John W. Davis, American Ambassador to Great Britain, left for the United States with his family today on the Olympic. He is on leave.

So Near And Yet So Far

PLAYERS THREATEN WAR TO OUST MAYS

Hold New York Pitcher Guilty Of Attempt To Injure Chapman, Who Died.

TRIS SPEAKER BELIEVES BLOW WAS UNINTENTIONAL

Owners Of Yankees To Back Mays To The Limit, Declaring Him To Be Innocent.

New York, Aug. 18.—Threats of a baseball war, to be waged by members of the American League teams, with the object of barring Carl Mays, pitcher for the New York Yankees, from organized baseball, have been made by Detroit and Boston players. Although Mays has been exonerated by the District Attorney's office in New York of any intention to injure Ray Chapman, shortstop of the Cleveland team, who died yesterday after having been struck by a pitched ball on Monday, American League players are not satisfied.

How much in earnest the members of the Detroit and Boston clubs are can only be ascertained when the plans of the campaign against Mays are made known. They are reported to have agreed on a plan of action against the underhand pitcher yesterday in Boston. If they persist, the New York club will back Mays to the limit, it was said, for Colonels Ruppert and Huston and Miller Huggins, his manager, declare the hitting of Chapman was purely an accident. Tris Speaker, manager of the Indians, said that he believed the blow was not intentional, but that he would give a detailed statement in reply to the Boston and Detroit complaint this morning.

Mays Much Depressed.

Mays went to the District Attorney's office after Chapman's death had been announced. He showed much depression, but told a straightforward story to Assistant District Attorney Joyce, in charge of the Homicide Bureau, asserting that he pitched a fast straight ball, aimed for the inside of the plate, to Chapman and with no intention of hurting him. Mr. Joyce heard his story, declared the occurrence an accident and formally released the pitcher from custody.

Mays says that he thought the ball hit Chapman's bat, and fielded it to first base with that idea, and did not know that the shortstop had been hurt until he saw him sink to the ground. He says he looked at the ball after the accident and found that it was slightly roughened on one side. He showed it to the umpire and called his attention to the spot. The roughening probably caused Chapman's death, for it made the ball "sail"—that is, take a freakish jump which the man throwing or the batter watching would not expect.

Owners Believe It Accident.

Col. T. L. Huston, of the Yankees, and Tris Speaker have discussed the accident. To the Colonel's expressed hope that the incident should not be allowed to increase any bad feeling that may exist between the two baseball clubs, Speaker said:

"It is the duty of all of us, for the welfare of baseball and for the sake of the poor fellow who is now dead, to dissipate all feelings of bitterness this terrible tragedy may have aroused."

Carl Mays saw the reporters at his residence in Edgecombe avenue last night. He said, among other things, that the injury to Chick Fewster, a clubmate, at Jacksonville last spring had affected him very much; that he had been unable to pitch "close"; batters for some weeks afterward, and he attributed some of his bad pitching early in the spring to getting the ball too far across the plate.

2-Cent Fare Fight Concerns 28 States

Legal Battle Begun By Illinois Anxiously Watched By 27 Commonwealths.

[*Special Dispatch to The Evening Sun.*]

Chicago, Aug. 18.—Twenty-seven States that at one time had 2-cent passenger rates laws on their statute books will join with Illinois in a fight against the 3-cent fare.

Railroad officials and attorneys-general of several States will watch the outcome of the Illinois fight closely.

The suit filed in Chicago by the railroads to restrain the State from enforcing an order of the Public Utilities Commission reducing the passenger rate from 3 cents to 2 cents is expected to furnish the greatest legal battle in the history of the State. The railroad realizes, it is said, that if the case is decided against them it will leave a loophole for 27 other States.

The case will be a long-drawn-out one. Both sides have declared that the matter will not be allowed to rest with the Federal Court, no matter in whose favor it is decided. The case undoubtedly will reach the Supreme Court.

LENINE AND TROTZKY IN ACCORD, SAYS KOPP

Unofficial Russian Ambassador To Germany Also Contradicts Report Czarist Officers Control Army.

FEELS SURE GREAT BRITAIN WILL REFUSE TO INTERVENE

Predicts Fate Of Denikin, Yudenitch And Kolchak For Wrangel—Says Russia Wants Corridor.

By George Seldes.
[*Special Cable to The Evening Sun and the Chicago Tribune. Copyrighted.*]

Berlin, Aug. 18.—An absolute denial of rumors of a split between Lenine and Trotzky and that the Bolshevist army was out of control of the soviet and was being led by Czarist officers was given in an interview yesterday by Wigdor Kopp, the unofficial Russian Ambassador to Berlin. At the same time Kopp affirmed that it was only a question of the restoration of diplomatic relations before prewar economic relations could be resumed with Germany.

Kopp talked plainly and quietly, but frankly, and without any attempt to evade questions or to introduce Bolshevik views or propaganda. He did not offer to give any information, but he answered every question asked of him precisely. He is dark-eyed, has a large head and is of medium stature. He is so immaculately attired that the English correspondents called him a "Bond street Bolshevik."

Sure Britain Is Hands Off.

The first question that I asked him concerned the Krassin negotiations in London. Kopp, replying to me, said:

"England, we are sure, will not intervene in Russia, and we do not believe that their threat of a naval blockade was meant seriously. There is too much common sense in England for that."

His answer inferred that British business men and politicians believe that their country's interests will best be

[Continued On Page 2, Column 1]

AMERICA KEEPS LEAD IN OLYMPIC GAMES

Still 56 Points Ahead Of Nearest Competitor, Despite Injuries To Several Contestants.

CANADIAN HURDLER SMASHES RECORD IN 110-METER EVENT

Earl Thompson Sets Up New Figures Of 14 4-5 Seconds For The Event.

Measuring By Meters.

A meter is equivalent to 39.37 inches in the United States.

With this as a basis, it is not difficult to figure out the distances of the various contests at the Olympic games. For example, the 10,000-meter walk covered a distance of 6.214 miles.

Antwerp, Aug. 18.—America maintained her lead today in the Olympic games.

At the end of the fourth day of the international athletic events the United States team was leading, with 102 points. Finland was second, with 46; Sweden third, 38; England fourth, 24; France, fifth, 12; Canada and South Africa tied for sixth, with 7; New Zealand, Esthonia and Norway tied for eighth, with 3 each.

Injuries undoubtedly kept the total of American points down. Pat McDonald, the huge New York policeman, who was counted a sure winner in the shotput, was able to take only fourth place because of an injured thumb. It was only through a heroic effort that McDonald was able to compete at all.

Sol Butler, the negro from Dubuque, recognized as one of the leading broad jumpers of the world, was unable to get into the finals because of the injuries sustained in the trials, and this event was won by Peterson, of Sweden.

Hurdle Race Day's Feature.

The feature of today's event was the performance of Earl Thompson, the champion Canadian hurdler, in the 110-meter hurdles. Thompson made a new world record for the event, 14 4-5 seconds. He finished two yards ahead of H. E. Barron, of Philadelphia, who took second place; F. S. Murray, of New York, third; Wilson, of New Zealand, fourth; Walker Smith, of Chicago, running despite an injured leg, fifth, and Christersen, Sweden, sixth.

Finland Wins Shotput.

The final in the shotput was won by Finland, Porolla, a Finn, throwing the shot 14 meters and 81½ centimeters. Nechlander, of Finland, was second; H. D. Liversedge, of the United States Navy, third; Pat McDonald, of New York, fourth; Nilsson, Sweden, fifth, and Tammer, Esthonia, sixth.

McDonald, who had been counted on to win for America, was hampered in the event by an injured thumb.

Sweden won the broad jump. Peterson, of that team, made the longest leap, 7 meters 15 centimeters. Johnson, America, was second; Abrahsom, Sweden, third, and R. L. Templeton, of the Olympic Club, San Francisco, fourth. Fifth and sixth went to Aastad, of Norway, and Franzon, of Sweden. Sol Butler, America's star broad jumper, was

[Continued On Page 2, Column 6]

Speaker Walker, Leading Fight Against Ratification, Will Try For Reconsideration.

GAINS RIGHT TO MOTION BY CHANGING VOTE TO AYE

Wild Scenes In State Capitol As Measure Is Pushed Through House.

Government Now "By The People," Mrs. Catt Says

Nashville, Tenn., Aug. 18.—Commenting on the suffrage victory, Mrs. Carrie Chapman Catt, president of the National Woman's Suffrage Association, who directed the fight for suffrage here, said today:

"For the country and the world this victory means this government, which purports to be 'by the people' is indeed by the people and not half of them.

"For women the suffrage victory means opportunity for more work and added responsibility. It is too belated to come with a shock or surprise. We have been ready for it. We are ready for the work that lies ahead."

Nashville, Tenn., Aug. 18.—The Tennessee House of Representatives today voted to ratify the Federal suffrage amendment. The vote was 49 to 47.

The State Senate having passed the ratification resolution last week the action of the House completed ratification on the part of Tennessee.

Tennessee being the thirty-sixth State to ratify, the amendment will become effective upon proclamation of its ratification by the Secretary of State at Washington, giving the women of the United States the right to vote at the Presidential election in November next and all elections thereafter.

Speaker Walker Makes Losing Fight.

Ratification by the House followed a spirited fight by Speaker Walker to kill the resolution.

Soon after the debate began at today's session, Walker took the floor and made a motion to table the resolution, at the same time giving notice that passage of the motion would kill the resolution. The vote on this motion was a tie, 48 to 48. Then was great confusion, and another vote was taken, without breaking the tie.

Vote For Ratification.

Then the Speaker announced the vote would be taken on the original resolution providing for ratification. When order had been restored the clerk began to call the roll slowly and the onlookers held their breath.

The vote was announced as 49 for suffrage, 47 against.

Speaker Walker was immediately on his feet, and the house was in confusion.

Then Walker said, "I change my vote."

This made the result 50 in favor of suffrage and 46 against. By changing his vote he gains two days during which a reconsideration may be had. The anti-suffragists immediately will begin work to get a reconsideration.

For a minute after the vote was called it looked as if it was a tie. It would have been, but Representative Harry Burns, of McMinn county, immediately announced he changed his vote from "no" to "aye." This gave victory for the resolution of ratification. Burns is the youngest Representative in the House.

Immediately after the vote the House went into adjournment on motion of Representative Riddick.

Leaders of the suffrage forces declared it would be "absolutely impossible" for Speaker Walker to change the result through a reconsideration.

Legislators Near Blows.

The session was one of the stormiest in the history of the Legislature. Time and again the sergeant-at-arms was employed to restore order. Speaker Walker and Representative Riddick, when the motion to table was up, engaged in an altercation that looked like it might develop into a fight, and the sergeant-at-arms and several members rushed to them.

Spectators hooted, cheered and hissed when the faction to which they adhered scored a point. This made the transaction of business difficult.

The Speaker threatened at one time to adjourn the House unless the members took their seats. Several had to be persuaded by the sergeant-at-arms.

Legal Battle Planned.

A legal attack will be made on suffrage, according to the officers of the Tennessee Constitutional League, which is composed of lawyers. The argument will be that the State Constitution forbade action by this session of the Legislature.

Aside from this and the possibility of a change in the result through a reconsideration, the only step remaining to make the Nineteenth Amendment operative is the promulgation of a decree by the Secretary of State.

Suffragists estimated there are 27,000,000 women voters in the country. Several million of those already had Presidential suffrage through State action and 17,000,000 had local suffrage.

State Honored, Says Miss White.

"Tennessee has ended our fight for political freedom, and our gratitude to her is boundless," said Miss Sue S. White, Tennessee chairman of the National Woman's Party. "We have had a close fight, but Tennessee men and Tennessee women have realized the great responsibility that was theirs, and added an additional honor to the story of their State by their work for the ratification of the nineteenth amendment."

Mrs. Catt Praises "Gallant Men."

Mrs. Carrie Chapman Catt, president of the National American Women Suffrage Association, said:

"Tennessee has triumphantly closed the 60 years of the women's struggle for the right to have their prayers counted on election day. The gallant men of the volunteer State, unafraid of the noisy threats to intimidate, have opened at last the long-locked door through which millions of grateful women will pass to political freedom.

"Ratification of the amendment is more than a victory for woman suffrage. It is proof of the inviolate integrity of the Tennessee Legislature, a fact which should fill every Tennessee heart with pride."

Fight Stirred Whole Country.

The Tennessee Legislature was called into special session a week ago to consider the suffrage amendment, by Gov. A. H. Roberts. State and national organizations advocating and opposing suffrage concentrated their efforts here because it was held the action of Tennessee would determine whether women shall vote in November.

Lobbyists by the score worked early and late and political leaders of both parties joined the struggle, among them President Wilson, Governor Cox, Senator Harding, Senator McKellar and several Congressmen and lesser lights. "Political pressure," as much as any other thing, is credited with having accomplished the suffrage victory.

Resolution Drawn In 1875.

Ratification of the amendment brings to an end a struggle to obtain votes for women which began before the Civil War and crowns with success the efforts of Susan B. Anthony, who was the pioneer in the suffrage movement in America. The resolution approved today was drawn by Miss Anthony in 1875 and was introduced in the United States Senate in 1878.

It went before the States in June, 1919, and women have since carried on a spirited campaign throughout the country to obtain ratification. A number of States acted favorably at special sessions of their Legislatures.

The two organizations most active have been the National Woman's Party, of which Miss Alice Paul is chairman, and the National American Woman's Suffrage Association, of which Mrs. Carrie Chapman Catt is president. Mrs. Catt has been established in Nashville for several weeks and the National Woman's Party has maintained headquarters and canvassed the State. Mrs. Catt has worked in behalf of suffrage for more than 30 years.

Miss Paul's group are the militants. They picketed the White House in 1918 and many times were arrested.

VOTE IN HOUSE URGED BY ANTIS AT RALEIGH

They Want Members Put On Record, Though Senate Killed Resolution.

[*From a Staff Correspondent.*]

Raleigh, N. C., Aug. 18.—Suffrage rejectionists are planning a vote in the House of Representatives on the Federal Amendment before the end of today's session.

Thus far the question has not been up in the House, and the antis insist that the members place themselves on record, though many of them, being candidates for re-election, are not anxious to do so. The intention is to bring to a vote the joint resolution of rejection, pass it and send it to the Senate.

THE WEATHER TODAY.

Fair and cooler; fresh west winds.

Detailed Weather Report on Page 6.

THE SUN

HEAVY REGISTRATION OF WOMEN VOTERS REPORTED FROM THE COUNTIES OF MARYLAND. See Page 5.

VOL. CLXVII—NO. 117 | 110,082 | SUNDAY 140,592 | BALTIMORE, WEDNESDAY MORNING, SEPTEMBER 29, 1920. | Published every week-day by The A. S. Abell Co. Entered as second-class matter at Baltimore Postoffice. | 20 PAGES. TWO CENTS.

TWO WHITE SOX PLAYERS CONFESS; 8 ARE INDICTED; COMISKEY CLEANS OUT TEAM

Cicotte Admits Getting $10,000 For Throwing Games—Jackson Promised $20,000, Got Only $5,000.

PROBE TO BE WIDENED

Replogle Promises Other Indictments To Include Men In Many Cities—Others Named In Chicago's True Bill Are Weaver, Risberg, McMullin, Felsch, Williams and Gandil—Season To Be Played Out.

[By the Associated Press.]

Chicago, Sept. 28.—Indictments were voted against eight baseball stars today and confessions obtained from two of them, when the Old Roman, Charles A. Comiskey, owner of the offtime champion Chicago White Sox, smashed his pennant-chasing machine to clean up baseball. The confessions told how the Sox threw last year's world's championship to Cincinnati for money paid by gamblers.

Seven Sox regulars and one former player comprise the players against whom true bills were voted by the Cook county grand jury and the seven were immediately suspended by Mr. Comiskey. With his team only one game behind the league-leading Cleveland Indians, the White Sox owner served notice on his seven stars that if they were found guilty he would drive them out of organized baseball for the rest of their lives.

Officials of Chief Justice Charles McDonald's Court, desirous of giving the national game the benefit of publicity in its purging, lifted the curtain on the grand jury proceedings sufficiently to show a great hitter, Joe Jackson, declaring that he deliberately just tapped the ball; a picture of one of the world's most famous pitchers, Cicotte, in tears, and glimpses of alleged bribes of $5,000 or $10,000 discovered under pillows, or on beds by famous athletes about to retire.

JUST BEGINNING, REPLOGLE SAYS

Assistant State's Attorney Hartley Replogle, in charge of the case, announced that the action taken today was only the beginning and that other indictments would be returned within a few days. He added he was now after the gamblers, and that men in Philadelphia, Indianapolis, St. Louis, Des Moines, Pittsburgh and other cities would be gathered in the net.

Around the courtroom at one time or another were some of baseball's greatest leaders, among them John J. McGraw, manager of the New York Giants, awaiting a call to testify tomorrow, and John Heydler, president of the National League, who went before the grand jurors this afternoon.

The exact nature of the information Mr. Comiskey got before the grand jury was not disclosed.

THOSE INDICTED.

The men whom the jury involved, as a result of testimony uncovered by their owner, were:

Eddie Cicotte, star pitcher, who waived immunity and confessed, according to court attaches, that he took a $10,000 bribe.

Arnold Gandil, former first-baseman.

"Shoeless Joe" Jackson, heavy-hitting left fielder.

Oscar ("Hap") Felsch, center-fielder.

Charles ("Swede") Risberg, shortstop.

Claude Williams, pitcher.

George ("Buck") Weaver, third baseman.

Fred McMullin, utility player.

Cicotte, according to court attaches, told the grand jury he received $10,000 from the gamblers, finding the money under his pillow when he returned to his hotel room on the night before the first game at Cincinnati.

"I refused to pitch a ball until I got it," they quoted him as saying.

Jackson, it was said, testified he was promised $20,000 by "Chick" Gandil, but he received only $5,000. Claude Williams, according to this testimony, got $10,000.

COMISKEY ACTS PROMPTLY.

Less than an hour after the grand jury voted their true bills the Old Roman, seated in the midst of the crumbling empire out at White Sox Park, issued the telegram suspending those involved, paid off Weaver, Cicotte and Jackson on the spot, and announced that checks for pay due the others would be sent them at once. With his voice trembling, Mr. Comiskey, who has owned the White Sox since the inception of the American League, said this was the first time scandal had ever touched his "family" and that it distressed him too much to talk about it.

Immediately after the indictments were returned, Alfred S. Austrian, attorney for the club, sent the following telegram to Risberg, McMullin, Jackson, Felsch, Weaver, Williams and Cicotte:

You and each of you are hereby notified of your indefinite suspension as a member of the Chicago American League baseball club.

Your suspension is brought about by information which has just come to me directly involving you and each of you in the baseball scandal (now being investigated by the present Grand Jury of Cook county) resulting from the world's series of 1919.

If you are innocent of any wrongdoing, you and each of you will be reinstated; if you are guilty you will be retired from organized baseball for the rest of your lives, if I can accomplish it.

Until there is a finality to this investigation it is due to the public that I take this action, even though it costs Chicago the pennant.

CHARLES A. COMISKEY.

CICOTTE TELLS ALL.

The rush of players to bare their part in the affair started today when Cicotte appeared at Criminal Court Building and asked permission to testify. Cicotte wept, court attaches said, and showed in anguish his sorrow for his two small children as he told how he did his utmost to lose rather than win the 1919 world series after he had "got" $10,000 be-neath his pillow, where it had been placed by professional gamblers.

He said he lobbed the ball to the plate so slowly "you could read the trademark on it" in the first game at Cincinnati, when he was taken out of the box after three and two-thirds innings had been played.

A court official who was present when Cicotte went on the stand described the scene when the star pitcher broke down and cried as he told the jury of his part in the series "fixing."

"My God, think of my children!" he cried. Cicotte has two small children. "I've lived a thousand years in the last year," the court official quoted him as saying.

DETAILS HIS CROOKED WORK.

"I never did anything I regretted so much in my life," the witness added, according to the State official. "I would give anything in the world if I could undo my acts in the last world's series. I've played a crooked game and I have lost and I am here to tell the whole truth."

The story Cicotte is said to have told the jury follows in every essential particular, as told at Philadelphia by Maharg last night.

"In the first game at Cincinnati I was knocked out of the box," Cicotte told the jury, according to the court official. "I wasn't putting a thing on the ball. You could have read the trademark on it when I lobbed the ball up to the plate."

"In the fourth game, played at Chicago, which I also lost, I deliberately intercepted a throw from the outfield to the plate which might have cut off a run. I muffed the ball on purpose. At another time in the same game I purposely made a wild throw. All the runs scored against me were due to my own deliberate errors. I did not try to win."

STORY OF THE GAME.

Last year's world series records show that in the first inning of the first game he started by hitting Rath, the first Cincinnati batter, in the back. Daubert followed with a single over second base and sent Rath to third and scored when Groh flied to Jackson. Rath beat the Jackson's throw to the plate.

Chicago tied this run in the next inning. Kopf putting Jackson on second with a wild throw. Felsch sacrificed him to third and Gandil dropped a little fly safely in center, scoring Jackson.

The end of Cicotte's pitching and the runs that ultimately won the game were scored by Cincinnati in the fourth inning. All the damage was done with two out. With Kopf on first, Neale and Wingo singled and Reuther, the hard-hitting Cincinnati pitcher, drove a three-base hit to the center-field bleachers. Rath doubled and Daubert singled, the combination resulting in five runs. Wilkinson took Cicotte's place after Daubert's single and Groh flied to Felsch. The final score of this game was 9 to 1.

FOURTH GAME THROWN AWAY.

The fourth game, played at Chicago, was also deliberately thrown away according to court officials who heard Cicotte's statement to the grand jury, 2 to 0. Ring pitching for Cincinnati, holding the American League champions to three hits. Both Cincinnati runs were made in the fifth inning, when two errors of Cicotte, one of them with a wild throw to first by Cicotte and a bad throw to the plate by Jackson, which the pitcher intercepted and muffed. The play of this inning was sent over the Associated Press wires as follows:

"Roush was out, Schalk to Gandil, the ball rolling half way to the pitcher's box. Duncan was safe when Cicotte threw his drive wide to first, the ball going to the stand and Duncan reaching second. Kopf singled to left and Duncan, Jackson threw wild to the plate. Kopf reached second. Correction: The official scorer gives Cicotte the error for muffing Jackson's throw. Neale sent one over Jackson's head and Kopf scored. Neale reached second. It was a two-base hit. Wingo out. Ed Collins to Gandil, Neale going to third. Ring drove a vicious grounder that Ed Col-

PROGRESSIVES LINE UP TO AID GOVERNOR COX

Former Bull Moose Leaders Issue Appeal To Roosevelt Followers.

THEY ARE EXPECTED TO HELP WIN WEST

15 Join In Scathing Assault Upon Harding And G. O. P. Platform.

By J. F. ESSARY.
Washington Correspondent of The Sun.

Washington, Sept. 28.—Democratic leaders have started a fresh offensive against the Harding-Coolidge lines. They have organized a campaign for the capture of what is left of the Progressive vote in the United States. While most politicians agree that only a small proportion of the men who left the Republican party under the leadership of Theodore Roosevelt have remained independent, the Democrats seem to believe that they are worth playing for.

ORGANIZATION IS FORMED.

It became known here today that the Democratic National Committee had created an all-progressive organization, the sole function of which is to take the insurgent Republicans into camp and to deliver the genuinely progressive vote of the country to Governor Cox and Franklin D. Roosevelt. This organization makes the broad claim that the Democratic ticket represents all that is forward looking in this campaign and is the only ticket for which any sincere follower of Colonel Roosevelt can afford to vote.

Democratic managers are strongly of the opinion that the progressives hold the balance of power in a number of Far Western States and that they are numerous enough in some of the States of the Middle West to make it worth while to appeal directly to them. In 1916 it was the progressive Republican vote which went very largely to Wilson west of the Mississippi and which turned the tide in his favor. This was undoubtedly true of Kansas, Nebraska, Colorado and California. Also Minnesota progressives went over in great numbers, as did those of Montana, Oregon and Idaho.

MAY AID IN WEST.

In that campaign the President had the benefit of enthusiastic support on the part of virtually every outstanding Progressive leader, with the exception of

(Continued on Page 2, Column 5.)

One-Legged Woman Is Arrested As Moonshiner

Hammond, Ind., Sept. 28.—Mary Misicke was arrested today for operating an illicit distillery and for bootlegging whisky. There is nothing unusual about catching moonshine artists, but Mary differs from the ordinary as she is a woman and has but one leg.

Mary had gone into the business on a large scale and was said to be doing a thriving business.

SINN FEIN CAPTURE BARRACKS IN BIG COUP

Carry Away Lewis Guns, Rifles, Ammunition And Stores From Military Depot.

GUARDS WERE OUT EXERCISING

British Government Officially Will Deny Conniving At Reprisal Policy Being Carried Out By Police.

[Special Cable to the Baltimore Sun. Copyright by the New York Tribune.]

London, Sept. 28.—Sinn Fein executed its biggest coup of the "Irish war" today when Republican raiders in a surprise attack on a military depot at Mallow, County Cork, captured the barracks and made away with Lewis guns and a large quantity of rifles, ammunition and stores.

"The depot was occupied by a company of the 17th Lancers, all but a few of whom were out in the fields exercising horses at the time of the raid. Sinn Fein raiding parties had the audacity to arrive in lorries and they took the depot with a rush. Only one shot, which wounded a sergeant, was fired.

One Lancer, clad only in his underwear, flung himself on a barebacked horse and galloped off to recall his comrades. Before he could arrive the Sinn Feiners had overpowered the few soldiers in the depot, made a clean sweep of all the ammunition and guns, and vanished.

The correspondent is informed by the highest authority that an official statement will be issued within a few days in which the British Government will formally deny connivance in the policy of reprisals being carried out by police in Ireland. Strong measures to prevent their continuance will be promised.

Meanwhile the inhabitants of many Irish towns are living in a constant state of terror. The police have affixed notices to houses in Kilkee, Kilcrush, Carrigaholt, Doonberg and Kilrupmahill, stating that the towns will be burned if Captain Lendrum, resident magistrate at county Clare, who is believed to have been kidnapped by Sinn Feiners, is not returned within 48 hours. All who are able to leave these towns are doing so.

The "Black and Tans" fired indiscriminately through the streets of Clonakilty Sunday, smashing windows and causing considerable damage.

After an attack on the police escort at New Ardrahan, County Galway, the local town hall was burned down by the police. Bayonet charges in Belfast last night together with the imposition of a curfew, helped to check the sectarian rioting there and to keep some semblance of order in most of the city, although there were lively clashes between mobs, in which 20 or more persons were hurt. Seven were wounded by revolver bullets.

An attempt by one London newspaper to start a scare story tonight of the discovery of a vast Sinn Fein plot in London involving well known persons drew only a scoffing denial from the Irish Office.

MRS. BERGDOLL FOUND GUILTY OF DRAFT PLOT

Conspired To Aid Her Two Sons To Evade Service, Jury Finds.

FOUR CO-DEFENDANTS ALSO ARE CONVICTED

All Are Released On $10,000 Bail Pending Motion For New Trial.

[By the Associated Press.]

Philadelphia, Sept. 28. — Mrs. Emma C. Bergdoll and her four codefendants were found guilty tonight of conspiracy to aid two of her sons, Grover and Erwin, evade the draft. The verdict was returned before Judge Dickinson, in the United States District Court.

JURY DELIBERATED 8 HOURS.

The case was given to the jurymen before noon today, but it was after 8 o'clock tonight before they reached a verdict. Mrs. Bergdoll, her son, Charles A. Braun and Former Magistrate James E. Romig were found guilty on every count under which they had been indicted.

Albert S. Mitchell and Henry Schuh were acquitted on the indictments in which they alone were defendants, but found guilty on the joint indictments, with a recommendation of mercy.

On application of their counsel, the defendants were released on $10,000 bail each pending a motion for a new trial.

TRIAL LASTED OVER WEEK.

The trial started last Monday and testimony was completed on Friday. There were seven indictments, including 56 counts.

In two of the indictments all five defendants were charged with conspiring with Grover and Erwin Bergdoll to assist them in evading the draft. The other five indictments charged each defendant separately with conspiring with the Bergdoll brothers to evade the draft.

During the trial automobile hunting and fishing trips enjoyed by the two Bergdoll brothers while they were being sought by the Government, were described by witnesses for the prosecution. It was testified that Mrs. Bergdoll was present at the start of several of these trips and prepared lunches to be eaten by her sons and their guests. Former Magistrate Romig, according to the testimony, was on several of these trips and together with Mrs. Bergdoll had drawn $105,000 in gold from the Treasury at Washington in exchange for bank notes.

BRAUN HARBORED BROTHER.

Braun, who changed his name because of his brothers' escapades, was accused of harboring Erwin at his home. Mitchell, an automobile salesman, and Schuh, formerly proprietor of a cafe in this city, were implicated in the furnishing of an automobile for Erwin's use.

In his charge today Judge Dickinson said:

"It is too much to expect any mother to surrender her own son." Then he added: "Pity and sympathy for a deserter are no excuse for harboring a deserter or aiding his escape."

The question confronting the jury, he declared, was whether the defendants conspired to block recruiting of an American army by keeping Grover and Erwin out of a uniform.

RADICALS SEIZE KING'S ESTATE NEAR NAPLES

No Opposition Offered To Taking Of Property, Is Report.

FIRES GUT PLANTS HELD BY WORKERS

Flames Said To Be Act Of Extremists, Who Refuse To Give Up Factories.

[By the Associated Press.]

London, Sept. 28. — Estates owned by King Victor Emmanuel of Italy at Santa Maria di Capca Vetre, near Naples, have been seized by members of local agricultural societies, according to a dispatch to the Exchange Telegraph Company from Rome. No opposition was offered to the persons seizing the property, it is said.

TWO FACTORIES FIRED.

Two serious fires occurring in Italian manufacturing plants which had been occupied by the workers are reported in dispatches to the Exchange Telegraph Company from Rome. One of the outbreaks occurred in the Ottiano munitions factory in Naples. The belief exists, says the message, that this fire was the work of extremists, who refused to evacuate the plant. The red flag floated over the flames, but eventually the blaze was conquered and the tricolor was substituted.

The other fire, in a Turin lace factory, causing a loss of 2,000,000 lire, also is suspected of being due to foul play. It occurred, the advices state, in a factory which the workers were to have evacuated on the day the blaze broke out.

TURIN PLANTS RETURNED.

Turin, Sept. 27.—Industrial plants which had been occupied by workmen were returned to the owners today. Before evacuating the works, the men filled trenches which had been dug around them, removed barbed-wire entanglements, filled up loopholes, dug in the walls and when they left carried with them their arms and ammunition, which were concealed in private homes.

Owners of plants reported that, after an inspection, they find there was a great waste of materials during the occupation of the works. It is asserted that the men used five times the amount of coal necessary to run the plants and that all reserves are exhausted. Losses amounting to 2,000,000 lire were caused by a fire which broke out in a large lace factory which had been occupied. It is not believed the fire was incendiary.

Statistics shown by the local section of the Federation of Labor prove that of 50,000 metal workers in the city only 36,000 voted during the referendum by which the men decided to return the occupied plants to their owners. The other 14,000, it is asserted, were prevented from going to the polls by the violence of the extremists.

FEW HOLD OUT IN GENOA.

Genoa, Italy, Sept. 27.—Only a small minority of the men occupying the Ansaldo industrial plant here refused to leave the establishment today, but it is believed that they will in the end yield to instructions from the Confederation of Labor. Men who have been taking part in the occupation movement celebrated the victory today by engaging in an immense procession, red flags being carried by many.

Reports from the Ligurian provinces show that no serious incidents occurred during the day, even in Sestri, where syndicalists and anarchists are very strong.

SYNDICALISTS HAVE WON.

Washington, Sept. 28. — The agreement reached between organized labor and the operators in the Italian metal industry "is a victory for the syndicalists," said a message to the Department of Commerce today from Alfred P. Dennis, American commercial attache at Rome.

"There is corresponding discouragement on the part of the stockholders and the so-called 'legitimate leaders of industry,'" said Mr. Dennis' cablegram. "It is generally apprehended by capitalists that the principles of this agreement will later be extended so as to apply to textiles and other industries.

"There is no warrant for the conclusion that the country has accepted a soviet control of industry and that confiscation is implied. Participation of labor in the control of industry as now conceded amounts to giving workmen a voice in financial and technical administration with facilities for ascertaining what profits are made, and how these profits are applied. Competent observers regard the settlement as the beginning of increasing production and checking an epidemic of strikes."

LEGION FACES BITTER FIGHT OVER POLITICS

Attempt Will Be Made Today To Open Door For Partisan Activity.

FAVOR NEUTRALITY TOWARD LABOR

General Wood Gets Ovation; General Fayolle and Admiral Grant Speak.

[From a Staff Correspondent.]

Cleveland, Sept. 28. — Former American fighting men, in an endeavor to complete a mass of proposed legislation governing matters of principle and policy concerning the American Legion, spent the second day of their second annual convention here today thrashing out discussions precipitated by resolutions offered by the myriad committees. The only recess taken was to welcome uproariously Maj.-Gen. Leonard Wood, Gen. Emil Marie Fayolle, of France, and Admiral William Lowther Grant, of the British Navy.

POLITICS OPENS FLOODGATES.

The legionnaires lost no time getting down to business this morning by unanimously indorsing the four-fold "bonus" plan now pending in the Senate, and walked over the troublesome organized-labor problem in an equally hobnailed manner, but when the Legion's participation in politics was brought up for debate there were frantic attempts on the part of many delegates to find shelter from the rhetorical barrage which burst forth.

Last year the faintest suggestion that the American Legion enter politics as an organization was howled down without ceremony. The Legion's constitution expressly forbids political activity by the Legion or any component part of it. Individuals are barred from Legion offices if they hold elective jobs.

THREE PROPOSALS UP.

This year it is different. The Committee on Amendments reported today through Eric Fisher Wood, its chairman, and one of the original organizers of the Legion, that it was wrestling with these three proposals:

1—That the constitution be amended to permit the submission of questionnaires to political candidates.

2—That the word "absolutely" be stricken from that part of the constitution which describes the Legion as "non-political."

3—That the constitutional prohibition against officers of posts, departments and the national headquarters holding political offices, be amended to eliminate "posts."

The majority of this committee was opposed to any amendment on political restrictions, Mr. Wood said, but he declared that "a respectable minority" wanted amendment or interpretations covering the above three points. The American Legion will make its decision about them within the next 24 hours.

WOOD GIVEN OVATION.

General Wood, speaking from the stage this afternoon, declared forcefully: "The American Legion is going to be the dominant force in this country for the next fifty years."

He was greeted with a thunderous staccato: "Wood, Wood, Wood," as he stepped from a box to the front of the stage. He said:

"Don't let any insidious influence drive a wedge between us and our allies, alongside of whom we fought. As both of them have said, the peace of the world and the happiness of mankind depend very largely upon keeping up that friendly spirit. And then, again, there is another thing we must remember. Don't let us make vain the death of all those fine fellows who lie wrapped in Flanders, and one might say all over the world; for they stretch from Siberia to the British channel. Don't let us permit anything to make that splendid sacrifice useless. Don't let any insidious distinctions creep in among us as to who won the war. We all won it all together.

"You've been fine fellows in war. Don't be slackers in peace. So long as we have a soul and a conscience we're going to fight. God pity us when we've neither.

"Keep away from the handy man in politics—the man with money. He is a low type of citizen. I hope you'll keep out of politics as an organization, but that, as you went over the top in the fighting, you will go over the top in civil affairs."

STANDING ARMY OPPOSED.

Adopting the report of the committee on military affairs today, the Legion pledged its efforts to help form, recruit and maintain the National Guard at the strength required by the adopted military policy of the Government. And while it condemned a large "standing army" as "uneconomic and un-American," it repeated its belief in compulsory training, recommending the adoption by Congress of a "system which shall include physical training, educational training and Americanization, as well as efficient military training to form a foundation for future extended military training in time of war."

The battle over organized labor began when a minority of the resolutions committee adopted a resolution recording the American Legion as neutral in labor disputes and as not being antagonistic to organized labor, whereupon the convention resolved itself into a pro and con debate of the question, Delegate Walsh, of Maryland, valiantly defending the action of the minority. Accusations were made that organized labor had refused indorsement of the Legion and likewise refused union cards to its members.

The debate ended when the convention voted down the minority report, but acted to indorse again the recent statement of Commander Franklin D'Olier, which embodied the same idea. R. S. T.

Bribes Ranged From $20,000 To $1,000

Chicago, Sept. 28.—Amounts alleged to have been given the men who threw the games in the world's series of 1919 follow:

Eddie Cicotte, pitcher, $10,000.

Claude Williams, pitcher, $10,000.

Joe Jackson, outfielder, $5,000.

"Buck" Weaver, third baseman, $5,000.

"Happy" Felsch, outfielder, $1,000.

Charles Risberg, shortstop, $2,000.

"Chick" Gandil, first base, $20,000.

Fred McMullen, utility, $15,000.

THREE CHILDREN KILLED BY POISON IN MILK

Arsenic Found In Bottle Of Beverage Taken From Home Of Kentucky Family.

CASE SENT TO GRAND JURY

Mother Tells Coroner's Jury She Was Made Slightly Ill By Drinking Some Of Fluid—Medicine Bottle Missing.

[Special Dispatch to The Sun.]

Lexington, Ky., Sept. 28.—That the three children of Carl Williams, prominent citizen of Newport, Ky., were poisoned by arsenic placed in their milk, is the declaration made by a coroner's jury. The children were Shirley, aged 4; Carl, aged 2, and Stanley, 4 months old. They died in convulsions soon after drinking milk from a bottle delivered by a dairy company. Blaine McLaughlin, prosecutor of Campbell county, brought a chemist before a jury who swore the milk taken from the Williams home following the children's deaths had contained a large percentage of arsenic, as his analysis showed. The coroner's jury referred the case to the grand jury for investigation.

McLaughlin made the following statement:

"The verdict of the jury clearly showed that a triple murder has been committed. We expect to make arrests within the next week, and already have several persons under surveillance. The crime is one of the most heinous ever committed in Kentucky, and county authorities and myself will lay aside all work and make every effort to bring the criminal to justice."

Coroner's Jury Hearing.

Interest centered about the testimony of the mother. Despite cross-examination by McLaughlin, Mrs. Williams remained firm in a statement that to the best of her knowledge only the two older children, Shirley and Carl, had drunk the milk.

"Shortly after breakfast on the morning of the day before my three children died," Mrs. Williams said, "I drank some of the milk myself. I noticed that I felt ill during the morning, but did not think of the milk at the time. I did not call in any physician, as I begun to feel better about noon.

"Mrs. Warner, my sister, had charge of the children during the day and had been giving Shirley, the youngest child, medicine prescribed for him by Dr. G. F. Sauter. Both I and my husband noticed that Stanley had been getting better during the day and we thought that he would recover. He had been ill about four days."

At this point in the trial McLaughlin called Mrs. Warner to the stand. He asked her what had become of a medicine bottle from which the child had been given doses.

"I threw the bottle away a few days after my nephew and nieces died," Mrs. Warner declared. She said that there was no further use after the deaths of the children.

Resuming her testimony, Mrs. Williams told of the children becoming ill and of summoning Dr. Sauter and his son, Dr. G. Sauter.

"The children, during their infancy, had been subject to spasms, and my husband and I did not attach any importance to their sudden attack. Although ill during the afternoon, Shirley and Carl did not go into convulsions until shortly after 6 o'clock in the evening. When both of them became ill we called the doctor," she said.

"Stanley, who had been subject to stomach trouble since birth, grew gradually worse as the evening progressed and seemed to lapse into unconsciousness shortly after 8 o'clock. Dr. C. F. Sauter, who was treating the two older children at the time, also gave Stanley soothing medicine before he died. The death of our 4-month-old baby was no surprise, as he had been a delicate child and ill almost continuously."

Mrs. Williams betrayed no emotion while on the stand and told of the death of her baby and two other children without hesitation and in a matter-of-fact way.

Chicago To Use Tanks To Baffle Hold-Up Men

Fleet Of Armored Cars Will Convey Payrolls From Banks To Various Factories.

[Special Dispatch to The Sun.]

Chicago, Sept. 28.—Armored cars and tanks that saw duty in France are to play a return engagement in the streets of Chicago, as a means of baffling the bandits who are now getting away with heavy payrolls almost every day in the week. This was decided upon at a conference of bank executives.

The fleet of armored cars that will convey the payrolls from the banks to various factories will consist of five units, each consisting of an armored truck and a high powered automobile. Two guards and a chauffeur will hold forth on the truck, with three guards and a chauffeur on the automobile. A loud gong and secret cutoff will be part of the equipment of the trucks. In the event the chauffeur is shot down by the bandits, the guards will operate the cut-off, stopping the truck automatically and starting the furious gong.

The crews of the "tanks" will be picked men, especially trained in the use of firearms, probably men who saw overseas service. The fleet of tanks and armored cars will cost $1,000,000 and will be ready within a few weeks. The Federal Reserve Bank already uses an immense armored car to carry its cash through the streets.

WEATHER FORECAST.
Fair today and probably tomorrow.
Detail Weather Report on Page 16.

THE SUN

BUSINESS REVIVAL SEEN BY WASHINGTON. SEE PAGE 3.
PRESIDENT HEARS OF DANGER TO AMERICAN SHIPPING. SEE PAGE 7.

VOL. 168—NO. 110 PRESS RUN WEDNESDAY { MORNING, 116,108 EVENING, 105,073 } 221,181 || SUNDAY 154,533 BALTIMORE, FRIDAY, MARCH 25, 1921. Published every week-day by The A. S. Abell Co. Entered as second-class matter at Baltimore Postoffice. 22 PAGES. 2 CENTS

RUSSIA'S HAND IS SEEN BEHIND GERMAN REVOLT

Communists Reported As Having Been Ordered To Join In Move.

OUTBREAKS SPREAD TO INTERIOR AREAS

Radicals Control Several Towns In Lower Harz Mountains.

[Copyright, 1921, by New York Tribune.]

Berlin, March 24 (By Wireless).—Terror grips Eisleben and some of the other industrial cities of the Elbe Valley in Central Germany, where Communist disorders broke out yesterday.

In Hamburg and other affected areas the police appear to have gained control, although strikes are still in progress and in several places there was severe street fighting, lasting far into the night.

THIRTY KILLED IN HAMBURG.

Thirty persons were killed and 50 severely wounded yesterday in Hamburg alone, and in other cities there were casualties when police clashed with groups of strikers who were seeking to foment trouble.

The belief prevails that the Russian Soviet Government precipitated the disorders with a demand that all Communists in Germany join in demonstrations against the "capitalist" Government. The labor unions of the country have issued an appeal to the workers denouncing the Reds for beginning an industrial strike without cause and charging that they are attempting a political overthrow.

The appeal says that the strikes are not in support of union aims, but were called for the sole purpose of bringing catastrophe on Germany at a time when the country's fate is in the balance.

WRECK CITY BUILDINGS.

The center of the uprising is in the lower Harz Mountains, west of the Elbe river, about 100 miles southwest of Berlin. In Eisleben, 23 miles west of Halla, the Reds are in complete control. They drove the police off the streets last night, threw hand grenades into the police station and town hall, wrecking them, and then looted the chief buildings of the city. The Communists ended the night's orgy by stopping a railway express train with a hail of missiles and looting it.

Mansfeld, which lies two miles northwest of Eisleben, is without police protection. Strikers there opened the city prison and liberated all the criminals. Several persons have been killed and others wounded in fighting at Mansfield and Eisleben.

NITROGEN PLANT SEIZED.

A Vorwarts dispatch from Naumburg reports that Communist workmen at the great nitrogen plant at Lauena, southwest of Merseberg, which employs 22,000 men, armed themselves with rifles and hand grenades, took possession of the factory and stopped all work there.

The trouble in the Hamburg area began when an army of unemployed forced its way into the Blohm & Voss Shipyard, across the river from the city. The Communist workers in the yards made common cause with these idlers and compelled the yards to shut down. When the workers who did not want to strike were leaving the yard, a fight developed in which eight persons were killed. Toward evening the police surrounded the yard and the 1,500 Communists spent the night there. The police established a blockade around them, preventing them obtaining food supplies or reinforcements.

In fighting at the Vulcan Shipyard, four were killed and many wounded. Martial law was established by the municipal authorities. Fighting continues, however, in different parts of the city. Fifteen civilians and two policemen were shot dead in these encounters.

CONFESS MOSCOW ORDER.

The connection of the Moscow Government with the disorders and strikers was believed to be definitely established by the arrest of several Communists who confessed their part in the plot. The persistent sympathetic campaign of agitation carried on by the Red Flag, and the proclamations published by Communist newspapers in different cities calling on the workers to rise against the present government, and Red documents that have fallen into the hands of the Bourgeoise press all lend color to the belief that the disorders were planned in Moscow and carried out through a central directing power in Berlin. The Red Flag says this morning:

"The white terror has begun. The bloodhounds of counter-revolution are rampant in Central Germany."

Nationalists Avenge Milan Bomb Outrage

Burn Anarchist And Communist Buildings—31 Killed By Explosion.

[Copyright, 1921, by New York Tribune.]

Milan, March 24 (Special Cable).—The Fascisti, or extreme Nationalists, fired the building where the anarchist newspaper is printed here late last night in retaliation for the explosion of a bomb earlier in the evening in the Diana Theatre, at an amusement park near this city. The Nationalists also tried to reach the Socialist newspaper, but were kept back by troops.

The Socialist headquarters building also was burned.

Thirty-one persons were killed and 100 wounded in the bomb outrage.

Austrian's Fortune Of 80,000 Kronen Shrinks To $84 In U. S.

Pittsburgh, March 24 (Special).—Martin Roster, formerly in the grocery and confectionery business in Donora, has returned to that place after a 12-year stay in Austria-Hungary. He left this country for Debreezen, Hungary, in 1909, and was in Europe all through the World War. He arrived in the United States last Saturday.

Rosner engaged in business in Hungary — busily piling up profits. When he decided to return to the United States he had amassed a fortune of 80,000 kronen.

When he arrived in New York he went to have his kronen exchanged for American dollars. The smiling clerk took his kronen, counted them and ascertained there were 80,000 of them—and then counted out $84 in United States tender.

GERMANY THREATENED WITH NEW PENALTIES

France Approaches Britain With Suggestions Of Additional Pressure.

ECONOMIC STEPS ARE FAVORED

Occupation Of Ports On North And Baltic Seas Among Proposals Advanced.

By RALPH COURTNEY.

[Copyright, 1921, by New York Tribune.]

Paris, March 24 (Special Cable).—Upon receipt of formal notice today from the Allied Reparation Commission that Germany had violated the Treaty of Versailles by failing to deliver the 1,000,000,000 gold marks demanded of her before March 23, Premier Briand approached the British Government through diplomatic channels, suggesting the immediate application of new penalties.

The Reparation Commission in its memorandum to the Allied governments on the situation advised them that an occasion had arisen for the application of force. Simultaneously the commission notified Germany that she must pay the balance of 12,000,000 gold marks due by May 1 or take the consequences.

German Unrest Is Factor.

The occupation by Allied armies of the city of Essen and possibly the whole Ruhr Valley shortly may take place. In view of the increased unrest in Germany some apprehension is felt here that a further Allied invasion of German soil may not be met with as meek resistance as heretofore.

Although some difference of opinion still exists in high French circles as to the exact punitive measures to be taken against Germany, the strongest current of opinion favors economic rather than military sanctions. It is still doubtful whether the extension of Allied sovereignty will go beyond Essen.

Measures Suggested.

Other measures of an economic nature understood to be under consideration are:

The Allied occupation of German ports on the North and Baltic seas and the taking over of German maritime customs and port duties. This administration would be undertaken by the British and French jointly.

The taking over by the Allies of more complete control and administration of government in the occupied areas.

The imposition of a heavy duty on all coal shipments leaving the Ruhr, either by land or water. Virtually all these shipments now go through the Allies' hands.

An extension of Allied administration in the occupied areas, which is expected to be taken in any event, would result in the collection by the Allies not only of customs duties along the Rhine frontier but of local land and income taxes as well. The Allies would impose new taxes to suit themselves and administer the municipal and provincial fiscal affairs.

Separate Customs State.

As soon as the customs frontier has been set up east of the Rhine and the local administration of the occupied areas is taken over by the Allies, a customs state, to all intents and purposes separate from Germany, will be established.

Bail Refused Man Held For Cronkhite's Death

Rosenbluth, Committed To Tombs, Protests His Innocence.

New York, March 24.—Robert Rosenbluth, former army captain, who was arrested yesterday on a warrant charging him with the murder of Major Alexander P. Cronkhite, a fellow-officer at Camp Lewis, Washington, on October 25, 1918, was committed to the Tombs without bail today after arraignment before United States Commissioner Hitchcock.

By consent of the United States Attorney's Office and Jonah J. Goldstein, Rosenbluth's lawyer, the pleading to the charge went over until Saturday morning. Rosenbluth declared his innocence. His lawyer said:

"Captain Rosenbluth is innocent and will assist the Government to bring on the trial as speedily as possible. He will enter no technical objections. He has no doubt of the outcome."

As nearly as can be learned, the Government will try to establish a conspiracy with Rosenbluth as its center and Roland Pothier, who admits "involuntary manslaughter," as the one who actually discharged the weapon which killed Cronkhite. No suggestion of the nature of the motive has crept out. One of the Government investigators permitted it to be inferred that further arrests were expected.

LANSING GIVES HIS STAND ON PEACEMAKING

Reveals In His New Book How Near He Came To Quitting Conference.

SPLIT WITH WILSON OVER SHANTUNG

Says He Opposed Article X Mandates And Self-Determination.

[By the Associated Press.]

Boston, March 24.—Robert Lansing, former Secretary of State and member of the American Peace Commission, in his forthcoming book on "The Peace Negotiations," which will be published tomorrow by Houghton-Mifflin Company, reveals how close he came to resigning from the commission because of differences with President Wilson over the Shantung decision and his belief that many of the terms of peace imposed on Germany were harsh, humiliating and seemingly impossible of performance.

FOR PRELIMINARY PEACE.

President Wilson, according to Mr. Lansing's belief, at one time during the Peace Conference purposed to negotiate a preliminary treaty which would start the League of Nations functioning without laying the document before the United States Senate, and evidently was much perturbed when his Secretary of State told him that the only way to change the status from war to peace was by a ratified treaty or a joint resolution of Congress.

A profound conviction that immediate peace was the primary need of the world, Mr. Lansing implies, was all that kept him from resigning from the Peace Commission because of fundamental disagreements with the President on principles. The former Secretary discloses that in 1916, shortly before a meeting in Washington of the League to Enforce Peace at which the President was to speak, Mr. Lansing wrote to Mr. Wilson objecting to the use of force to settle international disputes. In this letter he pointed to the menace to the Monroe Doctrine contained in such a plan.

Alarmed at the complications of war and foreign entanglements in the guarantee of territorial integrity and political independence of members of the League, a guarantee that finally was embodied in Article 10 of the Covenant, Mr. Lansing says that at Paris he tried to have substituted a negative pledge that the members would not infringe upon each other's territorial integrity or political independence. He became convinced that Col. Edward M. House, then President Wilson's closest adviser, was completely converted with regard to this question.

SHANTUNG CHIEF DIFFERENCE.

It is in relation to Shantung Mr. Lansing discloses the sharpest differences between himself and President Wilson. Mr. Lansing gives as his opinion that blackmail and bluff by Japan impelled the President to agree to surrender to that country such rights in Shantung as before the war were held by Germany and automatically annulled when China declared hostilities. In his

(Continued on Page 3, Column 2.)

Two Killed, 11 Injured By Tornado In Tennessee.

Nashville, Tenn., March 24.—Two persons were killed, one other probably fatally injured and 10 seriously injured in a tornado which started at Berlin, a village 10 miles west of Lewisburg, this afternoon and swept northeastward across Marshall county for 15 miles.

A stick was blown through the head of the man reported fatally injured.

Twelve residences and barns were blown away, many other residences were slightly damaged, much timber was destroyed and the railway station at Anes on the Lewisburg branch of the Louisville and Nashville was torn down.

Ten freight cars were blown off the Louisville and Nashville track at Anes and traffic on the Lewisburg branch was blocked until midnight.

GREEKS GAIN 20 MILES IN DRIVE ON TURKS

Nationalists Declare They Will Not Retreat Until All Means Of Defense Is Exhausted.

WEATHER FAVORING ATTACK

Constantine's Troops Number 120,000—Bagdad Railway Objective Of Attackers' Drive.

[By the Associated Press.]

Constantinople, March 24.—An advance of about 20 miles was made by the Greeks on both the Smyrna and Brussa fronts during the first day of their offensive against the Turks. The Turks, who are fighting hard, declare they will not retreat until every means of defense have been exhausted.

The offensive, which began after weeks of preparation, is proceeding under good weather conditions. The Greek line now runs some 12 miles east of Yenishehr, on the Brussa front, and also about 12 miles east of Ushak, on the Smyrna front.

Greek Trooos Number 120,000.

Greek troops numbering 120,000 are participating in the Greek offensive against the Turkish Nationalist forces in Asia Minor, it is reported here.

The Turkish Nationalists are believed to have about 90,000 effectives in the field, but have smaller supplies upon which to draw.

The most careful preparations were made by the Greeks in connection with the offensive which began yesterday, and it is anticipated here that the Greeks will win important positions with their first drive.

Apprehension is felt here that the advance of Greek forces east of the Smyrnah hinterland, will throw the Turks into the arms of the Russian Soviet Government of Moscow.

Bagdad Railway Objective.

The objective of the offensive is the Bagdad Railway, although Greek commanders have planned to reach the city of Eski-Shiehr. It is affirmed that British, French and Italian armies in the Near East will not participate in the campaign. General Selah Eddin Bey, commander of Turkish forces in Cilicia, has been transferred to the Smyrna front for the purpose of uniting the Turkish defense.

For the past two weeks the Greeks have been landing at Smyrna motortrucks, artillery and munitions, which had been stored at Saloniki.

Railroad Needs For Future As Presented By Each Side

W. Jett Lauck, For The Workers, And Samuel O. Dun, For The Roads, Closes Debate, With General Summing Up Of Changes Each Deems Essential.

The debate on the railroad controversy, which has been conducted in The Sun by W. Jett Lauck for the employes and Samuel O. Dunn for the roads, is closed today with a general summing up, in which these vigorous protagonists present what each side regards as the fundamental changes needed to bring peace and prosperity to the industry.

ARTICLE III.

By W. JETT LAUCK,
Consulting Economist for the Railway Employes.

The fundamental necessities of the railroad situation—the necessity of maintaining the solvency of the transportation industry and at the same time reducing and readjusting freight rates in order to stimulate a revival in traffic and business activity—will not be met by a reduction in the wages of railroad employes. As a matter of fact, because a smaller number of employes are handling a larger volume of traffic as compared with the prewar period, the productive efficiency of railway operating forces has increased and the increase in labor cost for each unit of traffic handled has been less than the advances in rates of pay since the beginning of the World War.

Wage reductions at this time would cause a further loss in the co-operative effort of railway workers, which is of such vital importance to the rehabilitation of the industry. It would be a grave injustice, as there can be no real justification for cuts in rates of pay until there has been a further decline in living costs. At the same time, the wage reductions which are now being sought, even if obtained, would afford no hope of a permanent solution of our transportation difficulties.

Cause Of The Problem.

The immediate occasion of financial trouble in the transportation industry has been the recent slump in industrial and commercial activity. The original and more fundamental cause is to be

(Continued on Page 6, Column 4.)

By SAMUEL O. DUNN,
Editor of The Railway Age.

The railways of the country are in a very serious financial condition. Month by month ever since the advance in freight and passenger rates was granted last August their net return has been declining. In January 160 large railways for which reports are now available failed by about $2,500,000 to earn enough to pay their operating expenses and taxes.

No intelligent person can examine the statistics without being convinced that unless they soon get relief a large part of the leading railroads of the country will become bankrupt.

This general condition is due to two causes: First, excessive operating expenses; second, an unprecedented decline in traffic. The railways within recent months have been carrying one-third less freight than in July, August, September and October.

Record Traffic; Small Earnings.

The present freight and passenger rates were put into effect late in August. The total traffic handled and the total earnings made in September, October and November were the largest in history for those months. In September, however, the railways earned only 4.1 per cent.; in October, 4.6 per cent.; in November, 3.3 per cent. This small net return was due entirely to the high operating expenses. In September it took 83 cents out of every dollar earned to pay expenses; in October, 82 cents, and in November, 86 cents. The railroad industry can never prosper and be adequately developed with such a rela-

(Continued on Page 6, Column 5.)

DEBS IS CALLED TO WASHINGTON BY DAUGHERTY

He Comes From And Returns To Atlanta Prison Unattended.

SPENDS THREE HOURS WITH JUSTICE CHIEF

Unprecedented Trip Is Made With Approval Of President.

By ARTHUR SEARS HENNING.

Washington, March 24 (Special).—Unaccompanied and unrecognized, Eugene V. Debs, the Socialist candidate for President last fall, who is serving a 10-year sentence in the Atlanta Penitentiary for obstructing the draft during the war, called at the Department of Justice today and conferred for more than two hours with Attorney-General Daugherty.

With the approval of President Harding, Mr. Daugherty sent for Debs and permitted him to come to Washington and return to prison absolutely alone. The Attorney-General questioned the prisoner as to his expressed views of opposition to the war which led to his conviction, as to whether he has changed his attitude in any respect, as to his physical condition and other matters pertaining to the question of releasing the aged radical from further confinement.

Mr. Daugherty declined to reveal what information he obtained from Debs or to indicate any conclusions therefrom, stating that he would advise the President whether, in his opinion, clemency should or should not be granted.

UNRECOGNIZED ON TRAIN.

Debs, furnished with a round-trip ticket to Washington, left the Atlanta Penitentiary yesterday, boarded a train and mingled with the passengers absolutely unrecognized, so far as is known. There was no one at the station to meet him when he arrived in Washington today and he hailed a taxicab and was driven to the Department of Justice.

Unrecognized at the department, he inquired his way to the office of the Attorney-General, sent in his card and soon was closeted with Mr. Daugherty and Col. Guy D. Goff, assistant to the Attorney-General.

After the conference Debs left the department, still unrecognized, and started back to Atlanta, where he is due to arrive tomorrow afternoon. The fact that Debs had been at the department did not become public until Mr. Daugherty received the newspaper correspondents an hour after the prisoner had departed.

"There is not much in the way of news," began Mr. Daugherty, "except that I wanted to tell you about Debs coming to Washington today. I have a prepared statement ready for you."

DAUGHERTY'S STATEMENT.

Thereupon the Attorney-General handed around this statement:

"In connection with the investigation of the Debs case and after conference with the President and with his approval I had Debs come here for the purpose of making some inquiries of him. He has returned to Atlanta. I have asked him to refrain from saying anything for publication or otherwise regarding the inquiries made of him. I am sure no well-meaning person will urge him to discuss this matter or anything that took place on his journey or during his stay here. Debs presented his own case to the trial court and jury. He was permitted to do so here.

"The Debs case, as I have said before, stands alone. I could not, of course, go to him. What took place and the information I have acquired will be reported in due time only to the President, and that in connection with any recommendations that may be made when the investigation is concluded. Debs came here without guard and so returns to Atlanta. Colonel Goff, assistant to the Attorney-General, was present during the inquiry."

Former President William H. Taft called upon Attorney-General Daugherty just before the newspaper men were ushered in and remained during their conference. He appeared extremely interested in the Debs case and the questions asked about it.

CLAIMS FULL AUTHORITY.

One of the very first inquiries put to Mr. Daugherty was where the authority lay for allowing a Federal prisoner to make the trip to Washington and return unguarded.

"I am satisfied there is full authority," said the Attorney-General. "I have not looked it up, but I am satisfied it exists."

"What precedent is there for it?" he was asked.

"Well, there is a precedent now," he replied. "I discussed the matter with the President and I am willing to take the full responsibility for my action."

As to the health of the prisoned, Mr. Daugherty said:

"He looked very well, although he appeared to be a little nervous."

NOT GENERAL POLICY.

There has been much pressure lately to force a general amnesty for political prisoners, comprising those who violated the Espionage law and who obstructed the Draft law through speeches and action. Mr. Daugherty was asked if the Debs case would be the basis of a general policy in this matter, but he said:

"No, this is an individual case; it stands alone."

"Did Debs display any change of mind?" asked a correspondent alluding to Debs' former attitude toward the Draft law.

"Naturally that was one of the things discussed, but just as naturally I cannot talk about it," was the reply.

G. O. P. Members Give Blood To Save Lone Democrat.

Salt Lake City, Utah, March 24 (Special).—Clyde A. Hammond, only Democratic member of the House of Representatives, died here after seven of his Republican colleagues had sacrificed several quarts of their own blood in transfusion operations in an effort to save the Representative's life.

He was taken suddenly ill a few weeks ago. Senator J. Will Knight yesterday contributed a pint of his blood to prolong Mr. Hammond's life, but the patient's condition was too weak and he died.

WOOD'S CAMPAIGN CHIEF SUES TREASURER OF FUND

Col. William Procter Seeks To Recover $110,000 From Major Albert Sprague.

ACTION BASED ON JOINT NOTE

Former Manager Says Sum Represents Money Borrowed By Sprague And Himself.

Chicago, March 24. — Col. William Procter, manager of Major-Gen. Leonard Wood's campaign for the Republican Presidential nomination and contributor of $50,000 to the campaign expenses, today filed suit to recover $110,000 from Major Albert A. Sprague, of Chicago, treasurer of the campaign.

The $110,000 was said to represent Major Sprague's liability on money borrower by him and by Colonel Procter for campaign expenses.

It was specified in the bill that one note for $100,000, due a bank, had become payable November 15, 1920, and that Major Sprague had refused to meet one-half of it, the amount Colonel Procter charged he had agreed to pay as co-signer of the note. Colonel Procter alleged that "repeated attempts to collect the money from Major Sprague had failed."

Money Due On Loans.

Colonel Procter charged that $50,000 was due him from Major Sprague on the note and in addition cited loans totaling $60,000, which, he said, had been made to Major Sprague during the campaign.

Major-General Wood said he "did not know a thing about it.

"It's a matter for the financial committee to settle," he said. "I didn't know there was any trouble over the financial matters. If the allegations of Colonel Procter are correct, I can't understand why Major Sprague should refuse payment."

Efforts to reach Major Sprague failed. At his office it was said he was out to lunch and later it was said he was out of town for the day.

No Obligation, Sprague Says.

Major Sprague was surprised when informed of the action of Colonel Procter and said that he felt under no obligation to return to Mr. Procter any money donated by him to the campaign fund.

"I feel that there is no personal obligation on my part to repay Mr. Procter," the Major declared. "There were several notes on the bank which I signed as treasurer and the suit is undoubtedly based on one of those. Colonel Procter undertook to finance the campaign and I acted as treasurer. I know of $60,000 that he advanced personally and probably that amount is included in the suit."

Policeman Given $27,000 For Injuries In Crash

N. Y. Supreme Court Jury Told Bluecoat Does Not Barter Life Or Body For His Wages.

New York, March 24.—A New York policeman was awarded $27,000 damages today by a jury which tried his complaint against a retired capitalist whose rented automobile crashed into the bluecoat's motorcycle on Fifth avenue, January, 1920.

Walter T. Menke, the policeman, had sued the capitalist, George F. Simons, of St. Mary's, Pa., for $50,000, charging that in the collision he was hurled to the pavement, causing a linear fracture of the skull.

In his charge to the jury, Supreme Court Justice Tierney said the fact that the plaintiff is a policeman, injured while performing official duties, does not prevent him from asserting his claim, for the policeman has the same right as a private person.

"It is no part of a policeman's contract of employment," he added, "that he barter his life or body for the wages he receives."

Naval Balloon And Crew Of Five Reported Missing

Craft Left Pensacola Tuesday. Last Message Said It Was Sinking To Sea.

Pensacola, Fla., March 24.—A naval balloon carrying five men was reported missing tonight by the naval air station here. The balloon, in command of Chief Quartermaster E. W. Wilkinson, accompanied by a machinist's mate and three marines as students, left here Tuesday night.

The last information from the missing aircraft was received early today, when two carrier pigeons returned with messages. One message was that the balloon was off St. Andrew's Bay, Florida, drifting toward the open sea. The other, arriving a little later, said that all ballast had been thrown overboard and that the balloon was then at an altitude of only 100 feet and slowly sinking.

A naval dirigible and a number of seaplanes and flying boats were sent in search of the missing balloonists, but up to a late hour tonight the searchers had been unable to find either the balloon or any of its crew.

Naval officials tonight frankly expressed fears for the safety of the missing men and ordered the search continued, with an Eagle boat added to the forces.

CARDINAL GIBBONS DEAD AFTER LENGTHY ILLNESS; THE END COMES GENTLY

Last Recorded Words Of America's Foremost Churchman Are A Blessing To His Household.

TO BE BURIED IN CATHEDRAL

Body, Which Will Lie In State Three Days, Will Be Interred Next Thursday In Presence Of Greatest Company Of Clergy In Country's History.

The story of the Cardinal's long life will be found on Pages 10 and 11.

James Cardinal Gibbons died at 11.33 o'clock yesterday morning, passing from sleep to lifelessness so quietly that even his nurse, a Bon Secours nun, could not be sure that it was the end. She had seen the change that betokened it, but it was slight, almost imperceptible, and five more minutes passed while she leaned over the slight, still form, watching.

Then from the gray house where he had lived and worked, in the shadow of the Cathedral of the Assumption of the Blessed Virgin Mary, whence he had sent unsparing gifts of himself and his love and care to a people that had learned to revere his name, went forth the news that he had died.

TO BE BURIED UNDER CATHEDRAL ALTAR

His grave will be a niche in the crypt under the high altar of the Cathedral. A slab of marble carved with an inscription in Latin in the north wall of the crypt will mark the resting place of all that is earthly of one of the greatest American churchmen of all time. Above this vault, dark as night in the daytime, behind whose south wall lie the six Archbishops of Maryland who preceded him, is the sanctuary of the Cathedral to which Cardinal Gibbons' parents brought him as a baby to be baptized, where he was consecrated a Bishop, where he was later consecrated an Archbishop, and where, on June 30, 1886, he was invested with the robes of the Cardinalate.

There, too, stands the throne of the Cardinal, and above the throne, above the white-walled niche in the crypt beneath, will hang the Cardinal's hat, symbol of princedom in the Catholic hierarchy to which man attains by godliness and good works. There it will hang so long as the Cathedral stands.

CALM AS END NEARS.

Cardinal Gibbons' last-remembered words from his death bed were words of affection and thankfulness for the services of his brothers in the church and gratitude for the peacefulness of his own death.

It was last Tuesday after dinner, and all the members of his household were in his room. The Rev. Louis R. Stickney, rector of the Cathedral, asked:

"Your Eminence, will you give us your blessing?"

Cardinal Gibbons smiled and inclined his head ever so slightly. Then the five priests—Father Stickney, the Rev. Eugene J. Connelly, chancellor; the Rev. Albert E. Smith, secretary to the Cardinal; the Rev. William J. Hafey, assistant chancellor, and the Rev. Edwin L. Leonard — knelt by the Cardinal's bedside and he blessed them. As they arose he whispered:

"What a devoted and loyal household! What noble, loyal priests!"

A moment or two before Bishop O. B. Corrigan, auxiliary Bishop for the Archdiocese of Baltimore and Vicar-General, had stepped from the sick room. The Cardinal added, weakly:

"There never was a more loyal, more devoted worker than Bishop Corrigan."

THE LAST RECORDED WORDS.

Then there was silence for a few moments, and the Cardinal moved his head to and fro slightly, seeming to be thinking deeply. Finally he spoke:

"How different an end from Cardinal Manning's!"

The sorrowing household was reminded that Cardinal Manning's last days were saddened by the forgetfulness of some of those upon whom he had counted to be his most loyal and unfaltering companions.

These were the last recorded words Cardinal Gibbons uttered. He knew then that he could not live long—that, in fact, he was dying. Thereafter he talked little, and only to his nurses or his physician, Dr. Charles O'Donovan. On Tuesday night he spoke to Sisters Columba, Ludovic, Reginald and Clare, the Bon Secours nuns who were his nurses, but not at length nor to any especial purpose.

Father Smith came to see him early Wednesday and asked him how he felt.

"I think I have had a good day," the Cardinal whispered, and his secretary knew then that his fine, keen mind, which had stanchly withstood the oncreeping weakness that assailed and was destroying his body, was being dulled. Then he lapsed into a coma, from which he slipped peacefully into death.

BODY LYING AT RESIDENCE.

The church's season of mourning for the death of the Saviour finds it mourning the death of its great American leader, and its rituals and prayers for that season will not be changed. Through the dark hours of Good Friday and Holy Saturday and the glorious dawn of Easter the body of Cardinal Gibbons will lie in his own room where he died.

But late on Eastern Sunday night, with the church's season of rejoicing over the Resurrection well under way, it will be moved to the Cathedral, to lie there throughout the masses of Monday, Tuesday and Wednesday, where his beloved people may see him for the last time; through the high requiem mass that will be his funeral on Thursday and from there to be borne to its niche in the crypt. And it will not be difficult for those who knew him to believe that he would have been rejoiced to pass on while his people were thanking the Creator for the Saviour's gift of life eternal.

GREAT CHURCHMEN COMING.

At the funeral will gather the greatest company of churchmen ever as-

(Continued on Page 3, Column 4.)

NEW CARDINAL UNLIKELY SOON FOR BALTIMORE

Purple, Instead Of Red, Will Adorn Throne In Cathedral.

Baltimore probably will continue to call the famous gray home at Mulberry and Charles streets "the Cardinal's residence" for many years. But it is likely to be a long time before the house will be able to claim as its permanent occupant another Cardinal.

Perhaps within the next six months a new archbishop will have been selected to take over the reins laid down by Cardinal Gibbons with his death yesterday. Baltimore will continue as the seat of the province which extends from Maryland down to Florida and out to West Virginia, and the prelate who sits here will be primate of that jurisdiction.

But the throne in the Cathedral, upon which Cardinal Gibbons, a picturesque and inspiring figure, performed the ecclesiastical functions of his high office in the church since receiving the red hat in 1886, will be divested of its brilliant hangings of cardinal red. It will be draped with the deep purple of an archbishop.

CARDINAL NAMED NO CHOICE.

If this archbishop should prove himself another Gibbons, whose voice and work attract attention of the whole church, he may, of course, be honored with elevation to the cardinalate. But, with two American cardinals now, and both on the Atlantic seaboard, such a probability seems remote.

There have been many rumors and reports, within and without Catholic circles, for years that Cardinal Gibbons had practically decided on his successor as Archbishop of Baltimore and that he had let the bishops of the Province of Baltimore know his wishes. There probably never has been any ground for these rumors other than the fact that, when he found a clergyman in his jurisdiction whose work was promising, the Cardinal invariably encouraged that clergyman with important assignments and frequent promotions.

When the Cardinal was elevated to the archbishopric, and to the head of the Archdiocese of Baltimore, in 1877, he received the office by right of succession, which belongs to a coadjutor bishop. There is, however, no coadjutor bishop in the Province of Baltimore at present. This province includes the dioceses of Charleston, S. C.; Richmond, Va.; St. Augustine, Fla.; Savannah, Ga.; Wheeling, W. Va., and Wilmington, Del., in addition to the vicariate of North Carolina. The heads of each of these jurisdictions are titular or auxiliary bishops, with no right of succession.

BISHOPS TO SUGGEST NAMES.

According to the usual formula, these bishops will meet in Baltimore within the next two months in secret conclave. They will discuss among themselves the merits of various candidates for the archbishopric. The result of this discussion will be the recommendation of

(Continued on Page 3, Column 6.)

WEATHER FORECAST

Increasing cloudiness today, followed by rain today and tomorrow; mild temperature; increasing southeasterly winds.

Detailed Weather Report on Page 17.

THE SUN

Incidents that throw light on the character of Woodrow Wilson. —*See Page 13.*

VOL. 174—NO. 67D PRESS RUN SATURDAY MORNING 133,817 BALTIMORE, MONDAY, FEBRUARY 4, 1924. Published every week-day by The A. S. Abell Company. Entered as second-class matter at Baltimore Postoffice. 22 PAGES 2 CENTS

WOODROW WILSON'S LIFE AT END; FUNERAL IS EXPECTED WEDNESDAY

FALL DEFIANCE HALTS NAVY OIL LEASE INQUIRY

Committee To Delay Action Until His Status Is Fixed.

WILL ADJOURN TODAY IN WILSON'S MEMORY

Gregory In Letter To President Makes Position Clear.

Washington, Feb. 3.—Albert B. Fall's challenge to the Senate oil committee, in which he disputed the authority of that body to examine him in connection with naval oil leases, resulted today in a decision by the committee to postpone the hearing of all other witnesses until the question of whether Mr. Fall will testify is definitely settled.

The committee will not meet tomorrow, because Congress will suspend its sessions in memory of Woodrow Wilson. On Tuesday it will assemble, but will adjourn immediately to await action of the Senate on its request for reenactment of the resolution under which it has been proceeding. Mr. Fall contended the committee's authority had expired.

Witnesses Must Wait.

A number of witnesses summoned in the inquiry are on hand to testify, including Washington brokers whose books have been subpœnaed to throw light on stock market operations in oil leases, but these must wait until the case of Mr. Fall is disposed of.

Thomas W. Gregory, Attorney-General in the Wilson Cabinet, who was one of those originally selected by President Coolidge to act as counsel in the Government's oil cases, called on the President today and gave him a letter explaining his position, both in respect to possible service in the proceedings and his connection with oil interests.

Mr. Gregory's Position.

Mr. Gregory said in the letter that in his telephone conversations with the White House prior to the announcement of his appointment he had no idea that he was accepting appointment or that the President had so construed it.

Mr. Gregory said also that if it had been in his mind at the time of his telephone conversation with Mr. Coolidge that he ever had been employed directly or indirectly by E. L. Doheny, whose company holds the leases to the California oil reserves, the matter would have ended at once.

Confirmed By President.

President Coolidge confirmed Mr. Gregory's understanding of the telephone conversations had with the White House as to the inferences to be drawn from the conversations.

The conference between the President and Mr. Gregory leaves the way open for the formal submission to Congress of another Democrat as a member of the special oil counsel and the name of former Senator Atlee Pomerene, of Ohio, will go forward within the next few days.

The Gregory Incident.

The letter of Mr. Gregory in regard to his acting as Democratic prosecutor in the naval oil lease case, together with a statement by the President, are given below:

The President's statement said:

> The statement in the letter of Mr. Attorney Gregory to me regarding the conversation between him and me over the telephone and the inferences to be drawn from it are correct.
>
> CALVIN COOLIDGE.

Mr. Gregory's Letter.

Mr. Gregory's letter follows:

"*Mr. President:* On last Tuesday night when I was in Austin, Texas, you stated to me over the long-distance telephone that you wished to employ me in the investigation of the leases of the naval oil reserves. You will recall that after expressing my appreciation, I stated that I was not in close touch with the developments in the matter, that nothing occurred to me that would prevent me from serving, but that I would be in Washington Saturday afternoon (today) and would then confer with you on the subject.

"I had no idea that in saying this I was accepting an appointment or that you so understood it. I assumed that would be decided when we conferred, and that in the meantime I would have an opportunity to go through my books

(Continued on Page 8, Column 8.)

All Ranks Of America Pay Tribute At The Passing Of The War President

At the announcement of Mr. Wilson's death there was an extraordinary spectacle in S street in front of the doorway where Dr. Grayson stood weeping. Without a word the heads of the throng were bowed, men removed their hats and a number of women, sobbing, knelt reverently in prayer in the open street. Then the crowd melted away silently, to be replaced by an unending throng throughout the day.

President and Mrs. Coolidge arriving at the S street house soon after receiving word of Mr. Wilson's death.

SEIZED JITNEYS RUSH MEXICANS TO BATTLE

Federals Requisition 500 Busses To Beat Rebels To Guadalajara.

[*By the Associated Press.*]

Mexico City, Feb. 3.—Five hundred jitney busses, seized in the most picturesque requisition Mexico City has ever witnessed, are playing an important part in an exciting race between Federal troops and rebels for possession of Guadalajara, second largest city of the republic.

General Amaro, Federal commander, filled the requisitioned jitneys with loyal troops and is trying to reach Guadalajara ahead of the rebels under Generals Estrada and Alvarado.

FOUR IN AUTO KILLED

Michigan Central Flyer Hits Car Near Dearborn.

Detroit, Feb. 3.—Four persons were killed late today when an automobile in which they were riding was struck by a Michigan Central flyer one mile west of Dearborn, Mich. The train, according to witnesses, struck the machine squarely in the center and demolished it.

Radical Meeting Is Broken Up With Forced Tribute To Wilson

"Bill" McCullough, Member Of American Legion, Demands That Heads Be Bowed And "America" Sung In Pittsburgh Hall.

Pittsburgh, Feb. 3 (Special).—Bill McCullough, who was secretary of the Pittsburgh team in the old Federal Baseball League and who during the World War went overseas as a member of a male quartet and sang for the soldiers in France, didn't receive any special invitation to attend the memorial meeting in honor of Lenine, held in the Lyceum Theater this afternoon, but decided to go anyway.

Many Soldiers There.

Bill—he's William Tice McCullough in the directory, but nobody would know him by that name—is an honorary member of American Legion Post here as a result of his work in France. He passed the word along to former soldiers, and when he strolled into the theater this afternoon and seated himself he glanced about and recognized several score of his soldier friends.

Addresses eulogizing Lenine had been made when the chairman of the meeting, a Russian radical, asked if there were others who might wish to say something or ask questions.

Time To Honor Wilson.

Before anybody else could speak Bill jumped to his feet with, "It strikes me that this would be an opportune moment for us all to rise and bow our heads in honor of our former President, who died in Washington today."

When the chairman found his voice, he protested that the suggestion was not in harmony with the purpose of the meeting. Bill intimated that it was so much the worse for the purpose. Then he and about 250 others rose and bowed their heads.

"America" Is Sung.

"Now we'll sing 'America,'" announced Bill, a bit huskily, as the heads were lifted.

Two hundred and fifty voices, led by Bill McCullough's tenor, were raised in the anthem. That broke up the meeting.

Woodrow Wilson

His Achievements And Their Permanence In American History

By JOHN W. OWENS.

WASHINGTON, Feb. 3.

Woodrow Wilson's chapter in American history will be one of the three or four that men will always read carefully.

Different, in personality and purpose, mysterious to the vast preponderance of his own people in his own time, he always will be the subject of debate, although time will provide a truer perspective upon his career and work than is now possible. But noticed, studied, recognized as the outstanding figure in American national life after Lincoln—that is assuredly his portion. And his different, mysterious personal quality will but stimulate study of him.

He moved swiftly to the peaks, as is often the way. When Theodore Roosevelt, William J. Bryan, William H. Taft, Elihu Root and Charles E. Hughes stood forth largely on the political horizon 15 years ago or so, Mr. Wilson was a college president, greatly admired among scholars but known only to few of the masses of the people. In those days there was talk of him for high office, for the Presidency. But it was the yearning, speculative talk, for the most part, of Southern men hoping to see a man of Southern birth in the Presidency and seeing in Mr. Wilson, in his Northern environment, the best chance.

Not Regarded "Likely" Candidate.

The odds were heavily adverse, even after George Harvey and others of influence perceived possibilities in Mr. Wilson and started systematically to educate the country in his favor. The country was not accustomed to taking its political leaders from scholastic fields, and it was not accustomed to putting in the White House men without training in practical politics and in office. Moreover, the period was one of deep suspicion of men whose lives had been spent in dealing with theories.

Yet when the sifting processes of history are done, all the great figures of the period just before Mr. Wilson's sudden rise to power will be subordinate to his. Mr. Roosevelt, the greatest of these other figures, may be known in another century chiefly as a critic of Mr. Wilson. In a sense, he will depend upon Mr. Wilson for an enduring and noted place in the records. For the thrilling political days of the Roosevelt Administration even now are seen to have presented not an epoch, as many believed at that time, but mere political phenomena. Viewed through the fleet decades, the Roosevelt upheaval will be seen as a minor convulsion.

The war days of the Wilson Administration and the peace-making days that followed, will bulk vastly above all that preceded. And hate or love Mr. Wilson as men may now and as they may in years to come, the unescapable fact is that he dominated the nation in those heroic days, and for a time dominated the world, not alone by virtue of his office but by virtue of the might of brain and will that he brought to his office in an hour of colossal things. The other figures of the time must revolve around him, as enemies or as friends. They will scarcely be seen otherwise. And for aught that the world knows now, the figures of other times must revolve around him in the work that he conceived to be his supreme contribution to the world, the League of Nations.

Preparation Was Generation Old.

The background and origin of the man, related to his development and the character of his service in office, make an engrossing study. It is easy to imagine that he was fashioned and destined for great things. There is a certain continuity about it all that gives rise to that thought, and to the thought that there was something approximating a steady, even progress through the generations of the Wilson strain until it came to full fruition in the boy who was born in Staunton, Va., December 28, 1856.

He came of that Scotch-Irish stock that loves God sternly, and imposes upon itself perhaps the most rigid self-discipline found among the English-

(Continued on Page 4, Column 1.)

NATION'S LEADER IN WAR SUCCUMBS WITH HAND HELD IN THAT OF WIFE

Hundreds Drop To Knees Before Residence As Announcement That Death Has Come To Former President Is Made.

COOLIDGE ORDERS FLAGS AT HALF-MAST 30 DAYS

Issues Proclamation, Instructing Army And Navy To Be Ready To Render Honors To Ex-Commander-In-Chief.

By J. F. ESSARY.

Washington, Feb. 3.—Woodrow Wilson, America's World War President, is no more. He has followed his achievements into history. He has gone to join the Unknown Soldier.

Death visited him at 11.15 o'clock this morning. It came at an hour when countless thousands of his countrymen were gathered in their places of worship to offer a prayer that he might linger longer upon the earth.

END PAINLESS AND PEACEFUL.

The end was painless and peaceful. He fell asleep late last night. From that sleep he was never to awake. A weary sigh passed his lips. There was a tremor of the eyelids. The heart ceased to beat. Life had left the broken body.

A few moments later word was passed to those waiting without that Woodrow Wilson was dead. It was flashed to the far corners of the world. Almost instantly the fluttering of flags descending to half-mast above the White House and all the Federal buildings of the National Capital gave mute expression to the grief of the Government he had served.

CROWD BEFORE HOUSE DROPS TO KNEES.

Men, women and children gathered before the house of death dropped to their knees in prayer. Tears were in the eyes of many of them. All day long a throng stood there silent and sorrowing and watching the long procession of callers coming to leave words of sympathy.

They saw the President and Mrs. Coolidge arrive within an hour of Mr. Wilson's death. Mr. and Mrs. Coolidge alighted, went to the door and personally gave their cards to an attendant. The people saw the Secretary of State and Mrs. Hughes come and go and many others of high and low degree, officials, diplomats and personal friends of the family.

COOLIDGE ISSUES PROCLAMATION.

Still later in the day the President issued a proclamation to the American people announcing the passing of the foremost private citizen of the republic and fixing a 30-day period of mourning. Tidings by wire and radio went forth from the War and Navy Departments to every military outpost and to every man-of-war and naval station of the nation that a former Commander-in-Chief was dead. Later in the day Mr. Coolidge wrote a personal message to Mrs. Wilson expressing his and Mrs. Coolidge's sympathy.

Arrangements for the funeral probably will be determined tomorrow when the time and place of entombment is selected. It is thought likely he will be buried temporarily in one of the local cemeteries pending the erection of a national memorial for his permanent resting place. Whether the funeral will be private or a great public ceremony has not yet been decided. C. Bascom Slemp, secretary to the President, called early in the afternoon to tender the services of the Government in arranging the funeral.

Mr. Wilson had been mortally ill for only four days.

But for nearly five years he had been disabled—a casualty of the conflict into which he led the greatest force of armed men ever mustered under the flag of his country.

Fought Grimly To End.

He received no wound in battle. He could not share the fate of the heroes beneath the battlefields of France or Flanders. The soldier died that peace among the nations of the earth might be restored. Woodrow Wilson went down fighting that peace and good will among men might endure.

For 48 hours the invalid had hovered between life and death. He fought as grimly against the inevitable as he had fought many times before. With all his waning strength he sought to overcome the ravage of disease. But it has been evident to his physicians, his family and his intimate friends since Friday that he must surrender.

Wife's Name Last On Lips.

All that medical science and tender nursing could do was to give the dying man a painless death. "I am ready," he had said when first told that in all human probability he could not live. He realized how slender was his chance of life. He haltingly observed to those at his bedside that he was "a piece of broken machinery." The mind and spirit might hold out, but the frail body refused to function.

The last name on his lips was "Edith," the name of his wife. It was just a whisper, yesterday afternoon, when Mrs. Wilson was out of the room, and Admiral Grayson sent for her, then withdrew as Mrs. Wilson hastened into the chamber. No other ear heard the few last whispered words exchanged between husband and wife. Aside from Mrs. Wilson, no one heard him speak again.

Grows Weaker As Night Passes.

Mr. Wilson thereafter lay scarcely conscious. He was profoundly prostrated as yesterday went into evening and lapsed into unconsciousness at about 8.30 P. M. and slept. At one time in the course of the night, in a moment of consciousness, he showed that he recognized Mrs. Wilson bending over him. Then he slept again, slept intermittently all night, growing weaker and weaker.

As the forenoon wore on Mrs. Wilson sat beside the bed and held her husband's right hand, the hand which retained feeling and power of voluntary motion when paralysis deadened Mr. Wilson's left side more than four years

WEATHER FORECAST

Partly cloudy today, colder by night; tomorrow, fair and colder; strong southwest and west winds.
Weather Report—Part 1, Section 3, Col. 1.

THE SUN

Railroad Peace Ends
Opponents of Esch-Cummins act resuming the offensive.
—*See Page* 11.

VOLUME 24—NO. 13D | PRESS RUN SUNDAY, March 23, 1924. } 182,908 | BALTIMORE, SUNDAY, MARCH 30, 1924. | Published every Sunday by The A. S. Abell Company. Entered as second-class matter at Baltimore Postoffice. | 124 PAGES | PRICE IN CITY AND SUBURBS 5c. ELSEWHERE 8c

FRENCH POLICY ON RUHR UPHELD BY NEW CABINET

Ministers For Continuation Of Poincare Program At Home And Abroad.

LOUCHEUR'S TARGET HIGH LIVING COSTS

Paris Newspapers See Maneuver To Assure Success In Elections.

[*By the Associated Press.*]

Paris, March 29.—The foreign and internal policies of the new Poincaré Government will be similar in their essential lines to those of the old Cabinet.

This was the unequivocal assurance given by the various Ministers at the close of the second Cabinet council of the day, which adjourned at 8 o'clock tonight.

Firm On Ruhr Policy.

Though no official announcement to that effect was made at the Foreign Office, it was learned that Premier Poincaré informed his new colleagues that there would be no change in the policy he has been following since he assumed power in January, 1922. He reaffirmed his will to maintain intact the Ruhr policy inaugurated 15 months ago. It was along these lines that the Premier asked his new collaborators to grant him their confidence.

Leading members of the new Ministry emphasized this position of the Government upon leaving their first meeting held just before Premier Poincaré presented his Cabinet to President Millerand at the Elysee Palace at noon.

Internal Policy Unchanged.

"The unanimous sentiment of the new Cabinet is to continue the policy of Premier Poincaré," said Justin de Selves, Minister of Interior.

"That goes for internal affairs as well as foreign policy," put in War Minister Maginot.

Louis Loucheur, Minister of Commerce, said his immediate efforts would be directed toward bringing down the cost of living. Frederic Francois-Marsal, Minister of Finance, said he would approve no expenditures unless they were covered by equivalent receipts.

Cabinet Meets Again Today.

The Premier informed the Cabinet members this evening that he would have the Ministerial declaration ready to submit to them at 4 o'clock Sunday afternoon, the document to be approved definitely in the Council of Ministers, which will assemble an hour later under the chairmanship of President Millerand.

The Presidential decree nominating the new members of the Government and outlining their respective functions will appear in the official journal tomorrow.

Paris Press Comments On Changes In Ministry

Paris, March 29 (Special Cable).—The almost complete change of Cabinet Ministers leads the Conservative *Journal des Debats* to remark that Premier Poincaré "judged it opportune to take a new crew on the eve of the elections" because the "old crew" had not a good enough record.

The *Intransigeant* comments on the difficulties of Henry de Jouvenel, editor of the *Matin*, who made a powerful speech against the financial measures fathered by Poincaré a week ago and now agrees to carry them out.

The general newspaper comment on Poincaré's action in picking so many men who voted against his financial reforms is that it can only be considered a maneuver to secure national union as the elections approach.

Butler's Crusading Tactics To Be Used In Washington

Capital Police Head Declares War On Rum And Vice After Seeing General.

Washington, March 29 (Special).—Periodic charges that Washington is the wettest city in the country led Major Daniel Sullivan, who heads the police force, to go to Philadelphia to take council with Brig.-Gen. Smedley D. Butler and when he returned today he announced an immediate vice-exterminating crusade.

"There will be no quarter," said the major. "Let the ax fall where it will, this city is to be swept clean. Rum running, drinking and gambling will be the first to go. If there is any vice rampant here its doom is sealed. We intend to clean house thoroughly this time."

Flying squadrons, "devil-dog" methods and sundry of the Butler battalion mopping-up ideas are to be adopted, in consequence of the conference with the Quaker City Director of Public Safety, Major Sullivan announced.

Daugherty's Job May Be Offered To Massachusetts Chief Justice

Judge Arthur P. Rugg Reported As Having Been Asked If He Will Accept Attorney-Generalship If Post Is Offered.

By J. F. ESSARY.

Washington, March 29.—It is well understood in Washington tonight that President Coolidge has inquired of Chief Justice Arthur P. Rugg, of the Massachusetts Supreme Court if the jurist would accept the Attorney-Generalship, should it be offered.

No word has been received in response to this feeler, it is said, in official quarters tonight, and it is unlikely that any word will be received before Monday or Tuesday. If the reply is favorable, it is probable that the Daugherty vacancy will be filled by the middle of next week.

President Turns To Bench.

Should Chief Justice Rugg decline the Attorney-Generalship, the chances are that it will be tendered to some other Federal or State judge. The President, it is said, has turned to the bench for the new cabinet official in order to be sure that the appointee, whoever he may be, has no corporate connection or association which would make trouble for him in the Senate.

Federal Judge William S. Kenyon, of Iowa, and Federal Judge Frank S. Deitrich, of Idaho, are among the jurists from whom the Executive might draw a new Attorney-General. The names of these men have been before Mr. Coolidge during the weeks he has looked forward to the time when he would have to replace Mr. Daugherty. Judge Wilbur, now Secretary of the Navy, might possibly be transferred to the Department of Justice.

Regarded Leader In New England.

Chief Justice Rugg is perhaps the foremost lawyer and jurist in the Bay State and one of the leading members of the bar of New England. He has long been looked upon at home as the logical successor on the United States Supreme Court of Associate Justice Oliver Wendell Holmes, should Mr. Holmes, also of Massachusetts, retire from active service.

Not only is Judge Rugg regarded as a learned lawyer but he has gained wide applause as an administrator, New Englanders here declare. He has almost completely overhauled the higher judiciary of his State, forcing through practical reforms of great value to litigants and practitioners alike. It is said of him that during his tenure of office he has swept the bench of musty cobwebs and put the judiciary of the State on a high-class businesslike basis.

Little Known Throughout Country.

At that the President's friends admit that the country at large has never heard of Judge Rugg and that the appointment of this jurist would not be capitalized politically. These same friends say, however, that the best politics Mr. Coolidge could play in this appointment is to play no politics at all.

Massachusetts already has one member of the Cabinet in Secretary of War Weeks. This has not been lost sight of in the consideration of Chief Justice Rugg. In that connection it is remarked that California now has two members of the Cabinet and that New York several times had had three members of that body at a time and once that State had four.

Wants To Avoid Fight In Senate.

The President is said to feel that the nomination of a new Attorney-General is perhaps the most important he will

(Continued on Page 2, Column 6.)

FIND MAN'S STOMACH FULL OF HARDWARE

Surgeons Open "Swallower's" Abdomen When He Complains Of Pains.

Chicago, March 29 (Special).—William Martell, a professional "swallower," was seized with peritonitis after swallowing a spike in a local theater last night.

Surgeons opened his abdomen today and found 12 tacks, nails of assorted sizes, 2 iron nuts, 12 safety pins, 22 paper clips, 2 iron washers, 1 dime, a can opener and bits of glass, brick and crockery.

The spike penetrated the wall of his stomach, and his condition is serious.

Gen. Barnett's Niece Elopes To Media And Weds

Miss Reisinger, Washington, And K. B. Carney, Philadelphia, Married March 8.

Philadelphia, March 29 (Special).—Despite parental protests that they were too young to wed, Kenneth Bostwick Carney, 20, this city, and Miss Laura Natalie Reisinger, 19, of Washington, it became known today, eloped to Media March 8 and were married.

The bride is a daughter of Dr. Emory Reisinger, prominent Washington physician; a niece of Brig.-Gen. George Barnett, former commandant of the Marine Corps, and a granddaughter of the late Capt. William Reisinger, a naval officer during the Civil War and for years thereafter.

Carney, a former midshipman, is a son of Lieut.-Com. Robert E. Carney, retired; a grandson of Commodore Frank M. Bostwick, retired; a nephew of Capt. Frank B. Upham, naval attache at Paris, and a brother of Lieut. B. Carney, an instructor at the Naval Academy.

The couple were accompanied to Media by Miss Sallie Fenwick, of Washington, a chum of the bride.

Lieut. Walter Hinton Sails To Explore Orinoco River

Transatlantic Flyer And U.S. Radio Inspector Leave For South America.

New York, March 29.—Lieut. Walter Hinton, who piloted the NC-4 across the Atlantic, and John Swanson, radio inspector of the Department of Commerce, sailed today on the steamer Southern Cross for Rio Janeiro, where they will soon be joined by Mr. and Mrs. Alexander Hamilton Rice in an exploration trip of the uncharted valley of the Orinoco river.

Hinton will pilot a plane over the valley wilderness, aiding the explorers in locating hitherto unvisited villages. Swanson, who has obtained an indefinite leave of absence from the Department of Commerce, will establish radio communication with the outside world at the source of the Amazon river.

CLARK HOWELL TO WED SOON

Atlanta Publisher's Bride To Be Widow Of Durham (N. C.) Man.

Concord, N. C., March 29.—Mrs. J. W. Cannon announced today the engagement of her daughter, Mrs. Margaret Cannon Carr, widow of Julian S. Carr, Jr., of Durham, N. C., to Clark Howell, editor and publisher of the Atlanta *Constitution*.

The wedding will take place April 5 at the home of Mrs. Cannon in this city.

FOLEY IS ACQUITTED IN JERSEY RUM CASE

Other Defendants Charged With Bribe Conspiracy Also Freed By Jury.

New York, March 29.—A Federal jury tonight acquitted J. Harry Foley, State Superintendent of Weights and Measures of New Jersey; Major Herbert I. Katz and the Paterson Brewing and Malting Company on charges of bribery and conspiracy to bribe Federal agents to permit the manufacture of liquor and beer in New Jersey.

The jury came to an agreement after approximately 13 hours of deliberation, including time taken to eat, only after Federal Judge Mack had informed them he would not accept a disagreement and that they would be given "plenty of time in which to consider the case."

Gen. Taufflieb Arrives To Visit United States

French Senator Well Pleased With Personnel Of Poincare's New Cabinet.

New York, March 29 (Special).—Gen. Adolph Taufflieb, French Senator from Alsace, arrived on the French liner Paris today, with Mme. Taufflieb, who was Miss Julia Catlin, of New York, for his second visit to the United States since the war.

He praised Premier Poincaré's appointments to the new French Cabinet and eulogized M. Poincaré himself, though he said he "needs a little oil in his system" to make him better understood throughout the world.

General Taufflieb commanded the Thirty-seventh French Army Corps during the war. He came to the United States in 1922 as an unofficial French envoy to sound American sentiment on the debt question and conferred with President Harding and Secretary Hughes.

French Arrest Four Men For Raising U. S. $1 Bills

Girl Complains When Bank Refuses $100 Note Given By Supposed Benefactor.

Paris, March 29 (Copyright).—The French police have arrested three Germans and a Pole, who were making their fortune by raising the figure on American dollar bills—making hundreds out of ones.

They admitted passing many such bills successfully in the occupied German territory on the Rhine, and might still be doing it if one of the group had not generously given a raised $100 bill to a girl. She was so furious when the bank refused her treasure that she led the police to the address of her benefactor.

Airplane Rum Runner Reported Near Arrest

Suspect Said To Carry Liquor From Bahamas To Chicago.

Chicago, March 29 (Special).—Arrest of "P. David Pinkijson," the admitted alias of an airplane rum-runner, who has been bringing choice liquor to Chicago through the clouds, is promised tomorrow by Federal prohibition agents. He flies all the way from the Bahamas to Chicago. In a warehouse 71 cases of imported Scotch that came by airplane have been seized.

The air rum-runner's real name is said to be known to Federal operatives, and he is declared to be under surveillance.

MOVIE TICKET TAX VOTED OUT BY COMMITTEE

Senate Body Agrees To Elimination As Did House.

WOULD END LEVY ON 50-CENT SEATS

Modifications In Proposed Appeal Board Also Accepted.

Washington, March 29.—The Senate Financial Committee today agreed to the repeal of the 10 per cent. admission tax on tickets selling for 50 cents or less, as voted by the House, and approved with some modifications the proposed board of tax appeals.

The admission tax to theaters and entertainments was the first of the rate schedules in the Revenue bill, aside from the income tax, taken up by the committee. Further study of the estimates and probable surplus available for tax reduction will be made next week before completing the various schedules. Chairman Smoot has invited Secretary Mellon to appear before the committee in this connection Tuesday.

Walsh Amendment Lost.

A motion today by Senator Walsh, Democrat, Massachusetts, to double the admission tax on tickets selling for $1.50 and over was defeated. Secretary Mellon had recommended repeal of this tax entirely, which he estimated would have reduced revenue about $70,000,000 annually. The proposed reduction is estimated to cut down receipts from admissions about $33,000,000.

Chairman Smoot repeated today in referring to the Treasury estimates that the Revenue bill as passed by the House would bring about a considerable Treasury deficit. This would have to be remedied, he declared, through raising the miscellaneous and excise tax rates, many of which were repealed or reduced by the House.

Frear Assails Smoot Figures.

In this connection Representative Frear, Republican, insurgent, Wisconsin, assailed the estimates of Chairman Smoot both on the Revenue and Soldier Bonus bills today on the floor of the House.

"The press was recently informed," Mr. Frear declared, "by a distinguished gentleman from a Western State that gave Mr. Taft half of his eight electoral votes that the House tax bill we passed would cause a deficit of $100,000,000. Secretary Mellon more recently testified before the Senate Finance Committee that any deficit from the bill we passed would reach only $55,000,000, and this was followed by Treasury estimates of greater receipts than previously offered in the House.

"Next, the press advised the country that the same authority had announced the Bonus bill would cost nearly $5,000,000,000, instead of $2,100,000,000, as shown by the legion actuary. In arriving at this figure numerous controverted items with accumulated interests for 20 years were added.

"Testimony, estimates and tax rates reached by proxy methods or such guesswork are willfully unfair and offered for the purpose of misrepresenting to the country the real facts in issue."

Praises Longworth.

Mr. Frear praised Representative Longworth, of Ohio, the Republican leader, and defended the latter's compromise tax-rate schedule, which was adopted by the House after the Republican insurgents had swung from the Democratic plan to its support. It was knocked out by the Senate Finance Committee in favor of the Mellon schedule.

The Senate Finance Committee received some additional data today from the army and navy regarding the number of veterans entitled to the bonus in an effort to determine the probable cost of the measure. This study will be completed also early next week, Mr. Smoot said.

Action of the House in transferring from the Treasury Secretary to the President the power of appointment of the members of the proposed board of tax appeals was approved by the committee. The salaries of the 28 members, however, were restored as first proposed to $10,000 instead of $7,500 as voted by the House. It was voted also to have the board consist of 28 members for two years only and after that of seven members on the ground that most of the back work on tax appeals could be disposed of in two years.

Mellon To Be Questioned.

Secretary Mellon on Tuesday will be asked particularly about the estate tax which was increased by the House, and the gift tax, placed in the bill by the House. Mr. Mellon previously has denounced both of these changes in the bill.

Other sections of the measure yet to be considered are corporation, tobacco and miscellaneous taxes, the proposal for a 25 per cent. reduction in income taxes payable this year and a provision relating to inspection of income tax returns by certain Congressional committees.

HOUSE SPEEDS RITCHIE'S NEW HOSPITAL BILL

$75,000 Fund Advanced. $500,000 Project To Go In Tomorrow.

AUTO CLUB MEASURE IS KILLED IN SENATE

Unfavorable Report On General Motor Proposal Adopted.

> Annapolis, March 29.—The Senate adjourned at 9.07 P. M. and the House at 6.10 P. M., both to meet at 11 A. M. Monday.

[*From The Sun Bureau.*]

Annapolis, March 29.—Governor Ritchie said tonight that he will send to the Senate and House of Delegates Monday morning amendments to his bill already introduced for the benefit of the University Hospital increasing the amount to be given to the hospital to $500,000, provided the relations between it and the school at College Park be severed. The amount named in the pending bills is $400,000. The Governor said that he is yet without information whether the board of regents will accept the proposition.

Present arrangements are for the Committees on Finance and Ways and Means to report the bills at once as amended. Unless the combination which passed the four bills which were vetoed by the Governor continues obstructive tactics the bills can be passed under suspension of the rules. The university authorities then would have until December 15 next to decide whether they will accept the provisions of the bill or not.

House Advances $75,000 Bill.

The Governor sent to the House this morning, through Delegate Given, Democratic floor leader, a bill giving the University Hospital $75,000 outright to make changes in the building to conform to the recommendations of the Building Inspector and the fire prevention bureau of the Baltimore Fire Department. He states that he has had an estimate made of the cost of the changes and has been advised that it will be well within the amount recommended.

The bill was passed to its third reading in the House, under suspension of the rules, but could not be finally passed because it was not printed. The Governor is having the printing done, and it is expected the bill will be passed finally by both houses before adjournment Monday night.

Committee Holds Two Vetoes.

As was stated in THE SUN this morning, the bills to issue a loan of $1,375,000 for the hospital and one of $750,000 for the proposed Baltimore-Eastern Shore Boulevard were vetoed by Governor Ritchie last night and the vetoes were sustained. The loan bills of $300,000 for the Salisbury Normal School and $100,000 for Allendale Training School and the accompanying vetoes were referred to the committee on finance through efforts of the Curran-Towers combination.

This committee, at a meeting this morning, decided to take no action on the bills and vetoes, as the measures already are dead. Should the advocates of the bills ask to have them reported out they will be handed back to the Senate with some statement tantamount to saying: "Here they are; we didn't want them in the first place." No one has any doubt that the vetoes will be sustained in case any action is taken.

The House adjourned this afternoon to meet at 11 o'clock on Monday and the Senate adjourned tonight to meet at the same hour. The session will finally adjourn at midnight Monday. But few bills of any importance remain to be acted upon by either body except the one fixing the State tax rate for the next three years. This measure, of necessity, must be held back until the last in order to provide for legislative appropriations.

Auto Club Bill Killed By 13-To-10 Vote In Senate

[*From The Sun Bureau.*]

Annapolis, March 29.—House Bill No. 55, the General Automobile bill, was killed in the Senate tonight through adoption of an unfavorable report by the Finance Committee.

The measure was one which had been contested in committee since its introduction early in January. It was sponsored by the Automobile Club and was the subject of numerous hearings before the House Judiciary Committee. J. Leroy Hopkins, assistant counsel for the club, followed the bill through the entire proceedings.

Senator Robb offered a motion to substitute the measure for the unfavorable report, but his motion was lost by a vote of 13 to 10. Just prior to the

(Continued on Page 6, Column 5.)

Former Russian Princess Narrowly Escapes Drowning

MRS. WILLIAM B. LEEDS

Brunswick, Ga., March 29.—Former Ambassador George Harvey; William B. Leeds, son of the late Princess Anastasia; his wife, formerly Princess Xenia of Russia, and other guests of Leeds narrowly escaped drowning late today when a launch in which they were riding sank in a strong southeast wind.

Some members of the party were thrown into the water, while others, after seizing life preservers, jumped into a small boat as the launch went down. A fishing boat went to their rescue as the small boat struggled in the heavy sea and finally brought the party safely ashore.

Young Leeds and his wife had been on Jekyll Island for two weeks as guests of Mr. Harvey, and the launch had been chartered by Leeds.

SCORE DEAD IN WAKE OF MIDWEST STORM

Rain, Snow, Hail And Lightning Spread Ruin In Ohio And Mississippi Valleys.

FLOOD MENACE IS GROWING

From Oklahoma To Minnesota Damage Running Into Hundreds Of Thousands Is Done.

Chicago, March 29.—Storms last night and today extending from the Ohio to the Mississippi valleys brought death to a score of persons, injured more than a hundred and caused damage estimated at hundreds of thousands of dollars.

More rain, probably turning to snow, was forecast for sections of the Middle West tonight, while the upper Ohio Valley faced the growing menace of flood waters.

Tornado In Oklahoma.

Dead in the wake of the storm included eight killed last night in a tornado at Shawnee, Okla., four known dead in Southeastern Missouri as the result of a windstorm and reports that four others had perished; a boy killed by lightning in Kansas, and two flood casualties at Pittsburgh.

The storm in various sections assumed the proportions of a tornado and elsewhere manifested itself by driving snow and hail. High winds with falling temperatures marked its progress.

Damage was widespread wherever the storm struck. In Southeastern Missouri live stock valued at thousands of dollars was killed, while three small towns

(Continued on Page 2, Column 3.)

Champions Dime Novel As Means To Education

Dr. J. Duncan Spaeth, Professor Of Literature At Princeton, Says Boys By Reading "Bad" Books Participate Vicariously In Evil And Are Bettered.

Philadelphia, March 29 (Special).—The dime novel, with its tales of blood and thunder wickedness, has found a champion in Dr. J. Duncan Spaeth, professor of literature in Princeton University. In an address before the annual spring conference of the high school teachers of the Philadelphia Teachers' Association today, Mr. Spaeth asserted that these so-called wicked books have a greater moral and educational value than "good" books.

The vicarious participation in wicked deeds that comes with reading books of piracy and bloodshed acts as an outlet for the normal child, Dr. Spaeth explained.

Would Give Bad Books.

"It's a fine thing to be vicariously wicked," he said. "I'd give boys bad books to read rather than the so-called good one. One does not become good from the reading of good books, but one doesn't become bad by dint of reading bad books. Rather the desire for wickedness is dispelled, because the boyish imagination actually participates in the evil deeds described in blood-and-thunder stories.

"Give boys bad books to read," he urged, "and let them have an imaginative outlet for their lawless instincts. That, along with the precepts and examples afforded by good books, constitutes a splendid educational method for the young."

Reading And Education.

That the reading of books is essential for a well-rounded education because men are able to have vicarious experiences which they otherwise could not have, but that, on the other hand, their experiences should not be confined entirely to the vicarious variety, but should be really lived, was emphasized by Dr. Spaeth.

$6,000,000 DAMAGE CAUSED, NINE REPORTED DEAD, IN WESTERN MARYLAND FLOOD

Raging Torrent Carries Away Houses And Railway Bridges In Stricken Area—Cumberland In Darkness.

TRAINS STRANDED IN HILLS; MILES OF TRACK SWEPT OFF

Automobiles Abandoned In Streets As Waters Rush At 40-Mile Rate—Boats And Rafts Aid Marooned Persons.

Cumberland, Md., March 29 (Special).—Flood waters of the Potomac river, sweeping with irresistible force today down the mountain gorge, inundated this city and several other nearby towns, swept away railroad bridges and cars, paralyzed traffic and caused more than $6,000,000 damage.

With half the city inundated, the waters began to recede from the streets at 8.40 o'clock tonight, after reaching a maximum depth of eight feet. The water had risen so rapidly that many people abandoned their automobiles in the street and fled. The city is without lights.

At least nine lives are believed to have been lost. Three men are thought to have perished when the torrents of water swept away the Western Maryland Railroad bridge here, and four in Garrett county. The interstate bridge connecting Westernport, Md., and Piedmont, W. Va., more than a half mile long, also was swept away.

The westbound Capitol Limited, crack Baltimore and Ohio passenger train between New York and Chicago, was floodbound eight miles east of here tonight. The train was halted when submerged tracks were encountered.

KEYSER AND PIEDMONT FLOODED.

Keyser, W. Va., and Piedmont, W. Va., were partly inundated and several scores rendered homeless in both towns, according to dispatches from Keyser. Officials of the State Roads Commission at Keyser estimated the damage to highways in that section at more than $1,500,000.

The Potomac river spread over an area of a mile from each bank around Westernport and Piedmont. Houses were loosened from their foundations and carried off downstream.

According to dispatches from Oakland several towns in Garrett county suffered heavily. Four of the Garrett county victims lived at Kitzmiller and two near that town. Oakland has been asked to send as many provisions as possible to Friendsville.

FOUR MILES OF TRACK WASHED OUT.

Four miles of Western Maryland Railroad track are reported to have been washed out between Kitzmiller and Piedmont and traffic is likely to be suspended for a week.

The entire village of McCool, Md., was flooded. Only one telephone in the village was in operation, and over this it was impossible to obtain confirmation of a report that a family of six had been drowned.

The Western Maryland bridge at McCool was swept away in the afternoon just before a passenger train reached it. When water invaded the coaches the passengers took refuge in the town. The village is without lights tonight and late in the afternoon the gas supply was cut off when a main was broken.

Twenty-six miles of tracks on the Baltimore and Ohio, west of this city, have been washed away.

Many freight cars on sidings of the Western Maryland Railway have been washed away. The freight office of this road stands in a lake of water.

Traffic on the two roads, as well as on the Cumberland and Pennsylvania, is at a standstill.

Railroad trains are stranded on the hills.

Marooned In Office Buildings.

Hundreds of persons were marooned in the darkness of office buildings, unable to reach their homes. Rowboats and improvised rafts were used to relieve these persons and shoppers from their plight.

The foundations of houses along the water front are crumbling and the structures are being carried downstream.

Towns in the entire George's creek mining region were in the path of the flood. Lonaconing, Westernport, Barton, Md., and Piedmont, W. Va., have several feet of water in their main streets. In Ridgeley, W. Va., across the river from Cumberland, some houses are submerged entirely.

Other Bridges Washed Away.

Tracks of the Cumberland and Westernport Electric Railway and the Cumberland and Pennsylvania have been washed away in the vicinity of Lonaconing and Westernport. The C. and P. Railroad bridge and the county bridge between Piedmont, W. Va., and Westernport, Md., were washed away.

In Cumberland the flood waters have turned Mechanic street, one of the principal business thoroughfares of the city, into a raging torrent. Mechanic street runs parallel with Wills creek a short distance from where the stream enters the Potomac river.

Forty-Mile Current In Street.

Pianos, barrels and boxes of provisions, furniture, carpets and debris of all kinds are being washed south on Mechanic street by a 40-mile-an-hour current. Scores of automobiles, abandoned by their owners, are surrounded by water up to their windshields.

Flood waters on Mechanic street had

WEATHER FORECAST
Partly cloudy today; warmer and unsettled tomorrow; moderate westerly winds.
Weather Report—Part 1, Section 3, Col. 1.

THE SUN

GIACOMO PUCCINI DEAD AT BRUSSELS.
See Page 9

VOLUME 24—NO. 48D | PRESS RUN, SUNDAY, November 23, 1924. } 183,946 | BALTIMORE, SUNDAY, NOVEMBER 30, 1924. | Published every Sunday by The A. S. Abell Company. Entered as second-class matter at Baltimore Postoffice. | 142 PAGES | PRICE IN CITY AND SUBURBS 5c. ELSEWHERE 8c

ARMY DOWNS NAVY, 12-0

SUDAN MUTINY IS PUT DOWN; 17 ARE KILLED

British Force Surrender Of Rebels By Shelling Khartum Hospital.

ENGLISH MINISTER FOR FIRM MEASURES

Persian Envoy At Geneva Ready For Possible Appeal To League.

[*By the Associated Press.*]

London, Nov. 29.—The Khartum mutiny, which has finally been put down, was much more serious than at first appeared and entailed numerous casualties, according to additional news received here tonight.

Two British officers were killed and eight men wounded. One officer and 14 men of the mutineers are believed to have been killed and their total casualties are estimated at about 60. There are still no precise details of the motives for the mutiny, but there appears to have been no repetition or extension of it.

Rebels Had Machine Guns.

The mutiny started Thursday evening when two platoons of the Eleventh Sudanese battalion became insubordinate and started to march on Gordon College in the center of Khartum. The mutineers had several rounds of ammunition each and had commandeered two machine guns.

The mutinous troops were met in the streets in front of the British Army Hospital by two platoons of Engl[illegible] troops. An officer of the latter [illegible] attempted unsuccessfully to p[illegible] the rebels to obey his orders[illegible]ey refused, declaring they di[illegible]ecognise Acting Sirdar Hudd[illegible]

British Shell [illegible]pital.

The acting Sirdar himself attempted to reason with the mutineers, but when they refused to obey his commands he ordered British troops to clear the street. When this was attempted fighting started. The rebels rushed into the hospital and British troops finally brought up artillery and by shelling the hospital compound, in which the main band of mutineers had taken refuge, forced their surrender.

According to the latest advices tonight both Egypt and the Sudan are now tranquil. The students' agitation in Cairo, however, is still threatening and all efforts by the authorities to pacify them are fruitless.

Official quarters profess no anxiety that anything serious may arise in the Sudan despite the comparative smallness of the British garrison, because the Sudanese troops are allowed only small supplies of ammunition and could not carry out a serious revolt unless they obtain supplies surreptitiously. As far as Khartum itself is concerned, any uprising would be easily suppressed because the layout of the streets, very wide, straight avenues, lends itself to effective military fire.

To Press For Sudan Mandate.

Ziwar Pasha and his Government appear to be doing their utmost to circumscribe the trouble in Egypt and aid the British authorities in effecting a peaceable settlement, and, with this intention, Ziwar has even risked trouble with the Egyptian Parliament over the question of parliamentary immunity in the case of those Deputies arrested on suspicion.

It is becoming evident that, when the British Parliament assembles, the Opposition parties, while lending general support to the Government policy of maintaining British rights as against the aspirations of the Egyptian Nationalists, will urge the Government to seek a mandate for British administration of the Sudan from the League of Nations and submit to the same authority the question of appointing a mixed commission to regulate the supply of Nile water to Egypt.

Explains British Policy.

In a speech at Birmingham today Neville Chamberlain, Minister of Health, declared that the British were not going to pursue an aggressive foreign policy in Egypt.

"Any suggestion that what has happened in Egypt is merely a veiled attempt to destroy the independence given some time ago is founded either on misunderstanding or else is deliberate misrepresentation," he said.

Warning To Other Powers.

"Nothing is more likely to lead Great Britain to friction or war with other powers," he added, "than to allow them

(Continued on Page 9, Column 7.)

SILKWORTH FOUND GUILTY OF FRAUD

Former President And Several Members Of Stock Exchange Convicted.

[*By the Associated Press.*]

New York, Nov. 29.—William S. Silkworth, former president of the Consolidated Stock Exchange, was convicted tonight in the United States District Court of the charge of using the mails to defraud.

Convicted with Silkworth are Blaine J. Nichols and Earl Truesdell, partners with Dewitt C. Raynor, in the defunct brokerage firm of Raynor, Nicholas & Truesdell, Louis Gilbough, floor broker on the Consolidated Exchange, for the firm, and a former member of the ways and means committee of the exchange, Edward A. McQuade and Francis X. Quillan, members of the former curb brokerage firm of McQuade Brothers and Quillan.

The jury was out for [illegible]ne hours.

C. Peter Owens, who was office manager for Raynor, Nicholas & Truesdell, was acquitted.

Judge Augustus N. Hand set Wednesday for sentence and motions.

OVER 40,000,000 SHARES TRADED DURING MONTH

November One Of Most Remarkable Periods In History Of N.Y. Exchange.

[*By the Associated Press.*]

New York, Nov. 29.—Spirited trading in the stock market, which lifted prices close to record high levels on an undiminished volume of business, today closed one of the most remarkable months in the history of the New York Stock Exchange.

Turnover Exceeds 40,000,000.

Today's sales of approximately 1,100,000 shares brought the total turnover for the month to more than 40,000,000 shares. To the achievements of the current stock market boom, which began the day after the election, was added another list of 55 new peak prices for the year, swelling the total number of 1924 high records established in November to almost 400.

The close of the month also saw the average price of representative industrial shares at the highest point in several years and that of leading railroad stocks hovering around the top level recently attained.

In maintaining its strength and activity throughout today's half-holiday session the market continued to ignore the absence of many brokers. who had forsaken Wall Street to attend the Army-Navy football game, and the 4 per cent. rate for call money, which held over the week-end.

Industrials Hold Lead.

Industrial shares, which supplanted the rail issues in public favor this week, continued to hold their lead today as the weekly mercantile reviews confirmed reports of current improvement in virtually all lines of trade. Despite the transfer of speculative interest, the most spectacular performance in today's trading was given by a leading railroad stock—Atchison—which led a last-minute rally, mounting 3 points to 115¼, the highest level in 18 years. Heavy buying of this issue was based on expectations of an early increase in the dividend rate.

The wide improvement in business conditions enabled leading stocks in the steel, motor, public utility, copper, leather and specialty groups to attain new high records.

Chinese Emperor Would Quit Country

Ousted From Palace Hsuan Tung Seeks Protection Of Japanese Flag.

[*By the Associated Press.*]

Tokio, Nov. 30 (Sunday).—The "boy Emperor" of China, Hsuan Tung, is seeking Japanese aid to reach Mukden and then Japan, according to a Japanese news agency.

Takes Refuge In Legation.

A Peking dispatch last night reported that Hsuan Tung, who was recently forced to leave the Imperial Palace by General Feng, the "Christian general," had taken refuge in the Japanese Legation. No reason was assigned why he had suddenly sought protection under a foreign flag. Hsuan has been making his abode in the home of the former regent, Prince Chun, since Feng's order.

CAUCUS ACTION MAY SET WEST AGAINST EAST

Outlawing Of Four Senators May Have Far-Reaching Effect.

POSSIBLE MENACE TO POWER SEEN

Attitude Of Democrats And Insurgents Still Uncertain.

[*From The Sun Bureau.*]

Washington, Nov. 29.—A shifting of alignment in the Senate because of yesterday's action of the Republican caucus in "reading out of the party" four insurgent Senators of the La Follette group eventually may array the West against the East in the Republican organization.

It conceivably might endanger the Republican margin of safety in the new Congress and affect the legislative program of the session which begins Monday. This is the political reaction today to the unexpected action of the Republican caucus.

Practical Effect Uncertain.

The situation still was somewhat beclouded as to the exact practical effect, because of two uncertain factors in the new equation created by the Republican regulars when, by the proposal of Eastern conservatives, the majority caucus struck off the party rolls the names of Senator La Follette, of Wisconsin; Ladd and Frazier, of North Dakota, and Brookhart, of Iowa.

The uncertain factors are, first, the attitude in the present session of the insurgent group, on which will depend in part whether the regular leadership will try to go further in the next Congress and remove the proscribed Progressives from all committee recognition, including the assignments they hold in the present Congress.

Democrats A Factor.

The second doubtful factor is the attitude of the Democrats, involving the question of whether they will go along with the Republican regulars to make effective the disciplining policy or will help the Progressives to resist it. No intimation has come from Democratic headquarters, but there is a possibility that the Democrats themselves will be split over the issue when the hour arrives to punish La Follette and others.

Cleavage along geographical lines has had profound influence in recent sessions of Congress, accounting in part for the development of blocs and enabling the West, particularly through the farm bloc, to accomplish a great deal in the way of legislation.

Men Ousted Westerners.

All four of the Senators read out of the Republican party belong to the West. Yesterday's caucus action was first proposed by Edge, of New Jersey, and was especially urged by Reed and Pepper, of Pennsylvania, the former being the author of the disciplining resolution adopted by the caucus.

Senator Spencer, of Missouri, an intense partisan, was the only Westerner who enthused over the proposition of disciplining the Progressives, and his proposal went no further than appointment of a committee to consider what action ought to be done.

In a general way the effect upon the Western representation in the Senate was disagreeable, and this extended outside the lines of the insurgent group itself—that is, the immediate La Follette group. The noticeable disposition today was for the Westerners, including men who supported Coolidge and who are counted as a part of the Republican majority rather than as part of the insurgent group, although some of them are more independent than Republican, to lean toward each other and away from the disciplining policy adopted yesterday at the instance of Eastern spokesmen.

Hints At Western Opposition.

One Western spokesman said today that the Westerners in the Senate had no intention of letting their solidarity be broken. The intimation was that the Western influence rather generally will be exerted in opposition to the policy of reading men out of the party at the instance of the Eastern leadership.

Should this sort of feeling crystallize in real action in the Senate, the West unquestionably would be able to back down the East.

The action of the Senate caucus came at a moment when, as a result of recent deaths and consequent reorganization and new assignment of committee chairmanship, the West has come into new

(Continued on Page 14, Column 2.)

His Kicking Won For Army Team

EDGAR GARBISCH, CAPTAIN AND CENTER OF WEST POINT TEAM

He was the one man the Navy couldn't stop. Four times he sent the pigskin sailing between the Navy's goal posts for a total of 12 points, the margin of victory. Three times he tried to do the same thing, but failed. Thus, "batting" over 500, he was the Babe Ruth of the game. His smile of victory was photographed before the contest. He still wears it.

Garbisch, Army Squad Captain, Regarded As Football Nugget

His Playing Against Navy Considered As Giving Him Place In Victory With West Point Heroes Of All Time.

West Point fell heir to a football nugget in June, 1921, when Edgar W. Garbisch, after playing several seasons on the Washington and Jefferson College eleven, decided to pursue the career of a soldier at the United States Military Academy.

Engaging in his last game for the Greylegs yesterday at the Stadium against Navy, and captaining his team, Garbisch took place with West Point heroes of all time by leading his team to victory and accounting personally for all of the 12 points scored by the soldiers.

Styled Real Leader.

Cadets at West Point say Garbisch is more than just the captain of the eleven; that he is a real leader, able to inspire his gridiron warriors to play to the limit of their ability.

Garbisch went to West Point after an excellent record at Washington and Jefferson, Washington, Pa. Garbisch's home town is Washington, and when he was old enough to enter college he naturally was found on the roster of the institution where he lived.

At Washington and Jefferson, Garbisch played both guard and center, showing marked strength in each position.

Garbisch was 21 years old when he went to West Point—he now is 25—and has been a tower of strength on a quartet of Army teams.

That poundage is not an essential requirement to football greatness is well exemplified in his case. He is exactly six feet in height, but weighs only 174 pounds, having been greatly outweighed by practically every center he has opposed in recent seasons. Playing against Osborn, of the Navy, yesterday, he faced a rival who tips the beam at 198, but Garbisch subscribes to a remark attributed to the late "Bob" Fitzsimmons, "the bigger they are the harder they fall."

In football toggery he is all over the field, encouraging and exhorting his players, pointing out where to strengthen the defense, suggesting more vital means of attack.

Wearing cadet grey, he seems moulded to the uniform. Young women who visit West Point for the hops refer to him as "that handsome Mr. Garbisch."

Tackling Hard And Fierce.

He means business when his team is playing. His off-the-field smile is replaced by a look which spells trouble to opposing gridders, and his tackling is hard and fierce.

West Pointers and Army followers naturally want their team to triumph, but this year there was an added incentive in victory over the Navy, for it was "Ed Garbisch's team."

Before the game a West Point first classman expressed the way the Cadet Corps felt about it when he said:

"If ever an Army football captain

(Continued on Page 2, Column 7.)

Bill Roper Diagnoses The Game

Princeton's Famous Football Coach Writes For The Sun His Opinion Of The Strategy And Tactics Of The Game.

—*Page 4*

PARADE GIVES THRONGS THRILL BEFORE GAME

Thousands See Cadets And Midshipmen March To Stadium.

Mars, devoid of the panoply of war and carrying a yellow megaphone instead of a sword, rode into Baltimore yesterday eating from a pasteboard lunch box and trailing a balky mule and a shaggy goat.

For the occasion the annual gridiron classic between West Point and the Naval Academy was a festive event, a contest of brain and brawn instead of blood and iron.

Parade Like Triumphal Procession.

Yet the march of the Annapolis midshipmen and the West Point cadets from the improvised railroad station in Clifton Park to the Stadium as a martial spectacle was as brave as any pictured by old Virgil, who centuries ago sang of arms and the man in the imperial city of the seven hills.

Although fate had decreed that later the midshipmen were to go down to defeat before the attack of the cadets that march to the Stadium along the broad stretches of the Alameda and Thirty-third street was as much a triumphal procession for the vanquished as the victors.

Tens Of Thousands Turn Out.

There were no vanquished nor victors when that march began. Baltimore had turned out its tens of thousands to welcome impartially the men who wore the gray of West Point and the blue of the Naval Academy—sturdy youths, who, to the crowd that swarmed the line of march, typified much of the might, the majesty and the power of these United States.

And although the sidewalks along the line of march seemed to surge with the swaying of the crowds, there was little

(Continued on Page 3, Column 1.)

FOUR GOALS FROM FIELD GIVE CADETS TRIUMPH; 80,000 WITNESS CONTEST

President And Mrs. Coolidge Among Notables Witnessing Annual Clash Between Academy Elevens In Baltimore.

CAPTAIN GARBISCH'S TOE REGISTERS ALL OF POINTS

Great Stadium, Filled To Last Seat, Provides Gorgeous Setting—Arrangements For Game Win High Praise From Visitors.

By HENRY M. HYDE.

Army, 12; Navy, 0; all due to the educated toe of Captain Garbisch, of West Point.

Four well-aimed boots between the Navy goal posts tell the whole story.

As the early evening shadows came down into the bottom of that wonderful bowl, the Baltimore Stadium, and the game drew near its end, 2,000 raging Midshipmen in blue, with golden sashes across their shoulders, barked the last desparing inspiration to their desperate team.

"Fight—fight—fight—like hell!"

NAVY PLAYERS FIGHT LIKE TIGERS.

The Navy players in gold sweaters did just that. They threw themselves into every scrimmage with fury. They blocked and tackled like demons. They fought like tigers.

But every now and then the terrible toe of Garbisch drew back for a kick. The ball went flying up to meet the lowering gray clouds. Four times it sailed over the bar between the goal posts.

And that was all.

CADET CORPS CELEBRATES VICTORY.

Then down from their high, steep seats swarmed the corps of cadets, gray and graceful and all aflame with victory. They charged the goal posts and every young soldier threw his cap over the bar, while the big army band played "Benny Havens, O!" The boys, a thousand at once, lockstepped and snake danced all over the torn playing field behind the music and celebrated their triumph with shrill chants.

Eighty thousands persons, massed about the high sides of the bowl, sat still to watch them.

GLORY ENOUGH FOR ALL.

To army posts in Asia and Central America word has already been flashed and the victory celebrated. And many ships at sea last night mourned the defeat of the gallant team from Annapolis.

Aside from the toe of Garbisch there was glory enough for all. Certainly no athletic spectacle ever had a more splendid setting.

The great stadium, filled to the last seat, was a gorgeous sight. Looked at from one end the steep sides of the huge bowl rose from the brown-green playing field like tapestries of reddish purple. Over the far end of the horseshoe hung a blue haze. Nearer by the red and yellow hats of the thousands of women made bright spots of color.

Even the weather, if not ideal, by no means did its worst. The West Pointers started south in a blizzard and came on through drenching rain as far as Philadelphia. Only in Baltimore did the storm clouds threaten and do no more. Once or twice the sun broke through for an instant and promised more than it fulfilled. The wind was sharp, the sky gray and as the afternoon wore on the cold grew more biting. But it was good football weather.

PRESIDENT AND MRS. COOLIDGE THERE.

President and Mrs. Coolidge and several members of his Cabinet honored first one side and then the other with their presence. All the local dignitaries were there: Mayor Jackson, Governor Ritchie, J. Cookman Boyd, president of the Park Board; a thousand others. Army men from all over the country; navy men from Washington and shore stations; nearly 80,000 plain citizens and football fans, gathered to watch the twenty-seventh battle in the long series.

Yesterday's victory gives the Army a lead of one in the ancient feud between the twin services.

MIDSHIPMEN FIRST TO ARRIVE.

Navy was the first to reach the Stadium. Its 2,000 men in blue marched in solid columns into the east gate with the splendid Navy band playing "Anchors Aweigh!" The Baltimore sections, which had filled earliest, welcomed their neighbors wildly. From the moment they filled the Navy sections on the west side of the Stadium the cheer leaders were busy. The Navy goat, with gold ribbons on its

THE WEATHER
Thunder storms this afternoon or tonight. Saturday probably fair; little change in temperature; light southwest and west winds.

THE EVENING SUN

5.30 FINANCIAL
GIVING CLOSING QUOTATIONS.

VOL. XXXI—NO. 71. PRESS RUN YESTERDAY { MORNING, 129,009 / EVENING, 114,061 } 243,070 || SUNDAY 186,439 BALTIMORE, FRIDAY, JULY 10, 1925. Published every week-day by The A. S. Abell Company. Entered as second-class matter at Baltimore Postoffice. 34 PAGES. PRICE TWO CENTS.

DANGER OF FEZ'S FALL THREATENS PEACE OF FRANCE

Factions Disagree On War Policy While Krim Draws Near.

COMMUNIST ISSUES WARNING OF STRIKE

Says General Walkout Will Follow Denial Of Moroccan Independence.

Paris, July 10 (Special Cable).—Heavy clouds are gathering on France's political horizon. Internal dissension, linked with the very precarious affairs in Morocco, where the present campaign threatens to become a long colonial war, is seriously worrying all French political leaders.

The military outlook in Morocco is very grave. Abd-el-Krim's army, which at the outbreak of the campaign counted not more than 70,000 rifles, is estimated now at well beyond 150,000. The plight of Taza, the important railway knot situated on the only line connecting Algiers to Morocco, is considered desperate and it is likely that the town will be abandoned within the next few days.

Fall Within Week Is Feared.

Abd-el-Krim's pressure against Fez becomes more accentuated daily, and, although the French have disposed large forces for the defense of the Holy City, it is believed that they will be unable to prevent its capture by Abd-el-Krim if he makes a daring effort within the course of the next week, before strong reinforcements arrive.

The strategical importance of Fez is quite negligible, but the moral effect of its occupation by the Riffians would be such that the French risk having the entire south, which so far has been quiet, rise up against them and then the number of troops required for coping with the conditions will be a whole army. This would necessitate partial mobilization. Whether this would be possible in France under present political conditions is doubtful.

$9,000,000 More Appropriated.

The Chamber of Deputies voted last night credits amounting to $9,000,000 to cover the extraordinary war expenditures of the last three months. Socialist and Communist speakers warned that this can be only a small installment of much heavier sums which the Government will be compelled to ask in the near future if peace is not made at once. They urged Premier Painlevé to make a public statement of what peace terms he is offering Abd-el-Krim and the Premier's refusal to comply created an unfavorable atmosphere among the Socialists.

Communist Threatens Strike.

M. Cachin, leader of the Communists, declared:

"I warn you in the name of the Communist party, as well as in the name of the General Federation of Workers, that a general strike will be proclaimed in France if the Government does not give the Moroccans the independence they have the right to ask and persists in throwing away moneys and lives of the proletariat for the sake of capitalists."

There is no doubt that people who understand how important it is for France to crush the Riffians and consolidate its position in North Africa want the Government to take drastic measures to defeat Krim, but the most of the nation, mainly the working classes who are insufficiently educated to the vital necessity for the country to preserve its colonial empire, is most unenthusiastic for war in Morocco.

New Jersey Detective And Nurse Found Dead In Parked Automobile

Both Shot To Death—Pistol And Blackjack Left On Floor Of Car.

Rumson, N. J., July 10.—William D. Walling, Jr., a detective-sergeant of the Long Branch police force, and Miss May Linzmayer, 19 years old, graduate nurse of the Monmouth Memorial Hospital, were found early today, dead from bullet wounds, on the rear seat of Walling's sedan. The automobile had been parked at the intersection of two roads.

A .32-caliber automatic pistol, from which two shots had been fired, a cartridge belt, holster and blackjack were found on the floor of the sedan. The windows were open, but the lights of the automobile had been extinguished.

Serge Merdendorff, watchman on a nearby estate, told the police he heard three shots fired in rapid succession, after which he found the bodies in the rear of the car. Both had been shot in the region of the heart.

Earthquake Shakes Montant Mountains Again; Terror Reigns

Returns For Half Minute To District Recently Visited—No Serious Damage Reported.

Great Falls, Mont., July 10.—An earthquake shock lasting about thirty seconds shook the Big Belt Mountain district at 7.45 A. M. today.

The shock apparently centered between White Sulphur Springs and Three Forks, the area which suffered most from the severe quakes on the night of June 27.

No serious damage was reported.

The people were momentarily terrorized and hastened from buildings into the open.

GOOD EVENING

Summer: That period of the year when we love winter.

Winter: That period of the year when we love summer.

If the Weather Man insists on killing the crops, wouldn't a frost do as well as a hot, dry spell?

WHAT'S IT ALL ABOUT?

It's obvious that man is like
The anthropoid ape;
One sees the similarity
In attitude and shape:
The only gap between the two
That's notable is thought,
And who can claim that mortals think
As often as they ought?

Perhaps we overestimate
And magnify the gap
And he who scorns the humble ape
But proves himself a sap:
Indeed, if thought divides the two
The gap's a merest chink,
For thought is often quite confined
To thinking that we think.

So why start up an angry roar
And tilt a haughty chin
Because the highbrows intimate
The apes and men are kin?
When man does more than think he thinks
His thoughts are mostly wrong
And though the ape thinks not at all
He somehow gets along.

Perhaps the populace will be persuaded there is something in evolution when man, in an asphalt street environment, develops asbestos feet.

SUN SQUARE DOIN'S Or The Diary Of A Traffic Cop.

8.30 A. M.—I was beginning to think women ain't as sensitive about their age nowadays as they used to be, but since last night

I've come to the conclusion that the only difference is they begin getting sensitive a little later. It used to be when a woman got to be 25 years old she got dern reluctant to talk about the flight of time. Nowadays, since this here bachelor girl idea has got stylish they keep up their courage till they're about 30 and then give up addition for subtraction. And I've got to give them credit, they sure can look any old age they decide on to be permanent, what with the clothes they pick out and the slick things they do with their hair and their complexions. But there's always two things that gives them away. One is the loose skin under their chins and the other is a woman never starts talking about how old she is till she is trying to create a impression she's younger than she really and truly is. It was that way with a friend of that there redheaded widow woman at the boarding house that called on her last night. I suspected she was getting along in years when she forgot Thursday night was beau night. I knowed she wasn't as young as she was making out she was when she started talking about her girlish inexperience and I thought I'd try her out. It didn't do no good, though. Before I got through it was dern clear our acquaintance wasn't going to ripen into friendship.

"You talk like you was 16 years old," I says to her.

"Well," she says, "I've only saw 24 summers. You wouldn't think it, would you?"

"No," I says, "I wouldn't. Is your recovery complete?"

"Recov...?" she says. "Recovery from what?"

"Blindness," I says.

10 A. M.—It's my ankles they seem to be fondest of most; but, after all, I guess there ain't no telling where a mosquito is going to puncture you. Anyway, a guy I know that lives out the York road just come along here a minute ago and I says to him in a social way:

"How is the mosquitoes out your way this summer?"

"Affectionate," he says.

"What do you mean, affectionate?" I says.

"They're fond of necking," he says.

11 A. M.—The sergeant just now told me the mosquitoes don't bother him none, but I don't believe

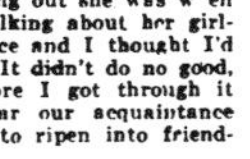

mosquitoes has got sense enough to be that discriminating.

Do you remember when there was a big coffee pot spouting steam on the front of a coffee-roasting house on Baltimore street near Marsh Market?

C. S. H.

Rain Makes Oriole Game Seem Dubious

Syracuse Drenched By Storm, Beginning Early This Morning. Tilt Not Definitely Off.

[Special Dispatch to The Evening Sun]

Syracuse, N. Y., July 10.—Rain, which fell in torrents during the early morning hours and which was still falling at 9 o'clock, made it seem likely that the final game of the series between the Baltimore Orioles and Syracuse Stars would be washed out today.

Secretary Mike Kelly said that the club would wait until 2 o'clock before calling off the game if the rain continued to fall.

Baby Eats Safety Pins.

Pottsville, Pa., July 10.—Vera Reninger, 4 years old, of Schuylkill Haven, made a meal yesterday on half a dozen safety pins. An X-ray showed one of the pins open in her stomach. Dr. E. C. Wallace operated on the child, removing the pin, and it is believed she will recover.

LEAGUE FORBIDS FREDERICK FAN TO WATCH GAMES

Charles Six Accused Of Leading Attack Upon Umpire.

BLUE RIDGE PRESIDENT FEARS ROOTER'S ARDOR

Trouble During Contest Became Near-Riot, Report Says.

[Special Dispatch to The Evening Sun.]

Hagerstown, July 10.—Because he is said to have led an attack on Umpire Ward during the Hagerstown-Frederick game at Frederick yesterday, Charles Six, Frederick baseball fan, has been barred from attending all games of the Blue Ridge League.

The bann was imposed today by J. Vincent Jamison, president of the league, who sent a telegram to Six, informing him that he was unwelcome at any of the games. A similar telegram was sent to the managers of the league's teams.

First Such Action Taken.

Jamison declared that this was the first time such action had ever been taken in the history of the league. He said that it is an unusual procedure which is only occasionally followed. He had taken it in Six's case, he said, because he feared that the fan's ardor might cause disastrous results.

Yesterday's trouble, it is said, developed into a near-riot that was only quelled when police were called to surround the park.

Followed Umpire's Decision.

The attack on Ward is said to have begun when he gave a decision in favor of George Scheminant, Hagerstown's center fielder, a former Baltimore boy, who picked up a low-liner fly that was knocked out by Frank Six, star left fielder of the Frederick team.

Player Six is said to be a relative of the man who has been barred from the games. There is keen rivalry between the two teams and a number of fans are said to have objected to Ward calling Six out.

Pitcher Sigman, of Frederick, also remonstrated with Ward and it was during this argument that Six, the barred fan, is said to have come on the field and attacked Ward. The umpire defended himself against Six with his mask, it was reported.

Was Removed From Field.

Six, it is said, was removed from the field, but returned. This time, it is reported, he was removed by policemen. Other patrolman surrounded the Hagerstown players to prevent them from being attacked.

Sigman, it is reported, was fined $20 for his part in the row with the umpire.

Workers Intimidated By Shanghai Strikers

Many Are Abducted, Beaten And Starved—Wives And Children Stolen.

Shanghai, July 10.—Intimidation, abduction and starvation are the newest weapons used here to force workers into joining the general strike. Many workers are being abducted and carried into Chinese territory, where they are beaten and starved, while wives and children are stolen.

The water company is threatening to cut off water in outlying sections as a measure of retaliation, hoping thus to check the growing activity of men engaged in intimidation.

British Would Retaliate.

London, July 10.—Deportation of unemployed Chinese in the strike-ridden city of Hongkong and flogging for men who use intimidation were threatened by Sir Reginald Stubbs, British Governor of the city, according to press advices today.

Inside Today---

PRESIDES OVER TRIAL OF EVOLUTION TEACHER

JUDGE JOHN T. RAULSTON

DIVORCE INCREASING, NINE STATES SHOW

Advances 3.7 Per Cent. In Maryland, With Marriages Decreasing 1.3 Per Cent.

GAIN IN SOUTH DAKOTA

Nebraska Only One Which Indicates Smaller Number Of Separations.

Washington, July 10.—Divorces are increasing and marriages rapidly decreasing, reports to the Department of Commerce from nine representative States revealed today.

A matrimonial census showed that in the year 1924 divorces had generally increased a little more than six per cent., while marriages had decreased about six per cent.

Decrease In Nebraska.

Out of the nine States Nebraska was the only one to show a decrease in divorces. This State had 183 less divorce cases in 1924 than the previous year, but marriages fell off 53.7 per cent.

South Dakota was the only State reporting an increase in marriages for last year. Cupid's darts were aimed correctly 6,401 times, an increase of 2.3 per cent, but 586 divorces were issued, an increase of 4.3 per cent.

The States reporting increases in divorce and decreases in marriage were:

	Marriage Decrease. P.C.	Divorce Increase. P.C.
Delaware	7.7	12.1
Connecticut	3.3	2.6
Rhode Island	9.3	8.8
Maryland	1.3	3.7
Maine	6.8	1.1
New Jersey	3.9	7.9
Wisconsin	10.5	9.1

The census of all the States will not be concluded for several weeks.

Anthracite Agreement Thought Far Distant

Subcommittees Confer After Operators Reject Demand For Higher Wages.

Atlantic City, N. J., July 10.—The joint anthracite wage conference settled down today to a battle in sub-committee, after a formal demand by the miners for higher wages and a formal rejection of the demand by Samuel D. W[illegible], spokesman for the operators.

A subcommittee, composed of six representatives of each group, is considering the men's demands. Unless an agreement is reached by July 18, and this is considered highly improbable, adjournment will be taken to permit the miners to attend a district conference at Scranton, after which negotiations will be resumed here.

COOLIDGE INVITES HIGH EXECUTIVES TO SWAMPSCOTT

Will Confer With Cabinet Heads And Others During Rest.

KELLOGG SOON TO COME WITH FOREIGN AFFAIRS

Secretary Of State Will Bring Problems Of China And Mexico.

By David Lawrence.

[Special Dispatch to The Evening Sun.]

Swampscott, Mass., July 10.—President Coolidge has arranged for a series of conferences with Cabinet officers and other important officials during the next few weeks, and now it will really not appear as all play and no work at the summer capital.

The President has let it be known that he always will be available to any member of the Cabinet or the head of any of the Government organizations who may want to consult him. Secretary Kellogg of the Department of State is the first to avail himself of the privilege. He asked for a conference and promptly was granted one.

China And Mexico Vital Problems.

The Secretary has had a number of things on his mind in the last two weeks and though none can be called critical, each is so important that the guidance of the President as well as his instruction is desired. Though Mr. Coolidge gives a free hand to his Cabinet officers, he remains nevertheless responsible for the broad principles of policy which they develop and carry to him for his approval.

There are two vital matters which have been commanding the attention of the Department of State. One is China and the other Mexico.

John V A. MacMurray, the newly appointed American Minister to China, has just reached Peking. His first reports have come through to the Secretary of State. Mr. MacMurry is to proceed with arrangements for a conference of powers interested in China, but before that he must exchange viewpoints with the diplomats in Peking. The American policy in the Far East is therefore at the incipient stage. Mr. Kellogg does not feel like deciding the questions involved without having a comprehensive talk with the President.

U. S. Seeks To Harmonize Powers.

In a sense the whole world is waiting on American initiative in the Chinese problem. Ever since the days of John Hay the American Department of State has pursued a policy of friendship for China which has in many cases amounted to mediation between China and European as well as Asiatic powers. The famous principle of the "open door" in commercial development was an American conception that has done much to keep the powers from diminishing the sovereignty of China. Although the revolution has complicated the problem in the last several years, the United States has endeavored to support the Central Government in Peking in the hope that ultimately the various elements in China might reintegrate.

The American purpose at the moment is to achieve unity inside China, to bring the outside powers into harmony on questions of foreign rights in China and to allay the anti-foreign feeling which has arisen in the treaty ports. It is a task of unparalleled difficulty and only by conspicuous demonstrations of friendship for the Chinese people can progress be made. Senator Borah, chairman of the Senate Foreign Relations Committee, has insisted upon American leadership in withdrawing from extra-territorial rights. He is a factor to be reckoned with in any policy that must be evolved at this time. Mr. Coolidge is inclined to listen to the liberalism of Borah whenever possible, and in this instance it may be remarked that the Borah influence is carrying weight.

No Response To Mexican Greetings.

Now, as to Mexico, the problem there has lately been one of concern. One of the Mexican newspapers points out, for instance, that the gracious message sent by President Calles to the United States congratulating it on the anni-

[Continued On Page 2, Column 8]

Impossibility Of Obtaining Fair Jury Insures Scopes' Conviction, Says Mencken

Dayton's Attitude Toward Evolution Makes Trial Only A Formality, With Outcome Foreordained, Critic Believes—Gray Pastor Teaches Him Lesson In Scripture.

By H. L. Mencken.

[Special Dispatch to The Evening Sun.]

Dayton, Tenn., July 10.—The trial of the infidel Scopes, beginning here this hot, lovely morning, will greatly resemble, I suspect, the trial of a prohibition agent accused of mayhem in Union Hill, N. J. That is to say, it will be conducted with the most austere regard for the highest principles of jurisprudence. Judge and jury will go to extreme lengths to assure the prisoner the last and least of his rights. He will be protected in his person and feelings by the full military and naval power of the State of Tennessee. No one will be permitted to pull his nose, to pray publicly for his condemnation or even to make a face at him. But all the same he will be bumped off inevitably when the time comes, and to the applause of all right-thinking men.

The real trial, in truth, will not begin until Scopes is convicted and ordered to the hulks. Then the prisoner will be the Legislature of Tennessee, and the jury will be that great fair, unimpassioned body of enlightened men which has already decided that a horse hair put into a bottle will turn into a snake and that the Kaiser started the late war. What goes on here is simply a sort of preliminary hearing, with music by the village choir. For it will be no more possible in this Christian valley to get a jury unprejudiced against Scopes than it would be possible in Wall Street to get a jury unprejudiced against a Bolshevik.

Bitterness Absent In Presence Of Town's Faith.

I speak of prejudice in its purely philosophical sense. As I wrote yesterday, there is an almost complete absence, in these pious hills, of the ordinary and familiar malignancy of Christian men. If the Rev. Dr. Crabbe ever spoke of bootleggers as humanely and affectionately as the town theologians speak of Scopes, and even Darrow and Malone, his employers would pelt him with their spyglasses and sit on him until the ambulance came from Mount Hope. There is absolutely no bitterness on tap. But neither is there any doubt. tI has been decided by acclamation, with only a few infidels dissenting, that the hypothesis of evolution is profane, inhumane and against God, and all that remains is to translate that almost unanimous decision into the jargon of the law and so have done.

The town boomers have banqueted Darrow as well as Bryan, but there is no mistaking which of the two has the crowd, which means the venire of tried and true men. Bryan has been oosing around the country since his first day here, addressing this organization and that, presenting the indubitable Word of God in his caressing, ingratiating way, and so making unanimity doubly unanimous. From the defense yesterday came hints that this was making hay before the sun had legally begun to shine—even that it was a sort of contempt of

[Continued On Page 2, Column 7]

MINERS LOSE HOPE OF EARLY AGREEMENT

Long Deadlock, With Lockout On September 1, Looms, Searles Declares.

THE SUBCOMMITTEE ARGUES

Workers "Will Not Arbitrate The Making Of A Contract," Spokesman Asserts.

[By the United Press.]

Atlantic City, July 10.—All hope of an amicable settlement of the wage controversy between the United Mine Workers and the anthracite operators has been abandoned by the miners, according to a statement today by Ellis Searles, editor of the *United Mine Workers' Journal* and spokesman for the miners.

Sees Long Deadlock.

While a subcommittee composed of six representatives from each side was seeking to effect an agreement at a conference here today, Searles issued the following statement:

"The miners fully expected the operators to take the stand they did take yesterday. The miners have no hope of reaching an agreement. Every indication points to a continued deadlock.

Sees Lockout September 1.

"If this situation continues to exist, there will be a lockout on September 1. Usually after such a lockout there is some new development or proposal that results in an agreement.

"The miners positively will not arbitrate the making of a contract. They are perfectly willing to arbitrate anything contained in a contract in order to have a proper interpretation, but they will not arbitrate the preparation of a contract."

Rescuers Seek Six Trapped In Desert

Routed By Cloudburst, Miners Are Struggling Over Blistering "Bad Lands."

Indian Wells, Cal., July 10.—Leaving Irish Jim's oasis, on the mirage-veiled trail toward Death Valley, a little rescue band struck out over the burning sands for Wild Rose Canyon today, bent on rescuing six miners routed by a cloudburst.

No word has been heard from the miners, who were reported by an Indian to be struggling on foot through the trackless, blistering wastes of the "Bad Lands." "Desert rats" say it is doubtful if the little group can withstand the terrific heat for more than a few days.

The miners were working claims in the valley sink when a cloudburst a week ago, destroyed their shacks and marauding Indians made off with their animals and most of their provisions.

Donald C. McDonald, owner of the mines, is leading the rescue party.

Rat Kills Baby In Cradle.

Boston, July 10.—A large rat attacked the two-week-old child of Mrs. Mary Shusinski, of East Cambridge, yesterday, inflicting injuries which caused his death. The baby's mother, awakened by a commotion in the crib, found a rat biting the face of the child. Her husband fought off the rat, which put up a desperate fight. The baby died before the arrival of a physician.

BUTLER WANTS SON TO READ EVOLUTION

Author Of "Anti" Bill Has Darwin's Books At Home.

HE PERUSED THEM HIMSELF

Tennesseean Says He Only Opposes Theory In State Schools.

[By the United Press.]

Dayton, Tenn., July 10.—Representative J. W. Butler, author of the famous Tennessee Anti-Evolution law, wants his sons to know all about evolution even if they have to read about it at home.

Butler, who has arrived here for the Scopes trial, said in an interview that he himself has read Darwin's "Origin of Species" and "The Descent of Man," and that they did him no harm.

Wants Son To Read It.

"I have a son, 19 years old, in the high school, and I want him to read about evolution," he said.

"But how will he learn about it now that teaching of evolution has been banned in the State?" he was asked.

Has Books At Home.

"He can read it at home," Butler replied. "I have the books at the house.

"I want him to know for himself how untrue it is," he added.

O. K. In Private Schools.

"I am not opposed to the teaching of evolution, but I don't think it ought to be taught in State-supported schools. If a man wants to put up his own school, let him teach all the evolution he wants."

Butler ridiculed a report that he didn't have enough money to come to Dayton to attend the trial. He has two farms of 120 acres and has a wheat thrashing outfit. He left in the middle of the thrashing season in order to attend the trial.

Butler and Bryan had their pictures taken today with their hands on a Bible.

Tot Starts Auto; Crashes; Dying

Philadelphia, July 10.—Daniel Sagerman, 4 years old, climbed into an automobile near his home, started the engine, causing the car to collide with another, and was so badly injured that he is reported dying.

Dancing, Swearing Pastor Wins Over His Traducers

Flock Rallies Round Mount Pleasant (N. J.) Cleric After He Admits Going To Dance And Saying $1,000 Was "Hell Of A Price" For Coffin.

[Special Dispatch to The Evening Sun.]

Mount Pleasant, N. J., July 10.—Modernist supporters of Mount Pleasant's dancing, swearing young pastor, the Rev. W. H. W. Rees, today were celebrating a victory which they hope will go far toward routing the unwritten, mid-Victorian blue laws which hedge about doings of small-town preachers.

The issue of whether a pastor is human, or must hold himself a little above the level of conduct he would prescribe for his flock, in order to set the best possible of examples, was resolved in favor of humanity, when the Rev. Mr. Rees was placed on trial before five members of the New Brunswick Presbytery last night, on charges of conduct unbecoming a minister.

Admits Dancing And Other Crimes.

The young pastor admitted he had been "guilty" of going to a dance and dancing with a woman other than his wife, and that he had agreed with a member of his flock, who had been overwhelmed by the $1,000 price paid for a coffin for a deceased member of his family, that he had paid "a hell of a price."

He contended that he had done no wrong, though he conceded he could see something in the viewpoint of those who held he should have set a shining example of rectitude for his congregation.

Accusers Rally To Support.

And then, right in the midst of what was supposed to be a trial, the foreman of the committee of eight elders who had accused the pastor admitted that

[Continued On Page 2, Column 4]

GRAND JURORS INDICT SCOPES SECOND TIME

Case Gets Under Way After Former Bill Is Thrown Out.

CLERGYMAN OPENS TRIAL WITH PRAYER

High School Pupils Give Evidence Again Before Talesmen.

Dayton, Tenn., July 10.—At 11.48 A. M. the court sitting for the trial of John T. Scopes was adjourned until 1.30 P. M., when the selection of jurors is to begin.

By George F. Milton.

[Special Dispatch to The Evening Sun.]

Dayton, Tenn., July 10.—The case of the State of Tennesseee versus John Thomas Scopes has opened and its first round has been a draw, but Dayton is disappointed.

The reindictment of the young high school teacher for violating Tennessee's Anti-Evolution law, for which Attorney-General A. T. Stewart set the wheels in motion just as soon as the court had listened to a Sprin City pastor's plea for the guidance of God for the judge and the lawyers, was desired with equal keenness by the defense and the State. Neither side wished any legal loopholes in the indictment itself through which the far-famed case would slip into disaster.

Crowd Fails To Materialize.

But Dayton's crowd, like that of Shelby, Mont., didn't materialize. The courtroom was well filled when Judge Raulston's gavel sounded. People filled it more and more as the trial got under way. But at no time this morning have there been more than 1,200 sweltering men, women and children in the courtroom.

Nor have the streets been particularly crowded. There has been a little knot of people on the Courthouse lawn, resting in comfort under the outspread arms of the spacious oaks, but not over a thousand more. Most of these are Rhea county folks. There are a scattering few from outside. Chattanooga's police commissioner, E. D. Herron, who hastened to Dayton with his detectives to aid the authorities here in keeping order, found the hardest job of the whole business that of keeping cool.

Concessionaires Sorrowful.

Expressed in the vernacular, the crowd is a "flop." The proprietors of the hot dog stands, the leaders of the soda pop brigade, are sorrowful.

Their 10,000 people didn't pan out.

But what a scene in the courtroom!

The large, well-lighted, newly painted room began filling early. Judge Raulston didn't appear until about 8.40. There was scattering applause as he took the bench and was presented a huge bouquet of rhododendrons from the nearby mountainside. Notables began coming in and the long deal tables set up for the press of the world began filling with sweating, nervous newspaper men. Cameramen with tripods clambered in every corner of the courtroom.

Bryan Heartily Cheered.

Bryan came in, to a hearty cheer. He walked over to his seat and then strode to the defense table, where Clarence Darrow, in his famous blue galluses and pale yellow shirt, greeted him cordially. Malone, Hayes and the others chatted respectfully with the great Commoner. It was the handclasp of the fighters just before the opening gong rang.

The judge rapped his gavel. Court opened with a fifteen-minute prayer in which God's divine blessing was invoked for the judge, the jury, the counsel and the case. It was an impressive and quite Fundamentalist prayer. The entire courtroom, bareheaded and coatless, except for Bryan's black alpaca and Malone's natty gray sack coat, listened to the divine appeal.

The Battle Begins.

Then the battle began. Attorney-General Stewart spring to his feet and asked for a recalling of the grand jury. The judge granted it instanter. The grand jurors, carefully parked in the courtroom for the emergency, filed to their seats and were sworn "to do no act through malice and all acts for the good of the State." The defense made no objection. It was quite as anxious to have the indictment airtight as was the State. It did not even plead for time. It didn't want the trial to be damaged by the State's tightening of its legal belt before getting to the real battle.

Court recessed until 11, while the grand jury was re-examining the school children whose testimony proves that young Scopes did really attempt to teach Hunter's "Bilology," the State-adopted text-book which has evolution in it. There was a flurry, for the State's chief grand jury witness had been mislaid. The young men of the State counsel ran around here and there looking for the boy who was needed to show up John Thomas. They found him. He went before the grand jury. The case was presented, the indictment was returned.

It's Airtight This Time.

This time it wasn't faulty. It was air-tight, rock bound, iron riveted. The court's process of calling the jury was entirely according to form. And the indictment returned mentioned the crime alleged to have been committed. So both legal loop holes were plugged. The State was now ready to go to bat. The first round had been a draw.

WEATHER FORECAST

Showers today and probably tomorrow; somewhat cooler tomorrow; moderate southerly winds.

Detailed Weather Report on Page 18.

THE SUN

WHERE MARK TWAIN'S GERMANY SURVIVES, DESCRIBED BY **S. Miles Bouton**

Page 11.

VOL. 177—NO. 57D PRESS RUN MONDAY { MORNING, 129,335 EVENING, 114,817 } 244,152 || SUNDAY 187,119 BALTIMORE, WEDNESDAY, JULY 22, 1925. Published every week-day by The A. S. Abell Company. Entered as second-class matter at Baltimore Postoffice 24 PAGES 2 CENTS

BERLIN INSISTS TERRITORY BE HELD NEUTRAL

Germany Will Make Terrain No Battlefield To Gain Pact.

DEMANDS EQUAL STATUS IN LEAGUE

Reich Wants Conference On Theory Nation May Gain Advantage.

Berlin, July 21 (Special Cable).—Germany will under no circumstances join the League of Nations, unless her territory is declared neutral in all emergencies.

Such is the essence of the German reply to France on security pact proposals, as distilled tonight by a high German official. He assented flatly, the Reich, eager as it is to have the pact, must, nevertheless, reject any proposal which would make its territory a battlefield for a European war; secondly, the Reich will not accept as a trustee of the pact any ally of France.

Attended All Meetings.

These two conditions Germany will insist upon, as it has in the weary months of preliminary negotiations. They are no mean obstacles. An official, who was present at all Cabinet meetings at which the proposed security pact was discussed during the past weeks, said:

"At the present moment, there is great tension between Great Britain and Russia. Any moment this may become a crisis. We can not be drawn into such a conflict. We can not permit troops to march across our territory.

Reich Wants Conference.

"If the Allies believe Germany must enter the League of Nations before the pack is concluded, we will concede this. But we cannot enter the league except with the same status as Switzerland. We are disarmed and the rest of Europe is heavily armed. We must remain out of all conflicts."

The speaker said the pact would undoubtedly have a reaction on the machinery of the occupation of the Rhineland, but that no one expected immediate results. What the Reich still wants is a conference, on the principal that there is nothing to lose and there is always the chance of gaining an advantage in any general discussion of Europe's troubles.

[Copyright, 1925, by the New York World.]

Three Ideas Underlie German Security Note

Berlin, July 21 (AP).—Three fundamental ideas underlie the German reply to the French note on the proposed security pact, Dr. Stresemann, the Foreign Minister, explained to the correspondents today—first, the relation of the pact to existing treaties; second, Germany's position on arbitration treaties, including guarantees, and, third, Germany's entry into the League of Nations.

Germany does not believe that the peace treaties can be regarded as sacrosanct for all time, but chinks that changes can be effected by peaceful agreement. This is guaranteed by Article XIX of the covenant of the league.

Fear French Guarantee Plan.

Germany, according to the minister, views with apprehension the French suggestion that a series of exceptions be legalized in connection with arbitration treaties, whereby forcible action can take place without previous judicial action, such as arbitration. Germany fears that this would leave her defenseless against possible military invasion whenever the Allies deemed such invasion justified.

Germany further fears that the system of guarantees suggested by France may cause injustice, as the guaranteers could decide for themselves without recourse to law who, in the event of a disturbance of the peace, was in the wrong.

Demands Equal's Treatment.

On the question of the League of Nations, Germany points out that her disarmament places her at a disadvantage as compared with other members of the league, so that until general disarmament is effected, it is essential that an interim solution be found, taking into account Germany's special military economic and geographic position.

The note insists that Germany must be treated on a basis of equality and reciprocity.

The first section of the note, delivered to France and Great Britain yesterday, deals with the Allied claim that the pact must not involve modification of the peace treaties. Germany maintains that she is not barred from attempting by peaceful agreement alteration of existing treaties to meet changed circumstances and that she is entitled to attempt to secure modification of the provisions of the Versailles treaty with respect to military occupation of German territories.

Germany, however, does not insist

(Continued on Page 11, Column 5.)

Many Hurdles Bar Pathway To Security Pact's Success

Disposition To Indulge In Old-Fashioned Diplomatic Jockeying Evidenced In Capitals Of Nations That Are Parties To Idea.

By JOHN W. OWENS.

[*London Bureau of The Sun.*]

[Copyright, 1925, by The Sun.]

London, July 21 (Special Cable).—There is a conflict of opinion in European capitals regarding the prospects of the security negotiations, now that they have entered the third stage with the delivery yesterday of Germany's reply to the French note.

The diplomatic correspondent of the Manchester *Guardian*, reflecting London views, says:

"The note is short but written in a way to show that the German Government wants the security pact to be carried through."

Many Hurdles Yet To Jump.

But that is not the tone of dispatches reaching London from Berlin and Paris. It is plain that there exists an opinion in both these capitals that many hurdles yet remain to be jumped, and a doubt whether there is sufficient desire to jump them.

Evidence develops that there appears a considerable disposition to indulge in old-fashioned jockeying, although there are also signs that this tendency may be mitigated by concern on the part of both France and Germany to keep in the good graces of the masters of international credit.

Moderates Growing Cold.

The news from Berlin is to the effect that the Nationalist critics of the security scheme have been increasingly aggressive and that Chancellor Luther and Minister of Foreign Affairs Stresemann have held them in check by concessions from day to day on such domestic questions as the tariff.

Meantime the Chancellor and the Foreign Minister are reported to be asking themselves whether they did not go too far. It is said that some of the German moderates are growing more cool toward the security pact idea.

French Reported Uneasy.

Consequently, it is reported, there would be no great sorrow exhibited in Germany if France upsets the apple cart in such a way as will relieve Germany of responsibility in the eyes of the world.

The Paris press, apparently, is behaving in such a manner calculated to give satisfaction to this reported German attitude. The French are reported uneasy and tending to become excited over the contents of the German note. They read into the note a sugestion for modification of the Rhineland occupation in return for a security agreement, and a question of the right of France to insist upon giving armed guarantee to treaties between Germany and the latter's eastern neighbors.

Far Removed From Briand's Idea.

The French are stated to believe that such suggestions project the security pact negotiations onto a plane far removed from that on which M. Briand carefully laid out his program in his June note to Germany.

His effort was to maintain the advantages contained in the Treaty of Versailles—to stereotype not only the frontiers between Germany, France and Belgium, but also Germany's eastern frontiers, through treaties between Germany, Poland and Czecho-Slovakia, guaranteed by France, with the right, apparently reserved by France, to move

(Continued on Page 11, Column 4.)

BOXER IS KILLED IN LOUISVILLE BOUT

Death Due To Head Striking Boards Of Ring, Physicians Say.

Louisville, Ky., July 21 (AP).—Mickey Shannon, Chicago light-heavyweight boxer, was killed during the fourth round of a boxing match here tonight with Harry Fay, Louisville, when Fay knocked him against the ropes so that he fell and struck his head against the floor. Physicians said death was almost instantaneous. Fay was arrested on a charge of manslaughter. Later he was released under $1,000 bond.

Shannon appeared to have the better of the fight in the first two rounds, but Fay pounded him with heavy body blows in the third and continued in the fourth. In this round Fay punished Shannon with body blows and then shifted to his head.

The Chicago boxer dropped under the constant pounding, falling over the ropes. His head struck the bare boards of the ring and as Referee Marvin Hart was counting the bell rang, ending the round. Shannon's seconds carried him to his corner and tossed in the sponge. Doctors were summoned and Shannon was rushed to a hospital, where physicians said he probably had died soon after his head struck the floor.

To Work Overtime, Minus Pay, To Further Exports

Canadian Steel Employes Stipulate That, If Profits Accrue, They Shall Get 75 Per Cent.

St. John, N. B., July 21 (AP).—Employes of James Pender & Co., Ltd., a subsidiary of the British Empire Steel Corporation, have agreed to work overtime without pay to enable the company to compete with foreign manufacturers in export markets.

The condition was made by the workmen that should profit accrue under the arrangement it must be shared between the company and the employes on a 75-25 per cent. basis, the big end of the division going to the men.

Start is to be made at once under the plan, eighty men giving three hours extra on alternate nights.

Policeman Whips Father For Beating Mother

Afterward Arrests Elder Man And Takes Him To Court.

New York, July 21 (AP).—Policeman James S. Monaghan today arrested his father, Patrick, and gave him a sound thrashing, when he found him beating his mother at their home in the East Side.

For fifteen years, with invariable monotony, the elder Monaghan has beat his wife, Patrolman Monaghan told Justice Delagi, in the Yorkville Court, when the father was arraigned.

Monaghan was held under $5,000 bail for examination on the charge of assault.

EARTH SHOCK IN SWITZERLAND

Buildings In Geneva Rocked By seismic Disturbance.

Geneva, July 21 (Special Cable).—Buildings here were perceptibly rocked by a seismic disturbance at 1.05 this afternoon. The center of the disturbance has not yet been determined.

Quakes are rarely felt in Switzerland.

1924 FARM INCOME PUT AT 12 BILLION

Gross Receipts Largest Since 1921, Agriculture Department Says.

Washington, July 21 (AP).—Farmers received a gross income of $12,136,000,000 for the year ended June 30, which, the Department of Agriculture estimated today, was more than they had taken during any year since 1921.

The income was $848,000,000 greater than last year and was attributed almost wholly to the increased value of grain and meat animals, particularly wheat and hogs.

The cost of production last year was placed at $6,486,000,000, or nearly two per cent. greater than the $6,363,000,000 estimated for the year before. The increase of gross income over the fiscal year 1924 was fixed at 7¼ per cent.

Talks From London With U. S. Ship Near Australia

Wireless Enthusiast Says He And Seattle's Operator Chatted About Twenty Minutes.

London, July 21 (Special Cable).—A wireless telephone conversation between England and the United States warship Seattle, 800 miles east of Australia, was carried on early this morning, it was learned tonight. Gerald Marcuse, a wireless enthusiast, of Osterham, near London, made the connection, as part of a test arranged by the American Relay Radio League.

"I got in touch with Lieutenant Schnell, wireless operator on the Seattle," Marcuse said. "We talked together about twenty minutes."

150,000 TROOPS READY IN DRIVE ON ABD-EL-KRIM

Two Marshals And Five Generals Lead French Forces.

RIFFS ABANDON ATTACK ON FEZ

Rebel Chief Reported To Believe His Days As Leader Numbered.

Paris, July 21 (AP).—Two marshals of France, Petain and Lyautey, and five generals, Naulin, Colombat, De Chambrun, Heusch and Bertrand, are leading 150,000 French troops arrayed against Abd-el-Krim, the rebel war lord in Morocco.

In French sources it was said today that the reorganized military command has caused the Riffian chief to see the handwriting on the wall and that there are indications that he believes his days as a leader are numbered.

Moors Abandon Attack.

The stupendous offensive across "the land of thirst" or "Taza and Wezzan" with the fertil plains of the sacred city of Fez as the objective, which had been threatening for the past two days, seems momentarily to have been abandoned by the Moors.

Marshal Petain's presence in the Riff is declared to have instilled fresh morale into the tired and dejected French troops. Faced by everincreasing French reinforcements the Riffian chief is endeavoring to raise revolt among all possible tribes as part of his last desperate effort to crush the Christian soldiers who stand between him and Moslem rule in Fez, it was asserted today.

Spread Propaganda.

Abd-el-Krim's brother and a number of his agents are credited with spreading propaganda with renewed energy among neutral tribesmen.

The battle facing Marshal Petain is similar to that which confronted him when he assumed the leadership of the French Army in 1917. It is one of the morale of the troops under his command more than of stopping the onslaughts of the enemy.

Weather Aids Riffs.

French official advices from Morocco continue to emphasize a general improvement in the situation. The correspondent of the *Temps* at the front telegraphs that trains loaded with troops and supplies passing toward the battle region day and night have so congested the road that traffic at Tunis was ordered stopped for several days.

"However," the correspondent adds, "the Moors have a strong ally in the climate, which is unbearable to Europeans. The Europeans chose the hottest season for the offensive. None but natives can live in the temperature around Taza, which averages a maximum of 108 degrees Fahrenheit and never is lower than 75. The average rainfall for July is three-quarters of an inch, in August two and three-quarters and in September two inches."

MONTH-OLD BABY BY AIR ROUTE

Infant Carried In Plane From Paris To Copenhagen.

Paris, July 21 (Special Cable).—The youngest air passenger is Axel Graham, one month old, who left Lebourget Flying Field for Copenhagen by aeroplane this morning, via Brussels, Amsterdam and Hamburg.

Axel was born in Paris June 20 and flew to his homeland in the arms of his Danish mother.

7,000 Guests At Garden Party Given By British King And Queen

About Hundred Americans Present—Two Famous Military Bands Play As Visitors Stroll About Buckingham Palace Grounds.

London, July 21 (AP).—One of the most successful and colorful royal garden parties given since the war was held in the beautiful grounds of Buckingham Palace this afternoon, with King George and Queen Mary as hosts to 7,000 of their subjects and distinguished guests from foreign countries, including about one hundred Americans.

Among the royal guests were the Queen of Rumania, the Queen of the Belgians and Prince Chichibu, of Japan. Princess Mary and the Duchess of York also were present.

King And Queen Mingle With Crowd

After passing through the palace proper, the guests strolled through the grounds and listened to the music of two famous English military bands until the king and queen arrived from their private apartments in the palace. Their majesties greeted as many guests as possible as they moved about in separate directions through the crowds. At tea time the king and queen retired to the royal pavilion while the guests were served refreshments at large marquees on the fringes of the lawn.

Among the few formal presentations were a number of State representatives of the National Society of Colonial Dames of America, who were introduced to King George and Queen Mary because of their activity in collecting $100,000 in the United States for the upkeep of Sulgrave Manor, Washington's ancestral home in England.

Several Americans Presented.

Among those presented were Mrs. Joseph R. Lamar, Atlanta, Ga.; Mrs. E. M. Townsend, New York; Mrs. T. T. Sherman, New York; Mrs. John Lowell, Boston; Mrs. N. T. Bacon, Providence, and Mrs. A. Crittenden Smith, Nebraska.

Other Americans attending the garden party included:

Mr. and Mrs. Howard C. Heins, Pittsburgh; Conde Nast and Miss Natica Nast, New York; Miss Louise Berid and Colonel and Mrs. Robert Roos, San Francisco; Mrs. R. F. Tucker, a daughter of Colonel and Mrs. E. M. House; Senator Arthur Capper, of Kansas, and Mrs. Capper; Representative Cordell Hull, of Tennessee, and Mrs. Hul Elisha C. Tower, New York; Mrs. Harry Brown, Pittsburgh, and Mrs. J. Corrigan, New York.

GENERALSTRIKE THREATENED BY SOFT COAL MEN

Appeal To Hoover And Davis To Uphold Jacksonville Pact.

CITE CONDITIONS IN WEST VIRGINIA

Charge Rockefeller And Bethlehem Companies With Breaking Faith.

Atlantic City, July 21 (AP).—Bituminous union coal miners here today asked Herbert Hoover, Secretary of Commerce, and James J. Davis, Secretary of Labor, to intervene in behalf of the Government in the Northern West Virginia fields to check abrogation of wage agreements which they said otherwise would force a general strike throughout the country.

Meanwhile, the anthracite scale parley was resumed after a three-day adjournment. Operators reconsidered their decision to open their books to the hard coal men, as announced Friday, and declined to furnish at this time data on salaries of company heads and officials.

Plea Sent By Bittner.

The joint telegram to Secretaries Hoover and Davis was sent by Van A. Bittner here, chief union representative in those fields.

Mr. Bittner also wired protests to John D. Rockefeller, Jr., and Samuel Untermyer, a New York attorney, in which he alleges repudiations of the "Jacksonville agreement," on the part of the Consolidation Coal Company and the Bethlehem Mines Corporation, in which the two men, respectively, are stockholders.

Plea To Hoover And Davis.

To Mr. Hoover and Mr. Davis, Mr. Bittner said:

Several large coal companies in Northern West Virginia, among whom are the Bethlehem Mines Corporation, a subsidiary of the Bethlehem Steel Corporation, and the Consolidation Coal Company, which is controled by the Rockefeller and Watson interests, have abrogated their wage contracts with the United Mine Workers of America and are attempting to put into effect a wage reduction approximating fifty per cent.

Defenseless miners, their wives and little children are being evicted from their homes by these coal companies because the miners will not agree to violate and abrogate the terms of the wage agreement which is effective until March 31, 1927.

Hundreds of armed gunmen are being employed to intimidate, coerce and force our people to accept this reduction in wages. In the interests of the coal miners and all the people of our country, the time has arrived when the Government of the United States should take a definite position against abrogation of wage contracts by the coal operators of Northern West Virginia.

The miners do not propose to have their wage agreements broken down by this method of guerilla warfare on the part of the Northern West Virginia operators and unless something is done to prevent this abrogation of wage agreements it will be necessary for the miners of the entire State of West Virginia to join with the United Mine Workers of America and of the rest of the country in a general strike.

Miners took up most of todays conference in reviewing their claims for a ten per cent. wage increase. Operators tonight showed signs of impatience at what they termed the "inability or failure" of the miners to focus their facts in the wage discussion.

Last Man's Club Is Now Down To Four Members

Three Of Original 34 Members At Forty-First Reunion Of Minnesota Veterans.

Stillwater, Minn., July 21 (AP).—Drinking a toast of water to their departed comrades, three members of the Last Man's Club ended their forty-first annual reunion here today with a prayer that they might meet again one year hence.

The club was organized in 1884 by thirty-four members of B Company, First Minnesota Volunteers, who purchased a bottle of wine with the proviso that its last survivor was to drink a toast to those who had died before him. Only four members survive—Peter Hall, 86, of Atwater, Minn.; Charles M. Lockwood, 82, Chamberlain, S. D.; John S. Goff, 81, St. Paul, and Emil Graff, 84, St. Cloud, Fla. The latter was absent because of illness.

Bee Stings Mother Killing Baby In Arms

Insect Strikes Woman On Breast And Infant's Death Results.

Peterboro, Ontario, July 21 (AP).—The shock of a bee sting transmitted from Mrs. Ethel Chapman, of Chilliwack, B. C., to her 3-month-old baby, which she was nursing, caused its death, Dr. Cronk, of Belleville, said today.

Immediately after the bee had stung the mother's breast the child lost consciousness and died within an hour.

Bloody Herrin Gives Up Pistols For Bibles At Call Of Preacher

Mississippi Evangelist, Called By Cincinnati Jew, Brings Klan And Flaming Circle To Peace While Gunmen Hit Sawdust Trail.

[*From a Staff Correspondent.*]

Herrin, Ill., July 21. — Peace has come to Herrin and "Bloody Williamson." From the belts of Herrin's two-gun men weapons no longer dangle. Hands that scarcely loosed their grip on pistol butts for almost three years now clasp leather-covered Bibles. Herrin, in short, has hit the sawdust trail.

Quiet reigns at the mouths of Herrin's cavernous coal mines. Machine guns no longer are mounted on coal cars. No raiding parties of union miners storm the pits, bind the guards and shoot them down in batches of four to the bloodthirsty cheers of a frenzied populace.

Love Displaces Strife.

The white robes of the klan have been put aside; the fiery cross is never lighted; the flaming circle has been allowed to burn itself out. The bloody raids on bootleg caches have ceased; the steady tramp of military forces no longer resounds through Herrin's streets. Peace, friendship and brotherly love now abide where only a short while since murder, assault, conspiracy and internecine strife held full sway. The lion has lain down with the lamb.

Strangely enough, this new tranquillity was heralded by the echoing reports when the pistols of S. Glenn Young, klan leader and free-lance dry raider, and his arch-enemy, Ora Thomas, deputy sheriff, spat fire in a cigar shop last January and both men fell dead.

Invoke Old-Time Religion.

At the funeral service for Thomas, the Rev. John Meeker, pastor of the Presbyterian Church in Herrin, said: "There is great need for the old-time religion. It is the only thing that will heal and save Herrin."

The words were read in Cincinnati by George Greenwood, an advertising salesman. Greenwood is a Jew, but he had been following with interest the evangelistic services then being conducted by Howard S. Williams, a layman, in Mississippi. He pondered the words of the Rev. Mr. Meeker and then reached the conclusion that Mr. Williams was the man to bring back the old-time religion and save Herrin.

Opposed By Elements.

Greenwood went to Herrin and made arrangements to have Mr. Williams conduct revival meetings in the town in May. Shortly before the arrival of the layman-evangelist a huge tent was erected. Two days later a terrific storm carried it away. Additional funds were borrowed and within a week a tabernacle that would seat 4,000 persons had been built.

Mixed feelings were aroused in Herrin by the news of the coming of the evangelist. Some persons thought it was just another attempt to "clean-up" Herrin, which was the avowed purpose of Young when he first swooped down on the town with his band of volunteer raiders. Others feared that it was a covert move on the part of the klan and that the klan would dominate the services. Others asked the question with cynical smiles: If State and country officials and detachments of troops can do nothing for Herrin, what good purpose will be served by bringing this evangelist here?

Talked Straight From The Shoulder.

But Mr. Williams came. Neither klansmen nor bootleggers interfered with him. Talking straight from the shoulder the evangelist did not hesi-

(Continued on Page 7, Column 8.)

GENERAL WAR SOON ON HIGH LIVING COST

Concerted Nation-Wide Action Will Take Form Of Appeal To President November 15.

INCREASE LAID TO TARIFF

Government Statistics Showing Rise In 51 Cities Will Be Submitted To Coolidge.

Washington, July 21 (Special).—The revival of the campaign to protest against high cost of living is set for November 15. Nation-wide organizations will appeal to Washington, filing with the President official figures, by the Department of Labor, to show that, since the enactment of the Fordney-McCumber tariff act, food, clothing and housing costs have increased materially, until now they are approaching wartime marks.

Statistics at the Bureau of Labor show a steady climb in living-cost figures for the last three years. In fifty-one American cities the cost of food and clothing has climbed steadily from 1922 to 1925, the increase each year having been marked.

Now Increases Show Up.

From May, 1924, to May, 1925, the per cent. increase in retail cost of food was as follows:

Atlanta, 8.1 per cent.; Baltimore, 9.6; Birmingham, 10.3; Boston, 4.1; Bridgeport, 4.7; Buffalo, 6.8; Butte, 4.7; Charleston, S. C., 7.2; Chicago, 5.6; Cincinnati, 6.3; Cleveland; 8.4; Columbus, 5.8; Dallas, 8.2; Denver, 6.5; Detroit, 8.3; Fall River, 4.5; Houston, Texas, 12.1; Indianapolis, 4.7; Jacksonville, 7.9; Kansas City, 7.9; Little Rock, 9.1; Los Angeles, 6.7; Louisville, 12.6; Manchester, 3.7; Memphis, 9.4; Milwaukee, 4.1; Minneapolis, 7.8; Mobile, 8.8; Newark, 4.0; New Haven, 2.9; New Orleans, 7.3; New York, 4.6; Norfolk, 9.1; Omaha, 7.9; Peoria, 8.8; Philadelphia, 6.6; Pittsburgh, 6.5; Portland, Maine, 4.0; Portland, Ore., 7.1; Providence, 4.2; Richmond, 7.8; Rochester, 5.7; St. Louis, 7.5, St. Paul, 7.4; Salt Lake City, 13.2; San Francisco, 9.0; Savannah, 10.3; Scranton, 7.6; Seattle, 8.1; Springfield, Ill., 5.9, and Washington, 7.5. This makes an average of 7.2 in the fifty-one cities.

Illustrations Given.

In 1922, when the Fordney-McCumber tariff bill was passed, a chuck roast cost $.197 per pound, but now it costs $.221; a dollar would have bought 5.1 pounds in 1922, but in 1925 it buys 4.5. Pork chops were selling for $.33 in 1922 and they are $.36 now. In 1922 lard cost $.17, now it is $.226.

The rise in bread and bread materials had been perceptible. In 1922 bread sold at $.0876 per pound; now it brings $.094. A dollar purchased 11.5 pounds in 1922 and buys 10.6 now. Flour advanced more rapidly and is selling for $.061 per pound, against $.051 in 1922.

During the first year after the passage of the Fordney-McCumber act there was greater increase in the cost of living than in any other year except during the World War.

Wheat flour rose with a bound after President Coolidge increased the import duty on wheat in 1924. It had reached a low mark after the war.

DARROW REPLIES TO QUIZ BY BRYAN

Answers Questions Former Secretary Of State Intended To Ask At Scopes Trial.

DOUBTS BIBLE TRUTHS

Declares He Has Been Unable To Find Any Proof Of Immortality Of Soul.

Dayton, Tenn., July 21 (Special).—William Jennings Bryan and Clarence Darrow continued their discussion of the Bible and religion today, but with positions reversed. Bryan today wrote the questions and Darrow supplied the answers.

They were made public simultaneously, in accordance with an agreement made after the Scopes trial was brought to an end without Bryan having had a chance to put Darrow and the other defense lawyers on the stand.

Wants Better Description Of God.

The questions by Bryan and the answers by Darrow follow:

Q.—Do you believe in God as described in the Bible?

A.—I do not know any description of God in the Bible, though we are informed in one part of it that He is a spirit. If Mr. Bryan would describe what he means by God I could probably tell whether I believe in his God. The question of what was meant by the word was directly put to counsel for the State, and one of them answered that God was made in the image of man. I do not believe in that kind of a God. As to the origin of the universe and what is back of it I do not pretend to know. I haven't the intimate acquaintance with it that Mr. Bryan says he has.

Much Of Value In Bible.

Q.—Do you believe the Bible is the revealed will of God, inspired and trustworthy?

A.—I think there is much value in the Bible. I do not believe that it was written or inspired by God. I believe it should be taken as every other book and that the portions in it that are sublime like such portions of every other great book might by a figure of speech be called inspired. I might even say this of Mr. Bryan's "In His Image," if I could find any such portion in it.

Q. Do you believe in the supernatural Christ, foretold in the Old Testament and revealed in the New Testament?

A.—I do not believe that any supernatural Christ was foretold in the Old Testament or revealed in the New. I believe that the Christ that was prophesied in the Old Testament was a great Jew who should deliver the Jews from their physical bondage and nothing else.

Does Not Believe In Miracles.

Q.—Do you believe in the miracles recorded in the Old and New Testaments?

Q.—If you believe in some, but not all of them, please name a few of those which you accept and those you reject with reasons for same.

Q. Do you believe that Christ was conceived of the Holy Ghost and born of the Virgin Mary, as recorded in Matthew and Luke?

Q. Do you believe that Christ rose

(Continued on Page 2, Column 3.)

SCOPES GUILTY JURY DECIDES IN THREE MINUTES

Case Appealed To State Supreme Court, Which Meets September 1.

LOVE FEAST MARKS CONCLUSION OF TRIAL

End Proves Most Amazing Part Of Proceedings At Dayton.

By HENRY M. HYDE.

Dayton, Tenn., July 21.—"Guilty!"—In three minutes.

Nothing is more surprising about this amazing trial of John T. Scopes for violating the Tennessee Anti-evolution law than its end.

There are no final arguments to the jury. Clarence Darrow, chief of defense counsel, his arms crossed behind his gallused shoulders, tells the twelve men that, under the rulings of the court, there is nothing for them to do but find his client guilty. Brawny "Tom" Stewart, the District Attorney-General, adds that Darrow would plead guilty save that such a plea would make it impossible to appeal the case.

Five-Minute Charge By Judge.

Judge Raulston reads a five-minute charge to the jury. If Scopes taught the theory that man descended from the lower animals they are to find him guilty.

In three minutes the jury returns from its conference room, with the agreed verdict in the hands of Capt. Jack Thompson, the big Methodist foreman, who "don't work at it much."

Young Scopes, slight of figure in his white shirt and gray flannel trousers, stands before the bar and tells Judge Raulston: "I feel I have been convicted under an unjust law. I shall continue to fight the law. I cannot do otherwise and be true to what I believe."

Judge Fixes Fine At $100.

Judge Raulston fixes his fine at $100. Notice of appeal is given and bail, pending the hearing by the Supreme Court, is fixed at $500, which is furnished by THE EVENING SUN, of Baltimore.

That is all—except for a farewell talkfest, in which almost everybody in the courtroom stands up on a chair and voices his abiding love and affection for everybody else. In all the flow of sweet oil there are two slight injections of discordant liquid. One is a drop of poison distilled by Clarence Darrow and another some large and bitter tears shed by Colonel Bryan.

"For their courtesy," drawls Darrow, "I thank the counsel for the State"—he halts an instant and glances at Bryan—"from Tennessee," he concludes.

Bryan To Appeal To Press.

"I shall appeal to the press," says Colonel Bryan, rising—he has been deprived of his chance of cross-examining Darrow by Judge Raulston's ruling this morning reversing his decision of yesterday and expunging all of Bryan's testimony from the record—"I shall appeal to the press to tell the world the questions I should have asked Darrow. I have been pilloried as ignorant and a bigot. I ask the chance of showing the other side of the picture."

It is Attorney-General Stewart who is responsible for transforming the three-ringed circus and open-air vaudeville show of yesterday afternoon into the orderly legal proceeding of this morning. He was outraged at what the court allowed to go on under the trees on the Courthouse lawn Monday. Half a dozen times he tried to stop it while it was still under way, with the great crowd of two or three thousand people cheering the dog fight between Bryan and Darrow. When the shocking exhibition was finally over "Tom" Stewart was ready to throw up the case. He was determined that at least no such further performances should be permitted to make the courts of Tennessee ridiculous.

Judge Considered Bryan Victor.

It is fairly certain he had his hardest work to persuade Judge Raulston to stop the shambles. For last night, after the shocking show was over, Judge Raulston is quoted as saying that he considered Bryan had utterly vanquished Darrow, the champion of the devil. He may not have been quite alone in that belief, though it is certain that most of the big fundamentalist audience was saddened and disappointed by the showing made by the colonel. His often-admitted ignorance of many subjects left them gasping. A good many of them were certainly convinced that their mighty man is hollow. They admit as much.

Within the next forty days the defense lawyers will perfect their appeal to the State Supreme Court, which

WEATHER FORECAST
Showers and thunder storms today and tonight, followed by clearing and cooler tomorrow; much cooler tomorrow night.
Detailed Weather Report on Page 23.

THE SUN

CAUSES OF DEPRESSION IN THE WOOLEN TEXTILE TRADE.
—Page 2.

VOL. 179—NO. 113D | PRESS RUN WEDNESDAY {MORNING, 128,201 / EVENING, 126,674} 254,875 ‖ SUNDAY 192,283 | BALTIMORE, FRIDAY, SEPTEMBER 24, 1926. | Published every week-day by The A. S. Abell Company. Entered as second-class matter at Baltimore Postoffice. | 30 PAGES | 2 CENTS

MOORE HAVEN'S DEATHS BLAMED ON LAKE DYKES

Okeechobee Folk Petition President To Bar Such Drainage System.

EVERGLADES BOARD IGNORANT, IS CHARGE

Editor's Criticisims Lead People To Ask U. S. Inquiry Into Disaster.

By JOHN DORMAN.
Staff Correspondent of The Sun.

Okeechobee, Fla., Sept. 23. — The storm tragedy at Moore Haven was attributed to faulty drainage methods and not to the wrath of the hurricane in a charge made today by William Griflis, editor of the Okeechobee *News*. In a signed editorial Mr. Griffis said the great loss of life resulted solely because dykes were being used to drain portions of the lake.

Against the dykes, Mr. Griffis said, was banked a surging flood. Waves ate through the earthen dyke so rapidly that villages spread along in the lowland under shelter of the dykes had virtually no chance to escape.

Rapidity Of Flood.

One man reported that seeing a little water spurt over the dyke he turned and ran, but before he had gone a hundred feet the water was above his head.

A petition signed by eighty Okeechobee residents has been sent to President Coolidge. This asks the President to use his influence to prevent building of more such dykes and that Federal investigation into the Moore Haven disaster be made. The petition says that a large proportion of more than a hundred lines lost in the lake region apparently is traceable to a condition created by the Everglades drainage board, and that the petitioners believe the board lacks understanding of existing conditions.

Editor Quoted.

Canvas of the town shows that Mr. Griffis is not alone in his opinion. Many others said dykes should not have been used but that the whole level of the lake should have been reduced.

"A short time ago," the editorial said. "I expressed the opinion that present methods of draining the Everglades would result in a failure that would be known as Florida's folly. That has occurred and we are stunned by the toll of life.

"Twenty years ago the flood waters of Lake Okeechobee flowed down the Hicpochee Canal and into the Caloosahatchee River, as well as over the natural rim of earth surrounding the lake to the south. At that time there were no locks in the Hicpochee Canal to stop and bank up the flood waters of the lake, nor was there any dyke on the south end of the lake to make of the ground thus dried a gigantic potential reservoir for flood waters.

Would Lower Lake Level.

"I believe in drainage and I believe that Lake Okeechobee can be drained, but it can only be done safely by lowering the whole lake level. I am no engineer, but common sense tells me the lake cannot be drained by erecting a dyke across the southern end where formerly the water had a natural overflow.

"Had there been no dykes and had the locks in all canals been open to allow flood water to escape, instead of piling up, there would not have been such loss of life. The assistant engineer at Moore Haven has stated he felt partly to blame for the tragedy because he did not open the locks.

Perished In Water.

"The loss of life there was caused from drowning.

"Had the canal locks been open there would not have been a sufficient head of water to have caused a wave of the terrible power of the tidal wave that swept over Moore Haven. No doubt the great velocity of the wind would have caused property destruction, but there would have been few, if any, lives lost by drowning.

"The lock at Moore Haven is a subterfuge to protect the Caloosahatchee River Valley. It's inadequacy is clearly shown by the fact that floods in the river valley are as bad as they ever were before the lock was constructed.

Says Dykes Are Futile.

"The dykes on the south side of the lake are equally futile. The dyke was built to give protection to favored interests. But it has resulted in adding to the flooded waters on the opposite or northern and eastern shores of the lake, so that for four years farms have been under water which formerly were tilled each year, with never a fear of floods.

"The dyke has ruined more farms on the north shore than it has made possible on the southern. The locks built to protect navigation, and keep dry the lowlands beyond the shores of the lake, have proved the most dismal failure ever recorded against any engineer. The locks have not protected the lowlands and they have ruined the higher lands bordering along the lake shore.

Blames Closed Locks.

"Had the locks been left wide open since last July the lake would have been lowered three feet and the rain

(Continued on Page 2, Column 5.)

Dempsey Ducks Left Lead, Tries To Get Under Tunney's Guard

—Photo by Henry Miller.

REAR-ADMIRAL WM. F. FULLAM DIES IN CAPITAL

Aviation Authority Succumbs To Pneumonia At Age Of 70.

Washington, Sept. 23 (AP).—Rear-Admiral William F. Fullam (retired), former superintendent of the Naval Academy, died here today of complications following an attack of pneumonia. He was in his seventy-first year.

Championed Air Defense.

Rear-Admiral Fullam was considered one of the leading authorities in the country on aviation and was a strong advocate of a huge air fleet as a first line of defense. He sided with Col. William Mitchell in the latter's controversy with the War and Navy Departments and testified in his behalf at the court-martial proceedings.

Rear-Admiral Fullam delivered two addresses in Baltimore last year on the subject of air navigation. In one of these, before the Sons of the American Revolution at the Hotel Belvedere, he prophesied that wars of the future would be fought on land and in the air rather than on the sea. He predicted that every type of auxiliary craft, aside from the capital ship, will be so constructed in the future as to permit the landing and launching of airplanes on its decks.

Predicted Battleship's Doom.

In another talk, before the Men's Club of Christ Protestant Episcopal Church, Rear-Admiral Fullam declared America was behind nearly every other nation in passing laws for the control and regulation of air navigation. At the Mitchell court-martial he forecast the doom of the battleship.

Rear-Admiral Fullam saw service at many stations during his forty years in the navy. He was born at Pittsford, N. Y., October 20, 1855, was appointed to the Naval Academy from that State and was graduated at the head of his class in 1877. In 1885 he married Miss Mariana Winder Robinson, of Kennedyville, Md., daughter of Chief Justice Joseph L. Robinson of the Maryland Court of Appeals.

Saw Duty In World War.

From 1883 to 1904 he served as instructor in different departments and as head of the department of ordnance at the Naval Academy. During the Spanish-American War he served on the New Orleans. From 1907 to 1909 he was commandant of the naval training station at Newport, R. I., and in 1912 was in command of the Great Lakes Naval Training Station. In 1914 he was superintendent of the Naval Academy. He was appointed a rear-admiral the same year and the following year was made commander in chief of the Pacific reserve fleet. In 1916 and 1917 he served as commander of the patrol force of the Pacific fleet. He was senior officer in command in the Pacific when he was retired for age, October 20, 1919.

Admiral Fullam is survived by his widow and two daughters, Mrs. Rhoda Welch, of Seattle, Wash., and Mrs. Austin Sands, of Washington.

PILSUDSKI FOE ACCLAIMED BY WARSAW POLES

Police Break Up Demonstration—Adverse Sentiment Grows.

Warsaw, Poland, Sept. 23 (Special Wireless).—Growing sentiment against the semi-dictatorship of Minister of War Pilsudski broke forth last night in a vast demonstration of support for General Malczewski, who opposed Marshal Pilsudski during his revolution of last May.

When Malczewski arrived at the Vienna station here a crowd of nearly 4,000 persons greeted him with cries of "Down with Pilsudski" and carried him on shoulders to his automobile. They followed him to his hotel and continued the demonstration there until dispersed by the efforts of almost the entire Warsaw police force. Several were slightly wounded.

Army Pay Raise Opposed.

Today the anti-Pulsudski movement again showed its strength when the Finance Committee of the Polish Diet voted against the War Ministry budget for the last quarter of the present year. One of the principal items objected to was the sixty per cent. increase in army pay, which Pilsudski obtained for the men last July.

If the Diet supports the veto of the Finance Committee when it votes on the War Ministry budget in two or three days, the Government will be faced with the alternative of resigning or of dissolving the Diet and calling a new election.

Financial Scandal Bared.

Some circles here today compare the present situation with that which existed in Warsaw just before the outbreak of the May revolution. The War Office is far from popular here now and the papers have just revealed a financial scandal which has brought it into further disfavor.

The Frankopol factory, in which a number of Polish industrialists and a French airplane motor company are interested, has for the last three years received a total credit from the War Ministry of approximately $1,000,000 for future delivery of airplanes and motors. But no deliveries have yet been made and out of this credit only the factory has been built.

The credit is now exhausted, and as the War Ministry has refused to grant further credit, negotiations are going on for the sale of the factory to the Skoda Works, a Czecho-Slovakian munitions concern.

[Copyright, 1926, by the New York World.]

LEAVES $2,000,000 FOR SICK

Incapacitated Professional Men Benefit Under British Will.

London, Sept. 23 (AP).—The will of Samuel William Farmer, of Wiltshire, who left $2,000,000, provides that the entire estate shall be used for the benefit of upper middle, or professional, class people, who, through ill health or advancing years, are unable to earn a living.

Comment of Victor And Vanquished

Ringside, Sesqui-Centennial Stadium, Philadelphia, Sept 23 (AP).

TUNNEY.

Dempsey is a sportsman and a clean fighter all the way. He fought me fairly. There was no suspicion of a foul blow, and don't let anyone tell you that he can't hit. His blows were terrific.

I was not hurt because I was in perfect condition. I am sure I hurt him.

I have realized my life's ambition and as the champion I will carry myself in a manner gratifying to my friends and becoming a Marine and champion.

I was never in doubt, but after the first and second rounds I knew it was all over but the shouting of my friends.

Tunney said he wished to give credit where it was due in his development as the champion—the United States Marines.

DEMPSEY.

It's the old story. The better man won. I have no alibis. Give all the credit to Gene. He's a great champion.

I couldn't seem to get going, but I have no complaint to offer. I knew I was going to get licked some time and I am glad I lost the championship to an American.

I defeated all the foreigners they could send over. I think I have given the public a run for its money every time I started. I licked Firpo, I licked Carpentier.

If I had to lose I am glad that a fellow like Tunney won the championship. He is a credit to the sport, a clean, fine fellow.

Dempsey said he knew that he was licked as early as the eighth round.

The fallen champion, badly battered as he was, rushed from his corner after the announcement of the decision and embraced Tunney in the middle of the ring.

Wilbur In Philadelphia, But Not To Attend Fight

Navy Department Says He Goes To Deliver Address At Y. M. C. A.

Washington, Sept. 23 (Special).—Secretary of the Navy Wilbur was among 5,000 or more Washington residents who left the capital today for Philadelphia. Dispatches from the Quaker City stated ringside boxes were being reserved for Mr. Wilbur, Vice-President Dawes and Secretary of War Davis.

Rumors that the Navy Secretary was going to attend the fight gave rise to some comment, since he recently forbade a boxing exhibition at an entertainment given for the relief of widows and orphans of sailors at Norfolk after protests were made by church organizations. Reports from the Virginia city stated resentment against this action led to the beating of a figure of the Navy Secretary in effigy.

Inquiries as to whether Secretary Wilbur intended to attend the Dempsey-Tunney fight elicited the information, however, that he had an engagement to deliver a religious address before the Philadelphia Y. M. C. A.

Frank Tinney Ordered Arrested For Contempt

Comedian Must Go To Jail Unless He Pays Back Alimony And Sheriff's Fees.

New York, Sept. 23 (AP).—Frank Tinney, blackface comedian, was today adjudged in contempt and his arrest ordered by Justice Dike, in Brooklyn Supreme Court. Justice Dike ordered the Sheriff to place Tinney in jail unless he pays forthwith $1,400 on back alimony and Sheriff's fees and other costs.

Mrs. Edna Tinney, his divorced wife, told the court that although she had made personal appeals to Tinney, he had failed to pay her anything since July 24, and that she and her son were in desperate need. When granted a divorce Mrs. Tinney was awarded $200 a week alimony.

Cloudburst Inundates Middletown Valley

Three Escape Death As Waters Wash Auto From Road And Man Off Porch.

Middletown, Sept. 23 (Special).—The Middletown Valley was flooded tonight when the Catoctin creek rose more than fifteen feet, following a terrific cloudburst.

Three men narrowly escaped death or serious injury when the rushing waters flooded the new concrete road from Middletown into Virginia, covering the road with a torrent six feet deep, hurling an automobile containing two men from the road and washing another man from the porch of his summer cottage into a treetop.

First Crown In Decades Lost On Points.

Ringside, Sesqui-Centennial Stadium, Philadelphia, Sept. 23 (AP).—The heavyweight title passed tonight from Jack Dempsey to Gene Tunney on a judges' decision for the first time in nearly four decades of glove fighting.

Every previous champion, from the days of John L. Sullivan's reign, has passed from the throne by way of a knockout. Down through an illustrious line—Sullivan, Corbett, Fitzsimmons, Jeffries, Burns, Johnson and Willard—the count of ten has been tolled to effect every shift of the scepter.

Dempsey's downfall ended a seven-year reign that shared the distinction of being the longest on record. Johnson was the only other titleholder to rule for as long a period.

25,000 WOMEN SURROUND RING TO SEE BATTLE

Range From Society Leaders To Phone Girls And Stenographers.

Ringside Stadium, Philadelphia, Sept. 23 (Special).—If the interest shown by women in this Dempsey-Tunney tiff really indicated any breathless absorption in fistic combat, men would have cause to worry.

It would mean that woman would give up such gentle diversions as channel swimming and politics for a little serious study of right jabs and left hooks. Careers and marriage alike would be junked. In brief, the era of the two-fisted hard-hitting she-woman would be upon us.

25,000 At Fight.

But men don't need to be afraid—yet. Not even though hundreds upon hundreds of women battled their way into the stadium tonight. Twenty-five thousand was the guess made by one of the men at Rickard's headquarters, although he had no definite basis for the figures. Be that as it may, it is certain women never before turned out in such large numbers for a prize fight.

Women of all sorts, from all ranks of society. Alice Roosevelt Longworth, whose favorite fights are usually the verbal battles of Congress. Mrs. Gifford Pinchot, another astute politician. Miss Anne Morgan, daughter of the late J. Pierpont Morgan, who promoted a boxing match herself once in the name of charity. Screen and stage stars galore, including Norma Talmadge and Mrs. Arthur Hammerstein, the former Dorothy Dalton. Mrs. Hanford MacNider, wife of the Assistant Secretary of War. School teachers and stenographers also were present.

Few Rabid Fans.

But, with the exception of a few really rabid women fans, they didn't come to see the fine points of prize fighting. They didn't come even because they wanted to see what they hoped would be the most thrilling ring battle in sports history.

They came for a much simpler reason. It's done. The tendency of the last ten years to make prize fighters fashionable, a tendency marked by no great growth hitherto despite the impetus given by the Walker boxing laws and Rickard's big bout sprouted overnight. From the ringside seats to the uttermost regions, the huge stadium was dotted with women wearing—but that's another story.

Variety In Costumes.

Lack of precedent as to what the well-dressed woman wears to a fight caused a lot of confusion. Left to themselves to decide. Women concluded, variously, that, as a place to parade fall wardrobes, a prize fight was on a par with:

A—Opening night of the opera.
B—A football game.
C—Spring house cleaning.

Until Paris settles the question once

(Continued on Page 14, Column 6.)

TUNNEY IS NEW CHAMPION; WINS DEMPSEY'S CROWN IN BATTLE THAT GOES LIMIT

Ex-Marine, Before 130,000 Fans, Who Paid $2,000,000, Dethornes Heavyweight King, Who Had Ruled Seven Years

JACK SEEKS RETURN MATCH; GENE REPORTED AS WILLING

Challenger In Sesqui Bout Outboxes, Outfights And Outgenerals Foe, Who Is Far From Fighter Who Slugged Way To Top.

$750,000 Purse Offered For Return Match

Los Angeles, Sept. 23 (AP).—A. T. Jergins and J. R. McKinnie, Long Beach oil operators, tonight announced they had telegraphed Jack Dempsey, former heavyweight champion, and Gene Tunney, the new titleholder, that they would hang up a $750,000 purse for a return fight between the pair to be held in an open-air arena near Los Angeles before January 30, 1927. If the offer is accepted they said they would post $100,000 at once to insure the match.

An Associated Press dispatch from Philadelphia last night said Dempsey wanted a return match with Tunney. His handlers were quoted as saying Tunney had agreed.

By GRANTLAND RICE.

Sesqui-Centennial Stadium, Philadelphia, Sept. 23.—Gene Tunney, the fighting ex-Marine, is the new heavyweight champion of the world.

In the presence of 130,000 people, who sat through a driving rainstorm in Philadelphia's big Sesqui-Centennial Stadium, Tunney gave Dempsey one of the worst beatings any champion ever took. He not only outpointed Dmepsey in every one of the ten rounds but the challenger hammered the champion's face almost out of shape.

DEMPSEY'S LEFT EYE IS CLOSED.

It was like nothing human when the tenth round ended.

Dempsey's left eye was entirely closed and there was a deep opening under his right eye. The falling champion was bleeding at both mouth and nose.

By a queer turn of fate he presented almost exactly the same ghastly sight at Philadelphia that Jess Willard had seven years before at Toledo.

He was beaten every bit as badly, although he was never knocked from his feet.

TUNNEY MEETS DEMPSEY'S RUSHES.

Tunney fought one of the most surprising fights of his career. With a pouring rain beating down on the ring, which left the footing slippery and treacherous, Tunney met Dempsey's wild savage rushes with stiff lefts and rights to the face. These jabs and punches were delivered from short range and carried terrific power. They cut Dempsey's face into a flutter of crimson ribbons.

They threw him off his balance and left him dazed and bewildered. Tunney appeared extremely confident from the start and he fought with the same confidence to the end of the battle.

FIRST SHOCK COMES IN OPENING ROUND.

The first shock to which the record-breaking crowd of more than 130,000 was treated came in the first round. This record crowd, which had paid over $2,000,000 to see the contest, saw a waning, fading champion before them before the first chapter in the new book had been written.

They saw the old champion come on with his same old savage attack, but after one or two furious rushes he blew up quickly and had to rest. While he was taking these rests Tunney came to him and simply knocked his face lopsided. Dempsey made at least five terrific charges, trying to end the fight in one punch, but as Tunney weathered each, a wan and listless champion had to back away to recuperate.

Tunney fought a great fight, but it was quite evident that when it came to a matter of pressure Dempsey had blown completely. Even when he crowded Tunney into a corner he had none of the old steam which formerly carried him to victories in the past.

Dempsey Lands Only Three Blows.

In the course of the entire fight Dempsey landed only three full punches on the much more clever boxer and none of these did any damage worth speaking of. A smashing right hook to the body and a left hook to the jaw plainly shook Tunney, but in each case he recovered so quickly that he was on top of Dempsey, jabbing him with a straight left hook to the face and hard rights to the nose and jaw.

There were three occasions during the contest when Tunney landed from five to seven clean punches with both hands without taking anything in return. As the rain-soaked crowd saw Tunney pass the fifth round far in the lead, they began to see a new heavyweight champion of the world.

Jack's Rushes Slow Up.

The excitement increased as the old champion's rushes became slower and more futile and his face began to swell as if some one had painted red oranges on either cheek. From the fifth round on they saw Dempsey's rushes take on a less aggressive part.

In the last three rounds he was peering at Tunney through a half-open eye. Only those who saw him can realize what an inhuman spectacle his face was. He was the gory and unsightly specter of Jess Willard at the end of the third round.

Gene Tunney fought his way to the

(Continued on Page 14, Column 1.)

THE WEATHER
Fair tonight and Saturday, colder tonight. lowest about 30 degrees; moderate westerly winds.

THE EVENING SUN

FINANCIAL
CLOSING STOCKS

VOL. XXXIV—NO. 29. PRESS RUN YESTERDAY {MORNING, 128,752 / EVENING, 131,641} 260,393 || SUNDAY 197,815 BALTIMORE, FRIDAY, NOVEMBER 19, 1926. Published every week-day by The A. S. Abell Company. Entered as second-class matter at Baltimore Postoffice. 62 PAGES. PRICE TWO CENTS.

EIGHT DEAD IN OIL-SHIP EXPLOSION SCORE HURT AT SPARROWS POINT DOCK

SIMPSON RESTS HIS CASE MINUS MYSTERY WOMAN

"Mrs. S," Who Wrote Him She Was In Lane, Fails To Show Up.

DETECTIVE MAKES COMICAL WITNESS

Dr. Hall's Sister Disappoints Crowd Expecting Vengeful Words.

[*By the United Press.*]

Somervile, N. J., Nov. 19.—The State today completed its case against Mrs. Frances Stevens Hall, Willie and Henry Stevens, charged with the murder of the Rev. Edward Wheeler Hall and Mrs. Eleanor Mills, and rested its case at 1.55 P. M.

The prosecution completed its case after Inspector Underwood, of the State police, had been perfunctorily questioned in regard to statements to newspaper men.

Way Cleared For Defense Case.

"That's our case," said Alexander Simpson, prosecutor.

"I understand the State has rested, then?" queried Robert McCarter, of defense counsel.

"Yes, we rest," reiterated Simpson, and the way was cleared for immediate beginning of the defense's testimony.

Mystery Woman Disappoints.

Simpson rested his case without having procured the testimony of the mysterious "Mrs. S.," of Brooklyn, who had written him that she was in De Russey's lane on the night of the murder with a male companion. She had been reluctant to reveal her identity, but Simpson had hoped up to the last moment that she might show up at the trial.

Dr. Hall's Sister On Stand.

For the first time since the trial began a member of the immediate family of the Rev. Dr. Hall has come to the witness stand.

And that witness today spoke but four words as a direct contribution to the State's evidence.

The witness was Mrs. Theodore Bonner, a sister of the dead rector. She is a rather attractive woman of middle age.

When asked if she attended her brother's wedding, she said "Yes." Then she was asked:

"Did you see Henry Stevens there?"

"I don't remember."

Courtroom Disappointed.

The courtroom was eager when Mrs. Bonner was called, believing that the spectacle of a sister, speaking out in vengeance for her brother's death, might follow. But the courtroom was disappointed.

Cancer Reported.

Today's session of the trial opened with Miss Barbara Tough, Scottish maid in the Hall home, recalled to the stand.

Dr. Hall's Razor Figures Again.

"How long were you a servant in the Hall home after the murder?" asked Prosecutor Alexander Simpson.

"Until February, 1923."

"Did you ever see the straight, old-fashioned razor used by the rector after the latter was murdered?"

She Denies She Used Razor.

"I don't know."

On cross-examination Senator Case, of the defense, asked:

"You never used the razor, did you?"

The Scottish woman blushed.

"No," she said.

The State has contended that Dr. Hall's razor might have been used to cut the throat of Mrs. Eleanor Mills.

Inspector Underwood Testifies.

Inspector John J. Underwood, of Jersey City, was called to the stand.

Underwood, who was put in charge of the murder investigation on August 8 this year, testified in regard to the calling card of Dr. Hall found near the

[Continued On Page 2, Column 3]

GOOD EVENING on this page in earlier editions will be found on Page 10.

HENRY M. HYDE'S daily article is printed on Page 8.

Airplane View Of Burning Tanker Made 15 Minutes After Blast

This photo of the oil tank ship Mantilla, burning in drydock at Sparrows Point, was made from an airplane less than fifteen minutes after the explosion which preceded the blaze. A number of workmen were killed and many injured by the explosion, which blew out both sides of the vessel.

"I AM READY TO DIE," MRS. GIBSON SAYS

Police "Hounded Me," But "I Told The Truth," She Affirms.

[*By the United Press.*]

Jersey City, N. J., Nov. 19.—"I have told the truth and am ready to die," Mrs. Jane Gibson, star witness in the Hall-Mills murder trial, said in a dictated statement from her cot in the Jersey City Hospital today.

Mrs. Gibson, who was taken to the trial yesterday and from a bed in the courtroom accused the three defendants of the murder, feels she is dying, she told doctors, and wanted her statement put on paper to justify herself to the world.

It was reliably reported today that she has cancer, that an operation is impossible and that her death within six months is probable.

The statement, signed by Mrs. Gibson, said:

> I have told the truth, now let justice take its course. I told it four years ago, but people did not and would not listen to me. It seemed to them as if everyone connected with the case was looking for money. They tried to poison my stock and burn down my home; they foreclosed the mortgage on my property right after the 1923 grand jury affair, and I was compelled to sell forty-one acres of land to clear the mortgage on the other twenty for less than I paid for it.
>
> **Police "Hounded Me."**
>
> A few days after I sold the land the man I sold it to was offered twice what he had paid for it. When

[Continued On Page 2, Column 1]

MEXICO BELIEVED HINTING SHE MAY SEVER RELATIONS

Angry Editorial Appears In Paper Said To Have Semi-Official Status.

[*By the United Press.*]

Mexico City, Nov. 19.—An angry editorial in which the newspaper *Excelsior* discussed United States and Mexican relations with Nicaragua today was interpreted by some observers to have semi-official status and to be the prelude to severance of diplomatic relations between Mexico and the United States.

So far there have been no official statements regarding the United States allegation that Mexicans have violated their international obligations by assistin the Liberal revolutionary party in Nicaragua, except Foreign Minister Saenz's denials that there had been any official Mexican assistance afforded the revolutionists.

Treaty Called Shameful.

"The author of the shameful Bryan-Chamorro treaty," said the *Excelsior*,

[Continued On Page 2, Column 5]

Queen Marie's Article

Another of the series of articles entitled "My Impressions of America," by her Majesty Queen Marie of Rumania, is printed in THE EVENING SUN today.

It will be found—

On Page 31

The Evening Sun Today Is Printed In Three Sections

RUM-CARRYING AIRPLANE FOUND AT FORD AIRPORT

Auto Maker, Indignant, Asks State Police To Investigate.

[*By the United Press.*]

Detroit, Mich., Nov. 19.—At the personal request of Henry Ford a sweeping investigation was launched here today into an alleged aerial rum-running ring, believed to have used his airport at Dearborn as a stopping-off place between Canada and interior States.

The investigation was prompted by seizure of a liquor-laden airplane at the airport early today and the arrest of P. W. Rodrick, alleged pilot of the craft, held on a charge of illegal possession and transportation. The seized

[Continued On Page 2, Column 4]

BOWIE RESULTS

FIRST RACE—Six furlongs.
Fabie, 103 (Peternell), $20.90, $12.10 and $5.70 ... 1
Greenback, 110 (Richards), $5.50 and $5.40 ... 2
Complaisance, 110 (Stevens), $5.70 ... 3
Time—1.19 1-5.
Scratched—Rig Jo, Rural Gossip, Hog King, Madlyn, Valdes, Red Light, Joan Shirley.

SECOND—For 3-year-olds and up; six and a half furlongs.
Knockany, 113 (Peternell), $3.60, $2.80 and $2.80 ... 1
Munge, 114 (Chalmers), $8.70 and $6 ... 2
Te Bal, 102 (Philips), $5 ... 3
Scratched—Darby, Courser, Lafonte, Margaret St. L., Aci, Everglade, Ten Sixty, Danger Signal, Immolator, Miss Rosedale.

THIRD—For 3-year-olds and up, six and one-half furlongs.
Kathleen Crosby, 110 (Church), $17.40, $6.80 and $5.40 ... 1
Saratoga Maje, 114 (Abel), $3.70 and $3.70 ... 2
Maxiva, 111 (Richards), $6.70 ... 3
Time—1.22 2-5.
Scratched—Glenister II, Briggs Buchanan, Grace A., Old Trick, Dawn Maker, Flying Al.

LEXINGTON RESULTS

FIRST RACE—Six furlongs.
[illegible] Schooler, 107 (Lynch), $8.40, $4 and $3.60 ... 1
Belfast, 102 (Watson), $5 and $4.20 ... 2
Meddling Seth, 107 (Dale), $6.60 ... 3
Time—1.12 4-5.
Scratched—Jedburgh Abbey.

CASUALTIES In Ship Blast

The following is an incomplete list of those injured in the ship explosion at Sparrows Point today:

JOHN HERGEL, 1514 Thames street.
WILLIAM WINCOPP, 523 South Bethel street.
MARTIN SABGINISKI, 28 Albemarle street.
ANTHONY HORTIK, 620 South Bond street.
WILLIAM BORKOFSKY, 723 South Bond street.
JOHN CARLSON, 211 South Eden street.
LARS LARSEN, second mate of the ship, burns on the faceand knee fractured.
LIND LESSEN, third mate, burns on the face and hands.
JULIUS HENDER, member of the crew, shoulder fractured.
ANDRE ANDERSON, another member of the crew.
HAROLD THOMPSON, burned on the hands.
SAMUEL PITTIT, 1112 North Bradford street.
CHESTER ROSTEN, 2400 Hudson street.
JOSEPH GEPHART, 424 South Seventh street, burned on face, wrist fractured.
ARUM WALTON, 10 West East street, Sparrows Point, face burned and fingers mangled so badly they had to be amputated.
CHRIS FISHER, Dundalk.

She Craves Hangman's Job.

Montreal, Nov. 19.—Sheriff J. T. H. Regan, of Hamilton, Ont., has received a communication from a woman asking permission to hang Joe Barty, who murdered Mrs. Nancy Cook last summer by hitting her on the head with a hammer. The Sheriff says that he will not consider the offer, although he is having some difficulty in finding an executioner. Barty is to be hanged on December 23.

10 TO 15 OTHER WORKERS BELIEVED DEAD IN HOLD AS FIREMEN FIGHT FLAMES

Fireboats And Special Oil Fire-Fighting Apparatus Called From Baltimore To Help Check Spread Of Blaze.

TWO BODIES RECOVERED FROM WATER; STEEL FRAGMENTS BLOWN INTO AIR

Hundred Workmen And Members Of Crew Aboard Vessel When Blast Blows Out Sides And Flames Follow.

Twenty-one men were killed and many more injured in the oil ship explosion and fire at Sparrows Point, it was declared late today by Marine officials who said they had inspected the ship. This information was not confirmed by police or Sparrows Point officials.

Eight men are known to be dead, ten to fifteen others are believed to have been killed and a score or more were hurt, some so seriously that their recovery is doubtful, following an explosion and fire aboard the oil tank ship Mantilla in dry dock at Sparrows Point today. Bodies of the eight known dead are at the morgue.

Approximately one hundred men, including shipyard employes and members of the ship's crew, were aboard the vessel when the explosion blew out the sides of the boat and shook buildings in Sparrows Point, more than a mile away.

Two Bodies Found In Water.

The bodies of some of the dead were blown into the water. Two corpses were found floating more than fifty feet from the wrecked Mantilla.

Practically all of the vessel's steel decking was ripped up. A twenty-five-foot steel girder from her interior was found on another dry dock several hundred feet away.

Another Vessel Damaged.

The Mount Clay, a steamship in an adjacent dry dock, was damaged in several places by pieces of steel hurled by the plast.

Parts of the bodies of some of the victims lay on the wrecked tanker's deck while firemen were fighting the flames.

Some of the braces holding the ship upright in the dock were knocked down by the blast. Firemen replaced them to prevent the vessel from toppling over.

The firemen said that only one of the ship's holds had exploded and that there was danger during the next twenty-four hours of another blast.

Scores Slightly Hurt.

More than 500 workmen in the shops near the dry docks were dismissed for the day. he explosion had shattered the windows in the shops, and officials decided it was too cold for the men to continue work.

Scores of men were slightly injured, but no record was made of their cases. Their hurts were dressed at the dispensary, and they were dismissed to make way for the more seriously wounded.

Members of the chip's crew who were hurt were taken to the Marine Hospital.

Checks May Identify Them.

Plant officials said an attempt would be made to identify the dead by means of their metal employes' checks. All of the dead recovered were white men.

A member of the chip's crew of thirty-six said eight of the crew were in the engine room and three in the pumphouse when the explosion occurred.

He said he did not know whether they escaped. After the ship had unloaded, it was said, about 1,500 gallons of oil remained in the tanks.

The seamen expressed the belief that an accumulation of gas in the center tank was set off by a spark.

They said the explosion seemed to center its force amidships.

The dispensary at the shipyards was overtaxed in caring for the injured and calls were made to Baltimore hospitals to look after those hurt.

Land and water fire fighting apparatus were sent from Baltimore to assist in fighting the fire which followed the explosion.

Workers Feared Still Inside.

Firemen fought hard to extinguish the flames because of the belief that many workers were still in the vessel.

A check was being made to determine the whereabouts of every man that was aboard the vessel.

Police were unable to learn the exact number hurt.

The explosion occurred at 11.45 o'clock, a few minutes before

WEATHER FORECAST.
Partly cloudy, slightly warmer today; cloudy tomorrow; moderate southeast and south winds.
Weather Report—Part 1, Section 3, Col. 1.

THE SUN

REORGANIZATION OF PROHIBITION FORCES AND PLANS FOR NEW ANTI-SMUGGLING CAMPAIGN.
Page 14.

VOLUME 27—NO. 21D | PRESS RUN SUNDAY, May 15, 1927. 200,372 | BALTIMORE, SUNDAY, MAY 22, 1927 | Published every Sunday bu The A. S. Abell Company. Entered as second-class matter at Baltimore Postoffice. | 144 PAGES | PRICE IN CITY AND SUBURBS 5¢

LINDBERGH IS IN PARIS

LINDBERGH DESCRIBES HOP; SAYS HE COULD HAVE MADE ANOTHER THOUSAND MILES

Trouble Expected Over Newfoundland Failed To Develop, But He Encountered Wide Area Of Sleet And Snow—Saw Ship Lights At Night.

FLIGHT ALTITUDES VARIED FROM TEN TO 10,000 FEET

One And a Half Sandwiches His Food For Entire Trip. Clad In Ambassador Herrick's Pajamas He Talks Of Experiences.

Paris, May 22 (Special Cable).—Captain Lindbergh was discovered at the American Embassy at 2.30 o'clock this (Sunday) morning. Attired in a pair of Ambassador Herrick's pajamas the aviator sat on the edge of the bed and talked of the flight.

At the last moment Ambassador Herrick had dismissed the plans of the reception committee and by unanimous consent took Lindbergh to the Embassy in the Place d'Iena. The staff of American doctors who had arrived at the Le Bourget field early to administer to an exhausted aviator found instead a bright-eyed smiling youth who refused to be examined and said:

"Oh, don't bother. I am all right."

ASKS FOR BATH AND GLASS OF MILK

"I'd like to have a bath and a glass of milk. I would feel better then," said Lindbergh when the Ambassador asked him what he desired. The bath was drawn immediately and in less than five minutes this amazing youth had disrobed in one of the Embassy guest rooms, taken his bath and was out again drinking a bottle of milk and eating a roll.

"There's no use worrying about me, Mr. Ambassador," instead Lindbergh when Mr. Herrick and members of his staff wanted him to be examined and to go to bed immediately. It was apparent the young man was too full of his experiences to want sleep and he sat on the bed and chatted with the Ambassador, and Mr. Herrick's son and daughter-in-law. By this time newspapermen who had been chasing the American airman from one false scent to another had finally tracked him to the Embassy.

DIDN'T CARE TO SLEEP

In a body they descended upon the Ambassador, who received them in the salon and informed them he had just left Lindbergh with strict instructions to go to sleep. As Mr. Herrick was talking with them the correspondents his son-in-law came downstairs and said Lindbergh had rung and announced he didn't care to go to sleep just yet and aould be glad to see the newspaper men for a few minutes. They were led upstairs. In a blue-and-gold room with a soft light glowing sat the conqueror of the Atlantic.

He immediately stood up and held out his hands. "Sit down, please," urged every one in the same voice, but Lindbergh only smiled in his famous boyish smile and said: "It's almost as easy to stand up as it is to sit down."

NO TROUBLE OVER NEWFOUNDLAND

Questions were fired from all sides about the trip across, but Lindbergh seemed to dismiss them all with brief nonchalant answers:

"I expected trouble over Newfoundland because I had been warned the situation there was unfavorable, but I got over that hazard with no trouble whatsoever. "However, it wasn't easy going. I had sleet and snow for over one thousand miles. Sometimes it was too high to fly over and sometimes too low to fly under, so I just had to go through it as best I could.

"I flew as low as ten feet in some places and as high as ten thousand in others. I passed no ships in the day time, but at night I saw the lights of several ships, the night being bright and clear."

"NODDED" SEVERAL TIMES

Everyone wanted to know if he had been sleepy on the voyage.

"I didn't really get what you might call downright sleepy," he said, "but I think I sort of nodded several times. In fact, I could have flown half that distance again.

"I had enough fuel left to go a thousand miles I think —certainly five hundred, although I had no time to examine fuel tanks, the crowds at Le Bourget were so terrific. If it hadn't been for soldiers and two French aviators I think I might have been injured by the wild enthusiasts in the throng. Anyway I paid no attention to economy of fuel during the voyage."

Mr. Herrick then asked the young aviator if he had any difficulty.

(Continued on Page 3, Column 6)

"Well, Here We Are!"

C.D. CHAMBERLIN CALLS OFF HIS PARIS FLIGHT

Attempt In Bellanca Plane Is "Indefinitely Postponed."

Roosevelt Field, N.Y., May 21 (AP).—The Paris flight of Clarence D. Chamberlin was "indefinitely postponed" tonight, when friends persuaded him not to make an immediate attempt.

Chamberlin had announced that he would take the hop-off tonight less than two hours after Charles Lindberg landed in Paris. He had his plane hauled to the runway and was telephoning officials for permission to use the runway when friends gathered about him to dissuade him.

May Give It Up Entirely.

They showed him that while weather was good tonight unfavorable conditions were predicted for tomorrow. Also Carl Schory, secretary of the contest committee of the National Aeronautical Society, was discovered to have gone to Washington, and it was said that the flight would not be official unless Schory sealed the barograph.

"All right, it's all off," Chamberlin said at length. "It's off indefinitely, and when we do take off it won't be for Paris in all probability. That has been done. We'll probably fly West instead of East. Perhaps Honolulu."

Shortly after Chamberlin had made his announcement, his plane had a narrow escape from destruction by fire. Gasoline spilled as it was being towed from Roosevelt Field to its hangar at Curtiss Field, caught fire and for a time threatened to spread to the plane.

Firemen rushed to the blaze, but when they arrived the gasoline fire had burned itself out. The plane was not damaged.

Gasoline that had been drained off formed a puddle and was believed to have been ignited by a cigarette.

Bellanca Breaks With Levine.

Coincident with Chamberlin's announcement that the flight was off, G. M. Bellanca, designer of the plane, announced complete severance of all relations with Charles Levine, head of the company which is backing the "Columbia" flight.

Bellanca attempted the role of peacemaker when dissension arose between Levine and Lloyd Bertaud, who was originally selected as navigator to fly with Chamberlin.

The Sun To Publish Lindbergh's Own Story.

By arrangement with the New York *Times*, THE SUN has obtained exclusive rights in Baltimore to Captain Lindbergh's own story of his flight across the Atlantic. This story is expected to be available for publication in THE SUN tomorrow morning.

Flyer's Triumph Stirs City To Enthusiastic Celebration

Demonstration Recalling Scenes Of Armistice Day Greets News Of His Success—State Guard Planes Present Circus Over Downtown Baltimore.

If all the world's a stage, Capt. Charles Lindbergh yesterday held, undisputed the center of that part which is Baltimore.

His successful non-stop flight from New York to Paris was celebrated with shrieking whistles, tolling bells, honking horns, hand clapping, shouts and soaring airplanes. Not since the World War armistice has the city shown such whole-hearted and united enthusiasm over any single event.

Five Hundred Hear Dispatch.

The news that the American flyer had arrived over Le Bourget flying field, near Paris, was read at 4.25 P.M. A few minutes later a dispatch, recording his safe landing at 4.21 P.M., Eastern standard time, was read to the crowd that had gathered in Sun Square. The news of his triumph spread quickly to distant parts of the city and everywhere and it was met with unusual demonstrations of feeling.

Even before the reading of the dispatch had been completed the bell in the dome of City Hall began to peal and as if its tones were a signal, whistles started their shrieking and horns their noise. The celebration was on in earnest and it lasted until supper bells rang and hunger called.

Under orders from Mayor Broening the City Hall bell was rung for five minutes. The bell started to ring at 4.30 P.M., eight minutes after the arrival of Captain Lindbergh in Paris on a signal given from The Evening Sun.

In virtually every city in the United States, according to dispatches, similar celebrations greeted the news of the success of the flight.

Nine Thousand Calls Received.

During the course of the day approximately 9,000 telephone calls for information concerning Captain Lindbergh were received at The Sun Building. Most of the inquirers used the pronoun "he" when referring to the flyer. The use of his name apparently seemed unnecessary—there were no other "he's"but Captain Lindbergh—and he held the center of the stage.

The day, however, did not pass without some misgivings. Baltimoreans, like the people of France in the unfortunate flight of Captail Nungesser and Captain Coli, snatched like 2 bass for a fly at false information broadcast throughout the city shortly after noon.

According to this information, Captain Lindbergh had already landed at Le Bourget Field. Noisy acclaim followed. Hundreds of shouting persons milled about the streets in the central part of the city. Office windows were opened and small pieces of paper thrown to the winds.

The central part of the city brought back memories of the false report of the Armistice in 1918. But in the case of Captain Lindbergh, as then, it became known that the rumor was unfounded. The premature celebrations halted and those who had taken part showed clearly that they resented being "fooled."

Similar false reports also caused demonstrations in New York and Lon-

(Continued on Page 3, Column 2.)

Log Of Lindbergh's Non-Stop Flight From New York To French Capital

(Baltimore Time.)

FRIDAY

6.52 A. M.—Left New York for Paris.
8.05 A. M.—Sighted over East Greenwich, R. I.
8.40 A. M.—Sighted over Halifax, Mass.
11.25 A. M.—Reported over Meteghan, Nova Scotia.
12.05 P. M.—Sighted over Springfield, Nova Scotia.
12.52 P. M.—Passed over Mulgrave, Nova Scotia.
3.00 P. M.—Sighted over Mainadieu, Nova Scotia, and started for Newfoundland.
6.15 P. M.—Passed over St. John's, Newfoundland, and put out over Atlantic for Ireland across 1,900 miles of open sea.

SATURDAY

7.10 A. M.—Cape Race, Newfoundland, receives wireless from Dutch schooner reporting Lindbergh was 500 miles off Irish coast.
8.50 A. M.—Sighted 100 miles off Ireland, London Press Association dispatch says.
9.00 A. M.—Reported over Valentia, Ireland, by Radio Corporation.
11.30 A. M.—Passes over Dingle Bay, Ireland, according to report from Belfast.
11.45 A. M.—Passed over Baltimore, County Cork, Ireland.
1.00 P. M.—Sighted off Plymouth, England.
2.00 P. M.—Arrives at French coast.
2.30 P. M.—Reported over Cherbourg, France.
4.21 P. M.—Arrives and lands safely at Paris.

Detroit, May 21 (AP).—Through tears of joy, Mrs. Evangeline Lodge Lindbergh, Spartan mother of an intrepid son, tonight expressed her relief that her boy, Capt. Charles Lindbergh, had arrived safely at the end of his daring flight from New York to Paris.

Mrs. Lindbergh plainly showed she had been under great strain, but her nerves did not give way.

"That's all that matters,"she said through tears that for the moment she could not restrain when told he had brought his big plane safely to earth at Le Bourget flying field, France.

Had Observed Rigid Silence.

Determined to have no share in the publicity that came to the youthful argonaut of the air, and to say nothing that could disturb or distract him while he prepared for his great adventure, Mrs. Lindbergh had observed a rigid silence since he hopped from the Pacific to the Atlantic Coast. A brief statement that she had every confidence in his ability to make the flight was all she permitted herself to say.

The epochal flight completed, however, she indicated fora moment that her confidence may have wavered after the take-off yesterday morning.

Decision Not Impulsive.

"How would anyone be confident," she replied to a question.

She then added:

"I know if it were possible for any pilot, given a good machine, to make the flight that he would."

Her son had been called "The Flying Fool,"but Mrs. Lindbergh made it plain she did not believe he had made an impulsive decision to fly across the Atlantic.

"He has always been cool, calm and collected,"she said. He was not of the daredevil type. Since he was a boy I have always permitted him to decide things for himself. He was taught to make his own decisions and abide by what he decided."

Leaves Career Up To Him.

Asked whether she wanted him to continue flying, she replied:

"That is entirely up to him."

The prime ambition of the flight, Mrs. Lindbergh said, "was an ambition to further aviation. He wanted to do the thing that should be done and had to be done for aviation."

Concerning aviation she said: "For the men who have adaption to it aviation is one of the best professions." Just a bit proudly she added that she believed her son had demonstrated his adaptability.

Mrs. Lindbergh is an instructor in chemistry in Cass Technical High School here and has frequently flown with her son.

SOLITARY FLYER MAKES NON-STOP FLIGHT FROM NEW YORK IN 33½ HOURS

French Crowd Of 25,000 Gives American Unprecedented Ovation When He Lands At Le Bourget Two And Half Hours Ahead Of Schedule.

DECLARES HE NODDED SEVERAL TIMES DURING HOP

Lucky Enough To Wake Himself Up At Once. Aviator Explains—Averaged 113 Miles An Hour On 3,800-Mile Journey.

Paris, May 21 (AP).—Capt. Charles A. Lindbergh, the young American aviator, who hopped off from New York Friday morning all alone in his monoplane, arrived in Paris tonight, safe and sound.

The sandy-haired son of the Middle West dropped down out of the darkness at Le Bourget flying field, a few miles from Paris, at 10.21 o'clock tonight (4.21 P.M. Eastern time) only 33½ hours after leaving Long Island—the first man in history to go from New York to Paris without changing his seat. He was about two and a half hours ahead of his schedule.

"WELL, HERE WE ARE," HIS GREETING

The wheels had scarcely ceased to roll, the propeller had barely come to a stop, when Lindbergh, weary eyed, but smiling, got up from the seat where he had so long sat and in a casual voice, almost drowned by the cheers of thousands, said with charming simplicity:

"Well, here we are."

To the young American it was seemingly merely the achievement of an ambition.

"It wasn't such a bad trip," he said later at the American Embassy. "I ran into some snow and ice in the early part; the rest wasn't so bad."

AFRAID OF SANDMAN ALL THE TIME

"The biggest trouble was staying awake. I nodded several times, but was lucky enough to wake myself right away. I was afraid of the sandman all the time."

Computing the distance as 3,800 miles, his speed averaged around 113 miles an hour. He also established a world's record for straight-line distance flying, breaking the record of 3,400 miles set by Coste and Rignot, of France, in their Paris-to-Yask, Persia, flight last October.

To Paris, to France, to America, to the world his landing tonight made him the greatest of heroes mankind has produced since the air became a means of travel.

A crowd of at least 25,000 surrounded his plane, the Spirit of St. Louis, when it came to earth after its epochal voyage from the new world to the old. The airman was lifted from the seat, where for two days and a night he sat fixed, guiding his plane over land and sea, and for 40 minutes he was hardly able to talk or do anything else, except let himself be carried along by a mass of men made delirious with joy at his achievement.

FRENCH RESPOND TO HIS RECKLESSNESS

Never has an aviator of any nation, even king or ruler, had a greater or more spontaneous welcome from the hearts of the common people of France. The very recklessness of his endeavor, as it appeared, appealed to the quick emotional imagination of Frenchmen, and they were quick to respond with everything their own hearts could give.

All ties of nationalism were forgotten by the Le Bourget throng. They saw in Lindbergh only a man who had brilliantly gambled with death, and won. There was regret, of course, for Nungesser and Coli, and regret, too, that the daring Frenchmen had not been the first. But there was no bitterness in their greeting of the American winner.

CROWDS SWEEP POLICE ASIDE

It was the common people of France who first hailed the intrepid Lindbergh as he emerged from what only yesterday morning he had called his "death chamber." Shortly after 10.10 tonight (French time) the roar of his motor, for which they had been waiting for hours, came out of the clear night sky to the ears of the multitude. Police lines were swept aside as thousands surged over the field to welcome the man who had won their hearts and had earned immortal fame.

"There he is!" the cry went up as the rays of searchlights gleamed upon the monoplane gracefully descending from the darkness which had enveloped all and through which only the sound of the motor gave warning of his approach. At this instant the crowds began their race across the field.

Smoothly the airplane, the Spirit of St. Louis, glided down upon the lighted ground. Even before it had come to

THE WEATHER
Probably showers tonight and Wednesday; cooler Wednesday. Fresh northeast and north winds, shifting to northwest.

THE EVENING SUN

FINANCIAL
COMPLETE STOCKS

VOL. XXXV—NO. 109. PRESS RUN YESTERDAY {MORNING 130,155 / EVENING 132,804} 262,959 || SUNDAY 198,039 BALTIMORE, TUESDAY, AUGUST 23, 1927. Published every week-day by The A. S. Abell Company. Entered as second-class matter at Baltimore Postoffice. 32 PAGES. PRICE TWO CENTS.

EUROPEANS RIOT OVER SACCO DEATH

BULK OF GARY'S ESTATE IS LEFT WITHIN FAMILY

Wife And Daughters Given Residue After Bequests Of $2,000,000.

EIGHT COLLEGES GET SCHOLARSHIP FUNDS

Personalty Estimated At From $25,000,000 To $100,000,000.

[*By the United Press.*]

Mineola, N. Y., Aug. 23.—The fortune which Judge Elbert H. Gary amassed as chairman of the United States Steel Corporation will remain, for the most part, within the control of the Gary family.

Gary's will was filed for probate here today, leaving to his family almost his entire fortune.

Trust funds of $800,000 each are set up for Gary's two daughters and of $300,000 each for his two grandchildren.

Establishes Scholarships.

Eight colleges are left trust funds of $50,000 each to pay tuition of deserving students.

The Gary Memorial Church (Methodist), Wheaton, Ill., is left $50,000.

Servants are remembered with small provisions. Then the residue of the estate, valued variously at from $25,000,000 to $100,000,000 by those who venture estimates, is left to Mrs. Gary and Judge Gary's two children by his first wife.

The will carefully specifies that Judge Gary is to be buried in the Gary mausoleum, Wheaton, Ill., which is bequeathed to his two daughters. Then it directs that the body of Judge Gary's first wife be placed in a crypt beside Judge Gary; that provision for similar burial of his widow be made, and that the bodies of his mother and father be placed in the mausoleum, thus gathering together for all time the Gary family.

Gary left to his two daughters, "share and share alike, all my personal wearing apparel, jewelry, personal belongings, including diplomas, decorations, memorials and gifts connected with my business career or otherwise."

$800,000 Each For Daughters.

The will creates two trust funds of $800,000 each for Mrs. Gertrude Gary Sutcliffe and Mrs. Bertha Gary Campbell, Gary's two daughters by his first marriage. They will receive the income from these funds for life. On the leath of Mrs. Sutcliffe the income from the fund set aside for her goes to her son, Elbert Gary Sutcliffe.

The income from the fund set aside for Mrs. Campbell, on her death, will go to her daughter, Julia Elizabeth Campbell. On the death of the children the incomes go to their children, or if they leave no children, then to other heirs.

A trust fund of $300,000 is set up for Elbert Gary Sutcliffe, grandson of the steel magnate, and a similar fund for Julia Elizabeth Campbell, granddaughter. They are to receive the income and on their deaths their heirs are to receive it.

Wife Gets Estate.

Mrs. Gary is bequeathed the Gary estate at Jericho, Long Island, New York, comprising 109 acres, together with the furniture and all the buildings contain.

The will adds that if Mrs. Gary does not care to occupy the estate, known as Ivy Hall, it may be sold and the proceeds added to the residuary estate.

A series of trust funds of $50,000 each is set up for scholarships at eight educational institutions. The trustees or governors of the schools are to name the students to benefit under the provision. The students are to be those "least able to pay their tuition" and "morally, mentally and physically competent." The money is to pay tuition.

Schools receiving these trust funds are:

McKendree College, Lebanon, Ill.
University of Pittsburgh, Pittsburgh, Pa.
Lafayette College, Easton, Pa.
Trinity College, Hartford, Conn.
Lincoln Memorial University, Harrogate, Tenn.
Syracuse University, Syracuse, New York.
Northwestern University, Chicago.
New York University, New York city.

A separate memorandum, the will said, would give directions for distribution of "articles of no considerable value." The memorandum was not filed.

Gives Legatees Advice.

Near the end the will said:

I earnestly request my wife and my children and their descendants to steadfastly decline to sign any bonds or obligations of any kind as surety for any other person or persons: that they refrain from anticipating their income in any respect,

[Continued On Page 2, Column 7]

GOOD EVENING

AIMED TO PLEASE.

"I want a suitable book to read on Sunday—something about an active church worker."

"Then I recommend this one, madam. It's about a minister who had two wives at the same time."—American Legion Monthly.

KNEW HER SIGNALS.

Betty—Have you any green lipstick?

Shop Assistant—Green lipstick?

Betty—Yes, a railway guard is taking me out tonight.—Everybody's Weekly.

THE POET TO HIS AUTO 2,000 FEET ABOVE SEA LEVEL.

Old bus, when first this hill you made
In high my heart beat loudly;
You darted up the nasty grade,
Your nickel gleaming proudly.
And finally when the slope was ended,
Exultingly I shouted, "Splendid!"

The second time we drove up here
You found the climb was not so easy.
I shifted into second gear
As on you panted, hoarse and wheezy.
The facts are plain beyond denying:
You found the hill was somewhat trying.

But now, you traitor, here you stall
With help 2,000 feet below you.
You will not creep, you will not crawl,
But beg for some kind soul to tow you.
And yet I really should not scold you. . . .
I guess I'll kill the guy who sold you!

—*Cyrano, in Judge.*

TUT, TUT!

Wife—Every time you see a pretty girl you forget you're married.

Husband—You're wrong, my dear. Nothing brings home the fact with so much force.—Chicago Tribune.

SEE!

Conductor of Orchestra—I don't know what's the matter with the cellos tonight. You seem to be quite lost.

Leader of Cellos—I'm sorry, sir; I'm afraid we are all at sea.

Conductor—That's just it! You ought to have been at B flat!—Christian Science Monitor.

HIS INDUSTRY THWARTED.

Arthur—It's always the same! Whenever I want to work I can't lay my hands on anything.

Wife—But, dear—I've just filled your fountain pen and put out plenty of paper.

Author—Yes—but what have you done with the corkscrew?—*Passing Show.*

IN WRONG.

"I want a bottle of iodine."

"Sorry, but this is a drug store. Can't I interest you in an alarm clock, some nice leather goods, a few radio parts or a toasted cheese sandwich?"—Penn State Froth.

PROGRESS.

"My wife has been using a flesh-reducing roller for nearly two months."

"And can you see any result yet?"

Yes—the roller is much thinner!"—Die Muskete (Vienna).

Ohio Wesleyan Bans Girls Who Smoke

Motor Cars And Student Marriages Also Barred—Dancing Allowed On Written Permits From Parents.

Delaware, Ohio, Aug. 23.—Coeds who desire to smoke will be requested not to enroll at Ohio Wesleyan University this fall.

Dr. John Hoffman, president of the institution, has written letters to parents of all prospective students, pointing out that coeds are not permitted to smoke. The letter asks the parents to send their daughters to other schools if the smoking habit is insisted upon.

Ohio Wesleyan also prohibits the use of motor cars by students and also student marriages. Women students may dance provided written permission is given by their parents.

Kills Her Husband And Wounds Self

Brooklyn Woman, Near Death, Says She Wielded Knife After Mate Attacked Her.

Brooklyn, Aug. 23.—Amelia Calino, bride of eighteen months, killed her husband with a knife today and was herself cut so severely that she may die.

Santo and Amelia fought behind locked doors while residents in the apartment pounded for admission. The door was broken open but Santo lay dead and Amelia was unconscious. She revived for a moment and whispered that Santo had attacked her with a knife.

NAVY FURNISHES 16 MORE SHIPS IN HUNT FOR FLYERS

Light Cruiser Omaha And 15 Destroyers Added To Already Large Group.

HOPE FOR MISS DORAN AND 6 OTHERS FADING

Pacific Search To Go On Until Thursday, Washington Announces.

[*By the United Press.*]

Washington, Aug. 23.—The extensive navy search of the Pacific for the seven missing Hawaiian flyers was augmented today by sixteen more ships—the light cruiser Omaha and fifteen destroyers.

The intensive search of the Pacific lanes will be continued until darkness Thursday, at which time, if no traces are found of Miss Mildred Doran and the six aviators lost in three planes, all vessels will start returning to duties interrupted by the hunt.

Fleet Commander Wires.

Word of these developments was given out today by the Navy Department in a dispatch from Admiral R. H. Jackson, Pacific fleet commander. Jackson ordered the sixteen new ships from Admiral Luke McNamee, commander of the destroyer squadron.

The sixteen ships engaged in battle fleet maneuvers, between Puget Sound and San Francisco, left the fleet yesterday and will arrive shortly after noon tomorrow at a point about 555 miles out of San Francisco, where Erwin's Dallas Spirit was last heard from.

After Thursday navy and commercial ships will be asked to watch for wreckage that may give a clue to the fates of the Dallas Spirit, the Miss Doran and the Golden Eagle.

Hope Nearly Gone.

Honolulu, Aug. 23.—Hope of eventual finding of Miss Mildred Doran and the six other missing aviators who were forced down on their mainland-to-Honolulu Dole air race, had been practically abandoned today.

Green flares seen above Nounakea, on Hawaii Island, offered a bit of hope last night, but little credence was given the report. It was pointed out that had any of the aviators landed there six days would have been sufficient time for them to have made their way across the mountains.

Another Woman Wants To Fly To Honolulu

Cleveland, Aug. 23.—With search going on for Miss Mildred Doran, the Michigan school teacher, and six other flyers lost in the Pacific Ocean, Miss Elizabeth Routson, a former Cleveland teacher, has wired T. M. Dobson, an Oakland (Cal.) flyer, asking permission to accompany him on a round-trip flight from Oakland to Honolulu.

Confident that her offer will be accepted, Miss Routson is making arrangements to fly from Cleveland to the Pacific Coast, and hopes to have the honor of being the first woman to fly to Honolulu.

Miss Routson has never been in the air, but she believes that almost any flight of which she was a party would be successful.

Gold Rush In Ohio.

Newark, Ohio, Aug. 23.—A gold rush has developed here following discovery of a quantity of gold quartz. The ore was found when workmen started excavating for a new building on the public square. Further "mining" is planned.

SEEKS LIGHT ON U. S. DRY LAW RESULTS

MRS. MARGARET WINTRINGHAM

New York, Aug. 23.—Mrs. Margaret Wintringham, the second woman to be elected to the British Parliament, expects to emerge from her three weeks' visit to this country with definite views on prohibition, she said yesterday just before departing for Lynchburg, Va. Mrs. Wintringham arrived on the Cunard liner Franconia on Sunday.

"I am a keen temperance reformer and would like to see some sort of scheme to reduce drinking put into effect in England," she said. "More than £3,000,000 a year are spent on liquors in Britain and they could be spent in better ways. I do not know if prohibition is the way to stop this waste, but I hope to find out."

Dutch To Reap Fruit Of Black's Air Voyage

Attempt Will Be Made To Establish Regular Passenger Service To East Indies.

Amsterdam, Aug. 23 (Special By Radio).—The recent successful flight to the East Indies in a Fokker plane by Van Lear Black, of Baltimore, has opened the possibility of the establishment of regular passenger and postal air service between Holland and her colonies.

Within the next few weeks Lieutenant Koppen, of the Dutch Air Forces, will start from Amsterdam in an attempt to fly to Batavia and return within one month. According to the agreement with the Dutch postal authorities, he will carry 500 kilos (more than a thousand pounds) of mail. A subsidy will be sought for commercial service. The manager of the Dutch Royal Aviation Company goes to the East Indies this week to open a colonial branch.

Russia Executes 18 Bandits.

Moscow, Aug. 23.—Eighteen bandits were sentenced to death and executed and prison sentences of varying lengths were meted out to twenty-eight others, as a result of a round-up in the town of Bierdiliev, in the Ukraine. They had carried on banditry for a year and had killed a police chief and a constable, as well as a score of citizens.

Tribute To Valentino.

Rome, Aug. 23.—The anniversary of Rudolph Valentino's death was observed today with a solemn requiem mass in St. Mary Majors. Movie celebrities and crowds of the late actor's admirers attended.

Chaplin Case Cost Actor Two Millions, Is Estimate

At Least Half Of That Amount Was Spent For Attorneys' And Receivers' Fees And Other Incidental Expenses.

Hollywood, Cal., Aug. 23.—Two million dollars was estimated today as the cost of the Charlie Chaplin divorce trial.

$1,000,000 In Fees.

The exact figure will be fixed at a hearing on receivers' fees late today.

At least $1,000,000 was spent for various attorneys' and receivers' fees and expenses during the months which intervened between the time Lita Grey Chaplin filed suit for divorce and her receipt of it from the famous comedian yesterday, attorneys said.

The itemized bill follows:

Property settlement, $625,000; children's trust fund, $200,000; receivers' fees, $10,000; temporary alimony, approximately, $15,000; interest on deferred property settlement, $17,000; $1,000 a month for maintenance of the children until the trust fund can be established. Attorneys' fees were not made public.

To Get $375,000 Now.

Mrs. Chaplin, it is understood, will receive $375,000 at once, with the rest of the settlement to be paid over a three-year period.

Infantile Paralysis Hits Town.

Lancaster, Pa., Aug. 23.—The third death in this city in nine days as a result of infantile paralysis occurred yesterday. The most recent victim is John Deichler, son of Mr. and Mrs. Milton Deichler.

YIELDS BODIES AFTER VANZETTI AND SACCO DIE

Massachusetts Has Thus Wiped The Case Off Her Books.

EXECUTIONS TAKE JUST 24 MINUTES

"Never Committed Crime, But Sometimes Some Sin," Bartolomeo's Adieu.

[*By the United Press.*]

Boston, Aug. 23.—The State of Massachusetts wiped the case of Nicola Sacco and Bartolomeo Vanzetti off its books this afternoon.

The anarchists, with Celestino Madeiros, were electrocuted at the Charlestown State Prison between midnight and 12.30 A. M.

In less than an hour the bodies rested at a city mortuary.

George B. Magrath, county medical examiner, came during the morning to perform the autopsy required by law. Then the State was through and ready to give the bodies to the relatives.

They Claim The Bodies.

Gardner Jackson and Aldino Felicani, of the Sacco-Vanzetti defense committee, claimed the bodies of the two anarchists.

An undertaker claimed that of Madeiros in behalf of his mother and sister.

Police vigilance has been relaxed. No crowds gathered at the morgue. Newsboys shouted extras telling of violence in other cities in the United States and abroad, but Boston was returning to normal.

Vanzetti's Body To Italy.

Vanzetti, student, philosopher and immigrant laborer, will be returned to Italy to be buried where he was born. His sister, Luigia, who came here from the little Italian village of Villafiletta to console him in his last moments, probably will accompany it.

Sacco, the shoe worker who "kept a beautiful garden" at Stoughton, will be buried by his wife, Rose, perhaps near a Massachusetts garden. He cannot lie in consecrated ground, as can neither of the others, for they refused to turn to religion for consolation before they died.

Testimonial Considered.

The body of Madeiros will be sent to New Bedford, Mass., where his mother lives.

The Defense Committee had not yet completed its plans for a testimonial to Sacco and Vanzetti. It was considered almost certain that a public memorial service would be held, "that Sacco would be buried with honor," and that perhaps a committee would accompany Vanzetti's body to Italy.

Bodies May Lie In State.

A proposal was made that the bodies lie in state at the headquarters of the defense committee here, and that they also be sent to New York to permit the public to pay its last respects, but the committee had decided nothing definitely.

The case which dragged through the Massachusetts courts for seven years, ended dramatically in the electric chair in just twenty-four minutes.

Stoically and with a flash of defiance, Sacco the shoemaker, and Vanzetti the fish peddler, went to their deaths protesting their innocence.

Madeiros went with them, and he, too, died a stoic.

Like An Ancient Fortress.

A gray old prison that resembled an ancient fortress was the scene of this closing chapter of the case that started as the conventional murder of a paymaster and his guard and ultimately became a world issue.

Up to the hour of doom weary attorneys who had battled relentlessly that the lives of the condemned anarchists might be prolonged, held the faintest glimmer of hope of staying the hand of death.

They Die Without Fear.

Once before—only twelve days since—these same lives had been spared by a midnight reprieve. But last midnight brought no respite, and in the minutes that followed, Sacco and Vanzetti paid with their lives for their alleged killing of Frederick Parmenter and Alexander Berardelli during a payroll hold-up on April 15, 1920.

The three men were ready for death and met it without show of fear.

Madeiros Goes First.

Madeiros, who played only a minor role in the drama, was stolid and resigned to the inevitable. At 12.02 A. M. he entered the death chamber. He walked to the chair, led by two guards, and sat down to die. At 9 minutes and 35 seconds past midnight the doctors announced he was dead.

Nicola Sacco was brought in next, at 12.11 A. M. A man of 36 years, he

[Continued On Page 2, Column 2]

Man Held After Bombing Of Monastery In Cleveland

Cleveland, Aug. 23.—One man was being held for investigation today in connection with the bombing last night which caused $10,000 damage to the Franciscan Monastery of St. Joseph's Church.

The man was arrested while loitering in the neighborhood of the church. He protested innocence.

No one was injured.

Windows in houses for blocks around were shattered. Residents were thrown from their beds.

Safety Director Edwin Barry was of the opinion that the bombing of the monastery of St. Joseph's Church last night was not the work of Sacco-Vanzetti sympathizers. He said his investigation of the case would indicate that a religious fanatic was responsible.

CHICK EVANS SETS BRISK PACE IN GOLF

Chicago Veteran Breezes In With Card Of 150 In Title Tourney.

Minikahda Club, Minneapolis, Minn., Aug. 23.—One of the old masters of American golf, Chick Evans, of Chicago, breezed home among the early qualifiers in the national amateur championship today with a total of 150 for his two rounds.

Evans, first of the favorites to finish, added a 75 today to his 75 of Monday and was certain to be among the lowest scorers of the thirty-two golfer. who will start match play tomorrow.

Evans Draws Crowd.

With Bobby Jones, George Von Elm and other favorites scheduled for late starts, Evans drew a large gallery and rewarded those who followed him with a brilliant exhibition. In 1916 Chick won the national open on this same course.

The popular Chicago amateur was not putting with his customary accuracy, but his remarkable play through the field enabled him to include three birdies in his card.

Dave Ward, Kent Country Club, Grand Rapids, Mich., turned in a 78 for today's 18 holes and was a probable qualifier with 156 strokes for the 36.

Ward scored a 37-41—78 today. Yesterday he scored a 41 on the first nine and a 37 coming in.

While Gene Homans, who will enter Princeton next fall, shot the best score of the opening day, and Philips Finlay, who will be a Harvard freshman, was next best, with Don Carrick, Toronto University senior, third, in the opening day's swing—"class" will tell.

Medalist Seldom Wins Title.

Golf students, mindful of the fact that the medalist seldom wins the championship, are looking for Bobby Jones, George von Elm, Francis Ouimet, Harrison (Jimmy) Johnston, Dexter Cummings or Ellsworth Augustus to supply the thrills of today's qualifying round.

Homans had a 71 yesterday, Finlay a 72 and Carrick a 73. The others were well satisfied with 75's and 76's. Von Elm confessed to a 79 and if he should do the same scoring today the present champion's chances of qualifying may be somewhat impaired.

Debate was violent on the breeze-swept Minikahda links today as to whether a 156, 157 or 158 would be required to qualify for the 144 holes of match play which starts tomorrow.

All the contestants must cover an additional eighteen holes today to the eighteen they traversed yesterday to come within the select thirty-two best who will go out in quest of the title over a 144-hole route starting tomorrow.

Amateur Golf Scores

Minikahda Club, Minneapolis, Minn., Aug. 23.—Scores for the full 36 holes of the qualifying round for the national amateur golf championship follow. The 32 lowest scores will qualify for the 144-hole match play rounds which start tomorrow and continue through Saturday.

A. M. Labatt, Minneapolis, Minn.	86	37	39—162
A. M. Hoxie, Boston, Mass.	83	42	40—165
G. F. Piper, Minneapolis, Minn.	80	48	43—171
J. D. Standish, Jr., Detroit, Mich.	79	47	42—168
David Ward, Grand Rapids, Mich.	78	37	41—156
A. P. Houghton, Washington, D. C.	82	41	43—166
Lee J. Chase, Buffalo, N. Y.	79	38	43—160
J. W. Hughes, Omaha, Neb.	81	42	43—166
H. W. Gardner, Milwaukee, Wis.	85	41	35—161
John McKinley, Chicago	77	38	39—154
"Chick" Evans, Chicago	75	38	37—150

ANTI-AMERICAN SENTIMENT GROWS IN WORLD CAPITALS; WORSE OUTBREAKS FEARED

Severe Fighting Occurs In Cities Of Switzerland, Germany And Denmark—One Killed, 25 Hurt In Geneva.

LONDON DEMONSTRATORS HALTED ON WAY TO BUCKINGHAM AND ST. JAMES PALACES

Ten Thousand March In Australia—Mob Scenes In Buenos Aires—Spain, Fearing Violence, Censors News From U. S.

[*By the United Press.*]

Disorder, mass protests, violence and one death were side shows last night and today to the drama of Nicola Sacco and Bartolomeo Vanzetti's execution.

Thousands of persons in America, Europe, Great Britain and Australia met to protest against the death sentence. Anti-American sentiment was especially prevalent in Geneva, seat of the League of Nations, where one person was killed and twenty-five were injured. American automobiles were attacked; stones were thrown at American delegates to the League's press conference; the council room of the League was wrecked.

Police dispersed protesting crowds in France, Germany, England, Denmark, Chicago and Detroit. Some heads were broken; no one was killed.

Paris Communists planned an attempt to prevent the American Legion convention meeting there next month.

London police dispersed demonstrators near Buckingham Palace and the United States Embassy.

U. S. Embassies In Europe Guarded.

Throughout Europe, United States embassies and consulates were under guard.

Italy was orderly although feeling was intense.

Pennsylvania State police sought the murderer of a State policeman who was shot after a Sacco-Vanzetti meeting yesterday.

Two bombs exploded in Montpelier, France, and another damaged a monastery in Cleveland, Ohio. There was no evidence to link these bombs with Sacco-Vanzetti sympathizers.

Amsterdam Consulate Stoned.

Police guarding the United States consulate in Amsterdam today arrested a man who had thrown stones through a window.

10,000 In Australia Hoot U. S.

In far-off Sydney, Australia, more than 10,000 sympathizers marched through the streets singing Communist songs and carrying banners. They jeered and hooted as they passed the office of United States Consul Lawton.

Fearing violence, the Spanish Government clamped a censorship on cable dispatches from the United States telling of the execution.

In Berlin the excitement reached fever heat as the hour of doom drew near. Thirty thousand workers assembled after factories and offices closed and paraded, carrying placards bearing anti-American slogans. A heavy police guard surrounded the American Embassy, and truckloads of police were concealed near the embassy. Numerous deputations from liberal and radical organizations were refused admittance.

Violence In Buenos Aires.

At Buenos Aires about a thousand persons were still on hand in front of newspaper bulletin boards when word came that Sacco and Vanzetti had been put to death. The crowd formed a parade, shouting and breaking windows of trolley cars as they marched. Police dispersed them.

Many were injured and a hundred arrested at Halle, Germany, where thousands of Communists clashed with police. Street fighting continued for four hours.

At Lyons, France, sympathizers attempted to enforce a boycott of movie houses showing American films. Three persons were arrested after a fight with police.

Two bombs exploded at Montpelier, France, today, one at the police station and another near the jail. Several policemen were injured and windows in neighboring houses were smashed.

Heavy Fighting In Denmark.

Several persons were wounded at Goteborg, Denmark, when thousands of sympathizers were dispersed by police from in front of the American Consulate.

There was heavy street fighting at Copenhagen, in which several policemen were wounded.

At St. Nazaire, France, police and sympathizers engaged in a revolver battle, but no one was injured. Twenty-five Communists attacked the police station, shouting "vengeance for Sacco and Vanzetti."

In London a thousand sympathizers attempted to march on Buckingham Palace, but were stopped 300 yards from the gates by foot and mounted police. Another crowd of demonstrators tried to reach St. James Palace, but was frustrated by police. A new demonstration was planned for tonight by Communists.

Firemen With Hose Guard Conference At Geneva After Riots

Geneva, Aug. 23.—Firemen with hose, backed by policemen, surrounded the building in which the League of Nations general communications and transit conference convened today. Americans were among the delegates participating in the conference and the guard was posted to prevent Sacco-Vanzetti demonstrators from indulging in violence.

1 Killed, 25 Hurt.

Sacco and Vanzetti sympathizers smashed property, killed one person and wounded twenty-five others last night. Another demonstration potentially violent was set for today.

Americans were the quarry sought by the rioters last night. American delegates to the League of Nations press conference were stoned. Windows in the council room of the league were smashed.

Americans' Car Wrecked.

the crowd as it approached a cafe where American tourists and delegates usually

[Continued On Page 2, Column 1]

Paris Radicals Plan Monster Parade For Tonight; Police Ready

By John Gunther.

Paris, Aug. 23 (Special by Radio).—In death Sacco and Vanzetti are assured of life forever, the Paris radical press says today, one journal even going so far as to compare the men to Christ.

Storms are gathering for a demonstration tonight which, if it goes forward as planned, will dwarf anything attempted while the two Anarchists were alive.

The first step in reprisal by radicals in general is a boycott of the American Legion convention. Dock workers and porters at Havre, Boulogne and Cherbourg are being urged to refuse to work on any boats discharging Legionnaires. Similarly all workers affiliated with radical unions as well as Communists are asked to have no association of any kind with any Legionnaire.

Failure Of This Is Predicted.

Responsible circles feel that this movement cannot be successful.

"Are you an American?" says the line under a cartoon in *L'Oeuvre* today. "I'll tell you tomorrow," is the cynical reply.

This indicates the belief of the radi-

WEATHER FORECAST

Cloudy today; fair, slowly rising temperature, tomorrow; strong northwest winds.

Detailed Weather Report on Page 22.

THE SUN

Registered United States Patent Office.

Weakness of Irish Labor Party Analyzed By George Young —*Page* 13.

VOL. 181—D | PAID CIRCULATION SEPTEMBER MORNING 126,710 EVENING 124,126 {250,836 ‖ SUNDAY 195,698 | BALTIMORE, WEDNESDAY, OCTOBER 19, 1927. | Published every week-day by The A. S. Abell Company. Entered as second-class matter at Baltimore Postoffice. | 28 PAGES | 2 CENTS

HOUSING IN TWO CAMPS IN STATE PAINTED AS BAD

Stables At Ft. Hoyle Found In Better Condition Than Homes Of Officers.

BUILDINGS AT MEADE HAVE LEAKY ROOFS

Men Complain That They Must Maneuver Cots To Escape Rain.

Charges by general officers of the army that officers and enlisted men are "living like immigrants or like prisoners of war, instead of soldiers of the United States," apply to at least two army posts in Maryland, it has been learned.

Dispatches from San Diego, Cal., last Tuesday quoted Maj.-Gen. Charles P. Summerall, chief of staff, as saying that the housing condition of the army was "deplorable" and that it was more fit for immigrants and prisoners of war.

As a result of the speech attributed to General Summerall, he was ordered by the President to return at once to Washington and last Friday it was learned the President was prepared to administer an oral spanking to the army chief of staff for his outspokenness.

Three Camps Described.

Dispatches yesterday said the San Diego speech was a "closed incident," since the President had been informed the statements which caused the controversy were not made by General Summerall.

But in view of the conditions complained of visits were made by a SUN representative Monday and yesterday to three large army posts—Camp Meade, Fort Hoyle and the Aberdeen Proving Grounds—to ascertain whether the remarks attributed to General Summerall applied to camps in Maryland.

Camp Meade, by far, presented the worst appearance. There every building was in need of paint and in many structures occupied by officers and men broken windows, rotting planks and boards were seen. All the structures at Camp Meade are wood, built for temporary use in the war days.

How Things Are At Fort Hoyle.

Conditions at Fort Hoyle and at the Aberdeen Proving Grounds are not comparable to those of Meade. Of these two, Fort Hoyle is in worse shape. Married non-commissioned officers there are quartered with their families in one-story structures in worse condition than the buildings used nearby as stables for the same unit—the Sixth Field Artillery. Other barracks are in permanent buildings of stucco and hollow tile.

The Aberdeen quarters are in good condition.

Timbers Found Rotted.

The most dilapidated buildings at Camp Meade are in the old part of the post, where the Quartermaster's Corps is living. The underpinning of one dormitory has partly rotted away and the enlisted men say that two weeks ago the floor in another dormitory was so rotted it was unsafe. The rotted planks were replaced with boards from a razed building.

Enlisted men said they were living with their wives in buildings which were drafty and leaked in heavy rains. In several instances the married men pointed out, the end of a huge building was their home, the remainder of the building, boarded off from the sections occupied, being without window panes and large cracks were showing in the walls.

Leaking roofs seemed to be the principal complaint at Camp Meade. In the section occupied by the Tank Corps, enlisted men asserted they usually spent rainy nights pushing their cots around the dormitory floor to escape the rain.

Dormitory Roof Leaks.

A man of Company C, Sixteenth Battalion, Tank Corps, pointed to a building affording sleeping quarters on the second floor for sixteen men. The roof was of a thin tar paper and the seams were covered with a tar mixture.

The covering failed to keep the rain out, this soldier said, the calcimined walls of the room showing streaks from the roof to the floor. Several streaks were just over the cots.

The panes in three windows in the room were broken.

Trying To Keep Warm.

In the center of the room a large stove glowed, but the chill wind prevented the heat from reaching more than five feet.

The soldier said that last winter, when he slept at one end of the room, he placed newspapers under his mattress and between each of six blankets to keep out the cold, but that often by midnight he would be so cold he could not sleep.

All the men quartered in that room usually would drag their cots as near as they could to the stove. The men in cots on the fringe of this circle spent uncomfortable nights, he said.

In walking past rows of sleeping

(Continued on Page 3, Column 1.)

The Great Game Of Politics

By FRANK R. KENT.

Mr. Bumble And The Law.

WASHINGTON, Oct. 18.

NO uninflamed person wants to be thought of as taking seriously the rollicking remark of the renowned Mr. Bumble that "the law is an ass." It is, however, true that the law at times baffles attempts of the average mind to reconcile it with logic and justice. It is further true that the technical defenses of legal procedure and ethics are not always convincing or even plausible.

—o—

FOR example, take these two famous criminal trials—that of Fall and Doheny a year ago and Fall and Sinclair now going on. It is, of course, too much to expect people to be again shocked over charges first made in 1923 and which are now very "old stuff" indeed. Even if the public had been stirred to great indignation by the original disclosures, the five years' delay would have blurred its memory of the facts and dulled the edge of popular resentment, never at any time particularly keen. It is not fair to expect the public to burn with anger that long.

—o—

THAT, however, should not prevent the thinking portion, concededly small, from taking an interest in certain phases of these cases which seem to stand them out as unique. Last year when Fall and Doheny were tried in the Criminal Court on the Elk Hill lease charges a jury acquitted both. They were proclaimed innocent of corruption and conspiracy. A few weeks later the Supreme Court, passing upon the civil suits growing out of these charges, unanimously branded the leases as "stained with corruption" and conceived in fraud and conspiracy.

—o—

IN other words, after a jury had declared them innocent the highest court we have denounced them as guilty, forced restitution of some $10,000,000 and returned to the Government its great oil reserve. To those who thought about this it seemed an extraordinary stroke of luck for Fall and Doheny that the Supreme Court decision, which crumbled their whole defense, should have come after instead of before the criminal trial. They could not, of course, be tried again. Yet that decision, removing the last doubt of their guilt, made it clear they had avoided conviction solely through an unusual combination of extremely smart lawyers and very befuddled jury.

No parallel to their escape could be recalled. In the light thrown on them by the Supreme Court the acquittal verdict could only be viewed as an amazing miscarriage of justice and the talk of "complete vindication" with which it was hailed by the defendants seem colossal impudence.

—o—

BUT, if the Fall-Doheny case was made unusual by the swift and ruthless completeness with which the highest court wiped off the jury whitewash and left these men in guilty nakedness, how much more unusual is the trial of Fall and Sinclair on the charge of criminal conspiracy which began in Washington yesterday? Because in this case the Supreme Court has spoken before the jury has rendered a verdict, not afterward. In this case, passing on the Teapot Dome leases, it unanimously declared they were corruptly obtained, the result of a conspiracy to defraud the Government between Fall and Sinclair.

It branded Fall as a "faithless public servant" and used the words sinister, corrupt and fraudulent in describing the transactions between him and Sinclair. In short, the highest tribunal in the land, in a civil suit involving the same issues and the same facts, declared two weeks ago that Fall and Sinclair are guilty of the conspiracy charge on which they are now being tried before a jury in the Criminal Court. Under the law this jury must be made up of persons who have formed no impression as to the guilt of Fall or Sinclair. It must be composed of those who either have not seen the Supreme Court decision, printed on the first page of every newspaper in the country, or, if they did see it, were unimpressed.

—o—

THE interesting thing about all this is the possibility that this jury, like the other, should declare Fall and Sinclair innocent, which would, in effect, slap the Supreme Court in the face. Undoubtedly the jury has a right to do that. There is nothing in the law or the Constitution to compel it to agree with the Supreme Court. Undoubtedly, too, there is a legal defense for such an absurdity should it occur, but it must be admitted the possibilities of the situation and the obvious deductions are a strain on the lay mind.

CADET COURT IGNORED, V. M. I. STRIKERS SAY

Class President Insists Gen. Cocke Assailed Students' Integrity.

SENIOR'S DISMISSAL STARTED TROUBLE

Honor Body Acquitted Accused Of Hazing Charges By Freshman.

Lexington, Va. (Wednesday), Oct. 19 (Special).—The board of visitors of the Virginia Military Institute, called to consider the strike of students, were still in session at 1 A. M. this morning. Jack West, president of the first class, was called before the board shortly after midnight.

Lexington, Va., Oct. 18 (Special).—Jack West, of Suffolk, Va., president of the first class at the Virginia Military Institute and spokesman for the entire cadet corps, who went on strike today, declared tonight that the real issue at stake was what the students considered an affront to the integrity of the honor court by Brig.-Gen. W. H. Cocke, superintendent, in suspending W. F. R. Griffith, a senior.

Griffith was suspended by the superintendent yesterday on charges of hazing preferred by a freshman and the strike was decided upon by the students at a massmeeting last night, to which General Cocke was invited, but which he failed to attend. The cadets remained in barracks throughout the entire day and all military activities and classes were suspended.

Faculty Backs Cocke.

The faculty and officers of the institute also met last night and indorsed the action of General Cocke in the Griffith case.

Townfolk say the suspension of Griffith marks the thirty-ninth instance since the present school year started in which a student either has been suspended or has withdrawn from the school. The board of visitors now holding sessions here is expected to go into the whole matter thoroughly.

The strike, however, did not interfere with football practice today in anticipation of the game between V. M. I. and the University of Maryland at Richmond next Saturday and no statement was made regarding any change in the original plans for the cadet corps to attend the game in a body.

Strike Not Personal.

Young West insisted the strike was not aimed either at General Cocke or Major R. S. Dodson, the new commandant, personally, nor as much at the dismissal of Griffith as at the fact that a decision of the honor court had been questioned and reversed for the first time in the school's history.

Cadet West pointed out that the honor court, an organization of the student body itself, which passes upon cases of conduct on the part of students, has been in existence practically ever since the school was founded in 1839.

Decisions Held Sacred.

It was merely an informal, voluntary body at first, but about 1880 became a recognized institution in the affairs of the school and its decisions—paralleling those of a court-martial in the army—were never questioned, Cadet West declared. Students found

(Continued on Page 4, Column 6.)

ERIE SUES RIDER FOR 92 CENTS

Forced By I. C. C. Rules To File Action For Unpaid Fare.

Hackensack, N. J., Oct. 18 (AP).—Suit to recover 92 cents was filed today in District Court by the Erie Railroad against Miss Cora Campbell, a commuter of Montvale.

The papers allege that Miss Campbell boarded a train for Jersey City, in December, 1925, and, finding herself with neither ticket nor money, promised the conductor she would mail her fare. The money has not been received, it was alleged, and the company was forced to file suit to comply with regulations of the Interstate Commerce Commission.

FIVE WITH STINSON MISSING IN PLANE

Aircraft Designer, Wife And Party Fail To Reach Boston From Hartford.

STORM OVER AREA

Report That Big Craft Had Been Forced Down In Woods Under Investigation.

Boston, Oct. 18 (AP).—Five hours' overdue on a short one-hundred-mile hop from Hartford, Conn., to Boston, Eddie Stinson, Detroit airplane designer and builder, and a party of five, including his wife and a German Baron, were missing late tonight, presumably forced down somewhere by a cold, blustering "northeaster" which has lashed the New England coast all day.

They hopped off from Hartford at 4 P. M. today on the last lap of an 18,000-mile air tour in the interest of airport promotion. They should have reached Boston in two hours, but at 11 P. M. they had not been heard from. At that hour state and local police in the vicinity of Natick, Framingham and Sherborn were investigating reports that a big plane had gone down in the woods near the Natick-Sherborn line.

Flares Lit At Boston Field.

Besides Stinson and his wife the plane carried Philip Ashby, J. T. Whittaker, Stinson's mechanician; Fred Koeler and Baron Ravene Barnekow, a German aviator.

At the airport here, which has no regular facilities for night flying, a ground crew lighted huge flares at dusk and settled down for a vigil that was to last until some definite news of the flyer had been received.

Reports of a plane heading east being sighted over Mansfield, south of here, at 4.30, and again over Natick, eighteen miles to the west, at about 7 P. M., led aviators to express the opinion that Stinson had been blown southward off his course and then begun to circle in search of a safe landing place.

Plane Sighted Flying Low.

Shortly after the time the plane believed to have been Stinson's was seen over Ashford the same plane was sighted over Pomfret, near Putnam, and over the village of East Thompson in the town of Thompson. Residents of East Thompson said the plane was flying low over the hills, apparently in an effort to keep below low hanging clouds. East Thompson is

(Continued on Page 8, Column 3.)

FIRST OIL CASE WITNESS TO GO ON STAND TODAY

Littleton Starts Defense Presentation In Fall-Sinclair Trial.

ROBERTS OUTLINES GOVERNMENT'S SIDE

Two Women Among Jurors—Only Forty Talesmen Examined.

[*Washington Bureau of The Sun.*]

Washington, Oct. 18.—With a jury of ten men and two women impaneled and opening statements of the case almost complete, the Government is ready to begin the presentation of evidence tomorrow morning in the conspiracy trial of Albert B. Fall, former Secretary of the Interior, and Harry F. Sinclair, millionaire oil developer and sportsman.

The former Cabinet officer and the wealthy New Yorker are charged jointly with having corruptly agreed to divert to private interests the rich naval oil reserves in Wyoming commonly known as Teapot Dome. They are being tried in Criminal Division No. 2 of the District of Columbia Supreme Court, with Associate Justice Frederick L. Siddons presiding.

Jury Secured Quickly.

It is the contention of the Government that Fall, fraudulently and secretly, leased the reserve to Sinclair for development and that the then Cabinet member was well repaid for the transaction which was to have resulted in enormous profits to Sinclair. The fact that the tract recently has been restored to the Government by nullification of the lease has served to emphasize rather than to mitigate the criminal charges against the two men.

In a surprisingly short time counsel for the Government and the defendants obtained a jury whose personnel was satisfactory to both. The selection was begun yesterday and was expected to consume three or four days. But after the fortieth prospective juror was examined just before the noon recess today both sides announced their satisfaction with the eligibility of the twelve persons then in the box.

After only a momentary delay for administration of the oath to the jurors, Owen J. Roberts, of special counsel for the Government, began his statement of the Government's case. With manner pronouncedly terse and aggressive, the tall dean of the University of Pennsylvania Law School took only twenty minutes to outline what the United States will attempt to prove in the case.

When the court reconvened for the afternoon session Martin W. Littleton, Sinclair's personal attorney, began a corresponding statement for the defendants. He was only part way through his remarks when court was adjourned for the day and is expected to ask for about three-quarters of an hour to complete the task tomorrow.

Announces Early Witnesses.

Mr. Roberts, who, with former Senator Atlee Pomerene, is assisting Peyton C. Gordon, United States Attorney for the District of Columbia, in the prosecution, announced at the close of court that George W. Holland, an attorney in the Department of the Interior, probably would be the first Government witness called tomorrow. Other early witnesses, he said, would include Stephen G. Quigley, a State Department clerk; George Otis Smith, chief of the United States Geological Survey; E. C. Finney, former Assistant Secretary of the Interior, and Capt. H. A. Stuart, United States Navy.

At the outset of his presentation Mr. Roberts said the Government would not offer witnesses professing actually to have overheard the alleged conspiracy between Fall and Sinclair, but that it would offer a series of circumstances from which the jurors must decide for themselves if any corrupt agreement took place.

Gives Preliminary Proceedings.

After a preliminary explanation of the creation of the Teapot Dome reserve and of its assignment to exclusive control by the Navy Department by Congressional action in 1920, Mr. Roberts began a detailed recital of the handling of the property subsequent to an executive order of 1921 which "purported" to transfer control from the Navy to the Interior Department.

Secretary Fall immediately began to assume full authority over the reserve, he continued, and by this time many persons wanted to take leases in this rich field. Sinclair was among the most eager. He gave first indication of his anxiety to get a lease during a special visit to Fall at the latter's home in Three Rivers, New Mexico.

Secret Conferences Held.

The conference at Fall's home, Mr. Roberts went on, was followed by others in Sinclair's Washington office—all of them conducted in strictest secrecy. As a result of these conferences, Fall, without consultation of his official associates, gave Sinclair the lease he desired.

That negotiation of this lease was accomplished through conspiracy is borne out by the fact that by reason

(Continued on Page 8, Column 2.)

Conveys 176 Acres To Coolidge, But With Farm Relief String

Indianan Stipulates Land Shall Revert To State When Congress Shall Have Provided "Curative And Equitable Policy."

Indianapolis, Oct. 18 (Special).—The President has come into unexpected possession of property, through conveyance today of 176 acres in Pulaski county, between Knox and Winamac, but the deed stipulates that when Congress shall have established "a real curative and equitable farm policy" the land is to revert to the State of Indiana.

The satiric instrument was filed by Luke Duffey, former Republican State Senator, who has taken a hand in efforts at farm relief.

Time Limit Set.

The farm is conveyed "to one Calvin Coolidge, as trustee for Andrew Mellon, James Reed, Simeon Fess, Julius Barnes, Pat Harrison, William Jardine, Herbert Hoover and Finis Garrett, to have and to hold, to maintain and support, during and throughout the period in which the Liverpool free trade price level, known in America as the Grover Cleveland plan of crop valuation, shall fix, un-Americanize, undersell or ruinously control the value of any and all commodities grown upon the within-described real estate.

"This title to endure and remain so vested as long as the paint-barren gloss shall remain upon the majority of the farm buildings of the United States. The trust shall not cease until American agriculture has been provided with a well-placed and effective niche in our national tariff scheme; until the farm life of the States has been wholly stripped of all the priority rights of our Eastern margin hunters; until the establishment of a protective farm policy by our Government which will make the farming industry anywhere within the sacred confines of the Stars and Stripes wholly free of free trade.

Must Bear General Burden.

"The farm shall be subject to all general liabilities of American farm ownership, accruing or prevalent under the official greetings of the grantees herein. It is subject to all general taxes levied on a valuation of eighty per cent. greater than the mortgage claim holding thereon, calling for $3,500 and accrued interest, which the grantees shall assume and agree to pay.

"It is also subject to a cashless squatter's tenancy of five years. In event the Administration does establish a real policy, then the land shall revert to the great Commonwealth of Indiana and become known and designated, with all its wooded beauty and good roads frontage, as the Coolidge Industrial Park, as a token and memorial evidence of the great service the trustee and his wards have rendered."

LINDBERGH CHEERED BY 1,200 AT DINNER GIVEN IN HIS HONOR

As Baltimore Saw Him In The Rain

COL. CHARLES A. LINDBERGH

URGES BACKING OF COMMERCIAL AVIATION HERE

Says Support Is Necessary If City Is To Keep In Foreground.

20,000 ACCLAIM HIM AT STADIUM

Crowds Brave Rain—His Plane To Go To National Museum.

Twelve hundred Baltimoreans last night rose as one man and cheered Col. Charles A. Lindbergh as the New York-to-Paris flyer, serious and self-contained, stood in the Lyric Theater to speak at a dinner given in his honor.

The young flyer, whose boyish face shows the strain of national adulation, bowed and smiled slightly. Then, belief in his mission evident in every expression, he urged Baltimoreans to support commercial aviation.

"Aviation has progressed so rapidly that we cannot keep up with it," he said. "So great is the interest in commercial flying today that manufacturers of planes and equipment cannot meet the demands made on their factories."

Airport Needed In Every City.

Colonel Lindbergh referred only indirectly to his own feat when he asserted that pioneer flying always would be dangerous, but he quickly added that the United States air mail, flying under "the worst possible conditions," had proved the practicability and safety of commercial aeronautics.

"If you citizens of Baltimore expect to keep in the foreground in the coming great air program," he said, "you must get behind your state and municipal aviation programs.

"We need airports in every town and city of the United States. We cannot operate without them. It is necessary for every citizen to get behind commercial flying."

Contrast Striking.

Colonel Lindbergh, tall and blond, in the black and white of formal evening clothes, was in striking contrast with the man whom thousands of Baltimoreans, massed at Logan Field, along the principal streets and at the Stadium, had hailed in the afternoon.

Last night his hair was combed smoothly, whereas in the afternoon the rain beat down on and tousled his light brown thatch as he rode through the streets bareheaded, perched high in the back of an open automobile and wrapped in a yellow slicker.

From Logan Field to the Stadium, where 20,000 persons stood in a driving rain to acclaim him, the young flyer was cheered by thousands.

Lands Lightly As Bird.

Lindbergh's famous plane, the Spirit of St. Louis, dropped from a leaden sky to the northern end of Logan Field at 2 P. M. The silver wings flashed out of the southwest at high speed, while 1,000 persons standing on the sodden field were held back by a cordon of soldiers. Lindbergh banked sharply and pancaked to the ground, landing as lightly as a sparrow on a telegraph wire. In a few moments he had taxied to the hangars. When mechanics had wheeled the plane inside the aviator stepped from the cockpit and was greeted by Mayor Broening.

While Lindbergh doffed his helmet and leather coat the crowd broke through the lines. Soldiers and policemen joined hands and forced the enthusiasts back, so that the transatlantic flyer might put on a slicker and climb into an automobile.

After the procession had left Logan Field a mechanic attached to Colonel Lindbergh's party gave the silver plane a close inspection. It was run out into an inclosure and the crowd was allowed to view it at close quarters. A company of soldiers kept guard while the plane was on exhibition.

Rides Through Streets.

Flanked by motor-cycle patrolmen and followed by a long line of official cars, Lindbergh rode through the streets. As he started, a light, insistent rain was falling. Thousands of persons, the majority of whom were women and girls, pushed their way from the sidewalks to cheer and toss flowers and confetti.

It was a gay crowd. Pushed back by policemen, women smiled and pressed forward again.

Along South East avenue to Balti-

43 Uplifters Meet To Save Morals Of Youth Of World

International Purity Congress Opens Sessions In La Crosse, Wis., With Small Attendance, But Extensive Program.

By W. A. S. DOUGLAS.

Staff Correspondent of The Sun.

La Crosse, Wis., Oct. 18.—Acceding to demands from every section of the world, taking the word of its publicity department, the World's Purity Federation and the Parents' International League today opened a three-day conference here under the title of the International Purity Congress. The sessions are being held in the First Baptist Church.

Despite the announced plea from all the civilized and uncivilized nations, attendance is not what one would expect. There were forty-three old and middle-aged men and women in the church when the conference was declared open by Dr. B. S. Steadwell, president of the Purity Federation. Fully fifteen of these delegates were from the No-Tobacco League, which is present in force under the leadership of Charles S. Fillmore, its general secretary.

Fervor Is Plentiful.

But what the congress lacks in numbers it makes up in fervor and in the strength of the subjects under discussion. The chief object is to arrive at means by which to purify the youth of the nation. Instances of the alleged rottenness of the youngsters of the world were not wanting. In fact, almost every paper went into this presumed condition in startling language. Members of the Purity Congress seem to delight in calling a spade a spade.

A resume of the titles of the speeches made will give the reader a rough idea of what is being talked about by these folk in the First Baptist Church of La Crosse. There is "The Economic and Sociological Effect of Venereal Infection Upon the Nation," by Dr. George E. Jorgenson, of Hollywood, Cal.

Some Of Topics Listed.

Margaret E. Luther, superintendent of the Ivakota Farm for Girls, takes up the subject of "Young People and the Social Evil."

William D. Upshaw, billed in the publicity matter as "Congressman, journalist, lecturer, orator, reform leader and the Georgia cyclone," discusses "National Purity, the Foundation of Enduring Greatness."

Other papers and speeches include the following:

"Social Education among the Northern Baptists."

"Social Morality Work for Girls."

"The Rights of God in Birth Control."

"Narcotic Drug Addiction, a Primary Cause of Immorality."

"Marriage and Parenthood."

"The Truth about Tobacco."

"Some Causes and Phases of our Recent War with Vice."

"Conformity with God's Law of Sex."

"The Social Evil Problem in Japan."

"Social morality and the Negro Race."

The announced intention of the

(Continued on Page 2, Column 5.)

Five On Barge Adrift Off Maryland Coast

Two Revenue Cutters And Towboat Standing By Ready To Render Assistance.

Lewes, Del., Oct. 18 (AP).—With four men and a woman aboard the coal barge Old Dominion is adrift eight miles off Ocean City, Md., having broken loose from the tug Jupiter, which was towing this and another barge down the Jersey coast. The people on the Old Dominion are not thought to be in serious danger as the revenue cutters Ruth and Gresham and towboat No. 193 are standing by. The heavy wind is abating and the barge is expected to be taken in tow again early tomorrow.

The tug Jupiter put in at the breakwater this morning and reported the plight of the Old Dominion, and the revenue cutters, cruising in nearby waters, were asked to aid.

Roosevelt's Assaults On Smith To Be Curbed

Own Party Leaders Fear Effect On Campaign For Election Of Albany Sheriff.

Albany, N. Y., Oct. 18 (Special).—Republican leaders are about to put the muzzle on Theodore Roosevelt and his vice crusade. No longer is the son of the late President to be permitted at his pleasure to hurl accusations at Gov. Al Smith to the effect that the Governor is in league with an underworld of corruption and red lights, which he shields through Tammany and its allied political interests.

The local Republican committee is up in arms over the affair. It has notified the State committee that Roosevelt must not come here to continue his attacks as scheduled. If he does come it is insisted that his speech be censored. The Republicans are trying to elect a Sheriff and the vice crusader's speeches are not going well.

WEATHER FORECAST

Partly cloudy today; increasing cloudiness and warmer, followed by rain tomorrow; moderate southwest and west winds.
Detailed Weather Report on Page 21.

THE SUN

Registered United States Patent Office

Harry Levin
Says Future Of Palestine Is Bright With Promise. —Page 13.

VOL. 184—C | PAID CIRCULATION JANUARY MORNING, 144,883 EVENING, 143,155 288,038 ‖ SUNDAY 192,930 | BALTIMORE, FRIDAY, FEBRUARY 15, 1929 | Published every week day by The A. S. Abell Company. Entered as second class matter at Baltimore Post-office. | 26 PAGES | 2 CENTS

HOOVER AIMING AT REPEAL OF ORIGINS CLAUSE

To Press For Action On Alien Act As Soon As He Returns To Capital

BUT DESIRES FIRST TO SEE COOLIDGE

If Agreeable To President, Leaders Will Be Urged To Pave Way

By J. F. ESSARY

Belle Isle, Miami Beach, Fla., Feb. 14—Immediately on his return to Washington President-elect Hoover will throw whatever influence he can bring to bear, without encroaching on the prerogatives of President Coolidge, in favor of a repeal of the national origins clause of the immigration act.

This is one of the measures that he feels should be dealt with decisively before the Seventieth Congress passes out of existence. If it is not repealed within the next two weeks a rule will be sought whereby that action can be taken in the extra session that is to begin in April.

Early Action Needed

The new and retiring Presidents are opposed to the national origins clause as basically unfair, as unworkable in practice and as calculated to give offense to millions of citizens whose origin was in the Irish Free State, Germany, Sweden, Norway, Denmark and France.

Twice operation of this act has been postponed, but unless the filibuster against it in the Senate is broken or the repealer is passed in the extra session Mr. Hoover will be forced, against his will, to issue a proclamation before July 1 placing the quotas of the national origins clause in effect.

To Press For Repeal

It is perhaps too much to say that the status of this piece of legislation is responsible for Mr. Hoover's decision to return to Washington two weeks ahead of his inauguration, but it is undoubtedly true he is deeply concerned over it and will lose no time in pressing Congressional leaders to enact the repeal measure before March 4.

Action, of course, might be invoked at the extra session, but both the President-elect and his Congressional advisers have taken a stand against any except farm relief and tariff legislation before the December session.

Urgency Emphasized

To let down the bars for one more bill may result in a rush of other bills to the calendar in which individual legislators are passionately interested.

Mr. Hoover has declined at this end to comment on the national origins clause, but he has been kept informed fully of the situation in the Senate over his private wire from Washington. He has been told something must be done or the repeal measure will be lost.

It was intimated today Mr. Hoover would consult the President the day after his arrival at the Capital and that, if it is agreeable to Mr. Coolidge, the President-elect will call in a group of Congressional leaders and urge them to relieve him of a serious embarrassment at the outset of his Administration.

Viewed As Nonpartisan

The view taken here is that the immigration situation is in no sense a party issue; that both candidates for the Presidency in the campaign went on record in favor of repealing the clause and that the Senate leaders of the two parties should cooperate to get early action.

Because of the delicate situation which always obtains between the election and the succession of a President, Mr. Hoover has refrained severely from interfering with pending legislation.

But the immigration question peculiarly concerns the new Administration rather than that which is about to pass. And Mr. Hoover is disappointed to find that a few Senate members are disposed to leave the national origins problem on his doorstep.

Gets Data For Inaugural

A mass of material for the inaugural address has been left with the President-elect by Edward Eyre Hunt, Clarence M. Wooley and A. W. Shaw, representing the committee on recent economic changes. Mr. Hoover is chairman of the committee, which is an outgrowth of the 1921 Harding conference on unemployment and which has made a nation-wide survey of economic developments.

The report laid before Mr. Hoover in conferences yesterday and today covers every phase of the economic life of the nation. Here is what the committee said about its report.

"The survey covers consumption and the standard of living, the growth of new and old industries, technical changes in manufacturing, the changing structure of industry, construction, transportation, marketing, labor,

(Continued on Page 8, Column 6)

Mellon For $2,500,000 More Dry Fund; Cannon Wins Edict

$1,500,000 Of Sum Would Be Used To Hire Extra Agents—Bishop Wants $100,000,000 If It Is Needed

[*Washington Bureau of The Sun*]

Washington, Feb. 14—Secretary Mellon let it be known today that the Treasury Department could use an additional sum of $2,500,000 for prohibition enforcement. Methodist dry leaders think he could use that much—and a whole lot more.

On February 5, it will be recalled, Bishop James Cannon, Jr., of the Methodist Episcopal Church South, issued a statement intimating that unless Mr. Mellon, who had opposed the proposed $24,000,000 dry fund, should ask Congress for "needed funds" for prohibition enforcement, drys would oppose his continuation as Secretary of the Treasury.

Drys Fail To Grasp Bait

If, as it is interpreted in some circles, Mr. Mellon's announcement that an additional $2,500,000 appropriation would be requested was designed to appease the elements represented by Bishop Cannon, it has failed of its purpose. For the Methodist drys are open to no compromise. This was evident in statements issued today by Bishop Cannon and by Eugene L. Crawford, general secretary of the Board of Temperance and Social Service of the Methodist Episcopal Church South.

Just before sailing for the Holy Land on the trip paid for by the *Christian Herald* Association as part of the award to him as the American "who during 1928 made the most significant contribution to religious progress," Bishop Cannon disclosed his views in the following message:

"I would emphasize the act of the College of Bishops of the Methodist Episcopal Church South, taken at Memphis January 2, calling upon Congress to provide what men and money may be necessary to develop and put into effect an adequate program of prohibition law enforcement. This means exactly what it says—whatever amount is necessary, even if it be $100,000,000."

Dr. Crawford, in releasing Bishop Cannon's message, said the people he represented would stand pat for "adequate" funds. He made it clear he did not consider the amount mentioned by Mr. Mellon adequate.

"Any amount appropriated by Congress at this time," Dr. Crawford said in a formal statement, "which would not adequately meet the needs for a vigorous enforcement of the prohibition laws until Congress can make additional appropriations would not satisfy the prohibition views of the Methodist Episcopal Church South."

House To Get Request

Secretary Mellon said the request for the additional $2,500,000 would be transmitted to the House through the Budget Bureau in the routine manner. It would be used in strengthening the Prohibition and Customs Bureaus.

The prohibition bureau would be allotted approximately $1,500,000 to be used chiefly in the employment of additional agents for distribution throughout the service. The additional funds for the Custims Bureau would be used in doubling the number of

(Continued on Page 8, Column 4)

NIGHT CLUB RAIDS IRK NEW ORLEANS

Threats Are Exchanged By Governor Long And Resort Proprietors

MAKE WOMEN UNDRESS

Militia Used In Descents On Alleged Gambling Houses After Mardi Gras

New Orleans, Feb. 14 (AP)—Following a series of raids early this morning, a day after the close of New Orleans' riotous Mardi Gras season, threats were hurled today between Gov. Hughey P. Long and proprietors and patrons of night clubs over the gambling campaigns of the State militia outside the city limits.

Several times in the last few weeks Governor Long has used the troops in raiding alleged gambling houses on the edge of the city, but a bitter controversy has arisen over the searching of patrons in the establishments in the latest three simultaneous raids.

Money Seized

Today's raids marked the first time the troops had seized money from patrons, and their authority has been challenged by both operators and guests. The first to complain was Fred P. Kriss, race-horse owner, of Detroit, who, with Mrs. Kriss, refused to submit to search when the troops descended on the Tranchina Night Club.

They were taken to Jackson barracks by the troops, where Kriss charges three guardsmen seized Mrs. Kriss and took her to a back room where non-commissioned officers' wives stripped her in search of money.

Wife Nervous

When they were released at 10 o'clock, Kriss said his wife required a physician's attention for nervousness.

He declared he will go to court, as neither he nor his wife had gambled and when the troops arrived they were dining.

Anticipating efforts of alleged gambling house operators to retrieve their losses of several thousand dollars seized in the raids, Governor Long deposited the money in New Orleans banks to the credit of the State Treasury, he said tonight.

Mrs. A. G. Stuart, of San Francisco, reported that she was forced by the soldiers to permit a matron to remove her clothing. The sum of $500 she said she had won at the races was confiscated, she asserted.

Long Answers Critics

Governor Long issued a defiant answer to his critics.

"Gambling has got to stop," he said. "If they proceed, the gambling houses are going to be construed as gambling paraphernalia and may be closed eternally by the courts. We are doing to do worse than raid. We haven't started yet. They can't continue to openly defy the law around here.

"They can't grab money out of the tables and put it in their pockets and throw it in to potato sacks, and have the women put it on their persons to keep the militia from getting it. In the raids last night the guardsmen obtained high-class, cultivated ladies to search the women found in the houses raided. Women will continue to be searched when they are found in gambling houses."

WRIGLEY SWITCHES TO STEWART'S SIDE

Wall St. Hears Chewing Gum Man Has Reassigned Proxies He Gave Rockefeller

TALK OF NEW COMBINE

Report Now Is Indiana Oil Co. Chairman Is To Quit And Head Refining Concern

[*New York Bureau of The Sun*]

New York, Feb. 14—William Wrigley, chewing gum manufacturer, owner of a large block of Standard Oil Company of Indiana stock, who had signed proxies in favor of John D. Rockefeller, Jr., in the ouster campaign against Robert W. Stewart, chairman of the corporation, has shifted his support to Mr. Stewart, it was reliably reported today.

Wall Street, interested in the duel for control of the company, reverberated with rumors, adherents of both sides as usual saying that their side was ahead in the number of proxies assigned by stockholders.

Resignation Rumor Revived

A report that Mr. Stewart would resign before the meeting on March 7, which has been denied repeatedly by his representativs, was revived in quarters that believed Mr. Stewart would be asked by a group of bankers to head a company to be formed as a consolidation of several small refining and producing units.

Mr. Wrigley, it was said, recently signed, before a notary public, duplicate proxies intended to supersede proxies he had signed in favor of Mr. Rockefeller. At Mr. Rockefeller's office it was said no notification had been received from Mr. Wrigley and that Mr. Rockefeller still had more than fifty-one per cent. of the stock assigned by stockholders.

A Wall Street report that Kenneth R. Kingsbury, president of the Standard Oil Company of California, was slated by the Rockefeller interests to succeed Mr. Stewart as head of Standard of Indiana, was denied in behalf of Mr. Kingsbury in dispatches from San Francisco tonight.

Friends Scoff At Rumor

Mr. Kingsbury's associates in this city scoffed at the rumor. Phillip Patchin, his assistant, said: "We haven't heard a thing about it. I hardly believe Mr. Kingsbury would accept the Indiana post if it were offered."

At. Mr. Rockefeller's office it was said no one had been chosen to fill Mr. Stewart's place and that the company may be without a chairman for a year.

Injured Girl Takes Food After 143 Hours In Coma

Captain Of Derita (N. C.) Basketball Team Was Knocked Unconscious In Practice Game

Charlotte, N. C., Feb. 14 (AP)—After living in a coma for 143 hours, Miss Nell Fincher, 17-year-old captain of the Derita High School basketball team, took her first solid nourishment at a hospital here today since she was knocked unconscious by a blow during a practice game Friday.

The girl passed her one hundred and forty-third hour in a coma at 3 o'clock this afternoon. Physicians, however, said she appeared to be nearer consciousness today and discontinued the liquid diet.

SHIPPING BOARD VOTES TO SELL ITS 2 FLEETS

United States And American Merchant Lines Go To P. W. Chapman

TO BE TRANSFERRED ON SIGNING OF DEAL

Contract Stipulates Present Routes Must Be Maintained

[*Washington Bureau of The Sun*]

Washington, Feb. 14—Immediately upon being informed that the Senate Committee on Commerce this morning had decided to interpose no objection to the deal, the Shipping Board went into session this afternoon and voted to sell the United States Lines and the American Merchant Lines to Paul W. Chapman, head of the Chicago and New York investment banking corporation that bears his name.

The Chapman bid for the eleven passenger vessels of the Government's two transatlantic fleets was $16,082,000, with an additional offer of $218,000 for the leaseholds on offices and terminal facilities of the two lines now maintained by the Shipping Board.

Transfer Due Soon

The transfer of the ships to private ownership will begin as soon as the contract of sale has been fully approved and signed. The terms provide for cash payment of twenty-five per cent. of the purchase price, or a little more than $4,000,000, with the remainder to be paid in equal annual installments over a period of fifteen years, the deferred payments carrying 4¼ per cent. interest.

Joseph E. Sheedy, formerly vice-president of the Merchant Fleet Corporation, who has been designated as the executive head of the operating company that is to be formed by the Chapman interests, caught the first train for New York after learning of the board's action. He said articles of incorporation for the operating company would be drawn up at once in New York and incorporated, for maritime purposes, under the laws of Delaware.

Two Ships To Be Built

The contract of sale will stipulate, it was announced at the Shipping Board, that operation over the present routes now covered by the two lines shall be maintained for a period of ten years, and that the purchaser shall construct, with the aid of the Shipping Board's construction loan fund, two new fast vessels of at least 45,000 tons each to round out the first-class service of the Leviathan, operated by the United States Lines. Under the terms of the contract, all of the ships involved will have been taken over within ninety days after the signing of the contract.

Plans for the construction of the two new liners, Mr. Sheedy said, will be expedited as soon as the operating company is formed. It is anticipated that work on these ships will be under way by the first of next year.

Operated For Seven Years

The United States Lines, consisting of six large vessels—the Leviathan, George Washington, America, Republic, President Harding and President Roosevelt—have been operated by the Government for seven years in the North Atlantic passenger trade.

The American Merchant Lines, consisting of the five combination passenger and freight vessels—the American Banker, American Trade, American Shipper, American Farmer and American Merchant—have been operated since 1924.

The Shipping Board's formal announcement of the vote to accept the Chapman bid described the deal as "involving one of the greatest ship sales in maritime history." In taking its action, it was announced the board was unanimous in its desire to place these vessels under private ownership for guaranteed operation under the American flag.

"The commissioners of the board," the announcement continues, "moreover, feel that this sale will be an outstanding step in the development of the American Merchant Marine and that with the increased interest in American flag-shipping the way will be paved for sale of the remaining cargo fleets still under Shipping Board control."

Commenting on the board's action, T. V. O'Connor, chairman, said:

"The Shipping Board has made the most outstanding sale in its career to an American citizen in whom it has the utmost confidence as to his ability to secure to the American merchant marine its position in the North Atlantic trade."

Mr. O'Connor represented the board as gratified that the Senate committee "which," he said, "has been in a large way responsible for the progress of American shipping during recent years," has seen fit to interpose no objection to the sale after hearings on the merits of the Chapman bid.

No Serious Doubts Raised

Touching on the Senate committee hearings, Mr. O'Connor said the arguments presented before the committee yesterday by William Francis Gibbs, representing one of the unsuccessful bidders for the lines, questioning the

(Continued on Page 2, Column 7)

COOLIDGE AGAIN OVERRIDDEN ON CRUISER BILL

Senate Group Votes For Immediate Start On Five New Warships

PRESIDENT SOUGHT DELAY OF ONE YEAR

Some Think He Was Trying To Escape Deficit On Retiring

[*Washington Bureau of The Sun*]

Washington, Feb. 14—President Coolidge today sent Congress a request for funds to begin construction on five of the fifteen cruisers and the airplane carrier recently authorized in the $274,000,000 naval building program. But, contrary to the terms of the authorization law and the anticipations of the bigger navy supporters, he asked that the entire sum requested—$12,370,000—be provided for the next fiscal year, beginning July 1, and nothing for the current year, the effect of which might be to postpone the whole construction program a year.

Immediately the request was received at the Capitol the subcommittee of the Senate Appropriations Committee, considering the Navy Department appropriation bill, voted to make $700,000 available immediately, so that the navy can let contracts for five ships before the present fiscal year ends. This action is expected to be approved tomorrow by the full committee and it is generally thought both houses will override the President's wishes.

Congress Ignored Coolidge

In authorizing the construction program Congress ignored Mr. Coolidge's repeated assertions that there should be no time limit in the bill. It specifically provided that five cruisers should be commenced in the fiscal year 1929 (the current year), five in 1930 and five in 1931, and that the aircraft carrier should be put under way prior to June 30, 1930. It stipulated further that, if construction of any vessel authorized to be undertaken in 1929 or 1930 were not undertaken in that year, it should be begun in the next succeeding year.

The action of President Coolidge in sidestepping the plain intent of Congress gave rise to speculation as to whether he was motivated by pique over the fact that Congress had ignored his recommendations with respect to the time limit or whether he feared his Administration might wind up with a deficit, as now appears certain unless he has gone far of the mark in his recent estimate of revenues and expenditures. At any rate, the effect of his policy would be, if carried out, to charge up to the Hoover Administration some $12,000,000 that ordinarily would have been debited to his own.

Fought Against Time Clause

When the authorization bill was pending in the Senate and Mr. Coolidge was desperately trying to have the time clause eliminated, it was intimated at the White House that, if his wishes were followed, the President would ask immediately for a substantial appropriation to begin work. It was explained the President opposed the time clause for budgetary reasons, since it might not be possible in each of the three years to allot the necessary funds.

The Congressional Committee in its report had contemplated that $13,000,000 would be appropriated in 1929, $43,000,000 in 1930, $71,000,000 in 1931, and larger amounts thereafter. It was anticipated Mr. Coolidge would ask the $13,000,000 to become immediately available and also a substantial sum for the next fiscal year.

$100,000,000 Deficit Possible

That Mr. Coolidge might have passed the burden over to Mr. Hoover in order to avoid a financial embarrassment in the closing year of his own Administration seemed possible in some quarters. For, if the President's estimate in his budget message two months ago that there will be a surplus of $36,990,000 on June 30 is cor-

(Continued on Page 8, Column 3)

"LITTLE BROWN JUG," BANDITS' DOWNFALL

Bank Robbers Pause In Flight To Drink Whisky And Are Captured

Independence, Kan., Feb. 14 (AP)—Two bank robbers, who tarried to drink from a jug of whisky after fleeing into Oklahoma with $1,000 loot from the Chautauqua State Bank at Chautauqua, Kan., were captured today by Marshal Harry McIntyre, of Elgin, Kansas.

Marshal McIntyre surprised the men while they were drinking from a jug in the brush across the Oklahoma line. The money was recovered and the prisoners were taken to the jail at Elgin without any formalities of extradition. McIntyre said the men were intoxicated.

Byrd's Operator Tells Of Antarctic Storm

North Carolina Amateur In Touch With Base Of Polar Expedition

Durham, N. C., Feb. 14 (AP)—A terrific gale is sweeping the camp of Commander Richard E. Byrd's Antarctic expedition, Radio Operator Grenlie with the expedition told F. M. Whitaker, of Durham, in their weekly exchange of messages here today.

Whitaker, operating amateur station WVOC, got into touch with the Byrd base at 6.05 o'clock this morning and talked with Grenlie for twenty-five minutes.

The gale has been blowing for five days, Grenlie reported. He expressed the opinion that it is now abating and said that during the storm communication with the civilized world had been difficult.

40 Injured In Boston Underground Gas Blast

Score Treated At Hospitals For Slight Hurts—Plate-Glass Windows Shattered

Boston, Feb. 14 (AP)—Terrific underground gas explosions, which hurled manhole covers skyward and shattered plate-glass windows, caused injuries to more than forty persons in the downtown mercantile district late today.

More than a score were treated at hospitals for their injuries, most of which were not serious. Only two persons remained in hospitals for treatment. The explosions occurred in the vicinity of Summer and Chauncy streets, when evening commuter traffic was at its peak. Many were trampled under foot in the confusion. Occupants of buildings shaken by the blasts fled to the streets.

Vienna Police Seize Arms At Socialist Offices

Inquiry Under Way To Learn Whether Revolutionary Attempt Was Planned

Vienna, Feb. 14 (AP)—The police today seized 30,000 cartridges, 300 modern rifles, machine guns, revolvers and army telephones in a raid at the headquarters of the Socialist Organization for the Defense of the Republic and the Republican Workmen's Union.

No arrests were made pending an investigation to determine whether the arms were intended for use in a *coup d'etat* against the present Christian Socialist regime headed by Chancellor Seipel. At Social Democrat headquarters it was asserted that the police had authorized the possession of the firearms for purposes of self-defense.

Box Car Painter Awarded First Prize For Canvas

John Kane, 60, Takes Honors At Carnegie Institute Annual Exhibition

Pittsburgh, Feb. 14 (AP)—John Kane, who paints houses and box cars for a living, but turns to the brush and palette for pleasure, today was awarded the Carnegie Institute prize in the nineteenth annual exhibition of the Associated Artists of Pittsburgh, which opened today.

Kane had passed his sixtieth milestone in life before he achieved his ambition of painting pictures. His advancement has been phenomenal and twice in recent years his paintings have hung in international exhibitions with the work of impotrant contemporary artists.

Cattle Man Says Beef Prices Are Down, But Not To Consumer

President Of Chicago Exchange Asserts $1,375,000,000 Has Been Written Off Live-Stock Value, With No Retail Price Drop

Chicago, Feb. 14 (AP)—Everett C. Brown, president of the Chicago Live-Stock Exchange, said today $1,375,000,000 has been written off the value of cattle in the United States in the last six months, yet the average consumer cannot buy beef any cheaper at retail markets than last summer.

At that time the buying public largely, he said, stopped buying beef, classed it as a luxury and substituted other food products. Now all beef distributing channels are choked with beef that cannot be moved. He attributed this situation partly to an excessive decline in prices for hides, amounting to ten cents a pound since a year ago.

Mr. Brown urged withholding cattle from the market to the greatest extent possible at present. He added:

"If bankers are calling loans on cattle in order to place the money at greater rates of interest on Wall Street, it is high time that they protect the great cattle industry, especially so after a break of $3 to $5 a hundredweight."

WAR TO END IS DECLARED ON CHICAGO GANGS AFTER SLAUGHTER OF 7 IN GARAGE

"Never Anything To Equal This," Commissioner W. F. Russell Says—New Underworld Round-Up More Extensive Than Any Other

MACHINE GUNS USED TO MOW DOWN AIDES OF LATE O'BANION

Trapped Victims Found Lying Face Upward—Presence Of Eye Specialist Among Dead Adds To Mystery—His Identification Proves Difficult

By D. L. FLEMING

[*Chicago Bureau of The Sun*]

Chicago, Feb. 14—Seven big-time Chicago gangsters—muscle men of the North Side booze racket and remnants of the once flourishing Dion O'Banion crew—met death as a unit today before a firing squad of rival desperadoes.

The apostles of the late O'Banion were wiped out without a fight. They simply were entrapped in their North Clark street rendezvous, relieved of their guns, lined up against a convenient brick wall and mowed down by a stream of lead and steel from machine guns and shotguns fired at close range. Six of them died instantly and the seventh within three hours.

SLAUGHTER UNPARALLELED

Having carried out the wholesale execution without a slip-up, the invading bandits sped away in an automobile, leaving police to solve a massacre which for audacity, novelty of method and extent of human destruction is without parallel in this city's long history of gangland slaughters.

The manner of the wholesale killing almost exactly reproduced the murder of one gang of bootleggers by another narrated in a recent serial story called "Hooch," printed in the *Saturday Evening Post*. In the fiction story the machine gunning also took place in a garage.

One of the mysterious features of the affair was the presence among the victims of Dr. Reinhart H. Schurmmer, eye specialist. The police had difficulty in identifying him and his presence in the garage was inexplainable.

ROUND-UP STARTED

Early speculation as to the identity of the murder squad connected it with the organization of "Scarface" Al Capone, czar of the West Side beer business and noted enemy of O'Banion and his successors. Another theory charged the assault against Detroit bootleggers from whom the O'Banion forces were reported to have hijacked two truck loads of Canadian whisky two weeks ago.

One of the first police moves in the case was the inauguration of an underworld round-up which Commissioner William F. Russell promised would be more thorough than the regular week-end scourings he has been making.

The commissioner said he was familiar with a good many gang killings in Chicago, "but never anything to equal this," and he pledged war to the finish, "no matter how long it takes.

"We're going to make this the knell of gangdom in Chicago," the chief warned.

Witnesses are not agreed as to the number of men in the murder party. Some say there were four; others, five. All concur, however, in the statement that two of the invaders were wearing what appeared to be police uniforms and that all were armed, some carrying shotguns and others machine guns.

Car Had Gong

As police have reconstructed the developments, what took place was about like this:

The slayers drove up to the O'Banion headquarters—a beer distributing plant just a block away from the fashionable hotel and apartment district along Lincoln Park West—in an automobile which resembled police cars, even to the gong that was clearing traffic out of its way.

They entered the one-story brick structure by a front door, beside which is a window bearing the legend: "The S. M. C. Cartage Company." Two men were sitting in the office, which occupies the front portion of the ground floor, and five were puttering around at various tasks in the large garage in the rear.

Lined Against Wall

Probably posing as policemen "making a pinch," the scene next shifts to the garage at the rear, with all seven men lined up against the brick side wall, their backs to their captors.

What word, if any, passed between the conquerors and the conquered are not known, but the neighborhood is full of persons who heard the roar of shotgun and machine gun fire that followed. A number of these persons also saw the invading party leave by the door they had entered taking flight in their automobile with artillery still smoking.

A mob of curious persons burst into the place immediately and there on the cement garage floor lay seven men in a row. They had fallen backward from the wall, their faces upturned. Silk shirts, flashy ties, and expensive watch chains draped over fancy vests, were blood stained. Red dust from the bullet-spattered wall was sprinkled over the scene.

One of the men was found to be alive. He was Frank Gusenberk, well-known gangster-bootlegger. He was taken to a hospital, where he died in less than three hours.

All Others Dead

All of the others were dead, and, while awaiting the arrival of a coroner, police readily identified them.

They were:

PETER GUSENBERG, brother of Frank Gusenberg and known to police as a professional slugger and bootlegger.

JAMES CLARK, brother-in-law of George "Bugs" Moran, leader of the O'Banion gang since the chief's death four years ago.

ALBERT WEINSHANK, owner of a Broadway saloon.

JOHN SNYDER, known as a minor politician.

JOHN MAY, mechanic.

DR. REINHART H. SCHWIMMER, eye specialist.

Where Is Moran?

Police tonight were concerned chiefly with establishing the whereabouts of Moran, leader of the mob. One theory was that he was in the Clark street headquarters when the raid took place and was taken away as a prisoner by the invaders.

Another was that he escaped as the attackers approached, and still another is that he was n near the place.

Coroner Arrives

Coroner Herman N. Bundesen arrived at the murder scene a half hour after the shooting and the searching of the bodies was begun. A large diamond ring was taken from one of Peter Gusenberg's fingers and his clothing yielded $447 in cash and some unimportant papers. Weinshank's fingers furnished another fine diamond ring but the money on his person amounted

THE WEATHER
Mostly cloudy tonight and Friday, probable showers Friday; slightly warmer tonight. Moderate east and southeast winds.
Detailed report on Page 2

THE EVENING SUN

Published every week day by The A. S. Abell Company

5 STAR ★★★★★ COMPLETE MARKETS

VOL. 39 | PAID CIRCULATION AUGUST MORNING 150,110 EVENING 141,356 291,470 ‖ SUNDAY 190,801 | BALTIMORE, THURSDAY, SEPTEMBER 12, 1929 | 46 PAGES | 2 CENTS

THOUSANDS SEE BIG MILITARY PARADE

Bullet Hole Found In Navy's New Blimp

THREE SENATORS TO INVESTIGATE SHEARER'S ACTS

Robinson, Shortridge And Allen Are Appointed As Subcommittee

SESSIONS EXPECTED TO BEGIN NEXT WEEK

Big-Navy Man And Shipbuilders Likely To Be Called First

By Henry M. Hyde

Washington, Sept. 12—No time is to be lost in exploring and exposing the activities of William B. Shearer, the blond mystery man of the big-navy lobby, and his employers.

At a meeting of the Senate Committee on Naval Affairs this morning Chairman Hale, of Maine, was instructed to appoint a subcommittee to start immediate hearings. It was left to the discretion of the chairman to appoint either three or five Senators to serve on the subcommittee.

Granted Full Authority

Senator Hale thereupon appointed Senator Shortridge of California, chairman, Senator Allen of Kansas and Senator Robinson of Arkansas.

Hale anticipates that the first meeting of the probers will not be held until early next week, though it is possible that there will be a preliminary session tomorrow or Saturday.

The subcommittee is empowered to act with full authority in conducting its hearings, and all details are left entirely in its hands.

None From States Concerned

The full committee decided to eliminate from appointment on the special body of investigators any Senators from States in which are located any of the plants of the Bethlehem Shipbuilding Company, the Newport News Shipbuilding and Dry Dock Company, or the American Brown-Boveru Electric Company, which were the three employers of Shearer in his various activities as a big-navy booster.

That rule prevented the following Senators from serving on the subcommittee—Tydings and Goldsborough, of Maryland; Walsh, of Massachusetts; Kean, of New Jersey, and Swanson, of Virginia.

Though this is a matter for final determination by the subcommittee it is expected that the first witnesses to be called for examination will be Shearer himself and the officers of the three shipbuilding companies named above.

Afternoon Meeting Called

Within half an hour of his appointment as chairman of the sub-committee, Senator Shortridge announced that he had called a meeting for 3 o'clock this afternoon, at which he expected that subpœnas would be issued for Shearer and for the officials of the three shipbuilding companies involved and their subsidiaries.

Shortridge went on to say that the first session of the sub-committee at which Shearer will, presumably, be heard will be held next Monday morning. All the meetings, which will be open to the public, will be held in a large room on the street floor of the Senate Building.

"Under the resolution which originated this investigation," said Senator Shortridge, "our hearings will be confined to the activities of Mr. Shearer at the fruitless Geneva conference on

[Continued On Page 2, Column 6]

Inside Today---

GOOD EVENING

By CLARK S. HOBBS

THEY WERE HEROES who drove the British down the North Point road back in 1814, and it's almost as great a test of courage to drive an automobile down that way now.

THEN AND NOW

Beating drums and tramping feet
As stalwart soldiers march the street
In nicely ordered ranks.
But smiles belie the grim display
Of deadly guns, and well they may,
For by Potomac's banks
No hostile fleet on plunder's quest
Has come to momentary rest
To threaten grievous harm.
Nay, smiles and laughter rule today
As marching hosts pass on their way—
There sounds no grave alarm.

Beating drums and tramping feet
As stalwart soldiers march the street
To make a brave display.
And happy we that smiles and cheers
Prevail instead of fears and tears,
As did one other day.
The foe that once assailed our peace
Is friend, nor must that friendship cease,
But ever stronger grow.
Let war no longer be the trade
Of soldiers; better they parade
To make a pleasant show.

OF COURSE, war leaves its wounds, but anniversary holidays are a splendid healing antiseptic.

DISARMAMENT is all to the merry, but we can't believe a procession of plowshares would give much of a thrill.

SUN SQUARE DOIN'S Or The Diary Of A Traffic Cop

8.30 A. M.—I've got to laugh when I think of what's going to happen to that there sorrel-top wife of mine and the boarding house lady and that good-looking little school teacher at the boarding house. I mean them females kept nagging at me so about a window for today's parade I practically was compelled to put one over on them to get a little peace. And when I think of where I've sent them and all that I could nigh bust.

I mean it tickles me pink to think of that there proud and haughty better half of mine explaining to a guy that never heard of me that she's my wife and expecting him at the mention of my magic name to give her the choicest window accommodations he's got in his place. I can sort of picture the guy looking at her dumb with astonishment and the sorrel-top beginning to get her dander up when the gink turns her away pitiful or maybe calls the police.

You see, the wife and the rest of them boarding house females got to pressing me so hard about getting some big business man friend of mine to give them a window I just had to do something, so I looked up a name in the telephone directory and give them that, remarking as how everything would be all right just as soon as they mentioned my name.

And then I had to go outside to keep from laughing right in their faces. And I've been chuckling to myself ever since because I've figured it out if I don't do my laughing between now and when I go home tonight I won't do none. I'm awful afraid along about that time I ain't going to have no cause for hilarity. You see, I give the wife a address on Eutaw street and I find out this morning the parade don't even go by there.

10 A. M.—Well, anyway, nobody can lose me when they start asking me history. I'm full of it. Just now a guy says to me:

"I guess it took a lot of courage back in 1814 for untrained citizens to go face the British soldiers."

"Absolutely," I says.

"The British were seasoned troops, wasn't they?" he says.

"Well," I says. "I don't know as to beforehand, but they was well peppered before they left."

11 A. M.—The sergeant don't know much about history. He says that North Point affair wasn't no more than a skirmish. Well, heck! even if it was a skirmish back in 1814 it would be a battle by this time.

BALTIMORE holds her head high. And that's doing well, for many a lady under 200 has had to have her face lifted.

BULLET HOLE IN NAVY'S NEW METAL BLIMP

Shot Pierces Main Helium Chamber Of ZMC-2

DIRIGIBLE LANDS AT LAKEHURST

Damage Discovered As Flight From Detroit Ends

[*By the Associated Press*]

Lakehurst, N. J., Sept. 12—The metal dirigible ZMC-2, being delivered to the Navy Department from Detroit, arrived shortly before noon today with a bullet hole in its main helium gas chamber.

The metal airship was manned by Capt. William E. Kepner, of the army; Lieut. H. J. Duggen, of the navy, and Sergt. Joseph Bishop, of the army.

Discovery Made In Hangar

Capt. William Kepner, of the army, who flew the ship from Detroit, was unaware that he had been shot at until the ship was safely in the hangar and the bullet hole was discovered by a member of the landing crew.

The hole was immediately plugged with rags to prevent further loss of the valuable helium until permanent repairs could be made.

It will be recalled that on the last leg of the Graf Zeppelin a bullet was found in the fabric covering when the ship landed at Lakehurst from Los Angeles.

Los Angeles Also Fired On

The navy dirigible Los Angeles also has been fired at upon several occasions.

Captain Kepner said that he could not say definitely where the metal ship had been when it was fired upon, but from the angle of fire, which could be determined by the line between the hole where the bullet entered and the one where it left he judged that the ship had been close over a mountain. He thought it probable that it had been somewhere in Pennsylvania.

The arrival of the ship had been awaited by naval officers here with keen curiosity. The idea for a metal dirigible was turned down by both the army and navy some years ago and this ship was finally contracted for by action of Congress.

Blimp Described

The metal ship is about the size of the non-rigid blimps, two of which are stationed here, but it is of much greater girth and has eight fins instead of the usual four. To those accustomed to airship designs, such as that of the Graf Zeppelin, Los Angeles and the army and navy blimps, this metal ship looked like some fantasy of an imaginative tinsmith.

There was a wind of about twenty-five miles an hour blowing and as the ship was driven toward the ground it rolled like a small boat in a heavy sea.

Captain Kepner was accompanied on the flight from Detroit by Lieut. H. J. Duggan, of the navy, and Sergt. Joseph Bishop, of the army. They expressed pleasure at the manner in which the ship had handled.

Tin Bubble Triumphs

The ZMC-2 is the first all-metal dirigible ever to fly successfully, although several others have been built, both here and abroad.

The sheath of the ZMC-2 is of thin aluminum alloy and the helium lifting gas is pumped directly into this tin bubble instead of being carried in cells as in the fabric dirigibles.

The ZMC-2 traveled the 550 miles from Detroit to Lakehurst at an average speed slightly more than forty miles an hour. This speed was made in spite of head winds which at times reached a velocity of thirty miles per hour.

Shipyards Aflame In Kiel, Germany

City's Entire Firefighting Force Battles Blaze At Krupp-Germania Plant

Kiel, Germany, Sept. 12 (AP)—A great fire broke out late this afternoon in the engineering plant of the Friedrich Krupp-Germania shipyards here and rapidly assumed dangerous proportions. All the city's fire brigades were engaged in fighting it.

Regulars On Parade For 200-Year-Old Baltimore

This photograph shows members of the Sixth Infantry, Regular Army, as they marched on Mount Royal avenue this afternoon in the big military parade marking Baltimore's Bi-Centennial. Other regular army units, as well as marines, naval detachments, militia organizations and veterans' groups, were represented in the line. Behind the infantrymen, not yet turned from Mount Royal avenue, is an artillery section.

MUSSOLINI QUITS 7 OF 8 POSTS HE HELD IN CABINET

Resulting Reorganization One Of Most Sweeping In Fascist History

[*By the Associated Press*]

Rome, Sept. 12—Benito Mussolini, Italian dictator, today relinquished seven of the eight cabinet posts he holds in the Italian Facist Government. He remains Premier and Minister of the Interior.

A royal decree announcing the action also contained notice of the replacement of two other Ministers, those of Public Instruction and of National Economy.

The Under Secretary for the Interior Ministry, which portfolio the Duce retained, also was changed in the move, which comprised probably the most sweeping reorganization of the Fascist Government since its inception.

New Cabinet Officials

The Cabinet officials taking the posts held by Signor Mussolini are:

Dino Grandi, Minister of Foreign Affairs, formerly Under Secretary for Foreign Affairs.

General Debono, Minister for the Colonies.

Gen. Pietro Gozzera, Minister of War, formerly Under Secretary for War.

Rear-Admiral Giuseppe Siriani, Minister of Marine, formerly Under Secretary for Marine.

Gen. Italo Balbo, Minister of Aviation, formerly Under Secretary for Marine.

Michele Bianchi, Minister of Public Works.

Giuseppe Bottai, Minister of Corporations; formerly Under Secretary in that Ministry.

The same royal decree announced the Ministry of Public Instruction henceforth will be known as the Ministry of National Education, and that the Ministry of National Economy will be known as the Ministry of Agriculture and Forests.

Prof. Deputy Giuliano Balbino will become Minister of National Education, replacing Signor Giuseppe Belluzzo, who held the old ministry.

Deputy Giacomo Acerbo will become Minister of Agriculture and Forests, replacing Signor Martelli, former Minister of National Economy.

Deputy Landro Arpinati will become Under Secretary for Interior, replac-

[Continued On Page 2, Column 2]

Jury Hears Last Stone Evidence, Then Adjourns

Panel At Bel Air Takes Testimony Of Six More Witnesses In Case Of Woman Charged With Poisonings—Decision Expected Tomorrow

[*From a Staff Correspondent*]

Belair, Md., Sept. 12—The last of a stream of thirty-eight persons bearing evidence and gossip about Mrs. Hattie Stone, suspected of having wiped out her family with poisons, filed through the grand jury room here today, and then the jurors adjourned without announcing any action they may have taken in regard to the accused woman.

It was reported at the Courthouse that the jury's decision in three mysterious deaths in the Stone family would be made known tomorrow, when a batch of indictments returned in other cases are to be presented to the court.

Six Witnesses Testify

Six witnesses moved into the secrecy of the grand jury chamber today, told their stories and disappeared. Most of them were Pennsylvania Railroad workers who were intimate with Ed Stone, husband of Mrs. Stone. His mysterious death on a train in January, 1928, has been the subject of much speculation. It was believed that the summoning of these men resulted from a determination of the jurors to probe into the death of the elder Stone as well as that of his 15-year-old son.

One witness who went before the inquest late yesterday was Bob Jordan, who, as trusty in the Belair jail, where Mrs. Stone is confined on a charge of murder, served her meals and overheard her conversations with

[Continued On Page 2, Column 5]

FLASHES

Heiress Killed By Ousted Gardener

Cleveland, Sept. 12 (AP)—Mrs. Barbara Diebolt Irr, 62, heiress of the Diebolt Brewing fortune, was shot and killed at her Euclid Village home today by a gardener angered because he had been dismissed, police said. Michael di Tirro, the gardener, surrendered after the shooting.

Tornado In France Wrecks Houses

Toulon, France, Sept. 12 (UP). A tornado struck Toulon and the neighboring countryside today, tearing up trees, lifting roofs, smashing windows and paralyzing the economic life of the city. Stores were flooded.

Will Ask Inquiry Into T. A. T. Crash

Albuquerque, N. M., Sept. 12 (UP)—A Senatorial investigation of the fatal crash of the T. A. T. plane, City of San Francisco, on Mount Taylor, will be demanded by Senator Sam G. Bratton, of New Mexico, he announced here today.

White Man Hanged For Attacking Girl

Raleigh, N. C., Sept. 12 (AP)—Willis Buckner, 32, a white man, was electrocuted at the State prison here today for attacking a young girl in Craven county several months ago. He was the second white man in the history of the electric chair in North Carolina to be executed for this crime.

Germans Find More Plots On Republic

Police Uncover Explosives And Correspondence In Alleged Communist House

Wiesbaden, Germany, Sept. 12 (UP). French army of occupation detectives and members of the Mainz Police Department raided the house of a Communist leader at Gonsenheim, near Mainz, and seized large quantities of explosives and a mass of correspondence allegedly dealing with plots to wreck public buildings and to cause a general uprising, dispatches from the occupation zone today said.

CAR DYNAMITED BY STRIKERS IN NEW ORLEANS

Acting Mayor Scores Use Of Tear Gas Bombs To Disperse Crowd

[*By the Associated Press*]

New Orleans, Sept. 12—The outbreak of fresh violence in the New Orleans street car strike has thrown the city into a state of alarm, with city officials striving to prevent further vandalism.

After several weeks of peace caused by the belief thatean amicable settlement of the strike, called July 2, would be effected, striking conductors and motormen voted yesterday to reject the settlement terms reached at the New York conference, and during the night either the strikers or their sympathizers attempted to check the operation of cars by non-union operators by placing dynamite on the tracks.

Shortly before midnight a car was blasted off the tracks at Washington avenue and Dupre street by running over a charge of explosive, and at 11 o'clock this morning another car ran over five sticks of dynamite in the fashionable St. Charles avenue and Elemore street section, but the wet charge failed to explode.

Wild Excitement Prevails

The Washington avenue explosion caused wild excitement in the neighborhood, thousands of persons gathering quickly. The police broke up the crowd by throwing tear gas bombs among them and Acting Mayor T. Semmes Walmsley, who was in the crowd, criticized the police and deputy marshals in a statement, in which he sai dthe bombs were thrown into the crowd without warning and without any previous attempt to disperse the people. He demanded an investigation.

The explosion threw the car off the track, split a front wheel, shattered the window panes, but the white woman, two Negroes and motorman and conductor escaped injury. The car was jacked back on the tracks and towed to the car barn.

Patronage of the cars fell off today and the strike situation was thrown back to the same status as at the start. Union officials said the men, who stood 1,446 to 87 for rejecting the peace proposals, would have accepted the terms if they could have received any assur-

[Continued On Page 2, Column 2]

TROOPS MARCH TO CELEBRATE BI-CENTENNIAL

Thousands See Soldiers, Sailors And Marines In Parade

BRIG.-GEN. GOWEN IS GRAND MARSHAL

Fifth Regiment Truns Out In Elaborate Dress Uniforms

Baltimore gave a military parade today as the first feature of its three-day party to celebrate its two-hundredth anniversary. The State's military outfit stepped out with soldiers, sailors and marines through streets lined with thousands of spectators and buildings draped with the national colors and the black and gold of Maryland.

The parade units formed in the streets intersecting Mount Royal avenue above the Mount Royal Station. Promptly at 2 o'clock drums rolled and the brassy voice of the bugle sounded the signal to fall in.

General Gowen Is Marshal

Down Mount Royal avenue, through St. Paul street, Read street, and the other streets on the parade route, solid lines of citizens awaited the coming of the marchers.

The procession was headed by a platoon of mounted police. Behind them rode Brig.-Gen. James B. Gowen of the U. S. Army, the grand marshal of the parade, and his escort, all on fast-stepping chargers. After the marshal and his staff came the First Division troops of the United States Army, led by Col. Thomas W. Darrah, chief of staff of the Third Corps Area.

The khaki-clad infantrymen paraded in broad lines, with the warm sunlight reflected from the tips of their polished bayonets. Behind the infantrymen clattered and clanked the artillery, with the gunners sitting stalwartly, with folded arms, on the gun caissons. After the artillery came the marines, marching in the same broad lines as the infantry, and after them the sailors, who, by comparison with the marines, seemed not to have quite gotten their land legs.

"Social Secretary" There

In the rear of the Marines strolled a small civilian figure with a streetcar conductor's cap, whose identity was a puzzle to all the spectators but one. That one shifted a chew of tobacco and announced to those around him, "that's the marine's social secretary." The sailors were followed by the Dandy Fifth Regiment, led by Col. Washington Bowie and other officers, whose elaborate dress uniforms were topped off with waving white plumes.

One point of interest in the parade was what appeared to be a traveling machine shop, mounted on a big truck from Camp Holabird.

Moving in four divisions, the troops, led by Brig.-Gen. James B. Gowen, grand marshal, passed through flag-hung streets to the City Hall, to be reviewed by Mayor William F. Broening, officials of the city government and visiting dignitaries.

Opened At Noon

The anniversary celebration was officially opened by Mayor Broening at noon when, after a short speech from a reviewing stand in front of the City Hall, he released a carrier pigeon which carried a message for President Herbert Hoover. Simultaneously the Memorial Plaza echoed with the whir of wings as approximately 300 other pigeons were freed, carrying messages of invitation and greeting to the Mayors of other cities.

"Lord Baltimore," the City Hall bell, marked the inaugural of the anniversary by tolling 200 times, once for each year of the city's existence. It was joined by other bells and whistles which helped to usher the anniversary in in a cacophony of sound.

Band Concert

Before the official inauguration spectators at the City Hall were entertained by a concert given by the Fifth Regiment Band and by the maneuvers of army, navy and marine airplanes which swung over the city and around around the City Hall.

The military and naval units formed on the streets west of Mount Royal avenue and moved out behind a platoon

[Continued On Page 3, Column 1]

WEATHER FORECAST
Cloudy and occasional rain today; rising temperature tomorrow; moderate east and southeast winds.
Detailed Weather Report on Page 22.

THE SUN

Registered United States Patent Office

Venezuela May Well Become A Latter-Day Mexico
Says Luis Munoz Marin
—Page 13.

VOL. 185—D | PAID CIRCULATION SEPTEMBER MORNING, 149,435 EVENING, 143,960 293,395 || SUNDAY 192,285 | BALTIMORE, WEDNESDAY, OCTOBER 30, 1929 | Published every week day by The A. S. Abell Company. Entered as second-class matter at Baltimore Postoffice. Copyright, 1929, by The A. S. Abell Company | 28 PAGES | 2 CENTS

MARKET STAMPEDE CHECKED

DALADIER GIVES UP ATTEMPT TO FORM CABINET

Radical-Socialist Leader Will Tell President Today Task Is Hopeless

BRIAND EXPECTED TO BE RECALLED

Mix-Up Over Ministry Due To Socialists' Refusal To Join Left Group

Paris, Wednesday, Oct. 30 (Special Cable)—The first week of the French political crisis has ended with a solution apparently as far off as on the first day. At 9 o'clock this morning Edouard Daladier, leader of the Radical-Socialist party, will go to the Elysee Palace to inform President Doumergue that he renounces the mission given him to form a Cabinet.

It is generally believed now that Aristide Briand, whose resignation as Premier and Foreign Minister was forced last Tuesday with unexpected abruptness, will be recalled and will form a Government including the Radical-Socialists and stopping short of the Louis Marin group of Republican Unionists.

Daladier Makes Announcement

M. Daladier announced his decision to desist from his task of forming a Ministry from his father-in-law's home in the Champs Elysees at 1 o'clock this morning to a group of bewildered newspapermen who had been informed at 7.30 P. M., that the Radical-Socialist leader had abandoned the task, and shortly before midnight that this was all a mistake and that he would have the list of his Cabinet Ministers ready this afternoon at latest.

Never in the history of France's Cabinet-making, fantastic as that operation has often been, has such confusion reigned in the shifting and reshifting of parties and groups.

First Out, Then In, Then Out

Special editions of the evening newspapers carried last night big headlines announcing that M. Daladier had abandoned his mission, to be followed by others announcing the opposite information.

Early editions of this morning's journals repeated the latter announcement, only to be quickly followed by second editions definitely reporting the exit of M. Daladier.

What has happened since 1 P. M. probably could not be paralleled in any other Parliamentary country in the world. At 1 o'clock the national organization of the Socialists called the national council, reversed its Deputies' vote in favor of coalition with the Radical-Socialists, and by a vote of 1,500 to 1,451, washed the Socialists' hands of inclusion in any Radical-Socialist Ministry.

Heavy Blow Struck

This seemed a heavy blow to M. Daladier's chances, and there was, therefore, little surprise when, early in the evening, close party associates of M. Daladier, such as Louis Jean Malvy, Joseph Caillaux and Edouard Herriot, let it be known that their party leader would inform President Doumergue at 9 o'clock tonight that it was impossible for him to inform a Government.

The evening extras of the Left newspapers carried M. Daladier's supposed renunciation in their headlines, and at 9 o'clock M. Daladier entered the Elysees Palace, with all Paris expecting that Aristide Briand would be called on tomorrow to take up the task at which the Radical-Socialist had failed.

It was reported that M. Daladier himself had told friends that he would not go on.

Reports Turned Around

But within two hours this information was absolutely turned around. The president of the Radical-Socialist party quit the Elysee Palace shortly after 10 o'clock and declared the report of his resignation was entirely unfounded. He asserted he had not resigned, but that he had told President Doumergue he would continue his efforts to form a government without the Socialists and would see the President at 10 A. M. tomorrow. At that time, it was intimated, M. Daladier might have the full list of his proposed Cabinet to submit to the President.

The part M. Briand himself has played in tonight's political operetta remains open to explanation. For the moment, the important fact is that M. Daladier has broken all sorts of political precedents, that he has paid court to the Socialists only to be rudely rebuffed, and that in so doing he has decidedly weakened his chances of forming any other combination of

(Continued on Page 17, Column 4)

The Great Game Of Politics

By FRANK R. KENT

Split Three Ways

WASHINGTON, Oct. 29.

A SWEETER MESS than the politics of the Grand Old Party these days is not easy to recall. It is usual enough for the party in power in state or nation to have a dissatisfied element. Always there is a disgruntled faction. Any such thing as complete harmony is impossible. You can have harmony in the minority but not in the majority. The possession and exercise of power and the distribution of patronage inevitably bring about division, for the simple reason that there are sure to be many to whom you cannot give what they want or do what they want. However, it is not customary to be split three ways, as the Republican party now is, within less than a year from the date of its greatest victory.

—o—

YET THIS IS the situation as revealed by the struggle over the tariff bill, the funeral services for which began yesterday in the Senate amid alibis and disclaimers from all factions and both parties as to responsibility for its demise.

First, there is the standpat group of regulars, most of whom were not for Mr. Hoover's nomination, who are inherently for the highest possible tariff, who rejected the Hoover recommendation for limited revision and sponsored the pending bill, doomed from the start. Some of these are in the Senate and some out, but few of them are in tune with Hoover's policies or like him personally. He isn't their type and they can be expected to pull in the other direction. They are the practical politicians of the old organization.

—o—

THEN THERE ARE the so-called Progressives from the West with a natural anti-Administration slant. Most of them, too, opposed the Hoover nomination and some were against him for election. They represent the other extreme from the regulars on tariff and on nearly everything else. There is a wider gap between regular Republicans and the Progressives than between Republicans and Democrats. Hostile to the Old Guard, they are, for different reasons, also unfriendly to Mr. Hoover, whose views on farm relief do not coincide with theirs. Hostility is their normal state between campaigns. They do not have to have real reasons. They have the sort of constituencies that make it good politics to oppose.

—o—

AND, THIRDLY, THERE are the newly developed Hoover Republicans, who, with White House backing, have taken over control of the national committee and are in charge of the party machinery. They were strongly for Hoover from the start and are strongly for him now. Some of them are helping him build up a new Republican organization in the South on a more decent foundation, but that is a job that bruises the feelings of men accustomed to kindly White House treatment from many Administrations. Others are advising him on patronage in different parts of the country and others are engaged in promoting his policies and playing politics along Hoover lines, which are the same sort of lines but more straightly drawn.

—o—

THESE HOOVER politicians are numerous, loyal, enthusiastic, and their activities are resented by both regulars and Progressives. Except in the Senate they are the most potent of the three divisions, largely, of course, because they capitalize the Presidential power and popularity. They constitute an element lacking in the two previous Administrations, lacking in fact in any Republican Administration that can be recalled. Both Mr. Coolidge and Mr. Harding were parts of the regular organization and had the unqualified regular support. They had, of course, Progressive hostility, but that was natural. Both relied politically upon the organization. Neither had the sort of personal following that in Hoover's case is developing a group of politicians in the party distinct from both regulars and Progressives.

—o—

THE NET RESULT appears to be more party discord than in previous Administrations. Certainly there are more party divisions and the amount of political bickering and back-biting going on in Washington is almost unprecedented. Scarcely any Republican is happy. On form, this would seem to promise well for the Democrats in the next campaign. It ought to, of course, but there are two reasons it probably will not work out that way. One is the extraordinary capacity of the Republican label to weld together all manner of absurdly incongruous and discordant elements in support of their ticket, once their national convention has acted. The other is the equally extraordinary incapacity of the Democratic label to do the same thing.

NORRIS DEFIES G. O. P. LEADERS TO DEFEAT HIM

Progressive Accepts Challenge Of Regulars, Who Plan His Destruction

DECISION TO RETIRE HAS BEEN CHANGED

Nebraskan Abandons Intention And Will Now Enter Primary Fight

By M. FARMER MURPHY
[*Washington Bureau of The Sun*]

Washington, Oct. 29—The understood intention of the Administration to attempt to defeat for renomination Progressive Republican Senators who have not followed orders has met with defiance from Senator George W. Norris, of Nebraska, who says he is one of those who has been singled out for political destruction.

In a long statement which he gave out tonight the Senator, who dared to go into Pennsylvania and support William B. Wilson, the Democratic candidate for Senator against William Vare and who repudiated the Republican candidate for President last year in favor of Governor Smith, announces he is ready to meet the threat of his elimination and give the stand-pat machine the fight they invite.

McKelvie May Oppose Him

Although he has not made any definite statement of his candidacy, the vehicle which the regular Republicans expect to use to defeat Senator Norris is said to be Samuel R. McKelvie, former Governor of Nebraska and now a member of the Federal Farm Board. The real purpose of the drive against him, Senator Norris says, is "to weaken and discredit progressive principles of Government by driving me out of public life and securing the nomination and election of a Senator from Nebraska who will be subservient to the political machine and its bosses, both inside and outside the State, who at all times can be trusted to be 'regular.'"

For the reason that such a scheme is being plotted, Senator Norris says he has abandoned his intention to retire at the end of his present term and considers it imperative that he enter the coming primary to fight "the virtual alliance that has been formed between the old guard stand at machine inside the State and those who control the machine from the outside."

Caused By G. O. P. Dinner

Senator Norris' statement was precipitated at this time, it is believed by the dinner of leading organization Republicans held at the University Club in New York last Thursday. It was given by Jeremiah Millbank, treasurer of the Eastern division of the national Republican organization, to be Claudius R. Huston, the newly chosen chairman of the national committee. Among those attending were several United States Senators, Wall street financiers and James Burke as directly representing the White House.

According to reports of the gathering, all the speeches were to the effect that the party must be purged of all Progressive Senators, or, as one speaker put it, in giving the sense of the meeting, "the pygmies and obstructionists" must be driven out. Some of those marked for the slaughter were named, including Senator Borah, Sen-

(Continued on Page 9, Column 2)

AIR LINER SAFE IN NEW MEXICO AFTER STORM

Plane Carrying Five Forced Down By Snow Near Lava Beds

CABIN SHELTERED PARTY FOR NIGHT

Ohio Mail Pilot Burned To Death As Craft Crashes Into Trees

Albuquerque, N. M., Oct. 29 (AP)—Fighting a snowstorm most of the way to Albuquerque from Trechada, Ariz., Pilot James E. Doles and his copilot, Allan C. Barrie, brought the Western Air Express plane No. 113 safely to the Albuquerque Airport this afternoon under its own power.

Doles, Barrie, R. L. Britton, steward, and Dr. A. W. Ward, of San Francisco, and W. E. Merz, of Mount Vernon, N. Y., passengers, were none the worse for their adventure and said the greatest inconvenience had been the loss of time.

Snowstorm Fought

The plane encountered a terrific snowstorm over Arizona yesterday morning and Doles circled until he found a safe place to land. He put the plane down at Trechada and the party spent the night there to await clear weather. Trechada is about seventy-five miles southeast of Gallup and is only about five miles south of the treacherous lava beds and extinct volcanoes.

Doles landed the large tri-motored plane at the airport here about 3.40 P. M. The search had been temporarily held in abeyance at that time until a snowstorm raging over the State had cleared.

Confident Of Pilot

The plane had been missing since 10.30 o'clock yesterday morning. At no time since it was reported overdue did officials doubt that Doles had safely landed it. Their confidence was based on his performance and the instructions issued to all pilots to seek safety in stormy weather. In three years of flying, the Western Air Express traveled 3,200,000 miles without an accident. Doles had been flying with the company since 1928 and had more than 2,700 hours in the air to his credit.

[Editor's Note—It was a Transcontinental Air Transport plane which crashed on Mount Taylor, near Grants, New Mexico, early in September with the loss of eight lives.]

"It was through the cleverness of Pilot Doles that a landing was made and we escaped injury," Dr. Ward said. "Doles ran into the storm but kept cool. He circled and searched the limited area visible and finally sighted a small clearing in some heavy timber land. He headed for this spot and brought the plane down safely.

"There was a cabin near by which provided us refuge for the night. Of course, we had no way of communicating with the outside world regarding our safety."

Passenger Is Nonchalant

Merz did not seem to think the forced landing was out of the ordinary.

"I have flown in France, Germany, India and other countries, and I see nothing to get alarmed about when a plane is overdue or has to make a forced landing. This the first forced landing I ever was in, but I have

(Continued on Page 17, Column 6)

Do You Mix Freely? Ad In Harvard Magazine Raises Rum Scare

Subtley Worded Notices Smacking Of Liquor Prompt United States To Investigate. Prosecution Not Planned

Boston, Oct. 29 (AP)—Elihu D. Stone, Assistant United States Attorney in charge of liquor cases in the Federal Court here, said tonight that no prosecutions would result from the publishing of alleged bootleggers' advertisements in the Harvard *Crimson* and the *Lampoon*, student publications at Harvard University. Stone said no reference to liquor was contained in the advertisements and therefore there were no grounds for prosecution.

The official expressed the belief that the advertisements might have been printed as a jest but, he added, "advertisements like this, however, do not tend to elevate American youth."

Puzzled Readers

The attention of the Federal authorities was directed toward the appearance in the last issues of the publications of advertisements which puzzled many readers. One of the advertisements in the *Lampoon* read:

"When an examination is over do you feel at a loss? Do you mix freely with your fellow man (Homo Sapiens), and if so, what do you mix with him? Well, we can give you one good answer. When you know it, you can easily spend $10 to $15 right at home and never miss it."

"Stocks And Bonds"

Another was: "Try the loan and mortgage game; fun for your friends; stocks now in liquidation." A name and telephone numbers were placed at the bottom of the page.

A quarter page of the *Crimson* yesterday carried another "stocks and bond" advertisement with telephone numbers corresponding to those in the *Lampoon*.

Matthew Luce, regent of the university, said he was astonished at the appearance, but said he did not know what action would be taken by the college authorities.

Decline In Quoted Values Of Leading Stocks

New York, Oct. 29 (AP)—The following table illustrates the tremendous decline in quoted values on the outstanding stocks of twelve of the country's leading corporations as a result of the recent break in security prices:

	Approximate Loss from Year's High.	*Approximate Loss Today.*
American Telephone	$1,399,500,000	$359,600,000
U. S. Steel	715,500,000	97,500,000
Consolidated Gas	1,064,000,000	80,100,000
Standard of New Jersey	645,900,000	173,900,000
General Motors	2,260,000,000	325,250,000
Du Pont	1,186,000,000	350,960,000
Union Carbide	584,900,000	96,000,000
Pennsylvania R. R.	309,650,000	88,450,000
Commonwealth & Southern	369,170,000	92,300,000
International Nickel	578,650,000	96,400,000
General Electric	1,300,000,000	201,900,000
United Gas Improvement	615,350,000	74,500,000

Nation's Vast Industrial Fabric Sound, Says Klein Over Radio

Normal Purchasing Power Not Appreciably Impaired Despite Market Slump, Assistant Commerce Secretary Comments

Washington, Oct. 29 (AP) — Julius Klein, Assistant Secretary of Commerce, in the first speech on the stock-market situation and business by a high Administration official since the startling price declines, informed a national radio audience tonight that "regardless of regrettable speculative uncertainties the industrial and commercial structure of the nation is sound."

He said the volume of purchasing power measured the heights of living standards and "basically our normal purchasing power has not been appreciably impaired."

Speaking over the Columbia network, Dr. Klein echoed the conviction recently expressed by President Hoover that the business fundamentals of the nation were on a firm basis. He dealt with the relation of business to the stock market, but refrained from forecasting the market trend.

Emphasized Confidence

"All of us are justified, in my opinion, in a profound confidence in the general economic future of the country," he said.

"The fundamental factor in the general situation of business is purchasing power. Real purchasing power is made up of wages, salaries, receipts of farmers, merchants, professional men and others and the profits of industry. These have not been changed by the drop in stock prices," Dr. Klein told his audience.

"The national income of the United States at this moment is hardly a fraction less than it was a month ago. Established indexes, such as the quantity of output of our farms, our mines and our factories, and the volume of our railroad transportation support this view."

"Stock exchange prices have gone down materially," Dr. Klein said, "but the stock market is not the major barometer of business, and a decline in security prices does not greatly affect the buying power of the community, on which buying power rests the activity of production, the earnings of corporations and other business enterprises and the employment of labor.

Extent Of Speculation

"No one knows the number of persons engaged in this speculative activity, but even if we accepted the apparently liberal estimate of some non-official observers, who place the speculative accounts at about a million, these would still involve less than four per cent. of all of the families in the entire nation. Or, if we put it on the basis of individuals, the ratio would be less than one per cent. of the total population.

"Please don't misunderstand me or think that I am belittling the hardships of even this small fragment of our people, but even if all of these speculators suffered—and there were untold thousands who did not—you would still have a vastly preponderant majority of the nation unaffected by these speculative gyrations. And remember, incidentally, to cite just one corrective of this situation, that these speculative accounts could be matched twice over by the more than two million families who derive their livelihood from export trade, which is almost entirely unaffected by this movement.

Finds Stocks Were Too High

"Stock prices have gone down suddenly because over the past two or three years, it seems to be generally agreed, they had risen much too rapidly. Throughout the last eight years, with very temporary and minor recessions, the production of goods and services in the United States has grad-

(Continued on Page 2, Column 5)

W. E. Scripps, Millionaire Publisher, Is Missing

Police Believe Detroiter Is On Business Trip And Neglected To Notify Family

Detroit, Oct. 29 (Special)—William E. Scripps, millionaire publisher of the *Detroit News*, has been missing from his home in the Detroit Towers, fashionable apartment house, since Friday, the police admitted today.

The police admitted they had first worked on the theory that the publisher had been kidnapped and was being held for ransom, but said they had dropped this theory. They consider it possible that Scripps merely had left the city on a business trip and had neglected to notify his family or business associates of his plans.

158,000 COAL MINERS IDLE

Anthracite Workers Take Day Off In John Mitchell's Honor

Hazelton, Pa., Oct. 29 (AP)—The 158,000 anthracite miners in this district were idle today in celebration of Mitchell Day, so named in honor of the late John Mitchell, former president of the United Mine Workers of America.

The day marks the anniversary of the successful termination of a six-week strike in 1900 under the leadership of Mitchell following establishment of the union in the hard-coal field. The strike won for the men a ten per cent. wage increase and other concessions.

STREET CARS DYNAMITED

Passengers On New Orleans Vehicles Are Uninjured

New Orleans, Oct. 29 (AP)—Two street cars were dynamited tonight in a resumption of the desultory bombings that have marked the duration of the local trolley strike.

The cars, blasted in different sections of the city a few minutes apart, carried few passengers. No one was hurt.

Wire Reputed To Smith Framed By Humorist

Read At Roosevelt Dinner, It Asked If Stock Market Would Be Blamed On Democrats

Springfield, Mass., Oct. 29 (AP)—An inquiry following reports that former Gov. Alfred E. Smith of New York had denied sending a telegram read last night at a banquet here tendered Gov. Franklin D. Roosevelt of New York, developed today that the message was framed by a local humorist while the banquet was in progress.

The telegram contained the laconic query, "Will they blame the stock market on the Democrats?"

The communication not only was a hoax so far as Governor Smith was concerned, but it also was a hoax on the large and representative Democratic audience present. Even the great majority of the Democratic leaders in attendance were unaware of the origin of the "message."

Fanatical Temperance Condemned By Roosevelt

Governor Of Porto Rico Warns W. C. T. U. Against Trying To Legislate Righteousness

San Juan, P. R., Oct. 29 (Special Cable)—Gov. Theodore Roosevelt, invited to address the annual convention of Porto Rico's Women's Christian Temperance Union, wrote:

"I most strongly commend temperance in the true sense of the word. I think, however, that all of us must bear in mind that when we say 'temperance' we mean temperance. There should be no fanaticism connected with it."

Asserting that laws could never take the place of character building, he advocated educating people to do right rather than trying to legislate righteousness.

A trip through the island prevented the Governor from attending the convention.

$25,000,000,000 LOPPED OFF STOCKS' HIGH PRICES SINCE THIS CRASH BEGAN

Bankers, Seeming To Let Slump Run Its Course, So Direct Selling That Recovery Comes When Disaster Appears Imminent

16,410,000 SHARES CHANGE HANDS IN $10 TO $70 DROP

U. S. Steel And American Can Declare Extra Dividends As Though To Instill Confidence—Insurance Cos. To Aid—Curb House Suspends

New York, Oct. 29 (AP)—Huge barriers of buying orders, hastily erected by powerful financial interests, finally checked late today the most frantic stampede of selling yet experienced by the securities markets—a stampede which at times threatened to bring about utter collapse in prices.

All trading records were eclipsed in a turnover of 16,410,000 shares on the Stock Exchange and 7,096,300 on the Curb Market. Last Thursday on the Stock Exchange 12,894,600 shares changed hands and on the Curb Market 6,148,500. These were the highest ever recorded until now. Yesterday the Stock Exchange turnover was 9,212,800 shares.

BANKERS AGAIN TAKE HAND

Extreme declines in the active issues ranged from $10 to $70 a share, but many of these were cut in two in the rally which started in midafternoon and continued until the close.

Bankers who had been called hurriedly into conference last night and again at noon, apparently stood aside at the opening as blocks of 10,000 to 80,000 shares were thrown into the market for any price they would bring. When this flood of selling had spent itself, supporting orders began to appear, not with the intention of wholly checking the streams of selling, but with the avowed purpose of regulating their flow.

MORGAN PARTNER EXPLAINS

Thomas W. Lamont, senior partner of J. P. Morgan & Co., announced, after a second conference of bankers tonight, leading New York bankers were supporting the market in a cooperative way and would continue to support it.

"It was not an attempt of the group," he said, "to maintain prices, but to maintain a free market for securities in good order."

Unofficially, it was ascertained large corporations, among them United States Steel, had stepped into the market to buy stock for their employes' stock-purchase plans, as well as for their investment accounts, and that these purchases had been supplemented by the buying of capitalists for their individual accounts. Rumors that the banking group was a seller of stocks were denied.

Bad Holes Plugged

Several times, particularly in the early afternoon and again toward the close, it looked as though a fresh collapse in prices, bringing ruin in its wake, was inevitable, but each time the holes were plugged and the disaster was averted.

Despite the fact that prices of probably half of the thousand stocks listed on the Exchange have been cut in two or more during the recent decline, and that the aggregate decline in quoted values of all securities from the high levels of the year exceeds $25,000,000,000, only one casualty has been reported among brokerage houses thus far.

Small Curb House Fails

Suspension of the Curb Exchange firm of John J. Bell & Co. for failure to meet its obligations was announced soon after the market opened. Inasmuch as this firm was not engaged in a general commission business, the failure had no serious consequences.

Directors of the United States Steel Corporation and the American Can Company, supplementing the efforts of bankers to restore confidence, which has been badly shaken by the price crash, declared extra dividends of $1 each on their common stocks, in addition to the regular quarterly payments. These special disbursements were made possible by the huge earnings piled up in the wave of general prosperity earlier in the year.

Moves Toward Compromise

The United States Steel Corporation, whose directors met after the close of the market, reported earnings

"Corner Is Turned," Leading Banker's View Of Market

New York, Oct. 29 (AP)—Thomas W. Lamont, of J. P. Morgan & Co., said tonight that New York's leading bankers had been supporting the Stock Market in a cooperative way and would continue to support it.

"I want to take occasion tonight," he said, "to explain again, as heretofore, that the banking group was organized to offer certain support in the market and to act, as far as possible, as somewhat of a stabilizing factor.

"It was not an attempt of the group to maintain prices but to maintain a free market for securities in good order. In other words, we aimed to correct the technical conditions which prevailed last Thursday. We have not been sellers of stock."

Banking Group Meets Twice

The banking group met twice today, once before noon and again after the close of trading. With the exception of Chellis Austin, president of the Equitable Trust Company, who called at the Morgan offices late in the afternoon to discuss general conditions, the same bankers composed the group as on last Thursday, Friday, Saturday and yesterday.

They were Mr. Lamont and George Whitney, of the Morgan bank; Albert H. Wiggin, of the Chase National Bank; William C. Potter, of the Guaranty Trust; George F. Baker, Jr., of the First National Bank, and Charles E. Mitchell, of the National City Bank.

Lessening Of Hysteria

A representative of the group said that various signs pointed to lessening of hysteria on the part of the public. He cited the action of the Stock Mar-

(Continued on Page 2, Column 8)

5 ★★★★★ Wall Street Markets

Rain.

Closing Baltimore Stocks—Late Wall Street Prices

THE EVENING SUN

Published every week-day by The A. S. Abell Company. Entered as second-class matter at Baltimore Postoffice. Copyright, 1929, by The A. S. Abell Company.

5 ★★★★★ Wall Street Markets

Detailed weather on Page 2

VOL. 40 | PAID CIRCULATION SEPTEMBER MORNING, 149,435 EVENING, 143,960 293,395 | SUNDAY 192,285 | BALTIMORE, WEDNESDAY, OCTOBER 30, 1929 | 40 PAGES | 2 CENTS

STOCK EXCHANGE TO CLOSE 2 DAYS

PROBERS HEAR GRUNDY O. K. EYANSON

GRUNDY THINKS EYANSON AIDED TARIFF SESSIONS

Says His Own Reputation Needs No Help From Blaine

ASKS WHO EXPECTS FARM LOANS BACK

Tells Caraway Tax-Exempt Manufacturing Might Help Arkansas

By Henry M. Hyde

Washington, Oct. 30—With the tariff bill dead and buried—its funeral oration already delivered by Reed, of Pennsylvania, its only efficient defender on the floor—with the Republican leader, that huge and shaggy shell of a man, Watson, of Indiana, driven into exile by the party debacle—the Caraway lobby investigating committee continued today what might well be called a post-mortem on the remains.

"Old Joe" Grundy, plump, rosy, with his very closely clipped white mustache and neatly brushed thatch of white hair, was on hand early.

He took the witness stand when the session opened. Senator Blaine started to examine him further on the steel schedule.

Blaine First Questioner

Blaine insisted that high tariff rates on steel shapes greatly increased the price of farm machinery and that while farm machinery is on the free list there are no imports coming into the United States. In the pending bill these tariff rates are increased by about forty per cent, and this puts an additional tax of $8,000,000 on the American people.

Grundy replied that if steel shapes to be used on the farm are imported there is no tariff imposed. The committee ordered him to file his authority for that statement.

"You won't be classified as a lobbyist if you do that," said Blaine. "I want to give you a reputation."

Feels Reputation Secure

"I don't worry about how I am classified," replied Grundy, with a wave of the hand. "Nor do I care to have you give me a reputation. My reputation will take care of itself."

Going on the tariff on wool blankets, Blaine said $28,000,000 worth were produced in the United States. The pending tariff bill increases the tariff on wool blankets, which would increase the tariff tax on the American consumer by $16,000,000 annually.

Grundy declared the increased duty on blankets was due to the increased duty on wool, which benefited the State represented by Senator Walsh, among others.

Skeptical About Half Billion

Grundy brought up the "half billion dollars of our money, so to speak, which you fellows voted to give the farmers."

Blaine wanted to know if Grundy thought the farmer was a poor creditor, but "Old Joe" replied:

"No, but I don't think any of us expect to get that half billion dollars back."

"Do you think," asked Blaine, "that the half billion dollars to be loaned to the farmers by the head of the farm machinery trust will enable that trust to collect the notes given it by farmers for farm machinery?"

"Well," replied Grundy, "if Mr. Legge was not the proper man to head the Farm Board you fellows should not have confirmed him. I understand you confirmed him almost unanimously."

Walsh, still smarting from "Old Joe's" classification of Montana as a "backward State," questioned Grundy sharply.

"Did not the people of the Far West by their enterprise contribute greatly to the wealth of Pennsylvania, of which you boast?"

"Oh, that is reciprocal. Pennsylvania sent many millions into the Far West for building railroads, for instance," replied Grundy, "a good deal of which never came back."

All the five members of the Lobby Committee were on hand this morning, with Borah at one end and Robinson on the other. Each of them sat with his chin supported on his hand, as Grundy lectured them at length on the difference between "compensatory" and "protective" tariff duties.

"There are at least three kinds of lobbying in Washington," said Blaine.

[Continued On Page 2, Column 6]

GOOD EVENING

By CLARK S. HOBBS

WONDERFUL THINGS come of having grit. Take the pearl, for instance. That's what comes of an oyster having it.

THERE'S A REASON

I'd like to be the talcum dust
That dulls my sweetie's nose;
Its role is one so intimate
It thrills me, goodness knows!
I'd like to be the lipstick, too,
That plays upon her lips
And leaves behind a ruddy hue
As back and forth it slips.

I'd like to be the dabs of rouge
Upon my sweetie's cheeks:
They have a more caressing touch
Than any known to sheiks.
I'd like to be the eyebrow muck
She pencils round her eyes
To give her that vampirish look
I fairly idolize.

I'd like to be these things I've named.
'Twould suit me very well.
For reasons I have hinted here
And others I might tell.
At any rate I'm free to say—
However you may scoff—
It's doggone tough to be the guy
Who merely wipes them off.

THE WORLD won't be a much better place to live in until the beauticians can do something for an ugly disposition.

SUN SQUARE DOIN'S Or The Diary Of A Traffic Cop

8.30 A. M.—I don't know what to make of it. This here business of trying to find out who it is that's trying to break up my happy home by calling me on the phone when I ain't around in a female voice and sending me picture postcards signed Sweetie has got me so dern flabbergasted I don't know my head from a hole in the ground.

And it's all because old man Googlefuss that keeps the drug store down on the corner from the boarding house ain't got as good a memory as he ought to have or this here domestic tangle I'm in is a dern sight more complicated than I ever thought it was.

When I got home last night I found the next door neighbor that got the phone company to trace the call for me and found out they was coming from Googlefuss' drug store, waiting for me in a terrible excited state. He could hardly say it fast enough that another call had come for me at 4 in the afternoon and not giving me time to calm myself he rushed me right down to Googlefuss'.

"If the old man has been on the watch for us like he promised," he says to me on the run, "at last we're getting somewhere."

"It's almost too much to expect," I says, all trembly inside with excitement.

And I don't know yet whether I was right about it or not.

"Positively there ain't been nobody unusual in here to use the pay station this afternoon," says Googlefuss when we told him what happened. "Most of them was men."

"But there was a woman or two?" I says.

"Only one, I'm pretty sure," he says, "but"——

"Who was it?" I says, not being able to restrain myself. "Did you know her?"

"Sure," says the old gent, "but"—

"Never mind the buts," I says, "who was it?"

"Your wife," says Googlefuss.

10 A. M.—The guy was leaning up against the trolley pole here for at least a hour and I got tired of looking at him.

"Young fellow," I says to him, why ain't you in a office somewhere working?"

"I've got a outside position," he says.

"Yeh," I says. "I see you have, and it's time for you to change it now. Beat it!"

11 A. M.—I told the sergeant about chasing that loafer, but he never gives me no encouragement. All he says to me was:

"You do hate competition, don't you?"

IF THE SKIRTS are lengthened probably this won't be such a shinful world.

5 LOST IN PLANE NONCHALANT ON RETURNING SAFE

Pilot Doles Brings Western Express To Port After 30 Hours

TWO OF PASSENGERS NEAR-STORM VICTIMS

Set Out To Seek Shelter. Only Noise Of Motors Guided Them Back

Albuquerque, N. M., Oct. 30 (AP)—A tri-motored Western Air Express plane piloted by James E. Doles today stood victor over elements and the rugged Southwest after hours of fear for the safety of the plane and its five occupants.

As a fine snow sifted down upon the airport here and men conferred about plans to locate the plane, thirty hours overdue, the ship roared onto the field, everyone healthy and happy and the plane in perfect condition. A very unconcerned landing and a very nonchalant quintet of men emerged from the cabin.

Sixty Miles Off Course

Doles, with Allan C. Barrie, copilot; R. L. Britten, steward; Dr. A. W. Ward, San Francisco dentist, and W. E. Merz, Mount Vernon, N. Y., passengers, took off from Los Angeles Monday morning and headed east.

After a refueling stop in Arizona the plane ran into a terrific snowstorm in the same region where recently a Transcontinental Air Transport liner crashed and burned, with loss of eight lives. It was forced down southeast of Tracheda, N. M., which is sixty miles south of the regular course.

Two Men Almost Lost

The men, however, had their share of experiences. Two of the five went out in search of shelter and it was only through the thoughtfulness of Pilot Doles that they were not victims of the storm. When they did not return in a reasonable time Doles started the motors of the plane and this noise was an auditory beacon to the wandering pair as darkness crept over the land.

Consuming what food they had in the plane, the party later found a cabin nearby that had been noted in circling for a landing. The night was spent there before a roaring fire.

Mrs. Bessie Mason, who lives about five miles from where the plane landed, discovered the flying party and cooked them a meal of eggs, ham and biscuits. Then, in the afternoon, the weather cleared sufficiently so Doles could take off.

Men Lost Three Hours

The two men who hunted for shelter were lost more than three hours in the biting snowstorm, it was revealed by Dr. A. W. Ward, one of the passengers, in an interview given the Albuquerque *Journal*.

Dr. Ward told how the passengers felt as their ship began to descend into the blinding snow, which made flying virtually impossible, and how the five men aboard smoked and swapped stories

[Continued On Page 2, Column 8]

Inside Today---

Flashes

Jury Discharged In Damage Suit

Chestertown, Md., Oct. 30 (AP). Unable to agree after seven hours of deliberation, the jury which heard the $25,000 damage suit brought by Vera Martin, 16, of Lyon Village, Va., against Wilmer F. Davis, of Denton, Md., for injuries received in an automobile accident in June, 1927, was discharged and the case continued until the next term of court.

Great Western Sugar In Anti-Trust Case

North Platte, Neb., Oct. 30 (AP). Charging violation of the Sherman anti-trust law, United States District Attorney J. C. Kinsler filed an information in Federal Court today against the Great Western Sugar Company of Denver, operating at Scotts Bluff, Bayard, Mitchell, Gering and Minatare, Neb.

Anslinger Becomes Assistant Commissioner

Washington, Oct. 30 (AP)—Harry J. Anslinger, chief of the Division of Foreign Control of the Prohibition Bureau, today was appointed Assistant Commissioner of Prohibition to succeed Alf Oftedal, who resigned to become Collector of Internal Revenue in San Francisco.

Kansas City Banker's Son Commits Suicide

Kansas City, Mo., Oct. 30 (U.P.). John D. Schwitzgebel, 45, son of the vice-president of the Commerce Trust Company, died today the victim of bullet wounds self-inflicted because of financial worries.

Federal Farm Board To Make Grape Survey

Washington, Oct. 30 (AP)—A survey is to be undertaken immediately by the Federal Farm Board of the grape situation in California to serve as a basis for a program to be applied to the grape crop of 1930.

Academy Heads Fail To Reach Agreement

Efforts To Resume Athletic Relations Between Army And Navy Produce No Result

Washington, Oct. 30 (AP)—The superintendents of the Military and Naval academies failed to reach an agreement today in their effort to resume athletic relations.

Major-General Smith, superintendent at West Point, after conferring with Rear-Admiral Robison, commandant at Annapolis, said West Point felt the disrupted relations over the three-year eligibility rule with the Navy to be deplorable.

He added that while no agreement had been reached today, the Army still was hopeful that the "Navy will in time agree to meet us on the gridiron man for man, as do other colleges."

Nothing was forthcoming immediately from Admiral Robison on the conference.

LAUREL

FIRST RACE—Purse $1,300; for maiden fillies; 2-year-olds; six furlongs.

Snappy Snub, 110 (Beishak)	$7.00	$5.00	$3.20
Aziz, 110 (Haines)		$5.40	$3.30
Snuntaft, 110 (Fisher)			$2.90

Time 1.14 4-5.

Rosatina, Sweet Yvette, Falona and Colmoor also ran.

SECOND—Purse $1,300; for maiden fillies; 2-year-olds; six furlongs.

Valenciennes, 110 (Rose)	$20.40	$7.90	$4.30
Keep On, 110 (Inzelone)		$4.30	$3.50
Donta, 110 (Barnes)			$3.30

Time—1.14 2-5.

Lucinia, Trapland, Black Curse and Miss Desmond also ran.

THIRD—Purse $1,300; claiming; for 3-year-olds and up; mile and an eighth.

Prairie Girl, 102 (Senor)	$39.70	$16.30	$10.30
Ecstasy, 109 (Fronly)		$6.60	$5.30
Laftar, 105 (Hughes)			$4.30

Time—1.56.

Manager Evers, Immortal, Highland Chief, Cornbelt, Blanco, Harry Carroll, Blue Flag also ran.

FOURTH—Purse $1,300; claiming; for 3-year-olds and up; mile and a sixteenth.

Equation, 103 (Carlisle)	$23.60	$12.50	$8.90
Rancona, 100 (Sere)		$27.20	$13.40
Blue Darter, 112 (Bollero)			$7.30

Time—1.47 1-5.

Nicodemus, Billy Baughn, Fair Class, Aregal, Rejuvenation, Croydon, Sanford also ran.

LATONIA

FIRST RACE—Purse $1,200; claiming; for 3-year-olds and up; six furlongs.

Updike, 106 (V. Smith)	$70.74	$15.48	$7.80
Peggy Lee, 103 (H. Schutte)		$3.12	$2.62
Governor Pratt, 106 (A. Greco)			$3.22

Time—1.17 4-5.

Boys Preferred, Doctor Fred, Crestwood, Prince Bulbo, Tannie, St. Charles, Sen. Miss Jimbill, American Coin also ran.

SECOND—Purse $1,200; the Visalia; for 2-year-old colts and geldings; maidens; six furlongs.

Billy Champ, 115 (V. Smith)	$7.48	$4.66	$2.98
Dark Entry, 115 (J. Heupel)		$4.16	$3.50
Vladimir, 115 (C. Turk)			$31.26

Time—1.19.

Bold Robin, Mint Sweepings, Workiesa, Rain Cloud, Gunner, Doman also ran

(Other Racing On Page 30)

FRENCH CABINET TASK NOW UP TO CLEMENTEL

Ex-Minister Of Finance Accepts Job Where Daladier Failed

KNOWN AS MODERATE MEMBER OF RADICALS

Newly Chosen Leader Has Confidence Of Financial Interests

[By the Associated Press]

Paris, Oct. 30—Etienne Clementel, chairman of the Finance Committee of the Senate and former Minister of Finance in the Herriot Cabinet, today accepted "in principle" the task of forming a Cabinet to succeed the recently defeated Briand Ministry.

Clementel is a member of the radical group in the Senate. He is regarded as one of the most moderate of that group and the most likely radical to be able to form a new union government more to the Left than the Poincaré combination, excluding Conservatives of the Republican Union group and replacing them by radicals

Has Confidence Of Bankers

Clementel has the confidence of the financial interests. This is chiefly because of his action when Minister of Finance in taking issue with Premier Herriot against a capital levy in 1925, resigning after making his position clear before the Senate. Since then he has been much interested in the International Chamber of Commerce, having been head of the French section.

Clementel, who is a veteran Radical Socialist, was summoned by the President after Edouard Daladier, leader of the Radical Socialist party, had definitely declined to continue further efforts to form a Government because he could not gain the support of the Socialists.

Only a short time before Clementel was summoned former Premier Aristide Briand went to the Elysee Palace and saw President Doumergue. It was first thought that he would be asked to form a government, but it later developed that he and the President had merely talked over the situation.

Held Many Portfolios

Although never Premier before, M. Clementel has long played a prominent part in French political life, having been a member of several governments, holding such portfolios as Finance, Commerce and Agriculture. He was Minister of Trade and Labor in the Clemenceau Cabinet of 1917-20 and was Minister of Finance in the Herriot Cabinet of 1924-25. He has since been a Senator.

As Minister of Finance in 1924 he played a large part in the Interallied debt negotiations in progress at that time. He is now first president of the International Chamber of Commerce, being head of the French section. M. Clementel is 65 years old.

Miami Has Six Airports

Miami, Fla., Oct. 30 (AP)—Miami, terminus of air lines to Latin America, boasts six airports and plans another, a combined land and seaplane base. Most of the airport development has taken place in the last three years.

Industry And Commerce Declared Sound Despite Stock Market Shocks

Together With Finance, They Will Emerge Substantially Undisturbed, Business Men Associated With National Government Assert

[By the Associated Press]

Washington, Oct. 30—After assessing all the effects of the shocks administered by the Stock Market during the last few days, experienced business men associated with the Administration of the national Government are a unit in the declaration that fundamentally, commerce, industry and finance will emerge substantially undisturbed.

The latest public word, as it was given late last night over radio by Julius Klein, Assistant Secretary of Commerce, has been echoed and re-echoed by officials of cabinet rank since President Hoover briefly outlined it.

Growth Definitely Upward

"The growth of the income of the nation, the advance in the well being of its business men, its wage earners and its farmers during recent years has not been due to temporary and fleeting causes," he said. "It has been a definite upward trend. Basically, our normal purchasing power has not been impaired. Regardless of regrettable speculative uncertainties, the industrial and commercial structure of the nation is sound."

An impressive array of considerations backing up that judgment, all pointing out that commodity prices have been kept clear from inflation in securities, was presented by Dr. Klein. As to the Stock Market performance of the last two years, he said that "profits of business justified an advance in stock prices, but they did not justify going up to the sky."

Reserve System Intrenched

Privately, two Cabinet members most associated with business and monetary affairs have indicated the

[Continued On Page 2, Column 3]

COURT SENTENCES THREE REPORTERS

Washington Judge Holds Them In Contempt In Liquor Investigation

SILENT ON BOOTLEGGERS

They Refused To Divulge Names In Liquor Probe, Citing Ethics Of Their Profession

[By the Associated Press]

Washington, Oct. 30—Three reporters for the Washington *Times*, afternoon newspaper, were sentenced today to forty-five days each in jail by Judge Peyton Gordon in the District of Columbia Supreme Court for refusing to reveal to the grand jury the names and addresses of persons from whom they claimed to have purchased liquor.

In passing sentence for contempt of court Judge Gordon told the trio—Gorman M. Hendricks, 35; Linton Burkett, 30, and Jack E. Nevin, Jr., 24—that the questions asked them by the grand jury were entirely proper. The law, he said, did not recognize ethics of the newspaper profession as sufficient grounds for a plea for immunity.

Bought In 49 Speakeasies

The men told the court they had bought liquor in forty-nine speakeasies in Washington. They explained they had gained admittance through friends and that they had promised not to reveal the names of the bootleggers, asserting their only purpose in going to the speakeasies was to develop news stories relating to crime conditions in Washington.

Hendricks testified that to comply with the jury's request would bring

[Continued On Page 2, Column 5]

OFFICIALS PAY LAST TRIBUTE TO BURTON

Body Brought To Senate Chamber After Private Service

RIVAL LEADERS TAKE PART

Watson And Robinson Head Senators That Escort Silver Casket

[By the Associated Press]

Washington, Oct. 30—In a drizzle of rain the body of the late Senator Theodore E. Burton, of Ohio, today was borne up the long flight of steps on the east front of the Capitol into the Senate chamber for a last tribute of honor from President Hoover, his colleagues in Congress, other high Government officials and the diplomatic representatives from foreign nations.

The massive silver casket was escorted by a delegation of Senators and Representatives headed by Senator Watson of Indiana, the Republican leader, and Senator Robinson of Arkansas, the Democratic leader.

Service At Home

The funeral party arrived from the home, where a private family service had been held.

The casket was placed on pedestals immediately in front of Vice-President Curtis' desk.

On top of the casket was a large wreath, fastened with a white ribbon. Palms were banked in front of the rostrum and around the chamber.

Tonight the body will be placed on board a train for Cleveland, where it will be interred. A large delegation from the House and Senate, in both of which branches of Congress Senator Burton served, will go to the Ohio city for the services there.

Service In Senate

The service in the Senate chamber was placed in charge of the Rev. Z. B. Phillips, chaplain of the Senate, and the Rev. James Shera Montgomery, champlain of the House, while the program included addresses by Senator Fess, of Ohio, and Representative Hawley, of Oregon.

Senator Burton and President Hoover were friends for many years. Several times the Chief Executive visited the legislator during the months of illness that preceded his death on Monday night, and he was unstinted in his praise and appreciation of Burton's public career.

Hoover To Attend

His decision to attend the funeral services at the Capitol was announced shortly after they were arranged. Similarly, President Coolidge attended services for Representative Martin Madden, of Chicago, which were held in the chamber of the House.

The announcement by Senator Fess of his colleague's death caused an im-

[Continued On Page 2, Column 4]

Prison Bars Powerless Against Woman's Sobs

Wails Of Mrs. Maloney Not Only Prevent Magistrate From Sentencing Brother, But Charm Two Other Kinsmen From Cells

Brooklyn, N. Y., Oct. 30 (AP)—Magistrate Mark Rudick, of the Adams Street Court, was about to sentence Morgan Boland, 58, today on a charge of intoxication when a woman, Mrs. Katherine Maloney, stepped forward and said she was Boland's sister.

"Oh, judge," Mrs. Maloney said, weeping. "My poor, unfortunate brother Morgan. He was injured while working several years ago. He takes a little liquor now and then and, of course, it affects him. Won't you please give him another chance?"

"All right," the magistrate said. "But will you take care of him if I let him go?"

"Oh, yes, judge!" said Mrs. Maloney. So sentence was suspended.

But Mrs. Maloney burst out weeping again.

"Oh, my other poor brother, Michael, is in there!" she sobbed, pointing toward the entrance to the jail. "Michael is all right. He works. And you know how it is when brothers get together."

Weeping Still Effective

Michael was brought in and told the magistrate he was serving a term for

[Continued On Page 2, Column 4]

2-DAY HOLIDAY DECLARED FOR N. Y. MARKET

Exchange To Be Closed On Friday And Saturday To Give Men Rest

ROCKEFELLERS INVEST AND HELP BRING RISE

Wide And Powerful Support Sees Issues Regaining Strength

[By the Associated Press]

New York, Oct. 30—Powerful buying support, supplied by some of the country's largest financial institutions and wealthiest individuals, including John D. Rockefeller, Sr., and his son, turned the course of stock prices definitely upward today after a week of selling by investors and speculators throughout the world had washed away more than $25,000,000,000 in quoted values.

Gains of $5 to $30 a share were quite general on the New York Stock Exchange and were well maintained, with corresponding advances on the New York Curb Market and other security exchanges of the country.

Bankers See Great Improvement

Leading New York bankers, meeting in informal conferences at the offices of J. P. Morgan & Co., reported that the situation was distinctly improved.

With every indication that the wave of selling had passed, governors of the New York Stock Exchange met this afternoon and decided to delay the opening of the exchange tomorrow from 10 A. M. to noon, and to suspend business on Friday and Saturday, in order to give overworked employes of brokerage houses and the Stock Clearing Corporation an opportunity to catch up on sleep.

The exchange will reopen for business on Monday at the usual hour, but will be closed again Tuesday, Election Day, which is a legal holiday in New York.

Action Duplicated In Chicago

The Chicago Stock Exchange also voted to delay tomorrow's opening and to close on Friday and Saturday. Similar action will be taken by the New York Curb Exchange.

John D. Rockefeller, Sr., who rarely speaks for publication, authorized the statement today that he and his son "for some days have been purchasing sound common stocks."

"We are continuing and will continue our purchases in substantial amounts at levels which we believe represent sound investment values," he added.

Brokerage Firm Falls

One more Curb Exchange firm fell by the wayside today for failure to meet its obligations, but, like the Curb member which was suspended yesterday, it was not engaged in a general commission business.

The New York Stock Clearing Corporation reported that all trades in yesterday's record-breaking 16,000,000-share session had been cleared at an early hour this morning. Check clearings through the New York Clearing House set a new high record today at $3,500,000,000, due largely to the tremendous volume of securities transactions.

Sales 8,738,800 At 2.10

Total stock sales from 10 A. M. to 2.10 P. M. were 8,738,800 shares, as contrasted with 13,838,000 in the same period yesterday, with indications that the day's total would run close to 11,000,000 shares.

A brief flurry of selling took place in some issues on the announcement that the exchange would be closed Friday and Saturday and only open three hours tomorrow, but offerings were quickly absorbed and prices bounded upward in impressive fashion in the last hour of trading. Some of the buying was attributed to Mr. Rockefeller's announcement.

Quotations At 2.30

Following are some of the 2.30 quotations and net changes of the leading issues:

United States Steel common, 184, up 10; General Motors, 48½, up 8½; Radio, 43½, up 5; General Electric, 242, up 20; Anaconda Copper, 92⅞, up 7⅞; American Telephone, 232, up 28; American and Foreign Power, 67,

WEATHER FORECAST
Fair and continued cold today; increasing cloudiness and warmer tomorrow; moderate to fresh northwest or west winds.
Detailed Weather Report on Page 18.

THE SUN

LECHARTIER SAYS FRENCH CATHOLICISM WELCOMES NEW HEAD —Page 13.

VOL. 186—D | PAID CIRCULATION OCTOBER MORNING, 149,487 EVENING, 150,307 299,794 | SUNDAY 195,060 | BALTIMORE, SATURDAY, NOVEMBER 30, 1929 | Published every week day by The A. S. Abell Company. Entered as second-class matter at Baltimore Postoffice. Copyright, 1929, by The A. S. Abell Company | 22 PAGES | 2 CENTS

BYRD RETURNS FROM POLE

RAIL MERGER PLANS OF I. C. C. EXPECTED SOON

Commission Said To Favor 18 Or 19 Big Systems For Country

MEMBERS DIVIDED ON EASTERN AREA

Majority Of Body Said To Be Inclined To Five-Group Program

By J. F. ESSARY

Washington, Nov. 29 — It was learned today in high official quarters that the Interstate Commerce Commission is preparing to submit an extended report to Congress, probably in December, proposing that the railroads of the country be merged into eighteen or nineteen great systems.

Also, it is learned that there is a division in the commission at present between a four and five party scheme of consolidations in the East of trunk-line territory, with indications that at least a majority of the commissioners will favor the five-system program.

Wabash Proposed Nucleus

In the latter event, the fifth system, it is said, will be set up around the Wabash and will be composed of that railroad, the Wheeling and Lake Erie, Lehigh Valley, Pittsburgh and West Virginia, Western Maryland, Delaware and Hudson, with a remote possibility that the Norfolk and Western will be included.

Should this set-up be recommended to Congress and to the railroads, the commission, it is believed, will make important concessions to each of the present trunk lines—the Pennsylvania, New York Central, Baltimore and Ohio and Nickel Plate in the hope of measurably satisfying those carriers.

Otherwise, the commissioners themselves well know, infinite delay will be encountered in putting the scheme into operation, a delay which already has run nine years since the passage of the Transportation act of 1920.

May Refuse Usual Order

Should the new commission plan go to Congress in the near future, as is predicted tonight, that body probably will reverse the usual order and grant the railroads hearings upon the scheme after its promulgation, instead of before.

The carriers, particularly those in the East, have been expecting hearings in advance of a commission plan and many of them have been preparing for weeks to make their presentations. In anticipation of such procedure, the Van Sweringen interests, the Baltimore and Ohio, and the Wabash each have submitted independent merger proposals and these are now pending along with many collateral consolidation propositions.

Although the transportation situation in the East, from a consolidation standpoint, is the more acute, and the commission's views upon it will be of greater interest, the plan which is now being worked out embraces the entire country.

Seaboard Air Line's Fate Question

It is said by those who believe they know the commission's mind that the situation in the South is not regarded as a problem, beyond the doubt in that body's mind as to the final disposition of the Seaboard Air Line. The Atlantic Coast Line and the Louisville and Nashville are regarded as one system, each complementing the other.

The Southern Railway is established, as its stands, it is declared, but will want to take over full ownership of its lines extending into New Orleans and Cincinnati, now known as the Queen and Crescent. The Central of Georgia may go to the Illinois Central, which would leave only a few small lines to be disposed of.

A problem is encountered in the Northwest in connection with the Northern Pacific, the Great Northern, the Milwaukee and the Burlington lines. How to set up two fully organized competitive systems through mergers in that quarter is not easy, it is said.

Difficulty In Southwest

Also there is said to be some difficulty in disposing of the lines in the Southwest as between the Southern Pacific, the Santa Fe, the Frisco, the Cotton Belt, the "Katy" and the Kansas City Southern.

Again, New England, which wishes competitive rail service, presents no plan which has as yet seemed altogether workable, as long as neither the Baltimore and Ohio or the Pennsylvania is willing to take over the New Haven.

Exactly how the commission stands regarding consolidations in the trunk-line territory is not known. That body, it is said, never has voted on the question. It has before it the plan worked

(Continued on Page 3, Column 2)

N. C. STRIKE CASE JURY LOCKED UP

Rioting Charges Against Four Labor Leaders In M[illegible]n Pondered

Marion, N. C., Nov. 29 (AP)—The jury in the case of four men charged with rioting and resisting officers in connection with a strike at the Clinchfield Mill village August 30, was locked up shortly after 10 o'clock tonight, after being unable to reach a verdict in deliberations that started at 5.30 P. M.

The defendants are Alfred Hoffman, organizer of the United Textile Workers of America; Lawrence Hogan, his associate here and a Brookwood Labor College student, and Del Lewis and Wes Fowler, local labor leaders.

Mauretania Scrapes Submerged Wreckage

Reports Sunken Ferry And Cars Menace To Navigation—They Will Be Salvaged

[*New York Bureau of The Sun*]

New York, Nov. 29—The nineteen freight cars and the railroad ferry sunk Wednesday night in a collision with the liner Mauretania in the lower bay constitute a menace to navigation, according to a radio message received from S. G. S. McNeil, commander of the liner, now at sea.

As a consequence, wrecking tugs in the next few days will attempt to salvage the submerged cars and ferry. The message was received after the Mauretania yesterday scraped the wreckage when she, after delay for repairs, passed over the point where the collision occurred.

Food Shortage Is Faced By 55 Because Of Storm

Refugees Living On Teachers' Private Supplies At Clark's Point, Alaska

Juneau, Alaska, Nov. 29 (AP)—Thirty Indians and twenty-five whites, together with the Government teacher at Clark's Point are facing a serious shortage of food because of the severe gale and tital wave which swept over the Bristol Bay region last Sunday, a cable from Dillingham revealed.

The cable from Judge E. Coke Hill, of the Third Division, to Gov. George Parks said the whites had come from the Ekuk and that all of them were living in the schoolhouse. All are living on the teacher's private supplies, Judge Hill cabled.

No Nobel Peace Prizes For Years 1928 And 1929

Committee Decides Against Awards—Kellogg Had Been Mentioned

Oslo, Norway, Nov. 29 (AP)—The Nobel Prize Committee has decided not to award the 1928 and 1929 peace prizes.

The 1928 prize money will be placed to the account of the committee's funds and the 1929 prize will be reserved for 1930.

Among the candidates whose names were reported to have come before the committee were Frank B. Kellogg, former American Secretary of State; Miss Elsa Brandstroem, Swedish Red Cross nurse; Archbishop Nathan Soederblom and Hansen Noeroemoelle, Danish legislator.

GEM BANDIT SUSPECTS HELD

Pair Accused In $250,000 Hold-Up Arrested In Buffalo

Buffalo, Nov. 29 (AP)—Clinton Duke, 30, alleged leader of the seven bandits who held up and robbed of $250,000 in jewelry guests at a dinner in the home of Edward L. Carson at Snyder, N. Y., on November 14, and Theodore Rogacki, another alleged participant in the robbery, are under arrest here, it was revealed tonight.

ZIHLMAN SAYS FIRM GAVE HIM SHARES FREE

Admits Holding 9,000 Shares In Company Under Investigation

ADMITS HE BOUGHT $5,000 OF PREFERRED

Organization Accused In Capital Of Mail Fraud And Embezzlement

[*Washington Bureau of The Sun*].

Washington, Nov. 29—Representative Frederick N. Zihlman, of Maryland, testified before a notary public today that he had paid nothing for the 9,000 shares of common stock which he owns in the F. H. Smith Company, which is under examination by the District of Columbia grand jury.

Mr. Zihlman, who is chairman of the District Committee of the House, is a director of the company, which until last week, when it removed to New York, had its principal office here. Mr. Zihlman's testimony was given in a civil suit brought against the company by N. E. Henderson & Co., Philadelphia, to recover money alleged to be due in connection with the construction of a Philadelphia apartment house. Mr. Zihlman testified he bought $5,000 worth of preferred stock.

Specialized In Financing

The F. H. Smith Company engaged in extensive real estate operations in Washington for some years and built hotels, apartments and other structures. The company specialized on financing rather than building, having taken several projects out of receiverships, reorganized and refinanced them.

Some investors in the company's securities complained that it was overcapitalized and that some of the officers participated in fees and bonuses to an unusual extent. This led to an investigation by the Department of Justice and later by the grand jury.

A considerable part of the company's transactions were outside the District of Columbia. A complaint from Washington, Iowa, caused Senator Brookhart to begin a campaign against the company and Washington real estate practices in general. Senator Brookhart accused the company of no specific indiscretions except circulating misleading advertising.

Investigator At Work

He put a private investigator to work and introduced a resolution calling for an investigation of real estate practices in the district, naming the F. H. Smith Company. The resolution was sent to the subcommittee of the District of Columbia, where Senator Blaine, Wisconsin, chairman, rewrote it and struck out the name F. H. Smith. Senator Blaine employed O. H. Brinkman, former clerk of the District Committee of the Senate, a lawyer, to make a study of real estate legislation.

Representative Zihlman made the following comment on his testimony:

"It is true, as I testified today, that I received 9,000 odd shares of the common stock of the F. H. Smith Company and that I paid nothing whatever for it. It is also true that 200,000 shares of this stock were issued to the directors and to employes of that company, none of whom paid anything for it.

50,000 Shares For Employes

"This stock was issued, in the case of the directors, to the holders of preferred stock. Of the total, 150,000 shares was issued to such preferred

(Continued on Page 6, Column 6)

SOVIET REJECTS NANKING PEACE NOTE PROPOSAL

"Superfluous," Russ Reply, Since Manchuria Is Already Negotiating

ACTION BY POWERS APPEARS UNLIKELY

U. S. Charge At Tokyo Confers With Japanese Foreign Minister

Moscow, Nov. 29 (AP)—Maxim Litvinoff, acting Commissar of Foreign Affairs, today handed the German Ambassador a note for China, saying that Gov. Chang Hsueh-liang, of Manchuria, already had agreed to the Soviet terms for peaceful settlement of their conflict and that Nanking's offer of negotiation was, therefore, "superfluous" and only delaying settlement.

[Editor's Note—Moscow officially announced Wednesday night that the Manchurian provincial government had agreed to a restoration of the status quo on the Chinese Eastern Railway and that peace negotiations were about to begin. Yesterday the central Chinese Government at Nanking, apparently ignoring the Soviet-Manchurian negotiations, sent Moscow a note proposing that both sides withdraw troops and submit their dispute to a joint board of inquiry. No mention was made of a return to the status quo on the railway.]

Nationalists Not Party To Present Discussions

Mukden, Nov. 29 (AP)—Despite denials and counter-denials of the negotiations reported to have been initiated by the Russian Government in Moscow and the Manchurian authorities at Mukden, it is generally believed here tonight that settlement of the Chinese-Russian controversy over the Chinese Eastern railway is near.

Authoritative sources in closest touch with Manchurian affairs stated today that the Mukden authorities had not yet fully accepted Moscow's terms for settlement of the Chinese Eastern Railway dispute.

The same source said further that the Nationalist Government at Nanking was not a party to the preliminary telegraph discussion between Moscow and Mukden now proceeding. The attitude of the Nanking Government thus far has not been revealed here.

Opposed To Intervention, Believing Peace Near

Tokyo, Nov. 29 (AP)—Edwin L. Neville, Charge d'Affaires of the American Embassy, conferred today with Baron Kijuro Shidehara, Foreign Minister of Japan. Although the nature of their conversation was not divulged, it was learned authoritatively that there was little chance of international action in the Chinese-Soviet situation.

This is because of Japan's conviction that prospects of an early settlement between Manchuria and Russia makes intervention by the world powers unnecessary and undesirable. This conviction, it is understood, is shared in other capitals.

Peace Prospects Bright

Information from Mukden, Manchuria, reaching authoritative quarters here asserts that Nanking has given Chang Hsueh-liang, Governor of Manchuria, full power to negotiate a settlement of the Chinese Eastern Railway controversy. Hence, prospects are believed brighter than for many months for termination of the long-drawn quasi-war situation on the Manchurian-Siberian border.

A dispatch to the Japanese Rengo News Agency from Mukden asserts that the coming Sino-Soviet parley will be conducted in the name of the Nanking Government, but actually by Mukden, with Tsai Yun-sheng as chief negotiator.

Chinese Officials Resign

The Manchurian Government, reports stated, had encouraged resignations of Gen. Chang Ching-hui, governor of the Harbin district, and Lu Yung-kuan, president of the Chinese Eastern Railway, who was responsible for the railroad's seizure by Chinese last July, and these resignations may be expected shortly.

The Russians are continuing their reminders that military pressure is still available if needed. Nineteen airplanes bombed Buchatu this afternoon, while another Soviet squadron bombed Chinese Eastern Railway trains near the crossing of the Yali river, sixty miles southeast of Buchatu.

U. S. Hears From Powers On Proposal For Action

[*Washington Bureau of The Sun*]

Washington, Nov. 28—Following receipt of news here today that Russia never really had invaded Manchuria, the State Department settled down to a policy of watchful waiting, not only to see what happens between China

(Continued on Page 13, Column 6)

Al Smith Appointed Head Of County Trust Company

Former Governor Takes Post Left Vacant By James J. Riordan's Death—Eventually Will Be Actually Named President

[*New York Bureau of The Sun*]

New York, Nov. 29—Former Gov. Alfred E. Smith, friend and associate of James J. Riordan, president of the County Trust Company, who ended his life November 8, today was elected chairman of the board of the bank and will hereafter [illegible] complete charge of its affairs.

Mr. Smith eventually will become president of the institution, but for the present he will control it with all of the powers invested in the president. To avoid a technicality he will function as chairman of the board, a position created after Mr. Riordan's death and filled temporarily by John J. Raskob.

To Continue As Member

William H. English, who was appointed president of the bank following Mr. Riordan's death, will continue as a member of the board of directors, as will Mr. Raskob.

Mr. Smith has been a director of the company since his retirement from the Governorship in January of this year.

$500,000 Deposited

Mr. Smith said more than $500,000 in deposits had been made since Mr. Riordan's death, and that forty-one new accounts had been registered in the bank.

"Banking is not exactly my line," he said, "but I've had some experience with it and, fortunately, am surrounded by authorities on the subject. I'm interested in the work and the institution and anticipate no difficulty in settling into the routine."

Adds New Laurels To His Fame

COMMANDER RICHARD E. BYRD

Byrd First Man In History To Fly Over Both Poles

Roald Amundsen And Robert Scott Reached Spot By Overland Route Few Days Apart In 1914

[*By the Associated Press*]

Commander Byrd's flight across the South Pole has made him the first man in history to fly across both the earth's poles.

In May, 1926, in the tri-motored Fokker airplane, the Josephine Ford, Commander Byrd flew from King's Bay, Spitsbergen, across the North Pole and return.

Other Flight In 15½ Hours

That springtime flight required a total of 15 hours and 30 minutes and the round trip covered 1,600 miles. In addition to being the first to fly across the North Pole, Byrd was also the first man to fly over it in a heavier-than-air machine. On that historic flight his pilot was Floyd Bennett, who died April 25, 1928, while attempting to rescue the crew of the transatlantic plane Bremen from Greenly Island. Bennett was second in command of the Byrd Antarctic expedition and had intended to accompany the commander on the trip.

The flight across the South Pole, begun Thursday, was the first attempt he had made to fly to the pole, although previously he had used airplanes in flights from his base at Little America in laying subbases on the route to the pole and in exploration trips.

He was the third man to reach the South Pole. The first was Roald Amundsen, a Norwegian, who reached it December 14, 1911, and a few days later he was followed by Capt. Robert F. Scott, British explorer. Both of them used overland methods of travel.

Bernt Balchen, pilot for Commander Byrd on the South Polar flight, also was a pilot on the commander's transatlantic flight of June 29, 1927. With Bert Acosta and Floyd Bennett, they flew the monoplane America from Roosevelt Field, N. Y., to Var-sur-Mer, France. Balchen, chief pilot of the expedition, is a native of Norway and has had extensive experience piloting planes under polar flying conditions. He assisted in all the tests to which the planes destined for the Byrd Atlantic expedition were subjected.

Harold I. June, radio operator of the flight, is a petty officer and pilot in the navy and was granted leave of absence to accompany the expedition. He was chief engineer in the famous "billion-dollar crew" of the Vanderbilt yacht during the war.

McKinley Also War Veteran

In addition to Balchen and June, Commander Byrd was accompanied on his South Polar flight by Capt. Ashley C. McKinley, an aerial photographer of St. Louis. Captain McKinley served from 1917 to 1926 in the United States Army Air Corps.

Commander Byrd's party reached the Antarctic in December of last year. After various reconnaissance flights from his base, he and his party established winter quarters on the ice barrier about the Antarctic continent. Only recently, with the coming of spring in that frozen territory, activity was resumed.

Hoover's Business Parley To Be Broadcast Dec. 5

Proceedings Of First Meeting To Go On Air At 10 A. M.—President To Speak

New York, Nov. 29 (AP) — The National Broadcasting Company today announced the proceedings of the first meeting of the permanent business conference, organized at the direction of President Hoover, would be broadcast over a nation-wide network December 5.

The broadcast, which will go on the air at 10 A. M., Eastern standard time, has been offered to all stations in the system. President Hoover will make an address.

TO USE SHIP-TO-SHORE PHONE

Leviathan Will Inaugurate New Service December 8

New York, Nov. 29 (AP)—The *Evening Post* says the first ship-to-shore telephone service on an ocean liner will be made available to passengers on the Leviathan on December 8, when she is a day out to sea on her way to Southampton.

Crosson Off In Quest Of Flying Mate, Eielson

To Join Two Other Alaskan Pilots For Hop To Wilds Of Siberia

Fairbanks, Alaska, Nov. 29 (AP)—Joe Crosson, copilot with Carl Ben Eielson in Sir Hubert Wilkins' first South Polar expedition, today took off from here to join in the quest along the Siberian border for his flying comrade and the latter's mechanic, Earl Borland.

Crosson was to join Pilots H. W. Barnhill and Ed Young at Ruby, halfway point to Nome. The latter took off several days ago, but have been held at Ruby because of damage to Young's landing gear.

COSTE FLIGHT IS RATIFIED

Distance In France-China Trip Put At 4,950 Miles

Paris, Nov. 29 (AP)—The Aero Club of France today ratified the non-stop record straight-line distance flight of Capt. Dieudonne Coste and Maurice Bellonte between France and China last October. The exact distance was placed at 7,905.14 kilometers.

AIRPLANE LANDS SAFELY AT BASE CAMP AFTER STOPPING AT MOUNTAINS

Party Forced To Dump Large Quantity Of Supplies To Enable Airship To Clear Top Of Glacier

CRAFT MAKES WIDE CIRCLE OVER SOUTH POLAR POINT

Part Of Return Journey Down Gorge Proves Rough. Round Trip Requires 18 Hours And 59 Minutes, Including Stop

By RUSSELL OWEN

Little America, Antarctica, Nov. 29 (By Wireless)—Conqueror of two poles by air, Commander Dick Byrd flew into camp at 10.10 o'clock this morning, having been gone eighteen hours and fifty-nine minutes. An hour of this time was spent at the mountain base refueling.

The first man to fly over the North and South Poles and the only man to fly over the South Pole stepped from his plane and was swept up on the arms of the men in camp who, for more than an hour, had been anxiously watching the southern horizon for a sight of the plane.

PLANE CLIMBS OVER GLACIER

Deaf from the roar of the motors, tired from the continual strain of the flight and the long period of navigation under difficulties, Byrd was still smiling and happy. He had reached the South Pole after as hazardous and difficult a flight as has ever been made in an airplane, tossed by gusts of winds, climbing desperately up the slopes of glaciers a few hundred feet above the surface.

His companions on the flight tumbled out stiff and weary also, but so happy that they forgot their cramped muscles. They were also tossed aloft, pounded on the back and carried to the entrance of the mess hall.

BALCHEN FIRST OUT OF CRAFT

Bernt Balchen, the calm-eyed pilot, who first met Byrd in Spitzbergen and who was with him on the transatlantic flight, came out first. There was a little smudge of soot under the nose, but the infectious smile which has endeared him to those who know him was radiant.

He was carried away and then came Harold June, who, between intervals of helping Balchen and attending to fuel tanks and lines and taking pictures, found time to send the radio bulletins which told of the plane's progress. And after him Captain McKinley was lifted from the doorway, beaming like a Cheshire cat because his surveying camera had done its work all the way.

Forced To Dump Food Supplies

Men crowded about them eager for the story of what they had been through, catching fragments of sentences. It had evidently been a terrific battle to get up through the mountains to the plateau.

"We had to dump food supplied for a month and a half to do it," said Byrd. "I am glad it wasn't gas. It was nip and tuck all the way."

"Yes," chuckled Balchen. "Do you remember when we were sliding around those knolls picking the wind currents to help us and there wasn't more than 300 feet under us at times. We were just staggering along, with drift and clouds and all sorts of things around us."

When the plane approached the mountains on the way south Commander Byrd picked out Livs glacier, a large glacier somewhat to the west of the Axel Heiberg glacier, as the best passage-way. The high mountains shut them in all around as they forced their way upward, Balchen conserving his fuel to the utmost, coaxing his engines, picking the up currents of the air as best he could to help the plane ride upward.

In Swirl Of Clouds

Clouds swirled about them at times, puff balls of mist driven down the glacier, drift scurried beneath them, it was a wicked place for an airplane to be, hemmed in by the hem of the towering peaks on either side. There was one time when they had to lighten ship, and Byrd, looking around for what could best be spared, decided to dump some food.

There was a dump valve in the fuselage tank, but he had determined to go

Byrd's Polar Flight As Given In Bulletins

Left Little America Nov. 28 (3.29 G. M. T.; 10.29 P. M., E. S. T.).

From Airplane Floyd Bennett via Little America, Nov. 29 (13.55 G. M. T.; 8.55 A. M., E. S. T.)—My calculations indicate we have reached the vicinity of the South Pole. Flying high for survey. Airplane in good shape. Crew all well. Will soon turn. Can see almost limitless Polar plateau. Are leaving South Pole. BYRD.

From Airplane Floyd Bennett via Little America, Nov. 29 (15.30 G. M. T.; 10.30 A. M., E. S. T.)—Flying well. Motors fine. Are over mountains. Starting down. JUNE.

From Airplane Floyd Bennett via Little America, Nov. 29 (16.33 G. M. T.; 11.33 A. M., E. S. T.)—We are going to land at the mountains now. JUNE.

From Airplane Floyd Bennett via Little America, Nov. 29 (18.06 G. M. T.; 1.03 P. M., E. S. T.)—Left mountains 6 o'clock for Little America. Flying well. Motors fine. JUNE.

From Airplane Floyd Bennett via Little America, Nov. 29 (19.00 G. M. T.; 2 P. M., E. S. T.)—About 100 miles north of mountains, flying well. Motors fine. JUNE.

From Airplane Floyd Bennett via Little America, Nov. 29 (19.57 G. M. T.; 2.58 P. M., E. S. T.)—About twenty miles south of crevasse. Flying well. Motors fine.

From Airplane Floyd Bennett via Little America, Nov. 29 (20.55 G. M. T.; 3.55 P. M., E. S. T.) — About sixty miles south of Little America.

From Airplane Floyd Bennett via Little America, Nov. 29—Are about ten miles out. JUNE.

Plane landed at Little America at 10.10 A. M., G. M. T.

[Copyright, 1929, by New York Times and St. Louis Post-Dispatch]

WEATHER FORECAST
Fair and colder today; cloudy, with slowly rising temperature, probably showers, tomorrow; north and east winds.
Detailed Weather Report on Page 21.

THE SUN

Registered United States Patent Office.

Robert Dell
SEES MORE CABINET CHANGES IN FRANC..
—Page 13

VOL. 186—D | PAID CIRCULATION FEBRUARY MORNING, 148,933 EVENING, 151,123 300,056 ‖ SUNDAY 198,204 | BALTIMORE, FRIDAY, MARCH 14, 1930 | Published every week day by The A. S. Abell Company. Entered as second-class matter at Baltimore Postoffice. Copyright, 1930, by The A. S. Abell Company. | 26 PAGES | 2 CENTS

NEW HARMONY PLAN FOR HAITI IS AGREED UPON

But Borno Refuses To Recede From Position On Congress Election

CONFERENCE HELD WITH COMMISSION

U. S. Group Drops Belligerent Attitude—President Less Defiant

By FRANKLYN WALTMAN, Jr.
Staff Correspondent of The Sun

Port au Prince, Haiti, March 13 (Special Cable)—Although President Borno, of Haiti, after an hour's conference with the Forbes Commission today, refused to recede from his position on the proposal to elect a Congress before January 10, 1932, a harmony plan of procedure was agreed on as a solution for the present critical situation.

The commission is losing its belligerent attitude and at the same time it is reported President Borno is less defiant. The conference late this afternoon at the palace was described as a mild affair, with President Borno in a conciliatory frame of mind. The suspicion here is that Washington has warned the commission to go slow on anything approaching strong-arm methods.

Commission Changes Attitude

It is known the commission has maintained close contact with President Hoover. There is no information that President Hoover has weakened the commission's determination to throw President Borno out unless he plays the game, but that the commission has changed its attitude overnight is noticeable to everyone.

This plan contemplates the selection immediately of a Provisional President who will not commit himself on the interpretation of the constitutional requirements for the legislative election until he assumes office.

Must Satisfy Both Factions

The man selected must be satisfactory to both the opposition leaders as well as to President Borno. If the candidate named is satisfactory to him, President Borno will sign the agreement pledging his support and will have the Council of State elect such a candidate as President.

The candidate must sign an agreement to call a legislative convention as soon "as possible" and on the convening of this Legislature resign the Presidency. In the minds of many of the opposition this plan is no settlement of the situation whatsoever, but the commission is willing to try it.

Plan Full Of Loopholes

The crux of the situation will be reached when President Borno signs the agreement pledging his support to the candidate chosen by the opposition.

This new plan is full of loopholes permitting deadlocks and also allowing double-crossing since, theoretically, and as far as actual records go, the candidate chosen is left with a free mind as to his course in the matter of calling elections.

Constitution Causes Impasse

The impasse has been created simply by differences in the interpretations of the Constitution. President Borno holds that a legislative election cannot be held legally until January 10, 1932. Many constitutional lawyers in the opposition contend that President Borno violated the Constitution by not carrying out the mandate to call an election for last January 10 and thus the Constitution should be interpreted for the benefit of the people, giving them an election as soon as possible.

On the surface all this appears trivial and boring, but under the surface it is of the highest importance, since the future course of the American foreign policy may be involved.

If the Haitian Congress elects a new President prior to 1932 the question of recognition by the United States Government will immediately arise. It is believed that both President Hoover and the State Department are anxious not to create a precedent recognizing as *dejure* any government which comes into power except strictly in conformance with constitutional requirements. A misstep here may return to haunt the United States' Latin-American policy in future years.

Believe Coup d'Etat Needed

The situation is muddled by the possibility that the opposition might throw the whole program over. Many reasonable observers here are unable to see their way out without a *coup d'etat*. They refuse to say that the danger of hostilities has passed.

It was learned on high authority that President Borno is incensed over the action of the Catholic bishops in repudiating him. He also made a vigorous defense of the occupation to the commission during the conference. He denied any unfriendly intentions by sending out Saturday a letter saying that enemies were maligning him and spreading stories of his resignation prior to May 15. He wanted to reassure his followers, he said.

In the meantime the opposition

(Continued on Page 5, Column 2)

The Great Game Of Politics

By FRANK R. KENT

He Eats Them Alive

WASHINGTON, March 13.

THE FEAR which Senator Thaddeus Caraway, chairman of the lobby investigating committee, inspires in the witnesses who come before him is one of the remarkable features of the investigation. His caustic and bitter tongue and the freedom with which he expresses himself in asides, and directly, regarding the character of the witness and the nature of his answers, set a record. Nothing like it has been heard before in a Senate committee.

—o—

AN EXAMPLE occurred yesterday. Mr. Claudius Huston was on the stand. Mr. Huston is in something of a jam and scarcely anyone has much sympathy with him. He is chairman of the Republican National Committee and has been an extremely poor one. Though he denied he had any idea of resigning, so intense is the dissafisfaction with him among party people that it is difficult to see how he can stay. A great many rough stories have been spread around Washington about him. His name has been up in the lobby committee at various times and some of his activities have seemed to need explanation. His account of why the Tennessee River Improvement Association kept no records other than on its check stubs of the large sums it received and expended was obviously thin.

—o—

NEVERTHELESS the remark made to him by Senator Caraway was startling. Some years back, Mr. Caraway said, it had been stated before the Senate Judiciary Committee that Mr. Huston had collected money to pay the expenses of delegates to the 1924 Cleveland convention, but the delegates had paid their own expenses.

"That," said the chairman, "must have been embarrassing to you?"

"No, Senator," replied Mr. Huston, "it was not."

"Well," said Senator Caraway, "it would have been to almost any honest man"—and he emphasized the word honest.

—o—

IF A ROUGHER or more insulting thing was ever said to a witness it cannot be recalled. It is, in fact, difficult to imagine a more direct insult. It is the sort of thing a police court judge might say to a Negro chicken thief, but from the chairman of a Senate committee to the chairman of the Republican National Committee it is almost incredible. The direct intimation was that Mr. Huston is not an honest man. If there is any other deduction it is hard to think what it could be. The marvelous thing is that Mr. Huston took it without blinking and without a word.

—o—

ONE EXPECTED him to leap to his feet in indignation and denounce Mr. Caraway for gratuitously reflecting upon his integrity. One, at least, expected him to tell the committee that he refused to answer further questions until and unless it repudiated the deliberately offensive remark of its chairman. No court in the world would send him to jail for contempt under such circumstances. Had Harry Sinclair had half that excuse for refusal to answer he would never have served a day. But Mr. Huston did neither of these things. He said nothing at all, calmly answered the next question with no outward evidence of perturbation.

—o—

WHY, IT IS HARD to say. He may not have felt insulted. He may not have wanted to pursue the subject. He may have thought the better policy was to ignore the insult and that to lose his temper would be to play into the Caraway hands. And he may have been, as many others have, just plain afraid of Mr. Caraway and the authority with which he is clothed. It is perfectly true that Mr. Caraway would not have apologized. No one who knows him thinks that. On the contrary, he would undoubtedly have elaborated and sustained his contention. Further, there would have been a sensational scene in which Mr. Caraway would have had all the advantage.

—o—

NOT ONLY is he chairman of the committee, with the power and prestige of the Senate behind him, but he has an extraordinary talent for rough and tumble conversational battling and a genuine love of it. He is a master of invective and satire, an adept at cutting phrases and rough repartee, behind which lurks an unusual concentration of venom. If he had no positional advantage and were on the level with the other fellow in this sort of game he would beat any ordinary man. He would have liked nothing better than for Mr. Huston, or any of the other witnesses whom he has blistered with that scathing tongue of his, to fight back. They would be his meat. He would chew them up.

—o—

REALIZATION of this is probably why so many have kept silent while flayed by that biting tongue. Mr. Caraway has said a good many sneering and offensive things to witnesses since he took on his job, but none quite as raw as the thing he said to Mr. Huston. You could not go much beyond that.

HEARING ON DRY LAW ADJOURNED TO STOP ROW

Chairman Graham Acts To Allow Committeemen To Cool Off

INSULT TO WOMAN LEADER IS ALLEGED

Celler, A Wet, Had Accused Mrs. Peabody Of Coaching Witnesses

[*Washington Bureau of The Sun*]

Washington, March 13—Friction between wet and dry members of the House Judiciary Committee, more and more in evidence as the hearings on repeal or modification of the Eighteenth Amendment have advanced, generated so much heat today that Chairman Graham had to adjourn the session to stop the row and allow members to cool off.

Just before adjournment Representative Celler, Democrat, New York, a wet, charged that Mrs. Henry W. Peabody, leader of the delegation of women appearing before the committee yesterday in support of prohibition, had coached some of her fellow-witnesses while they were on the stand. The stenographer had caught some of Mrs. Peabody's suggestions to witnesses and had inserted them in the record. Mr. Celler insisted the committee ought to take cognizance of such attempts to influence the witnesses.

Snipe At Each Other

This charge was thrown out in an atmosphere already heated by repeated clashes earlier in the day. The wets and drys had begun to snipe at each other during the examination of Carlton M. Sherwood, secretary of the citizens committee of one thousand for law observance, who was hard pressed by Representative LaGuardia, Republican, New York, on cross-examination.

The cross-fire had been suspended during the testimony of Alonzo A. Stagg, for many years football coach at the University of Chicago; of John A. McSparran, of Furness, Pa., Democratic candidate for Governor in that State four years ago, and of Arthur H. Hood, a representative of federated Bible classes in Philadelphia.

LaGuardia Attacks Hay

But it had been resumed when Charles H. Hay, of St. Louis, Democratic candidate for the Senate in Missouri two years ago and former attorney for the Anti-Saloon League, took the stand.

Mr. Hay had several tilts with Representative LaGuardia, who interrogated him as to his service as attorney for Heber Nations, recently convicted of violating the dry laws in St. Louis.

Coming after a day of such interchanges, Mr. Celler's charge about Mrs. Peabody brought Representative Stobbs, Republican, Massachusetts, to his feet. Stobbs objected that Mr. Celler obviously intended to humiliate Mrs. Peabody, and that while he held no brief for her he wanted to see that she received fair treatment. Mr. Stobbs said Mrs. Peabody's remarks were in the record and would form a proper subject of argument when the time for argument arrived, but insisted that the committee refuse to discuss the issue at that time.

Stobbs Objection Upheld

Representative Graham, the chairman, ruled with Mr. Stobbs. Mr. Graham pointed out that the committee was not sitting in a judicial capacity, and that it was not permissible in an investigation such as the committee is holding to call attention of witnesses to matters like that of which Mr. Celler had alluded.

It seemed for a time that the chairman's ruling had restored the temperature of the committee room to normal, but Representative Sumners, of Texas, ranking minority member of the committee, reopened the whole subject by coming to the defense of Mrs. Peabody.

"I have been in Congress eighteen years," affirmed Mr. Sumners, "and I have never heard witnesses insulted as this lady has been insulted here this afternoon. I insist that the chairman ought to protect those who come here to testify before us against such unfair treatment as she has received."

Graham Adjourns Hearing

With this demand half a dozen members of the committee, including Mr. Celler, sought recognition from the chairman. In the confusion, Representative Hammer, Democrat, North Carolina, made himself heard with a motion that the criticism of Mrs. Peabody be stricken from the record.

Before this motion could be seconded and before a single other remark could be interjected, Mr. Graham shouted that the meeting was adjourned, adding in lower tones that the adjournment would allow time "for us to cool off."

The stenographer's transcript of the evidence at yesterday's hearing showed, among other things, that during the cross-examination of Mrs. Hilda L. Olson, of Cambridge, Mass., Mrs. Peabody had once told her to "stick to her statement," and again had cautioned her "don't go into that."

It also showed that Mrs. Peabody

(Continued on Page 2, Column 4)

Planet, Sought For 25 Years, Discovered Beyond Neptune

Whereabouts, Size And Age Still Unknown—Its Presence Predicted By Late Dr. Lowell. "Sighted" On Lens Developed For Purpose

Flagstaff, Ariz., March 13 (AP)—In that cluster of orbs which swings across the siderial abyss under the name of the solar system there are, be it known, nine instead of a mere eight worlds.

The presence of a ninth marcher in the retinue of the sun, long suspected, was definitely announced here today by Dr. V. M. Slipher, of the Lowell Observatory, who headed a group of eminent astronomers whose gropings in the Milky Way with telescopes and cameras located the new sphere.

Size And Age Unknown

Way out beyond Neptune, tagging bashfully behind his brothers, the new planet's exact whereabouts, size and age are still unknown, and it hasn't even got a name. Its presence was mathematically predicted years ago by the late Dr. Percival Lowell, noted scientist, who founded the observatory here, partly for the very purpose of identifying it. Other noted astronomers, notably Dr. W. W. Campbell, director of Lick Observatory, verified Lowell's calculations.

Today the faith in those calculations was rewarded by an announcement by Dr. Slipher that the new planet had been "sighted" January 21 by an extremely delicate photographic lens, developed for the search. Announcement was withheld, Dr. Slipher said, "until we were absolutely sure."

The discovery revealed that the planet is about forty-five times as far from the earth as the earth is from the sun. Although its size has not been definitely determined, the announcement said, it was at least no smaller than the earth.

Greatest Find Since Neptune

Astronomically, the discovery is regarded as the greatest since the location of Neptune, eighth member of the solar system, in 1846. The astronomers who participated with Dr. Slipher in the discovery are: C. O. Lampland, E. C. Slipher, J. C. Duncan, K. P. Williams, E. A. Edwards and T. B. Gill.

Until some one entitled to do so gives the sphere a name it is to be known as "The Trans-Neptunian Planet." First notice of the body was made by C. W. Tombaugh, photographer at the observatory, who saw a tiny spot on one of his plates. Astronomers soon declared it to be the long-sought planet.

Astromoner Predicts It Is Smaller Than Neptune

Cambridge, Mass., March 13 (AP)—Announcing the discovery of the ninth major planet of the solar system by astronomers at the Lowell Observatory, Flagstaff, Ariz., Prof. Harlow Shapley, director of the Harvard College Observatory, predicted that the planet, as yet unnamed, is probably larger than the earth and smaller than Neptune.

The discovery was made by means of photographs through a new thirteen-

(Continued on Page 5, Column 4)

WETS TAKE LEAD IN DIGEST VOTING

Nine Of Ten States, Sending In 291,588 Ballots, Overwhelmingly For Law Change

KANSAS DRYS AHEAD

New York And New Jersey Lead In Request For Modification Or Repeal

New York, March 13 (Special)—The vote for repeal of the prohibition amendment outnumbers that for either modification or strict enforcement in the first scattering returns from ten States in the *Literary Digest's* current nation-wide straw poll on prohibition.

Twenty million ballots are being distributed throughout the country to obtain a referendum on the three questions:

1. Do you favor the continuance and strict enforcement of the Eighteenth Amendment and Volstead law?
2. Do you favor a modification of the Volstead law to permit light wines and beers?
3. Do you favor a repeal of the prohibition amendment?

291,588 Votes Received

Of the total of 291,588 votes received for this first tabulation, 80,739 expressed their favor for enforcement; 91,915 voted for modification, and 118,934 were for repeal.

The ten States represented in the first returns of the poll include Illinois, Indiana, Iowa, Kansas, Minnesota, Missouri, Nebraska, New Jersey, New York and Ohio.

In this first tabulation Kansas seems to indicate a pronounced stand on the dry side, while New York and New Jersey show a distinctly opposite opinion. Returns from all other seven States imply a less decisive stand.

The *Literary Digest*, however, issues a warning of caution that these first returns are so small in comparison to the final vote anticipated that all now apparent tendencies may be completely overturned.

No Result Indicated

"These early figures," the magazine states, editorially, "interesting as they may be, are by no means to be regarded as a sure-fire indication of the poll's final results, even in the ten States involved in the tabulation.

"No one should be elated or discouraged by them. Many fluctuations, perhaps startling ones, may be expected to occur in the voting before the last gun is fired.

"Every incoming mail brings a greater flock of votes to be sorted out by our army of tally clerks, while the outgoing waves of blank ballots are still running high.

"Extraordinary public interest, meanwhile, is being focused on the poll and everything connected with it. This is largely due, of course, to the dominance of prohibition as a burning question."

A previous national prohibition poll of considerably smaller magnitude was taken by the *Literary Digest* in 1922. The first tabulated returns of that poll showed 94,657 votes counted. Of these 32,445 favored strict enforcement; 39,665 favored modification, and 22,547 voted for repeal of the prohibition amendment.

Drys In Delaware Find Solace In Questionnaire

Wilmington, Del., March 13 (Special)—Members of the W. C. T. U.,

(Continued on Page 2, Column 7)

LIFE-TERMER SLAIN; HAD KILLED GUARD

Prisoner, 29, Shot Down In Trenton Penitentiary In Seeking Freedom

TWO OTHERS WOUNDED

Tear Bomb Hurled Into Institution To Quiet Others Locked In Cells

Trenton, N. J., March 13 (AP)—A desperate break for liberty tonight by a 29-year-old prisoner, who had completed eleven years of a double life sentence in State Prison, was terminated by his death, the fatal wounding of a guard and injury to two other guards.

Cornered in a cell by three keepers, Charles F. Evans, who had been a trusty since 1923, shot it out with them until a bullet from the gun of Ernest L. Gordon, a guard, killed him.

The slain guard was Frank Butcher, who received a number of bullet wounds in the exchange of shots. Gordon received a superficial shoulder wound and Thomas Foren was struck on the head with an improvised blackjack.

Prisoner Seizes Pistol

Evans' single-handed revolt came at sundown. T. P. Leydon, a guard on duty, heard a call for help and the sound of a falling body. In a second, in the words of Leydon, Evans had the pistol of the man he slugged. The victim was Foren.

Leydon climbed up two tiers to the sounds of the scuffle, but, being unarmed, he returned to the first floor, locked up two cookhouse prisoners and obtained a pistol from another officer.

Guards Shield Themselves

When Butcher appeared with another guard Evans slipped into a vacant cell and the firing began, with the guards shielding themselves behind a locker.

"The first thing we knew," Leydon related, "we smelled gas and heard a bomb drop. Foren grabbed my hat and hastily wrote a note and then threw it out the window. What was on that note I don't know yet, we were so excited. The three of us stayed back out of range for a while, and we saw several guards in the center coming on, armed. We came out in time to see them pull Evans' body from the cell."

When the disturbance was heard throughout the prison considerable shouting and excitement resulted among the prisoners, who not long before had been locked in their cells for the night. Leydon believed the gas bomb quieted the inmates.

Prison Surrounded

A cordon of Trenton police surrounded the prison, and for the next half hour what was known outside the prison walls was conveyed by the shouts of the prisoners. It was this noise which warned officers in the prison yards and caused them to hurl in the tear bomb through a window.

500 AT BRIDGE OPENING

Many Attend Dedication Of New Hooper's Island Span

Cambridge, Md., March 13—The new bridge between Upper and Middle Hooper's Island over what is known as Hooper's Island Narrows was dedicated yesterday.

Addresses were delivered by former Governor Harrington and John A. Baker, president of the Board of County Commissioners. About 500 people were present and enjoyed an oyster roast.

LIBERALS HELP LABOR DEFEAT TORY ATTACK

Attempt To Overthrow MacDonald Beaten By Majority Of 73

PROTECTION FAILS TO RALLY SUPPORT

Baldwin Predicts Ousting Of Goverment On Unemployment Issue

London, March 13 (AP)—The Labor Government tonight beat off a Conservative attack in the House of Commons, defeating a motion of censure brought by former Premier Baldwin, Conservative leader, with a margin of more than seventy votes to spare. The figures were 308 to 235 in the division.

After six hours of debate, in which Winston Churchill, former Chancellor of the Exchequer, led the Tory attack, about a score of Liberals filed into the Government lobbies and voted with Labor. The Labor strength of 287 votes, however, would have been sufficient alone to defeat the Tories. The figures indicated many abstentions among both opposition parties.

Baldwin Urges Tariffs

Mr. Baldwin's motion to censure the Government for its refusal to extend safeguarding duties as a means for reducing unemployment and protecting British industries had from the beginning little chance of success. It was not drawn up in such a way as to attract support from the Liberals, who are as much at odds with the Conservatives on the question of protection as are the Laborites.

Mr. Baldwin himself admitted that the Government would probably win. The victory became certain when Sir Herbert Samuel, one of the Liberal leaders and chairman of the party organization since 1927, rose and pledged "the unhesitating support of the Liberals to the Government today in resisting the motion of censure." The active Liberal support was not so "unhesitating" as Sir Herbert predicted, but it was enough, and taken with the absences among the Conservatives it was overwhelming.

Victory Was Expected

The Government's victory had been expected in all quarters of the House as well as in naval conference circles.

In opening the attack Mr. Baldwin asserted that eventually the cold fact of unemployment would mean the defeat of the MacDonald Ministry. He asked whether the Laborites intended at any time to have recourse either to any single duty or to a general duty as a remedy for unemployment.

Philip Snowden, Chancellor of the Exchequer, who acted in behalf of Prime Minister MacDonald, in reply to Mr. Baldwin's criticism said:

"It is a fact that ever since this Government came into office there has been an organized conspiracy. It has been the deliberate policy of certain interests to prevent employment in order to discredit the Government."

Blames Newspapers

He declared that British newspapers had been chiefly responsible for spreading a feeling of pessimism, daily printing stories about the closing of factories and the laying off of men, attributing the whole increase of unemployment to the actions and policy of the Labor Government.

The Chancellor attributed the uncertainty existing today to the late Conservative Government in leading industries to believe they could get protection and thus preventing them from reorganizing themselves.

In concluding the Tory attack, Mr. Churchill went for Snowden, his old opponent and successor at the Treasury. He declared that Mr. Snowden's "persistent refusal" to divulge the Labor party's policy on safeguarding duties had "created uncertainty which had been harmful to trade and to employment." He also asserted that Snowden had "wantonly and callously"

(Continued on Page 13, Column 8)

WEALTHY REALTOR KIDNAPPED IN N. J.

Samuel Barron, Of New York, Beaten And Carried Off In Auto

Asbury Park, N. J., March 13 (AP)—Samuel Barron, wealthy New York real estate operator, was slugged and kidnapped almost in front of his home in Interlaken last night, police revealed tonight.

Persons living near heard him shouting for help and ran out to see him being beaten by three unmasked men and then pushed into a car driven by a fourth.

Herman Goodstein, an associate of Mr. Barron, said in New York tonight that no demands for ransom had been made by Barron's captors. Barron, who is 48 years old, is senior partner of the Barsam Real Estate Corporation on Broadway.

Texas Legislature Asks Boycott On Wisconsin

Requests People It Represents Not To Buy Goods Produced In That State

Austin, Texas, March 13 In a resolution adopted by the Legislature today the people of Texas are requested to boycott all articles produced or manufactured in Wisconsin. It was estimated by members of the Senate and House who advocated the passage of the resolution that more than $20,000,000 of machinery and general equipment manufactured in Wisconsin are sold annually in Texas.

The boycott had its origin in the fact that the Wisconsin State Real Estate Brokers' Board had discharged its secretary, John L. Newman, because he purchased a ten-acre citrus fruit orchard in the lower Rio Grande valley while on a visit to that section recently.

Bugs Bother Senators In President's Room

Moths Found On Couches Of Office In Capitol Where Conferences Are Held

Washington, March 13 (AP)—Bugs invaded the President's room in the Capitol just off the Senate chamber today.

An alarm was sounded quickly by agitated Senators who frequent the room to rest during conferences with newspaper men.

The excitement was quelled somewhat by a pronouncement that the insects were a species of moths.

Nevertheless, demands were rushed to Chairman Moses, of the Rules Committee, for a hasty cleaning of the furniture. He referred the protests to cleaners in the Senate Office Building, who reported proudly just last week that the Capitol finally had been rid of roaches.

240 Miles An Hour Is Goal Of Kaye Don, British Racer

Mechanics Pronounce Huge Silver Bullet Ready For Preliminary Runs

Daytona Beach, Fla., March 13 (AP). Four miles a minute—240 miles an hour—is the goal Kaye Don, British racer, hopes to attain when he sends his powerful 24-cylinder Silver Bullet roaring over the ocean speedway soon in an effort to shatter the world's automobile speedway record.

He expressed that opinion tonight, shortly after mechanics pronounced his huge, stream-lined machine ready for a series of preliminary runs to test out the performance of the car before he attempts his official trials, probably early next week.

SPANISH JOBLESS PARADE

Disband Voluntarily When Madrid Governor Reassures Them

Madrid, March 13 (AP)—A demonstration of about 1,000 unemployed disbanded voluntarily without disorder here today when the civil governor gave assurance that he would do everything possible to supply jobs.

The unemployed paraded in orderly fashion to the Governor's palace carrying banners inscribed "we want work." When the Governor told them that it was little enough to ask and that they were entitled to work, the demonstrators cheered.

PARLEY HOPES REVIVED AFTER STRENUOUS DAY

Briand Abandons Pessimism—Professes To See Chance For Treaty

ITALY IS PRESSED TO REDUCE CLAIMS

U. S. And Britain Warn France Not To Disrupt Conference

By DREW PEARSON
Staff Correspondent of The Sun

London, March 13 (Special Cable). The naval conference having touched the rock bottom of discouragement yesterday, strenuous efforts were made today to revive the possibility of a five-power pact, and a reasonable degree of success was achieved.

Many Conferences Held

These efforts consisted of:

1. An early two-hour conference between Aristide Briand and Secretary Stimson and Ambassador Morrow, during which they dissuaded the French Foreign Minister from making pessimistic statements to the press and persuaded him to radiate a little optimism.
2. Cancellation of a meeting of heads of the delegations and instead a meeting between Dino Grandi, chief of the Italian delegation, and Premier MacDonald, at which the latter brought all possible pressure to bear on Italy to state her figures and to state them at a low level.
3. Telephone conversation before breakfast between Premier Tardieu, in Paris, and Briand and Francois Pietri, Minister of Colonies, in London, followed by a meeting between Grandi and Pietri, who speaks Italian, in an effort to get Italy to publish her figures.
4. A meeting between Senator Reed, of the American delegation, and Reijiro Wakatsuki, Japan, which was followed by a meeting of the entire American delegation to discuss the Japanese negotiations and the conference situation in general.
5. Talks between MacDonald and Wakatsuki and between MacDonald and Briand.
6. A meeting of the British Empire delegation.
7. Finally, and just to show that technicalities hadn't been lost in the rush to save the conference, there was a meeting of the experts' committee on submarines.

Parley Hopes Revived

The result of all this undoubtedly most strenuous day of the conference was not merely a general feeling that a flicker of new life had been injected into the negotiations but two concrete, detailed developments. The first was that Briand postponed issuing a polemic on security, which had been promised for some days, and gave a decidedly optimistic press interview, reversing the pessimism of last night, and, second, the British and American delegations joined the French in trying to batter down Italy's resolve not to state her figures, but to retain the right of parity with France.

Part of this Anglo-American-French drive is to persuade Italy to place her total naval needs at 400,000 tons, in which case France is willing to reduce to 600,000 tons, which would be a material concession to the British and probably make possible a five-power pact.

The chief question, of course, is whether Italy will do this, and so far it does not seem likely. Grandi has maintained that Italy could not state her figures, even though reserving the right to parity with France. The reason, of course, is that she wants to state exactly the same figures as France in order to attain parity and yet does not want to place them so high now as would be beyond her financial abilities to attain.

Duce Must Be Cautious

Mussolini is further handicapped by the fact that the liberal Government which preceded him and which he accuses of being unpatriotic brought back parity with France from the Washington Disarmament Conference and he cannot well afford to achieve less than that at London.

The Anglo-American combination, which is resolved to secure some kind of an agreement or bust, resorted to something akin to strong-arm tactics to change the pessimistic views of the French. One thing Briand has constantly harped upon is that the London conference, after all, has made some progress since it settled the old feud between the British and French regarding global tonnage, established a method of measuring disarmament, and achieved other technical victories which could be taken to Geneva for foundation of the League's program.

At this morning's session between Stimson and Morrow on the one hand and Briand, however, it is understood the former intimated to the aged French Foreign Minister that unless a real reduction treaty was concluded the United States was entirely unwilling to agree to anything on these technical problems, since they had made material concessions to France with a view to securing something in return. These counter-concessions not being forthcom-

(Continued on Page 13, Column 3)

Poincare Asked To Referee Monaco Rulers' Marital Row

Former French President Also May Pass On Dynastic Controversy—France, As Overlord, Expected To Uphold Prince Louis

Paris, March 13 (AP)—Little Monaco, famed chiefly for the gambling casino at Monte Carlo, is giving almost more trouble to France than all her other problems put together.

Should the Monacan elections March 30 result in the proclamation of a republic, France—which exercises domination over the principality—will be placed in an embarrassing situation, because her treaty with Monaco recognizes only the dynasty headed by Prince Louis.

France To Back Dynasty

If the people vote to overthrow the dynasty, it is believed that France will assure Louis' place as Prince, or, if he abdicates, probably will arrange a regency for his grandson.

A report reached Paris today that Prince Pierre, husband of Princess Charlotte, is liked by the party which is striving for a republic, and that in the event of a republic he might even be proclaimed the first president.

Poincare Possible Referee

At the conclusion tonight of a meeting of the Paris Bar Association, it was announced unofficially that former President Poincaré had been requested to referee the matrimonial controversies of Princess Charlotte—who is Prince Louis' daughter—and Prince Pierre; and also the dynastic controversies between Prince Louis and Monaco's two organized legislative and administrative bodies.

WEATHER FORECAST
Fair today; rain tomorrow; not much change in temperature.
(Details on Page 21.)

THE SUN

Henry W. Nevinson
Britain's Old Guard Still
Fights Tariff—Page 11

VOL. 190—D | PAID CIRCULATION FEBRUARY MORNING, 145,749 EVENING, 145,290 291,048 || SUNDAY 190,064 | BALTIMORE, WEDNESDAY, MARCH 2, 1932 | Published every week day by The A. S. Abell Company Entered as second class mailer at Baltimore Postoffice. | 22 PAGES | 2 CENTS

LINDBERGH BABY STOLEN

Note On Sill Believed Ransom Demand

CARRIED IN SLEEPING GARB FROM FLYER'S JERSEY HOME

World's Most Famous Baby Kidnapped From Nursery

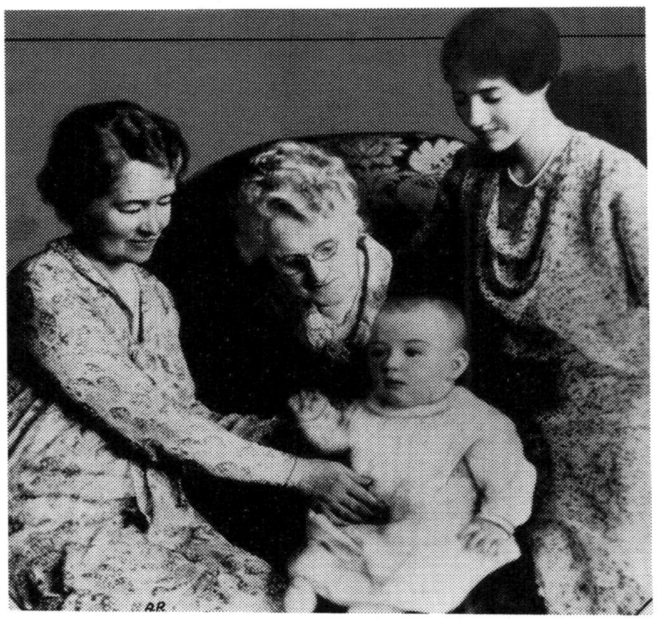

This photograph, taken when Charles Augustus Lindbergh, Jr., was about 8 months old, shows four generations on the maternal side. Mrs. Lindbergh (right), Mrs. Dwight W. Morrow (left) and the baby's great-grandmother. Mrs. Charles Long Cutter (center), of Cleveland.

STATE'S HIGHWAYS COMBED BY POLICE UNDER ORDERS TO STOP AND SEARCH CARS

Child Spirited From Hopewell Nursery Through Window By Means Of Ladder—Abductors Leave Note On Sill—Contents Not Revealed

SERVANT DISCOVERS CHILD MISSING FROM HIS CRIB

Alarm Over Disappearance Of America's Best-Known Infant Spread Quickly—Holland Tunnel And New York Ferries Guarded

[*By the Associated Press*]

New York, March 1—Friends in this city of Colonel and Mrs. Charles A. Lindbergh said tonight that Mrs. Lindbergh was expecting another child within about three months.

[*New York Bureau of The Sun*]

New York, March 1—Charles Augustus Lindbergh, Jr., 20 month-old son of Col. Charles A. Lindbergh was kidnapped between 7.30 and 10 o'clock tonight from his nursery in the Lindbergh home near Hopewell, N.J.

His abductors, who apparently carried the child in his night clothes down a ladder from a second-story window, left a note on the window sill of the nursery. Its contents were not divulged but it was reported to demand ransom.

MAID DISCOVERS DISAPPEARANCE

Both Colonel Lindbergh and his wife, the former Anne Morrow, were in the house at the time.

A maid discovered the absence of the child at about 10.30 o'clock. He had been in his crib asleep three hours earlier. Colonel Lindbergh was expected at a dinner of New York Universit Alumni here tonight and the dinner as delayed half an hour for him but he did not appear.

LINDBERGH NOTIFIES POLICE

As soon as the maid reported to the Lindberghs the disappearance of their child, Colonel Lindbergh telephoned to the New Jersey State police. Three troopers were sent to his home and the teletype system by 10.30 o'clock had carried the alarm throughout New Jersey and to New York and Pennsylvania.

Everywhere State troopers and local police were on the lookout for speedingmotor car containing a drowsy and perhaps petulant boy of under two years. All over New Jersey the police had orders to stop every motorist of whom they had the slightest suspicion.

GREEN SEDAN CLUE FAILS

Almost immediately reports bgan to come in from zealous policemen who thought they had discovered a clue. At first the search centered upon a green sedan, the license number of which was given. It had been stolen earlier in the evening in Atlantic City. Before the night was over that car was found in a locality which eliminated its driver from the search.

A report came from Hammonton, N.J., where the State police have barracks, that a man driving a car painted black or dark blue and carrying New York license plates had been seen in Princeton early in the evening making inquiries as to where Colonel Lindbergh lived. The Lindbergs home is not far from Princeton.

"NO ONE HAS TIME TO TALK NOW"

Efforts to reach the Lindbergh home immediately after the kidnapping was reported met with the response: "No one has time to talk now." The chief operator at the Hopewell telephone exchange said that although the Lindbergh home had a private telephone she had been instructed by Colonel Lindbergh to "keep my telephone line clear all night." She said he had asked particularly that no calls from newspapers be put through until morning.

Mrs. Morrow, the baby's grandmother, was notified of the kidnapping a few minutes before midnight. She was unde-

(Continued on Page 2, Column 1)

CHINESEROUTED BY JAPANESE STORM TROOPS

Vicious Battle Results In Capture Of Tachang, Invaders Claim

NIPPONESE PLANES DESTROY RAILWAY

Both Sides Locked In Artillery Conflict On Chapei Front

Evacuation Of Chapei Termed Imminent

Shanghai, March 2, *Wednesday* (AP) — Chinese evacuation of Chapei and the area to the west, including army headquarters at Chenju, seemed imminent this afternoon. Persons coming in from around Chenju said a majority of the Chinese already had departed toward Nanziang, five miles west of that point.

By MORRIS J. HARRIS
(*Associated Press Copyright*, 1932)

Shanghai, March 2 *(Wednesday)* — Fresh Japanese storm troops beat China's army into rout on the Kiangwan front and took Tachang, four miles to the west, today in a great and bloody onslaught over Shanghai's entire battleline.

The Chinese Nineteenth Route Army was flung back toward Kunshan, west of Shanghai, at a cost of 1,800 lives, the Japanese said, while they lost only 60 dead. A retreat of other Chinese troops in Nantao, south of Shanghai, also was reported.

Battle Rages Near Liuho

Another battle was under way near Liuho, twenty miles north of Shanghai, where Japanese flyers bombed Chinese troops attempting to block thousands of landing Nipponese reinforcements fighting their way through Chinese fire to join the left flank of their comrades.

Six Japanese airplanes bombed the Shanghai-Nanking Railway near Kunshan, thirty-five miles west of Shanghai, and cut the line apart, the flyers said, with their rain of 250-pound missiles. They had threatened to destroy the railway if the Chinese continued to transport reinforcements over it. The threat was carried out on schedule.

Whole Of Shanghai Jarred

Thus Japan's mounting power of armaments and men broke the Chinese lines about midway between Shanghai and Woosung, sixteen miles away.

At the Shanghai end, in Chapei, both sides were locked in artillery combat, neither giving any ground. The duel of big guns jarred the whole city.

The Japanese, the superiority of their war machines and men felt more strongly with every blow, said they had crushed the Chinese defenses on the Kiangwan line.

Japanese Army authorities said Tachang, an important objective, was occupied by Japanese troops at 12.30 P.M. today.

Chinese Forces Give Way

The Japanese pushed relentlessly on as the Chinese forces fled toward Kunshang and Tatsang. The Japanese right wing was closing in from the north in a similar advance.

Toward Chapei the Japanese line bent eastward as the Chinese continued to hold the devastated battleground of the conflict's beginning more than a month ago.

Liuho Not Yet Occupied

Japanese officers said their forces in the vicinity of Liuho totaled 12,000. Their landing was virtually completed, they said, and the soldiers had begun a southward movement. Although Liuho itself was not yet occupied, the Japanese expected to take it over during the day or tomorrow.

The Japanese seemed headed for Kating, as well as Tachang. Kating is a short distance north of Tachang.

In event the Japanese continued westward while the army near Liuho advanced southward, a great enveloping movement would result, threaten-

(Continued on Page 4, Column 3)

The Great Game Of Politics

By FRANK R. KENT

Arguments And Answers

Dallas, Texas, March 1.

IT WAS INCORRECT to say that every local leader in Texas has now joined in the Garner movement. There is one exception—the well-known Tom Love, once national committeeman, the close friend of William G. McAdoo and the man most responsible for Texas going Republican in 1928, when Al Smith was the candidate.

—o—

THERE IS A GREAT deal of feeling here against Mr. Love because of that campaign. Most Texas Democrats are thoroughly ashamed of the State's bolt of the party at that election. They ascribe it—and rightly— to the prejudice against Mr. Smith's religion and not to either his wetness or his Tammany affiliations. Mr. Love is the recognized dry leader of the State, and he was the most conspicuous absentee at the big Garner rally in San Antonio last week. He is understood to take the position that he will not support any candidate who does not flatly stand for upholding the Eighteenth Amendment.

—o—

WHETHER MR. LOVE supports Mr. Garner or not is an unimportant matter. He is completely impotent to affect the Texas attitude or the Garner chances. Rather he enhances them. In the first place, wet sentiment has increased in four years in Texas as it has everywhere else and the State is not inflammable against a wet Democrat now, so long as he is a Protestant. In the second place, the Ku Klux Klan has shriveled and almost disappeared. In the third place, the announcement of his peerless leader, Mr. McAdoo, for Garner, has left Mr. Love away out on the limb.

—o—

MR. LOVE IS NOT important politically any more, but his attitude does serve to call to attention that Texas, though wetter in sentiment and awfully wet in fact in the cities, is still a dry State and that there is the keenest interest here as the Garner position on prohibition — far more keen than about anything else. Not long ago, it is said, the W. C. T. U. here wrote Mr. Garner requesting him to state his position. They got a letter back saying that his record spoke for him. So far as it is known that record is this—he voted against the adoption of the Eighteenth Amendment, but since has voted in the House for every dry legislative proposal. It is not believed Mr. Garner personally favors prohibition, but he has been since its adoption a consistent political dry. A few days ago it was announced he would say no word on the subject, holding that there are a lot more vital things to attent to now.

—o—

HIS POLITICAL friends believe he will adhere to this position—that he will say nothing unless he is nominated. If and when that happens, they argue, he will then come out for repeal. The contention is there will be nothing else he can do. He could, of course, hold the dry South if he does that, and his only chance of carrying the great indispensable wet States of the East is to do it. Politically he would be compelled to. As the practical politicians see it here, to be nominated Mr. Garner must convince the leaders in the Eastern States that he can be elected —or at least that he will run as well as any other man who could be put up. There are plenty of arguments for him —only three, as it is viewed here, against him.

—o—

THE FIRST IS that the Democratic party cannot possibly carry the New York group of States, whose electoral votes are essential to sucess—or Massachusetts, Illinois or Ohio — with a dry. The answer to that has already been given. Mr. Garner, it is said, will be for repeal if he is nominated. He will not be unless he is. The second is that a Southern man cannot be elected. The answer to that is that the Civil War has been over seventy years, that the feeling between North and South has faded, that this is one

(Continued on Page 3, Column 2)

HOUSE MAY GET NEW TAX BILL BEFORE NIGHT

Approval Of Draft By Ways And Means Committee Expected Today

SALES LEVY YIELD PUT AT $625,000,000

Rate Understood To Be 2 Per Cent.—Excise Impost Kept Secret

By DEWEY L. FLEMING

[Washington Bureau of The Sun]

Washington, March 1—With the nation's budget-balancing tax bill virtually written, Representative Crisp, acting chairman of the House Ways and Means Committee, has called the full committee to meet tomorrow to consider the final draft.

Because of its bipartisan character, Mr. Crisp is hopeful that the measure will receive the committee's approval before nightfall and it is his plan to introduce it in the House "without a minute's delay."

Full Debate Promised

What will hapin to the program when the House takes hold of it is a matter of conjecture, but the committee is disposed to permit full and free debate within reasonable limits Mr. Crisp, author of the newly liberalized House rules, said he had no intention of asking cloture to limit debate, as was done with President Hoover's emergency relief measures.

Being privileged legislation, the tax bill could be brought up next Tuesday without resort to a special rule, and the acting committee chairman indicated that he favored that course. Under ordinary procedure in the House, the measure, upon introduction, would be referred automatically to the Ways and Means committee, which already had approved it, and would be back the following day with the committee's recommendation that it be considered immediately. Every effort is to be made to expedite the bill's passage.

Sales Tax Plan Approved

A completed draft of the manufactures sales tax, which is to be the chief feature of the new tax program, was approved by the Rainey subcommittee today and will be laid before the full committee tomorrow with recommendations that it be approved. The levy would apply to all manufactured articles save a limited number of staple foods, farm products and certain farm requisites, schoolbooks, newspapers and magazines, and a sew other items not yet disclosed.

The rate of the tax has not been made public, but the expectation is that it will be about two per cent. Until today the subcommittee has estimated the expected yield of the new tax to be about $600,000,000, but word came out of the committee room that it is now anticipated the return will be nearer $625,000,000.

New rates on income, inheritance and estate taxes are understood to have been framed to produce some $250,000,000 of added revenue, while budget cuts and certain administrative changes in the tax law are expected to account for at least $125,000,000. Slight modification of postal rates, chiefly in the parcels-post field, are expected to yield about $20,000,000.

Items On Excise List

Items most prominently mentioned in the list likely to be subjected to an excise tax are gas, electricity, gasoline, industrial alcohol and amusement tickets. Today's boost in the estimated yield of the manufactures tax was interpreted in some quarters as an indication that one or more of these items would bear the manufacturers' sales tax instead. In the case of gasoline, this would mean that instead of paying the suggested tax of one cent per gallon, motor fuel would be considered an ordinary manufactured commodity and would bear the two per cent tax.

In a speech addressed to the nation, Representative Crisp tonight appealed to all citizens to "ponder and consider well" the emergency tax situation, and "be willing in this emergency for a year or two to bear additional tax burdens in order to balance our budget, upon the accomplishment of which rest the peace, happiness and stability of our Government and the welfare of us all."

Treasury Gives Up Campaign For Sale Of New Baby Bonds

$50 Securities Will Be Issued, But No Special Effort Will Be Made To Dispose Of Them Due To Objection Of Bankers

by J. F. ESSARY

Washington, March 1—All special efforts for the sale of the new $50 Government bonds as a part of the nationwide anti-hoarding campaign, have been called off by Treasury officials.

These officials have decided not to press the sale of these "baby" securities, and although they will be issued on March 7, as announced, it will make no difference to the Treasury if the country forgets about them.

The secret of this is that the banks have objected. They objected first to the bond issue as a whole, complaining that the Government was going into competition with them for cash at a time when cash is none too plentiful.

Fear Loss Of Deposits

They objected again to high-pressure salesmanship in connection with the sale, particularly to patriotic appeals, on the grund that the people who might yield to such appeals would draw $9 out of banks to buy the bonds for every dollar of hoarded money that would be beguiled from its hiding place.

This has sounded reasonable enough to the Treasury, with the result that all special campaigning for the sale of bonds is being discouraged, all private tenders of assistance in that connection are being rejected and all local anti-hoarding committees are being coached to subordinate the bond argument in their drive for the hoarded and hidden millions.

Big Drive Due Sunday

On Sunday night the emergency reconstruction committee, organized by Frank Knox, of Chicago, at the President's solicitation, will put on its biggest effort to induce owners of the $1,300,000,000 now in hiding, to put it

Continued on Page 3, Column 7)

WORLD'S MOST FAMOUS BABY BORN JUNE, 1930

International Interest Centered On Child's Birth At Englewood

Charles Augustus Lindbergh, Jr., most famous baby in the world was born at 4:15 P.M. June 22, 1930, his mother's twenty-fourth birthday.

His birthplace was the Englewood (N.J.) estate of his grandparents, the late senator Dwight W. Morrow and Mrs. Morrow, it was there that his parents, Col. Charles A. Lindbergh and the former Miss Ann Morrow, had been married May 27, 1929.

World Awaited Event

The baby weighed at birth 7-¼ pounds and had blue eyes and curly hair.

Heralded in advance in a manner the world heretofore had associated only with the nativity of princes, his birth drew worldwide attention. A corps of newspaper men had waited all night and through the day at the gates of the Morrow estate for the word Senator Morrow slipped out to give them late that afternoon.

World Speculated On Name

Congratulations came flooding in to the parents and grandparents by telephone wireless, telegraph and cable from kings and presidents, royalty and commoners.

Then began an anxious speculation on the name the parents would choose for their child whom the headline writers already had dubbed the Eaglet. Even the filing of his birth certificate June 25 failed to allay that speculation for the paper showed a blank space where the name was to be written. Not until July 8, seventeen days after the infant's birth, was the name chosen for him officially announced.

Lindbergh Distributed Pictures

The following day Colonel Lindbergh distributed to the press the first pictures of his son, which he had taken.

Colonel Lindbergh early announced his determination to protect his son from publicity. Attendants reported him as having been calm when the child was born, remarkably so in contrast to Senator Morrow, who made no

(Continued on Page 2, Column 7)

INJUNCTION BILL PASSED BY SENATE

Norris Wins Eight-Year Fight To Curb Authority Of U. S. Courts

[*Washington Bureau of The Sun*]

Washington, March 1—By a vote of 75 to 5, the Senate late today adopted the Norris Anti-Injunction bill substantially as it was eported from the Judiciary Committee, thus marking the first major victory in the twenty-five-year fight of labor leaders to curb the authority of Federal courts in issuing labor injunctions.

It was a foregone conclusion last week that the Norris measure would pass the Senate by a substantial margin and earlier in the day the last of the Hebert amendments was voted down, 58 to 16. But when the roll call on the final vote there was a gasp of

(Continued on Page 3, Column 4)

JUSTICE IS SWIFT IN HAWAII CRIME

Ex-Convict Admits Attack On Woman And Is Sentenced To Life In Prison

by RUSSELL OWEN

[*Special Dispatch to the Sun*]

Honolulu, March 1 (By Cable) —Another attack case here today was followed by swift police action, which resulted in the capture of the alleged assailant within a few hours.

Today's victim was a Japanese woman, Mrs. Miwa Watanabe, mother of four children, who was attacked near her home on the Kanehoe side of the island. She is employed as a servant by Harold Castle, one of the wealthiest men of the islands and a cousin to William R. Castle, Jr., Under Secretary of State.

Mrs. Watanabe, the wife of a steward on the Castle estate, had

(Continued on Page 18, Column 2)

Watson, Smoot, Moses, Bingham And Jones Beaten For Senate

THE SUN

6.15 A.M.

VOL. 191—F | PAID CIRCULATION OCTOBER MORNING, 140,519 EVENING, 138,080 278,599 ‖ SUNDAY 183,152 | BALTIMORE, WEDNESDAY, NOVEMBER 9, 1932 | Published every week day by The A. S. Abell Company. Entered as second-class matter at Baltimore Postoffice. | 20 PAGES | 2 CENTS

New Congress Wet, Democrats In Control

ROOSEVELT IS ELECTED

Democrats Capture Maryland By 125,000

ROOSEVELT 80,956 AHEAD IN BALTIMORE RETURNS; ADDS 43,335 IN COUNTIES

Senator Tydings Has 148,940 Advantage Over Williams, But Runs 21,561 Votes Behind National Ticket

PALMISANO AND KENNEDY CAPTURE SEATS IN HOUSE

Former Defeats Ingram By 23,217 And Latter Downs Sweezey By 23,790—Election Of Other Four Representatives Assured

By LOUIS J. O'DONNELL

Gov. Franklin D. Roosevelt yesterday smashed all precedents for a Presidential candidate's majority in Maryland by rolling up a lead over President Hoover which at 6 o'clock this morning had reached 124,291, with 68 precincts still to be tabulated.

He led the Democratic ticket in Baltimore city to victory with a majority of 80,956 over his Republican opponent.

TYDINGS IS 148,940 VOTES AHEAD

Senator Tydings — with the same 68 precincts out — had established an all-inclusive record for majorities in the State by overwhelming his Republican opponent—State Senator Wallace Williams—by 148,940 votes.

The six Democratic candidates for the House of Representatives were reelected.

The voters of the entire State decisively approved the proposed amendment to the Constitution prohibiting the extension of judges' terms after they have reached the age of 70 years.

PALMISANO AND KENNEDY WIN

Representative Vincent L. Palmisano was reelected in the Third district over R. Palmer Ingram, Republican, by 23,217 votes. Ambrose J. Kennedy, Democrat, defeated Col. Claude B. Sweezey, U. S. A. (retired), the Republican candidate, by a vote of 46,352 to 22,562 in the Fourth district.

Leads they obtained in Baltimore city alone were almost enough to elect Representatives William P. Cole, Jr., Second district, and Stephen W. Gambrill, Fifth district, over their Republican opponents, David L. Elliott and A. Kingsley Love, respectively.

Cole's lead in Baltimore was 26,953, to which 16,985 was added by the incomplete returns from the county territory of the Second district—Baltimore, Carroll and Harford counties—to bring his total lead to 43,938. Mr. Gambrill's city lead over Love was 8,272, to which Southern Maryland added enough to bring his final majo[illegible] to 25,560.

Representative David J. Lewis in the Sixth (Western Maryland) district in 193 of a total of 245 precincts had taken a lead of 8,402 votes over Harold C. Smith, Republican.

On the Eastern Shore Representative T. Alan Goldsborough, running as a dry, in reports from 168 of 175 precincts was leading Harry T. Phoebus, who adopted a dripping wet platform in preference to the Republican plank, by 16,325. In only his home county—Somerset—did Phoebus defeat Goldsborourh, and there by 518 votes, with one precinct missing.

G. O. P. Leads In Three Counties

The Roosevelt-Garner ticket had carried thirteen of the twenty-three counties from which complete returns were received by 6 A. M., and unless there is a tremendous and unlooked-for swing to President Hoover in six of the others, they also will fall in the Roosevelt column. Hoover was leading by a narrow margin in Washington and Allegany, and complete returns gave the Republican ticket Calvert

(Continued on Page 6, Column 1)

Tydings Swamps G.O.P. Senate Rival By More Than 2-1

Piling up a majority which created a new record for the State, Senator Millard E. Tydings last night had swamped his opponent, Wallace Williams, by a count of more than two to one.

With reports from all sections of the State virtually completed the return of the six Democratic Congressmen to the House of Representatives with Senator Tydings was assured.

Mr. Tydings leaped into the lead with the first returns and when the complete figures of the 672 polling places in Baltimore were announced had amassed 150,022 votes to the 54,375 polled by Mr. Williams, his lead of 95,647 being about 1,500 short of the record city majority of 97,000 rolled up by Herbert R. O'Conor, State's Attorney, in 1930. His total vote in the State of 277,025 fell 21,561 below that for President-elect Roosevelt. He lost only Garrett county to Mr. Williams.

Has Big Lead In Counties

With all but 68 polling places in the counties reported, the Democratic candidate was leading Mr. Williams by 148,940 early this morning.

In returns from nineteen precincts in Cecil, the Republican candidate's home county, Mr. Tydings was leading by 813, and in Harford, his own stronghold, he had amassed 6,122 votes to his opponent's 2,832.

The four Democratic Congressional

(Continued on Page 7, Column 1)

VICTOR HEARS GOOD NEWS MID JOYFUL THRONG

Headquarters Goes Wild As Governor Becomes President-Elect

FAMILY AT HIS SIDE AS RETURNS COME IN

Al Smith, J. W. Davis And Raskob Congratulate Roosevelt

"I Am Grateful With All My Heart"

New York, Nov. 9 (AP)—The New York *Times* today quoted President-elect Franklin D. Roosevelt as saying:

"While I am grateful with all my heart for this expression of the confidence of my fellow-Americans, I realize keenly the responsibility I shall assume and I mean to serve with my utmost capacity the interest of the nation."

By FRANKLYN WALTMAN, JR.
Staff Correspondent of The Sun

New York, Nov. 8—A jubilant Democracy gathered at the party's headquarters in the Biltmore Hotel tonight worked itself into a frenzy of enthusiasm as returns from all parts of the nation assured election to the Presidency of Gov. Franklin D. Roosevelt.

Governor Roosevelt, barricaded in a room guarded by a dozen police officers, declined to make any public comment on the outcome of the election, explaining through his aides that he wished to see returns from the Pacific Coast before speaking. Apparently he wished to avoid Charles E. Hughes' mistake of thinking he had been elected before California reported.

Thanks Party Workers

Although adhering to his determination not to make any statement claiming his election to the Presidency, based chiefly on courtesy to wait for President Hoover's telegram of congratulation, Governor Roosevelt a few minutes before midnight tonight made a brief speech to several thousand persons in the Biltmore ballroom.

The President-elect said::

"My friends, I have come out here to bid you God speed and to thank you each and every one for all you have done in this campaign, and especially all the men and women who have worked so faithfully at headquarters. It has been because of their work that the great majority we have

(Continued on Page 2, Column 6)

FRANKLIN D. ROOSEVELT

Hoover, Conceding Defeat, Congratulates Roosevelt

Extends His Felicitations On Latter's Opportunity To Serve Country—Blackboard In Home, Meanwhile, Shows Mounting Tide Of Defeat

[By the Associated Press]

Palo Alto, Cal., Nov. 8—In a telegram, President Hoover tonight extended to Franklin D. Roosevelt his congratulations.

While a gathering of friends and neighbors lingered in the big living room of his home one of the Chief Executive's secretaries handed to the press the following message to the New York Governor:

Hon. Franklin D. Roosevelt, Biltmore Hotel, New York City:

I congratulate you on the opportunity that has come to you to be of service to the country and I wish for you a most successful administration. In the common purpose of all of us I shall dedicate myself to every possible helpful effort.

HERBERT HOOVER.

The President sent this telegram from his study after watching the returns pile up increasing majorities for his opponent.

Cheered By Students

When the announcement of the President's conceding came, shortly after 9.30 P. M. (Pacific Standard Time), a throng of Stanford University students filled his driveway. They waited opportunity to stage a rally for him.

Shortly, the Chief Executive, with Mrs. Hoover by his side, appeared on the front balcony of their Pueblo dwelling, and a burst of cheering that lasted for four minutes was started. Large powder candles were set off, lighting the driveway bright as day. Smoke from the candles swirled upward, almost completely enveloping the President and First Lady, but they stood, smiling until it cleared away.

Someone called for "another yell for the President and Mrs. Hoover" and a "siren" consisting of a whistle or two

(Continued on Page 4, Column 5)

Returns In Baltimore City

The following are complete returns from the 672 Polling Places in Baltimore city:

FOR PRESIDENT AND VICE-PRESIDENT

ROOSEVELT and GARNER (Dem.)	159,928
HOOVER and CURTIS (Rep.)	78,972
THOMAS and MAURER (Soc.)	6,835
Roosevelt plurality	80,956

FOR UNITED STATES SENATOR

TYDINGS (Dem.)	150,022
WILLIAMS (Rep.)	54,375
TOOLE (Soc.)	5,700
Tydings plurality	95,647

FOR HOUSE OF REPRESENTATIVES

Second District (Complete)		*Fourth District* (Complete)	
COLE (Dem.)	51,227	KENNEDY (Dem.)	46,352
ELLIOTT (Rep.)	24,274	SWEEZEY (Rep.)	22,562
Cole majority	26,953	Kennedy plurality	23,790
Third District (Complete)		*Fifth District* (Complete)	
INGRAM (Rep)	11,361	GAMBRILL (Dem.)	12,257
PALMISANO (Dem.)	34,478	LOVE (Rep.)	3,717
Palmisano plurality	23,117	Gambrill majority	8,540

CONSTITUTIONAL AMENDMENT

Judges' Term Extension Abolishment

For	71,033
Against	16,113

NEW YORK GIVES ITS 47 VOTES TO ROOSEVELT

Entire Democratic Ticket Elected In Tidal Wave Of Ballots

[By the Associated Press]

New York, Nov. 9 (*Wednesday*)—In an unparalleled landslide, Franklin D. Roosevelt seized New York's 47 electoral votes for himself while the complete Democratic State ticket rode into office in the quadrennial Presidential election.

Coasting to victory on a plurality of 862,000 amassed in the Metropolitan area, Roosevelt overcame an up-State advantage of 230,000 which accrued to President Hoover.

The Vote In Detail

With only 448 of the State's 8,837 election districts missing, an early morning tabulation gave:

Roosevelt	2,455,560
Hoover	1,823,912

Swinging the State of his birth into the Democratic Presidential column for the first time since 1912, Roosevelt almost doubled the New York city margin registered by Alfred E. Smith in 1928, and cut in half the Hoover up-State lead of four years ago. For the first time in history the total vote cast in the metropolitan area exceeded 2,000,000.

In New York city's 3,794 districts the count was: Roosevelt, 1,437,231; Hoover, 575,031. In 4,595 of the remaining 5,043 districts Roosevelt received 1,108,324 to 1,248,881 for Hoover.

Lehman Chosen Governor

Lieut.-Gov. Herbert H. Lehman, commanding the joint support of

(Continued on Page 2, Column 5)

DEMOCRATIC CANDIDATES ARE SWEPT INTO POWER BY VOTES OF ALL SECTIONS

East, Middle West And South Unite In Repudiating President Hoover, And Far West Returns Indicate Landslide

CONTROL OF BOTH HOUSES OF CONGRESS ASSURED

President Concedes Defeat And Wires Congratulations And Best Wishes To Victor—Wets Gain In Legislative Branch

Loser's Congratulatory Message To President-Elect

Hon. Franklin D. Roosevelt, Biltmore Hotel, New York city:

I congratulate you on the opportunity that has come to you to be of service to the country and I wish for you a most successful administration. In the common purpose of all of us I shall dedicate myself to every possible helpful effort.

HERBERT HOOVER.

By J. F. ESSARY

The Roosevelt-Garner ticket was swept to overwhelming victory in yesterday's election.

East, West and South alike united in repudiating the Administration of President Hoover.

Even the Pacific Coast, on a basis of partial returns, received early this morning, contributed to the landslide.

DEMOCRATS CONTROL CONGRESS

The Democrats not only captured the Presidency but, in addition, assumed undisputed control of both houses of Congress.

Anti-prohibitionists, moreover, firmly intrenched themselves in power, with modification of the Volstead act, if not immediate repeal of the Eighteenth Amendment, now in sight.

The Roosevelt electoral vote is well over 400 and an early morning Associated Press compilation fixes it at 453, or nine more than were accorded Mr. Hoover four years ago.

Early this morning President Hoover conceded his defeat and sent a cordial message of congratulation and good wishes to Governor Roosevelt.

Still earlier in the evening Vice-President Curtis bowed to the inevitable and mournfully told interviewers at Kansas City that this is the only popular election he had ever lost.

Most of the President's faithful supporters yielded to the overwhelming evidence of party disaster long before midnight and gave up the fight.

Joining in that chorus of despair were the New York *Herald Tribune*, Chicago *Daily News* and Senators Hastings, of Delaware, and Hebert, of Rhode Island, in charge of the Republican headquarters in New York.

Maryland For Roosevelt

Maryland put in her oar for Roosevelt with a big splash early in the evening. Governor Roosevelt had a lead in the State of 111,000 votes, apparently assuring him an unprecedented majority.

Senator Tydings had a lead over State Senator Williams of 129,000.

New York Defeat Decisive

The decisive defeat of Mr. Hoover in New York, assured when the Roosevelt plurality in New York city mounted to [illegible], shattered the Hoover hope of even a near-solid East. No Hoover victory could be calculated without those 47 votes.

And the New York returns had barely become conclusive when reports were flashed from Chicago that Roosevelt had taken a 3-to-1 lead over his rival in Illinois, thereby

Democratic Sweep Gives Them Control Of Both Branches

By DEWEY L. FLEMING

The Democratic party yesterday established a firm grip on both branches of the new Congress in the avalanche of votes which swept Franklin D. Roosevelt into the Presidency. Indications were, too, that the anti-prohibition vote in the new body would be heavy, although it was impossible to ascertain the extent of this change.

The most sensational result of the cannonading on the Congressional front was the routing of such veteran Republican Senate leaders as Watson, Indiana, the party floor leader; Smoot, Utah, chairman of the powerful Finance Committee; Jones, Washington, chairman of the Appropriations Committee; Moses, New Hampshire, president pro tem., and Bingham, of Connecticut.

Glenn And Oddie In Doubt

Other prominent Republican Senators who appeared to have gone down to defeat were Glenn, Illinois, and Oddie, Nevada, chairman of the Committee on Postoffices and Roads.

Incomplete returns from the far flung balloting indicated that the Democrats probably would capture twenty-eight of the thirty-four Senate seats offered. This would bring the party division of the body to sixty Demo-

(Continued on Page 3, Column 1)

THE WEATHER

Increasing cloudiness, with rain or snow late tonight or early Tuesday, followed by rain Tuesday; rising temperature.

[Detailed report on Page 2]

Closing Prices On N. Y. Stock, Curb, Bond And Baltimore Exchanges

THE EVENING SUN

6 STAR ★★★★★★ Wall Street Close

VOL. 46 | PAID CIRCULATION DECEMBER MORNING 135,417 EVENING 134,324 269,741 ‖ SUNDAY 181,374 | BALTIMORE, MONDAY, JANUARY 30, 1933 | Published every week-day by The A. S. Abell Company. Entered as second-class matter at Baltimore Postoffice. | 24 PAGES | 2 CENTS

HITLER CHANCELLOR, 2 NAZIS GET JOBS

Senate Finance Group Approves Beer-Wine Bill

BEER, WINE BILL AGAIN IS PLACED BEFORE SENATE

Committee Scraps Hearing Idea, Gives Okay By 12 To 5

MILLS SEES $5 TAX WORTH $125,000,000

Action Expected As Soon As Parliamentary Situation Permits

[*By the Associated Press*]

Washington, Jan. 30—Brushing aside proposals for further hearings, the Senate Finance Committee sent the Collier-Blaine 3.05 per cent. beer and wine bill speeding back to the Senate today with a favorable report.

The Volstead modification bill was was approved, 12 to 5, within little more than an hour of consideration in executive session.

Chairman Reed Smoot, (Rep., Utah) said he would submit the committee's report today, which will put the bill before the Senate, ready for action as soon as the parliamentary situation permits.

Bill Left Unchanged

No changes were made in the bill as approved a week ago by the Senate Judiciary Committee.

The committee turned down Smoot's proposal for hearings and agreed to confine its consideration to the revenue features of the bill.

Smoot said the vote to report the bill favorably was on its revenue features only. These provide for a tax of $5 a barrel.

Secretary of the Treasury Ogden L. Mills appeared before the committee in executive session and estimated that this tax would raise from $125,000,000 to $150,000,000.

Prefers $5 Tax Rate

The $5 a barrel rate, Mills said, would produce more revenue than any other tax level.

The vote by which the bill was reported follows:

For—Watson, Indiana; Reed, Pennsylvania; Shortridge, California; Bingham, Connecticut; La Follette, Wisconsin, and Hastings, Delaware, all Republicans; and Harrison, Mississippi; King, Utah; George, Georgia, Walsh, Massachusetts; Barkley, Kentucky, and Hull, Tennessee, Democrats.

Against: Smoot, Utah; Keyes, New Hampshire, Republicans; Connally, Texas; Gore, Oklahoma, and Costigan, Colorado, Democrats.

Senator Connally issued a statement explaining his vote against the bill. "Three and two-tenths per cent. beer by weight is equal to four per cent. beer by volume," it said. "This is substantially the same percentage as ordinary beer sold before the adoption of the Eighteenth Amendment, which I regard as intoxicating. So long as the

[Continued On Page 2, Column 2]

Today On Inside Pages

Bitz Held With Spitale In Murder

Lindbergh's Underworld Aides Suspected Of Shooting Antonio Fantaino On August 25

New York, Jan. 30 (AP)—Salvatore Spitale and Irvin Bitz, emmissaries retained by Col. Charles A. Lindbergh in his effort to find his kidnapped son, were arraigned today on suspicion of homicide and were held without bail.

They were arraigned as suspects in the murder of Antonio Fantaino, who was shot as he walked along a Lower East Side street in the early morning of August 25. They had been taken into custody early Sunday in a restaurant.

Each Carried Gun

An adjournment until Wednesday was granted by a magistrate today at the request of the police. Counsel for Spitale and Bitz strongly objected, accusing the police of being "on a fishing expedition."

Spitale and Bitz will be given a hearing in Tombs Court tomorrow on a charge of violating the Sullivan Anti-Firearms law. Each had a revolver when they were arrested, but Spitale produced a permit signed January 13 by Judge William E. Thorp, of Greene county.

Saturday night some anonymous person called a police station, saying that if authorities wanted to prevent a "coupla guys" from getting "bumped off," they should lose no time in getting to the Red Devil Restaurant.

At a table in the restaurant, sat the two "square-shooting guys from the underworld" who rose to headlines underworld" who rose to headlines when they were commissioned to try to get the Lindbergh baby back.

Detectives weren't sure, however, whether the arrest really forestalled a killing or whether some one with a distaste for Spitale and Bitz decided to get the police to annoy them.

Flashes

Insull And Firm's Directors Sued Again

Chicago, Jan. 30 (AP)—Samuel Insull and the entired directorate of the bankrupt Corporation Securities Company were made defendants today in a suit filed in Federal Court seeking an accounting of $23,233,000 due the bondholders of the investment concern. Similar action against the directors of the Insull Utility Investments, Inc., involving $40,000,000 alleged to be due its bondholders, was taken last week.

Woodchopper Reveals Year-Old Murder

Caribou, Maine, Jan. 30 (U.P.)—A conscience-stricken young wood chopper today led officers deep into the snowbound backwoods and showed them the hidden body of a man he slew with an ax a year ago. The confessed slayer was Rolando King, 18-year-old French-Canadian, who speaks no English.

Poet's Death Held Accident

New York, Jan. 30 (AP)—The death of Sarah Teasdale, lyric poet, was the result of an accident, Dr. Charles Norris, chief medical examiner, found today after an autopsy. The body of the poet was found yesterday in a partially filled bathtub in Miss Teasdale's apartment at 1 Fifth avenue.

South Bend Police Rout 5,000 Jobless

South Bend, Ind., Jan. 30 (U.P.). A small army of police and deputies wielding clubs broke up a demonstration by 5,000 unemployed in the business district today, arresting twenty and driving the others to the outskirts of the city. None was hurt.

Woman Sentenced To Death For Murder

Sunbury, Pa., Jan. 30 (U.P.)—Mrs. Mary Stancavage, 49, of Shamokin, today was sentenced to death in the electric chair after she pleaded guilty to killing her husband, Jacob Stancavage.

BLIZZARD VISITS SAN BERNARDINO, BLOCKING AUTOS

California Rushes Effort To Open Roads To 2,000 Marooned

HOMES FLOODED IN THE LOWLANDS

Reno Still In Darkness As Storms Continue On West Coast

[*By the Associated Press*]

San Francisco, Jan. 30—Caught in a sudden and terrific blizzard, more than 2,000 persons were snowbound in the San Bernardino Mountains of Southern California today as winter stormed the Pacific Coast for the seventeenth consecutive day.

In the lowlands of Long Beach, Cal., fifty families waited for flood waters to leave the homes from which they were rescued by life boats yesterday. Nearby Los Angeles expected more rain after experiencing the greatest precipitation in seventeen years—8.41 inches since January 1.

Reno Still In Darkness

Reno, Nev., was without power for the third day as a result of broken lines in the high Sierra Nevada Mountains which darkened the city Saturday night.

Snowfall broke all records for Yosemite National Park with a season's total of 148 inches, since settled to much less.

Every available snowplow in Southern California was turned to the rescue of the hundreds marooned along the rim of the World Drive in the San Bernardino Mountains after they watched the Lake Arrowhead winter sports carnival yesterday.

500 Autos Abandoned

Approximately 500 automobiles had started the trip down from the mountains when caught in the fury of the storm. Automobiles were abandoned and motorists walked back to Lake Arrowhead. Cabins, ordinarily closed to the public during the winter, were opened and check-up today disclosed occupants of all stranded machines were accounted for at the lake.

At several other mountain points rescue parties struggled to reach persons cut off from sources of supplies by ever increasing snow drifts.

Historic Donner Summit, transcontinental railroad and highway pass over the Sierra Nevada Mountains, lay under more than twelve feet of snow.

Nine Fort Bragg (Cal.) youths, members of a basket-ball team, were rescued from a snowbound ranch home where they took shelter Saturday after their automobile, in which they were traveling to another town, stalled in the drifts.

The coast highway between Santa Monica and Ventuja was blocked by a landslide.

The United States Weather Bureau predicted the Pacific Coast States and Nevada and Idaho might expect more snow and rain.

Boston Fishing Boat Cancels Call For Aid

Boston, Jan. 30 (AP)—As the Coast Guard cutter Mojave fought her way through angry seas in response to a radio call for help from the Boston trawler P. J. O'Hara today a second message was received which announced the trawler had repaired her engines and no longer required assistance.

Fears aroused by reports from Canadian ports that the Gloucester schooner Rhodora had foundered were set at rest when it was learned the schooner had been storm bound in Provincetown harbor since Saturday.

The Nantucket lightship, which had been driven many miles from her station by the gales, returned to her position early today.

Communities that have suffered to the extent of approximately $2,000,000 went to work on battered sea walls that line a much-changed coast line.

Monomoy Point, eight miles down a narrow peninsula from Chatham, was cut off from the mainland by a 600-foot channel. The new waterway made an island of a four-mile tip of the peninsula.

At the Pamet River Coast Guard Station, near Truro, tides and pounding surf had undermined the building and toppled over the lookout and signal towers.

Firm Grants Moratorium To Farmers

New York Life Insurance Company Suspends Foreclosures In Iowa

New York, Jan. 30 (AP)—The New York Life Insurance Company announced today that it had suspended foreclosure on mortgages on farm properties in Iowa.

The company's action was explained in the following statement issued by Thomas A. Buckner, president of the company:

"Pursuant to the request contained in the proclamation of the Governor of Iowa, the New York Life Insurance Company has issued instructions to suspend the foreclosure of mortgages on Iowa farms pending further consideration of the farmers' difficulties by the Legislature of that State.

"For some time past it has been the practice of the New York Life Insurance Company not to foreclose farm mortgages for nonpayment of rent or taxes, although they may be long past due, provided the company is satisfied that the owner living upon the farm is endeavoring to keep up the property and is doing his best to meet his obligations.

"It has not been the company's practice to institute foreclosure proceedings for non-payment of curtailments of principal. The company is fully aware of and is deeply interested in the problems confronting the farm population today, and has long since notified its correspondents of its willingness to renew farm mortgages upon the most liberal terms consistent with the company's obligations to its policyholders."

The company did not disclose whether it contemplated similar action in other districts.

Baby On Back Seat, Thieves Abandon Car

Police Believe Robbers Became Frightened Upon Discovering Child's Presence

Washington, Jan. 30 (AP)—Mary Eagleston, 7, slept in the back seat of her father's sedan while her parents stopped at the home of Mary's grandmother.

Fifteen minutes later the parents, Mr. and Mrs. Harry E. Eagleston, came out. The automobile was gone and so was Mary.

Police searched for the car while neighbors tried to comfort the Eaglestons. An hour and a half passed and then there was a telephone call: "Mary is found!"

The car with Mary inside, just awakening from her sleep, had been found a mile from grandmother's home. Police believe that automobile thieves became frightened when they saw the girl a little while after taking the machine.

7, Unhurt, Halt Hunt For Their Own Bodies

Out Of Chicago House Wrecked By Explosion And Fire, They Return To Ruins

Chicago, Jan. 30 (U.P.)—Seven persons escaped death by a few minutes here today when their two-story brick home was demolished by explosion and fire.

They arrived at the home just as firemen were entering the ruins in search of their bodies. They said they had been visiting relatives since late yesterday.

Buries Jar Of Cash And Dog Digs It Up

Master Returns From Trip, Finds $1,400 Lying In Yard, In Sight Of Passers-By

Empire, Ore., Jan. 30 (AP)—Andy Kelley buried his $1,400 cash savings in a glass jar alongside his house to foil thieves while he was away on a trip.

Kelley's dog thought his master had buried a bone. He dug up the "treasure." Kelley came home several days later to find his money intact, but lying in the yard in sight of every passerby.

Court Refuses To Pay Bill

Eugene, Ore., Jan. 30 (U.P.)—"No taxes, no pay," said the Lane County Court firmly when a bill for $2,300 was submitted by a hospital here for services to Lane county needy during December, 1932. Records showed the hospital had received $17,000 from the county for such treatment of indigents and that it owed approximately $4,000 in taxes for two years.

FARM BILL SEEN DOUBLING PRICE OF HAM, BACON

Would Affect All Pork Products, Says Packers' Spokesman

LOWER SALES HELD INEVITABLE RESULT

Senators Told Allotment Plan Would Hurt Producers, Too

[*By the Associated Press*]

Washington, Jan. 30—A prospect of a 100 per cent. increase in the price of ham and bacon if the Emergency Domestic Allotment Farm Relief bill becomes a law was presented to the Senate Agriculture Committee today by a spokesman for the meat packers.

G. F. Swift, chairman of the committee on public relations of the Institute of American Meat Packers, told the Senators that such a price boost would hurt rather than help the country's hog producers by greatly reducing consumption of pork.

Would Tax Packer

The bill would tax the packer of hogs and the processors of six other selected products to provide a bounty for the farmer.

Destruction of the daily cash market for hogs if the bill should pass was predicted by Swift.

"You can get a fixed price for a portion of the hog supply," he said, "but you simply make the balance of the supply unmarketable.

"Inasmuch as fresh pork is highly perishable, the packer is always in the position of having to sell, and sell promptly, but the consumer is never in the position of having to buy pork. He can always substitute other foods.

"I hope you realize what the effect of artificially advancing the cost of hogs to the packing industry by law would be. The packing industry would necessarily be obliged to reduce materially its purchase of hogs.

"It would be absolutely impossible to buy all of the hogs at the higher price and sell the product at the higher price because the public would not buy it and would go to substitutes.

Expects Double Price

"Pork loins now selling wholesale from 6 to 8 cents a pound would probably sell at twice the current figure or more and the same would doubtless be true of hams and bacons and the more expensive cuts.

"A law of this kind would not only arouse the resentment of consumers; it would be resented by the producers. They would be left with unsalable hogs on their hands."

Swift, who is president of Swift & Co., was questioned closely concerning circulation of a pamphlet asking recipients to write members of Congress in opposition to the measure.

Produces Pamphlet

The pamphlet about which Swift was questioned in the Agriculture Committee was produced by Chairman Charles T. McNary (Rep., Ore.), who said it had been left with him by Senator Lynn J. Frazier (Rep., N. D.). It was dated January 11 and said, "Cash market for hogs would be eliminated."

Recipients of the pamphlet were advised to write Chairman Marvin

[Continued On Page 2, Column 6]

Fascist Chief Leads Germany

—Associated Press Photo

ADOLF HITLER

SENATE RUBS OUT SEATRAIN SUBSIDY

Cuts $240,000 Mail Contract From $961,000,000 Supply Bill

By Frederick R. Barkley

Washington, Jan. 30—The Senate today accomplished a saving of something like a quarter of a million dollars on the first regular appropriation bill to come before it—but did it only after an hour of acrimonious and taunting debate, in which the Tydings economy exploit of last week played a conspicuous part.

The saving, of course, amounted to only a small fraction of one per cent. of the amount carried in the appropriation bill, which provides $961,000,000 for the Treasury and Postoffice departments. Nevertheless, it took two years to accomplish even this little paring down, for a similar onslaught on the same item last year met with failure.

Mail Subsidy Involved

The item involved is a $240,000 mail subsidy to a concern known as Seatrain, Inc., which operates two new-type car ferries between New York, Havana and New Orleans.

This company, whose venture was ardently defended by Senator David A. Reed (Rep., Pa.) as of great military value, apparently has been a governmental pet from the beginning. It

[Continued On Page 3, Column 4]

PHILADELPHIA GETS ELECTRIC RATE CUT

Consumers To Be Saved $1,800,000 In Year By Reduction

Philadelphia, Jan. 30 (U.P.)—A general revision of electric rates throughout its entire territory was announced today by the Philadelphia Electric Company.

The new rate schedule, filed with the Public Service Commission at Harrisburg, becomes effective March 2. It will reduce the revenue collected from consumers during the next twelve months by at least $1,800,000, the announcement said.

Customers in Philadelphia, Delaware and all eastern Pennsylvania counties will benefit by the reduction.

Economies Effected

In making the rate reductions, the company said, an upturn in business is expected. Increased efficiency and economy of operation and a revision in the practices, rules and regulations of the company make possible the lower tariff schedule.

The practice of supplying free electric lamp renewals to customers will be discontinued under the new regulations.

A statement from the company said, in part:

"It is estimated that the bills to customers who use the domestic rate will be reduced approximately $780,000 annually under the new program. This reduction is to be accomplished by lowering the rate in the second block from 6 cents to 5½ cents per kilowatt hour, and by adding a fourth block applicable to residence customers at 2½ cents per kilowatt hour as a new rate feature, in order to stimulate a greater use of household electrical appliances."

Leaps Out Of Danger And Dies Of Exertion

Fireman Avoids Falling Chimney, Only To Drop Lifeless At Feet Of Companions

Philadelphia, Jan. 30 (AP)—Fireman Joe Kasper's desire to live cost him his life. While fighting a fire that destroyed a vacant house, Kasper was endangered for a moment by a falling chimney.

As his companions shouted a warning, he leaped toward safety—and fell dead at their feet. Exertion had proved too much for his heart.

Files On The Thirteenth

St. Louis, Jan. 30 (U.P.)—John C. Meyers, who had lived here 13 years, picked Friday, the 13th, to file his candidacy for the Democratic nomination for 13th Ward Alderman.

Scott Finds Three Poets In Technocrats' Parade

Benson Sings How Bolbels Wangle And Sisten Goes Hist—Kemp And Holmes Stick Closer To Traditional English

New York, Jan. 30 (U.P.)—Technocracy, hitherto praised and condemned exclusively in prose, became the subject today of three minstrels of the moment determined to let who will make energy surveys as long as they can write its poems.

The three candidates for the poet laureateship of erg and joule are Harry Kemp, veteran Greenwich Village bard, who usually devotes himself to the "open road"; Ira Benson, a column contributor, and John Haynes Holmes, civic reformer and churchman.

Benson's sonnet, titled "A Song of Technocracy," appeared today in Franklin P. Adams' Conning Tower column in the *Herald-Tribune*.

An excerpt:

The toggling bolbels wangle on the blump,
Convecting brittled turbumps to the freat;
The dumpfel-bearings wheezer, and the flump
Burrybangles with a quiver-brinking jeet.
Hist goes the sisten and the jank of four
And all is placid at the factory door.

"Poor Among Riches"

Kemp rendered his "vision of technocracy (technocracy speaks)" at a

[Continued On Page 2, Column 7]

CHIEF OF NAZIS HEADS MINISTRY IN COMPROMISE

Surrounded By Conservative Leaders In New Line-Up

BAVARIAN PARTY AND CENTRISTS EXCLUDED

Must Tolerate Regime Or Reichstag Will Be Dissolved

[*By the Associated Press*]

Berlin, Jan. 30—Adolf Hitler, picturesque leader of the German Fascists, was made Chancellor of Germany today, succeeding Gen. Kurt von Schleicher, who resigned last week.

But in granting him the ambition of his political lifetime President von Hindenburg surrounded him with a Cabinet of conservatives. Franz von Papen, the former Chancellor and confidant of the President, is Vice-Chancellor; Konstantin von Neurath remains Foreign Minister; Alfred Hugenberg, the Nationalist leader, has an important Cabinet post.

Places Two Best Men

Hitler placed his best men, Wilhelm Frick and Hermann Goering, in the Cabinet, Frick as Minister of the Interior and Goering as Minister Without Portfolio.

The new Chancellor, who is only 43, took the appointment in his stride.

"Well, we shall see," was all he said to the correspondents as he returned to his hotel from the President's office. "Now, let's eat."

He had been up all night and until 5 o'clock this morning working out a detailed program to submit to the President.

With his new associates he went over to the executive offices.

Taken To The President

Otto Meissner, the President's secretary, met him. They talked for a little while. Meissner assured him that the President in his talks with Colonel Von Papen over the week-end finally had been persuaded to overcome his last scruples against placing Hitler at the head of the Government. Then Hitler was taken to the President.

One of those who was there described the meeting.

The venerable field marshal was kindliness itself, he said, when Col. von Papen, in the presence of Alfred Hugenberg and several others, proposed Hitler for Chancellor.

"Yes, yes indeed," the President nodded.

Hindenburg Greets Him

Then he rose, towering above the others, grasped Hitler's hand and formally made the appointment.

The word got around quickly and when Hitler got back to his hotel the streets were jammed.

His own close friends waited to shake his hand, and there were hundreds of others, cheering as they lifted their hands in the Nazi salute. Hitler grinned and waved. He went into the hotel for luncheon with Herr Frick and his other associates.

The Reichstag Council of Elders, meeting this afternoon, adopted a motion by the National Socialist members to reconvene the Reichstag on or before February 7.

"Generals' Putsch" Rumored

There was a startling rumor that a group of high army officers headed by General von Schleicher had threatened to take the law into their own hands and set up a "directorate" as a prelude to restoration of the monarchy.

This rumor, emphatically denied in official circles, was offered in explanation of the unprecedented haste with which the Hitler Cabinet was formed.

The story was that General von Hammerstein, chief of staff, warned President von Hindenburg yesterday that unless the period of political uncertainty were ended quickly there was the greatest danger of a "generals' putsch."

Cabinet Line-Up

The Cabinet personnel includes:

Chancellor, Hitler.

Vice-Chancellor and Prussian Commissar, Franz von Papen.

Foreign Minister, Konstantin von Neurath.

Finance, Lutz Schwerin von Krosick.

Interior, Wilhelm Frick.

Defense, Gen. Werner von Blomberg.

Economics and Agriculture, Alfred Hugenberg.

Labor, Franz Seldte.

Posts and Transportation, [illegible]

[Continued On Page 3, Column 1]

WEATHER FORECAST
Generally fair today; fair tomorrow; not much change in temperature; moderate northerly winds.
(Details on Page 17.)

THE SUN

Registered United States Patent Office

5.30 A. M.

VOL. 192—E | PAID CIRCULATION FEBRUARY MORNING. 136,911 EVENING. 136,037 272,948 || SUNDAY 180,261 | BALTIMORE, SATURDAY, MARCH 4, 1933 | Published every week day by The A. S. Abell Company. Entered as second-class matter at Baltimore Postoffice. | 18 PAGES | 2 CENTS

Roosevelt To Take Oath Of Office Today

N. Y., ILLINOIS BANKS CLOSE

General Assembly Passes Bank-Aid Bill

HOUSE VOTES EMERGENCY MEASURE; AMENDMENTS ARE APPROVED BY SENATE

State-Control Legislation Expected To Be Signed By Governor Ritchie And Made Law This Morning

WAY NOW CLEAR TO END BANKING HOLIDAY MONDAY

New Amendment Adds Jurisdiction Over Salaries In Maryland Financial Institutions To Broad Powers Given To Ghingher

By LOUIS J. O'DONNELL
[*Annapolis Bureau of The Sun*]

Annapolis, March 4 (*Saturday*)—Maryland's General Assembly this morning, before the day was many minutes old, placed the final stamp of approval on the emergency banking legislation without a dissenting vote in either house.

Not ten minutes after the legislators had enacted the measure, the final draft was on its way to the State Printer's in Baltimore. It will be reprinted and back in Annapolis for the Governor's signature at 9.30 this morning and, becoming law at that time, will clear the way for the opening of the banking institutions under the State-control plan most probably on Monday morning.

GHINGHER'S POWERS BROADENED

The House of Delegates, under suspended rules, passed the bill at 12.05 A. M., with some twenty minor amendments and one major change, giving the State Bank Commissioner, in addition to the other sweeping powers conferred on him, jurisdiction over the salaries and expenses of all banking institutions within the jurisdiction of the new law.

A few seconds after receiving the House's approval, the measure was returned to the Senate, where in a few seconds all the amendments met with the concurrence of that body and, with the legislative end of the financial reconstruction plan completed after a hectic week's deliberations, the administrative officers of the State turned their attention to the working out of the machinery to put it into operation.

An audience even larger than that which crowded the legislative halls Thursday night when the emergency bill first was brought to the floor in the Senate crowded the House chamber this morning as the measure was sped through to final passage.

It was 11.45 P. M. exactly when the House Judiciary and Ways and Means Committees returned to the chamber after a four-hour executive session for the preparation of the amendments.

Report Adopted Unanimously

The committees' favorable report with amendments was adopted almost at once by a *viva voce* vote, and then Delegate James J. Lindsay, Jr. (Dem., Baltimore county), moved for suspension of the rules and final passage of the bill, which was effected by a roll call, with 111 votes in the affirmative and none in the negative.

Speaker T. Barton Harrington (Dem., Third Baltimore district) did not adjourn the House, however, but held the Delegates in readiness to act at once on any further changes which the Senate might decide to make.

As in the case of the House, the Senate by *viva voce* vote adopted all the amendments made by the lower branch's committees without a hitch.

The Senate's approval was voted unanimously at 12.45 A. M.

Errors Corrected

Virtually all the amendments to the bill were corrections of printers' errors and eliminated unnecessary words and punctuation.

Advised of the Senate's complete concurrence, the House adjourned at 12.50 A. M. until 8 o'clock Monday night, while the Senate remained in session a short while longer to pass a resolution by Senator Lansdale G. Sasscer (Dem., Prince George's), majority floor leader, empowering the Governor to distribute as emergency funds to the various counties approximately $48,000 in the State Treasury from the proceeds of charity racing days.

Meetings Called

Almost as soon as the bill was received by the House yesterday afternoon, Delegate Lindsay and Delegate George Hofferbert (Dem., First Baltimore district), chairman of the Judiciary Committee, called meetings of their two committee groups and started the hearings immediately.

Mr. Lane, the Attorney-General, and Mr. Jones again went over the provisions of the entire bill and explained the seventeen amendments and three new sections tacked on while the measure was in the hands of the Senate Finance and Judicial Proceedings Committee yesterday.

Status Of National Banks

Not until the bill has been made a law can the Comptroller of the Currency, acting under the Couzens resolution, order national banks in Maryland to abide by it. As soon as the bill has been signed copies will be rushed to the Comptroller at Washington and by him referred to the Attorney-General. If the measure passes that scrutiny with approval, the Comptroller at once will issue the order.

E. Brooke Lee, member of the State Roads Commission and the administration's legislative field marshal, said the reorganization provisions of the bill alone would permit of the salvage of between $35,000,000 and $40,000,000 of depositors' funds, which otherwise would go by the board if the banking institutions too weak to stand without

(Continued on Page 4, Column 4)

PLANS TO END FARM BOARD'S PRICE PEGGING

Henry Morgenthau, Jr., Its New Head, To Stop Grain Stabilization

REORGANIZATION SCHEME OUTLINED

Four Divisions To Be Created To Take Over Seven Agencies

[*By the Associated Press*]

Washington, March 3—The end of the Farm Board's price-pegging experiment was heralded today, as two men on whom the incoming Roosevelt Administration will rely in its efforts to provide a "new deal" for agriculture outlined their programs.

Henry Morgenthau, Jr., of New York, revealed plans for a sweeping reorganization of the Government's farm credit agencies, which will be centralized under his direction, and will include absorption of the Farm Board and retirement of its members to private life soon.

Morgenthau placed emphasis on what he gave as his "first objective," taking "the Government out of the stabilization business"—a declaration of policy which soon after swept through the nation's grain markets and was credited in part for the day's rise of 3 cents in wheat prices.

Wallace Forms Farm Plan

Henry A. Wallace, of Iowa, who, as Secretary of Agriculture, will share direction of the Roosevelt farm policies, inspected the department and announced he had planned the groundwork of a program of farm legislation. Through it he hopes to bring about "an orderly retreat from production of farm lands now devoted to surplus crops."

Wallace, contemplating the department over which his father presided as Secretary during the Harding Administration, refused to reveal the details of his plans. He has been an enthusiastic supporter of the original domestic allotment plan and a critic of the form given it by the Senate Agriculture Committee. He brought with him Prof. Rexford Tugwell, of Columbia University, expected to be named Assistant Secretary.

To Create Four Divisions

Morgenthau's reorganization plan contemplates the creation of four divisions which will assume functions now divided between seven units. Each will be headed by one man, who will be personally responsible to Morgenthau, who has tentatively styled the unified agency the "Farm Credit Administration."

The functions of the Farm Board in making loans to cooperative marketing groups will form the basis of the activities of one division. Another will take over Federal farm loan activities now centered in the Federal Farm Land Bank Board and its affiliates.

The third division will take over the Crop Production Loan Bureau of the Department of Agriculture, now engaged in disbursing $90,000,000 in Federal funds, and the regional farm agencies established by the Reconstruction Finance Corporation—both described as "emergency functions" by Morgenthau.

To Aid Mortgage Situation

The fourth division is planned for the activities of the Federal Government in aiding the farm mortgage situation—activities for which Roosevelt is expected to recommend Congressional approval and details of which remain to be worked out.

Soon after Morgenthau's announcement, the Senate adopted a resolution permitting its Agriculture Committee

(Continued on Page 15, Column 3)

EX-FOOTBALL STAR BROKE

Edward H. Coy Files Petition In Bankruptcy

New York, March 3 (AP)—Edward H. Coy, former Yale football star and husband of the late Jeanne Eagels, actress, filed a voluntary petition in bankruptcy in United States District Court today.

He gave his occupation as an insurance broker, of 68 William street, and listed liabilities of $13.872 and assets of $730.

GOVERNORS ISSUE ORDERS FOR SHORT HOLIDAYS IN BOTH COMMONWEALTHS

Lehman Takes Action After Early Morning Conference With Leading Financiers—To Last Until Tuesday Morning

MID-WEST EXECUTIVE SETS REOPENING FOR WEDNESDAY

New Yorker Says Suspension Should Give Officials Time To Consider Situation Calmly And Adjust Difficulties

[*By the Associated Press*]

New York, March 4—A bank holiday until close of business Monday night was declared for New York State today.

The holiday was proclaimed by Gov. Herbert H. Lehman after an early morning conference with New York bankers.

"Until early this morning it was my hope," the Governor said in his proclamation, "that it would not be necessary to interrupt the continuous operation of the banking system of New York State.

SAYS DRASTIC ACTION NECESSARY

"The spread of hysteria and the restrictions imposed upon the banking facilities of the country through measures adopted in so many States have at last placed upon the New York banks a burden so great that it has finally rendered drastic action imperative here.

"Therefore, at a meeting late this evening the clearing house committee of the New York Clearing House, with the advice and recommendation of the Federal Reserve Bank of New York, has asked me to proclaim a banking holiday lasting until the close of business Monday, March 6th.

CALLS FOR COOLNESS AND LEADERSHIP

"I make this proclamation with complete conviction that the best interests of the people of the State are being served thereby. This is a time for coolness and leadership. The people of this State and of the whole nation have shown a splendid spirit to date in meeting all the trying problems of the depression. I am confident that this spirit will be maintained.

"The interval which these holidays afford should give responsible officials the necessary opportunity to consider the situation calmly and to prepare the way for an adjustment of our difficulties.

"Now, therefore, I, Herbert H. Lehman, Governor of the State of New York, do hereby proclaim and set apart Saturday, March 4th, and Monday, March 6th, as holidays on which all banking institutions will be closed."

EXPECT EXCHANGES TO CLOSE

While the statement did not mention the Stock Exchange, a high banking authority said he "did not see how the exchange could be opened," and that "it is the practice to close the exchange in these circumstances."

He said the Chicago exchange "doubtless would be similarly affected."

THREE-DAY HOLIDAY IN ILLINOIS

Chicago, March 4, *Saturday* (AP)—A general three-day bank holiday affecting all Illinois banks was ordered early today after an extended conference between leading Chicago financiers and Gov. Henry Horner. M. A. Traylor, president of the First National Bank, made the announcement. The order will be in effect today, Monday and Tuesday.

Traylor said that the three-day closing order is mandatory upon all banks in Illinois by virtue of a proclamation signed by Governor Horner.

The proclamation said that the banks must reopen Wednesday, March 8, but that withdrawals may be limited to five per cent. during the following eight days.

Close In Iowa

Des Moines, March 4 (AP)—Following New York and Illinois, a temporary bank holiday affecting all Iowa banks was proclaimed early today by Lieut. Gov. Nelson Kraschel.

N.Y. Savings Banks Weigh Plan For 60-Day Notice

[*New York Bureau of The Sun*]

New York, March 3—The sixty-day clause which requires depositors in savings banks to give notice for that length of time of their intention to make withdrawals from their accounts has been considered by the mutual institutions of New York in recent days and undoubtedly will be invoked by them to save the majority of depositors from the hysteria of a minority, it was learned tonight.

The clause, which is printed in every passbook and has been invoked in past times to quiet panic, allow normal

(Continued on Page 5, Column 2)

SENATE SPEEDS FUND BILLS AS HOURS WANE

Only Two Appropriation Measures Remain For Final Vote

WIDE AUTHORITY GIVEN PRESIDENT

Legislation Empowering Cut In Federal Expenses Approved

By DEWEY L. FLEMING
[*Washington Bureau of The Sun*]

Washington, March 3—Congress concentrated today on appropriation measures and with adjournment tonight had disposed of all but two—the second deficiency and the bill carrying funds for the District of Columbia.

Outstanding in the day's achievement was final action on the Treasury-Postoffice measure, to which is attached an economy rider giving President-elect Roosevelt sweeping authority to reorganize the Federal governmental machine in the interest of national retrenchment. The bill went to the White House after the Senate adopted a conference report approved by the House last Wednesday.

Can Merge Or Abolish Agencies

The reorganization instrument gives Mr. Roosevelt power to consolidate, transfer or abolish executive agencies wherever he believes a saving can be effected, the sole restriction being that he may not abolish an entire executive department. A two-thirds vote of both Houses of Congress would be required to upset the President's program, now being worked out for him by a group headed by Representative Douglas (Dem., Ariz.), who will be director of the Budget Bureau in the new Administration.

When Congress met this morning for the last full working day of the Seventy-second session five of the eleven bills carrying money for the operation of the Government during the next fiscal year awaited final action.

Conferees Agree On Two Bills

Conference committees and the House continued their labors until almost midnight, with the result that the House disposed of the second deficiency and District of Columbia bills and sent them to the Senate for action tomorrow morning.

The House started the ball rolling by speedy adoption of conference reports on the War Department and independent offices measures, an action duplicated a short while later by the Senate. As finally passed the War Department bill carried $349,840,749, compared with an appropriation of $456,742,513 for this department last year.

Couzens' Amendment Dropped

The final item of the War Department bill in dispute was the proposed appropriation of $22,000,000 for the purpose of operating all-year Citizens' military training camps to absorb about 88,000 unemployed youths. The item was inserted by the Senate at the insistence of Senator Couzens (Rep., Mich.), and was rejected by the House. The Senate finally receded from the amendment and allowed it to be dropped.

The Senate won its controversy with the House on the appropriation for the Federal Trade Commission which held up the independent offices bill many days. As finally passed the bill carried the Senate's figure of $1,089,000 for continuation of the work of the trade body.

Adopts Conference Report

The independent offices bill carries $1,003,314,981 for twenty-nine Federal boards, bureaus and commissions, $966,838,634 of which goes to veterans' administration. Last year Congress appropriated $1,024,286,041 for these agencies.

The Treasury-Postoffice bill cleared Congress when the Senate today adopted the conference report on items in dispute. The House had taken similar action last Wednesday.

This bill carries $957,416,597 for the work of the two departments. The final dispute occurred over the amendment inserted in the Senate by Senator Bratton (Dem., N. M.), which would have directed all Federal departments to make an executive cut of five per cent. in their appropriations in addition to the slash already made by Congress.

The Senate receded from its insist-

(Continued on Page 15, Column 2)

BECOMES NATION'S CHIEF FACED WITH BURDEN OF UNPRECEDENTED NATURE

Expected To Issue Call For Special Session Of Congress To Deal With Situation Arising From Banking Crisis

CONFERS WITH PRESIDENT AND ADVISERS FOR HOUR

Hoover Later Calls Into Consultation Secretary Mills And Attorney-General Mitchell—Federal Reserve Board Meets

By J. F. ESSARY

Washington, March 3—Franklin D. Roosevelt will be inaugurated President tomorrow and will assume the power of his high office under conditions perhaps unprecedented in the history of the country.

And in order to meet in a measure the emergency that has arisen through a limited suspension of banking operations in more than thirty States, he conferred first today with President Hoover for more than an hour and was closeted tonight with a group of his most trusted advisers.

EARLY CALL OF EXTRA SESSION EXPECTED

It remained in doubt at midnight whether he would put forward a concrete plan of action in his inaugural address, but there was no doubt that he would issue a quick call for a special session of Congress, maybe on Monday, and then, if not sooner, he would be prepared to declare the Administration's purposes.

While he was yet in conference in his Mayflower suite with William H. Woodin, the new Secretary of the Treasury; Senator Hull, of Tennessee, Secretary of State-designate; Senator Glass, of Virginia, and Jesse H. Jones and Harvey Couch, members of the Reconstruction Finance Corporation Board, a hurried conference was called at the White House by Mr. Hoover and a special meeting of the Federal Reserve Board was in progress.

WOODIN CONFERS WITH BOARD

The White House conference, participated in by the President, Secretary of the Treasury Mills, Henry M. Robinson, Los Angeles banker; Attorney-General Mitchell and Mr. Jones, adjourned just before midnight and Mr. Mills rushed away to attend the Federal Reserve Board meeting.

Mr. Woodin, after leaving the President-elect's apartment just before midnight, also dashed to the Treasury to meet with the reserve board members. He left an hour later wtihout making any statement.

A few minutes later, howover, word was issued from the office of Eugene Meyer, governor of the board, that the special meeting was continuing and that it was not improbable that a statement would be issued by the board before morning.

Also Consults With Mills

Half an hour after Mr. Meyer's office made this brief announcement Mr. Woodin returned to the Treasury accompanied by Professor Raymond Moley and passed quickly into the office of Secretary Mills.

It was assumed that he had conferred again with President-elect Roosevelt and that he was the bearer of Mr. Roosevelt's advice as to a course of action.

It seemed probable to observers here, from the meager information available late tonight that a national bank holiday would be demanded within the next twenty-four hours, probably through action of the Federal Reserve Board.

What other steps may be taken to prevent a collapse of the country's banking structure cannot yet be foretold. Something more than a temporary suspension seemed imperative, however, and there were suggestions in every official quarter of Congressional action that would in some manner insure certain of the bank deposits, if not all of them.

While the conferences were in prog-

Ogden Mills Silent Pending Word From N. Y. and Chicago

By FRANKLYN WALTMAN, JR.
[*Washington Bureau of The Sun*]

Washington, March 4 (*Saturday*)—Secretary of the Treasury Ogden L. Mills, on leaving the Treasury at 3.30 A. M. today, declined to reveal what had been done in the three-and-one-half-hour meeting of the Federal Reserve Board. He said that any announcement, if any, would come from New York and Chicago.

Mr. Mills declined to give any intimation of what action was taken, but he admitted that the Reserve Board members had been in constant telephone communication with banking officials in both New York and Illinois during this morning's extraordinary meeting.

Indicates Decisive Action

William H. Woodin, Secretary of the Treasury-designate, on leaving the meeting forty-five minutes earlier, distinctly intimated that decisive action had been taken in regard to the banking situation, but he contended it would be improper for him to make the announcement.

He said, "see the chief and he will tell you." This was taken to mean Mr. Mills.

The Reserve Board members entered

(Continued on Page 2, Column 6)

WEATHER FORECAST

Fair today; cloudy tomorrow, with slowly rising temperature, followed by rain. (Details on Page 11.)

THE SUN

Registered United States Patent Office

8.00 A.M.

VOL. 192—E | PAID CIRCULATION FEBRUARY MORNING, 136,911 EVENING, 136,037 272,948 ‖ SUNDAY 180,261 | BALTIMORE, MONDAY, MARCH 6, 1933 | Published every week day by The A. S. Abell Company. Entered as second-class matter at Baltimore Postoffice. | 12 PAGES | 2 CENTS

Mayor Cermak Dies In Florida Hospital

NATION IMPOUNDS GOLD

Extra Session Of Congress Meets Thursday

NAZI FORCES GAIN CONTROL OF REICHSTAG

Victory Of "Nationalist Right" Paves Way For Fascist Dictatorship

MANY CITIES OUST SOCIALIST MAYORS

Hitler To Deny Communists Right To Sit In New Reichstag

[By the Associated Press]

Berlin, March 6 (*Monday*)—Seventeen million voters out of 39,290,000 manifested their confidence in Chancellor Adolf Hitler in yesterday's Reichstag election, and demonstrated to President von Hindenburg that he sensed the desires of the German people rightly when he asked the chief of the Nazi Brown Shirts to take the helm of the ship of State.

Germany now is well on the way to Fascist dictatorship. Chancellor Hitler, by the vote of the people, has been given the legal tools to annihilate the last vestiges of the democracy which he considers a failure.

Nazis Command Majority

The Nazis alone will command nearly forty-four per cent. of the votes in the new Reichstag and can dictate to their Nationalist co-workers in the Government what must be done to shape a new Germany in accordance with Nazi ideals.

The Cabinet assembled after midnight to adopt an "appeal to the German people," and Chancellor Hitler expressed himself as unusually well pleased with the outcome.

The Chancellor said that an indorsement of a Cabinet of national concentration by more than 20,000,000 voters—that is the ballot totals of the National Socialists and the Nationalists—was an unheard of thing.

So far as could be learned, Hitler will stick to the Nazi preelection campaign contention that the Communists must not take their seats in the Reichstag, and this means that the Government would have an almost two-thirds majority to change the Constitution and the Nazis would have a regular majority without aid from any other party.

In Prussia, which elected a State Diet yesterday, the Nazi victory was equally sweeping. Thus in both the Reich and in its largest State no popular election may be expected for a long time to come.

Party Standing Given

Hitler's National Socialists and their Nationalist allies polled 51.7 per cent. of the votes cast yesterday. The following table shows the party standings compared with the last previous Reichstag election November 6, 1932:

	March 5	Nov. 6
National Socialists	17,264,000	11,705,000
Nationalists	3,131,000	3,061,000
People's Party	432,000	660,000
Christian Socialists	382,000	412,000
Centrists	4,289,000	4,228,000
Bavarian People's Party	1,206,000	1,081,000
State Party	335,000	338,000
Socialists	7,176,000	7,231,000
Communists	4,746,000	5,970,000
Scattered	329,000	....

Party Allotments Given

The Wolff News Agency estimated that the new Reichstag will reach record size, with 640 to 650 seats. The size of the Legislature is flexible, in general a seat being allotted on the basis of each 60,000 votes obtained by each party.

The Wolff Agency said the following allotments were definite:

	New	Old
National Socialists	288	196
Nationalists	52	51
Centrists	71	69
Bavarian People's Party	20	19
State Party	6	2
Socialists	120	121
Communists	79	100

In accordance with the promise he gave President von Hindenburg when he was appointed Chancellor, Hitler does not intend to make any effort to rid himself of Vice-Chancellor Franz von Papen, Baron Konstantin von Neurath, Dr. Alfred Hugenbeg, Franz Seldte and other non-Nazi members of

(Continued on Page 5, Column 2)

Assassin's Bullet Wound Is Fatal To Chicago Mayor

Miami, Fla., March 6 (AP)—Mayor Anton Cermak, of Chicago, who was wounded February 15 by Giuseppe Zangara, the man who tried to assassinate President Roosevelt, died at 6.55 A. M. (E.S.T.) today in Jackson Memorial Hospital.

The announcement was made by Alderman Edward F. Kelly, South Park commissioner.

Cermak died quietly. He did not emerge from the coma in which he sank last night.

Rallied From Three Crises

The Mayor rallied from three crises in a gallant stand against complications of colitis, pneumonia and heart trouble that set in after the wound, but gangrene appeared in the lower lobe of his right lung Saturday night and he grew steadily worse. The lung was the one grazed by Zangara's bullet.

Yesterday a third blood transfusion was given Mayor Cermak and neo-arsphenamin was administered to combat the gangrene area, but he failed to respond and his condition continued to grow more and more grave.

Late last night physicians pronounced the Mayor's condition "definitely critical" and the family was called into his room. They came out weeping and Mayor Cermak's physicians shortly after midnight said he could live but a few hours. He was 59 years old.

Family Summoned To Bedside

Shortly after 11 o'clock last night the Mayor's family was summoned to his bedside.

The Mayor lay back on his pillow, hands folded over his chest, breathing heavily. His color, however, seemed fairly good.

Dr. Frank Jirka and Dr. E. S. Nichol were attending the Mayor.

"While there is life there is hope," said Dr. Jirka, who is Cermak's son-in-law.

Recognized Members Of Family

Dr. Jirka said the Mayor recognized members of the family.

"My wife asked him if he knew her. He told her 'Yes; kiss me.'"

The greatest air of concern prevailed in the little sun porch where a heavy guard of police and detectives was maintained.

The Mayor's right lung, punctured on the night of February 15 by a bullet from the pistol of the assassin, Giuseppe Zangara, was aspirated yesterday as physicians sought further information on his condition.

They said they found a gangrenous condition, basing their findings on the presence in the lung of "foul gas." They said they found no pus in the lung cavity.

Members of the family, summoned to the bedside, emerged weeping.

After the blood transfusion yesterday afternoon Cermak suffered a "slight reaction," causing a weakening of the pulse and irregular respiration, the doctors said.

Later it was announced the symptoms improved. Neo-arsphenamin was administered to combat the gangrene area discovered in the lower lobe of the right lung last night.

The physicians said that the gangrene was diagnosed by means of aspiration of the chest, but that at no time had Cermak shown a fetid breath or sputum, or expectorated blood.

Saves Inauguration From Mourning Sign

Next Speaker's Wife Calls Attention To Flags At Half-Staff Before Ceremony

Washington, March 5 (AP) — Quick thinking and effective action by the wife of the next Speaker of the House kept President Roosevelt from taking his oath of office yesterday under flags at half-staff.

The flags on the Capitol had been lowered in memorial to the late Senator Walsh, of Montana. Mrs. Henry T. Rainey, a few minutes before the oath was administered, noticed the emblems at half-staff. She called the proper officials, and for the duration of of the inauguration ceremony all Capitol flags, save that over the Senate, were raised to the top of the staff.

"It was the President's day and the instant of his inauguration certainly was not an instant of mourning." was Mrs. Rainey's explanation.

ASKS STATE AWAIT DETAILS OF PLAN

Ritchie Asserts Effect Of President's Action Cannot Yet Be Told

HE LAUDS ROOSEVELT

Governor Declares Outstanding Thing Is "He Has Not Hesitated"

The effect of President Roosevelt's banking proclamation on trade and industry in Maryland cannot be determined until the Federal Treasury rules and regulations governing the proclmation have been put into effect, Governor Ritchie indicated in a statement which he issued shortly after last midnight.

The Governor's statement, issued at 12.40 A. M., follows:

"The President's proclamation is an amazing instance of instant action to meet a tremendous crisis. There has of course not been the opportunity to consider the exact effect of this action, and, indeed, before doing that it is necessary to await the promulgation of the regulations prescribed by the Secretary of the Treasury.

"Has Not Hesitated"

"The outstanding thing is that the President has not hesitated a moment to proclaim the course which he and his advisers consider the nation must follow in order to meet the emergency."

The Governor issued his statement in his suite at the Belvedere Hotel, where during the afternoon and part of the evening he had been closeted

(Continued on Page 2, Column 8)

MEETING DATE ADVANCED BY BANK CRISIS

Roosevelt Reaches Decision At Conference With Leaders Of Both Parties

EMERGENCY BILLS WILL BE RUSHED

Executive To Ask Cooperation Of Governors At Meeting Today

By J. F. ESSARY

Washington, March 5 — Swinging swiftly into action, just as he promised in his inaugural address yesterday, President Roosevelt tonight issued a call for an extra session of Congress. This was followed a few hours later by his proclamation taking command of the nation's supply of gold and currency.

And tomorrow, after only two days in office, he will preside over a conference of Governors in the course of which he will call for unstinted cooperation on the part of the States in dealing with the present crisis.

Members Given Hint Saturday

The Congressional call was expected. Only the day when it would become effective was remotely in doubt. And the fact that the House and Senate are to reassemble on Thursday indicates clearly the speed with which the new Executive proposes to meet emergency conditions.

Word was passed to House and Senate leaders an hour after the inaugural ceremonies were concluded yesterday that all members of the two houses who were in Washington should be warned to remain in the Capital and all those not here should be given notice that their presence soon would be required.

The first decision of this tense and dramatic day was that which calls Congress to meet Thursday. Before the present financial crisis developed, it was presumed that the legislative session would not come until some time in April.

Other Issues Overshadowed

But all such questions as balancing the budget, reorganization of the governmental structure, legalization of beer and farm relief have now been completely overshadowed by a new and to some an appalling emergency. Other matters of moment might wait. Total suspension of banking service cannot wait.

This was realized days ago. It was accepted without question at the White House conference today between the President and those Democratic and Republican Congressional leaders whom he drew together.

Also the President satisfied himself that he had the legal power to call

(Continued on Page 2, Column 4)

Social New Deal At White House Inaugurated By Mrs. Roosevelt

She Greets Guests At Door, Serves Tea In East Room And Kisses Relatives, Thereby Playing Hob With Etiquette Of Old Order

[By the Associated Press]

Washington, March 5—The century-old White House wore a startled air today, as though listening to the sound of shattering precedents.

One day with dynamic Mrs. Franklin D. Roosevelt as mistress, and the pattern of red-tape-embroidered official etiquette was snipped into as many pieces as a jigsaw puzzle.

A first lady who greeted her dinner guests at the door, instead of waiting for them to assemble and then make ceremonious descent!

A White House hostess who served tea in the East Room!

A President's wife who had invited in the women of the press, with the promise that she'd "talk for publication," and who, indeed, already had been "interviewed" in her new home!

A woman of proudest place who did not hesitate to kiss in greeting the relatives who came to her first tea

Washington had never seen the like, and Anna Eleanor Roosevelt's tall figure became symbolic of an exclamation point as the Capital dwellers talked of the social transformation that apparently had taken place with the "new deal."

The first function was that afternoon "tea," originally planned for 1,000, but assuming the proportions of a formal reception, 3,000 came—or at least food for that number was consumed.

Though as an afternoon affair it was not truly comparable with a nocturnal one, nevertheless that tea made prophetic contrast with the last big function of the Republican regime.

Only a week and a day ago that was, the reception for army, navy and department officials.

It was a smartly formal symbolic show that has "always been done."

But Mrs. Roosevelt's tea guests

(Continued on Page 5, Column 6)

GOLD PROCLAMATION

[Washington Bureau of The Sun]

Washington, March 5—The President's proclamation was as follows:

Whereas there have been heavy and unwarranted withdrawals of gold and currency from our banking institutions for the purpose of hoarding; and

Whereas continuous and increasingly extensive speculative activity abroad in foreign exchange has resulted in severe drains on the nation's stocks of gold; and

Whereas these conditions have created a national emergency; and

Whereas it is in the best interests of all bank depositors that a period of respite be provided with a view to preventing further hoarding of coin, bullion or currency or speculation in foreign exchange and permitting the application of appropriate measures to protect the interests of our people; and

Whereas it is provided in Section 5 (B) of the act of October 6, 1917 (40 Stat. L. 44) as amended, "That the President may investigate, regulate, or prohibit, under such rules and regulations as he may prescribe, by means of licenses or otherwise, any transactions in foreign exchange and the export, hoarding, melting, or earmarkings of gold or silver coin or bullion or currency . . ."; and

Whereas it is provided in Section 16 of the said act "That whoever shall willfully violate any of the provisions of this act or of any license, rule, or regulation issued thereunder, and whoever shall willfully violate, neglect, or refuse to comply with any order of the President issued in compliance with the provisions of this act, shall, upon conviction, be fined not more than $10,000, or, if a natural person, imprisoned for not more than ten years, or both . . .";

Now, therefore, I, Franklin D. Roosevelt, President of the United States of America, in view of such national emergency and by virtue of the authority vested in me by said act and in order to prevent the export, hoarding, or earmarking of gold or silver coin or bullion or currency, do hereby proclaim, order, direct and declare that from Monday, the sixth day of March, to Thursday, the ninth day of March, Nineteen Hundred and Thirty-three, both dates inclusive, there shall be maintained and observed by all banking institutions and all branches thereof located in the United States of America, including the Territories and insular possessions, a bank holiday, and that during said period all banking transactions shall be suspended.

During such holiday, excepting as hereinafter provided, no such banking institution or branch shall pay out, export, earmark, or permit the withdrawal or transfer in any manner or by any device whatsoever, of any gold or silver coin or bullion or currency or take any other action which might facilitate the hoarding thereof; nor shall any such banking institution or branch pay out deposits, make loans or discounts, deal in foreign exchange, transfer credits from the United States to any place abroad, or transact any other banking business whatsoever.

During such holiday the Secretary of the Treasury, with the approval of the President and under such regulations as he may prescribe, is authorized and empowered (a) to permit any or all of such banking institutions to perform any or all of the usual banking functions, (b) to direct, require or permit the issuance of clearing-house certificates or other evidences of claims against assets of banking institutions, and (c) to authorize and direct the creation for such banking institutions of special trust accounts for the receipt of new deposits which shall be subject to withdrawal on demand without any restriction or limitation and shall be kept separately in cash or on deposit in Federal Reserve banks or invested in obligations of the United States.

As used in this order the term "banking institutions" shall include all Federal Reserve banks, national banking associations, banks, trust companies, savings banks, building and loan associations, credit unions, or other corporations, partnerships, associations of persons engaged in the business of receiving deposits, making loans, discounting business paper, or transacting any other form of banking business.

In witness whereof, I have hereunto set my hand and caused the seal of the United States to be affixed.

Done in the city of Washington this 6th day of March, 1 A. M., in the year of Our Lord one thousand nine hundred and thirty-three, and of the independence of the United States the one hundred and fifty-seventh.

(Seal) FRANKLIN D. ROOSEVELT,

By the President:

CORDELL HULL,
Secretary of State.

Bank Holiday Delays Wedding

Los Angeles, March 5 (AP) — Because they could not obtain a license during the bank holiday, Louis Brock, film producer, and Helen F. Collins, of Washington, D. C., have postponed for several days their wedding.

Senator Howell Improved

Washington, March 5 (AP)—Senator Robert B. Howell, of Nebraska, was reported today at Walter Reed Hospital to have shown a "distinct gain" for the day in his battle against pneumonia.

ROOSEVELT PROCLAIMS NATIONAL BANK HOLIDAY TO LAST UNTIL FRIDAY

Immediate Embargo Placed On All Exports Of Gold And Currency—Issuance Of Clearing-House Scrip Is Provided

DECREE SERVES AS STOPGAP UNTIL CONGRESS CAN ACT

"Managed Currency," Secretary Woodin Says, Denying U. S. Is Off Metallic Basis—Decree Issued Under Trading-With-Enemy Act

By FRANKLYN WALTMAN, JR.
[Washington Bureau of The Sun]

Washington, March 5—Acting under war-time dictatorial powers, President Roosevelt, one day in office, tonight issued a proclamation taking absolute control of the nation's entire financial structure.

Coming as the climax of a day and evening spent in a series of conferences at the White House and Treasury, the President's unprecedented action was his first stroke to end the hoarding of currency and gold.

WHAT PROCLAMATION PROVIDES

The proclamation provided that:

1. All banks in the country shall be closed until Friday.

2. All banking transactions shall be suspended, except those specifically authorized by the Secretary of the Treasury.

3. No bank "shall pay out, export, earmark or permit the withdrawal or transfer in any manner whatsoever, of any gold or silver coin or bullion or currency."

4. No bank shall take "any other action which might facilitate the hoarding" of gold or currency.

5. No bank shall pay out deposits, make loans, deal in foreign exchange, transfer credits from here to any place abroad.

6. The Secretary of the Treasury may require and take control of the issuance of clearing-house certificates during this holiday period.

CONGRESS CALL TO MEET THURSDAY

Six hours before this action was announced to be effective at 1 A. M. tomorrow, President Roosevelt issued a proclamation for an extra session of Congress at noon Thursday to deal with a program as yet unannounced to stabilize the country's banking and monetary system.

The sweeping restrictions imposed on the country by the President will be only a stop-gap until Congress in the new session can adopt remedial legislation. It was intimated tonight that Congress on Thursday will prescribe the course of action for banks, starting Friday.

APPLIES TO ALL BANKING INSTITUTIONS

The President's proclamation applies to all commercial banks, Federal Reserve banks, trust companies, savings banks, building and loan associations, credit unions and all "other corporations, partnerships, associations or persons engaged in the business of receiving deposits, making loans, discounting business paper or transacting any other form of banking business."

Mr. Roosevelt invoked the provision of the war-time Trading With the Enemy Act which gave the President discretionary power to declare an embargo on the export of gold and currency. His power to control domestic money transactions flowed as a corollary from his authority to prohibit gold export, it was contended.

Not all authorities agree that the Trading With the Enemy Act remains in force, several holding that the President's authority under this statute ended with the official termination of the war with Germany. But that is a controversy which can be settled only by the courts.

WOODIN DRAFTS MACHINERY

As the Presidential proclamation was issued Secretary Woodin, Ogden L. Mills, Secretary of the Treasury until yesterday, and members of the Federal Reserve Board with their

WEATHER FORECAST

Generally fair and cooler today; fair, with rising temperature, tomorrow; fresh west and northwest winds.

(Details on Page 21)

THE SUN

Registered United States Patent Office

Four-Power Pact Rejected By Daladier, Premier Of France—Page 11

VOL. 192—D. PAID CIRCULATION MARCH MORNING, 140,009; EVENING, 137,762; 277,771 || SUNDAY 180,651

BALTIMORE, FRIDAY, APRIL 7, 1933

Published every week day by The A. S. Abell Company. Entered as second-class matter at Baltimore Postoffice.

22 PAGES 2 CENTS

ROOSEVELT BID IS ACCEPTED BY M'DONALD

Premier To Discuss World Situation With President And His Aides

FOUR OTHER NATIONS MAY SEND EXPERTS

France, Italy, Germany And Japan May Take Advantage Of Opportunity

By M. FARMER MURPHY
[*Washington Bureau of The Sun*]

Washington, April 6—A formal invitation from President Roosevelt to Premier Ramsay MacDonald of Great Britain to visit Washington this month to discuss world affairs was dispatched through the State Department today, and within six hours an acceptance of the invitation had been received.

In his message to Premier MacDonald, President Roosevelt emphasizes the importance of the world economic conference, and, since the preparations for it "are entering a more intensive stage," he believes that the world situation calls for "realistic action." The people in every nation are calling for it, he says. And not only is this an urgent matter but there is need also for "making further progress toward practical disarmament."

To Sail For U. S. April 15

Premier MacDonald's reply is a cordial acceptance without comment and says he will sail for this country by the Berengaria on April 15.

Although Great Britain is the only country to which a formal invitation of this character has so far been sent, there is reason to believe that others may follow. At any rate, other nations have been made aware that the attitude of this Government is one of willingness to receive representatives of any country interested in the subjects of the world conference and to discuss these with them in a preliminary way.

Other Representatives Expected

As a result all the principal nations may soon be sending delegates to Washington for an exchange of views on current world problems or carry on such conferences through their accredited envoys here. It is thought that France, Italy, Germany and Japan may take advantage of the opportunity offered. If any of them should indicate a desire to do so it is expected formal invitations to them will follow.

The absence of any reference to debts in President Roosevelt's invitation is in accordance with the position constantly taken by the Administration that the great problem which must be attacked is the world economic situation, of which intergovernmental indebtedness is only a part and not a predominating factor at that.

This idea has been reiterated by Secretary Hull, who has said that there could be no general economic recovery until the choking of world trade had been stopped and the restrictions on international trade removed.

Advance Preparation Sought

With this conception of the primary importance of a successful outcome of the world economic conference the Administration is obviously trying to avoid the mistake of plunging into it without preparation and without knowing the feelings of other countries toward the subjects with which it will deal.

If, therefore, Premier MacDonald's visit is but the forerunner of visits from representatives of other nations, Washington will be the scene of a kind of preparation for the world economic conference and this and other governments will have gained in advance a fair notion of what can be accomplished.

Would Welcome French Envoy

As President Roosevelt's invitation to Premier MacDonald indicates, the idea of having him come over had its inception in the visit of Sir Ronald Lindsay to Mr. Roosevelt at Warm Springs; so, also, may an invitation to France result from a similar informal meeting. At the time President Roosevelt asked the retiring French Ambassador, Paul Claudel, to come to see him to say good-by before his departure it is understood he intimated to him that if France should desire to send some one to this country to discuss general economic questions this Government would be pleased to receive him.

Despite the prospect of a number of countries engaging in discussions with this Government on the general economic situation this will not result in a conference in the sense that they will all participate at the same time. All such exchanges will be conducted separately.

Parley To Be Held In London

The world conference is to be held in London, and there is no intention to attempt to usurp its functions, to take the edge off it or to forestall its conclusions. The intention of this Government is understood to be simply that of getting the opinions of other governments and in so doing impress on them the vital necessity of reach-

(Continued on Page 11, Column 2)

The Great Game Of Politics

By FRANK R. KENT

No Cause Yet To Shudder

WASHINGTON, April 6.

THE AMAZING reductions in the cost of the Federal Government, which President Roosevelt has made within six weeks of taking office, are without precedent in any country. The estimate is fairly close to a billion dollars that will have been cut out of the operating expenses of the Government when the executive orders, already issued, have taken full effect.

—o—

IT IS REALLY an unparalleled performance and completely redeems the most basic of his campaign pledges—the pledge which it was said could not be redeemed—to wit, a flat 25 per cent. reduction. The bulk of this saving is contained in the $400,000,000 pared from the veteran load. The rest comes from the fifteen per cent. cut in salaries of all Federal employes, and in economies made in all Federal departments. With the revenue of $150,000,000 from beer, and the imposition of a few new taxes it is clear a real balance of the national budget is in sight.

—o—

THIS IS SO without counting upon the large additional revenue that will flow from liquor, once the ratification of the Eighteenth Amendment has been achieved. The vote of Michigan and Wisconsin seems to forecast this within a year. Thus, it would seem that the national solvency has already been restored, and the future holds promise of an even greater financial solidity.

—o—

NOW, IT IS INCREDIBLE that having achieved so epochal a victory over the great organized groups, whose unchecked progress was breaking the financial back of the nation—it is incredible that, having done this in the first weeks of his Administration, Mr. Roosevelt will deliberately unbalance the budget and nullify his economies by a program of expenditures. To think that, one must believe Mr. Roosevelt and his advisers are without sense enough to know what they are doing. Hence the apprehensions of those who, while cheering the economy accomplishments, shudder at the other side of the Roosevelt program, seem unfounded.

—o—

YET THERE ARE plenty of shudderers. For example, it is pointed out that $500,000,000 of the savings has already been offset by the $500,000,000 Federal grant to the States for distress relief. This proposition is the same one the Senate voted down two months ago. Then, there is the farm relief bill, which, it is held, means a great increase in Federal employes and a vast outlay of money. To it now has been attached the mortgage relief proposal, which involves a $2,000,000,000 bond issue.

—o—

THE REFORESTATION employment bill, which will cost many millions, is already in force, and a great public works program, which will entail more bond issues, is soon to make its appearance. The question is asked as to how the budget is to be kept in balance if economies are thus to be offset by expenditures; if Federal employes are to be reduced with one hand and increased with the other; if we are to deflate and inflate at the same time.

—o—

THE ADMINISTRATION answer to all this is conclusive. It can be summed up in the statement that an Administration intelligent enough to do what this one has done in the way it has done it, is too intelligent to turn right around and undo the job. The idea of such a switch from intelligence to stupidity is ridiculous. In the first place, the Federal grant of $500,000,000 for State relief was imperative and unavoidable. It is not a recurring item of expense and not properly chargeable to the normal budget. In the second place, Mr. Roosevelt has stated that the farm bill will not be permitted to create a "great army" of jobholders and the expense will not be vast. How he proposes to avert this is not revealed, but it is clear he knows the danger and intends to avert it.

—o—

AS TO THE BIG BOND issues involved in the public works program, it is said, vital as is economy and budget balance, no real recovery can be hoped for by reducing purchasing power. Real recovery must come through an increase in employment and thus an increase in purchasing power. The public works program, like the farm and mortgage program, is designed to do those things. As to the soundness of the future Government financing, every bond issue will provide for its own amortization. In brief, the budget once balanced, will not be unbalanced; the Federal credit now reestablished by Mr. Roosevelt will not be impaired by Mr. Roosevelt. It does seem that the shudderers are unduly alarmed. They might wait until there is something concrete to shudder about.

GIRL RETRACTS SCOTTSBORO ATTACK STORY

Witness, Long Missing, Reappears To Deny Earlier Testimony

CALLED TO STAND IN NEGRO'S DEFENSE

Says Rev. Dr. Harry Emerson Fosdick Advised Return To Alabama

[*By the Associated Press*]

Decatur, Ala., April 6—Ruby Bates, long missing witness in the "Scottsboro case," appeared dramatically and unexpectedly in the courtroom today and denied her testimony in previous trials in which eight of nine Negroes indicted for an attack on two girls were sentenced to death.

The girl, missing since February 27, appeared just as the defense was prepared to rest its case in behalf of Heywood Patterson, 19-year-old Chattanooga Negro, and the first of the nine to face retrial.

Lays Story To Excitement

"No, sir," she replied, raising her voice slightly, in reply to a question from Samuel S. Liebowitz, of New York, chief of defense counsel, who asked, "Were you attacked aboard the freight train that afternoon?"

"I told it because I was excited," she replied to Leibowitz's question as to why she testified in the trials in Jackson county two years ago that she had been attacked by six Negroes.

Through a long cross-examination, in which at times she was obviously flustered and hesitated on some questions, she reiterated that she was not attacked.

"I can't remember," she replied to several questions propounded by Attorney-General Thomas E. Knight, Jr., particularly as to the surname of a woman for whom she said she worked while in New York. "Marguerite is all I remember," she said.

Says Mrs. Price Fainted

The Bates girl on cross-examination said that Victoria Price had fainted when she left the train at Paint Rock, Ala., and she sat holding her head in her lap.

She said she "could not say" whether Mrs. Price had been attacked.

Court Grants Delay

The court was in informal recess at the time she entered. Judge James E. Horton, presiding, but a minute or two before had said "the court will wait eight minutes" to a whispered request from Leibowitz.

That remark was the only inkling the spectators had that something unusual was impending.

To Summon Minister

The girl, wearing a gray coat and close-fitting hat to match, was accompanied by Miss May Jones, social worker of Birmingham, who testified she had driven her here at the request of the Rev. Charles Clingman, rector of the Episcopal Church of the Advent there. Attorney-General Knight immediately asked a subpœna for the Birmingham minister.

Taking the stand, the Bates girl identified herself. Then in a hushed courtroom she faced Mrs. Victoria Price, whom Patterson was charged with attacking, and identified her.

Testifies Of Intimacies

Lester Carter, of Knoxville, Tenn., who was on the stand during the morning, was brought in and the girl identified him.

Carter in the forenoon, in a three-hour recital during which he gestured almost constantly, told of a clandestine meeting with the Bates girl at which Mrs. Price and Jack Tillery were present, and of intimacies with her.

Taking up a recital of her movements from March 23, 1931, until she was taken from a Southern Railway freight train at Paint Rock, Ala., she

(Continued on Page 5, Column 2)

Legal Flow Of Beer Starts In 19 States And Nation's Capital After 13 Years

Soft-Drink Era Bade Farewell At "Watch-Night" Parties But "No Rowdyism" Is Keynote Everywhere

[*By the Associated Press*]

New York, April 7 (*Friday*)—Beer broke through a 13-year-old barrier at 12.01 A. M. and openly foamed once more into the glasses of waiting thousands today.

Approved by Congress, a brew—3.2 per cent. alcohol by weight and 4 per cent. by volume—was legal again immediately in nineteen States and the District of Columbia, embracing more than half the population of the United States.

The reception was as varied as the control systems of the States.

New York Compelled To Wait

A warning word from President Jacob Ruppert of the United States Brewers' Association against intemperance in the early morning hours postponed deliveries from most New York city breweries until 6 A. M.

Along Broadway and in private parties there was a scattered celebration—steins topped with soft white collars. White Way restaurant and night club proprietors were reticent about the source and some observers who postponed their imbibing until breakfast said only bootleg beverage was available at the stroke of midnight in the metropolis.

In nearby Newark beer trucks roared out of their home sheds at 12.01 A. M. with assortments of barrels, half barrels and cases. None of the new brew was served to individuals immediately, since a State law in New Jersey prohibited dispensing until 7 A. M.

In Philadelphia the fresh beer began to flow at once.

Westward The Tide Moves

Quickly the welcoming festivity spread toward the Central time belt where one hour later brewing centers such as St. Louis, Chicago and Milwaukee flared into new activity. Plenty for breakfast but not a drop for midnight revelry was the watchword at San Francisco.

Holding the new beer non-intoxicating as defined by Congress, brewing interests set forth the belief that the revived industry would entail important construction and employment for the jobless.

Ranged on the opposite side were prohibition advocates ready to challenge the brew as intoxicating and argue that no benefit to the nation would result.

Long before the hands of clocks

(Continued on Page 4, Column 2)

Two Cases Of Beer Hauled To White House

Washington, April 7 (AP)—Under police escort a truck, gayly decorated, delivered two specially wrapped cases of beer at the White House at 12.05 A. M. today.

A marine guard also was riding on the truck as it pulled up to the West Executive avenue entrance to President Roosevelt's mansion.

The truck bore this sign:

"Here's to you — President Roosevelt. The nation's first real beer in years."

MRS. JUDD AGAIN SEEKS NEW TRIAL

Jury-Tampering Charges Hurled Anew In Motion Filed In Court

AFFIDAVITS PRODUCED

Action Follows Denial Of Reprieve By Pardon Board—Hanging Set For April 21

[*By the Associated Press*]

Phœnix, Ariz., April 6—Charges of jury tampering were hurled anew tonight by counsel for Winnie Ruth Judd in another and perhaps final legal move to save her from death on the gallows April 21 for the murder of Agnes Anne LeRoi.

Earlier in the day the Arizona Board of Pardons and Paroles had denied her application for a reprieve, which she had asked to gain time to reorganize her forces in a last desperate battle for life.

Walter Wilson, clerk of the Maricopa county Superior Court, accepted filing of a motion by O. V. Wilson, chief of Mrs. Judd's attorneys, which prays for setting aside of the judgment and sentence, setting aside of a previous order denying a new trial and asks that a new trial be granted.

Affidavits By 3 Jurymen

The motion, supported by affidavits in corroboration of an alleged jury "deal" to make Mrs. Judd "talk," was placed by the court clerk on next Monday's law and motion calendar of Superior Judge Howard C. Speakman. Judge Speakman presided at the trial which resulted in Mrs. Judd's conviction February 8, 1932. He recently dismissed an information, which had been pending since November, 1931, charging murder of Miss Hedvig Samuelson.

Affidavits attached were sworn to by three members of the jury of twelve men which voted the death penalty. They were: T. T. Kunze, Ed

(Continued on Page 5, Column 4)

Minister Would Rather See Dog Killed Than Church Disturbed

Oklahoma City Pastor, Who Forcefully Ejected Mongrel From Tabernacle, Severely Injuring Him, Is Center Of Heated Controversy

[*By the Associated Press*]

Oklahoma City, Okla., April 3—Injuries suffered by a mongrel pup in its ejection from the Faith Tabernacle by the Rev. William Kitchen caused widespread controversy here tonight.

Mr. Kitchen said he threw the dog out of the church Sunday night "because it was disturbing services," but advised it was near death and denied he intended to treat it brutally.

Prosecution of the pastor was threatened by Abe Aronson, Pooch's master, who identified the dog in a hospital for pets.

"I would sooner see a dog killed than a church service interrupted," Mr. Kitchen said when asked about the incident.

"Pooch was not a mean dog and I want this man prosecuted whether she lives or dies," said Aronson after the injured animal had licked his hands in recognition.

"It is ridiculous," said Mrs. Warder White, president of the local humane society. "Coming from a minister, it is even worse."

The congregation of Mr. Kitchen's church was divided in sentiment, some backing their pastor in his statement that he did not intend to injure the dog and others criticizing him.

A group of the latter gathered over the injured dog after it fell upon the sidewalk outside the church and prayed for its recovery. Late today hospital attendants said the pup probably would die.

NAZIS WOULD MOLD GERMAN RELIGION

Advocate Ousting Old Testament And Erecting In Its Stead Nationalist Sagas

LUTHERANS IN PROTEST

Rosenberg Says 2,000,000 War Martyrs Form Living Mythology And Are Basis For New Faith

[*By the Associated Press*]

Berlin, April 6—The religion of Germany under Hitler rule, as defined today by the Protestant Nazi "German Christian Movement," would oust the Old Testament and would erect in its stead the sagas and fairy tales of Germany and the leading personalities from German spiritual, philosophical and artistic life.

At their first national convention the members of this movement named a commission to amend German church life in conformity with Nazi ideas and "in a pure Aryan spirit."

The Nazi urge for a realignment of religious values was further stressed in an address by Alfred Rosenberg, new head of the foreign political division of the party, who declared that 2,000,000 German World War martyrs form a living mythology and a new religion for uncounted millions in the new Germany.

Lutherans Protest To Hitler

The Supreme Council of the Evangelical Church, disturbed by Nazi attempts to reorganize the Lutheran communion to coordinate it with Naziism, reminded Chancellor Adolf Hitler that he had promised not to touch the nation's independent ecclesiastical institutions.

The policy the Nazis will adopt toward the Catholics remained uncertain. Vice-Chancellor Franz von Papen will discuss the situation with the Pope when he visits Vatican City within the next few days.

Observers holding the theory that the Nazis plan further to nationalize the church saw evidence to that effect in a press report that the Government intends to abolish the church tax, substituting a "culture tax" in its place.

Rosenberg Paraphrases Voltaire

The "German Christians" adopted resolutions asking "equal fusion of the church with the Nazi movement in a pure Aryan spirit, equalization of organist and pastor, and the living language to the exclusion of the ancient, dismissal of the Old Testament basis and substitution of the German inheritance; instead of prophets, sagas and fairy tales to take the leading personalities from German spiritual, philosophical and artistic life."

Herr Rosenberg, who is expected by some political observers to become the moving force in the Foreign Office, paraphrased Voltaire in his speech, saying there was no world history, only the recitation of the various fights peoples and races had with one another. Through racial histories he developed an Aryan-Germanic mythology of "liberty and honor."

Hitler Cites U. S. Action

"Our fate is to fight for new times and for new futures," he said. "The new mythology cannot be downed. The personifications of this mythology are the World War heroes, and the new German movement shows that uncounted millions are beginning to

(Continued on Page 11, Column 5)

HOUSE TO OPEN AKRON CRASH PROBE TODAY

Three Survivors Of Fatal Flight To Give Testimony To Committee

INQUIRY BY NAVY HEADED BY BUTLER

Replaces Admiral Phelps In Investigation Starting Monday At Lakehurst

By DEWEY L. FLEMING
[*Washington Bureau of The Sun*]

Washington, April 6—The House Naval Affairs Committee today determined to take the lead in investigating the tragedy of the navy dirigible Akron.

The inquiry will begin in the House Office Building tomorrow morning, with the three survivors of the disaster—Lieut.-Com. Herbert V. Wiley, Richard E. Deal and Moody E. Erwin—giving the first testimony.

Plans for the navy's own investigation of the crash, which will begin Monday at Lakehurst, N. J., were completed today by Secretary Swanson and other officials of the department. The final arrangements were accompanied by two substitutions in the personnel of the official court of inquiry.

Admiral Butler Heads Court

Rear-Admiral Henry V. Butler, commandant of the Washington Navy Yard, was named president of the court in the place of Rear-Admiral W. W. Phelps, previously designated, who was reported unable to serve on account of illness, and Commander Sydney M. Kraus, manager of the naval aircraft factory at Philadelphia, was selected to take the place yesterday assigned to Commander Garland Fulton. The third member of the court will be Capt. Harry E. Shoemaker, commandant of the Sunnyvale (Cal.) naval air station. Lieut.-Com. Ralph G. Pennoyer will be judge-advocate.

While plans for these two inquiries were going forward, resolutions for yet three more investigations of the Akron's destruction were pending in Congress. Senator King (Dem., Utah) was sponsoring a resolution in the Senate and Representatives McClintic (Dem., Okla.) and Fish (Rep., N. Y.) were supporting similar requests in the House.

To Seek Special Committee

Representative McClintic, who thinks the House investigation should be made by a select committee rather than the Naval Affairs or other service committee, plans to go before the Rules Committee tomorrow morning in support of his resolution for a special committee of seven to be drawn from various standing committees of the House.

Although the investigation, which begins at the Capitol tomorrow, will be under the technical direction of an aeronautics subcommittee, headed by Representative Delaney (Dem., N. Y.), Representative Vinson (Dem., Ga.), chairman of the full Naval Affairs Committee, said all members of that body would participate.

Wiley Tells His Story

At a preliminary meeting today the committee heard the first-hand stories of the disaster from the lips of Commander Wiley, Boatswain's Mate Deal and Metalsmith Erwin. The survivors made only direct statements and were preparing to answer questions at tomorrow's session. Earlier in the day the three were received by President Roosevelt at the White House, and related their experiences to their Commander-in-Chief.

Although today's committee meeting was held behind closed doors, Representative Vinson curtly denied there was any secret about the talks of the members with the crash survivors and declared that the formal inquiry to be started tomorrow would be "wide open" to the public.

"We are going to investigate every phase of this disaster," Mr. Vinson elaborated, "and we are going to do it publicly so that Congress and the whole country may know all of the facts as they are developed.

To Probe Sabotage Charge

"We shall inquire not only into the facts of the accident itself but we will review the whole history of this and other lighter-than-air craft of the navy. We will endeavor to get all the facts connected with the construction of the Akron, including the charges that attempts were made to sabotage her during the building. We shall also inquire into the military and commercial values of such aircraft, with the view of determining what shall be the policy of the future with regard to their use in the United States Navy."

Mr. Vinson asserted the committee would try to get direct testimony from "everyone" having pertinent information about the Akron and its fatal accident, civilians as well as members of the navy. He said all witnesses would testify under oath, and that if civilians exercised their right to refuse appearance the committee would ask the House for authority to subpœna them.

The committee chairman said Wiley, Deal and Erwin today gave them only information already transmitted to

(Continued On Page 2, Column 3)

THIRTY-HOUR-WORK-WEEK BILL PASSED BY SENATE, 53-30, AND SENT TO HOUSE

Amendment Of Senator Robinson, Democratic Leader, To Raise Limit To 36 Hours And Permit Eight-Hour Day Is Rejected

6,000,000 JOBLESS WILL FIND WORK, BACKERS ESTIMATE

Milk And Farm Products Processed By Producers Are Exempt—Hatfield Move To Impose Ban On Exports Loses By Margin Of Two

By FRANKLYN WALTMAN, JR.
[*Washington Bureau of The Sun*]

Washington, April 6—By the overwhelming vote of 53 to 30, the Senate late today approved the Black thirty-hour work-week bill, the most revolutionary piece of social legislation to be passed by either branch of Congress in peacetime.

The measure was adopted several hours after the Senate rejected by 41 to 48 votes the proposal of Senator Robinson, of Arkansas, the Democratic leader, to modify the measure by permitting a thirty-six-hour work-week with eight hours of labor in any one day.

FIRST DEFEAT FOR ROBINSON

Rejection of his amendment was the first defeat Senator Robinson has suffered in the present Congress. In some quarters it was counted as President Roosevelt's first set-back in Congress. Senator Robinson yesterday declined to say, however, that the President had inspired the amendment. The Arkansan said before offering the amendment he had consulted "a higher authority" and that the proposal was "agreeable" to the President.

At all events, the Senate appeared in no mood to modify the drastic provisions of the Black bill, voting down along with the Robinson proposal a list of other amendments which would have exempted certain commodities or manufacturers. Milk and milk products and farm products when processed by the original producers and products of a perishable nature when used in canning, however, were exempted.

MEANS 30-HOUR WEEK IN UNITED STATES

Invoking the interstate commerce powers of Congress, the bill makes it illegal to ship in interstate commerce any commodity "produced or manufactured in any mine, quarry, mill, cannery, workshop, factory or manufacturing establishment in which any person was employed or permitted to work more than five days in any week or more than six hours in any day."

This virtually means a compulsory thirty-hour week for all American industry. The bill was designed to force a partition of existing employment among the jobless of the country. It is estimated that if it is passed by the House and approved by the President its provision will make possible absorption of one-half of the 12,000,000 unemployed in the country.

House Action In Doubt

The fate of the bill in the House remains in doubt. Speaker Rainey indicated that the measure would not be pushed unless President Roosevelt requested such action. At the White House it was explained the President would have nothing to say in respect to the bill until he read the text as approved by the Senate.

As soon as the Black bill was approved the Senate made the Roosevelt farm-relief bill, with the agricultural credit program attached as a rider, its unfinished business. This measure, one of the major points in the President's emergency rehabilitation program, will remain before the Senate until passed, probably some time next week.

May Turn To Insurance Bill

An effort will be made to lay the farm-relief bill temporarily aside tomorrow to permit passage of a bill authorizing the Reconstruction Finance Corporation, on recommendation of the Secretary of the Treasury and approval of the President, to subscribe to preferred stock, notes, bonds or debentures of insurance companies needing funds for capital purposes.

Senator Smith (Dem., S. C.), in charge of the bill, agreed to take up the Reconstruction Finance Corporation insurance measure tomorrow provided it does not inspire protracted debate and can be disposed of within a short time.

Of the fifty-three Senators who voted for the Black bill forty-one were Democrats, eleven Republicans and one a Farmer-Laborite. The opposition to the bill on the final roll call comprised ten Democrats and twenty Republicans.

Senator Tydings (Dem., Md.) voted

Congress Session To End By June 1, Leaders Predict

[*Washington Bureau of The Sun*]

Washington, April 6—Belief that the extra session of Congress might be terminated by the middle of May or the first of June was expressed today by Speaker Rainey and Representative Byrns, majority floor leader of the House. The Speaker suggested the possibility of cleaning up emergency legislative tasks by the first of June, while M. Byrns thought the job might be concluded two weeks earlier.

Both the Speaker and the majority leader tempered their forecasts with observations that the legislators would have to work at a fast pace to wind up on either of the dates mentioned and said, too, that their predictions were based on the presumption that only legislation now pending in the Congress or to be recommended by the White House in the near future would receive consideration in the extra session.

12 Big Measures Pending

It was pointed out that no fewer than twelve pieces of important legislation yet remain to be acted upon, and almost any one of them is capable of tying the Legislature in knots.

At the top of the list is the farm-relief bill, passed by the House and now about to start through the Senate. To it has been appended the farm-mortgage measure, which would necessitate its return to the House for further consideration. Whether attached to the farm-price bill or not, the mortgage measure still remains to be considered in both branches.

Relief Bill May Start All Over

The Wagner-Costigan-La Follette direct-relief bill has passed the Senate, but it now appears that it will have to start anew as a House measure because of the lower body's refusal to take such a money-bearing bill from the Senate.

The thirty-hour-week bill, passed today by the Senate, is expected to come before the House in its turn, but leaders have not determined when that turn will come. The House ex-

(Continued on Page 2, Column 2)

NRA MEMBER U. S. WE DO OUR PART

THE EVENING SUN

6 STAR ★★★★★★ Wall Street Close

THE WEATHER—Clear to partly cloudy, little change in temperature tonight and Saturday. Detailed report on Page 2.

VOL. 47 | PAID CIRCULATION JULY MORNING. 138,062 EVENING. 128,770 266,832 ‖ SUNDAY 176,667 | BALTIMORE, FRIDAY, AUGUST 25, 1933 | Published every week-day by The A. S. Abell Company. Entered as second-class matter at Baltimore Postoffice. | 38 PAGES | 2 CENTS

STORM TOLL 50; BOAT STILL MISSING

Liner's Rescued Passengers Tell Of Gale In Bay

56-HOUR WEEK PROPOSED FOR DRUGGISTS' CODE

Hearings Open On Plan To Affect 150,000 Employes

BALTIMOREAN CALLS LONG DAYS NECESSARY

N. R. A. Prepares Drive To Enroll Employers And Consumers

[*By the Associated Press*]

Washington, Aug. 25—A fifty-six-hour work week, the longest that has been sought in any important code so far presented to the Recovery Administration, was advocated by retail druggists today in formal hearings.

The code, designed to cover 60,000 druggists with about 150,000 employes, called for a ninety-hour store week at wages of from $14 to $15 for regular employes in large towns.

Regular employes would earn $15 a week in towns over 500,000, $14.50 in towns between 250,000 and 500,000, $14 a week in towns between 2,500 and 250,000 and a twenty per cent. increase in towns under 2,500, this wage not necessarily to exceed more than $12.

Pharmacists Excluded

Registered pharmacists, executives earning more than $35 a week, outside salesmen and employes in towns under 2,500 would be excluded from the minimum hour provision, and pharmacists from the wage provision.

Primary among the unfair trade practices listed was a prohibition of selling at less than cost plus 5 per cent., plus overhead Other bans forbade trading allowances to consumers, substitution of articles, using imitative trade names or designs, misbranding and defamation of competitors.

Baltimorean Heard

Dr. R. L. Swain, of Baltimore, secretary of the Maryland State Board of Pharmacy, said the retail drug store industry could not hope to reduce hours beyond the limits of the self-preservation.

He testified that sixty-five per cent. of the nation's drug stores were run by one man and that forty-five per cent. were in towns under 10,000 population.

Swain said there had been no acute unemployment among registered pharmacists. All druggists, he added, regarded the necessity for price raising and stabilization as essential for the preservation of the industry.

In defense of the proposed fifty-six-hour week, which is eight hours longer than the maximum proposed for other retail trades, Swain emphasized it often was necessary for druggists to act in a professional capacity regard-

[Continued On Page 2, Column 6]

Today

On Inside Pages

Provisional Blue Eagle Use Okayed

Administration Rules Company Claiming Exemption Can Display Striped Bird

Washington, Aug. 25 (AP)—A provisional use of the Blue Eagle insignia by stores and factories claiming special hardships would be wrought them by full compliance with the President's agreement was decreed today by the Recovery Administration.

Thomas S. Hammond, executive director of the N. R. A. campaign division, ruled that a white stripe with the word "provisional" printed upon it should be pasted across the Blue Eagle in such establishments pending decision on whether the exemptions asked would be accepted. After decision, either the bar may be removed or the Eagle will have to be taken down.

The order by Hammond of the provisional bar for the Blue Eagle said sufferers of special hardships might ask exemptions from specific requirements, even though their industry had obtained modifications of the voluntary agreement by submitting a code with wage and hour terms of its own.

The exemption petitioner, he said, should make his application in the same manner as those whose trade was under the blanket voluntary agreement, obtaining the consent of their trade associations or local Chamber of Commerce before requesting exemptions.

SECRET INDICTMENT OF INSULL REVEALED

Government Starts Move To Return Magnate From Greece

[*By the Associated Press*]

Chicago, Aug. 25—A suppressed indictment charging Samuel Insull, Sr., and ten others with violation of the bankruptcy law was released today by

[Continued On Page 4, Column 3]

Wets And Drys In Texas Bring Drive To End

Appeals By Farley, Garner For Repeal Feature Last Day Before Voting

Dallas, Texas., Aug. 25 (U.P.)—Texas wets and drys today wound up their campaigns for votes in tomorrow's election to determine whether the State will be the twenty-third to ratify the Twenty-First (repeal) amendment.

The drys carried on their fight to the zero hour with rallies on college campuses and in schools throughout the State. They concentrated their last minute attacks on beer legalization, which also will be decided at the election.

The wets expressed confidence the fight is as good as won. Both sides estimated at least 500,000 votes would be cast tomorrow. Repealists and advocates of beer forecast a wet majority of 100,000 votes. Drys made no estimate of how many votes their cause would poll.

A statement issued by the united forces for prohibition said:

"All that is needed to assure a dry victory in Texas is for dry voters to go to the polls."

The statement was signed by Senator Morris Sheppard, coauthor of the Eighteenth Amendment, and former Gov. Dan Moody, one of the outstanding dry campaigners, and nearly a hundred other prominent drys of the States.

Behind the wet drive, led by former Gov. James E. Ferguson and State Democratic leaders, was President Roosevelt's appeal for a repeal victory. The appeal was broadcast throughout the State by Postmaster-General James A. Farley in a telephone-radio hookup from Washington. The President's stand has been seconded by Vice-President John Nance Garner, who issued a statement urging ratification of the repeal amendment and legalization of beer.

Sea Carves New Inlet Through Ocean City

The photographs, taken at storm-swept Ocean City, show the smashed boardwalk and the inlet which was cut through from the Atlantic Ocean to the Sinepuxent Bay by the pounding waves on Wednesday. The photograph at the botton shows the Yorktown Ferry, which works between Norfolk and Gloucester, Va., piled high by the waves and high wi...

PRISON COUNTERFEIT PLOT IS FRUSTRATED

Materials Found At Leavenworth—Psychologist At Institution Is Suspended

[*By the Associated Press*]

Washington, Aug. 25—The Justice Department today disclosed the discovery and frustration of a plot to manufacture counterfeit money by inmates of Leavenworth Penitentiary.

Dr. H. D. Powers, assistant psychologist of the Public Health Service, was reported by the department to have been suspended from duty at the institution pending a further investigation, as some counterfeiting material had been found in a portion of the prison under his direct supervision.

Waterproof Colors Found

The department said counterfeiting materials, including waterproof fluids of various colors, had been found. It added that other materials and instruments, apparently intended for use in counterfeiting, had been discovered in various parts of the prison.

No paper was found, it was said, that could be used for making currency, and the department thought it probable the plot had been broken up before actual operations could begin.

"There are a large number of very skillful counterfeiters incarcerated in the institution at Leavenworth, and constant vigilance is required to prevent incipient attempts to make counterfeit money," the department said.

Oregon Fire Fighters Close To Exhaustion

2,000 Work On, Nevertheless. Forest Blaze, Worst In State's History, Still Spreading

Portland, Ore., Aug. 25 (AP) — 'Although almost exhausted by their days of ceaseless effort, nearly 2,000 men today kept up their fight against the worst forest fire in Oregon's history.

At one place 110 men were forced to drop their tools and hurry to safety when the flames jumped the fire line ahead of them.

Tillamook reported that the blaze leaped the Wilson river last night and was crackling down both banks. Residents feared that a shift in the wind might send the flames toward Tillamook.

Ware Funeral Sunday

Charles Town, W. Va., Aug. 25 (Special)—Funeral services for John F. A. Ware, who died at his home near here yesterday, will be conducted Sunday at 2.30 P. M. in the Baptist Church here by the Rev. Goodwin Frasier. Mr. Ware, a farmer, 43 years old, is survived by his widow and three sons. Death followed a long illness.

PENNSY TRAIN KILLS FIVE IN MOTOR CAR

Sixth Victim Hurt, Probably Fatally, In Crash Near Columbia, Pa.

[*By the Associated Press*]

Lancaster, Pa., Aug. 25—Five persons were killed and another probably fatally injured today when a special Pennsylvania Railroad inspection train crashed into their automobile at Brooms Landing, along the Susque-

[Continued On Page 2, Column 7]

Cutters Seeking Vessel Missing With 12 Aboard

[*By the Associated Press*]

New York, Aug. 25—The Atlantic seaboard's storm had blown itself out today, but from northern New York to North Carolina there remained devastating floods, stupendous property damage and a mounting death list.

The death toll reached fifty as reports from hard-hit areas trickled in and the prospects were that it would go even higher.

Coast Guard cutters still sought the motor ship Solarina, a 225-ton craft missing off the Carolinas with twelve persons aboard. The ship, bound from Winyah Bay, S. C., to Southport, S. C., first was reported safe in a South Carolina cove, but today a check-up disclosed nothing of her.

Airport Under Water

There also was a possibility that some smaller craft off Virginia were missing and that a thorough investigation of some waterlogged resorts would disclose additional casualties.

Hundreds were made homeless in southwest Philadelphia as the swirl-

[Continued On Page 2, Column 5]

PLANE SPEEDS TO ISLANDS STILL CUT OFF; NINE FROM BALTIMORE GET OFF SHIP

2 Other Marylanders Safely Taken From City Of Norfolk With Rest Of Passengers—Virginian Praises Skipper

CARRIES BABY FROM BATTERED CRAFT; VOYAGERS PLAYED BRIDGE AWAITING AID

A mounting toll of fifty dead was counted today in the widespread and battered wake of the runaway hurricane now blowing itself out in the valley of the St. Lawrence after a devastating rush along the Atlantic seaboard from Cape Hatteras northward.

The passengers on the Chesapeake Line steamer City of Norfolk, on the bay since Tuesday with the vessel on a shoal in Pocomoke Sound, reached Norfolk aboard the City of Baltimore during the day.

Coast Guard cutters put out to seek the missing motorship Solarina, with twelve aboard, off the Carolina coast and unsighted since the hurricane.

Apparently complete reports showed thirteen storm dead in Maryland.

Property damage in the seaboard States on which the hurricane visited its fury was estimated at $3 000,000.

A seaplane put out from the Naval Academy today for a flight to a group of islands in the Chesapeake Bay to learn whether the inhabitants were in need of outside aid. Naval craft were reported ready to carry food and medical supplies if the plane discovers the islanders in distress.

The passengers landed in Norfolk from the City of Norfolk related harrowing experiences during more than thirty hours while the vessel was grounded.

Associated Press dispatches today said the City of Baltimore picked up the thirty-two passengers early this morning from her sister ship which went aground during Wednesday's terrific storm while en route from Baltimore to Norfolk.

Crew Stays Aboard

With the exception of Purser Keely and his assistant, R. H. Bland, waiters and stewardess, the remaining thirty-odd members of the crew of the City of Norfolk remained aboard, as she is in no immediate danger of breaking up on the hard bottom of the mouth of the Pocomoke river. No news is available as yet as to plans to float the liner, which is in ten feet of water.

The tugs Helen and Peerless established contact with the stranded steamer shortly before midnight last night, but they were unable to get within a quarter of a mile of the steamer.

Steaming swiftly along through the starlight night, the City of Baltimore sighted two lights dead ahead at about 2.45 A. M. and at 4 A. M., Capt. C. L. Brooks and his crew as well as many passengers received an answering signal from the City of Norfolk.

As day was breaking Captain Brooks ordered lifeboats lowered. Without further incident the passengers and several members of the crew were brought to their rescue craft.

"We are well and unharmed," said Burwell Wimmer as he and his family clambered aboard the City of Baltimore on the quarter deck. His tiny baby was clasped in his arms while his wife saw that the other children were taken from the lifeboat. Mr. Wimmer, in common with all the rescued passengers, were high in their praises of Capt. Edward James, whose skill in navigation is credited with saving the City of Norfolk from destruction.

Played Bridge

According to the varied stories told by the stranded ship's passengers, those on the boat spent their time in playing bridge and wondering how quickly aid would reach them. A number of boats passed near the grounded ship, but the storm prevented it being reached until that feat was made possible by the lifeboats of the City of Baltimore.

"I've got my work cut out for me and that is about all I can say at the present time," said A. L. Stephens, president of the Chesapeake Line, who left Baltimore last night on the City of Baltimore and was active in the work of rescue this morning.

Nine From Baltimore

Passengers on the City of Norfolk, all of whom are uninjured, follow:

Mr. and Mrs. Burwell Wimmer;

[Continued On Page 3, Column 8]

STATE'S STORM DEATH TOTAL CLIMBS TO 13

Fears Rise For Isolated Islands—Ocean City's Rebuilding Begins

A seaplane was sent today from the Naval Academy to survey the needs of inhabitants on islands in the Chesapeake Bay cut off from the mainland by the devastation of storm and flood.

The plane set out this afternoon while the storm-stricken sections of the State were setting to work at clearing away the wreckage of Maryland's worst storm. At that time the count of dead in the State stood at thirteen. A body was reported sighted near Millers Island today, and Essex police who went to search for it said it might be that of an unidentified man believed to have been lost in flood waters near Bear Creek.

Rebuilding Under Way

Rebuilding got under way in the devastated sections and Ocean City, which bore the brunt of the gale in Maryland, announced that it would "open for business" tomorrow.

Communication was restored at a number of points isolated since Wednesday, bringing new reports of damage, but many outposts were still unheard from and a possible large loss of life on small islands believed to be under water was feared. Floods continued in many places over which the storm had passed.

Admiral Thomas S. Hart, superintendent of the Naval Academy, assigned the seaplane to the island rescue flight after a conference with Gov. Albert C. Ritchie concerning the plight of the inhabitants of Hoopers, Taylors and Bloodsworth Islands, lying close to the Eastern Shore peninsula near the Virginia line.

Islands Flooded

A squadron of National Guard planes surveyed the storm territory yesterday under the command of Major Charles D. Masson and one of these passed over the three islands. Major Masson reported to the Governor that the normal connections between the mainland and the islanders seemed to have been destroyed and the islands flooded. The National Guard planes, not equipped for landing on the sea, were unable to alight and learn the needs of the islanders.

Governor Ritchie said it was feared

[Continued On Page 3, Column 1]

WEATHER FORECAST
Rain and warmer today; fair and colder tomorrow.
(Details on Page 25)

THE SUN

Registered United States Patent Office

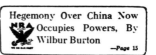

Hegemony Over China Now Occupies Powers, By Wilbur Burton —Page 15

VOL. 194—D. PAID CIRCULATION NOVEMBER MORNING, 137,131 EVENING, 133,411 270,542 || SUNDAY 184,438 BALTIMORE, WEDNESDAY, DECEMBER 6, 1933 Published every week day by The A. S. Abell Company. Entered as second-class matter at Baltimore Postoffice. 26 PAGES 2 CENTS

PROHIBITION ENDED

Lindbergh And Wife On Atlantic Hop

COUPLE LEAVE WEST AFRICA FOR BRAZIL

Flyers, Becalmed Since Saturday, Face 1,900 Miles Of Open Sea

HOMEWARD-BOUND AFTER LONG TRIP

Flight, Longest Yet Attempted, Expected To Take 14 Hours

Wireless Reports Give Lindberghs' Position

[*By the Associated Press*]

Colonel and Mrs. Charles A. Lindbergh reported their position by wireless at brief intervals. The position reports follow, in Eastern standard time:

10 P. M.—12.17 north latitude, 17.50 west longitude (115 miles at sea).

11 P. M.—11.05 north latitude, 19.05 west longitude. "All well."

11.50 P. M.—Making 100 knots per hour (about 116 land miles).

The message did not give position.

12.30 A. M.—Position 446 miles southwest of Bathurst, speed 100 knots. Altitude 1,200 feet.

1.27 A. M.—Skies overcast. Weather squally. Visibility three miles. Daybreak. All well.

[*By the Associated Press*]

Bathurst, Gambia, *Wednesday*, Dec. 6—Col. Charles A. Lindbergh lifted his heavily-laden red monoplane into the air at 2 A. M. today (9 P. M. Tuesday, E.S.T.), and, with Mrs. Lindbergh at the radio, headed across 1,900 miles of open sea toward South America.

After a score or more unsuccessful attempts to lift the heavily-laden plane in an almost dead calm, he was helped on his way by a light breeze from the interior which rippled the surface of the lower Gambia river.

It was a still, clear night and the moon was shining brightly when the Colonel and Mrs. Lindbergh took off from the marine moorings at Halfie, across the river from Bathurst.

Plane Rises Gracefully

There were about a dozen spectators who had foregone sleep for the purpose of wishing the American flying couple luck and of witnessing a sight most unusual here.

In a strong, fresh wind, the plane rose gracefully to be followed by the eyes of the watchers as it sped swiftly westward.

The visibility was good and conditions altogether favorable, while the strength and direction of the wind promised to aid the flyers' progress.

Becalmed For Four Days

For four days the Lindberghs had been balked by inability to lift the heavy load of fuel required for the longest hop yet attempted in their aerial survey tour of Atlantic Ocean airways.

Excess fuel and baggage was jettisoned, and at 4.30 P. M. today the colonel went to the plane for a final inspection. Ready for the flight, the craft bobbed in a gentle swell before a picturesque row of native shacks bordering the river.

The colonel was informed that weather indications insured a bright, clear tropical night for the take-off.

Westfalen Offers Security

The German steamer Westfalen, which had been in Brazil securing supplies, was due to return to its mid-Atlantic post yesterday, affording further security for the Lindberghs on their long flight. The Westfalen is used by the German Lufthansa Line as a base for transatlantic flights, and officials of the line previously had offered the Lindberghs use of their facilities.

By veering slightly northward off a direct course to Natal, Brazil, they could also stop at St. Paul's Island, a French possession in mid-Atlantic. Fernando de Noronha, a volcanic

(Continued on Page 10, Column 4)

The Great Game Of Politics

By FRANK R. KENT

Just Dumb

WASHINGTON, Dec. 5.

THE REPUBLICAN attack today upon the Roosevelt program is a fine illustration of the lack of political intelligence that characterizes the management of that befuddled and enfeebled party. It comes pretty close to the height of futility. They might just at well whistle in the face of an eighty-mile gale.

—o—

FOR ONE THING, there isn't anyone anywhere, in any way, at this time, interested in what the Republican party has to say on any subject. There might be some interest in what some outstanding man of character and reputation in that party had to say for himself. But there isn't so much as a trace of interest in anything emanating from the Republican National Committee, or in anything said through that committee. The best evidence of this is that the committee could not get its own party organs—the recognized Republican papers—to carry the emanation of today on their first pages.

—o—

IN THE SECOND PLACE, everything said about the Roosevelt program in the committee's statement had been said very much more forcefully and very much better by Democrats. It would seem that a 6-year-old child would have political gumption enough to let those Democratic attacks alone, instead of taking the curse off of them for the Administration by imparting a partisan flavor and chilling the spirit of the Democratic critics, who have nothing in common with the Republican party and a complete distaste for being associated with it in any way.

—o—

IN THE THIRD PLACE, even if the committee had had anything effective to say, which it had not, the thought might have occurred that the day on which the repeal of the Prohibition Amendment became effective and some very burdensome taxes removed was no day for the Republican party to speak. It is perfectly true that Mr. Roosevelt was not for straight-out repeal, prior to his nomination; that the repeal plank was forced into the platform over the protest of his friends, who had brought out a very different and much less clean-cut plank.

—o—

IT IS ALSO TRUE that, at his direction, there has now been set up in Washington a complete Federal control over liquor which is in direct conflict with the party pledge. What the party promised and what the people thought they were voting for was the complete return of the liquor problem to the States. The big point made in the campaign was that the Federal Government would confine itself to protecting dry States from wet, and exercise power over importations. Otherwise the whole business was to be returned to the States. That was the idea, but it hasn't worked out. Instead, a rigid system of Federal regulation and direction has been imposed, of which there was not the slightest Democratic hint during the campaign. On the contrary, Federal control was supposed to be the Republican idea and it came in for the bitterest sort of denunciation from Democratic spokesmen.

—o—

HOWEVER, these are matters of detail and theory, about which a lot will be heard later on, and which, unfortunately, will keep the controversy alive. At the moment the people generally are far too pleased at being free from the restrictions of a hated law, which had become intolerably obnoxious, to bother about things of this sort. Whether or not Mr. Roosevelt was originally for straight repeal; whether or not the new Federal control clashes with his promises; whether or not the real leaders in the repeal movement are sore about what he has done—these things make no real difference.

—o—

THE FACT IS THAT, today, people who want a drink can buy one legally and drink it openly. The credit for this

(Continued on Page 6, Column 4)

HOUSE GROUP PLANS TO RAISE $237,000,000

Would Increase U. S. Receipts By Changes In Revenue Act Of 1932

INCOME TAX USED AS NEW SOURCE

Increase Made In Some Rates While Eight Loopholes Are Plugged

By PAUL W. WARD

[*Washington Bureau of The Sun*]

Washington, Dec. 5—Promising to file at a later date suggestions as to new Federal revenue sources, a House Ways and Means subcommittee today issued some recommendations on how to squeeze an additional $237,000,000 from an old source, the income tax.

Representative Doughton (Dem., N. C.), discussing the report tonight, said he expected to receive the subcommittee's final report, including its recommendations on new revenue sources, when the full committee, which he heads, meets again at 10 A. M. tomorrow.

Public hearings on the subcommittee's proposals will be held, Mr. Doughton said, after the House Ways and Means Committee completes the liquor-tax hearings which, sitting in joint session with the Senate Finance Committee, it will inaugurate Monday.

Changes Proposed

The subcommittee proposes to raise $36,000,000, or fifteen per cent. of the $237,000,000 additional revenue it envisions through changes in the Revenue Act of 1932 that would:

Raise the rates on net taxable income in excess of $6,000.

Slightly decrease income taxes paid by married men and offset the reduction by an increase in taxes paid by single men.

Substantially increase taxes on unearned income but still leave those taxes lower than those paid on earned income.

Substitute a flat four per cent. rate for the present graduated "normal," or basic, income tax and raise surtax rates approximately seven per cent.

To Plug Loopholes In Law

The subcommittee proposes to raise the remaining eighty-five per cent., or $201,000,000, by plugging eight loopholes in the Federal income-tax laws. The spotlight of the Senate stock-market investigation has been focused on four of those loopholes, and by plugging that particular quartet, the House subcommittee predicts, Congress would add $80,000,000 to the Federal income. The four are those revenue act provisions pertaining to capital gains and losses, personal holding companies, exchanges and reorganizations, and partnership losses.

The other loopholes which the subcommittee proposes to seal are the depreciation and depletion, the foreign tax credit, the consolidated returns and the "dividends out of pre-March, 1913 earnings" provisions of the revenue act.

The subcommittee proposes that the allowance granted under the first of those four provisions be reduced

(Continued on Page 6, Column 1)

Text Of President's Repeal Proclamation

[*By the Associated Press*]

Washington, Dec. 5—The text of President Roosevelt's repeal proclamation follows:

Whereas the Congress of the United States in second session of the Seventy-second Congress, begun at Washington on the 5th day of December in the year one thousand nine hundred and thirty-two, adopted a resolution in the words and figures following, to wit:

JOINT RESOLUTION

Proposing an amendment to the Constitution of the United States.

Resolved by the Senate and the House of Representatives of the United States of America in Congress assembled (two-thirds of each House concurring therein), that the following article is hereby proposed as an amendment to the Constitution of the United States, which shall be valid to all intents and purposes as part of the Constitution when ratified by conventions in three-fourths of the several States:

ARTICLE

Sec. 1. The Eighteenth article of Amendment to the Constitution of the United States is hereby repealed.

Sec. 2. The transportation or importation into any State, territory, or possession of the United States for delivery or use therein of intoxicating liquors, in violation of the laws thereof, is hereby prohibited.

Sec. 3. This article shall be inoperative unless it shall have been ratified as an amendment to the Constitution by conventions in the several States, as provided in the Constitution, within seven years from the date of the submission hereof to the States by the Congress.

Whereas, Section 217 (A) of the act of Congress entitled "an act to encourage national industrial recovery, to foster competition and to provide for the construction of certain useful public works, and for other purposes" approved June 16, 1933, provides as follows:

Sec. 217 (A) The President shall proclaim the date of:

(1) The close of the first fiscal year ending June 30 of any year after the year 1933, during which the total receipts of the United States "excluding public-debt receipts" exceed its total expenditures (excluding public-debt expenditures other than those chargeable against such receipts), or

(2) The repeal of the Eighteenth Amendment to the Constitution, whichever is the earlier.

Whereas, it appears from a certificate issued December 5, 1933, by the Acting Secretary of State that official notices have been received in the Department of State that on the fifth day of December, 1933, conventions in thirty-six States of the United States, constituting three-fourths of the whole number of States, had ratified the said repeal amendment;

Now, therefore, I, Franklin D. Roosevelt, president of the United States of America, pursuant to the provisions of section 217 (A)

(Continued on Page 2, Column 2)

RITCHIE SIGNS STATE-WIDE LIQUOR BILL

Gordy Issues 16 Licenses As Law Becomes Effective

By LOUIS J. O'DONNELL

[*Annapolis Bureau of The Sun*]

Annapolis, Dec. 5—The State-wide liquor-control bill became a law at 8.28 o'clock tonight when Governor Ritchie signed the measure in the reception room of the executive offices in the State House. The law became effective immediately.

Before pens of the Governor and presiding Assembly officers had been affixed to a final printed copy of the bill as passed yesterday by both the House and Senate, William S. Gordy, Jr., State Comptroller, had issued nine licenses to manufacturers and seven to wholesalers at a cost of $405.53 each. These will be good until April 30.

He also had collected $26,398.97 for State excise tax stamps, which must be affixed to bottles of fortified wines and liquors before they can be sold legally, and had contracted for the delivery of approximately $200,000 worth of the stamps tomorrow.

Printed To Meet Demand

These stamps were being printed as fast as demanded in the office of the Comptroller here. Nearly a dozen of the State tax machines which will be installed in all distilleries and wholesalers' establishments already have been delivered.

They are of the type furnished by the United States Government to business houses with great mailing output.

(Continued on Page 3, Column 4)

Return Of John Barleycorn Finds Gotham Crowds Blase

Times Square Throngs Refuses To Get Excited At News, But Millions Say "Here's How." Hotel Bars Jammed

[*By the Associated Press*]

New York, Dec. 5—John Barleycorn came back to Broadway tonight from his fourteen-year exile. The town had changed, so had he.

He was not the bleary-eyed old man they drove into the wilderness fourteen years ago, but a restrained patriarch who realized apparently that his popularity depended on his decorum.

Dusk was here when he came tearing across the country from Utah but even then the multitudes had gathered at Times Square to welcome him.

They watched the story unfold in the lights that tell the news on Broadway. There was no shouting, only the usual noises—the rumble of traffic, the clang and bustle of the street.

Ten thousand eyes were glued on Times Square's lights—

"Utah voting!" the sign flashed.

A lull. The multitude shifted, swayed and sighed.

"Prohibition is dead!"

The lights flickered the flash. The crowd whooped a few "hoorays," but it didn't roar. The let-down was obvious. It was all over but the shouting but the throng didn't shout—it milled about and waited.

Newsboys took up the peal—"Pro

(Continued on Page 4, Column 3)

'No Glasses, No Bottles,' Booms Al, Who Says He's Too Busy To Celebrate

New York, Dec. 5 (AP)—Alfred E. Smith spent a busy day today—but it was not celebrating repeal of the Eighteenth Amendment.

"I don't drink in the daytime, and I am not going to start today," Smith told a group of photographers.

"No glasses, no bottles," Smith boomed in response to a suggestion he pose with a drink—even if it were only ice water.

"And I haven't any plans for a celebration tonight."

Things were different on April 7 when 3.2 beer became legal. A huge beer truck, drawn by six horses, pulled up in front of the building housing Smith's offices and a case was presented to him.

U. S. PROCLAMATION SIGNED BY PHILLIPS

Acting Secretary Formally Notifies Nation Of Repeal Of Prohibition

LIBRARY WILL GET PEN

Appeals Of Dry Leaders Fall On Deaf Ears In District Of Columbia Court

By DEWEY L. FLEMING

[*Washington Bureau of The Sun*]

Washington, Dec. 5—Sitting beneath a large oil portrait of Chief Justice Charles E. Hughes and facing another of Bainbridge Colby, who announced the advent of national prohibition thirteen years ago, William Phillips, Acting Secretary of State, today put his signature to the official proclamation that the Twenty-first Amendment had been ratified by three-fourths of the States and that the Eighteenth Amendment was dead.

The Acting Secretary used a serviceable but inelegant pen of the two-for-a-nickel variety which will go to the Congressional Library if officials there desire it—and David Hunter Miller, State Department historian, is sure they will.

Signing Customary

The signing took place in the diplomatic reception room of the State Department in the presence of a handful of department officials and a legion of photographers, radio men and newspaper correspondents. Although it was a procedure required by custom of the department, it had absolutely no effect upon the validity of the repeal amendment.

Repeal, according to legal experts, became effective at 5.32 P. M. (Eastern standard time), when Utah became the thirty-sixth State to ratify, and liquor would have flowed legally in wet States from that moment regardless

(Continued on Page 2, Column 5)

UTAH DEALS DEATH BLOW TO PROHIBITION

Becomes Thirty-Sixth State To Ratify Repealing Amendment

[*By the Associated Press*]

Salt Lake City, Dec. 5—Utah today added the thirty-sixth ratification to the Twenty-first Amendment and thereby terminated Federal prohibition throughout the nation.

Final action came at 3.31 P. M. (mountain standard time), when Sam D. Thurman, Salt Lake City, one of the leaders of the repeal campaign in this State, cast the twenty-first vote on a roll call of the State convention after having called attention to the fact his vote would place the Twenty-first Amendment into effect, thereby repealing the Eighteenth.

Cheers Delay Announcement

Prolonged cheering by delegates and guests who taxed the limited seating capacity of the chamber of the House of Representatives in the Utah State Capitol, interrupted proceedings and it was not until 3.32.30 o'clock that Ray L. Olson, Ogden, president of the convention, formally announced ratification had been effected.

Meeting at noon today, the convention was torn between a program calling for a lengthy recess and final action this evening and immediate ratification. Insistence of Eastern States and a feeling among delegates, as expressed by Mr. Olson afterward, that Utah "owed it to the rest of the country to act without delay" finally won, however, and the recess was limited to an hour, and at 2.48 P. M. the convention resumed its deliberations prepared to carry them to a cilmax.

Wet Leader Made President

Organization of the convention had been affected prior to the recess with election of Mr. Olson, head of the repeal campaign in Utah, as president; Clarence Bamberger, Salt Lake City, State commander of the Crusaders, vice-president, and Mrs. Paul F. Keyser, Salt Lake City, director of the women's repeal organization, secretary.

Adoption of the routine report of the credentials committee was followed by an address by Franklin Riter, chairman of the Utah League for Prohibition Repeal and head of the resolutions committee. He read the committee's report, which incorporated the language of the Twenty-first Amendment, the Congressional resolution submitting it and recited the action of the Utah Legislature in bringing it to a vote of the people, and a result of that vote.

The delegates and spectators sat attentively through the reading of the lengthy report awaiting the conven-

(Continued on Page 4, Column 6)

PRESIDENT PROCLAIMS REPEAL EFFECTIVE AFTER UTAH CASTS FINAL VOTE

Thirty-Sixth State Acts At 5.33 P. M., And Seven Minutes Later Phillips Certifies Ratification Of 21st Amendment

ROOSEVELT URGES PEOPLE TO BAR RETURN OF SALOON

Pennsylvania And Ohio Clear Way—News Greeted By Nation-Wide Demonstration—Great Experiment Lasted 13 Years, 10 Months And 19 Days

By J. F. ESSARY

Washington, Dec. 5—National prohibition, as ordained by constitutional enactment, came to an end in this country at 5.33 o'clock this afternoon (Baltimore time). Thus ended the great experiment after 13 years, 10 months, 19 days, 17 hours, 27 minutes and 30 seconds.

At that hour Utah cast the vote of the thirty-sixth State for ratification of the Twenty-first Amendment, thereby erasing the Eighteenth Amendment from the organic law of the land.

A few hours earlier Pennsylvania and Ohio, in order, recorded their decision and rushed official notification of that fact to the Department of State by the swiftest means at their command.

PHILLIPS CERTIFIES RATIFICATION

William Phillips, Acting Secretary of State, was advised by the Utah convention of its action three minutes after the vote was counted. At 49½ minutes after 5 o'clock he affixed his signature to the State Department's formal certification that the Twenty-first Amendment had been ratified.

Turning from the paper before him, while the ink upon it was still wet, Mr. Phillips reached for a telephone to advise officially President Roosevelt of the fact that ratification had been consummated.

PRESIDENT PROCLAIMS REPEAL

The President, on his part, issued a proclamation to the effect that the Eighteenth Amendment to the Constitution had been repealed and that emergency taxes of $220,000,000, with which to service the public works expenditures, were automatically blotted from the statute books.

In the course of this proclamation, the President went a step farther. He spread before the country his sentiments on the question of temperance and called upon the American people to exercise restraint in the use of alcoholic beverages.

CALLS FOR BAR ON SALOON

The President admonished the people to cooperate with the Government "to restore greater respect for law and order"; he called upon the people to use only liquor that has passed Federal inspection in order that illicit manufacture and sale may be broken up, and he reminded the people that transportation of liquor into dry territory is still prohibited.

He spoke of his own revolt at the "repugnant conditions" which came in the wake of the Eighteenth Amendment, and he pleaded with the States not to authorize the return of the saloon "either in its old form or in some modern guise."

PROCLAMATION HELD UNIQUE

No document comparable to this, so far as could be recalled, was ever issued by a President of the United States. It is true that no occasion similar to this had ever arisen, but to preach what amounts to a temperance and law-enforcement sermon to the country in a formal Presidential proclamation is more than a mere incident in official life.

And in denouncing the saloon the President has not hesitated to fly in the face of action already taken by more than one State. The saloon or the "tavern" has been authorized in several of the State enforcement codes and has been proposed in still others.

While these official functions were being enacted in Washington the word that the prohibition experiment had been abandoned was flashed to the four corners of the country, if not also the four corners of the earth.

NATION-WIDE CELEBRATIONS HELD

And in communities from coast to coast the brief bulletin that Utah had cast the decisive ballot was a signal for demonstrations reminiscent of the signing of the Armistice on a November day fifteen years ago.

Sirens were sounded on land and sea. Bell were rung. In

WEATHER FORECAST
Mostly cloudy and not quite so warm today; fair tomorrow.
(Details on Page 15)

THE SUN

Registered United States Patent Office

Marshal Petain Warns French Reservists "Prepare For War" —Page 7

Vol. 195—D. PAID CIRCULATION JUNE MORNING, 138,949 EVENING, 137,061 276,010 || SUNDAY 186,200 BALTIMORE, MONDAY, JULY 23, 1934 Entered as second-class matter at Baltimore Postoffice. Copyright, 1934, by The A. S. Abell Company 16 Pages 2 Cents

15 U.S. AGENTS KILL DILLINGER

ARMY AIR CORPS IS INADEQUATE, REPORT SAYS

Baker Committee Blames Congress For Lack Of Appropriations

PLANE DEFICIENCY AND TRAINING CITED

Recommends Corrective Measures For Many Defects Found

By DEWEY L. FLEMING
[*Washington Bureau of The Sun*]

Washington, July 22—Lack of money was put down as a major reason for the present "unsatisfactory situation" in the Army Air Corps in the report of the special civilian-military investigating committee which for the last three months—since the army's experience with carrying the mails—has been studying the corps from stem to stern in an effort to find out, if anything, what is wrong.

As a direct result of Congressional stinginess with respect to army aviation, the committee holds, the Air Corps is deficient in airplanes, in personnel and in training, to a point where it is "inadequate to meet the army requirements of the national defense."

Only Money Needed

The committee, headed by Newton D. Baker, President Wilson's Secretary of War, found many defects within the corps itself and made recommendations for their correction. In general, however, it approved the present organization scheme and took the position that with adequate funds army aviation could be developed to the superior position already enjoyed by American Navy and commercial aviation.

An airplane strength of 2,320 serviceable craft—820 more than the corps now possesses—and expansion of personnel to the full strength now authorized by law, were among the committee's primary recommendations. Along with that it advised more thorough training of army flyers, particularly as to cross-country, instrument, night and radio beam flying, to mastery of aviation and communication instruments, and to the study of meteorology.

Against Single Department

It emphatically recommended against consolidation of all aviation—civil, military and naval—into a single Federal department of air defense, saying that such a plan, while popular and apparently satisfactory in Europe, was unsuited to the United States. To set up such a system here, the committee averred, "would be a serious error, jeopardize the security of the nation in an emergency and be an unnecessary burden on the taxpayer."

One member of the committee, James H. Doolittle, former army speed pilot, dissented from majority opinion on the consolidation proposal, saying he was convinced that the required air force could be more rapidly organized, equipped and trained if completely separated from the army and developed as an entirely separate arm. If that could not be accomplished, he said, then he would at least like to see the Army Air Corps have a separate budget, a separate promotion list, and be removed from control of the general staff.

Members Of Committee

Besides Mr. Baker and Mr. Dolittle, members of the investigating committee were:

CIVILIANS

KARL T. COMPTON,
GEORGE W. LEWIS,
EDGAR S. GORRELL,
CLARENCE D. CHAMBERLIN,

MILITARY

MAJ.-GEN. H. A. DRUM,
MAJ.-GEN. BENJAMIN D. FOULOIS, chief of the Air Corps.
MAJ.-GEN. GEORGE S. SIMONDS,
BRIG.-GEN. C. E. KILBOURNE,
BRIG.-GEN. J. W. GULICK,
MAJOR ALBERT E. BROWN.

Hundreds Testify

The Baker committee was the fifteenth which, within the last sixteen years, has made an intensive study of national aviation defense problems, including those presented in the Army Air Corps. It spent three months on the task, examined 105 witnesses and received the written views of more than 500 Air Corps officers.

Called to the task by President Roosevelt and the Secretary of War immediately following the Air Corps' unfortunate experiences with the carrying of mails during temporary suspension of private air-mail operations the committee spent much of its time inquiring into that particular chapter of Air Corps history. It concluded that

(Continued on Page 13, Column 2)

Committee Completes Army Air Corps Report

NEWTON D. BAKER

$100,000,000 FARM BONDS TO BE SOLD

Treasury For First Time To Act As Fiscal Agent For Another Unit

PREMIUM IS EXPECTED

Mortgage Corporation Head Explains Borrowers Need Cash To Pay Some Obligations

[*By the Associated Press*]

Washington, July 22—The Treasury tomorrow will offer to the public $100,000,000 of 3 per cent. Federal Farm Mortgage Corporation bonds, marking the first time it has ever acted as the fiscal agent for another Government agency.

The bonds, maturing from 1944 to 1949, will be fully guaranteed by the Government. The proceeds will be used largely to repay Treasury and Reconstruction Finance Corporation advances.

Hopes To Get Premium

Sale will be to the highest bidders. The Government hopes to obtain a premium, inasmuch as similar obligations closed on the New York Exchange Saturday at 101 6-32.

W. I. Myers, governor of the Farm Credit Administration, today explained that, while the bulk of the corporation's advances to Federal Land Banks for relending to farmers were in the form of the corporation's bonds, cash requirements also were substantial.

Borrowers need cash to pay taxes, insurance premiums and other items, and all the corporation's disbursements of $500 or less are paid in cash.

Cash Obtained By Deposit

In recent months, Myers said, most of the cash for both Federal Land Bank and Land Bank Commissioner loans has been obtained by Treasury deposit of money in the Federal Land Banks. This is secured by the corporation's bonds, and by sale of its bonds to the postal savings system and institutions operating under the supervision of the Farm Credit Administration.

The Farm Mortgage Corporation has $500,490,700 of bonds outstanding, Myers said. Since March 26, he added, more than 51,000 Land Bank loans, totaling $197,000,000, and more than 85,000 Land Bank Commissioner loans, aggregating $156,000,000, have been placed.

82 Per Cent. In Bonds

Eighty-two per cent. of the amount of loans made since that date has been in the form of the corporation's bonds, in exchange for mortgages, he said.

Applications for the new issue will be received at the Federal Reserve Banks and branches until 2 P. M. July 25, in the same manner as are the usual Treasury offerings. Tenders by persons other than banks, trust companies and recognized investment dealers must be accompanied by a deposit of five per cent. of the face of the amounts bid for.

Stratosphere Flight Held Up By Weather

Lack Of Favorable Reports And High Humidity Delay Uncrating Of Balloon

Rapid City, S. D., July 22 (AP)—Uncertainty today still marked plans for the start of the Stevens-Kepner stratosphere flight as the weather report showed no favorable developments.

A bulletin issued by Major William E. Kepner, pilot, said there was no promise of satisfactory weather for the take-off for at least twenty-four hours.

Plans to remove the balloon from its crate and attach Reggins ropes were postponed because of moisture in the air.

NRA IS URGED TO 'GAMBLE' UPON UPTREND

Business Improvements By Autumn Are Prophesied

SUMMER DECLINE REPORTED SLIGHT

Blue Eagle Authority Points To Steady Conditions

[*Associated Press Copyright, 1934*]

Washington, July 22—The NRA has been informed by its experts to "gamble" on a substantial rise in business and a less than usual slump during the remainder of the summer.

Leon Henderson, chief of the Blue Eagle's Research and Planning Division, held this conclusion today on the basis of a mass of statistical and other data. His advice to NRA is based upon an expectation of an upswing.

Henderson's researchers have reported to him that the decline thus far this summer has been less than normal, and that there are now numerous signs of an upward trend in business generally.

Boom Not Expected

There is no expectation, however, of a boom development. Henderson employs most careful language in his estimate of the future. He himself referred today to his attitude as a "gamble" on the basis of the best facts available.

The research chief is paying especial attention to what he describes as his "homely indicators." For instance, there has been a gain in the sale of living-room rugs, one of the first things which housewives like to replace when funds are available.

There also has been a decline in the number of bachelors, he points out. In one city, for instance, the number of bachelors before the depression was 10,000. This increased to 29,000 at the height of the depression, and is now about 22,000, the expert conclusion being that men with funds are less fearful of marriage.

Rentals Are Improving

For another thing, Henderson's "doubling up" indicator in reference to housing shows that families which have been crowded now are spreading out and filling vacant apartments and houses.

Small personal loans, his figures show, are being paid up in full at an increasing rate. The index on the indicator shows the rate of repaying at a record high for the depression, and higher even than in the month when soldiers' cash bonus payments were largest. Similarly, the rate of repayment of building and loan obligations is up, and the amount of unrented property held by building and loan associations is down. Repayments to the Home Owners Loan Corporation and Farm Credit Administration are also holding up well.

Henderson said he was paying increasing attention to this type of statistical indicator because, first, it shows the status of the ordinary person better than the customary type of business statistics, and second, because it tends to get at the beginning of the buying process rather than at the end.

Personal Debts Reduced

Of particular significance, Henderson said, are the indicators showing a reduction in personal debt. He holds this to be one of the first develop-

(Continued on Page 12, Column 7)

14 BALL FANS DIE IN BLAZING SING SING BUS

25 Hurt As Car Plunges Over Embankment And Gas Tank Explodes

FLAMES SPREAD TO LUMBER YARD

Songs Change To Screams As Wreck Brings Tragic End To Gay Outing

[*By the Associated Press*]

Ossining, N. Y., July 22—Fourteen Brooklyn men and women were burned to death and twenty-five were injured today when a bus carrying them to a Sing Sing Prison baseball game plunged down a twenty-five-foot embankment and trapped them in a sheath of flame.

Screaming passengers, their clothing ablaze, fought their way out of broken windows after the gas tank exploded, igniting the bus and a large lumber yard into which it had toppled.

Flames Force Rescuers Back

Some were frantically hauled to safety by onlookers but the flames engulfed the bus so rapidly that rescuers were forced back.

Twelve bodies, all burned beyond recognition, were taken to morgues as soon as the wreckage cooled. Another woman died in Ossining Hospital of burns.

The identified dead:

MRS. ROSE THOMPSON, 40, of 9 Woodbine street, Brooklyn.
MRS. WILLIAM HAYES, 27 Cornelius street, Brooklyn.
JOHN MCNICHOLS, 413 Irving avenue, Brooklyn.

Death Toll May Be Heavier

The possibility that the death list might be increased with the discovery of additional bodies in the ruins was considered by Medical Examiner Amos O. Squier.

Reports came to him that Kate, Bernadotte and Joseph McDonald—all in their 'teens—were missing. He said that on the basis of estimates of the number of passengers the number of missing might reach six.

The bus, last in a procession of seven carrying a gay party of Young Democratic League members and their friends, picked the wrong road as it entered Ossining.

Instead of turning left, it went straight ahead down a steep hill. Apparently the driver tried to slow down, the medical examiner said after an examination of the tranmission.

Witnesses, however, testified the bus continued at a good speed.

Songs Change To Screams

With its passengers singing and laughing, it sped up a long ramp over the New York Central Railroad tracks. At a sudden right turn the heavily laden vehicle swerved and crashed through a rail fence.

Four passengers, sensing disaster, jumped through the windows just before the bus hurtled down the sheer drop.

The songs changed to screams as the vehicle landed right side up in the midst of piles of lumber. There was a sharp report and flaming gasoline spurted up.

Bus Enveloped In Flames

Before the panic-stricken men and women could climb from their seats the entire bus was in flames. The first few to escape ran to the Hudson river

(Continued on Page 3, Column 2)

Adolf Hitler Enjoys 'Parsifal,' First Of Wagner Performances

Chancellor And Goebbels Cheered By Crowds Upon Attending Festival—Strauss Conducts Before Distinguished Audience

[*By the Associated Press*]

Bayreuth, Germany, July 22—Chancellor Adolf Hitler, accompanied by Propaganda Minister Joseph Goebbels, both in civilian evening dress, were the cynosure of all eyes tonight at the opening of the annual Wagner festival.

It had been announced the Chancellor would attend one or more of the performances, but the date had not been set. He chose the first of six presentations of "Parsifal," with Richard Strauss conducting.

The beaming Chancellor occupied a private box. Frau Winifred Wagner, daughter-in-law of the famous composer, who supervised the festival, was there, amid a multitude of ardent Wagnerites. Her name has been connected in speculation as to the future of the bachelor Chancellor. The two Government leaders were cheered by the distinguished audience and again by a Bavarian crowd outside when during an interval in the performance they appeared at a window. Hitler generously applauded the performance and appeared to enjoy himself thoroughly.

Among the notables present were Prince August Wilhelm, son of the ex-Kaiser; Grand Duke Hesse of Prussia, the Duke of Coburg and Hjalmar Schacht, president of the Reichsbank.

The Sunday presentation of "Parsifal" will be followed by four performances of the Meistersing and three of the Nebelungen series, in all twenty-two performances before August 23.

Dead Outlaw---Nemesis

JOHN DILLINGER

MELVIN H. PURVIS

ONE DIES, 3 FLEE IN PRISON BREAK

Two Other Convicts' And Guard Wounded In Gun Battle

PAL OF BARROW FREE

Raymond Hamilton One Of Trio To Escape In Autos Of Friends Waiting Outside

[*By the Associated Press*]

Huntsville, Texas, July 22—The three most desperate killers in the Southwest—Raymond Hamilton, Blackie Thompson and Joe Palmer—escaped from the death house of the State Penitentiary here today in a daring break in which one convict was killed, two others were wounded and a guard was shot.

The three convicts who were shot, all bank bandits and life-termers, were mowed down by the gunfire of guards as Hamilton, Thompson and Palmer scampered over the wall to two waiting automobiles.

Killed By Guards' Shots

Whitey Walker was killed by the shots of guards whom the convicts engaged in battle. Charlie Frazier, the man who engineered the break, was shot from the ladder with which he was scaling the wall and was believed to be fatally wounded. Roy Johnson, the third bank robber, was shot and less seriously hurt.

H. E. George, the guard was momentarily stunned as a bullet creased his scalp. He was not seriously hurt.

The break occurred while the prison yard was almost deserted. All officials and guards not actually on duty, and practically all convicts were attending a ball game between the prison team and a Conroe team at the athletic field beside the walls.

Unparalleled In Daring

The escape was the first ever made from the death house, which is located in the center of the prison. In daring and cool execution, the break has no parallel in the annals of the penitentiary.

At 4.30 P. M. Lee Braswell, inside guard, approached the death house to feed the five inmates. Inside guards are not permitted to carry weapons, as they come closely into contact with the convicts, and it would be possible for the latter on occasion to overpower and disarm them.

As Braswell approached the door, Frazier, crouched against the wall, stepped forward and thrust the muzzle of a .45-caliber revolver against his ribs. In his other hand the convict held another pistol.

Locked In Hamilton's Cell

Frazier marched Braswell into the death house and compelled him to unlock the cells in which Palmer, Hamilton and Thompson were incarcerated. These convicted murderers came out, and Frazier handed Hamilton his extra gun. Braswell was locked in Hamilton's cell.

The quartet of desperadoes sped from the death house and were joined at the door by Walker and Johnson. A few feet from the death house they encountered W. T. McConnell, also an unarmed inside guard, and compelled him to go with them to the back wall

(Continued on Page 2, Column 6)

DILLINGER EXPLOITS WORST OF DECADE

Death Marks Journey's End Of Most Dangerous Of All Desperadoes

MADE JEST OF JUSTICE

Outlaw Leader And His Uhlans Escaped Jails And Robbed With Impunity

[*By the Associated Press*]

Chicago July 22—The death of swashbuckling John Dillinger today marked the journey's end for the most dangerous desperado of the decade.

The machine-gunning outlaw and his pals ranged the country for months, raiding banks, looting police station arsenals, clashing with officers, vanishing and reappearing like so many modern headless horsemen.

Escapades of the head man and his henchmen crowded police annals. Dillinger bullied his way from the Crown Point (Ind.) jail; drove through an elaborate official ambush in Chicago; shot his way out of a Federal trap in St. Paul; mocked the largest army the law ever assembled in the Middle West. With his aides he was captured under dramatic circumstances in Tucson, Ariz., only to take to the crime trail again and blast to freedom through a ring of Government operatives at the Little Bohemia Lodge in Wisconsin.

Name Was Byword

The report, "Dillinger Sighted," was bulletined from coast to coast. His name was bruited in the Senate chamber and mouthed on the stage. He was the subject of endless editorials, an object lesson to law enforcement officials, a factor in politics. Humorists found in him a fruitful source of gags, and some civic authorities the cause of chagrin.

On May 23, 1933, he was paroled from the Indiana State Prison at Michigan City. He was virtually unknown—a leering man of 31 with a hatred for law engendered during his nine years of incarceration. A year

(Continued on Page 2, Column 2)

INDIANA OUTLAW FELLED BY HAIL OF LEAD AS HE LEAVES CHICAGO THEATER

Squad Of Justice Marksmen, Lying In Wait For More Than Two Hours, Opens Fire When Fugitive Draws Gun, Officials Say

SHOOTING ENDS GREATEST MANHUNT OF RECENT YEARS

Desperado's Last Stand Witnessed By Throng Of Spectators—Two Women Passers-By Wounded Slightly By Stray Bullets

[*By the Associated Press*]

Chicago, July 22—John Dillinger, arch criminal of the age, was shot to death tonight by a group of Department of Justice operatives as he walked out of a Chicago movie theater.

He whipped an automatic revolver out of his pocket and had it half raised when the operatives loosed a withering blast of revolver fire that dropped him mortally wounded. He died a few minutes later.

RUNS INTO CORDON OF OFFICERS

Fifteen operatives had surrounded the theater, after information had reached Melvin H. Purvis, Chicago agent for the Department of Justice, that Dillinger would attend the theater. Not a word was spoken as the outlaw ran into the cordon of officers.

Dillinger knew what was coming. He gave a hunted look, reached quickly into his pocket and the guns roared.

The end of the greatest man hunt in contemporary criminal annals came in the swift tempo in which the notorious outlaw had lived.

LIE IN WAIT FOR TWO HOURS

The Federal men watched him buy his ticket, and then for more than two hours, "the longest two hours I ever spent," Purvis said, kept the theater surrounded.

"It was late yesterday when I received undercover information that Dillinger would attend the movie, 'Manhattan Melodrama,' at the Biograph Theater," Purvis said. "I hurriedly made arrangements to surround the theater with picked men from among my investigators. They were armed only with pistols. No shotguns or machine guns were issued, for I wished no general firing that might endanger passers-by.

AGENTS STATIONED IN DOORWAYS

"I stationed myself in my own automobile, parked two doors south of the theater, on the same side of the street and facing north. My men were stationed in doorways about the theater.

"It was shortly before 9 o'clock when I first noticed Dillinger. He had passed my car before I saw him, but I have studied every available photograph of him so carefully that I recognized the back of his head immediately.

"As he bought a ticket I got profile and front views of him, and I knew I was not mistaken. Those two hours that he spent in the theater—two hours and four minutes, to be exact—were the longest I ever spent.

GIVES PREARRANGED SIGNAL

"By the time he left the show our plans were complete, and my men were covering the neighborhood about the show so thoroughly that a cat couldn't have gotten through.

"When Dillinger left the show he started south, and again passed my car without noticing me. As soon as he had gotten a step past my car I thrust my right arm out of the car, dropped my hand and closed it, the prearranged signal for closing in. Instantly my men appeared from all sides.

DRAWS GUN AS HE RUNS

"Dillinger gave one hunted look about him and attempted to run up an alley, where several of my men were waiting. As he ran he drew an automatic pistol from his pocket, although I have always been told that he carried his weapons in his waistband.

"As his hand came up with the gun in it several shots were fired by my men before he could fire. He dropped, fatally wounded. I had hoped to take him alive, but I was afraid that he would resist to the last.

SCAR REMOVED WITHOUT TRACE

"I was surprised to notice that the scar on the left side of his face had been removed without a trace, a nice piece of plastic surgery. It was one of the identification marks that I had impressed on my men.

"I'm glad it's over."

The theater faces on Lincoln avenue, on Chicago's North-

THE WEATHER

Overcast, with probably occasional rain tonight and Friday; little change in temperature.
[Detailed report on Page 21]

THE EVENING SUN

6 STAR ★★★★★★ Wall Street Close

Vol. 54 — Paid Circulation November: Morning 144,371 Evening 152,703 297,074 — Sunday 207,267 — BALTIMORE, THURSDAY, DECEMBER 10, 1936 — Entered as second-class matter at Baltimore Postoffice — 52 Pages — 2 Cents

King Abdicates For Mrs. Simpson, Baldwin Reveals Whole Story Of Two-Month Secret Struggle

PRIME MINISTER DESCRIBES HIS TASK AS "REPUGNANT"; YORK TO RULE AS GEORGE VI

Monarch's Decision Called Final And Irrevocable. Premier Tells Of Stressing Danger Of American's Divorce Case

CORONATION DATE STANDS; EDWARD LOSES EVERY TITLE; SPECIAL ONE TO BE CREATED

Dunkirk, France, Dec. 10 (AP)—The chief of special police of the port of Dunkirk said tonight he had received orders to station extra guards at the water front in preparation for the possible arrival of Edward.

[By the Associated Press]

London, Dec. 10—King Edward of England abdicated his ancient, mighty throne today.

He will marry Wallis Warfield Simpson as man, not monarch.

Albert Frederick Arthur George, the tall, 40-year-old Duke of York, will rule over the 495,000,000 subjects of the greatest Empire on earth.

He will reign as George VI.

In "a message from his Majesty the King, signed by his own hand," Capt. Edward Algernon Fitzroy, Speaker of the House of Commons, announced the abdication to a House in which tension and hysteria were breathing, living things.

"My Final And Irrevocable Decision"

Around the globe, to all who bear allegiance to England's King, flashed this message from their sovereign:

"After long and anxious consideration, I have determined [to re]nounce the throne to which I succeeded on the death of my father, and I now am communicating this, my final and irrevocable decision."

In that epochal moment of eight centuries, the Commons, the people and the Empire saw their Government victorious in a tremendous constitutional struggle with a monarch who has reigned for less than a year.

Rather than give up the twice-divorced American woman who waited today in a villa at Cannes, France, balked by state and church in his desire for morganatic marriage, Edward VIII signed the decree of abdication today.

Brothers Witness His Abdication

The actual abdication papers, it was learned, were signed at Fort Belvedere at 10 A. M. today.

As the signatures were affixed, the flag of the Duchy of Cornwall, which had been flying over the estate since the crisis began, was lowered on its staff. Then it was raised—an indication, some thought, that the King might retain the title, Duke of Cornwall.

York, his heir, and his other two brothers, the Dukes of Gloucester and Kent, witnessed the historic deed. And the swift machinery to make a new King began throbbing in London and throughout the empire, while the King, through Baldwin, told the Parliament assembled:

"I can only hope that I shall have the understanding of my peoples." . . .

A report received by the Exchange Telegraph Agency said Edward intends to leave the country, probably tomorrow night. There was no indication where he would meet Mrs. Simpson or when they would marry.

Not Allowed To Stay In Empire

No law exists covering the situation, but it generally was considered true that Edward may not stay in Great Britain or any Dominion of the empire.

The passage of time may change that situation, if the Government becomes convinced his return would not be embarrassing politically. Many thought he would return to England within a few years and live the quiet life of a country gentleman—a life he so greatly prefers to the duties of state.

If Edward does go to the Continent, his friends said, he undoubtedly will meet Mrs. Simpson at an early date.

Hopes For York's Speedy Accession

Black-clad and somber, Stanley Baldwin, the Prime Minister, moved immediate consideration of the abdication by Parliament. That was the King's own wish, for his message said:

"I am most anxious that there should be no delay of any kind in giving effect to the instrument which I have executed, and that all necessary steps should be taken immediately to secure that my lawful successor, my brother, his Royal Highness the Duke of York, should ascend the throne."

In the deep, breathless hush, Baldwin then pleaded for an understanding of his part in the most "repugnant task ever imposed on a Prime Minister," and told the story of the momentous weeks of struggle between King and Prime Minister.

Parliament To Remain In Session

Parliament will remain in session, it was indicated, until all the necessary steps are taken for the abdication of one King and the making of another.

The members of Parliament are expected to take their new oath of allegiance on Monday.

A bill to make the abdication law is ready for introduction, here and in the Dominions.

Coronation Date Stands; Edward Loses Every Title

Unofficially, it was stated there would be no alteration in coronation plans or the May 12 date.

By abdication, Edward relinquished all his many titles, but it was expected that a special dukedom would be created for him.

Whether he will await April 27—the date Mrs. Simpson's decree of divorce from Ernest Aldrich Simpson becomes final—to marry her was not known. Many, however, thought such a delay likely. There has been no move, as yet, to accelerate the time of the decree's finality, which may be accomplished only with the assent of the trial court and the King's Proctor.

The new King's reign will begin after this act is finally passed and signed, whereupon the lords, the Privy Council, the High Commissioners of the Dominions and India, the Lord Major and the Aldermen will gather to approve proclamation of the new sovereign.

Steps in the accession of the new King will be swift after the proclamation of accession, to be read Saturday to the court at St. James's Palace.

Proclamation To Be Read

Following the accession council, the proclamation of the new King will be read at Friary Court in the Palace by officers at arms, garbed in their medieval tabards.

Trumpets will sound a double fanfare as the garter principal king of arms intones the proclamation.

Afterward a procession, formed by the king of arms, heralds, pursuivants and other ancient officials, their prerogatives established by precedent old and obscured, will move through London streets to the law courts, to the Royal Exchange in the heart of the City, proclaiming a new monarch for the second time within the year.

After Speaker Fitzroy had finished the King's message, Baldwin said:

"I have to move that his Majesty's most gracious message be now considered.

"No more grave message has ever been received by Parliament and no more difficult and I might almost say more repugnant task has ever been imposed upon the Prime Minister.

"I will ask the House, which I know will not be without sympathy for me, now to remember that in this last week I have had little time in which to compose a speech for delivery today.

"And so I must tell what I have to tell, truthfully, sincerely

[Continued On Page 2, Column 1]

He said:

DAVID WINDSOR

After long and anxious consideration, I have determined to renounce the throne to which I succeeded on the death of my father, and I am now communicating this, my final and irrevocable decision.

Realizing as I do the gravity of this step, I can only hope that I shall have the understanding of my peoples in the decision I have taken and the reasons which have led me to take it.

I will not enter now into my private feeling, but I would beg that it should be remembered that the burden which constantly rests upon the shoulders of a sovereign is so heavy that it can only be borne in circumstances different from those in which I now find myself.

I conceive that I am not overlooking the duty that rests on me to place in the forefront public interest, when I declare that I am conscious that I can no longer discharge this heavy task with efficiency or with satisfaction to myself. I have accordingly this morning executed an instrument of abdication in the terms following:

"I, Edward VIII, of Great Britain, Ireland and the British Dominions beyond the Seas, King and Emperor of India, do hereby declare my irrevocable determination to renounce the throne for myself and for my descendants and my desire that effect should be given to this instrument of abdication immediately. In token whereof I have hereunto set my hand this tenth day of December, 1936, in the presence of the witnesses whose signatures are subscribed."

I deeply appreciate the spirit which has actuated the appeals which have been made to me to take a different decision and I have before reaching my final determination most fully pondered over them.

But my mind is made up. Moreover, further delay cannot but be most injurious to the peoples whom I have tried to serve as Prince of Wales and as King and whose future happiness and prosperity are the constant wish of my heart.

I take my leave of them in the confident hope that the course which I have thought it right to follow is that which is best for the stability of the throne and empire and happiness of my people.

I am deeply sensible of the consideration which they have always extended to me both before and after my accession to the throne and which I know they will extend in full measure to my successor.

I am most anxious that there should be no delay of any kind in giving effect to the instrument which I have executed and that all necessary steps should be taken immediately to secure that my lawful successor, my brother, his Royal Highness the Duke of York, should ascend to the throne.

She said: (*through Lord Brownlow*)

WALLIS SIMPSON

LORD BROWNLOW

There is not the remotest possibility that King Edward will join Mrs. Simpson at Lou Viei villa either now or later. Not only is the King not coming to the villa, but he is not coming to the Riviera. What his definite plans are we do not know, but we do know that much.

There are no changes so far as Mrs. Simpson's plans are concerned. She plans to stay here at least until after Christmas.

Concerning the abdication of King Edward, Mrs. Simpson has no statement. There is no statement; there will be no statement.

The Lawful Heir

GEORGE, DUKE OF YORK

THE WEATHER

Mostly clear tonight and Saturday, with little change in temperature.

Detailed Report on Page 12

THE EVENING SUN

6 STAR ★★★★★★ Wall Street Close

Vol. 55 | PAID CIRCULATION APRIL MORNING, 143,276 EVENING, 157,921 301,197 || SUNDAY 211,754 | BALTIMORE, FRIDAY, MAY 7, 1937 | Entered as second class matter at Baltimore Postoffice | 60 Pages | 2 Cents

30 KILLED; CAPTAIN MAY DIE; SURVIVORS TELL OF ESCAPES

WIREPHOTO—*Hindenburg Survivor Runs For Life Out Of Flaming Wreck*

LAKEHURST, N. J.—This picture, one of the most dramatic to come out of the explosion and crash of the giant Zeppelin Hindenburg, shows a survivor (lower right) racing from the blazing mass of twisted girders to save his life. In the left foreground are rescuers, held back by the intense heat of the blazing German luxury airliner.

THROWS SONS OUT WINDOW TO SAVE THEM

Mexico City Woman Relates Own Story Of Zeppelin Crash

DAUGHTER DIES LATER IN HOSPITAL

One Slides Down Rope To Safety; Man Shuts Eyes And Leaps

[By the Associated Press]

Lakehurst, N. J., May 7—A skeleton of charred and twisted metal was all that remained of the silver sky liner Hindenburg today in the wake of an explosion that sent the transatlantic giant plunging to earth at 6.23 o'clock last night.

Thirty persons were known dead or missing.

Of the ninety-seven passengers and members of the crew aboard when the greatest of all airships exploded, burst into flames and crashed to earth last night—just as it was lowering to the mooring mast and only 200 feet above the ground—sixty-eight persons survived.

Spectator Killed

One of those killed was a spectator, burned to death in the falling, fiery debris.

Dozens of the survivors, catapulted or stumbling dazedly from the holocaust, hovered between life and death today in hospitals nearby the scene of the disaster.

Capt. Max Pruss, commander of the Hindenburg, was reported by the Ocean county coroner today to be in a "critical condition" at Paul Kimball Hospital.

The coroner, Dr. Raymond Taylor, said the condition of Capt. Ernst A. Lehmann, whom Pruss succeeded as commander, was also serious and he "was not out of the woods yet."

Girl Dies In Hospital

Miss Irene Doehner, 16, who was burned in the disaster, died today at Beach Borough's Hospital, Point Pleasant.

The daughter of Mr. and Mrs. Hermann Doehner, a prominent Mexico City family, Miss Doehner made the trip with her parents and two brothers. Her mother and brothers survived the disaster and are now in the hospital where she died. Her father is among the missing. Besides her burns, Miss Doehner suffered several fractures.

One of two bodies found in the wreckage was that of a small woman. It was taken from the ruins of the control cabin.

Members of the crew suggested she might have been the stewardess, a Mrs. Imhoff. They said she normally should not have been in the cabin, however, especially when the ship was coming to land.

A woman who slid an estimated thirty feet down a rope from the blazing ship was identified today as Mrs. Elsa Frost, who was placed in an oxygen tent at a hospital.

Threw Sons Out Window

Mrs. Doehner told Point Pleasant Hospital aides that she and two sons were in the dining room when the first blast occurred. She threw her sons out of the window and then, with the ship six feet off the ground, jumped herself. Her daughter died later, and her husband was not reported in the family survival list.

"I landed on my stomach and crawled 30 or 40 yards to escape the flames," Philip Mangone of New York said in Paul Kimball hospital.

Shut Eyes And Jumped

Alfred Groezinger, 20-year-old chef on the Hindenburg, shut his eyes and leaped just before the great ship sank to earth, a blazing wreck.

"I jumped," he kept repeating dazedly, in German, when he was placed on a hospital bed. "I jumped—and I'm alive!"

A cheerful, sandy-haired youth with freckles Groezinger sat up in bed

[Continued On Page 12, Column 2]

MRS. SIMPSON TAKES DUKE ON VINEYARD TOUR

Couple Taste Wines Of Vouvray District And Lunch At Inn

Competition

London, May 7 (AP)—The Hindenburg disaster had to share the front pages of London's afternoon newspapers today with pictures of "the world's happiest couple"—Edward of Windsor and Wallis Warfield Simpson.

Pictures of the beaming couple in several newspapers were only slightly smaller than wired pictures of the flaming dirigible.

News of the coronation of King George VI next Wednesday and the strike of 25,500 busmen was buried inside.

[By the Associated Press]

Monts, France, May 7—Wallis Warfield Simpson guided the Duke of Windsor on a wine-tasting excursion in the famous Vouvray wine district today.

Deserting the Chateau de Cande together for the first time since their reunion, the couple explored the wine cellars of several castles on a short trip through the verdant countryside.

They lunched on chicken, lobster *a la bretagne* and old Vouvray wine at a little inn in the village of Semblancay. The proprietor said Mrs.

[Continued On Page 22, Column 1]

Wirephoto Makes History

Today, for the first time in history, it is possible to tell in pictures the complete story of a great disaster step by step, from beginning to end.

Turn to the next page of *The Evening Sun.* In 4 successive pages, WIREPHOTO tells the story of the arrival of the Hindenburg at Lakehurst, the first explosion, the fall of the flaming ship, the flight of the ground crew as the burning wreck plunges toward it, the rescue efforts and the debris, and on Page 30 the aftermath—rescuers and rescued.

On The Inside Today

Death notices and late classified advertising will be found on Page 12.

Weather report on Page 12.

General News on Page 12.

Race results and entries on Page 41

HAD HIS CAMERA ALL POISED FOR ZEPPELIN BLAST

Photographer's Finger Was On The Trigger As Crash Came

By Murray Becker

Associated Press Photographer

Lakehurst, N. J., May 7 (AP)—I have been a news photographer for years, covering major events, but never in my life have I had such a tragic and spectacular picture as the destruction of the Hindenburg appear before my eyes.

I had taken several "shots" as the Hindenburg approached the landing field and had backed away for a general view when the first explosion occurred.

I had my camera up to the eye level when the ship burst into flames. Like a hunter, I had my sights on the target and my finger on the trigger. I shot the picture showing the first puff of flames.

Changing my plates, I got a second picture of the airship striking the ground with the flames shooting the length of the ship, and then started running for it.

It is hard to explain my feelings. I was in a daze and yet I was trying to get all the pictures possible in the least time. One of them was of a man half-naked, his clothes burned from him, stumbling from the ship.

ECKENER HINTS AT SABOTAGE IN AIRSHIP CRASH

Says He Hopes It Isn't A Factor But Tells Of Receiving Threats

[By the Associated Press]

Vienna, May 7—Dr. Hugo Eckener said today the possibility of sabotage must be considered in investigation of disaster to the Hindenburg, which he designed, but that he considered such explanation most unlikely.

"Mind, I did not say sabotage was responsible, but that it must be considered as a possibility, especially in view of many threatening letters received by our firm," he asserted upon his arrival from Graz, Austria.

"We have received several anonymous warnings of possible efforts to damage the ship," the doctor added. "One mysterious warning told us not to attempt landing in America. Every precaution was taken but the only rational conclusion was that the veiled threat came from cranks."

Finds Some Comfort

"In this unhappy moment I find some comfort in the thought that a natural and explainable cause brought about destruction of the ship to which I contributed a lifetime of study, work and love."

He turned to the future.

"I will go ahead with construction of

[Continued On Page 6 Column 1]

Experts Theorize On Cause Of Crash

Eckener Blames 'Spark' From Three Sources—Lehmann Dumbfounded—Thunder Storm And Landing Rope Cited By Others

[By the Associated Press]

What caused the crash of the Hindenburg?

Dr. Hugo Eckener, the airship's designer—"I should say that if this disaster was caused by sabotage, only the firing of a burning bullet into the bags could have accomplished it. That seems highly unlikely."

Dr. Eckener, in Austria, outlined three possible causes.

1. When the ship is lowered, some hydrogen usually is released. This free hydrogen in the air might have been sufficiently concentrated to be ignited by lightning or by a spark. It would not necessarily have to be a great flash of lightning; perhaps it wasn't even seen by observers.

Current From Earth?

2. When landing, the water ballast is released from the tanks. A stream of water, connecting with the earth, might have served as an electrical conductor to bring a spark up from the ground. It is possible that an electric charge, so to speak, stabbed the Hindenburg from the earth.

3. Someone aboard may have made a fire, a spark possibly from a cigarette lighter. I regard this also as unlikely, for the conduct of the passengers and crew is watched carefully."

[*Smoking on the Hindenburg was allowed only in a spark-proof compartment.*]

Capt. Ernst Lehmann, its commander: "I don't know what happened. She just went up."

Gill Robb Wilson, New Jersey State aviation director: "Something strange caused that tragedy."

Capt. Frank McCarthy, once commander of the Shenandoah, which crashed twelve years ago: "It is more reasonable to assume that a flame from one of the Diesel engines ignited the hydrogen."

James C. Mars, American pioneer in lighter-than-air craft: "Static electricity. The hydrogen gas bag would have gathered static in the electrical storm, and one of its landing ropes touching the wet ground could complete the circuit."

F. W. von Meister, vice-president of the American Zeppelin Transport Company: "The rain may have caused a spark of static electricity when the landing ropes were dropped. Or there may have been a spark from one of the engines."

Other experts said airplanes frequently pick up electrical charges while flying in thunderstorms; that this very fact eliminates most of the danger of an airplane being struck by lightning, since it carries relatively the same charge as the surrounding clouds. Passengers inside an airplane flying under such conditions have no sensation of the phenomenon whatever.

WEATHER FORECAST
Generally fair and slightly cooler today; cloudy tomorrow; showers in afternoon or night.
Yesterday's Temperatures: Max., 73; Min., 53.
(Details on Page 13)

THE SUN

LIGHT FOR ALL
Registered United States Patent Office

Paris Traffic, Pedestrians And Canines, By
Thomas W. Wilson—Page 11

Vol. 201—D. | PAID CIRCULATION APRIL MORNING, 143,276 EVENING, 157,921 301,197 || SUNDAY 211,754 | BALTIMORE, MONDAY, MAY 17, 1937 | Entered as second-class matter at Baltimore Postoffice. Copyright, 1937, by The A. S. Abell Company, Publishers of The Sun. | 20 Pages | 2 Cents

NICE CHOOSES LAWSON FOR COMMISSIONER OF POLICE; DEFENDS PICK

PREMIER FAILS IN EFFORT TO FORM CABINET

Largo Caballero Quits Because Of Communist Opposition

INSISTED ON KEEPING WAR MINISTRY POST

Rebels Gain Half-Mile After Basque Attack Near Bilbao

[By the Associated Press]

Valencia, Spain, May 16—Francisco Largo Caballero tonight refused to make further efforts to form a new Government to replace the Cabinet whose resignation he turned in yesterday.

His refusal, announced to President Manuel Azana, who had commissioned the stern, gray-haired leader to form a "Win-the-War" Ministry, was based on strong opposition to his proposals on the makeup of the new Cabinet.

A stalemate was reached largely because of the veteran's insistence on retaining the War Ministry portfolio with the Premiership.

Communists Are Opposed

This plan met the determined opposition of the Communists who announced they were intent on reorganization of the war machine for an intensive drive to victory against Gen. Francisco Franco's Insurgents.

It was believed President Azana would select one of four persons to attempt to form a Cabinet—Julio Alvarez del Vayo, Minister of Foreign Affairs in the last Ministry; Indalecio Prieto, Minister of Marine and Air; Dr. Juan Negrin, Minister of Finance; or Julian Besteiro, former Minister to the Hague and president of the Constituent Assembly.

The Communists were supported in their opposition to Largo Caballero's proposals by Socialists who refused to join any government in which there were no Communists, and by the Left Republicans who backed the Communists' demands for a stronger war policy.

Syndicalists Denounce Plan

On the other hand, the C. N. T. (Confederacion Nacional del Trabajo, a syndicalist organization of workers) denounced the Premier Designate's plan to reduce the number of anarchist seats in the Cabinet from four to two.

The C. N. T. also charged Largo Caballero's proposed ministry gave the Socialists too strong an economic grip on Spain through the ministries accorded them.

Under his plan, the U. G. T.—Socialist - Communist - Labor party, with which he is affiliated—would have held the Premiership and the important portfolios of public defense, interior and foreign affairs.

The C. N. T. would have been represented by Ministers of Justice and Health.

Supported By Republicans

Largo Caballero was supported also by the Union Republicans.

His chances for success in forming his third Cabinet of the civil war diminished through the day as the Communists stood steadfastly behind the conditions they had outlined for participation in the Government.

These included separation of the War Ministry from the Premiership, reorganization of the general staff and the initiation of "a consistent war policy."

The Communist and Socialist executive council after a meeting tonight told Largo Caballero their attitude remained unchanged and he quickly informed President Azana by telephone he was compelled to abandon his effort to form a Government.

Country Remains Calm

Despite the difficulty encountered in settling the discords among factors in the People's Front Government, the country outside the war zone was calm.

The C. N. T., in a statement, accused the Communists of causing the governmental crisis and formally announced its rejection of the Premier Designate's plan of reducing the number of C. N. T. Ministers.

While political leaders strove to achieve order out of the welter of conflicting party demands, Sunday crowds surged through the sunshine to view the destruction wrought by Insurgent air raiders at nightfall yesterday.

The number of dead in that raid—most destructive yet suffered by the temporary capital—rose to thirty-eight as victims in hospitals died. Among them was the cook of the British Embassy, Justine Garcia. Sixty-six were listed as wounded.

City Regains Calm

Seven Insurgent bombers swooped down on the city last night just as dusk fell. One bomb fell in front of the British Embassy, wounding a doorman in addition to Garcia. Another fell in front of the Ministry of Marine and Air.

Valencia was calm today. Socialist and Communist leaders appealed to

(Continued on Page 11, Column 2)

1837---1937

One hundred years ago this morning, Arunah S. Abell published the first issue of *The Sun*. Since that day, this newspaper has met varying fortunes and, with the rest of the community, has enjoyed and endured a variety of experiences. During all this time of war and peace, prosperity and depression *The Sun's* successes and failures, its championship of truth or consortings with error, have been weighed and judged by successive generations of Maryland people. To that continuing jury *The Sun* cheerfully submits, confident that during the next hundred years its critics will be as generous as they have been over the century just ended.

KING MAY DECIDE ON WALLIS' TITLE

Court Circles Report "H. R. H." Dispute Must Be Settled By George Himself

Paper Says Ruler Will Announce Duke's Engagement To Mrs. Warfield

[By the Associated Press]

London, May 16—King George VI, his coronation just over, today found reason for the uneasy rest of crowned heads in the vexing problem of his prospective sister-in-law, Baltimore-born, twice-divorced Wallis Warfield.

In quarters close to the court it was generally held the King himself must settle the question of whether the bride-to-be of the former King Edward is to be fortified with the rank of "Her Royal Highness" when she and Edward return to move in semi-hostile London court and society circles.

The *Sunday Referee* predicted the King himself will announce the engagement of the Duke of Windsor and Mrs. Warfield, but even that will not settle the question of her rank.

Announcement Tomorrow

With the Duke's wedding plans to be announced Tuesday, it was believed King George's decision would be forthcoming this week.

In London this controversy takes rank as a crisis only behind that of last December, which led to the abdication of King Edward.

It was generally agreed Prime Minister Stanley Baldwin was leading the opposition to bestowing the "H. R. H." and that he had the backing of strong church and court circles. On the other hand the strong-willed Edward, Duke of Windsor, was equally insistent that his royal but younger brother do the handsome thing by his duchess-to-be.

The *Sunday Referee*—whose startling predictions have not always come true—said:

"The King this week will announce the engagement. It will be the royal family's first public recognition of the Duke's association with Mrs. Warfield.

In Government Organ

"The Duke has asked the King if he will make an announcement. The King has agreed and it will appear in the London *Gazette*, the Government's official organ, probably on Thursday.

"There are several ways of making such an announcement, and the likely form is:

"'The King learns with pleasure of the betrothal of his brother to . . .'"

The *Referee* said the Duke of Kent, the Duke's youngest brother, will be best man at the wedding, and that the Princess Royal, Edward's sister Mary, countess of Harewood, also will

(Continued on Page 3, Column 4)

MAJOR BATTLE IMPENDING ON SUGAR QUOTAS

Domestic Producers Will Try To Break Down Import Allotment Plan

ACT PASSED IN 1924 EXPIRES THIS YEAR

Cuban Interests Are Being Supported By Administration

By J. FRED ESSARY

Washington, May 16—A battle over sugar as desperate as any of the score or more that have raged in Congress during the fifty years that this product has been an issue, is just ahead.

It will involve first, an effort on the part of domestic producers—cane and beet—to break down the quota system set up in an Administration bill, in order that home growers may have a larger slice of the business.

And it will involve next, a campaign on the part of American refiners to reduce, or perhaps wipe out entirely, the importation of refined sugar from offshore regions, particularly from Cuba.

Two Lobbies Organized

Two powerful lobbies have been organized to defeat or to defend the Administration bill. On one side are the domestic interests which are working through a number of well-financed and highly experienced organizations.

These interests start out with an initial advantage of about 140 members of Congress from sugar-producing States, ready to throw themselves in the way of the Administration's program.

On the other side, are the Cuban sugar interests, equally well-financed and experienced, with a counter advantage of the Secretary of State, Secretary of Interior and Secretary of Agriculture in league with them and in effect making their fight.

Administration Backs Cuba

The Administration has made the Cuban fight its own chiefly to give fuller effect to the reciprocal trade policy which blossomed most successfully in the agreement reached with the Cubans more than two years ago.

To keep that agreement in operation as Cordell Hull, Secretary of State, argues, is not merely a matter of good faith, but it is far more important to the country at large to keep trade channels open than it is to subsidize greater sugar production in the United States.

And in this, Mr. Hull finds both Henry A. Wallace, Secretary of Agriculture, looking at the matter from a domestic sugar standpoint, in agreement with him. The interest of Harold L. Ickes, Secretary of the Interior, is mainly that of protecting the sugar producers of those of our insular possessions which come under his supervision. They, too, are affected by the demands of the domestic growers.

1924 Act Aided Industry

The issue comes up at this time because the Jones-Costigan Act of 1924 will expire this year. That act sets up sugar quotas in an effort to alleviate widespread depressed conditions in the sugar industry.

This act did, in fact, bring relief to the industry both at home and abroad. Also it banned child labor in the beet fields and brought on a general increase in wages to all sugar workers. Cuban conditions improved along with those in this country.

Although when the AAA processing tax was declared unconstitutional and subsidies to sugar interests paid out of that tax went by the board, the quota system remained.

Urged Permanent Quotas

Some months ago the President in a special message urged that legislation be enacted which would provide that a permanent quota system be

(Continued on Page 16, Column 5)

Throngs Choke Streets Of London To View Coronation Decorations

In Place Of Usual Exodus Over Holiday Week-End, Residents Stay In Town While Country-folk Flock Into City

By PHILIP WAGNER
[London Bureau of The Sun]

London, May 16—Today London has seen greater crowds than on any day during the current jubiliations, probably excepting only coronation day itself.

The huge throngs which have choked the streets of this city all day are being likened to those on Armistice Day, 1918, but without the frantic character of the crowds on that historic occasion. Today they have been curiously sedate, almost gentle, and content merely to inch along the pavements and gape at the decorations and take a quiet satisfaction in being units of the swarm.

The size of the influx is partly explained by the fact it is Whitsuntide and tomorrow is a bank holiday. Normally, on a bank holiday week-end people leave London is great numbers for field, stream and the seashore, and the city gives the impression of being deserted. This time, though the railroads report some exodus, it quickly became evident that most of the population were staying in the city to see what would happen.

Their number was constantly swelled as the day wore on by the influx of people from the suburbs and the outer ring of London's satellite towns, bringing their children into town to see what they could not see earlier in the week.

On top of all this there has come an incursion of people from all parts of

(Continued on Page 3, Column 2)

Where Revolution Hit Little Kingdom Of Zog I

Revolutionists Saturday seized the town of Argyrokastro, near the Greek border, in what was called a civilian uprising.

TOWN IN ALBANIA SEIZED BY REBELS

Civil Authorities Made Captive By Revolutionists In Argyrokastro

Belgrade Hears Troops Have Been Sent Near Greek Border To Quell Rising

[By the Associated Press]

Tirana, Albania, May 16—A revolt at Argyrokastro, in southern Albania near the Greek border, created a tense situation here tonight as the Government moved to end the uprising, in which a gendarme officer was killed.

A brief official news agency dispatch said a group of civilians occupied the town and imprisoned civil authorities late Saturday.

They cut communication lines and staged a battle with police and gendarmes in which the officer was killed. Former Minister Efan Toto, a former gendarme officer, and a former army captain led the uprising, the dispatch said.

Argyrokastro also is called Gjinskastra.

Report Town Still Held

Belgrade, Yugoslavia, May 16 (AP)—Reports from the Albanian border tonight said revolutionaries remained in possession of Argyrokastro. Police, the reports said, were made prisoners.

The Tirana administration was said to have sent troops to the town. Most of Argyrokastro's inhabitants are Greek.

Italy Watches Developments

Rome, May 16 (AP)—Italy found particular interest in news of insurrection from Albania tonight because it came soon after a visit to King Zog, of Albania, by Count Galeazzo Ciano, Italian Foreign Minister.

Count Ciano assured King Zog late in April that Italy's recent treaty with Yugoslavia did not mean Italy's abandonment of her protection of Albania.

Independence Guaranteed

A 1930 census set Albania's population at 1,003,068. The country is bounded by Yugoslavia on the north and east, Greece on the south, and is separated from Italy on the west by the Ariatic Sea.

Albania's independence was assured under a treaty with Italy in 1920. Under its constitution the nation is a democratic, parliamentary independent monarchy. King Zog assumed the crown in 1928.

An Italo-Yugoslav exchange of letters guaranteeing the independence of Albania was one of the topics of conversations between Count Ciano and King Zog at Tirana in April. The exchange followed signing of a five-year Italo-Yugoslav pact.

Italian Influence Strong

Italian influence has been strong in Albania since 1935, when Premier Benito Mussolini and King Zog patched up differences.

Italians have played an important part in organization of the present Albanian Government. Important rights to participate in development of Albanian oil resources have been obtained by Italy.

For many years Albania has been largely supported by annual loans from Italy. Original agreement for these loans was made in 1931, partially suspended in 1933, and revived in 1935.

Says Roosevelt Favors Textile Wage Measure

House Labor Committee Head Announces Bill Will Provide $18 Minimum

Lawrence, Mass., May 16 (AP)—United States Representative William P. Connery, Jr., (Dem., Mass.), tonight declared the House Labor Committee, of which he is chairman, would report favorably "with Presidential approval" a bill which would provide an $18 minimum wage and thirty-five-hour week for the textile industry throughout the country.

Connery declared the committee would also report favorably "with Presidential approval" a bill which would provide minimum wages, maximum hours and no child labor for all industries throughout the United States.

He said he had discussed the measure with President Roosevelt before the President left for his recent vacation "and the President told me to go to it," he added.

COURT CHANGE FIGHT GROWS IN BITTERNESS

Opponents Of Bill Declared Strengthened By President's Stand

McGILL REPORTED IN HOSTILE GROUP

Kansas Senator Says He Is Not Ready To Announce His Position

By C. P. TRUSSELL
[Washington Bureau of The Sun]

Washington, May 16—The eve of another Supreme Court opinion day found the "no compromise" Congressional fight over the reorganization of that tribunal growing in bitterness as its first test vote came nearer.

Accompanying the speculation upon whether the court session tomorrow will produce a decision on another major New Deal program, Social Security, were reports that the President's determination to fight to the end for his original reorganization plan had strengthened, rather than weakened, the opposition forces.

Hears McGill Has Shifted

With ten of the eighteen members of the Senate Judiciary Committee committed openly against the Administration's six-justice program, word came from a usually authoritative source that one of the two uncommitted members of the committee—Senator McGill (Dem., Kan.)—would cast his lot with the opposition Tuesday when the long-anticipated vote is taken.

Asked about this tonight, Senator McGill replied:

"I haven't said anything."

Not Ready To Give Stand

Asked whether he was ready to announce his position, he answered:

"I am not. I cannot help what reports are going around."

Until today Senator McGill virtually had been conceded by opposition forces to the Administration group. Senator Hughes (Dem., Del.) is the other member of the committee who is listed as uncommitted.

Reports today also had it that Senator Bankhead (Dem., Ala.), might be found in the opposition ranks when the issue reached the Senate floor. Senator Bankhead is not a member of the Judiciary Committee.

Await Court Session Today

Anticipation of the Supreme Court session tomorrow was particularly keen in the Capitol tonight in view of the possibility that the opinions might again disclose a liberal majority on the day before the Senate committee votes. A decision upholding the old-age pension and unemployment provisions of the Social Security Act would have distinct repercussions at the Capitol, it was conceded.

Whether the court will rule on this statute tomorrow, however, was a question that only the justices themselves could answer. There will be at least two other opinion days before the close of the present court term.

Committee Procedure In Doubt

It had not been decided tonight whether the Senate Judiciary Committee would vote Tuesday upon the Administration's court reorganization bill only, or ballot also upon some or all of the twenty-five to thirty substitutes and amendments which have been offered.

Senator Wheeler (Dem., Mont.), leader of the Senate opposition, is pressing for a yes-or-no vote on the bill itself, with no attempt at compromise. However, he is not a member of the committee.

Compromise Believed Dead

Senator McCarran (Dem., Nev.), author of a substitute bill which would compromise on two additional justices and a member of the committee, has suggested a withdrawal of all compromises as "more in keeping with the attitude of the other side."

Until the non-compromise declaration came from the President, through

(Continued on Page 2, Column 5)

New Commissioner Of Police

"I deeply appreciate the confidence of the Governor in my ability to conduct the affairs of the Police Department of Baltimore. I am sensible of the responsibilities involved and will exert every effort, in the interest of the people, to keep the department on the highest plane possible." —WILLIAM PRICE LAWSON

CAPITAL DEBATES ABATTOIR ERECTION

Proposed Slaughter House Is Warmly Opposed By Many In District

Senator Tydings, However, Fights Bill Forbidding "Nuisance Industries"

[Washington Bureau of The Sun]

Washington, May 16—A new civic issue has arisen in Washington to overshadow, at least temporarily, the controversy over the proposed Jefferson Memorial and the removal of the cherry trees lining the tidal basin.

At perhaps the opposite extreme, esthetically, to cherry blossoms, the new issue centers about a slaughter house which a company hopes to open in the eastern part of the city, and which many citizens and several Government officials are vigorously opposing.

Committee Heads Sponsor Bill

For the past week the issue has been debated during hearings on a bill sponsored by Senator King (Dem., Utah) and Representative Mary T. Norton (Dem., N. J.), chairmen, respectively, of the Senate and House District of Columbia committees.

The bill is designed to restrict certain so-called "nuisance industries" in the District and thus to prevent the packing company from completing and opening its proposed plant.

Marylander Leads Opposition

Thus far the opponents of the bill have been led by Senator Tydings, of

(Continued on Page 16, Column 4)

Number Of Federal Employes Is Largest Since World War

Records Show 829,193 Civilians In Addition To Members Of Legislative And Judiciary Branches Are Drawing U. S. Pay

[By the Associated Press]

Washington, May 16—The Government's official family is larger than at any time since the World War.

Civil Service Commission statistics showed a total of 829,193 persons on Federal pay rolls April 1, in addition to the legislative, judicial and military branches of Government, which remain relatively constant. The figure includes both Civil Service and non-Civil Service officials and workers.

This classification stood at 917,760 on November 11, 1918, dropped to 515,772 on June 30, 1923, then began a ten-year gradual climb to 572,091 on June 30, 1933. It stood at 824,259 eleven months ago.

Available fiscal year totals of Federal executive Civil Service follows:

1920	691,116	1929	559,579
1921	562,252	1930	580,494
1922	527,517	1931	588,296
1923	515,772	1932	583,196
1924	521,641	1933	572,091
1925	532,798	1934	673,095
1926	528,542	1935	719,440
1927	527,258	1936	824,259
1928	540,867		

The April 1 total of 829,193 persons did not include the thousands of

(Continued on Page 2, Column 7)

SISTER, 6, SLAIN, BOY'S THROAT CUT

Lad, 4, And Dying Girl Crawl From Funeral Pyre In Long Island Thicket

"Joe Did It," Child Says At First Later, "Mommy Hit Me With Baseball Bat"

[By the Associated Press]

Brookhaven, N. Y., May 16—A 6-year-girl was slashed and bludgeoned to death today in a heavily wooded section near this Long Island village, and her 4-year-old brother seriously wounded by an assailant he alternately described as a man named "Joe" and as a woman.

After attacking the children, their assailant apparently saturated their clothes with gasoline, covered them with leaves and set the mound afire. For some reason the fire went out, District Attorney J. Barron Hill theorized, and the little girl crawled a few feet away and died, while the boy managed to struggle 200 feet from the funeral pyre.

Boy Mumbles Name "Jimmy"

The feverish ramblings of the boy and a report by a resident of the neighborhood that a woman with two children had been seen in the vicinity yesterday sent police on a hunt for the knife-killer who slashed the throats of both victims.

The boy, between lapses into a coma at the Patchogue Hospital, was able to tell police that his name was "Jimmy"—and to mumble a family name that his questioners said sounded like "Kiernan," "Keane," or "Keenan."

The girl's name, he said, was Helen.

Says "Mommy Hit Me"

Questioned by James Padula, special investigator for the Suffolk county district attorney, the boy said, "Mommy hit me with a baseball bat," and later declared, "Mommy hit me with a handle."

Previously Jimmy had said:

"Joe did it. Mommy's hurt, too. Joe bought us ice cream and then hurt us."

The child was found in woodlands about eight miles from Brookhaven by police officers summoned by 18-year-old May Savage, of Brookhaven, and Warren Brady, of East Patchogue, who stumbled on the body of the slain girl as they walked through the woods.

Knife, Scissors And Ax Near By

Near the girl's body police found a blood-stained butcher knife, a stained pair of scissors and an ax unstained.

About 175 feet northeast of the body Deputy Sheriff Richard Stradtner came across the boy lying unconscious.

"Here's another body," Stradtner shouted.

The boy opened his eyes and sat up. He was taken to Patchogue Com-

(Continued on Page 2, Column 4)

GOVERNOR SAYS SELECTION IS THAT OF PARTY

Calls Issue Republicans "Versus Sunpapers And Mrs. Bauernschmidt"

PLEDGES HE'LL RID FORCE OF POLITICS

Criticizes System Under Gaither—Hits Number Of Unsolved Crimes

By N. T. KENNEY

Governor Nice last night announced he would appoint William Price Lawson police commissioner of Baltimore.

Thus ended months of speculation—speculation that reached a fever pitch in the last few days—as to who was to succeed Gen. Charles D. Gaither, retiring June 1 after seventeen consecutive years of service as head of the city force.

The issue, the Governor said, is "the Republican party, with its 200,000 members, versus the Baltimore Sunpapers and Mrs. Bauernschmidt," an issue, the executive said, that was created "very recently."

"Overwhelming" Choice

The chairman of his Republican State Central Committee, the Governor said, is the "overwhelming" choice of the party to which he belongs.

"I am a Republican," Governor Nice continued, "and intend to stand by the Republican party.

"Mr. Lawson is the overwhelming choice of my party, and I shall appoint him Police Commissioner of the city of Baltimore, being responsible for my action to the people, and to the people alone."

Criticizes Present System

Charging the present police system was far from good, the Governor pledged his new appointee to elimination of all traces of politics from the department, presented a resume of his qualifications and asked for the "suspended judgment of the public."

The Governor's statement is as follows:

"Until very recently the issue in regard to the Police Commissionership of Baltimore city was Eierman vs. Lawson. Today, the issue as to the appointment of a Police Commissioner is the Republican party, with its 200,000 members, vs. the Baltimore Sunpapers and Mrs. Bauernschmidt.

"Both Mr. Lawson and Mr. Eierman (J. George Eierman, head of the Baltimore Board of Elections Supervisors) are members of the Republican organization, members of the Republican City Committee. Both are high type, reputable citizens, and neither, if appointed, would introduce or permit politics in the department.

Position "Irrevocable"

"On the issue thus created my position is clear-cut, definite and irrevocable. I am a Republican and intend to stand by the Republican party. Mr. Lawson is the overwhelming choice of my party and I shall appoint him Police Commissioner of the city of Baltimore, being responsible for my action to the people and to the people alone.

"He goes into office with a determination to accomplish two objectives: service to and protection of the lives and property of the citizens of this State and the elimination of politics within the department as it now exists, a condition well known to every person familiar with its inner workings.

"The department can be and will be improved. Many murders remain unsolved. Traffic problems have not been met. The numbers racket still flourishes, and illegal bookmaking is alleged to be rampant.

"They Should Know"

"If the members of the department do not know of these things, then, to use the language of a member of the Supreme Bench of Baltimore city, they should know. The Federal Government finds it necessary to stage spectacular raids to prevent the sale of narcotics and to eliminate the traffic in white slavery, both of which are offenses against Maryland law, and these the department should likewise have known.

"As to the charge that politics will be introduced, everyone knows that the department is under the Merit System. No appointment or promotion should be made except through the Merit System, and there should be no removals or demotions except upon charges preferred and after a public hearing. Mr. Lawson will abide and be guided solely by the Merit System of Maryland, and politics will not be tolerated.

"Mr. Lawson's reputation, his ability as an organizer, and in the handling

(Continued on Page 4, Column 1)

WEATHER FORECAST
Fair and slightly warmer today and tomorrow.
Yesterday's Temperatures: Max., 82; Min., 69.
(Details on Page 25)

THE SUN

Registered United States Patent Office

H. L. Mencken
Deals With Clinics In Another Article On Johns Hopkins Hospital —Page 13

Vol. 201—D. | PAID CIRCULATION JUNE MORNING, 147,274; EVENING, 154,617 301,891 ‖ SUNDAY 210,928 | BALTIMORE, WEDNESDAY, JULY 7, 1937 | Entered as second-class matter at Baltimore Postoffice. Copyright, 1937, by The A. S. Abell Company, Publishers of The Sun. | 26 Pages | 2 Cents

EARHART HUNT TRANSFERRED TO NEW AREA

U. S. S. Colorado Changes Course For Locality East Of Howland

NAVY COORDINATES SEARCHING UNITS

Putnam Says Radio Signals Would Indicate Plane Is Ashore

[By the Associated Press]

Honolulu, July 6—The battleship Colorado changed its course and sped toward Winslow Bank, one hundred miles east of Howland Island, today in the hunt for Amelia Earhart, and the navy moved to coordinate the far-flung searching efforts.

The tactical shift coincided with an apparently growing belief that if Miss Earhart and her navigator, Frederick J. Noonan, were alive they had reached an island or a coral reef.

Small islands are numerous beginning some 200 miles to the south, east and northwest of Howland, but virtually are unknown in the previously searched area to the north.

To Release Planes Today

The Colorado, which had been heading from Honolulu toward the area north of Howland, where the Coast Guard cutter Itasca, the navy mine-sweeper Swan and the British freighter Moorby had been searching, planned to release its three catapult planes over the Winslow Bank area late tomorrow.

Special lookouts were stationed on the battleship late today to watch for any floating objects and officers said they would light searchlight beacons beginning tonight. The Colorado plans to contact the Itasca tomorrow morning.

In Washington the Navy Department announced that direction of all American vessels engaged in the search had been placed in the hands of Rear Admiral Orin G. Murfin, Fourteenth naval district commandant in Honolulu. This includes the Itasca, the Swan, the aircraft carrier Lexington and three destroyers.

Winslow Bank lies on the northern fringe of the Phœnix Islands, which center at about 280 miles southeast of Howland.

Believes Craft On Land

Shortly before the search plans were changed, George Palmer Putnam, husband of Miss Earhart, reported the directional bearings taken on the most likely of the mysterious radio signals from that region all pointed to the Phœnix Islands.

Putnam stated if any of the numerous radio reports seemingly from the lost world-girdling plane were genuine, the ship must have been down on a reef or an island.

He said he had determined definitely that the plane would not have been able to send signals if down in the water.

Putnam expressed appreciation of the naval and Coast Guard efforts, which included sending of the Lexington and the three destroyers from San Diego.

Roosevelt Concerned

"They have done everything possible," he said, "and I am grateful for their extensive efforts."

President Roosevelt expressed concern for Miss Earhart's safety. He said the searchers had been ordered to cover as much territory as possible.

Despite the unprecedented mobilization of naval forces for the hunt, the Navy Department said it was impossible to estimate whether it involved costs in addition to regular operating expenses.

Officers said the normal daily operating cost of the five naval vessels involved was about $13,750, but pointed out this expense had to be borne whether the ships were in port or under way.

Moorby Quits Search

The Moorby, which had been assisting the Itasca and the Swan, decided to proceed to its next port of call.

Belief Miss Earhart and Noonan might have fallen short of Howland instead of overshooting it followed navigators' reports indicating they may have been bucking brisk head-winds.

Hopes were raised, but quickly dashed, early today when the Itasca sighted lights it at first believed were flares, but which officers later concluded were meteors or heat lightning.

Radio Report Probed

San Francisco Coast Guard authorities investigated without comment the report of Charles Miguel, of Oakland, radio amateur, that he heard a woman's voice at 9.35 A.M. (E.S.T.) call "S O S" giving the signature of Miss Earhart's plane and mentioning a position 281 miles north of Howland.

The area was searched in vain previously by the Itasca seeking the source of a similar message. No other stations reported the call Miguel said he heard.

From the South Pacific the Japanese airplane carrier Kamoie and the Jap-

(Continued on Page 2, Column 5)

Earhart Rescue Ship At Howland Island

—Courtesy U. S. Navy

The above photograph, taken at Howland Island, shows the Coast Guard cutter Itasca, now cruising in the South Pacific in the thus far unsuccessful search for Miss Earhart and her navigator, Frederick J. Noonan.

PARIS DEMANDS RENEWAL OF SPAIN PATROL

Threatens To Open Way To Aid To Loyalists Unless Action Is Taken

[Special Dispatch to The Sun]

Paris, July 6—If naval control around Spain by the non-intervention patrol is not restored at the next session of the non-intervention committee, scheduled to meet on Friday in London, France will announce her decision to open her Spanish frontier, thus allowing arms and munitions to be shipped from France to Loyalist Spain by the shortest and easiest route, it was stated today in official circles.

Although the French Government is extremely anxious to maintain the non-intervention setup, it was said, she cannot allow continuation of the present state of affairs, under which an important section of the Mediterranean, from the Franco-Spanish border to Gibraltar, is unguarded by the international patrol and is open to a blockade by the rebels.

Wants Patrol On Portugal's Border

Portugal's desire to walk out of the control system, on the heels of Germany and Italy, is also considered inadmissible by France, which demands equal patrolling all around Spanish territory. If there were no neutral observers along the Portuguese frontier there should be none along the French border, it is argued.

Statements in official circles today would indicate that stiffer instructions have been given to Charles Corbin, French Ambassador at London, who returned to his post after a conversation with Yvon Delbos, Foreign Minister, over the week-end.

It would be erroneous to conclude that France wishes to drop the non-intervention agreement and begin openly helping the Loyalists. More likely, she wants to intimidate Germany and Italy into resumption of the naval patrol and prevent Portugal from throwing open her frontier to the passage of Italian or German troops.

Another Policy Shift Hinted

However, if her threats to open her own border fail to persuade the two dictatorships and their satellite, Por-

(Continued on Page 6, Column 3)

De Valera's Party Loses Control Over Lower House

President Of Irish Free State May Call New Election In Effort To Get Clear Majority—Labor Now Holds Balance Of Power

[By the Associated Press]

Dublin, Irish Free State, July 6—President Eamon de Valera's Fianna Fail party failed to gain even a majority in the Free State's Dail Eireann election, complete returns showed tonight.

The announcement was a sharp blow to the New York-born President, and political observers predicted he might call another election within a few months in an effort to get a clear mandate.

Constitution Wins By 157,746

De Valera, however, won his fight for a new Constitution cutting Ireland's last ties with Great Britain. The country accepted the proposed charter by 686,042 to 528,296, the final tabulation showed.

De Valera's party won sixty-nine places in the Dail Eireann (lower house of Parliament), the same number taken by all the other parties together. But one of the President's adherents will be speaker of the Dail, who votes only in case of a tie.

The party of William T. Cosgrave, former President, the Fine Gael, took forty-eight places. Laborites won thirteen and Independents eight. In the old house, De Valera had a majority of four over all the other parties and a majority of twenty-four over Cosgrave's party.

Labor gained five seats over the number it held in the previous house, fulfilling its prediction it would hold the balance of power, as Cosgrave's group and most of the Independents probably will oppose the Government.

Labor Against New Constitution

If he decides against calling a new election, De Valera will have to seek cooperation from the Laborites. In the past they often have worked with him, but they flatly opposed his pet creation—the proposed new Constitution for Ireland.

The charter would sever the last link between the Free State and Great Britain, even ignoring the British King, and would change the country's name to *Eire* (pronounced "Airy"). It was designed to permit the eventual adherence of northern Ireland. It recognizes the "special position" of the Catholic Church in the Free State but permits all other religions.

Grenville Emmet Named As Minister To Austria

Roosevelt Nominates New Yorker, Now At Netherlands Post, To Succeed Messersmith

Washington, July 6 (AP)—President Roosevelt sent to the Senate today the nomination of Grenville T. Emmet, of New York, to be Minister to Austria. Emmet, now Minister to The Netherlands, will succeed George S. Messersmith, recently appointed Assistant Secretary of State.

Ray Atherton, of Illinois, was nominated to be Minister to Bulgaria, succeeding Frederick A. Sterling. No announcement was made regarding Sterling.

Norris Is Reported Better

Washington, July 6 (AP)—A "no-visitors" sign hung on Senator George Norris' room in Naval Hospital today to permit the Nebraska Progressive to get "a complete rest" before returning to his legislative duties. Relatives said Norris, who suffered an intestinal disturbance, is "getting stronger daily."

Drags Injured Brother From Path Of Express

Brooklyn Man Saves Washingtonian When Car Crashes On Tracks At New Haven

New Haven, Conn., July 6 (AP)—Irving Capell, 22, dragged his injured brother, Bernard, 23, from the wreckage of an automobile today a few minutes before the vehicle was tossed by a speeding New Haven Railroad train into the pathway of a second express.

The automobile, failing to round a curve, plunged through a fence to the railroad tracks thirty feet below, where it was struck by a train bound from New York to Boston.

The brothers, Irving, a resident of Brooklyn, N. Y., and Bernard, of Washington, D. C., were taken by bystanders to a hospital, where attendants said both would recover.

Latest Giannini Opera To Be Given In Germany

Work Will Have Premier In Reich Next May, Composer Announces

New York, July 6 (AP)—The Giannini corner on the Central European music market, so far as Americans go, is further strengthened by Vittorio Giannini's announcement today that his latest opera, "The Scarlet Letter," will be given its premier next May by a German opera house.

Giannini, brother of the famous soprano, Dusolina Giannini, just has returned to this country after four years at the American Academy in Rome.

He has been commissioned, he added, to do a concerto for organ and orchestra by the venerable Gesellschaft der Musikfreunde of Vienna.

POWELL RETURNS TO WORK

Abandons Seclusion He Has Kept Since Jean Harlow's Death

Hollywood, July 6 (AP)—William Powell returned to his work before the cameras today after spending almost a month in seclusion following the death of his fiancee, Jean Harlow.

For several days after her funeral Powell remained at home. He spent some days on Ronald Colman's yacht. Several times he has visited the mausoleum where Miss Harlow's body lies in its crypt.

Soldier In Unscheduled Leap From Plane Lands In Cornfield

Langley Field Private Takes To Parachute When Army "Flying Fortress" Sideslips At Altitude Of 12,000 Feet Or More Over North Carolina

[By the Associated Press]

Winston-Salem, N. C., July 6—Private J. H. Shealey, who bailed out of one of the army's "flying fortresses" from Langley Field, Va., today near Dobson, N. C., in Surry county, arrived in Winston-Salem early tonight.

Shealey said he made his unscheduled parachute leap when the plane sideslipped. Except for slight scratches on his hand which he said he received in the plane before making the jump, he was uninjured.

Shealey estimated the plane was flying at 12,000 or 13,000 feet when he jumped. He landed in a cornfield.

The bombing plane, attached to the Ninety-sixth Squadron, was on an instructional flight. Shealey was in the armament-control apartment under the nose of the ship when it sideslipped. He was one of a crew of eight.

"Just as my chute opened I saw that the plane had been brought under control," Shealey said.

"I passed through a rain cloud on the way down. There were several open fields around there. I picked the closest one and 'dish-ragged' the parachute so as to hit it. I came down without a jar, and out of the rain through which I had passed on the way down."

Shealey was given a ride on a lumber truck to Mount Airy and from that city, forty miles west-northwest of here, he came to Winston-Salem by bus.

3,000 WORKERS RESUME JOBS WITH REPUBLIC

Three Mills In Cleveland Reopen As Troops With Bayonets Stand Guard

[By the Associated Press]

Cleveland, July 6—Steel mills in another major salient in the seven-State strike opened here today. An estimated 3,000 workers returned to their posts at three Republic Steel Corporation plants after forty-one days of idleness.

Jeers and shouts of "scab!" marked the maneuver—the latest in a series of back-to-work marches—but there was no violence. National Guard bayonets and machine guns kept the peace.

The Cleveland mills, closed since the strike began May 26, had been regarded as one of the C. I. O.'s stoutest strongholds.

1,000 Guardsmen On Hand

The reopening, carried out under the protection of 1,000 Ohio National Guardsmen, left only two steel plants still shut down in the Great Lakes strike area extending from Johnstown, Pa., to Indiana Harbor, Ind.

Youngstown Sheet and Tube's mills at Indiana Harbor, employing 7,000 workers, and at East Chicago, employing 700, remained closed.

An estimated 3,000 pickets patroled Sheet and Tube's East Chicago plant to prevent any attempt at reopening as State and union officials predicted settlement of the strike there "within the next day or two."

Claim Operations Up

All other strike-affected mills in the dispute between the Committee for Industrial Organization and Republic, Bethlehem, Inland and Youngstown Sheet and Tube claimed they were speeding operations back to near-peak production once more.

The controversy, which arose over the refusal of steel producers to sign labor contracts, found strike leaders still maintaining they would "fight to the last ditch."

Thousands of men trooped back to work at Bethlehem Steel's Cambria works at Johnstown, which reopened without interference.

Crowds Seek Jobs

At Youngstown, in the Mahoning Valley, crowds of men gathered at the

(Continued on Page 8, Column 1)

ROOSEVELT ASKS 10% CUT IN ALL GRANTS

President Calls On Department Heads To Set Aside Reserve Fund

$400,000,000 SAVING FOR YEAR ESTIMATED

"Layman's Balance" At End Of Year Foreseen By Executive

By GERALD GRIFFIN
[Washington Bureau of The Sun]

Washington, July 6—President Roosevelt has requested the heads of all the Federal departments and agencies to save ten per cent. of the funds apportioned to them during the present fiscal year, he disclosed this afternoon.

This saving, he estimated, would amount to approximately $400,000,000 if the cuts are made as directed, and would bring about a "layman's balance" of this year's budget.

Although he emphasized that items such as the interest on the public debt, the wage scale of Government employes and the pay of the army and navy could not be trimmed, the President said he believed that an average saving of ten per cent. could be made on other disbursements.

Some Activities To Be Reduced

Asked if this would not involve a reduction in the personnel of some agencies, he stated that some activities would have to be curtailed. He did not explain what agencies or activities he had in mind, however.

The savings plan outlined by Mr. Roosevelt was patterned somewhat after the economy plan fostered by Senator Byrnes (Dem., S. C.), who has been urging that a ten per cent. cut in all appropriations be effected. Senator Byrnes has stated that he will attempt to have his plan incorporated into the last appropriation bill of the present session.

Under the President's plan, department heads would establish a reserve fund designed to amount, in the aggregate, to ten per cent of the total funds allotted to each unit of the Government. The reserve would revert to the Treasury at the end of the year.

Text Of President's Letter

In his letter to the heads of the departments and agencies, which was dated June 23, Mr. Roosevelt said:

"In preparing the apportionments of funds available for the fiscal year 1938, as called for by Treasury Department Circular No. 494, Revision No. 4, of June 11, 1937, it is my desire that there be set up such reserves as will amount in the aggregate to not less than ten per cent. of the total amount of all funds that are properly susceptible to the establishment of reserves for that fiscal year.

Budget Chief To Keep Check

"It will not be possible, of course, to establish a reserve in such an appropriation as the one for payment of interest on the public debt, and there will be numerous appropriations where it will be impracticable to establish a reserve of as much as ten per cent.

"In the aggregate, however, the reserves should equal that percentage of all apportioned funds susceptible to the establishment of such reserves, and I have asked the acting director of the budget to see that the apportionments for the fiscal year reflect that accomplishment."

The heads of the regular departments, constituting the Cabinet, already have gone over the savings plan with him, the President said. The heads of the various independent agencies will be summoned to the White House within the next few days to discuss the plan as it affects their units, he added.

During the discussion of the plan at his afternoon press conference the

(Continued on Page 2, Column 7)

Hanfstängl Plans To Remain In Voluntary Exile In London

Former Personal Aide To Hitler Will Make Statement To This Effect Today, His Friends Announce

[By the Associated Press]

London, July 6—Dr. Ernst F. S. Hanfstängl, former confidant of Reichsführer Adolf Hitler and for a long time head of foreign press affairs for the Nazi party, has no intention of returning to Germany, it was stated authoritatively today.

Friends of the former personal aide to the Reichsführer said he would make such a statement in appearing in court tomorrow in connection with settlement of a libel action instituted by him against the British magazine *Cavalcade*.

The magazine was alleged to have published a statement giving the impression that Hanfstängl was forced to leave Germany.

The Harvard-educated Putzi objected to the article and sued. A settlement was reported reached under which *Cavalcade* would retract the statement.

Hanfstängl came to London about three months ago, but has declined to discuss his plans.

Hanfstängl left Germany last February. At the time, he was believed by his German friends to have gone on a secret mission to Spain. He turned up at Zurich, Switzerland, on March 18, and announced he would return to Berlin after a "vacation."

Subsequently, Col. Karl Bodenschatz, aide to Hitler, visited Hanfstängl in London, but Hanfstängl turned a deaf ear to pleas that he return home. His post as press chief was abolished but he was offered a "scientific task."

ROBINSON, OPENING COURT BATTLE, DEFIES THREAT OF FILIBUSTER BY FOES

Majority Leader Serves Notice He'll Keep Bill Before Senate Continuously Until It Is Disposed Of

FIRST ROUND OF DEBATE FILLED WITH PERSONALITIES

Hatch Denies Adverse Report On Administration Plan Was Meant To Humiliate President Or Damage Democratic Party

By DEWEY L. FLEMING
[Washington Bureau of The Sun]

Washington, July 6—The long-anticipated "constitutional debate of the century" got under way in the Senate today with unexpected speed and fury.

To the mutual delight of packed galleries and a Senate that had not had a first-rate fight all year, the President's court reorganization bill was called up for debate shortly after noon and the opposing forces went to it hammer and tongs for almost five hours in the first clash.

Robinson Opens Debate

Senator Robinson (Ark.), majority leader, opened the Administration's case with an hour-and-a-half speech, which he delivered with such vigor that at one stage Senator Copeland (Dem., N. Y.), who is a physician, moved over to his side and cautioned him against overexertion.

Besides his technical and political defense of the Administration's revised plan for rejuvenation of the Supreme Court and inferior Federal courts, the veteran Democratic floor leader roared out defiance of opposition threats to filibuster the legislation to its death.

Defies Filibuster Threat

He served notice that it would be his purpose to keep the court bill before the Senate continuously until it was disposed of, "making reasonable allowance for such emergency measures as may be brought to the attention of the Senate." He prophesied, too, that the advocates of filibuster would not be as "cocky" after the fight had run for a time as they appeared to be today.

Senator Hatch (Dem., N. M.), principal author of the revised or substitute court plan now being debated, took the floor as soon as Senator Robinson had concluded and held it for the remainder of the day against steady fire from the opposition.

Personalities Indulged In

There was no pulling of punches in the opening engagement of the forces that have been preparing for this fight since the first Administration bill on the subject was transmitted to Congress in February. Debate was sprinkled liberally with personalities from beginning to end and there was every indication that the practice would grow as the argument continued.

As was expected, the controversy was not confined to the merits of the bill under consideration and Senators thundered away with abandon on such other matters as the effect of the fight upon the Democratic party, the effect upon President Roosevelt, the motives of the opposition and the sincerity of the Administration.

Fight Hot Over Revised Plan

This phase of the fight waxed warmest during Senator Hatch's exposition of the revised plan for reorganization of the Supreme Court—a program of appointing one new justice each year for each sitting justice over the age of 75. The original Roosevelt bill had called for appointment at one time of one new justice for every sitting justice over 70.

The New Mexico Senator related how he had been compelled from the start to oppose the first bill, and how he had labored to produce a less objectionable measure to accomplish the same objective—a younger Supreme Court.

Urged To Beat Roosevelt

Senator Hatch said that since the filing of the majority report of the Judiciary Committee on the original court bill, an adverse report, he had received a flood of letters from persons who complimented him for subscribing to that document. In many of the letters, he continued, the authors counseled him in almost identical language: "Now is the time to humiliate the President. Now is the time to beat Franklin D. Roosevelt."

"I want to say here at the beginning of this debate," the Senator continued,

(Continued on Page 14, Column 8)

Loopholes In Tax Laws Blamed On Supreme Court

[Washington Bureau of The Sun]

Washington, July 6—While Capitol Hill's spotlight, which has been playing upon those who have found tax-saving flaws in revenue laws, was turned off momentarily today, the United States Supreme Court was cited from the floor of the House of Representatives as the provider of loopholes that had cost the Federal Government nearly $16,000,000,000.

"Is the Congress to blame?" asked Representative Lewis (Dem., Md.), a member of the revenue-raising Ways and Means Committee. "No, sir; not ours the guilt. These egregious items, delinquent, have their origin not here but in the courthouse.

Tells Of Discouragement

"I confess, as one member of the Committee on Ways and Means, charged with the duty of initiating revenue measures, a feeling of complete discouragement.

"The court's revenue decisions make it impossible for me to draft a revenue bill which does not grossly and unjustly discriminate in favor of large classes able to pay at the expense of other citizens whom I must make pay taxes for both."

Gives List Of Losses

The $16,000,000,000 delinquent taxpayers' list, the Marylander said, could be laid at the door of the Supreme Court, bearing the following notations of revenue losses they effected:

Repudiation of the income tax 1894 (25 years)	$1,500,000,000
Exemption of public securities	2,000,000,000
Exemption, employes, officers of counties, cities, states	1,000,000,000
Tax exemptions, community property (in 8 States)	200,000,000
Exemption of income of State-leased oil lands	200,000,000
Exemption of income from stock dividends	1,000,000,000
Evasion of surtaxes	7,000,000,000

Calls Tax Stepchild

"And now you ask, my colleagues, 'what of it?'" Mr. Lewis concluded after citing Supreme Court decisions in tax cases for an hour. "I should say that the tax situation created by the attitude of the judicial department toward the other departments cannot be fully commented on in a single address—but res ipsa loquitur, one comment forces utterance: Verily, verily,

(Continued on Page 15, Column 1)

THE WEATHER

Mostly cloudy and warmer tonight ... Saturday partly cloudy to clear and warmer. ... Page 51

THE EVENING SUN

6 ★★★★★★ FINANCIAL Closing New York Stocks

Vol. 56 | Morning 142,016 Evening 158,584 Paid Circulation February 300,600 ‖ Sunday 212,250 | BALTIMORE, FRIDAY, MARCH 11, 1938 | 52 Pages | 2 Cents

GERMANY INVADES AUSTRIA, HITLER SENDS ULTIMATUM

ORDERS RICHARD WHITNEY REARRESTED ON SECOND CHARGE OF GRAND LARCENY

New York Attorney General Acts On Complaint Of Yacht Club Head That He Unlawfully Took $103,000 In Bonds

Broker Already Free In $10,000 Bail In First Case And Faces Arraignment Within Week Or Dewey Indictment

Wirephotos on Pages 2 and 28

[By the Associated Press]

New York, March 11—The immediate arrest of Richard Whitney, five times president of the New York Stock Exchange, on a new charge of grand larceny, was ordered today by State Attorney General John J. Bennett, Jr.

Whitney was at liberty in $10,000 bail on another grand larceny charge on which he was indicted yesterday through the efforts of District Attorney Thomas E. Dewey.

Facing Arraignment

He was arrested yesterday on that charge and is to be arraigned within a week.

The present charge is based on a complaint of Commodore William A. W. Stewart, of the New York Yacht Club, that Whitney "unlawfully" took from a safety deposit box $103,000 worth of bonds belonging to the club, of which Whitney had been treasurer.

Whitney, notified through his counsel, Charles H. Tuttle, of Bennett's intention of rearresting him, said he would surrender immediately at Bennett's office.

Accused In $105,000 Theft

The Dewey indictment against Whitney is based on a complaint by Whitney's sister-in-law that he took between $105,000 and $110,000 worth of securities, belonging to a family trust fund established by his father-in-law. She, Mrs Whitney and his alma mater, Harvard University, were losers by his alleged misappropriations.

Financial difficulties of the bankrupt firm of Richard Whitney & Co. were traced back today by a member of the firm to an unsatisfied demand last fall of the New York Stock Exchange that Whitney surrender funds in the exchange "gratuity fund," maintained for the benefit of widows and orphans of exchange members.

F. Kingsley Rodewald, senior partner under Whitney, told investi-

[Continued On Page 28, Column 1]

DEFIES ROOSEVELT IN TVA SQUABBLE

Morgan Declines Request To Produce Evidence To Back Charges

[By the Associated Press]

Washington, March 11—Chairman Arthur E. Morgan, of the Tennessee Valley Authority, declined today to meet President Roosevelt's request for factual evidence to support charges that Morgan has made against the two other members of the TVA board.

"I am of the opinion that this meeting is not, and in the nature of the case cannot be, an effective or useful fact-finding occasion," Chairman Morgan told the President in a conference with the Chief Executive and the toher two directors of TVA.

Evidence Requested

Morgan's statement came after President Roosevelt had asked him "what evidence of dishonesty or malfeasance on the part of your colleagues have you in regard to the so-called Berry marble case."

This followed an opening statement by Mr. Roosevelt that he had been convinced reluctantly that the work of the TVA board members was impeded and real issues of public policy obscured by their personal recriminations.

Claims Involved

The case to which Mr. Roosevelt referred in questioning Chairman Morgan involved claims by Senator George L. Berry (Dem., Tenn.), for payment from the TVA on marble land in the Norris Dam Basin.

In a statement to the press some days ago Morgan accused his TVA associates, Directors H. A. Morgan and David E. Lilienthal, with bad faith in their handlinng of the Berry claim.

Earlier in the day President Roosevelt told the quarreling TVA directors he had been convinced reluctantly that their work was impeded and real issues of public policy obscured by personal recriminations.

"It is intolerable to the people of the United States," the President told the directors in his statement, "that issues of fundamental public policy should be confused with issues of personal integrity and misconduct. . . .

"I have called this hearing," he said, "to investigate charges of dishonesty, bad faith and misconduct. . . . This is not an inquiry to determine a national power policy, a national conservation policy, a national flood policy, or any other straight matter of policy. It is an inquiry into charges of personal and official misconduct."

Hearing Recessed

After asking the three directors a few questions concerning their faith in the TVA project and making his statement to them, the President recessed the hearing until after luncheon.

All three directors said they believed in the feasibility and wisdom of the

[Continued On Page 28, Column 8]

On The INSIDE

Tax Bill Is Passed By House

Declines To Restore Special Levy On Family Owned, Closely Held Concerns

Washington, March 11 (AP) — The House passed the tax bil and sent it to the Senate today after declining to reinsert a special surtax on family owned and closely held corporations.

It refused also to go back and eliminate an undistributed profits tax or impose a flat levy of 12½ per cent. on capital gains.

Described by its supporters as a measure to provide "a very substantial stimulation to business," it would revise the entire corporate and capital gains tax structures.

Smoother Path Seen

The levy on closely-held corporations had been the biggest point of controversy in the bill, and with that removed the legislation was expected to find a somewhat smoother path through the Senate.

For the present corporate income taxes of 8 to 15 per cent. and undistributed profits surtaxes of 7 to 27 per cent. the bill would substitute a system to:

Impose an income tax of 72½ to 16 per cent. on all corporations with net incomes of $25,000 or less, thereby removing their undistributed profits tax.

Subject the majority of corporations with larger incomes to a sixteen per cent. income tax and a four per cent. surtax on undistributed profits.

Rates Explained

The legislation would fix maximum rates of 16 to 39.2 per cent. on gains on capital assets held by a taxpayer more than thirteen months.

Under present law capital gains are included with a taxpayer's other income and subjected to income-tax schedules. The taxable portion of the gains so included graduates downward

[Continued On Page 10, Column 1]

MADRID RISKS MAIN ARMY TO STOP FOE

Forced To Take Stand When Insurgent Offensive Gains Momentum

[By the Associated Press]

Hendaye, France, At The Spanish Frontier, March 11—With Belchite lost, the Government's Aragon army moved up to meet the Insurgents' great offensive today in a battle for control of eastern Spain.

Military advices said the Government, which had been withdrawing steadily before the three-day-old thrust, had been forced by Insurgent gains to take a stand, risking its main army in a major clash to decide the fate of the Mediterranean seaboard.

Rebels Reach Codo

Insurgents said a Moorish corps, commanded by Gen. Juan Yague occupied Belchite after a day-long bombardment and thus demolished a seventeen-mile deep salient established by the Government last September. American and British volunteers were among the prisoners taken.

Insurgent officers expressed belief the Government's international brigade was used in the Government's last stand defending Belchite.

Strewn in the olive groves where the battle was fought were badges with the picture of Abraham Lincoln and inscribed, "Friends of the Lincoln Battalion."

New Yorker Captured

Insurgent officers said one prisoner identified himself as John Berserie, 22, of New York, a member of the Lincoln brigade.

The main body of Government troops retreated to the plateau of El Saso, just east of Belchite.

Government reserves were rushed forward along the Valencia-Zaragoza highway between Alcaniz and Hijar, taking positions around Hijar, seventeen miles southeast of Belchite.

Insurgent forces also converged on Hijar, indicating the shock would come there.

CHIEF EXECUTIVE TALKS ON TAX REBUFF IN HOUSE

Denies Family Levy Was Designed As A Punitive Measure

President Contends He Sought To Restore Equality In Taxation

By Henry M. Hyde

Washington, March 11—President Roosevelt was asked at his press conference today if he had any comment to make on the action of the House in throwing out the proposed supertax on closely held corporations.

He replied that there was perhaps a simple explanation which might interest some newspapers.

Sought Equalization

He said that what the Administration was seeking is the ending of special privilege in matters of taxation. He instanced Mr. A and Mr. B, both of whom have large and equal incomes in the upper brackets. If they make the same profits, have the same incomes, should not A and B pay the same tax?

To secure such equality was the object of the proposed tax. Headlines and leads in newspapers should not, therefore, refer to it as a punitive tax. That, the President said, was the last word which should be used. It was simply an attempt to restore equality in taxes between two people.

Plans Monopoly Talk

Asked just what he meant by saying that this information might be of special interest to some newspapers, the President urged his questioner not to press him.

President Roosevelt said that he was now working on three or four special messages to Congress. One of them is on the subject of monopoly. He declined to state the subjects of the others.

Hopes For Reorganization

Asked if he had given up hope of getting his reorganization bill through Congress, the President shook his head. He explained that he had become interested in the reorganization twenty-five years ago, when he was Assistant Secretary of the Navy. The subject has been discussed off and on ever since. It has been recommended by both Republican and Democratic Presidents. The President hopes that something will be done about it at this session.

The President had a busy morning. At 10 o'clock he addressed the National Conference on Human Needs. His press conference began half an hour later. At 11 o'clock he started his conference with Dr. Arthur Morgan, chairman of the TVA commission, and Dr. Harcourt Morgan and David Lilienthal, the other two members, in an effort to prevent the feud between the two factions from breaking into open warfare.

Promises Record Of Parley

He was asked if he expected it to be a Kilkenny cat session, and replied that he hoped not. The President announced that a stenographic record of the conference would be taken and would be made public as rapidly as it could be turned out.

Dr. Harcourt Morgan and Mr. Lilienthal reached the White House five minutes ahead of time. Chairman Arthur Morgan drove up at exactly 11 o'clock.

Chairman Morgan was asked, as he entered, whether he expected to resign.

"One does not say anything as one goes in," he replied with a grin.

Traffic Defendant Blames Occupation

Distillery Employe Says He Had "Too Many Tastes"—Judge Fines Him $50

Seattle, March 11 (AP)—Vernon Fields, 30, blamed his occupation for reckless driving.

He told Police Judge Jacob Kalina his sensitive sense of taste had won him a job in a distillery, and "I guess I had too many tastes."

Judge Kalina fined him $50.

Line Crossed At Passau; Vienna Troops Retreat

Schuschnigg Himself Announces Surrender To Fuhrer's Deman For New Regime "To Prevent Spilling Of German Blood," And Adds, "Goodbye; God Protect Austria"---Nazi In Cabinet Calls On Country To Make No Resistance

Paris, March 11 (AP)—High officials of the Foreign Office declared today that Italy had refused to join France and Britain in "any action whatsoever" to defend Austrian independence.

A spokesman for Foreign Minister Yvon Delbos said that, even without Italy, France was determined to act in a "most vigorous manner," providing Britain supported her. He ruled out protests as "worse than useless."

The spokesman added that Count Johannes Welczeck, German Ambassador to France, whom Delbos had called in earlier, had told the Foreign Minister flatly that "Germany will not make the slightest concession in regard to Austria."

In London the Austrian Legation announced tonight that Chancellor Kurt Schuschnigg had resigned.

[By the Associated Press]

Vienna, March 11—The Austrian Government Press Bureau announced tonight that German troops had crossed the Austrian border at Passau.

Austrian troops were ordered to fall back without resistance.

Nazi throngs virtually took possession of Vienna.

A high official said the resignation of Chancellor Kurt Schuschnigg was expected.

The official declared the next Austrian Government would be completely satisfactory to Germany. He added that Schuschnigg might be retained in some capacity.

Schuschnigg announced by radio that Germany had presented an ultimatum with a time limit demanding the reorganization of the Austrian Government.

Austria, said Schuschnigg, had yielded to Germany's demands and "the object is to prevent the spilling of German blood."

The Chancellor said the ultimatum had been presented to President Wilhelm Miklas, and that the President thereupon had conferred with army officers.

At the end of his short announcement Schuschnigg said:

"I say good-by with the wish that God protect Austria."

Seysz-Inquart Asks "No Resistance"

It was not known immediately whether the "good-by" meant his resignation.

Arthur Seysz-Inquart, the Hitler-approved Austrian Minister of the Interior, in a broadcast asked that there be no resistance to the German troops coming in. He urged Austrian Nazis to maintain strict discipline.

At the Chancellery it was said that the Government was being reorganized and that a new Cabinet list would be announced shortly.

Two Other Border Crossings

Two German regiments were reported to have crossed the border at Kufstein-Salzburg and Rosenheim-Salzburg. It was reported that they met with no resistance and were greeted with cheers.

The Austrian War Minister ordered the mobilization of 100,000 reserve troops, called 30,000 National Guardsmen to immediate duty and strengthened the Chancellor's bodyguard because of Nazi threats against his life.

The Vienna Government ordered all soldiers and police to remain in barracks, without even the daily leave of one or two hours.

Asked whether today's intensive precautions meant that martial law was being declared, army circles answered: "It is a matter only of a technical name."

The total number of troops, police and reserves on protective duty is believed to be 500,000. These forces have varying equipment, including tanks, machine guns, howitzers and sabers.

German Mobilization Under Way All Day

[By the Associated Press]

Munich, March 11—Mobilization of German troops in the Seventh Army Corps Area—near Austria's border—was in full swing today. Munich is army corps headquarters.

Bavarians believed the purpose was to scare Chancellor Schuschnigg, who had called for a plebiscite Sunday on Austrian independence, a move which Nazi leaders consider unfriendly to their cause.

Because there was no effort to hide mobilization, Bavarians believed it was not intended actually to send troops to Austria.

Sources close to the German Government, while confirming the mobilization, vigorously denied that the purpose was to intimidate Schuschnigg.

"Bolshevist Chaos" In Austria Alleged

"Various border garrisons on the Austrian frontier have been slightly reinforced," said a source close to the Chancellor. But it was insisted this was merely a precaution "which in view of the turbulent indignation prevailing among the Austrian public and the passionate sympathy felt by the German population on this side of the border scarcely needs explanation."

The same sources had denied that any ultimatum was presented to Schuschnigg demanding cancellation of the plebiscite.

German newspapers which for a few days had played down Austrian news, were wide open today.

Der Angriff, Propaganda Minister Paul Joseph Goebbel's newspaper, banner lined:

"Schuschnigg No Longer Able To Control Situation. Bolshevist Chaos Threatens Vienna."

That Bolsters Invasion Idea

Der Angriff's heavy emphasis on "Bolshevist chaos" heightened the belief of many that German troops might enter Austria to put down the "Bolshevist" danger.

German troops are moving toward the border carrying pontoons for making bridges and also field artillery, said motorists who encountered them on a highway south of here.

One motorist said he saw 130 military motor trucks on the road to Salzburg.

Hundreds of motor-cycle troops were moving southward.

Mobilization "Going On All Night"

Motorized engineer detachments carried pontoons, motor boats and other material used in military crossings of wide streams. Numerous commandeered brewery trucks helped carry this material.

Peasants along the highway said this had been "going on all night."

Near the border troops impressed peasants for work and commandeered horses and automobiles.

The border near Salzburg is marked by the Rivers Inn,

[Continued On Page 4, Column 1]

THE WEATHER

Clear and not quite so cold tonight; Wednesday clear to partly cloudy and warmer.

Detailed report on Page 35

THE EVENING SUN

6 STAR ★★★★★★ Wall Street Close

Vol. 58 | Paid Circulation October — Morning, Evening 304,195 Sunday 190,411 | BALTIMORE, TUESDAY, NOVEMBER 1, 1938 | Entered as second class matter at Baltimore Postoffice | 36 Pages | 2 Cents

MATCH RACE DRAWS 40,000

Forty Thousand Spectators Jam Pimlico for Opening Day and the Big Match-Race Between War Admiral and Seabiscuit

BOY'S CAP LEADS TO ARREST IN HIT-RUN DEATH

Found On Running Board And Identified As Property Of Victim

A cap found on the running board of an automobile in Seat Pleasant, Md., last night resulted in the owner of the car being charged, technically, with the death of a boy in a hit-and-run accident.

The accident had occurred only about an hour earlier on Carmody road, approximately one mile out of Seat Pleasant. A coupe speeding toward the town struck three of four boys who were trudging along the road in the same direction.

One Dies In Washington

Bernard Randolph, Jr., 11 years old, one of three who was struck, died early today at the Provident Hospital in Washington. The other boys, Douglas Sparks, 14, and his brother Robert, 9, were only cut and bruised.

They and Allen Foster, the fourth boy in the party, said the coupe continued on after the accident and disappeared in the direction of the town. The Sparks boys and young Foster telephoned for police and Officer Edward Cissel, of the Prince George's county force, went out from Upper Upper Marlboro.

Cap Identified

After Bernard had been taken to the hospital his friends went on into Seat Pleasant. There, they said, they found a sailor's cap on the running board of a coupe and identified it as one Randolph had been wearing. His parents also identified it, reported the police.

The coupe owner, Eugene W. C. Lyons, who said he is employed as a private policeman by a Washington utility company, was arrested and first charged with simple assault. He denied

[Continued On Page 19, Column 4]

27 Races In British Colony Oppose Reich

Tanganyika Mine Workers Hold Massmeeting To Protest Any Absorption; Nazis Forbid Germans To Attend

[By the Associated Press]

Nairobi, Kenya, Nov. 1—Lupa Goldfield miners of twenty-seven races held a massmeeting today to advocate keeping Tanganyika within the British Empire, but Germans were forbidden to attend by local Nazi headquarters.

The meeting approved resolutions demanding that Tanganyika, former German East African colony which adjoins Kenya, remain under British mandate and pledged resistance to cession to Germany "by every conceivable means."

The resolutions were read in the English, Afrikaans, Greek, Gujerati and Kishwahili languages, among others.

Mandates Gave British Control Of Tanganyika

Although Adolf Hitler in *"Mein Kampf"* denounced the pre-war German policies of colonies and trade as "foolish," the Colonial question, vibrant for years, has come still further into the foreground since the Munich consortium strengthened the Führer's hand.

The mass-meeting at Nairobi, Kenya, today is the latest action of a series reported from many places in Europe and Africa in recent weeks. Only yesterday, for instance, Albert de Vleeschauwer, Belgian Minister of Colonies, returned a flat "No" to suggestions that Belgium might contribute in a general redistribution of colonial territory to meet German demands.

Conquered In 1918

The Tanganyika territory discussed at Nairobi was formerly German East Africa and was conquered in 1918. Subsequently, it was divided by Belgium and Great Britain, but in March, 1921, two districts formerly administered by

[Continued On Page 19, Column 6]

CZECHS AND POLES AGREE ON BORDER

Exchange Of Notes Ends Dispute; Commission To Meet Soon In Prague

[By the Associated Press]

Prague, Nov. 1—Czechoslovakia's frontier dispute with Poland was ended today by an exchange of notes between Czechoslovak Foreign Minister Frantisek Chvalkovsky and Casimir Papee, Polish Minister to Prague.

The notes said the two governments were in agreement on their common border and that only slight rectification was necessary before a formal treaty could be signed.

Commission To Meet

Official Polish sources declared the accord excluded the possibility of a plebiscite in the Frydek district, disputed area near the regions of Teschen and Frystat which Polish troops already have occupied.

A joint Czechoslovak-Polish commission is to meet at Prague soon to draw up documents necessary for conclusion of the border agreement.

The Polish-Czechoslovak border in Silesia is to be decided by November 15 and the two Governments bound

[Continued On Page 19, Column 2]

ANSWERS PRANK WITH SHOTGUN; 2 IN HOSPITAL

Resident Of Berwyn, Md., Denies Knowing Weapon Was Loaded

[By the Associated Press]

Berwyn, Md., Nov. 1—Halloween's aftermath found three boys nursing shotgun wounds today and George A. Godey facing charges of assault with a dangerous weapon.

The boys were shot after pranksters stoned Godey's house and he replied with a shotgun blast. At a hearing before Magistrate George Phillips, Godey said he thought he had a blank shell in his gun, and meant only to frighten the pranksters. He was released under $1,500 bond for a hearing tomorrow.

Two Go To Hospital

Two of the boys, Milton Wood, 11, and his brother, Roland, 16, were taken to a Washington hospital, where it was reported their wounds were not serious.

The third youth, Jack McManus, 15, was treated at home. All three denied participating in the prank which aroused Godey.

The shooting was the only reported casualty of a Hallowe'en that was celebrated in colorful style by many towns. Hagerstown and Frederick contributed gala parades to the Western Shore's celebration, and Berlin and Easton were merrymaking centers on the Eastern Shore.

Thousands jammed the streets and sidewalks at each place and participated in street dances after the parades and awarding of prizes.

First Lady Buying Dresses

New York, Nov. 1 (AP)—Mrs. Franklin D. Roosevelt came to New York today to select several new gowns in preparation for the Washington social season. She set aside an hour during the afternoon to try them on

SPY COURT BARS TESTIMONY ON FBI RESIGNATION

Silences Lawyer For German Girl, Renewing Frameup Charge

[By the Associated Press]

New York, Nov. 1—An accusation that the German espionage trial now proceeding in Federal court was the result of a "frameup" was made today by George C. Dix, counsel for Fraulein Johanna Hofmann, who is one of three persons on trial.

"I charge that there was a frameup and corruption on the part of the Government in this case," said Dix, turning angrily to Judge John Knox when Government attorneys objected to his cross-examining Reed Vetterli, former special agent of the Federal Bureau of Investigation in New York.

The prosecution contended that Vetterli's testimony, which dealt with a statement signed by Otto Hermann Voss, another defendant, did not affect Dix's client.

Dix, in his opening statement at the start of the trial, asserted that Miss Hofmann was "framed" by Leon G. Turrou, former F.B.I. agent, who was in charge of the espionage investigation.

Cross-Examination Permitted

Judge Knox permitted Dix to cross-examine Vetterli, but sustained an objection when the attorney asked Vetterli to describe the circumstances of Turrou's resignation after the grand jury returned the espionage indictments.

Voss' statement, read into the record yesterday over the objection of his counsel, which charged it was obtained under duress, quoted him as saying he gave secret information about United States military planes to

[Continued On Page 19, Column 2]

5 Risk Jail In Dayton School Row

Dayton, Ohio, Nov. 1 (AP)—Five Board of Education members, risking citations for contempt of court, stood pat today on their determination to keep the city's schools closed at least until December 3 as the only way out of a financial jam.

While a twelve-man committee requested by Common Pleas Judge Null M. Hodapp "to work in conjunction with the board" prepared to report to him the details of a five-hour conference ending early today, the board members faced the expiration of a day of grace on contempt warrants.

The indefinite holiday went into its second day with only thirty-three caretakers at the buildings which last week held 34,000 boys and girls and 1 300 teachers and other employes.

The five majority members held applications for habeas corpus writs to avoid going to jail.

Says U. S. Has Mass Jitters

Psychologist Links Radio Scare To Shag Dancing. Blames World War

Terre Haute, Ind., Nov. 1 (AP)—Dr. Rudolph A. Acher, Indiana State Teachers' College psychologist, traces Sunday night's widespread hysteria over a radio play to the same thing he says causes "jitterbugs."

He said the alarm spread by a dramatization of H. G. Wells' "War of the Worlds" and the antics of "shag" dancers both grew out of a "mass case of jitters" started by the World War and aggravated by "persistent economic chaos."

WAR ADMIRAL, SEABISCUIT FIND PIMLICO TRACK FAST

Jervis Spencer, Umpire Of Test, Rules Strip Meets Requirements—Fans Start Arriving For Match Race At Dawn

Summoned by the compelling prospect of the greatest race in the history of Pimlico, avid turf fans from all parts of the East and from many other sections of the nation crowded into the race plant today to watch War Admiral and Seabiscuit match strides in their long-awaited match for the American track championship.

Forty thousand fans assembled under almost perfect weather conditions.

Although the real crowd didn't show up until the day was well along, the fall season at Pimlico—from the point of view of many enthusiasts—started about 5.30 A. M., when the two contenders ducked out for a last minute gallop.

Many Out Early

Making certain they would be on hand for the flag-fall this afternoon when George Cassidy yells to the two great thoroughbreds to "come on," many race fans nosed their cars out of their garages and headed them toward Pimlico to watch these early performances of the horses.

Scarcely had the two animals been wrapped up again and put on the shelf for a few hours rest, when Jervis Spencer, Jr., chairman of the Maryland Racing Commission and umpire of the track condition today, appeared at the club house clad in gray overcoat and black derby.

Tours Track

Sticking his hands deep in his pockets and accompanied by Al Weston, former steward at the track, Mr. Spencer began the walk around the mile stretch of turf.

About thirty minutes later, their inspection complete, the two men strolled to the winners' circle in front of the stands and Spencer nodded to Alfred

[Continued On Page 8, Column 2]

CATAPULT, BROTHER OF ADMIRAL, WINS

Good Chance First To Score Over New Pimlico Jump Course Before 40,000

By William Boniface

Pimlico's Fall meeting, with the War Admiral-Seabiscuit race as a special lure, opened this afternoon with 40,000 spectators in the grounds and more pouring in through the gates every minute.

By post time for the opening event all the seats were occupied and the overflow thronged the promenade and covered a good section of the infield on the grandstand side.

As its opening attraction Pimlico offered the running of the Battleship Steeplechase Handicap of two miles, and it was Rokeby Stable's Good Chance, ridden by Eddie Roberts, which scored the initial victory over a brand-new jumping course.

The race was marred by three mishaps. T. T. Mott's The Hour, the early

[Continued On Page 28, Column 3]

Weather Forecast
Generally fair today and tomorrow; little change in temperature.
Yesterday's Temperatures: Max., 84; Min., 67.
(Details on Page 25)

THE SUN

Registered United States Patent Office

7:00 A.M.

Vol. 205—E | PAID CIRCULATION JULY MORNING, 145,960 EVENING, 154,913 300,873 || SUNDAY 190,554 | BALTIMORE, FRIDAY, SEPTEMBER 1, 1939 | 26 Pages | 2 Cents

NAZI ARMY INVADES POLAND

"Victory Or Death For Me"---Hitler

CITIES BOMBED; DANZIG SEIZED

POLISH HARBOR CUT OFF; GERMAN SOLDIERS TOLD TO "FIGHT FOR HONOR"

Führer Asserts Warsaw Has Rejected His "Efforts To Establish Neighborly Relations And Has Appealed To Weapons"

[*By the Associated Press*]

Berlin, *Friday*, Sept. 1 (Filed Berlin, 5.55 A. M.)—The German radio announced today a blockade of the Polish harbor of Gdynia as Adolf Hitler ordered his army to meet force with force as a result of Polish "violations" of the German frontier.

Neutral ships in the Baltic were warned they entered Danzig harbor or nearby harbors at their own peril.

The announcement said military operations necessitated these measures.

"Use Force Against Force"

Hitler gave his orders to his army at 5.30 A. M. (11.30 P. M., E.S.T., Thursday) to use "force against force."

The command was issued as the order of the day to the army massed on Polish frontiers from the Baltic to the **high Tatra Mountains,** and in East Prussia.

No instruction was made public, however, for any action except for German soldiers to "conduct a fight for honor and the right to the life of the resurrected German people."

It was not known immediately whether the army had orders to make an advance along the frontiers.

Text Of Hitler's Order

The text of the order read:

> The Polish state has rejected my efforts to establish neighborly relations, and instead has appealed to weapons.
>
> Germans in Poland are victims of a bloody terror, driven from house and home.
>
> A series of border violations unbearable for a great power show that the Poles no longer are willing to respect the German border.
>
> To put an end to these insane incitations, nothing remains but for me to meet force with force from now on.
>
> The German Army will conduct a fight for honor and the right to the life of the resurrected German people with firm determination. I expect that every soldier, mindful of the great traditions of the eternal German military, will do his duty to the last.
>
> Remember always that you are representatives of the National Socialist great Germany. Long live our people and our Reich!

Schools Closed Indefinitely

The radio announced immediately an indefinite closing of all schools in Germany.

Rapid fire orders followed commanding masters of German vessels to get out of the Baltic Sea and not to enter the Danzig or Polish harbors.

The radio warned all foreigners that Polish territory is a danger zone and their presence was at their own peril because of the likelihood of military action.

Civil Air Flights Prohibited

Another order issued shortly before 6 A. M. prohibited all except military plane flights over Germany.

A moment later came the radio order declaring the Polish harbor Gdynia blockaded by the German Navy.

Gdynia and Danzig are but a few miles apart in the same harbor.

The Government announcement said German warships would meet foreign vessels steaming into the danger zone and instruct them where to go.

Ships were warned to stay out of waters between 18 degrees 5 minutes (the German-Polish border) and 20 degrees, east longitude.

Warlike orders issued by the War Ministries to the German

(Continued on Page 2, Column 2)

Bulletins

Reaction In London

[*By the Associated Press*]

London, Sept. 1 — King George summoned the Privy Council to a meeting today and Parliament was called to meet at 5 P. M. as reports were received here of a German offensive against Poland.

The Cabinet met at 11.30 A. M. and the Privy Council was to meet at noon (7 A. M., E.S.T.)

The Polish Ambassador conferred with Prime Minister Chamberlain before the Cabinet meeting.

Reservists Called

Athens, Aug. 31 (AP) — All French reservists in Greece were ordered to proceed to France at the first opportunity tonight.

Two hundred Americans left Piraeus for the United States aboard the American steamer Exorchorda.

Canadian Troops Movmg

Calgary, Alta, Aug. 31 (Canadian Press)—Thirty-one members of No. 1 Fighter Squadron, Royal Canadian Air Force, carrying gas masks, left Calgary tonight on an east-bound Canadian Pacific Railway train for an undivulged destination.

The men left less than twelve hours after two squadron planes, capable of 400 miles an hour, soared away to eastern Canada.

Poland Needs Copper

New York, Aug. 31 (AP)—Poland was reported in trade circles today to be attempting to buy copper in the United States market.

Copper dealers said that because of difficulty in obtaining transportation for the metal to Europe, all quotations to foreign countries now are at the refinery prices, leaving it up to the buyer to obtain shipment.

Japanese In Rome

Rome, Aug. 31 (AP)—A Japanese mission headed by Admiral Baron Mineo Osumi and Gen. Count Juichi Terauchi, former Navy and War Ministers, which arrived at Naples yesterday, remained there today awaiting fresh instructions from Tokyo.

They were en route to Germany to attend the Nürnberg annual Nazi party congress, which was to have opened Saturday, but was canceled because of the European crisis.

Lightning And Dynamite

Brussels, *Friday*, Sept. 1 (AP) (Passed by the British Censor). Two bridges over the River Meuse at Liege, one a railway bridge, collapsed during a violent thunder storm late last night, and latest reports placed the total dead at ten and the injured at thirty-seven.

Investigators said the accidents apparently were due to lightning striking charges of dynamite such as have been placed at all bridges for defensive purposes.

The bridges were the Val Benoit and the Ougree.

ROOSEVELT ORDERS NAVY SHIPS AND ARMY POSTS NOTIFIED OF HOSTILITIES

Receives Word By Telephone From United States Ambssadors At Warsaw And Paris Of Invasion Of Poland And Bombing Of Four Cities

Washington, Sept. 1 (AP)—President Roosevelt today asked all potential participants in a European war to pledge themselves against bombarding civilian populations or unfortified cities from the air. The Chief Executive's appeal was sent at 4.30 A. M. to the governments of Great Britain, France, Italy, Germany and Poland. He requested "an immediate reply."

[*By the Associated Press*]

Washington, Friday, Sept. 1—President Roosevelt directed today that all naval ships and army commands be notified at once by radio of German-Polish hostilities.

The White House issued the following announcement:

> **The President received word at 2.50 A. M. (E.S.T.) by telephone from Ambassador Biddle at Warsaw and through Ambassador Bullitt in Paris that Germany has invaded Poland and that four Polish cities are being bombed.**
>
> **The President directed all naval ships and army commands be notified by radio at once.**
>
> **There probably will be a further announcement by the State Department in a few hours.**

May Aid In Evacuating Americans

The announcement was issued by William Hassett, acting White House press secretary, after the President telephoned him at his home.

There was speculation that naval vessels in European waters might be ordered to lend a hand to merchant ships in evacuating Americans.

Reports Warsaw Bombed

Ambassador Bullitt telephoned the State Department that he had official information that the Polish cities of Warsaw and Krakow were being bombed.

State Department officials said the President got in touch immediately with Secretary Hull and Under Secretary Welles by telephone, and they came to their offices before Adolf Hitler delivered his Reichstag speech.

FREE CITY IS ACCEPTED INTO REICH BY HITLER

[*By the Associated Press*]

Berlin, *Friday*, Sept. 1—Adolf Hitler today accepted the Free City of Danzig into the Reich.

The Führer acted after Albert Förster, Nazi Chief of State of the Free City and Nazi district leader there, had proclaimed the reunion of the Baltic city with Hitler's Germany, and begged the Führer to accept it.

Thanks Him For Loyalty

In a telegram to Förster, Hitler acknowledged the reception of Förster's proclamation and thanked him for "the loyalty of Danzig to Germans."

He declared a newly proclaimed law by Förster for the reunion of Danzig to Germany "immediately effective" and named Förster, already chosen by the Danzig Senate as Chief of State, to head the city government.

Förster notified Adolf Hitler, Führer of Germany, of his action by telegram.

Article 1 of Förster's decree suspended the constitution of the Free City immediately.

[Editor's Note—Under the city's League of Nations status its constitution was guaranteed by the League, and changes without its consent were declared illegal.]

Article 2 of the decree placed all legal and administrative

(Continued on Page 8, Column 3)

DOESN'T COUNT ON ITALIAN AID, FÜHRER SAYS

Names Goering Successor If He Should Be Killed In Conflict

Declares Versailles Treaty Is "Not A Law For Us Germans"

Reichstag Approves

Berlin, Friday, Sept. 1 (AP)—The Reichstag voted today, immediately after Hitler's speech, to annex the Free City of Danzig.

[*By the Associated Press*]

Berlin, *Friday*, Sept. 1—Adolf Hitler declared to the German nation today he would achieve the return of Danzig and Pomorze (Polish Corridor) and halt Polish attacks on Germans or die fighting.

As a sign of his determination to "live henceforth more than ever for Germany alone," the Führer and his adjutants appeared at the momentous session of the Reichstag in grey army uniforms.

"I am putting on the uniform and I shall take it off only in victory or death," Hitler vowed in his impassioned thirty-six-minute speech.

Goering His Successor

The Führer dramatically disclosed his wishes as to his successors in the leadership of the Reich—Field Marshal Hermann Goering and Rudolph Hess, Hitler's deputy, were first and second choices, respectively.

After Goering and Hess, Hitler said, the nation would be led by men chosen as the bravest by the senate of the Nazi party.

Germany does not count on Italian support, the Führer said, while on the other hand Soviet Russia now is the Reich's eternal friend.

[Editor's Note — A transcript of Hitler's speech as taken down in London showed that at this point he thanked Italy for support and said: "I will not appeal to foreign help in this fateful hour. We will carry out this task ourselves."]

"Modest And Loyal"

In essence, Hitler's speech was a reiteration of the German plea that every attempt at peaceful revision of "intolerable conditions" had failed and that Germany's demands were "modest and loyal" but that the reply of Poland and the Western powers was only provocation.

To neutral nations Hitler pledged scrupulous respect so long as Germany's opponents do likewise.

In a last-minute effort to stave off action by the Western powers (Britain and France) Hitler renounced all claims on them. By implication, this included renunciation of Germany's colonial claims.

Ask Nothing From West

"We want nothing from the Western powers and we have formally declared we have no claims against them," Hitler said. "Our west wall (of fortifications) is also our west border."

Hitler refrained from declaring war on Poland but said he would continue to fight until Poland's government yields or is supplanted by a government which would yield.

Greeted by a great ovation from the Reichstag that had been summoned at 3 A. M. for a special 10 o'clock meeting, plunged directly into the subject of Poland and Danzig by declaring:

"We meet to solve the problems raised by the Versailles Treaty."

Denies War Inclinations

Denying the Reich is not peaceably inclined—the Führer less than five hours before had announced his army was meeting "force with force" because of alleged border violations by the Poles—declared that we "tried to solve many problems peacefully."

"Fifteen years of peaceful effort to

(Continued on Page 2, Column 4)

WARSAW ANNOUNCES RAIDS FROM AIR AND ATTACKS ON ITS DEFENSES NEAR MLAWA

Foreign Office Confirms That Fighting Has Started In Danzig—Army Ambulance Carries German Wounded To Gleiwitz

[*By the Associated Press*]

Warsaw, Sept. 1—The Foreign Office said today that German planes had bombed Krakow and Katowice, in southwestern Poland.

German planes also bombed Czestochowa, Tczew and Grudziadz early this morning, the Foreign Office said.

It was reported officially that German troops had attacked Polish defenses near Mlawa, bordering the southern part of east Prussia.

Action Against Munitions Base

It also was officially announced that Germany began an air and land action against Westerplatte, a Polish munitions base in Danzig harbor, at 5 A. M. (The Polish Legation in Budapest said the attack had been repulsed.)

Simultaneously she started an air action against Puck, the Polish naval base in the Bay of Gdynia.

Artillery shelling was reported on a line between Grudziads and Mlawa on the southern border of east Prussia.

It was pointed out that all points bombed except Westerplatte have civilian population which had not been evacuated.

Wounded Reach Gleiwitz

[*By the Associated Press*]

Gleiwitz, Germany, Sept. 1—An army ambulance carrying wounded soldiers arrived at the emergency hospital here today at 9.10 A. M. (3.10 A. M., E.S.T.).

The men, carried in a wagon, were on stretchers. One had on a first aid field bandage. It could not be ascertained where the ambulance came from.

Warsaw Bombed, London Hears

London, Sept. 1 (AP)—Reuters (British News Agency) said it had learned from Polish sources in Paris that Warsaw was bombed today.

Reuters also said in a Warsaw dispatch that the official Warsaw radio announced German troops had launched a full-scale attack against towns in the Polish Corridor.

Berlin, Sept. 1 (AP)—A radio announcement from army headquarters said today the German air force was in action over Polish territory.

French Cabinet Called

Paris, Sept. 1 (AP)—Edouard Daladier, Premier and War Minister of France, informed that German troops crossed the Polish frontier today, summoned an urgent meeting of his Cabinet for 10.30 A. M. (4.30 A. M., E.S.T.).

It was probable that Parliament would be called tomorrow.

Reports of the German invasion came from Berlin and from the Polish Embassy here. The Ministers were called to Elysee Palace to meet with President Albert Lebrun.

Upon receipt of word of the German operations, Daladier rushed to the War Ministry and called Generalissimo Maurice Gustave Gamelin, supreme commander of land, sea and air forces, into consultation.

A little later Daladier summoned Foreign Minister Georges Bonnet.

The Polish Embassy said Germans violated the Polish frontier at four points and at the same time it characterized German charges that Poles had crossed into Germany as "pure invention."

Havas, French news agency, announced that "a German declaration of war against Poland probably will lead France and Great Britain to take new military measures."

Weather Forecast
Partly cloudy and continued warm, with local afternoon thunder showers today and tomorrow; moderate southwest winds.
Yesterday's Temperatures: Max., 94; Min., 69.
(Details on Page 25)

THE SUN

Registered United States Patent Office

6 A. M.

Vol. 207—No. 17—E | PAID CIRCULATION MAY MORNING 148,229 EVENING 162,594 310,823 || SUNDAY 202,519 | BALTIMORE, WEDNESDAY, JUNE 5, 1940 | Entered as second-class matter at Baltimore Postoffice. | 26 Pages | 3 Cents

NAZIS RENEW ATTACK

France Must Meet Onslaught Alone

BRITAIN WILL NEED TIME TO REPLACE LOSSES IN FLANDERS, LONDON SAYS

Churchill Vows England Will Fight On To Bitter End, Unsupported If Necessary—Cable Service To Paris Interrupted

Wednesday Morning Communique 4.45 A. M.

Paris, Wednesday, June 5 (AP)—The French high command announced today that a new German attack had begun.

Its communique said:

"All information received from the front this morning announces that a new battle has begun.

"The enemy's violent effort has carried so far between the sea and road from Laon to Soissons."

Soissons is on the Aisne river, about fifty-three miles northeast of Paris, air line, and eighteen miles southwest of Laon. It is approximately one hundred miles inland from the English Channel.

BULLETIN—5.25 A. M.

Zurich, Switzerland, Wednesday, June 5 (AP)—Allied warplanes early today bombed Friedrichshafen and other objectives on the German side of Lake Constance and dropped six bombs on the Swiss side of the border.

BULLETIN—4.33 A. M.

Paris, Wednesday, June 5 (AP)—Paris was out of touch with the United States by cable this morning, but communication was maintained by wireless. There was no immediate explanation of the cable disruption.

[By the Associated Press]

London, June 4—British spokesmen said tonight that France must stand alone, or virtually alone, against the German onslaughts until British industries can replace the vast quantities of guns, tanks, trucks and munitions abandoned by the British Expeditionary Force in the retreat from Flanders.

There are some British troops south of the Somme and the War Office made it clear that others would be sent to France as soon as possible, but the fact remains that in the meantime the French army stands almost alone across the Channel.

By RAYMOND DANIELL
[Copyright by New York Times]

London, June 4—In a moving, dramatic speech to the House of Commons this afternoon, Premier Winston Churchill declared that even if the motherland had to fight alone and was brought to her knees by the German military machine, the British fleet and the empire would fight on to the bitter end until "in God's good time" the New World came to the rescue of the Old.

These were brave, prescient words uttered by a man in whose veins flows British and American blood, for while he is a descendant of Marlborough, his mother was a Jerome of New York.

Recites Story Of Heroism

None who heard the Prime Minister, who foresaw it all and warned the nation and the world where appeasement was leading, could doubt the dire extremity in which this country finds itself today, with no effective allies save France, which lies partly under the invader's boot, and with Italy threatening the life line of its empire in the Mediterranean.

He led up to his grim peroration with a recital of the story of heroism and sacrifice of the British army in Flanders, making no bones about the extent of its losses. While it was true that the navy and air force had been able to rescue the bulk of this encircled army betrayed by the treachery of Leopold, Mr. Churchill said, wars are not won by retreats and withdrawals of armies.

Although most of this army is home again, prepared to defend these sea-surrounded islands or to depart again for the battle front in France, the Prime Minister said it had left 30,000

(Continued on Page 9, Column 5)

Churchill's Speech Shatters Delusion Of Victory, Paper Says

By FRANK R. KENT, JR.
[London Bureau of The Sun]

London, June 4—The public here is reacting to two salient points in Prime Minister Churchill's speech, namely, the fighting tone of it and his unsparing presentation of the cold facts.

Churchill gave unstinting praise to the men of all three services for the fight they put up, giving special mention to the Dunkerque evacuation and the holding of Calais. At the same time, he did not pull punches in describing the situation which the Allies face. It was a realistic speech with indomitable undertones.

"Gravest Speech"

The Manchester *Guardian's* Parliamentary correspondent says that many members of the House of Commons

(Continued on Page 8, Column 6)

Waiting For Ships At Dunkerque

ALLIED SOLDIERS line up on the beach at Dunkerque waiting for ships to take them off while the Germans pressed forward on three fronts and attacked from the air those trying to debark. (By radio from London.)

ARMY AND NAVY DEFENSE BILLS ARE ADVANCED

House Approves Report On One, Sends Another To Conference

By J. FRED ESSARY

Washington, June 4—The House late today approved the conference report on the huge naval appropriation bill, providing for $1,308,171,000 for an increase in that arm of the service.

At the same time it defeated a move led by Republicans to earmark $68,000,000 of the amount instead of issuing a "blank check" for the sum.

In addition to this the House sent to conference the companion army appropriation bill carrying a total appropriation of approximately $1,500,000,000.

Breakdown Of Program

In that general connection the President sent to Congress a breakdown of the $1,277,740,000 supplemental program which he asked in his second defense message.

In other words, this was essentially a day of action in dealing with defense issues. In another two or three days it is expected that the financial end of the program will have been enacted by Congress.

The Senate passed the aviation expansion bill carrying large authorizations for the naval flying service.

Bureau Of Ships Set Up

Also the Senate passed a bill consolidating the Naval Bureau of Construction and Repair with the Bureau of Engineering, to be known hereafter as the Bureau of Ships.

Finally the Senate sent back the conference report on the War Department civil functions bill which includes $114,000,000 in appropriations and contract authorizations for construction of a third set of Panama Canal locks as part of the defense program.

The naval bill must go back to the Senate for consideration of a few amendments agreed upon after that body had originally passed it. It is not assumed that the army bill will remain long in conference.

Marshall Backs Guard Plan

On top of all this Gen. George C. Marshall, chief of staff of the army, told the House Military Affairs Committee how important it was that the President be given power to order out the National Guard.

And the White House authoritatively stated that the importance of this lies in a possible emergency in which it will be necessary for the Guard to relieve regulars at various outposts such as the Canal Zone, Puerto Rico and elsewhere.

It was also stated with reference to the Guard that the Presidential power to use it should be given before Congress adjourns, against the possibility

(Continued on Page 5, Column 3)

House Committee Votes Four Billion Debt Rise

Ways And Means Body Raises Proposed Increase By Billion To Finance National Defense

By C. P. TRUSSELL
[Washington Bureau of The Sun]

Washington, June 4—A $4,000,000,000 increase in the Governmental debt limit, instead of the $3,000,000,000 decided upon only last week, was voted late today by the revenue-raising House Ways and Means Committee in the light of new financial demands for national defense.

This action, taken after Treasury Department conferences and in the midst of the committee's consideration of the pending $656,000,000 five-year amortization tax bill, necessitated an abrupt readjustment of its program.

There were indications, plain ones, that before the present measure leaves committee custody and is sent to the House for floor action, it will call for at least another $200,000,000 of additional taxes, and may, in the end, become a bill whose mission will be to yield $1,000,000,000 of new revenues annually over a period of five years.

Must Reach Deep

To raise just the extra money needed to amortize the additional $1,000,000,000 debt limit rise—which would increase the total to $49,000,000,000—the committee, which had planned to report the bill out promptly, will have to reach deep into other sources.

Many revenue yielding fields were explored today in executive session. No decisions were reached, but it was said by members that a broadening of the income tax base was not beyond the realm of possibility. It had been suggested previously that something in excess of $200,000,000 could be realized by reaching for incomes as low as the $800-a-year bracket.

Roosevelt Mentions It

As the House committee deliberated its new move at the Capitol, President Roosevelt observed, in the course of his semi-weekly press conference, that the more revenues raised for contribution to the pay-as-you-go emergency defense program, the better it would be.

At the same time Mr. Roosevelt held out little hope for more than a $250,000,000 to $300,000,000 saving—in contrast with the $500,000,000 estimate of Senator Byrd (Dem., Va.) and sponsors of his horizontal expense reduction program—even though a proposed ten per cent. cut-back were effected.

Doubts Percentage Cut

There were a number of items of expense and benefit, the President said, that could not be cut. Hence, he maintained, savings estimates could not be made on a straight-out percentage schedule.

Pensions to veterans, Mr. Roosevelt observed, could not be reduced without an act of Congress. Social security benefits, he added, could not be reduced without impairing the program. Nor, he held, could public roads expenditures be lowered, as they were a matter of contract between Federal and State governments. Public debt interest payments, he said, must proceed at full volume in the interest of national credit.

Would Preserve CCC

The President went further. He did not think, he said, that the Government could cut farm parity and soil conservation payments or allotments to the Civilian Conservation Corps and the National Youth Administration. Nor, he went on, could the work-relief funds be reduced, as it was not yet known how much employment would be created.

Without making detailed breakdowns, President Roosevelt concluded that, of total budgetary and extraordinary expenses, there would be only about $250,000,000 or $300,000,000 left to be subjected to savings-for-defense cuts.

Most of these, he explained, were regular departmental expenses—running expenses—and he hoped, he added, to save around ten per cent. of them through economies. During the present fiscal year, Mr. Roosevelt explained, approximately $184,000,000 was saved the same way.

Meanwhile, the way had been cleared for a recapitulation of funds

(Continued on Page 13, Column 3)

ALLIES BOMB MUNICH, RUHR AND FRANKFORT

Launch Reprisal Raids On Reich As Paris Death Toll Hits 254

[By the Associated Press]

Paris, Wednesday, June 5—An air-raid alarm was sounded from 9.55 P. M. to 10.45 P. M. in the northwestern region of France last night. The alarm was in the same region which the Germans bombed Monday night.

[By the Associated Press]

Paris, June 4—The Allies wrote off the Battle of Flanders with the abandonment of Dunkerque today and slashed back at the Germans in grim bomb-for-bomb reprisals for the raid on Paris Monday which left 1,000 French dead or wounded.

With most of their troops out of the besieged Channel port, the French announced the end of the northern campaign and turned swiftly to the task of replying to the German air forays which continued today with new assaults on the Rhone Valley and the port of Le Havre.

Allies Strike Back

Less than twelve hours after the Germans loosed 1,000 bombs on Paris and vicinity yesterday, the War Ministry announced that Allied bombers had started striking back "with great

(Continued on Page 4, Column 5)

Mrs. Morrow Again At Odds With Lindbergh On Allied Aid

She Urges All Help, Saying Nazi Victory "Would Endanger Our Way Of Life For A Generation"

[By the Associated Press]

New York, June 4—Mrs. Dwight W. Morrow, widow of a one-time United States Senator and Ambassador to Mexico, appealed tonight for United States aid to Britain and France "as a matter of self interest" because, she said, a Nazi victory would mean that "our peaceful way of life will be endangered for a generation at least."

"Short of actually declaring war," she said, "I believe that everything we have which we could give without impairing our own safety—'all that is within us'—should go to help them win on the field of battle."

Thus again she differed with her son-in-law, Charles A. Lindbergh, on this country's policy in the European conflict. She has several times urged help for the Allies, while Lindbergh last fall favored an embargo on offensive weapons to belligerents and last month declared Americans need not fear a foreign invasion unless they "bring it on through their own quarreling and meddling with affairs abroad."

Mrs. Morrow, the acting president of Smith College, spoke over the air under the auspices of the Committee for American Defense Through Aid for the Allies.

She said there was "no thought of our sending an army abroad" but contended that "the best means of avoiding this type of involvement" was the sending of munitions and supplies.

(Continued on Page 3, Column 8)

HITLER GIVES COMMAND WHICH HURLS LEGIONS AGAIN AGAINST FRENCH

Eight-Day Celebration Of Battle Of Flanders Proclaimed In Reich — 1,200,000 Prisoners Claimed To Have Been Taken

[By the Associated Press]

Berlin, Wednesday, June 5 — Adolf Hitler announced from his headquarters on the Western front today that "beginning today the West front will resume the march."

This declaration was contained in the Führer's order of the day to his army.

In a special appeal to the nation, Hitler asked the German people to stage an eight-day celebration of the German victory in the Battle of Flanders.

The text of the order of the day follows, in part:

"Soldiers of the West front:

"Dunkerque has fallen. Forty thousand Frenchmen and Englishmen have been taken prisoner as the remainder of one-time great armies. An untold amount of material has been captured.

"Thus the greatest battle in world history has been concluded.

"Soldiers! My confidence in you is boundless.

"You did not disillusion me.

"The most audacious plan of war history was realized through your unexampled courageousness, through your energy of withstanding the greatest strain and through hardest exertion and hardships.

"Soldiers, in a few weeks you have in the hardest fight, often against really valiant opponents, forced two states to capitulate, destroyed France's best divisions and defeated the British Expeditionary Force, taking it prisoner or chasing it from the continent.

"The plutocratic rulers of England and France, however, who pledged each other to avoid with all means the bloom of a new and better world, want a continuation of the war.

"Their desire shall be realized.

"Soldiers, beginning today the West front is ready to march again."

[By the Associated Press]

Berlin, June 4—Adolf Hitler's high command announced tonight the conclusion of "the greatest destructive battle of all times," with the capture of hard-held Dunkerque along with 40,000 prisoners, and then threatened the French and British with "total destruction."

It told the German people that they could be certain "that final victory is ours," now that Flanders is won.

Suggestions that a big offensive might thus be in the making in the south toward Paris were accompanied by a jubilant recapitulation in which the high command said that English, French, Belgian and Dutch prisoners numbered 1,200,000 since May 10, exclusive of an undetermined number killed and wounded.

"Total Destruction" Threatened

The message from the front—a message which was read over all German radio stations after the public had for an hour been told repeatedly to listen in, thus directly challenged the Allies:

"Inasmuch as the enemy still spurns peace, the fight will be carried on to his total destruction!"

The message follows:

"The great battle in Flanders and Artois is ended. It will go down in war history as the greatest destructive battle of all times.

"When the German army entered upon its decision in the West on the morning of May 10 the strategic goal as given by the Führer and supreme commander in chief was to force a break-through in the enemy border fortifications south of Namur and thereby create a precondition for destruction of the French and English armies north of the Aisne and Somme.

"At the same time Holland was to be occupied swiftly and thereby eliminate it as a base for a planned English opera-

(Continued on Page 2, Column 7)

Weather Forecast
Mostly clear and moderately cold today; fair, with slowly rising temperature, tomorrow; fresh northwest winds.
Yesterday's Temperatures: Max., 59; Min.; 39.

THE SUNDAY SUN EXTRA

Vol. 41—No. 49— 4 Pages PAID CIRCULATION NOVEMBER MORNING EVENING 317,773 SUNDAY 233,019 BALTIMORE, SUNDAY, DECEMBER 7, 1941

JAPS DECLARE WAR ON U. S

Honolulu, Manila Bombed

NAVAL BATTLE OFF HAWAII

By the Associated Press

Tokyo, Moday, Dec. 8– Japanes e headquarters announced at 6 A. M. today that Japan had entered a state of war with the United States and Britain in the Western Pacific as from dawn to day.

By the Associated Press

Honolulu, Dec. 7– A naval engagement is in progress off Honolulu, with at least one black enemy aircraft carrier in action againt Pearl Harbor defenses.

By Eugene Burns

Associated Press Staff Correspondent

Honolulu, Dec. 7—Japanese bombs killed at least five persons and injured many others, three seriously, in a surprise morning aerial attack on Honolulu today.

Unverified reports said a foreign warship appeared off Pearl Harbor and began firing at the defenses in that highly fortified post.

The sound of cannon firing can be heard here in Honolulu, as this story is telephoned to the San Francisco Associated Press office.

Reports say that the Japanese bombers scored two hits, one at Hickam Field, Air Corps post on Oahu Island, and another at Pearl Harbor, setting an oil tank afire.

Shortly before I started talking on the transpacific telephone, I saw a formation of five Japanese planes flying over Honolulu.

American anti-aircraft has set up a terrific din and the sky also is filled with American battle aircraft. The sound of cannonading coming from the direction of Pearl Harbor has been continuing for an hour and a half. So far, there are no reports of casualties. No bombs have fallen in Honolulu itself, so far as I could determine before making this call.

Some aerial dogfights are in progress in the skies over Honolulu. At 9.30 A. M. Honolulu time (3 P. M. Eastern standard time) the attack still was in progress.

What damage was done by the swift surprise raid was not immediately apparent. But reports said enemy bombers scored a hit at Hickam Field, army airport, and another on an oil tank at the Pearl Harbor naval base.

At least two nine-plane formations of four-motored black bombers flew over Honolulu and Pearl Harbor. Each plane bore Japan's Rising Sun insignia.

There was a report from persons who came past Pearl Harbor that one ship there was lying on its side in the water and four others were on fire. This could not be confirmed immediately.

The sky was filled with puffs of smoke from exploding shells fired by American army and navy anti-aircraft units.

Whether surface vessels of the United States fleet were in action against the enemy could not be learned at once, but columns of water rising from the sea as shells hit the water indicated a naval action.

Viewed from the hills back of Honolulu, where many city folk went to view the fight columns of heavy black smoke went skyward from Pearl Harbor.

The citizens of Honolulu have been cleared from the streets by military and naval units, assisted by civilian volunteers, all carrying arms.

But a lot of citizens have left the city for hills, to watch the planes and anti-aircraft, and get a general view of the excitement.

LONDON HIT BY AMAZEMENT BY WAR NEWS

Official British Reaction To Attack Expected Quickly

[By the Associated Press]

London, Dec. 7—Prime Minister Churchill and John G. Winant, United States Ambassador to Britain, were in conference tonight a short time after President Roosevelt's announcement that Japanese planes had attacked Hawaii and the Philippines.

[By the Associated Press]

London Dec. 7—An authoritative British source declared tonight that Britain reaction to President Roosevelt announcement that the Japanese had attacked Hawaiian and Philippine lines of the United States "could be expected fairly soon."

Prime Minister Churchill, who promised November 10 that Britain would declare war on Japan "within the hour" if she attacked the United States, was presumed to have been informed immediately.

British sources, however, could not disclose when or where he had heard it.

Winant Not At Embassy

United States Ambassador John G. Winant was away from the embassy but aides said he "wa in a position to hear the news immediately, and it be presumed he was informed."

Most of the British Cabinet was believed to be in London tonight.

The Prime Minister's promise, made

(Continued on Page 2, Column 3)

BULLETINS

New York, Dec 7 (AP)—Japanese warplanes killed 350 men at Hickman Field and set fire to the United States battleship Oklahoma today in a suden raid on Pearl Harbor and Honolulu, an NBC observer radioed direct from the scene today.

Berlin, Dec. 7 (AP)—A German spokesman declared tonight there could be no reaction from Germany to the announced Japanese air attack on Pearl Harbor until all sides of the case were at hand.

Hawaiian Defenses

(By the Associated Press)

The Hawaiian Islands stand at the crossroads of the Pacific, approximately one third of the way across the vast ocean separating the United States and Japan.

In these islands the United States has constructed a great naval fortress, centered in the naval base and drydock at Pearl Harbor on the picturesque island of Oahu. This harbor, sixty feet deep and home ten square miles in area, can accommodate the entire United States fleet.

Major Key To East

The strategic location of Hawaii and the great defense works centered there make the territory a major key to war in the Far East.

Honolulu, the principal city of Hawaii, lies a dot in the ocean approximately 2,000 nautical miles from California, 3,500 from Japan, almost 5,000 from the Philippines, and the naval base at Hongkong.

To the average American Hawaii may mean hula dancers, ukuleles and pineapples; to the army and navy and air force it is one of their major outposts, dotted with guns, sinewed with the most modern machinery for all types of warfare.

In combined area the islands, although only slightly larger than Connecticut, are the only major group in the North Pacific. Most of the population of 423,000 are Orientals, slightly more than a third of them of Japanese stock. One —seventh are Polynesian, one-eighth Filipinoes, one-fifteenth Chinese.

Pearl Harbor lies on the southern shore of Oahu. A narrow channel provides the only entrance from the sea and makes it one of the world's best natural havens. Ships in the harbor cannot be seen from the open water.

Army Strength

Thousands of soldiers, their numbers increasing steadily recently, are housed in the Schofield barracks on the center of Oahu. There also is on the island a big army air field to which a mass flight of twenty-one bombing planes was made secretely from California earlier this year.

The Hawaiian Islands politically are territory of the United States, ceded to the United States by the Republic of Hawaii in 1898 and made a territory by the Congress of 1900.

SOVIET ARMY WILL FIGHT ON, LITVINOFF SAYS

To Continue Stout Resistance Against Nazis, New Envoy Asserts

[By the Associated Press]

Washington, Dec. 7—Maxim Litvinoff, the new Russian Ambassador, arrived in Washingon today to assume an important part in troubled world affairs, and assured the American people that the Red Army would continue its stout resistance against the Nazi invasion.

Looking after a month of travel, but affable as always, the diplomat landed at the Washington National Airport with his English-born wife at his side, to be greeted by officials of the embassy, their wives and their children and a group oattired in Russian military uniforms.

Bring Huge Bouquets

The embassy wives and children bore huge bouquets of roses, snapdragons and chrysanthemums, which they thrust upon Mr. and Mrs. Litvinoff as they stood smiling on the plane ramp.

Then the Ambasador, wearing a battered felt hat and a rusty dark blue overcoat, made a brief statement.

"I am very happy to be once more in the Capital of the remarkable country, the United States of America," he said. "My first visit here was of great importance. But still more important is my arrival now at a moment when the destiny of all mankind is being settled.

Assures American People

"I know of the great interest and sympathy with which the American

(Continued on Page 2, Column 4)

Untold Damage Done Honolulu, Witness Says

[By the Associated Press]

Washington, Dec. 7—The White House announced today that heavy damage had been inflicted in the apanese attack on Hawaii and that there probably had been heavy loss of life.

(By the Associated Press)

New York, Dec. 7—Untold damage has been done to the United States naval base at Pearl Harbor and to the city of Honolulu itself by unidentified bombing planes, an NBC observer reported today in a broadcast direct from Honolulu.

The observer, standing on the roof of a building in Honolulu, said the planes, undoubtedly Japanese, made the raid unexpectedly. His report was suddenly broken off.

"It Is A Real War"

Before its interruption, his report said:

"We have witnessed this mornng the attack of Pearl Harbor and a severe bombing of Pearl Harbor by army planes, undoubtedly Japanese.

"The city of Honolulu has also been attacked and considerable damage done.

"This battle has been going on for nearly three hours.

"One of the bombs dropped within fifty feet of the KGU tower.

"It is no joke; it is a real war.

"The public of Honolulu have been advised to keep in their homes and away from the army and navy. There has been severe fighting going on in the air and on the sea."

At this point the broadcast was interrupted.

The speaker continued a few minutes later:

"We have no statement as to how much damage has been done, but it has been a very severe attack.

"The army and navy, it appears, now have the air and sea under control."

Here the broadcast again was cut off without explanation.

Roosevelt Gives Navy Orders

(By the Associated Press)

Washington, Dec. 7—Japanese airplanes today attacked American defense bases at Hawaii and Manila, and President Roosevelt ordered the army and navy to carry out undisclosd orders prepared for the defense of the United States.

The White House said that Japan had attacked America's vital outposts in the Pacific—Hawaii and Manila—at 3.20 P. M. (E.S.T.) and that so far as was known the attacks were still in progress.

Announcing the President's action for the protection of American territory, Presidential Secretary Stephen Early declared that so far as is known now the attacks were "made wholly without warning—

THE WEATHER

Cloudy and warmer tonight, with lowest temperature 33. Tuesday cloudy and colder.

Detailed report on Page 39

THE EVENING SUN

6 STAR ★★★★★★ Wall Street Close

Vol. 64—No. 44 | PAID CIRCULATION NOVEMBER MORNING, 151,220 EVENING, 166,553 317,773 || SUNDAY 233,019 | BALTIMORE, MONDAY, DECEMBER 8, 1941 | Entered as second-class matter at Baltimore Postoffice | 42 Pages | 3 Cents

U.S. DECLARES WAR

Senate Unanimous, House 388 To 1

1,500 KILLED IN HAWAII

Old American Battleship Lost, One Destroyer Blown Up, Our Plane Loss Heavy

By Ben H. Miller

Washington, Dec. 8—Japan's *Blitzkrieg* against the Hawaiian Island of Oahu struck the United States with damage more serious than at first believed and caused the loss of at least one "old" battleship, a destroyer, several smaller ships, a large number of airplanes and at least 1,500 lives, the White House revealed today.

In the first official communique of the second day of this country's shooting war, Presidential Secretary Stephen T. Early issued the following statement, which he said had been approved by President Roosevelt:

"American operations against the Japanese attacking force in the neighborhood of the Hawaiian Islands are still continuing.

"A number of Japanese planes and submarines have been destroyed.

"Several Hangars Destroyed"

"The damage caused to our forces in Oahu in yesterday's attack appears more serious than at first believed.

"In Pearl Harbor itself, one old battleship has capsized and several other ships have been seriously damaged.

"One destroyer was blown up.

"Several other small ships were seriously hit.

"Army and navy fields were bombed with the resulting destruction of several hangars and a large number of planes were put out of commission.

3,000 Oahu Casualties Feared

"A number of bombers arrived safely from San Francisco during the engagement—while it was under way.

"Reinforcements of planes are being rushed and repair work is under way on ships, planes and ground facilities.

"Guam, Wake, the Midway Islands and Hongkong have been attacked.

"Details of these attacks are lacking.

"Two hundred marines—all that remained in China—have been interned by the Japanese near Tientsin.

"The total casualties on the island of Oahu are not yet definitely known, but in all probability will mount to about 3,000.

1,500 Are Wounded

"Nearly half of these are fatalities, the others being wounded.

"It seems clear from the reports that many bombs were dropped in the city of Honolulu, resulting in a small number of casualties."

This concluded the formal statement, but Early was asked if there was any explanation how the Japanese appeared to have been able to get inside of this country's outer defenses.

The secretary said there was no official explanation, but that the consensus of the experts was that probably all, if not all, of the planes which struck out of the dawn yesterday morning had been airplane-carrier borne.

They apparently were dive-bombers, he said, and had struck about daylight.

Coasted On Targets, Is Belief

This meant, he went on, that the carriers would have had all night in which to approach under the cover of darkness.

It seemed that they thus were able to take off at a considerable distance, attain a high altitude, and then coast in to loose their destruction.

Prior to Early's communique the Capital had been gripped in a tight and ominous silence since about midnight.

All news, all major activities, centered around the White House, where President Roosevelt sat until far into the night with the Cabinet, Congress leaders and his closest advisers, and contemplated the epochal message he delivered this afternoon to a joint session of the House and Senate.

Sea Supremacy Won, Tokyo Claims

Tokyo, *Tuesday*, Dec. 9 (Official Radio Picked Up by AP)—The Japanese asserted today they had won naval supremacy over the United States in the Pacific, claiming by official or unofficial reports the destruction of two American battleships and an aircraft carrier and the damaging of four battleships and six cruisers.

These, declared the Japanese, were the principal results of the first shock of their air-naval offensive.

The claim to supremacy appeared in a commentary resume broadcast by Domei, which said that any force the United States now could muster "would be regarded as utterly inadequate to accomplish any successful outcome in an encounter with the thus-far intact Japanese fleet."

Reports Heavy Blows Dealt

Imperial headquarters, in an announcement broadcast by Domei, said that two battleships and a minesweeper had been sunk, four heavy cruisers damaged, many merchant ships seized and scores of planes destroyed aground and in the air in Hawaii and the Philippines.

The communique said also that a United States aircraft carrier had been sunk by submarine off Honolulu "although this is not confirmed."

So far as naval losses went, the Japanese said they had escaped unscathed and they acknowledged the loss of only two planes in Philippine actions.

The Japanese said that the mine-

[Continued On Page B, Column 7]

Welders Planning Strike

[By the Associated Press]

Washington, Dec. 8—The United Brotherhoods of Welders, Cutters and Helpers, an independent labor union, today rescinded an order of yesterday calling off a nation-wide strike and instructed all local officers to get their men ready "for a sudden and determined walkout."

A strike which had been set for tomorrow was called off because of the war situation.

National leaders said the new call came because members of the union had been refused permission to work by members of the American Federation of Labor at two ammonium plants being constructed for the War Department at Morgantown, W. Va.

Officials said a strike would involve 125,000 men throughout the nation.

No time or date for the walkout was set.

Latest War Bulletins

Manila Damage "Terrific"

New York, Dec. 8 (AP)—An NBC reporter, broadcasting in the midst of an early Tuesday morning air attack on Manila, said that "terrific damage" had been left by the Japanese attackers, including the apparent destruction of the gasoline supply at Nichols Airfield.

State Guard To Be Called Out

A decision to call out the State Guard for the first time was made at Gov. Herbert R. O'Conor's conference at Annapolis this afternoon with military and police officials and leaders of civilian defense organizations. The Governor said the guard would be called out in numbers to be determined by its leaders and Third Corps Area officers to guard vital defense spots in Maryland.

Pecautions At Oakland

Oakland, Cal., Dec. 8 (AP)—All schools in metropolitan Oakland were ordered closed today as an air raid precaution on reports that a Japanese airplane carrier may be off the Pacific Coast.

Axis Roundup In Canal Zone

Cristobal, C. Z., Dec. 8 (AP)—Police began rounding up Germans and Italians in the Canal Zone today in a drive coordinated with the roundup at Colon where Panama police have taken eleven Germans into custody and are combing the city for more Axis nationals.

Guatemala Backs United States

Guatemala City, Guatemala, Dec. 8 (AP)—President Jorge Ubico sent a message today to President Roosevelt to express Guatemala's solidarity with the United States against Japan. A declaration of war was expected during the afternoon.

Egypt Breaking With Japan

London, Dec. 8 (AP)—Exchange Telegraph reported today that the Egyptian Government has decided to break off diplomatic relations with Japan.

Honduras Declares War On Japan

Tegucigalpa, Honduras, Dec. 8 (AP)—Honduras declared war on Japan today and the Government established martial law throughout the republic.

[More War Bulletins on Page 2]

Philippine Forts, Harbors Bombed

[By the Associated Press]

Manila, Dec. 8—Japanese bombers struck at military bases and ports the length of the Philippines today, smashing at big Fort Stotsenburg, Clark Field, the summer mountain capital at Baguio, the ports of Davao and Aparri and the far northern Batan Island group.

Manila had heard no air-raid alarms and saw no raiding planes early tonight although Japanese warcraft were reported within forty miles of the city.

Manila, which has no public air-raid shelters, was blacked out beneath heavily overcast skies from soon after dusk. Other ports also shut off lights and waited tensely.

One Clipper Reported Damaged

It was reported here reliably that the Hongkong Clipper of Pan American Airways was damaged in a Japanese air raid on Hongkong.

The huge flying boat left Manila yesterday with a number of prominent Manila residents aboard and apparently was at the airways base on the Kowloon side of Hongkong harbor at the time of the raid. Reports here said passengers and crew were uninjured.

Three Japanese Planes Downed

The army headquarters announced that Davao, a center of concentrated Japanese population on the southernmost of the large islands, and Baguio, summer-time mountain capital of the Philippines north of Manila, had been bombed by daylight.

During the afternoon Japanese bombers struck at Fort Stotsenberg, one of the biggest army encampments in the Philippines, and nearby Clark Field.

Numerous buildings were said to have been set afire and the army's telephone communications to Manila were cut.

Private advices said three Japanese planes were shot down during the attack.

(Domei broadcast what it described as a reliable report from neutral sources that the Japanese air force attacked Fort Stotsenburg, headquarters of the United States Army in northern Luzon, heavily damaged an airfield and blew up numerous oil reservoirs during afternoon attacks on the Philippines.)

13 And 17 Planes In Attacking Squads

The Mayor of Davao reported later that the Japanese had made a second assault on that city.

(An NBC report from Manila said one Japanese plane was shot down in Davao Bay.)

Army officials said they were investigating reports that the Japanese had also bombed Tarlac on the island of Luzon.

Thirteen planes took part in the attack on Davao and inflicted some damage, the official announcement said.

Seventeen raiders were reported to have struck at Baguio

[Continued On Page B, Column 3]

'Unprovoked And Dastardly,' Roosevelt Terms Japan's Sea And Air Attack

New York, Dec. 8 (AP)—The Rome radio said today in a broadcast that the Japanese declaration of war "involves, in accordance with the three-power pact, the existence of a state of war between the two Axis powers and the United States." CBS heard the broadcast.

[By the Associated Press]

Washington, Dec. 8—Congress voted a formal declaration of war against Japan today after President Roosevelt requested immediate action as an answer to Japan's "unprovoked and dastardly attack" on Hawaii.

A united Congress acted swiftly after the President had revealed that American forces lost two warships and 3,000 dead and wounded in the surprise dawn attack yesterday.

The Senate vote was 82 to 0.

The vote for war in the House was 388 to 1.

The single adverse House vote was that of Miss Jeannette Rankin, Republican Congresswoman from Montana, who was among the few who voted against the 1917 declaration of war on Germany.

The speed with which the two Houses granted President Roosevelt's request for the declaration was unprecedented.

Text Of President's Message

The full text of President Roosevelt's message follows:

"To the Congress of the United States:

"Yesterday, December 7, 1941—a date which will live in infamy—the United States of America was suddenly and deliberately attacked by naval and air forces of the Empire of Japan.

"The United States was at peace with that nation and, at the solicitation of Japan, was still in conversation with its Government and its Emperor looking toward the maintenance of peace in the Pacific.

"Indeed, one hour after Japanese air squadrons had commenced bombing in Oahu, the Japanese Ambassador to the United States and his colleague delivered to the Secretary of State a formal reply to a recent American message. While this reply stated that it seemed useless to continue the existing diplomatic negotiations, it contained no threat or hint of war or armed attack.

Calls Attack Deliberate

"It will be recorded that the distance of Hawaii from Japan makes it obvious that the attack was deliberately planned many days or even weeks ago. During the intervening time, the Japanese Government has deliberately sought to deceive the United States by false statements and expressions of hope for continued peace.

"The attack yesterday on the Hawaiian Islands has caused severe damage to American naval and military forces. Very many American lives have been lost. In addition, American ships have been reported torpedoed on the high seas between San Francisco and Honolulu.

"Yesterday the Japanese Government also launched an attack against Malaya.

"Last night Japanese forces attacked Hongkong.

"Last night Japanese forces attacked Guam.

"Last night Japanese forces attacked the Philippine Islands.

"Last night the Japanese attacked Wake Island.

"This morning the Japanese attacked Midway Island.

Defense Measures Ordered

"Japan has, therefore, undertaken a surprise offensive extending throughout the Pacific area. The facts of yesterday speak for themselves. The people of the United States have already formed their opinions and well understand the implications to the very life and safety of our nation.

"As commander in chief of the army and navy I have directed that all measures be taken for our defense.

"Always will we remember the character of the onslaught against us.

"No matter how long it may take us to overcome this premeditated invasion, the American people in their righteous might will win through to absolute victory.

Speaks Of "Inevitable Triumph"

"I believe I interpret the will of the Congress and of the people when I assert that we will not only defend ourselves to the uttermost, but will make very certain that this form of treachery shall never endanger us again.

"Hostilities exist. There is no blinking at the fact that our people, our territory and our interests are in grave danger.

"With confidence in our armed forces—with the unbounding

[Continued On Page 3, Column 3]

Britain Declares War Against Japan

[By the Associated Press]

London, Dec. 8—Britain, like the United States under Japanese attack, declared war today on the Tokyo Government, without waiting for Washington first to formulate an American declaration.

Said Prime Minister Churchill:

"It only remains now for the two great democracies to face their tasks with whatever strength God may give them."

At the same time Britain made allies of Thailand and Free China.

Fighting In Malaya

Churchill said the Japanese began landing in British territory in northern Malaya at 6 A. M. yesterday and were engaged immediately by British forces.

Prime Minister Churchill told the House of Commons that instructions had been forwarded to the British Embassy at Tokyo and that at 1 P. M. a note was handed to the Japanese charge d'affaires here "stating that in view of Japan's wanton acts of unprovoked aggression the British Government informed them that a state of war existed between the two countries."

Colonial Secretary Moyne made the statement in the House of Lords.

Churchill recalled that "with the

[Continued On Page B, Column 1]

Weather Forecast
Somewhat warmer this afternoon and evening; gentle to moderate winds. Yesterday's temperatures: Maximum, 83; minimum, 68; mean, 76........Page 29.

THE SUN

FINAL

Registered United States Patent Office

Vol. 213—No. 100—F | PAID CIRCULATION AUGUST MORNING, 166,686 EVENING, 177,758 344,444 || SUNDAY 258,263 | BALTIMORE, THURSDAY, SEPTEMBER 9, 1943 | Entered as second-class matter at Baltimore Postoffice | 30 Pages | 3 Cents

7TH ARMY LANDS AT NAPLES

U. S. Troops Move In After Italy Gives Up

ITALIAN WAR THOUGHT FAR FROM ENDED

Large German Force Still To Be Overcome, It Is Pointed Out

Delaying Action Expected—Allies Are Confident Of Success

By JOSEPH H. SHORT
[Washington Bureau of The Sun]

Washington, Sept. 8—Despite the surrender of the Italian Government and armed forces, the Allied military campaign in Italy is far from concluded, experts here believed today.

Because of the continued presence of a large German force in the peninsula, Allied commanders are preparing to meet—and overcome—delaying actions of high intensity at one or more points on their march toward Brenner Pass, the narrow southern gateway to Germany.

Although this enemy resistance may not be dissolved for weeks, even months, United Nations authorities were confident of a successful campaign which would give them access to short water passages across the Adriatic to the Balkans—and the German rear.

Allied Forces Strong

Available Allied forces in the Mediterranean are too large and too well-equipped to be thwarted in their northward push, these authorities said, but time probably will be required and many lives lost. The Germans have an estimated eight to fourteen divisions in Italy and upward of 750 aircraft.

Because of the natural defenses they afford, the most likely lines of enemy resistance are the Apennines, the mountain range which cuts Italy in two parts north of Rome, and the Po river valley, still closer to Germany, and Brenner Pass.

Except for rear guards to slow down the Allied advance, the Germans may well withdraw into one or the other of those lines and battle it out there until further resistance is impossible.

Mountain Line Vulnerable

The mountain line would be much more vulnerable to a flanking attack than the Po river, leading many unofficial observers to speculate that the latter probably will be the line on which the Germans make their last stand in Italy.

The Allies control the sea and the air in the Mediterranean and forces could be taken by sea and air routes to points back of the mountain line to encircle the German defenders.

Whatever line of resistance is chosen by the retreating enemy, an important unknown factor is the degree of cooperation given the Allies by the Italian people.

Would Help Eisenhower

Their failure to cooperate in supplying the Germans will be a great help to Gen. Dwight D. Eisenhower's men, but should they break into open hostility against what Allied headquarters in North Africa called "the eternal enemy" the German position much sooner will become untenable.

Officials here were quite hopeful that a high degree of assistance will come from the newly freed Italian people and that, in pursuance to the demands of Allied commanders, Italian troops in the Balkans also will cease to take their commands from German generals.

Stronger In North

The largest force of Germans probably is in the north of Italy, where the supply lines are shorter and much less difficult than to the southern region. Rome constitutes a railroad bottleneck, which is a serious hazard to any army south of that point receiving its food and ammunition from the north.

The strength of German air forces in Italy is known to have varied widely at different times,

(Continued on Page 7, Column 6)

Reds Clear Donets Basin

[By the Associated Press]

London, *Thursday*, Sept. 9—The Soviet army captured Stalino, steel-making center, wiped out the entire German salient in the Donets basin and drove against the retreating German army along a 600-mile front north to Smolensk, Moscow announced today.

As 224 Moscow guns saluted the Stalino victory, tank spearheads were stabbing forty miles northwest of the city—so swiftly they captured German planes still parked on an airfield and seized trainloads of supplies.

In the Donets basin area the Soviet forces were reported to be one hundred miles from Dnieperopetrovsk, on the Dnieper river line to which the Germans appeared to be retreating. Far to the north, near captured Konotop, the Red army slashed to Borzna, one hundred miles from Kiev.

Generals Named

[A report from Moscow said that two Red armies—the southern under Gen. Feodor Tolbukhin and the southwestern under Gen. Rodion Y. Malinovsk—carried out the full restoration of the Donets region to the Soviet Union.]

The Germans, now menaced by the capitulation of Italy, the sagging of the Balkans and threat of an Allied invasion from the west appeared to be falling back to their last-ditch line in Russia, abandoning gains now in more than two bitter years of war.

Capture of the Donets basin returned to Russia an area rich in mines and factories and straightened the line south from Kharkov to the Sea of Azov.

The Moscow midnight communique, recorded by the Soviet monitor, said more than 200 towns and hamlets were captured in the day's advances around Stalino, south of Bryansk, west of Kharkov and toward Smolensk.

Fierce Street Fighting

Stalino fell yesterday after fierce street fighting, the communique said, although the Germans announced earlier they had abandoned the city and destroyed its installations. The Russians said they captured large dumps of ammunition, many guns and mortars and other war materials in the city.

Borzna, northwest of Bakhmach, was captured in the push toward Kiev as 1,000 Germans fell before the advancing Russians and stores of military goods were captured.

On the Bryansk front Soviet forces swept up through the forests to capture Navlya, thirty miles south of Bryansk, penetrating the flank and rear of the Germans. Twelve hundred Nazi soldiers were killed and twenty-five guns captured.

Stalin, in a special order of the day, announced the recapture of Stalino and the Donets basin.

The Russian victory toppled Russia's twelfth largest city of nearly 500,000 which the Germans described as the "Essen of the Soviet Union" when they first overran the

(Continued on Page 8, Column 4)

WILSON NOW GIVES ORDERS IN BALKANS

Italians There Obeying Him, Not Germans, Says Allied General

Greece And Yugoslavia Told To Await Signal For Uprising

[By the Associated Press]

Cairo, Sept. 8—General Sir Henry Maitland Wilson, Allied commander in chief in the Middle East, announced tonight that Italian troops in the Balkins "are now obeying my, not German, orders."

Giving an indication of the still secret Italian armistice terms, Wilson said in a message broadcast to occupied Greece and Yugoslavia that the Italians in the Balkans "according to my order must cease all hostile acts to the Greeks and Yugoslavs."

"Their ships must be handed over to the United Nations, their aircraft must be flown to Allied airfields," the message continued. "They must not hand over their arms and equipment or defended points to the Germans."

Await Our Signals

Wilson called upon the two countries to "await our signal for a general uprising," adding that the hour of liberation had not yet arrived.

In a second proclamation to Italian troops in the Balkans by radio, General Wilson asked them to prevent "by force of arms" the Germans from taking their weapons and supplies. The broadcast was recorded by CBS.

"The war between Italy and the United Nations has come to an end," said Wilson. "All attempts made by the Germans or their vassals to disarm Italian troops or to dissolve them, take over their arms, supplies, transports and water supplies must be prevented by force of arms. All German orders are to be disregarded."

[A third proclamation by General Wilson to Italian troops in the Aegean Islands urged them to "take possession by force of all fronts occupied by the Germans in the Dodecanese."

[The Cairo radio broadcast in Arabic a fourth Wilson message to Italian ships, ordering them to report to Alexandria, in Egypt, or Haifa, in Palestine, and to Italian aircraft ordering them to proceed to Nicosia, Cyprus.

Text Of Wilson's Message

The text of General Wilson's message to the Greeks and Yugoslavs follows:

"A message from the commander in chief of Middle East forces to the Greeks and Yugoslavs:

"The Italians have been beaten to their knees. The armistice was

(Continued on Page 2, Column 3)

BULLETINS

Allied Headquarters in North Africa, Thursday, Sept. 9 (AP)—Allied troops landed early today in the Naples area, a third of the way up the Italian boot, a few hours after the surrender of Italy was announced.

The occupation of the bomb-battered area presumably places Allied forces behind at least some of the German troops retreating from southern Italy.

The Allied announcements said merely that "further operations have started on the Italian mainland in the vicinity of Naples."

Seventh Army Identified

New York, *Thursday*, Sept. 9 (AP)—Merrill Mueller, National Broadcasting Company correspondent, reported in a broadcast from Allied headquarters in North Africa at 1.19 A. M. (Eastern War Time) today that the American Seventh Army has landed at Naples.

Reported At Genoa And On Sardinia

London, Sept. 8 (AP)—American troops were reported in a Reuters dispatch from Stockholm tonight to have landed at Naples and Genoa and on Sardinia. The dispatch quoted the Stockholm newspaper *Svenska Dagbladet*.

Landing Reported North Of Leghorn

London, *Thursday*, Sept. 9 (AP)—The Swiss radio reported today that large forces of the American Seventh Army had landed on the Tyrrhenian coast of southwest Italy and also to the north at Leghorn.

The broadcast, recorded by Reuters, added that "hundreds of Allied planes are about to land on Italian airfields."

Three Other Cities Named

Stockholm, *Thursday*, Sept. 9 (AP)—Allied invasion forces have struck Gaeta, Civitavecchia and the Calabrian town of Pizzo in an effort to cut off German troops following the capitulation of Italy, the newspaper *Dagens Nyheter* reported today in a dispatch from the Italian frontier.

Tunis Radio Reports Invasion

New York, Sept. 8 (AP)—American, British and Canadian armies "are landing at various points in the heart of Italy," the United Nations radio at Tunis announced tonight in an Italian-language broadcast reported to the Office of War Information.

A German radio broadcast recorded by CBS said that four or five Allied infantry divisions were reported to have landed on the Gulf of Eufemia, about thirty miles ahead of the British Eighth Army's lines.

The text of the broadcast to the Italians follows:

"Take vengeance on the Germans.

"Powerful British, American, and Canadian armies are landing at various points in the heart of Italy.

"Arrival of these armies, powerfully equipped and protected by an invincible Allied air force and by the full might of the Mediterranean Allied naval forces, gives you, Italians, a last great opportunity.

"Supported by the might of the Allies, Italy now has the possibility of avenging itself on the German oppressor and to cooperate in repelling the traditional enemy from Italian soil.

"Italians! These are your fighting orders for this phase of the war for the liberation of Europe.

"Wherever Allied forces are to be found, give them your support and obey the orders of the commanders to the letter. Wherever German forces are to be found, refrain from assisting them in any way.

"Give proof of your national unity and of your will to resist by refusing unanimously and in perfect discipline, to be accomplices of the Germans."

Allies Landing Now, Roosevelt Asserts

Washington, Sept. 8 (AP)—A possibility that new invasion operations may have got under way shortly before President Roosevelt's war-bond address tonight was indicated by a last-minute change in the Chief Executive's words.

Telling his radio audience that the "war does not and must not stop for one single instant," the President said fighting men who "are landing at this moment in barges moving through the dawn up to strange enemy coasts" know that the war is a full-time job.

His original text as distributed to newspaper offices a few hours earlier, did not include the phrase "at this moment."

Nazi Troops Stationed On Corsica Overpowered

London, *Thursday*, Sept. 9 (AP)—Reuters correspondent in Stockholm quoted reports received there today that the Italian garrison on the island of Corsica, off the southern coast of France, had overpowered German troops stationed with them.

TREACHERY, NAZIS CALL SURRENDER

Prepared Since July 25 And 'Criminal Plot Will Fail,' Berlin Says

German Government Not Informed Of Step, Broadcast Adds

London, Thursday, Sept. 9 (AP). A proclamation read over the German radio announced the establishment of a national Fascist Italian Government in the name of Benito Mussolini, Reuters said today.

[By the Associated Press]

London, Sept. 8—The German radio screamed "betrayal" in giving the German people news of Italy's unconditional surrender tonight.

The official German news agency, DNB, made it plain that the Nazis had not been taken into the confidence of King Vittorio Emanuele and Marshal Badoglio when the Italian Government decided to get out of the war.

Shifting its propaganda line to keep up with events, Berlin said an American - British "plot" overturned the Fascist regime of Premier Mussolini, which it described as loyal to Berlin. Just after July 25, when Mussolini fell, Berlin said that Fascism in Italy had proved sterile and was quite properly ousted. Then the Germans obviously hoped to keep Italy in the war through the Badoglio Government.

Expected Since July 25, They Say

"Since the criminal plot against Il Duce of July 25 and the coup *d'etat* prepared in cooperation with the British and Americans for removal of the Fascist regime, which was loyal to the alliance, German authorities were prepared for such open treachery and they therefore took all the measures required by the situation," said the broadcast, recorded by the Associated Press.

"The criminal plot against the defenders of Europe will fail ultimately, just as all similar actions."

Blame Put On Badoglio

Quoting Allied announcements on the capitulation and stating that an armistice was now in effect, Berlin added bitterly:

"Marshal Badoglio, in the meantime, confirmed the capitulation in a broadcast from Rome, although the King of Italy only on September 8 had rejected as slander the suggestion that Italy was thinking of capitulation.

"Badoglio admitted that he had asked General Eisenhower for an armistice."

All telephone communication between Berlin and Italy have been severed, Berlin announced tonight, declaring that the Italians had re-

(Continued on Page 2, Column 6)

BADOGLIO ORDERS ARMY TO FIGHT BACK IN EVENT OF ATTACK BY GERMANS

Eisenhower Reveals Armistice Was Signed Day Invasion Began But Effective Date Delayed Until Moment Favorable To Allies

[By the Associated Press]

Allied Headquarters in North Africa, Sept. 8 — War between the United Nations and Italy ended at 6.30 P. M. (12.30 P. M., E. W. T.) today, as Gen. Dwight D. Eisenhower accorded a military armistice following unconditional surrender of Marshal Pietro Badoglio's Government. Eisenhower's announcement was coupled with an appeal to the Italian people to drive the Germans from their soil, and a promise of help from the Allies in doing so.

But there is a powerful German army in Italy, giving prospect of a gigantic battle and no hope that all Italy itself will fall like a plum to the Allies.

There is every likelihood the Nazis will fight desperately to hold the country and that one of the most critical phases of the battle of Europe is about to begin.

To Oppose Attack From "Other Quarters"

Badoglio in a proclamation issued simultaneously called on Italian soldiers to cease fighting the American and British forces but to "oppose attacks from any other quarter."

This could only mean to fight back if the Germans attack them.

The military armistice, approved also by Russia, actually was signed in Sicily last Friday, on the day Italy was invaded, with the stipulation it would "come into force at a moment most favorable to the Allies."

"That moment has now arrived," headquarters asserted.

Eisenhower pledged the aid of the United Nations to Italians who help to "eject the German aggressor."

Allied bombers immediately roared over the war-weary nation, dropping pamphlets declaring that, "Backed by the might of the Allies, Italy now has the opportunity of taking vengeance on the German oppressor and of aiding in the expulsion of the eternal enemy from Italian soil."

Call Issued To Italian Workers

It called on workers to prevent the movement of German troops or supplies by ship, rail or road, and Admiral Sir Andrew Browne Cunningham, Allied naval commander, broadcast an appeal to seamen to save their vessels from Germans.

Official statements here did not specifically say Allied forces would occupy Italy, but the assertion that they would smash at the Germans in Italy made this seem obvious.

Italy accepted all the terms imposed by the Allies—they were not disclosed—and will be obliged to "comply with political, economic and financial conditions" which will be imposed later.

The surrender was announced simultaneously by Allied headquarters and by Marshal Pietro Badoglio's Government.

The leaflets dropped by Allied planes announced the news of the armistice to Italian civilians, and gave them these "battle orders for this phase of the war for the liberation of Europe."

Complete And Absolute Defeat

To obey all orders of Allied commanders in occupied areas.

To do "nothing whatsoever to assist the Germans."

"He who wins the battle of transport wins the war" in Italy, the message declared, and transportation workers "can and will play a decisive role."

The war adventure into which Italy was embarked by Benito Mussolini, the creator of Fascism, who was himself deposed last July 25, thus ended in complete and absolute defeat—but with the promise that the Allies would help in freeing the country of the German yoke.

As the armistice was announced, British and Canadians of the Eighth Army were already installed on the Italian toe, widening their invasion hold with scant opposition.

Italy was primarily important to the Germans because of her position in the Mediterranean and other geographical advantages. These now are lost except in so far as the Nazis may be able to keep some hold on the nation.

Considerable Nazi Force In Italy

Germany still has considerable forces in Italy.

In the coming hours events may continue to move swiftly.

Italy's collapse represents the greatest victory so far scored by the United Nations in four years of the second World War, and reduces the opponents worthy of consideration from three to two.

An additional communique issued late tonight said "the armistice is strictly a military instrument signed by soldiers. No political, financial or economic terms are included. These will be imposed later.

"Granting of the armistice means only cessation of

(Continued on Page 2, Column 1)

Red Approval Of Armistice For Italy Excites Comment

Signs Of Big Moscow Role In Post-War Settlement Seen In Diplomatic Circles

By PAUL W. WARD
[Washington Bureau of The Sun]

Washington, Sept. 8—Combined with the reported creation of a tripartite Mediterranean commission, today's official disclosure that the Italian armistice terms had been approved in advance by the Russian as well as the American and British governments caused excited speculation in diplomatic circles here.

A part of the excitement was due to the reading into the situation of signs that Russia—which did not participate in the Versailles peace conference's shaping of the post-World War I Europe—has made long strides during the last few days toward assuring the Kremlin a powerful role in the political architecture of the Western world after the present war.

It was recalled that, after the invasion of Sicily and the subsequent peace negotiations with Rome, Moscow complained publicly that the U. S. S. R. had not been granted by her British and American allies any voice in either the peace negotiations or in shaping the military government of Sicily.

It also was recalled that these complaints were synchronized—in the midst of the Roosevelt-Churchill conference at Quebec—with the Kremlin's sudden recall of the Soviet Ambassador here, Maxim Litvinoff, whose displacement as Russia's Foreign Minister in May, 1939, had been a prelude to the Russo-German pact.

These and other diplomatic proddings by the Kremlin, including repeated "second-front" demands and Stalin's holding aloof from the Roosevelt-Churchill conferences, have produced sudden and quick

(Continued on Page 7, Column 2)

Italian Ship Captains Urged To Save Vessels From Nazis

Admiral Cunningham's Broadcast Gives Directions For Gaining Haven In Allied Ports

[By the Associated Press]

Allied Headquarters in North Africa, Sept. 8—Italian naval and merchant marine commanders were asked today by the Allied naval commander in chief in the Mediterranean, Admiral Sir Andrew Browne Cunningham, to avoid letting their ships fall into German hands and to sail immediately for Allied ports.

A message, broadcast by the United Nations radio in Algiers and recorded by the Associated Press, gave the Italians detailed instructions as to their course of action. It said:

"Sailors of the Italian navy and the mercantile marine! Your country has terminated hostilities against the United Nations. The German armed forces have become the open enemy of the Italian people and intend to seize your ships.

"Your ships are urgently needed to assist in the work of pouring supplies to Italy and your warships to protect them from the Germans. Take heed, therefore, that you do not scuttle your ships or allow them to be captured.

"The forces of the United Nations are watching out to receive you and protect you.

"Sail your ships and follow the directions now given to you by the United Nations.

"Ships in the Mediterranean: Sail to a place safe from the interference of the German armed forces. Sail if you can to North Africa or Gibraltar, to Sicily or Malta, to Haifa or Alexandria, or to Sicily, there to await the outcome of events.

"Ships in the Black Sea: Sail to Russian ports. If you have not the fuel to do this then proceed to neutral ports.

"When you meet forces of the United Nations identfy yourselves

(Continued on Page 6, Column 4)

Weather Forecast
Cooler today and this evening, with moderate winds and lower humidity. Yesterday's temperatures: Maximum, 85; minimum, 64; mean, 74 ....Page 25

THE SUN

Registered United States Patent Office

FINAL

Vol. 213—No. 101—F | MORNING, 166,686 / EVENING, 177,758 — PAID CIRCULATION AUGUST 344,444 || SUNDAY 258,263 | BALTIMORE, FRIDAY, SEPTEMBER 10, 1943 | Entered as second-class matter at Baltimore Postoffice | 26 Pages | 3 Cents

MUSSOLINI REPORTED HELD BY ALLIES

Yanks And British Battling Germans, Gain On Naples

F.D.R.'S TAX STAND LEFT TO TREASURY

Vinson Is Expected To Serve On Program As An Adviser Only

Ways, Means Of Raising Revenue To Be Up To Congress, Belief

War Department official tells House committee Government has saved $3,955,845,000 under renegotiation law........Page 9

By RODNEY CROWTHER
[Washington Bureau of The Sun]

Washington, Sept. 9—The long-standing quarrel within the Administration over the nature of the new tax program and who will take the lead in the fight for it finally was settled at the White House today by President Roosevelt himself, according to word which spread following a conference of the President with his anti-inflation and fiscal advisers.

Although the White House maintained silence, and Treasury officials refused to talk about the matter, word got around quickly that the meeting definitely decided who will be tax spokesman for the Administration.

Vinson's Expected Role

At the same time members of Congress began hearing that Fred M. Vinson, economic stablization director, whose views on tax matters have differed considerably from those of the Treasury, will serve only in an advisory capacity on the program, confirming inferentially word in other quarters that the President decided to depend upon the Treasury to offer whatever views the Administration decides to offer Congress.

Present at the White House meeting were Secretary Morgenthau; James F. Byrnes, war mobilization director; Vinson, Randolph Paul, Treasury general counsel, and Judge Samuel I. Rosenman, personal adviser of the President.

The presence of Judge Rosenman lent color to the word circulated in unusually well-informed quarters that there had been a showdown and a solution of the quarrel which has prevented the Treasury so far from formulating a definite tax program for submission to Congress.

To Be Up To Congress

Meanwhile, members of Congress heard that the Treasury intends to leave it pretty much up to Congress itself to find the ways and means of meeting the $12,000,000,000 of additional revenue the President wants to help meet the rising costs of the war program.

Neither members of the Administration nor members of Congress are eager to bear the onus of increasing tax rates on individuals sharply—to become effective in a national election year—and an increasing number of Congressmen incline to the belief that it may be late next spring before any sort of legislation can be enacted. Whatever measure comes forth, they believe, will be geared to impose only a very small additional extra burden on the lower income groups.

Parley Slated Soon

A further meeting of the President and his advisers is planned to be held within the next few days, it was heard, at which time some of the definite details of the Federal revenue situation will be discussed.

Some members of the Ways and Means Committee, who declined use of their names, said they had learned today that the present plan is for Secretary Morgenthau to appear before the committee, when hearings are opened September 20, and offer a series of revenue possibilities without giving Administration approval or support to any of them.

Iran Declares War

London, Sept. 9 (AP)—Reuters reported from Teheran tonight that Iran, which for many months has permitted the Allies to use its territory in sending supplies to Russia, had declared war on Germany.

Segundo Storni Resigns After Letter From Hull

Argentine Foreign Minister Takes Step After U. S. Refusal To Grant Lend-Lease Aid

Other Argentine developments reported by *Sun* correspondents in Buenos Aires, Santiago and Montevideo..............Page 8

[By the Associated Press]

Buenos Aires, Sept. 9—Segundo R. Storni, retired vice-admiral who was a pro-democratic member of Pedro Ramirez' Government, resigned as Foreign Minister tonight following disclosure of a sensational exchange of letters with Secretary Hull. His resignation was accepted.

Withdrawal of the bluff old officer came as the Argentine press, profiting by Government authorization to comment on the diplomatic incident, generally critcized the Foreign Minister for having placed Argentina in a position to receive a public admonition from the United States Government.

It came with rejection of a bid for United States lend-lease aid for Argentina, the only American nation which still maintains relations with the Axis.

Tried To Collaborate

Storni told President Ramirez his resignation was motivated by a desire to facilitate "the forward progress" of the Government.

"I have tried to collaborate in the best manner possible to me," he said. "In resigning, I am moved only by patriotic interest in removing every obstacle which my person may present to the success of the Government of your Excellency, which in these grave moments represents the hope of the country. I fervently hope for this success."

Among the last of Storni's acts as Foreign Minister was a conference with Japanese Ambassador Shu Tomii.

Storni told newspapermen the Japanese envoy inquired whether publication of the Storni-Hull notes foretold a change in Argentine foreign policy.

No Change Now

Storni said he replied "not for the present."

Although Storni stated in his letter asking for lease-lend aid that he was acting with the authority of President Ramirez, it is known that some Cabinet members considered the note ill-advised and ineptly phrased and its publication unwarranted.

Storni was severely criticized by the nationalist press, the pro-Axis newspaper *Pampero* going so far as to state it was evident the Government contained a representative who failed to express Argentina's sentiments or those which inspired the June 4 revolution.

Resignation No Surprise

Washington, Sept. 9 (AP)—News of the resignation of Argentina's Foreign Minister, Segundo R. Storni, came as no surprise to official and diplomatic quarters here after the recent disclosure of Storni's appeal to Secretary Hull for lend-lease aid and Hull's rejection.

Certain officials emphasized that Storni was regarded here as the most pro-Allied member of the Argentine Cabinet and that he apparently had been made the "goat."

CABINET FALL HELD LIKELY

Publication Of Hull's Letter Seen As Defeating Government's Purpose

By JOHN W. WHITE
[Special Correspondent of The Sun]

Santiago, Chile, Sept. 9 (By Cable)—The United States State Department's publication of the notes exchanged between Argentina's Foreign Minister, Vice-Admiral Segundo R. Storni, and Secretary of State Cordell Hull, is likely to cause the resignation of the Argentine Cabinet and may even cause the downfall of the entire military regime of President Pedro P. Ramirez.

This is the opinion of well-informed Argentines here, who base their belief on information received from reliable sources close to the Buenos Aires Government.

These Argentines believe that the publication of the notes is certain to defeat the one main purpose of the Ramirez Government in sending Gen. Arturo Rawson, leader of the June 4 *coup d'etat*, instead of former President Ramon Castillo to Rio de Janeiro as Ambassador.

Sent To Make Deal

According to reports from Buenos Aires, Rawson was being sent to Rio de Janeiro to "try to make a deal" with Washington through Jefferson Caffery, United States Ambassador to Brazil, for lend-lease provisions and armaments in exchange for a rupture with the Axis.

It was believed, according to these reports, that in Rio, Rawson and Caffery might be able to work in an atmosphere more conducive to success than in Buenos Aires, where, it is said, every visit of any American Embassy official to Storni arouses a renewed outbreak against the United States by pro-Nazi newspapers, making it almost impossible to carry on negotiations of such delicacy.

According to Buenos Aires reports, pro-Nazi newspapers there, known to be financed by the German Embassy, are continually making the charge that "pressure and threats of foreign agents are being

(Continued on Page 8, Column 6)

Japanese Defenses At Lae Reduced 'To Practical Ruin'

Australian Troops Advance To Within Two Miles Of Airdrome After Heavy Bombing

[By the Associated Press]

Allied Headquarters in the Southwest Pacific, *Friday*, Sept. 10—Australian troops have closed to within two miles of the Malahang airdrome at Lae, New Guinea, and the Japanese defenses of Lae have been reduced "to practical ruin" by more than 500 tons of bombs dropped by Allied planes in less than a week.

Allied Liberators and Mitchells have demolished enemy artillery, destroyed or disrupted installations and heavily punished the Japanese garrison, headquarters said today.

New big guns are also being brought to bear on the isolated enemy garrison.

The Malahang airdrome is on the eastern outskirts of Lae. To the northwest, Allied troops which parachuted into the Markham valley Sunday and seized an airstrip twenty miles from Lae now are approaching fortified Japanese positions only eight miles from the town.

An estimated 20,000 enemy troops are trapped in the Lae-Salamaua sector.

Every day that weather permits, air transports are flying across the Owen Stanley Mountains to land men and equipment on the captured Markham valley airfield of Nadzab.

Allied warships ventured once more into narrow waters between New Guinea and New Britain to shell the Huon peninsula coastal area around Finschhafen. Warships previously had entered these waters to escort the Australians in their landings northeast of Lae September 4.

Finschhafen is sixty miles above Lae.

Allied warships also put in an appearance near Salamaua, bombarding the water front and shooting down at least two of the enemy planes which attacked them. A third plane probably was downed. The communique said the warships which shelled the Finschhafen area were "light surface units," probably destroyers.

MARAUDERS STEAL SHOW IN NEW RAIDS

Marylanders Score In Forays Against Targets At Boulogne And Lille

Dress Rehearsal For Invasion Held In English Channel

London, Friday, Sept. 10 (AP). The Daily Express quoted a Swiss frontier report today as saying that Berlin had officially announced that the great cities of southern Germany and Austria would be evacuated as soon as possible. They include Vienna, Munich, Augsburg, Graz and Stuttgart.

[By the Associated Press]

London, Sept. 9—Allied naval and landing craft filled the Strait of Dover today in an unprecedented dress rehearsal of a cross-Channel invasion.

The Channel show, biggest of the kind ever held, was conducted under cover of the largest daylight air fleet ever assembled in Britain.

So tremendous was the demonstration that many British coastal dwellers were convinced the invasion of France was actually under way.

But a terse official summary said only: "Full-scale amphibious exercises were most successful. Valuable lessons were learned."

Marauders Steal Show In Cross-Channel Raids

By LEE McCARDELL
[London Bureau of The Sun]

A United States Bomber Station Somewhere in England, Sept. 9 (By Cable)—For the last forty-eight hours Baltimore-built medium bombers—Martin Marauders—have been carrying the ball in a full-scale tactical aerial assault against German positions on the French and Belgian coasts.

The attack, apparently marking the climax of the past week's almost continuous air offensive, also was part of a full-scale amphibious exercise in the English Channel. During the concluding phase of that exercise the largest formations of Marauders ever seen in any theater of war have been taking off from this and other United States medium bomber fields.

Marauders' Targets

Targets for the Marauders yesterday and today were two enemy airdromes near Lille and heavy coastal defenses in the Boulogne area. The defenses included large caliber dual-purpose guns, which can be used either as long-range artillery against the British coast, or as anti-aircraft weapons against Allied planes.

Although Marauder crews reported the flak over Boulogne the heaviest they had ever encountered, few German fighters were seen. Those few were handled without difficulty by RAF, Dominion and Allied Spitfires which covered the Marauder attacks.

Luftwaffe's Failure

Failure of the *Luftwaffe* to offer a more determined resistance may be regarded as another indication that recent persistent bombing of enemy airfields near the coast may have driven the German air force inland.

Yesterday's attack was continued last night by aircraft of the British bomber command. Flying Fortresses supported by United States Thunderbolts went out over France again today. So did British fighter-bombers.

A few enemy aircraft dropped a few bombs on the east and southeast coast of England last night. That foray, in which three of its planes were destroyed, was the *Luftwaffe's* only reply.

Marylander In Raid

One group of Marauders taking off from this field yesterday to attack the Lille airdromes was commanded by Col. Herbert B. Thatcher, of Chevy Chase, Md. Another taking off later to bomb the Boulogne defenses was commanded by Capt. George Gould, of Minneapolis, Minn. Both missions were highly successful.

The bombing looked "mighty good" to Lieut. Luther Hargroves, of Richmond, Va., piloting the Marauder named "Shirley Bee" after his best girl. Said Lieut. C. H.

(Continued on Page 2, Column 4)

SOVIETS TAKE BAKHMACH, AIM FOR KIEV

Troops In South Press To Within Sixty Miles Of Dnieper River

300 Villages Recaptured In Fighting, Moscow Report Says

[By the Associated Press]

London, *Friday*, Sept. 10—Russian armies have stormed into Bakhmach, key railroad junction on the road to Kiev, squeezed a vise on Bryansk and driven to within sixty miles of the Dnieper river in a swift advance from the Donets basin in the south, Moscow reported today.

More than 300 towns and villages were captured and more than 4,100 Germans killed in the day's victories that saw the Soviet armies push into the town of Nedrigailov, twenty miles east of Romni, and capture Lyudinovo, forty-five miles north of Bryansk.

The Moscow communique, recorded here by the Soviet monitor, told of Soviet aircraft pounding the German retreat road, destroying eighteen locomotives and attacking eighty trucks and several railway bridges. More than twenty enemy planes were destroyed or burnt in one airdrome.

Azov Landings Cited

A German radio report, meanwhile, told of a new Russian threat in the south. It said Soviet troops made landings along the Sea of Azov coast south of Stalino, which would be in the vicinity of Mariupol. The Germans said the beachhead was "sealed off" and the Russians were "facing annihilation."

Soviet troops had driven eighty miles in two days as Nazi resistance appeared to be collapsing in this sector. Petrovka, thirty miles southwest of Stalino and forty-four miles northwest of Mariupol, was taken yesterday, the Soviet communique said, and a total of 180 populated places were captured in advances up to ten miles.

A BBC broadcast reported Russian patrols thirty-one miles from Pavlograd, which is forty miles east of Dnieperopetrovsk.

Crimea Endangered

These advances in south Russia mean increasing peril for the Germans in the Crimea.

With the capture of Bakhmach and Nedrygailov, the Soviets were moving toward Priluki, eighty miles east of Kiev. A general Soviet advance of six miles took eighty hamlets in this area, the communique said.

Moving on Bryansk from the north and south, the Red army captured forty villages.

The victory at Bakhmach, announced by Marshal Stalin in an order of the day to Gen. Constantin Rokossovsky, virtually split the

(Continued on Page 2, Column 3)

Italian Army In Greece Ordered To Be Neutral

General Vecchiarelli Tells Troops To "Have No Dealings With Americans, British Or Germans"

[By the Associated Press]

Cairo, Sept. 9—Italian General Carlo Vecchiarelli told Italian garrisons in Greece via the Athens radio last night to "have no dealings with either the Germans, British or Americans," General Sir Henry Maitland Wilson, Allied Middle Eastern commander, disclosed tonight.

Smiling grimly, General Wilson said: "He'll get nowhere with that policy. If the Italians persist in that policy, their food and all supplies can and will be cut off."

General Wilson had asked Italians in the Balkans to go home and surrender their arms to Allied soldiers, and others to "take possession by force of all fronts occupied by the Germans in the Dodecanese islands." He made his broadcasts from here last night, and said Italian troops "are now obeying my, not German, orders."

First Reaction To Wilson's Order

Today Wilson told a press conference that Vecchiarelli's passive instructions were the first reaction to his own orders.

Wilson said the Italian general was tasting bitter fruits of the war since he was a representative on the Italian Armistice Commission which dealt with France after that nation collapsed in 1940.

Wilson said that no Italian aircraft or ships had arrived in Allied territories as yet to comply with his broadcast orders.

This, however, was not taken as an indication that the Italians were attempting to evade fulfillment of the armistice terms, the press conference was told by Richard Gardiner Casey, the Australian who is Minister of State in the Middle East.

Italians In Control In Athens

The impression prevailed in Cairo that things might move swiftly in the Balkans, where Italians are in considerable numbers. In Greece alone, it is estimated, there are between twenty and thirty Italian divisions.

There is a German commander in Athens, but Vecchiarelli outranks him. The fact that the Italian was able to make the broadcast was significant in that the Italians could control a broadcasting station when Germans were around.

Casey said all arrangements were made in the armistice terms for getting back British prisoners of war, numbering about 59,000. He said most of them were in northern Italy, from Pisa up.

As To Cirenaica's Future

Discussing the Italian colonies, Casey said the British military ad-

(Continued on Page 3, Column 4)

RED ARMY CREDITED FOR FALL OF ITALY

Izvestia Says Defeats On Soviet Front Wiped Out Pick Of Italian Troops

British press appraises advantages gained from surrender of Italy.................Page 2

[By the Associated Press]

Moscow, Sept. 9—News of Italy's capitulation was received jubilantly in the Soviet Union, where it was attributed largely to the Red army's victories on the eastern front.

It was interpreted to mean that the way is now open for the early defeat of Germany. The broken Axis camp, said the Government newspaper *Izvestia*, "is approaching its catastrophe."

Izvestia Explains Surrender

The official *Izvestia* said in explaining the Italian surrender:

"It is because of defeats on the Soviet front in which all contingents of picked Italian troops were exterminated.

"The victory of the Red army gave our allies the possible opportunity to land troops in Sicily."

Mussolini appealed to Hitler on July 18 and 19 for arms, *Izvestia* said, but the Germans were tied up on the Orel and Belgorod

(Continued on Page 2, Column 2)

PEOPLE JOIN FIGHT ON NAZIS IN ITALY

Men Of 70 Reported Demanding Arms—Garrisons Hold Firm, Bern Hears

By ROALD NERDRUM
[Special Correspondent of The Sun]

Bern, Switzerland, Sept. 9 (By Cable)—The Italian people today, wherever possible, are celebrating the break with the Axis by joining army volunteers in order to take part in the last phase of the battle on Italian soil.

It was reported from Milan that men of 70 were demanding arms to fight the Germans. While Allied troops were landing all along the Mediterranean coast, Italian garrisons were making desperate efforts to hold firm in the interior.

Fight In Genoa Reported

Most of the big cities are still firmly in Italian hands, including Milan and Turin in the north. Unconfirmed reports here tonight were that fighting is going on for possession of Genoa.

The Germans seem to have prepared for the eventuality of the Italians breaking away, but all the same it was learned here there is much confusion in the German army in Italy because it doesn't know where to expect a blow from the American Seventh Army.

No doubt the Germans decided to fight in northern Italy, but how far they will be successful seems to depend on the swiftness of the Allied moves in the next few days.

A diplomat arriving today from Rome told me that the German envoy, Rudolph von Rahn, who arrived in Rome a few days ago to take over the German Embassy, has a special mission

But Rahn came too late. Known as Hitler's "bridgehead specialist," Rahn is a most unfortunate man who always seems to have the habit of arriving too late.

Croats Eye Dalmatia

Dispatches reaching here say the Croatian leader, Ante Pavelic, ordered his troops to invade Dalmatia with the blessing and support of Hitler. Pavelic complains the territory was robbed by Italians when Yugoslavia parted.

Italian garrisons in Dalmatia are reported putting up a stiff resistance, but, facing modern German tanks, the Italian commander is appealing for swift help from the Allies. Croat Partisans joined in the fight with the Italians.

The Germans also are reported advancing toward the coast of Albania, while in Greece many Italian units are trying to join Partisans in the mountains.

Fighting has been going on in southeastern France between Italians and Germans. Hundreds of Italian soldiers have been streaming into Switzerland since yesterday for internment. There even were some Germans with them.

Rush By Exile Governments To Stake Out Claims Expected

French Protest Over Italian Armistice Likely To Herald Many Headaches For United Nations

By PAUL W. WARD
[Washington Bureau of The Sun]

Washington, Sept. 9—French protests over the failure of the Allies to consult the French Committee on National Liberation on Italian armistice terms were regarded here today as typical of the diplomatic headaches expected by State Department officials to accumulate rapidly in the wake of Badoglio's surrender.

A rush by the nine duly-recognized "governments in exile," by the French committee and by various "free" movements to stake out their post-war European claims is anticipated.

Some of their representatives here were privately inclined today to the belief that, if they do not take steps immediately to strengthen and perfect their judicial positions within the United Nations structure, they may find themselves without seats and a voice at the eventual European peace conference.

Now that the first break in the Rome-Berlin-Tokyo Axis has been achieved, they reasoned, the end of hostilities in Europe may follow as rapidly as the German armistice in November, 1918, followed Bulgaria's unconditional surrender forty-three days earlier.

They do not seriously expect such a rapid turn of events but, they said, their groups, or governments, cannot afford to gamble otherwise lest they find their conflicting claims and interests have been composed for them on an *ex parte* basis by some such tripartite organization as the Mediterranean Commission with only British, Russian and American members.

That handling the anticipated push will exercise to the full the diplomatic talents of the State Department is generally conceded, for the stakes are big, the controversies—especially within the "governments in exile"—are violent, and any misstep might lead to

(Continued on Page 7, Column 1)

ALLIES STILL LAND AT NEW BRIDGEHEAD

Clark's Progress Called "Satisfactory"—Nazi Prisoners Taken

Enemy Headquarters At Frascati Destroyed By Fortress Bombs

London, Friday, Sept. 10 (AP) — A Reuters dispatch from Stockholm quoted the Italian newspaper Corriere Della Sera as saying that Benito Mussolini, deposed Fascist Duce, had already been delivered to the Allies and transported to North Africa.

London, Friday, Sept. 10 (AP)—The Rome radio reported today that planes had dropped bombs on the Italian capital during the night, causing casualties and damage.

A broadcast recorded by the Ministry of Information said:

"Some planes of unknown nationality dropped bombs on Rome last night. One bomb hit and damaged workers' lodging in the district of San Lorenzo and caused some victims among the inhabitants. Another bomb damaged an arch of the Aqua Marcia (Rome water supply)."

[There was no indication from Allied sources that Rome had been bombed.]

[By the Associated Press]

Allied Headquarters in North Africa, Sept. 9—Strong American and British forces under United States Lieutenant General Mark W. Clark hammered out a bridgehead near Naples today in a dawn landing that overpowered a number of stoutly resisting German troops embittered by Italy's unconditional surrender.

Allied reinforcements were still streaming ashore tonight, it was reported

"Operations are proceeding satisfactorily," said an Allied communique of the new landings one third of the way up the Italian peninsula.

"In Contact With Germans"

The troops led by Clark, hero of the submarine mission to North Africa that paved the way for the successful Allied invasion there last November, "are in contact with German forces and prisoners have been taken," the bulletin added. "The disembarkation of troops with their guns and vehicles is proceeding according to plan."

Before the troops struck the shore near Naples, three waves of Flying Fortresses had destroyed the German military nerve center at Frascati, twelve miles outside Rome.

Nazi Quarters Leveled

The blow at Frascati occurred six hours before yesterday's announcement of the Italian surrender. Nearly every building in the resort city, famous for its wine, had been occupied by German military authorities. These were leveled by American bombs, official reports said.

American Liberators from the Middle East also dumped 150 tons of explosives on the Foggia expanse of airdromes, less than one hundred miles east of Naples, to facilitate the big amphibious operation.

Warships Lay Barrage

The landing occurred a few moments after 4 A. M. (10 P. M. Wednesday, E. W. T.) under cover of a powerful barrage laid down by the American and British navies. This rain of explosives hammered wooded hills overhanging the invasion coast and left great columns of smoke as th

(Continued on Page 2, Column 5)

7 A.M. THE SUN EXTRA

Registered United States Patent Office

Vol. 215—No. 18—F | PAID CIRCULATION MAY MORNING. 162,501 EVENING. 183,442 345,943 ‖ SUNDAY 268,914 | BALTIMORE, TUESDAY, JUNE 6, 1944 | Entered as second-class matter at Baltimore Postoffice | Zone 3 | 24 Pages | 3 Cents

ALLIES INVADING FRANCE, TROOPS LAND IN NORMANDY

BULLETINS

London, June 6 (AP)—Prime Minister Churchill told the House of Commons today that an immense Allied armada of 4,000 ships with several thousand smaller craft had carried Allied forces across the Channel for the invasion of Europe. Churchill also said that massed air-borne landings had been successfully effected behind the Germans' lines.

"The landings on the beaches are proceeding at various points at the present time," Churchill said.

"The fire of shore batteries has been largely quelled."

He said that 'obstacles which were constructed in the sea have not proved so difficult as was apprehended."

The Prime Minister said the American-British Allies are sustained by about 11,000 first-line aircraft, which can be drawn upon as needed.

"So far," he said, "the commanders who are engaged report that everything is proceeding according to plan."

"And what a plan!" he declared.

Churchill said the vast operation was "undoubtedly the most complicated and difficult which has ever occurred."

New York, June 6 (AP)—The Berlin radio broadcast a DNB dispatch today saying that one Allied cruiser and a large landing vessel carrying troops had been sunk in the area of St. Vaast La Hougue, 15 miles southeast of Cherbourg.

ALLIES PURSUE FLEEING NAZIS NORTH OF ROME

Rome, June 5 (AP)—Allied armor and motorized infantry roared through Rome today—not pausing to sight-see—crossed the Tiber, and proceeded with the task of destroying two battered German armies fleeing to the north.

Allied fighter-bombers spearheaded the pursuit, jamming the escape highways northward with burning enemy transport and killing and wounding many Germans.

The enemy was tired and disorganized by the Allied assault, which in 25 days had inflicted a major catastrophe on German forces in Italy and liberated Rome almost without damage.

Rail Yards Bombed

Joining the program of destruction, 500 American heavy bombers blasted rail yards at five points in northern Italy between Venice and Rimini along which the Germans might attempt to move reinforcements and equipment to bolster Marshal Albert Kesselring's armies.

At 10 A. M. today Lieut. Gen. Mark W. Clark, commander of the Fifth Army, entered Rome in a jeep and drove to the city hall, where he formally proclaimed the Allied occupation and praised the valor of his troops.

Addressing his corps commanders and looking out over thousands of cheering Italians, Clark declared that both the 10th and 14th German armies had been at least partially destroyed, more than 20,000 prisoners taken and untold quantities of Nazi equipment captured.

Allied Troops Praised

He lauded individually the French, British and American troops of the Fifth Army and paid tribute to the "gallant men and women who made the supreme sacrifice" that made today's occupation possible. Mussolini's famous balcony in the Palazzo Venezia, a few blocks from where Clark spoke, looked empty and deserted.

Pope Pius XII, addressing an enormous crowd including many Fifth Army soldiers in St. Peter's Square, expressed thanks to God that Rome had not been destroyed by war.

The inhabitants' reception to the troops approached hysteria as the day wore on and homemade confetti soon littered the streets. There was an almost carnival atmosphere. Little damage to the city was visible, the Nazis having limited demolitions to a few installations of no artistic or religious importance.

Much Material Taken

The speed of the enemy's flight once his lines before Rome burst was evident in the great quantities of war material left behind, stock piles sufficient to equip several divisions. An Allied spokesman expressed the official opinion that the tremendous pressure exerted by the Allies in the final phase of the battle for Rome had forced the enemy to flee beyond the capital rather than make a protracted fight for the city itself.

Just 24 hours after the first Allied troops made their way through

(Continued on Page 2, Column 8)

KING TURNS RULE OVER TO UMBERTO

Naples, June 5 (AP)—King Vittorio Emanuele III stepped aside as monarch of Italy today as he previously had said he would upon the liberation of Rome and handed to his 39-year-old son, Crown Prince Umberto, all "royal prerogatives."

Italian political pressure had been brought to bear against him since the conquest of Naples.

In a decree signed by himself and countersigned by Premier Marshal Pietro Badoglio, head of the Italian liberation government, the King named his son lieutenant general of the realm.

Still Heads House Of Savoy

The monarch, however, retained his title as head of the House of Savoy and remains as King without power.

King Vittorio Emanuele, who became ruler July 29, 1900, had announced last April 12 his "irrevoc-

(Continued on Page 2, Column 5)

Army In Rome Is Greeted By Thousands Of Flags

By PRICE DAY
[Sunpapers War Correspondent]

With the Fifth Army in Rome, June 5—Weary soldiers of the victorious Fifth Army are slogging through and around Rome toward the front, but for the people of this lovely city, today is a day of festival.

Streets which all night seemed full today flow with streams of citizens of the capital where the word "citizen" came into being.

Now and then one says: "Welcome to you, welcome," stressing the second syllable, or "Hello, boss." But for the most they don't talk or cheer.

Sound Of Clapping

Instead they clap their hands. Rome today is filled with the staccato sound of clapping.

Tens of thousands of flags fly in the brilliant sunshine. They are of almost every kind—except Nazi—and size and even shape.

Some in windows wave the British Union Jack. A great American flag is draped over the balcony near Pincia Gardens.

From the flagpole on Corso del Popolo flies another American flag. It is home-made and has only 20 stars, and the background of stars is green instead of blue but the intention is right or at least expedient.

Somebody with an eye to profit has printed thousands of Italian green, white and red flags, seven by ten inches in size, and of the quality of small cotton flags sold in America before each Fourth of July.

Description Of Flags

These flags have the arms of the House of Savoy in the center but a huge flag flown from the front of an American engineer jeep is without this embellishment. It is a Fascist flag, but the men in the jeep, unschooled in the niceties of politics, are very proud of their prize.

Some Italian civilians are more politically minded. A few Soviet flags with hammer and sickle are along the streets. A small speeding civilian car flaunts a banner of the

(Continued on Page 2, Column 6)

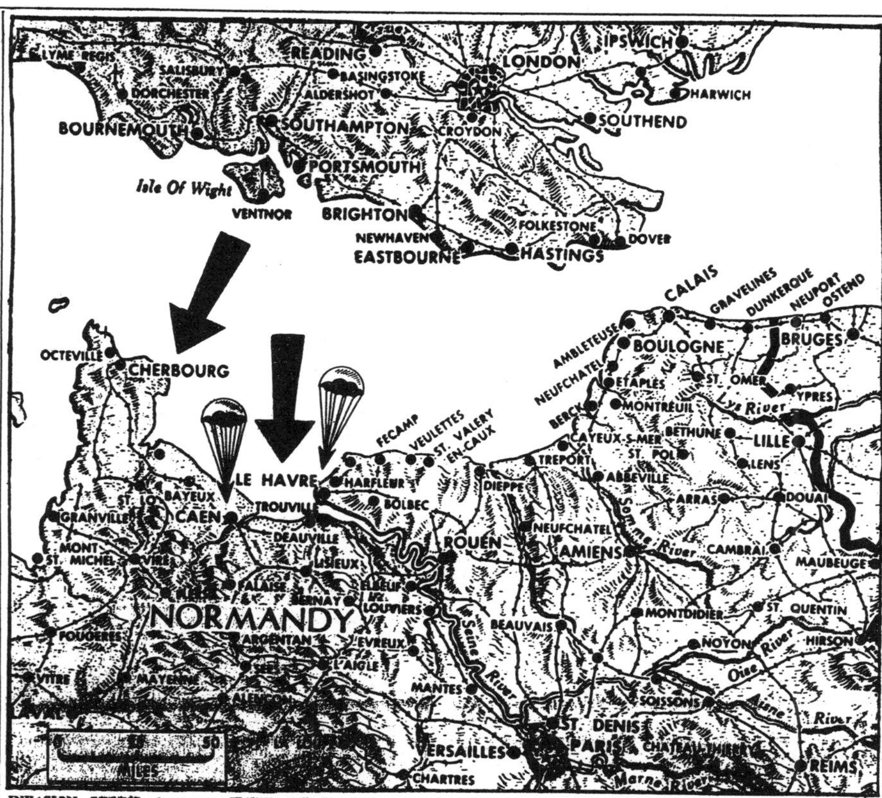

INVASION BEGINS—American, British and Canadian troops landed this morning in France. According to the Germans, landings were made all along the coast between Cherbourg and Le Havre, as indicated on the map by the arrows and parachutes.

VICTORY NOT NEAR ROOSEVELT WARNS

"Fiercer Fighting" Before Nazi Defeat Forecast

By DEWEY L. FLEMING

Washington, June 5—President Roosevelt tonight hailed the liberation of Rome by armed forces of the United Nations, but warned against "inflated" estimates of the accomplishment.

In a radio speech heard around the world, the Executive emphasized that the Allies must endure a long period of "greater effort" and "fiercer fighting" before the Nazis are crushed; that the campaign will be "tough" and "costly"; that total victory lies "some distance ahead."

Distance Will Be Covered

But, he said:

"That distance will be covered in due time—have no fear of that."

The President's only reference to forthcoming blows at other parts of Hitler's European "fortress" was the observation:

"Our victory comes at an excellent time, while our Allied forces are poised for another strike at western Europe—and while armies of other Nazi soldiers nervously await our assault."

"One up and two to go!" was the way he referred to the capture

(Continued on Page 3, Column 2)

WAR DEPARTMENT WORKS ALL NIGHT

General Marshall In Office Almost Continuously

Washington, June 6 (AP)—Key offices of the War Department were fully manned and working feverishly when the long awaited invasion of Europe began early today.

Gen. George C. Marshall, the chief of staff, was in his office continuously since yesterday except for a brief interlude last evening when he went to the Russian Embassy to receive from Ambassador Gromyko the Order of Suvorov, First Degree—the Soviet Union's highest military decoration.

The operations section of the general staff, the Signal Corps message section and the Military Intelligence Division were islands of frantic activity in the otherwise dark vastness of the Pentagon Building, and officers and messengers scurried through the dim corridors relaying messages between them.

Assistant Arrives At 10

Secretary of War Henry L. Stimson was not in his office, but the Assistant Secretary John J. McCloy came in about 10 P. M.

The German broadcasts on the invasion began to bring news reporters and radiomen into the department in the early hours of this morning.

Maj. Gen. Alexander D. Surles, director of public relations, and his deputy, Col. Stanley J. Grogan, told the waiting reporters about 3.20 A. M., that the announcement was expected at 3.32 o'clock.

Copies Distributed

As soon as the news was flashed from General Eisenhower's headquarters duplicate copies of his first communique were distributed in the Pentagon, along with the text of the statement by the General of the Armies John J. Pershing and a background information discussing the general terms of invasion preparations.

The White House was dark, except for the usual points where guards are stationed.

Elmer Davis, director of the Office of War Information, was at his office, helping check on incoming radio reports through the night hours.

King George Speaks Tonight

New York, *Tuesday*, June 6 (AP). The London radio, in a broadcast recorded by the Federal Communications Commission, said that King George VI would deliver a special broadcast tonight at 9 P. M. London time.

Eisenhower's Order Of Day

London, June 6 (AP)—Gen. Dwight D. Eisenhower issued the following order of the day to his invasion troops today.

"Soldiers, sailors and airmen of the Allied Expeditionary Force:

"You are about to embark on a great crusade. The eyes of the world are upon you and the hopes and prayers of all liberty loving peoples go with you.

"In company with our brave allies and brothers in arms on other fronts you will bring about the destruction of the German war machine, elimination of Nazi tyranny over the oppressed peoples of Europe, and security for ourselves in a free world.

Will Not Be Easy Task

"Your task will not be an easy one. Your enemy is well trained, well equipped and battle hardened. He will fight savagely. But in this year of 1944 much has happened since the Nazi triumphs of 1940 and 1941.

"The United Nations have inflicted upon the Germans great defeats in open battle, man to man. Our air offensive has seriously reduced their strength in the air and their capacity to wage war on the ground, our home fronts have given us overwhelming superiority in weapons and munitions of war, and have placed at our disposal great reserves of trained fighting men. The tide has turned and free men of the world are marching together to victory.

"I have full confidence in your courage, devotion to duty and skill in battle. We will accept nothing less than full victory. Good luck and let us all beseech the blessing of Almighty God upon this great and noble undertaking."

American Paratroopers Land In Back Of Foe's Defenses

By HOWARD COWAN

With United States Parachute Troops, June 6 (AP)—American paratroopers—studded with battle-hardened veterans of the Sicilian and Italian campaigns—landed behind Hitler's Atlantic Wall today to plant the first blow of the long-awaited western front squarely in the enemy's vitals.

The Allies' toughest, wiriest men of war cascaded from faintly moonlit skies in an awesome operation.

By Plane And Glider

Twin-engined C-47s — sisters of America's standard airline flagships—bore the human cargo across the skies, simultaneously towing troop-laden CG4A gliders—to merge in a single sledgehammer blow paving the way for frontal assault forces.

Armed with weapons from the most primitive to the most modern, the paratroopers' mission was to disrupt and demoralize the Germans' communications inside the Nazis' own lines.

There was no immediate indication that their dynamite and flashing steel and well-aimed fire was not succeeding in the execution of plans rehearsed for months in preparation for the liberation of occupied Europe.

The steel-helmeted, ankle-booted warriors wore a red, white and blue American flag insignia on the sleeve and camouflaged green-splotched battle dress.

Series Of Feints By Allies Revealed

Supreme Headquarters, Allied Expeditionary Force, June 6 (AP)—It can now be revealed that the Allies have been conducting a series of feints in advance of the invasion today.

These feints were predicted some time ago by Prime Minister Churchill, and were designed to lull the Germans so they would never know when the blow was coming.

AMPHIBIOUS OPERATIONS AIMED FROM CHERBOURG TO LE HAVRE, NAZIS SAY

General Montgomery In Charge Of Assault, Eisenhower's Headquarters Reports—Strong Naval And Air Support Backs Troops

London, June 6 (AP)—The German radio reported today that four British parachute divisions had landed between Le Havre and Cherbourg in France.

This was four times the size of the Nazi parachute force dropped on Crete in the Mediterranean.

By THOMAS M. O'NEILL
[Staff Correspondent of The Sun]

Allied Expeditionary Force Headquarters, England, June 6—Allied forces launched the assault on Europe today.

Air-borne troops, naval forces and infantry combined in a thrust at northern France, opening the invasion for which troops have been massing in the British Isles for months. The fighting men were Americans, Britons and Canadians. General Sir Bernard L. Montgomery was in command of the army group.

The "This Is It" Communique

A 26-word communique from the supreme headquarters of the Allied Expeditionary Force brought the announce that meant "This is it." The communique, No. 1 from the Allied camp, said:

"Under the command of General Eisenhower, Allied naval forces, supported by strong air forces, began landing Allied armies this morning on the northern coast of France."

Another announcement disclosed that the Allied troops were under the command of the Briton with the winning ways, General Montgomery, and that the American, British and Canadian troops were taking part in the assault.

Giving No Secrets To Enemy

There was no more—no suggestion as how the troops were faring, no clue to the number of separate landings, no inkling as to the numbers of the fighting men involved in the attacks by land, sea and air. All that is information the command left for the Germans to discover by themselves, the hard way.

There had been signs the long-awaited communique was about to appear. For hours aircraft had roared out to sea—fighters, bombers and transports—in clouds surpassing even the fury of the sustained bombing attack with which the air command has been softening the invasion coast and crippling German communications.

First Announced By German Radio

Then the German radio said that landings had been made, though that was no proof since the Germans have frequently made that announcement.

Both navies, British and American, sent ships to sea to protect the soldiers, to put them ashore, to blast the enemy fortifications. Some of the landing ships flew the red duster of the British merchant navy. Air and naval forces jointly scoured the waters for German craft—torpedo boats, destroyers, E-boats and U-boats.

Minesweepers went ahead of the landing craft, aware that the Germans in the many months at their disposal had done their best to make the waters impassable.

Ships Of Other Allies In Armada

Among the naval forces were ships flying the ensigns of Norway, Poland, Holland, France and Greece.

It was said at headquarters that the operation provided the first example in the centuries of northwestern Europe's warfare of "triphibious" strategy in which sea and air forces move as a unit with the armies, the ships and planes to aid the army gain a foothold, the army in turn to seize ports for the ships and airfields for the planes.

Superiority at sea had long been held by the Allies, but today's undertaking could never have started without control of the air above the Channel.

Fighting In France Heavy, Nazis Say

Supreme Headquarters, Allied Expeditionary Force, June 6 (AP)—Gen. Dwight D. Eisenhower's headquarters announced today that Allied troops began landing on the northern coast of France this morning strongly supported by naval and air forces.

The communique was read over a transatlantic hookup direct from General Eisenhower's headquarters at 3.32, E. W. T.

The Germans said the landings extended between Le Havre and Cherbourg along the south side of the bay of the Seine and along the northern Normandy coast.

Parachute troops descended in Normandy, Berlin said.

Berlin first announced the landings in a series of

(Continued on Page 2, Column 1)

THE WEATHER
Fair and warmer this afternoon. Fair and cooler tonight and Wednesday.
Detailed report on Page 23

THE EVENING SUN

7 STAR SPORTS

Vol. 69—No. 43 | MORNING, 162,501 / EVENING, 183,442 PAID CIRCULATION MAY 345,943 || SUNDAY 268,914 | BALTIMORE, TUESDAY, JUNE 6, 1944 | Entered as second-class matter at Baltimore Postoffice | Zone 3 | 30 Pages | 3 Cents

INVASION 9 MILES INLAND

Opposition Weak, Losses Below Expectations

By J. W. Gallagher

Supreme Headquarters, Allied Expeditionary Force, June 6 (AP)—The Allies landed in the Normandy section of northwest France early today, and by evening had smashed their way inland on a broad front, making good a gigantic air and sea invasion against unexpectedly slight German opposition.

Prime Minister Churchill said part of the record-shattering number of parachute and glider troops were fighting in Caen, nine miles inland and 120 miles from Paris, and had seized a number of important bridges in the invasion area.

Four thousand ships and thousands of smaller landing craft took the thousands of American, British and Canadian sea-borne forces from England to France under protection of 11,000 Allied bombers and fighters who wrought tremendous havoc with the whole elaborate coast defense system that the Nazis had spent four years in building. Naval gunfire completed the destruction, and the beachheads were secured quickly.

Allied Losses Far Under Expectations

Allied losses in every branch were declared to be far less than had been counted upon in advance.

The grand assault found the highly vaunted German defenses much less formidable in every department than had been feared.

Air-borne troops who led the assault before daylight on a history-making scale suffered "extremely small" losses in the air, headquarters disclosed tonight, even though the great plane fleets extended across 200 miles of sky and used navigation lights to keep formation.

A headquarters officer declared this air-borne operation was "carried out with great precision. It was a fine job—very fine indeed." The air-borne troops bore the brunt of early battle, creating a large diversion and many demolitions.

Naval losses for the sea-borne forces also were described at headquarters as "very, very small."

Warships Virtually Silence Nazi Coastal Guns

Coastal batteries were virtually silenced by the guns of the British, American and Allied fleets, including battleships, and the beachheads were speedily consolidated.

The German radio said the scene of the landings was a 100-mile stretch of coast from Cherbourg to Le Havre, around the bay of the Seine and the northeast shore of the Normandy peninsula.

Britain's Prime Minister Churchill, in announcing the successful invasion to the House of Commons at noon—six hours after the first sea-borne troops landed—said the landings were "the first of a series."

It was Churchill who disclosed that 11,000 Allied planes were available as needed for the battle. The Allied bombers, climaxing 96 hours of steady pounding, lashed German coastal defenses this morning with 10,000 tons of explosives.

Only 50 German Sorties Against Beaches

Fighters who went out to guard the beaches had little to do, however, as the German air force up till noon had flown only 50 sorties against the invading forces.

The Germans were known to have probably 1,750 fighters and 500 bombers to meet the attack. Why they did not use them at the start was not apparent, but Allied airmen warned that a violent reaction might be expected soon, noting that Air Minister Goering, in an order of the day, had told his forces: "The invasion must be beaten off, even if the *Luftwaffe* perishes."

Prime Minister Churchill told Commons tonight that Allied troops had penetrated in some cases several miles after their effective landings on a broad front, and happily asserted: "Many dangers and difficulties which this time last night appeared extremely formidable are behind us."

He and all other sources agreed that the operation was going according to plan. The air forces, to which he paid high tribute for their work in smashing coastal defenses, estimated that between midnight and 8 A. M. alone more than 31,000 airmen were over France, not counting parachute and glider troops.

Allies Gain Between Caen And Isigny

German broadcasts said the Allies penetrated several kilometers in between Caen and Isigny, which are 35 miles apart and respectively 9 and 2 miles from the sea. Caen is 120 miles from Paris.

The sea-borne troops, led by General Sir Bernard L. Montgomery, were preceded across the Channel by massed flights of parachute and glider forces who landed inland during the dark.

The German radio, after reporting landings from Cherbourg to Le Havre, later said additional landings were being made "west of Cherbourg," indicating that the Allies intended to seize the Normandy peninsula with its ports and airfields as the first base of their campaign to destroy the power of Nazi Germany.

Heavy Allied Raids On Dieppe Reported

The initial landings were made from 6 to 8.25 A. M., British time (midnight to 2.25 A. M., E.W.T.). The Germans said subsequent landings were made on the English Channel isles of Jersey and Guernsey and that invasion at new points on the Continent was expected hourly.

The Berlin radio, in a broadcast picked up in New York by the NBC, said strong Allied air attacks had been launched on the Dieppe area.

Aside from confirming that Normandy was the general area of the assault, supreme headquarters of the Allied Expeditionary Force was silent concerning the location, for tactical reasons.

From Moscow came word that the Russian army was massing in preparation for another great attack from the east as its part in defeating Germany.

All reports from the beachhead, meager though they were in specific detail, agreed that the Allies had made good the great gamble of amphibious landing against possibly the strongest fortified section of coast in the world.

Some Troops Advancing At A Run

Reconnaissance pilots said the Allied troops had secured the beaches and were slashing inland, some of them actually running in a swift advance. The unofficial word at headquarters confirmed this, while the Vichy radio admitted that the Allied drive inland was going right ahead.

The Paris radio also said the battle in the Normandy peninsula appeared to be gaining depth.

More than 640 naval guns, ranging from 4 to 16-inch, hurled many tons of shells into the coastal fortifications that the Germans had spent four years preparing against this day.

Allied planes preceded the landings with a steady 96-hour bombardment which reached its peak in the hour before the troops hit the beaches.

The air attack was thrust home through cloud banks 5,000 feet high.

Nazi Naval Opposition Limited

German naval opposition was confined to destroyers and motor torpedo boats which headquarters said succintly were being "dealt with." The Germans, as expected, blared on their radios all sorts of claims of vast destruction done to Allied fleets and forces, but with no confirmation.

In one defiant gesture, some of the German cross-Channel guns opened a sporadic fire on Dover during the afternoon.

Unconfirmed reports said Adolf Hitler was rushing to France to try his intuition against the Allied operation. Presumably Field Marshals Karl Gerd von Rundstedt and Erwin Rommel were directing the defenses from their headquarters in France.

Caen And Barfleur Called 'Chutist Targets

German accounts through Sweden admitted that steady streams of Allied troops were continuing to land, particularly in the vicinity of Arromanches, about midway between Le Havre and Barfleur, and that tanks were ashore at several places. They said there was especially bitter fighting at the mouths of the Orne and Vire rivers.

The air-borne troops' principal scenes of operations were placed by the Germans at Caen and Barfleur. The Germans said the American 82nd and 101st Parachute divisions

[Continued On Page A, Column 8]

Battle In Caen Reported By Churchill

London, June 6 (AP)—Prime Minister Churchill announced today that Allied air-borne troops had captured several strategic bridges in France before they could be blown up and that "there is even fighting proceeding in the town of Caen.".

(Caen in 120 miles from Paris.)

"Air-borne troops are well established and the followups are proceeding with very much less loss than we expected," Churchill reported in a second statement of the day to the House of Commons.

Allied troops had penetrated in some cases several miles inland after effective landings on the coast on a broad front, he said.

"Thoroughly Satisfactory"

The Prime Minister said he had visited the various centers where latest information was received and could state that "this operation is proceeding in a thoroughly satisfactory manner."

"Many dangers and difficulties which appeared at this time last night extremely formidable are behind us," the war leader reported.

"Passage of the sea has been made with far less loss than we apprehended.

Batteries Weakened

"The resistance of batteries has been greatly weakened by bombing by the air force and the superior bombardment of our ships quickly reduced their power to dimensions which did not affect the problem."

Churchill, addressing the House of Commons after a visit to Gen. Dwight D. Eisenhower's headquarters in company with King George, described the landing of air-borne troops on the European continent as an outstanding feat "on a scale far larger than anything there has been so far in the world."

"These landings took place with extremely little loss and great accuracy."

Earlier he told the cheering House that the Allied liberating assault was "proceeding according to plan—and what a plan!"

First Step

"All this, of course, although very valuable, is a first and vitally essential step and gives no indication whatever of what may be the course of battle in the next days and weeks because the enemy will now probably endeavor to concentrate on this area."

"In that event heavy fighting will soon begin and will continue. It is, therefore, a most serious time that we are entering upon and we enter upon it with our great Allies all in good heart and all in good friendship."

4,000 Ships

In tones of confidence he reported that the Allied forces had been transported across the Channel to the shores of France by "an immense armada" of 4,000 ships with several thousand smaller craft—"probably the greatest fleet ever assembled."

Mass air-borne landings also have been successfully effected behind the enemy's lines, he said.

"Tactical Surprise"

"There are already hopes that actual tactical surprise has been attained," he continued, "and we hope to furnish the enemy with a succession of surprises during the course of the fighting.

"The battle which is now beginning will grow constantly in scale and intensity for many weeks to come, and I shall not attempt to speculate upon its course.

"The landings on the beaches are proceeding at various points at the present time," Churchill said.

"The fire of shore batteries has been largely quelled."

He said that "obstacles which were constructed in the sea have not proved so difficult as was apprehended."

The Prime Minister said the American-British Allies are sustained by about 11,000 first line aircraft, which can be drawn upon as needed.

"Most Complicated"

Churchill said the vast operation was "undoubtedly the most complicated and difficult which has ever occurred."

To cheers by Parliament members, Churchill took "formal cognizance of the liberation of Rome," and added:

"American and other forces of the Fifth Army broke through the enemy's last lines and entered Rome, where Allied troops have

[Continued On Page A, Column 7]

Invasion Leaders

With the start of the invasion of western Europe today, the greatest military leaders on the sides of the Allies and Germany are locked in a mighty battle of wits and resources. Look today for informative thumbnail sketches of the ten top men in the Allied High Command and the ten leaders of Germany's forces on Page 17.

Flashes

Invasion Front Placed

London, June 6 (AP) — The Transocean News Agency in a Berlin broadcast today said the Allies had established a 15-mile front from a mile to half a mile deep between Villers-sur-Mer and Trouville.

This area is about seven miles south of the big port of Le Havre and takes in the beach resort area of Deauville.

Secret Weapons Used

London, June 6 (Reuter)—Many secret weapons were used today for the first time by the liberating armies, the Ministry of Supply revealed.

Russians Rejoice

Moscow, June 6 (AP)—Russians who learned of the invasion today literally danced with glee. For them it meant the end of three years of anxious waiting for the thrust from the west. Newspapers which had not announced the landings still were carrying glowing accounts of the fall of Rome.

F. D. R. To Read Prayer On Air

Washington, June 6 (AP)—President Roosevelt called upon a hopeful nation today to join him in a prayer for divine aid in speeding the invasion to victory and "a peace that will let all men live in freedom, reaping the just rewards of their honest toil."

The Chief Executive wrote the prayer last night as he sat up late at the blacked-out White House to hear up-to-the-minute reports on progress of the great battle of liberation.

He will read it over a nation-wide broadcast at 10 P. M. tonight, but its text was issued at midday to permit Americans to familiarize themselves with its wording so that they might join him in the recital.

Prayer Read In House

Mr. Roosevelt dispatched the prayer to the House by motorcycle messenger, and it was read on the floor shortly after Dr. James Shera Montgomery, House chaplain, departed from custom to ask members to join in the opening invocation.

Again the members stood, this time in silent prayer. At its conclusion Minority Leader Martin, of Massachusetts, reminded his colleagues that "many heartbreaking days lie ahead."

Senate Opens With Prayer

The Senate, meeting an hour later, at noon, opened its D-day session with a moment of silent prayer and the recital of the 23d Psalm by the Rev. Frederick Brown Harris, the chaplain.

Then, to the hushed and solemn chamber, Majority Leader Barkley, of Kentucky, said:

"It seems that all we need, or ought, or can do is pray fervently and devoutly for the success of our troops and those of our allies in whatever direction they may be moving."

During the morning Mr. Roosevelt summoned the army and navy high command to the White House for his first personal conference with the commanders since troops began hitting the beaches during the night.

Gen. George C. Marshall, army chief of staff; Gen. H. H. Arnold, head of the Army Air Forces, and Admiral Ernest J. King, chief of

[Continued On Page B, Column 1]

Sunpaper Men Report

O'Neill---H-Hour

By Thomas O'Neill
[Sunpapers London Bureau]

London, June 6—An officer looked intently at his watch, remarked in five seconds the news would be released. It was then 29 minutes and 55 seconds past 9 o'clock, British double daylight saving time.

American, British and Allied troops were storming the hostile and bristling beaches of the Continent.

This Was It

Airborne troops were dropping to earth behind the enemy coast defenses, laden with explosives to blast his roads and railways, ready to disrupt the movement of reserves as the foe undertook to shuffle his men, to guess the next move on the great checkerboard of war.

Allied naval vessels were hammering shore emplacements, covering the landing troops, casting tons of high explosives far inland against the concrete shelters of the West Wall. This was it.

Message To The French

Excitement was shown in the faces of the military men who had taken part in the long months of planning for this, the vital day. Excitement was reflected among the war correspondents, many of them veterans of that other June, four years ago, that marked the retreat from Dunkirk, others who had witnessed the seesaw of Africa, the victories of Italy. This was the big day.

The invasion was on.

Messages flashed around the world. Another message went by radio broadcast, direct from the Allied headquarters to the people of France who for four years have lived under the tyranny of the conqueror. Now, they were told, the hour had come, the hour to hamper, to halt, to hamstring the oppressor. D-day had arrived and H-hour.

Sea Was Rough

They had arrived three hours and thirty minutes earlier. At dawn the first wave had struck by the light of the moon and the rising sun. The date, probably dictated by the terrible tides of the Channel coast, had also been selected with an eye on the moon, which becomes full tonight.

(The Associated Press reported today that the Allied landings in France were postponed 24 hours, due to bad weather. They were originally scheduled for yesterday morning.)

The unpredictable Channel weather had not been kind. A gale had been blowing at the beginning of the week, and the narrow sea was still rough. Many soldiers in landing craft must have been seasick at the invasion's start. The skies, though, were clear, the temperature, coolish, "the outlook, favorable."

Hours beforehand, light sleepers had surmised that the big push was on. Aircraft filled the pre-dawn skies of Britain—all going the same way. Fighters, bombers,

[Continued On Page B, Column 6]

M'Cardell--In Air

By Lee McCardell
[Sunpapers War Correspondent]

London, June 6—Marauders of the Ninth Air Force led one Allied air attack early today when our armies began landing on the northern coast of France.

The Marauders swept in over the Channel at daylight to bomb and strafe one long stretch of sandy beach, while warships were bombarding the shore from the sea and landing craft were speeding in to put the first tanks ashore.

With three other American correspondents I flew over the beach with the first group of bombers making the attack. We had taken off before dawn. It was about breakfast time when the returning formation landed at its base. An army car brought us direct to London, arriving here a few minutes after Supreme Headquarters of the Allied Expeditionary Force had released the first invasion communique.

Attack At Dawn

The Marauders made the attack at dawn—at what is known as "first bombing light." They roared in at a much lower altitude than that from which they usually bomb. From the windows of the pilot's compartment and the waist gun windows the crews and the correspondents who flew with them looked down on the curtain-raiser of the battle for western Europe.

At briefing at their base a few hours earlier the Marauder men had been told they would spearhead the air attack. Fighter cover of thousands of Allied fighter planes had preceded us.

Nazi Batteries Blaze

We saw one of our aircraft shot down in flames over the target. We saw but one enemy aircraft during our mission. German anti-aircraft batteries blazed away at our formation while we were on the bombing run, but we saw no enemy troops in the dawn's early light.

The guns of our warships lying off the coast were blazing. Their shells were bursting in a belt a mile or more deep along the shoreline. Fiery tracers of the Marauders' .50-caliber machine-gun bullets, the blinding twinkle of Marauder bomb bursts and the muzzle bursts of enemy flak batteries provided the sort of vast fireworks display that all of us knew we probably would see but once in a lifetime.

Smoke And Flash

We heard nothing but the roar of our planes' motors and the rattle of their machine guns. All the rest was merely smoke and flash. Our formation turned out of its bombing run at a speed in excess of 200 miles per hour as it streaked for home.

On our way in we passed over great fleets of landing craft and other vessels, all headed toward the beach where our target lay. In the wide sweep we executed to

[Continued On Page B, Column 3]

Watson--Tactics

By Mark S. Watson
[Sunpapers Military Correspondent]

London, June 6 (By Cable)—The prompt establishment of bridgeheads by British and Canadian troops and the apparent continuance of Allied air superiority gives assurance that the first phase of the grand invasion by sea, air and land is a success.

The first phase is only a small part of the mighty effort, but it is an essential part and to that extent a vastly encouraging part.

Besides the landings on the Continent which the German radio identified as on broad beaches between Le Havre and Cherbourg, the Germans now state that our attack is methodically widening towards the southwest and that our landing parties are already ashore on the Channel islands.

Two Vital Needs

The occupation of the islands would serve two vital needs: first, to eject the enemy from seaward positions which enable him to observe our ship movements and intercept our forces; and second, to make use ourselves of those invaluable positions whose airfields might serve our short-range fighter planes and whose limited anchorages could be of great value to surface patrols and other auxiliaries.

The ground forces already engaged are British, Canadian and American elements composing a group of armies of which General Montgomery is the commander under the supreme Allied command of American General Eisenhower.

Overhead Cover

The air forces which are providing the overhead cover are composite and in tremendous number; Prime Minister Churchill says 11,000 planes are available.

The extent and composition of the huge naval forces employed in clearing the Channel of enemy mines, in transporting our landing elements and waves of supplies and in protecting the whole force from interception by the enemy is presumably mingled British and American.

The coordination of all three combat elements and the secrecy with which the vast enterprise was initiated appear fully up to the highest hopes.

Weight Of Assault

Despite the German declaration that the defense was ready for our attack, it is far from certain that they expected such a weight of assaul as fell upon the French coast before dawn and throughout the succeeding day.

The most visible and audible

[Continued On Page 2, Column 1]

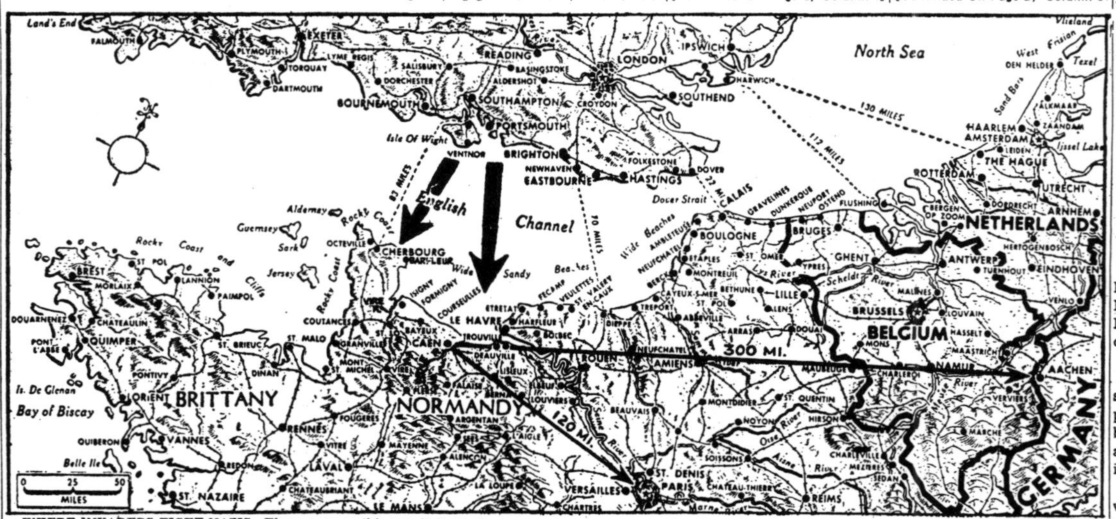

WHERE INVADERS FIGHT NAZIS—The arrows on this map indicate the general area of the French coast where Allied invasion forces landed today and are now pushing inward against German defenders. The black lines show the approximate distance from Caen to Paris and from Caen to German border.

Weather Forecast
Cloudy today; warm, with showers tomorrow afternoon or night. Yesterday's temperatures: Maximum, 72; minimum, 59; mean, 66.........Page 21

THE SUN

Registered United States Patent Office

Roosevelt's Presidency: Page Of Pictures: Page 5

Vol. 216—No. 125—E | PAID CIRCULATION MARCH MORNING, 167,054 EVENING, 190,378 357,432 || SUNDAY 275,245 | BALTIMORE, FRIDAY, APRIL 13, 1945 | Entered as second-class matter at Baltimore Post Office | Zone 3 | 24 Pages | 3 Cents

Roosevelt Dies At Warm Springs; Truman Takes Oath As President

9TH ARMY ACROSS ELBE AS 1ST AND 3D SPEED IN LEIPZIG DIRECTION

Patton's and Hodges's Tank Columns Close To Key Center In Central Reich; 'Chutists Reported 30 Miles From Berlin

By PRICE DAY
[*Sunpapers War Correspondent*]

SHAEF, Paris, April 12 [*By Radio*] — Five armored divisions of the United States 1st and 3d armies, breaking loose on the Thuringian Plain, have swept to the east and southeast to cross the Saale River in two places and tonight stand within 23 miles of Leipzig, 55 of Chemnitz and 90 miles of Dresden.

Meanwhile, it was reported from the front that troops of the 9th Army have crossed the Elbe River near Magdeburg and are less than 70 miles from the center of Berlin.

Weimar, Schweinfurt, Heilbronn, Rastatt and Baden Baden have fallen. Erfurt is surrounded and will go soon, if it has not already gone. Halle and Bamberg are directly threatened.

Airborne Landing Unconfirmed

There is no confirmation here of reports that Allied airborne troops have been dropped near Brandenburg, 30 miles from Berlin.

The crossings of the Saale River were made by the 3d Army's 6th Armored Division somewhere south of Naumburg, which lies 23 miles southwest of Leipzig, and by the 4th Armored Division south of Jena.

Armored spearheads moved forward under a security silence which may still obtain for their further movements beyond the Saale.

The reports of the crossings of the river and of the points at which the crossings were made were purposely delayed in order to keep the information from the enemy.

East Front Supplies Hurt

At the river our troops were 90 miles due south of Madgeburg and appeared ready to drive a wide wedge eastward or southward toward, and to break into, the rear areas of the German forces in tactical contact with the Red Army.

Already Allied advances from the west have seriously impaired the supplying of the Eastern front. Once we are well within the network of communications leading to the east, the *Wehrmacht* will begin to lose effective control of its troops there.

It is too early to predict the date on which the western and eastern allies will join to cut Germany through the middle. It is certainly their purpose to join at the earliest reasonable moment.

Erfurt Entered

How quickly this can be done depends on the plans of the Red Army and on whether our armor can carry through on its impetus or must stop again for supplies and consolidation. This last, in turn, depends partly on the German strength encountered.

To the rear of the armored breakthrough in the center of the front, the 80th Infantry Division surrounded Erfurt and, after a three-hour artillery and air preparation, has entered the city where the opposition is, so far, not heavy.

While this action was in progress,
(Continued on Page 2, Column 3)

FRANCE SENDS CONDOLENCES

De Gaulle Writes To Truman; Eisenhower At Front

By PRICE DAY
[*Sunpapers War Correspondent*]

Paris, *Friday*, April 13 [*By Radio*]—The free peoples of Europe and the people of Europe who hope to be free will be shocked and saddened to learn, when they arise this morning, that Franklin Delano Roosevelt is dead.

When word of the President's death was confirmed here shortly before 12.30 A.M., General Eisenhower was in the forward battle area and could not be reached at once for a statement.

De Gaulle's Message

General de Gaulle, at 2.10 o'clock, sent the following message to President Truman:

"Mr. President, it is with great emotion and deep sadness that the French Government and people learn of the death of the great President Roosevelt.

"He was in the eyes of all humanity the symbolic champion of the great cause for which the United Nations have suffered so much and fought so hard—the cause of liberty.

'An Undying Example'

"He did not live long enough to see the triumphal ending of this war in which his noble country is fighting in the front rank.

"At least the decisive success to which he has so powerfully contributed will have given him the certainty of victory before he succumbed at his post. He leaves the world an undying example and an essential message. This message will be heard.

"He was from his first to his last day the faithful friend of France. France admired and loved him. I send you, Mr. President, her fervent tribute to the memory of President Franklin Roosevelt and her expression of deep sympathy and afflicted friendship for the great American people."

It is not only the great and the articulate, however, who will sorrow at this news. As deep and
(Continued on Page 2, Column 6)

PRESIDENT ROOSEVELT

Frisco Parley To Go On As Set, Truman Says

Washington, April 12 (AP)—Harry S. Truman, who eleven years ago was a Missouri county judge, became the thirty-second President of the United States at 7.09 P.M. tonight and solemnly pledged himself to the policies of Franklin Delano Roosevelt.

Sworn in 2 hours and 34 minutes after Mr. Roosevelt's death in Warm Springs, Ga., as a shocked capital sought to weigh the import of the sudden change, Truman announced in quick succession:

1. He will try to carry on as he believes President Roosevelt would have done.

2. The San Francisco United Nations conference will go on as scheduled April 25.

3. He has asked the Roosevelt Cabinet to stay on with him.

4. The war will be pressed to a "successful conclusion."

The new Chief Executive issued this statement:

"The world may be sure that we will prosecute the war on both fronts, east and west, with all the vigor we possess, to a successful conclusion."

Acts To Steady Nation

Thus Mr. Truman acted immediately to steady a stunned nation and drive forward toward victory and a lasting peace.

About the White House crowds stood silently at the tall iron fence. Flags there, and on embassies and other public buildings, dipped to half staff.

After the brief and solemn induction ceremony, President and Mrs. Truman went from the Cabinet room to the White House residential quarters to speak with Mrs. Roosevelt, who was leaving to fly to Warm Springs.

Shortly after 7.30 P.M. they left by a rear entrance and motored to their apartment on Connecticut avenue in northwest Washington.

Secret Service men and District police threw a cordon around the apartment building and visitors to the Truman suite were barred. All telephone calls, and they were myriad, were rejected except one from Mrs. Truman's brother, Frank Wallace.

Senator Denied Audience

Senator Green (D., R.I.) was among those who called in person to congratulate the new President, but he, too, was denied an audience.

Guards patrolled the third-floor corridor. The neighborhood was quiet in contrast to the throngs which stood across from the White House for hours, far into the darkness.

It was Mrs. Eleanor Roosevelt who summoned Mr. Truman from his Capitol office to the White House and told him her husband was dead.

While waiting she sent messages to the four Roosevelt sons in the armed forces—James, Elliott, Franklin, Jr., and John—telling them of their father's passing.

"He slept away this afternoon," she told them. "He did his job to the end, as he would want to do. Bless you all and all our love." She signed it Mother.

Funeral On Saturday

Funeral services will be held Saturday afternoon in the East Room of the White House. Burial
(Continued on Page A, Column 4)

End Due To Cerebral Hemorrhage; Funeral At White House Tomorrow

By DEWEY L. FLEMING

Washington, April 12—President Roosevelt died of a cerebral hemorrhage at 4.35 o'clock this afternoon at the "little White House" in Warm Springs, Ga. Two hours and 34 minutes later—7.09 P.M.—Vice President Harry S. Truman, of Missouri, took the oath of office as President. The President collapsed while sitting for the sketch of a portrait. He had been resting at his Georgia home for the last ten days, gathering strength for official duties he expected to perform at the opening of the world security conference scheduled to begin in San Francisco week after next.

A few minutes after taking the oath as the thirty-second President of the United States, Mr. Truman authorized Edward R. Stettinius, Jr., Secretary of State, to announce that the San Francisco parley would proceed as arranged.

Truman Pledges Prosecution Of War

The new President also announced:

"The world may be sure that we will prosecute the war on both fronts, east and west, with all the vigor we possess to a successful conclusion."

The country will be without a Vice President until the next presidential election, in 1948. In the event of Truman's death, Secretary Stettinius would succeed to the presidency. Senator Kenneth McKellar, of Tennessee, president *pro tempore* of the Senate, succeeds Truman as the presiding officer of the Senate.

4.35 P.M. Announced As Time Of Death

Word of the President's sudden death at 4.35 P.M. (E.W.T.) reached Washington a moment later, but was not made public for a little more than an hour. The official announcement was made by Stephen T. Early, only surviving member of the President's official family as it came into office in 1933.

To Mrs. Roosevelt, who was attending a Washington club meeting when the news came, fell the lot of advising her four sons, all in the armed services, of their father's unexpected death. She dispatched messages saying the President had "slept away" this afternoon.

"Had Done His Job To The End"

Secretary Early said the message to the sons added that their father had done his job to the end, as he would want them to do.

First news that the President was in distress reached the White House at 3.05 P.M. when Vice Admiral Ross T. McIntire, the Executive's personal physician, was advised by telephone that the President had fainted while sitting for his portrait.

Admiral McIntire, who had planned to go to Warm Springs tomorrow, said that until that moment all reports from Warm Springs indicated that the President was in the best of health.

"Bolt Out Of Clear Sky"

He said a report from Warm Springs this morning was to the effect that "everything is fine," and that the afternoon report, therefore, was "a bolt out of a clear sky."

After the report of the fainting spell, Admiral McIntire telephoned Dr. James Paullin, of Atlanta, asking him to go to Warm Springs immediately.

A half hour later Commander Howard G. Bruenn, who was attending the President personally, called Admiral McIntire and reported that what had happened in Warm Springs was "a very serious thing." He said undoubtedly the President had suffered a cerebral hemorrhage.

"I of course notified everyone here," said Admiral McIntire, who related the details personally to reporters who gathered at the White House a few moments after the death flash came.

"I contacted Steve (Early) first and as he and I were
(Continued on Page A, Column 1)

President Stricken While Being Sketched

Warm Springs, Ga., April 12 (AP). President Franklin D. Roosevelt died unexpectedly here today at 4.35 P.M. of a cerebral hemorrhage.

Mr. Roosevelt's last words were: "I have a terrific headache."

He spoke them to Commander Howard G. Bruenn, naval physician.

Presidential Secretary William D. Hassett said Mr. Roosevelt's body would leave here around 9 A.M., (E.W.T.) tomorrow for the approximately 22-hour run to Washington.

Mr. Roosevelt, 63, was sitting in front of a fireplace in the Little White House here atop Pine Mountain when the attack struck him.

Described As Massive

Bruenn described it as a massive cerebral hemorrage.

The President's Negro valet, Arthur Prettyman, and a Filipino messboy carried him to his bedroom. He was unconscious at the end. It came without pain.

Mr. Roosevelt, in the third month of his fourth term as President, came here three weeks ago to rest.

Dr. Bruenn said he saw the President this morning and he was in excellent spirits at 9.30 A.M.

Complains Of Severe Headache

"At 1 o'clock," Bruenn added, "he was sitting in a chair while sketches were being made of him by an artist. He suddenly complained of a very severe occipital [back of the head] headache.

"Within a very few minutes he lost consciousness. He was seen by me at 1.30 P.M., fifteen minutes after the episode had started.

"He did not regain consciousness and he died at 4.35 P.M."

Only others present in the cottage were Commander George Fox, White House pharmacist and long an attendant on the President; Hassett, Miss Grace Tully, confidential secretary; and two cousins, Miss Laura Delano and Miss Margaret Suckley.

News Services Notified

Bruenn said he called Vice Admiral Ross T. McIntire, United States Navy Surgeon General and White House physician in Washington and that McIntire in turn called Dr. James E. Paullin, of Atlanta, an internal medicine practicioner and honorary consultant to the navy surgeon general.

Paullin was present when Bruenn gave the statement of the cause of death to reporters of the three national news services.

In response to a question, Dr. Bruenn said the President died without pain.

News of the President's death spread quickly and caused many a tear among the 125 infantile paralysis patients at the foundation here.

Mayor Frank W. Allcorn of Warm Springs was giving a barbeque at his mountain cabin this afternoon for the President and about 50 other guests.

Allcorn was awaiting the President's arrival when reporters got word through the Army Signal Corps radio telephone and summer White House telephone communication to rush to the foundation.

Miss Louise Hackmeister, veteran White House chief telephone operator, could hardly talk in her excitement to round up those who had to be informed.

Tears and quivering voices accompanied the announcement of the President's death by Hassett.

Had Been Underweight

Miss Tully, Mrs. Alice Winegar, Hassett's secretary, and Mrs. Dorothy Brady, presidential stenographer, sat tense on a sofa as Hassett gave the news.

Mr. Roosevelt arrived at Warm Springs March 30. He had been underweight and his doctors wanted him to take it easy to see if he could not regain the poundage at which he felt comfortable.

Rumors had been heard the last few days that the President was not picking up as much as his doctors would have liked.

He received reporters last Thursday and, in the presence of Sergio Osmena, President of the Philippine Commonwealth, told of his desire to grant full independence to the islands by autumn.

Outlines Postwar Plans

Mr. Roosevelt also outlined ambitious postwar plans for American participation in the Western Pa-
(Continued on Page A, Column 3)

Stalin, Churchill Mourn Roosevelt

London, *Friday*, April 13 (AP)—Premier Marshal Stalin expressed his sorrow at the death of President Roosevelt today in a message to Mrs. Roosevelt in which he characterized the President as "a great organizer of the struggles of the freedom-loving nations against the common enemy."

The text of the note as broadcast by the Moscow radio:

"*Mrs. Eleanor Roosevelt*, Washington:

"Please accept my sincere condolences on the occasion of the death of your husband and an expression of my sympathy in your great sorrow.

"The Soviet people highly valued President Roosevelt as a great organizer of the struggles of freedom-loving nations against the common enemy and as the leader in the
(Continued on Page B, Column 7)

FRANCES PERKINS HENRY A. WALLACE JAMES V. FORRESTAL (UNIDENTIFIED) HARRY S. TRUMAN MRS. TRUMAN HARLAN F. STONE FRED M. VINSON ROBERT RAMSPECK
HENRY L. STIMSON J. A. KRUG CLAUDE R. WICKARD FRANCIS BIDDLE EDWARD R. STETTINIUS, JR. HAROLD L. ICKES SAM RAYBURN JOSEPH W. MARTIN, JR. JOHN W. McCORMACK

Harry S. Truman, of Missouri, is sworn in as the thirty-second President of the United States at 7.09 P.M., April 12, in the Cabinet room of the White House. Chief Justice Harlan F. Stone administers the oath.

Weather Forecast
Cloudy and warm today, with showers in afternoon or evening; fair tomorrow. Yesterday's temperatures: Maximum, 79; minimum, 48; mean 64 .... Page 19

THE SUN

FINAL

Registered United States Patent Office

Vol. 216—No. 146—F | PAID CIRCULATION APRIL MORNING, 168,851 EVENING, 192,089 360,940 ‖ SUNDAY 275,260 | BALTIMORE, TUESDAY, MAY 8, 1945 | Entered as second-class matter at Baltimore Post Office | Zone 3 | 22 Pages | 3 Cents

KING GEORGE SENDS EISENHOWER CONGRATULATIONS ON VICTORY

London, Tuesday, May 8 (AP)—King George VI today sent a message to General Eisenhower congratulating him and his armies on the "complete and crushing victory" in Europe. Text of King George's message:

"Eleven months ago you led the Allied Expeditionary Force across the English Channel, carrying with you the hopes and prayers of millions of men and women of many nations. To it was entrusted the task of annihilating the German armies in western Europe and of thus liberating the peoples whom they had enslaved.

"All the world now knows that after fierce and continuous warfare this force has accomplished its mission with a finality achieved by no other such expedition in history.

"On behalf of all my peoples I ask that you, its supreme commander, will tell its members how deeply grateful we are to them and how unbounded is our admiration for the courage and determination which, under wise leadership, have brought them to their goal of complete and crushing victory.

"I would ask you also to convey a special message of congratulation to my own forces now under your command. Throughout the campaign they have acquitted themselves in all services with a valor and distinction for which their fellow countrymen will forever hold them in honor.

"(Signed) George, R. I."

NATION TO HEAR TRUMAN ON AIR AT 9 A. M. TODAY; LONDON OFF ON BIG SPREE

President Is Expected To Read Proclamation Of Victory In Europe; British Capital's Liquor Stocks Demolished By Celebrants

President Truman will make a broadcast address to the nation at 9 o'clock this morning. An official proclamation on the achievement of victory in Europe is expected to be read by the President.

Londoners satisfied without such official confirmation that Germany actually has surrendered, have gone on a spree that is said to have depleted all available liquor stocks.

Washingtonians Take Surrender News In Stride

By DEWEY L. FLEMING

Washington, May 7—President Truman will speak to the nation by radio at 9 o'clock tomorrow morning and is expected to ready an official proclamation that victory has been achieved in Europe.

The White House announcement of the Chief Executive's plan, made late this evening said:

"On the basis of reports now received, the President confidently expects to make an announcement to the nation by radio at 9 o'clock tomorrow morning.

Press Conference Slated

"Unless unforeseen developments cause the President to change his plans, a White House press conference will be called at 8.30 A.M., at which time the press and radio will be given in confidence the text of the President's radio remarks."

When asked whether it was a fair assumption that the President would announce V-E day, Jonathan Daniels, White House press secretary, replied:

"The statement speaks for itself."

The announcement was construed as

(Continued on Page A, Column 4)

England's Stock Market Slumps As Spirits Rise

By THOMAS M. O'NEILL
(London Bureau of The Sun)

London, May 7 *(By Cable)*—Whatever the official attitude that postpones the proclamation of peace, the people of London decided today that the war was over and huge celebration was gathering tonight.

There were more people on the streets that at any time since the war began and carnival was abroad. Public houses prospering to an extent that wrecked their carefully hoarded stocks. Spontaneous celebrations took place in the streets.

Traffic police joined in the spirit and gravely shook hand with all those celebrants who thought that a particularly proper method of signalizing the curtain up on 2,074 days of war.

To Be Proclaimed Today

The Stock Market slumped in true end-of-hostilities style as business looked forward to a long and difficult period of adjustment and reconstruction.

It now appears that the formal anouncement will be heard about midafternoon tomorrow (midmorning, Baltimore time). The delay probably arises from a Russian request that all formalities of the German surrender on the Eastern front be attended to before the victory signals are hoisted.

[The Associated Press carried the following announcement from the Ministry of Information:

["It is understood that in accordance with arrangements between the three great powers, an official announcement will be broadcast by the Prime Minister at 3 o'clock tomorrow afternoon the eighth of May, 9 A.M. E.W.T.

["In view of this fact tomorrow Tuesday, will be treated as Victory-in-Europe day and will be regarded as a public holiday.

["H.M. the King will broadcast to the peoples of the British Empire and commonwealth tomorrow Tuesday at 9 P.M. B.D.S.T. (3 P.M. E.W.T.)

["Parliament will meet at the usual time tomorrow."]

The Rest Is Mummery

London took the view, however, that what it had been waiting for has been done in the war and not in officials' statements, and if went ahead in the belief that the war is over and that the rest is mummery.

This belief took hold in mid-

(Continued on Page A, Column 3)

8 Japanese Ships Sunk, 5 Damaged

By PHILIP S. HEISLER
(Sunpapers War Correspondent)

Advanced Fleet Headquarters, Guam, Tuesday, May 8 *(By Navy Radio)*— While the last sparks of the war flickered out in Europe today, the furious fighting of the Pacific war flamed undiminished as United States forces, tightening an aerial blockade on Japan, sank eight and damaged five Jap ships off Korea and Honshu and flame-throwing tanks led another push against the Japs on the southern Okinawa front.

Search aircraft of Fleet Air Wing 1, attacking at masthead height with bombs and machine guns, sank four Jap cargo ships and tankers and damaged five Jap cargo ships in the waters around Korea yesterday, Admiral Chester W. Nimitz's communique revealed.

On the same day planes of Fleet Air Wing 18 in searches over Japanese

(Continued on Page 5, Column 4)

DUMBARTON ISSUE RAISED BY MOLOTOV

Russian Opposes Treaty-Revision Power For New League

San Francisco, May 7 (AP)—Senator Vandenberg (R., Mich.) agreed tonight with Soviet Foreign Commissar Molotov that the proposed new world organization will have no powers to revise treaties. [Details of Senator Vandenberg's stand will be found on Page 9.]

By PAUL W. WARD
(Conference Bureau of The Sun)

San Francisco, May 7—During a press conference which he abruptly terminated when questions were raised about Russia's arrest of sixteen Polish underground leaders, Stalin's Foreign Minister Vyacheslav M. Molotov, tossed a delayed action bomb today into the United Nations discussions here on world security organization.

Mr. Molotov also evaded—along with questions about the Polish issue—a query as to whether, with V-E day at hand, Russia was ready at last to state its position in the Japanese war.

Interpretation Differs

Soviet spokesman's potentially explosive utterance occurred when—after announcing Russian acceptance of the so-called Vandenberg amendment to the Dumbarton Oaks plan for a new league—he placed upon the amendment an interpretation contrary to that of its American proponents.

He did so, moreover, although he had been warned by American delegates in behind-scenes conferences that the Senate might refuse to ratify United States participation in the new league if their version were not accepted.

He had warned them in turn that

(Continued on Page 9, Column 2)

Associated Press News Ban Lifted By SHAEF

Suspension Of Filing Privilege Limited To Writer Of Report On Surrender

Paris, May 7 (AP)—A Supreme headquarters order suspending filing facilities of the Associated Press in the European theater was lifted tonight except as it applied to Edward Kennedy, chief of the AP's Western front staff, who sent the Reims dispatch telling of Germany's unconditional surrender.

The earlier order of supreme headquarters public relations division had halted all AP filing from here for several hours.

Order Addressed To Kennedy

Brig. Gen. Frank Allen, Jr., chief of the division, addressed this order to Edward Kennedy, chief of the Associated Press bureau here:

"The Associated Press is suspended from filing copy by any means in their theater (European theater of operations) effective 1640 hours (10.40 A.M. E.W.T.) this date until charges are investigated in connection with the filing of a story under Reims dateline that SHAEF had officially announced the unconditional surrender of all German forces as of 0241 hours this date.

"Signed, Frank Allen, Jr., brigadier general, U.S.A., director public relations division."

Word "Official" Not In Dispatch

In fairness to Kennedy it must be stated that nowhere in his dispatch as received via London and issued by the Associated Press in the United States did he say the surrender was officially announced.

A flash which moved just before Kennedy's by-lined dispatch said: "Reims, France—Allies officially announced Germany surrendered unconditionally."

This was based on an assumptoin that since the story came from General Eisenhower's headquarters at Reims it was official.

The word "official" did not appear in the printable story under Kennedy's byline which followed the flash.

Issue Put Before Eisenhower

New York, May 7 (AP)—When the Associated Press was cut off today from filing facilities throughout the European theater of operations by an order from Supreme Allied Headquarters, Kent Cooper, executive director of the Associated Press, immediately dispatched messages to General Eisen-

(Continued on Page A, Column 7)

PHONE TO LONDON GAVE OUT REPORT

Associated Press Tells How Dispatch Was Relayed

London, May 7 (AP)—The Associated Press London Bureau tonight gave out this account of how Edward Kennedy's dispatch on the surrender was received and sent to the Allied public:

The London staff was sweating out the peace news in an atmosphere loaded with rumor, expectancy and cigarette smoke, when one of many telephones in the main news desk rang about 3.24 P.M. London time (9.24 A.M. E.W.T.) and Russell Landstrom dropped his job of herding copy to the cable and radio channels to answer it.

Voice On Phone Fades

"This is Paris calling," came a faint, muffled voice. Then it faded and came back so Landstrom could catch the word "Paris" again and he turned the telephone over to Lewis Hawkins.

Very dimly, the voice said that Germany had surrendered unconditionally

(Continued on page A, Column 8)

NORWAY NAZIS GIVE UP; YANKS NEAR PRAGUE

Allied Fleet Reported Off Oslo; Bohemia Chief Won't Quit Fight

With U.S. 7th Army, Tuesday, May 8 (AP)—Leopold III, King of Belgium, and his Queen have been liberated by the United States 7th Army, it was announced today. [Details will be found on Page 3.]

London, May 7 (AP)—The root of the German power was dead, but its branches were still dying today, sometimes violently, as in Bohemia, sometimes passively, as in Norway, but always swiftly.

In Bohemia, the Partisan held Prague radio announced tonight that American tanks, racing to the relief of patriots in the Czechoslovak capital, had driven into the city's suburbs within 4 miles of its limits.

A Partisan leader, identifying himself as the "military commander of greater Prague," said American staff officers already were in contact with his forces as the Germans burned and sacked the city and shelled its hospitals.

[The FCC reported that the Czech-controlled radio at Prague announced that German troops in the city and "the whole of Bohemia" have been ordered by their commander to cease fighting.]

Norway Surrender

In Norway, General Boehme, German commander in chief broadcast an order of the day over the Oslo radio tonight commanding his troops, to lay down their arms, in obedience to Foreign Minister "von Krosigk's announcement of unconditional surrender of all German fighting troops."

Boehme said the surrender order "hits us very hard because we are un-

(Continued on Page 3, Column 2)

Watson Given Pulitzer Prize For World News

Mr. Watson depicts French reaction to Nazi surrender, *Page* 2,

New York, May 7 (AP)—Mark S. Watson, military correspondent of the Baltimore *Sun*, has been awarded the Pulitzer prize of $500 for "a distinguished example of telegraphic reporting on international affairs," it was announced today.

Mr. Watson, currently in Paris, was cited for dispatches written out of Washington, London and the fronts in Sicily, Italy and France.

Chief of the *Sunpapers'* staff of war correspondents, Mr. Watson now is stationed at the Supreme Allied Headquarters.

Officer In World War I

Being with a fighting expeditionary force in France was not a new experience for Mr. Watson. In World War I he was an officer in the AEF.

When he went to the Normandy beachhead to report on the activities of the invasion forces it was the fifth war front he had covered for the *Sunpapers*.

He was in London during part of the German *blitz*. He toured battlefields in North Africa, was with Allied troops in the invasion of Sicily and accompanied the assault waves at Salerno.

War News Interpreted

Between assignments in Italy and his return to England to cover the invasion of France, Mr. Watson came back to Washington for several months to interpret the war news through daily contact with officials of the War and Navy departments.

Mr. Watson was a major of artillery when World War I ended. Shortly after the armistice was signed he was sent to Paris as officer in charge of the army newspaper, *Stars And Stripes*, remaining on that duty until the papers wound up its affairs in July, 1919.

Returning to this country, he became associated with *The Sun* in 1920, and has been with the paper ever since, as assistant managing editor, as editor of *The Sunday Sun* and, for a time, acting editor of *The Sun*, which post he left to become military correspondent.

Baltimore Author Honored

Another Baltimorean who was honored was Sergt. Karl Shapiro, author of "V-Letter and Other Poems." It was cited as the most "distinguished volume of verse published during the year by an American author."

Sergeant Shapiro was graduated from City College.

Except for one poem, it was said at the time the verse was published last summer, the entire book was written in the South Pacific, where Sergeant Shapiro has been stationed since the early days of the war.

Won Prize While At Camp

His first book of poems, "Person, Place and Things," was written in Australia and helped him win the Guggenheim fellowship in poetry.

In 1941, while stationed at Camp Lee, Va., before being sent abroad, Sergeant Shapiro won one of six $100

MARK S. WATSON

prizes awarded by the magazine *Poetry*.

His "V-Letter" was dedicated to his mother, Mrs. Irwin Shapiro, who formerly lived in the 3600 block Copley road, but who now is a resident of Arlington, Va. Sergeant Shapiro was a librarian at the Enoch Pratt Free Library before joining the Army. He is 32 years old.

The Pulitzer prize committee announced that the prize for distinguished correspondence during 1944 was awarded to Harold V. (Hal) Boyle, Associated Press war correspondent, who told the day-by-day story of the American foot soldier in the battle for Europe.

AP Photographer Honored

Another $500 award went to Joe Rosenthal, Associated Press photographer who made the historic picture of the Marines raising the United States flag on Iwo Jima.

Rosenthal's photograph — made for the wartime still-picture pool — was taken in February, 1945, and normally would not have been eligible for a 1944 award, but the rule was suspended "for this distinguished example." it was announced.

The Pulitzer prize for the most distinguished novel of 1944 went to John Hersey, for "A Bell for Adano," and to Mary Chase for "Harvey," the best original American play.

Awards Since 1917

Established under the will of Joseph Pulitzer, the awards have been made annually since 1917 by Columbia University trustees on the recommendations of the graduate school of journalism's advisory board.

The award which Boyle received was based on "distinguished correspondence, the test being clearness and

(Continued on Page 2, Column 2)

BIG THREE ARE EXPECTED TO PROCLAIM VICTORY SIMULTANEOUSLY TODAY

Generals Smith, Susloparov, Sevez And Jodl Sign Terms In Eisenhower's Headquarters In Red Schoolhouse At Reims, France

London, May 7 (AP)—Complete victory in Europe was won by the Allies today with the unconditional surrender of Germany.

President Truman, Prime Minister Churchill and Premier Stalin are scheduled to proclaim the historic conquest simultaneously at 9 A.M. (Eastern War Time) tomorrow from Washington, London and Moscow.

Germany's formal capitulation came at 2.41 A.M. (French Time) in the Reims schoolhouse, headquarters of Gen. Dwight D. Eisenhower, supreme commander of the Allied armies in the West. The crowning triumph came just five years, eight months and six days after Hitler invaded Poland.

It marked the official end of war in Europe, but it did not silence all the guns, for battles raged on in Czechoslovakia.

There, Gen. Ferdinand Schoerner, who has been designated a war crimnial, defied the orders of Grand Admiral Karl Doenitz, successor to the dead or missing Hitler, to lay down arms.

May Be Named Guerrilla Outlaws

But this force — all that remains of what once was the mightiest military machine on earth — faced inevitable liquidation or surrender.

Presumably, the victoious powers soon will label these troops guerrilla outlaws, subject to execution unless they yield.

The only details of Germany's end came from Edward Kennedy, chief of the Associated Press staff on the Western front, who was the first to flash the word the world had long awaited.

His story said:

"Germany surrendered unconditionally to the Western Allies and Russia at 0241 (French time) today in the big Reims red schoolhouse which is the headquarters of Gen. Dwight D. Eisenhower.

"The surrender which brought the war in Europe to a formal end after five years and eight months of bloodshed and destruction was signed for Germany by Col. Gen. Gustaf and (Alfred) Godl. Godl is the new the chief of staff of the *Wehrmacht*.

Eisenhower Not Present At Signing

"It was signed for the supreme Allied command—the United States and Britain—by Lieut. Gen. Walter Bedell Smith, Eisenhower's chief of staff; for Russia by Gen. Ivan Susloparov, member of a military mission on the Western front, and for France by Gen. Francois Sevez."

Thus to the very end did the Allies deny to the Germans their hope of concluding a separate peace.

"General Eisenhower was not present at the signing," Kennedy said, "but immediately afterward Jodl and his fellow delegate, General Admiral Hans Georg Friedeburg, were received by the supreme commander."

It was Friedeburg, named commander in chief of the German Navy after Doenitz took over he Third Reich, who negotiated last week the unconditional surrender of 1,000,000 German soldiers in Denmark, Holland and northwestern Germany.

"They were asked sternly if they understood the surrender terms imposed upon Germany and if the would be

(Continued on Page A, Column 1)

EXTRA THE EVENING SUN EXTRA

Vol. 71—No. 17 PAID CIRCULATION APRIL MORNING, 168,851 EVENING, 192,089 360,940 ‖ SUNDAY 275,260 BALTIMORE, MONDAY, MAY 7, 1945 Entered as second-class matter at Baltimore Post Office Zone 3 4 Pages 3 Cents

SURRENDER

FLASH

Reims, France, May 7 (AP)—Germany surrendered unconditionally to the western Allies and Russia at 2.41 A.M. French time today.

(This was at 8.41 P.M., Eastern War Time Sunday).

The surrender took place at a little red schoolhouse which is the headquarters of General Eisenhower.

The surrender which brought the war in Europe to a formal end after five years, eight months and six days of bloodshed and destruction was signed for Germany by Col. Gen. Gustav-Jodl.

Jodl is the new chief of staff of the German Army.

It was signed for the Supreme Allied command by Lieut. Gen. Walter Bedell Smith, chief of staff for General Eisenhower.

It was also signed by Gen. Ivan Susloparoff for Russia and by Gen. Francois Sevez for France.

General Eisenhower was not present at the signing, but immediately afterward Jodl and his fellow delegate, General Admiral Hans George Friedeburg, were received by the supreme commander.

They were asked sternly if they understood the surrender terms imposed upon Germany and if they would be carried out by Germany.

They answered yes.

Joy at the news was tempered only by the realization that the war against Japan remains to be resolved, with many casualties still ahead.

The end of the European warfare, greatest, bloodiest and costliest war in human history—it has claimed at least 40,000,000 casualties on both sides in killed, wounded and captured—came after five years, eight months, and six days of strife that overspread the globe.

Hitler's arrogant armies invaded Poland on September 1, 1939, beginning the agony that convulsed the world for 2,319 days.

Shifting Men, Supplies To The Pacific Won't Be An Easy Job

By James D. White
[Associated Press Staff Writer]

Victory in Europe turns American eyes to the Pacific.

But our two-way war effort cannot be recast overnight into a single surge against Japan. The farther we push Japan back, the longer grow our supply lines, and the shorter Japan's become.

Best estimates are that it will take at least six months to reverse our European supply system and transfer the full weight of American armed might to the Pacific. Not only are Pacific distances already the longest in military history but the reversal itself presents special problems.

Gen. Brehon Somervell, chief of Army Service Forces, disclosed months ago that 40 per cent of the Army's overseas shipments had been going to the Pacific theater. The remaining 60 per cent presumably were going mostly to Europe. What now happens?

The Broad Outlines

Here are broad outlines foreseen by army experts.

Maj. Gen. Charles P. Gross, the Army's chief of transportation, says that our transport fleet is larger this time than after the last European war, but he points out that part of it is already being used in the Pacific and British shipping will be less widely available this time than last.

General Gross expects that after an early direct movement to the Pacific via the Panama and Suez canals, mostly of service forces, the remaining flow of men will be mainly through this country.

So he looks for a shortage of shipping, just at a time when the troops not going directly to the Pacific all want to come home on the first boat. Some of these men will be coming home to stay, others for short furloughs before going on to the Pacific.

Cargo Ships Uncomfortable

"The job probably will require the reconversion of every ship that can be employed," he predicts. "Cargo ships will be uncomfortable, but experience in the last war indicates the boys will be glad to get on anything that floats. Also from the last war, we know that by the time they get to the home port they'll be sore about the boats they came home on.

"As for the half million or so who may remain as occupation troops, we must figure on having to replace them before too long—that's an added problem to think of."

But this is just the beginning of the huge complicated business of "redeployment" — moving troops from Europe to the Pacific.

Troop transports are faster than the freighters which will carry equipment. Somewhere the troops will have to wait to let their equipment catch up with them. It would be ideal to give them entirely new equipment, but this is too much to hope for throughout, says General Gross.

Problem Of "Remarrying"

After equipment catches up with soldiers, the problem of "remarrying" them remains. Different types of equipment will be required in some instances. Although the Pacific war has moved out of the jungle to a certain extent, it still is being fought largely in warmer climates than was the case in Europe. Tropical clothing, medicines and other items must be provided and troops instructed in their use.

The Pacific war is expected to require relatively less heavy equipment because of the inferiority of Japanese equipment. Thus, the Army may use less artillery ammunition on its way to Tokyo than across Europe. But as fighting moves up from the beachheads of China and Japan it can be expected to increase its appetite.

Although the Pacific is the world's largest ocean, General Gross says it lacks large base areas from which to stage offensives.

"You can't use every little Pacific island as a base for this mass 'marriage' which must take place between troops and equipment," he says. This takes room, for great storage areas and training grounds.

Specialized Training

As to training, Gen. Joseph W. Stilwell, chief of the army ground forces, said recently that there would be specialized training, but relatively little need for intensive retraining of soldiers from Europe for combat against the Japanese. He declared that the basic training and discipline was the main thing; that methods change through the years, but that the principles remain the same.

In moving men and equipment westward, army authorities expect "choke points" all along the line.

The movement will tax Western ports and the transcontinental railways, predicts General Gross. He says an effort will be made to avoid using East Coast and Gulf ports, except for the overflow; but other army statements have mentioned that such ports already are being used to load Pacific shipping which travels through the Panama Canal, particularly when Atlantic shipping is transferred for service in the Pacific.

Some Congestion Foreseen

Pacific ports have increased their handling capacity since 1942; but, even so, some congestion can be looked for.

Pacific distances are such that one naval authority estimates that if we have 200 ships going out with supplies, 200 more are on their way back and another 200 are either loading or unloading. Once materials get to the Pacific, unloading and storage is a problem. That may cause costly delays. Before the war there was no port between Australia and Manila which could berth and unload a Liberty ship.

Port facilities in Japan are good if they can be captured intact. But on the China coast Shanghai is the only really great port between Hong Kong and Dairen.

Total German Disarmament Is Urged

(How shall the victorious United Nations treat a beaten Germany? As the views of a man with practical experience in promoting peace, here are the opinions of Viscount Cecil of Chelwood, president of the League of Nations Union, chief draftsman of the old League Covenant and winner of the 1937 Nobel Peace Prize for his work in the League and in promoting international good will.)

London (AP)—For a lasting peace, I believe that close cooperation of the Big Four is essential.

It should, in my view, be provided for in part by the organization of an international authority, of which all peace-loving countries should be members.

Germany should be totally disarmed, apart from what may be necessary for police purposes to maintain internal order.

However, I do not think that to split Germany into separate states would give any additional security, nor could it be made permanent practically, and when it disappeared the position would be worse than it is now.

Occupation Of Reich

There will certainly have to be some kind of international occupation of Germany by the Allied forces, and probably occupation of strategic points may have to be permanent or lasting for a considerable number of years.

As soon as militarily possible, the Germans should be encouraged to form their own government, subject to the maintenance of disarmament.

As to Germany's post-war relationship to the rest of the world, the essential thing is to take precautions against any revival by Germany of her aggressive policy, and any proposals made for dealing with her should be judged by that test.

Revenge or even retribution is not likely to be a useful guide. Ultimately, one hopes that Germany may be restored to the community of nations, but when that can be done must depend on the attitude of the German people.

Wartime Trials

Germans guilty of war crimes—by which is meant actions which any civilized system of law regards as crimes and which are not justified by any rules of international law as to military proceedings—should be tried by impartial courts and those guilty should be punished according to the discretion of the court.

Germany certainly should be made to restore all property her troops or officials have stolen and should, as far as that can be done without doing harm to the economic interests of injured countries, be made to repair or rebuild the property she has damaged.

Nothing but the reeducation of Germany and her genuine abandonment of the whole of the Nazi policy—based as it is on much of Germany's pre-war teaching—can give any real security that she will act in a peaceful way in the future.

WHEN AXIS TIDE WAS HIGHEST—How the great shadow of Axis oppression lay over Europe and parts of Africa at the high-water mark of German-Italian military success is illustrated by this map. Black area represents the territory occupied or dominated by the Axis when the United Nations were on the defensive on all fronts. Late in 1941 Axis hordes held all of France, Norway, Poland, Yugoslavia and Greece and dominated the satellite states of Finland, Romania, Hungary and Bulgaria. German armies stood at the gates of Stalingrad and Moscow and the British in Africa were engaged in bitter struggle to escape annihilation by Rommel's Afrika Korps. The United States entered the war late in 1941. The tide turned the next year when the British stopped the Nazis at El Alamein and the Russians held at Stalingrad. Then came the Normandy invasion June 6, 1944.

Sunpaper War Writers Turn To New Tasks

Sunpaper war correspondents in Europe wrote "finis" to the their battle chapters today and rolled clean sheets of paper into their typewriters to report the important developments still to come.

To cover the war in Europe, five staff members of *The Sun* and *The Evening Sun* were sent into the battlefields and news centers in that theater while two other correspondents are covering the battle areas of the Pacific and the military centers in Washington.

Mark S. Watson, dean of the *Sunpaper* corps of war correspondents, arrived in London when the Germans were still blitzing the British capital with nightly bombing raids.

Went To North Africa

From England he went to North Africa to tour the battlefields there and then accompany American troops when they invaded Sicily and Italy.

Meanwhile, Lee McCardell, Price Day and Holbrook Bradley, who had been training with American troops in this country, arrived in England to report the invasion preparations and await the day when they could accompany the troops on the invasion of France.

Thomas M. O'Neill, veteran political reporter on Maryland State and national affairs, was also sent to England to take charge of the *Sunpapers'* London Bureau and report the diplomatic and British home-front news.

To get the correspondents experienced in battle-front reporting, McCardell was sent to Italy. There he accompanied the American Fifth Army as it slowly fought its way up the Italian boot. From a hilltop he watched the historic bombing of Cassino.

After a tour of duty in Italy, McCardell was transferred back to England to concentrate on the Allied air might which by then was softening up Germany and France in preparation for the invasion.

Price Day took up where McCardell left off in Italy just in time to push through with the Fifth Army when it cracked the German defenses at Cassino, drove up through Rome and continued up through Italy to the north.

Bradley With Marylanders

Meanwhile, Watson had returned to the United States, inspected the war progress here and returned to England to await D-day, which by then was fast approaching.

All this while Bradley was living, eating and training with the Maryland men of the Twenty-ninth Division in England and reporting to the people back home the news of their friends and relatives who had by this time been away from their homes for more than two years.

Covering the growing offensive in the Pacific was Howard M. Norton and from Washington, Philip S. Heisler reported the official views and interpretations as seen from the War Department and Navy Department.

Then came June 6—D-day.

Bradley was with the Maryland troops of the Blue and Gray when they approached the beachhead of France and fought their way inland against the toughest opposition of the whole landing operation.

McCardell was high over the invasion landing barges in a Martin B-26 Marauder bomber.

From SHAEF, somewhere in England, Watson cabled and radioed back to Baltimore the historic news that all the world waited for.

Advance In Italy

Almost simultaneously, the American forces broke loose again in Italy and Day reported their advances. A few days later, a powerful American task force attacked Saipan and invaded that island only 1,500 miles from Tokyo. Norton was aboard a ship in that fleet and accompanied American marines and soldiers as they fought their way onto the island.

Watson soon joined the Allied forces in France and O'Neill was on hand in England to report on the robot-plane attacks which were then unleashed against southern England.

In addition to seeing and reporting the exciting events of the fighting men, the *Sunpapers'* war correspondents had considerable excitement of their own.

Into St. Lo On Tank

Bradley rode into battered St. Lo in an American tank, was knocked to the ground by a shell explosion and later wounded in the leg when a mortar shell burst close to him during the battle of Vire.

McCardell accompanied American troops as they pushed into Cherbourg, and was riding in a jeep with an Associated Press photographer when the photographer was killed by fragments from an American bomb.

In Italy Day had his helmet blown from his head when a German shell landed close by.

Hurt On Sub Chaser

And out on the Pacific, Norton was aboard a sub chaser when a Jap shell hit the small vessel and killed or wounded 21 out of 25 persons aboard. Norton suffered only a torn ligament in his shoulder when thrown to the deck by the explosion. When Norton returned from the Pacific theater in September, Heisler took over in that theater and is now covering operations of the fleet. Norton is now on assignment in Italy.

Battles in France were nothing new to Watson. During the World War he had fought there as an officer in the AEF. Before going abroad to cover this war, Watson was editor of *The Sunday Sun*.

McCardell was one of the first American newspapermen to go abroad during this war. He was one of a few newspapermen selected to accompany American troops to Iceland.

Watson recently returned to the United States to cover war developments as a military analyst in Washington. McCardell rode with Patton's 3d Army across the heart of Germany. Day moved to Paris, to cover the broad front of Allied operations in Europe from supreme headquarters there. Bradley has been with the American 9th Army.

Strength That Won Took Over 4 Years To Build

By James D. White
[Associated Press Staff Writer]

The strength that beat Germany was more than four years in the building.

America's entry into the war at the time of Pearl Harbor saw this effort already uncertainly begun—moving toward goals then considered fantastic but long since outstripped in the greatest production feat the world has known.

The process was begun in the summer of 1940 with the program announced by President Roosevelt to make this country the arsenal of democracy.

Astronomical Goals

He laid down goals which seemed astronomical—50,000 planes a year where we then were building 6,000; a two-ocean navy; an army of 1,725,000 men where we then had 250,000; critical items for an army of three million, with a system of factories capable of supplying four million; a vastly expanded merchant marine to carry the weapons of war to the beleaguered democracies fighting the Axis.

By Pearl Harbor planes were being produced at the rate of 2,000 a month; the two-ocean navy, badly needed because of losses at Pearl Harbor, still had to be built—but the Government had 11 of its own yards and 110 private yards busy with naval construction which already had launched the world's two most powerful battleships—the North Carolina and the Washington.

Ship A Day

The Maritime Commission shortly was able to launch a merchant ship a day, mostly tankers and the war-emergency Liberty ship which was assembly-line produced on both coasts, the Gulf and along some inland waterways.

THE WEATHER
Occasional thunder storms tonight and Tuesday; cloudy and a little warmer Tuesday; fair at night.
Detailed report on Page 17

THE EVENING SUN

7 STAR SPORTS

Vol. 71—No. 94 | MORNING 175,213 / EVENING 190,130 } PAID CIRCULATION JULY 365,343 || SUNDAY 275,960 | BALTIMORE, MONDAY, AUGUST 6, 1945 | Entered as second-class matter at Baltimore Post Office | Zone 3 | 22 Pages | 3 Cents

Atomic Bomb Hits Japan: 2000 Times As Powerful As Largest Used Before

Called Reply To Rejection Of Ultimatum

Washington, Aug. 6 (AP)—An atomic bomb, hailed as the most terrible destructive force in history and as the greatest achievement of organized science, has been loosed upon Japan.

President Truman disclosed in a White House statement at 11 A.M. today that the first use of the bomb—containing more power than 20,000 tons of TNT and producing more than 2,000 times the blast of the most powerful bomb ever dropped before—was made sixteen hours earlier on Hiroshima, Japanese army base.

The atomic bomb is the answer, President Truman said, to Japan's refusal to surrender. Secretary of War Stimson predicted the bomb will "prove a tremendous aid" in shortening the Japanese war. Mr. Truman grimly warned that "even more powerful forms (of the bomb) are in development. He said:

"If they do not now accept our terms, they may expect a rain of ruin from the air the like of which has never been seen on this earth."

The War Department reported that "an impenetrable cloud of dust and smoke" cloaked Hiroshima after the first atomic bomb crashed down. It was impossible to make an immediate assessment of the damage.

Suggests U.S. Commission For Control

President Truman said he would recommend that Congress consider establishing a commission to control production of atomic power within the United States, adding:

"I shall . . . make . . . recommendations to Congress as to how atomic power can become a powerful and forceful influence toward the maintenance of world peace."

Both Mr. Truman and Secretary Stimson, while emphasizing the peacetime potentiality of the new force, made clear that much research must be undertaken to effect full peacetime application of its principles.

The product of $2,000,000,000 spent in research and production—"the greatest scientific gamble in history," Mr. Truman said—the atomic bomb has been one of the most closely guarded secrets of the war.

Franklin D. Roosevelt and Winston Churchill gave the signal to start work on harnessing the forces of the atom. Mr. Truman said the Germans worked feverishly but failed to solve the problem.

Harnesses Basic Power Of Universe

Mr. Truman added:

"It is an atomic bomb. It is a harnessing of the basic power of the universe. The force from which the sun draws its power has been loosed against those who brought war to the Far East."

The base that was hit is a major quartermaster depot and has large ordnance, machine tool and aircraft plants.

The raid on Hiroshima, located on Honshu Island on the shores of the Inland Sea, had not been disclosed previously although the 20th Air Force on Guam announced that 580 Superforts raided four Japanese cities at about the same time.

The city of 318,000 also contains a principal port.

The President disclosed that the Germans "worked feverishly" in search of a way to use atomic energy in their war effort but failed. Meantime American and British scientists studied the problem and developed two principal plants and some lesser factories for the production of atomic power.

The President disclosed that more than 65,000 persons now are working in great secrecy in these plants, adding:

"We are now prepared to obliterate more rapidly and completely every productive enterprise the Japanese have above ground in any city. We shall completely destroy Japan's power to make war."

Answer To Rejection Of Ultimatum

The President noted that the Big Three ultimatum issued July 26 at Potsdam was intended "to spare the Japanese people from utter destruction" and the Japanese leaders rejected it. The atomic bomb now is the answer to that rejection, and the President said, "They may expect a

[Continued On Page 3, Column 1]

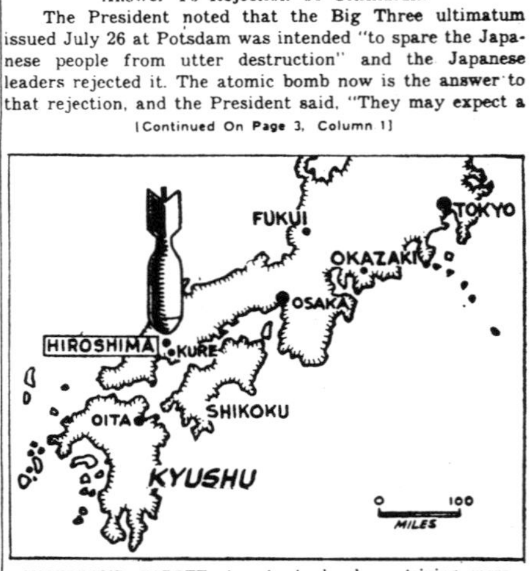

SUPERBOMB TARGET—An atomic bomb containing more power than 20,000 tons of T.N.T. and producing 2,000 times the blast of the largest bomb ever before used, has been dropped on the important Japanese army base of Hiroshima.

Stimson Predicts Atomic Bomb Will Speed End Of War

London, Aug. 6 (AP)—Germany possessed some atomic power secrets, Winston Churchill said tonight, but "by God's mercy, British and American science outpaced all German efforts."

Washington, Aug. 6 (AP)—Secretary Stimson predicted today that the atomic bomb will "prove a tremendous aid" in shortening the war with Japan.

The War Secretary made his statement as the Army reported that an "impenetrable cloud of dust and smoke" cloaked Hiroshima after it was hit by the new weapon from the air.

An accurate assessment of the damage inflicted by the bomb is not yet available, however, the War Department said. As soon as details are learned they will be released.

"Staggers Imagination"

Stimson said in his statement that the explosive power of the bomb is such as to "stagger the imagination." He added that scientists are confident of developing even more powerful atomic bombs.

Stimson said that security requirements do not permit disclosure of the exact methods of producing the bomb or the nature of its action. He did say, however, that uranium ore is essential to the production of the bomb.

Development of the bomb culminated three years of work by Allied scientists, industry, labor and military forces, Stimson said, adding that he was convinced Japan will not be in a position to use a similar weapon. While Germany worked "feverishly" to develop an atomic bomb, Stimson said, the Nazi defeat has now erased danger from that source.

More Details Later

Stimson promised, that further statements will be released in the future to give additional details concerning scientific and production aspects.

He disclosed that development of the bomb was carried out by thousands of persons "with the greatest secrecy." The work has been so divided, he said, that no one has been given more information concerning the bomb than was absolutely necessary to his particular job.

The possibility of using atomic energy in the manufacture of weapons, Stimson said, was brought to President Roosevelt's attention late in 1939. The Chief Executive named a committee to investigate, and by June, 1942, Stimson said, sufficient progress had been made to warrant a big expansion of the project.

Three Plants Started

Three plants to produce the bombs were started in December, 1942. Two of these are located at the Clinton Engineer Works, in Tennessee, and a third at the Hanford Engineer Works, in Washington State. The Clinton Engineer Works is located on a Government reservation 18 miles west of Knoxville, Tenn. The Hanford Engineer Works is located on a 430,000-acre reservation 15 miles northwest of Pasco, Wash.

In addition, a special laboratory to deal with technical problems has been established near Santa Fe, N.M. The laboratory is directed by Dr. J. Robert Oppenheimer, whose "genius and inspiration," Stimson said, has been largely responsible for development of the bomb.

Peacetime Uses Seen

Stimson said that the fact that atomic energy can now be released on a large scale in an atomic bomb raises the prospect that such energy may have a big place in peacetime industrial purposes. The Secretary added:

"Already in the course of producing one of the elements much energy is being released, not explosively but in regulated amounts.

"This energy, however, is in the form of heat at a temperature too low to make practicable the operation of a conventional power plant. It will be a matter of much further research and development to design machines for the conversion of atomic energy into useful power."

Co-Operation Of Britain

Stimson said the atomic bomb had been developed with the full knowledge of and co-operation of Britain and Canada and substantial patent controls on the weapon had been obtained in those countries. Presidet Roosevelt and Prime Minister Churchill many months ago decided that all work on the bomb should be concentrated in the United States in order to bring about quicker development of the weapon and to eliminate duplication.

As a result of that decision, a group of British scientists who had been working on the problem were transferred to the United States late in 1945 and since that time had participated in the development of the project in this country.

In addition, Stimson disclosed, one of Denmark's great scientists—Dr. Neils Bohr—was whisked from the grasp of the Nazis in Denmark

[Continued On Page 3, Column 3]

—Atomic Power—

What T.N.T. Did At Halifax

New York, Aug. 6 (AP)—A faint idea of the power within the atomic bomb:

On June 6, 1917, a munitions ship blew up in a collision in the harbor of Halifax, N. S.; 1,500 persons were killed, 4,000 injured, 20,000 made homeless, two and one half square miles of the city devastated.

That munitions ship carried 3,000 tons of T.N.T.—about one seventh of the equivalent of the new bomb.

Belgian Regent On Holiday

Brussels, Aug. 6 [Reuter]—Prince Charles, the Belgian regent and brother of King Leopold, left by air for London today. He intends to spend a few days in Britain on holiday.

A Punch Like 2,000 B-29's

Washington, Aug. 6 (AP)—The atomic bomb announced by President Truman today packs a punch equivalent to that normally delivered by 2,000 B-29's.

The President said the missile has an explosive force equal to 20,000 tons—40,000,000 pounds—of T.N.T. Assuming a B-29 carries a bombload of ten tons of T.N.T., four 500-plane raids by the world's biggest bombers would be necessary to equal in destructice power the exploding fury of one atomic bomb.

The atomic bomb dwarfs by 2,000 times the blast power of the British "grand-slam" bomb, which weighed approximately eleven tons.

Japs Mention No Unusual Blast

San Francisco, Aug. 6 (AP)—The Tokyo radio announced that the city of Hiroshima, target of the American atomic bombing announced by President Truman, was raided at 8.20 A.M. today (7.30 P.M. Sunday, United States Eastern war time.)

President Truman said the powerful new bomb was dropped about that time, but the Tokyo broadcast heard here made no mention of any unusual destruction.

It reported only that "a small number of American B-29's" attacked the city on southwestern Honshu with incendiary and explosive bombs.

B-29's Hit Four Cities

Guam, Aug. 6 (AP)—Four more Japanese cities were left in a mass of flames by 580 Superfortresses today, and their destruction appeared certain, returning crewmen reported.

Waves of B-29's dropped approximately 3,850 tons of incendiaries on the industrial cities of Nishinomiya, Maebashi, Imabari and

[Continued On Page 2, Column 8]

Hitler's V-3 Was Atomic Bomb

London, Aug. 6 [Reuter]—The atomic bomb which, according to President Harry S. Truman, rocked Japan today was Hitler's V-3 weapon and would have been used by him but for a British and Norwegian raid on laboratories in Norway in February, 1943, the British press association reported tonight.

The agency said that the raid was carried out by paratroopers whose success was due to the co-operation of a Norwegian workman at Rjukan laboratories who did not raise the alarm but allowed the Allied soldiers to go about their work.

Laboratory Destroyed

Twenty minutes after he wished the paratoopers "good luck," the laboratory with its radium, uranium and heavy water was destroyed.

June 29 Atom Forecast Recalled

[By the Associated Press]

Commander Herbert Agar, aide to John G. Winant, the United States Ambassador to Great Britain, said on June 29 that "If the war (European) had gone on for another six months it is quite possible that this planet would have ceased to exist because it was probable that someone would have learned to break the atom without controlling it."

Agar said "there was a danger that the Germans would learn how to split the atom first," and added: "I sincerely believe that in a very few years human beings will know how to destroy the human race."

Previously, Lieut. Col. John A. Keck, of Greensburg, Pa., chief of the Enemy Equipment Intelligence Section of the United States Army Ordnance Division in the European Theater, had told of many highly advanced German secret weapons which had not yet reached the perfection stage, when the war ended.

Peace-Time Military Training Backers Losing Hope

Washington, Aug. 6 (AP)—Congressional backers of universal military training said privately today they have all but abandoned hope of winning their fight.

They plan to make an effort, when Congress reconvenes, to put through a program of compulsory training for all able-bodied youths, but they don't expect to get far.

The House Postwar Military Policy Committee, headed by Representative Woodrum (D., Va.), has recommended the program. It has the backing of the Army, Navy and veterans' groups, but is opposed by most churchmen, educators and organized labor.

Delay Is Blamed

Proponents, who contend a peacetime draft is necessary as a defense measure, blame delay in action and the current low ebb of army sentiment on Capitol Hill for the dark outlook.

Another factor involved is President Truman's attitude. Pending a promised message to Congress this fall, the Chief Executive has declined to state his views.

Some Capitol Hill friends of the President, however, say Mr. Truman is much more likely to suggest an enlarged and modernized National Guard rather than universal training legislation.

"We had a fighting chance up to about a month ago," one of the backers of postwar conscription said, "but recent actions of the Army have just about ruined that chance.

"Army relations with Capitol Hill are at their lowest in history because of dissatisfaction with their manpower policies, their food program and other things. There are many of us who believe the Army has gone too far in hoarding manpower, in cornering food, in imposing too severe sentences for violations of rules, and in the general treatment of personnel."

May Loses Ardor

Only last week Chairman May (D., Ky.) of the House Military Committee lambasted the Army for what he referred to as "brutal" treatment of soldier prisoners. May is one of the universal training legislation backers who has lost much of his enthusiasm for the plan.

Even should Congress decide on a program of compulsory training it is doubted that the Army would be allowed to run the program. Original advocates of army control already are advancing proposals for strict civilian direction, with the Army providing only the necessary officers for such things as drill practice and supervision of field maneuvers.

Hiram Johnson, Cal. Senator, Dies At 79

Washington, Aug. 6 (AP)—Senator Hiram W. Johnson, of California, militant opponent of the League of Nations and the San Francisco Charter for a United Nations organization, died today at the age of 79.

The veteran Republican Senator expired at the Bethesada (Md.) Naval Hospital, where he had been confined for two and one half weeks. His physician, Capt. Robert E. Duncan, USN, said he died from a thrombosis of a cerebral artery.

Mrs. Johnson was with her husband when he died. His son, Lieut. Col. Hiram W. Johnson, Jr., left San Francisco last night by plane, but failed to arrive before the Senator died.

His political activities extended over a third of a century, covering some of the most stirring events in the nation's history.

Elected To Congress In 1916

A striking figure in the Senate since he was first elected to Congress in 1916, he played a leading part in defeating President Wilson's League of Nations covenant and later in opposing United States's adherence to the World Court.

Senator McKellar (D., Tenn.), president of the Senate, today will appoint a committee to attend the funeral of the silver-haired veteran.

Fought Teen-Age Draft

One of his last great Senate fights was against passage of the teen-age draft bill. He told his colleagues, with tears in his eyes, that he opposed "calling children to fight our battles."

He had been expected to take a lead in opposition to the recently

[Continued On Page 2, Column 5]

Sinatra Saves Boy's Life

Hollywood, Aug. 6 (AP)—Frank Sinatra, belying his reputation for emaciation, highlighted the Hollywood happenings of the week by making a spectacular dive into the harbor at near-by San Pedro to save the life of a 3-year-old boy.

Frank's feat occurred when the boy, Duke Jones, fell 13 feet from a railing onto a yacht dock, then rolled unconscious into the water. The singer, who had spent the day as crewman for a sailing boat in a match race, rushed across the dock, leaped into the water and pulled the youngster to safety.

Army's 'Doctor Hoard' Probe Is Asked

Chicago, Aug. 6 (AP)—A 2-year-old organization of doctors, the Association of American Physicians and Surgeons, today sought an investigation into "rumors" that the armed services are retaining doctors above need in order to "force" them into "the socialized medicine program" and into the Veterans Administration and Public Health Services.

In a letter to President Truman, members of Congres, and military and naval officials, the association asserted that "immediate release should be given to as many doctors as is consistent with the successful execution of the war effort."

Rumors Are Cited

But, the letter asserted, "disquieting rumors persist that:

"Since V-E day there is a tremendous surplus of physicians in the armed forces.

"Medical officers will be kept in the services against their consent even after the war is terminated.

"Medical officers were being retained in the services and eventually will be forced into the Veterans Administration.

"Older medical officers will be . . . forcibly transferred to the Veterans Administration; young physicians will be released from their interneships to form a nucleus of doctors who would accept the political control of their practices and start the socialized medicine program proposed in the Wagner-Murray-Dingell bill. . . .

"By keeping more than 40,000 physicians in the military service and thus silencing this large group of opposition to regimented medicine, the ranks of the American medical profession will be so divided and weakened that schemes for controlling physicians and their patients can be made more easily operable.

Thorough Probe Asked

"Physicians are being kept in the services for the purpose of eventual transfer to the public health services, and then using them to staff large Government hospitals which have been built during the war.

"The above stories have been spoken and written with enough consistency and frequency to cause grave concern, and in the opinion of the Association of American Physicians and Surgeons warrant thorough and exhaustive investigation."

Dr. Andrew J. Sullivan, Chicago, president, and Dr. H. W. Detrick, Hammond, Ind., secretary, signed the missive. Officials of the association said the group was organized two years ago with 250 members.

Letter To Hitler From Petain Introduced

Paris, Aug. 6 (AP)—A letter which Marshal Pétain sent to Hitler three weeks after the Allied landings in Africa telling of conversations between the two about "reconquering" French colonies was introduced suddenly by the state today at the treason trial of the old soldier.

The letter, dated December 5, 1942, apparently surprised the defense. It contained this phrase:

"I am aware, Mr. Chancellor, of the personal intentions that you have expressed to me concerning your resolution to collaborate with France and to assist her in reconquering her colonial domain."

"Ghost Army"

The letter came after a number of French generals testified they were organizing a "ghost army" without German knowledge.

Once, while Gen. Charles Lafargue was testifying for Pétain, a violent discussion broke out in the courtroom and several jurors jumped in anger to their feet when Lafargue declared: "There are many undesirables among the Maquis."

Gen. Pico Andart testified that French troops were ordered by Gen. Maxine Weygand at the time of the armistice to hide all military equipment. They concealed 18,000,000,000 francs' worth of matériel from the Germans and an equal amount of food and raw materials by the end of 1942, he asserted.

Andart said underground factories, at the order of Pétain, started building machine-gun carriers as early as 1941 and produced 270 of them in one year. The General said Pétain congratulated him for his part in the activity and ordered him to continue his work.

"Pierre Laval knew of this but he did not appear to be interested," the witness said. Andart said the French hid and produced enough equipment for 24 divisions, except for heavy artillery and tanks. General Weygand, a previous witness, was French commander at the time of the armistice.

Praise From Frisco Delegate

Pierre Merillon, French delegate to the United Nations Conference at San Francisco, sent a cable to the trial from Santa Barbara, Cal., describing Pétain as a man who served France with "perfect patriotism and loyalty" and "with all his power and energy."

Merillon was a former member of the French Embassy in Madrid, where Pétain served.

The telegram was read as the third week of the trial opened, just before Gen. Henri Lacaille testified that Winston Churchill had told a Vichy representative to Great Britain:

"We have been momentarily separated. Let us try not to damage each other any further."

Envoy For De Gaulle

The representative was a Colonel Groussard, whom the defense described as a former member of the pro-Fascist Cagoulard and at presen representative of the de Gaulle Government in Switzerland. The general said Groussard was sent to London to inquire if Great Britain could assist the French with military aid in North Africa.

Lacaille did not say whether the British made commitments. Most of his testimony was concerned with the material weakness of the French Army in the years immediately preceding the war.

A heated argument developed when Prosecutor Andre Mornet asked Judge Paul Mongibeaux to

[Continued On Page 4, Column 4]

29 Nurses Of Hopkins Unit On Way Back From Pacific

By Robert B. Cochrane
[Sunpapers War Correspondent]

Tacloban, Leyte, Aug. 6 [*By Cable*]—Twenty-nine nurses of the 118th General Hospital (the Johns Hopkins Hospital unit) left recently for home and are now en route via steamer. All of them have been overseas at least two years. Eighteen of them were among the unit's members when it left Baltimore April 20, 1942.

Fifteen of the group trained at Johns Hopkins, one at Union Memorial and one at Church Home and Infirmary. Although only four are native Marylanders, all are Baltimoreans by adoption.

The lone native Baltimorean in the group is First Lieutenant Mary Brun, daughter of Edwin F. Brun, 5104 Midwood road, and the niece of Dr. B. Lucien Brun. Lieutenant Brun announced that she was engaged to Capt. Thomas Wann, of St. Paul, Minn., shortly before leaving for home.

Other Marylanders are Lieut. Vista Boyd, of Big Spring; Lieut. Anna West, of Forrest Hill, Harford

[Continued On Page 4, Column 2]

Weather Forecast

Considerable cloudiness and continued warm today, with showers in afternoon. Yesterday's temperatures: Highest, 85; lowest, 74; mean, 80............Page 17

THE SUN

FINAL

Registered United States Patent Office

Vol. 217—No. 77—F | PAID CIRCULATION JULY MORNING, 175,213 EVENING, 190,130 365,343 || SUNDAY 275,960 | BALTIMORE, WEDNESDAY, AUGUST 15, 1945 | Entered as second-class matter at Baltimore Post Office | Zone 3 | 18 Pages | 3 Cents

THE WAR IS OVER

BIG CUT IN DRAFT CALL; 2-DAY WORK HOLIDAY; MANPOWER CURBS END

Truman Foresees Release Of 5 Million GI's; Induction Of Men Over 25 Ordered Halted; Navy Cuts Nearly 6 Billion In Contracts

Truman forecasts release of 5,000,000 soldiers.
President sets today and tomorrow as holidays.
U. S. revokes all wartime manpower controls.
Navy cancels nearly $6,000,000,000 in contracts.
Congress will reconvene on September 5.

Washington, Aug. 14 (AP)—President Truman tonight forecast that 5,000,000 to 5,500,000 men now in the Army may be returned to civilian life within the next twelve to eighteen months.

Furthermore, he said in announcing Japan's surrender, only the lowest age groups will now be drafted into the Army. Preliminary estimates indicate only those under 26 will be called, Mr. Truman added.

Urges Cut In Inductions

His recommendation was that selective service reduce inductions immediately from 80,000 a month to 50,000.

Maj. Gen. Lewis B. Hershey, selective service director, following Mr. Truman's instuctions, tonight telegraphed all state directors ordering them to stop at once the induction of all registrants 26 years of age or older.

"It is too early to propose a definite figure for the occupation forces which will be required in the Pacific twelve months from now or what reduction it may be possible to make in the strength of the army force now allotted to occupation duties in Europe," the President said in a statement.

"It is apparent, however, that we can release as many men as can be brought home by the means available during the next year."

Army releases will be speeded by air and sea transportation in an effort to attain that 5,000,000 to 5,500,000 figure, he said.

Mr. Truman said that, in justice to millions of men who have given "long and faithful service under the difficult and hazardous conditions of the Pacific war and elsewhere overseas, a constant flow of replacements to the occupational forces is thought to be imperative."

He added that inductions of 50,000 a month in the lowest age groups "will provide only sufficient men to support the forces required for occupational duty and to permit the relief of long-service men overseas to the maximum extent transportation makes possible."

Present Problem Cited

The present problem, he said, centers on the readjustment of personnel now in uniform and induction of new men through selective service to "permit the earliest possible release from the Army of those men who have long records of dangerous, arduous and faithful service."

The President did not mention the Navy draft call, currently about 20,000 men a month.

General Hershey said he had no word of the Navy's plans, but that it would be "reasonable to expect a cut there, too."

Actually men through 37 previously were subject to the draft, but in practice the calls the last few months have been confined to men under 30.

Hershey said he regarded the President's instructions "as a flat prohibition" on drafting of men 26 and over.

President Proclaims Holidays

Washington, Aug. 14 (AP)—Tomorrow and Thursday are legal holidays and days off for Government workers, and holidays for pay purposes for workers in general.

And V-J day, when it comes, will be a premium pay day, too.

President Truman announced both rulings tonight.

He directed agency heads throughout the Government to cut their forces down to a bare skeleton staff August 15 and 16 and not to charge the two days against the employés' annual leave.

"Inadequate" Recognition

He said it was in "inadequate" recognition of the four-year efforts of "one of the hardest-working groups of war workers."

For other workers under wage control, Wednesday and Thursday count like Christmas and the few other accepted holidays for purposes of overtime pay and in figuring the number of days worked in a week. Many employers already have gotten approval for regular-time pay to workers who take the day off.

Postal service for the next two days will "approximate holiday service," the Post Office Department said.

V-J Day Holiday Expected

Local postmasters will have wide discretion in carrying out the President's wishes, it was indicated, and those postal employés required to work tomorrow and the next day will have compensating time off at a later date.

It was presumed, but not specifically stated, that government workers generally will be off on V-J day, too.

The White House said the next two days are to be regarded as legal holidays.

Navy Drops 6 Billions In Orders

Washington, Aug. 14 (AP)—The Navy announced tonight it is canceling nearly $6,000,000,000 in prime contracts.

This is in addition to a recently announced $1,200,000,000 cut in the shipbuilding program.

The cancellations were ordered the Navy said, to bring production into line with requirements of the postwar navy and to free men, materials and productive capacity for manufacture of civilian goods.

Some Orders To Remain

Many types of procurement will be reduced in percentage, the Navy said, with some orders remaining on the books.

Large numbers of aircraft scheduled for production will be cut back, together with engines and propellers. However, as long as the fleet is kept at its present size, a certain number of replacement planes must be procured.

Since it is no longer necessary to maintain munitions stocks at war levels, cuts were ordered in procurement of ordnance materials—particularly projectiles, explosives, bombs, mines and torpedoes.

Other Ordnance To Be Cut

Other ordnance also will be cut, but production will be maintained on items required for vessels under construction or repair, and for research and experimental work.

Large shipbuilding cutbacks have already been announced, but other reductions are being made in components for ships, propulsion machinery and spare parts.

Preparation has been under way for several months for termination of navy contracts with the war's end.

Manpower Controls Revoked

Washington, Aug. 14 (AP)—The Government today revoked all wartime manpower controls, effective immediately, and set forth a plan aimed at speedy re-employment of veterans and released war workers.

In an action timed to coincide with Japan's surrender, the War Manpower Commission announced a seven-point program which it said would stimulate "reconversion activities and the speedy re-employment of displaced workers, at the same time restoring a free labor market."

48-Hour Week Out

Among the controls lifted are those providing for hiring through the United States Employment Service, employment ceilings to channel workers to essential industries and the requirement for certificates of availability in changing jobs.

Eliminated also was the mandatory feature of the 48-hour week in areas or industry where it is in effect, an official said. However, the Little Steel formula for general wage stabilization is not affected by the action of the WMC, which has no jurisdiction over it.

Specific Provisions

Frank L. McNamee, acting WMC chairman, said regional directors have been instructed to put the new program into effect at once in

(Continued on Page 7, Column 2)

PEACE COMES TO BALTIMORE—Sun Square after proclamation of Japan's surrender.—Photo by LeRoy B. Merriken.

JAPS ACCEPT ALL TERMS, FIRING TO END AT ONCE, PRESIDENT ANNOUNCES

General MacArthur Is Named To Receive Surrender Of Enemy, Who Is Ordered To Comply With Any Requests He May Make

Guam, Wednesday, July 15 (AP)—Japanese aircraft are approaching the Pacific Fleet off Tokyo and are being shot down, Admiral Nimitz announced today. Five enemy planes have been destroyed since noon.

New York, Wednesday, Aug. 15 — Gen. Douglas MacArthur, in his first communication to Japan, has just ordered the Japanese Government and imperial general staff to put a radio station at his continuous disposal for communication of his orders to Japan, NBC's Merrill Mueller, radioed from MacArthur's headquarters in Manila today.

By DEWEY L. FLEMING

Washington, Aug. 14—The war with Japan ended tonight.

Japanese acceptance of Allied surrender terms, and orders for suspension of hostilities, were announced by President Truman at 7 P.M.

The news was announced in other Allied capitals at the same hour.

Gen. Douglas MacArthur, commander of United States Army forces in the Pacific, has been named supreme Allied commander to receive the formal Japanese surrender—at the earliest possible moment.

To Sign Surrender On Battleship

It is expected that the signing of the surrender instrument will take place aboard an American battleship.

The official proclamation of V-J day will await the formal signing of the surrender terms by Japan.

Although this proclamation may not come for several days, the President immediately granted a two-day holiday—tomorrow and Thursday—to all Federal employes in Washington and throughout the country.

This normally sedate capital went wild at the authentic news of the Japanese surrender. The downtown section was packed in anticipation of the announcement and the ensuing uproar was indescribable.

Truman Is Calm As He Calls Reporters

Perhaps the calmest person in the city, or so it seemed, was President Truman as he called reporters into his office at 7 P.M. and announced the news for which the world had been waiting.

Seated at his desk and showing no more excitement than if he were about to announce the appointment of a new postmaster at a Missouri village, he read a brief introductory statement before handing out the text of the Japanese reply to the Allied surrender ultimatum.

"I have received this afternoon a message from the Japanese Government," he began, "in reply to the message forwarded to that Government by the Secretary of State on August 11.

"I deem this reply a full acceptance of the Potsdam declaration which specifies the unconditional surrender of Japan. In the reply there is no qualification.

Arrangements Under Way For Signing

"Arrangements are now being made for the formal signing of surrender terms at the earliest possible moment.

"Gen. Douglas MacArthur has been appointed the supreme Allied commander to receive the Japanese surrender. Great Britain, Russia and China will be represented by high-ranking officers.

"Meantime, the Allied armed forces have been ordered to suspend offensive action.

"The proclamation of V-J day must wait upon the formal signing of the surrender terms by Japan."

Hull Arrives Late, Congratulates Truman

At that point the President began reading the text of the Japanese reply, as transmitted through the neutral Swiss Government. He said reporters need not try to take down the words in their notes as copies had been prepared for immediate distribution.

The text of the Japanese reply follows: "With reference to the Japanese Government's note of August 10 regarding their acceptance of the provisions of the Potsdam declaration and the reply of the governments of the United States, Great Britain, the Soviet Union and China sent by American Secretary of State Byrnes under the date of August 11, the Japanese Government have the honor to communicate to the governments of the four powers as follows:

"1. His Majesty the Emperor has issued an imperial rescript regarding Japan's acceptance of the provisions of the Potsdam declaration.

"2. His Majesty the Emperor is prepared to authorize and insure the signature by his Government and the imperial general headquarters of necessary terms for carrying out the provisions of the Potsdam declaration. His Majesty is also prepared to issue his commands to all the military, naval and air authorities of Japan and all the forces under their control wherever located to cease active

(Continued on Page 2, Column 1)

TORPEDO SINKS INDIANAPOLIS

883 Of Cruiser's Crew Lost; 315 Rescued After 5 Days

Peleliu, Palau Islands, Aug. 5 [*AP—Delayed*]—The 10,000-ton cruiser Indianapolis was sunk in less than fifteen minutes, presumably by a Japanese submarine, twelve minutes past midnight July 30—and 883 crew members lost their lives in one of the Navy's worst disasters.

She went down in the Philippine Sea, within 450 miles of Leyte, while on an unescorted high-speed run from San Francisco.

She had completed the trip to Guam and was bound for the Philippines.

Without A Second's Warning

There were 315 survivors.

[The Navy in Washington, first to announce the tragedy, said there were "100 per cent casualties" and listed 5 Navy dead, including one officer; 845 Navy missing, including 63 officers; 307 Navy wounded, including 15 officers; 30 Marine Corps missing, including 2 officers, and 9 enlisted Marine Corps wounded.]

The fatal torpedo attack came without a second's warning. Two explosions flashed out of her bow. She quivered while flames streaked down passageways all through her hull.

In less than fifteen minutes the Indianapolis was gone; 10,000 tons of "proud and happy" ship plunged headfirst into the sea.

315 Survive 5 Days In Sea

Nobody outside the oil-covered circle of men and debris in the water knew her fate until after a Peleliu search plane led the way to the rescue of the 315 men who survived five days in the sea.

Nearly 700 men went down with the ship. Hundreds more jumped off the cruiser's rearing side in time—but many were without life preservers or rafts, without clothing, without hope of remaining afloat for long.

Survivors believe two underwater torpedoes smashed into the starboard side near the bow of the 14-year-old cruiser, setting off one of the 8-inch gun magazines.

Radio Efforts Futile

Gun crews manned their stations and stayed there while the ship pitched over violently. Radiomen tried desperately to get out a message to all ships' stations—"Hit. Position longitude — latitude —. Need immediate assistance." But it was no use; the ship's power was dead and radio keys clicked futilely the words that might have saved hundreds of lives.

When the skipper, Capt. Charles Butler McVay 3d, of Washington, D.C., saw the badly listing ship was going fast, he had the "abandon ship" order passed by word of mouth through the darkened, fire-scaled compartments of the 610-foot ship.

What happened in the last 15 minutes aboard the Indianapolis was a living nightmare of flames, explosions, of men screaming, of others making near-miraculous escapes, of watching the one-time 5th Fleet flagship of Admiral Raymond A. Spruance founder helplessly, and disappear.

Spruance was not aboard when she was hit.

For the nearly 500 men who

(Continued on Page 3, Column 2)

Flood Of Joy Sweeps Through Allied World

Baltimore cuts loose with bang as 200,000 fill downtown streets to celebrate............Page 18

New York, Aug. 14 (AP)—A couple of false starts didn't dim New York's enthusiasm for celebrating victory tonight.

There were almost 500,000 persons—police figures—in Times Square when the announcement came. The noise then, with no particular provocation except the day's mounting tension, was so great that the blare of the news from a radio sound truck almost was drowned out. But the flashing lights of the bulletin board on the *Times* Annex Building told the story.

The tremendous roar that went up then made the previous clamor sound like the squeal of an ungreased axle. New York let loose with all the shenanigans for which it had trained since the first intimation last Friday that Japan was willing to talk peace.

Paper Salvage Drive Flouted

As in all celebrations in New York, paper cascaded from windows all over town. It came in streamers, in pieces, in packets, in rolls. It came in Chinatown, and in Harlem, in Little Italy and Hell's Kitchen, from Broadway to the Battery, in a midsummer snowstorm that covered the streets in an unmelting blanket which said nuts to the paper salvage drive.

The entire police department—14,000 men—was mobilized, as was the fire department. Mayor LaGuardia was out in his radio patrol car when the news broke and even he promised himself "a couple of hours of relaxation and celebration." Then he hurried to a radio, proclaimed tomorrow and Thursday as victory holidays, and named Sunday as "world peace day" for giving thanks to God "for the complete victory."

On the East Side, in Little Italy, a barrage of firecrackers was loosed. On upper Broadway windows sprouted flags. Harbor boats set up a great din.

10 Cents For A Paper

On Forty-second street newsboys were getting 10 cents apiece for papers, the buyers seeking only tearing-up privileges. Chinatown brought out its sacred dragon, usually seen only in the Chinese New Year, and paraded with clashing cymbals, beating of drums, and popping firecrackers.

One thousand WAVES poured onto Broadway from their barracks at 76th street for a mass celebration. At 43d street, a sailor "shinnied" up a light pole. At Times Square, a Marine and a Brooklyn boy succeeded in raising a flag on the monument replica of the Iwo Jima picture. It was against regulations to raise a flag after sundown but officers told the two to go ahead.

Traffic was snarled. Motorists paid no attention to police and police paid no attention to motorists. Bars were busy but it was on the basis of in-for-a-quick-one-and-out-again. Some restaurants saw their customers gulp the last gulp of their coffee and race out the door without paying their checks.

Fire Hydrants Go On

On the East Side, celebrators devised a special trick of turning on fire hydrants. The same section saw a succession of bonfires in the streets. All the wounded men who could walk streamed out of the United States Veterans Hospital in The Bronx and stood at the gates in pajamas and bathrobes to cheer at civilians who cheered at them.

One temporary blank spot in the hubbub was the theaters. Managers did not announce the news of the surrender, fearing a stampede that might cause injuries.

Amid all the exuberance, though, there were many who turned their first thoughts to giving thanks to God. More than 2,500 attended a special victory mass at St. Patrick's Cathedral, just one hour after the Truman announcement. Other churches, too, held services but most of these were held off until Wednesday. The Fifth Avenue Presbyterian Church, for instance, announced hourly services from 11 A.M. through 5 P.M.

Building Up All Day

New York had been building up for the explosion all day. At noon, police figured there were 150,000 persons in Times Square, most of them just milling around. Three hours before the news came, the city collection department said 2,560 tons of paper had been frittered onto the streets. Twenty-five persons were in hospitals because of celebration accidents.

But all that was only the burning of the fuse to the explosive.

Peace! Shoot Only In A Friendly Way

San Francisco, Aug. 14 (AP)—"It looks like the war is over," Admiral Halsey said. "Cease firing, but if you see any enemy planes in the air, shoot them down in friendly fashion."

The hundreds of navy pilots, but a few seconds from their targets in the Tokyo area, heard and obeyed.

Honolulu Celebrating Ever Since Friday

Honolulu, Aug. 14 (AP)—The same air-raid sirens which signaled the Japanese attack on Pearl Harbor, starting the war, sounded the end

(Continued on Page 4, Column 5)

On Other Pages

Rodney Crowther says King's speech at opening of Parliament today will set forth Labor's program................Page 6

Philip Potter cables that Chinese puppet troops may decide allegiance of country's liberated areas....................Page 3

Thousands roar welcome at appearance of Truman...Page 2

American air forces stage around-clock raids.............Page 3

Chinese troops cut Jap link with Kwangsi province.......Page 3

Navy describes principle of radar, "silent weapon" credited with changing character of the war ....Page 7

Baltimore lets loose with a bang as President announces the Japanese surrender........Page 18

HIROHITO TELLS FOE OF DEFEAT

Says 'Most Cruel Bomb' Could Destroy Civilization

New York, Wednesday Aug. 15 (AP)—The Japanese Cabinet issued today a "proclamation to the nation" calling on the Japanese people to obey Emperor Hirohito's imperial rescript announcing Japan's surrender to the Allied powers and pledging itself to do likewise, the Japanese Domei agency reported.

San Francisco, Aug. 14 (AP)—A Domei dispatch broadcast by the Tokyo Radio said tonight that Emperor Hirohito had told the Japanese people by radio that "the enemy had begun to employ a new and most cruel bomb" and should Japan continue to fight "it would lead to the total extinction of human civilization."

"The enemy has begun to employ a new and most cruel bomb, the power of which to do damage is indeed incalculable, taking the toll of many innocent lives," the Emperor was quoted as saying.

"Should we continue to fight, it would not only result in an ultimate collapse and the obliteration of the Japanese nation, but also it would lead to the total extinction of human civilization.

"Such being the case, how are we to save the millions of our subjects; or to atone ourselves before the hallowed spirits of our imperial ancestors? This is the reason we have ordered the acceptance of the joint declaration of the powers."

The Text Of The Rescript

The text of the rescript follows:

"To our good and loyal subjects:

"Pondering deeply the general trends of the world and the actual conditions of . . . (indistinct word) in our empire today, we have decided to effect a settlement of the present situation by resorting to an extraordinary measure.

We have ordered our Govern-

(Continued on Page 2, Column 4)

BULLETINS

London, Aug. 14 (AP)—King George VI will make a victory broadcast tomorrow (Wednesday) night at 9 P.M. (4 P.M. E.W.T.), following a thanksgiving service on the BBC at 8.15 P.M. (3.15 P.M. E.W.T.).

Manila, Wednesday, Aug. 15 (AP)—"I thank a merciful God that this mighty struggle is about to end," Gen. Douglas MacArthur commented this morning after receiving official notification of the Japanese capitulation and of his appointment as supreme Allied commander of occupation forces.

"I shall at once take steps to stop hostilities and further bloodshed.

New York, Wednesday, Aug. 15 (AP)—Japanese War Minister Korechika Anami has committed suicide, the Japanese Domei agency reported today. The English-language wireless broadcast was recorded by the Federal Communications Commission.

Weather Forecast
Sunny and warm, with highest temperature around 80 degrees today; clear tonight. Yesterday's temperatures: Highest, 79; lowest, 63; mean, 71....Page 31

THE SUN

FINAL

Registered United States Patent Office

Vol. 221—No. 134—F | MORNING. 172,962 EVENING. 188,273 | PAID CIRCULATION SEPTEMBER 361,235 || SUNDAY 300,501 | BALTIMORE, TUESDAY, OCTOBER 21, 1947 | Entered as second-class matter at Baltimore Post Office | Zone 3 | 32 Pages | 5 Cents

Writers Called Worst Hollywood Communists

STRIKE ENDS IN PARIS AS RPF LEADS

Union Action Follows Close On Heels Of Victory By De Gaullists

Paris, Oct. 20 (AP)—The week-old strike in Paris's transit system, led by the Communist-bossed General Confederation of Labor, appeared ended tonight on the heels of the emergence of Gen. Charles de Gaulle's new anti-Communist party, Rally of the French People (RPF), as the strongest political force in France.

Service on the capital's subway system and business, a spokesman said, is to be resumed early tomorrow. At the same time, the threat of a general strike in the Paris area faded when the Paris Federation of Labor unions adjourned a meeting without voting on a walkout.

Confer With Strikers

Representatives of Socialist Premier Paul Ramadier's Cabinet conferred all day today with strikers' delegates, despite the announcement last week that the Government never would negotiate while the strike continued.

The Government had denounced the strike as politically motivated and observers had seen it as a struggle between the non-Communist coalition Cabinet and Communist-led labor.

Both the Cabinet and Communist positions were weakened today by the apparent sweeping victory scored by de Gaule's followers in Sunday's municipal elections.

Began October 11

The transport strike began October 11, when a small independent union of subway motormen, opposed by the National Confederation, struck for recognition and shorter hours.

Subway service was slowed then, but the General Confederation did not issue a strike call to its 30 000 transport workers until Monday, October 13, and all busses and subways in Paris stopped the next day.

Emergency service, hurriedly organized by the Government with trucks and busses, gave some relief and today carried about a million passengers in 1,200 vehicles.

Generators Sabotaged

Nine of the twelve big generators supplying subway power were sabotaged, emergency bus drivers were threatened and at least two busloads of passengers were "kidnapped" by strikers.

No one could say with certainty whether the success of de Gaulle's RPF in Paris was the result of the strike. However, it was noted that the RPF triumph marked the first time in this century that Paris has given a single party a clear majority.

Long before returns were complete, a delegation of the strike committee was talking with a spokesman of the Ministry of Public Works.

While the Paris federation union delegates met to consider a general walkout in sympathy with the transport workers, an agreement was reached at the Ministry and the strikers won most of their demands.

Pay Raises Granted

Annual raises of $82 to $208 were granted, the Government promised there would be no punishment of strikers and transit management is to find a means through overtime to permit the employes to make up pay they lost while striking.

There were indications and predictions that de Gaulle's big vote in the municipal elections would be reflected in the composition of the non-Communist Government headed by Ramadier.

De Gaulle remained silent, but a long-time follower, Andre Malraux, noted author and former Cabinet minister, declared that the General would take power only after a referendum demonstrating his support and in no case would he try to seize authority by force.

Less than twenty per cent of the

(Continued on Page 7, Column 4)

On Other Pages

Hurricane lashes Bermuda, causing heavy damage, but no loss of life..........Page 3

Harriman assails Russ anti-U.S. campaign, begun, he says, shortly after VJ-Day..........Page 7

Strike affecting 125,000 workers called on Canadian railroads for November 3..........Page 12

Europe declared to need more than U.S. "tonics"....Page 13

Baltimore gains tonnage at New York's expense, Commerce Association reports........Page 32

Billboard regulation measure passed by City Council after bitter debate..........Page 32

$240,000,000 In Silver And Gold Sold By Britain

Former Bought By International Fund, Latter By U.S., But All Exchanged For Dollars

London Bureau of *The Sun* reports that the British Home Fleet will be drastically cut as an economy move..........*Page* 14

King George tells Parliament Britain is grateful for the United States' initiative in setting up the Marshall plan......*Page* 14

By GERALD GRIFFIN
[*London Bureau of The Sun*]

London, Oct. 20—Two financial announcements of the sort called "danger signals" by Hugh Dalton, Chancellor of the Exchequer, were made tonight by the British Treasury.

The Treasury disclosed that it purchased today an additional $120,000,000 from the International Monetary Fund. It drew $60,000,000 from the same source in September.

Also, confirming earlier unofficial reports, it announced that during the past month it has sold in New York $120,000,000 worth of gold taken from reserves of the sterling area.

Gold Sold In September

On September 15 $80,000,000 in gold was sold in New York. Tonight's announcement raised to $200,000,000 the amount of gold taken from so-called final reserves, leaving a balance estimated at somewhat over $2,000,000,000.

The $240,000,000 raised by sale of gold and purchase of dollars from the Monetary Fund, announced tonight, will be used for purchase of food and materials which Britain must make in the dollar area.

Transaction's Charge

Dalton has referred to such transactions as "danger signals" because in each instance the source of dollars available to Britain is limited, and each step of this kind brings this country that much closer to the end of its dollar resources.

In its transactions with the International Monetary Fund, the British Treasury gives sterling to the fund in exchange for dollars. It has now purchased $180,000,000 of a total of $217,000,000 which it can obtain from the fund by paying a transaction's charge of three fourths of one per cent.

Gold Sale Limited

If it went beyond $217,000,000 (which represents largely Britain's initial gold subscription to the fund), the Treasury would begin to pay interest on this additional sum.

Similarly, there is a limit on the amount of gold the Treasury can sell, although it has arranged a gold loan of $320,000,000 from the Union of South Africa during the period

(Continued on Page 14, Column 5)

Italians Appeal For More U.S. Aid

Washington, Oct. 20 (AP)—Alberto Tarchiani, Italian Ambassador, today presented the United States another urgent appeal for financial help to buy American food and fuel.

He said later that Italy "has no more dollars and no raw materials of any kind."

Tarchiani conferred 40 minutes with Robert Lovett, Under Secretary of State. He said Lovett told him this Government is studying the situation intensively and that he hoped for a possible answer within a few days.

Government officials said the United States will turn over $10,000,000 to the Italian Government shortly. It is the last of funds owed by the War Department for services and supplies to American troops in Italy.

Pietro Campilli, Italy's chief delegate on the Marshall plan discussion, said Italy's problem now has grown so urgent that "it is not a question of how we go on to the end of the year, but how we go on to the end of the week." Campilli accompanied Tarchiani.

RUSSIA HOLDS BACK DECISION ON BALKANS

Bloc's Speeches Put Off Assembly Vote On American Proposal

Russia tries to depict Mrs. Roosevelt as defending white slave traffic..........*Page* 5

By PAUL W. WARD
[*Sun Staff Correspondent*]

New York, Oct. 20—Making a last-ditch fight to keep the United Nations from abetting the United States' efforts to prevent sovietization of strategically located Greece, the world organization's Slav bloc forced its General Assembly into a fruitless overtime session here tonight.

All that the striving—led by the Kremlin's Andrei Y. Vishinsky—accomplished was to put off until tomorrow settlement of the question: Will the required two thirds of the world organization's 57 members indorse the American plan for ridding Greece of the guerrilla warfare that is preventing her restoration to economic and political stability?

Calls For Watchdog Unit

The American plan involves a formal demand on the Assembly's part that Yugoslavia, Albania and Bulgaria—Greece's northern neighbors—cease aiding the guerrillas.

It also involves creation of an international commission to watch and report on the extent to which the three Soviet satellites comply with that request and they—plus Greece — fulfill recommendations by the world organization for peaceful settlement of their differences.

The plan was indorsed nine days ago by 63 per cent of the members of the Assembly's Political Committee "present and voting" and—to be given full effect—now needs to get the ratifying votes of 66 per cent of the Assembly itself.

Repeats Arguments

To stave off, if possible, that result, Mr. Vishinsky began here late today an hour and a half speech that repeated all the arguments that he and other Soviet bloc spokesmen had adduced in the Political Committee against the American plan.

Meanwhile, the United States' Herschel V. Johnson was telling his countrymen in a nation-wide broadcast that the issue was "crucial for the people of Greece and crucial for the future peace of the world."

Recalling that the Soviet Government had used its power of unilateral veto to "frustrate" efforts of nine of the United Nations Security Council members to "solve this question," Mr. Johnson added:

"Therefore, the United States has submitted the question of threats to Greece to the General Assembly, the forum of all the people of the world, in which no veto can stop action."

U.S. Ready To Co-Operate

The resolution embodying the American plan, which is before the Assembly and awaiting a vote, he said, provides that, if the "aggressive acts" by Greece's northern neighbors continue, the investigating commission may call "a special session of the General Assembly to consider the matter."

"The United States delegation," he added, "has told the United Nations that should this become necessary, the United States would be prepared to co-operate with other members in putting into effect whatever measures are recommended by the General Assembly for the protection of Greece."

ENGLISH-SPEAKING POLES ROUNDED UP

Ministry Asserts Arrests Are To Destroy Underground

Warsaw, Oct. 20 (AP)—A Polish Foreign Ministry spokesman said today his Government intends to continue the drive to exterminate its underground opposition as security police increased arrests of English-speaking Poles who have shown friendship with Americans and Britishers.

Among the latest arrested were three editors of the Western Press Agency, a nonprofit co-operative journalists' organization specializing in the dissemination of news from Poland's western territories.

Earlier, two employes of the British and American embassies were seized.

Embassies Make Protests

The American Embassy made representations to the Foreign Ministry against the arrest and five-hour detention of Mrs. Wanda Sroka, an American citizen and embassy clerk. The British Embassy acted similarly in connection with the arrest and imprisonment of Charles Whitehead, a native Pole and commercial aide at the embassy.

[Dispatches from London said that Britain had warned Poland the British may break off discussions of Polish compensation for British property nationalized unless Whitehead is released. He represented Britain in the talks. The protest charged that his arrest Friday was "yet another example of Poland's desire to cut off contact between her people and the people of western Europe," a British Foreign Office spokesman said.]

Linked To Underground

The Polish Foreign Ministry spokesman told a news conference that no one had been arrested merely for association with the British and Americans but because of suspected connection with the underground or for other charges.

The increased activity of the security police appears to be centered on Poles particularly friendly with the British and Americans.

Ike's Elephant Emblem Is Danish—Not GOP

Washington, Oct. 20 (AP)—Gen. Dwight D. Eisenhower hooked up with an elephant tonight—but it had nothing to do with the Republican party.

It came in the form of Denmark's highest decoration—the order of Knight of the Elephant—awarded to the United States Chief of Staff at a Danish Embassy dinner.

Embassy officials said the diamond-encrusted medal, one of the oldest decorations in the world, is usually awarded only to princes of royal blood. They said the knighthood title of "Sir" does not go with it, however, and so it will not conflict with regulations barring Americans from accepting foreign titles.

ARMY KEEPS RULE IN OCCUPIED AREAS

State Department Drops Plans For Taking Control

By WILLIAM KNIGHTON, JR.
[*Washington Bureau of The Sun*]

Washington, Oct. 20—The State Department announced tonight it had dropped its plans, for the time being at least, of taking over administration of occupied areas from the Army.

Earlier, the department made it known that the United States had formally turned down Russia's proposal for the withdrawal of American and Russian troops from Korea at the beginning of next year.

The announcement concerning the occupied areas—Germany, Austria, Japan and Korea—was made by Michael J. McDermott, special assistant to the Secretary of State.

Administrative Matter

He added that the decision was made by Gen. George C. Marshall, Secretary of State, and was not influenced in any way by the "present world situation," but rather on "administrative matters," such as the necessary obtaining of a large number of employes by the department to carry on the duties

(Continued on Page 4, Column 4)

Wallace Is Visitor At Shrines Of Three Faiths In Jerusalem

By PHILIP POTTER
[*Sun Staff Correspondent*]

Jerusalem, Oct. 20—Henry Wallace, like any tourist, spent his first full day in Palestine visiting the shrines of the three faiths which have made this the Holy City—Moslem mosques, Jewish temples and Christian churches.

That there are political implications in his visit to Palestine, however, was indicated when he spent two hours over luncheon with David Ben-Gurion, chairman of the Jewish Agency, which speaks for the country's 675,000 Jews.

Ben-Gurion told the former Vice President of the plans of world Jewry to settle another 1,000,000 Jews in the promised land once the country has been partitioned into Arab and Jewish states.

Believes Capacity Unlimited

Ben-Gurion holds that Palestine's absorbtive capacity is unlimited if enough capital is invested to develop the hydro-electric and irrigation potentialities of the Jordan River.

Wallace, on his arrival here last night, said he had come as a newspaper man to study the situation for the *New Republic*, of which he is editor, and was particularly interested in what has been accomplished in agriculture. He would make no comment on Ben-Gurion's views, but he asked several questions during his tour around Jerusalem's holy spots regarding the country's crop yields.

At the Catholic Church of Saint Catherine in Bethlehem, adjoining another church which encloses the manger where Christ lay in swaddling clothes, he looked across at the field of Boaz, which in Biblical parable had yields of as much as a hundredfold.

Close To Average Yield Now

"What does it yield today? he asked Revero Camillus Liska, of Terra Santa convent, a native of Houston, Texas, who has been in Palestine since 1926 and wants nothing more than to return to the Franciscan monastery in Washington, D.C., where he served for many years.

He was told it was not far above the average yield in Palestine today, about five bushels to an acre. Wallace noted that was only one third of the average yield in the United States.

Later, in conversation with Joseph Yuja, of the Catholic faith, who was born in El Salvador and returned here a few years ago because of the ill-health of his 95-year-old grandfather, Wallace ex-

(Continued on Page 6, Column 3)

'Angel' Echoes Being Picked Up By Army Radar

Washington, Oct. 20 (AP)—"Angels" are being picked up by radar, members of the International Scientific Radio Union were told today.

"Angels" are unidentified echoes from the atmosphere which have been observed to a maximum range of about 3,000 yards above the earth's surface, said a report prepared by William B. Gould, Herbert B. Brooks and Raymond Wexler of the Army's signal laboratory at Belmar, N.J.

That's the same laboratory that bounced radar signals off the moon some time ago—but this "angel" business has nothing to do with the moon project.

Radarman Gould, who presented the report, said the mysterious echoes were different from those which are obtained when radar signals are returned by dust particles in the atmosphere or by the influence of certain turbulence in the atmosphere.

Studies still are under way to determine the cause of the unidentified echoes.

BANKERS TOLD TO CURB CREDIT

Federal Reserve Member Cites Rising Tide Of New Money

Liberalization of credit buying in Baltimore indicated after removal of Federal controls on November 1..........*Page* 32

By RODNEY CROWTHER
[*Washington Bureau of The Sun*]

Washington, Oct. 20—A member of the Federal Reserve Board tonight warned American bankers that a heavy responsibility rests upon them to "help restrain further monetary expansion based on private debt creation."

M. S. Szymczak, of the Federal Reserve Board, in an address before the fall meeting of the District of Columbia Bankers Association, stated that there no longer exists any effective controls on money inflation and that the Federal Reserve system is so "handicapped by its present responsibilities and by the limited scope of its authority" that it cannot stem the rising tide of new money.

"The total money supply," Szymczak told the District of Columbia bankers, "is currently increasing at approximately $9,000,000,000 a year.

Private Demands Still Rising

"This increase in the money supply is directly inflationary and is seriously accelerating the upward spiral in prices."

The problem now facing the country, he said, is not the money which came into being in an inflationary process during the war, but the new money and credit which is coming into being through an influx of gold from abroad in payments for exports. So far this year the gold stock has increased $1,800,000,000, "providing the banks with the reserves necessary to support additional deposit expansion."

Heavy private demands for credit from business, property owners, consumers and state and local governments sent bank loans up $5,000,000,000 in nine months—almost as much as the entire 1946 expansion, and they are still rising, Szymczak pointed out.

Self-Restraint Urged

But there is not much the Federal Reserve system can do at the moment to hold back the flood, although "the system will do all it can, directly and indirectly, to restrain further credit expansion," he declared.

The system did bring some counterpressure by selling some Government securities, he said, but it can do little because of "a fundamental change in the financial situation."

"This fundamental change is the ability of the banking system to continue credit expansion that the Federal Reserve system is not in a position to offset because of its responsibility for maintaining orderly and stable prices of Government securities," the Reserve Board member pointed out.

Because of this handicap on the Reserve system, Szymczak added, "a heavy responsibility devolves upon individual banks to submit to self-restraint."

Credit Expansion Risks

"Under present conditions, banks are incurring large risks in private credit expansion and they should be constantly aware of those risks.

"Banks that conserve their credit resources and stubbornly maintain a high degree of liquidity will have less to regret and fewer losses to write off than institutions that ride the crest of the inflationary wave.

"This is particularly true," Szymczak warned, "for banks specializing in real estate and consumer credit, but it is also true for banks engaging in extensive business and agricultural lending."

The speaker told the bankers that "greater alertness" on their part regarding the inflationary effects of their individual credit advances can do much to restrain the current rate of bank credit and monetary expansion. It also can do much to fortify the banks, he added, against the inevitable day when inflation ends.

POULTRYLESS DAY QUESTION IS STILL IN AIR

Luckman And Industry's Representatives Meet Again Today

By JOSEPH H. SHORT
[*Washington Bureau of The Sun*]

Washington, Oct. 20—The question of whether poultryless Thursday would be dropped from the food-for-Europe program was still up in the air tonight.

Charles Luckman, chairman of the Citizens Food Committee, rejected a poultry industry program which included ending the campaign to induce the public to eat less chicken and turkey.

However, the industry promised to bring back a new program tomorrow.

Thinks Plan Is Acceptable

"We think it will be acceptable," said a spokesman for the National Poultry Producers Federation. He said it would be in Luckman's hands by 9 A.M.

At the same time, Luckman offered to meet the poultrymen again tomorrow afternoon and that offer was accepted. The food committee chairman stated that he did not "regard the issue as closed," adding that "it will be constantly reviewed and reconsidered when the industry's representatives bring back a set of more specific proposals."

The main premise of the National Poultry Producers Federation was that poultryless Thursday was keeping chickens alive to consume grain so desperately needed for Europe.

Luckman Not Convinced

Luckman countered that he was not convinced the poultrymen's plan would save more grain for export than the Government's poultryless Thursday program now in effect. He and his agricultural advisers were holding to the theory that if poultry consumption were increased, it would cause producers to enlarge their flocks.

After arguments had passed back and forth for five hours, Don M. Turnbull, executive secretary of the International Baby Chicks Association, made this statement for the poultrymen's group:

"The industry cannot reconcile itself to believe that poultryless Thursday has any value in conserving grain being eaten by mature poultry on farms."

Pledges Called For

The industry plan called for slaughter within 90 days of 340,000,000 fowls, including all old and unproductive hens and pullets and all roasters, fryers, and roosters.

The program, which also called for indefinite pledges of grain conservation by the poultry producers and feed manufacturers, would save up to 4,250,000 bushels a week, they claimed.

After the industry group became certain that the Government would not accept their plan as presented today, it was suggested informally that the breeders and hatchery men might pledge a 25 per cent reduction in use of all grain. This may be incorporated in the new offer expected from the industry tomorrow.

The poultrymen, in presenting their case this evening contended that many chickens were being kept on the farm (and thus required continued feeding) because of what the producers considered low prices.

Wheat Highest Since 1917

Chicago, Oct. 20 (AP)—The cost of living inched upward today as wheat futures for December delivery sold at a 30-year high of $3.07 a bushel on the Chicago Board of Trade and the Associated Press price index of commodities broke previous all-time records for the fifth consecutive day.

December wheat advanced 6¾

(Continued on Page 2, Column 5)

PRODUCERS MAKE CHARGE IN TESTIMONY IN FIRST ACT OF FILMDOM PROBE

AP Wirephoto
JACK L. WARNER

FILM INQUIRY LACKS DRAMA

Audience Is Disappointed As Movie Stars Fail To Appear

By N. T. KENNEY
[*Washington Bureau of The Sun*]

Washington, Oct. 20—The stage was all set, the lights went up, the audience settled back in its seats and the actors strode tensely to the microphone. Right there, as far as drama went, the first day of the highly touted communism-in-Hollywood investigation by the House Committee on Un-American Activities could just as well have ended.

Instead of such glamorous figures as Clark Gable and Lana Turner, the committee gave top billing to the more prosaic Louis B. Mayer and Jack Warner.

"Willing" Witnesses

Obviously, these gentlemen were in that group that the committee had warned would be "willing" witnesses. In prepared statements and extemporaneously, they swore they hated communism, loved the American way of life and wouldn't for an instant permit any Russian propaganda in any movies they made.

Mr. Mayer even went so far as to assure the committee he would fire three of his best writers, to whom it was revealed his company had paid fabulous sums of money for their efforts over a period of years, should it be revealed to him they held cards in the Communist party.

Some Suspect For A Time

Just why the committee brought up that subject was pretty obvious. Members already have disclosed, unofficially, that they have Communist party cards issued to some ten Hollywood figures, including writers, so the audience waited hopefully—and in vain—for some cards to be produced, and some high-priced heads to roll.

The audience itself, by the way, probably was a disappointment to itself. Its members almost twisted their necks off, when they first filed in, trying to spot some of the faces they can see on the silver screen of an evening for 80 cents, including tax, but there were no such faces.

A few people in smoked glasses and one tall youngish man with a square jaw and wavy hair were suspects for a while. Then it developed that the wearers of the glasses had donned them only as a far-sighted protection against the bat-

(Continued on Page 2, Column 4)

Jack L. Warner Charges 'Slanted Lines' Are Put Into Scripts

By HOWARD NORTON
[*Washington Bureau of The Sun*]

Washington, Oct. 20—Two leading motion picture producers—Jack L. Warner and Sam Wood—told the House Committee on Un-American Activities today that the most dangerous Communists in Hollywood are screen writers.

A third movie executive—Louis B. Mayer, Russian-born head of Metro-Goldwyn-Mayer studios—refused to pin the Communist label on any of his writers, but declared he would fire any writer of proved Communist allegiance.

The three executives testified at the opening of an investigation to determine the extent of Communist infiltration into Hollywood. They were summoned here by committee subpoenas, along with about 50 other Hollywood figures, including actors and writers. It is estimated that three weeks will be required to hear them all.

Republicans Assailed

The charge that the current probe is a smear organized by Hollywood Republicans to embarrass Hollywood Democrats was made by Robert Kenny, former attorney general of California and counsel for nineteen subpoenaed writers, in a press conference during recess at noon.

Reading from today's paper the announcement of a new Hollywood Republican committee, Kenny declared that most of the movie people who have testified against the alleged Communists are members of the new GOP group while "the people they are smearing are Democrats—almost to a man."

Kenny's motion to quash the subpoenas issued to his clients was set aside at the opening of today's session and he was told he would have to wait until his clients were called—probably early next week—to argue his point.

Shouted Down By Thomas

Kenny tried to inquire whether he would have the privilege of crossquestioning witnesses, but he was shouted down by Chairman J. Parnell Thomas (R., N.J.).

"This is certainly American" Kenny shouted back. He was silenced by the gavel.

Warner, who is vice president of Warner Brothers Studios, testified that he had let twelve of his writers go because they had tried to inject what he considered "un-American ideas" into their scripts. Warner repeatedly sidestepped the use of the term "Communist," using "un-American" instead.

"Slanted Lines" Charged

He declared the writers had been putting in "slanted lines," but denied that they had "attacked the Government or advocated overthrow of the Government by violence."

Wood said it wasn't so much what the writers put into the script as what they leave out.

"Their chief interest," Wood said "is in underselling the American way of life."

Questioned by the committee counsel, Robert E. Stripling, as to what he thought the Hollywood Communists were up to, Wood answered:

"I think they're agents of a foreign country, myself."

Mayer, the last of the three to testify, said it was impossible for Communist ideas to slip into his pictures because the scripts were checked and rechecked by so many people.

He admitted that the names of one or two writers had been suggested to him as pro-Communist, but declared that he "couldn't find any propaganda in their pictures."

He named these writers as Dalton Trumbo, Lester Cole and Donald Ogden Stewart.

"I Think They're Cracked"

Representative Vail (R., Ill.) asked him what would make such high-salaried writers embrace an ideology that would tear down the system that gave them their opportunity.

"In my opinion," Mayer answered, "I think they're cracked."

Mayer read a prepared statement before answering questions.

In it he revealed that the movie, "Mrs. Minniver," was "rushed into release at the urgent request of the United States officials to meet the rising tide of anti-English feeling that followed the fall of Tobruk."

Defends "Song Of Russia"

Concerning the wartime film, "Song of Russia," which was criticized by its star, Robert Taylor, in earlier hearings in Hollywood, Mayer denied that it was intended as pro-Russian propaganda, and said:

"It seemed a good medium of entertainment and at the same time offered an opportunity for a pat on the back for our ally, Russia. It also offered an opportunity to use the music of Tchai-

(Continued on Page 2, Column 1)

Wife Sues To Bar Husband's Visits To 'Test Tube' Daughter

New York, Oct. 20 (AP)—A mother's legal effort to keep her estranged husband from visiting her daughter, on the grounds that he had no right to do so since the child was born as the result of artificial insemination, was disclosed by attorneys today.

Principals in the case are Mrs. Julie Strnad, 31, her 4-year-old daughter Antoinette, and her estranged husband, Antoine, a chauffeur.

At Request Of Husband

The mother's claim that Antoinette is a "test-tube baby" and that the mother is the sole legal parent was the basis on which she sought amendment of a State Supreme Court separation decree handed down October 8, which granted Strnad the right to visit the child on Sundays. She maintains that her husband was not the father of her child.

Through her attorney, Jerome Horowitz, Mrs. Strnad declared:

"The daughter of the parties is a test-tube baby. I submitted to artificial insemination at the request of my husband, and he paid the physician."

Philip Wolfson, attorney for Strnad, said that "biologically and physically, it is impossible for a child to have only one parent."

"Also," Wolfson said, "there is no way of proving that the mother conceived artificially, since the doctor could not be called as a witness. The doctor could only testify regarding such confidential services if the husband waived his rights, which he has no intention of doing."

Rehearing Denied

Mrs. Strnad related that last spring, after she and her husband had agreed to separate, he took the child to Czechoslovakia, where he has relatives. She flew there and brought the child back.

Her motion for a rehearing was denied on technical grounds by Justice Samuel H. Hofstadter, but Horowitz said a new petition would be filed before Justice Henry Clay Greenberg, who had decided the original suit.

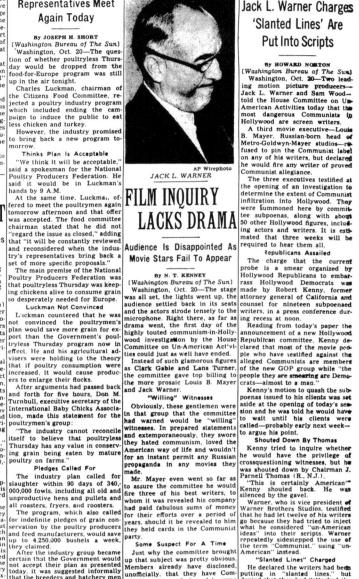

Weather Forecast
Fair and mild today and tonight; highest temperatures in mid-80's. Yesterday's temperatures: Max., 85; min., 63; mean, 74............................Page 29

THE SUN

FINAL

Registered United States Patent Office

Vol. 223—No. 79—F | PAID CIRCULATION JULY MORNING 171,365 EVENING 188,586 359,951 ‖ SUNDAY 299,625 | BALTIMORE, TUESDAY, AUGUST 17, 1948 | Entered as second-class matter at Baltimore Post Office | Zone 3 | 30 Pages | 5 Cents

Truman Signs GOP Anti-Inflation Measure

Babe Ruth, Baseball's Home-Run King, Dies Of Cancer

ENVOYS HOLD PARLEY WITH MOLOTOV

Longest Session Of Series Ends With Silence On Discussions

Moscow, Aug. 16 (AP)—Envoys of the United States, Britain and France met with Vyacheslav M. Molotov, Soviet Foreign Minister, again tonight in the current negotiations to settle East-West differences in Berlin and Germany.

The meeting in the Kremlin was the longest since the negotiations began July 31, lasting three hours and 40 minutes. None of the Western diplomats would comment as they left the Kremlin. They refused even to say whether they thought there would be another meeting.

Walter Bedell Smith, United States Ambassador, and Yves Chataigneau, French Ambassador, went immediately to the British Embassy with Britain's special envoy, Frank Roberts, for a conference.

Seems In Good Spirits

Smith seemed in good spirits as he sent his chauffeur to get something to eat. But the envoys themselves went right into the meeting without stopping for food.

Tonight's conference was the sixth with Molotov. The Western envoys met with the Soviet Foreign Minister July 31. He was present also at the August 2 meeting with Prime Minister Stalin, which was followed by meetings with Molotov on August 6, August 9 and August 12.

The three Western diplomats met among themselves at the British Embassy before they left for the Kremlin.

There has been no indication in Moscow as to how the talks are going. The Western diplomats have been silent on the progress of the conferences throughout the negotiations.

Most Moscow observers were of the opinion, however, that today's talks were crucial.

Together For 6 Hours

The Western powers representatives conferred in the British Embassy for an hour and fifteen minutes. They had been together uninterruptedly for six hours from the time they met for a short conference before going to the Kremlin.

After the last session in the embassy broke up, Smith, Roberts and Chataigneau presumably each took a brief period out for dining and then went to work separately on their reports of the conference to their home governments.

Experienced observers in Moscow commented on the apparent fact, judging from the length of the conference, that the four power representatives still have plenty to talk about.

The length of the session with Molotov and the unexpectedly long parley at the British Embassy indicated to some that concrete, detailed questions were discussed.

Molotov Answer Forecast

London, Aug. 16 (AP)—A responsible diplomatic informant said today Vyacheslav M. Molotov, Soviet Foreign Minister, was to give Russia's reply to the Western envoys' proposals for a Berlin settlement at today's four-power meeting in Moscow.

Meanwhile, Herbert Morrison, Acting Prime Minister, met today with members of the British Cabinet and several British service chiefs. Ernest Bevin, Foreign Secretary, attended. There was no indication from official sources of the nature of the discussion.

On Other Pages

Anti-Communist Relates Aid To Mrs. Kosenkina

Teacher Sought Russian Editor's Advice On How To Escape Returning To Homeland

Soviet consul charges "White Russians" are responsible for Mrs. Kosenkina's leap....Page 2

By ROBERT W. RUTH
[*Sun Staff Correspondent*]

New York, Aug. 16—Mrs. Kosenkina's story—why she jumped to freedom—was told today by the man who knows it best.

He is Mark Weinbaum, editor of the Russian-language daily here, *Novoye Russkoye Slovo* (New Russian Word). He knows it best because he got it straight from Mrs. Oksana Stepanovna Kosenkina herself, the Russian schoolteacher whom Soviet authorities tried to hold inside the consulate here.

Weinbaum's Account

Weinbaum was the first person she sought out and the first to hear her tearful tale of hardship, misery, frustration of soul and how she resolved never to return to the land of the Communists.

Here is what Weinbaum said:

On the morning of July 29 at about 11 o'clock he was seated at his desk—a paper-cluttered desk in a second-floor office overlooking West Fifty-sixth street—when a woman came in and said in Russian, "I would like to see the editor."

She closed the office door rapidly, which Weinbaum thought unusual. Shaking and excited, she almost ran into the room. She said:

"I came to ask your advice."

She sat down and then added:

"I will be frank with you. I am a Soviet teacher. Our school has been closed and I have to go back on the ship Pobeda (Victory).

"I do not wish to go back. What shall I do?"

Weinbaum was picked as her first contact with the outside world because Mrs. Kosenkina had been reading his newspaper in secret. While she sat in his office she took

(Continued on Page 2, Column 2)

N.Y. Police Refute 'Kidnap' Charge

New York, Aug. 16 (AP)—The New York *Times* said tonight it had learned "from trustworthy sources" that an exhaustive report by the New York Police Department on the Kosenkina case had been made to Mayor William O'Dwyer and turned over to prosecuting agencies.

The *Times* said the report declares flatly that Soviet charges that Mrs. Kosenkina was kidnapped are "unfounded."

A copy of the report, "the contents of which are secret," according to the *Times*, has been forwarded to Attorney General Tom C. Clark in Washington.

It is on this report, the *Times* said, that the United States Government will rely for its answer to the formal protests made by Russia.

CLAY CONFIDENT PLAN WILL STAND

General Doubts Parley Will Bar New German State

Frankfurt, Germany, Aug. 16 (AP). Gen. Lucius D. Clay, American military governor in Germany, said tonight he expects no change of the Western powers' plans for Germany to come out of the four-power talks in Moscow.

He said he expects the Western diplomats to stand firm and added: "I know of no intention by anybody to deviate from the present program."

General Clay indicated at a news conference that the West will continue with plans for a west German government until there can be a unified Germany, reflecting the political and economic views of the German people.

Always Hopes For Treaty

Asked about an eventual peace treaty with Germany, Clay said "our Government has always hoped for a quadripartite treaty." At another point he said he expects eventual economic unity in Germany.

Asked whether he considers himself a policy maker or an administrator, Clay answered "policy has always been made in Washington, the operations are in our hands."

Told of reports in Berlin that he and his top advisers will resign if plans for a west German government are abandoned, Clay said: "Soldiers don't resign."

He was asked: "Just what do the Russians want as a condition for lifting the Berlin blockade?"

Quotes Sokolovsky View

He said Marshal Vassily D. Sokolovsky, Russian commander in Germany, had described it as a question of what type of currency should be used in Berlin and what type of government Germany should have.

"But that was never official," Clay added. "It still rests officially on 'technical difficulties.'"

Clay rejected socialization for any one part of Germany, saying the American Military Government is "not prepared to see socialization on a state basis until a German government is established in which the German people have a chance to express their views."

Communists Reported Planning Berlin Purge

Berlin, Aug. 16 (AP)—A Berlin Liberal newspaper, *Montags Echo*, said today a Communist "fifth column" is at work in the Soviet-blockaded western sectors of the city—preparing for the day they hope the Western powers will leave.

The *Montags Echo* said the Communists had prepared a purge list of "hundreds of thousands" of anti-Communists upon whom they will take revenge if the Western allies quit Berlin.

"The Communist spy system has worked its way into industrial workers' councils, into commerce, into postal and telegraph systems of western Berlin, and there makes systematic preparation for 'X-day'—the day the Communists hope the Western allies will leave Berlin," the newspaper said.

The newspaper appealed again to

(Continued on Page 13, Column 2)

REBELS FLEEING, GREECE REPORTS

Guerrillas Leave Wounded On Battlefield, Stratos Says

Athens, Aug. 16 (AP)—George Stratos, War Minister, told the Cabinet tonight the Greek Army has captured the highest peak of the Grammos Mountains.

He said divisions of the 1st Army were pushing forward unimpeded by the Communist-led guerrilla forces. The guerrillas were routed and abandoned their wounded and war material in their unorganized flight from the battlefields, he said.

A general staff spokesman said earlier that the Communist defense along the entire southwestern sector of the Grammos front had crumbled under the Greek army's drive.

No Reports On Casualties

Lycorrahi and Aetomilista, both of which had been headquarters for Communist General Markos Vafiades in earlier campaigns, were captured along with Zerma in the Greek army sweep along the whole southwestern front.

There were no indications of the number of guerrilla casualties of the past two days, and it is not clear whether main guerrilla forces are running to Albania or being mopped up by the Greek army.

A general staff statement said 1,140 square miles had been cleared in the big general offensive launched June 21 on the Grammos front. Only 135 square miles containing fifteen villages are still left to the guerrillas, the statement said.

Big Blow To Markos

During the offensive, the general staff said, 3,830 guerrillas had been killed or captured. Greek losses were described as 49 officers and 502 men killed, 230 officers and 2,600 men wounded, and 30 missing.

Territorial gains are large, and the loss is a big political blow to Markos, who is trying to hold territory for the flag of "Free Greece."

The perimeter has been reduced to about 22 miles. Guerrillas still had about 12 miles of Albanian border to use as a crossing, but there are only three beaten trails left in the sector. Other main roads have been taken or closed by Greek army fire. Markos's frontal wedge into Greece from Grammos is about 6 miles across.

Some military observers expect Markos to pull as many men as possible out of the Grammos line into Albania, despite the severe handicaps of military movement, and then reform to attack later north and east of Alevista to regain some Greek territory.

Raid Over Border Charged To Slavs

Vienna, Aug. 16 (AP)—Yugoslav border guards crossed into Austria Sunday, critically wounded one person and abducted two others of a party of four, the Ministry of Interior said tonight.

The ministry said the four Austrians, who were on a hiking party, were drinking at a spring about 150 yards north of the border when they were fired upon. The wounded man was reported left where he lay on the ground, and the fourth man escaped. The ministry said the other two, including a girl, were taken into Yugoslavia.

SPY PROBERS MAY TURN TO LIE DETECTOR

Alger Hiss Is Questioned Secretly; Will Meet Accuser Aug. 25

By HOWARD NORTON
[*Washington Bureau of The Sun*]

Washington, Aug. 16—A tight lid was clamped on the spy probe of the House Un-American Activities Committee today, but there were indications that a lie-detector might be used to determine which of two key witnesses is telling the truth.

For three hours behind closed doors this afternoon the committee cross-questioned Alger Hiss, ex-Baltimorean and former State Department official, who is accused of being a key figure in the wartime Communist underground.

Hiss has denied the charges under oath and has declared, moreover, that he never "laid eyes on" the man who accuses him—Whittaker Chambers, a senior editor of *Time* Magazine.

Hasn't Changed Story

Hiss told reporters as he left the closed session today that he had not changed his story.

At a press conference a few minutes later, Chairman Thomas (R., N.J.) said that:

1. The committee still doesn't know which one is "telling the truth."

2. "Confrontation Day" — The day when the two will be brought face to face before the committee—has been set for August 25 at 10.30 A.M.

3. Every detail of corroborative evidence of Chambers's story of his alleged association with Hiss in the Communist underground is to be checked, in the meantime, by committee investigators.

Asked to confirm a report that Leonarde Keeler, noted criminologist, had been asked to bring his lie-detector to Washington to help resolve the case, Thomas replied:

"I have nothing to say about that."

To Come To Washington

In Chicago, meanwhile, Keeler announced he had been contacted by the committee, and that he would come to Washington soon for a conference with them.

Thomas said the committee already had talked to Chambers in closed session to get corroborative data to support his accusations.

He indicated that an unusual policy of secrecy has been imposed on the committee members, all of whom in the past have been known to pass out hints as to what took place in secret sessions.

"I don't think it will be worth your while," he warned newsmen, "to ask any member of the committee or the staff what happened here today."

Though Chairman Thomas declared that Hiss had been told he was "on his own" and might make any statement to the press, the witness had nothing to say as he strode from the committee room.

Referred To Committee

Brushing newsmen aside, he said:

"Any statement at this point will have to come from the committee."

"Would you submit to a lie-detector test?" he was asked.

Hiss shrugged and walked on.

Earlier, a member of the committee said one of the two men had agreed to such a test.

Thomas said he didn't know, yet, whether the "confrontations" of the two would be in a public or closed session.

"From the testimony of the two

(Continued on Page 2, Column 5)

U.S. ACCUSES A 'TOKYO ROSE' OF TREASON

Iva D'Aquino Ordered Arrested In Japan, Sent To San Francisco

Washington, Aug. 16 (AP)—The Justice Department today decided to go ahead with a treason prosecution in the so-called "Tokyo Rose" broadcasts of World War II.

Tom C. Clark, Attorney General, asked United States Army authorities in Tokyo to arrest 32-year-old Iva Toguri D'Aquino and send her to San Francisco to face a Federal grand jury there "at as early a date as possible."

[In Tokyo, officers said they have not yet been ordered to arrest Mrs. d'Aquino.

[Her landlady said she was away visiting relatives.]

3-Year Investigation

The action follows more than three years of investigation. The inquiry, Clark said, indicated that Mrs. D'Aquino, born in Los Angeles July 4, 1916, was one of six English-speaking Japanese women who broadcast over Radio Tokyo between 1943 and 1945.

The Attorney General said she was the only American-born woman in the group to which the American armed forces in the Far East applied the collective nickname "Tokyo Rose."

The feminine broadcasts over Tokyo's powerful radio station became a legend among United States fighting men in the desolate places of the Pacific to which they were beamed.

Nightly Reminders

The programs were elaborately planned. Soft-voiced and sexy in appeal, they were employed as nightly reminders to American combat men on lonely islands of what they were missing by not going back home.

Often, the broadcasts included imaginary descriptions of the scenes in famous American good-time centers, with heavy emphasis on how much fun stay-at-homes were having.

Throughout the war, the Japanese women broadcasters used the latest American dance recordings as a backdrop for their patter.

Just how Radio Tokyo got this up-to-the-minute stuff has never been fully explained. However, one theory is that pickup stations spotted in South America made transcriptions from United States broadcasts and sent them to Japan by submarine.

Mrs. D'Aquino went to Japan shortly before the war broke out and was married there to a Portuguese. She has been in custody in Tokyo previously in connection with the investigation of the "Rose" broadcasts, but has been at liberty recently.

15 Japs To Be Witnesses

As late as last December, the Justice Department said a two-year effort had failed to turn up the two witnesses needed under the Constitution to support filing of a treason charge.

However, today's announcement said that both American and Japanese witnesses will be called to testify. For this purpose, Clark disclosed that some fifteen Japanese nationals will be brought to San Francisco from Japan for the grand jury hearing.

Mrs. D'Aquino will make the trip to the West Coast by steamship and is expected there within 30 days.

Justice officials wanted to fly her across the Pacific, but there were legal complications. The treason

(Continued on Page 2, Column 6)

Saudi Arabia Refuses U.S. Loan Because Of Palestine Stand

Washington, Aug. 16 (AP)—The Government of Saudi Arabia has refused to accept a $15,000,000 American loan because of its displeasure with alleged United States support of the Jewish cause in Palestine.

"We feel we would like to get assistance from a friend and not from someone helping our enemy," a spokesman for the Saudi Arabian legation announced.

Saudi Arabia deliberately permitted a $15,000,000 credit earmarked for it at the Export-Import Bank to expire July 15, he said, "because of the attitude of the American Government in the Palestine situation."

For Modernization

The Export-Import Bank said the loan has been avaliable to the Saudi Arabian Government since January 10, 1946.

The $15,000,000 is part of a total $25,000,000 authorized for reconstruction and modernization in Saudi Arabia. About $10,000,000 was used by the Saudi Arabians shortly after the money became available.

The Saudi Arabian spokesman said his country now has "no intention" of asking the bank to reinstate the credit.

"We will use our own money for the projects we have in mind," he said.

State Department officials said the Saudi Arabians never have given them a reason for not submitting projects to the Export-Import Bank, which could draw on the $15,000,000 loan held for them.

These officials said if political motives influenced this decision, they did not mention it to the State Department.

King Ibn Saud Anxious

The Export-Import Bank credit was scheduled to be used to pay for a long-planned program of expanding, and modernizing Saudi Arabian ports, highways, airports, hospital and electrical facilities.

King Ibn Saud of Saudi Arabia has been described as particularly anxious to finish the modernization program in his lifetime.

The new Jewish state of Israel has an application for $100,000,000 loan pending for the Export-Import Bank. Gen. George C. Marshall, Secretary of State, said last week this request is receiving exhaustive consideration.

Former Yankee Star Passes Away In Sleep

Death Follows Lengthy Illness — Career Began In Baltimore As Member Of Orioles

AP photo
BABE RUTH

Jesse Linthicum tells of seeing Ruth hit his first home run, pitch his first game and get his nickname "Babe"..........Page 15

Boys at St. Mary's here will attend special mass this morning for Babe Ruth..........Page 30

New York, Aug. 16 (AP)—Babe Ruth, who rose from the obscurity of an orphanage to become one of baseball's immortals, died tonight of cancer.

The once-mighty Yankee slugger, his frame and strength weakened by a long and painful illness, lapsed into unconsciousness shortly before death came to him—peacefully.

"The Babe," said a Catholic priest at the bedside of the long-time home-run king, "died a beautiful death."

"He said his prayers," the priest added, "and lapsed into a sleep—and he died in his sleep."

End Comes At 8.01 P.M.

Death came to one of baseball's brightest stars at 8.01 P.M. (E.D.T.) in New York city's Memorial Hospital Center for Cancer and Allied Diseases.

At the end of Ruth's prayers, the priest, the Rev. Thomas H. Kaufman, of the St. Catherine of Siena parish, administered the last rites of the Catholic Church.

It was the Catholic Church which took over the training of George Herman Ruth when he was 7. Six years after Ruth entered the orphanage, his mother died.

Tonight in the hospital room with Ruth at the time he died was a last tribute from the youngsters who, throughout the world, had idolized the Babe.

Signed By Jack Dunn

The final tribute, typical of the many which had come from Ruth's millions of admirers, was a wreath of 37 orchids, fashioned in the shape of a Hawaiian lei.

With the wreath came a message from Hawaiian schoolchildren who sent their "best wishes for a speedy recovery to our all-time baseball favorite."

The flowers were shown to Ruth before he became unconscious. He said nothing.

The Babe got his baseball start in Baltimore when Jack Dunn, of the Baltimore Orioles, signed him out of St. Mary's Industrial School as an 18-year-old youth with an uncanny ability to throw and bat a baseball.

Had Rallied Sunday

Throughout Ruth's long illness of nearly two years, the exact nature of his sickness never had been disclosed. But tonight, Dr. Hayes Martin, the Babe's personal physician, announced that Ruth's death was caused by cancer.

Throughout the day, Ruth's condition had grown steadily worse. His fever had soared, and he had been unable to take nourishment.

Yet only the previous day he had surprised everyone by leaving his bed and sitting in a near-by easy

(Continued on Page 16, Column 5)

DEWEY, WARREN PLAN WIDE TOURS

Albany Campaign Conference Quiet On Most Strategy

State-rights Democrats in North Carolina go to court in effort to get place on ballot........Page 5

By THOMAS O'NEILL
[*Sun Staff Correspondent*]

Albany, N.Y., Aug. 16—Wide swings across the country by both the candidates of the Republican national ticket were decided upon today in discussion between Gov. Thomas E. Dewey, nominee for President, and Gov. Earl Warren, his running mate, with the aim of presenting their cause in person to the greatest possible number of voters.

The dates and routes of their tours, which will be made separately, remained indefinite.

With a number of aides, the two governors conferred today and again tonight on all aspects of their campaign. The meetings are to continue tomorrow.

Most Plans In Hiding

Only the decision to have both candidates crisscross the country was revealed, the conferees remaining silent on any additional business that was disposed of at their meetings. The strategy being followed requires the hiding of most of the campaign plans from the Democrats.

Governor Dewey's campaign manager, Herbert Brownell, Jr., announced the crosscountry campaign agreement. He said:

"Both Governor Dewey and Governor Warren will conduct very active campaigns and travel country-wide during the course of the campaign. They propose very intensive and extensive coverage."

To Aid Senate Candidates

Although the candidates will travel separately, their routes may cross and both may speak in the same areas. This is especially likely to occur in states where Republican candidates for the United States Senate appear to be hard pressed and it is considered that the national candidates can bolster the weaklings.

"Where Senate races are close the states will have plenty of attention," Mr. Brownell said. "It is the aim to strengthen and increase our majority in the Senate."

The campaign manager insisted that there had been no discussion of the situation presented in West Virginia, where Senator Revercomb, who is up for re-election, defied Governor Dewey's request during the special session of Con-

(Continued on Page 5, Column 3)

MCGRATH DENIES PRESS-GAG REPORT

Democratic Leader Explains Criticism Of Truman Foes

[*Washington Bureau of The Sun*]

Washington, Aug. 16—Senator McGrath (D., R.I.), chairman of the Democratic National Committee, today said he has no desire to suppress some radio commentators or newspapers, even though they "untruthfully" attack the man his job it is to return to the White House—President Truman.

Nor, he added, does he favor the transformation of our Government into the kind of a "democracy" which would prohibit such actions.

But he appeared to be advocating both yesterday, when in an address to a Democratic rally in Rhode Island he declared that "in months that have recently passed you have found a campaign in your papers and on the part of radio commentators to pour into your ears the most anti-democratic philosophy."

Made Out To Be Stupid

"These $100,000-a-year commentators," he added, according to an Associated Press dispatch, "would not be allowed to exist under a truly democratic form of government. They make your President out to be an erroneous fellow and a stupid man."

Senator McGrath did not deny that he made the above statement but said it was "taken out of context" and was not complete. Neither would he attempt to reconstruct the entire section of his statement made extemporaneously in the heat of a political speech.

Neither yesterday, nor today when questioned about the quotation, did he name any names, either commentators or newspapers, to which he objected, but while he said he would not muzzle them, he gave every indication that he wished they would support his candidate instead of being critical of him.

Intended To Be Plea

What he was "trying to say" in his address yesterday, he explained, was that some of the high-salaried radio commentators appeared to be "working more in the interest of their wealthy sponsors than in the interest of their country and democracy."

That portion of his address, he added, was intended to be in the form of a plea that they should think of their trust as requiring them to disseminate unbiased news rather than the distribution of propaganda.

Some of the attacks on the Presi-

(Continued on Page 5, Column 2)

PRESIDENT HOLDS BILL INADEQUATE

Charges Congress Fails To Meet Responsibility To Nation

By WILLIAM KNIGHTON, JR.
[*Washington Bureau of The Sun*]

Washington, Aug. 16—President Truman today signed the Republican anti-inflation bill into law with another attack on Congress.

He said he had done so "even though it is clear that the Congress in passing this law failed to meet its responsibility to the American people."

In a 1,200 word statement, the President reviewed the details of his eight-point program which he submitted to the legislators for dealing with inflation, but he declared that Congress passed a bill limited to only one subject—credit controls — "which is but a tiny fraction of what we needed."

"Ends Of Special Privilege"

The Chief Executive used the word "Republican" only when he quoted Senator Wherry (R., Neb.), the party whip, as saying that "it was Republican leadership in the Senate and the House that was responsible for ending OPA," but he took another shot at the GOP leaders without naming them when he declared:

"The failure to take adequate measures in this critical situation is final proof of the determination of the men who controlled the Eightieth Congress to follow a course which serves the ends of special privilege rather than the welfare of the whole nation."

Mr. Truman said he had proposed a "balanced program." It consisted of restoration of the wartime excess-profits tax, price and wage controls, rationing, allocations of scare materials and credit controls.

Did Nothing To Control It

"The Congress said 'no' to my program," the President declared. "They had no program of their own. They made excuses and called names and argued about who was to blame for inflation, but they did nothing effective to control it."

The measure which the President signed today gives the Federal Reserve Board the authority to revive installment buying controls and increased bank reserves.

The Chief Executive said he had recommended methods which would halt inflation and were known to work, adding:

"They worked in wartime when inflationary pressures were much greater than they are now."

Invite Economic Collapse

The President said that "prices are pulling away from the incomes of most of our people," with the result that "millions of housewives throughout the country are finding it impossible to pay today's high prices for the food and clothing their families need.

"Unless inflation is checked, the situation will get even worse and we shall invite economic collapse," he added.

The "right way" to fight inflation, the President continued, is to "strike hard at the trouble spots which represent the excesses of inflation, and at the same time help the people who are its victims."

He said his program would have done that by preventing "some people from getting too much," and helping "others to get enough."

Bear The Brunt

"Then there is the wrong way to deal with inflation," the President continued. "That is to let the plain people bear the brunt of its burdens, while special interests reap the benefits of excessive profits. We have heard a lot lately from people who advocate this method.

"These people say it would be inflationary to increase the pitifully inadequate benefits provided by our present social security laws. They say it would be inflationary

(Continued on Page 6, Column 3)

Five Beating Homes Shortage

When an ex-Marine, an aviation engineer, a white-collar man, a horse trainer and a professional photographer decide that the housing shortage doesn't have them licked, they get results.

Five Baltimoreans are taking their example from the pioneers of 1748 and building their own homes, stone by stone and brick by brick.

The story, with pictures, will appear in today's issue of

The Evening Sun

Weather Forecast

Considerable cloudiness and warmer today, scattered showers likely this afternoon or tonight. Yesterday's temperatures: Highest 61, lowest 45. Page 33

THE SUN

6 A. M.

Registered United States Patent Office

Vol. 224—No. 110—F | PAID CIRCULATION FEBRUARY: MORNING 168,061, EVENING 195,845 = 363,906 ‖ SUNDAY 310,015 | BALTIMORE, FRIDAY, MARCH 25, 1949 | Entered as second-class matter at Baltimore Post Office | Zone 3 | 34 Pages | 5 Cents

FIRE AT LEXINGTON MARKET WIPES OUT ENTIRE SECTION

8 Women In Nearby Hospital Evacuated

Lexington Market was wrecked today by fire that swept its principal section, the block-long area between Eutaw and Paca streets.

The flames broke out near Paca street and raced through the block of stalls, leaping southward to several business buildings on Lexington street.

Patients were evacuated from the Volunteers of America Hospital north of the market, at 418 West Lexington street, as a precaution, but the hospital was untouched.

Frank J. Bauer, president of the Board of Fire Commissioners, pronounced the market area a complete loss.

Roof Caves In, Interior Ruined

Although the walls were still standing after the flames died away, the roof had caved in and the interior was destroyed.

The section burned was that in which the market's first buildings were erected at the time it was established in 1803.

Firemen attributed the outbreak to an electric flash from an undetermined source that was observed shortly after 3.30 A.M. in a poultry stall near Paca street. It was seen by two employes of the American Ice Company, William Bayne, 1001 Riverside avenue, and Charles Greene, 3811 Hayworth avenue, who were icing a produce stall in the center of the block.

"The flash was back of us," Bayne and Greene told police. "When we turned around to see what it was, flames started shooting up all around right up to the roof."

Six Alarms Sounded

They ran half a block to No. 2 Truck Company, at Paca and Fayette streets, and sounded the alarm. Six alarms in all were sounded in the next eleven minutes by Fire Department officials.

The narrow streets of the market area were crowded with 33 firefighting vehicles, and five ambulances added to the jam when they arrived to take out eight women and five infants from the maternity ward of the Volunteers of America Hospital.

Fifteen hundred spectators thronged the area while firemen turned dozens of streams of water on the flames.

Women Put In Ambulances

The women patients were loaded in ambulances which waited in Clay street, behind the hospital, to remove the patients to the University Hospital if a transfer was needed. The infants, the youngest of whom was born at 10 o'clock last night, were bundled by attendants, but were kept in the building.

Immediately after the first alarm identified the fire as in the Lexington Market area, a longtime nightmare to Fire Department officials, heads of the department turned out.

Chief Travers In Charge

The battle against the blaze was directed by Howard Travers, chief engineer of the department, and Deputy Chief Clarence W. Smith, head of the first division. They said that 165 firemen took part in the fight before the fire burned out.

These were from 24 engine companies, six truck companies, two high pressure units, and a water tower.

Flames leaped hundreds of feet in the air from the roaring stalls.

Cornices on Lexington street buildings opposite the market caught up the tongues of flame and blazed out.

Windows Smashed

High pressure streams quelled these outbreaks, but windows all along the block were smashed. The largest casualty among the windows was the plate glass of the Purity Creamery Company, at Paca and Lexington streets.

A burglar alarm in midblock along Lexington street was set off

(Continued on Page 6, Column 1)

SOVIET UNION RELIEVES MARSHAL BULGANIN AS ARMED FORCES MINISTER

Vasilevsky, His Deputy, Appointed To Top Military Post

London, March 24 (AP)—The Soviet Union announced tonight that Marshal Alexander M. Vasilevsky, 49, has succeeded Marshal Nikolai A. Bulganin as Minister of the Armed Forces, the highest military post in all of Russia.

This was the first big change in Soviet military leadership since Prime Minister Stalin stepped down as Minister of the Armed Forces in 1947 and appointed Bulganin to succeed him. Stalin ran the armed forces during the war.

The new shift followed top-level changes in the Soviet political hierarchy in the last few weeks. The most important was the release of Vyacheslav M. Molotov as Foreign Minister to be succeeded by Andrei Y. Vishinsky. Molotov remained as first Deputy Prime Minister—right at Stalin's side.

Strengthen Policy Makers

Western observers in Moscow viewed these changes as measures to strengthen the highest ranks of Soviet policy makers.

Bulganin is also a vice chairman of the Council of Ministers of the Soviet Union—a deputy prime minister.

Bulganin, 53, is an alternate member of the all-powerful Politburo of the Central Committee of the Communist party.

Was Bulganin's Deputy

Into the post of Minister of the Armed Forces comes a relatively young man who has carved out a distinguished career in Soviet military annals. Vasilevsky was deputy minister under Bulganin and therefore is closely associated with the workings of the office.

Vasilevsky had been relieved of his duties as chief of staff of the general staff of the Soviet Army last November but retained his job as Deputy Minister of the Armed Forces. The Russians said they wanted to relieve Vasilevsky of an excessive burden of work.

Bulganin's last declaration to bring him world-wide notice was his order marking the thirty-first anniversary of the Red Army last month.

Called U.S. Policy Aggressive

He said Soviet fighting men must maintain a constant battle of preparedness at a high level because of the "policy of aggression" pursued by the United States.

The Moscow broadcast announcing the promotion of Vasilevsky said:

"The Presidium of the Supreme Soviet of the U.S.S.R. has relieved Marshal N. A. Bulganin, a vice chairman of the Council of Ministers of the U.S.S.R., of his duties as Minister of the Armed Forces of the U.S.S.R.

"The Presidium of the Supreme Soviet of the U.S.S.R. has appointed Marshal of the Soviet Union Alexander M. Vasilevsky as Minister of the Armed Forces of the U.S.S.R."

Holds High Decorations

Vasilevsky became first deputy minister of the armed forces after a distinguished military career that brought him some of the highest Soviet decorations.

These included the Order of Victory, Hero of the Soviet Union, the Order of Lenin and the coveted Order of Suvorov.

He was deputy commissar for defense in 1942 and top planner of the Voronezh offensive in 1942 and

(Continued on Page 6, Column 2)

AP photo

MARSHAL BULGANIN

DANISH HOUSE BACKS TREATY

Lower Branch Of Parliament Registers 119-23 Vote

Copenhagen, March 24 (AP)—The lower house of the Danish Parliament today approved the nation's entry into the North Atlantic alliance by a five-to-one margin. The action was referred to the upper house, where similar approval is regarded as certain.

Denmark would join an alliance made up of at least eight other nations.

Two Others Invited

Iceland and Portugal also have been invited to join. Subject to final ratification procedures, present members of the alliance are the United States, Canada, Britain, France, Belgium, the Netherlands, Luxembourg and Norway.

The decision of Denmark's lower house (Folketing) had been expected. It supports the foreign policy of Premier Hans Hedtoft's Government and is in line with Norway's stand.

Its vote of 119 to 23 not only approved Denmark's adherence to the Atlantic treaty but also authorized the Government to ratify the pact, after signature, without further reference to Parliament.

Britons Honor 'Decent' Nazi Prison Commander

London, March 24 (AP)—A German prison commander is going to be honored by Britons he kept under guard because he was "so decent" to them during the war.

Prince Wilhelm von Hohenlohe, who commanded the prison at Blechhammer, Upper Silesia, has accepted an invitation of a committee arranging a reunion to honor him next October.

THOUSANDS SPY ON U.S., PROBERS SAY

Agents Serving Russia, House Un-American Committee Warns

Washington, March 24 (AP)—The House Un-American Activities Committee said today "thousands of Russian agents" and more thousands of Americans are spying in the United States right now.

It said some of the spies "may" be attached to the Russian Embassy or the United Nations. And in a time of national crisis, the committee said, "the United States would have nearly 825,000 persons who are either spies, traitors or saboteurs working against us from within."

The statements were made in a pamphlet entitled "Spotlight on Spies."

Based On Old Figures

The House committee's 825,000 estimate was based on some old figures of J. Edgar Hoover, FBI director—74,000 Communist party members and Communist claims that for every member "there are ten others ready, willing and able to do the party work."

What the current crop of spies wants most, the committee said, are "production secrets of the atom bomb."

The committee said it had uncovered recent secret orders from abroad to spy leaders here, listing twenty-odd classes of information wanted on America's armed strength.

Secrets Reported Stolen

It said it knew of cases in which Russian agents or Americans working with them had made off with secrets on aviation, submarines and industrial processes.

Because we let our Russian allies inspect this country and its defense industries during the war, the committee said, the Soviets have been able to print "a thick book which can easily be used as a handbook for bombing and sabotage against the United States."

The committee said it had "confessions to prove" that treasonable Americans are the actual thieves for Communist spy networks in this country. But it said Communists trained in espionage actually direct the work.

Urges Efforts Be Redoubled

The FBI and military and naval intelligence are on the job, the committee says. But it wants every patriotic American to be "on the alert and report all suspicious activities."

The committee says efforts to root out spies and send them to jail or Russia should be redoubled.

The committee says it knows of a Russian agent who collected a "huge store of confidential aviation data" with the help of other spies. It was said to contain photos, blueprints and notes "which were personally flown to Moscow by the chairman of the then Soviet purchasing commission."

It says blueprints, photos and technical descriptions have been sneaked out of American submarine companies.

Other developments today bear

(Continued on Page 2, Column 1)

Chinese Ship Hits Mine; 100 Killed Or Seriously Hurt

Canton, *Friday*, March 25 (AP)—Authorities estimated more than 100 persons were killed or injured seriously today when the motor ship Miss Orient struck a mine between here and Hong Kong.

The ship was en route to Hong Kong from Canton when the explosion occurred.

[A dispatch from Hong Kong said there were 500 passengers aboard.]

The injured were being brought to Canton. It was believed here that the mine was laid by pirates after the owners refused to pay extortion money.

The explosion occurred in Eliot Passage, six miles east of Canton. The Orient is a ship of 1,200 tons.

[Hong Kong said the explosion took place near the spot where the river steamer Shihmen narrowly missed an exploding mine Wednesday.]

CANCER TESTS POINT TO VIRUS

British Say Research May Advance Study Of Disease

London, March 24 (AP)—The British *Medical Journal* said today new experiments indicating definitely that a virus is the cause of cancer may lead to "the biggest advance in cancer research for many years."

The experiments were carried out by Dr. W. E. Gye, director of the Imperial Cancer Research Fund, and three colleagues. They were reported in the *Medical Journal*, the official journal of the British Medical Association.

Tumors Transmitted

Dr. Gye wrote how he and his research workers transmitted tumors in mice by means of dried tissues. They subjected the tissue of a chemically fostered tumor from a mouse to the temperature of 110.2 degrees below zero Fahrenheit for five to eight weeks before drying.

All that could have lived through that treatment would have been an ultra-microscopic microbe known technically as a virus, they said.

They then used the material left to transmit the disease to other mice.

Dr. Gye reported:

"The experimental evidence points to the conclusion that cancer has a continuing cause and that this, in mammals as in birds, is a virus."

Advance Is Indicated

Many researchers have held that cancer is mainly produced by chemical agents.

If researchers can "safely accept the conclusion that tumors in general can be propagated in the absence of viable tumor cells (that is, cells capable of growing or developing), where does this lead?" the *Journal* asked in its leading article. "It leads certainly to the biggest advance in cancer research for many years."

China Delegate's Wife Asks U.N. Aid In Suit

Lake Success, N.Y., March 24 (AP)—Mrs. Ting Fu Tsiang, estranged wife of China's chief delegate to the United Nations, asked the agency's Commission on Human Rights today to look into her suit for a separation.

She has accused Tsiang of adultery. The New York Supreme Court rejected her suit on grounds that Tsiang enjoys diplomatic immunity.

She asked the commission to "spare a moment from its work on the rights of people all over the world in order that it might look into a situation concerning members of its official family." She said she could get relief only through the United Nations or through United States congressional action, voiding her husband's immunity.

Chicken In Pan Kicked Her In Eye, His Alibi

Detroit, March 24 (AP)—Johnny H. Franklin told the judge today that his wife got that black eye when a chicken she was cooking reared up and kicked her.

"I didn't do it, judge," he said. "She was frying chicken. The heat made the chicken muscles quiver and it kicked her."

Incredulous, Judge John P. Scallen found Franklin guilty of assault and battery anyway. He put Franklin on six months probation.

PENSION BILL IS SHELVED BY 1-VOTE MARGIN

House Sends Rankin Measure Back To Committee For More Study

Maryland House blocks move to kill bonus, recommits bill *Page 34*

By PHILIP POTTER
[*Washington Bureau of The Sun*]

Washington, March 24—Administration forces in the House, with substantial Republican support, today shelved by a one-vote margin the Rankin veterans pension bill.

The House, in one of the heaviest votes ever recorded, adopted, 208 to 207, a motion offered by a Purple Heart veteran of World War II to send the pension measure back to committee "for further study."

President Truman at a press conference said the House had taken constructive and forward-looking action. He added that it made him exceedingly happy.

GOP Aids In Shelving Bill

One hundred and fifty-one Democrats and 57 Republicans voted to recommit. The vote came at the start of today's session, following two days of debate which saw many confusing and complicated amendments written into the original Rankin bill.

Voting against the motion were 100 Democrats, 106 Republicans and Representative Marcantonio (A.L., N.Y.).

Three Maryland Democrats, Garmatz, Fallon and Sasscer, voted with the Administration forces. Their Democratic colleague, Bolton, and the two Maryland Republicans, Miller and Beall, voted with the Rankin forces.

Rankin Shows Anger

Rankin stalked angrily from the chamber following the vote to say "this ends the battle for veterans pensions at this session of Congress."

He said there would be "no further hearings on the bill."

A number of his opponents, including Administration leaders, discounted the remark.

Representative Priest (D., Tenn.), majority party whip, said he felt "certain" the Veterans Affairs Committee, of which Rankin is chairman, "will bring out a sensible pension bill."

Two Switched Votes

The Administration victory was made possible by two Pennsylvania Democrats, Barrett and Granahan, who changed their votes from "nay" to "yea."

Both Pennsylvanians said amendments adopted by the House yesterday left the pension bill in such shape they believed further committee consideration essential.

They cited the amendment by Representative Jacobs (D., Ind.) which would have based payments to veterans on length of service, with some veterans of World War I getting as little as $13 monthly, while some World War II veterans would have drawn $250.

Rankin beamed when, on the basis of a tally clerk's error, Representative McCormack (D., Mass.), majority leader and acting speaker, first announced the recommittal motion had been defeated, 209 to 208.

A tense House awaited a retabu

(Continued on Page 2, Column 5)

HOUSE GIVEN SECURITY PLAN

Would Extend To 50,000,000, Raise Benefits, Taxes

By RODNEY CROWTHER
Washington Bureau of The Sun

Washington, March 24—The Administration today proposed to Congress an enlarged social security program to cover virtually every worker in the land, and to raise everybody's benefits and everybody's taxes.

Arthur J. Altmeyer, social security commissioner, outlined before the House Ways and Means Committee President Truman's "fair deal" social insurance program as follows:

1. To raise the number of insured from about 30,000,000 to more than 50,000,000 by extending old-age and survivors' insurance to self-employed persons, farmers, farm labor, domestics, members of the armed forces, employés of nonprofit concerns and some State and Federal workers.

2. To inaugurate a new system of temporary and permanent disability insurance.

To Double Old Age Aid

3. To double old-age and survivor benefits.

4. To raise employer and employé contribution rates 50 per cent on July 1 and another 33⅓ per cent next January 1 and beginning next January to raise the tax base from $3,000 to $4,800.

5. To inaugurate a system of stamp-book taxes to collect contributions of agricultural and domestic workers.

6. To give all members of the armed forces during the last war wage credits toward old-age and survivors' insurance for the period of service.

7. To lower the retirement age for women when they can claim old-age benefits—from 65 to 60 years.

Mr. Altmeyer told Congress that the cost of the expanded program

(Continued on Page 2, Column 6)

TRUMAN CALLS OFF SPEECHES

Cancels All Out-Of-Town Dates For April Due To Work

By DEWEY L. FLEMING

Washington, March 24—President Truman today cleared his calendar of all out-of-town engagements for April.

He said his object was to concentrate on business that had accumulated and to confer with members of Congress who have been trying to see him.

The revision of plans caused cancellation of two speeches in New York city—at the laying of the cornerstone of the new United Nations headquarters, April 10, and at a testimonial dinner for Dr. Chaim Weizmann, head of the Israeli Government, on April 23.

Earlier this week the Executive called off engagements to speak at the mid-century convocation of the Massachusetts Institute of Technology, Cambridge, Mass., on April 1, and at Boston College on April 26.

Has Plenty Of Work

The President announced the latest speech cancellations at his press conference today. He said he was so covered with work since his return from Florida, and was facing so many interviews with senators, representatives and others who wished to discuss matters with him that he expected to be working from daylight until dark for the next several weeks.

Asked whether his program amounted to the holding of an "at home" for members of Congress, the President replied it would be better to describe it as an at-home for the business of the Government.

Silent On Civil Rights

Except for remarking he was exceedingly happy that the House had recommitted the veterans pension bill, the President declined to comment on Congress developments. Specific inquiries for his reaction to changes in the Administration's rent control bill and to the bogging down of preliminaries to civil-rights action in the Senate brought replies that the President had nothing to say at this time.

In response to another specific question the President said he was standing by his appointment of Mon C. Wallgren to be chairman of the National Security Resources Board, notwithstanding adverse action by the Senate Armed Services Committee.

To Attend Signing Of Pact

The President said he planned to attend the ceremony of the signing of the North Atlantic pact on April 4, but pointed out that Dean G. Acheson, Secretary of State, would do the signing for the United States.

The appointment of Dr. Frank P. Graham as a Senator from North Carolina was hailed by the Executive. He said Graham was a great American and a great citizen who had carried out many missions for the Government in exemplary fashion.

Questioned about the reported desire of Lieut. Gen. Walter B. Smith to give up his post of Ambassador to Russia, the President said he still was trying to per-

(Continued on Page 2, Column 8)

Marseille Just Doesn't Know Extent Of Marshall Plan Aid

Mr. McCardell is abroad to report on what is happening to Marshall plan goods. His dispatches appear from time to time.

By LEE McCARDELL
[*Sun Staff Correspondent*]

Marseille, France, March 24—More than $200,000,000 worth of wheat, flour, coal, petroleum and petroleum products were imported by France last year under the Marshall plan.

In terms of dollars these commodities represented the largest import items on the French recovery program. In terms of tonnage, wheat, flour, coal and petroleum were the biggest bulk cargoes unloaded here at Marseille, the leading port of France.

But nobody in Marseille seems to know how much of this cargo was financed by Marshall plan dollars. A Swiss firm of accountants, retained by the ECA mission to France to make spot checks of incoming shipments, doesn't know. The American consulate doesn't know.

Coal Cargo In Doubt

A Greek tramp freighter, in from Norfolk, Va., has just unloaded a cargo of coal here. Was this coal Marshall plan coal? Presumably, but no one on the dock knew for sure.

Port authorities assume that most of the wheat, coal and petroleum imports unloaded here last year were Marshall plan goods. If that is true, Marseille received in the neighborhood of 3,000,000 tons of petroleum, 800,000 tons of coal and 400,000 tons of wheat and flour purchased with American aid.

Altogether these imports accounted for more than half of the port's incoming freight traffic of 6,609,635 metric tons.

Bulk Cargo Can't Be Marked

"But no one knows when Marshall plan commodities of this sort are coming in," says Georges E. Reavel, commercial attache of the port authority. "It is rather practical that we should know. But bulk cargoes cannot be marked, and so we have no means of telling whether or not they represent American aid.

"I would say that the education of the people of Marseille in regard to the Marshall plan is just beginning. For a long while they did not know what it meant. It looked to them like a donation—like UNRRA goods. It is difficult to

(Continued on Page 8, Column 3)

Laurence Olivier, Jane Wyman Win Oscars For Movie Acting

Hollywood, Cal., March 24 (AP)—"Hamlet," which William Shakespeare wrote and Laurence Olivier brought to film life, almost swept the boards tonight for 1948's Academy awards.

It took the coveted Oscars as the best picture, for Olivier as the best actor, for art direction, set decoration and costume design.

Lovely Jane Wyman won the feminine award for her plain but appealing deaf mute in "Johnny Belinda," for Warner Brothers.

Olivier Not Present

"Hamlet" is the first British picture to win this country's top award. It was made for J. Arthur Rank, the English film mogul, and released in this country by Universal-International.

Douglas Fairbanks, Jr., accepted the Oscar for "Hamlet," and said "I am sure that Larry (Olivier), who lived and worked among us so long, must feel that of all the awards he has received, none can be more gratifying than this one by his chosen profession."

Olivier was not present to receive his award. Miss Wyman declared: "I accept this award very gratefully for keeping my mouth shut once. I think I'll do it again."

12-Year-Old Honored

A miniature statuette, a special award, went to Ivan Jandl for the best juvenile performance of the year. The 12-year-old was the sensation of the Swiss-made "The Search." He is the son of Mr. and Mrs. Klement Jandl, of Prague.

John Huston was named the best director for "The Treasure of Sierra Madre."

Walter Huston won the Oscar for the best male supporting performance of the year in this same film, which was directed by his

(Continued on Page 4, Column 4)

Britain In The Air

Britain's Royal Air Force thinks it has the best fighter planes in the world. It has placed the emphasis upon jet engines and is trying out all possible designs.

Look for a full page of pictures with explanatory text by Gerald Griffin, chief of the London Bureau of *The Sun*, in the Features Section of

THE SUNDAY SUN

On Other Pages

Weather Forecast

Some cloudiness and milder today; generally fair; little change in temperature tomorrow. Yesterday's temperatures: Highest, 73, lowest, 52 Page 39

THE SUN FINAL

Registered United States Patent Office

Vol. 225—No. 111—F | PAID CIRCULATION AUGUST MORNING 172,053 EVENING 187,767 359,820 ‖ SUNDAY 301,535 | BALTIMORE, THURSDAY, SEPTEMBER 22, 1949 | Entered as second-class matter at Baltimore Post Office | Zone 3 | 40 Pages | 5 Cents

Vishinsky Rebuffs U.S. Plea On Greek Issue

FINDS FAULT IN RULE OF THAT NATION

Also Calls For An End To Anglo-American 'Intervention' There

By PAUL W. WARD
[Sun Staff Correspondent]

Flushing Meadow, N.Y., Sept. 21 Andrei Y. Vishinsky, Stalin's Foreign Minister, rebuffed here this afternoon an appeal that Dean Acheson, Secretary of State, had made a few hours earlier for Soviet co-operation in settling the Greek problem.

Fighting in the steering committee of the United Nations General Assembly to keep that problem from being discussed by the world organization, Vishinsky declared that Greece's territorial integrity is not threatened.

He added that, instead of the measures advocated by Acheson to ease the situation there, what is needed is an end to the "monarcho-fascist" regime in Greece and of British and American "intervention" there.

Same Line Indicated

Meanwhile, with Vishinsky addressing himself to this and other pending issues in a fashion suggesting he will follow in this 1949 session of the General Assembly the same intransigent line the Stalinites have pursued at past annual meetings, there were these other developments here:

1. The United Nations' nine-power Balkans commission filed a report declaring "the Greek armed forces have eliminated organized guerrilla resistance along the northern borders of Greece" and noting "with concern the increased support being extended to the Greek guerrillas by certain states not bordering upon Greece, in particular Romania."

Slavs Seek Council Post

2. The delegation from Yugoslavia, which the commission said "has implemented its recently declared policy of closing its frontier with Greece, was found maneuvering behind the scenes here to get one of Tito's envoys elected to a United Nations Security Council seat which is now held by the Ukrainian S.S.R. and normally would go to a Soviet satellite.

3. Assembly anterooms buzzed with speculation on whether Mao Tze-tung's proclamation today of a Communist government for China would be followed by a move to supplant the Chinese Nationalist Government's representatives in the United Nations General Assembly and Security Council with envoys of Mao's regime.

Calendar Plan Dropped

4. It was noted in that connection that in anticipation of such a possible move the United States yesterday—along with Russia—had maneuvered itself into a seat on the Assembly's credentials committee which the big powers ordinarily eschew and where the non-Communist states now hold seven out of nine votes.

5. To the delight of the Israeli delegation, the steering committee, at American behest and by a tie vote, dropped from the Assembly's agenda a Panamanian proposal to establish throughout the world a fixed, uniform and invariable calendar.

Anti-Veto Move Withdrawn

6. To the delight of members of the United Nations secretariat and others professionally interested in keeping the Assembly's 1949 session as placid as possible, Argentina withdrew its proposal for a general conference to revise the world organization's Charter and get rid of the unilateral veto power it gives to Russia and the other

(Continued on Page 10, Column 5)

On Other Pages

Maybe Waldorf Guest Just Has Tomato Surplus

New York, Sept. 21 (AP)—Somebody at the Waldorf-Astoria Hotel either likes Ernest Bevin, dislikes Irishmen, hates noise or just has a basketful of tomatoes to get rid of.

For the third night in a row, chanting "American-Irish Minutemen of 1949" paraded around the big hotel where the British Foreign Minister is staying.

For the second night in a row, from a high window of the Waldorf, the pickets were greeted with tomatoes.

The Irish have said they will picket every day Bevin is here, which will be about five or six more days.

Since the police were unable to find out which window the tomatoes came from, it was not known whether the supply will last that long.

REDS SET UP CHINA REGIME

Early Bid For International Recognition Expected

San Francisco, Sept. 21 (AP)—The Chinese Communists, with more than half of China's 457,000,000 population under their red banner, announced today they had established "the Peoples Republic of China."

The long-expected announcement was made in Peiping by Mao Tze-tung, Communist leader and a peasant's son who 27 years ago helped to found the Chinese Communist party.

An early bid for international recognition is expected. This Communist regime now holds dominion over roughly half the land mass of China proper.

Must Unite With Soviet

Mao declared in an address that the "Peoples Republic" must unite internationally "first of all (with) the Soviet Union and the new democratic countries." He meant the Soviet satellites of eastern Europe.

Mao spoke before the opening session of the "Chinese Peoples Political Consultative Conference." The conference was called to set up a central government.

The broadcast was heard here by the Associated Press.

The conference's 635 delegates are a mixture of Communists and non-Communist politicians. They enabled the Communists to raise the facade of a conference representing all phases of Chinese life.

Communists Run Show

But Communist delegates are in the majority, and it is the Communists who run the show.

The conference will select the "Government Council" of the "Peoples Republic," and adopt its "organizational statute" or constitution. If the Central Government follows the pattern of regional Communist governments in China, this council will do the ruling.

Nationalist observers in Canton expect the Communist government to be proclaimed formally on October 10. That is the anniversary of Sun Yat Sen's revolution of 1911 which overthrew the Manchu dynasty. Mao was a teen-age worker in that revolution.

Forerunner Of Revolution

Mao in his speech referred to Sun's revolution as the forerunner of "the peoples (Communist) great revolution."

The Communist leader boasted that Communist armies several million strong had "defeated the Kuomintang (Nationalist party) reactionary government, which is led by American imperialism."

"Our national defense will be consolidated," Mao said, "and no

(Continued on Page 6, Column 3)

WEST GERMAN REPUBLIC BORN IN CEREMONY

Rites Held In Hotel Where Chamberlain Stayed Before War

By HAROLD A. WILLIAMS
[Sun Staff Correspondent]

Konigswinter, Germany, Sept. 21. The Federal Republic of Germany, the world's newest state, was officially created shortly after 11 o'clock this morning in a simple, dignified ceremony during which Konrad Adenauer, Chancellor of the Republic, announced to the Allied high commissioners that his Government was formed.

The Republic was born in a small reception room of Petersberg, a former resort hotel near here, atop one of the storied *Siebengebirge* (Seven Mountains).

From the windows of the reception room the participants could see the historic Rhine below and the town of Bonn, capital of the new Government.

It was here that former Prime Minister Chamberlain stayed just before he conferred with Hitler at the Hotel Dresden in Bad Godesburg, across the Rhine. This talk many historians claim, led to the downfall of Czechoslovakia, a factor in the beginning of World War II which culminated in the surrender of Germany four years ago.

Ministers Presented

Germany formed a Government, after four years occupation by the Allies, when Adenauer and the three Allied high commissioners, standing on a small oriental rug atop a brilliant red carpet, shook hands and the 73-year-old Chancellor, in the stiff, sober fashion of an old-school German, presented his Vice Chancellor and four of his ministers.

The historic event, for which the chairs and tables in the room had been pushed against the paneled walls, was witnessed by members of the high commissioners' staffs and a small group of newspaper men and photographers representing the world's press.

The only American observer present was Paul Patterson, president of the A.S. Abell Company, publishers of the Baltimore *Sunpapers*, who was the guest of John J. McCloy, the United States high commissioner.

After presenting his ministers, Chancellor Adenauer read a short speech which then was translated into French and English.

Stands On Carpet

Adenauer stood on one corner of a small carpet, with the three high commissioners near the other end. Just above his head were two carved figures in the paneling of a pillar. One was a buffoon playing a flute, the other a small flute player standing on the back of a man who was holding his ears and grimacing.

The Chancellor concluded his speech by saying: "If we now turn back to the sources of our European civilization, born of Christianity, then we cannot fail to succeed in restoring the unity of European life in all fields of endeavor. This is the sole effective assurance for maintaining peace."

André Francois-Poncet, French high commissioner, who was the spokesman for the commissioners, replied by saying:

"We are persuaded that you will know well how to guide her (Germany) for the well-being of the individual and for the collective prosperity of her inhabitants through ways of liberty and peace where she will recover the confidence of the other peoples to whom she is united in a community of culture."

During Francois-Poncet's talk,

(Continued on Page 10, Column 1)

Blackmer Ends His 25-Year Exile, Fled Teapot Dome Probe

Boston, Sept. 21 (AP)—Henry M. Blackmer, the Colorado oil tycoon who ran away 25 years ago to escape testifying in the Teapot Dome scandal, came home today to face charges still pending against him.

Quietly, the millionaire fugitive slipped into Boston aboard an Air France trans-Atlantic plane—ending a quarter of a century of self-imposed exile in Europe.

The Justice Department announced the 80-year-old Blackmer was on his way immediately to Denver to enter pleas to 21-year-old income tax evasions, six indictments still pending against him there.

To Answer Charge Next Week

Max Bulkeley, United States district attorney, announced in Denver that Blackmer would appear there early next week to answer charges of income-tax evasion and perjury.

The perjury charges grew out of a Government claim Blackmer's secretary signed and swore to the income-tax returns during the years 1920-21 and 23. The wealthy oil man has maintained his innocence through his years of exile on the grounds he had nothing to do with computing the tax or signing the forms.

Air France officials reported a woman they identified as Blackmer's wife, Kaja, was with him on his flight from France. They said she was traveling on a Norwegian passport.

Since fleeing to Europe in 1924, Blackmer has purged himself of some charges against him—paying $60,000 in fines for contempt and settling one income-tax dispute with the Government for $3,670,784.

To Fight Other Charges

Blackmer — whose financial wizardry once brought him the nickname "Child of the gods"—has indicated he would fight the other charges.

There were reports several months ago that negotiations were being conducted with the Justice Department for an understanding which would permit the aged exile to return to the United States.

Tom Clark, the then Attorney General, said at the time that the department had made every effort to extradite Blackmer from France.

Clark added that the department would be glad to see him back in this country any time he was ready

(Continued on Page 3, Column 4)

London Railmen Ignore Slowdown Strike Call

But Threat Of Walkouts Remains In Britain And France In Wake Of Devaluation

Lord Winster says opposition to devaluation of the pound will be based on its timing .... Page 22

U.N. official proposes $5,000,000,000 world food agency for moving farm surpluses to needy nations .... Page 22

London, *Thursday*, Sept. 22 (AP)—London's railwaymen appeared to be working normally early today despite a slowdown strike call for more pay to balance rising costs of living.

The threat of a strike arose both in Britain and France in the wake of currency devaluation.

In London the strike threatened to throw freight yards and subway systems into confusion and delay. But as the midnight deadline passed a British Press Association survey showed that thousands of workers were ignoring the strike call.

Normal At Most Stations

The press association said the station staffs were working normally with the exception of the Bricklayer Arms Station in South London, where some delays appeared. The real test of the strike call, however, was expected to come later in the morning when the underground trains begin to transport millions of workers to their jobs.

The workers want a weekly pay hike equal to $1.40.

Two more nations—Portugal and Luxembourg — joined the devaluation column, which now lists 24 nations.

Belgian Charges Selfishness

Western Germany's Cabinet also decided to devalue, but the decision must be ratified by Allied authorities.

More growls of anger at the steepness of Britain's pound cut last Sunday, when she devalued sterling from $4.03 to $2.80, came from Europe. A Belgian financial expert, who declined use of his name, said the sudden British move was selfish. Maurice Petsche, French Finance Minister, had called the 30.5 per cent British devaluation "commercial war."

The European Parliamentary Union, a private body of legislators of eleven nations, proposed in convention at Venice that western European nations establish a common currency based on the gold standard. The action was suggested by Ferruccio Parri, former Italian Premier.

Disappointed By TUC

Heavy weather faced Britain's Labor Government on the political front. The higher cost of living resulting from devaluation, coupled with a year-old wage-freeze policy, threatened to divorce the Government from many of its 8,000,000 unionized supporters.

However, a Government spokesman said he no longer expected a Conservative motion of censure in Parliament

Sir Stafford Cripps, Chancellor of the Exchequer, was reported disappointed at the lukewarm wait-and-see attitude of the Trades Union Congress, whose general council failed to back devaluation last night. He is to meet the bosses of the congress next Monday to tell them labor must be satisfied with present wages to keep

(Continued on Page 22, Column 5)

350 PROTEST RIOT PROBE IN ALBANY

Crowd Charges 'Whitewash' Of Robeson Concert Battles

Former Communist secretary on trial tells jury there were thousands of Communist clubs while he held office .... Page 4

Albany, N.Y., Sept. 21 (AP)—Paul Robeson partisans marched on the State Capitol today and protested what they called Governor Dewey's "whitewash" of recent mob violence near Peekskill.

There was no disorder here, although a crowd estimated by police at about 3,000 booed and heckled the 350 marchers, most of them from New York City.

Spokesmen for the marchers charged that Dewey, the Ku Klux Klan, Catholic war veterans and "reactionary elements" of the American Legion tried to provoke disorder.

Charge Dewey "Sympathy"

They also accused Dewey of having "deep sympathy" for what they termed "un-American and subversive conduct" by anti-Communist veterans' groups and others who clashed with persons who turned out to hear Robeson, Negro baritone, sing near Peekskill August 27 and September 4.

A five-member delegation of the Peekskill protesters conferred for fifteen minutes in the capitol with Lawrence E. Walsh, Dewey's assistant counsel. They submitted a demand that Dewey remove the Westchester county district attorney, George M. Fanelli, and appoint a "nonpartisan" citizen's committee to investigate the Peekskill riots.

The delegation was headed by O. John Rogge, former United States assistant attorney general, and Paul L. Ross, assistant State chairman of the American Labor party.

Walsh Declines Comment

Walsh had no comment after the conference. Ross said the session was unsatisfactory and that Walsh was "as silent as a Sphinx."

The governor was in New York city. He has ordered a grand jury investigation of the Peekskill incident.

More than 200 city police, armed with riot clubs, screened the marchers from the hecklers in the trudge from the railroad station through the business district to Capitol Hill.

A shoulder-to-shoulder police cordon blocked off the hooting spectators while the marchers held a rally on the Capitol steps. There was no attempt to force the police line.

4 Die In Philadelphia Rooming-House Fire

Philadelphia, *Thursday*, Sept. 22 (AP)—Firemen said four persons including two children, were burned to death in a rooming-house fire early today.

The dead, in addition to a 5-year-old boy and 4-year-old girl, included a man about 40 and a woman about 35, firemen said. The bodies were not identified immediately.

At least three other children and several adults were burned in the blaze which broke out in a four-story rooming-house at 468 North Fourth street.

SYMINGTON SHUNS NAVY B-36 PROBE

Says Previous Engagement Keeps Him From Testifying

By HOWARD NORTON
[Washington Bureau of The Sun]

Washington, Sept. 21—W. Stuart Symington, Secretary for Air, today sidestepped an invitation to answer questions before a navy board of inquiry investigating the B-36 "smear" letter.

The board wanted to ask Symington who he was talking about when he told the House Armed Services Committee that a group of navy men helped concoct the letter.

The invitation was extended after Symington's testimony was flatly contradicted today by Cedric R. Worth, suspended navy official and confessed author of the letter.

Worth testified that the letter was entirely his own work and that no one else in the Navy knew anything about it.

Out-Of-Town Engagement

Symington told the navy board that a previous out-of-town engagement prevented him from appearing tomorrow morning as requested.

Though he did not refuse outright to appear at another time, he suggested instead that the board submit to him questions they desired him to answer and he would consider them on his return to Washington tomorrow.

Admiral Thomas C. Kinkaid, chairman of the inquiry board, earlier had expressed hope that the hearing could be closed if Symington testified tomorrow.

Worth, in his testimony today, also contradicted the sworn testimony of Glenn L. Martin, Baltimore plane maker, that he (Martin) contributed none of the items in the smear letter, and simply verified one minor fact.

Lists Seven Items

Worth listed seven items—some fact and some rumor—which he said Martin supplied.

And he declared that the whole letter originated from a request by Martin for a memorandum on the information contained in it.

Worth said it was his "clear understanding" that Martin wanted the material for Senator Tydings (D., Md.). Tydings has stated that to his knowledge he never saw a copy of the letter.

Revolves On Secret Report

The Symington-Worth conflict apparently revolves around a still-secret report on an Air Force investigation into the authorship of the smear letter.

The Air Secretary, testifying before the House Armed Services Committee, said an Air Force investigation had determined the letter was the product of "a series of individuals who organized themselves into a group."

The "individuals," he indicated, were Navy officers or officials.

But Representative Vinson (D., Ga.), committee chairman, refused to permit him to name the individuals publicly.

The Navy then asked the Air Force for a copy of the report on its B-36 investigation, so that any individuals named in it might be called before the board of inquiry which is currently trying to determine whether any navy personnel helped Worth.

But the Air Force declined to re-

(Continued on Page 2, Column 7)

SENATORS ACT TO BLOCK CUT IN ARMS AID

Morse Will Be Brought On Stretcher To Vote On Military Fund

Johnson eases secrecy on U.S. mobilization program .. Page 12

By PHILIP POTTER
[Washington Bureau of The Sun]

Washington, Sept. 21—Bipartisan foreign policy leaders today were anxiously mustering all their strength against an "economy bloc" drive to cut in half the arms-for-Europe allocation in the $1,314,010,000 foreign military aid bill.

Senator Morse (R., Ore.), who voted with the bipartisan majority when a similar cut was defeated in the combined Foreign Relations-Armed Services Committee by a narrow 13-to-10 margin, will come to the Senate floor on a stretcher tomorrow, presumably to cast his vote for the full $1,000,000,000 asked for European signatories of the Atlantic pact.

He will be brought to the Capitol from the Bethesda Naval Hospital, where he has been recuperating from a fall from his prize-winning stallion at the Oregon State Fair.

See Grave Threat

Indications were that Administration forces and Republican supporters of the arms bill as it came out of committee saw a grave threat in the $500,000,000 cut proposed by Senator George (D., Ga.).

Many observers believed speeches today by George and Senator Byrd (D., Va.) in behalf of the reduction had vastly improved the prospects for at least some cut in the $1,000,000,000 allocation for Western Europe.

Senator Vandenberg (R., Mich.), who supports the full allocation, is known to have told Senator Connally (D., Texas), chairman of the combined committees which worked on the bill, that many Republicans who ordinarily follow his lead on foreign affairs were "wobbly."

Wants Full Amount

Connally, who believes the full amount for our pact allies is "vitally" needed to equip existing Western European forces so they can play their role in the common defense of the North Atlantic area, almost immediately went into a huddle with Senator Lucas (D., Ill.), majority leader.

There was no doubt that they were worried.

Observers noted that many senators were out of the city, some of them—including Senator Tydings (D., Md.), one of the arms program's staunchest supporters—on trips abroad, and believed this might have a vital bearing on the outcome when the George amendment is voted on tomorrow evening.

To Start At 6 P.M.

Senator Lucas obtained unanimous consent today for votes starting at 6 P.M. tomorrow on amendments and final passage of the measure under an agreement dividing the time from noon on equally between supporters and opponents of the full amount.

Senator Dulles (R., N.Y.), who teamed with Vandenberg in securing in committee the adoption of an amendment lopping $160,990,000 off the $1,160,990,000 asked by the President for pact nations, interrupted his campaign tour of New York to appear before the Senate today in support of the $1,000,000,000 figure.

"I think that the amount proposed is reasonably related to the

(Continued on Page 9, Column 1)

Pittsburgh's Golden Triangle New Rockefeller Center Site

Pittsburgh, Sept. 21 (AP)—Twenty-three acres of blighted area in Pittsburgh's celebrated Golden Triangle are going to be turned into a Rockefeller Center far more elaborate than New York's.

The biggest development program in this steel and coal capital's history became a reality today with disclosure the Equitable Life Assurance Company of New York agreed to help finance it.

This "Gateway Center," as it will be called because of Pittsburgh's fame as Gateway to the West, will cost $50,000,000 as a starter for three new 20-story skyscraper office buildings alone. Additional millions will go into ultimate construction projects with the total reaching possibly $100,000,000.

Located Between Rivers

The gigantic new commercial center will be located in the historic point carved out by the Allegheny and Monongahela rivers merging to form the Ohio.

Here on the point is located historic Fort Pitt dating back to pre-Revolutionary War days when the English finally succeeded in driving out the French and claiming the rich western Pennsylvania territory.

This downtown section of a few square miles became known as the Golden Triangle with Pittsburgh's development into a steel and coal metropolis. The Mellon financial empire and other family fortunes were made there.

Already nine major industrial firms headed by Mellon National Bank and Westinghouse are seeking space in the proposed three new commercial center office buildings which will provide 60 acres of office and store space. Completion and occupancy is expected in 1952.

Project consultants won tentative approval of a plan to "outdo New York's Radio City" by separating the buildings with parks and not using more than twenty per cent of the land for buildings.

Robert Dowling, of City Investing Company of New York, adviser to Equitable on the undertaking, explained:

"In this project, the architects will be released from the straight-jacket of 60-foot streets and 200-foot city blocks.

Room For 9 Skyscrapers

"We want Gateway Center to be as far ahead of Rockfeller Center as that development was ahead of other buildings when it was built.

"We have open minds about everything — plan, exterior design and materials."

The entire redevelopment area stretching from river to river will have room for nine skyscrapers. Plans have been two years in the making.

5,000 Halt Work At 3 Pittsburgh Area Steel Plants

Pittsburgh, Sept. 21 (AP)—More than 5,000 CIO United Steelworkers quit work today in three district steel plants.

Officials of two of the companies said they believed the walkouts are unauthorized. One spokesman said he thought the men are "jittery over the whole situation in the steel industry."

Union spokesmen could not be reached for comment. Many of the steelworkers' top executives, including President Philip Murray, are en route to Pittsburgh. Tomorrow they will act on President Truman's request that the midnight Saturday strike deadline be extended six days.

The walkouts occurred at Universal Cyclops Steel Company at near-by Bridgeville, where 1,400 are employed; Superior Steel Company in suburban Carnegie, which has 1,050 employés, and at the Ambridge Bridge Company's works at Ambridge, where 2,800 went out.

MINE OWNERS LIMIT TALKS

Tell Lewis New Contract Must Await Steel Settlement

Clearfield, Pa., Sept. 21 (AP)—State Police Sergeant James Stuck said tonight a score of additional State policemen have been ordered here to preserve order in the Clearfield county coal fields. The order, Stuck said, came from Gov. James H. Duff after motorized roving pickets today closed four non-union mining operations near Shawville.

White Sulphur Springs, W.Va., Sept. 21 (AP)—It looked today as if a settlement of the current crisis in coal may wait until after the steel industry labor dispute is decided.

Northern and Western coal operators resumed negotiations for a new contract with John L. Lewis and his United Mine Workers here.

However, they told him quickly that they would not discuss specific terms on any new contract until the dispute in the steel industry has been cleared up.

These operators, representing about one half of the nation's soft-coal production, feel that any new steel contract might set a pattern for industry as a whole.

Stand Provokes Lewis

The stand of the operators provoked Lewis at a three-hour session but he refused to comment on the development.

The chief negotiator for Northern operators, George H. Love, of the huge Pittsburgh Consolidation Coal Company, was absent. He is expected to attend tomorrow's meeting. Union and industry representatives expect Lewis to deliver one of his famous verbal blasts at the operators then.

Meanwhile, there were reports from Bluefield, W. Va., that the few Southern producers, who withheld their 20-cent-per-ton royalty payments to the Miners' Welfare Fund in the absence of a contract, now intend to pay up.

Suspension Voted By Trustees

The 480,000 soft and hard coal miners walked out of the pits Monday after trustees of the fund announced suspension of pension and distress payments.

The suspension was voted by the trustees of the fund. Lewis and Senator Bridges (R., N.H.) voted to suspend payments. Ezra Van

(Continued on Page 2, Column 2)

U.S. STEEL O.K.'S TRUCE EXTENSION

Union Plans To Follow Suit—Strike Deadline Now October 1

Ford negotiators hold first night parley .... Page 2

Industries of ten states feel effect of rail strike .... Page 2

By JOSEPH H. SHORT
[Washington Bureau of The Sun]

Washington, Sept. 21—President Truman's request for a six-day extension of the steel strike truce was accepted immediately today by United States Steel Corporation, and labor circles indicated the United Steel Workers (CIO) would follow suit.

It thus appeared that the threatened strike would be postponed until October 1 and Government circles felt there was a good chance it never would occur.

The union's formal response to Mr. Truman would not be made, it was said, until after Philip Murray, USW president, met in Pittsburgh at 10 A.M. tomorrow with the union's wage policy committee.

Both Sides Pleased

Union leaders, however, appeared happy over the presidential intervention. Murray himself said, before leaving for Pittsburgh, that he interpreted the Chief Executive's letter to himself and the steel companies as supporting the union's demand for a 10-cent pension-insurance formula.

At the same time, United States Steel was pleased with Mr. Truman's request for immediate resumption of collective bargaining.

The strike truce was to have ended at 12.01 A.M., Sunday, shutting down the nation's largest manufacturing industry. Prior to the President's latest move some of the companies had commenced to bank their fires.

Ching Calls On Truman

Against this depressing background, Cyrus S. Ching, Federal mediation director, made a late-morning unannounced call on Mr. Truman.

Ching came out of the President's office with a big grin on his face. "Just quote me as saying, 'I came out smiling.'" Ching said.

Shortly afterward, the White House press office disclosed that the Chief Executive had given Ching a letter addressed to the parties in the steel dispute.

The letter asked for a postponement of the strike deadline until 12.01 A.M., Saturday, October 1, to permit a resumption of bargaining and commended to the disputants the recommendations of Mr. Truman's Steel Industry Board.

Board Rejected Wage Boost

That board turned down the union's request for a 12½-cents-an-hour wage increase, saying a national fourth round of wage rises would be unwise, but recommended a social insurance-pension program to cost the companies no more than 10 cents per hour per man.

The United Steel Workers, whose original demands would have cost the companies 30 cents, accepted the board formula in full but the companies refused to go further than agree to resume bargaining on social insurance and pensions.

Murray thereupon announced the union would strike. There would be no further bargaining, the USW president declared, until the companies accepted the board's report.

Pensions A Stumbling Block

The stumbling block was the board's suggestion that social insurance and pensions be provided solely from company funds, with no contribution from employés. The board proposed this as "a part of normal business costs to take care of temporary and permanent depreciation in the 'human' machine."

Even with the prospect of an immediate resumption of bargaining that obstacle must be surmounted. The union indicated it would not budge from the principle of company-financed security.

On the other hand, the companies described this as "the major issue" between the disputants and took the position that "any lasting plan of social insurance must be

(Continued on Page 2, Column 5)

I Christened The Emma Giles

More than 62 years ago a 5-year-old girl swung a champagne bottle against the side of a steamer named after her.

The band played "Whoa, Emma" and the Emma Giles, one of Baltimore's most popular excursion boats, slid down the ways.

Emma Giles Parker recalls those days and the launching of her namesake in The Magazine section of

THE SUNDAY SUN

Weather Forecast
Partly cloudy, warm and humid today; scattered showers in afternoon and night. Yesterday's temperatures: Highest, 78; lowest, 65; mean, 72 .... Page 33

THE SUN

FINAL

Registered United States Patent Office

Vol. 227—No. 31—F | PAID CIRCULATION IN MAY MORNING, 174,827 EVENING, 197,366 372,193 ‖ SUNDAY 312,326 | BALTIMORE, WEDNESDAY, JUNE 21, 1950 | Entered as second-class matter at Baltimore Post Office | Zone 3 | 34 Pages | 5 Cents

Senate Votes 100% Increase In Social Security Benefits

Governors Hail Acheson Defense Of State Department

DEMOCRATS, REPUBLICANS SAY SECRETARY INSPIRED CONFIDENCE BY ANSWERS

Hurley Tells Senate Probers There Would Be 'No Point' In Testimony Unless Government Releases Official Documents To Him

San Francisco, June 20 (AP)—Federal Judge George B. Harris today signed a formal decree revoking the United States citizenship of Harry Bridges—convicted in April of making a false statement in his 1945 naturalization proceedings.

But the longshore leader's lawyers immediately filed notice of appeal. Judge Harris said this automatically postponed Bridges's reverting to alien status while the appeal was in the courts.

Acheson

By DEWEY L. FLEMING
[*Chief of the Washington Bureau*]

White Sulphur Springs, W.Va., June 20—Dean Acheson, Secretary of State, today apparently went a long way toward relieving, if not removing, fears of the country's state governors on the score of Communist influence in the department over which he presides.

For nearly three hours the Secretary submitted to searching examination by the governors, here for their forty-second annual conference, and when the session was over no governor could be found who was critical of the Cabinet officer's presentation or who professed any lingering apprehension about the loyalty and trustworthiness of his department personnel.

Governor Lane Presides

On the contrary, Republican and Democratic governors alike declared the Secretary had been extremely frank and informative and expressed the opinion that he had inspired the confidence of the group in himself and his department.

Governor Lane of Maryland presided over the session, two hours of which were conducted behind closed doors, and at its conclusion he commented:

"The governors feel a definite confidence in the State Department and its leadership. It was the frankest discussion of the foreign situation we have ever heard, and we have a desire to help in the unification of public opinion sorely needed today."

Formal Motion Possible

The unanimity of the verdict in Acheson's favor suggested the possibility that a formal expression of confidence in him will figure in resolutions in preparation for consideration at the final conference session tomorrow.

One Republican governor who keeps himself well informed on the conduct of foreign policy but who did not wish to be quoted on today's session said Mr. Acheson "swept them all" with his handling of the barrage of questions, some of which he described as "pretty tough."

Governor Dewey of New York pronounced the discussion "very informative" and remarked that it "covered a lot of ground." Governor Warren of California said it was "a wholesome experience."

Driscoll Sees Confidence Rise

Governor Driscoll of New Jersey gave it as his opinion that confidence in the State Department had been "increased" by the frank exchange of information.

This was the tenor of all comment, and governors took pains to point out that the Secretary responded frankly, explicitly and patiently to all manner of questions.

They also noted appreciation of the fact that Mr. Acheson brought staff experts with him to assist in answering questions, including Philip C. Jessup, Ambassador at Large; John Sherman Cooper, special adviser to the Secretary, and Carlyle Humelsine, assistant to John Peurifoy, State Department security officer.

Tells Of "Point Four"

Secretary Acheson, whose preliminary talk to the Governors was an exposition of so-called "Point Four" — technical assistance in

(Continued on Page 6, Column 4)

Hurley

By WILLIAM KNIGHTON, JR.
[*Washington Bureau of The Sun*]

Washington, June 20—Maj. Gen. Patrick J. Hurley, USA (retired), former Ambassador to China, today informed Senate loyalty investigators there would be "no point" in his testifying before the Tydings subcommittee unless the State Department released to him documents denied him five years ago.

Hurley, in a telephone conversation with Senator Tydings (D., Md.), also said he had "no direct information" concerning the *Amerasia* stolen documents case upon which the committee now is concentrating.

Simultaneously with the Tydings release of the two-paragraph telephonic statement dictated to him by Hurley, the Marylander approved a recommendation that Philip Jaffe, former editor of the defunct magazine *Amerasia*, be cited for contempt for refusing to answer questions before his committee.

Follows Accusations

The Hurley statement came just 24 hours after he had issued a blast at his home in Santa Fe, N.M., in which he said that "certain officials and employés of the State Department did steal and give or sell top-secret documents to the *Amerasia* Communist-front, anti-American group." Committeemen immediately announced that Hurley should be called to testify.

But this afternoon, Tydings, in a typewritten statement said:

"General Hurley just advised me by telephone as follows:

"'I have no direct information concerning the *Amerasia* matter as I was out of the country most of the time when this affair took place.

"No Point In My Coming"

"'In regard to the testimony on other matters before your committee, unless the State Department makes available and decodes the documents which I requested be furnished five years ago, there would be no point in my coming and telling a second time what I have already told without the documents five years ago to the Senate Foreign Relations Committee.'"

Under the circumstances, Tydings said, the soldier-diplomat, who has twice unsuccessfully run for the United States Senate in New Mexico on the Republican ticket, would not be called to testify.

Hurley was referring to his appearance before the committee shortly after he had resigned as Ambassador to China in 1945 after charging that certain State Depart-

(Continued on Page 6, Column 6)

Religion Lacks Humor, Lords Told

London, June 20 (AP) — Baron Mountevans told the House of Lords tonight religion is suffering from a lack of humor.

This could be overcome, he said, by "snappier prayers." He suggested the following:

"God, *give me sympathy and common sense*

"*And help me home with courage high.*

"God, *give me calm and confidence*

"*And please—a twinkle in my eye.*"

SCHUMAN PLAN MOVE STARTED BY CHURCHILL

Resolution Of Tories And Liberals Asks British Participation

Janetta Somerset reports from Paris that the first six-nation Schuman meeting discusses broad policy .... *Page 5*

By HOWARD NORTON
[*London Bureau of The Sun*]

London, June 20 — Winston Churchill tonight launched an effort to take part in the Schuman-plan conference which opened in Paris today.

The Conservative leader is attempting to accomplish this by having the House of Commons, in effect, order the Government to join the talks by a majority vote.

He has the full support of the Liberal party, and it is confidently believed that he will also get support from some Labor party members, who will at least refrain from voting against the proposal.

Given Even Chance

He is given about an even chance of putting it across.

Churchill opened his maneuver tonight by introducing a resolution in Commons. After a conference this afternoon, Clement Davies, parliamentary leader of the Liberal party, agreed to be co-sponsor of the motion with the Tory chief.

The motion is on the calendar to be debated and voted on Monday.

As introduced by Churchill, it reads:

"*Be it resolved*, That this House requests his Majesty's Government, in the interests of peace and full employment, to accept the invitation to take part in discussions on the Schuman plan, subject to the same condition as that made by the Netherlands Government; namely, that if the discussions show the plan not to be practicable, freedom of action is reserved."

Most Unpredictable Vote

Uncertainties on both sides of the House combine to make this forthcoming vote the most unpredictable of the present session.

Differences within the Labor party already have broken into public print. One prominent member, Ronald Mackay, denounced the Labor party's rejection of European co-operation in the bitterest terms in a letter to a London paper yesterday.

He called the document "deplorable in every respect," and branded it as dogmatic, inaccurate and complacent.

After that public outburst, observers do not see how he could possibly vote with his party against the Tory motion. And it is known that there are others in the party who feel the same way, though they have not spoken up so boldly.

Only Three Or Four Needed

If all the Tories and all the Liberals vote, it will take only three or four disaffections among the Laborites to put the motion across.

But there are also chances of disaffections among the Tories. Some of them do not like the Schuman plan and probably would vote for the Churchill motion only if they are convinced by doing so that they are not committing Britain to any part of it but are merely helping strengthen the chance of defeating the Government.

It is the most wide-open situation that has arisen in the present Parliament and nobody will predict the outcome beyond saying that it could go either way.

King's Nephew Selling Third Of His Estate To Pay Taxes

Leeds, England, June 20 (AP)—A nephew of King George, the Earl of Harewood, started selling off one third of his ancestral estate at auction today to pay inheritance taxes.

Most of the happy buyers were his old tenants—farmers and tradespeople. One item up for sale is the village pub at Rigton, population 364.

The 27-year-old Earl is eleventh in the line of succession to the throne through his mother, the Princess Royal, daughter of the late King George V and sister of the reigning George VI.

The royal mother and son are keeping the ancestral seat, Harewood house.

51 Parcels Sold In Day

Announcements that 7,000 of his 22,000 acres would be put on the block said the Earl was forced to break up his holdings by "the burden of death duties"—inheritance taxes.

Such assessments against the estate that went to the young Earl when his father died in 1947 amounted to about one third of the estate's valuation of 549,120 pounds sterling—$2,196,480 at the rate of exchange then prevailing.

Fifty-one parcels sold today for the equivalent of $426,272, and 48 others will be disposed of later.

The Earl had told tenants he would like to have them bid in the homes and fields they have rented.

Family Worked Area 300 Years

Mrs. Annie Mary Ridsale, 83, bought the cottage she has lived in for 40 years. When it was knocked down to her for $588, she said: "I am so happy I could walk home the 10 miles from Leeds."

The cottage is in East Keswick, a village of 490 people. The Post Office there with 6½ acres went for $7,420 and the shoemaker bought his shop for $168.

One tenant paid $33,880 for two farms his family has worked on or around for 300 years.

Single farms brought as much as $23,100 for 175 acres with a house. Two others were withdrawn from sale because bidding was too low. Two tenants were unsuccessful bidders for their farms. A King George III-period stone house, dating from American Revolutionary times, brought $5,880.

The Earl lives with his Vienna-born bride of eight months in London, where he is editor of an opera magazine.

108 Globe-Circling D.P.'s Win Hope Of U.S. Refuge

Truman Extends Citizenship Possibility To Band Now Awaiting Return To Germany

By ROBERT W. RUTH
[*Washington Bureau of The Sun*]

Washington, June 20—President Truman today extended the possibility of United States citizenship to 108 European refugees who fled Germany under Nazi persecution, trekked across Asia to Shanghai, fled the Communists there, and are now in New York city awaiting return to the Germany most of them left twelve years ago.

When they get back they will have circled the globe in search of a home. As dismal as their return to Germany might seem, it will be gladdened by the knowledge that the highest American authorities are keeping an eye on their welfare.

And on some bright tomorrow many of these much-displaced refugees will move on for the last time: To come back to the United States to acquire citizenship here.

Orders Temporary Haven

The President intervened today to direct that John J. McCloy, High Commissioner for Germany, prepare a temporary haven in an International Refugee Organization camp until they can be processed under the new Displaced Persons Act.

The amendments to the law which the Executive signed last week require issuance of visas by consular officers after extensive screening. But provisions stipulating that immigrants must obtain United States visas outside the country still stand.

None of the 108 refugees—all but three of them Jews—has a visa. The Government canvassed all the courses open and came to the conclusion that the "most convenient and expeditious method of processing this group would be to send them on an IRO vessel to a camp in Germany where they could be accommodated satisfactorily during the period of processing."

Contrary To Interests

The White House said other possible destinations, some closer than Germany, were considered but were dropped for various reasons. Some countries refused permission for temporary entry. Problems of transportation and the inadequacy of processing facilities were weighed.

A further stay—the refugees have already been granted two—was regarded as contrary to their interests. It would lead only to a delay in arrangements now going on under Donald Kingsley, IRO director.

The story of these wanderers started when Hitler began his pogroms around 1938. According to Herb McGushin, of the IRO office here, the 108 fled Germany, Austria and Italy and headed eastward. He said they utilized "underground" methods of travel and finally arrived in Shanghai.

Impossible To Hold Jobs

Taking only the belongings they could carry, they traveled overland. McGushin, who accompanied the group across this country, knew of no cases of passage by sea.

However, once established in Shanghai they met new reverses. The Chinese Communists descended on the city. Although there was no persecution from then on it was impossible to do business or to hold jobs.

Not long ago the refugees arrived

(Continued on Page 2, Column 2)

EISENHOWER'S O.K. OF INSURANCE CITED

Army Finance Probers Told Of 1946 Action

Washington, June 20 (AP)—House investigators were told today that Gen. Dwight D. Eisenhower approved the formation of a private group insurance plan for army officers in 1946.

There was evidence, too, that Eisenhower, who then was Chief of Staff, was invited to head the organization but turned it down because of the press of other duties.

A House Armed Services subcommittee is looking into the insurance plan as part of its investigation of alleged irregularities at the army finance center at St. Louis.

Managed By Finance Chief

A House Civil Service subcommittee, which also investigated the finance center, reported that the insurance business was managed for more than two years by Maj. Gen. William H. Kasten, now retired but then on active duty as army finance chief.

Kasten testified at today's hearing that he never devoted any of his regular duty time to the insurance organization, but did work on it at nights and during week ends.

The organization, known as the Armed Forces Mutual Benefit Association, now is a $44,300,000 concern handling $10,000 life insurance policies for 4,430 officer members.

Kasten, now secretary-treasurer of the association at a salary of $12,000 a year, testified that the association was formed December 5, 1946 "with the knowledge and approval of the Chief of Staff."

Always Paid Own Bills

At first it had headquarters in an army structure near the Washington Airport, and later at finance section headquarters in the Pentagon Building. But Kasten said the association always paid for its stationery, postage and secretarial help, and since last year has had its offices in a Washington office building.

He said that none of the army officers on the association's board of directors receive any compensation. He said he himself began drawing a salary only after he retired from the Army and took the secretary-treasurer position.

Through Regular Companies

The association arranges for group insurance through regular life insurance companies. At the start, Equitable Life Insurance Company wrote the insurance, but later the association switched to the John Hancock and the State Mutual Insurance companies.

Lieut. Gen. Edwin Rawlings, Air Force Deputy Chief of Staff and now president of the association, testified that $525,000 has been paid out in benefits.

The committee will go into the matter further Thursday. Kasten was instructed to return for additional questioning.

LAUSCHE SHOCKS OHIO DEMOCRATS

Party Chiefs Fear Pro-Taft Talk Will Hurt Governor

Columbus, Ohio, June 20 (AP)—Ohio Democrats were stunned today by a hint that their party leader—Gov. Frank J. Lausche—might vote for the Republican senator, Robert A. Taft.

Lausche in a frank statement didn't say he would; but he didn't say he wouldn't.

He said in White Sulphur Springs, W.Va., that "my general disposition would be to vote for the Democratic candidate for United States senator," Joseph T. Ferguson. Then he added:

"I will vote, when I determine the issues, for the candidate I believe will serve the nation best. If I decide that candidate is Ferguson, I will vote for him. If I believe it is Taft, I will vote for him. I will not allow my party interest to overcome my interest in my country."

Held Political Heresy

Everybody granted that Governor Lausche is privileged to vote for whom he pleases.

But in the opinion of Democratic party workers, striving to elect all their candidates, Lausche's position amounted to sheer political heresy.

And the position was taken by their titular State leader, who is asking them to give him a third term as Governor.

At White Sulphur Springs, Lausche tonight shrugged off thinly veiled Democratic criticism of his hint that he might support Taft for re-election.

To Keep Them Confused

At the same time, Lausche made it plain in remarks that he intends to keep confused for some time to come, everybody in Ohio and elsewhere who is interested in his unorthodox statement that he might not vote for Ferguson.

Lausche only grinned when he was told that William Boyle, Jr., the Democratic National Chairman, had said in Columbus that "any official has a right to vote for anyone he wants."

"That's nice of him to say that," Lausche said.

Albert A. Horstman, Ohio national committeeman, and India Edwards, vice chairman of the Democratic National Committee, followed Boyle's line publicly. But there was little doubt they didn't have much patience with Lausche's statement.

Declines To Comment

The Ohio Governor, who is known for his independence, wouldn't comment on Ferguson's statement that "if I quit campaigning now Taft never could catch up with me—but I'm not going to quit."

The Lausche statement dropped like a bomb on a conference of national and State Democratic leaders in Columbus. The meeting

(Continued on Page 5, Column 4)

CORPORATION TAX SPEEDUP IS APPROVED

House Group Would Bring In $4,200,000,000 Ahead Of Time

Washington, June 20 (AP)—A corporation income tax "speedup," to channel about $4,200,000,000 into the Treasury ahead of time over the next five fiscal years, was approved today by the House Ways and Means Committee.

This completed committee action on the $1,010,000,000 excise tax slashing bill, whose authors now consider it veto-proof. The measure, which took almost five months to write, was headed toward the House for a vote there probably on next Wednesday.

Cuts May Come Sept. 1

The excise cuts, if the bill becomes law, probably will be effective September 1.

The speedup of corporation tax payments was approved one day after the committee voted to put $433,000,000 new taxes a year on big corporations.

Somewhat similar to the pay-as-you-go system now in effect for individual taxpayers, the corporation speedup would not, in the long run, bring more cash into the Treasury. But it would bring it in sooner and help brighten the Government's annual book-balancing.

Gradually Changes Due Dates

Offered by Representative Mills (D., Ark.), the speedup would gradually change the dates that corporation taxes are due, so that by the end of five years corporations on a calendar year basis would pay all their income taxes by June 15 on their income of the previous year.

The corporations now can spread their taxes on last year's income over four quarterly payments during the following year. The speedup would ultimately require payment of last year's taxes within six months, instead of a year.

Although the plan involves no new tax obligations its effect would be to crowd about $800,000,000 extra into the Treasury during the fiscal year ending June 30, 1951. This, together with other new revenue found by the committee, is figured to bring in about $600,000,000 more than the proposed $1,010,000,000 excise cut.

Thus, the bill would more than meet President Truman's requirement that any excise cut must be accompanied by new revenue to offset the excise loss. He has said he will veto any tax bill that doesn't do that.

House Leaders Confident

House leaders confidently predicted House passage of the legislation next week. Senator Lucas (Ill.), Democratic leader, said he believes the Senate will pass it also—in time for Congress to adjourn by July 31.

There may be some lively debate, however.

The excise cuts cover fur coats, movies, jewelry, travel tickets, luggage, telephones, tires, tubes, baby bottle warmers and scores of other items.

Under Mr. Truman's threat to veto the bill, unless it made up in new revenue the amounts lost by excise cuts, the committee turned to corporations as the principal source for such offsetting income.

The Mills speedup is a complicated plan that moves the corporations gradually from the present system of four quarterly payments this year on last year's tax to a

(Continued on Page 2, Column 8)

Judy Garland Slashes Throat With Glass; Wound Is 'Minor'

Hollywood, Cal., June 20 (AP)—Despair over career troubles drove Judy Garland to slash her throat with the shattered edge of a water glass, her studio disclosed today.

The troubled star is resting under the care of her physician, who calls the wound "very minor." No stitches were taken.

Dr. Francis Ballard later said that he believed that "there was no intent of self-injury."

He issued this statement:

"I have been treating Miss Garland for several months, during which time she has suffered several emotional reactions. Last evening I was called and, upon examination, discovered several minor scratches on her neck.

Drew Suspension

"I was informed she had inflicted them in a moment of vexation. These required no treatment, and in my opinion there was no intent of self-injury."

The doctor did not enlarge upon his opinion, but a friend said it was based on the fact that Miss Garland readily opened a locked bathroom door on her husband's insistence.

Here's how her studio, M.G.M., told the story:

"Miss Garland had been under

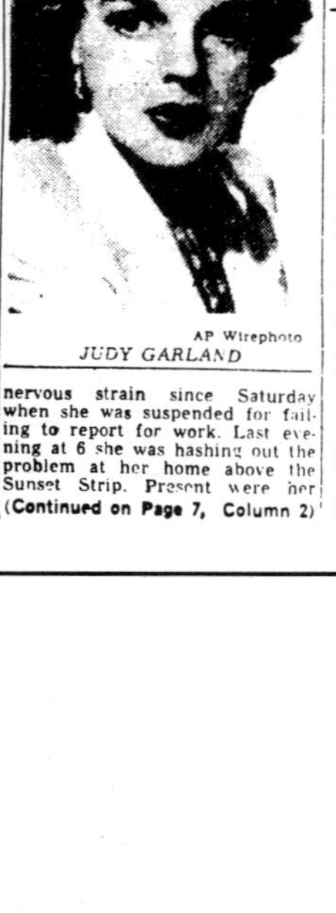

AP Wirephoto
JUDY GARLAND

nervous strain since Saturday when she was suspended for failing to report for work. Last evening at 6 she was hashing out the problem at her home above the Sunset Strip. Present were her

(Continued on Page 7, Column 2)

BILL, PASSED BY 81 TO 2, TAKES 10,000,000 MORE INTO FEDERAL SYSTEM

Boosts Yearly Payments Beyond $2,000,000,000, Raises Pay-Roll Tax Base To $3,600 And Freezes Contribution Rate At 1½%

By RODNEY CROWTHER
[*Washington Bureau of The Sun*]

Washington, June 20—The Senate, by a vote of 81 to 2, today passed legislation to widen the existing social security system and to boost old-age retirement benefits more than 100 per cent.

The two dissenting senators were Butler (R., Neb.) and Cain (R., Wash.).

The bill accepted a House-approved proposal raising the tax base on which social security pay-roll contributions are paid from the present $3,000 to $3,600.

It freezes the pay-roll contribution rate for both employers and employés at 1½ per cent to the end of 1955. The House had voted for a boost to two per cent next January 1.

To Exceed $2,000,000,000

As approved, the legislation will lift benefit payments from the present $900,000,000 a year to well over $2,000,000,000 a year.

It brings into the Social Security system for the first time domestic servants, farm workers, the self-employed and persons working for nonprofit and religious organizations.

The bill, which grants substantially more liberal benefits for retired workers than those in the House bill, now goes to conference between the two bodies. Except for some battles over technical issues and a possible fight over the wider coverage voted by the upper body, the House is expected to accept most of the provisions of the Senate bill.

Before the final vote, the Senate decisively rejected a series of proposals which would have added more than $4,000,000,000 a year to the cost of social security.

What Senate Refused

The Senate refused:

1. To add total and permanent disability coverage to the old-age and survivor insurance system at an estimated additional cost of some $500,000,000 to $750,000,000 a year. The House approved this proposal and the matter will be before the conferees between the two houses when they meet to iron out differences in their respective bills.

2. To approve a special bonus, now in the law at the rate of one per cent, as a special increment, to boost the retirement benefits of workers in accordance with the length of time they have worked in covered employment. The House bill carried a special one half per cent increment for length of coverage. It was estimated that a one per cent increase would cost $1,000,000,000 a year.

3. To reduce the retirement age of all workers, male and female, from 65 under the present law, to 60 years. It was estimated that this would have added at least $3,000,000,000 a year to the cost.

4. To provide that the Federal Government pay one half of the medical costs incurred by states for the recipients of old-age assistance, aid to the blind, and aid to dependent children. This would have boosted the Federal load by $70,000,000 a year.

Bridges Proposal Rejected

One of the final acts of the Senate before approving the bill was to reject a proposal by Senator Bridges (R., N.H.) which would have excused from further payments of social-security taxes persons insured in the system who wish to go on working.

The bill represents the first dras-

(Continued on Page 2, Column 5)

Security Bill Points Listed

[*Washington Bureau of The Sun*]

Washington, June 20—Major provisions of the social-security bill as it passed the Senate late today were:

I.—Coverage:

It extends coverage to about 10,000,000 persons not now insured, lifting the total to about 45,000,000 covered jobs.

The particular groups added included about 5,000,000 self-employed, about 1,000,000 domestic servants, about 1,000,000 agricultural workers and about 1,400,000 employés of state and local governments not now covered by retirement plans, and some 600,000 employés of nonprofit and religious institutions.

It excludes from coverage of the self-employed, physicians, lawyers, dentists, osteopaths, veterinarians, chiropractors, optometrists, Christian Science practitioners, professional engineers, architects, naturopaths and certified public accountants.

II.—Benefits:

Benefits for the 2,900,000 beneficiaries now receiving old-age and survivors insurance benefits would have their monthly payments increased about 85 to 90 per cent on the average.

The average payments for workers now retired would be boosted from $26 a month to $48 or more.

The minimum payments, now $10 under present law, would be increased to $25 except for those workers with a monthly average wage of less than $34 a month, and for them the minimum would be $20.

A new benefit formula is provided under which monthly payments will amount to 50 per cent of the first $100 of average monthly wages plus fifteen per cent of the next $200.

For workers who retire in the next few years the average benefit will be boosted under the bill to around $50 to $55 a month.

Maximum family benefits under the bill are set at $150 compared with a present maximum of $85.

Other benefit liberalizations contained in the bill include those for dependent husbands of women workers and more liberal treatment for children of women workers.

Retired workers, who now are allowed to earn no more than $14.99 a month in any covered em-

(Continued on Page 2, Column 6)

On Other Pages

Weather Forecast
Mostly sunny and cooler today; tomorrow cloudiness and warmer with showers likely. Yesterday's temperatures: Highest, 92; lowest, 72; mean, 82....Page 37

THE SUN

Registered United States Patent Office

FINAL

Vol. 227—No. 37—F | PAID CIRCULATION IN MAY MORNING, 174,827 EVENING, 197,366 372,193 || SUNDAY 312,326 | BALTIMORE, WEDNESDAY, JUNE 28, 1950 | Entered as second-class matter at Baltimore Post Office | Zone 3 | 38 Pages | 5 Cents

U.S. JETS LAUNCH ROCKET, MACHINE GUN ATTACKS ON NORTH KOREA COMMUNISTS

TRUMAN PUTS FUTURE PEACE UP TO STALIN IN KOREAN WAR NOTE

Orders Sea And Air Support For Seoul; Congressmen Give Almost Unanimous Backing To President's Decision

New York, June 27 (AP)—The four major radio broadcasting networks (NBC, CBS, ABC and Mutual) made program changes tonight in order to broadcast President Truman's speech tomorrow at 4.30 P.M. at Washington before the annual convention of the American Newspaper Guild.

There was no indication in Washington of what the Chief Executive's subject would be although it seemed likely he would make some reference to the Korean situation.

Truman

By PAUL W. WARD
[*Washington Bureau of The Sun*]

Washington, June 27—President Truman today ordered United States sea and air forces to the "support" of Communist-beleaguered Korea and almost simultaneously invited Stalin's aid in stopping the fighting there.

By the latter note, which he had the American Ambassador in Moscow deliver to the Soviet Foreign Office, he sought to pin more firmly on the Kremlin responsibility for ensuing events.

The note, in effect, put squarely up to Stalin for decision the issue of whether the Korean crisis shall remain a localized conflict or fan out into a multinational war. It was, accordingly, a rigidly polite note that eschewed the character of an appeal to Stalin and at the same time was devoid of recriminations or ultimata.

Reversal Of Policy

But it formally served notice on the Kremlin of all five of the decisions toward halting the Communist wave in the Pacific area that President Truman—in an abrupt reversal of his Administration's Far Eastern policy—had announced to the world at noon.

Six hours later—when the United States Navy and Air Force had long since swung into action and Stalin presumably had retired for the night—the official Soviet press and radio still kept silent on both the forcing bid President Truman had put before the boss of the Kremlin and on his decisions with respect to the Far Eastern situation.

Taken 14 Hours Earlier

Those decisions — proclaimed some 62 hours after this Government learned of the Communist invasion of South Korea but apparently taken fourteen hours earlier —comprised:

1. Orders for the "United States air and sea forces to give the Korean Government troops cover and support."

2. Abandonment of the policy President Truman announced January 5 of leaving Formosa to its fate and the substitution, instead, of one calling for the United States 7th Fleet to proceed at once to the defense of that island refuge of Chiang Kai-shek and his Nationalist regime, stopping the latter's bombing and blockade of the Chinese mainland in the process.

Mission For Indo-China

3. Directives that United States forces in the Philippines be "strengthened" and American military supplies be rushed to the Philippine Republic's own forces.

4. Orders for a similar speeding up of American military supplies—plus the dispatch of an American "military mission"—to the French

(Continued on Page 10, Column 1)

Congress

By WILLIAM KNIGHTON, JR.
[*Washington Bureau of The Sun*]

Washington, June 27—Visibly aroused by the decision to send military aid to South Korea and Formosa, Congress today rallied behind the action of President Truman almost to a man.

The national legislators, both Republican and Democrats, through statements on and off the floor, showed they were collectively more united on the crisis than at any time since Pearl Harbor.

The consensus of the members was that this country had to make a definite stand against Communist armed aggression at some point and the sooner the better.

The next move, determining whether the "cold war" would in fact become a world-wide "hot war", and not an incident that might be resolved through short military action, was up to the rulers in the Kremlin.

Kem, Watkins Disagree

Senator Lucas (Ill.), Democratic leader, fresh from a White House conference, informed the Senate that negotiations with other nations for their co-operation had been progressing.

In the Senate, only two, both isolationists spoke out flatly against the military action ordered by the President. They were Senators Kem (R., Mo.) and Watkins (R., Utah).

In the House, only Representative Marcantonio (A.L., N.Y.) went on record as opposing it. The New Yorker is a consistent follower of the Communist party line.

It was noted that the three dissenters—Kem, Watkins and Marcantonio—all took the same line: that the action of the President, in ordering military action without the consent of Congress, was unconstitutional.

Bridges Gives Support

Marcantonio, however, went farther in his speech in the House than did the senators, declaring that the effort will fail because the "will for national liberation will not be stopped."

But more significant were the statements by several Republicans, who, while they have supported the bipartisan foreign policy program as far as it went, have been sharply critical of the Administration's policy in the Far East.

One of these, Senator Bridges (R., N.H.) said on leaving the White House conference:

"I approve completely what has been done, it has my support."

On the floor of the Senate, another, Senator Knowland (R., Cal.), told his colleagues:

"I believe the President should have the overwhelming support of all Americans in spite of their party affiliation."

Democratic members praised the sentiments expressed from the GOP side of the chamber with the statement that "this is the time to close ranks."

The President's statement was read to the Senate by Lucas, some of the members learning of the decision then for the first time.

The galleries were crowded, with a section being occupied by large groups of Boy Scouts who came into the chamber in relays.

Speaks In Low Voice

Lucas spoke in such a low, tense voice that upon the first reading it is doubtful that more than a few in the galleries were able to learn of its import.

Questions from members, however, particularly by Kem and Watkins, brought out the details. There was no demonstration—they are banned in the Senate—at any time.

In the House, the statement was read by Representative McCormack (D., Mass.), majority leader. It drew applause from the members twice—when he read that the United States Navy would prevent an attack on Formosa and at its conclusion.

Lucas and Senator Morse (R.,

(Continued on Page 10, Column 5)

On Other Pages

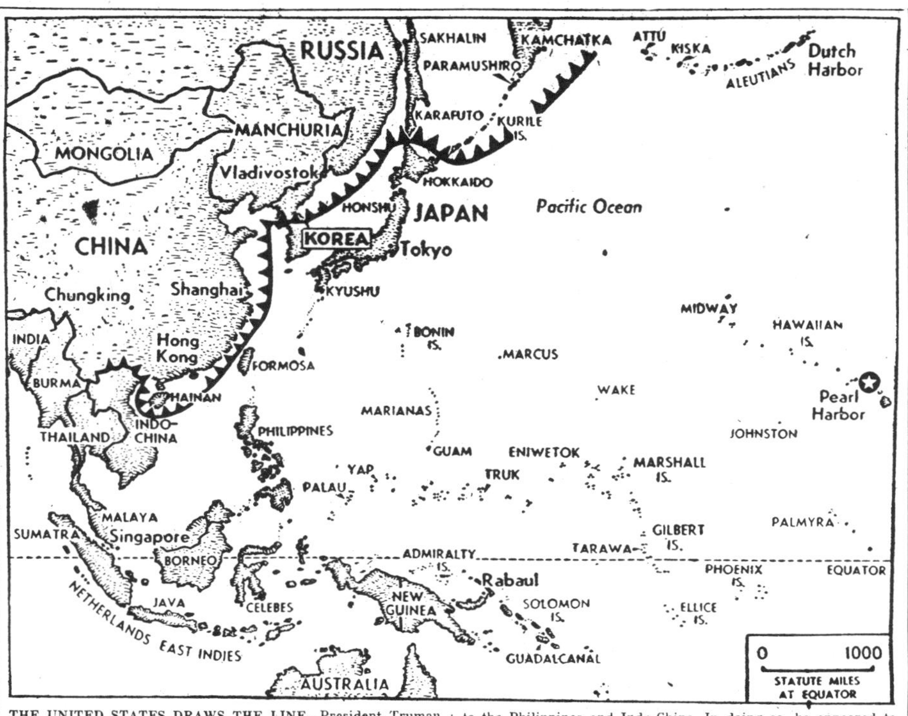

THE UNITED STATES DRAWS THE LINE—President Truman yesterday ordered United States air and naval forces to the assistance of the embattled South Koreans, directed the 7th Fleet to protect Formosa, and announced increased military assistance to the Philippines and Indo-China. In doing so, he appeared to draw a 6,000-mile line against further Communist penetration of the Western Pacific. The line, shown on the above map, extends from the Bering Sea to the northwestern corner of Indo-China.

Political Situation

By PAUL W. WARD

Washington, June 27—Another 385,046 square miles of territory and some 53,000,000 Asiatic peoples were put under the United States protecting wing as President Truman today drew what some diplomats here called a new Communist balkline in the Pacific area.

He did so, they inferred, in the series of Korean crisis decisions he announced and which included new commitments to keep out of the Communist grasp:

SOUTH KOREA with its 85,426 square miles of land and some 20,000,000 people.

FORMOSA, the Chinese Nationalist refuge with its 13,800 square miles of island and some 8,000,000 people off the China mainland.

INDO-CHINA, with its 25,000,000 people and 286,000 square miles of land.

Changes Security Line

Those additions compelled a change in the line which had defined the previously declared limits of American security in the Far East and drew upon the map of the Eastern Hemisphere what some United Nations Security Council members referred to as a new "Pacific front."

The new line—roughly estimated by one professional cartographer as between 5,800 and 6,000 miles long—extends from the Bering Straits between Alaska and Russia at least to the juncture of the China, Burma and Indo-China borders.

All of Korea below the thirty-eighth parallel plus Formosa and Indo-China were put behind that line which previously had run west only of the Aleutians, Japan, Okinawa and the Philippines.

Greater Extent Suggested

There were some diplomats here who felt the full implications of President Truman's midday announcement were such as to project much further afield that line at which Communist aggression may be sure henceforth to meet American armed resistance.

In their view, the line extends on across the northern frontiers of Burma, Pakistan, India and Afghanistan to Iran, Turkey and Greece, all three of which already are recipients of American military assistance.

On that basis there would be sheltered behind that line not only 153,500,000 Koreans, Japanese, Formosans, Filipinos and Indo-Chinese but also 554,000,000 residents of Australia, New Zealand, India, Pakistan, Indonesia, Ceylon, Malaya, Siam, Burma, and Afghanistan.

Officials Less Positive

Responsible American officials, however, did not feel free to project the line in any such wholesale fashion. The aforementioned diplomats were themselves in doubt as to whether what they called the implications of the President's policy statement could be extended to include, for example, the British crown colony of Hong Kong, near Canton.

No line of any sort has ever been officially proclaimed by this Government with respect to the Pacific area. It has avoided any hard and fast commitments in that part of the world, while concentrating mainly, until today, on steps to insure that western Europe's non-Communist states shall not be engulfed and swell the Soviet warmaking potential by the addition of their highly developed industries and skilled workers.

Out of the latter endeavor has come last year's twelve-power North Atlantic treaty which in precise terms marks off about a quarter of the globe as a prohibited area for forces—of any origin—bent upon aggression.

Bound To Repel Attack

In that treaty the United States, Britain, France, Italy and eight other countries bound themselves to repel jointly any attack upon any of their number or upon their occupation forces and communications in Germany and Austria, including Berlin and Vienna.

Thus an officially proclaimed line has existed for approximately a year in the Western Hemisphere. Furthermore, the Atlantic treaty line extended in the European and Near Eastern area that was established by President Truman's March 12, 1947, message to Congress on military aid to Greece and Turkey.

A similar line also has been drawn around the United States and the Latin-American republics by the treaty of Rio de Janeiro which some five of those republics have yet to ratify but which, nevertheless, is in full force and effect.

Not On Official Documents

All comparable lines in the Pacific area have had to be built up not on the basis of similarly official documents but out of fragments of official statements. Thus President Truman in a statement last January 5 put Formosa to the west of the Pacific line by proclaiming that this Government

(Continued on Page 11, Column 5)

Military Situation

By MARK S. WATSON
[*Sun Staff Correspondent*]

Washington, June 27—The President's orders provide Gen. Douglas MacArthur with powers over enlarged forces throughout the Far East and apparently with broad authority in performing his mission. They also set up a firmly drawn boundary beyond which Communist military strength is not to pass.

The designated barrier to further Communist advances in the Orient is much more than the line across the Korean peninsula.

Rather, in addition to ordering Communist forces to go back of that thirty-eighth parallel in Korea, it bars them from Formosa, the Philippines and from Indo-China.

Military Strength Necessary

That military strength is necessary—whether by its actual exercise or by a warning display of arms—is thoroughly understood. The President's orders provide military force, either active or potential, for each area of the Far East which his statement mentions, in these respects:

KOREA—"Cover and support" by United States air and sea forces for the South Korean Government troops, to enable them to push the Communists back to the boundary line.

FORMOSA—United States naval forces (the powerful 7th Fleet) to prevent Chinese Communists from attacking Formosa, and to stop the Chinese Nationalists from harassing the Communists.

PHILIPPINES — Strengthening of United States forces in the Philippines, and military assistance to the new Philippine Government in its persistent internal war with the Hukbalahaps (largely Communist)

INDO - CHINA — Acceleration of United States military aid to the French and their native associates. Dispatch of a United States military mission to that land, which obviously goes much further than the American military aid previously given.

Forces Impressive

The forces already at General MacArthur's disposal are impressive, briefly estimated as follows:

ARMY (UNDER LIEUT. GEN. WALTON WALKER)—123,000 men, including four infantry divisions.

NAVY (UNDER VICE ADMIRAL CALVIN T. JOY)—Until today the Far East Navy Command was only the cruiser Juneau and four destroyers. To Admiral Joy's force now has been added the whole 7th Fleet (previously based in the Guam-Philippines area) including the 27,000-ton carrier Valley Forge the cruiser Rochester, eight destroyers (including two of the new anti-submarine type), three submarines, and auxiliaries.

AIR FORCE—One medium bomber group (30 B-29's), five fighter groups (375 F-80's), one all-weather fighter group (36 twin-Mustangs), two light bombing squadrons (32 B-26's).

Due For Field Command

The field command of the South Korean forces seems likely to go to Maj. Gen. John H. Church, lately in command in the Ryukyus, but a wartime infantryman in the Mediterranean and European campaigns. General MacArthur has sent him to President Syngman Rhee as a senior military adviser, which under the circumstances begins to look much like a command for the duration of the current hostilities in South Korea.

Of the course of fighting in South Korea, invaded three days ago on three sides by Communist task forces, not much new information is at hand, save that—in the words of General MacArthur's curt summary—"combat missions" are being conducted by American air and naval forces.

The American operation in Korea, it must be borne in mind, is to be wholly protective. That is, General MacArthur is instructed to eject the Communist invaders from every position they have taken south of the thirty-eighth parallel. How he does it, by air, naval, or, ultimately, ground forces, is for him to determine.

Limited In Operations

But he is not to conduct any operations north of the parallel, whether by sea, air or land. In this he is to follow strictly the implied mandate of the United Nations Security Council, which last Sunday ordered the Communists to withdraw to that boundary line and then called upon United Nations members to "render every assistance to the United Nations in the execution of this resolution," as President Truman's statement recites.

The military limitation which this implies is a real one. It is understood, for instance, that the Communists have reserve forces in waiting, north of the parallel, ready to push south in exploitation of a

(Continued on Page 11, Column 8)

BULLETINS

Oslo, Norway, Wednesday, June 28 (AP)—Moscow radio made its first mention—without comment—today of President Truman's declaration that the United States would give military protection to South Korea.

The report of the President's statement was broadcast first at 7.15 A.M. Moscow Time (12.15 A.M. E.S.T.).

Hong Kong, Wednesday, June 28 (AP)—The Chinese Communists today were reported attacking tiny Lintin Island, last Chinese Nationalist base for the dwindling blockade of Red Canton.

Lintin, largest of the Lintin island group, is 5 miles west of Hong Kong and only 3 miles from British territorial waters.

Lansing, Mich., June 27 (AP)—Industrial Michigan set up an emergency air-raid alarm system tonight and began whipping together a civilian defense organization.

Michigan, "arsenal of democracy" in the last war, is believed the first state to take these extensive steps in the present Korean situation.

BOMBERS ALSO THROWN INTO BATTLE FOR SEOUL; RED SETBACK REPORTED

MacArthur Starts Airlift Of Supplies To South Korea; Yugoslavia Casts Lone Vote Against O.K. On Armed Intervention

London, Wednesday, June 28 (AP)—The Communist party organ Pravda charged the United States today with a "direct act of aggression against the Korean People's Democratic Republic and the People's Republic of China."

The editorial, broadcast by Moscow Radio and heard in London by the Soviet monitor, was the first Russian comment on the United States decision to use American military forces to aid the South Korean Republic and the Chinese Nationalist regime on Formosa.

Support

By THOMAS O'NEILL
[*Sun Staff Correspondent*]

Lake Success, N.Y., June 27—International armed aid for the Republic of Korea was called for tonight by the Security Council of the United Nations.

It was the first time in the five years since it was established that the organization for international peace had been driven to indorse the use of armed force against aggression.

All member nations in a position to put combat supplies at the disposal of Korea were asked to do so. In effect, the Council action was **ratification by the United Nations of the step** announced by President Truman slightly more than ten hours earlier today.

Vote 7 To 1 On U.S. Motion

On a show of hands on a resolution sponsored by the United States, the Council voted 7 to 1 to give Korea all possible material assistance. The lone objector was Yugoslavia.

Neither Egypt nor India voted, both because instructions from their governments were unobtainable. The eleventh member of the Security Council, Russia—was unrepresented at the session in pursuance of a boycott it instituted 23 weeks ago when it was unsuccessful in a demand that Nationalist China be ousted from the Council.

Until the last moment the possibility was considered that the Soviet delegate might put in an appearance for the purpose of vetoing Council adoption of the American proposal.

Assembly Plan In Reverse

The Soviet stayed away. This obviated the use of a plan the American delegation had in reserve against the possible use of the veto.

Had the Russians put in an appearance, the Americans intended to withdraw their resolution and move instead for an immediate call of the General Assembly of the United Nations. A two-thirds vote of the General Assembly is sufficient to bypass the Security Council, and the United States delegation was confident the necessary backing could be won.

There was a disappointment for the American delegation in the failure of India to cast a vote on the question of arms aid for an Asiatic nation which is the victim of an unprovoked attack.

Attributed To Phone Trouble

The absence of instructions to the delegate from India, Sir Benegal Rau, was officially attributed to the inability to complete satisfactory communication with New Delhi by radio telephone. Cables were available, however, and it was understood that the Nehru Government had been unable to reach a decision on a matter constituting a direct challenge to Russia, now spread close to Indian borders by conquest in China.

The Egyptian delegate was unable to get any reply from his Government.

Several hours were given over to attempts to have India represented in the voting. The Council session, which began at 3.16 P.M. and continued until 11 o'clock, was recessed for five hours while these attempts were under way.

Overnight Recess Opposed

Telephones in the office of Trygve Lie, secretary general of the United Nations, were used by the Indian and Egyptian delegates in the attempts to talk to their capitals. Standing by with Lie and the two delegates was Ambassador Ernest A. Gross, of the United States delegation.

Several times, the two delegates suggested that they might be able to get directives from home if the

(Continued on Page 11, Column 2)

Action

Tokyo, *Wednesday*, June 28 (AP)—American-manned jet fighters and light bombers have bombed and strafed North Korean forces, it was announced today.

This new American support, reliable reports said, enabled South Korean troops to drive the Communist invaders out of Seoul.

Gen. Douglas MacArthur's headquarters announced that 500-pound bombs were rained down on the troops from the Communist North who plunged Korea into war with an invasion Sunday.

The swift jets and attack bombers of MacArthur's command were thrown into the swaying battle at the express orders of President Truman, who acted to halt now a conflict leading the world to the brink of war.

Headquarters Echelon Set Up

An advance echelon of MacArthur's general headquarters was set up in South Korea. His generals were in continuous conference.

Headquarter's latest summary of the situation said southern troops still held Seoul and the capital was quiet. A concentration of about 40 North Korean armored vehicles was reported several miles to the north.

It declared the situation on the front was "substantially unchanged."

The summary declared the initial northern advantage of "surprise and shock action" had been eliminated and the invaders had run into "considerable difficulty in their various attempts to resume the offensive."

Moscow Broadcast

It made no further mention of United States air or sea activity.

A Moscow broadcast had said that the northerners knifed into Seoul, capital of the United States-sponsored South Korean Republic, at four points this morning.

But an American informant said that later reports indicated a southern counterattack had thrown the tank-led troops from the north all the way back to the key city of Uijongbu.

This city sits astride the invasion valley 12 miles north of Seoul. Southern Korean reports yesterday said the city had been recaptured. Accounts early today indicated the Communists had swept back through the city and on to the limits of Seoul.

Naval Units In Action

The American informant, who said he was in communication with the South Korean army, declared the counterattack pushed the northerners out of Seoul at about 11.30 A.M.

[Editor's Note—Events in Korea are fourteen hours ahead of Eastern Daylight Time. When it is midnight, Eastern Daylight Time, it

(Continued on Page 11, Column 1)

Other Korean News

Weather Forecast
Some cloudiness with sunshine and milder today; showers late tonight and tomorrow. Yesterday's temperatures: Highest, 54; lowest, 45.........Page 35

THE SUN

FINAL

Registered United States Patent Office

Vol. 228—No. 123—F | PAID CIRCULATION IN MARCH MORNING, 175,550 EVENING, 198,601 374,151 || SUNDAY 309,397 | BALTIMORE, WEDNESDAY, APRIL 11, 1951 | Copyright, 1951, The A. S. Abell Company Entered as second-class matter at Baltimore Post Office | 36 Pages | 5 Cents

TRUMAN FIRES MACARTHUR, PUTS RIDGWAY IN COMMAND

Finds General 'Unable To Give Whole Support' To U.S. And U.N.

Washington, Wednesday, April 11 (AP)—President Truman early today forced Gen. Douglas MacArthur from all his commands.

The President said he had concluded that MacArthur "is unable to give his wholehearted support" to United States and United Nations policies. Mr. Truman immediately designated Lieut. Gen. Matthew B. Ridgway as MacArthur's successor as Supreme Commander, Allied Powers; Commander in Chief, United Nations Command; Commander in Chief, Far East, and Commanding General, United States Army, Far East.

In a statement, Mr. Truman asserted that "military commanders must be governed" by policies and directives of the Government and "in time of crisis, this consideration is particularly compelling."

The President appointed Lieut. Gen. James A. Van Fleet to succeed Ridgway to take over active command of the 8th Army.

[General Van Fleet is the commanding general of the 2d Army at Fort George G. Meade, Md. He went on leave a few days ago and was not on the Meade reservation early this morning.]

Announcement of the almost unprecedented dismissal of the hero-general was made at a rare news conference at the White House at 1 A.M. (E.S.T.). The time was fixed to coincide as nearly as possible with the delivery to MacArthur at Tokyo of the order relieving him of his commands, "effective at once."

Memorandum Released

The White House released, with the President's statement, a memorandum purporting to show differences between MacArthur's statements and action and presidential policy.

The President's order, telegraphed to MacArthur over the army network, was brief and pointed.

"I deeply regret that it becomes my duty as President and Commander in Chief of the United States military forces to replace you as Supreme Commander, Allied Powers; Commander in Chief, United Nations Command; Commander in Chief, Far East; Commanding General, United States Army, Far East.

Ridgway To Command

"You will turn over your commands, effective at once, to Lieut. Gen. Matthew B. Ridgway. You are authorized to have issued such orders as are necessary to complete desired travel to such places as you select.

"My reasons for your replacement will be made public concurrently with the delivery to you of the foregoing order, and are contained in the next following message." (This referred to the President's statement.)

The President's action came as the aftermath of a series of differences with MacArthur over policy in the Far East and raised prospects that MacArthur might return to this country to deliver a series of blasts against the Administration, probably under auspices of Republican supporters of the General.

MacArthur Praised

The President's statement asserted that General MacArthur's place in history "as one of our greatest commanders" is fully established.

"The nation owes him a debt of gratitude for the distinguished and exceptional service which he has rendered his country in posts of great responsibility," the President's statement said.

"For that reason I repeat my regret at the necessity for the action I feel compelled to take in his case."

Aware of political reverberations certain to follow in the wake of his actions, the President made public a series of heretofore secret directives tending to show how MacArthur failed to follow administrative foreign policy.

Directive Disclosed

These included one from the Joint Chiefs of Staff to MacArthur and other commanders on December 6, 1950, embracing a presidential order that: "No speech, press release, or other public statement concerning foreign policy should be released until it has received clearance from the Department of State.

"No speech, press release, or other public statement concerning military policy should be released until it has received clearance from the Department of Defense."

Full Text Of Statement

Following is the text of President Truman's statement:

"With deep regret I have concluded that General of the Army Douglas MacArthur is unable to give his wholehearted support to the policies of the United States Government and of the United Nations in matters pertaining to his official duties.

"In view of the specific responsibilities imposed upon me by the Constitution of the United States and the added responsibility which has been entrusted to me by the United Nations, I have decided that I must make a change of command in the Far East. I have, therefore, relieved General MacArthur of his commands and have designated Lieut. Gen. Matthew B. Ridgway as his successor.

"Full and vigorous debate on matters of national policy is a vital element in the constitutional system of our free democracy. It is fundamental, however, that military com-

(Continued on Page 2, Column 2)

GENERAL MACARTHUR

MacArthur Reaction

Washington, *Wednesday*, April 11 (AP)—Removal of General MacArthur may be "a preliminary step to a Far Eastern Munich," Senator Knowland (R., Cal.) said today.

The Senator, a strong MacArthur supporter, saw in President Truman's replacement of the General "a great victory for Secretary of State Acheson and his Far Eastern policies."

"By his action," Knowland said in a statement, "the President has yielded to British and American critics of General MacArthur. Our position in Japan and the whole Far East is placed in jeopardy by an action which most observers will interpret as a preliminary step to a Far Eastern Munich."

Looks To American People

He added, "when General MacArthur arrives home the American people will have an opportunity to pay him the great honor and respect in which he is held by them."

Representative Van Zandt (R., Pa.) said General MacArthur's ouster "will further divide the American people."

Interviewed by phone, he added the action "will also give the people an opportunity to receive an unvarnished and uncensored first hand report on the situation in the Far East."

Representative Martin (Mass.), House minority leader, said early this morning he had no comment on the sensational move by President Truman. He implied he would have something to say later on.

"A Tragic Error"

Senator Taft (R., Ohio) called the decision "a tragic error."

"It is an error not only because of the loss of one of the greatest military leaders in United States history, but because it indicates a determination to continue the wavering, planless course in the Far East which points toward either a stalemate or ignominious concession to the Chinese Communists," declared the Republican leader.

MacArthur's Staff Bitter

Tokyo, *Wednesday*, April 11 (AP)—President Truman's removal of General MacArthur struck this headquarters like a thunder clap today.

The news broke here in a broadcast over the Armed Forces radio.

MacArthur was at his American Embassy residence for

(Continued on Page 2, Column 7)

BUTLER PROBERS LEARN THAT FBI DROPPED SURINE FOR 'DISREGARD OF RULES'

Subcommittee Hears Hoover Statement That McCarthy Aide Was Discharged; Resignation Was Not Accepted

By GERALD GRIFFIN
[*Washington Bureau of The Sun*]

Washington, April 10—Donald A. Surine, an investigator for Senator McCarthy (R., Wis.) and a major witness in the Senate Elections subcommittee's investigation of Senator John M. Butler's campaign, was shown today to have been dropped as an FBI agent last year for disregard of rules and regulations.

Surine, testifying before the subcommittee this afternoon, repeated his previous statement that he resigned voluntarily from the FBI in February, 1950, before he went to work for McCarthy.

Edward A. McDermott, the subcommittee's chief counsel, read into the record a letter dated April 3, 1951, from J. Edgar Hoover, FBI chief, stating that Surine's resignation was not accepted and that the FBI's records show that he was dropped from the rolls.

"I think you will agree with me that if you had given us this information when you first appeared we would all be more comfortable about this at this moment," Senator Hendrickson (R., N.J.) commented to Surine.

One Of 4 Witnesses

Surine was one of four witnesses heard today. The others were:

MILLARD E. TYDINGS, former Maryland Senator, who asserted that his charges of violation of Maryland and Federal election laws by Senator Butler and his associates have been proved, and who sought to warn the subcommittee members that the tactics used against him in the Maryland campaign might be employed elsewhere, if nothing is done to check them.

F. TROWBRIDGE VOM BAUR, a partner in the law firm of Ralph E. Becker, the subcommittee's Republican assistant counsel. Von Baur testified that he has been assisting Becker in the Republican side of the investigation, with Hendrickson's approval, but Senator Margaret Smith (R., Maine) declared that she has been "kept in the dark" about his services.

Defends Tabloid

MISS JEAN KERR, a research assistant in McCarthy's office, who defended the four-page campaign tabloid, "From the Record," as a "truthful" piece of campaign literature and testified about her part in taking financial contributions from Washington to the Butler headquarters in Baltimore

Surine, according to his own previous testimony, as well as that of other witnesses, figured in the Butler campaign in connection with the "ride" of William H. Fedder, a Baltimore printer, around the streets of Baltimore in the early hours of last November 6.

Surine, Ewell Moore and George Nilles accompanied Fedder on the ride, but vehemently denied his complaint that they had intimidated him and seriously frightened him. Surine accused Fedder of telling malicious lies to the subcommittee about the ride.

With Surine recalled to the witness chair this afternoon, McDermott inquired into the testimony

(Continued on Page 4, Column 5)

FEARED JAIL, WITNESS SAYS

Mississippian Reticent About Talking In U.S. Jobs Probe

Jackson, Miss., April 10 (AP)—A witness told a Senate committee investigating sale of Federal jobs in Mississippi today she had been "afraid to tell all I knew" for fear "we'd probably all go to the pen."

The witness was Mrs. Claude V. Murphy, of Winona, a member of the pro-Truman Mississippi Democratic Committee and identified by previous witnesses as their contact with the committee in purchasing Post Office Department jobs.

Senator Karl Mundt (R., S.D.) asserted during the hearings now in their second day that handling of Post Office patronage in Mississippi is "one of the most vicious job selling rackets I've ever heard of."

Mrs. Murphy and her husband, a rural mail carrier, were sworn in together.

Mrs. Murphy Testifies

She told the Senate Committee that Curtis Rodgers, secretary of the Mississippi Democratic Committee and Forrest Jackson, an attorney at Jackson, "told us we could accept contributions up to $5,000. I understood that if the contributions were made and I recommended them the people would get the jobs."

She said Rodgers would not accept any checks other than her own, and that "he told me he couldn't run the office on hot air."

She said she had collected $2,630 in contributions for the committee. "I've been afraid to tell all I knew," she testified. "Mr. Rodgers told me that if we told everything we knew we'd probably all go to the pen."

Her husband, explaining that he is a Republican while his wife is a Democrat, added "but you know a Republican in Mississippi has about as much chance as a snowball in hell." He said he had contributed

(Continued on Page 4, Column 2)

OPS OFFICIAL QUITS OVER U.S. 'SEA OF WASTE'

Thompson Not Consulted In 12 Weeks On Job As Consultant

Washington, April 10 (AP)—Former Governor M. E. Thompson of Georgia today quit as a consultant with the Office of Price Stabilization, charging that "official Washington is drifting in a sea of confusion, inefficiency, waste and extravagance."

Thompson said in a statement that he came to Washington as co-director for territories for OPS.

"Knowing that it was impossible to have two directors for the same job," Thompson said, "I offered to resign and accept another assignment."

On Pay Roll 12 Weeks

But, he added:

"For twelve weeks I have been carried on the pay roll as a consultant at a salary plus expense account of $53.48 per day. Yet, during this time, I have been consulted about nothing. I have had no assignment to do anything.

"On February 19 at the White House, I told the President the story up until then. He called Don Dawson (presidential assistant) and instructed him to see that the mess was straightened out immediately. It hasn't been done.

"Under the circumstances, I refuse to accept salary and expense money from the taxpayers when I am rendering no public service.

"I am resigning and returning to my home in Valdosta, Ga. I refuse to be a parasite on the American tax payers."

Michael DiSalle, price stabilization chief, who has been Thompson's boss said:

"In an organization the size of the price stabilization agency, a speedy job has to be done. It is understandable that some people may be brought in, in the haste of organization, and their talents not utilized fully.

"We had planned a more demanding job to make fuller use of Mr. Thompson's talents. This had been discussed with Mr. Thompson and we had planned to set up the position shortly. In the meantime, Mr. Thompson said that he had another position in mind."

White House Declines Comment

The White House declined comment on Thompson's statements. President Truman's press secretary, Joseph H. Short, said he was not familiar with the former governor's resignation and hadn't had an opportunity to look into it."

Thompson said there are "thousands upon thousands of others rendering no service but are on the public pay roll, not only in Washington but throughout the United States."

He charged that no real effort has been made to stabilize prices.

"Even those charged with this

(Continued on Page 4, Column 3)

MOVE TO SCARE TOBEY IS LAID TO PRESIDENT

Senator Is Reported To Have Told Of Threat In RFC Probe

Appeals court charges Sawyer, 9 others with contempt in Dollar steamship case..........Page 4

Washington, April 10 (AP)—Senator Tobey (R., N.H.) was quoted tonight as saying President Truman called him up and tried to intimidate him by saying the White House "had the goods" on various Congress members in connection with RFC loans.

Later, however, the President is reported to have talked to Tobey a second time and to have withdrawn the charges he had made against the legislators.

Highly placed congressional sources said Tobey told a Senate subcommittee yesterday that he had made recordings of both conversations with the Chief Executive. Tobey himself could not be reached tonight.

Told Story To Senate Unit

The New Hampshire Senator, according to persons who cannot be named, told his story to a Senate banking subcommittee headed by Senator Fulbright (D., Ark.). It is this subcommittee which has charged that an influence clique extending into the White House has exercised undue influence on lending operations of the Reconstruction Finance Corporation.

The Senate subcommittee, it was learned, treated Tobey's remarks about his conversations with the President as "off-the-record" and did not include them in the official records of its session.

Several Capitol Hill sources gave this version of Tobey's testimony:

The President telephoned the Senator and charged that certain members of Congress had taken fees for exerting improper influence on the RFC in connection with the granting of Government loans.

The President said he "had the goods" on the legislators because he had copies of letters they had written to the RFC.

Fulbright Dispute Cited

The time of the conversation was not given exactly, but it presumably was about the time Mr. Truman was in vigorous controversy with the Fulbright Committee, whose report he had called "asinine!"

One source said Tobey telephoned Mr. Truman some time later—again recording the conversation—and that this time the President told him he had found there was no basis for the charges of congressional influence on RFC loans.

The subcommittee was stirred to wrath several weeks ago when RFC board members, testifying in a public hearing, disclosed that President Truman had called for copies of House and Senate members' letters to the lending agency concerning loan applications.

Fulbright and other members promptly charged the President's action was an attempt to intimidate the Senate investigators.

The White House later issued a statement that it had obtained the letters for its guidance in proposing a reorganization of the RFC and that Mr. Truman knew of no evidence in the documents of any improper congressional conduct.

Earlier today, David K. Niles, White House aide, and former Senator Burton K. Wheeler identified themselves as men who made other moves interpreted by Senator Tobey as an effort to interfere in the RFC investigation.

Each of the two, interviewed separately, said all that really happened was that word went to Tobey through Wheeler that Donald Dawson, another White House official, is a "good guy" and the senatorial investigators ought to "go easy" on him. Both denied there was any effort to apply pressure.

Senator Tobey said at a news conference tonight, however, that the way he interpreted it, "the White House palace guard" tried to interfere in a Senate investigation "affecting one of its men."

He said he considers Wheeler's role was "simply that of a voice relaying a message" and that he is not resentful against the former senator.

But he said of the reported role of Niles in arranging the call from Wheeler:

"I thought the thing irregular and improper, so I went before the subcommittee and told the story."

Senator Fulbright (D., Ark.), chairman of the banking subcommittee, said that Wheeler had told his story at a secret meeting of the subcommittee yesterday.

Wheeler said the "go easy" sug-

(Continued on Page 4, Column 3)

Lose Snore Or Lose Her, Wife Tells Mate In Divorce Court

The snorer and his snore-allergic wife.

Chicago, April 10 (AP)—If Richard Michalak wants his wife back, he must cure himself of snoring within 30 days.

Mrs. Florence Michalak, a 20-year-old blonde, told Judge Rudolph F. Desort of Superior Court today she would go back to her husband if he could learn to snooze quietly in that time.

Blood Test, Neck Tube Suggested

Mrs. Michalak has a separate maintenance suit pending on the grounds that Michalak's snoring wrecked her health.

Her attorney, Charles C. Colley, gave Michalak a number of suggestions for curing snoring he said he had received from "several hundred" persons.

Michalak glanced at the list and mopped his brow.

Some of the snore lore included suggestions that he take a blood test for possible sleeping sickness, take a "brain wave test" under supervision of a psychiatrist, or place a rubber tube around his neck.

One person suggested he train himself to keep his mouth closed at night by keeping it closed during the day.

Another person wrote that Michalak's head "is too flat on the

(Continued on Page 7, Column 5)

MacArthur's War Record Praised

Sydney, Australia, April 10 (AP)—Prime Minister Robert G. Menzies today praised General MacArthur's conduct of United Nations operations in Korea and said he is "a man entitled to great honor in Australia."

"There are some people who say that, as the aggression by the North Koreans consisted of crossing the Thirty-eighth Parallel, all you have to do is push them back to the parallel and discontinue the battle," Menzies said in a speech before the Australian-American Association.

"This is a queer conception to me and it must strike MacArthur as sheer midsummer madness. The United Nations went into South Korea under enormous disadvantages. But never was a campaign conducted with more skill."

Weather Forecast
Cloudy today, with light rain and highest around 50 degrees. Yesterday's temperatures: Highest, 59; lowest, 43.
(Details, Page 10; Map, Page 25)

THE SUN

FINAL

Registered United States Patent Office

Vol. 230—No. 38—F | PAID CIRCULATION IN NOVEMBER MORNING, 176,255; EVENING, 198,529 | 374,784 ‖ SUNDAY 311,464 | BALTIMORE, WEDNESDAY, JANUARY 2, 1952 | Entered as second-class matter at Baltimore Post Office | 26 Pages | 5 Cents

Maryland Routs Tennessee, 28-13, In Sugar Bowl Game

All 28 Aboard Air Force C-47 Found Dead In Arizona

19 WEST POINT CADETS AMONG GROUP KILLED IN WRECK ON MOUNTAINSIDE

Transport Plane Had Vanished In Storm On Sunday Near Phoenix; Party Plans To Climb Peak To Remove Bodies

Nine West Point seniors among victims of plane crash....Page 5
CAB officials open probe into crash of C-46 in N.Y..........Page 5

Phoenix, Ariz., Jan. 1 (AP)—The wreckage of a missing Air Force C-47 plane and the bodies of the 28 persons aboard were found today on the face of a central Arizona mountain.

A cowboy who had made his way up the steep mountain, 65 miles northeast of Phoenix, reported "bodies and wreckage were scattered all over." The plane, carrying nineteen West Point cadets, a crew of four and five other passengers, vanished in a storm Sunday. The wreckage was sighted from the air today.

Arnold Johnson, 50, foreman of the Jack Shoe Cattle Company, climbed to the scene on horseback after spotting the wreckage through field glasses.

He said he couldn't tell how many bodies there were, but he said there was no indication that anyone could have survived. Only the tail section of the burned twin-engine plane was intact.

"Was Awful," He Says

"Some of the bodies were in two groups," Johnson related at the base camp set up by the ground party sent out from Williams Air Force Base. "Others were scattered. I have never seen anything like it. It was awful.

"Most of the plane was in small pieces," Johnson said. "I didn't see the engine at all."

Johnson said the plane smashed into a bluff on Armer Mountain, which is on the Jack Shoe Cattle Company's range.

The wreckage is about 150 feet below the crest of the 7,000-foot-high mountain.

The wreckage was located early this afternoon by 1 of more than 60 planes which had been flying over a 24,000-square mile area for two days in search of the lost craft.

Sets Up Camp

The ground party, headed by First Lieutenant Donald C. Humphrey, sped to the foot of the mountain and set up camp about 5 miles from the crash scene before dusk.

Rock and ice slides prevented the airmen in the party from going up the mountainside tonight. They plan to set out about 7 A.M. tomorrow. It was estimated it will take at least an hour and a half to reach the wreckage on horseback.

Removal of the bodies down the precipitous mountain was expected to be a slow and difficult task.

There is some snow on the mountain, and the ground is wet from heavy rain which fell during the week end.

The C-47, which took off from Hamilton Air Force Base, Cal., for Goodfellow Air Force Base, Texas, was last heard from at 3.34 P.M. Sunday when the pilot radioed for landing instructions. He reported he was near Phoenix. The plane was not heard from again.

Were Going Back

The cadets were returning to the United States Military Academy at West Point, after spending Christmas vacation with their families in northern California.

They had hitchhiked the ride upon finding that space was available in the C-47.

Among the other passengers was a woman, WAF Sergt. Jeane Garafalo, 20, of Plainfield, N.J. She was going home to surprise her mother.

Pilot of the plane was Major Lester Carlson, flying safety officer for the 4th Air Force. The copilot was First Lieutenant Walter Boback, 29, former Los Angeles county (Cal.) deputy sheriff.

A passenger was Second Lieutenant George Ahlgren, a member of the University of California crew that won the Olympics rowing championship in 1948.

On Other Pages

DIMES MARCH OF '52 OPENS

California Governor, Daughter, O'Connor Launch Drive

Los Angeles, Jan. 1 (AP)—Three persons who have known polio as an "unwelcome house guest" launched the 1952 March of Dimes tonight.

Gov. Earl Warren, of California, his daughter Nina and Basil O'Connor, president of the National Foundation for Infantile Paralysis, spoke over a coast-to-coast radio network.

Nina and O'Connor's daughter, Mrs. Sidney Culver, both recovered from polio. Their fathers described the shock to which a family is subjected when a member is stricken.

Governor Comments

Nina told her radio audience that she was "lucky" enough to recover "without any serious after-effects." The Governor, introducing O'Connor, said:

"I don't think any man can know what the word polio really means until it strikes in his own family. It wasn't until my own daughter Nina lay stricken in a hospital isolation ward that I began to understand not only what the polio patients themselves have to suffer but what thousands upon thousands of parents have had to go through—the helpless standing by, the waiting, the desperate hoping."

O'Connor said the Foundation starts 1952 with $5,000,000 in unpaid 1951 bills, adding:

"Forty-five thousand people at this very moment are still directly dependent upon March of Dimes for help."

State March Of Dimes Drive To Start Today

The 1952 March of Dimes campaign in Maryland begins at noon today, with a parade of volunteer workers in Baltimore and a Statewide appeal for contributions to the fight against polio.

Maryland's goal this year is to exceed the 1951 contributions of half a million dollars, according to former Senator George L. Radcliffe, State chairman for the March of Dimes.

"It's vital that we do pass last year's contributions," Senator Radcliffe said, "because the March of Dimes has not kept pace with the march of polio." The National Foundation for Infantile Paralysis, he explained, ended 1951 with a $5,000,000 debt.

MARYLAND TOUCHDOWN—Bob Shemonski, right, Maryland halfback, waits for ball, in the air, for the Terps second touchdown. Others in the picture are Francis Holohan (54) Maryland; Bill Barbish (18) and Pug Pearman (60), both of Tennessee.

ALLIES APPROVE PRISONER TRADE

Displaced Civilians Included In 'All-For-All' Plan

Dulles holds "dependable peace" unlikely in Korea........Page 2
Two top Communist commanders in Korea issue harsh and threatening statements........Page 2

Munsan, Korea, Wednesday, Jan. 2 (AP) — Allied delegates today agreed to an "all-for-all" exchange of Korean war prisoners and displaced civilians.

But in making the proposal, Rear Admiral R. E. Libby told the Communists they must strip the Red army of all former South Korean troops who have been "conscripted" into Communist fighting ranks since their capture.

The Red delegates who heard Libby read the six-page Allied proposal previously had expressed fears that the United Nations command wanted a "man-for-man" exchange.

Demand By Libby

The Allies hold about 120,000 prisoners and the Reds maintain they have only about 11,000 prisoners including 7,000 South Koreans.

In addition, the Allies suggested that each prisoner should be given the right to refuse repatriation.

This right of choice, however, should be supervised by the International Red Cross to make sure that "the decision of the individual is made freely and without duress," the Allies insisted.

Libby accused the Reds of "incorporating into your army many

(Continued on Page 2, Column 4)

Maxim Litvinoff, Once Russia's Foremost Diplomat, Dies At 75

London, Wednesday, Jan. 2 (AP)—Maxim Litvinoff, Russia's top diplomat between the wars, died today, Moscow Radio announced.

He was 75 years old.

Litvinoff dropped out of sight as a Russian official after August 23, 1946, when Moscow announced he had been "released from his duties."

At that time, he was deputy minister of foreign affairs.

Malik Was Given Post

Jacob Malik was appointed to the job.

Litvinoff always had been known for friendliness to the West, a reputation he earned as Ambassador to the United States after America first recognized the Soviet regime in 1933.

His eclipse in 1946 was widely interpreted as finally ending much likelihood of easy Soviet-Western co-operation.

Litvinoff had been Russia's leading figure in foreign affairs for a decade before the second World War broke out.

His policy was peace and he was distinguished for his debates in the League of Nations. One phrase—"peace is indivisible"—set the tenor and told the meat of his arguments for collective security.

But as war clouds gathered, Litvinoff suddenly resigned from the Russian Foreign Office on May 3, 1939, in the middle of Russian negotiations for a mutual-assistance pact with Britain and France.

Three months later, when the Russian nonaggression pact with Germany was announced, the mystery of his sudden resignation was solved. He had become a victim of changing Kremlin policy.

After he resigned, there were rumors he had been arrested, but they appeared without foundation. Litvinoff took a spacious Moscow apartment, retained his chauffeur and luxurious car and appeared in public occasionally.

Stalin Liked Him

He came back to prominence in November, 1941—five months after Germany's attack on Russia brought the Soviet Union into an alliance with the Western powers—when he was appointed Ambassador to Washington.

Stalin liked him, and fifteen years ago, when he pinned on Litvinoff's breast the Order of Lenin, one of Russia's highest decorations, Stalin called him "*Papasha*" (dear fahter).

U.S. Defense Gains Reviewed; Outlook For 1952 Is Weighed

By MARK S. WATSON
[*Sunpapers Military Correspondent*]

Washington, Jan. 1—There are two factors in providing a measurement of America's defensive position at any specific time.

One is the military resources (and these include economic and political and moral resources as well) of the United States and its allies. The other factor is the task to be accomplished, or the situation to be faced.

For in an era and region of good feeling, military resources can be reduced to a minimum—indeed, in such an area as the frontier between the United States and Canada they long ago were reduced to zero.

May Last For Years

In an area of threatened conflict and a period of baldly stated hostility—which threatens to last for years—defensive forces, actual and potential, must be brought to a high level and maintained there.

This building up of American military resources has made impressive advances in the last year, is still under way, and is scheduled to continue under way for fully two years before our defensive establishment reaches a temporary plateau.

Even then, when it no longer appears necessary to expand our powers (if peace prevails, or merely today's cold war), it still will be necessary to replace some of them with new forms of equipment and new techniques.

Seapower Substitutions

To think that this recurring substitution of new weapons for old is limited to airpower would be a delusion. We simply know that airpower is taking on new forms almost monthly as scientists make new discoveries and technologists develop new applications.

But seapower also is making its own rapid substitutions (note the atomic submarine now scheduled for completion in 1954, with its certainty of transforming underseas warfare, and hence all warfare) and landpower's adaptation to guided missiles will transform army tactics and strategy quite as much.

Production Time Lag

Yet all these things come slowly (there is a two-year lag even when an airplane model is approved) and while they are developing, military chiefs must maintain the strength of such an organization as they already have, and make best use of it. Korea has demonstrated this, because until very recently when jet airplanes appeared, the enemy was using World War II weapons and techniques, and he could be coped with, to a large degree, with our own weapons of that period.

Europe, too, has demonstrated it, for regardless of the deterrent powers of our known atomic bomb resources, the immediate threat to western Europe has been very largely that of Russia's World War II resources in the form of tanks (mostly of World War II type) and artillery and 175 divisions of infantry, supported by aerial fleets including (like our own) numerous attack planes of obsolescent types.

In figuring what could deter, if not defeat, Russian aggression, Western statesmen may have leaned too heavily upon the American atomic bomb, with its presumed powers of bombarding interior Russia at will and doing enormous damage to Russian industrial resources. A thoughtful American officer, of extremely high rank, has pointed out that the atomic bomb, so used, could indeed shatter Russian industry.

"But Russian industry is limited anyway, and we must assume that it already has produced vast stores of tanks, guns, planes and ammunition," he said. "This would suffice

(Continued on Page 2, Column 5)

NEW BUDGET FACES CONGRESS PARING

Rep. Cannon Spearheading Drive For Fiscal Balance

By RODNEY CROWTHER
[*Washington Bureau of The Sun*]

Washington, Jan. 1—A congressional drive to cut President Truman's 1953 budget to make income and outgo balance already has begun with Representative Cannon (D., Mo.), chairman of the powerful House Appropriations Committee, spearheading the movement.

Cannon declared on his return to Washington yesterday that he is determined that both defense and nondefense appropriations must be trimmed enough to avoid a deficit.

Meanwhile, word has come from the White House that the returning legislators may have to wait an extra week or ten days for a look at the President's budget proposals.

Usually the budget message follows closely on the heels of the message on the state of the Union—it had originally been set down tentatively for January 14.

Delay Is Indicated

But Joseph Short, presidential press secretary, has indicated that there will probably be a delay this year because of difficulties experienced in getting all the departmental estimates together.

The particular delay has been in getting the detailed figures on the defense needs from the Pentagon authorities.

Cannon indicated, however, that he has no intention of waiting for the budget message before going to work on 1953 appropriations. Some subcommittee men will get down to work next week, he said, hearing departmental justifications for the funds they are seeking.

The Missouri Democrat, who led last year's movement in the House for economy, said he plans to pull the purse strings so tight this year that neither new taxes nor an increase in the Federal debt limitation will be needed.

Unofficial reports for weeks have indicated that the President himself

(Continued on Page 4, Column 2)

TAFT FORCES SURE OF HIS NOMINATION

Backers Say He Will Get GOP Nod On Early Ballot

By DEWEY L. FLEMING

Washington, Jan. 1—A flurry of activity on the part of Republican presidential hopefuls and faint signs of animation in the Democratic camp marked the advent of the 1952 election year.

Headquarters of Senator Robert A. Taft, Ohio, celebrated New Year's Day with the issuance of a statement saying the Senator's nomination for the presidency of the GOP on an early ballot "now seems a certainty."

Important News Promised

Champions of Gen. Dwight D. Eisenhower stimulated interest and curiosity with an announcement that they would dispense important news of their man's intentions at an extraordinary press conference scheduled for Sunday noon.

The supposition was that in one way or another the forthcoming announcement in behalf of the General would serve to clarify the question of his availability, and it was expected that it would have direct relation to the year's first presidential preference primary election March 11, in New Hampshire.

From Nashville, Tenn., came word that Charles Neese, former administrative assistant to Senator Estes Kefauver (D., Tenn.), planned to open a national "Kefauver-for-President" headquarters in Washington later this week.

The near-victory claim of the

(Continued on Page 4, Column 3)

U.S. Ship Captain Riding Out Hurricane Alone In Atlantic

Captain Carlsen is well-known in Baltimore shipping circles as the "Mercy Radio Skipper"..............................Page 26

London, Jan. 1 (AP)—Capt. Kurt Carlsen rode out New Year's Day alone on his hurricane-beaten, heavily listing ship, the Flying Enterprise, 250 miles out in the Atlantic.

The storm, which sent three sizable ships to the bottom and took at least 63 lives at sea and in western Europe, was abating and seamen said the 6,710-ton ship had a chance of surviving the six-day storm.

When the hurricane struck, the Flying Enterprise was en route from Hamburg, Germany, to New York.

Remains Company's Property

The United States destroyer John W. Weeks was expected to reach the scene tomorrow to relieve the United States Navy supply ship, Golden Eagle, which was watching over the helpless vessel. But there was no hope that a rescue tug would arrive before tomorrow.

The 37-year-old skipper from Woodbridge, N.J., ordered the crew of 40 and ten passengers to abandon ship Friday, but stubbornly stuck to his bridge alone. As long as he was aboard, the ship was the property of its owner, the Isbrandtsen Company of New York. If he abandoned ship it would be classed as a derelict and anyone taking her in tow could claim extra salvage money.

A radio amateur, Carlsen tapped out cheerful messages to his family until today when his radio was silent. A company spokesman said no effort was being made to intercept his messages.

The sixteenth survivor from the Flying Enterprise was landed at Liverpool from the rescue ship Arion last night. He was George Miterko, 33-year-old greaser from Cleveland. The body of one crewman and all other passengers and crew were picked up by other ships.

"Please, God, Protect Our Skipper"

Members of the Arion's crew quoted Miterko as telling them:

"Captain Kurt was simply wonderful. He insisted on staying with his ship to the end. Please, God, protect our skipper."

Miterko was rescued after he had

(Continued on Page 2, Column 8)

COLLEGE PARK ELEVEN SCORES THREE TIMES IN FIRST HALF OF CONTEST

Ed Modzelewski, Terp Fullback, Awarded Warren V. Miller Trophy As Outstanding Player; Ed Fullerton Tallies Two Touchdowns

Full page of Sugar Bowl pictures on Page 13

By LOUIS M. HATTER
[*Sun Staff Correspondent*]

New Orleans, Jan. 1—An alert and aggressive University of Maryland defeated Tennessee, the nation's top-ranked 1951 football power, 28 to 13, in the eighteenth annual Sugar Bowl classic here this afternoon.

The College Park eleven outclassed its favored rival in almost every department of play as it scored once in the opening quarter, twice in the second period and again in the third. Ed Fullerton, 190-pound halfback, was the all-around standout for the Terrapins, scoring two touchdowns; intercepting two Tennessee passes — running 46 yards with one for the longest scoring play of the day; passing to a third Old Liner tally, and recovering an enemy fumble that set up another Maryland drive to the end zone.

Payne Leads Tennessee

Jack Scarbath, junior quarterback from Baltimore, and Bob Shemonski, left-halfback in Coach Jim Tatum's split-T attack, registered the other Maryland six-pointers. Don Decker successfully place-kicked all four of his extra-point attempts.

For the Tennessee Volunteers of General Bob Neyland, the nation's foremost teacher of the single-wing attack, Herky Payne, understudy to the heralded All-America, Hank Lauricella, was the hero in a losing cause. Payne passed five yards to Bert Rechichar for one six-pointer and tallied the other himself on a two-yard buck.

Maryland's triumph today in this battle of undefeated gridiron titans, before a capacity Sugar Bowl audience of 82,500, stamps the Terrapins as unquestionably the foremost football team of the last season.

Ranked Number 3

The Terps entered the contest with a No. 3 ranking in the final nation-wide Associated Press poll. Maryland had won nine and Tennessee ten games during the regular season, and the Terps had an 11-game winning streak and the Volunteers a 20-game string.

Individually, there were Maryland standouts on both offensive and defensive platoons in every position. Ed Modzelewski, the Terps' crushing 210-pound fullback, was the big gun of the attack, piling up 153 yards rushing in 28 carries, almost double Tennessee's net ground attack of 81 yards.

For his performance, greatest seen here by a fullback since Jarrin' John Kimbrough led Texas A.& M. to a 14-to-13 victory over Tulane in 1940, Ed Modzelewski was voted the Warren V. Miller Memorial Trophy. He took the honor in a close vote over Fullerton, who also received many ballots in recognition of his all-round play on both offense and defense.

But it was a great team victory for Maryland, the nearest thing to a Yankee in the Southern Conference and treated like one two weeks ago when the conference ordered a one-year football-schedule boycott because Maryland accepted the invitation to this very Sugar Bowl game against the wishes of the other schools.

Ball Handling Superb

The ball handling and passing of Quarterback Scarbath, who completed 6 of his 9 passes for 57 yards, was superb. His selection of plays was brilliant.

Maryland's offensive line outcharged Tennessee's vaunted forward wall throughout the bruising battle, played in sweltering 82-degree heat. Defensively, the names of Bob Morgan, Bill Maletzky, Ed Kensler, Dick Modzelewski and John Alderton were constantly being repeated in the press row and credited with stopping the Volunteers' great running and passing threat, Lauricella.

Lauricella's final game for Tennessee, played before home-town New Orleans fans, was almost a complete anti-climax to a sensa-

(Continued on Page 15, Column 3)

MARYLANDERS STORM FIELD

Fans Surround Athletes After Sugar Bowl Victory

Football scores over politics at McKeldin reception.....Page 26

By CHARLES G. WHITEFORD
[*Sun Staff Correspondent*]

New Orleans, Jan. 1—Maryland stood on top of the football world today.

And the view turned thousands of Terp rooters here in the Sugar Bowl dizzy with elation.

With the sounding of the horn that spelled a 28-to-13 victory over Tennessee, some of the younger Maryland fans stormed the field and surrounded the athletes in red and white uniforms who had made the whole thing possible.

Many of the older alumni simply slumped in their seats, completely exhausted.

Maryland Band Struts

One old timer, his red and white cap on the back of his head and his pennant drooping, just lolled back and muttered, "It's grand, it's grand, it's grand."

The 100-piece Maryland band took to the field on which the "big team" had just proved its right to the game and strutted to the tune of "A Hot Time in the Old Town Tonight."

There was not a doubt in the world that it was going to be exactly that—a hot time in old New Orleans tonight.

Dr. H. C. Byrd, president of the university, was grinning all over himself. He must have shaken 1,000 hands during and after the contest.

He was obviously as happy as it is possible to get. "Curley" himself was a Terp football coach for 23 seasons, and before that was an outstanding quarterback for Maryland.

Dr. Byrd Happy

There was just one little cloud on the horizon for Marylanders. They had to watch dyed-in-the-wool Tennesseeans go through the throes of their team's first defeat in 21 games.

The Tennesseeans had been fully confident that the Vols would lick Maryland—just as Marylanders were fully confident that what did happen would happen.

Maryland rooters know how Tennesseans feel tonight—and they can sympathize.

Nevertheless, hundreds of Marylanders were keeping appointments with an equal number of Tennessee supporters in hotel lobbies, rooms and bars. They are not sympathetic

(Continued on Page 15, Column 2)

Bowl Game Scores

Sugar Bowl	
28—Maryland	Tennessee—13
Rose Bowl	
40—Illinois	Stanford— 7
Orange Bowl	
17—Georgia Tech	Baylor—14
Cotton Bowl	
20—Kentucky	T.C.U.— 7
Gator Bowl	
14—Miami	Clemson— 0
Sun Bowl	
25—Texas Tech	Pacific—14

Weather Forecast
Partly cloudy with a chance of scattered showers and thunder storms. Yesterday's temperatures: High, 88; low, 71.
(Details, Page 10; Map, Page 31.)

THE SUN

FINAL

Registered United States Patent Office

Vol. 231—No. 64—F | MORNING, 179,030 EVENING, 197,505 PAID CIRCULATION IN JUNE 376,535 SUNDAY 308,451 | BALTIMORE, THURSDAY, JULY 31, 1952 | Entered as second-class matter at Baltimore Post Office | 32 Pages | 5 Cents

2,300 CARS CROSS BAY BRIDGE IN 6 HOURS

66 B-29'S HIT HUGE KOREAN METAL PLANT

Red Fighters Attack U.S. Planes Making Biggest Night Raid Of War

Seoul, Korea, *Thursday*, July 31 (AP)—Waves of B-29 Superforts, flying in darkness without fighter escort, smashed a huge North Korean metals plant early today in the biggest overnight air blow of the Korean war.

The 66 B-29's ran a gantlet of Communist night fighters and anti-aircraft fire to dump 660 tons of bombs on the sprawling 12½-acre plant near Sinuiju in Northwest Korea. Pilots reported at least 25 to 30 Red fighter planes and 19 searchlights in the target area.

Every bomber which took part in the huge raid returned safely to its base, the Air Force said. Two B-29 wings from Okinawa and one from Japan hit the big aluminum processing installation, but bomber crews were instructed to avoid hitting nearly 300 barrack-type structures near the target.

The Far East Air Force described results of the raid as "excellent."

Smoke Rises 4,000 Feet

Col. Winton R. Close, of Los Angeles, who directed the attack from one of the bombers, said smoke was rising 4,000 to 5,000 feet over the shattered aluminum plant when the last B-29 finished its bomb run.

Close said almost every other bomber was attacked by Red jet and propeller-driven night fighters as they swept over the target area. Nine of ten enemy fighters made firing passes at Close's plane during the five hours he spent over the area.

The light metals plant, a fat military target, was at Yangsi, 3 miles east of the mouth of the Yalu River. Only 11 miles west of the target was Antung, home base of hundreds of Red jets in Manchuria.

None Crosses Border

Lieut. Col. Fred W. Grindle, of Westbury, N.Y., deputy air commander for the Yangsi strike, said no Allied planes crossed the Manchurian border, but they flew so close he could see "lights all over Manchuria."

The biggest raid of the war was a daytime strike June 23 by more than 500 Air Force, Navy and Marine planes at five North Korean hydroelectric plants forming the nucleus of Asia's largest power system.

No B-29's participated in that strike. That was the opening of a new "get tough" policy of which today's raid was another installment.

Brig. Gen. Wiley D. Ganey, commanding general of the Far Eastern Air Force bomber command, said the big raid would have a "psychological impact" on the Communists. Gen. James A. Van Fleet, 8th Army commander, has often said the Reds would agree to an armistice in Korea only if sufficient military pressure were applied.

Pull Troops Back

Van Fleet said yesterday the Reds had pulled 60,000 troops out of the rain-sodden front lines to escape punishing blows by Allied artillery and fighter-bombers.

Both sides waited out the ground war today as rains and floods left the front a water-soaked morass.

It was the first blow at the factory—the Oriental Light Metals Company. The sprawling plant lies 10 miles southeast of Sinuiju.

For three shattering hours the big bombers from Japan and Okinawa blasted the plant with 500 bombs. Some were delayed bombs timed to explode hours or days later.

The B-29's came in at 20,000 feet through an almost moonless night and dropped their deadly loads through electronic techniques.

Are No Saucers, Says Vandenberg

Seattle, Wash., July 30 (AP)—The top man of the Air Force tossed cold water today on the latest flying-saucer phobia, saying he doesn't believe such things exist.

Gen. Hoyt S. Vandenberg, Air Force Chief of Staff, said in an interview with a *Post-Intelligencer* reporter:

"I don't believe there is any such thing as a flying saucer. But apparently there are physical phenomena which make people say they have seen the saucers.

"They are not machines flown by men from Mars, nor from any foreign powers. Nor does the Air Force or any United States military agency have a flying saucer.

"I don't like this continued, long-range occurrence of what might be called mass hysteria about flying saucers. The Air Force has had teams of experts investigating all reports for several years, since the end of World War II, and they never have found anything to substantiate existence of such things as flying saucers."

Sunpapers photo—Kniesche

THE OLD AND THE NEW—A motorcade heads east to complete the opening of the Chesapeake Bay bridge while a ferry sails west, and into oblivion, as the ferry transportation service comes to end.

CHESAPEAKE SPAN OPENED IN CEREMONY

5-Hour-Plus Dedication Attended By 10,000 On Both Shores

By RUSSELL W. BAKER

The first surge of what Marylanders hope will be an endless stream of traffic across the Chesapeake began flowing through the toll gates of the new Chesapeake Bay Bridge at 6.01 o'clock last night.

The regular flow of toll traffic, which will eventually help pay the $45,000,000 bill for the world's third-longest bridge, began after a double-header dedication ceremony that may well have been the longest in history.

Early Business Brisk

Business was brisk last night. Louis J. O'Donnell, director of bridges, estimated early today that between 2,300 and 2,500 vehicles paid charges between 6.01 P.M., when the toll lanes were opened, and last midnight.

Figuring an average of a little more than four to a vehicle, that would mean about 10,000 persons used the bridge during its first six hours of business.

So prolonged was the job of dedicating the bridge that one State trooper was felled during the ceremonies—by the heat—and the amplifier system which bore a day-long barrage of oratory to the visitors eventually collapsed under the strain and forced curtailment of the program.

The Silent Star

The bridge itself, the silent but overshadowing star of the day's proceedings, proved it is made of sterner stuff. When all the excitement subsided and the orators and the politicians departed, it got down immediately to the job of whisking motorists across the bay faster than they have ever gone before.

Subordinated only slightly to the bridge's role in the ceremonies were Governor McKeldin and former Gov. William Preston Lane, Jr.

Mr. Lane held the spotlight because it was his work, during the 1947 session of the Legislature, that got the bridge started.

Governor McKeldin earned top billing because he happened to be the Governor when the bridge was finished. As he, himself, put it, "I did nothing. Time took care of that."

Program Lasts 5 Hours

From beginning to end, the marathon dedication program lasted 5 hours and 27 minutes. It began on the shadeless, broiling highway near the Sandy Point toll booths at 10.40 A.M. and ended 4 miles away in a county-fair atmosphere at Matapeake on the Eastern Shore at 4.07 P.M.

In the hours between, approximately 10,000 people on both sides of the bay milled about, drank soda pop, chased babies, perspired, watched parades, admired the bridge and ignored most of the awesome oratorical barrage.

From all the speechmaking, two points which may be of significance to the bridge's future were raised.

Mr. Lane, in his dedication speech, again raised the question of a formal name for the bridge and revived an old suggestion of City Councilman Joseph Bertorelli's that it be named to honor the State's dead fighting men of World War II.

"Our Deepest Debt"

"Our deepest debt of gratitude," he said, "we owe to those who made the greatest sacrifice for us and all mankind.

"I hope the bridge will be called the Memorial Bridge in memory of those who gave their lives that we might continue to live as free people."

The second problem for the future was raised by Governor Mc-

(Continued on Page 19, Column 1)

Laborites Heckle Churchill As He Tells Economic Plans

Acheson blames Congress in defense slowup............Page 2

By RODNEY CROWTHER
[London Bureau of The Sun]

London, July 30 — Winston Churchill, who once in Britain's darkest hour was called on to become her war leader, today had a dark hour of his own.

He heard an unruly and noisy opposition loudly demand "Resign," "Resign," as he painted a picture of his nation's economic peril and told the House of Commons that Britain must shift its production emphasis from defense to export items in order to avert bankruptcy.

He said the nation will also have to sell munitions to other countries to pay their way in the world.

Calls Plight "Tragic"

He called the economic plight of Britain "tragic." While there have been gains in the past half year, reserves are still too perilously low for comfort, he said, and "further effort to restore the balance between exports and imports by substantial economies" is necessary.

But the Prime Minister had a rough time of it. He was heckled by Labor opposition from start to finish. He was frequently taunted from opposition front benches.

Throughout the speech the chamber resounded with almost every sort of noise the human voice can devise. And throughout the whole uproarious hour Mr. Churchill looked the picture of an uncomfortable man who was being bullied for reasons he could not understand.

Refuses To Back Down

Despite opposition charges that he and his Government have painted the nation's plight in darker hues than justified, Churchill refused to retract one word of warning he has given about the peril of standing on a dangerous trapdoor.

The House later voted to support Churchill's economic program. It rejected by a 302-to-277 vote a Labor motion to censure the Government for failure to safeguard Britain's economic security. It then adopted, 299 to 277, a Conservative motion [illegible] those policies.

In his [illegible] Churchill said:

"Fifty [illegible] of us standing at a level of civilization not surpassed in the world and yet barely able to earn our living and pay our way and dependent for food for two fifths of our people on how we can do all this in this vast swirling world.

"Tragic, indeed—surely it is not a party matter. Tragic is the spectacle of the majesty, dominion and power of this once magnificent and still considerable British Empire having to worry and wonder how we can pay our monthly bills."

Drowned Out By Noise

Churchill's eloquent words were virtually drowned in the loud noise and boos from opposition benches. But he went on doggedly:

"I fully admit I am tortured by the thought. I will do everything in my power"—from the opposition benches came loud shouts of "Resign," "Resign" — "to bring home to the masses of our race and nation a sense of peril and the need for grave and far-reaching activities."

The 77-year-old statesman, who looked at times bewildered by the noise and sometimes angrily defiant, then leaned over to Clement

(Continued on Page 2, Column 3)

Red Radio Urges Iranians To Oust Shah, Mossadegh

By PAUL W. WARD
[Washington Bureau of The Sun]

Washington, July 30—The Kremlin has started its own propagandists beating the drums for the Iranian masses and soldiery to revolt and thrust their monarch, the Shah of Shahs, into exile behind Egypt's recently-ousted King Farouk, it was learned here today.

Its openly revolutionary agitation for the overthrow of not only the Shah but also Premier Mohammed Mossadegh, his National Front and the Iranian Parliament, it was further learned, is:

1 Being carried on by a radio station which keeps up a superficial pretense of being a "clandestine" one inside Iran but actually is located in the U.S.S.R.

Would Turn Flank

2. Being conducted in a fashion suggesting that the Russians see in the current Iranian situation an opportunity to turn the flank of the Atlantic community's eastern defenses.

Meanwhile, invited to discuss that situation at his regular weekly press conference here this forenoon, Dean Acheson, Secretary of State, confessed he found it less than encouraging.

He asked to be excused from further discussion of it on the ground that no attempt by him to make a public appraisal of the situation

(Continued on Page 2, Column 6)

ARMY SAYS RUSSIA DISTORTED DIARY

Points To Falsified Quotations From Grow's Notes

Washington, July 30 (AP) — The Army charged tonight that Soviet propagandists completely falsified and twisted excerpts from Maj. Gen. Robert W. Grow's famous diary for which the General was court-martialed.

In a surprise development, less than 24 hours after General Grow was convicted of improperly jotting United States military secrets in his personal journal, the Army said flatly that the diary did not contain the statement:

"War! As soon as possible! Now!"

Called Fabrications

The Army's official spokesman said excerpts as published by the Soviets were "complete fabrications."

The spokesman said the Russian version of what Grow allegedly wrote in his diary "twisted" the General's statements in such a way as to make the United States instead of Russia appear as the potential aggressor.

The spokesman said the Army had been unable to make any portion of the diary text available earlier because publication might have prejudiced the findings of the court-martial.

A court of eight top ranking generals convicted General Grow yesterday and sentenced him to a formal reprimand and suspension from command for six months.

The basic charge, in effect, was

(Continued on Page 9, Column 3)

LODGE EYES PLANS FOR IKE STRATEGY

Flies To Denver; Argues For Stronger Civil-Rights Stand

Summerfield predicts Taft will stump for GOP.........Page 7

By THOMAS O'NEILL
[Sun Staff Correspondent]

Denver, July 30—Senator Henry Cabot Lodge, manager of the preconvention campaign that brought the Republican nomination for President to Gen. Dwight D. Eisenhower, flew to Denver today with a portfolio of strategy suggestions for the campaign.

Shortly after his arrival, it was reported that he was arguing for a stronger civil rights stand than is contained in the party platform or in statements so far made by the nominee.

This was coupled with a counsel to fight for the election in the populous industrial states without placing too great reliance on victory in the South.

Goes Into Conference

Immediately upon his arrival, Senator Lodge went in to a luncheon conference with General Eisenhower. He said he will remain at the campaign headquarters until the end of the week taking part in a busy schedule of strategy and organization talks scheduled by the Eisenhower staff.

Under questioning at the campaign headquarters, Senator Lodge indicated a conviction that the trend of the Democratic National Convention dictated a change in

(Continued on Page 7, Column 2)

U.S. Jury Charges Bribery, Perjury In Army Contracts

Brooklyn, N.Y., July 30 [*Special*]—Six indictments were returned today by a Federal grand jury charging bribery, conspiracy and perjury in connection with Army Transportation Corps contracts.

Named in three of the indictments, presented before Judge Harold M. Kennedy in United States District Court, was Louis L. Fragala, 38, of Newport News, Va., a civilian Transportation Corps employé.

Gannon Also Named

Fragala, formerly deputy chief of the Technical Publications Unit of the Transportation Corps in Brooklyn and reported to be doing similar work at Fort Eustis, Va., was charged with bribery and two cases of conspiracy.

Also named was Edgar T. Gannon, 41, of Fort Lee, N.J., a former first lieutenant discharged from the Army July 28, 1946, while serving as chief of the Technical Publications Unit here. Gannon faces two conspiracy charges.

The alleged conspiracies involved contracts for composition of technical manuals for use of equipment by army personnel.

To Expedite Payments

One contractor had subcontract arrangements with a corporation in which Gannon and another man named in the indictments had an interest.

Fragala, according to the charges, was to approve and expedite work submitted by the contractor and expedite partial payments requested by the contractor.

In another instance where a sim-

(Continued on Page 9, Column 1)

Stevenson Makes It Clear He's No 100% 'Fair Dealer'

By HOWARD NORTON
[Sun Staff Correspondent]

Springfield, Ill., July 30—Gov. Adlai E. Stevenson tossed off the mantle of the "reluctant candidate" today, announced that he is "quite content with the Democratic convention and its results," and made it clear he is not a 100 per cent Trumanite "Fair Dealer."

The Democratic standard bearer turned up at his first big press conference in a confident, fighting mood.

Taft-Hartley Views

He let it be known that:

1. He intends to run his own campaign in his own way—even to controlling the extent of President Truman's participation in it.

2. He personally feels the party's labor plank goes unnecessarily far in demanding repeal of the Taft-Hartley law, and believes the same results could be achieved by mere revision of the law. But he will go along with the platform.

3. He agrees with Gen. Dwight D. Eisenhower "substantially" on foreign policy as it concerns western Europe, and doesn't think that portion of foreign policy will be a campaign issue.

4. He feels it is "foolish and irresponsible" to talk of definite cuts in either arms or taxes.

5. He is convinced "a tax cut must be obtained as soon as possible in keeping with the nation's needs."

Plans Many Speeches

6. He believes his biggest political "hazard" is that he is not well known over the country. To remedy this he intends to travel "extensively" and speak as often as he can.

"I'm feeling more aggressive every moment," he told a reporter who asked whether he had undergone any change of heart about running for President.

"Do you feel that you reflect a different philosophy than has prevailed in Washington the last twenty years?"

"That," he said after pondering a moment, "would have to be judged objectively.

"I have expressed views which certainly are not consistent with what the people think is the prevailing philosophy in Washington.

"But in other respects," he added quickly, "we are in agreement."

Hasn't Talked To Truman

Stevenson said he had not talked to the President since he saw the Chief Executive in Chicago, and has had only one or two brief conversations with Frank McKinney, chairman of the Democratic National Committee.

Observers here are remarking on the notable absence of visitors or calls from Washington.

Everything, so far, has been in the hands of the Governor and the staff he had collected around him here before he was nominated.

And aides report that the Governor has not yet begun even to get financial help from the National Committee toward handling his public relations.

Asked About Truman Aid

Someone asked Stevenson whether he welcomed President Truman's plans to make some "whistle-stop" campaign tours on his behalf.

He gave a "yes—but" answer, qualifying it because he said he doesn't know yet to what extent President Truman plans to cam-

(Continued on Page 4, Column 3)

Klan Wizard Gets 4-Year Sentence In North Carolina

Whiteville, N.C., July 30 (AP)—A four-year prison sentence today cut short the empire plans of Thomas L. Hamilton, pudgy imperial wizard of the Ku Klux Klan who masterminded the flogging of a Negro woman.

Hamilton and 62 of his night-riding Klansmen were sentenced in Columbus Superior Court in one of North Carolina's largest mass trials. The trial, one of several involving the Klan in recent months, was aimed at destroying the anti-Catholic, anti-Negro and anti-Jewish secret society in the Carolinas.

Residents Bolted Doors

Judge Clawson L. Williams gave the 45-year-old, bespectacled Leesville (S.C.) ex-grocer the maximum term. He had pleaded guilty last week to two counts of conspiracy to assault in the flogging of Evergreen Flowers, a Negro woman. Klansmen testified that they beat her because she had been "running around with white men."

Judge Williams commented tersely in passing sentence against Hamilton:

"The day has not come in North Carolina when a man has to barricade himself in his home with the setting sun."

This was in obvious reference to the wave of terror that gripped this southeastern North Carolina tobacco-growing section last year after the Klan spread across the

(Continued on Page 9, Column 2)

On Other Pages

Weather Forecast
Sunny in the morning, becoming cloudy and colder toward night. Yesterday's temperatures: High, 49; low, 37.
(Details, Page 16; Map, Page 35.)

THE SUN

FINAL

Registered United States Patent Office

Vol. 232—No. 93—F | PAID CIRCULATION IN FEBRUARY MORNING 175,398 EVENING 201,317 376,715 || SUNDAY 313,897 | BALTIMORE, FRIDAY, MARCH 6, 1953 | Entered as second-class matter at Baltimore Post Office | 36 Pages | 5 Cents

Stalin Is Dead But Kremlin Keeps Silent On Successor

PARTY AND GOVERNMENT LEADERS GIVE OFFICIAL ANNOUNCEMENT BY RADIO

Doctors Attribute Death To Heart Failure—Medical Bulletins Marked Decline After Brain Hemorrhage Sunday

London, *Friday*, March 6 (AP)—Joseph Stalin died last night behind the 12-foot-thick walls of Moscow's Kremlin. He dominated a third of the world's peoples as the most powerful dictator in history.

The Prime Minister of the Soviet Union and the supreme chief of the Communist party succumbed at 9.50 P.M., four days after suffering a brain hemorrhage (stroke).

He had been in a coma since he was stricken Sunday night, and his condition grew progressively worse. Yesterday his ten physicians said his heart was faltering.

Broadcast Six Hours Late

The announcement of his death was broadcast from Moscow at 4.07 A.M. Moscow time today—more than six hours after his doctors had given up their struggle.

The official announcement said:

"The heart of the comrade and inspired continuer of Lenin's will, the wise leader and teacher of the Communist party and the Soviet people—Joseph Vissarionovitch Stalin—has stopped beating."

There was no immediate indication from Moscow who was taking over control of the country, but the announcement was issued in the name of the Communist party's Central Committee, the Council of Ministers and the Presidium of the Supreme Council.

All these are organs which Stalin dominated and among those next to him in power have been Georgi Malenkov, Lavrentt P. Beria, Vyacheslav M. Molotov and Nicholas Bulganin.

Malenkov Called Most Prominent

The most prominent leader of the Communist party, next to Stalin, has been Malenkov. He keynoted the all-party Congress last October, laying down the law to all segments of the party in matters of discipline.

The Soviet regime holds sway across a sixth of the surface of the earth—from the Baltic Sea to Bering Strait.

Stalin's fatal illness became known on Wednesday, more than two days after he was stricken in his Kremlin apartment.

An official announcement issued from the Ministry of Health and signed by the ten physicians said Stalin "had a sudden hemorrhage of the brain" the night of March 1. This "affected vitally important parts of the brain" and paralyzed his right leg and arm. He lost consciousness and the power to speak.

A Striking Coincidence

Two more bulletins were issued—early yesterday Moscow time, and again last night only an hour and a half before the announced death hour. The third bulletin told of Stalin's failing heart.

By a striking coincidence, Stalin's fatal illness came only two months after his regime had announced the uncovering of a plot by nine doctors. These doctors plotted to kill A. A. Zhdanov, once a Stalin heir-apparent, and indeed had killed him in 1948, the charges said.

Stalin ruled Russia as undisputed dictator for nearly 30 years. Through communism, he extended his sway beyond the borders of the Soviet Union and its 200,000,000 people to areas encompassing another half billion people.

He reached the height of his power when he led the Soviet Union against the Nazis of Adolf Hitler as an ally of the United States and Great Britain. He was one of the "Big Three" of the world — with Britain's Winston

(Continued on Page 6, Column 1)

U. S. TO FIRE HUNDREDS OF JOBHOLDERS

New Order To Hit Department Of Justice And FSA Hardest

Agency seeks cut in every item in Truman budget......*Page* 2

By THOMAS O'NEILL
[*Washington Bureau of The Sun*]

Washington, March 5—An Administration ax swung down today on the job security of several hundred highly placed holdover officials in governmental departments.

Most of those whose doom was declared are in top salary brackets where they assist in policy making and act in confidential relationships to the agency heads.

President Eisenhower directed the preparation of an executive order repealing earlier directives that bestowed civil service protection upon jobholders in positions which the White House declared are not legitimately of civil service classification.

"More Than Several Hundred"

An official estimate put the number at "more than several hundred."

Announcing the order, James C. Hagerty, the White House press secretary, said it was aimed at jobholders who had been "frozen into the civil service over the last twenty years"—the period of unbroken Democratic administration. He said it was the Administration view that these officials are improperly in the civil service. Asked if it was the aim to strip that protection from as many as several hundred employés, he replied:

"You bet your life."

Mrs. Hobby Protests

Newly appointed department heads under the Eisenhower administration have uniformly expressed shocked surprise at the limited number of appointments available in their agencies because of civil service barriers permitting removal only for cause, barriers extending high in the departments.

Mrs. Oveta Hobby, new Federal Security Administrator, protested bitterly after a look around her department that she was restricted to the appointment of but a single subordinate of her own choice because of civil service limitations, but it was later ascertained that her fears were exaggerated.

In that department, however, the chief assistant administrator, ranking next to Mrs. Hobby, is under civil service protection. That is one of the jobs at which the new executive order is aimed.

Congressmen Insist On Action

A White House statement said the step will strengthen the civil service by bringing about more efficient administration.

Congressmen have been especially insistent upon action to make more appointments available to the new Administration. Their complaints led recently to a statement by Wesley Roberts, the Republican national chairman, that jobs would be found and made available.

"Questions have arisen relative to the attitude of this Administration toward the career civil service," said the White House announcement of the impending executive order.

"During the campaign the President assured the people that he would do everything possible to strengthen the civil service system. That is and will continue to be the policy of this Administration.

"From the beginning of the civil service system in 1883 it has been recognized that there are certain types of position that do not belong in the civil service system."

On Other Pages

Prince Charles Plays Cupid For His Pet 'Harvey'

London, March 5 [*Special*]—Prince Charles has added a furrow or two to the brow of Tommy, a gardener and handyman at Buckingham Palace.

Prince Charles was afraid that his Angora rabbit, Harvey, was lonely and wanted a wife, so "Mrs. Harvey" is arriving in about a fortnight's time.

The other day Prince Charles handed Tommy three brushes.

"I want Harvey to look nice when he meets his wife," he explained. "You brush him first with this hard brush and then with the soft one. And this," he added, "is Harvey's toothbrush. I want you to clean his teeth morning and evening just as I clean mine."

Another amenity Prince Charles has introduced into Harvey's life is a blind for his electrically heated hut—so he will not be frightened by stray cats.

[N.A.N.A.—Kemsley]

KIN OF TYDINGS FACES CHARGE

Probers Ask Justice Department To Study Conflicts

Washington, March 5 (AP)—House investigators asked the Justice Department today to study the testimony of Donald S. Tydings, an $8,700-a-year tax official, and determine whether he should be prosecuted for perjury.

Tydings, 56, is a cousin of former Senator Millard E. Tydings of Maryland.

In a two-week investigation of his career as an agent of the Alcohol Tax Unit of the Internal Revenue Bureau, a House Ways and Means subcommittee turned up evidence that Tydings used the good offices of his cousin and at least three other senators to advance his fortunes in the revenue bureau.

Says Conduct Was Probed

The subcommittee also heard testimony that Tydings was in frequent trouble with his superiors and that his official conduct was investigated several times.

When he appeared before the subcommittee Tuesday, Tydings acknowledged that he was buying diamond-studded jewelry for a woman friend at the time he was in trouble over a $3,000 bank loan guaranteed by a man described as a bootlegger.

He also admtited that an explanation he gave Federal agents concerning the use of the loan money was a "figment of imagination."

Snyder Blamed

Today the subcommittee, headed by Representative Kean (R., N.J.) heard that it was John Snyder, former Secretary of the Treasury, who was directly instrumental in putting a "stop order" on impending disciplinary action against Tydings and promising a promotion instead.

Dwight E. Avis, chief of the Alcohol Tax Division, testified that this was after Senator Tydings issued "an ultimatum" to promote his cousin rather than discipline him for alleged misdeeds, under the threat that he would "carry the matter to the President."

VAN FLEET SAYS GI'S ARE SHORT ON AMMUNITION

Byrd Demands Pentagon Punish Those Responsible For Lack

Washington, March 5 (AP)—Gen. James A. Van Fleet told Congress today American troops in Korea have been handicapped by a "serious shortage" of ammunition including hand grenades needed for close-in fighting on the battle front.

Senator Byrd (D., Va.) promptly dispatched an urgent message to Charles E. Wilson, Secretary of Defense, demanding that the Pentagon punish officials responsible for what he termed "this criminal inefficiency."

Wilson's office said he has already been giving "urgent attention" to the reported serious shortage of ammunition in Korea.

"Given Full Consideration"

A defense spokesman said that Wilson received Byrd's letter late this afternoon. The spokesman said that the letter "will be given full consideration, that the points raised will be looked into thoroughly and a factual reply will be made."

Maj. Gen. Floyd Parks, army chief of information, said later that he had checked Pentagon records and he declared:

"I find no immediate evidence of a shortage of hand grenades in Far East command depot stocks since the beginning of the Korean war. No doubt there have been local or short-term shortages due to distribution difficulties."

Parks estimated there are enough hand grenades stocked in Far East depots to last 90 days under normal combat conditions.

Fire Power Exceeds Reds'

Parks also said that even at the height of the heavy fighting in Korea last fall, when Communist artillery fire was five times heavier than ever before, Allied guns hurled back more than five times as many shells as the Reds fired into Allied lines.

Bristling with anger, Byrd said that in all his twenty years in the Senate he had "never been more shocked" than he was by testimony given by the former commander of United Nations forces in Korea at a closed-door session of the Senate Armed Services Committee.

Reported It Almost Daily

"General Van Fleet testified this shortage (of ammunition) has been continuous since he took command and that almost daily he had reported it officially and through channels," the Virginia Senator wrote Wilson.

"Failure to supply these munitions, according to General Van Fleet, seriously handicapped not only the prosecution of the war against Communist Chinese and North Koreans, but also the protection of our own troops.

"Shortage of munitions inevitably leads to greater loss of life and prolonged conflict. To me such a situation as this, extending over 22 months, represents criminal inefficiency."

Byrd called on Wilson to make a thorough investigation and advise him "what action you will take to punish those officers who have

(Continued on Page 17, Column 3)

U.S. Removes Price Controls From More Consumer Items

By HOWARD NORTON
[*Washington Bureau of The Sun*]

Washington, March 5—Price ceilings were removed today from items on which the American people spend $25,000,000,000 a year—including automobiles, bread, laundry and dry cleaning services and many home appliances.

Immediate price rises in some of these lines are expected.

Today's action was the fifth in a step-by-step program to decontrol all prices by April 30, and it leaves less than four per cent of common goods and services still under price controls.

The only consumer items still under restraint are coffee, beer, food waste disposal units, hot water heaters, hardware items and home heating fuel sold mainly in the northeast.

Bread Price To Rise

In announcing the action, Joseph Freehill, the price stabilizer, warned that consumers may expect to pay about a half-cent more per loaf of bread, but said he didn't think other bakery products would be affected.

Freehill also predicted price boosts by laundries and dry cleaners, and said that makers of home appliances have told him that higher copper prices may force them to charge more for their products.

Decontrol of laundry and dry-cleaning prices also means decontrol of linen and diaper supply services.

Home appliances removed from the control list today included refrigerators, stoves, dishwashers, clothing washers, dryers and ironers.

Action Set Later

Freehill said that waste disposal units and hot-water heaters would be decontrolled later.

Today's decontrol list also included: repair parts for autos, trucks, busses and aircraft; X-ray and therapeutic equipment, industrial and commercial services, copper chemicals and all items in the shipbuilding field on which controls had remained until today. These included mainly used ships and boats.

With the release of these items, only about 21½ per cent of the items on the Government's wholesale price index were still under control.

The Senate Banking and Currency Committee, meanwhile,

(Continued on Page 4, Column 4)

U.S. Watching Russian Crisis, President Says

Eisenhower Declares Free World Must Cling To Determination To Make Progress Toward Peace

By DEWEY L. FLEMING

Washington, March 5—President Eisenhower today described the Administration attitude toward the Soviet governmental crisis as one of very definite watchfulness.

The Executive chose his words carefully, and after a moment's reflection, in reply to a questioner at his weekly news conference who wanted to know if "events in the last day or so" had caused a feeling of "misgiving" or of "optimism" around the White House.

Earlier in the conference, which was held before the announcement of Joseph Stalin's death the President had observed on his own initiative that the subject uppermost in most minds around the world today was the illness of the Russian Premier and its possible effect upon the long struggle between the free world and the Communist world.

Bohlen's Departure Speeded

He stated bluntly that he could not foresee what the effect would be or what the results of a change of leadership in the Soviet Union might be. He said he and his intimate advisers had been trying to explore many possibilities in the situation, and that usually they ended up where they started.

But whatever the results within Russia and the whole Communist world, he counseled, Americans and free men everywhere must pursue the goal of peace seriously and must cling to determination to make progress along this line.

Meanwhile, the State Department moved to speed the departure of Charles E. Bohlen, newly appointed Ambassador to Russia, to his post in Moscow, in order that he might observe and report on developments resulting from the Russian crisis.

Quick Action Asked

Specifically, the Department asked the Senate to expedite Bohlen's confirmation. Hearings on his nomination already have been conducted by the Senate Foreign Relations Committee, and the chairman Senator Wiley (R., Wis.), said a vote on confirmation would be sought on Tuesday.

John Foster Dulles, Secretary of State, who asked that the confirmation procedure be speeded up, also requested the Senate committee to postpone "until a more appropriate time" the intended publication of an edited version of Bohien's testimony before the committee in a closed session last Monday.

The Secretary wrote that "the announcement of the serious if not mortal illness of Stalin, and the impossibility of prediction at the pres-

(Continued on Page 6, Column 5)

SMITH ANALYZES RUSSIA SITUATION

Senate Unit Hears Under Secretary Behind Closed Doors

By WILLIAM KNIGHTON, JR.
[*Washington Bureau of The Sun*]

Washington, March 5—Walter Bedell Smith, Under Secretary of State, today gave the Senate Foreign Relations Committee his expert analysis of the situation inside Russia.

For more than two hours he frankly discussed the potentialities of Premier Stalin's death as it might affect the future of the Soviet Politburo and of the free world.

The conference was held behind closed doors and the members, most of whom stayed to the end, were tight-lipped as to what specifically the State Department official had said. Smith's general views of the crisis were "substantially unchanged" from those expressed in his book, "My Three Years in Moscow."

Top-Secret Data

But Senator Wiley (R., Wis.), committee chairman, reported these sentiments were buttressed by "more recent intelligence reports," top-secret data which are at the official's disposal.

Smith was United States Ambassador to Moscow from 1946 to 1949 and directed this Government's Central Intelligence Agency before his recent appointment to the State Department by President Eisenhower.

The committee chairman reported that Smith had expressed the view that the situation in Russia is "in the laps of the gods."

According to Wiley, the Under Secretary commented on reports that three of Stalin's present associates, Georgi M. Malenkov, V. M. Molotov and L. P. Beria, might possibly engage in a struggle to become his successor.

Comments On Successors

In his book, copyrighted in 1949, Smith said those three men at that time appeared to be sharing the major portion of the power Stalin had delegated to his subordinates. But, the author stated:

"It is inconceivable to me that any one of these men can take Stalin's place. During the war years his stature became so great that it dwarfed all his associates. His mantle is now too large for any one of them to wear.

"My own belief is that when Stalin dies his power will be divided among these three. Or possibly, there may be associated with them the other two who appear to be next to them in prestige—Kaganovich and Bulganin."

The former Ambassador wrote that it now is impossible to state, when that time comes, whether "personal antagonisms and ambitions, suppressed in Stalin's presence, may assert themselves and disturb the co-operative relationship."

"I think it is quite likely that one or more of the directorate which succeeds Stalin, or even some new leader whose name is still unknown, eventually will be tempted to make a bid for

(Continued on Page 6, Column 6)

VISHINSKY RUSHING BACK TO MOSCOW

United Nations Observers Left Confused By Tactics

By PAUL W. WARD
[*Sun Staff Correspondent*]

New York, March 5—Andrei Y. Vishinsky, Soviet Foreign Minister, again today stayed away from the United Nations meeting halls, and this afternoon his aides let it be known that he is dropping his tasks here in favor of more important business now awaiting him in Moscow.

Vishinsky, who as prosecutor of Moscow's prewar purge trials helped Joseph Stalin rid himself of all rivals among the old Bolsheviks, is rushing back to the Soviet capital to protect his own interests in the new succession struggle that impends there, it is understood.

Conflict On Details

After Stalin's death was announced Vishinsky confirmed reports that he planned to leave tomorrow. But until then there had been only a series of remarks by his aides that predicted his early departure but conflicted as to how and when.

Valerian A. Zorin, No. 2 member of the Soviet delegation, when asked if Vishinsky were leaving tomorrow, replied: "I think so."

Georgi M. Zarubin, No. 3 member, made the same reply to that question.

But to the next: "By air or by sea?" Zorin answered: "By sea, I think," whereas Zarubin said: "By air, I think."

Later another Russian diplomat said Vishinsky definitely would sail on the French liner Liberte.

Reasons Left In Doubt

The difference between Zorin and Zarubin left reporters guessing as to the degree of Vishinsky's haste and, in particular, as to whether his concern is to avoid repeating the mistake of Trotsky, who missed Lenin's funeral in 1924, or, instead, to take care of less ceremonious matters.

Their puzzlement was not lessened by Zorin's reply when asked if Vishinsky would later return to New York and the General Assembly

It was again: "I think so."

Sir Gladwyn Jebb was moved at one point in the Korean debate this afternoon to refer to the puzzle, but he suppressed the desire and deleted from the prepared text of his speech the following lines:

"Mr. Vishinsky is not here. He has other preoccupations and no doubt they are very real ones."

Would Defer Debate

Sir Gladwyn kept, however, the line—"I feel that now is not the moment for a full-dress debate"—that had followed in his prepared text and added:

"We all know where we are and nothing we can say at this time can really change the facts of the situation. Instead, therefore, I would say only this: It is still essential for the free world, as represented in this Assembly, to remain united, confident and calm.

"Sure in the knowledge that aggression in Korea has been repelled, we must continue to stand on the various offers for an hon-

(Continued on Page 6, Column 3)

U.S. SENDS ITS CONDOLENCES TO RUSSIANS

Eisenhower Tells Dulles To Dispatch Message Of Official Regret

[*By The Associated Press*]

President Eisenhower last night ordered John Foster Dulles, Secretary of State, to send America's official condolences to the Soviet Government. The President acted within minutes after hearing of the death of Prime Minister Stalin.

The message follows:

"The Government of the United States tenders its official condolences to the Government of the Union of Socialist Soviet Republics on the death of Generalissimo Joseph Stalin, Prime Minister of the Soviet Union."

Observers in Washington noted immediately that Mr. Eisenhower strictly adhered to the requirements of international courtesy and omitted any words of personal tribute.

Lie Sends Message

Trygve Lie, secretary general of the United Nations and long-time adversary of Stalin, also sent a telegram to the Soviet Union's Foreign Minister tonight regretting Stalin's death.

"I have the honor," Lie told Andrei Y. Vishinsky, Soviet Foreign Minister, "to extend my personal condolences on the death of Generalissimo Joseph Stalin.

"On those occasions on which I have had the honor of meeting Mr. Stalin, I have been deeply impressed by the qualities which made him one of the outstanding statesmen of our time."

Lie was Justice Minister of Norway when Stalin demanded—and Lie refused—that Leon Trotsky be turned over for "trial." Trotsky had fled to Norway for refuge.

1950 Quarrel Reported

In the Spring of 1950 Lie visited Moscow where he was reported to have had a quarrel in the Kremlin with Stalin. Later Lie went all out in support of the United Nations in Korea and the Soviet Union has refused to recognize him as secretary general of the United Nations ever since.

In recognition of this, Lie signed his telegram without his title—there was no mention of his being connected with the United Nations.

William Z. Foster, chairman of the Communist party in the United States, called Stalin's death "a tremendous loss to the Russian people."

"Greatest Living Statesman"

He called Stalin "by far the greatest living statesman, the greatest statesman of our time. He was also the greatest leader for peace in the world." Foster scoffed at reports that there might be a struggle for the succession to Stalin.

Canadian officials said Prime Minister Louis St. Laurent would not comment until he had received official news of Stalin's death from the Canadian Embassy in Moscow.

Lester B. Pearson, Canada's Foreign Secretary and president of the United Nations General Assembly, told Vishinsky:

"With his passing the United Nations has lost one of its founders and the Soviet peoples the man

(Continued on Page 7, Column 6)

Son Of Cobbler, Stalin Rose To Be Reds' Undisputed Ruler

[*By the Associated Press*]

Joseph Stalin, the son of a cobbler, emerged out of the chaos of the Russian Revolution to master the forces unleashed by the upheaval—and became the undisputed ruler of the Soviet Union and the world Communist movement.

Successively theological student, revolutionary agitator, journalist, military leader and political administrator, he fired a downtrodden and war-shattered conglomeration of varying races into a crusading host. Under iron discipline they fulfilled in four years a five-year plan begun in 1928. Then he launched them upon an even broader effort which carried them into the front rank of nations.

Constitution Of 1936

The 1936 report of the International Labor Office at Geneva said that the Soviet Union had then attained a level equivalent to 300 per cent of its 1929 industrial output. Its grain, oil and timber were afloat to ports in all parts of the world. It was producing much of its own machinery from raw materials mined, smelted and fabricated within its own borders. It was supporting an army and air force deemed adequate to hold back possible foes in Europe and to check Japanese expansion in the

AP Wirephoto
MARSHAL STALIN
In Red Army uniform in 1944

Orient. It was rapidly building a navy to replace the czarist fleet destroyed by the Japanese 30 years earlier.

On top of this, Stalin, in 1936, gave the U.S.S.R. a new constitution, calculated to strengthen socialism but instituting a system which was called "Soviet democracy." It granted universal suffrage,

(Continued on Page 7, Column 1)

Stalin Had Stooge, London Paper Says

London, *Friday*, March 6 [*Reuter*]—The right-wing London *Daily Sketch* today carried on Page 1 a story headed "The Greatest Stalin Hoax Yet"—claiming that the Russians have been using a healthy double for Stalin to prevent rumors of his ill health.

The last person from this side of the Iron Curtain to see Stalin was India's Ambassador Krishna Menon, on February 18. The Indian said Stalin seemed fit.

"But this was not Stalin," said the *Sketch*. "The Russians, who have used a double to stand in for Stalin at public meetings, had now planted a stooge at all personal interviews.

"The double, says a report from an underground source in Moscow, spoke in a Caucasian dialect—no Georgian like Stalin's.

"Naturally, Mr. Menon could not be expected to know the difference."

Weather Forecast
Partly cloudy and warmer today and tonight; high near 87 degrees. Yesterday's temperatures: High, 80; low, 66.
(Details, Page 10; Map, Page 25.)

THE SUN FINAL

Registered United States Patent Office

Vol. 233—No. 60—F | MORNING, 179,056; EVENING, 199,328; PAID CIRCULATION IN JUNE 378,384 SUNDAY 308,448 | BALTIMORE, MONDAY, JULY 27, 1953 | Entered as second-class matter at Baltimore Post Office | 26 Pages | 5 Cents

Armistice Signed; Communists Order End Of Fighting; Rhee Will Keep Peace Until Political Conference; President And Dulles Hail Truce But Urge Caution

CHIEF EXECUTIVE GIVES FREE WORLD WARNING TO KEEP POWDER DRY

Secretary Of State Promises Vigilance In Korea Will Not Be Relaxed; 'Armistice Without Victory,' Some Legislators Say

By PAUL W. WARD
[Washington Bureau of The Sun]

Washington, July 26—President Eisenhower joined tonight with his Secretary of State and Democratic as well as Republican congressional leaders in hailing the achievement of a cease-fire in Korea, and simultaneously warning the free world's 1,600,000,000 people to keep their powder dry.

They themselves had kept their fingers crossed about the reaching of an armistice right up to the moment official word was flashed them from Panmunjom that—after 757 days of off-and-on negotiations that started July 10, 1951—the Communists finally had signed there.

With an eye to the fragilities of the truce thus effected and the possibilities that, even if it does not break down, it may produce to the Communists' benefit more divisive strains among the forces opposing them than the war itself has done, they urged upon the free world in general and Americans in particular an attitude of caution rather than elation.

"Prayers Of Thanksgiving"

Addressing the nation for five minutes by radio and television at 10 P.M. on the armistice signed "almost an hour ago," President Eisenhower, who had driven back to Washington from Quantico, Va., in midafternoon, asserted he and his compatriots greet the truce with "prayers and thanksgiving."

But, before closing with a repetition of the "with malice toward none, with charity for all" from Lincoln's second inaugural address at the Civil War's end, he warned his countrymen: "We have won an armistice on a single battleground, not peace in the world." They "must be vigilant," he added, "against the possibility of untoward developments."

Dulles Hopes For Good Faith

Following the Chief Executive on the air, John Foster Dulles, Secretary of State, said:

"The Communist commanders have signed for their commands. We hope that they have acted and will proceed in good faith. However, until that is demonstrated, the present armistice is by no means the equivalent of assured peace. So, we shall not relax our vigilance nor shall we reduce our strength in Korea until future events show that this is prudent."

Neither the Chief Executive nor Dulles sought to claim for the Eisenhower Administration exclusive credit for a truce that ends the fighting in Korea.

Doubts And Misgivings Voiced

Nor did Republican leaders in Congress assert any such claim. Instead, they joined with their Democratic opposite numbers in voicing doubts and misgivings about the truce that President Eisenhower and Secretary Dulles had merely implied.

Thus Representative Short (R., Mo.), chairman of the House Armed Services Committee, declared himself "anything but pleased" with the armistice terms and added that American prestige had been damaged by this first instance of the country's failing to fight a war to a finish. It could have ended in victory over the Communists, he maintained, if either Gen. Douglas MacArthur or his immediate successor, Gen. James A. Van Fleet, had been given "a green light."

Similarly, Senator Johnson (D.,

(Continued on Page 2, Column 6)

Text Of Talk By President

Washington, July 26 (AP)—Following is the text of President Eisenhower's address to the nation tonight on the signing of the Korean armistice:

My Fellow Citizens:

Tonight we greet, with prayers of thanksgiving, the official news that an armistice was signed almost an hour ago in Korea. It will quickly bring to an end the fighting between the United Nations forces and the Communist armies.

For this nation the cost of repelling aggression has been high. In thousands of homes it has been incalculable. It has been paid in terms of tragedy.

Sorrow And Gratitude

With special feelings of sorrow—and of solemn gratitude—we think of those who were called upon to lay down their lives in that far-off land to prove once again that only courage and sacrifice can keep freedom alive upon the earth.

To the widows and orphans of this war, and to those veterans who bear disabling wounds, America renews tonight her pledge of lasting devotion and care.

Our thoughts turn also to those other Americans wearied by many months of imprisonment behind the enemy lines. The swift return of all of them will bring joy to thousands of families. It will be evidence of good faith on the part of those with whom we have signed this armistice.

Decisive Purpose

Soldiers, sailors and airmen of sixteen different countries have stood as partners beside us throughout these long and bitter months. America's thanks go to each. In this struggle we have seen the United Nations meet the challenge of aggression—not with pathetic words of protest—but with deeds of decisive purpose.

It is proper that we salute particularly the valorous armies of the Republic of Korea, for they

(Continued on Page 2, Column 3)

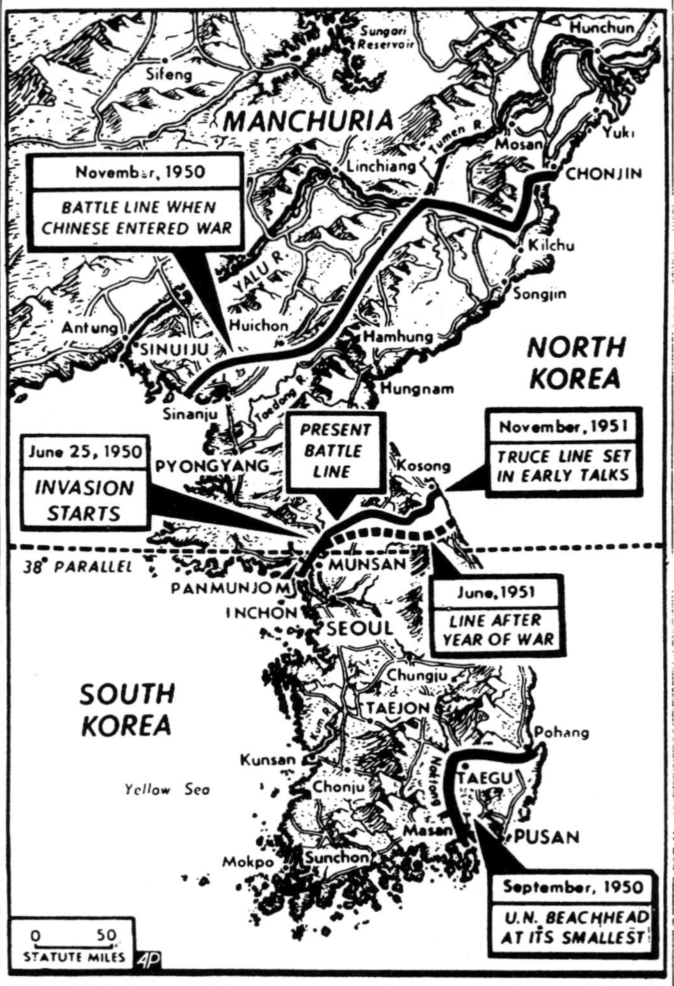

THE KOREAN WAR—Map indicates the various stages of the Korean conflict from its inception in June, 1950, to eve of armistice signing. The present battle line, which is expected to be the truce line, has shifted only a few miles in isolated areas from the truce line delineated by agreement in November, 1951, talks by United Nations and the Reds.

48 Rebels Killed In Cuban Uprising

Santiago de Cuba, July 26 (AP)—Col. Alberto de Rio Chaviano, commander of the Monchada army barracks here, reported that 48 men were killed early today when rebels attempted to storm the barracks.

Chaviano reported that 29 others were wounded in the short-lived uprising which took place as this city was celebrating a three-day carnival.

Attack Guard Post

He said a group of 200 men, dressed in uniforms resembling those of the United States Army, attacked the undermanned barracks at 5.30 A.M. in an effort to seize it for the purpose of starting a revolution to oust President Fulgencio Batista.

He reported that 33 of the attackers and 15 members of the army were killed in the fighting.

At the same time, 30 men attacked a rural guard post in the city of Bayamo, resulting in the death of two of the attackers and a police sergeant who tried to halt them.

An army corporal and two soldiers were also killed at the Bayamo post, Chaviano reported.

He said that the leader of the attacking forces in the Monchada barracks assault was Fidel Castro, a student leader, who escaped in the shooting.

The attackers were members of the opposition Autentico and Orthodox parties, Chaviano said.

Assault On Barracks

The rebels—taking advantage of the carnival holiday in which soldiers were used in the city to keep order—attacked on three sides of the barracks, swarmed into the building and killed two musicians of an army band while another group penetrated the military hospital and killed seven hospitalized soldiers, Chaviano said.

Chaviano said the attacking forces used hand grenades, pistols, automatic rifles and machine guns. He added that ammunition seized from the attacking forces had Montreal (Canada) markings on it.

He said that captured rebels admitted they had come to Santiago de Cuba in 50 automobiles over the last three days and had concentrated at a farm called Siboney owned by a man named José Vazquez who was storing equipment for the attack.

The number of prisoners captured and the identity of Vazquez was not made known immediately.

Prio Denies Revolt Role

Miami, Fla., July 26 (AP)—Ex-President Carlos Prio Socarres, of Cuba tonight said he had nothing to do with today's uprising in Cuba against the Government of President Fulgencio Batista.

He ridiculed a charge of Batista that Prio was behind the uprisings. Batista ousted the Prio Government in a bloodless revolution March 10, 1952.

"The only time it could be said that I was directing such a movement would be when I am on the ground leading such a revolution," Prio said.

"I have said before the people of Cuba will never tolerate a dictatorship. For that reason, we may see at any time an uprising by the people and the army itself against Batista.

"The year and some months Batista has been in power has been marked by an abuse of power, a destruction of Cuba's economy, and by Batista's chamminess (*coqueteo*) with Communist leaders.

"There will be other uprisings such as today's as long as Batista usurps power. In Cuba there is a struggle between the entire people and one man. The people will lose battles from time to time, but they will win the war.

"Batista often says he enjoys the solid support of the army. But the army is a part of the nation itself and it thinks and feels as the Cuban people feel. And the people are opposed to seeing a whole nation enslaved so a group of unscrupulous military officials and chiefs and a few pals of Batista can make themselves millionaires."

Arizona Governor Directs Polygamy Colony Roundup

Short Creek, Ariz., July 26 (AP).—A big task force of law officers swooped down on this historically polygamous community on the Arizona-Utah border before dawn today and seized virtually every man, woman and child.

Carrying warrants for 36 men and 86 women, they moved in to put down what Arizona's Gov. Howard Pyle proclaimed "an insurrection against the State" directed by "a hard core of greedy and licentious men."

Some patriarchs of the strange cult dwelling in unworldly isolation below the Vermillion Cliffs have as many as six wives, the State charged.

No Unwed Girl Over 15

They have spawned a total of 263 children, and, Governor Pyle said, in the last decade no girl has reached the age of 15 "without having been forced into a shameful mockery of marriage."

The two-pronged motorized raiding party, 100-strong and operating under the elaborate secrecy of a military maneuver, burst into little Short Creek from the north and east after having been deployed overnight in the pine and aspen forest north of mile-deep Grand Canyon.

But despite the secrecy, word of the impending raid had reached Short Creek, and the inhabitants were waiting quietly in the schoolyard, dressed in their Sunday best.

There was no resistance.

They're "Tired Of Running"

"We're tired of running," said one of the cult leaders.

Three of the leaders immediately were placed under bond of $2,500 each. Bonds for the others ranged downward.

As officers moved in, a truckload of men and women fled across the border into Utah.

Others, on a prearranged signal, left their homes and gathered at the schoolhouse. They sang "America."

Some Stay In Homes

Some women stayed in their homes and were taken into custody there.

A deputy sheriff marched up to the schoolyard assemblage and announced, "You are under arrest."

"We have run for the last time," shouted one of the men. "We are going to shed our blood here."

The warrants charged these offenses:

Conspiracy to commit adultery;

(Continued on Page 4, Column 6)

On Other Pages

Truce Just Agreed On—'Next Thing I Knew I Was Hit'

Western Front, Korea, *Monday*, July 27 (AP)—Three hours after a Korean armistice had been agreed upon, the 19-year-old United States Marine warily raised his head over the trench and searched for a Communist sniper.

"The next thing I knew, I was hit," he said softly, without bitterness, as he lay on a litter at the aid station.

This is the kind of war the men on the front fear most, in the final, nervous hours of the shooting in Korea—the kind of war that will last twelve hours after the official armistice signing.

"The thing you never expect gets you," the young Marine said. He considered himself lucky. It was not a bad wound and by the time it healed the shooting would be over.

"I Just Got Word"

There were four other Marines at the station, just a trickle compared to normal nights, but a tragic trickle. They had been in mortar range of Panmunjom, site of the armistice signing.

"I just got word that the war was supposed to be over. They ought to get the word around," said another Leatherneck, as he waited to get his legs patched up and the shell fragments removed.

He was one of two who hadn't heard of the armistice agreement when they were hit. But it wouldn't have made any difference. They were living in a fox-

(Continued on Page 3, Column 4)

A Frightful Toll In Human Life

Panmunjom, *Monday*, July 27 (AP)—The three-year war in Korea took a frightful toll in human life.

It cost the Allies approximately 72,500 killed in action, including 24,965 Americans as of last Wednesday, 45,000 South Koreans, 600 British and 1,900 from other nations.

Some 250,000 Allied soldiers were wounded and about 84,000 captured or listed as missing.

The United Nations Command estimated 1,350,000 Reds were killed or wounded.

The war kept the United States fighting longer than in World War I and cost the American people more than $22,000,000,000.

Return Of Prisoners To Begin Within Week

Panmunjom, Korea, Monday, July 27 (AP)—United Nations Command and Communist senior truce delegates signed the long-awaited Korean armistice in a crisp ten-minute ceremony today, halting three years and one month of undeclared war.

Scheduled for 10 A.M. (Korea time), the signing began at 10.01 A.M. and was over at 10.11 A.M. Eighteen copies of the historic document were signed.

All shooting along the 155-mile battlefront was to stop twelve hours from the time of the signing at Panmunjom.

North Korean Marshal Kim Il Sung broadcast on the Pyongyang radio at 11 A.M. a message to all Chinese and North Korean forces to stop fighting at 10 P.M. tonight.

Gen. Mark W. Clark signed the armistice at Munsan and sent the historic document back to Panmunjom for relay to the Communist high command. He signed at 1.05 P.M.

Lieut. Gen. William K. Harrison, Jr., signed for the United Nations command. North Korean Gen. Nam Il signed for the North Koreans and Chinese Communists.

The signing went like clockwork, in contrast with more than two years of bitter debate that led up to it.

Minutes after the historic document was signed and blotted, an authoritative source announced that the Communists had promised to return 3,500 American prisoners of war in a prisoner exchange to begin in a week or less.

South Korea Not Represented

The Communists and Allies last week exchanged lists of war prisoners, which included those captured since original lists were exchanged in December, 1951.

The total the Reds said they would return was approximately 12,200, this source said.

Of the new list of prisoners to be returned by the Communists, just under 1,000 are British Commonwealth troops with the remaining 7,700 all South Koreans, except for a scattering of small groups of other nations.

The Republic of Korea, which opposed a truce that leaves Korea divided with Chinese Red troops in the north, was not represented at the signing.

But following the signing President Syngman Rhee declared that the Republic of Korea would not disturb the truce for "a limited time" while a political conference attempts to liberate and unify Korea.

Sees Rehabilitation Gains

The south Korean leader said the republic still holds this promise for her countrymen in North Korea:

"Do not despair. We shall not forget nor neglect you. The fundamental aim of the Korean nation remains and will be accomplished—to reclaim and redeem our provinces and our people in the north—with the definite pledge of the United Nations co-operation to this end.

"We shall not disturb the armistice while a political conference undertakes within a limited time to solve peacefully the problem of the liberation and reunification of Korea," Rhee went on.

"Our understanding with the United States insures effective co-operation between our two nations in maintaining the security of the area of our mutual interests.

"Rehabilitation of South Korea will proceed promptly and effectively.

"Will the Communists do as much for the north?"

Controversy Recalled

Rhee recalled his long controversy with her allies over whether Korea could best be unified by war or through peaceful means.

"I have opposed the signing of the truce because of my conviction that it will prove to be the prelude to more war, not less; to more suffering and ruin; to further communist advances by war and by subversion," Rhee said.

"Now that it is signed, I pray that my judgement of of its effects may turn out to be wrong."

The 78-year-old President said his government would issue some time later "a detailed explanation of why we have adopted this changed policy of not disrupting the truce."

The armistice was signed in a pagoda-like structure hastily built by the Communists in this wide place in the road near the Thirty-eighth Parallel.

Harrison Shows No Emotion

It was that historic parallel which the North Korean Communist Army crossed at dawn on June 25, 1950, in a surprise assault aimed at unifying Korea by force under the Red flag.

When the representatives of the warring sides entered the building the eighteen copies of the truce document were placed on an empty table in the middle of the one large room.

General Harrison signed in a businesslike manner, with Col. J. C. Murray, veteran United Nations command liaison officer, handing him the drafts.

Harrison signed nine of the eighteen documents and Nam signed nine. Then they exchanged sets and each

(Continued on Page 2, Column 1)

KEEP ALERT, CLARK URGES

General Says There Will Be No Immediate Withdrawal

Seoul, *Monday*, July 27 (AP)—Gen. Mark W. Clark, in a message to United Nations forces in Korea, said today that the armistice agreement just signed does "not mean an immediate or even early withdrawal."

The general said, "It does mean that our duties and responsibilities during the critical period of the armistice are heightened and intensified, rather than diminished."

"This is why," he continued, "an armistice is a military agreement between opposing commanders to cease fire and to permit the opposing sides to attempt a solution of the conflict by political conferences."

A Reminder To Enemy

The United Nations commander pointed out that under the terms of the armistice, "the commanders of each side have agreed to recommend to their respective governments that a political conference be held within three months, at which a peaceful settlement of the Korean problem will be sought."

"But," he continued, "I must, at the same time, make it plain that although the thunder of the guns dies down and a welcome silence descends upon the battlefield, the conflict will not be over until the governments concerned have reached a firm political settlement.

"Meanwhile, we remain—in strength—a reminder to the enemy and his emissaries that our might and power stand behind the pledges of the United Nations to defend the Republic of Korea against any aggressor."

Warning By Taylor

Seoul, *Monday*, July 27 (AP)—Lieut. Gen. Maxwell D. Taylor, United States 8th Army commander, warned today that the armistice signed this morning at Panmunjom "is not a definite end of the war."

Taylor said the armistice period would be "a stern test for the discipline and soldierly qualities of every man in the 8th Army."

Taylor warned his soldiers that "we must constantly be on the alert and ready for a resumption of hostilities in case the political discussions break down or the enemy breaches the terms of the armistice."

Weather Forecast
Sunny and warm today with highest temperatures near 90 degrees. Yesterday's temperatures: High, 89; low, 58.
(Details, Page 18, Map, Page 39)

THE SUN FINAL

Registered United States Patent Office

Vol. 233—No. 116—F MORNING 178,723 / EVENING 193,304 PAID CIRCULATION IN AUGUST 372,027 SUNDAY 305,460 BALTIMORE, WEDNESDAY, SEPTEMBER 30, 1953 Entered as second-class matter at Baltimore Post Office 40 Pages 5 Cents

BIG LEAGUE BALL BACK IN CITY AS BROWNS DEAL IS APPROVED

RUSSIA ASKS PARLEY BID FOR PEIPING

Says Red China Must Have Role In Stabilizing Peace

Washington, Sept. 29 (AP)—Russia told the Western powers in a note released tonight that a first consideration in stabilizing peace in the Pacific and lessening world tensions is "re-establishing the legal rights" of Red China in the United Nations.

Moscow said that international regulation of Asian and Pacific problems as well as efforts to ease global frictions require "continual participation" of Communist China.

The Soviet note proposed that a conference of big-power foreign ministers should now be called for the purpose of dealing with general international tensions and the problem of German unification, with the Chinese Communists to sit in on the international tensions phase.

Note Called Obscure

American officials, reportedly including John Foster Dulles, Secretary of State, called the Soviet note obscure and confusing. The State Department charged it was evasive and represented "dilatory tactics" in response to western proposals for a Big Four meeting on Germany.

The action part of the Soviet note, the proposal for a conference, was read by some experts as actually calling for two conferences. Others thought it called for one conference of two parts. The idea was that Big Four foreign ministers would talk about Germany, which is the heart of East-West problems in Europe, while Red China would sit in and make the meeting a Big-Five session when the talk turned to broader world problems, including Asian matters.

Repeats Previous Stand

The note was similar to previous messages from Moscow on the subject of a high-level meeting. Whatever else it may have been 'esigned to do, it certainly seemed aimed at putting pressure on the United States with respect to Red China and probably to make that a major issue in bickering on American calls for early talks on German unification.

Officials here said one thing which is clear is that it is highly unlikely a Big Four foreign ministers meeting can be held at Lugano, Switzerland, October 15, as the Western nations proposed in a note to Russia on September 2.

Ready "To Continue"

As for another problem in East-West debate—that of concluding an Austrian independence treaty—the Soviet note said Moscow is ready "to continue discussions of this question in normal diplomatic channels."

Much of the 3,000-word note was a repetition of Soviet ideas about Germany, particularly emphasizing that the Russians give priority to a peace treaty with Germany while the Western powers give priority to unification of Germany.

In the new note, Moscow said discussions at the proposed con-

(Continued on Page 10, Column 3)

On Other Pages

First Of Army 'Buddy Teams' Reaches Japan

Sasebo, Japan, *Wednesday*, Sept. 30 (AP)—The first of the United States Army's four-man "buddy rifle teams" has reached here on the way to Korea.

The Army hopes to prove that training men in groups of four and keeping them together throughout their army careers will pay off in the field.

Three companies of four-man teams arrived Friday at Sasebo replacement depot after training since last fall in the United States.

Each four-man unit will be assigned to Korea as a team rather than as single replacements.

The men took their basic training at Camp Roberts, Cal., Fort Riley, Kan., and Camp Breckenridge, Ky.

P.O.W. RULES ANNOUNCED

Provide For Individual Interviews For All Captives

Panmunjom, Korea, *Wednesday*, Sept. 30 (AP)—The Korean Repatriation Commission announced today the "ground rules" under which the Allies and Communists will seek to persuade reluctant war prisoners to return home.

The rules—providing for individual interviews and requiring all prisoners to listen to the "explanations" regardless of their wishes—evoked bitter comment from a United Nations command spokesman.

"The commission bought everything the Communists wanted," he said.

The United Nations command has vigorously opposed both points. It contended that prisoners could be intimidated in individual interviews and that no prisoner should be forced to hear a sales talk on returning home.

Slated Tomorrow

The explanations were scheduled to begin tomorrow, but a further postponement appeared likely because of a dispute over the location and design of "explanation centers." The explanations had been postponed from last Saturday.

The centers, in the demilitarized zone, were built for the processing of nearly 23,000 prisoners, 22,600 of them prisoners of the Allies who have repeatedly refused to return to Red rule. The rest are Allied P.O.W.'s.

The major provisions of the rules include:

"Explanations and interviews can be given to groups or individual prisoners of war as requested by the explaining representatives of the nations to which the prisoners of war belong. Every one of the prisoners of war shall attend the explanations and interviews.

"Any act on the part of prisoners of war impeding the work of explanations and interviews is prohibited.

"Several explanations and in

(Continued on Page 7, Column 4)

MEAGER CLUE REPORTED IN KIDNAP CASE

Child Answering Description of Missouri Boy Seen In Truck

Kansas City, Sept. 29 (AP)—A meager clue, and intimations the kidnappers of 6-year-old Bobby Greenlease were trying to make contact, brought a faint bit of hope today to parents, desperate for word of their missing child.

The faint clue was word received by the Johnson county (Kan.) sheriff's office that a child answering the description of the missing boy was seen in a pickup truck near Overland Park, Kan., yesterday, accompanied by a man and a woman. Bobby was abducted about 11 A.M. yesterday.

Robert C. Greenlease, the father, gave the intimation that a contact with the kidnappers was a possibility.

Close associates said that if a ransom demand were made, arrangements had been made to obtain the currency to meet it, at any time of day or night.

No Contact Reported

At midday Greenlease and Robert Ledterman, a business associate, left the Greenlease home in suburban Mission Hills, Kan.

"We think they are trying to make contact," the father said. He was sobbing.

On his return a short time later he said no contact had been made. He added that he and Ledterman had been in his office briefly.

If the child reported seen was Bobby it would indicate that the kidnappers had crossed the Missouri-Kansas State line. The school from which the boy was taken is in Missouri.

Greenlease Quoted

"About all we can do is sweat, wring our hands and hope," Greenlease, millionaire automobile distributor, said.

Bobby was taken from the fashionable Notre Dame de Sion School yesterday morning by a woman who claimed to be Bobby's aunt. She told the nun in charge at the school that the boy's mother had suffered a heart attack and that it was necessary to take him to the hospital.

Before the nun went to get the boy, she suggested to the "aunt" that she step into the chapel and pray for the child's mother.

"I'm not a Catholic, but I hope God heard my prayer," the woman told the nun as she and Bobby left the building.

A cab driver told police the woman had him take her and the child to a parking lot near the school. There they left the cab and entered a car with a Kansas license. That is the last word police have of them.

Bernard Brannon, chief of police, said his department is taking all routine measures usually taken in such cases, but "otherwise, we are sitting tight."

"Until the boy is returned alive we'll do what the family wants us to do. The boy's life is paramount. We don't want to do anything that

(Continued on Page 5, Column 2)

IN LEAGUE—This was the scene in a New York hotel after the American League voted to transfer the Browns to Baltimore. Left to right are Thomas N. Biddison; Charles C. Comiskey, vice president of the Chicago White Sox; Bill Veeck, Browns head; Mayor D'Alesandro; Walter O. Briggs, Jr., president, Detroit Tigers; Clarence W. Miles; Del Webb, of Yankees.

120-WING GOAL LIKELY IN '54

Wilson Says Air Force 'May' Reach Aim By Midyear

By MARK S. WATSON
Sunpapers Military Correspondent

Washington, Sept. 29—Charles E. Wilson, Secretary of Defense, clearly gratified by reports on defense production, today stated cautiously that the Air Force "may" attain the 120-wing target by midyear of 1954.

While he emphasized the possibility, rather than the certainty, of any such achievement, his hopes are impressive. Until today there had been no official hint that the Air Force's twice deferred target could be reached before mid-1955.

Whether the 120-wing "interim" target will soon be altered up or down still awaits the judgment of the new Joint Chiefs of Staff, whose "new look" has required six weeks thus far and whose belated recommendations Wilson now expects within a week.

Air Force Favors 143 Wings

The Air Force itself has not weakened in its devotion to the original 143-wing target. Roger Lewis, Assistant Air Secretary, stated firmly, although fully aware that the views of Gen. Nathan F. Twining, Air Chief of Staff, on that subject may be beaten down by his army and navy colleagues.

Lewis repeated that all combat elements of the 143-wing schedule are contained in the 120-wing plan, and that economizing and deferment measures have affected only the support elements.

Secretary Wilson discouraged any expectation of a large drop in the defense budget for fiscal year 1955, now in course of preparation with completion required by mid-December.

25% Cut Seen Impossible

A drop of anything like $10,000,000,000 from current expenditures, or roughly 25 per cent, he indicated was out of the question; even a 5 per cent cut in this year's funds, which might be possible through increased operating efficiency, he remarked might be canceled through a high-level decision to increase our strength instead of merely maintaining it.

His "purely personal opinion" was that the 1955 defense budget should be about that of 1954, or less. Whether this will permit a balance of the entire national budget he did not know, and he added that it was not his business.

Equally cautious on most other matters, Wilson expressed a continuing doubt that Russia is planning a war, and a belief that Russia's much talked-of MIG, so far as disclosed, is an "overrated" plane, far inferior to our Sabre.

Warns Of Complacency

He remarked quickly that our improved strength does not justify complacency, but that neither is this a time for panicky thinking. Even Russia's progress with nuclear bombs, he suggested, is not ahead of American anticipations.

President Eisenhower is to get a new presidential plane, Assistant Air Secretary Lewis announced. Like the President's present plane it will be of the Super Constellation type, made by Lockheed.

Baltimore Captured Last Big League Pennant In '96

By EDWARD C. BURKS

The last time Baltimore won a major league pennant telegraphy had been invented, to be sure.

But on the air waves there wasn't even a crystal set around to bring the play-by-play account of the post-season world series that has since become standard October fare for the American baseball fan.

That last big pennant was back in 1896, back in the days when the rough and ready Orioles were the terrors of the National League.

But there was a lot of baseball in Baltimore long before the terrible Orioles roughed up the league in the 90's.

In Game From Start

Records show that Baltimore was interested in the national pastime practically from its beginnings.

At the end of the Civil War, Maryland had something like twenty amateur baseball clubs in existence, including the old Baltimore Pastimes, who played on the Madison avenue grounds near North avenue.

Professional baseball first got a foothold here in 1872 and has been around most of the time ever since. There have been times, however, when that foothold was just a good jumping off place for a Baltimore club to move along to another city.

Beaten 47 To 7 In 1869

The unbeatable Red Stockings of Cincinnati gave Baltimore its first view of a professional club when the Sox came here in 1869 and licked the Marylands, champions of the South, 47 to 7.

In 1871 the first league, known as the National Association of Professional Baseball Players, was founded. A year later Baltimore joined the circuit with an outfit known as the Lord Baltimores and finished third both in '72 and in '73.

The club played only a few more than 50 games each year.

The 1874 Lord Baltimores didn't fare too well, and it was later discovered that some of the players were throwing games. That discovery put baseball in a bad light in these parts and Baltimore was out of organized ball until 1882.

In American Association

When the city returned to organized ball, it was in the old American Association, a major league in those days and a competitor of the National League, then seven years old.

The story goes that Harry Vonderhorst, a Baltimore brewer, set up the team in the six-club association as a means of selling beer to patrons in Union Park at Huntingdon avenue (now Twenty-fifth street) near Greenmount avenue.

Baltimore's foothold in organized ball that year was a deep one. The local dandies finished in the cellar.

The next year the Brooklyn Atlantics were brought to Baltimore and for the first time the local club was known as the Orioles. However, in that 1883

(Continued on Page 6, Column 3)

N.Y. MAYOR SAYS HE'LL RUN AGAIN

Impellitteri To Campaign On Experience Party Ticket

New York, Sept. 29 (AP)—Mayor Vincent Impellitteri, beaten two to one by Robert Wagner, Jr., in the recent Democratic mayoral primary, said today he will try again as an independent in the November 3 general election.

In a statement, Impellitteri said he had accepted a "call" to run for re-election because of "the choice of candidates being offered to the voting public if I don't make the race."

Impellitteri will run under the banner of the "Experience" party, the same one under whose flag he won the mayoralty in 1950 after failing to get the Democratic nomination.

Opponents In November

His opponents, besides Wagner, will be:

RUDOLPH HALLEY, City Council president, enrolled Democrat running on the Liberal party ticket.

HAROLD RIEGELMAN, Republican.

CLIFFORD MCAVOY, American Labor party.

Impellitteri declared that "up to now there isn't a real Democrat in the race." He accused both Wagner and Halley of representing not Democratic principles but "a brand of Socialistic thinking."

Riegelman, he said, is just a "do-gooder" who "has done good in the past mostly for himself."

Scoffs At Primary Vote

As for the primary, the Mayor said he was convinced most of the people who voted for Wagner were "liberal party supporters who have infiltrated the Democratic party . . . for the purpose of forming a fifth column."

West Berlin's Mayor Reuter Dies Of Heart Attack At Home

Berlin, Sept. 29 (AP)—Lord Mayor Ernst Reuter, militant leader of West Berlin's fight against communism, died unexpectedly at his home tonight of a heart attack. He was 64.

A Social Democrat who once dabbled in Communist party affairs, Reuter was world famed for his defiance of the Russians who surrounded the war-ravaged Allied sectors of Berlin, isolated within the Soviet zone. He rallied the people to resistance against the Russian blockade of 1948-49.

Often mentioned as a possible next president of the West German Republic, Reuter worked closely with the conservative Bonn Government in trying to reunite a free Germany.

"Great Loss For Cause"

Expressions of the grief for his loss and the esteem for the figure he had made in the post-war world began to pour in after the sudden fatal attack.

Chancellor Konrad Adenauer said the death "is a great loss for the German cause."

Maj. Gen. Thomas S. Timberman, United States commandant in Berlin, said: "I feel that he died like a soldier, in the line of duty. His devotion to the cause of freedom has become symbolical throughout the world."

James B. Conant, United States high commissioner, said Reuter's leadership of "the brave community of Berlin has been a symbol

(Continued on Page 7, Column 2)

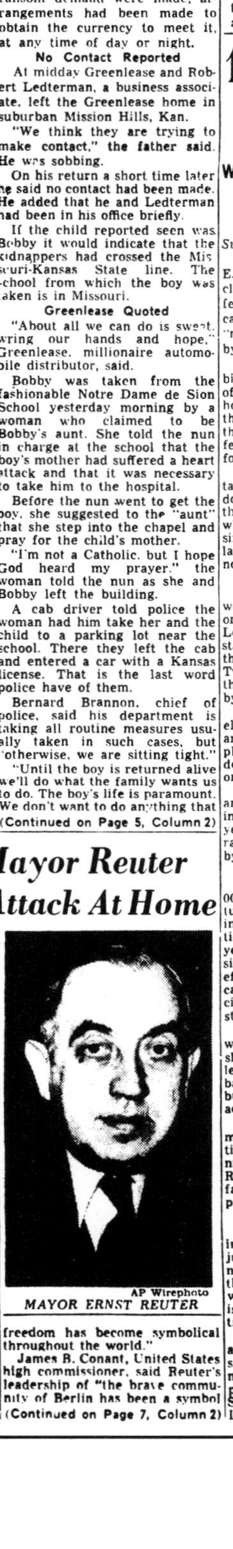

AP Wirephoto
MAYOR ERNST REUTER

AMERICAN OWNERS VOTE 8-0 TO O.K. TRANSFER; CLUB'S FARMS INCLUDED

Local Group Will Purchase 80 Per Cent Of Stock For $2,475,000; Decision Comes After Mayor, Miles Make Further Appeal

By JESSE A. LINTHICUM
[*Sports Editor of The Sun*]

New York, Sept. 29—After a lapse of 51 years, big-league baseball returned to Baltimore tonight.

The American League transferred the franchise of the St. Louis Browns to Baltimore by an 8-to-0 vote of the club owners.

A fighting Mayor D'Alesandro and a Baltimore attorney, Clarence W. Miles, neither of whom would take no for an answer Sunday night and again yesterday, finally won the big fight shortly before 6 P.M.

The offer of Mr. Miles to buy 80 per cent of the Browns' stock for about $2,475,000 was accepted.

It will be an all-Baltimore operation, with Baltimore business and industrial leaders in complete control.

To Become Orioles

The St. Louis Browns will become the Baltimore Orioles — a name that was last seen in American League box scores in 1902.

With the purchase of the Browns, Baltimore also gets the St. Louis club's twelve minor-league farms, including Class AA San Antonio, of the Texas League.

Mr. Miles, Mayor D'Alesandro and Thomas N. Biddison, city solicitor, made two appearances before the American League club owners during the long, hectic day, last in a series of three long, hectic days for all concerned.

Originally, Mr Miles and his associates had offered to buy 40 per cent of the Browns stock. About that much was to have been retained by Bill Veeck and his Chicago and St. Louis backers who had held control for two years.

When the Baltimore attorney and civic leader learned the plan could not gain approval of the league, he conferred by telephone with members of his Baltimore group, and a counterproposal was made.

Would Purchase 80%

The second plan—the one that gained acceptance—calls for purchase of 80 per cent of the stock for approximately $12 a share.

It means an investment of more than $1,350,000 above what Baltimore had been prepared to offer.

But it also means that the new Baltimore Orioles baseball team will be strictly a Baltimore institution.

Mr. Miles, in all probability, will be chairman of the board and general counsel of the team and will cast Baltimore's votes in future American League meetings.

Asked if Bill Veeck, the controversial leader of the Browns, would be included in the new setup, Mr. Miles said:

"I don't want to talk about that."

However, it was learned from another source that Mr. Veeck, under present plans, will be with Baltimore temporarily in order to help get things rolling.

Mill Outside Room

Many Baltimoreans—all of them with pulses racing—milled outside the meeting room in the Hotel Commodore, waiting impatiently for the American League owners to reach the big decision.

The Mayor, Mr. Miles and Mr. Biddison were called in to the room shortly before 6 P.M. to get the word.

Five long minutes passed.

Then Earl Hilligan, secretary of the league, came out with a piece of paper in his hand.

He started to read from the paper.

The Baltimoreans waited only to hear the word "approved," followed by the word "Baltimore."

Then they whooped.

Mayor D'Alesandro emerged from the meeting room a moment later, dancing and jumping up and down.

He got some lusty yells and whoops out of a system which had been tightening by the hour as the long battle against Del Webb, part owner of the New York Yankees, who wanted to shift the franchise to Los Angeles, was being waged.

Then he settled down to a stage of merely bubbling over.

It was Webb who threw the Sunday roadblock up against Baltimore—and who had just about every Baltimorean except D'Ales

(Continued on Page 6, Column 1)

Mayor's Statement

New York, Sept. 29 [Special]—The text of a formal statement issued tonight by Mayor D'Alesandro hailing the return of big-league baseball to Baltimore:

This day will go down in history.

It marks the official return of Baltimore to big-league status after an exile of 51 years.

Nothing else that could have occurred in our city could mean so much in advancing Baltimore to its deserved place in the sun as a great American metropolis. Far too long Baltimore has been psychologically handicapped and held down by its designation as a minor-league town.

"On Road Back"

In the early days of our great country Baltimore competed with New York, Philadelphia and Boston for leadership among American cities. For some time, we have been on the road back with respect to industry, commerce and civic improvement. Now, with our return to big-league baseball, which will bring Baltimore the recognition it deserves as the sixth largest American city, nothing can stop us in our efforts to revitalize our beloved old city.

Nothing can stop Baltimore from climbing back to her once proud position as a leader among cities.

Bid For Co-operation

On behalf of all Baltimoreans and the many thousands of Marylanders who supported the effort to bring big-league baseball back, I give my sincere thanks—to Clarence W. Miles and his associates, to Jim Anderson, president of the Park Board, to Thomas N. Biddison, city solicitor, and to everyone who helped to bring about this great day.

And now I ask for the co-operation of every organization and individual in Baltimore and the surrounding counties in planning the greatest official reception and parade that can be devised to greet our big-league Orioles when they come home next spring.

St. Louis Singing Blues

St. Louis, Sept. 29 (AP)—St. Louis baseball fans were singing the blues today over the loss of the St. Louis Browns to Baltimore as business men concerned with the baseball operation estimated the city would lose about $500,000 a year because of the shift.

EDITORIAL

All Baltimore will rejoice today at the happy news. The St. Louis Browns will soon be the new Baltimore Orioles. After half a century, this city once again will be a full member of a major baseball league.

It has been a long and bitter struggle. Twice the prize was snatched away at the very moment when success seemed assured. This time the victory is ours.

We have won against selfish opposition chiefly because of the persistent optimism of Mayor D'Alesandro and the resourcefulness of Mr. Clarence W. Miles. These two men refused to be discouraged.

Their determination was contagious. Between them they procured such backing, moral and financial, as has been given to few local enterprises. Carefully and methodically they surmounted obstacle after obstacle. Carefully and methodically they argued their case. In the end there was no denying them.

And, lest it be forgotten, give them credit, too, for the generous fashion in which they have looked after the legitimate interests of Mr. Jack Dunn and the old Orioles, a mighty deserving aggregation. The whole proceeding, from start to finish, leaves a pleasant taste in the mouth.

Weather Forecast
Occasional drizzle and light rain today, with the high about 58 degrees. Yesterday's temperatures: High, 65; low, 46. (Details, Page 22; Map, Page 47.)

THE SUN FINAL

Registered United States Patent Office

Vol. 236—No. 125—F | PAID CIRCULATION IN MARCH MORNING, 186,113 EVENING, 212,610 398,723 ‖ SUNDAY 320,899 | BALTIMORE, WEDNESDAY, APRIL 13, 1955 | Entered as second-class matter at Baltimore Post Office | 48 Pages | 5 Cents

U.S. Licenses Polio Vaccine For Public Use

Red Sox Beat Orioles, 7-1, Before 38,085 At Stadium

LEPCIO HITS TWO HOMERS FOR BOSTON

Sullivan Holds Birds To Five Safeties In Home Opener

Full page of pictures . . . *Page* 27

Other pictures, news and comment . . . . *Pages* 22, 25, 48

By LOU HATTER

An unco-operative weatherman and a boisterous band of Red Sox applied the damper to Baltimore's 1955 American League home inaugural yesterday as Ted Lepcio and Jimmy Piersall sponsored Boston to a one-sided 7-to-1 victory over the Orioles at Memorial Stadium.

A throng of 38,085 topcoated fans watched in anguish while Paul Richards's punchless Birdmen shunned scoring opportunities through the first five innings, then subsided before Frank Sullivan's five-hit pitching to absorb their second straight defeat.

Lepcio became the first player ever to hammer two home runs over the boundaries of the Thirty-third street arena in a single major league game, and the fleet Piersall contributed a perfect three-for-three to a 13-hit Boston assault against a trio of Oriole hurlers.

Red Sox Take Lead

While the Flock was leaving eight runners orphaned upon the bases during the opening five chapters, the Red Sox jumped into a three-run advantage in the first two frames to lead for the remainder of a damp and disagreeable afternoon.

From the outset yesterday, it was evident that Joe Coleman, Baltimore's comeback hero of 1954, didn't have it. His mound successors—Lou Kretlow and Rookie Don Ferrarese—were scarcely any improvement.

Sullivan, tallest chucker in the American League at 6 feet 7¼ inches, was in almost constant hot water during the game's early stages.

Sullivan In Trouble

But, after yielding five of his six bases on balls and all of the Flock's safeties over the first five innings, the big right-hander was in complete command from there to the conclusion.

Considering the damp, penetrating wind whipping across from right field to left and the threat of rain right up until game time, yesterday's turnout was remarkable.

Some 41,000 seats had been sold prior to the contest, so only a relative few were frightened off by adverse weather conditions that sent the temperature dipping into the lower 50's.

The enthusiastic inaugural crowd milling in the flag-decked Stadium was full of expectation from the time that Mayor D'Alesandro, flanked by Governor McKeldin and Club President Clarence W. Miles, officially tossed out the first baseball to Catcher Les Moss.

Miranda Fields Well

Frustration, though, summed up the reaction thereafter. A couple of fielding gems by Shortstop Willy Miranda and a third inning tally—product of a base on balls to Don Leppert, Gil Coan's double into the right-field corner and Gene Woodling's run-scoring fly to left—provided just about the only concrete basis for cheering their new heroes.

The 32-year-old Coleman, offering no alibis but obviously still handicapped from a severe spring head cold, was in trouble after

(Continued on Page 30, Column 1)

Yale Senior Seeks To Give Up Trust Fund Of $350,000

New York, April 12 (AP)—A Yale University senior, stating he has "two hands and a head of his own," has moved to renounce a $350,000 trust fund left by his father, it became known today in Surrogate's Court.

The petition of Eugene F. Suter, Jr., 23, upon which Surrogate William T. Collins reserved decision, posed a legal question whether he has a right to renounce the trust fund.

The student is the son of Eugene F. Suter, Sr., machinery manufacturer, who died February 20, 1943, leaving an estate estimated worth $1,000,000. This included the $350,000 trust fund for the son, which has since increased to about $385,000.

Although he has no other source of income, papers on file said Suter seeks to renounce the legacy because "he has two hands and a head of his own."

DULLES BARS BID TO RUSSIA

Calls Stevenson Idea Of Formosa Move Impractical

London Bureau of *The Sun* reports Manchester *Guardian* approval of Stevenson's speech on Formosa . . . . *Page* 12

By PAUL W. WARD
[*Washington Bureau of The Sun*]

Washington, April 12—John Foster Dulles, Secretary of State, turned thumbs down today on a suggestion that the United States Government try to get the Kremlin to state publicly whether it prefers a negotiated settlement of Formosa's future to the war risks created by Communist China's threats to make a grab for the island.

A public approach to Russia to make a public declaration on that subject would not be an advisable step, Dulles asserted without amplification under press-conference questioning about a speech in which Adlai E. Stevenson, the Democrats' 1952 presidential nominee, made the suggestion last night.

Charges Ignoring Of Chiang

Earlier Dulles had volunteered a 400-word statement charging the Democratic party's titular leader with:

1. Failure to take Chiang Kai-shek into account in projecting a Far Eastern settlement based on a formula that might require Chiang to surrender the Chinese Nationalists' island refuge either to the Communists or to the United Nations.

2. Attempted theft of what, in all other respects, is the Eisenhower Administration's own program for solving the Formosa question without resort to war.

Dulles's elaboration of the latter point put him at odds with some of his fellow Republicans, including Senator Bridges (N.H.), Senator Hickenlooper (Iowa), and Representative Short (Mo.).

Given Defeatism Label

Bridges, who heads the Senate Republican Policy Committee, said that Stevenson had preached "appeasement." Hickenlooper called it "defeatism" and Short said the Democrat had given "aid and comfort to the enemy."

Dulles said:

"In relation to Formosa, he (Stevenson) suggests, as original ideas, the very approaches which the Government has been and is

(Continued on Page 12, Column 1)

TWO STATES DEFIANT ON INTEGRATION

Will End Public School System If Date Is Set, Southerners Say

Baltimore and Maryland given until May 1 to decide on segregation ruling appeal . . *Page* 48

By JOHN VAN CAMP
[*Washington Bureau of The Sun*]

Washington, April 12—Attorneys for Virginia and South Carolina told the Supreme Court today that free public education in their states would be abolished if the court set a deadline for the ending of racial segregation.

In speeches that came near defiance, the four Southern lawyers said white citizens would refuse to support desegregated schools. Enforced integration, they threatened, would not affect tax-paying whites, but would "set the clock back for the poor whites and the Negroes."

S. E. Rogers, of Clarendon county, South Carolina, said the integration of whites and Negroes could not be achieved until traditional attitudes were changed. He said this might not come about until "2015 or even 2045."

J. Lindsay Almond, Jr., Attorney General of Virginia, speaking in a voice that shook, said in the court, "There will not be enforced segregation [in Virginia] during the lifetime of those of us who are now hale and hearty."

"Bleak Prospect"

"We are facing," he said, "the bleak prospect of serious impairment or the destruction of our free public school system."

Rogers, speaking for a school district in which there are nine Negro school children to every white pupil, asked—as did the other Southern attorneys—for an "open decree."

Such a decree would not set any limit on the time given states to comply with the Supreme Court decision of May 17, 1954, in which the court held the school segregation is unconstitutional.

The "open decree" would leave the supervision of desegregation up to the local courts which, according to the Southern interpretation, would be given wide latitude in dealing with each local situation.

Chief Justice Earl Warren asked Rogers, "Is your request for an open decree predicated on the assumption you will try to conform or is it not?"

Rogers replied, "I will be frank to tell you it depends on the type of decree. . . . We will not send white children to Negro schools. But we hope to work something out where there is compliance. But it won't come today or tomorrow."

The Chief Justice asked if there was any basis to assume an immediate attempt to comply with the May 17 (1954) decision.

Presses Point

Rogers repeated that if the problem were passed down to the district courts the "people would work something out."

Chief Justice Warren pressed the point. "You are not willing to state you would try to comply?" he asked Rogers.

"We will not send whites to Negro schools," Rogers answered.

Justice Felix Frankfurter asked Rogers if he was asking the court to reconsider its decision of last May. Rogers said he was not.

"You are not saying the deci-

(Continued on Page 2, Column 2)

Senate Group Plans Probe Of Corsi Case

Public Is Entitled To Know The Truth About Refugee Dispute, Langer Says

Washington, April 12 (AP)—Senator Langer (R., N.D.) announced tonight that a Senate Judiciary subcommittee he heads will "conduct a full and complete" investigation into Edward J. Corsi's charges that the refugee law was being "sabotaged."

Langer's announcement came after Secretary Dulles had swapped hot accusations with Corsi, his one-time good friend whom he fired as his immigration expert.

"Mr. Corsi has asked for a complete congressional investigation of the operation of the whole Refugee Relief Act and he is entitled to it," Langer said, adding:

"Everyone connected with this important matter will be requested to testify and to testify under oath."

Hearing To Be Arranged

The actual setting up of the hearing, Langer said, will be worked out at a meeting of the subcommittee tomorrow afternoon.

Commenting on Dulles's charge that Corsi sought to circumvent the law and take over administration of the refugee program, Langer said "the country is entitled to the truth." And if Corsi was removed to placate Representative Walters (D., Pa.), as Corsi has charged, the senator said, "the people likewise are entitled to know the truth."

EDWARD J. CORSI
"Shocked and astounded"

Dulles Backs Refugee Program In Corsi Row

By PAUL W. WARD
[*Washington Bureau of The Sun*]

Washington, April 12—Faced with demands for some sign that the Eisenhower Administration's refugee relief and immigration programs will soon be liberalized, John Foster Dulles, Secretary of State, maintained today that they already are working reasonably well.

Stirred up by the departure of Edward J. Corsi, whose addition to Dulles's staff had been ballyhooed in January as evidence of a liberalizing intent, the demands came from:

1. Nine Catholic, Protestant and Jewish agencies, including

(Continued on Page 2, Column 6)

BONN IS PROMISED ALL-OUT DEFENSE

U.S. Would Fight For 'Every Inch,' McAuliffe Says

By EDWARD C. BURKS
[*German Bureau of The Sun*]

Bonn, Germany, April 12—The American General who once derisively said "nuts" to a Nazi surrender demand today declared the United States now stands ready to defend "every inch" of German soil it holds.

General Anthony C. McAuliffe, at a press conference here today, extended a hand of welcome to the new German Army-to-be and told of substantial increases to be made in American forces.

Instead of the existing four infantry divisions and one armored division, the United States will have one airborne, two armored and two infantry divisions to defend West Germany, he said.

Now Ground Force Commander

McAuliffe was making his first Bonn appearance since taking over as chief of the United States forces in Germany.

McAuliffe, the hero of Bastogne in the Battle of the Bulge a little more than ten years ago, declared the United States will help in training the new German Army. America "will assist, at least initially, say for a year or so, in its training," he said.

Then, speaking as a man who ought to know, the general told correspondents, tongue-in-cheek, "My experience is that Germans are splendid soldiers. . . . It would be presumptuous on our part to think we should train them. They are pretty good at this business themselves as the record will clearly show."

Debunks Superman Idea

McAuliffe asserted any Soviet aggression into western Europe would be a costly venture and he debunked the idea that Russians are super soldiers.

"I see no reason to paint Ivan as suddenly a mighty military superman," the general said. "He pulls on his trousers one leg at a time as we all do. And I bet that if we could have a peek behind the Iron Curtain we would see problems that would make ours seem small by comparison."

At the same time he promised the Russians would receive a rugged fight, McAuliffe warned that the new American tactical atomic weapon "will not be decisive" in itself.

As the new German Army comes into existence, 56-year-old McAuliffe said he can foresee the necessity of sharing with the Germans certain existing firing ranges and maneuver areas.

Holds Out The Cup

"We shall certainly lose to the German Army some of the skilled German employés who are contributing so materially to support of our operations," he said.

Not only did McAuliffe extend a hand to the new German soldiers but he held out the cup to them. Said he: "I look forward to the day when Private Joe Doakes, of Brooklyn, and Grenadier Hans Schmidt, of Stuttgart, get tossed

(Continued on Page 6, Column 1)

REDS THREATEN NEW BERLIN CURB

Charge West Makes City Sector A Spy Center

Berlin, April 12 (AP)—Red East Germany tonight threatened to take "security measures" against West Berlin, claiming the city had been made a spy center by the Western powers. The nature of the security measures was not stated.

The East German Cabinet issued a declaration announcing the arrest of 521 "Western agents" and the liquidation of "a considerable number of espionage and terror groups" which it said were being directed from Allied West Berlin.

This, the statement said, "threatens the security of the [East] German Democratic Republic and cannot remain unanswered."

"Undesired Consequences"

The Government said it would take "all necessary measures" to protect the East German state against what it called the West's criminal activities from the West Berlin base.

"The fact that West Berlin is used as a center of various espionage and sabotage groups which engage in underground activity against the German Democratic Republic creates a tension in Berlin which must lead to undesired consequences and special difficulties for the population of West Berlin," the statement said.

West Berlin circles speculated that movement between the Allied sectors on one side and East Berlin and the surrounding Soviet zone on the other probably would be further restricted.

Sector Movement Still Free

Any West Berliner who wants to visit relatives or friends in the East zone must obtain a special permit from the East Germany Ministry of the Interior. If he crosses the border without it, he is arrested.

Movement between the western and Soviet sectors of the city, however, is still free.

Eastern sources said last December that a plan existed to seal off West Berlin as soon as it is clear that the Western drive to include Germans in the North Atlantic pact becomes fact.

To Cut Desertion Rate

They gave these reasons for such a move:

1. The Eastern bloc, organized by Moscow, must protect itself from penetration by Western allied agents.

2. Tough controls are needed to cut down the high desertion rate from the East.

The Soviet strategy was described by Eastern circles as something different from the blockade of 1948-49 which was broken finally by the allied airlift. This time, these informants said, West Berlin would be allowed contact with West Germany.

But, these officials added, the frontier separating the Western sectors and the Soviet portion of Berlin is a different matter. This 28-mile long stretch can be

(Continued on Page 6, Column 2)

FOES LEARN ARMS DATA, WILSON SAYS

Secretary Promises To Check Leaks By Careful Scrutiny

By HOWARD NORTON
[*Washington Bureau of The Sun*]

Washington, April 12—The Secretary of Defense, Charles E. Wilson, said today that "potential enemies" have been getting too much information "about the performance and capabilities of our new weapons."

And he emphasized that he is going to try to stop the leakage by scrutinizing information not only for security violations but also to determine whether release of such information would be a "constructive contribution" to the mission of the Defense Department.

He told 90 newsmen at a conference this afternoon that in the future their inquiries might be rejected if they were not judged "constructive"—whether or not any security matter is involved.

Stevens Issues New Order

Admitting that the term "constructive" is "a little hard to define," Wilson indicated that defense officials would be the judges of what falls in that category.

But he insisted that he has no intention of interfering with "the proper flow of information to the public regarding the country's defense activities."

A few minutes before the Secretary's conference, however, the Secretary of the Army, Robert T. Stevens, issued a new order to all field commands which appeared to impede considerably the flow of information to the public.

Stevens directed the field commands to submit "all defense information" to Washington for clearance not less than three days before it is released to the public.

Authority For Manuscripts

The only information permitted to be released on the ground by field commanders is that which concerns purely local or regional matters.

Stevens instructed the commanders that his order applies to "the entire field of information" concerning the military services, including speeches, manuscripts, press releases and photographs.

Manuscripts may be published, Stevens asserted, only with the approval of himself or Wilson, except in the case of military journals where the proper review is customary procedure.

The field commanders were told that they might hold press conferences and issue news to the newspapers, radio and television stations only if their information does not have "overriding defense policy implications" and is in keeping with Army and Defense Department directives.

The Army Secretary's order appeared to be even tighter than the original, handed down to him by Secretary Wilson March 29.

The Defense Secretary's memorandum had called only for central review of "certain public information matters."

But Stevens specifically made it read "all defense information."

Wilson declared it was "our whole system" and not any particular leakage or incident which led to the current tightening of security restrictions.

The system has resulted in

(Continued on Page 5, Column 4)

ACTION SIGNALS START OF VAST CAMPAIGN TO GIVE CHILDREN SHOTS

Salk Treatment In 1954 Tests Reported Up To 90 Per Cent Effective; 1955 Aim Is 100 Per Cent Prevention

Other news of battle against polio . . . . *Page* 4

Washington, April 12 (AP)—The Government tonight signaled the start of a vast campaign to treat America's children with the Salk vaccine, hailed as a potent foe of polio.

The vaccine was officially licensed for general public use by Oveta Culp Hobby, Secretary of Welfare, who signed licenses in Washington only hours after it had been found safe, effective and powerful in preventing paralytic polio.

Mrs. Hobby announced that six pharmaceutical concerns were given licenses to manufacture and distribute the vaccine.

The licenses were signed on the recommendation of Dr. Leonard A. Scheele, surgeon general of the Public Health Service. Scheele based his action on an evaluation report made in Ann Arbor, Mich., by Dr. William G. Workman, chief of the biologics control laboratory of the National Institutes of Health.

Up To 90 Per Cent

The vaccine in mass tests last year proved its ability to prevent up to 90 per cent of cases of paralytic polio.

But since then it has been improved, and this new 1955 model vaccine is the one which the public will begin to get very soon, perhaps within a few days time.

This vaccine is far better than the vaccine tested last year, and it can theoretically prevent paralytic polio 100 per cent, declared Dr. Jonas E. Salk, young Pittsburgh scientist who developed it.

Children would get only two shots of this newer vaccine—spaced two to four weeks apart—if Dr. Salk's recommendations are followed.

They would get a third shot no earlier than seven months after that.

Dr. Salk finds this spacing best pulls the trigger of the body's gun mechanism, flooding billions of protective antibodies into the bloodstream. It is these antibodies which build a wall between children and paralytic polio

Secret Research

"Grave consideration will be given" to Dr. Salk's two-shot recommendation, said Dr. Hart E. Van Riper, medical director of the National Foundation for Infantile Paralysis. The present plan is three shots, given within five weeks time.

The historic news that the Salk vaccine works was announced, after long months of secret research, by Dr. Thomas Francis, Jr., University of Michigan epidemiologist, who headed the task of determining its effectiveness.

Children, kept living and well, tell the full import of his story:

Only 71 children were paralyzed by polio last summer, out of the 440,000 vaccinated.

But 445 children were paralyzed among the 1,400,000 surveyed who didn't receive vaccine.

A total of only 113 youngsters were stricken by polio—paralytic and nonparalytic types—among all those vaccinated.

But a total of 750 were felled by polio among the nonvaccinated.

No dead among the children who took the full series of shots.

But fifteen dead among those not vaccinated.

There was one death from polio in a child—not named—who had taken only two shots and had a tonsillectomy during an epidemic of polio in his community.

Brothers and sisters were spared when polio virus struck down one member of a family. Only one of 233 vaccinated chil-

(Continued on Page 4, Column 2)

POLIO SHOTS BEGIN MONDAY

140,000 Schoolchildren In Maryland To Get Vaccine

Maryland's health authorities, organized in advance for one of the most far-reaching preventive programs in medical history, yesterday were ready to proceed as early as Monday with giving the first injections to halt development of paralytic poliomyelitis in about 140,000 young schoolchildren in the State.

In Baltimore county, doctor-nurse-teacher and volunteer teams will begin the series of inoculations of first and second-grade children in public schools on Monday, Dr. William H. F. Warthen, county health officer, announced.

City Start Set For April 20

In Baltimore city, the first injections are scheduled for 9 A.M. next Wednesday at Public School No. 22, Scott and Hamburg streets, Dr. Huntington Williams, health commissioner, announced.

Also eligible to receive free inoculation with the Salk vaccine—yesterday declared both safe and effective—will be first and second-graders in all parochial and private schools in Maryland.

The drug will be provided these groups through the National Foundation for Infantile Paralysis, and the program will be administered by the State Health Department through its county and Baltimore city organizations.

Written Permission Of Parents

Written permission of parents is required before schoolchildren can receive injections, it was explained. Because the initiation of the program had been anticipated, about 90 per cent of the Maryland parents involved already have granted this permission, authorities reported.

The first step of others who want the protection for their youngsters is to sign the authorization, both State and city officials suggested.

Priority Plan Suggested

A limited amount of the vaccine will be available this year for the distribution of private physicians to their patients.

Because the supply will be restricted this year, health authori-

(Continued on Page 4, Column 5)

Priest Gives FBI Bank Loot; Vows Forbid Telling Source

Denver, April 12 (AP)—An unidentified Catholic priest, whose lips are sealed by his vow not to reveal anything heard in the confessional, today turned over to Federal Bureau of Investigation agents $6,850 he said was part of the loot taken in a Denver bank holdup last February.

Donald E. Kelley, United States district attorney, said the priest "asked that he [the priest] not be named and I respect that confidence."

Officials of the Colorado State Bank said the priest had come to them earlier in the day, saying he had some of the money taken in the daring daylight robbery. They notified FBI agents and took the priest to them.

Is Fingerprinted

The priest was fingerprinted and whisked away by FBI agents.

Kelley quoted the priest as saying: "My lips are sealed. I have a sacred obligation by which I must abide even if it means my life."

Kelley would not disclose how the priest got the money. From the clergyman's statement about the seal of the confessional, it was assumed he had obtained it from the robber after hearing his confession.

The FBI would make no statement on the matter.

The bank was robbed of $7,780 in currency February 17 by a short, squinty-eyed man, who walked in shortly before noon, showed a woman clerk what he said was a bottle of nitroglycerin and threatened to blow up the building if she did not obey his orders.

He told her to hand over a stack of bills, shoved the money in his pocket and walked out the bank door. He cut through a parking lot and disappeared in the crowd on the street. Until today, the investigation of the robbery had produced no results.

A Down Payment On Some Shuteye

Chicago, April 12 (AP) — An anonymous letter arrived at the income-tax office today. It was clipped to four $100 bills and read:

"Enclosed find $400 for my income tax. My conscience bothers me and I can't sleep. If I still can't sleep I will send you the balance."

Peiping Blames Plane Crash On U.S. And Chiang Sabotage

Tokyo, Wednesday, April 13 (AP)—The pilot of a Communist-carrying Air India plane that crashed into the South China Sea argued for two hours the day before the flight that the plane was not airworthy, a passenger said today.

Luigi Pirola, Italian businessman, said the plane was delayed 4½ hours at Bombay Monday, "during which time the plane captain and ground maintenance engineers had a heated discussion over the plane's condition.

"The captain argued that the plane was not airworthy and at first refused to take it off," Pirola said.

Singapore, *Wednesday*, April 13 (AP)—Communist China charged last night that the crash of an Indian air liner Monday with a Chinese delegation aboard was "murder . . . prearranged by secret agents" of the United States and Nationalist China.

Peiping radio said the Red Chinese Government knew of a plot to sabotage the plane and had warned British authorities before the plane left Hong Kong Monday.

Precautions Taken

British Colonial government officials met today in Hong Kong to discuss the charges made by Communist China.

After the meeting a British spokesman said a warning had been received to "watch for an expected incident" during the plane's arrival and departure at Hong Kong Monday. He said precautionary measures were carried out.

Among the nineteen persons aboard the plane were members of the Peiping delegation to the forthcoming African-Asian conference at Bandung, Indonesia. Three persons were rescued yesterday. Sixteen others were still missing.

The plane was a four-engine Constellation of Air India International, owned by the Indian

(Continued on Page 10, Column 2)

Congress Medal For Salk Urged

Washington, April 12 (AP)—Representative Derounian (R., N.Y.) today proposed that Congress award a medal to Dr. Jonas E. Salk, who developed the anti-polio vaccine.

Derounian said it would be a "fitting expression of the tremendous gratitude of the people . . . to this great doctor and humanitarian for his brilliant achievement."

He added in a statement that he would formally offer in the House tomorrow a bill to award the medal.

"Dr. Salk's contribution to mankind, through the successful development of his polio vaccine, is one of the greatest in modern history, and I feel that I am voicing the gratitude of all America in presenting this bill," Derounian said.

On Other Pages

The Weather
Partly cloudy, windy and cooler today. High about 66 degrees. Yesterday's temperatures: High, 74; low, 48. (Details, Page 20; Map, Page 43.)

THE SUN FINAL

Registered United States Patent Office

Vol. 239—No. 125—F | PAID CIRCULATION IN SEPTEMBER (Daily--Mon. to Fri.) MORNING, 195,378 EVENING, 213,697 409,075 ‖ SUNDAY 324,110 | BALTIMORE, TUESDAY, OCTOBER 9, 1956 | Entered as second-class matter at Baltimore Post Office | 44 Pages | 5 Cents

West's Suez Plans Hit Russo-Egyptian Stone Wall

Stevenson Outlines Federal-Aided Health Program

LARSEN HURLS PERFECT GAME, FIRST IN HISTORY OF SERIES, AS YANKS WIN

Ex-Bird Beats Dodgers And Maglie, 2-0; New York Leads, 3-2

Other news of World Series on *Pages 23 and 26.*

By LOU HATTER
[*Sun Staff Correspondent*]

New York, Oct. 8—Don Larsen created baseball history here today by pitching a perfect no-hit game, the first in 53 years of World Series competition, as New York defeated Brooklyn, 2 to 0, before 64,519 Yankee Stadium spectators.

The feat by the 6-foot, 4-inch right-hander, during which Larsen retired in order all 27 Dodger batsmen to oppose him, boosted the Yankees into a 3-to-2 lead in the 1956 series which shifts tomorrow to Brooklyn's Ebbets Field.

Fans Seven Dodgers

Never before had a no-hitter of any description been achieved in the annual postseason championship.

Larsen, a cool, deliberate workman who two years ago was a chronic loser for the Baltimore Orioles, hurled a masterpiece.

The 27-year-old native of San Diego struck out seven Dodgers and issued not a single base on balls while the Yanks were posting their third straight victory over the National Leaguers on the strength of Mickey Mantle's fourth-inning homer off Sal Maglie and a run-scoring single by Hank Bauer in the sixth.

Had 3 Balls On Reese

Only once did Larsen come close to giving up a walk. This occurred in the opening frame, when he issued three balls to Peewee Reese before retiring the Brooklyn shortstop on a called third strike.

Otherwise, backed up superbly by the infield defensive skill of Gil McDougald, Billy Martin and Andy Carey and by Mantle i.. the New York outfield, Larsen was in command from start to finish.

When Larsen, his teammates on the tips of their toes and the huge throng in a state of breathless anticipation, sneaked a third-strike fast ball past pinch-swinger Dale Mitchell for the final out, bedlam broke loose in this vast baseball arena.

Yogi Berra, Larsen's batterymate, leaped upon his widely-grinning teammate with a flying leg scissors sufficient to crush a boa constrictor and other Yankees mobbed him in delirious excitement en route to the dugout.

He had it all coming to him, and more in a wild dressing-room celebration which only the greatest of performances seems capable of extracting from New York's baseball professionals.

Maglie Somber Figure

While all eyes and all voices were directing their tributes to this new Yankee hero, a somber, 39-year-old mound veteran was trudging wearily up the runway leading to the Dodger clubhouse.

He was Maglie, 6-to-3 opening-game victor over the Yanks, who today was touched for just five hits—four less than New York collected off him last Wednesday at Ebbets Field.

Maglie, baseball's 1956 "Cinderella Man" whose crucial mound triumphs led to a pennant for Brooklyn on the final two days of the last season, twirled well enough this afternoon to win most normal games.

The fierce old bluebeard from Niagara Falls himself fanned five Yanks—including the last three

(Continued on Page 26, Column 1)

DON LARSEN
The happy history-maker

LARSEN HITS PEAK FOR N.Y.

Ex-Oriole Hurler, At 3 And 21, Was At Worst Here

City's Brooklyn rooters take Larsen feat hard......*Page 44*

By LOU HATTER

New York, Oct. 8—The closest Don Larsen ever came to a no-hit game prior to this afternoon's 2-to-0 World Series feat against Brooklyn was for the Baltimore Orioles in 1954, the Yankee hero recalled late today.

And Larsen could thank the incumbent Baltimore manager, Paul Richards, for creating the opportunity of finally achieving that goal today in the greatest of all series mound performances.

It was in a mammoth 17-player deal during November of 1954 that Larsen became a Yankee, along with Bob Turley — at the time regarded as the prize of the package—Shortstop Billy Hunter, and five others.

Had 3-21 Record

Richards hardly could have been criticized for dealing off Larsen, although most certainly he was rapped for swapping Turley in exchange for Gus Triandos, Hal Smith, Willy Miranda, Gene Woodling, Harry Byrd, Jim McDonald, Kal Segrist, Don Leppert and Bill Miller.

Larsen had been anything but a roaring success for the Birds of '54. He had beaten the Yanks twice that season and Cleveland on one occasion. But interspersed was the dismaying total of 21 defeats.

It seemed almost inconceivable this afternoon that, only two years ago, Larsen was the losingest pitcher in the major leagues of baseball with a final 3-21 won-and-lost record.

As recently as the spring of 1955, too, Larsen's status with New York was much in doubt because of what was described at the time as an "indifferent attitude."

Later last season, in fact, Lar-

(Continued on Page 26, Column 4)

IKE FINISHING WORK ON TALK FOR TV, RADIO

White House Says He'll 'Answer' More 'Misstatements'

By WILLIAM KNIGHTON, JR.
[*Washington Bureau of The Sun*]

Washington, Oct. 8—President Eisenhower spent much of today putting the finishing touches on his political speech for Pittsburgh tomorrow night, when he will "answer" more of the "misstatements" made by the Democratic opposition during the campaign.

Some of these "misstatements" have been made by Adlai E. Stevenson, the Democratic presidential candidate, James C. Hagerty, the White House press secretary, said.

Mr. Eisenhower took some time out from work to watch television and saw baseball history made when Don Larsen pitched a perfect game for the Yankees.

The President will fly from Washington to Pittsburgh and spend the few hours before his address in the same hotel with former President Truman, who is campaigning against him.

To Be Televised

The address will be broadcast and televised over the facilities of the National Broadcasting Company beginning at 8 P.M. Baltimore time. The President will fly back to the capital following his address, and is expected to arrive here before midnight.

Mrs. Eisenhower will miss this trip, the first one during this campaign. She has a cold, and while she is able to keep her engagements in the White House, her physician advised her not to make the trip.

Senator Knowland (Cal.) Republican leader in the Senate, just back from a 10,000-mile campaign swing through ten states, reported to the President that there had been a "definite upswing" in the last ten days in GOP strength.

This swing to the Republicans applies both to the presidential and congressional campaigns, he said as he left Mr. Eisenhower's office.

Cites Major Factor

A major factor in the "swing" toward the GOP is the fact that Mr. Eisenhower has stepped up his campaign and has taken off his "kid gloves" when dealing with the opposition, the Senate leader said.

Knowland said his reports indicated Republicans were "stronger" where they were "generally safe" before, had picked up strength in close areas, and were closing the gap where the Democrats generally are considered in front. He would not define those areas, however.

He predicted that besides winning the presidency again, his party would regain both the House and Senate, although he thought the latter "still is close."

Ike Gets Some Bean Soup

Washington, Oct. 8 (AP)—A supply of Civil War style bean soup was presented to President Eisenhower today by a group of Pennsylvania Republicans. The soup, two gallons of it, prepared from a Civil War recipe, came from the annual bean soup celebration held at McClure, Pa., on September 15. It was frozen.

Democrat Opposes Socialized Medicine

Favors Money For Research, New Hospitals, Doctor Scholarships And Those Unable To Pay

Kefauver blames GOP for living-cost................*Page 4*

By BRADFORD JACOBS
[*Sun Staff Correspondent*]

Chicago, Oct. 8—Adlai E. Stevenson today outlined a full program for improving the nation's health. It was built on Government money for research and new hospitals, for doctor scholarships and for medical subsidies for those who cannot pay.

Stevenson drew a firm line at socialized medicine. He also opposed any form of compulsory health insurance and suggested a voluntary system of insurance instead.

"I am opposed to socialized medicine," he said. "I am equally strongly in favor of a program to make comprehensive private health insurance available on a voluntary basis to all Americans, so that no American will be denied good medical care for financial reasons."

No Cost Estimate

Several times Stevenson complained of President Eisenhower's efforts in this field as "inadequate." He also cited occasions when he said the Eisenhower Administration resisted Democratic progress toward better national health.

No estimate was offered as to the final cost of the Stevenson proposals. He noted, however, that illness costs the nation some $30,000,000,000 a year and indicated that expenses to curb such "social wastefulness" would be repaid in saved doctors' bills and in increased productiveness.

This was the third in a series of half-a-dozen policy papers, or "major affirmations," by which Stevenson hopes to make clear his program for what he calls "a new America."

Previously he has urged a guaranteed "customary" standard of living for the aged and, to cure the school "crisis," a program running to $500,000,000 or even $1,000,000,000.

Mass Phone Calls

Today's health program was set forth while Stevenson enjoyed a day's rest between his campaign in the last week and a Western swing, beginning early tomorrow morning. Stevenson remained at his Libertyville farm, 40 miles outside of Chicago.

His only public activity was to telephone, via two mass conference calls, to the 49 Democratic chairmen in the states and the District of Columbia. His purpose was to pep up the collection of money for the Democratic campaign. As a special wrinkle, he promised to go out doorbell ringing himself on October 16, which is "Dollars for Democrats" day.

"We are winning the cam-

(Continued on Page 4, Column 3)

'PRESSURE' IS LAID TO WHITE HOUSE

Senator Says Lobbying By Executive Is Growing

By BYNUM SHAW
[*Washington Bureau of The Sun*]

Washington, Oct. 8—A Republican senator participating in a special investigation of lobbyist activities declared today that Congress is going to have to find some way to resist the "extreme pressures" brought to bear by the executive department when it is interested in the passage of a particular legislative proposal.

Senator Goldwater (Ariz.), who resigned as chairman of the Republican Senatorial Campaign Committee last summer when he was appointed to the lobbying investigation, said that over the years the White House gradually has eased its way more and more into legislative functions.

"I personally resent any executive pressure in my office," he said.

"It's Another Thing"

Goldwater said he believes it is a necessary and proper function for a representative of an executive agency to testify before a committee in support of a bill, but "it's another thing to come up here from the White House and put on pressure for a piece of legislation."

Goldwater's comments were in response to a question raised by Charles B. Shuman, president of the American Farm Bureau Federation, who today was discussing the farm organization's legislative conduct.

Shuman said the executive branch engages in "myriad activities . . . for the sole purpose of influencing legislation."

Unauthorized Telegrams

"We appreciate the fact that the executive branch of the Government has a responsibility to make recommendations to Congress," Shuman said. "We believe, however, that the public at large might be as interested in knowing how much time and money the executive branch of the Government is spending on legislative activities as it is in knowing what the American Farm Bureau Federation spends on such activities."

In another development today the sales manager of a Boston insurance agency admitted sending unauthorized telegrams urging both Massachusetts senators to vote against an amendment liberalizing the social security law.

The insurance official, Albert H. Stoddard, said he used the names of some of his agents without their permission in sending 80 telegrams to Senators Saltonstall (R.) and Kennedy (D.), both of Massachusetts.

Passed By The Senate

The amendment he sought to defeat would have lowered the retirement age for the totally disabled to 50. It passed the Senate, 47 to 45, with Saltonstall opposing it and Kennedy favoring it.

Senator McClellan (D., Ark.), chairman of the special committee, condemned the use of unauthorized signators as "an imposition" on Congress. He said steps should be taken to stop it.

Stoddard said he had found it

(Continued on Page 5, Column 3)

MILWAUKEE BLAST KILLS 2, HURTS 21

Malfunctioning Boiler Blamed For Metals Foundry Mishap

Milwaukee, Oct. 8 (AP)—An explosion ripped through the administration building at the Ampco Metals, Inc. foundry on the city's Southwest Side today, killing two persons and injuring 21 persons.

All 30 people who were in the building at the time of the blast have been accounted for.

Fire department authorities said the blast was caused by a malfunctioning boiler for the hot water heating system.

The explosion blew out two floors of one corner of the modernistic glass and brick building. The firm makes special castings for industry and does gas and extrusion welding.

Two Are Killed

Mrs. Clara Baxter, 35, an office worker, was killed in the blast. Charles Plenke, 49, a clerk, died in a hospital several hours later. Ten others in the hospital were listed in poor to fair condition.

Paul A. Knudsen, secretary of the firm, said:

"I was sitting upstairs in the comptroller's office when all of a sudden I thought a bomb struck the place . . . I ran outside and saw the building had collapsed."

Knudsen said that a few minutes before the blast he talked with two maintenance men who told him they were going into the boiler room to find out why there was so much steam down there.

Radiator Began To Hiss

The export manager for the firm, Frederick Opipz, said he was in his second-floor office when a radiator started to hiss, the floor heaved up and upset his chair and threw him under his desk as the roof collapsed.

The explosion left an 86-foot-square pile of debris. Part of the second floor collapsed onto the first floor and then into the basement.

For over an hour more than 100 rescue workers feverishly dug at the rubble believing at least six persons were trapped.

"I knew the building was blowing up," F. E. Garriot, office worker, said, "and I ducked under my desk. After that there was nothing I could do. I just rode the floor down to the basement."

Not Seriously Hurt

Garriot was not seriously injured.

There was no fire following the explosion.

The part of the administration building destroyed by the blast was a new annex that housed the mimeographing and filing departments in the basement and sales departments on the two upper floors.

A girl who escaped from the basement seconds before the blast said she heard a "loud hissing noise." Buildings near by were not damaged.

Broken Bowl Kills Boy

Gary, Ind., Oct. 8 (AP)—A 3-year-old boy bled to death today when he tripped, broke his dog's glass food bowl and suffered a slashed jugular vein. Roger Allen Harris was dead in two minutes.

LABORITES' VIEWS SAID TO FOSTER EOKA

Cyprus Governor's Aide Says Terrorists Hope For Eden's Fall

By PATRICK SKENE CATLING
[*Sun Staff Correspondent*]

Nicosia, Cyprus, Oct. 8—British Labor party statements advocating a give-away colonial policy if Labor regains power have been encouraging EOKA terrorists to continue their campaign against the British in Cyprus, according to a spokesman for Sir John Harding, Governor of the island.

Cypriots who support union with Greece have demonstrated their belief that if they can hold out against security forces longer that Britain's Conservatives can maintain their parliamentary majority the cause of *Enosis* will have been won.

Effective Timing

Credited with shrewd understanding of British domestic politics and with an effective sense of timing, the terrorists are believed to have intensified their efforts in recent days to add extra force to sentiments expressed just before and during last week's Labor party conference and so to try to hasten overthrow of the Eden Government.

However, the Laborite prodigal liberality is easier to indorse in opposition to a government than it would be to practice in the administration of one, the Governor's spokesman added in interview here yesterday.

The Eden Government remains unwavering in its conviction that Britain must keep Cyprus as a military base for possible operations in the Middle East.

Stated In Leaflets

This conviction was reaffirmed on Saturday night when British troops in Nicosia distributed leaflets, printed in Greek, declaring that maintenance of the base is "in the interests of Cyprus, Greece, Turkey and all the Western powers and the free world."

The spokesman acknowledged that security forces on Cyprus have not been as successful as Governor Harding had hoped they would have been by now. In London late last spring, he said that the back of the Cypriot movement had been broken and that he expected a significant change for the better here by autumn.

But conditions now seem generally just as bad, if not worse.

The greatest unforeseen factor that upset Governor Harding's hopeful prognosis was the Suez crisis, the spokesman explained.

Drop-School Refresher

Cyprus-based British paratroops, whose crosscountry manhunts forced the terrorists into hiding in remote mountain caves, had to be rushed to England for a drop-school refresher course and then had to stand by for possible operations against Egypt.

Their airborne preparations completed and with the present international emphasis on negotiations rather than military coercion, the paratroopers are back on the job of crosscountry hunts for EOKA.

The spokesman said that official hopes are again rising, although the terrorists are still boldly taking initiative by day as well as

(Continued on Page 2, Column 5)

U. N. SPEECHES SHOW NO PRESSURE OF WORLD OPINION UPON NASSER

Shepilov Attacks United States, Accusing Oil Monopolies

By PAUL W. WARD
[*Sun Staff Correspondent*]

New York Oct. 8—The Western Big Three's current Suez "peace offensive" ran into a stone wall of Soviet and Egyptian construction here today and the impact threw the drive at least momentarily into neutral if not reverse.

The latest effort to push Egypt into negotiations on British-French-American terms also failed to enlist any ardent support from four countries — Belgium, Nationalist China, Cuba and Peru — whose governments had not taken an official position until their representatives on the United Nations Security Council spoke out today.

Lacks Pressure On Nasser

In consequence, when the Council recessed no such pressure of world opinion on Cairo had been registered as that which John Foster Dulles, Secretary of State—who is to speak in the morning—counts upon to make the regime of Egypt's President Gamal Abdel Nasser ultimately recant its July 26 Suez coup.

Instead, developments during the Council session were suggestive in general that, if an end is to be put to the Suez crisis in the near future, not Nasser but Britain, France, and the United States will have to retreat.

Otherwise, developments indicated the Security Council will fail to pass what Dulles calls the "crucial test" in the Suez case.

The first of the afternoon's speakers, Victor Andres Belaunde, of Peru, voiced deep concern on that score. And the last speaker, Paul-Henri Spaak, Belgium's Foreign Minister, warned that the United Nations might collapse and "chaos" ensue.

Cites Aswan Dam

An hour-long speech by Mahmoud Fawzi, Egypt's Foreign Minister, besides making clear that Nasser's stand has not been altered, invoked in support of it the United States' recantation of its Aswam dam offer to Egypt and in such a way that Dulles issued a defensive statement.

Another hour-long speech by Dimitri T. Shepilov, Soviet Foreign Minister, applied such epithets as "sinister" and "bankrupt" to the Big Three's tactics and served notice, in effect, that a Soviet veto awaits the American-backed Anglo-French proposal if it be pressed to a vote.

Speeches by five Council members raised doubts that the Anglo-French resolution could command, in any event, the majority support necessary to turn a Soviet "nay" into a veto.

Attacks Oil Monopolies

Shepilov attacked the United States as well as Britain and France, charging that American oil "monopolies" are working behind the screen of the Eisenhower Administration and the Suez crisis to gobble up British or French interests in the Middle East.

In a sharp rejoinder, Henry Cabot Lodge, Jr., permanent United States delegate, said:

"Having been here almost four years and heard the speeches of the late Mr. (Andrei Y.) Vishinsky, Mr. (Andrei A.) Gromyko, Mr. (Valentin) Zorin and Mr. (Arkady A.) Sobolev, I can only conclude, after hearing Mr. Shepilov's speech today, that the man

(Continued on Page 2, Column 2)

Beauty Bridges Canal Crisis

London, Oct. 8 (AP) — Buxom Miss England tonight agreed to share a room with beautiful Miss Egypt.

Sponsors of a "Miss World" contest here next Monday emphasized this was important in view of the Suez Canal crisis.

"The girls say beauty comes before politics—they don't care if the Suez Canal dries up," said Eric Morley, organizer of the annual competition.

Miss Egypt, 17-year-old Norma Dugo, of Alexandria, gave an agreeing shrug which echoed all the way down her 35-24-36 statistics.

"Yes, yes, no politics," she purred in her limited English.

Miss England, 21-year-old Iris Waller, settled her 36-23-36 into a nearby chair and put on a display of international good will:

"It makes no difference to me about that canal. I think Miss Egypt is lovely. Of course we'll share a room."

SULTAN CLAIMS TANGIER HOLD

Says International Role Is Now Just Advisory

Rabat, Morocco, Oct. 8 (AP)—Sultan Sidi Mohammed ben Youssef made clear today to nations on the control committee that has ruled the international zone of Tangier that he now considers their role as purely advisory.

Representatives of the United States, Britain, France, Belgium, Portugal, the Netherlands, Spain and Italy — the eight nations which have held actual rule in Tangier in recent years—met at the port of Fedala to consider the future of the 225-square-mile international zone.

"Morocco," said the Sultan at their opening session, "has just established full and complete sovereignty over all its territory, including Tangier, which was long the diplomatic capital of independent Morocco."

Committee Ruled For 50 Years

But, he added, he wished to consult the interested countries on what measures should be taken to meet the desires of Tangier residents and favor development of their interests.

Tangier has been ruled by an international committee for 50 years because of its strategic position at the entrance to the Mediterranean opposite Gibraltar.

The United States became one of the ruling powers in 1945 when it joined Britain, France and Russia in a conference that demanded Spain withdraw troops that had been sent in 1940 when Adolph Hitler controlled most of Europe. Spain, which occupied the zone avowedly "to guarantee its neutrality," agreed and Russia be-

(Continued on Page 2, Column 8)

GOP To Outspend Democrats 2-To-1 For TV-Radio Time

By JOHN VAN CAMP
[*Washington Bureau of The Sun*]

Washington, Oct. 8—The Republicans will be outspending the Democrats 2-to-1 for network television and radio in the last month of the campaign, according to the latest figures supplied today by Senator Gore (D., Tenn.).

Other statistics, on campaign contributions in 1952, showed that the big-corporations money went to the Republicans.

Gore made an up-to-date report on television-radio spending by the national parties as he opened the second in the series of hearings on campaign expenditures being conducted by his Senate Elections and Privileges subcommittee.

Up to last Saturday, the two parties were fairly even—the Republicans having paid out $411,650 for TV-radio (mostly TV) time as compared with $384,600 for the Democrats.

GOP To Step Up Pace

But the Republicans have a big jump on the amount of air time reserved for their use between now and November 6.

Planning to step up the pace, the Republicans have reserved $1,490,000 worth of network time between now and election day while the Democrats have reserved about half that amount—$703,000—according to figures supplied by the American, Columbia and National broadcasting companies.

Senator Curtis (R., Neb.), minority member on the three-man subcommittee, said he believed the Democrats will find more TV-money if they decide they really need to spend it.

The only purely radio network is the Mutual Broadcasting Company and testimony from its president, Jack Poor, indicated how little use is being made of national radio in the 1956 campaign.

One Half-Hour Period

The Democrats thus far have bought one half-hour period of network radio, at a cost of $6,000, and have contracted for only two more at the same price.

Most national radio coverage, Poor pointed out, is on the TV-radio networks. The big show is on television and radio almost goes along just for the ride.

No figures have been presented

(Continued on Page 4, Column 6)

Rescue Attempt Turns Turtle

Norfolk, Va., Oct. 8 (AP)—The Coast Guard received a report that two men were clinging to a capsized boat in Lynnhaven inlet

By sea, by land and by air the Coast Guard sped to the rescue.

A 30-foot vessel was dispatched from the Little Creek lifeboat station.

An amphibious truck was dispatched from the Virginia Beach lifeboat station.

A plane was dispatched from the Elizabeth City (N.C.) air station.

One hour later yesterday Coast Guard headquarters ordered all units to return to their stations, and added this explanation:

"Source of report had mistaken dead floating sea turtle with two seagulls aboard for a capsized boat."

Russia Orders Its Gypsies To Quit Roving, Go To Work

By HOWARD NORTON
[*Moscow Bureau of The Sun*]

Moscow, Oct. 8—Russian gypsies can't be gypsies any more.

The Supreme Soviet has decreed that they have to settle down and do some "socially useful labor."

It is doing this, the Supreme Soviet declared, for the gypsies own good, in order to improve their living standard and raise their cultural level.

And any gypsy who resists this uplift movement, who insists on continuing his wanderings and avoiding work, will be subject to "five years' banishment" and to "reformatory work," the top Russian legislative body has ordered.

Published In Armenia

There is no indication in the Government order that it has any connection with the admitted shortage of labor in industry under the current sixth five-year plan.

Although the order was issued October 5, it was not made known here until today when copies of the Armenian newspaper *Kommunist* reached this capital from Yerevan. Armenia is a center of the Russian gypsy world.

The Supreme Soviet noted, by way of explanation of its decree, that most Soviet gypsies already have settled down to useful work. Only a minority, it said, continue to be vagrants and commit crimes.

"Forbidden To Wander"

"In order to put these vagrant gypsies to socially useful labor," the order reads, "the Supreme Soviet decrees:

"1. That gypsies be forbidden to wander, and that they shall be offered a settled, working way of life instead.

"2. That the Councils of Ministers of the various Soviet republics be ordered to take measures to settle vagrant gypsies, see to their employment and attend to their cultural and living conditions.

"3. That any adult gypsies who maliciously avoid socially useful work and persist in being tramps shall be punished by the people's courts with sentences of five years' banishment and reformatory work."

There were 61,000 gypsies in the Soviet Union in 1926, the latest count available here.

On Other Pages

The Weather
Mostly sunny and mild today, with the high near 70 degrees. Yesterday's temperatures: High, 68; low, 56.
(Details, Page 16; Map, Page 33.)

THE SUN

FINAL

Registered United States Patent Office

Vol. 239—No. 148—F | PAID CIRCULATION IN OCTOBER (Daily—Mon. to Fri.) MORNING, 196,697 EVENING, 217,667 414,364 || SUNDAY 326,874 | BALTIMORE, MONDAY, NOVEMBER 5, 1956 | Entered as second-class matter at Baltimore Post Office | 34 Pages | 5 Cents

Hungary's Bid For Freedom Lies Crushed; U.N. Votes To Send Observers To Scene; British, French Paratroops Land At Suez

CYPRUS SAYS AIRBORNE ATTACK BEGINS ACTION OF INVASION FORCES

'Chutists Covering For Landing Troops. Russia Accuses Allies Of Violating Pacts. U.N. Creating Mid-East Police Force

London, Monday, Nov. 5 (AP)—British and French paratroopers landed on Egyptian soil today, launching an invasion to take over the Suez Canal zone.

The paratroop operation was announced by the British-controlled Cyprus radio and confirmed by a spokesman for the British Defense Ministry.

Neither the Cyprus broadcast nor the ministry spokesman gave any details.

Invasion

London, *Monday*, Nov. 5 (AP)—The British on Cyprus announced early today that a British-French "airborne operation" against Egypt has begun. Earlier an invasion force bent on occupying the Suez Canel Zone embarked at Cyprus.

The Cyprus radio announcement of the airborne operation did not give any details, but presumably it referred to the dropping of paratroopers to support troop landings.

At the British War Office, a spokesman said no report of the operation had been received so far in London. He added, however, that Cyprus radio should be a "perfectly reliable source," since it is being operated by the British.

There was no immediate comment from the Defense Ministry, but callers were told a press information officer might have something to say "a little later."

Invasion On, Egypt Says

Egypt insisted the invasion attempt already had begun.

Omar Loutfi, Egyptian delegate to the United Nations, told the General Assembly Sunday night "forces of aggression" tried to land in Egypt Sunday and "were engaged."

A member of the Egyptian United Nations delegation said British and French ships were approaching the canal from both the Mediterranean and the Red Sea.

Cairo communiqués claimed the invasion attempt had started and that a French battleship and a British destroyer had been sunk. News dispatches from the Egyptian capital last night told only of more air raids east and north of the city.

The British and French said they had no news of any vessel of either country being sunk. The British added: "It seems unlikely."

Report No Air Opposition

British-French headquarters said the Egyptian air force has ceased to exist.

A communiqué issued on Cyprus said, Allied planes roamed the length and breadth of Egypt without air opposition. It gave no word of troop landings, reporting only air bombing of shore batteries on Agami island off Alexandria and attacks on Egyptian motor torpedo boats in the same area.

The Foreign Office in London announced a British frigate had shot down an Israeli plane interfering with a British patrol in the Gulf of Suez.

The Soviet Union protested to Britain and France that closing the Eastern Mediterranean to

(Continued on Page 4, Column 3)

Intervention

By PAUL W. WARD
[*Sun Staff Correspondent*]

New York, *Monday*, Nov. 5—Another United Nations deadline for a Suez-Sinai cease-fire having passed unheeded at midnight, the 76-nation agency this morning adopted a resolution setting up an international peace-police force.

Henry Cabot Lodge, Jr., abetting that move and trying to turn back a tide of Arab-Asian demands that the Assembly vote punitive action against Britain, France and Israel, announced that the United States Government would "airlift" any such peace-police force to its scene of operations.

It would also back it, he said, with "shipping, transport and supplies."

Adopted By 57 To 0

The Canadian-Colombian-Norwegian resolution for an "emergency international force" was adopted over the protests of Britain and France, which abstained along with Israel, Egypt, and fifteen other United Nations members, including the Soviet bloc and most of the Arab states.

No date or time was set for the Assembly's next meeting on the Middle East situation.

The police force was to be recruited from the small powers and commanded by Maj. Gen. E. L. M. Burns, the Palestine truce supervisor.

The assembly specifically excluded the big powers, the United States, the Soviet Union, Britain, France and Nationalist China, from contributing to the police force.

The police force resolution, requested by Dag Hammarskjöld, the world organization's secretary-general, was so worded as to exclude American, Soviet and Nationalist Chinese as well as French and British soldiers, sailors and airmen.

Deadline Extended

He made the request without waiting to obtain commitments from any United Nations member government to contribute to such a force which, according to the preliminary report about it that he made to the Assembly, would not, in any event, be put to use until Britain, France and Israel have complied with the cease-fire-

(Continued on Page 4, Column 1)

WAR-TORN CITY—This scene in a Budapest street is reminiscent of World War II European photos. It was made after recent fighting in which anti-Soviet rebels gained temporary control of Hungary, and before Russians sent additional forces.

DULLES FOUND WITH CANCER

Condition 'Good' Following Abdominal Operation

Washington, Nov. 4 (AP)—Emergency surgery on John Foster Dulles, Secretary of State, revealed that the 68-year-old Cabinet member was stricken with an intestinal cancer, the State Department said today.

Lincoln White, press officer, disclosed this to newsmen at the Army's Walter Reed Hospital, where Dulles was reported in "good" condition after yesterday's 2½-hour operation.

White declined to say whether Dulles had been informed of the malignancy, discovered in preliminary studies of a portion of the large intestine removed during the operation.

No Evidence Of Extension

The State Department aide emphasized that doctors had "no evidence whatsoever" that the cancer had extended to other organs in the abdomen.

"A complete removal of the diseased tissue was accomplished," White said in a statement handed to newsmen in mid-afternoon.

Doctors held to their prediction of yesterday that the Secretary should be able to return to his State Department desk in about six weeks.

A few hours before the nature of Dulles's illness was revealed,

(Continued on Rage 2, Column 8)

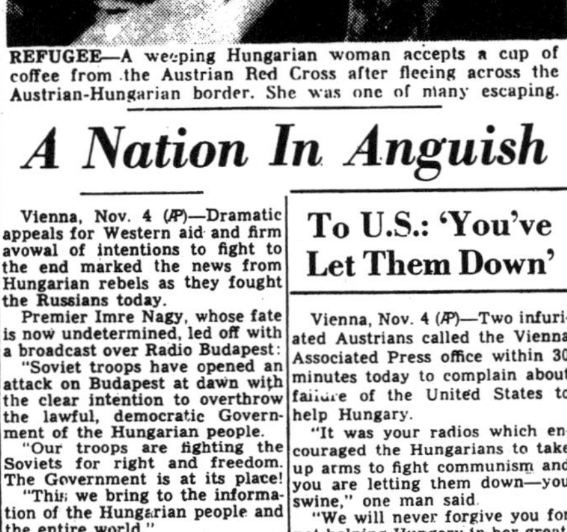

REFUGEE—A weeping Hungarian woman accepts a cup of coffee from the Austrian Red Cross after fleeing across the Austrian-Hungarian border. She was one of many escaping.

A Nation In Anguish

Vienna, Nov. 4 (AP)—Dramatic appeals for Western aid and firm avowal of intentions to fight to the end marked the news from Hungarian rebels as they fought the Russians today.

Premier Imre Nagy, whose fate is now undetermined, led off with a broadcast over Radio Budapest:

"Soviet troops have opened an attack on Budapest at dawn with the clear intention to overthrow the lawful, democratic Government of the Hungarian people.

"Our troops are fighting the Soviets for right and freedom. The Government is at its place!

"This we bring to the information of the Hungarian people and the entire world."

Series Of Messages

Then came a series of messages by various routes:

Radio Budapest:

"Russian officers, Russian soldiers, stop shooting. Avoid a blood bath. We are your friends and will remain so."

A Hungarian news agency message by printer line to the Associated Press Bureau in Vienna:

"Russian gangsters have betrayed us. The Russian troops suddenly attacked Budapest and the whole country. They opened fire on everybody in Hungary. It is a general attack. . . .

"I speak in the name of Imre Nagy. He asks help. . . . Nagy and the Government and the whole people ask help.

"If you have anything from the Austrian Government, tell me. Urgent, urgent, urgent. . . .

"Long live Hungary and Europe: We shall die for Hungary and Europe. . . .

"Any news about help? Quickly, quickly, quickly. . . .

"The Russian attack was started at 4 A.M.

"Russian MIG fighters are over Budapest. Russian MIG fighters are over Budapest. Gyoer [rebel stronghold in Western Hungary] is completely surrounded by the Russians. Szekesfehervar does not answer.

"Associated Press Vienna, if you have something, please pass it on to me. The Government waits for your answer!

"We have no time to lose, we have no time to lose. . . .

"At A Safe Place"

"The news of the capture of the Hungarian military leadership [which had been negotiating with the Russians] was confirmed by the Government spokesman, Mr. Hamori.

"Mr. Nagy is at a safe place now. Mr. Zolan Tildy [non-Communist member of the Nagy Government] is in the Parliament now.

"The time is [5.45] A.M. and the Russians stopped their fire

(Continued on Page 8, Column 2)

To U.S.: 'You've Let Them Down'

Vienna, Nov. 4 (AP)—Two infuriated Austrians called the Vienna Associated Press office within 30 minutes today to complain about failure of the United States to help Hungary.

"It was your radios which encouraged the Hungarians to take up arms to fight communism and you are letting them down—you swine," one man said.

"We will never forgive you for not helping Hungary in her greatest need and distress," a woman said.

Israeli Officers Interview Captured Egyptian General

By PATRICK SKENE CATLING
[*Sun Staff Correspondent*]

Somewhere in Israel, Nov. 4—A captured Egyptian general attributed Israeli victory to Anglo-French suppression of Egyptian air power.

Maj. Gen. Yosef Abdullah El Agrouly, 44-year-old commander of the Egyptian 8th Division at Khan Yunis, in the Gaza strip, also blamed his defeat on the recent withdrawal of Egyptian troops to guard the Suez Canal.

General El Agrouly and some of his Egyptian staff officers were taken prisoners yesterday morning when Israeli soldiers overran his headquarters. He denied Israeli reports that some other officers had fled from the Gaza strip in advance of Israeli attackers.

He made his statements in a bizarre press conference in a room with blacked out window at a secret secluded location.

With him was another high-ranking Egyptian officer, Maj. Gen. Mohammed Fuad el Digwi, military governor of Gaza.

An Israeli sergeant with a submachine gun unlocked the back door of the conference room and a civilian policeman and an Israeli major ushered the first prisoner, General El Agrouly, to a table with a tape-recorder microphone.

The general was smartly groomed in his dress khakis, a British-style uniform, with a star and crossed swords on each shoulder, the red shoulder tabs of general rank, and three rows of medal ribbons. His decorations were Libyan, Iranian and Egyptian, including one for commanding a battalion in the Arab-Jewish war of 1948.

As he sat down to confront his questioners, his manner was calm, except for light tremors of his fingers when he smoked a cigarette.

He is a massive man with black

(Continued on Page 5, Column 4)

On Other Pages

IKE APPEALS TO BULGANIN

Calls For Troop Withdrawals From Hungary Areas

By GERALD GRIFFIN
[*Washington Bureau of The Sun*]

Washington, Nov. 4—President Eisenhower today called on Premier Nikolai A. Bulganin to withdraw Soviet troops from Hungary.

The President sent an urgent message to the Soviet Premier, covering this point as well as an appeal for Hungary's right to self-government, after an unusual Sunday afternoon meeting with top diplomatic and intelligence officials.

Eisenhower and his advisers also discussed the Middle East situation and the efforts in the United Nations to obtain a cease-fire.

Declines Answers

James C. Hagerty, the President's press secretary, declined at this time, however, to answer questions about the possible assignment of American military units to a proposed United Nations force in the Middle East.

Hagerty stressed the point that the United Nations General Assembly early today asked the Secretary General, Dag Hammarskjöld, to report back on such a proposed international force by Tuesday. Until Hammarskjöld makes his report, Hagerty said, he could not say whether the United States would contribute military units or whether the

(Continued on Page 9, Column 2)

Stevenson Suggests Sending Of U.N. Teams Into Satellites

By BRADFORD JACOBS
[*Sun Staff Correspondent*]

Chicago, Nov. 4—Adlai E. Stevenson today recommended that the United Nations immediately dispatch to Hungary and to Poland peace observation teams as "protection" from the Russian invaders.

Stevenson wired his suggestion to President Eisenhower in a gesture above their battle for the presidency, due to be settled Tuesday.

Machinery is already prepared in the United Nations, Stevenson noted, for carrying out such missions. It was set up as the Peace Observation Commission shortly after the outbreak of the Korean War.

"Restraining Influence"

"This would make it possible," Stevenson wired the President, "for the United Nations to mobilize large teams of official observers and fly them into Hungary, or at least the still free parts of Hungary."

Any of the other satellite nations, such as Poland, which might "welcome or consent to" the presence of these observer teams could also be included, Stevenson said. In Poland's case, he said, this step might save the nation from a fate like Hungary's.

As to Hungary, he said the teams should prove a "restraining influence" on the invaders and might also be of "benefit to that suffering country." An added feature, he pointed out, is that the move is "beyond veto."

Seeks "To Be Helpful"

Stevenson emphasized that his recommendation is made on a nonpartisan basis. He told the President that, "like all Americans," he is "shocked" by the Russians' "brutal, treacherous" attack on the Hungarians.

"I would like to be as helpful as I can," he said. ". . . It may be, Mr. President, that some better plan will occur to you but I ear-

(Continued on Page 9, Column 4)

NEW RED REGIME SET UP IN BUDAPEST; FRANTIC REBELS STILL FIGHT ON

Core Of Revolt Smashed By Guns, Tanks, Planes — Any U.N. Team Will Be Barred, Russ Delegate Warns

Vienna, Nov. 4 [*Reuter*]—Budapest Radio said tonight that Ernoe Geroe, former First Secretary of the Hungarian Communist party, had been "murdered in a barbarous fashion" by Hungarian rebels.

Geroe, right-hand man of the arch-Stalinist Matyas Rakosi, was thrown out of office October 25 at the height of the Hungary riots. He was replaced by Janos Kadar, head of the new Government announced today.

Post-Mortem

By PAUL W. WARD
[*Sun Staff Correspondent*]

New York, Nov. 4—A United Nations General Assembly post-mortem on the corpse of Hungary's Soviet-aborted democracy ended here tonight in a 50-to-8 vote to try to send "observers" to view the remains.

Arkady A. Sobolev, of the U.S.S.R., made it abundantly clear just before the vote that any "observers" the world organization sends to Hungary under the United States proposal the Assembly adopted will be turned back at the frontier by Moscow's Budapest satraps.

The vote taken at 8.08 P.M. was, in consequence, less a matter of action to restore Hungary's Soviet-smashed bid for freedom than a test of the *bona fides* of that 85 per cent of the Assembly's members who less than 72 hours earlier denounced British, French and Israeli armed intervention in Egypt.

Arabs Deny Support

Less than 66 per cent of the Assembly's 76 member delegations voted to pass condemnatory judgment on what, as proposed by the United States, was called the Kremlin's "use of Soviet military forces to suppress the efforts of the Hungarian people to reassert their rights."

All the Assembly's Arab delegation, including Egypt, denied the United States resolution their support, either abstaining, instead, along with India, Indonesia, Afghanistan, Burma, and Ceylon, or letting themselves be recorded "absent" as happened in the cases of Laos, and Lebanon.

All the Communist delegations voted against the United States resolution except Yugoslavia's, which abstained, and Hungary's, which, pleading lack of instructions from Budapest, let itself be recorded "absent."

The 50 member delegations that voted for the United States resolution tonight included those of Britain, France, and Israel who had voted against the American resolution that, adopted by a 64-to-5 vote at 2.30 A.M. Friday, demanded in vain that they throw into reverse the military operations they had just begun against Egypt.

Tonight's 50 also included

(Continued on Page 8, Column 5)

Holocaust

Vienna, Nov. 4 (AP)—Soviet military might apparently smashed Hungary's freedom movement today. The Russians installed a Communist Government patterned after the new Polish regime.

Communist radio stations asserted the anti-Communist revolt was crushed under the weight of Soviet tanks, guns and planes.

They trumpeted that the Government of Premier Imre Nagy, the nationalistic Communist, "fell apart and has ceased to exist."

But the Communists acknowledged Hungarians still fought Russians in the rubble of Budapest. The Hungarian capital was caught in a vise of armor by the sudden Soviet onslaught launched before dawn today.

Rebel radios still operated furtively as Soviet columns sought them out. The radios called for Western help.

"We will hold out to our last drop of blood," the rebels pledged.

In Hands Of Regime

Budapest Radio, which carried Nagy's frantic early morning appeals for world help, was in the hands of the Soviet-supported regime.

The radio said the new regime had repudiated Nagy's appeal to the United Nations to guarantee a free and neutral Hungary.

The appeal, said Budapest Radio, "has no legal force and cannot be regarded as an appeal sent by Hungary as a state."

Moscow and other Communist radios denounced Nagy as a tool of "reactionary enemies of Hungary." They boasted Nagy was a prisoner, but the rebels said he was safe.

The Communist radio at Nyireghyaza in eastern Hungary acknowledged indirectly the frantic resistance of battered rebel units.

"Deeply Convinced"

It said the new Government of the Hungarian Communist boss, Janos Kadar, "is deeply and sincerely convinced that order and calmness will be restored in the whole country in the next few days."

The radio pleaded with workers to go back to their jobs.

Budapest Radio said Peter Kos, fired by Nagy as Hungary's delegate to the United Nations, had been restored to his post. The Nagy regime said he actually was a Russian, not a Hungarian.

Moscow Radio's political commentator, Viktor Shragin, made clear the Soviet Union's determination to maintain a Communist one-party government in Hungary.

Nagy had proposed free elections with a number of parties to be represented. He strove for neutrality, independence from the Warsaw Pact, and freedom from Soviet occupation troops in Hungary.

Kadar, who became Communist party secretary last week, was supposed to be working with Nagy.

Shragin said Kadar had asked Soviet troop commanders "to crush these mutineers." He said

(Continued on Page 9, Column 5)

Voting Suggestions

On today's editorial page *The Sun* brings together the various recommendations which it has made in connection with the election.

See Page 16

Weather Forecast
Considerable cloudiness today. Chance of a few showers. High about 78 degrees. Yesterday's high, 70; low, 64. (Details, Page 16; Map, Page 35.)

THE SUN FINAL

Registered United States P

Vol. 241—No. 100—F | PAID CIRCULATION IN AUGUST (Daily—Monday to Friday) MORNING, 198,536 EVENING, 212,438 410,974 || SUNDAY 314,136 | BALTIMORE, TUESDAY, SEPTEMBER 10, 1957 | Entered as second-class matter at Baltimore Post Office | 36 Pages | 5 Cents

Judge Orders Injunction Suit Against Faubus; Government Will 'Comply As Soon As Possible'; Eisenhower 'Deplores' Violence At Dixie Schools

SYRIA SAYS AMERICAN WARSHIPS PROVOKE BY APPROACHING COAST

Charge Meets Denial By Navy–State Department Official Warns Moscow And Damascus Not To Underestimate U.S.

Washington, Sept. 9 (AP)—A Navy spokesman said "no United States navy ships have been operating in the immediate vicinity of the Syrian Coast."

He reported the bulk of the United States 6th Fleet is now in the Aegean Sea, between Greece and Turkey and hundreds of miles from Syria.

Some United States destroyers may have been cruising in the eastern Mediterranean in recent days, he said, but none have been within sight of the Syrian Coast.

Syrian

United States begins airlift of arms to Jordan.......Page 2

Damascus, Syria, Sept. 9 (AP). A Syrian Army spokesman charged five United States warships provocatively approached Syria's coast yesterday and two unidentified jet fighters flew high over the port of Latakia today.

The Syrian spokesman said the Syrian army is "firmly determined to resist . . . by cold nerves" any American provocations.

"No sooner was the Dulles statement on Syria announced," the spokesman said, "than provocative, irritative operations were begun with the aim of stirring Syria into taking such measures as to be used as a pretext to launch aggression against her.

Called Open Challenge

"Five United States warships yesterday approached the Syrian coast in a way that constitutes an open challenge and violates international protocol.

"Furthermore, two unidentified jet fighter planes today flew at an extremely high altitude over Latakia port.

"What we want from announcing these provocations is to acquaint world public opinion with the means used by imperialism to infringe on the sovereignty of a free United Nations member country and force her to abandon her freedom.

No Protest Yet

"The Syrian Army of the People's Government is firmly determined to resist these provocations by cold nerves."

Asked whether Syria had protested to Washington, the spokesman said: "So far, no."

From the Foreign Ministry came charges that the United States is interfering in Syria's domestic affairs and "preparing an atmosphere for anti-Syrian aggression."

This was in reply to a statement Saturday by John Foster Dulles, Secretary of State, on the Syrian situation. The Dulles statement was a report on a White House conference in which President Eisenhower urged the Syrian people to do something to ease the fear of Communist-inspired attacks by Syria on her neighbors.

Eisenhower pledged to use his full power as needed under the congressionally approved resolution for blocking Com-

(Continued, Page 2, Column 6)

American

New York, Sept. 9 (AP)—The United States warned Russia and pro-Soviet Syria today not to miscalculate American military power or "misinterpret our determination" to block communism in the Middle East.

The State Department's No. 3 official, Robert Murphy, Deputy Under Secretary, voiced the warning in a speech at the annual conference of United States mayors. He said "it is entirely possible" that the American Government's readiness to negotiate an international disarmament agreement "has been misinterpreted in some quarters."

Murphy called attention to big Soviet arms shipments to Syria, Egypt and Yemen, as well as arrival of "substantial numbers" of Russian technicians in the area. These have been accompanied, he noted, by "a series of Soviet boasts" about advances in intercontinental missiles, naval and air power.

In words clearly aimed at Kremlin rulers, Murphy declared:

"It . . . would be unwise to underestimate the industrial and military power of our country, and to misinterpret our determination."

The State Department diplomat, one of Secretary Dulles's key advisers, denounced Moscow's policy of offering weapons "at bargain prices to certain countries with military ambitions." He did not identify these countries but said they "run the grave risk of absorption" and loss of their independence to Russia.

Murphy's speech, it was learned, reflected top-level State Department worry over the possibility that Russia and Syria were "misreading" American willingness to fight, if necessary, to check further Red expansion. The Deputy Under Secretary's blunt words were aimed, officials said, at preventing any Kremlin miscalculation which might plunge the Middle East into war.

The remarks were in line with

(Continued, Page 2, Column 6)

On Other Pages

Algeria: The Rebels' Side—VIII

French Air Attack Answers Raid

The following article is the eighth in a series by Mr. McCardell on the activities of the Algerian rebels. The articles were written in Rome on his return there from Africa.

By LEE McCARDELL
[*Rome Bureau of The Sun*]

Rome, Sept. 9 —We got little sleep that night. Officers, soldiers, couriers kept coming and going in the *gorbi*. About 3 A.M. somebody shook me awake.

"Come quickly," I was told.

Three mules were harnessed and waiting in the dark outside the *gorbi*, one for each of the three correspondents with the troop. Ariel Sutter and Karl Breyer, my Swiss and German newsmen colleagues, mounted. I said I preferred to walk.

"No, no! You must ride." I was told. "It is faster."

One Leads, One Beats Mule

I had no choice. Up I went into the straw saddle.

There were two soldiers for each mule, one to lead and one to beat it. We set out at a smart clip—for mules. We were heading across the valley toward another mountain. I tried to find out where we were going but my impatient muleteers spoke only Arabic.

Later I realized that we were racing against the dawn. The officer leading our party was anxious to cross the bare valley and reach the foot of the mountain before sunrise. Brush and stunted cedar grew at the foot of the mountain and along its lower slope. We were running for that cover.

A French answer to the night attack was a certainty. It would probably come from the air. The two Algerian troops were dispersing and taking up new positions for the next phase of their operation. They hoped to lure French ground forces into the valley. We correspondents were being conducted to grandstand seats, a new post on another mountain.

We crossed the valley without difficulty, thanks to the mules, which negotiated gullies, loose stones and shadowy hollows in the darkness with more confidence and dispatch than I would have shown if walking. We dismounted at the foot of the mountain and day broke behind us as we puffed and panted up a 1,500-foot climb.

The trail was a narrow, one-man path, switching back on the steepest slopes. It led to a rocky cleft at the top of the mountain. Not too long ago it had been shelled by the French. Our guides pointed out blasted cedars and fractured rock where the artillery shells had landed or burst. I did not find this reassuring.

We reached our perch, a rocky slot between two forbidding crags, commanding a magnificent view of the countryside. We could see the French post attacked last night. We could look for miles in three directions.

Planes' Search Begins

Part of Baba's troop was in position on the mountain. They had set and camouflaged a mortar and two machine guns. The place was impregnable to attack from below. Its precipitous outcroppings of black, ferrous rock, its huge boulders made it a natural stronghold.

Captain Mustapha's company was across the valley, concealed in a ripple of low sand hills. The *gorbi* from which we had started out in the dark that morning was now deserted. It sat out in the middle of the

(Continued, Page 2, Column 2)

Tunis Proclaims Zone Emergency

Tunis, Tunisia, Sept. 9 (AP)—President Habib Bourguiba declared a state of emergency today in five provinces bordering on Algeria.

French authorities have acknowledged that five Tunisians were killed by French troops tracking down a rebel group in the territory of this former French protectorate. The French maintain they have a right to pursue rebels into Tunisia when it is used as a base in the nationalist rebellion in Algeria. The Tunisian Government in a sharply worded protest claimed seven—not five—Tunisians were killed.

The proclamation of emergency affects the border areas of Souk-el-Arba, Kef, Sbeitla, Gafsa and Tozeur.

3 Executions In Red China Seen Lesson In Coexistence

By PHILIP POTTER
[*Sun Staff Correspondent*]

Hong Kong, Sept. 9—The Chinese Communist regime three days ago gave the world and its own fellow-traveling liberals an object lesson on the meaning of coexistence.

The execution of Wang Chien-ko, vice principal of the Hanyang middle school, and two alleged fellow "counter-revolutionaries" blamed for a two-day student riot last June has given sharper definition to slogans Mao Tze-tung coined a year and a half ago to mark a new stage in progress toward communism.

Last February Mao elaborated on what he had meant a year earlier when he promulgated the slogans.

Invited Criticism

One, "letting a hundred flowers bloom and a hundred schools of thought contend," invited intellectuals to speak up and constructively criticize the practice of arts and sciences in the country so as to awaken the country from the Marxist torpor that had set in following victories over what the Communists call the Kuomintang reactionaries of Chiang Kai-shek, the landlord and capitalist classes.

The other less widely heralded slogan was an assurance to the eight puppet parties with which most of the country's 5,000,000 intellectuals are identified that the Communist party believed in "long-term coexistence" with them and a policy under which the so-called democratic parties and the Communist party would exercise "mutual supervision."

Both Were Hedged

Mao, in that February speech, hedged both the invitation and the assurance, but intellectuals and minor party members, neglecting apparently to read all the fine print in his long speech, rode off with lances atilt and let the Communist party have it in an orgy of criticism which did not stop short

(Continued, Page 6, Column 1)

Student Red China Ousted Advised To Quit Russia Soon

By HOWARD NORTON
[*Moscow Bureau of The Sun*]

Moscow, Sept. 9—The first American youth to return here from an illicit trip to Red China was "advised" today to leave Russia at once and report to the American Embassy in London.

The advice was given Shelby Tucker, 22-year-old college senior from Pass Christian, Miss., by the American Ambassador to Russia, Llewellyn Thompson, in a 40-minute interview this morning.

No Specific Instructions

Thompson said he had "no specific instructions" in the Tucker case, and his action, in effect, passes the buck to the Embassy in Britain.

Tucker is registered at the London Embassy as an American resident of Britain. He is a student at Oxford University.

Presumably it is now up to the London Embassy to decide whether to indorse Tucker's passport as good only for a one way trip to the United States—an action which was threatened by the State Department before Tucker and 40 other young Americans went to Red China last month.

Any such action might mean an end to Tucker's studies in Britain unless the British authorities are willing to let him stay temporarily without a valid passport.

May Finish Studies

[A State Department spokesman in Washington said it was conceivable that Tucker would be permitted to remain at Oxford under some special provision in his case, but that as a general, policy that department in due course will stamp the passports of the other students so that they are valid only for a trip home.]

The young Mississippian was deported from China after spending a week in Peiping. The grounds for his deportation, he said here, are that he refused

(Continued, Page 6, Column 3)

HUNGARY MOTION ASSAILS RUSSIA

36 Nations Ask U.N. To Condemn Soviet Action

New York, Sept. 9 (AP)—The United States and 35 other nations tonight called on the United Nations to condemn Russia for depriving Hungary of liberty and political independence.

The request was in a resolution submitted on the eve of the 81-nation special Assembly on Hungary.

The resolution asked also that Prince Wan Waithayakon, of Thailand, Assembly president, be named special representative on the Hungarian problem.

Power To Take Steps

He would be empowered to take steps he deems appropriate to see that previous United Nations resolutions on Hungary, including demands for withdrawal of Soviet troops from Hungarian soil, are carried out.

The resolution indorses the report of the five-nation inquiry committee on Hungary. On the basis of the committee's finding, the resolution draws up a scathing indictment of the Soviet Union and the present Hungarian regime of Premier Janos Kadar. Among the accusations:

1. The Soviet Union in violation of the United Nations Charter has deprived Hungary of its freedom and its people from exercising fundamental human rights.

2. The Kadar regime was imposed on the Hungarian people by armed intervention of the Soviet Union.

3. The Soviet Union has carried out mass deportations of Hungarian citizens to Russia.

The resolution calls on the Soviet Union and the Kadar

(Continued, Page 9, Column 1)

RUSSIAN MISSILE CLAIMS DOUBTED

Quarles Says U.S. Will Not Be Outdistanced In Race

By MARK S. WATSON
[*Sun Military Correspondent*]

Washington, Sept. 9—Donald A. Quarles, the Deputy Secretary of Defense and a recognized authority on missiles research, today evinced no alarm over Russia's recent announcement of the successful testing of an intercontinental ballistic missile.

"I am confident," he said, "that we will not be outdistanced in this so-called ballistic missiles race." He added that until the actual production of long-range missiles on an operational basis is at hand, the manned bomber will remain supreme as a long-range tool of destruction. At present America is thought to have a wide lead both in heavy bombers and in the technique of using them.

"Exceeded The Truth"

Quarles, speaking before the United States Conference of Mayors in New York, supported President Eisenhower's description of the Moscow announcement as a "boastful statement," and remarked that, while not untruthful, the Russian communication sought to create "an impression that substantially exceeded the truth."

In explanation he quoted the essential items of the Moscow

(Continued, Page 4, Column 3)

WHITE HOUSE 'SUPPORTING' COURT ACTION

President Keeping In Touch With Brownell On Arkansas Case

By WILLIAM KNIGHTON, JR.
[*Sun Staff Correspondent*]

Newport, R.I., Sept. 9—President Eisenhower "deplores" the new outbreaks of violence over attempts to integrate the public schools at several points in the South.

The Chief Executive also is "supporting the action of the District Court" at Little Rock, Ark., where Judge Ronald N. Davies has three times ordered the end of segregation. But State Guardsmen, under orders of Gov. Orval E. Faubus, have prevented it.

Except for keeping in touch with the situation by telephone conversation with Herbert Brownell, Jr., Attorney General, and his aides, the vacation White House here is taking a "watch-and-wait" attitude now that the Justice Department report of the incidents which brought on the Little Rock crisis has been submitted to Judge Davies.

Position Reiterated

Before injunction proceedings against Governor Faubus were ordered by Judge Davies today, James C. Hagerty, White House press secretary, had reiterated that the next move in this clash between Federal and state power was in the hands of the Federal jurist.

Hagerty, at his late afternoon press conference, offered only the facts that the temporary White House at the Newport naval base had been in touch with the Justice Department officials three times today.

The first was a talk between the press secretary and William P. Rogers, deputy Attorney General, this morning. Then early this afternoon the President personally discussed the growing crisis with Brownell, and Hagerty was on the telephone about 4 P.M. with Brownell in Washington.

The only fact that Hagerty either could or would discuss was to reveal that Brownell informed him that the 400-page FBI report was at that moment being submitted to the judge.

Sharp Questioning

Under sharp questioning, the White House spokesman said the President had been informed of the other outbreaks of violence at North Little Rock, Birmingham and Nashville. Asked what the Chief Executive's reaction was, Hagerty replied:

"I think that like every other American the President deplores violence wherever it occurs." Newsmen pressed the press secretary for some hint as to what the next move of the President, or the Department of Justice, might be, but they got nowhere.

Hagerty was asked what the President was going to do to suppress the violence. "I believe local officials have already done that," was the reply.

"Does the President intend

(Continued, Page 5, Column 5)

COURT ACTS TO BRING HALT TO INTERFERENCE IN INTEGRATION PLAN

2 Guard Officers Also Named In Directive; White Students Shove 6 Negroes Away From North Little Rock High School

Little Rock, Ark., Sept. 9 (AP)—Mayor Woodrow Mann tonight said telephone callers had threatened his life and heaped "plain filth" on his family because he sharply criticized the action of Gov. Orval Faubus in the Little Rock school dispute.

Little Rock, Ark., Sept. 9 (AP)—United States District Judge Ronald N. Davies today ordered injunction proceedings against Gov. Orval Faubus at the climax of a day which saw the first outburst of violence in the Arkansas integration process.

In Washington, a Justice Department spokesman said the department would "comply as soon as possible," possibly tomorrow. Announcement of the compliance came also from the vacation White House, at Newport, R.I.

Davies's directive also specified that Maj. Gen. Sherman T. Clinger, head of the Arkansas National Guard, and Lieut. Col. Marion E. Johnson also be named as defendants.

Johnson commands the troops which now surround Central High School and have forcibly prevented nine Negro students from attending classes.

Must Have Petition

Davies's order asked Federal attorneys to file a petition for an injunction to prevent interference with court-ordered integration in Little Rock. A judge cannot draw up a petition but may impose an injunction once the petition is presented.

At neighboring North Little Rock, a separate city not involved in the judge's order to the attorneys, white students shoved and jostled six Negroes and kept them from entering the previously all-white high school.

The North Little Rock School Board meantime announced it was standing firm on its intention to postpone integration indefinitely.

The Governor at a press conference tonight parried numerous questions about the effect of the injunction proceedings.

"Legal Question"

"I have not yet received official notice, and it will be a very important legal question," Faubus said. "I'd like to see the official notice to see just what it involves."

Asked whether Federal marshals would be allowed through the gates of the mansion guarded by National Guardsmen to serve a summons, Faubus said the guards could forcibly prevent entry of any unauthorized person to the mansion grounds.

Davies's order told the attorneys to bring action immediately against Faubus, who has kept armed National Guardsmen at Central High School for a week to prevent Negroes from attending the school.

The order was directed to Herbert Brownell, Jr., United States Attorney General, and Osro Cobb, United States attorney, of Little Rock.

Davies three times before had in effect ordered the Little Rock School Board to proceed with its plan of limited, gradual integration.

Today his brief order said that the court had received a report from the United States attorney that Negro students were not being permitted to at-

(Continued, Page 5, Column 2)

ALABAMIANS BEAT NEGRO

Minister Attacked After His Integration Attempt

Birmingham, Ala., Sept. 9 (AP). A Negro minister was beaten today in an outbreak of mob violence set off by his attempt to enter Negro students at all-white Phillips High School.

The Rev. F. L. Shuttlesworth, 35, was knocked down several times and threatened with death by members of a white group which had gathered outside the downtown school.

Shuttlesworth's daughter, Ruby Fredericka, 12, suffered a bruised ankle when a car door was slammed against it during the melee.

Three white men were arrested by police who battled a dozen or more men until the minister was able to break away and make his escape.

Two hours after the incident, a car containing four Negro men drove past the block-square Phillips building and threw rocks into a window. No one was hurt. The Negroes escaped.

Will Try Again

Police Commissioner Robert E. Lindbergh ordered Birmingham police to prevent persons "who have no lawful reason to be at the schools" from entering school grounds. This would include Negroes who have not been registered.

Shuttlesworth said, after Lindbergh's letter, that he would try to enroll the Negroes at Phillips again tomorrow, "whether they kill us or not."

After the violence, Lindbergh said, "The Negroes will not enter our schools. We will use police to keep them out."

"There is no parallel between this case and the one in Arkansas," he added.

"The Governor of Arkansas is acting in direct conflict with a Federal court order. We are acting under the authority of

(Continued, Page 4, Column 4)

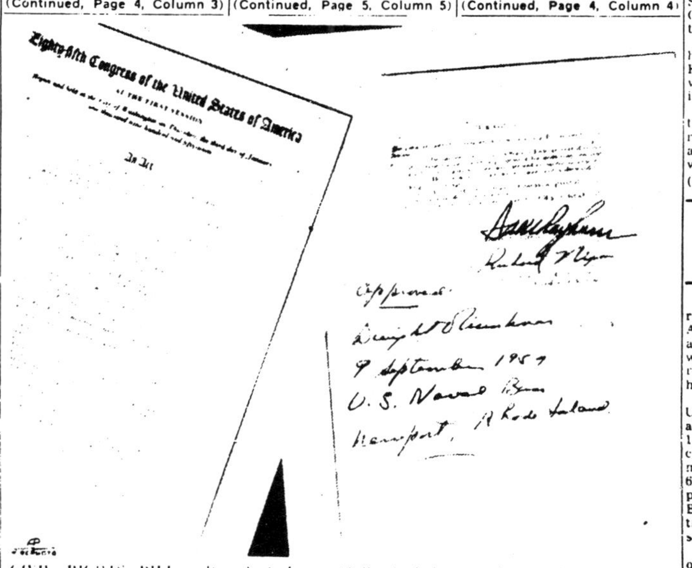

CIVIL RIGHTS BILL — President Eisenhower's signature is shown on civil rights bill which he signed yesterday morning at Newport, R.I. "Approved" precedes signature.

Carrie's Course Still Unchanged

Miami, Fla., Sept. 9 (AP)—Hurricane Carrie roared over the Atlantic tonight, still traveling about 10 miles an hour on its west-northwest course but carrying top winds of 160 miles an hour, a new high.

An advisory issued by the United States Weather Bureau at San Juan, Puerto Rico, at 11.08 P.M. indicated the hurricane had reached a point 1,000 miles east of San Juan, a gain of 60 miles in six hours since a previous advisory. The Weather Bureau said the big storm continued to be a menace only to shipping.

Miami, Fla., the nearest point on the North American continent, lies about 1,000 miles west-northwest of San Juan.

The Weather
Cloudy and windy with some rain. High about 67 degrees. Yesterday's temperatures: High, 65; low, 54. (Details, Page 18; Map, Sports Section, Page 40.)

THE SUNDAY SUN

LIGHT FOR ALL

New Tips Being Checked In Police Probe: Page 40

Vol. 57—No. 40—D* | PAID CIRCULATION IN SEPTEMBER (Daily—Mon. to Fri.) MORNING, 199,232 / EVENING, 214,631 } 413,863 ‖ SUNDAY 318,158 | BALTIMORE, SUNDAY, OCTOBER 6, 1957 | Entered as second-class matter at Baltimore Post Office | 284 Pages | Price 20 Cents

Russian Satellite Still Whirling Around Earth; Symington Urges Probe Of Why Soviet Beat U.S.

YANKS WHIP BRAVES, 12-3, LEAD SERIES

Kubek Belts 2 Homers, Mantle Another In Third Contest

Pictures and other news of Series in *Sports Section.*

By LOU HATTER
[*Sun Staff Correspondent*]

Milwaukee, Oct. 5—The New York Yankees answered the derisive jeers of Milwaukee's baseball populace with an explosive clutch-hitting assault here today that buried the Braves under a 12-to-3 score in the third game of the 1957 World Series.

Rookie Tony Kubek dismayed his hometown fans, hammering a pair of homers and a single to drive in four Yank runs as the American Leaguers assumed a 2-to-1 edge in this best-four-out-of - seven - games post - season classic.

Mickey Mantle likewise slammed a four-master, his ninth in series competition, and whacked a single to figure prominently in the rout of the Braves before 45,804 County Stadium spectators.

Yanks Get Only Nine Hits

The Yanks wreaked their destruction on the hapless Braves this blustery afternoon on a total of only nine hits, as a procession of six Milwaukee hurlers contributed to their own downfall by issuing eleven bases on balls.

The Braves had their chances, a bushelful of them, against the pitching of Bob Turley and Reliefer Don Larsen, who emerged with his second triumph in post-season play against one loss.

Including three safeties by Second Baseman Red Schoendienst and two blows apiece by Shortstop Johnny Logan and Center Fielder Hank Aaron, Milwaukee collected eight hits.

Aaron Hits 2-Run Homer

One of these, a fifth-inning four-master by Aaron, accounted for two of the National League champions' three tallies.

But sluggers like Joe Adcock, Eddie Mathews, Wes Covington and Bob Hazle—the hitters whose bats had driven Milwaukee to its first pennant—were not functioning at the critical junctures.

On four occasions, eight walks having been doled out by the two Yankee chuckers, the Braves left three runners stranded.

Altogether, fourteen Milwaukee runners representing potential runs were left on base, tieing a long-standing World Series record.

Cubs Held Record

On October 18, 1910, the Chicago Cubs orphaned fourteen men on the paths in the second game against the old Philadelphia Athletics.

This was anything but a well-played series encounter, as evidenced by another record which was eclipsed this afternoon.

While the Milwaukee pitchers—Bob Buhl, Juan Pizarro, Gene Conley, Ernie Johnson, Bob Trowbridge and Don McMahon—were giving up 11 free passes, Turley and Larsen each were handing out four walks.

The combined total of 19 bases on balls was three higher

(Continued on 2d Sports Page)

Other Major Sports Results

COLLEGE FOOTBALL

13—N. Carolina	Navy—	7
14—Duke	Maryland—	0
13—F.& M.	Hopkins—	6
26—Notre Dame	Indiana—	0
27—Army	Penn State—	13
47—Princeton	Col'mbia—	6
40—Okla.	Iowa State—	14
19—Mich. State	Calif.—	0
20—Cornell	Harvard—	6

PRO FOOTBALL

21—Colts	Chicago Bears—	10
23—Cleveland	Pittsburgh—	12
24—New York	Phila'phia—	20

GOLF

England crushes U.S. in Ryder Cup golf, 7 to 4.

RACING

Reneged won the $50,000 Manhattan 'Cap at Belmont and Terra Firma was the victor in the $25,000 Juvenile Handicap at Hawthorne.

Atlantic City closed its race season with My Warrior taking the Home Bred 'Cap and Derry the Handicap Stakes.

Gromyko And Dulles Hold 'Helpful' Talk

But Russian Foreign Minister Refuses To Consider Reunification Of Germany

By JOSEPH R. L. STERNE
[*Washington Bureau of The Sun*]

Washington, Oct. 5—John Foster Dulles, Secretary of State, and Andrei Gromyko, Russian Foreign Minister, held a long conference today that was described as "helpful" and "useful."

Chatting face to face in the library of Dulles s home, the two foreign-policy chiefs discussed Middle East tensions, disarmament differences, the situation in Europe and American-Soviet "contacts."

While a joint communiqué said the talks were designed to provide a "clarification of the intentions" of the rival nations, it contained no hint that any of the issues dividing East and West had been resolved.

"Not Proper Subject"

In fact, Gromyko refused to talk about one of the world's key problems—reunification of Germany.

Andrew H. Berding, Assistant Secretary of State, said Dulles brought up the subject but "Gromyko said he could not accept this as a proper subject of discussion by him."

This was in line with Russia's stand that negotiations on reunification should be conducted directly between West Germany and East Germany. The United States takes the view that unless the Soviet Union and America can come to agreement, German-to-German talks would be useless and unrealistic.

Today's meeting, which went on for 3 hours and 45 minutes, was the first between Dulles and Gromyko since the latter succeeded Dimitri T. Shepilov as Foreign Minister in the course of the Kremlin shakeup earlier this year.

State Department officials had anticipated that the conference would last two hours. But Gromyko insisted on the use of a translator despite his command of the English language.

Zarubin In Conference

The Russian Foreign Minister had a characteristic scowl on his face when he arrived at Dulles's Tudor-style home at 4.02 P.M. He moved his arm in what seemed like a curt salute, then walked quickly into the house, trailed by Georgi Zarubin, Soviet Ambassador in Washington, and Oleg Trozanovski, a translator.

According to Berding, six men were in the Dulles library during the talks. In addition to the Secretary of State and the

(Continued, Page 7, Column 1)

2 SCUFFLES MAR ARKANSAS PEACE

Little Rock Paratroopers In Minor Incidents

Little Rock, Ark., Oct. 5 (AP). This capital city in the old South was under military occupancy today for a second week end. A couple of minor ruckuses involving the occupying troops marred an otherwise placid scene.

One regular army paratrooper tangled with a teen-ager during the night on the campus of Central High School, center of a great integration crisis. Two off-duty paratroopers were picked up by city police during a disturbance at a fair.

By contrast, scores of other paratroopers mingled with local citizens on a polite, if not friendly, basis.

Central High was closed, its green campus patrolled by a skeleton guard of troops, its corridors and classrooms silent until Monday.

Youth Accuses Paratrooper

Nine Negro students, the first ever integrated in Little Rock, finished a second week of classes yesterday. Some of their days at Central have been hectic. Others, like yesterday, have been quiet.

A 19-year-old alumnus of Central claimed he was knocked down last night by a paratrooper's rifle and menaced with a bayonet.

The youth, Robert King, with four companions, left a dance at the high school fieldhouse for a quick smoke. Two paratroopers of the 101st Airborne Division, on duty in the area, told them to move on.

King claimed he politely declined to move. He said one of the paratroopers fixed a bayonet to his rifle, knocked him down with the butt of the rifle and stuck a bayonet in his midriff, without, however, breaking the skin.

Order Defied, Army Says

The youth said the soldiers finally released him to a male schoolteacher who had emerged from the fieldhouse.

An Army spokesman said King defied the trooper's order to move on and grabbed at his rifle. The soldier shoved the weapon against King's chest, the Army account continued, and the youth fell down. There was no mention of any bayonet.

The Army added that a faculty witness said King had been drinking.

The dance followed a Friday night football game in which Central's crack team won its twenty-fifth straight victory, beating Hot Springs, Ark., 46 to 6. A couple of hundred off-duty paratroopers—minus weapons—were among spectators.

About 90 other off-duty paratroopers were given passes to attend the Arkansas Livestock Show, Little Rock's annual State fair. Two of them fell afoul of local police, who accused them of being drunk and resisting arrest.

The Army said Sergt. James D. Holt's scalp was cut by a police billy club during what

(Continued, Page 22, Column 4)

RUSSIA ASSAILS LODGE'S CHARGE

But U.S. Stands By His Accusation At U.N.

By PAUL W. WARD
[*Sun Staff Correspondent*]

New York, Oct. 5—While United Nations circles here buzzed with talk about the Soviet's earth satellite as a new Communist triumph in "peaceful competition with other systems," the Kremlin's delegation here rang some more changes today on a related theme.

It issued a four-page statement rebuking Henry Cabot Lodge, United States Ambassador, for having charged the Soviet hierarchy five days ago with a "desire not to coexist peacefully with the United States."

"Good Of All Nations"

The Soviet statement, which drew a reply from the United States delegation that left Lodge standing by his charge, served as a curtain-raiser to the talk that Andrei A. Gromyko, Soviet Foreign Minister, was to have with John Foster Dulles, Secretary of State, in Washington this afternoon.

It ended with a reminder that Nikita S. Khrushchev, No. 1 Soviet Communist, said in an American telecast four months ago:

"We want very much peace and friendship with the American people. We want friendship, not in order to have our two great countries combined

(Continued, Page 6, Column 1)

MOB STONES RIOT POLICE IN WARSAW

Students Off Streets, But Others Clash With Militia

Warsaw, Oct. 5 (AP)—Communist riot police charged angry crowds in Constitution Square again tonight with tear gas and noise bombs in new disorders after two nights of student freedom uprisings.

The students, targets of beatings and bombing Thursday and Friday nights because they protested suppression of their paper *Po Prostu*, stayed off the streets tonight.

But their anger at Government and party heads had spilled over into the general population. Crowds gathered in Constitution Square, scene of violent attacks on the students Friday night.

The riot squads moved into the square from their stations. The crowds picked up stones and bricks from wartime rubble areas and hurled them at the steel-helmeted police.

Crowd Gathers Again

The police then charged with noise bombs and tear gas grenades. The crowd gave way, then formed again in defiant groups of about 50 each on one side of the square.

Other groups clustered in the courtyards of undamaged homes in neighboring streets.

The police threw a cordon around the square.

But even while the gas clouds billowed, traffic kept moving. Yachts sailed under bleak gray skies on the Vistula River. Parents accompanied students to a university ceremony a half mile across town from the Warsaw Polytechnic School, center of the student resistance.

A Western witness said the Constitution Square rioting began when a crowd of boys, 12 to 15 years old, threw stones at the police. The police charged them without clubs while about 2,000 persons watched from the edge.

Clubs, Tear Gas Used

Then more stones began to fly. Demonstrators pulled crates off passing trucks and threw bottles, at one time forcing the police to retreat. They fashioned clubs from timbers torn from food stalls and kiosks. With the tear gas loosed, the crowds fell back up Marshalkowska street into the wooded square surrounding the skyscraper Palace of Culture.

Reinforced militia used clubs and more tear gas to disperse them.

At least ten policemen and fifteen civilians have been injured in the three nights of rioting. Some hospitals refused to divulge any information about casualties.

The students kept to their boarding-houses on Narutowicza Square, adjoining the school, after renewed warnings that all 6,000 might be expelled and new students enrolled if they kept up their resistance.

The decision to keep indoors was made after a five-man delegation representing all Warsaw University departments and

(Continued, Page 2, Column 4)

Hoffa Calls For Teamster Unity, Favors AFL-CIO Tie

Miami Beach, Fla., Oct. 5 (AP)—James R. Hoffa worked today to get rival teamsters union factions to close ranks and gird for a coming battle to avoid expulsion from the AFL-CIO.

Dave Beck, retiring union president, proposed a $10,000,000 teamsters battle fund to be ready for use against rival unions in the event the teamsters are ousted from the parent labor body on corruption charges.

But Hoffa, now in full command of the 1,500,000 member teamsters organization, said he is opposed to Beck's plan and intends to work hard to keep the teamsters inside the AFL-CIO family.

Never "Fire 1st Shot"

Hoffa was overwhelmingly elected by a 3-1 margin as Beck's successor by teamster convention delegates yesterday and actually is to take over from Beck on October 15.

Plainly irked at Beck's proposal, Hoffa said he would never "fire the first shot in a civil war in the American labor movement," and there would be time enough, when and if the teamsters get booted out of the AFL-CIO, to plan then what retaliatory actions and funds may be necessary.

Beck, in his apparent open break with Hoffa, said he expected to propose the multimillion dollar fund at the closing teamsters' convention session, where the principal remaining business is filling eight union vice presidential posts.

Labeled As Corrupt

Hoffa and Beck are deeply involved in scandals developed in Senate rackets committee hearings. Both have been labeled by the AFL-CIO's powerful Executive Council as corrupt and unfit to remain in organized labor.

Hoffa said he hopes to get the AFL-CIO to reverse its findings and withdraw a threat to suspend and later expel the teamsters from AFL-CIO ranks.

But George Meany, AFL-CIO president, and fellow federation chiefs repeatedly have stated their determination to rid labor's ranks of corruption and to co-operate with the Senate rackets committee headed by Senator McClellan (D., Ark.).

Frank W. Brewster, dumped by Hoffa as the teamsters' West Coast boss, meanwhile, said he feels the teamsters' unit that

(Continued, Page 22, Column 1)

Reds' Moon-Launching Also Stirs Up American Service Rivalries

White House Insists Russ Action Was 'No Surprise'

Washington, Oct. 5 (AP)—A demand was heard today for a congressional investigation of why Russia beat the United States into the realm of space with an earth satellite.

It was voiced by Senator Symington (D., Mo.), long-time critic of Eisenhower Administration policy in the military and scientific fields.

Stirs Hot Rivalry

The Soviet feat also stirred the hot embers of rivalry between the armed services. Rumblings were heard from backers of the Army that if that branch of the service had charge of the satellite program, it could have beaten the Russians to the punch. The Navy has principal responsibility for the baby-moon undertaking.

Meanwhile the White House insisted there was no race and that the Soviet satellite launching came as no surprise. James C. Hagerty, press secretary, who gave out this word, did not elaborate on his "no surprise" remark.

Causes Great Interest

He said the event is "of course of great scientific interest" and should contribute much to the world's knowledge.

Symington, a former Secretary of the Air Force and a member of the Senate Armed Services Committee, gave his views in a telephone interview from Missouri.

"This is a very serious matter that cannot be laughed off," he said.

Relating the satellite launching to Russia's claims of great progress in the military missiles field, Symington said:

"Unless our defense policies are promptly changed, the Soviets will move from superiority to supremacy. If that ever happens, our position will become impossible."

Symington said he would ask Senator Russell (D., Ga.), chairman of the Senate Armed Services Committee, to call in top defense officials and scientists for questioning.

Butler Comments

Senator Butler (R., Md.) said in a radio interview that he was "very much surprised" by news of the Soviet earth satellite but he did not feel the congressional investigation proposed by Symington was necessary.

"The Soviets have gotten the jump on us," he said, "but I don't think that we need to have a congressional investigation.

"I think we have to go to work now. I know our work is progressing satisfactorily on our satellite program. We'll just have to keep ahead in other fields."

Senator Wiley (R., Wis.), one of the few senators here in the capital, took a less alarming view of the latest Soviet surprise. "It's nothing to worry us," said Wiley, a member of the Foreign Relations Committee. "It's something to tell us to keep on our toes."

Research Cutback Seen

Senator Mansfield (Mont.) assistant Democratic leader called the development "a major victory for the Soviet Union in the field of science."

Mansfield recalled that the Kremlin leaders also had announced successful firing of an intercontinental ballistic missile.

"This is additional proof that we must not understimate the scientific skill and the technical know-how of the Soviet Union," he said.

"We appear to have cut back on vitally needed research and development. At the same time we have failed to develop a centralized organization in these fields to replace the interservice rivalries in missile production."

"Anger And Distress"

At the Army's Redstone Arsenal in Huntsville, Ala., a scientist expressed belief that if the Army had been put in charge a couple of years ago it could have launched an earth satellite before the Russians did.

The scientist, asking that his name not be used, said his first reaction to the Russian announcement was "anger and distress."

He said the Army a year ago fired a test vehicle which could have been refined to a point where it could have launched a baby moon. He evidently referred to reports that a Jupiter-C was fired 640 miles high and a distance of more than 3,000 miles at a speed of about 15,000 miles an hour.

A contention that Russia won

(Continued, Page 3, Column 8)

Analysis

By MARK WATSON
[*Sun Military Correspondent*]

Washington, Oct. 5—From the viewpoint of American defense there is a most useful aspect of Russia's successful launching of the first world satellite, months ahead of the American scientists' schedule and apparently six times as large as America's projected "Vanguard."

It demonstrates unmistakably the advanced state of Russian scientists and technologists in the numerous areas involved—both as to elaborate scientific calculation and highly satisfactory technologic design, construction, and operation.

Skeptical Expressions

It therefore should compel American defense authorities to look with a good deal more respect on Russia's possible attainments in related fields.

Ever since Moscow's announcement of success of some sort in the launching of an intercontinental ballistic missile there have been skeptical expressions from American authorities—the President, the Secretary of State, and the Deputy Secretary of Defense among them—and complacent assurances that the Russian statement sought to create "an impression that substantially exceeded the truth."

Maybe.

But military men have not had quite as much complacency. They have remembered that in certain fields of military technology, as in some nonmilitary sciences, Russian performance has been high for decades.

Past Russian Achievements

The Russian Army has made better use of artillery projectiles than others, for example. The best Russian tank in World War II was far better than the best German tank.

The new Russian jet-transport which lately went into service is in successful large-scale operation earlier than any that American aviation has been talking about.

Most significant, however, is a fact often stated but widely ignored, namely, that Russian exploration of the missile-rocket field (in which the new satellite is at the moment the most distinguished item) has been determined and continuous.

Lag Laid To Economy

America's has not. Our post-1945 "economizing" halted some of our most important arms research almost in its tracks. And our post-Korean "economizing" brought fresh disaster to military research in several fields.

Russia and the Western Allies engaged in 1945 in a scramble for the German missile plants and their personnel. America, for example, brought home a

(Continued, Page 3, Column 5)

Russia Sets Moon Timetable

Moscow, Oct. 5 (AP)—The Soviet Union gave the Russians an almost continuous timetable of the first earth satellite today as the tiny Russian-conceived sphere hurtled around the globe with unprecedented speed.

Moscow Radio, whose first announcement to Russian citizens of the Soviet scientific victory came hours after the Kremlin told the rest of the world, rallied interest among its listeners as the day went on.

The magnitude of the Soviet achievement grew here with appreciation of the feat of Soviet scientists. Russians began to congratulate themselves as the radio announcer reeled off the names of world cities over which the satellite had passed and a Soviet rocket expert told the world that passenger travel to the moon was just another long step away.

18,000 Miles An Hour

Moscow Radio broadcast calmly the timetable of the satellite which is circling the globe, invisible to the unaided human eye, at the highes speed—about 18,000 miles per hour—ever attained by any man-made object, once every 96.2 minutes. The broadcast said:

"Since the moment of its passage over the city of Moscow at 1.46 A.M. Moscow time, it has circled the earth about six and a half times. According to precise calculations the period of its circling the earth lasts 1 hour, 36.2 minutes. The radio transmitters in the satellite are working without interruption on wave-lengths of 7.5 and 15 meters."

Then, after giving the baby moon's schedule for today over Eurasia and America, the broadcast told where it would be Sunday:

"On October 6 the satellite will be over the following places: Yakutsk, at 0025; Prague, 0149; Riga, 0151; Moscow, 0152; Oslo, 0327; Rangoon, 0528; Bandung, 0535; Leningrad, 0649; Moscow, 0650; Bombay, 0703; Damascus, 0834; Manchester, England, 1005; Paris, 1006; Rome, 1009."

[Times are all Moscow time which is seven hours ahead of Eastern Daylight Time.]

This schedule shows that the satellite orbit, at a 65-degree angle to the equator, would not carry it over Moscow each trip.

North American Passage

The Moscow broadcast gave the times of the satellite's passage over North America Saturday as follows: Halifax, 0752 E.D.T.; Detroit, 0930 E.D.T.; Washington, 0931 E.D.T.

The newly-announced time of 96.2 minutes replaced an earlier Soviet estimate that it was making the circuit in 95 minutes. The radio announcement gave no reason for the revision—but apparently resulted from reports being constantly piped into the central satellite headquarters from dozens of Soviet observation stations.

The satellite is 58 centimeters, or about 22.835 inches, in diameter and weighs 83.6 kilograms, or about 184.306 pounds.

Russian Sees Moon-Bound Flight In 'Several Years'

By HOWARD NORTON
[*Moscow Bureau of The Sun*]

Moscow, Oct. 5—Russia's victory in the race to launch the first earth satellite is due to the merits of the Communist system, the Soviet people were told today.

This explanation was carried on a nation-wide broadcast and credited to Prof. Kirill P. Stanikovich, who is believed to be one of the scientists who took part in the project.

The professor also hailed the launching of the satellite as the first stage in a flight to the moon, and predicted confidently that it will be possible to send instruments to the moon within "several years."

Amateurs Get Signals

His remarks were the first official comment on the project since the launching was announced at 2.30 A.M. today.

It is reported here tonight, meanwhile, that radio amateurs from all over Russia have been reporting receipt of signals from the satellite.

And the official news agency, Tass, says that "a rich store of information already has been gathered as a result of these reports."

Professor Stanikovich is quoted by Moscow Radio as saying that the initial success makes it possible now to build bigger and better satellites which will carry more and improved equipment.

"The launching is a big victory," the professor said, "not only for Soviet science but for the Soviet [Communist] system."

Ability Was Questioned

He said that a few years ago Russia's ability to put a satellite into the air was seriously questioned in the West.

"The launching of the satellite is not only a great event for all mankind," he declared, "but it is also the necessary first stage in a flight to the moon.

"Now it can be stated with confidence," he added, "that in several years a flight to the moon with instruments will become as possible as the launching of the first satellite."

Evening papers here today are publishing detailed time schedules for the appearance of the sphere over various cities of Russia and Europe.

It is due to pass over Moscow twice tomorrow morning, but probably will not be seen, since the area has been under heavy clouds for several days.

WEST PICKS UP SIGNALS FROM 'MOON'

Sphere Reported Sending Messages In Secret Code

Washington, Oct. 5 (AP) — Russia's epoch-making earth satellite sped around and around a fascinated world today, sending what may be messages in secret code back to its creators in the Soviet Union.

As it circled the globe every 96.2 minutes, 560 miles out in space, the Western world's scientists knew it was there because they could pick up its radio signals.

But they experienced great difficulty in spotting it visually. Although there were some scattered reports that it had been seen, these were disputed, and there was some feeling that it might never be spotted except by Russians.

7 Times Every Day

The satellite's course around the globe from north to south brings it over the United States seven times every 24 hours, as the earth spins beneath it.

The Naval Research Laboratory here said it would be impossible tonight to estimate approximate times at which the baby moon would pass over specific areas of the country tomorrow.

A laboratory spokesman said that the satellite would have to complete another orbit before computers could start figuring the time schedule which it probably will follow tomorrow. The laboratory said it hoped to have the time estimates tomorrow morning.

U.S. Sightings Discounted

Two American scientists said the Soviet-launched sphere was sending back coded messages that they were unable to decipher.

A Cambridge (Mass.) astronomer said it was obvious the Russians had chosen to launch the satellite at such an angle to the sun as to prevent visual observations in the free world.

There were a number of reports of sightings from different parts of the United States, but officials at the Smithsonian Astrophysical Observatory in Cambridge said the baby moon is not yet visible to observers in this country.

Japanese Report Sighting

A Japanese scientist said he saw the satellite by telescope as it passed over Niigata, 160 miles northwest of Tokyo. He said it was "barely visible," though much brighter than he had expected.

Cambridge scientists said the satellite can be seen only in the North and South polar regions at present because of its relation to the earth and sun. They said it might become visible in other parts of the world if it changes direction in two or three weeks.

How long it will continue to whirl through the heavens in its north-south orbit was a subject of the greatest speculation. Estimates ranged from a few days to 1,000,000 years.

A Soviet scientist attending a meeting in Washington said the batteries operating the satellite's

(Continued, Page 3, Column 1)

On Other Pages

The Weather
Rain ending by afternoon today. High near 50. Yesterday's temperatures: High, 53; low, 34.
(Details, Page 10; Map, Page 25.)

THE SUN FINAL

[Registered United States Patent Office]

Vol. 244—No. 36—F | PAID CIRCULATION IN NOVEMBER (Daily—Mon. to Fri.) MORNING. 196,863 EVENING. 219,356 416,219 || SUNDAY 321,258 | BALTIMORE, MONDAY, DECEMBER 29, 1958 | Second-class mail privileges authorized at Baltimore, Md. | 26 Pages | 5 Cents

COLTS WIN CHAMPIONSHIP

DE GAULLE ANNOUNCES AUSTERITY BUDGET TO REDUCE FRENCH PERIL

Says Nation Is In Dangerous Straits, Must Tighten Financial Belt To Survive; Cuts Include Veterans Pensions

Paris, Dec. 28 (AP)—Premier Charles de Gaulle told the French people tonight the nation was in a dangerous strait and must accept sweeping financial reforms and belt tightening.

Explaining a sharp devaluation of the franc, partial convertibility of the franc in international trade and announcing the freeing of quota restrictions from 90 per cent of France's imports. De Gaulle addressed a nation wide radio and television audience.

He outlined an austerity budget cutting into everything from rail fares to politically touchy veterans pensions.

Pinay Supports Pledge

However, de Gaulle promised funds to raise the lowest minimum wage levels as well as unemployment benefits to give bottom-rung workers a guaranteed, if low, annual wage.

Antoine Pias, de Gaulle's conservative, bespectacled Finance Minister, followed him on the nationwide hookup and backed up the de Gaulle promise by saying:

"I solemnly assure you that the standard of living for the lowest paid will not be reduced and that legislation protecting them will be applied with loyalty and exactitude."

Pinay also promised to hold the line on the new franc, which was devalued 17.55 per cent yesterday to 493.7 to the dollar.

No Algeria Proposals

The messages by de Gaulle and Pinay were heard through France and its dwindling empire by millions who had been braced for the bad news by black headlines telling of the nation's financial troubles.

It was one of the longest and meatiest addresses the 68-year-old Premier has made since returning to power seven months ago. He held out no immediate prospects of a better life to the French.

He gave no solutions or ending the nationalist rebellion in Algeria which is the cause of much of France's financial trouble. On the contrary, the cost would likely increase, de Gaulle sald. "We have undertaken to transform while pacification advances,' he said in his sole reference to the troubled terrtory.

"Way Toward Catastrophe"

The tall, erect leader of the French in World Was II told citizens of his Fifth Republic "I accept the mandate which you confided in me "by electing me president, the office he assumes January 8.

"The national task which fell upon me eighteen years ago thus finds itself by this fact, confirmed," he added.

He recalled that when he returned to power seven months ago, with Algeria's settlers and the Army up in arms against the weak Paris Government, France was "on the way toward catastrophe."

"The movement of the month of May, while it first appeared in Algeria, proceeded in reality from the general conviction that the public powers were impotent against the wave of menaces, which comprised, naturally those striking our economy.

"The confidence of the country has permitted us, in this realm, as in others, to reverse the tendency and ward off the

(Continued, Page 4, Column 1)

MONEY MOVES STIR EUROPE

Uncertainty About Long-Term Effect Voiced

London, Dec. 28 (AP) — Western Europe's leap towad freer finance triggered political arguments today—and some uncertainty about the long term effect on people's pocketbooks.

By the time banks open their doors tomorrow morning the continent's main trading nations, in the hope of encouraging wider trade, will have relaxed the regulations for converting their money into foreign currencies.

At the same time, France is grabbing for a bigger share of international markets by devaluing the franc and making its goods cheaper for foreign buyers.

Businesss leaders generally welcomed the decisions announced Saturday, although some were reluctant to forecast the consequences.

Socalist newspapers and left-wing leaders like Britain's Hugh Gaitskell called the currency relaxations serious mistakes and forecast possible depression and increasing unemployment.

Austrian Move Expected

Under the changes, most of the West European governments guarantee to exchange foreign holdings of their currencies into dollars or any other form of cash.

This limited convertibility was announced by Britain, West Germany, Holland, Belgium, Luxembourg, Denmark, Sweden, Norway, Italy and France.

Newspapers in Vienna predicted today that the Austrian Government shortly would announce free convertibility of its schilling.

Business interests in the countries that already have taken the stepacknowledged it will mean tenser and tighter competition, but were optimistic about their ability to meet it.

The West Berlin Sunday paper *Der Tag* commented:

"Convertibility has been in preparation for a long time. Its importance exists in the fact that from now on the participating countries will be forced to coordinate their policies

(Continued, Page 4, Column 2)

THE RUN THAT WON THE GAME — Alan Ameche, Baltimore Colt fullback, has plenty of running room as he booms over for the winning touchdown that beat the New York Giants, 23 to 17, in "sudden death" overtime for the National Football League championship. Lenny Moore (24), at left on the ground, is effectively blocking Emlen Tunnell (45), while Johnny Unitas (19), in rear, watches the action as does Giant Jim Patton (20) in Yankee Stadium.

NEWSPAPER STRIKE ENDS

N.Y. Delivery Union Votes Heavily For Settling

New York Dec. 28 (AP) — Newspaper deliverers today voted overwhelmingly—2,091 to 537 —to end New York's costliest newspaper strike. Morning papers started their presses rolling almost immediately.

The nineteen-day strike was the longest in the city's history involving all nine major New York newspapers.

A loud cheer went up from a crowd of about 1,500 union members and newspaper-starved spectators as the result of the vote was announced at the Manhattan Center.

"We are now ready to go back to work with the best wages and working conditions ever had by the members of our union," said Sam Feldman, president of the Mail and Newspaper Deliverers Union. The union's membership had twice turned down negotiate agreements before today's vote.

Happy At End

Asked if he thought the strike had been worthwhile, Feldman said only that he was happy to see it over. A spokesman for the Publishers Association of New York, which represented the newspaper management, said: "The drivers tonight accepted what they twice earlier rejected after prolonged negtiatins and despite the advice of their officials.

He estimated that the strike cost the publishing business alone $25,000,00 in revenues. Other millions were lost outside the newspaper business.

"The effect of the strike has been felt in industry trade, cultural life, and almost every ele-

(Continued, Page 7, Column 2)

New York Shudders As Colt Fans Romp

By ERNEST B. FURGURSON
[Sun Staff Correspondent]

New York, Dec. 28 — Within seven seconds after Alan Ameche crossed the goal line and the Colts became football's world champions, a Baltimore fan in a blue knit hat was swinging from the crossbar of the goal post.

Backing up ths fast enthusiast was a "bench"of about 15,000 Colt rooters, who made Yankee Stadium, the north-south subway lines and Pennsylvania Station shudder to a chant that went like this:

Gimme a C!" "C!"
"Gimme an O!" "O!"

And so on—but the difference today was that when C-O-L-T-S was all spelled out, the fans' rejoinder to "What does that spell? "was:

"CHAMPS!"

The sudden death victory sent the mass of Baltimore backers swarming out of their biggest stronghold along the erstwhile right-field bleachers to mob Ameche.

Then some of them played ring-around-the-rosy.

Some pushed toward the Colt band at the far end of the field and just stood there yelling. No words, jut yelling.

Others fought for pieces of the goal posts. Big clusters of fans, showing only a spot of flailing fists at their center, marked the struggle for each big piece of post.

Shortly afterward, smaller clusters marked the scraps over smaller scraps, some of them as small as pocket size.

The battle of the goal posts was nearly over when it reached the point at which one young fellow ran out of a pileup yelling, I got some, I got some!"

He was holding up his index finger and pointing to a precious splinter in it.

Goal Posts Demolished

But while the goal posts were finally demolished, the stadium still stood, and the Baltimoreans set to work to shake it as much as their thousands of lungs could manage.

The team band, led by majorettes, sassier than ever, marched down the field trailing thousands of yellers, then swung in a very roogh pivoting movement and stormed back up—and back and forth some more.

Among the more conservative

(Continued, Page 16,Column 5)

COULDN'T LET TEAM DOWN

Myhra Thought Tying Kick Would Be Good

By EDWIN H. BRANDT
[Sun Staff Correspondent]

New York, Dec. 28 — "I couldn't let these guys down. If I got a good snap and hold I thought it would go through."

It was Steve Myhra talking above the noise of the Colt dressing room as a milling crowd desperately sought elbow room among the players, coaches, photographers, reporters, lockers, equipment and benches of the suddenly small room.

Gino Marchetti lay stretched out on a table, his broken right ankle in a cast, the game ball clutched under one arm. The players wandered around, somewhat subdued and dazed except for Johnny Sample, who was chanting, "we are the best in the world. We are the best in the universe."

Not Aware Of Time

Weeb Ewbank whirled around in the arms of Don Kellett and Carroll Rosenbloom and Mayor D'Alesandro, red-faced and puffing, shouted, "It was the greatest, it was the greatest."

It was the greatest.

Myhra congratulated Marchetti, and shouted over his shoulder, "I knew we were pretty shy of time, but I didn't know it was only nine seconds." He was talking about his 20-yard field goal, which sent the game into overtime and on into a 23-to-17 Colt victory.

It was Myhra's most important kick in his life, and about all he could do was grin for a while, at a loss for words.

"I knew it was the big one

(Continued, Page 16, Column 3)

YULE ROAD TOLL MOUNTS TO 577

Rate Increases Rapidly As Motorists Return Home

Chicago, Monday, Dec. 29 (AP)—The holiday death toll at 2 A.M. this morning as compiled by the Associated Press:

Traffic	**577**
Fires	**91**
Miscellanous	**92**
total	**760**

Chicago, Dec. 28 (AP) — The homeward rush of Christmas vacationers today sent the country's death toll surging toward a pre-holiday estimate of 620.

Millions of autos jammed roads and generally good weather invited high speeds, one of the major factors in the bloody highway slaughter.

In a statement, the National Safety Council said, "Only the greatest care by motorists could hold the death toll down to our estimates."

New Record Unlikely

The Council added, however, that only an unusual upswing in the death rate in the weekend's closing hours would bring the toll close to the all-time record of 706 traffic deaths set in the four-day 1956 Christmas holiday.

A heavy toll of casualties at the start of this Christmas holiday posed the possibility a new record would be set.

Multiple death smash-ups studded the roll of highway accidents.

In Illinois, four lives were snuffed out early today when one motorist sought to pass another on a hill in fog and collided with an oncoming car.

Four Milwaukee men were killed near Racine, Wis., and a fifth was injured today when their car plowed through a construction barricade.

The National Safety Council predicted before the holiday that the auto death toll would be 620 for the 102-hour period from 6 P.M. (local time) Wednesday to midnight tonight. This would be the second highest holiday traffic toll on record.

DEFEAT GIANTS, 23-17, AS AMECHE SCORES IN SUDDEN-DEATH PERIOD

Myhra's Field Goal With Nine Seconds To Go In Regulation Game Ties Score, 17-17; Berry Breaks Playoff Record

Full page of pictures and other news of Colt victory . . . *Pages* 13, 16, 17 and 26

By CAMERON C. SNYDER
[Sun Staff Correspondent]

New York, Dec. 28—Six years of sweat and frustration bore fruit today as the Colts stormed 80 yards in thirteen plays to win the National Football League championship, 23 to 17, in a sudden-death playoff with the New York Giants at Yankee Stadium.

Propelled by John Unitas's passes and Raymond Berry's catches, the Colts forced the game into the first sudden death extra period in pro history when Steve Myhra place kicked a 20-yard field goal with nine seconds left in the regulation time.

Placekick Ties Score At 17-17

That placement evened the game at 17-17 and gave the Colts their winning chance, which Alan Ameche cashed on a 1-yard scoring plunge after 8.15 minutes had elapsed in the sudden-death period.

The first team to score in a sudden-death period is the winning team, no matter how the score is achieved.

Actually the Colts almost allowed the title to slip through their fingers, much to the dismay of 16,000 Baltimore rooters and the delight of a larger New York crowd composing a surprising attendance of 64,185. Pre-game forecasts had predicted a capacity gathering of 70,000-plus.

Helped By Strong Defense

It was only the cold, calculating and deadly play-calling of Unitas and the clutch catching of Berry, who set a championship game record with twelve receptions, that brought the Colts back from what would have been a dismal and disappointing defeat.

This pair, augmented by a stout offensive line and the likes of L. G. Dupre, Ameche and Lenny Moore were just too much for the Giants. Fortified with luck and a burning desire after their defensive unit had staged a magnificent goal-line stand in the third period, the New Yorkers struck twice within the space of five minutes to pull ahead of the Colts.

Giants Trail In Statistics

Until their defense ignited the rest of their team, the Giants were appearing completely outclassed as the smoother functioning Colts compiled an overwhelming statistical edge.

But a team that has thrived on adversity during its entire pro history, dating back to 1947 in the old All-American Conference, and recently in 1953 when the present management took over, thrived on adversity this time.

After the Colts blew their half-time lead of 14-3, they rose to their greatest heights behind Unitas.

Unitas raced the clock in the last minutes of the regulation time and won.

Trailing, 17-14, the Colts got possession of the ball with just 2 minutes and 25 seconds left and 86 yards away from the promised land.

It was enough time, but just enough. Unitas passed and passed again. His first two were incomplete and only 1 minute and 50 seconds were left. He hit Moore for an important first down on the Colt 25, missed another, and then Berry became the target to the 50.

Giants Win Extra-Period Toss

Another Berry connection and the ball was on the Gaint 35 with 43 seconds left and time running on.

It was Berry again on a diving catch to the 13. Fifteen seconds were on the clock as the Colt place-kicking unit lined up or the most important kick in Baltimore football history. Myhra, from the hills of North Dakota, a cool customer under tremendous pressure, lifted the pigskin and the Colts into the sudden-death period.

It wasn't over. The game was just tied. The captains came out for the important coin-flipping ceremonies. The Giants were represented by Kyle Rote and Bill Svoboda, the Colts by Unitas, subbing for the injured Gino Marchetti.

Luck was with the giants again. They won the toss and elected to receive.

But even luck can't overcome a determined defense, which the

(Continued, Page 16, Column 1)

THE KICK THAT SAVED IT — All eyes watch the ball after Steve Myhra's (No. 65) crucial kick that enabled the Colts to tie Giants, 17 to 17, and then go on to win in overtime.

Showdown Believed Near As Cuban Rebels Advance

Havana, Dec. 28 (AP)—Cuban Government forces and insurgents were engaged in violent offensives in central and eastern Cuba today.

The pay-off day of the two-year-old civil war appeared close at hand.

Four of Fidel Castro's rebel columns were reported marching on Santiago de Cuba in the east after smashing blows at the Army in Oriente Province.

The rebel radio triumphantly broadcast this report and said the purpose was to set up a separate government in the eastern province soon.

But in central Cuba, President Fulgencio Batista's Government forces apparently have opened a ferocious offensive to stem a tide of rebel successes which seriously threatened Santa Clara, the capital of Las Villas Province.

Planes, Artillery Sent

While the rebels in Oriente claimed they had begun their drive to smash the bulk of Batista's 10,000-man force there, Batista was sending bombing planes, tanks and heavy artillery against the rebels in Las Villas.

The Government offensive apparently was in the area of Cuba's main central highway east of Santa Clara, possibly in the area of Ranchueio, one of the towns the rebels claimed to have taken.

Reports from Las Villas pictured the Army as delivering smashing blows at rebel positions. army planes and artillery heavily bombed and shelled rebel concentrations in the area surrounding Santa Clara.

The rebels have attempted to declare these places open cities in order to stifle a Government counterattack.

Government forces also were on the move in the eastern areas of Las Villas. A rebel radio broadcast from Jatibonico, in Camaguey province near the Las Villas border, said the insurgent-held town was heavily bombed by four Army planes.

The Army had warned civilian populations in towns held or threatened by rebel forces there would be all-out counterattacks on populated places to rout the insurgents.

In Oriente Province, the rebel

(Continued, Page 2, Column 5)

On Other Pages

The Weather
Most sunny but with some cloudiness today. High, 32. Yesterday's temperatures: High, 32; low, 22.
(Details, Page 12; Map, Page 27.)

THE SUN FINAL

Registered United States Patent Office

Vol. 244—No. 66—F PAID CIRCULATION IN DECEMBER (Daily—Mon. to Fri.) MORNING, 194,165 EVENING, 217,153 411,318 || SUNDAY 318,570 BALTIMORE, MONDAY, FEBRUARY 2, 1959 Second-class mail privileges authorized at Baltimore, Md. 28 Pages 5 Cents

SHIP SURVIVOR'S SIGNAL BELIEVED HEARD

Integration Of Schools Begins In Virginia Today

PLANS MADE TO HANDLE ANY STRIFE

No Violence Expected But Foes Ready To Demonstrate

Richmond, Feb. 1 (AP)—The first public school integration in Virginia history will start tomorrow at Norfolk and Arlington, where plans are being readied to quell any possible violence.

City and school officials in both communities say they expect no violence.

However, a segregationist group at Arlington has announced plans for a demonstration in connection with the integrated opening of Stratford Junior High where four Negro students will enroll along with 1,076 white youngsters.

The Arlington school will open its doors at 8.45 A.M.

Arlington police said nearly 100 signs were posted today on the school grounds warning against unauthorized entry.

Special Policemen

They read: "No Trespassing. Authorized Persons Only. By Order of Arlington County School Board."

A special detail of 80 policemen, in addition to the regular area patrol, will form a backdrop for the 9 A.M. opening of six secondary schools in Norfolk, closed by State order since last September. White student leaders will also assist in maintaining order.

Seventeen Negroes and nearly 7,000 white students will enroll for classes. Many of the 10,000 white students originally enrolled at the six schools are attending private schools or public schools in nearby communities, and are not expected to return to Norfolk public schools this semester.

To Close At 12.30

The schools will close at 12.30 P.M. after registration.

As desegregation becomes an accomplished fact—four years and 261 days after the May 17, 1954, Supreme Court decision banning public school segregation—the Virginia Legislature will be standing by in Richmond to gauge the effect. The Legislature has reluctantly accepted token integration as inevitable.

The Arlington chapter of the pro-segregation Defenders of State Sovereignty and Individual Liberties announced its members would follow school buses en route to Stratford High Monday morning and attempt to talk white pupils out of boarding the buses.

The organization's president, Jack Rathbone, said signs bearing anti-integration messages also would be available for distribution to any white students desiring them.

85 Members

The Arlington chapter has about 85 members. Rathbone is a plumbing contractor.

But Ray E. Reid, Arlington school superintendent, said he believes "there will be a smooth transition" to integration at Stratford. Negro and white students will be forbidden to congregate outside the school, and police will block off an area a half-mile wide around the school grounds.

Charles Jennings, president of the Norfolk chapter of the Defenders, said the organization had no plans for any demonstration there.

The Norfolk police chief, Harold Anderson, said there will be a special detail of 80 policemen on duty tomorrow, in addition to 160 men on regular duty.

All On 12-Hour Shifts

Anderson said he had placed the entire Police Department on two 12-hour shifts in lieu of the usual three 8-hour shifts.

Student leaders will join in the effort to discourage violence. Wayne Bedser, a member of the 40-member Monogram Club and the 25-member Key Club at Maury High—one of the six schools to be integrated—said members of the two clubs will be at the school tomorrow morning doing everything they can to stop trouble before it can start.

Norfolk's school superintendent, J. J. Brewbaker, joined white student leaders today in urging citizens to keep the peace.

Brewbaker called for "sympathetic understanding and full cooperation on the part of everyone" so the Norfolk schools may reopen "in a calm and dignified manner."

His plea was echoed by 63

(Continued, Page 7, Column 5)

BULLETIN

Kerrville, Tex., Feb. 1 (AP)—An ice-ladened C-47 military transport plane carrying 25 National Guardsmen from Idaho, crashed and burned tonight 17 miles Southeast of here in the Central Texas Hill country.

First reports from the crash scene said that 25 of the 28 men aboard had survived the crash. Three men—two of them crew members and a National Guardsman—were still missing.

The pilot was injured and was taken to a Comfort, Tex., hospital.

The plane had earlier attempted without success to make an emergency landing at the Schreiner airport here.

FOOD CHAIN DATA SOUGHT

FTC Asking About Mergers, Interlocking Directorates

Washington, Feb. 1 (AP)—The Government is ordering the nation's largest food merchants to help determine whether too few hands hold too much power over the housewife's food dollar.

The Federal Trade Commission said today it is requiring more than 1,000 major food retailers to supply detailed data on mergers, acquisitions, interlocking directorates, distribution trends and industry growth patterns.

Mailing of questionnaires marks the beginning of a broad study of the food industry, the nation's largest business with annual retail sales of about $47,000,000,000.

Announced In October

The FTC announced in October it was planning the inquiry. The commission said it had received many complaints of collusive price action, unfair competitive methods and concentration of economic power within the industry.

At present, the FTC is focusing its study on concentration of power. It may look later into other aspects of food retailing, depending perhaps on what its current inquiry turns up.

Investigations of this sort normally continue for months, even years. They frequently are climaxed by the filing of formal complaints against some members of the industry studied.

Questionnaires have been sent to 1,050 food chains, retail food cooperatives and groups of grocery wholesalers formed to service independent food stores. These account for the great bulk of annual food sales.

Each organization will have to fill out at least three separate question forms. Some will answer four sets of questions. All forms must be returned by March 31 and failure to comply can result in court action.

CHANGE SEEN IN PROPOSED BUDGET CUTS

Mansfield Says They Will Be Made So Arms Can Be Increased

'The Hole We're In'

Washington, Feb. 1 (AP)—Just what is space?

Dr. James A. Van Allen, of the State University of Iowa, for whom the newly discovered Van Allen radiation belt encircling the earth is named, offers this definition:

"Space is that in which everything else is."

Or, he suggested this:

"Space is the hole we are in."

Washington, Feb. 1 (AP)—Senator Mansfield (D., Mont.) predicted today the Democrats will offset a prospective increase in defense spending by economies in other parts of President Eisenhower's budget.

Noting that Vice President Nixon and other Republicans appear to be preparing to make a political issue in 1960 of their efforts to balance income with outgo, Mansfield said the Democrats are ready to meet the GOP on this battlefield.

"The Democratic Congress has reduced President Eisenhower's money requests in every one of the last four years," the Montana Senator said.

"We cut his recommendations by $5,000,000,000 last year while we were increasing the allowances for national defense, health, education and welfare. We intend to use the same responsible discrimination in going over the budget this year.

"Won't Sacrifice Security"

"If we believe it is in the national interest, we will raise the defense appropriations because the Democrats don't intend to sacrifice security in the name of economy."

Senator Keating (R., N.Y.), said the budget battle will "be a tough fight" because the Democrats dominate Congress as a presidential election year approaches.

"I am for a balanced budget if we can possibly achieve one without undermining our defenses," Keating said in a television program for New York stations. "A lot of people don't realize how important it is in keeping prices down to balance the income and outgo of the Government."

Deficit Government spending, Keating said, causes inflation which pushes living and other costs higher.

Mansfield, who is the assistant Democratic floor leader, said he thinks his party will support revisions which will cut the cost of the farm program. He suggested that subsidy payments may be ended for large-scale farm producers.

Foreign-aid outlays could be

(Continued, Page 6, Column 6)

Willie Hoppe Dies At 71, Billiard Champ 50 Years

The form of a champion.

Miami, Fla., Feb. 1 (AP)—Willie Hoppe, whose name was synonymous with billiards almost from the day he mounted a wooden box to reach the table in the rear of his father's barber shop, died today after a long illness. He was 71.

Hoppe had suffered from cancer for many months. He was in St. Francis Hospital at Miami Beach for the last four months but, as late as last night, was able to receive visitors.

William Frederick Hoppe was his full name but he was known the world over as just plain "Willie" from the time he showed the town boys at Cornwall on the Hudson, N.Y., how to control the ivory balls. He gave his last exhibition two years ago in Chicago.

He was quiet, unassuming and always immaculate in dress. Poised, self-assured and courteous to friend and foe alike, the man who ruled the green baize world for so many years looked more like a man of the church than of the kaleidescopic sports world of which he was a definite part for a half century.

Yet Hoppe, who began his career by touring dirty, smoke-filled pool rooms, so dignified the game that he drew Metropolitan Opera stars, ranking members of world society, kings and princes to see him weave a spell with a cue. He probably

(Continued, Page 13, Column 4)

Dulles Plans Pre-Trip Parley With Fulbright

Secretary To See Frequent Critic Before Leaving For Conferences On Germany

Washington, Feb. 1 (AP)—Secretary Dulles plans to confer with Senator Fulbright (D., Ark.) before leaving for German policy talks with Allied leaders in Europe this week.

In the State Department the meeting with Fulbright is viewed as having more than ordinary importance because it constitutes Dulles's first move to set up a close working relationship with the incoming chairman of the Senate Foreign Relations Committee.

Senator Green (D., R.I.) decided last week to step aside from the Foreign Relations chairmanship because of defective eyesight and hearing. Fulbright, who will succeed him as the next ranking Democrat, has been a frequent and bitter critic of Dulles.

Two Aspects Of Problem

Dulles is tentatively slated to leave by air late Tuesday, with his first round of talks scheduled for Wednesday in London. He will see French leaders in Paris and West German leaders in Bonn before returning here about February 11. His meeting with Fulbright is expected to take place late Monday.

In an airport interview on returning today from a New York speaking trip, Dulles said his mission to Europe will deal with two aspects of the German-Russian problem, which has been the focus of East-West conflict for more than two months and which threatens to develop into a full-blown cold war crisis in May.

One aspect, Dulles said, "is the problem of Berlin and the Western reaction to possible Soviet moves."

To Achieve Harmony

"The other," he added, "is the possibility of having talks about Germany with the Soviet representatives."

His words indicated that he will be talking with Prime Minister Harold Macmillan of Britain, President Charles de Gaulle of France and Chancellor Konrad Adenauer of West Germany in an effort to remove disagreement and achieve allied harmony on these questions:

1. What the Western powers can hold out to Russia—and to world public opinion—in the way of new ideas for reuniting Germany and thereby resolving the problem of divided Berlin.

2. Specifically what line the Western governments should take in making specific proposals to Moscow for East-West talks on Germany and possibly some other issues.

3. What measures the Western powers should take—such as an airlift or a show of military ground forces—if a new

(Continued, Page 2, Column 6)

GOP FAVORS NIXON IN POLL FOR 1960

Congressmen Vote Almost 5-1 Against Rockefeller

By GERALD GRIFFIN
[Washington Bureau of The Sun]

Washington, Feb. 1 — Among Republican senators and representatives, Vice President Nixon is strongly favored over Governor Nelson Rockefeller of New York for the party's Presidential nomination in 1960, as indicated in a poll taken by the *Congressional Quarterly*.

Rockefeller appeared to be the leading choice for the vice presidency, although by a smaller margin, over such other men as James P. Mitchell, Secretary of Labor.

Yesterday the *Congressional Quarterly* reported that its poll of Democratic senators and representatives showed Senator Symington (Mo.) as the favored prospect for the Democratic Presidential nomination, with Senator Kennedy (Mass.) favored for the Vice Presidency.

38 Per Cent Answer

The Democratic poll was based on replies from 13? legislators, about 38 per cent of the party's total membership.

The Republican poll favoring Nixon was based on replies from 76 senators and representatives—40 per cent of the total Republican members.

In the polling on the Presidency, Nixon was mentioned 59 times as the party's strongest choice for the nomination, whereas Rockefeller was named thirteen times. Senator Bridges (N.H.), the chairman of the Republican Policy Committee, was named on one ballot. Three Republicans said they didn't know who the strongest candidate would be.

Nixon Leads In West

Nixon had a wide margin over Rockefeller in the returns from Western and Midwestern Republicans, and he led Rockefeller two to one even in the East, the *Congressional Quarterly* found. Among the few Southern Republicans in Congress, the two men were rated about the same.

Whereas Nixon and Rockefeller drew all the attention among possible Presidential candidates nineteen men were mentioned as vice presidential prospects. One fifth of the replies indicated no choice.

Rockefeller was named sixteen times as a Vice Presidential prospect. Secretary Mitchell was named four times. Nixon was listed in six replies as the second member of a ticket headed by Rockefeller.

Others mentioned in two or more replies as possible Vice Presidents included Senator Dirksen (Ill.), the GOP floor leader; Representative Halleck (Ind.), Republican leader in the House; Senator Goldwater (Ariz.), Senator Keating (N.Y.), Representative Simpson (Pa.), and Henry Cabot Lodge, Ambassador to the United Nations.

MIKOYAN BRANDS NIXON 2-FACED

Says U.S. Officials Changed Tune After He Left

By HOWARD NORTON
[Moscow Bureau of The Sun]

Moscow, Feb. 1 — Anastas I. Mikoyan has accused some top American Government officials of being two-faced in their dealings with him.

According to the text of his address to the Communist party congress, as released in this morning's *Pravda*, he charged them with giving one story to him while he was in the United States and quite a different story to the American people after he left.

He also declared that the State Department is sending prominent speakers to talk to the same groups he addressed in America in order to counteract the goodwill Mikoyan created.

Nixon And Dillon Named

These charges were not included in the summary of Mikoyan's speech to the closed congress which was given to Western newsmen here last night.

He said that Secretary Dulles, Vice President Nixon, and two Under Secretaries of State, C. Douglas Dillon and Robert Murphy, are among those who have changed their tune since he left America.

The reason for their change, he alleged, is that "somebody in the United States got scared" that Mikoyan was making too favorable an impression.

"Campaign Of Exhortations"

"After my departure," he told the congress, according to *Pravda*, "the American press started a campaign of exhortations in an attempt to paralyze the positive influence which was exerted by my visit on public opinion in the United States.

In the "campaign to unleash the cold war" since his return to Russia, Mikoyan said, "the most prominent representatives of the Government and cold war experts have taken part."

"Two able deputies of the Secretary of State, Dillon and Murphy, are making a tour around the United States, going to the same cities I visited and talking before the same audiences I addressed, and delivering speeches in the spirit of the cold war."

"About To Feel Thaw"

These speakers, Mikoyan charged, are "throwing cold water on the same business circles which were about to feel the warm wind of a thaw in our relations."

When Dillon and Murphy did not bring about the desired results, Mikoyan told the 1,269 party-congress delegates, Dulles himself joined in with his heavy artillery.

He quoted Dulles as telling his January 27 press conference that all Soviet proposals aim at

(Continued, Page 2, Column 7)

BRITISH FORM NEW GROUP TO BOOST TRADE

Common Market Hurting Sales After Only A Month

Tighter NATO curbs on Red trade urged . . . . Page 2

London, Feb. 1 (AP)—British industrialists, fearful of an approaching trade war, announced today first counter-measures against Europe's six-nation common market.

After just a month's operation, the market already is hurting British manufacturers. Industry and Government fear the outlook is bleak.

An influential group led by Raymond Gordon, of Fairey Aviation, announced it is forming an organization called the Commonwealth Union of Trade. Its aim is to build up Commonwealth trade as an insurance against possible loss of European markets.

Switch To German Machines

Topline British manufacturers, big names in the auto and engineering industries among them, already have lost sales outlets carefully built up in Europe since World War II. Their continental agents, dealers and merchants who had been importing British machines, are switching to German products, which they believe will benefit most from the common market scheme.

The common market started operating January 1 in France, Germany, Italy, Belgium, Holland and Luxembourg. The six nations cut tariffs and increased quotas for imports from fellow members.

About 12 per cent of all Britain's trade is with the six. And although it is too early to assess detailed figures, the British are clearly anxious.

'Our Agents Are Worried"

A spokesman for the Society of Motor Manufacturers said:

"Our agents on the continent are as worried as we are.

"If an agent is handling a British car in France and sees that in ten years time his chances of selling it will be reduced, he naturally gets worried."

France is the focal point of British worries. It has more barriers against imports than other members of the six. And that makes the tariff-reduced German product an even bigger attraction for French buyers.

The British still are pressing a rival scheme which would extend common-market advantages to all seventeen members of the Organization for European Economic Cooperation. France is the main objector to this all-European free trade area. One objection is that the British, while seeking equal treatment in Europe, refuse to give up their preferential trade arrangements with the Commonwealth.

The newly formed Commonwealth Union of Trade will be largely an advisory group, pooling know-how on ways to increase sales. Its basic aim is to remove tariffs and other trade barriers such as import quotas inside the Commonwealth.

Business men expect similar groupings to follow.

The powerful Federation of

(Continued, Page 2, Column 5)

Constitutional Crisis Fails To Upset Monaco Gambling

By LEE McCARDELL
[Sun Staff Correspondent]

Monte Carlo, Monaco, Feb. 1 — Monaco's "grave crisis" brought about by the temporary suspension of part of its Constitution has caused no interruption to business.

The casino's roulette wheels, card tables, crap games and one-armed bandits may not be operating at top speed tonight but they are doing all right for Sunday night in an off-season February.

The lyric opera season opened this afternoon with a performance of Gounod's "Faust." The house was sold out. Gina Lollobrigida's new film, "La Loi," will have its Cote d'Azur premiere tomorrow night in the big cinema at the International Sports Club.

Posters Complete

Colored posters advertising "Faust," Gina and assorted dinnertime and cabaret attractions calculated to appeal to the winter tourist trade outnumber and outshine the white posters bearing the Constitution-suspension decrees signed last Thursday by Prince Rainier III.

The *Nice-Matin*, the principal daily newspaper circulated here, today published "as a matter of information" a statement to Monegasques by Councilor Max Brousse. Brousse is one of the eighteen members of the National Assembly which Rainier dissolved.

The Chancellor called upon his fellow-citizens for a "a calm and cool acceptance" of the "grave action" by the Prince. Only in a serene political state of mind could the principality find a solution, said the Councilor.

As far as outward appearances are concerned, Councilor Brousse is pouring oil upon a calm, untroubled sea. If any Monegasque was refusing to accept the situation calmly he was doing so in strict privacy.

The absence of any general excitement is easily explained. Less than 3,000 of the principality's 22,000 permanent resi

(Continued, Page 2, Column 2)

BULLETIN

A 37-year-old woman was found stabbed to death in the front seat of an automobile in the 3500 block Keswick road early this morning.

The woman, identified by Northern district police as Mrs. Anna Blevins, of the 3500 block Keswick road, was found dead from a knife wound through the heart at 1.20 A.M. by Patrolman William Wright of the Northern district.

Police said they were questioning a 34-year-old man at the Northern police station in connection with the stabbing. The man was arrested by Patrolman Wright at the scene.

SUICIDE FAILS; CUBAN IS SHOT

Batistan Tries To Kill Self Hour Before Execution

Havana, Feb. 1 (AP)—Capt. Pedro Morejon, first to die in Havana's revolutionary trials, attempted suicide an hour before he was executed by a six-man firing squad, authoritative sources said today.

The execution of the 38-year-old veteran of fifteen years service in the army of Fulgencio Batista was carried out in almost complete secrecy shortly before midnight as the provincial Government stepped up the pace of its trials of alleged war criminals.

No Government announcement was made of the execution—the two hundred and sixty-fourth, by unofficial count, since the rebels won a month ago—and it was witnessed by no newsmen. Only a priest, besides the firing squad and officers, was present.

Execution Confirmed

Revolutionary sources confirmed the execution, however, and a witness reported seeing Morejon taken from his cell in the converted prison chapel, loaded in a jeep with a squad of six soldiers and driven into the interior of Spanish-built La Cabana fortress.

Soon the sound of firing and then a single shot were heard. Presumably he was placed against the 20-yard thick wall surrounding the grassy interior. Disposition of the body was not made known.

The secrecy contrasted with the publicity given his trial in a small courtroom just outside Libertad army camp and some of the executions witnessed by crowds.

Visited By Priest

It also contrasted with Government promises that newsmen would be admitted to all trials and executions.

The lone outside witness of Morejon's death, Franciscan Father Javier Arzuaga, had two long visits with him yesterday and said his spirit was serene.

But an hour before he was led out, prison sources said,

(Continued, Page 2, Column 4)

SEARCHERS FIGHT GALE, HEAVY SEA

Report Stirs Flagging Hopes For 95 Aboard Danish Ship

Copenhagen, Denmark Feb. 2 (AP)—Greenland coast stations and a rescue vessel today picked up weak radio signals believed to be from a lifeboat of the missing Danish Arctic ship Hans Hedtoft.

The report stirred flagging hopes for the 95 persons aboard the ship which hit an iceberg Friday in the North Atlantic off Greenland.

Ships and planes which searched the frigid, stormy seas had found no trace of the ship or its lifeboats. A lone patrol plane kept up the search last night, and more planes were to go out at dawn today.

The Danish motorship Umanak reported the radio signals had been sent by an untrained operator and were very weak and irregularly spaced. The Umanak's radioman said it appeared the sending operator was trying to transmit distress signals or a homing beacon.

Halifax, N.S., Feb. 1 (AP)—Two big United States Air Force patrol planes cruised above the stormy seas off Greenland today, searching in vain for a trace of the little Danish ship Hans Hedtoft.

Surface rescue vessels were forced out of the immediate area where the Hedtoft was believed lost with all 95 aboard after striking an iceberg Friday. The search ships were fighting 40-foot waves and freezing 60-mile-an-hour winds.

Although hope has been virtually abandoned for the Danish passenger-freighter, one of the search planes reported spotting an object it said could possibly have been an overturned lifeboat near the Hedtoft's last reported position in the North Atlantic.

Black Stripe Reported

The United States Coast Guard in New York said the plane reported the object appeared to be a double-ended lifeboat with a lengthwise black stripe.

A spokesman for the Royal Greenland Trading Department in Copenhagen said the object described could hardly have been a lifeboat from the Hedtoft. He said its lifeboats all were made of aluminum and unpainted.

The United States Coast Guard cutter Campbell said the object was seen by the Air Force fliers only once and that tomorrow's air and sea search would be conducted in the area where it was sighted—"weather and sea conditions permitting."

Joined In Search

"The reported overturned lifeboat was the only significant result of the air search," the Coast Guard said.

The Campbell was joined during the night by two Danish ships, the Tiesten and the Rink.

Along with the German vessel Poseidon, which has already criss-crossed a wide area of ocean with the Campbell, they steered clear of the smashing ice floes around the Hedtoft's last known position.

The 2,318-ton Danish motorship Umanak, carrying 85 passengers and 40 crewmen, was diverted from its Greenland-Denmark run to join the search but later withdrew because of the weather, the Greenland Trading Department said.

Other Planes Due

A Coast Guard spokesman in New York said the aerial search would continue all night. An American T-24 search plane was over the area, he said, and a Canadian Air Force Lancaster was to go up later. The two Air Force C-54's have returned to their bases.

"There is bad weather up there all right," the spokesman

(Continued, Page 4, Column 2)

WEATHER
Fair, colder tonight, lows near 32 some suburbs, near 40 downtown.
Detailed report on Page 2.

THE EVENING SUN

7 STAR ★★★★★★★ 2 30 STOCKS

Vol. 100—No. 13 | PAID CIRCULATION IN SEPTEMBER (Daily—Mon. to Fri.) MORNING, 197,963) EVENING, 215,682(413,645 || SUNDAY 316,643 | BALTIMORE, MONDAY, NOVEMBER 2, 1959 | Published daily except Sunday by The A. S. Abell Co. Calvert & Centre Sts., Baltimore Md. Second class postage paid at Baltimore, Md. | 38 Pages | 5 Cents

VAN DOREN ADMITS DISHONESTY IN TELEVISION QUIZ SHOW ROLE; CONFESSES LYING TO GRAND JURY

Conciliator Meeting Separately With Steel, Union

Washington, Nov. 2 (AP)—Federal mediators met separately with both sides in the 111-day-old steel strike for 75 minutes today with no indication a settlement was near.

Federal conciliator Joseph F. Finnegan set further meetings for this afternoon with management negotiators, and with negotiators for the striking United Steelworkers Union.

Finnegan showed no particular optimism. David P. McDonald, steelworkers' president, had only a glum appraisal of settlement prospects.

Finnegan refused to say whether he anticipated further meetings with negotiators tomorrow.

Asked why he was not scheduling joint bargaining sessions today, Finnegan said "because I think it's better to do it separately."

Industry Statement

R. Conrad Cooper, chief industry negotiator, said, "It is now apparent that the union is determined to force a 'S' Kaiser-high' settlement on the steel industry and the nation.

"Clearly, they are interested only in perpetuating inflation in America and wasteful practices in the steel industry," Cooper stated.

McDonald, asked whether he saw any reason for optimism, replied: "What happened? We waited and we were dismissed. We will meet again at 4. I have nothing further to add."

Before going into session with the mediators, McDonald complained that many of the top steel company officials were absent, declaring:

"I don't think a summit conference could be held if the presidents and premiers were not present. Nothing can happen if they sulk in their homes and their offices."

Supreme Court Hearing

Cooper declined to comment or make any appraisal of prospects for an agreement. "We're here to find out," he said.

Finnegan, chief of the Federal Mediation and Conciliation Service, met first with union negotiators.

Federal mediators moved back into the strike picture, shifting the deadlocked negotiations from Pittsburgh to Washington a day before the Supreme Court is to hear arguments in the Government's suit to halt the strike with an 80-day Taft-Hartley Act injunction.

McDonald said that "if some of the great bankers would give the signal to the Bloughs and the Whites and the Homers, etc., it wouldn't take long to reach a Kaiser type settlement."

The reference was to the separate peace negotiated between the union and Kaiser Steel Corporation a week ago. Edgar F. Kaiser said yesterday he expects a final agreement will be reached ultimately which will not be far different from the Kaiser settlement terms.

USW Contends T.-H. Provision Is Invalid

Washington, Nov. 2 (AP) — The United Steelworkers contended to the Supreme Court today the 80-day injunction provisions of the Taft-Hartley Labor Act are unconstitutional.

In a 97-page legal brief filed with the court, the steelworkers said the law attempts to give Federal courts powers which go beyond the limits of the Constitution. It asserted:

"The simple contention is, simply, that under the Taft-Hartley Act, Federal courts are asked to issue an injunction which is no part of 'the judicial function of adjudicating justiciable controversies.'"

Government's Reply

The Government, in a reply brief, held that the law is constitutional.

The Government told the court the steel strike already has resulted in such unemployment as to "fully establish the imminence of great economic disruption."

The Supreme Court has scheduled oral arguments for 11 A.M. tomorrow on validity of the 80-day injunction issued by District Judge Herbert Sorg in Pittsburgh, and upheld by the United States Court of Appeals in Philadelphia.

The union's brief again challenged the District Court's finding that the strike imperils the national health or safety.

Question Of Necessity

And it repeated its argument that an industry-wide injunction was not necessary to meet defense needs for steel.

The Government's brief rejected the union's contention that the impact of the strike on the economy as a whole was immaterial, and that justification for the injunction could be found only in shortages of steel for defense projects.

The Government argued that the Taft-Hartley Act provides simply that if the court finds a strike is industry-wide and will imperial the national health or safety, it should have jurisdiction to send the workers back to their jobs under an 80-day cooling-off period.

Flash

Fire On Charles St.

Firemen battled a blaze in the basement of the Mazor Furniture Galleries, 345 North Charles street, late this afternoon. Twenty employees were forced to flee before the flames were brought under control. No injuries were reported.

CRASH SURVIVOR—Ernest Philip Bradley, 33, of Clifton Forge, Va., only survivor of the Piedmont airliner which crashed in the Blue Ridge Mountains, is recovering in a Charlottesville hospital. He spent 40 hours with 26 lifeless bodies on the mountain.

36 Hours Of Quiet, Survivor Says

Waynesboro, Va., Nov. 2 (UP)—"Things were all quiet, no moans, no groans."

This was the way a 33-year-old union official described the immediate aftermath of a crunching impact against a Virginia mountainside in which 26 persons aboard a twin-engine airliner lost their lives and he alone survived.

"I yelled to see if anyone else was alive, but no one answered," said E. Phil Broadley, of Clifton Forge, Va., as he told of his 36-hour ordeal in the wilderness following the crash of the Piedmont Airlines DC-3 Friday night.

He suffered a dislocated hip and minor cuts.

Within a few hours after Bradley was taken to a hospital yesterday at Charlottesville, 26 bodies, wrapped in tarpaulins, were laboriously carried to the summit of cliff-studded Bucks Elbow Mountain near Virginia's famed Skyline Drive.

Found By AF Man

Bradley, who said he noticed his watch showed 8.45 P.M. moments after the crash, was first reached at the wreck scene by Air Force Sgt. John Weis, of Pittsburgh.

The plane, en route from Washington to Roanoke, was last heard from at 8.24 P.M. Friday, when the pilot requested landing instructions at Charlottesville. At that time the plane was believed to be about six minutes from touchdown.

The wreckage, 18 miles west of Charlottesville, was not sighted until 8.30 A.M. yesterday.

Bradley, who was seated near the rear of the plane was thrown from the cabin still strapped in his seat. Because of his dislocated hip, he remained upright in the seat some five feet from the wreckage until rescuers arrived.

Finds Blanket, Coat

With [illegible] he managed to fish for a coa[illegible]d blankets to warm him in the chilly mountain air.

Weis reported Bradley's first words were:

"I'm all right. Go on up and see if anybody else is alive."

Bradley said the pilot never gave any indication there was anything wrong.

Of the actual crash, it "sounded like the roaring of an ocean," he said. "The only sensation was the wings cutting the tops of trees."

Asked when he realized he was the only survivor, he said:

"I can't say I ever really knew."

As to his own chances of survival, he said, "I hoped always that I'd be found."

IAM Representative

He is a district representative of the International Association of Machinists.

Investigators expect no early explanation as to why the plane failed to land safely at Charlottesville.

"It probably will be at least a month before we know the cause of the crash," said David Thom-

[Continued, Page 2, Column 7]

Jet Hits Home; 2 Girls Killed

Wirephoto on Page 2.

Dayton, Ohio, Nov. 2 (UP)—A jet F-104 Starfighter crashed broadside into a house near here today and buried itself in the ruins. Two young sisters were killed. The pilot ejected to safety.

The girls' mother, Mrs. Grace Shoup, 37, ran from the house, her clothing in flames after the supersonic craft crushed the house and exploded. She is in critical condition.

The sisters were Lynn Shop, 12, and Laura, 2. Their brothers, Billy, 10, and Tommy, 8, were in school. Lynn, a sixth-grader, was to have reported for her half-day session of school at noon. Their father, John, was at work at the National Cash Register Company.

Wallace McCormick, 27, of Xenia, was driving past the house when the plane hit.

"Flames from the blast shot clear across the road, more than 50 feet away, and completely enveloped my car," McCormick said. The fire was all over the car. I could feel the heat.

"I lost control and hit the ditch about 50 yards down the road. When I got a look at the house, it was a complete wreck and Mrs. Shoup was running across the yard with her clothing afire."

McCormick was uninjured.

Railroads Claim Outmoded Working Rules Cost $500 Million Yearly

By JOHN T. WARD

(This is the first of two articles)

This week railroad managements and unions representing operating employees begin talks about revision of working rules. A three-year moratorium ran out Saturday.

The railroads claim outmoded practices are costing them $500,000,000 annually.

At the same time, the unions are seeking wage increases and fringe benefits which may cost an additional $750,000,000. (The railroads have proposed a pay cut to bring rail pay in line with some other industries.)

Last year the railroads of the nation with assets reaching $28,000,000,000 had a profit of only $601,000,000.

As an example, the giant Pennsylvania with assets of $2,403,641,998 had net income of but $3,544,073 on revenues of $844,232,093, a narrow squeak in a difficult year.

Cost Estimated

The railroads charge they are hampered by "featherbedding," that is, being forced to pay unneeded workers, or to pay for duplicate jobs which only serve to stretch out work at excessive cost.

They estimate the $500,000,000 annual "unnecessary" cost this way:

$232,000,000 for firemen on freight trains;

$150,000,000 on crew assignment problems;

$50,000,000 on failure to use road crews in yard service;

$68,000,000 in other expenses brought about through "obsolete" working practices begun at least 40 years ago and maintained ever since.

The steel strike has slashed revenues by 20 per cent, (the furloughed crews lost their wages,

[Continued, Page 4, Column 4]

Ike Calls For Letters On Inflation

Washington, Nov. 2 (AP)—President Eisenhower today urged the public to flood Congress and his office with demands that America's economy be kept sound.

Eisenhower, warning against the dangers of inflation, called for the demonstration of support in an informal talk at a conference designed to promote economic growth and stabilize living costs.

He told the conference sponsors that one of the greatest helps that the President and Congress get in the handling of great problems is millions of letters and other communications from the public.

Eisenhower called on the sponsors to promote a flood of such communications in the interest of a sound dollar.

That, he added, would be "one of the greatest services you can accomplish for the United States of America."

Eisenhower spoke at a breakfast meeting of representatives of 48 national organizations. The one-day conference was arranged by H. Bruce Palmer, president of the Mutual Benefit Life Insurance Company.

Introduced By Publisher

The President was introduced by D. Tennant Bryan, president of the American Newspaper Publishers Association and head of Richmond (Va.) Newspapers, Incorporated.

In stressing the need for a sound economy and an intensive fight against inflation Eisenhower repeated a story he has told before.

A year ago, he said, he thought it would be a good idea to write a letter to his 11-year-old grandson, David Eisenhower. The President indicated he never got around to putting the letter in final form, but said this was the gist of the idea he wanted to put across:

"He should stop supporting me."

Get Them Peeved

Explaining, Eisenhower said that every time the big national debt is boosted by a single dollar, the youngsters of America actually are supporting their elders.

Because the debt some day must be paid by the younger generation, they are the ones who will have to "pick up the tab," Eisenhower said.

He urged his audience of about 85 persons to stir up the young people of America to a point where they will get really peeved about having to shoulder the growing national debt.

Today, Eisenhower said, there is need for big spending for defense, for scientific developments and for other things.

In a free government such as America's, Eisenhower said, public opinion runs the Government.

In urging that public support be rallied in a fight against inflation, Eisenhower said without such support a government of imposed discipline results.

"And in the long run, no matter how you cut it, imposed discipline is dictatorship," he said.

As for inflation, Eisenhower said, "there is no particular villain" in the picture. He said all segments of the economy—industry, labor, farmers and everyone else—must join in the fight for a sound dollar.

$129,000 Winner Testifies On Coaching, Learning Script

ANOTHER QUIZ—Charles Van Doren sits in the witness chair of the House subcommittee on Legislative Oversight to answer questions on his participation in a nation-wide TV quiz show.

Washington, Nov. 2 (AP)—Charles Van Doren confessed tearfully today that his television appearance as a mental giant was a dishonest role in a great deception on the American public.

He also confessed that he gave false testimony to a New York grand jury investigating quiz shows.

His boyish face drawn and his eyes bloodshot, Van Doren, 33, told House investigators he followed a prepared script in giving the answers that made him a national celebrity.

Collected $129,000

The most famous of big money winners on TV quiz shows—Van Doren collected $129,000—testified he was coached not only in what to say but how to say it—groping agonizingly for answers he already knew in order to build up suspense.

"I was deeply involved in a deception," Van Doren admitted in telling how he played the part of genius on the old "Twenty-One" quiz program.

When he had completed his story of collusion, followed by fear and shame, Van Doren acknowledged to newsmen who asked if he won the small fortune honestly: "I didn't come by it honestly."

He said he didn't know whether he would return any of the money.

But he said he was relieved now that the hoax had been revealed.

The intellectual scion of a noted literary family admitted he had given the wrong answers in denying previously the show was rigged in his favor.

Van Doren's appearance before the House subcommittee conducting its own quiz into TV question and answer programs was as dramatic as his weekly displays of mental wizardry on the since abolished "Twenty-One" show.

The hearing, under House rules, was neither televised nor broadcast.

Van Doren said he is now aggrieved that he gave in to the persuasive arguments of Albert Freedman, a producer of the show—that he was creating new respect for the teaching profession and that, after all, it was only entertainment for the millions of TV viewers.

"Learned A Lot"

"I learned a lot about good and evil," Van Doren said, "and I learned that things are not always the way they appear to be."

Answering questions posed this time by the congressional investigators, Van Doren later testified that in late January, 1957, while he still was on "Twenty-One," Freedman demanded $5,000 of his potential winnings.

Van Doren hurriedly added that he didn't think Freedman meant it. Nothing came of it, he said.

The incident occurred, Van Doren related, when Freedman approached him one night "and told me I was to be the first contestant to win more than $100,000."

"Exact Words"

"I think these are his exact words," Van Doren said:

"'Charlie, I think I ought to have $5,000 of that money.'"

"I'm very sorry to have to mention this," he said.

Freedman "never repeated it."

[Continued, Page 3, Column 4]

Van Doren Speaks Of Panic, Greed

By DAVID CULHANE

(Staff Correspondent)

Washington, Nov. 2—The voice of Charles Van Doren, sounding as if it could never speak anything but profound truths, today confessed to an elaborate series of lies.

In a voice that sounded quiet, precise and controlled, he spoke of fright, panic, desperation and greed.

A gum-chewing capacity audience spilled out of the House hearing chamber as he revealed what one official called "the whole sordid mess" of the television quiz shows.

Opera Glasses

The crowd was made up predominantly of women and they were well prepared for the 'show' some even carrying opera glasses.

In a dark gray suit, a white button-down shirt and a dark tie, a smiling, controlled Van Doren read a prepared statement for about one-half hour.

"The Only Person"

He said at one point that he knew very little about entertainment, but the dramatic reading he gave his statement belied his professed lack of knowledge.

His perfect timing during the reading reminded many spectators of his television presentations of Seventeenth Century poetry with all its cadences and pauses.

At one point he said, "I may be the only person who ever read Seventeenth Century poetry on television."

Today he added several others to this one distinction.

He seemed familiar and at ease with the atmosphere of blinding lights, press cameras and an audience anxious for entertainment.

A good number of those in the press section were reporters and executives from the National Broadcasting Company, which suspended him when a question arose concerning the validity of his fourteen week stand on the quiz show "Twenty-One."

"Hurry Up, Hurry Up"

Van Doren smiled and accommodated the battery of photographers time and again as the committee went promptly into session at 10 A.M., but finally Congressman Harris, committee chairman, rapped for order, saying "hurry up, hurry up."

A dozen congressmen sat in a row facing the Columbia University assistant English professor as he prepared to read his statement.

A few nervous titters rose from the audience and one voice said quietly, "And now for $64,000. . . ."

Van Doren first said, "May I ask, first, if I can have a glass of water. I'm sorry to bother you."

Presumably an honest request, his statement only added to the tension of anticipation and then he finally began:

"I would give almost anything I have to reverse the course of my life in the last three years. . . .

Teacher And Writer

He spoke of his career as a teacher and writer, and spectators looking at him could see, indeed, that he looked to be exactly that, a teacher and writer.

The engaging, calm and alert manner which endeared him to his television audiences produced

[Continued, Page 4, Column 2]

Cardinal Tedeschini Dies At 86 In Rome

Vatican City, Nov. 2 (AP)—Federico Cardinal Tedeschini, 86, archpriest of St. Peter's Basilica, died early today.

First reports said death was due to intestinal cancer for which he recently underwent surgery.

He was one of the senior members of the College of Cardinals, having been named a prince of the church by Pope Pius XI in 1933.

His death reduces the College of Cardinals to 71 members. Pope John XXIII increased the college to 74 a year ago after its size had been limited to 70 members for nearly 400 years.

Tall, handsome and of stately bearing, Cardinal Tedeschini won recognition for his work as the Vatican's nuncio in Spain from 1921 until 1935, a period which saw the overthrow of the monarchy and an anti-church campaign by the republican government that followed. His elevation to the College of Cardinals was considered to be at least partly in recognition of his work in Spain.

Cardinal Tedeschini was born at Antrodoco, a mountain hamlet in central Italy. He was ordained a priest in 1896 and soon after was called to the Vatican, where he rose to the office of Assistant Secretary of State.

On Inside Pages

The Weather
Mostly cloudy today. High near 40. Some snow or sleet tonight, changing to rain. Yesterday's high: 42; low, 33.
(Details and map, Page 32.)

THE SUN FINAL

(Registered United States Patent Office)

Vol. 250—No. 82—F | PAID CIRCULATION SIX MONTHS ENDING 9/30/61 MORNING, 191,090 EVENING, 214,354 405,444 || SUNDAY 318,537 | BALTIMORE, WEDNESDAY, FEBRUARY 21, 1962 | Published daily except Sunday by The A. S. Abell Co. Calvert & Centre Sts., Baltimore, Md. Second class postage paid at Baltimore, Md. | 48 Pages | 7 Cents

ELATED, GLENN SAFE AFTER 3 ORBITS; NATION AND WORLD HAIL HIS FLIGHT

PRESIDENT, CONGRESS SEND CONGRATULATORY MESSAGES TO OFFICER

Peoples Of Almost Every Land Share In Tension, Relief And Enthusiasm Of Astronaut's 'Super Goodwill Tour'

London, Feb. 20 (*Reuters*)—Prime Minister Macmillan tonight sent a special message of congratulations to President Kennedy on Lt. Col. John H. Glenn's space flight.

The message said:

"My most sincere congratulations to you and to all concerned in your achievement of manned orbital flight.

"This is an outstanding and well deserved achievement."

U.S. Reaction

By WILLIAM KNIGHTON, JR.
[*Washington Bureau of The Sun*]

Washington, Feb. 20—"We have a long way to go in this space race. We started late. But this is the new ocean, and I believe the United States must sail on it and be in a position second to none."

President Kennedy made these remarks as soon as he was officially notified that Lt. Col. John H. Glenn, Jr., had stepped, well and hearty, from the Mercury capsule onto the deck of the destroyer Noa which had plucked him from the Atlantic on schedule.

Within another few minutes Mr. Kennedy had reached the astronaut by telephone and personally congratulated him on his successful three-orbit flight.

"It was a wonderful trip," Glenn told the President. "Almost unbelievable, thinking back on it right now.

"But it was really tremendous."

The President expressed what the nation felt, and what Congress put into a resolution—deep pride at his achievement and thanksgiving for Glenn's safety.

Invited To White House

And the Chief Executive arranged to fly to Cape Canaveral Friday for a public ceremony honoring the Marine officer. The President invited Glenn to visit him at the White House Monday or Tuesday.

A parade from the executive mansion to the Capitol will be held the day of his visit here, with a hero's reception in the halls of Congress.

Congratulatory messages to Glenn streamed out of Washington from Government officials. Congressmen rushed to get their jubilant statements into print and on the air even before it was certain that the Marine flier was safe.

Like the Chief Executive, this capital of the free world continued the work required of it, but kept one eye on television coverage of the space shot.

Leaders of both parties in the Senate and House emphasized before applauding lawmakers that the successful orbiting was accomplished for all to see, in sharp contrast with Russia's secret

(Continued, Page 5, Column 1)

On Other Pages

World Views

London, Feb. 20 (*F*)—The peoples of the world raised an almost universal cheer from the heart tonight for Lt. Col. John H. Glenn, Jr.'s, epic voyage into space and his safe return.

From Vatican City to Tokyo, from government ministries to workingmen's bars, in homes and offices from the Arctic to the equator, mankind thrilled at the news of the 40-year-old American's triple orbit of the globe.

Expressions of sympathy, pride and praise arose in a babel of tongues, but the meanings were clear—"congratulations . . . well done."

Super Goodwill Tour

It seemed that people of almost every land, following Glenn's exploit through news dispatches, radio and TV, shared in the tension, relief and enthusiasm of the United States and the joy that yet another human being had ventured successfully into the uncharted reaches of space. It proved to be a sort of super goodwill tour.

Even the Russians, sometimes disdainful of United States failures, appeared sympathetic toward the American triumph, though it was part of the United States effort to trim their lead in the space race.

Moscow Radio and TV outlets carried factual accounts of the launching and the flight and were swift to announce Glenn's safe return.

Muscovites seemed genuinely pleased and even delighted. "I hope he gets back," said a typical citizen at the news of the blastoff. *Horozho! horozho!* (good! good!) exclaimed a Russian policeman when Glenn came back to earth.

Russian Lauds Feat

In Ottawa, Amasap Aroutunian, Russian Ambassador, voiced praise for Glenn, for the American people, their technicians and workers.

"I believe this remarkable achievement is another step toward better cooperation of scientists of the world and in particular of the Soviet Union and the United States," he declared.

In Europe, a flood of congratulatory messages flowed from capital cities to Washington.

Britain's Queen Elizabeth cabled President Kennedy: "On behalf of my peoples throughout the commonwealth I send you my warmest congratulations on Colonel Glenn's historic achievement."

Italians Rejoice

Italian Premier Amintore Fanfani messaged that the Italian Government "rejoiced . . . in the happy result of the astronautic feat."

Konrad Adenauer, West German Chancellor, wired President Kennedy: "I wish to congratulate you and the American people wholeheartedly on behalf of the German people."

Praising "that courageous" man Glenn, Mayor Willy Brandt of West Berlin said he hoped the space flight would make an important contribution "to the building of a peaceful, free and progressive world."

Sweden's Premier Tage Erlander sent a message of con-

(Continued, Page 19, Column 3)

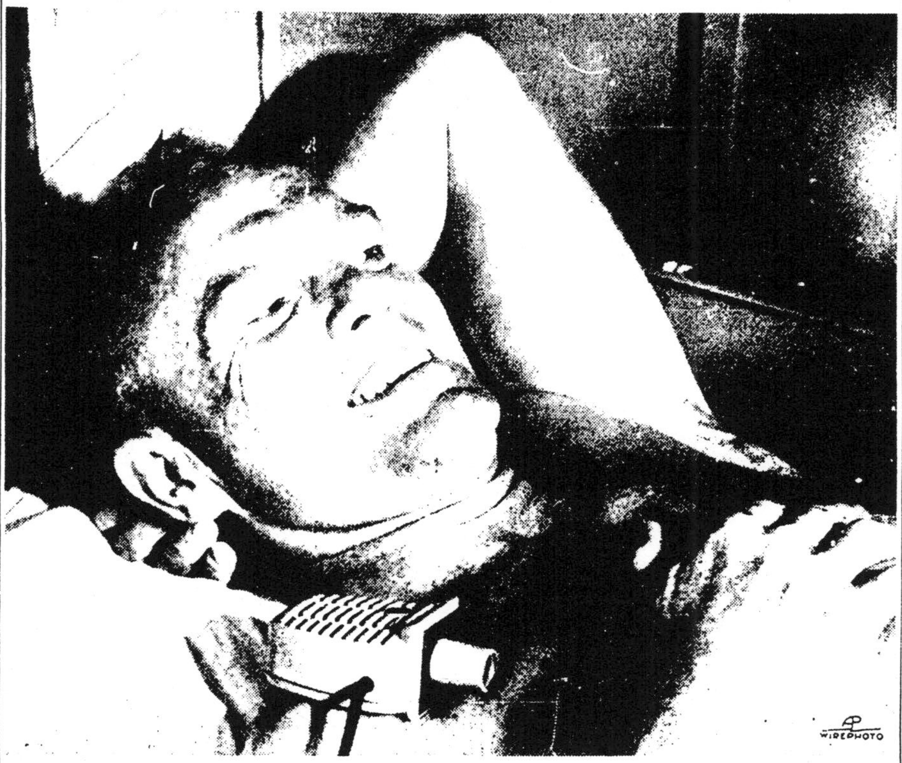

ALL SMILES—Astronaut John H. Glenn, Jr., rests on bunk during examination on ship after being picked up at sea.

OUT OF THE DRINK—The Mercury space capsule with Glenn still inside is pulled out of water by the destroyer Noa.

ASTRONAUT IS PICKED UP AFTER JOURNEY OF 4 HOURS 56 MINUTES

Recovery Made In Atlantic By Destroyer; Marine Calls His Condition 'Excellent'; Speed Of 17,545 M.P.H. Attained

By ALBERT SEHLSTEDT, JR.
[*Sun Staff Correspondent*]

Cape Canaveral, Fla., Feb. 20—America sent its first man into orbit today.

Lt. Col. John H. Glenn, Jr., sped three times around the world in 4 hours and 56 minutes. Then he was recovered safely in the Atlantic.

Glenn, at the controls of his Friendship 7 space capsule, attained an orbital speed of 17,545 miles an hour. His altitude varied between 100 and 160 miles.

The 40-year-old Marine Corps officer was in regular contact with eighteen ground tracking stations around the world as he swung across the Atlantic Ocean, Africa, the Indian Ocean, Australia, the Pacific and the United States.

Glenn, reporting his positions in a firm, often enthusiastic voice, passed from morning in Florida to the afternoon of Africa and the night of Australia.

Braking Rockets

He saw the lights of the city of Perth on the island continent and watched the sun come up over the horizon as he crossed the broad Pacific.

Nearing the end of his third orbit, the spacecraft's braking rockets were fired. The capsule then began falling through a long, easy arc across the southern half of the United States.

His big parachute (63 feet broad) opened on schedule as the capsule descended toward the Atlantic recovery area approximately 800 miles southeast of here.

Glenn had seen the world three times in one day but, judging by reports received here, nothing looked so good as the opening of that parachute.

The elated astronaut was picked up by the destroyer U.S.S. Noa, one of the ships in the naval recovery forces operating with the aircraft carrier Randolph.

Glenn hit the water at 2.43 P.M.

Calls Condition "Excellent"

The Noa, 6 miles away, sped to the floating capsule. The ship hoisted the Friendship aboard a few minutes past 3 P.M.

The marine described his condition as "excellent."

After taking a shower aboard the Noa, Glenn talked to his wife and then to President Kennedy by radio telephone.

At 5.44 P.M., he was transferred by helicopter to the anti-submarine carrier, Randolph, for a brief physical examination and at 8.04 P.M. was sent by helicopter to Grand Turk Island, arriving about 9 P.M. There he will stay for 48 hours and undergo a more exhaustive physical examination and questioning about his flight by a team of scientists and doctors.

Back at Cape Canaveral, officials of the National Aeronautics and Space Administration seemed weary but jubilant.

Dr. Hugh L. Dryden, deputy administrator of NASA, said, "This is a very historic day, which we have been looking forward to for more than three years."

NASA's manned space flight program, Project Mercury, was inaugurated in October, 1958.

Dryden said today's success was "just the beginning, just the first step."

He said that in years to come people will look back on Glenn's flight as they do today at the Wright Brothers' first successful airplane flight.

Robert R. Gilruth, director of NASA's Manned Spacecraft Center, said he was "very proud" of Glenn.

Glenn "Very Sharp"

"It was a very good flight," Gilruth added. "We got a tremendous amount of information about space flight from it."

He said Glenn was "very sharp" in his performance on the 81,000-mile trip.

Gilruth also was high in his praise of Walter C. Williams, associate director of the Manned Spacecraft Center, who played a leading role in the planning and execution of the three-orbital mission.

Williams himself said Glenn's flight was significant for several reasons.

He first noted that the United States has now put a man in orbit.

Williams also pointed out that today's mission demonstrated man's ability to work in space. He said

(Continued, Page 11, Column 1)

The Weather
Partly sunny and breezy today. High near 62 degrees. Yesterday's temperatures: High, 70; low, 50.
(Details and Map, Page 30)

THE SUN FINAL

(Registered United States Patent Office)

Vol. 251—No. 137—F | PAID CIRCULATION SIX MONTHS ENDING 3/31/62 MORNING 186,226 EVENING 215,740 401,966 ‖ SUNDAY 321,955 | BALTIMORE, TUESDAY, OCTOBER 23, 1962 | Published daily except Sunday by The A. S. Abell Co. Calvert & Centre Sts., Baltimore, Md. Second class postage paid at Baltimore, Md. | 40 Pages | 7 Cents

U.S. Orders Arms Blockade Of Cuba; Russia Turning Isle Into Atom Base Able To Bomb Nation, Kennedy Says

CHINESE TANKS PUSH WITHIN 6 OR 7 MILES OF LADAKH AIRFIELD

8 Posts Reported Fallen; New Red Offensive In Northeast Cited; U.S. Bids Russia At U.N. To Restrain Peiping

London, Oct. 22 (AP)—Britain accused Communist China today of aggression against India and stood ready to hurry weapons and other military aid to her threatened Commonwealth partner.

The Foreign Office went out of its way to remind newsmen that Britain regards India as the victim of Red Chinese aggression.

Meanwhile, the Defense Ministry announced that Admiral of the Fleet Earl Mountbatten, chief of the defense staff, will visit New Delhi among other Asian capitals early next month.

In India

By PHILIP POTTER
[*New Delhi Bureau of The Sun*]

New Delhi, Oct. 22—Chinese tanks are within 6 or 7 miles of the Chushul airfield, southern anchor of India's line in Ladakh, an official Defense Ministry spokesman announced here tonight.

He said eight posts had fallen in the Ladakh area and that the Chinese have opened a new offensive in India's North East Frontier Agency, 900 miles to the southeast.

Near Burma

The thrust, he said, began at 3 A.M. today at the far eastern end of the McMahon Line, presumably close to the Burma border.

The spokesman said the Kibitoo post there was engaging the Chinese in heavy fighting.

In that general area a recent Sino-Burma border treaty showed the Diphu Pass as the three-way junction with India.

India lodged protests with both countries, claiming the border with Tibet was 5 miles to the north.

Chinese forces, the spokesman said, also have been concentrating since yesterday in Longju.

It is about 140 miles east of the Thagla ridge sector of the McMahon Line, where there has been heavy fighting since early last Saturday.

Advance South

The Chinese, who crossed the boundary ridge September 8 and used the north bank of the Namkhachu River just below it as the springboard for their Saturday attack, are now reported about 3 miles south of the stream.

The spokesman said Tsang Dhar, a half-mile south of Dhola, had fallen and the fighting was now in mountain pockets to the south.

Altitudes in the area range from 12,000 to 14,000 feet.

The spokesman said the Chinese now were about 40 miles by trail from the Towang Monastery, their possible objective.

They are operating on a 15-to-20-mile front, having overrun In-

(Continued, Page 2, Column 2)

At U.N.

By PAUL W. WARD

New York, Oct. 22—Resisting a new Soviet attempt to squeeze Communist China into the United Nations line-up, the United States Government challenged the Kremlin today to prove its devotion to peace by "demanding that Peiping renounce the use of force."

Uttered here in Washington's behalf by Adlai E. Stevenson, the challenge highlighted the opening round of the United Nations Assembly's thirteenth annual squabble as to whether Communist China deserves the place now held by Nationalist China in the society of "peace-loving states."

Indians Silent

India's delegation, a consistent champion of Communist China's admission for the last twelve years, sat mute throughout the opening round this afternoon, which was further highlighted by:

1. A display of reluctance on the part of all participants save the delegates of Washington and Manila to take any note of the fighting going on between Indian and Communist Chinese troops.

2. A total avoidance of the Sino-Indian conflict by Valerian A. Zorin, who, speaking for Moscow, elected to turn his defense of Peiping into a Soviet offensive against the United States.

Pro-Peiping Nations

3. A series of declarations by representatives of Afghanistan, Finland and Somalia to the effect that their Governments are as strongly pro-Peiping now as they were a year ago.

Reflecting not only the unreadiness of India to seek United Nations assistance against the Chinese Communists but also the

(Continued, Page 2, Column 6)

On Other Pages

U.S. ASKS U.N. TO MAKE CUBA END BUILD-UP

Bids Security Council Send Observers To Check On Order

By PAUL W. WARD
[*Sun Staff Correspondent*]

New York, Oct. 22—The United States is asking the United Nations' Security Council to order "immediate dismantling and withdrawal from Cuba of all missiles and other offensive weapons."

And to "assure and report on compliance" with such an injunction, it is also asking the council to send "a United Nations observer corps" to Cuba.

A petition to both effects was sent to Valerian A. Zorin, a Deputy Soviet Foreign Minister who is the council's current president, while President Kennedy was telling Americans tonight that launching sites for Soviet missiles that could hit any point between Hudson Bay and Lima, Peru, have been spotted in Cuba within the last six days.

Filed in the form of a letter to Zorin from Adlai E. Stevenson, United States Ambassador to the United Nations, the petition also asked for an "urgent meeting" of the council.

Council Meeting Asked

United States delegation attachés, who gave newsmen copies of the petition just as President Kennedy began his telecast, said Stevenson is pressing to have the council meet tomorrow.

A spokesman for U Thant, acting Secretary General, said half an hour later that he also had received a copy of the American request and added that Zorin would have to confer with other council members before setting a date and hour for the meeting.

Communist delegates intimated that Zorin will not try to delay a council meeting.

Counter-Proposal Due

They also intimated that he will counter the United States' proposals for council action by putting forward a long-standing demand for the dismantling of the whole system of North Atlantic Treaty Organization bases—including those maintained by the United States in Europe, the Middle East and Far East—and the withdrawal of all "foreign troops" to their homelands from such places as West Germany and West Berlin.

Along with the United States request for an "urgent meeting" of the Security Council, Stevenson sent Zorin a copy of the action resolution that he will urge the council to adopt and that Zorin has power to veto.

The council—currently comprising representatives of Chile,

(Continued, Page 6, Column 7)

"This secret, swift and extraordinary build-up of Communist missiles (in Cuba) . . . is a deliberately provocative and unjustified change in the status quo which cannot be accepted by this or any other country."—President Kennedy.

Kennedy, Johnson Cancel Remaining Campaign Trips

By GERALD GRIFFIN
[*Washington Bureau of The Sun*]

Washington, Oct. 22 — President Kennedy and Vice President Johnson have canceled the remainder of their election campaign trips, the White House announced tonight.

Because of the weapons quarantine around Cuba ordered by the President, plus the chance of additional and graver action, Mr. Kennedy intends to remain in Washington for the foreseeable future. So does Johnson.

This brought a sudden and dramatic end to the President's active part in the 1962 election campaign, which he himself has been describing as one of the utmost importance to the Democratic party.

Whether the President's action in the case of Cuba, together with his own withdrawal from further participation in the electioneering, will remove Cuba as a political issue from the rest of the campaign was somewhat uncertain.

Senator Mansfield (Mont.), the Senate Democratic leader who was one of the congressional leaders summoned to meet with the President this afternoon, said he thinks this will take Cuba out of the campaign.

Republican congressional leaders were quick to indorse the measures taken by the President and to pledge their support. At least one of them, however, had argued for tougher action during the White House meeting.

"Any Strong Stand"

Representative Wilson (Cal.), the chairman of the GOP Congressional Campaign Committee, said in advance of Mr. Kennedy's speech that Republicans would give him their whole-hearted support for "any strong stand" on Cuba and Berlin.

Wilson was one of the three Republican campaign chairmen who declared, only six days ago, that Cuba was the dominant is-

(Continued, Page 6, Column 5)

U.S. 'QUARANTINE' FACES FAST TEST

Soviet Ships Now At Sea Get 24-Hour Warning

By HOWARD NORTON
[*Washington Bureau of The Sun*]

Washington, Oct. 22 — Soviet ships already at sea and destined for Cuba are being given 24 hours to change course and head back home.

The United States is delaying the proclamation of a limited blockade or "quarantine" until tomorrow night.

The Soviet vessels, meanwhile, are being watched and followed.

If they do not reverse course, they will be halted and searched.

"Offensive" Arms Barred

They will not be permitted to go on to Cuba if they are found to be carrying "offensive" weapons.

If they decide to turn back, then the first explosive showdown will be averted.

This is the way the naval blockade of the island will go into effect, according to a responsible Government official.

The 24-hour delay in proclaiming what the President called a quarantine also serves another purpose, of interest mainly to international lawyers.

OAS To Meet

The delay will give the Organization of American States time to meet and approve the quarantine as an action of the OAS.

This would give the move, announced unilaterally by President Kennedy tonight, the mantle of a United Nations action, taken collectively by the American states.

The OAS is the United Nations organization with the responsibility for guarding the peace of this hemisphere.

A State Department official said

(Continued, Page 9, Column 1)

U.S. IS READY TO SINK SHIP IF NECESSARY

'We Will Use Force' To Enforce Quarantine, Pentagon Says

Ottawa, Oct. 22 (AP) — Canada has stopped Soviet planes en route to Cuba and the Caribbean from landing at Canadian air bases such as Gander, Nfld., Howard Green, Foreign Secretary, said tonight.

By MARK S. WATSON
[*Sun Military Correspondent*]

Washington, Oct. 22 — Immediately after the President's announcement tonight of the quarantining of Cuba, a Defense Department spokesman outlined in plain terms the steps already taken to make the quarantine effective.

The immense operation by sea and air, reaching "as far east as necessary in the Atlantic," is designed to warn all ships on apparent course for Cuba that they will not be allowed to deliver any offensive weapons to that island. Defensive weapons will be permitted—initially.

If the ship continuing on course is believed likely to be carrying offensive weapons (a list of which will be published) it will be hailed, stopped, boarded and searched — not only as to its cargo manifest but as to the cargo itself.

"Force" Is Promised

If the foreign ship refuses to halt "we will use methods necessary to hold it," said the spokesman. If it refuses to permit a search, "we will use the force necessary to search."

The blunt question then was put: "Are you prepared to sink a Soviet ship if necessary?"

"Yes," replied the Pentagon spokesman.

The hazards attached to the enforcement of a quarantine in these absolute terms are clearly recognized. This too was made clear by the Pentagon official.

"We must assume, as we move into this kind of operation, that we must face losses," he said.

Steps Are Listed

The steps already taken or ordered include these:

1. The command at sea is given to Adm. Robert L. Dennison, head of the United States Atlantic Fleet and also NATO's supreme commander in the Atlantic. Dennison reports directly to the Joint Chiefs of Staff and all Atlantic and Caribbean units report to him.

2. Forces in the Caribbean have been strengthened. The Marine Corps garrison of the United States naval base at Guantanamo Cuba, has been "more than

(Continued, Page 9, Column 2)

AMERICA WILL HALT ALL SHIPS CARRYING OFFENSIVE WEAPONS

President Warns Any Missile Launched By Castro Against Any Hemisphere Nation Will Be Regarded As Attack By Moscow

Text of President Kennedy's speech ....Page 8

By WILLIAM KNIGHTON, JR.
[*Washington Bureau of The Sun*]

Washington, Oct. 22—The United States today threw a sea-and-air blockade around Cuba to cut off shipments of "offensive weapons" from Russia or its Communist satellites.

Announcement of the military action came from President Kennedy tonight, just a week after he had first obtained "unmistakable evidence" that bases for the use of nuclear weapons against the Western Hemisphere had been established on the Soviet-backed Communist island.

Missiles with atomic warheads that could reach almost every major city in the United States, Central America and South America are either in place in Cuba or their launch sites are under preparation, President Kennedy declared tonight on all national television and radio networks.

Further, he said, jet-powered atomic bombers are being uncrated and assembled and air bases to handle them are under construction.

Warns Khrushchev

The President announced he had ordered all ships—"from whatever nation or port"—found to contain offensive weapons to be "turned back." If necessary, they will be sunk, he said.

The Chief Executive also flatly warned Soviet Premier Khrushchev on two counts:

1. If any nuclear missile is launched from Cuba against any nation in the Western Hemisphere, the United States will consider it an attack upon itself and launch a retaliatory attack of the same type on Russia.

2. America will take "whatever action is necessary" should Moscow use United States preoccupation with the Cuban crisis to "move anywhere in the world against the safety and freedom of peoples to whom we are committed." West Berlin was emphasized by the Commander in Chief as a case in point.

The situation was so critical that the President tonight announced that neither he nor Vice President Johnson would participate further in the election campaign. Each canceled political speeches in nearly a dozen states between now and November 6.

Meets With Cabinet

The President spent almost the entire day working on the Cuban emergency, as he had most of the weekend.

The decision to address the nation was made this morning.

At 3 P.M., the President received the advice of the National Security Council on handling the crisis, and at 4.30 P.M. he held a meeting with his Cabinet.

A half hour later more than a score of leaders of Congress, both Republican and Democrats, were briefed on the situation and told what the President had decided to do.

Most of them were out in their districts campaigning for reelection when notified of Mr. Kennedy's request for them to come back to Washington immediately. Air Force jet planes were dispatched to bring them back. They agreed, at the President's request, to remain in the capital for possible further consultations.

Talks With Predecessors

The President also conferred with his three predecessors by telephone during the day—former Presidents Hoover, Truman and Eisenhower. The latter was in the city yesterday and was briefed on the latest developments by John A. McCone, director of the Central Intelligence Agency.

After the address, the Chief Executive also announced he had named John J. McCloy, New York attorney and former banker, to be special adviser to Adlai E. Stevenson, United States representative to the United Nations, during the period the Cuban situation is before the General Assembly.

McCloy's most recent Federal post was as Mr. Kennedy's adviser on disarmament matters.

In his address, the President warned that if the present limited blockade was not effective in preventing more of a military build-up of nuclear weapons

(Continued, Page 8, Column 7)

DC-7C Ditches Off Alaska; All 102 Aboard Are Saved

Sitka, Alaska, Oct. 22 (UPI)—A swift, skillful rescue at sea saved 102 persons aboard a military-chartered passenger airliner that ditched today in the ocean off this southeast Alaska city.

The Northwest Airlines DC-7C with 95 passengers, including women and children, came down with propeller trouble this afternoon off the entrance to Sitka Sound.

Four persons were reportedly injured.

The ditching was so adept that the plane stayed afloat 22 minutes, while those aboard calmly got into 25-man life rafts.

Panic Is Doubted

"Apparently there was no panic," said Jim Jaqua of KSA-TV, who reached the scene before the plane sank.

"It looked to me like the pilot did a beautiful job. The top of the wings were just starting to be awash when I got there. The nose went down first and when the tail went over. It headed straight for the bottom just like a big whale going down."

A Coast Guard plane alighted at the scene within three minutes of the ditching. An Alaska Coast-Ellis plane circled overhead. But it was a Federal Aviation Agency supply boat from a nearby station that took the passengers from the rafts.

By the time the DC-7C went down, Jaqua said, everyone was aboard the FAA boat, the Fedair. Later the 102 persons were transferred to the Coast Guard cutter Sorrel.

Pilot Gives Alert

The pilot's radioed report of trouble gave time for planes and rescue boats to head for the scene, about 7 miles south of here.

Fairly calm water contributed to the rescue's success.

"Everybody got out and into the life rafts with no trouble at

(Continued, Page 5, Column 3)

Leaders Of Both Parties Support Decision On Cuba

British view word of Cuba build-up as a shock ....Page 8

By PETER J. KUMPA
[*Washington Bureau of The Sun*]

Washington, Oct. 22 — Congressional leaders of both parties, flown here today from the far corners of the country, expressed their full support tonight of President Kennedy's decision to block arms shipments to Cuba.

Within minutes after the President concluded his solemn television report to the nation, strong statements of support from Democrats and Republicans, political leaders and hopeful candidates and ordinary citizens were rolling into Washington.

During a full and frank 90-minute White House briefing for the leaders, one top Republican legislator, however, felt President Kennedy was not going "far enough" to meet the danger of the Communist build-up in Cuba.

He asked for "more specific and direct action" by the United States. The next step, presumably would be direct military intervention in Castro's Communist-dominated island.

Other Republicans at the meeting reportedly did not agree that more drastic action was now required. The lone GOP dissenter was left as a "minority of one" offering his tougher alternative.

A brief GOP statement by seven of the leaders participating in the White House discussions was issued tonight after their own party meeting on Capitol Hill.

"Americans will support the President on the decision or decisions he makes for the security of our country," it said.

Signed by four senators, Dirksen (Ill.), minority leader; Hickenlooper (Iowa), Saltonstall (Mass.), Wiley (Wis.), and three congressmen, Halleck (Ind.), minority leader; Arends (Ill.), and Chiperfield (Ill.), the statement said the GOP leaders "were

(Continued, Page 8, Column 6)

EXTRA THE SUNDAY SUN EXTRA

Vol. 62—No. 43—F | PAID CIRCULATION SIX MONTHS ENDING 3/31/62 MORNING, 186,226 EVENING, 215,740 401,966 ‖ SUNDAY 321,955 | BALTIMORE, SUNDAY, OCTOBER 28, 1962 | Published every Sunday by The A. S. Abell Co. Calvert & Centre Sts., Baltimore, Md. Second class postage paid at Baltimore, Md. | 4 Pages | Price 7 Cents

RUSSIA ORDERS MISSILES OUT OF CUBA; KENNEDY HAILS MOVE

INDIA EXPECTS ARMS PLUS SUPPLIES FROM FRIENDLY COUNTRIES

Nehru Tells Party Members Arrangements Are Already Made; Forces Seen 'Offering Better Resistance' To Chinese Reds

By PHILIP POTTER
[New Delhi Bureau of The Sun]

New Delhi, Oct. 27—Prime Minister Jawaharlal Nehru today assured the country arrangements already had been made with friendly countries for the supply of arms and equipment to India.

He gave this assurance to 50 Congress party members of Parliament as a Defense Ministry spokesman said Indian forces were now "offering better resistance" to Chinese invaders.

The spokesman indicated the enemy had seized control of Jang, a small village 5 miles east of fallen Towang in the North East Frontier Agency, as Indian forces withdrew to higher ground leading to the Sela Pass, but he added that Indian forces had beaten back two Chinese attacks at Walong Coa at the far eastern end of the Frontier Agency.

Still Resisting

He said Walong, on the Lohit River not far from the Burma border, is still in Indian hands, with fighting going on in the outskirts.

The Chinese there have thrust 15 miles south of the McMahon Line, which today was formally acknowledged by the United States as the "accepted international border."

Ambassador John Kenneth Galbraith, who worked all day with his staff at the embassy, possibly on supply as well as diplomatic problems, issued the statement on the disputed Sino-Indian boundary tonight to make sure that "there should be no ambiguity in our position."

The McMahon Line, it said, "is the accepted international border and is sanctioned by modern usage. Accordingly we regard it as the northern border of the North East Frontier Agency area."

Withdrawal Offer

Red China contends the McMahon Line is illegal, but it has now indicated that it would be prepared to withdraw to its version of where the line runs providing India recognizes Chinese seizures in Ladakh, 900 miles to the northwest. This indication came in a Peiping broadcast of a Peiping *Peoples Daily* editorial elaborating on a three-point Chinese peace proposal sent here last Wednesday by Premier Chou En Lai and replied to by Nehru today.

He said that India's terms for talks are Chinese withdrawal to lines they held as of last September 8.

The proposal suggested a meeting of the two prime ministers at a time appropriate to both, a cease-fire and a 20-kilometer (12 miles) withdrawal by troops of

(Continued, Page 2, Column 8)

Analysis

By MARK S. WATSON
[Sun Military Correspondent]

Washington, Oct. 27—The Indian Government's years-long delusion, even after the engulfment of Tibet, that Communist China would respond graciously to gentle protests against further aggression, now has been rewarded with actual invasion by assault forces.

More serious than the loss of territory, a blindly optimistic India has for years deliberately squandered time, which never can be recovered.

China has followed the established Communist pattern of conquest—first moving small forces over a border on the pretext that the map is wrong, and counting on the victim nation's regarding the offense as too small to go to war over; then moving forward at another place with like expectation; then pushing still harder, linking up the stolen sectors, setting up roads and storage points and strongpoints and meantime charging the victim with hostile actions.

Withdrawal Asked

The next Red step, in India as in Korea and elsewhere, has been to call for peace, accompanied by a withdrawal of both nations' troops 12 miles or so from a stated line—not the original line, but the new line.

By this, the Chinese forces would be permanently assured a large part of their stolen territory, and the abused Indians would be faced with an inability to defend an additional 12-mile strip, including strategically critical points.

If India's faith in its own peaceful aims and its confidence in a notorious aggressor's promises have been shattered and its own defensive strength weakened by its delay in putting up armed

(Continued, Page 2, Column 4)

Major Sports Results

COLLEGE FOOTBALL

13—Maryland . . S. Carolina—11
32—Navy . . . . . . Pittsburgh— 9
15—Hamp.-Sydney. Hopkins— 0
30—W. Maryland . . . Upsala— 0
21—Morgan N. Caro. A.&T.—14
23—Penn State . . California—21
14—Ohio State . . Wisconsin— 7
35—Northwest. Notre Dame— 6
28—U.S.C. . . . . Illinois—16
21—Duke . . . . N.C. State—14
42—Georgia Tech . . Tulane—12
14—Yale . . . . Colgate—14
35—Cornell . . . . . . Princeton—34
24—Dartmouth . . . Harvard— 6

RACING

Dr. Giddings wins $23,000 added Maryland Futurity at Laurel.

Beau Purple breaks Belmont course record in taking $114,800 Man O' War Stakes.

Main Swap takes $159,995 Gardenia at Garden State Park.

GOP LOSES ISSUE; RIVALS LOSE LEADER

President Ends Reproof Of Mildness And His Own Campaigning

By GERALD GRIFFIN
[Washington Bureau of The Sun]

Washington, Oct. 27—With the elections only ten days away, the Republicans have lost their chief campaign issue and the Democrats have lost their campaign leader.

The two parties are faced with different problems as they go into the final week of their schedule.

For the Democrats the danger is that many citizens, with public attention focused on Cuba and Russia rather than on the elections, will neglect to vote. The Democrats need a heavy vote, to take advantage of their registration majorities, and their task is to get out the vote without President Kennedy's active assistance.

GOP Still Needs Votes Against

For the Republicans the problem is, while they declare their support for the Democratic President on the Cuban issue, to persuade citizens to go out and vote against the domestic policies which the President represents.

These are what could be called the national phases of the national congressional elections.

But, as veteran congressmen and senators have long since learned, many election campaigns are decided on local personalities and local issues rather than national questions, and hence to a certain extent it is every man for himself.

Capehart Asks Toughness

For example, the veteran Senator Capehart (R., Ind.) is campaigning for reelection – and favored to win—on his own platform of urging a tougher policy toward Cuba than Mr. Kennedy's.

The veteran Senator Wiley (R., Wis.) is seeking another Senate term—and he, too, is favored to win—making the most of the fact that Mr. Kennedy summoned him to Washington for consultation on Cuba, along with other congressional leaders.

Senators and congressmen already in office have an edge over their opponents on the Cuban issue.

Van Zandt Scores Beat

Representative Van Zandt (R., Pa.), a candidate for the Senate, was able to come out of an official briefing and get on the press-service wires ahead of the Pentagon with the news that a Soviet tanker had been questioned and allowed to proceed.

Official Britain To Back Rejection Of Bases Deal

By LOUIS R. RUKEYSER
[London Bureau of The Sun]

London, *Sunday*, Oct. 28 — The British Government will support the American rejection of a "Cuba for Turkey" deal on bases, authoritative sources said early today.

Officials here regard the proposal by Soviet Premier Khrushchev as "irrelevant." Wider issues cannot be discussed until the Cuban missile build-up is halted, it was said.

A broader agreement was not ruled out for the future, however.

Public Opinion Lag

There were growing indications that the Government's resolute support of the United States—signaled Friday by Prime Minister Macmillan—was still ahead of the bulk of British public opinion.

British Sunday newspapers gave considerable support to a deal that would end the Caribbean crisis.

The Conservative *Sunday Times* described the Khrushchev proposal as "a hopeful offer" and said:

"As this deal is reasonable in itself and can be carried out without any weakening of the military defense of the West, there can be no good argument against accepting it."

"Already Obsolete"

The left leaning *Observer* agreed. Is it really insulting, it asked, to suggest that the United States should offer to give up one of her own missile bases, say in Turkey, which are already obsolete?

A notable exception to this trend of opinion was the pro-Government *Sunday Telegraph*, which warned against "standing a little apart from the Americans, whispering in their ear and tugging at their coat-tails.

Recalling the attempted appeasement of Adolf Hitler by Prime Minister Neville Chamberlain, the paper declared:

"Fear and confusion about Cuba have set walking the ghost of appeasement . . . The face of

(Continued, Page 2, Column 6)

BULLETIN

Text of Khrushchev's message to Kennedy . . . *Page 2*

Moscow, Sunday, Oct. 28 (AP)—Premier Khrushchev said today he has ordered Soviet rocket bases in Cuba dismantled and the rockets returned to the Soviet Union.

The Soviet Premier said the order had been issued "in the interests of peace."

The information was contained in a letter sent to President Kennedy and broadcast over Soviet radio and television.

Premier Khrushchev also proposed that negotiations should start between NATO and the Warsaw Pact powers.

"We are not threatening," the Premier said. "We only want peace."

President Kennedy welcomed Khrushchev's willingness to dismantle missile bases in Cuba and called it an important contribution to peace.

Mr. Kennedy, in a statement issued shortly after noon, described Khrushchev's decision as "statesmanlike" and said he hopes a solution of the Cuban crisis could lead to steps to end the world arms race.

"This is an important and constructive contribution to peace," Mr. Kennedy said.

He added that United States diplomats would get in touch with U Thant, Acting Secretary General of the United Nations, "with respect to reciprocal measures to assure peace in the Caribbean area."

In Washington, the Pentagon said it is keeping up its pace of activities and preparations in the Cuba crisis, hours after Khrushchev's order.

A Pentagon spokesman said that "there has been no order, at this time, for any relaxation of the activities that we had been carrying on."

The President did not say when the United States would be ready to work out an arrangement for solving the Cuban crisis in cooperation with the United Nations. But in a letter to Khrushchev last night he said negotiations could begin this weekend.

"It is my earnest hope that the governments of the world can, with a solution of the Cuban crisis, turn their urgent attention to the compelling necessity for ending the arms race and reducing world tensions," Mr. Kennedy said.

"This applies to the military confrontation between the Warsaw Pact and NATO countries, as well as to other situations in other parts of the world where tensions lead to the wasteful diversion of resources to weapons of war."

Following is the text of the statement by President Kennedy:

"I welcome Chairman Khrushchev's statesmanlike decision to stop building bases in Cuba, dismantling offensive weapons and returning them to the Soviet Union under United Nations verification.

"This is an important and constructive contribution to peace.

"We shall be in touch with the Secretary General of the United Nations with respect to reciprocal measures to assure peace in the Caribbean area.

"It is my earnest hope that the governments of the world can with a solution of the Cuban crisis turn the urgent attention to the compelling necessity for ending the arms race and reducing world tensions.

"This applies to the military confrontation between the Warsaw Pact and NATO countries as well as to other situations in other parts of the world where tensions lead to the wasteful diversion of resources to weapons of war."

In New York, U Thant was said today to be "ready for all eventualities" that might arise from Premier Khrushchev's offer to withdraw Soviet missiles from Cuba.

That is what the United States chief delegate, Adlai E. Stevenson, told reporters after an hour's conference with Thant, who has been holding separate talks on the Cuban crisis with the United States, the Soviet Union and Cuba.

Stevenson declined comment on Khrushchev's new letter. But, in response to a question, Stevenson said he had no evidence that work on the Soviet missile bases in Cuba had been halted.

Khrushchev, in his message, warned that the Soviet people "are not divesting ourselves of the responsibility of granting help to the Cuban people" and said violations of Cuban air space could have "dangerous consequences."

He indicated that Moscow was concerned about any harm befalling Soviet officers, instructors and technicians working in Cuba.

Khrushchev said he was calling off the Soviet military build-up in Cuba "to liquidate with greater speed the dangerous conflict, to serve the cause of peace . . . and to calm the American people."

The Soviet installations are no longer neces-

(Continued, Page 2, Column 6]

D.C. EXPECTED KHRUSHCHEV TURKISH BID

Success In Such Deal Seen As A Real Red Triumph

By GERALD GRIFFIN
[Washington Bureau of The Sun]

Washington, Oct. 27 — Premier Khrushchev's attempt to trade off Russian bases in Cuba for NATO bases in Turkey had been expected here for several days.

It was one of the obvious moves open to him. To obtain the removal of the long-established bases in Turkey in exchange for the not-yet-completed Soviet bases in Cuba would be a real diplomatic and military bargain for the Soviet Premier, it was pointed out.

Cuba is of little real importance to the Soviet Union, as Khrushchev's message to President Kennedy made clear today.

Record Of Admissions

He thus far has backed away from a clash at sea, has acknowledged that Russia has installed weapons in Cuba which the United States considers offensive, has announced that Soviet officers control the missiles and has proclaimed his ability to direct Castro.

The Soviet admissions, in any case, have abruptly changed the picture of Premier Fidel Castro and Cuba which the Soviet Union had drawn, a change which other Latin Americans were expected to notice.

The Castro regime, ostensibly looking to Moscow for help to maintain its independence, was shown to be so fully in the Soviet Union's grip that it could be traded off to serve Moscow's interests.

Propaganda Move Seen

In other words, Khrushchev showed himself ready to give up something of little importance to him to get something of great importance.

Some observers thought that Khrushchev was seeking primarily to gain a propaganda advantage in asserting his willingness to pull his missiles out of Cuba in return for an American withdrawal from Turkey.

The propaganda, it was noted, could be effective with countries and individuals already looking for an easy way out of the crisis built up by the Soviet Union's operations in Cuba.

Reasons Are Different

But the history of the bases is different, the reasons for the bases are different and the results of the suggested withdrawals would be different.

In 1947, less than two years after the end of World War II, it will be recalled, the Soviet Union

(Continued, Page 2, Column 6)

U.S. PUTS 24 RESERVE UNITS ON DUTY; PLANE IS 'LOST' OVER CUBA

14,214 Men In 20 States Involved; Maryland Not Included; President Insists Russia Must Inactivate Missiles

Key West, Fla., Oct. 27 (AP)—Military sources who conducted a search from about 1 P.M. until dark for the missing American surveillance plane, said tonight they also did not know if the aircraft had been shot down over Cuba.

"We kept hoping for some time the plane would come back or had landed at another field," one source said, indicating that no word had reached here from the plane before it disappeared.

U.S. Terms

By PETER J. KUMPA
[Washington Bureau of The Sun]

Washington, Oct. 27—President Kennedy told Premier Khrushchev tonight that the United States was prepared to seek a prompt and permanent solution to the Cuban crisis, provided Soviet missile bases there were quickly "rendered inoperable" under effective United Nations supervision.

Mr. Kennedy said that if—and it's a big if—the Russians pulled their medium and intermediate range rockets out of Cuba and kept them out under proper safeguards, the United States would be willing to lift its blockade and give assurances against an invasion of Cuba.

N. Y. Parleys Urged

The Chief Executive proposed quick talks in New York this weekend between the two world powers in cooperation with U Thant, acting United Nations Secretary General.

If Premier Khrushchev agrees, Mr. Kennedy said, an agreement can be reached in a couple of days.

The President's proposals came in a direct reply to two letters from Premier Khrushchev, one delivered last night and one this afternoon. The text of Mr. Kennedy's answer was made public by the White House this evening shortly after a copy was handed over here to the Soviet Embassy.

First Requirement

The President again ruled out any suggestion that withdrawal of NATO rocket installations in Turkey could be swapped for similar Soviet action at its offensive missile bases in Cuba.

He insisted that dismantling of Rusian missiles on Fidel Castro's island was the first requirement.

Mr. Kennedy warned the So-

(Continued, Page 2, Column 7)

Call-Up

By ALBERT SEHLSTEDT, JR.
[Washington Bureau of The Sun]

Washington, Oct. 27—Following Cuban firing on reconnaissance aircraft, the Defense Department said tonight it was calling to active duty 24 troop carrier squadrons of the Air Force Reserve.

The announcement was made by Robert S. McNamara, Secretary of Defense, following an earlier Pentagon report that a military aircraft on a surveillance mission over Cuba was "missing and presumed lost."

A Pentagon spokesman was asked if McNamara's move was a "prelude to invasion."

14,214 Are Involved

"I wouldn't go beyond what I have said," responded the spokesman, Arthur Sylvester, Assistant Secretary of Defense for public affairs.

The call-up affects 14,214 Air Force reservists in approximately 20 states. Maryland is not one of the states.

McNamara preceded his announcement of the call-up with the following statement:

"Today United States unarmed reconnaissance aircraft, conducting surveillance of the build-up of the offensive weapons secretly introduced into Cuba by the Soviet Union, were fired upon.

Under Resolution

"Such surveillance operations were in accordance with the resolution adopted on October 23, 1962, by the Organ of Consultation of the Inter-American System under the provisions of the Rio Treaty of 1947.

"To insure that the nations of the Western Hemisphere continue to be informed of the status of the threat to their security, it is essential that such reconnaissance flights continue.

"The possibility of further attack on our aircraft and the continued build-up of the offensive weapons systems in Cuba require that we be prepared for any eventuality.

"Therefore, tonight, acting under the authority granted me by Executive Order 11,058, dated October 23, 1962, I have instructed the Secretary of the Air Force to order to active duty 24 troop carrier squadrons of the Air Force Reserve with their associated units."

The executive order mentioned by McNamara referred to recent congressional action which empowered the President to call members of the ready reserve to active duty at any time up to February 28, 1963.

McNamara's announcement was made at 9.45 P.M.

Approximately three hours earlier the Defense Department issued the first report about the missing reconnaissance aircraft over Cuba.

No details of that incident have yet been made public.

Speculation On U-2

There was some speculation here that the missing aircraft was a U-2 high-altitude reconnaissance plane. The Defense Department had no comment to make about the type of aircraft involved.

At 10.15 tonight the Pentagon identified the pilot of the missing aircraft as Maj. Rudolf Anderson,

(Continued, Page 2, Column 5)

Castro Vows 'Defensive Fire' On Any U.S. Planes

Key West, Fla., Oct. 27 (AP)—Fidel Castro tonight bluntly countered a firm United States stand on aerial surveillance of Cuban missile bases with a promise of ready defensive fire.

Slightly more than an hour after Castro's statement was broadcast by Havana Radio, the United States Defense Department said one of its surveillance planes was missing and presumed lost.

"Defensive Fire"

In a broadcast statement, Castro said war planes violating Cuba's air space would do so "at the risk of confronting defensive fire."

Castro's statement followed a Defense Department warning that interference with surveillance, which will be continued, would be met with counter-action.

The United States warning came on the heels of a vague Cuban Government announcement that anti-aircraft batteries drove off unidentified war planes from western Cuba this morning.

The Cuban communique heard at Key West via Cuban radio did not say specifically that fire was opened on the so-called war planes.

Shortly after the broadcast, Arthur Sylvester, Assistant Secretary of Defense, announced the firm United States stand on surveillance and said he did not know about the Havana warplanes claim.

The Defense Department's information chief said, however, that so far as he knew no American had been injured in surveillance operations.

Text Of Statement

The text of Castro's statement follows:

"By declaration formulated today, the Government of the United States tried to claim officially the prerogative of invading our air space.

"Cuba will not accept the vandalistic, and piratical privilege of any war plane to violate its air space because it essentially affects its security and facilitates

(Continued, Page 2, Column 1)

WEATHER
Fair and cooler tonight, lows in 50's. Sunny and continued cool tomorrow.
Detailed report on A 2

THE EVENING SUN

7 STAR ★★★★★★★ 2:30 STOCKS

Vol. 107—No. 48 | PAID CIRCULATION SIX MONTHS ENDING 9/30/62 MORNING 188,156 | EVENING 212,245 | 400,401 || SUNDAY 321,686 | BALTIMORE, WEDNESDAY, JUNE 12, 1963 | Published daily except Sunday by The A. S. Abell Co. Calvert & Centre Sts., Baltimore, Md. Second class postage paid at Baltimore, Md. | 84 Pages | 7 Cents

3 Shot, 3 Places Fire-Bombed In Cambridge Racial Violence

Cabinet Backs Macmillan In Profumo Case

London, June 12 (AP)—Prime Minister Macmillan held an emergency Cabinet meeting today and reportedly persuaded his shaken ministers to back his handling of the Profumo vice scandal.

None of the ministers would speak publicly about the dramatic Cabinet meeting and, in fact, none of them looked very happy about it.

But the usually well-informed British Press Association said it was evident that the meeting "was a harmonious one and that there may well be a unanimity of view."

Three Facts Leaked

These facts leaked out:

The Cabinet received the report of an inquiry into whether resigned War Minister John Profumo violated security in his relations with model Christine Keeler who was having an affair at the same time with Soviet navy captain, Yevgeni (Eugene) Ivanov.

Decisions were reached on tactics to restore Conservative party confidence, at its lowest ebb since the Suez crisis which brought down Sir Anthony Eden (Lord Avon), then Prime Minister.

. Strategy was planned for Monday's parliamentary session when the Labor opposition is certain to attack the Government on its handling of the entire scandal.

Cleared By Lord Chancellor

Official sources said the Lord Chancellor, Lord Dilhorne, after a two-week inquiry, cleared former War Minister John Profumo of suspicion that he leaked security secrets while he was seeing model Christine Keller at the same time she was having an affair with a Soviet naval attache in 1961.

Dilhorne's report is expected to bolster Macmillan's position in a House of Commons debate Monday on the scandal.

Political observers said it would be the most gruelling and momentous debate since the Suez crisis of 1956 that drove Sir Anthony Eden from office.

More Unsavory Cases?

The Conservative Daily Mail joined in the clamor for a fuller investigation, reporting new rumors that more unsavory disclosures would come into the open soon.

Profumo and his wife, former actress Valerie Hobson, remained in hiding. His brother, Philip, an army major, appealed to him last night to come forth with a personal statement to the nation.

While the Cabinet was meeting, Dr. Stephen Ward, Miss Keeler's mentor who introduced her to Profumo, was refused bail for the second time in as many days.

The osteopath was ordered held in Brixton Prison to await trial on charges of living off the earnings of prostitution. The police, in objecting to bail, said they may make other charges against Ward.

Russia Staying Out

Sydney, Australia, June 12 (Reuters)—The United States will exhibit at the trade fair here July 26 to August 10, but Russia, which exhibited last year, will not participate.

PREMIER CARAMANLIS
Resigns in bitter dispute

King Of Greece Conferring On Crisis Plans

Athens, June 12 (AP)—King Paul opened a round of consultations today designed to bring Greece out of its first real government crisis in seven years.

The Monarch conferred with Constantine Rodopoulos, president of Parliament, and then invited two leading opponents of Constantine Caramanlis to a palace conference.

Caramanlis resigned as premier last night, protesting the refusal of the royal family to postpone a state visit to London next month.

Conferring On Next Step

King Paul's talks with political leaders were preliminary to his decision on his next step: Whether to ask someone to form a new government, or dissolve Parliament and call for new elections.

Official sources said the Monarch preferred the formation of a new government, but wanted to consult political leaders before making a final move.

Caramanlis, who has been premier since 1956, said after resigning that the only solution to the crisis was the calling of new elections. He was hoping for a chance to submit his policies to the electorate. He won a resounding election victory in 1961.

A new government could only come from Caramanlis's National Radical Union party, which has a 60-seat majority in Parliament. But the party's high command, at a meeting yesterday, advocated new elections.

Streets Patrolled In Swazi Strike

Mbabane, Swaziland, June 12 (Reuters)—Armed police and civilians carrying tear gas grenades and clubs patrolled the capital of this British protectorate today as a general strike entered its third day.

The African Nationalist Ngwane National Liberatory Congress, sponsoring the strike domands the release of twelve strikers arrested Saturday, a minimum wage of $2.80 a day for Swazi workers, and rejection of the new constitution.

Mercury Orbit Program Ends

Spending billions on race to moon "is nuts," Eisenhower says. [Page A 2.]

Washington, June 12 (AP)—Space chief James E. Webb announced today that there will be no additional Project Mercury orbital flights.

Instead, Webb said, the National Aeronautics and Space Administration will move ahead with the program for the two-man Gemini spacecraft, which will practice the space-docking maneuvers that will be required later for Apollo flights to the moon.

Webb told the Senate Space Committee that the decision against another Mercury flight was reached this morning at a conference with associate director Robert Seamans, Jr., and deputy administrator Hugh Dryden.

Project Mercury directors and the seven original Mercury astronauts had urged that one more Mercury flight be attempted, this one of about 100 hours.

1965 Expectation

But Webb said plans and preparations for another Mercury flight would slow up development of the Gemini program, the first flight in which is now expected early in 1965.

"We cannot conduct a flight in the Mercury program with a second team, or plan for a flight operating up to two weeks and make the changes in the work on the ground, without delaying the Gemini program," he said.

"It will require the first team in the manned spaceflight program to do the work we must do in the Gemini project."

The 22-orbit flight of Air Force Maj. L. Gordon Cooper, Jr., last month completed the scheduled series of planned Mercury flights. But the astronauts and others immediately started urging still another one-man orbital flight.

More Data Sought

They argued that such a flight would provide enough useful new information on man's ability to perform usefully for a long period in a weightless condition to justify the additional cost.

They also argued that such a flight would help fill in the gap before the first Gemini flight, keeping public interest alive and maintaining the technical staff intact.

But Webb announced the decision to end the Mercury program and concentrate on Gemini.

Ship Hits Iceberg And Calls For Aid

New York, June 12 (AP)—The Coast Guard reported today that a French fishing trawler, the 250-foot Alex Pleven, has struck an iceberg about 40 miles off the northwest coast of Iceland and needs immediate assistance.

Three ships were bound for the distress area: Latitude 67.00 North, Longitude 21.40 West.

The Coast Guard said it had not learned how many persons were aboard the Alex Pleven, which operates out of St. Malo, France.

NEGROES pray in county court yard at Cambridge, Md., before skirmishes that erupted between Negroes and whites.

Negroes Attend Ala. Classes

Wirephoto on Page A 2.

Tuscaloosa, Ala., June 12 (AP)—Two Negroes—a girl and boy—went to their first classes at the University of Alabama today and white students extended friendly hands in an atmosphere of tranquillity.

Three girls walked with Vivian J. Malone as she went from her dormitory to a classroom building. They chatted as they strolled.

And a white youth addressed James A. Hood as Jimmy in advising him that he had taken the wrong turn along the tree-lined campus at one point.

Across from Comer Hall, where Miss Malone went to study business administration, a National Guardsman in green fatigue uniform stood. Nearby were three Federal marshals.

"I Have Been Accepted"

"I feel that I have been accepted here, the same as any other student," Hood said when he left class.

"I think the University of Alabama should be a model to the nation. I think the faculty, the students and the people of Tuscaloosa are to be commended.

"I am grateful and gratified. This is basically the way I feel. All of the universities should take note of this situation here."

A co-ed fainted during the first class attended by Hood but university officials said similar instances had happened previously and that the incident was not related to his presence.

Prof. Harold Nelson, teacher of the sociology class, said the woman suffered a muscle spasm causing pain and fainted. The study session was cut short. Her name was not made public.

Few Curious Glances

Miss Malone sat through her class taking notes while her classmates cast a few curious glances in her direction. The subject was "government."

She left, walking with a co-ed.

Meanwhile, Wallace wire President Kennedy that he is withdrawing most State law enforcement officers from the campus today and the rest Sunday.

In a telegram to the President, Wallace said:

"At all times since the Federal District Court ordered the admission of Negro students to the University of Alabama, State law enforcement officers under my control have maintained absolute peace and order at the university campus.

"At 3.33 P.M. (C.S.T.), June 11, 1963, through the use of Federal troops you assumed full responsibility for the presence of Negro students and for preserving peace and order on the campus of the University of Alabama.

"Phased Withdrawal"

"In order that there might be complete coordination as you assume this responsibility I am furnishing you and your local military commander with the following schedule of phased withdrawal of State law enforcement personnel.

"June 12 effective 3 A.M. 300

[Continued, Page A 2, Column 7]

Negro Leader In Integration Drives Slain In Mississippi

Another Wirephoto on Page A 3

Jackson, Miss., June 12 (AP)—Medgar W. Evers, one of the Negro leaders in the massive civil-disobedience campaign against racial discrimination in Jackson, was mortally wounded in the driveway of his home early today.

Police launched a widespread search for his assassin.

The Highway Patrol broadcast a State-wide alert calling for a check on any "suspicious cars" leaving the State. Patrolmen were ordered to take names, addresses and destinations.

Chief of Detectives M. B. Pierce said today that police have found the murder rifle in bushes near the scene of the killing.

The 37-year-old Evers, Mississippi field secretary of the National Association for the Advancement of Colored People, died at University Medical Center about 50 minutes after he was shot.

In a recent interview, Evers said:

"I do not believe in violence either by whites or Negroes. That is why I am working tirelessly with the N.A.A.C.P. in a peaceful legal struggle for justice," he said.

"I'm a native of Mississippi. I don't ever intend to live elsewhere, but I'm determined we can gain some equality and be accepted as human beings with dignity."

MEDGAR EVERS
Killed after leaving rally

Wilkins On Air

Chief of Detectives M. B. Pierce called the shooting "most unfortunate." He asked the FBI to assist in the investigation.

In New York, Roy T. Wilkins, executive secretary of the N.A.A.C.P., said Evers's death "demonstrates anew the blind and murderous hatred which obsesses too many Mississippians.

"In their ignorance they believe that by killing a brave, dedicated and resourceful leader of the civil-rights struggle they can kill the movement for human rights," Wilkins said.

In Jackson, Gloster B. Current, appearing on the "Today" show on television today, said he hoped the slaying would not provoke violence among Negroes.

But, he said, "my guess is the people will be angry and resentful and will have a tendency to strike back. I hope not."

He also said that no one should delude himself into thinking Negroes will forever take the kind of treatment they have been getting, and adding: "Evers went overseas to fight for his country and what did he get for it—a bullet in the back."

$10,000 Reward Posted

The N.A.A.C.P. leader said his organization was posting a $10,000 reward for Evers's murderer.

Negro director of branches for the N.A.A.C.P., challenged city officials "to match our reward offer."

"The cowardly ambush murder

[Continued, Page A 3, Column 5]

President 'Appalled By Barbarity' Of Slaying Of Negro Leader

Washington, June 12 (AP)—President Kennedy "was appalled by the barbarity" of the slaying of Medgar W. Evers, Mississippi Negro leader, the White House said today.

The Justice Department had told Kennedy "that its full investigatory machinery has been placed at the disposal" of police officials at Jackson, Miss., "in an effort to uncover the assassin," a White House statement said.

FBI Put At Disposal

The first word to the White House about the shooting came at 3 A.M., Andrew T. Hatcher, assistant press secretary, reported. Hatcher said the call came to a White House staff member from an acquaintance in Jackson.

Kennedy was notified of the shooting at 7 A.M.

Hatcher said the Justice Department had learned of the killing earlier, and, even before the President was notified, placed the facilities of the Federal Bureau of Investigation at the disposal of Jackson police.

He said Kennedy is keeping in touch with the Jackson situation through reports from his brother, Attorney General Kennedy, and through reports relayed from Jackson.

It was understood that several Justice Department attorneys have been in the Mississippi city for several weeks, acting as observers of the racial tension there.

White House Text

Here is the text of the White House statement on the Evers killing:

"The President was appalled by the barbarity of this act. He has been assured by the Justice Department that its full investigatory machinery has been placed at the disposal of the Jackson police in an effort to uncover the assassin."

Attorney General Kennedy in an earlier statement said he was "saddened and shocked."

"We have asked the FBI to offer

[Continued, Page A 3, Column 4]

Wallace May Escape Jail Term For 2d Time In Defiant Career

Tuscaloosa, Ala., June 12 (AP)—For the second time in his turbulent career, Gov. George Wallace may escape a jail term in his running battle with the Federal Government.

Whether his stand in the doorway yesterday at the now-integrated University of Alabama will bring a contempt of court citation remained to be seen.

State Sovereignty

But there were indications that the Justice Department will make no effort to prosecute Wallace for his conduct in the face of a non-interference injunction. He had been told by a Federal Judge to refrain from barring two Negro students from the university.

The Governor, once again invoking the sovereign power of the State against what he called the onrushing march of an omnipotent central Government, refused to budge from the path where the two Negroes later walked into the university.

But despite his defiant gesture, Wallace did not come face to face with the Negroes himself.

He addressed his remarks to three Federal officers headed by Deputy Attorney General Nicholas Katzenbach while the waiting students sat in automobiles nearby.

When Katzenbach returned five hours later with Federalized National Guard troops, the Governor again voiced a protest, then walked away. The two Negroes, Vivian Malone and James A. Hood, entered the doorway where Wallace had stood and quietly registered for classes.

Consequently, said Justice Department spokesmen, the Governor did not actually turn back the Negro students because at that time they did not try to enter the building.

When Miss Malone and Hood finally did walk through the doorway, with troops escorting them, they were admitted. Wallace had left the campus.

One Attempt

Said Edwin O. Gutman, the Justice Department's chief information officer: "We consider that only one attempt at registration was made." And, he added, that was successful.

Technically, the injunction is-

[Continued, Page A 2, Column 4]

Red Nations Take Public Polls, Too; Sometimes Don't Like Findings

Washington, June 12 (AP)—Taking a leaf from the American book, Communist nations have started conducting their own public opinion polls. And sometimes they don't like what they find out, the United States Information Agency reports.

Communist pollsters have sampled public opinion in Poland, Yugoslavia and the Soviet Union, the USIA said in a report on its own research activities submitted to a House Appropriations subcommittee and made public today.

Marxist Doubts

Poll reports published in Communist newspapers usually are not complete enough to permit accurate judgments about the findings, the agency said, but do "tell us something about what people are thinking behind the Iron Curtain, where USIA has an important audience."

The agency cited a report on 1961 poll of Yugoslav students conducted by the Zagreb Union o Communists, which indicated that "a large percentage of students had serious doubts about the validity of Marxist ideology."

"The poll reports also said that despite long indoctrination efforts, Yugoslav young people still are oriented largely toward private and personal pursuits in life," the USIA said.

Views Of Communism

The agency commented that recent studies of its own show "people in developing areas do not express deep concern for democracy and such abstractions as free speech and personal independence.

"Avoiding communism usually is considered of little importance in underdeveloped areas," the USIA report said.

Such peoples are far more concerned with improved living conditions and better education, the USIA said its surveys showed.

The agency also told of these findings:

Opinions of Castro-style communism among rural workers in Latin America "ranged downward from cool neutrality to strong rejection." Such workers favored land reform instituted by their governments, a seven-nation study showed.

Student surveys in the Near and Far East, Africa and Latin America indicated that "a majority professed to dislike communism as a system, but in each country they always ranked socialism highest."

Four Hurt; 100 State Police On Alert

Negro demonstrators announced today they will stage another protest march to the Cambridge jail tonight to renew their integration demands. The demonstration is planned between 8 P.M. and 9 P.M. At the same time, assistant police chief James Leonard charged that the Negro demonstrators were responsible for last night's rioting.

By Jerome Kelly
[Staff Correspondent]

Cambridge, Md., June 12—Three men were shot, at least four other persons were injured by flying bricks and three business places were fire-bombed last night as racial violence erupted in this tense Eastern Shore community.

Today, as more than 100 State troops stood by outside the city, ready to intervene against any new violence, the Baltimore Congress of Racial Equality announced it would send teams of demonstrators to Cambridge over the weekend to reinforce the efforts of local Negroes.

Police patrolled the streets for the first few early-morning hours after the riot. Later in the day, the town went about its business under an uneasy quiet.

Meanwhile, members of both the State interracial commission and the Civic Interest Assistance Committee, an integrationist group, called upon Governor Tawes to intervene in the racial crisis. There was no immediate response from Mr. Tawes.

Mrs. Gloria Richardson, of the Cambridge Non-Violent Action Committee, sent a telegram to Attorney General Robert F. Kennedy today asking him to send Federal troops to Cambridge.

"The prevailing climate is such that a state of riot could occur at any second without warning," the telegram said. It charged also that State Police "have proven as intolerable and prejudiced as local police."

Last night's violence erupted following demonstrations earlier in the evening by Negroes at the courthouse and jail. They were protesting arrests and sentencing some of their number for earlier protest marches.

Negroes have been demonstrating for weeks to seek more rapid integration of school classes, desegregation of the town's twenty or so restaurants and for better employment opportunities.

Crowd Of Whites

When the crowd of nearly 100 Negroes finished the praying and singing at the jail, another crowd of about the same number of whites followed them back to the Negro section of town.

City police tried to keep the two groups apart and shepherd the Negroes toward their homes, but the whites swarmed across the street toward the Negroes just as they reached the Negro section.

Bricks began to fly between the two groups.

Two Identified

Integrationists said the fight began when two white college students who had joined the Negro protest marches were knocked down and kicked by hostile whites.

The two youths, who were not hurt, were identified as Mark Suckle, 20, of Philadelphia, a

[Continued, Page A 3, Column 1]

On Inside Pages

The Evening Sun today is printed in four sections.

The Weather
Mostly sunny today, with the high near 72. Cool tonight and warmer tomorrow. Yesterday's high, 75; low, 62.
(Details and Map, Page 43.)

THE SUN FINAL

[Registered United States Patent Office]

Vol. 253—No. 24—F PAID CIRCULATION SIX MONTHS ENDED 9/30/62 MORNING 188,156 EVENING 212,245 400,401 || SUNDAY 321,686 BALTIMORE, THURSDAY, JUNE 13, 1963 Published daily except Sunday by The A. S. Abell Co. Calvert & Centre Sts., Baltimore, Md. Second class postage paid at Baltimore, Md. 54 Pages 7 Cents

Kennedy, Eisenhower Discuss Racial Problems; Southern Senators Map Fight On Rights Program; 5-Point Plan Gets Backing Of Nation's Mayors

MACMILLAN HANDLING OF CRISIS O.K.'D

Approval Is Given In Emergency Meeting Of Full Cabinet

London, June 12 (AP)—Four of Britain's Cabinet ministers tonight were reported considering resignation as a moral protest against the John Profumo scandal and Prime Minister Macmillan's handling of it.

By DAVID M. CULHANE
[*London Bureau of The Sun*]

London, June 12—Prime Minister Macmillan won approval of his handling of the Profumo affair from his full Cabinet at an emergency meeting today.

A few ministers privately were reported to be less than completely satisfied. However, they made no overt moves during the day to make public their discontent.

But actions and atmosphere in political, press and church circles made it clear that the national crisis triggered by the resignation of the Secretary for War still continues to threaten the Macmillan Government.

There is strong speculation that Prime Minister Macmillan will order a formal investigation by a three-judge tribunal in a bid to satisfy the House of Commons during the formal debate of the Profumo affair Monday.

Resigned Week Ago

John D. Profumo, 48, resigned one week ago because of a previously denied improper relationship with a 21-year-old girl allegedly involved in a simultaneous liaison with a Soviet diplomat.

A successful outcome to the two-hour Cabinet meeting today was essential to the Prime Minister's counterattack against his critics, but the negative terms in which it was presented were ominous in themselves.

Qualified sources said that the Prime Minister has no intention of resigning, that no other minister had resigned and that there were no indications of such action in the Cabinet.

Still in a somewhat negative vein, informants said that the Prime Minister and the Government are now confident that the doubts, queries, and misgivings raised by the affair can be answered Monday to the satisfaction of the House of Commons.

Security Risk Stressed

A so far unpublished report from Baron Dilhorne, the Lord Chancellor, is believed to show that there was no actual breach of security involved in the case.

The Labor party is now stressing the security risk that existed and arguing that Macmillan should have known and done something about it.

Several other indicators of the level of tension over the affair were made known today:

1. The Conservative party has issued a three-line whip, that is,

(Continued, Page 2, Column 2)

10 Cubans Bring 3 Prisoners To Florida In Boat

Marathon, Fla., June 12 (AP)—Ten Cubans, one wounded; brought a commandeered boat and three prisoners into port today after what they said was a battle with a Fidel Castro gunboat.

The apparent leader was identified by the State Department as Manuel Quiza Docal. It was Quiza who led his tiny anti-Castro action force in an October, 1962, foray that netted them two Castro militiamen.

The wounded Cuban was hospitalized with a bullet in his back.

Before United States authorities clamped on a security lid, his comrades told local officers the gunboat suffered casualties in a blazing action yesterday but sank both their light craft off Çayo Blanco.

The men were questioned and their commandeered 36-foot auxiliary sailboat was impounded at Marathon, in the Florida Keys south of Miami.

RUSSIA PRINTS KENNEDY VIEW

Paper Carries Text On Disarmament, Peace, A-Tests

By ERNEST B. FURGURSON
[*Moscow Bureau of The Sun*]

Moscow, June 12 — The Soviet Government newspaper *Izvestia* tonight made the rare gesture of printing the text of President Kennedy's American University speech on peace, disarmament and nuclear testing.

Some observers saw it as a move to create an impression of Soviet reasonableness and objectivity before the atomic test ban talks scheduled to begin here next month.

The text covered four full columns in the four-page edition of the Kremlin paper, and included several Kennedy remarks on Soviet propaganda, dogma, information policy and lack of freedom which are directly opposed to what Russians normally read in *Izvestia*.

New Disclosure

Mr. Kennedy's report on the progressing negotiations on a direct emergency line for top-level use between Moscow and Washington was among the disclosures new to Soviet citizens.

Izvestia made no editorial comment on the speech, which was delivered Monday. But subsequent criticism of some of the President's statements is almost certain.

It was noted here that by giving valuable newspaper space to the American President, as well as by agreeing with him on the test-ban talks set for mid-July, the Kremlin was taking still another step likely to alienate the Chinese Communists.

The announcement that Premier

(Continued, Page 8, Column 1)

6 In Crowd Shot By Jagan Guards

Georgetown, British Guiana, June 12 (AP)—With bodyguards firing pistols from both sides of the car, Marxist Prime Minister Cheddi Jagan's automobile burst through a hostile crowd outside the Parliament building today. Six persons were reported shot.

The incident occurred after Trades Union Council squatters, increasingly menacing in their 8-weeks-old general strike, had trapped Jagan, United States-trained dentist of East Indian origin, and the rest of his Cabinet in the building.

The strike was called to protest against a labor bill which Jagan's foes say would give the Prime Minister control over workers in a move toward a Castro-like dictatorship.

BETANCOURT TELLS OF PLOT ON HIS LIFE

He Orders Arrest Of All Communists In Venezuela

Caracas, Venezuela, June 12 (AP). President Romulo Betancourt announced in a broadcast tonight that terrorists plotted to assassinate him with a time bomb in an archbishop's palace and that he has ordered the arrest of all Communists in Venezuela.

The incident occurred in Ciudad Bolivar, a river port 275 miles southeast of Caracas, shortly before Betancourt was scheduled to arrive for the inaugural of the new palace.

Police guards captured two of the terrorists, but a third got away, the announcement said, and a high-powered bomb was taken from the captives.

An Extensive Tour

Betancourt, who has escaped several previous attempts on his life, is currently on an extensive tour of the interior of Venezuela inaugurating public works projects.

Leftist enemies of his regime have been conducting almost daily terrorist attacks in various parts of the country.

A special committee of the Organization of American States stated in a report June 5 that "there is no doubt" Cuba's Prime Minister Fidel Castro, has selected Venezuela as a prime target for a Communist takeover.

Underscored By Attack

That warning was quickly underscored by an attack on a United States installation in Caracas by pro-Communist terrorists a few hours later. Screaming "Yankee imperialists," eight gunmen burned the headquarters of a United States military mission after forcing twelve mission employees, including six United States Army officers and enlisted men, to strip off their clothing

The OAS committee's report cited a speech by the Cuban Communist spokesman, Blas Roca, in January as indicative of the Castro regime's position toward Venezuela. The report quoted Roca as saying:

"When the people of Venezuela . . . gain full independence from imperialism . . . then all America will be inflamed, all America will advance, all America will be freed once and for all from the ominous yoke of imperialism."

Reported Planting Bomb

Authorities said the terrorists were captured at the rear of the archbishop's palace while planting a dynamite bomb.

The two captured men were identified by police as Vicente Barrios and Jose Santana Rivas. The man who escaped was identified as Roger Antonio Figueroa.

Betancourt denounced the terrorists in a speech broadcast from the palace.

U.S. Acts To Avert Flooding Of Ancient Temples In Egypt

By PAUL W. WARD
[*Washington Bureau of The Sun*]

Washington, June 12—President Kennedy committed the United States today to help keep a Soviet-financed power and irrigation project in Egypt from destroying two sun-god temples built 3,200 years ago by a Pharaoh known as "the Oppressor of the Hebrews."

The Chief Executive's decision, announced by the State Department, involved a commitment of up to $16,000,000 or four times the sum approved by Congress in September, 1961, when the project was first broached.

It also presented a number of ironic facets, including these:

1. The United States will be paying for one of the after-effects of Egypt's $1,300,000,000 Aswan Dam Project, which Washington once offered and then refused to finance and for which Moscow has since been getting the credit as successor-financier.

2. Some 40 other United Nations members are slated to help pay for the save-the-temples undertaking, including several that are also engaged in raising an African "liberation" fund, but refuse to pay their assessed shares of the world organization's peace-keeping operations in the Congo and along the border between Egypt and Israel.

The temples in question are at Abu Simbel on the Nile in Egyptian Nubian about 180 miles south of the Aswan Dam site and 25 miles from the Sudan's Egyptian border. Unearthed little more than 150 years ago, they were built by order of Rameses II (circa 1,250 B.C.), whose successor was "the Pharaoh of the (Hebrew) exodus."

Carved out of a sandstone cliff

(Continued, Page 8, Column 4)

Civil Rights Leading Problem For Kennedy

It May Be 'The' Issue Of President's First Term Due To Commitment For Immediate Program

By GERALD GRIFFIN
[*Washington Bureau of The Sun*]

Washington, June 12—In its full scope, as discussed by President Kennedy last night, the civil rights issue is by far the most important domestic issue the President has tackled.

Present indications are that it will be "the" issue of the President's first term. If he succeeds in handling it, in leading the country toward real progress out of this long-smouldering problem, he will be on his way not only to a second term but to a place in history.

His failure, on the other hand, could mean a disastrous outbreak of bitter feeling, racial violence and mob action with consequences only to be guessed at.

Mr. Kennedy, who chooses his language carefully, used such words as "moral issue," "moral crisis," "great change" and "revolution" to bring the matter before the American people.

"Now the time has come for this nation to fulfill its promises," he said in his talk last night.

The impression here today is that the President now is committed fully to work for a broader and more immediate, answer to the Negroes' demands for equal rights and opportunities than he had contemplated only a few weeks ago.

He has taken the active leadership of an Administration effort to meet the problem without violence and within the framework of voluntary community cooperation and essential new Federal laws.

In political terms, his task is to give national direction to the great body of moderate opinion, both North and South, both white and Negro, which looks for progress. At the same time his task is to hold down the excesses of the extremists among Negro and white citizens.

One of the most encouraging developments for the Kennedy Administration last night was a telegram sent to the President by the Rev. Martin Luther King, Jr., one

(Continued, Page 7, Column 1)

MERCURY SHOTS ARE TERMINATED

Resignation Of NASA Aide Also Announced

By MARK S. WATSON
[*Sun Military Correspondent*]

Washington, June 12—Today's announcement by the National Aeronautic and Space Administration that the series of Mercury satellite shots is terminated herewith was followed abruptly with the announcement that Brainerd Holmes, the NASA deputy administrator largely responsible for Mercury, is quitting.

Whether the first decision is wholly responsible for the second is not stated officially. But it has long been known that Holmes, as director of NASA's office of Manned Space Flight, has been in disagreement with James E. Webb, the top NASA administrator.

The Mercury program itself was a prime point of difference, it being understood that Holmes strongly desired to continue it with at least one more flight, lasting longer than any orbiting flight to date, on the reasoning that this would add significantly to the nation's knowl[illegible]ge of s[illegible]e and hence appreciably advance the later space programs.

Higher Sums Urg[illegible]

It also has [illegible] reported that t[illegible] deputy [illegible] larger space expenditu[illegible] Webb was willing to recommend to Congress—and larger, incidentally, than Congress is likely to authorize when the NASA allotment is finally determined.

The official statement observes that NASA's manned flight program is being "realigned . . . so as to permit (Holmes) to return to industry within the period of two years which was understood to constitute his obligation for Government service."

Holmes added nothing to this. He has long been conspicuous in space matters, with a large prior responsibility to the Air Force for setting up B-Mews (ballistics missile early warning service), the costly Arctic installation whose immense radar system is expected to detect the approach of missiles coming across the Arctic area toward the United States.

Gemini Is Next

Whether his exact duties will be taken over by someone else in the "realignment" is not clear. Dr. Robert Seamans, associate administrator of NASA, apparently will devote much of his time to the Gemini and Apollo programs (sequels to Mercury).

The Webb decision, which so far has stirred no objections from military scientists at the Penta-

(Continued, Page 9, Column 1)

HOUSE DEFEATS JOB LEGISLATION

Kennedy Loses Bid To Enlarge Redevelopment Plan

By PETER J. KUMPA
[*Washington Bureau of The Sun*]

Washington, June 12—The House tonight rejected an Administration proposal to enlarge the area redevelopment program designed to help communities plagued by chronic unemployment, thus dealing President Kennedy an important legislative defeat.

It was the President's first loss in the Congress, a startling one for House leaders had predicted victory by a small margin and were coasting along, turning back repeated Republican moves to cut back or tighten up the New Frontier legislation.

The roof fell in on the final roll-call. By a tense vote of 209 to 204 that saw votes switched at the last minute and urgent whispered pleas for more changes, the Administration bill was defeated.

Coalition Credited

Credit for the defeat went to a GOP-Southern Democratic, coalition. A combination of 152 Republicans and 57 Democrats, virtually all Southerners, opposed the bill that would have added $455,500,000 in Federal aid to distressed areas over the next two years.

There were 189 Democrats and 15 Republicans favoring the Administration's recommendations. The number of Republican supporters fell short of expectations. At least twenty GOP members were expected to back the Federal aid program which would have been enough to pass it.

Maryland's two Republicans split on the vote. Representative Morton voted for it. Representative Mathias skipped the first two calls and then at the last minute voted against the bill.

Democrats Back Bill

The State's six Democrats—Fallon, Friedel, Garmatz, Lankford, Long and Sickles—all supported President Kennedy's bill.

One Democrat attributed the defeat to the accumulation of small mistakes in the program's administration which had irritated congressmen. Representative Patman (D., Texas), Banking Committee chairman and floor manager for the bill, conceded the program had not worked perfectly and did not defend some specific criticisms.

Another possibility for the defeat might have been resentment by some Southern Democrats of President Kennedy's strong civil rights stand.

There was a last-minute amendment offered by Representative Waggoner (D., La.) that would

(Continued, Page 5, Column 2)

CONFERENCE O.K.'S RIGHTS RESOLUTION

Controversy Had Been Expected At Group's Final Session

Honolulu, June 12 (AP)—The nation's mayors without objection today approved President Kennedy's five-point program aimed at reducing racial tension in cities.

An equal opportunities resolution, expected to set off controversy, went through at the final business session of the United States Conference of Mayors. Twenty seven other proposals ranging from urban renewal to more Federal aid for municipal projects also passed.

3 Others Rejected

Three others, on recommendation of the Resolutions Committee, were rejected.

Several Southern mayors, notably Haydon Burns, of Jacksonville, Fla., opposed the civil rights plan but no one denounced it directly.

Burns said that late introduction of civil rights and four other resolutions represented a "departure from precedent." These programs were submitted to the conference after it had convened.

An effort was made to block voting on all poposals at one time. However, Mayor Richard C. Lee, of New Haven, the conference president, overrode objections and forced a voice vote.

Vote Carries, 70 To 45

He ruled adoption of the resolutions, but bowed to a request for a "division of the house" revote made by Mayor Herbert A. Smith, of Maison Heights, Mich. The standing vote carried 70-45.

The civil rights program was drawn up after the President addressed the gathering of nearly 1,000 mayors Sunday. The resolution contains the five points outlined by Mr. Kennedy plus a provision that "all citizens be encouraged to recognize the correlation of responsibility and duty with right and that equality of responsibility be encouraged along with equality of opportunity."

The sixth point was added on recommendation of Mayor Herman W. Goldner, of St. Petersburg, Fla., who criticized the President's speech as overemphasizing rights and not considering duty, Goldner was a member of the Resolutions Committee.

Some Not Happy

Some Southern mayors were not happy with the civil rights program. It calls for biracial committees, nondiscriminatory hiring, ordinances for equality in housing, employment, recreation and public accommodations, alteration of city laws that do not conform to the Constitution and efforts to halt school drop-outs. However, conference officials said any objection from the floor could be classified as "just for the record."

Southern mayors objected vigorously to a resolution opposing

(Continued, Page 6, Column 1)

PARLEY OF PRESIDENT, PREDECESSOR LASTS MORE THAN AN HOUR

Dixie Bloc To Use Filibuster And Other Means Against Chief Executive's Integration Plan, Sees 'Step' Toward Communism

Washington, June 12 (AP)—The slaying of a Negro leader in Jackson, Miss., was cited at a Senate Judiciary subcommittee hearing today as an additional reason for extending the Civil Rights Commission and passing other civil rights measures.

Paul Cooke, national chairman of the American Veterans Committee, said it had become almost mandatory for Congress to continue the commission in the light of last night's killing of Medgar W. Evers and other evidence of racial strife.

Senators

By JOSEPH R. L. STERNE
[*Washington Bureau of The Sun*]

Washington, June 12—Southern senators declared war today against President Kennedy's civil-rights program.

From a 90-minute caucus there emerged a battle strategy based not only on the filibuster but on accusations that the President is making a Marxist attack on private property rights and is using the threat of mob violence to rush his legislation through Congress.

Senator Russell (D., Ga.), leader of the Southern bloc, made it clear after the meeting that the rest of the Administration program — including economic measures that would help Negroes —is in trouble.

Russell Quoted

"When a man is knocked down and choked, he won't embrace the man who did it," the Georgian remarked, thus undercutting the President's long efforts to obtain Southern support.

Seventeen Democrats and one Republican — Senator Tower of Texas — met at short notice to plan their all-out fight against the proposals President Kennedy announced last night in a speech to the nation.

One measure would ban discrimination in hotels, restaurants, theaters and stores classified as being engaged in interstate commerce.

"Bitterly Opposed"

Another would give the Attorney General powers to intervene on behalf of complaints in school desegregation cases.

Russell said Southerners were so "bitterly opposed" to these proposals that he had no doubt they would "resist to the end."

Describing the public accommodations bill as "a long step to-

(Continued, Page 6, Column 5)

White House

By PHILIP POTTER
[*Washington Bureau of The Sun*]

Washington, June 12—President Kennedy, striving to enlist bi-partisan support for his forthcoming civil-rights legislative program, invited former President Dwight Eisenhower to the White House this afternoon for a long talk on the subject.

Also present at the hour and ten-minute session was Vice President Johnson, Senate majority leader during all but two years of Mr. Eisenhower's two-term regime. As such, he played a key role in securing passage of two civil-rights acts, the first in 80 years.

A White House spokesman disclosed only that Mr. Kennedy had invited Mr. Eisenhower and that "they discussed the President's civil rights speech and civil-rights problems in general."

Meets With GOP Leaders

After a morning meeting with Republican congressional leaders on Capitol Hill, Mr. Eisenhower said that priority in solving civil-rights problems should be given to the guarantee of voting rights, which would eventually lead to local solutions of most difficulties.

"While some additional laws may be necessary," he said, he is skeptical about trying to achieve solutions through "a bundle of laws."

"No one can be sure he's got the right answer," Mr. Eisenhower said.

In his nation-wide television-radio address last night, Mr. Kennedy committed the Administration to a package legislative program to speed school desegregation and open facilities in hotels, theaters, restaurants and stores to Negroes, as well as to strengthen voting-rights provisions already in the law.

"Appalled By Barbarity"

The White House meeting between the Chief Executive and his predecessor occurred shortly after Mr. Kennedy issued a statement that he was "appalled by the barbarity" of the slaying of Medgar W. Evers, top Negro integrationist leader in Mississippi, at Jackson early today.

The statement, echoed by many members of Congress—both

(Continued, Page 6, Column 6)

Jackson Pressing Search For Negro's Sniper Killer

By CHARLES WHITEFORD
[*Sun Staff Correspondent*]

Jackson, Miss., June 12—State and city authorities worked frantically against time and the growing outrage of the Negro community today to find the sniper who felled Mississippi's civil rights leader.

Medgar W. Evers, state director of the National Association for the Advancement of Colored People, was ambushed early this morning and mortally wounded outside his home here.

His slaying has already resulted in one demonstration of Negroes. More than 100 of them were seized by police and placed in a special compound set up by local authorities at the State fair grounds some weeks ago.

Fourteen Negro ministers also were arrested on a charge of parading without a permit but in fear of touching off another explosion with the Negro community police released them on their own recognizance.

Negro leaders were openly fearful that the "non-violent" movement for civil rights would soon shift into something much more dangerous.

Mrs. Ruby Hurley, southeastern regional secretary of the N.A.A.C.P., who rushed here from Atlanta after Mr. Evers was shot, said, for example: "Everybody I've talked to is just plain mad.

"Our big job is to keep that anger from getting out of control

"I don't know how long the Negro is going along with non-violence. That is the frightening thing about it."

Mrs. Hurley said she was so frustrated and angry this morning that "I don't know what I would have done if I'd seen a white face."

Mrs. Myrlie Evers, wife of the

(Continued, Page 6, Column 3)

On Other Pages

The Weather
Cloudy with the high near 80 today. Fair tonight and tomorrow. Yesterday's high, 78; low, 60.
(Details and Map, Page 31)

THE SUN FINAL

[Registered United States Patent Office]

Vol. 253—No. 25— F | PAID CIRCULATION SIX MONTHS ENDING 9/30/62 MORNING, 188,150 EVENING, 212,251 400,401 ‖ SUNDAY 321,686 | BALTIMORE, FRIDAY, JUNE 14, 1963 | Published daily except Sunday by The A. S. Abell Co. Calvert & Centre Sts., Baltimore, Md. Second class postage paid at Baltimore, Md. | 44 Pages | 7 Cents

Johnson, Boykin, Two Others Convicted

Labor Chiefs Back Kennedy Rights Plan

RUSS PRESS HAILS TALK BY KENNEDY

Sees Chances For 'Improvement Of International Climate'

By ERNEST B. FURGURSON
[Moscow Bureau of The Sun]

Moscow, June 13 — The Soviet press said today that President Kennedy's American University speech showed that "opportunities have emerged for a radical improvement in the international climate."

But the Kremlin's leading theoretician indicated to Harold Wilson, British Labor party leader, that the West would be unwise to suppose Russia would rush into any compromises because of a need to demonstrate the success of policies opposed by Red China.

Mikhail A. Suslov, party secretary, Presidium member and senior ideological expert, received Wilson and voiced criticism of an idea he attributed to Lord Home, British Foreign Secretary.

Wilson's View

He said Home had proposed that the West wait for an open Soviet breach with Communist China, then step in to offer a policy of peaceful coexistence with the Russians.

Suslov also turned down Wilson's view that the West should move quickly to reach some kind of agreement with the Kremlin because advocates of the "hard line" toward capitalism are pressuring Premier Khrushchev.

These influences against any compromise with the West, both inside Russia and in Peking, may make it much more difficult for Khrushchev to reach any agreement if action is postponed, Wilson told Suslov.

But Suslov, first of the officials visited here by Wilson to take up the subject of China, rejected his idea. He apparently did not convince Wilson that his idea of a prompt agreement was wrong however.

First Comment

Mr. Kennedy's speech on peace, nuclear testing and the need for Americans to reexamine their attitudes toward these subjects as well as the Soviet Union was printed this morning by *Pravda*, Communist party paper, and last night by the Government newspaper *Izvestia*.

Sovietskaya Rossiya, party and Government organ of the Russian federation, issued the first comment on the international aspects of the talk.

Its commentator, Eduard Baskakov, called it a "very significant" speech.

"For the first time in twenty years of cold war, the United States President publicly came out for the need of basically reevaluating Soviet-American relations and recognized to a certain extent the need for a peaceful coexistence.

"Significant also is the fact that the speech coincided with

(Continued, Page 2, Column 2)

Nazi-Fascist Network Seen

London, June 13 (*Reuters*)—The World Jewish Congress claimed here today there was fresh evidence of the active existence of an internationally linked network of Nazi-Fascist anti-Semitic groups in many countries.

The London headquarters of the congress said the evidence was brought to light at a conference of the European executive of the congress in Paris Sunday.

A congress spokesman said: "Deep concern was expressed at the report of plans by former members of Nazi S. S. formations to hold an international rally at Hammeln, West Germany, in September.

"The report stressed that the purpose of such rallies was to maintain and foster the spirit of Nazism and to stimulate a Nazi-Fascist revival."

Laotian Rightist Post Is Attacked By Pathet Lao

Vientiane, Laos, June 13 (*AP*)—Pro-Communist Pathet Lao troops attacked a Rightist outpost in southern Laos today, but were reported repulsed with heavy losses.

The action could mean broadening of a war so far restricted to the area of the Plaine des Jarres.

The target was a company-strength garrison based 8 miles southeast of Attopeu, a Rightist stronghold itself about 350 miles southeast of the embattled plain.

The Defense Ministry said a night artillery barrage was followed up with an attack by two Pathet Lao battalions — perhaps 1,200 men.

The ministry said the Pathet Lao left 32 dead and "we recovered an important amount of armament." Of Rightist casualties, it said only that a company commander was killed.

U.S. MISSILE GROUP READY

Titan II Able To Reach Any Spot On Earth

By MARK S. WATSON
[Sun Military Correspondent]

Washington, June 13—The nation's first squadron of "all-global" missiles—capable for the first time of reaching any spot on earth—became operative today.

The readiness of the 570th Strategic Missile Squadron, at Davis-Monthan Air Force Base near Tucson, Ariz., with nine of these 12,000-mile Titan II missiles in firing position, was announced by Lt. Gen. T. P. Gerrity, deputy chief of staff.

A second such squadron at that field, two more at Little Rock, Ark., and two more at McConnell base near Wichita, Kan., will be installed before the end of the year, adding impressively to the nation's deterrent powers.

Doubles Launch-Power

The previous ICBM's—that is, the thirteen Atlas, six Titan I-type, and two Minuteman squadrons—have a reported range of up to 6,000 miles.

Titan II doubles their launch-power, making possible either a doubling of the size of the missile (to provide greater penetration of the target area) or a comparable increase in range, by adding to the fuel-load rather than to the missile's destructive powers.

In two other respects Titan II marks a great advance: 1. It employs the new packaged-liquid fuel which can be stored in an ever-ready state, whereby the missile can be fired in less than a minute of the signal. Titan I, like Atlas, requires a fifteen-minute warning.

2. It employs a new launching system, whereby it can be fired

(Continued, Page 5, Column 7)

CASTROITES, REDS SEIZED IN VENEZUELA

Raids Are Prompted By Announced Plot On Betancourt's Life

Caracas, Venezuela, June 13 (*AP*)—Police seized Communists and Castroites throughout Venezuela today in raids prompted by an announced plot against the life of President Romulo Betancourt.

In the midst of the manhunt, terrorist gunmen staged a daring hold-up in Caracas.

Some 250 persons were in custody by mid-day, a Government source estimated. Police suspected that hundreds of others fled to the autonomously ruled campus of the University of Caracas, shielded from raids by political sanctuary.

Deputies Protected

Communist and Castroite deputies were protected from arrest through parliamentary immunity.

Bandits invaded the offices of a bus company, held 16 employees at gunpoint and escaped with $2,000 from the safe, claiming they needed the money for anti-Government operations.

President Betancourt, meanwhile, cruised off the coast in a heavily armed destroyer.

Betancourt Infuriated

Betancourt, infuriated by the latest of a series of attempts on his life, last night ordered the arrest of all Venezuela's estimated 40,000 Communists and members of the Movement of the Revolutionary Left, known as the MIR.

The MIR is a party which gets its inspiration from Prime Minister Fidel Castro of Cuba.

The Communist and MIR congressmen are the persons Betancourt has charged with directing terror operations and the assassination attempts.

Communist Sought

Police efforts were concentrated on a search for Roger Antonio Figueroa, a young Communist who escaped during a gun battle after the attempt to kill Betancourt at the Archbishop's palace in Ciudad Bolivar failed.

The Interior Minister, Carlos Andres, declined to say how many, if any, Communists have been rounded up.

Meanwhile, the pro-Communist tabloid *Clarin* said it had learned the Red terrorist organization, FALN (Armed Forces of National Liberation), may be ready to call a truce in its raids on United States-owned installations.

Betancourt On Tour

The story said the FALN was responding to pleas by anti-Betancourt organizations and by business men. It did not say what the FALN would demand in return.

Although the attempted assassination took place Tuesday, Betancourt kept it secret until he issued his round-up orders from the Orinoco River village of San Felix while he was visiting.

He has been on a tour dedicat-

(Continued, Page 17, Column 3)

Macmillan Awaiting Battle, Gets Uneasy Cabinet Truce

By DAVID M. CULHANE
[London Bureau of The Sun]

London, June 13 — Prime Minister Macmillan achieved an uneasy truce within his party today so that he can prepare for opposition attacks over the Profumo affair in the House of Commons Monday.

A second Cabinet meeting in two days given over entirely to the Profumo crisis left Macmillan still in charge and with his Cabinet intact.

Profumo Quit June 5

A source close to the Prime Minister volunteered the information tonight that Macmillan has "absolutely no intention of following John D. Profumo into retirement."

Profumo resigned as Secretary for War June 5 because of a previously denied affair with a 21-year-old girl who was being equally generous with her favors at the same time with a Soviet diplomat then stationed in London.

A few of his Cabinet ministers are not satisfied that Macmillan did enough to avoid the scandal, but they today they continued to hold their peace in public.

However, continuing criticisms from several important Conservative party figures made it clear again today that a single false step could bring Macmillan down.

Lloyd Makes Speech

Selwyn Lloyd, fired as Chancellor of the Exchequer by Macmillan last July, made a speech tonight that only thinly veiled his readiness to look for new leadership for the Conservative party.

But the Prime Minister gained strong support tonight from Viscount Hailsham, the senior Cabinet minister who will represent Britain in the nuclear test ban talks in Moscow next month.

Lord Hailsham said on television that the Conservative Government "is not to be brought down because of a squalid affair between a woman of easy virtue and a proved liar."

Parliament is in recess until Monday, and most ministers have

(Continued, Page 2, Column 5)

Senate Liberals Vow Fight For Civil Rights

Members Of Both Parties Plan Around-The-Clock Battle Against Filibuster

By JOSEPH R. L. STERNE
[Washington Bureau of The Sun]

Washington, June 13 — Senate liberals in both parties vowed today they will stay in session around the clock to break the impending Southern filibuster against President Kennedy's civil rights legislation.

Senator Morse (D., Ore.) said he is ready to eat his Christmas dinner on Capitol Hill if it takes that long to "deliver the Constitution to the Negroes of this country."

Senator Cooper (R., Ky.) said the Senate should be kept in session straight through the long end-of-the-year vacation period if such means are necessary to enact civil rights measures.

Sole Concentration

The Kentuckian held that an Administration willingness to subordinate other legislative proposals — no matter how important they might be — would be the first step toward insuring passage of a civil rights program.

Today's pledges by the liberals constituted a response to Southern senators who have voiced their readiness to fight civil rights with every legislative weapon at their command.

In a related development, senators began speaking out publicly about the prospect of Negro demonstrations and sit-ins designed to influence Congress.

Senator Robertson (D., Va.) raised the question when he noted on the Senate floor that the Rev. Martin Luther King, Jr., a Negro leader, had proposed a mass demonstration at the Capitol when the Southern filibuster begins.

Robertson cited Federal laws forbidding mass gatherings on the Capitol grounds and then declared:

"Before the demonstrations, being whipped into a frenzy by Martin Luther King, reach our capital city, I think someone in authority should publicly announce whether or not the law against illegal parades and assemblages is going to be enforced."

Another Southerner, Senator

(Continued, Page 7, Column 1)

Kennedy's Defeat In House Called Rights Bill Skirmish

By GERALD GRIFFIN
[Washington Bureau of The Sun]

Washington, June 13—President Kennedy came back fighting today after his defeat yesterday in the House of Representatives.

"The tragic death of area development legislation could not have come at a worse time," the President said, referring to the 209-204 vote by which a combination of Republicans and Southern Democrats blocked an Administration bill to enlarge the redevelopment program.

"Unemployment persists — our distressed areas need help — and scores of hard-hit communities in Pennsylvania, Michigan, West Virginia, eastern Kentucky, upstate New York, upstate Minnesota and southern Illinois were counting on an expansion of this program," Mr. Kennedy's statement continued.

"More Than Speeches" Asked

"The people of these and other affected states need more than speeches to help their depressed communities and jobless workers. This program must not be allowed to die—and it is my intention to give the Congress another opportunity to support it."

Mr. Kennedy's quick response indicated that more battles with Congress are coming up. In fact, some responsible authorities here think that the House vote can be regarded as the first round in the approaching contest over new civil rights legislation.

Others think that the House might well have rejected the Administration's bill, even if the President had not already pledged himself to recommend new civil rights legislation.

Alliance Powerful

In any case, the vote was a jolting reminder to the President of the strength of the conservative Southern Democrats when they can find an alliance with the Republicans.

In the House yesterday 189 Democrats and 15 Republicans voted for the Administration bill, while 57 Democrats and 152 Republicans voted against it.

This vote did not kill the area redevelopment program, which was designed to help bring new industries into communities affected by chronic unemployment. The program will go on, but without the additional funds that the

(Continued, Page 7, Column 6)

POLICE BREAK UP NEGRO PROTEST

By CHARLES WHITEFORD
[Sun Staff Correspondent]

Jackson, Miss., June 13 — City police used their billy clubs this afternoon to break up a Negro demonstration in this Mississippi State capital where the State's Negro civil rights leader was shot to death yesterday.

Among those beaten to the ground by police was a white professor from Tougaloo Southern Christian College — who was dragged from a porch and hit from behind while two policemen had his arms pinioned.

100 Arrested

An estimated 100 persons were arrested and placed in a "concentration camp" at the nearby fairgrounds.

It brought the total arrested to more than 900 since a series of nonviolent demonstrations sponsored by the National Association for the Advancement of Colored People started here May 13.

Those demonstrations had been tailing off. However, Medgar Evers, 37-year-old Mississippi field director for the N.A.A.C.P., was shot and killed by a sniper as he stepped from his automobile at the carport of his home early yesterday morning.

It is difficult to describe the deepness of the outrage among the Negroes of this area over the assassination.

State, city and Federal authori-

(Continued, Page 7, Column 2)

U.S. IS BLAMED IN EVERS DEATH

By PETER J. KUMPA
[Washington Bureau of The Sun]

Washington, June 13 — Clarence Mitchell, Washington director of the N.A.A.C.P., today blamed the death of Medgar Evers on a "too little and too late" policy of the Government in protecting the rights of Negroes in the South.

He told a House subcommittee that is nearing the end of its hearings on civil rights legislation that Evers's home had been bombed and his life threatened on several occasions.

Numerous Pleas Recalled

"In spite of the arrests, the assaults, the humiliations and numerous pleas to the Department of Justice the Government did not make massive charges that it could have earlier until the television cameras were focused on the burned buses and maimed humans in the dreadful action on the freedom riders," Mitchell said.

Mitchell urged enactment of far-reaching, anti-discrimination legislation that would include fair employment practice provisions, injunctive authority to permit the Attorney General to intervene in all bias cases, congressional support for faster school desegregation and the lowering of discrimination bars in all public facilities.

With Mitchell and Representative Diggs (D. Mich.), a Detroit Negro, came Dr. Aaron E. Henry, the head of the Mississippi

(Continued, Page 6, Column 3)

300 UNIONISTS HEAR OUTLINE OF PROGRAM

President Also Briefs Group Of Leaders In Congress

Military sets review on Negro civilians ....Page 7

By WILLIAM KNIGHTON, JR.
[Washington Bureau of The Sun]

Washington, June 13 — President Kennedy received unanimous support for his civil rights program from nearly 300 labor leaders today.

Their only complaint was that the proposed legislation was not tough enough. Their spokesmen told the President at a meeting at the White House that a fair employment practices commission should be included in his coming proposals to Congress.

In another White House conference earlier today, Mr. Kennedy presented his proposals to a group of Democratic and Republican congressional leaders.

Only Outline Given

At both meetings, only a general outline of the Administration's plans was discussed.

No draft bill was submitted to the congressional leaders because the legislation has not been completed. Therefore no commitment was sought by the President and none was given.

At the President's meeting with the labor leaders, however, a succession of union and department heads arose and pledged to Mr. Kennedy their personal support and that of their unions for his program and specifically for his appeal to wipe out discrimination in the labor movement, down through the locals.

James B. Carey, president of the International Union of Electrical Workers, reported later that the unionists included many from the South and representatives of the building trades unions — one of those most accused of discriminating against Negroes.

After outlining his program and asking their help in removing segregation from their unions and in job employment, Mr. Kennedy heard their pledges of support and requested that they submit to him in writing the suggestions they had made.

Carey, David J. McDonald president of the United Steelworkers of America, and others said they would emphasize their demand for a fair employment practices commission.

Former President Harry Truman went to the White House to pay a courtesy call on Mr. Kennedy while the meeting still was in progress. Mr. Kennedy met him and led him before the union leaders.

They gave him a standing ovation and he told them he was happy to see a Democrat in the White House and hoped one would be there always.

Although the Administration's

(Continued, Page 7, Column 6)

22 CHILDREN FLEE BUS AFTER CRASH

Vehicle Quickly Evacuated; Truck Driver Killed

Orangeburg, N.Y., June 13 (*AP*)—Twenty-two children, superbly trained for just such a crisis, evacuated their burning school bus today after it collided with a tractor-trailer truck. Not a hair singed so rapid was their exit.

The driver of the truck, John Fost, 31, of Piermont, N.Y., was killed. There were no casualties on the bus.

The children had been trained monthly in the use of emergency exits and other evacuation methods, since all of them regularly travel to and from school by bus. The pupils, most of whom are 9 years old, are fourth-graders.

They were returning from an outing in New York city when the collision occurred. Both vehicles burst into flames.

Almost instantly, one of the children opened the emergency

(Continued, Page 6, Column 5)

Ike Hits 'Democrat' Party And Some GOP Politicians

By PHILIP POTTER
[Sun Staff Correspondent]

Hershey, Pa., June 13 — Former President Dwight Eisenhower tonight lashed out at the current "Democrat" Administration as one that got into office and then engaged in a "headlong retreat on matters of national survival."

His indictment was delivered at a "citizens workshop" dinner sponsored by the Republican Citizens Committee of the United States, an organization founded by an agency to recruit volunteers and "amateurs" for Republican congressional and Presidential campaigns.

Amateur Role Urged

Mr. Eisenhower's strongest denunciation to date of the Kennedy regime was coupled with a strong plea that "amateurs" and "idealists" move in on the professional politicians in his own party, whom he accused of belittling the formation of his "citizens" group.

"Politics is becoming far too important in our individual and corporate lives to be monopolized by politicians," the former President told his 65 fellow participants in the two-day citizens' workshop, many of them representing the nation's great corporations.

Political "amateurs," he declared, "bring verve, sparkle and fresh ideas which perk up a political party the way a well-advertised medicine does tired blood."

Nixon Quoted

Mr. Eisenhower's statement that he was "partial to so-called 'amateurs'" came the day after Richard M. Nixon told shipboard reporters as he sailed for Europe with his family that "among the professional politicians, Senator Goldwater (Ariz.) has the lead, and they have more influence on nominations than anyone else."

Goldwater drew a critical bead on the Republican Citizens Committee when it was founded by his backers since have been charging that Mr. Eisenhower's

(Continued, Page 5, Column 1)

FORMER CONGRESSMEN GUILTY OF CONSPIRACY, CONFLICT OF INTEREST

THOMAS F. JOHNSON

FRANK W. BOYKIN

Federal Grand Jury Finds Misuse Of Influence

By THEODORE W. HENDRICKS

Thomas F. Johnson, a former Maryland congressman, was convicted by a Federal jury yesterday on conspiracy and conflict-of-interest charges that accused him of the misuse of his congressional influence.

Three other defendants, tried in the eleven-week case, were also convicted on all eight counts of the Federal grand jury indictment.

All four were charged with conspiracy in depriving the Government of its right to conduct its affairs without undue influence and pressure.

Fourteen Terms In House

The other defendants were:

Frank W. Boykin, a former Alabama congressman, who was defeated last year after fourteen terms in the House of Representatives.

J. Kenneth Edlin, a Maryland savings and loan operator who formerly backed two associations whose assets were seized by court actions.

William L. Robinson, an attorney and Edlin's chief associate in the operation of the Maryland firms and a Miami (Fla.) mortgage company.

Only 3½ hours after the jurors were locked up to deliberate on the evidence they returned to tell Chief Judge Roszel C. Thomsen that they had reached a verdict.

Menzies Is Foreman

The jury foreman, John T. Menzies, a Baltimore industrialist, repeated the guilty verdict 32 times—once for each charge against each defendant.

During the trial, which started April 1, the jury heard an estimated total of 1,500,000 words of testimony supporting and rejecting charges that the congressmen were paid to do illegal favors for Edlin.

Despite Judge Thomsen's warning that no demonstrations would be allowed while the long verdict was being recorded, there was an audible gasp when the first guilty finding against Johnson was announced.

Family In Court

Mrs. Johnson, a daughter and a son and the aged mother of the former congressman crowded on a front row bench to hear the verdict.

At first, Mrs. Johnson appeared to fight back tears. She later discussed the chances of reversing the jury finding on appeal.

The 54-year-old former Eastern Shore representative appeared tired. He refused comment.

Johnson's lawyer, George Cochran Doub, bowed his head and rested it on his hand after the verdict. He said he would file a motion for a new trial and, if

(Continued, Page 9, Column 1)

On Other Pages

The Weather
Variable cloudiness today. High near 92 degrees. Fair, not so warm tomorrow. Yesterday's temperatures: High, 96; low, 80.
(Details and Map, Page 20.)

THE SUN FINAL

(Registered United States Patent Office)

Vol. 253—No. 56—F | PAID CIRCULATION SIX MONTHS ENDED 3/31/63 MORNING, 186,944 EVENING, 215,427 402,371 ‖ SUNDAY 329,670 | BALTIMORE, SATURDAY, JULY 20, 1963 | Published daily except Sunday by The A. S. Abell Co. Calvert & Centre Sts., Baltimore, Md. Second class postage paid at Baltimore, Md. | 28 Pages | 7 Cents

Tawes Hits 'Irrational Demands' Of Negro Leaders In Cambridge; Gwynn Oak To Be Integrated Aug. 28

KHRUSHCHEV OFFERS TO ALLOW OBSERVERS ON SOVIET TERRITORY

Reciprocal Plan Aims To Prevent Surprise Attack; U.S. Views Test Ban Talks With Cautious Hope, Will Consult Allies

Peking, July 19 (*Reuters*)—The Chinese Communist party today published in full the texts of the latest ideological exchange between Moscow and Peking.

A spokesman of the Central Committee of the Chinese Communist party, announcing the publication, said the latest Soviet letter to Peking was "superlative material for learning by negative example."

Moscow

By ERNEST B. FURGURSON
[*Moscow Bureau of The Sun*]

Moscow, July 19 — Premier Khrushchev offered today to allow Western observers at key points on Soviet territory as part of a reciprocal East-West program to prevent surprise attack.

The unexpected proposal was considered the most meaningful indication yet of a Soviet turn toward accommodation with the West as a result of the increasingly hopeless split between Moscow and Peking.

It was one of a series of steps Khrushchev suggested to follow up a modified nuclear test-ban treaty, which is now under negotiation here by the United States, Britain and the Soviet Union.

"Hope" Seen

Khrushchev said, "We are gaining the impression that there is now hope" of a test-ban agreement "unless there is some special turn in the stand of the British and American representatives."

He strongly implied that a non-aggression treaty between NATO and the Warsaw Pact nations could be worked out without the features that previously have prevented Western approval.

The Premier's major foreign-policy speech, including new condemnation of his Red Chinese comrades, was delivered at a Soviet-Hungarian "friendship rally" in the Kremlin Palace of Congresses.

Plan Is Surprise

Janos Kadar, the Hungarian Communist chief who is winding up an official visit, also spoke and indorsed Khrushchev's position against that of the Chinese.

Soviet support of the plan to prevent surprise attack was itself a surprise. It contradicts Russia's insistent contention that foreign observers on Soviet soil would be merely espionage agents—a position Khrushchev repeated in regard to on-site inspections of suspected underground nuclear shots.

The Soviet Union included a similar proposal in one of its documents tabled at Geneva five years ago, but later backed away from discussing it.

The United States spelled out such a proposal in its general disarmament plan, introduced at Geneva last August 18.

Although it has not been fully argued, Soviet reaction to it had been generally negative until today.

Khrushchev went from the current test-ban talks into his other East-West proposals.

He said it was now rather clear that no agreement banning under-

(Continued, Page 2, Column 3)

Washington

Washington, July 19 (AP)—The United States viewed with cautious hope today the Moscow test-ban talks and said the Western allies will be consulted on Soviet Premier Khrushchev's optimistic-sounding pronouncements on the cold war.

The American reaction was expressed by the State Department's press officer, Richard I. Phillips. He said items mentioned by the Soviet leader in his speech today already have been discussed in the closed United States-British-Russian conference, as an aside from the test-ban discussions.

Addressing a Soviet-Hungarian friendship meeting in Moscow, Khrushchev lambasted the Red Chinese hard line toward the West and saw hope for reaching a limited nuclear test-ban agreement in the negotiations now underway at the Soviet capital.

Post Proposals Brought Up

The Russian leader also brought up several proposals the Kremlin has advanced in past discussions on easing cold war problems.

Among them, he mentioned setting up observation posts at airports, railway junctions, highways and major ports inside Communist and Western territories to guard against sneak attack.

Observers from the other side would be at points where they could report suspiciously large military movements.

The United States view as given by Phillips was this:

"We shall, of course, give careful study to the various suggestions outlined by Chairman Khrushchev today in his speech at the Kremlin Palace of Congresses and we will be consulting with our allies about them.

"Practical Means"

"The United States for its part has long sought practical means by which progress in arms reduction could be achieved.

"On the test-ban issue specifically, the talks in Moscow directed toward working out a mutually satisfactory limited ban are proceeding in a businesslike manner.

"While caution about the outcome of these negotiations is still

(Continued, Page 2, Column 6)

RUSSIAN SAYS 'SOME' WANT NEW LEADERS

Khrushchev Sees Aim Of Chinese As Stalin-Type Soviet Chiefs

By ERNEST B. FURGURSON

Moscow, July 19—"Some people" want to install new leadership in the Soviet Union by "putting Stalin back on his pedestal," Premier Khrushchev asserted today.

He warned them—clearly meaning the Chinese Communists—not to interfere in Soviet affairs.

His 1½-hour speech in the Kremlin was studded with charges aimed at the Chinese "comrades."

The talk came as the Soviet-Chinese party "reconciliation" conference ended its second week with no apparent result except a further stiffening of the positions of both sides.

Delegates Meet Again

Ranking party delegates met again this morning at the House of Receptions on Lenin Hills. As usual, there was no official report of their session.

Khrushchev's comment that some people are trying to replace Soviet leadership—meaning the Premier himself and his supporters—was perhaps his most direct reference thus far to the intensely personal challenge being pushed by China's Mao Tse-tung.

The Chinese clearly date the deterioration of Soviet-Chinese relations from the time Khrushchev ousted the "anti-party group" and began to put his own policies into effect.

Khrushchev said he dared his challengers to take their own program and his Soviet party program to the workers of any factory or collective farm in the Soviet Union.

They would listen to both politely, then tell the outsiders to take their ideas and go away, he maintained.

Throughout his speech he avoided identifying "some people" as the Chinese comrades, but there was no doubt of his target.

"Democratic Order"

No such reticence has been practiced in recent statements by the Soviet party Central Committee—or its Chinese counterpart. Some "wizards" think they can tell the Soviet people that Khrushchev was wrong in exposing Stalin's "personality cult," the Premier said.

But they will not be believed, he went on.

"I receive many letters from workers, peasants, and employees, and they support the line of our party," he stated.

Khrushchev said the Stalin cult had not been exposed in 1956 just for the sake of exposure, but to warn the party that such a mistake must never be made again.

"The democratic order, forgotten under Stalin, now prevails in the party," he insisted.

Again quoting "some people,"

(Continued, Page 2, Column 2)

A-Ban Won't Stop Spread Of Weapons, Jackson Says

By GERALD GRIFFIN
[*Washington Bureau of The Sun*]

Washington, July 19 — Senator Jackson (D., Wis,) said today that it is "utterly unrealistic" to take the position that a test-ban agreement signed by the United States, Great Britain and the Soviet Union would stop the spread of nuclear weapons.

Jackson is a member of the Armed Services Committee and the Joint Atomic Energy Committee whose knowledge and opinions are generally respected. He set forth some of his views today in a speech at the National Editorial Association convention at Seattle, and his office distributed copies of his remarks for examination here.

"Matter Of First Importance"

The Senator discussed a number of "wrong assumptions" which, as he put it, have worked their way into public thinking.

One of the assumptions he listed, which has special application to the talks going on in Moscow, was that "some people tell us that we should make whatever concessions are necessary to get a test-ban agreement in order to halt the spread of nuclear weapons."

After saying this is unrealistic, in the light of the steps being taken in France and Communist China to develop nuclear weapons, Jackson declared that, for the United States, the matter of first importance is to "protect our military deterrent."

Takes Issue

"If there is a conflict between a test-ban agreement and a credible deterrent," he said, "the deterrent must come first.

"To me the order of priority is crystal clear."

But Jackson took issue with suggestions that the United States Senate is the big obstacle to a test ban agreement. A two-thirds majority vote of approval in the Senate is necessary for a treaty to become effective.

"If a test-ban agreement is

(Continued, Page 2, Column 7)

On Other Pages

Bid To Cut Spending Abroad Is Expected

Congressional Effort Is Seen In Wake Of Plan To Tax Buyers Of Foreign Stocks

By RODNEY CROWTHER
[*Washington Bureau of The Sun*]

Washington, July 19—Heavier demand for deeper slashes in United States spending abroad, particularly for foreign aid, is expected to be the most immediate result of President Kennedy's proposal to impose a special tax on United States purchasers of foreign stocks and bonds.

Capitol Hill sources said today there was considerable disappointment over the President's failure to plan big retrenchments in overseas spending.

Byrd Gives View

This view was strongly expressed by Senator Byrd (D., Va.), chairman of the Senate Finance Committee, one of the two groups which must consider the plan to tax Americans who buy foreign capital issues.

The proposal will get its first hearing before the House Ways and Means Committee shortly after that body finishes its work on Administration tax reduction and reform programs.

Representative Mills (D., Ark.), Ways and Means chairman, said his group would conduct public hearings on the foreign securities tax plan after the tax reduction bill.

This may be three weeks away, as the committee already has arranged to take a few days off to consider an Administration request for another boost in the national debt ceiling. Opening hearings on this have been set for July 29.

Meanwhile, there have been growing doubts that Mr. Ken-

(Continued, Page 8, Column 4)

$240,000,000 Aid Slash Made

Washington, July 19 (AP)—The Senate Foreign Relations Committee sliced another $240,000,000 from President Kennedy's foreign aid requests today and approved making research funds available for overseas birth control projects.

The latter action, taken on a voice vote, is likely to stir added controversy when the much-disputed measure reaches the Senate floor.

Senator Fulbright (D., Ark.), chairman, sponsored the amendment which would make funds available, on request of the recipient governments, "to conduct research into problems of controlling population growth and to provide technical and other assistance to cooperating countries in carrying out programs of population control."

A member said the committee adopted the amendment with little discussion.

X-15 PILOT SOARS RECORD 67 MILES

Says 'I Thought My Altimeter Had Gone Wacky . . .'

Edwards Air Force Base, Cal., July 19 (AP)—Joseph M. Walker, ace space pilot, shot to an unexpectedly high X-15 altitude mark of nearly 67 miles today—presumably towing a small balloon—then landed with these picturesque comments:

"I thought my altimeter had gone wacky. . . ."

"It sure is dark up there . . . like a black velvet photographer's curtain. . . ."

"It was the smoothest flight I've ever had . . ."

"I could see farther than I could see. . . ."

"It's all in a day's work."

Exceeds Expectations

Walker, who flies for the National Space Agency, was supposed to soar to but 315,000 feet (about 60 miles), barely surpassing the old X-15 record of 314,750 set a year ago by Air Force Maj. Joseph M. White.

Instead, the edge-of-space research rocket plane soared 35,000 feet higher, to 350,000 feet, or nearly 67 miles. Why?

Walker attributed it to the fact the engine burned 85 seconds instead of the programed 83, giving it a harder kick as it zoomed skyward.

Plunging back from the nearly airless realm of near space into the thicker earth's atmosphere, Walker hit a top speed of 3,886 miles an hour, no threat to his X-15 speed mark of 4,104 miles an hour.

To determine air density, the X-15, was to eject a 30-inch-diameter balloon at 250,000 feet and trail it at the end of a 100-foot fishline as it arched over the desert. Experts assume this happened, but will have to check data to be sure. Walker's view of it was blocked.

Designated As Warm Up

By soaring to 350,000 feet, Walker stole his own thunder in a way. Today's flight had been described as a warm-up for a 350,000-footer later in the summer. Will another to that altitude be necessary?

Walker and other experts said they won't know until results of this one are analyzed.

The 350,000-foot-altitude area is regarded by some as the probable safe maximum for X-15's as they are presently constructed. The engine has power to shoot them far higher, probably 100 miles or more. The problem is heating due to air friction as they return to earth.

One of the three X-15's is due to be equipped with new heat

(Continued, Page 9, Column 3)

PRESIDENT GETS TIE CLASP BACK

Remorseful Student Returns Pin, Receives Another

By WILLIAM KNIGHTON, JR.
[*Washington Bureau of The Sun*]

Washington, July 19—A possible diplomatic breach between the United States and the Republic of Indonesia was averted today—the remorseful Indonesian high school student who snitched President Kennedy's tie clasp yesterday personally returned it to him with apologies.

The President gave him another pin—one in the form of his World War II PT-109—to replace the one he had taken from him during the mob scene of 2,500 American Field Service foreign exchange students on the White House south lawn yesterday.

Last night, after reading about what had happened at this reception, the handsome, 19-year-old youth, Bowo Soerjosoedarmo, wrote a letter to Mr. Kennedy, and this morning he showed up at a White House gate and told the member of the White House police on duty he wanted to give the President his letter and return the tie clasp.

Sees President

The policeman phoned the Secret Service, which informed Pierre Salinger, the President's press secretary, of the teen-ager's request, and Salinger had him brought in. He also arranged a short interview with Mr. Kennedy.

The letter he handed to the Chief Executive stated:

Dear Mr. President:

All of the A.F.S. students are very happy that you could meet and give a brilliant speech to us on Thursday, the 18th. I am only one of the 2,500 A.F.S. students who are so anxious and excited to meet you.

In that exciting moment I could not handle myself correctly; without thinking any longer I took your tie pin.

I apologize for what I've done to you and realize that I should not do that either as an individual or as a representative of a country. I hope that this happening won't have any effect at all to the A.F.S. students in the years to come.

Very sincerely yours. . . .

He also expressed his regret for his actions orally when he saw the President who, he reported, asked him, "Did you have a good time or not?"

Handkerchief Return Due

The White House also reported that the Japanese girl who pilfered Mr. Kennedy's pocket handkerchief during the near riot, phoned and said she would return it. It is expected by mail.

Earlier, the President person-

(Continued, Page 9, Column 2)

JOB BIAS BAN ASKED IN CIVIL RIGHTS BILL

Reuther Urges 'Single, All-Inclusive Package' At House Hearing

By JOSEPH R. L. STERNE
[*Washington Bureau of The Sun*]

Washington, July 19 (AP)—Walter Reuther, president of the United Automobile Workers Union, said today that a bill banning racial discrimination in labor unions and in private employment should be included in the omnibus civil rights package.

"A single, all-inclusive package" would be the best kind of bill that the House could send to the Senate, he told the House Judiciary Committee.

Reuther thus took issue with the Administration decision to have fair employment practices legislation considered as a separate item.

Action Held Unlikely

Although the House Education and Labor Committee has passed an employment practices bill of the type advocated by Reuther, the measure seems destined to wind up in a House Rules Committee pigeonhole.

This dim outlook, according to congressional sources, is due to two key factors:

First, the Administration will have to expend most of its efforts on getting the main civil rights bill around or through the Rules Committee; little leverage will remain for a push on fair employment practices.

Second, the Administration did not want to attach an employment practices title to the main civil rights bill for fear this would jeopardize the entire program.

Control Over Locals

Reuther said today that a Federal law in the employment field would give national unions greater control over locals that practice bias and would require private industry to end discrimination.

In assessing other parts of President Kennedy's bill, which he lauded vigorously, the labor leader said he would like several provisions to be strengthened.

Persons wrongfully excluded from public accommodations should be entitled to recover a flat sum in damages from the offending proprietors, Reuther contended.

Federal voting registrars should be appointed to accelerate Negro voting rights on a "wholesale" basis in contrast to the "retail" approach of the Administration, he added.

And the Attorney General, the witness held, should be empowered to intervene on behalf of complainants in all civil rights cases—not just a designated few.

Asserting that the executive and judicial branches of Government have acted more "boldly" than the legislative branch in promoting civil rights, Reuther pleaded with congressmen not to weaken the President's proposals.

The United States, he said, "must bridge the gap between our noble promises and our ugly practices."

GOVERNOR ALSO RAPS 'INTIMIDATIONS,' SEES PROGRESS IN EQUALITY

Terms Integration Leadership 'Fragmented'; Park's Owners To Drop Charges; Protest March Canceled

Hollywood, Cal., July 19 (AP) — Integration leaders outlined today their demands on Hollywood's movie-television industry, including a demand that a Negro role be written into every television series.

"We demand recognition of one simple truth," said Herbert Hill, labor secretary of the National Association for the Advancement of Colored People. "One out of every nine persons in this country is a Negro. We demand that films reflect that Negroes do not perform only menial tasks in film portrayals, but that among them are professionals who offer great value to America and the world."

Gwynn Oak

By STUART S. SMITH

Gwynn Oak Amusement Park will be integrated August 28, the park's owners announced last night.

Civil rights leaders simultaneously promised to halt all demonstrations against the park's discriminatory admittance policy.

In addition, the owners stated they would "make known" to the Baltimore county prosecutor their "wish that all charges against the demonstrators be dropped."

The agreement was tentatively negotiated by Spiro T. Agnew, Baltimore county executive, during hours of telephone conferences yesterday with both sides of the racial dispute.

Meeting Called Hastily

The formal announcement came at a hastily called night meeting in the Baltimore County Office Building.

Present, in addition to Mr. Agnew, were the park owners, James, Arthur and David Price some of the clergymen and others who were arrested at the park during the July 4 and 7 demonstrations, and a number of members of the County Human Relations Commission.

The eleventh-hour settlement was reached during clear indications that today would have been too late.

Protest Marches Canceled

Plans for holding massive protest marches, which would surely have ended in further arrests and possible violence, were canceled a little more than twelve hours before the marches were scheduled to begin, at noon today.

Thus far, 383 white and Negro men and women, including many prominent leaders of the Catholic, Jewish and Protestant faiths, are awaiting Circuit Court trials on charges of violating the Maryland trespass law in the earlier protests.

Earlier this week the Prices turned down a proposed July 26

(Continued, Page 15, Column 5)

Governor

Bar unit sets terms for Cambridge intervention ....*Page* 28

By ADAM CLYMER

Governor Tawes criticized Negro leaders in Cambridge last night for "intimidations and irrational demands."

Speaking on State-wide radio and television, the Governor said Negro demands for equality in the Eastern Shore city "have been met to a very large degree."

But he specifically attacked pleas that he free two teen-age demonstrators held as juvenile delinquents, issue an executive order banning discrimination, and call a special session of the General Assembly to broaden the public accommodations law.

The Governor complained that integration leadership in Cambridge is "fragmented" and "one never really knows which individual is speaking for the Negro community at any one given time."

Saying that "both sides are closer to agreement than their emotions allow them to admit" and that "only in a calm atmosphere can settlement be achieved," Governor Tawes called for further negotiations with the newly appointed Cambridge Human Relations Committee, and said he had asked a special committee of the Maryland Bar Association to help resolve the dispute.

The Governor said no broadened public accommodations bill could pass at a special session, "and its failure could result in greater frustration that could lead to more violence and to more bloodshed."

But he said he hoped the next regular session of the General Assembly would pass "broadened civil rights legislation."

"Torn By Strife"

The Governor began by saying "some areas of our State are torn by strife, by racial strife. During the last several weeks, we have seen our sons in the National Guard forced by circumstances to occupy a city on the Eastern Shore."

"We have witnessed prominent members of the clergy jailed because they protested racial discrimination in facilities which serve the public.

"We have seen bitterness and rancor replace reason and good will," he noted. But "we have come to learn that there is no solution—no lasting solution—to the problem of race discrimination to be found in the streets.

"Unless all the citizens of this State begin to appreciate the magnitude of the social revolution now under way, we will face not weeks nor months of racial strife, but years," the Governor said.

Reviews Passage

He reviewed the passage of the State public accommodations law in the last General Assembly and said that "although the bill was weakened by exemptions, it still covers 90 per cent of the State's population and includes the troublesome U.S. Route 40 corridor."

"Surely, many of us thought, this progressive and enlightened step would serve to insulate Maryland, temporarily at least, from the racial troubles that were affecting other sections of the country," he said.

Turning to Cambridge, Gover-

(Continued, Page 15, Column 4)

The Sun Will Star Today As Millions Watch Eclipse

Experts caution on viewing today's eclipse directly ......*Page* 17

New York, July 19 (AP) — The star known as the sun will really star tomorrow.

Jet airplanes will chase the shadow it casts. Rockets and radio waves will poke up toward it. Hundreds of scientists will carry out special photography and measurements. And perhaps millions of Americans will look up to see the sun become totally or partially eclipsed.

Scientists Busy

It is a rare enough event when the moon moves along in just the right path to cover the face of the blazing sun for observers on earth. The last total eclipse visible in the United States occurred June 30, 1954, and the next will not come until March 7, 1970.

This is expected to be the most scientifically observed eclipse in history. The eclipse, brief as it is, provides opportunities to study phenomena of the sun, the space between sun and earth, and the earth's high atmosphere itself.

Some findings might be helpful in guarding future astronauts from dangerous radiation loosed by terrific storms on the sun.

The scientists will be concentrated largely within a narrow belt, averaging 60 miles wide, in Japan, Alaska, Canada and Maine, the only land areas where the eclipse will be total.

The sun will rise eclipsed in Japan, and the path of totality will cover about 10,000 miles in 2¾ hours. Totality, which will last about a minute, will occur at 5.42 P.M. to 5.44 P.M., in localities in Maine.

5,700-Mile Orbit

From start to finish, the earth will have sped more than 1,600,000 miles in space, rotating through 41¼ degrees, while the moon travels about 5,700 miles along its orbit.

For observers in the total path, night will fall, with sunlight reduced to half the intensity of a full moon. Stars will become visible — and so may faint comets. Observers in the total path will

(Continued, Page 9, Column 2)

The Weather
Cloudy today, high near 85. Showers this afternoon into tonight. Clearing tomorrow. Yesterday's high, 85; low, 64.
(Details and map on Page 36)

THE SUN

FINAL

(Registered United States Patent Office)

Vol. 253—No. 90— F | PAID CIRCULATION SIX MONTHS ENDED 3/31/63 MORNING, 185,944; EVENING, 215,427; 402,371 || SUNDAY 329,670 | BALTIMORE, THURSDAY, AUGUST 29, 1963 | Published daily except Sunday by The A. S. Abell Co. Calvert & Centre Sts., Baltimore, Md. Second class postage paid at Baltimore, Md. | 46 Pages | 7 Cents

200,000 Attend Peaceful D. C. March

Kennedy Says 'Nation Can Be Proud'

President Signs Bill Averting National Rail Strike

PLAN SETS MANDATORY ARBITRATION

Kennedy Says Action Reaffirms Priority Of Public Interest

By RODNEY CROWTHER
[Washington Bureau of The Sun]

Washington, Aug. 28—President Kennedy at 6.14 P.M. today signed into law the emergency legislation averting the threatened nation-wide railroad strike and submitting to a special arbitration board the two major disputed issues between rail management and labor.

Well before the strike deadline set for 12.01 A.M. tomorrow, the President acted, less than two hours after the House approved by a nonrecord vote the legislation to require compulsory arbitration of the two issues which had been in dispute for four years.

"By its joint resolution adopted almost unanimously in both Houses, the Congress has now eliminated this threat and reaffirmed the essential priority of the publi' 'nterest over any narrower interest," the President said in a statement issued shortly after the signing.

Virtual Unanimity

"The virtual unanimity of the votes on this joint resolution, by members of Congress completely committed to the preservation of private freedoms, is the firmest assurance that free collective bargaining is not being eroded," he said.

Before approving the final measure by voice vote, the House after several hours of debate approved by a 286-to-66 vote its own Commerce Committee's bill with amendments and then agreed to the bill which had been overwhelmingly approved in the Senate last night.

After that only a number of procedur:' steps remained, such as getting signatures of the Senate and House presiding officers, before rushing the measure to the White House.

The speedy action of Congress lifted from the nation the fear of a major shutdown after midnight tonight of the railroads from coast to coast.

Warning Issued

Both President Kennedy and leading lawmakers of the two Houses had warned that if a strike had been permitted to occur the consequence would have been wide-spread unemployment and serious consequences to the economy.

Soon after the House acted W. Willard Wirtz, Secretary of Labor, announced that the railroads had withdrawn promulgation of their disputed work rules—which would have triggered the strike—and in a message to the presidents of the railway brotherhoods he urged that they "take necessary steps immediately to cancel the strike order."

The Association of American Railroads in a statement ex-

(Continued, Page 9, Column 1)

200,000 FOR FREEDOM—View from top of Lincoln Memorial shows civil rights marchers in Washington yesterday. (Page of rally photos . . . Page 10).

SPACE FUND BILL PASSED

$5,350,820,400 Authorized For Civilian Program

Washington, Aug. 28 (AP) — A bill to authorize a $5,350,820,400 civilian space program for the current fiscal year was passed today by Congress and sent to President Kennedy.

The House acted first, 248 to 125, and the Senate then completed congressional action on a voice vote.

It was a compromise of bills passed previously by the two branches and included $1,147,000,000 for the Apollo project designed to send a man to the moon and bring him back alive by 1970.

The final version was about $362,000,000 less than the President requested, $160,000,000 less than the Senate had voted earlier

(Continued, Page 9, Column 4)

D.C. Rally Described As Flawless

By GERALD GRIFFIN
[Washington Bureau of The Sun]

Washington, Aug. 28—The greatest achievement of the march on Washington today, as shown in the comments of those who watched it and were in it, was its powerful, but orderly, demonstration of the Negroes' responsibility and determination.

They came to the nation's capital as citizens exercising their right of peaceful assembly and their right to petition their Government for a redress of grievances, as it was pointed out.

Humphrey Lauds "Manners"

Their performance, and the performance of their leaders which was reflected in the organization and conduct of the marchers, was generally described as flawless.

Senator Humphrey (D., Minn.), the assistant Democratic leader of the Senate and an ardent advocate of new civil rights legislation, set the tone of the reaction of members of Congress who went to the Lincoln Memorial to have a part in the ceremony.

Humphrey praised the huge crowd for its "good manners, good intentions and determination."

Humphrey, like other members of Congress, said it was unlikely that the demonstration had changed any votes for the civil rights bill. But, he said, the march was "a good thing for Washington and the nation and the world."

At the other end of congressional reaction was that of Senator Thurmond (D., S.C.), as strong in his opposition to the civil rights program as Humphrey is for it. When Thurmond was asked what he thought about the march, he said:

"I think it's uncalled for and unnecessary."

Thurmond said he thought the march would not affect Congress. He added, "At least it should not."

The Rev. Martin Luther King, Jr., one of the Negro leaders, said the march will be remembered as "the greatest demonstration for freedom in the history of our nation."

Representative Hawkins (D.,

(Continued, Page 11, Column 8)

Europe Sees March On TV

London, *Thursday*, Aug. 29 (AP)—From stately manors in the English countryside to coffee bars in Rome, Western Europe surveyed the equal rights march in Washington with interest and cautious reluctance to sermonize on other people's problems. Even the Communists in the Soviet Union and elsewhere were relatively restrained.

Live television coverage via the Telstar satellite took the scene of tens of thousands of American Negroes and whites demonstrating peacefully in Washington yesterday into the homes of West Europeans at peak evening viewing hours.

The television coverage penetrated the Iron Curtain to Warsaw, Poland, but Moscow television canceled plans to screen the march five minutes before the program was due to go on. Instead, it relied on voice description and comment and presented a panel discussion on "the Negro revolution" in America.

Praises Administration

Moscow Radio also featured the march in a three-minute report that called it the biggest political event in United States history. Soviet newspapers published thousands of words on the March. Although sympathetic to American Negroes, Russian news media notably refrained from criticizing the American people as a whole and praised the Administration for its efforts in the civil rights field.

The Soviet Government newspaper *Izvestia* devoted its main editorial to the march, asserting: "The patience of twenty million Negroes has given way. All progressive mankind, all the honest-minded people in the United States, wish them success.

"The march on Washington is only the beginning of a long and difficult road. But having once embarked upon it, people fighting for their human dignity will not leave it, will not turn back."

No Reason Given

The Soviet television network gave no reason for its cancellation of the scheduled pickup from the Eurovision network in the West.

But as the marchers gathered without police hindrance and demonstrated peacefully, Soviet television directors may have decided that such fare might not be received well in a land where mass demonstrations are forbidden except with official sanction.

In Warsaw, however, Poles saw the demonstration on television screens in the first Telstar transmissions received in Communist Poland.

"How Prosperous They Seem"

The image was often jerky during two fifteen-minute telecasts but viewers could clearly make out closeups of the participants.

One Pole was impressed at the sight of the crowd at the foot of the Lincoln Memorial.

"It looks like Lincoln is embracing them all with his arms," he said.

"How prosperous they seem," a viewer commented as the Polish announcer related that the marchers were being asked to "return to their buses and cars."

The Polish announcer declared: "This is a great moral protest . . .

(Continued, Page 11, Column 7)

Utah Mine Rescue Stalls After Two Are Brought Up

Moab, Utah, Aug. 28 (AP)—The bodies of 8 dead miners were reported found tonight after 2 of 7 known survivors were brought up safely from a mine where an explosion had trapped 25 miners more than 2,700 feet underground.

Moab, Utah, Aug. 28 (AP) — A frustrating breakdown in communications temporarily stalled further attempts tonight to rescue more of the 25 miners trapped by an explosion more than 2,700 feet underground.

Two of seven known survivors were brought up to safety shortly before noon, but as dusk fell there was still no further contact with the other five. Three are known dead, the fate of the other fifteen a mystery.

"Cost Us More Time"

Rescuers, who themselves have been trapped for up to an hour in the shaft by mechanical failures of the "lift bucket," almost reached the bottom of the main shaft again about 6 P.M., then lost communications with teams at the top.

"We had to bring them back up. It's cost us more time," said Hugh Crawford, chief engineer of the Texas Gulf Sulphur Company which owns the potash mine.

"But the air is good where the five men are and it's getting better," he said. "We aren't too worried about them. They're still behind a lot of debris. They piled up some of it themselves to keep out the gas. That might have saved their lives."

No Voice Contact

He did not speculate on the other fifteen. There has been no sign of them.

Workers spent two hours this afternoon trying to set up a simple bell-system communications line. It failed. Walkie-talkie radios, used earlier with only spotty success, were brought back into service.

No one would even guess when

(Continued, Page 5, Column 1)

RIGHTS BILL AIMS GIVEN

13 Leaders Hold Talks With Congressional Chiefs

By JOSEPH R. L. STERNE
[Washington Bureau of The Sun]

Washington, Aug. 28—Thirteen civil rights leaders were given a cordial but cautious reception on Capitol Hill this morning before they took part in the mass march from the Washington Monument to the Lincoln Memorial.

In private talks with the Democratic and Republican leaderships, they stressed their desire for a civil rights bill even stronger than the omnibus package President Kennedy has sent to Congress.

The organizers of the march on Washington placed special emphasis on the need for a section

(Continued, Page 11, Column 7)

City And State Contingents Swell Throng On D.C. March

Thousands of marchers flood Maryland roads returning from demonstration in capital .... *Page* 46

By CHARLES WHITEFORD
[Sun Staff Correspondent]

Washington, Aug. 28—The pilgrims gathered early at St. Peter Claver Catholic Church in Baltimore.

After a mass, coffee, doughnuts and an admonition to try to duck if they saw bricks flying their way during the day, they boarded buses for the trip to Washington and the great civil rights demonstration.

Priests Ride On Buses

Some 50 priests, many of them bus riders, were in the contingent of several hundred who were to march under the banner of the Baltimore Catholic Interracial Council.

Mayor McKeldin was there to see them off. Three nuns waved a "God be with you" to the pilgrims.

The cavalcade grew as it swung past Lafayette Square and Metropolitan Methodist Church. Religious differences were forgotten. Before the cavalcade hit the Washington expressway, Catholic, Protestant, Jewish, labor and civic contingents were rolling along together.

Like a stream hitting the Mississippi, the Baltimore buses were intermixed with a seemingly endless flood of vehicles bearing "March on Washington" signs moving south on the expressway.

The 40 Negroes and whites on the bus sponsored by St. Pius V Church cracked jokes, munched on buns and drank orange juice as they moved along.

Only Unsympathetic Note

A passing car, bearing the legend, "National Association for the Advancement of White People," drew nothing but smiles.

That one sign, incidentally, was the only unsympathetic note encountered during the day.

The Baltimoreans encountered many familiar faces as they joined

(Continued, Page 12, Column 4)

ORDERLY CROWD HEARS APPEALS FOR FREEDOM, RACIAL 'TOGETHERNESS'

President Sees Cause Of U.S. Negroes Advanced, Calls Civil Rights Gathering 'Contribution To All Mankind'

As of early this morning, no reports had been received from any part of the country of violence or disturbances involving the participation of thousands of demonstrators homeward-bound from their civil rights march on Washington.

President

By WILLIAM KNIGHTON, JR.
[Washington Bureau of The Sun]

Washington, Aug. 28—President Kennedy declared tonight that the "nation can properly be proud" of the massive civil rights demonstration here today.

Not only was the cause of this country's 20,000,000 Negroes advanced, but the program was even more significant in its "contribution to all mankind," the President asserted.

The Chief Executive issued a formal statement praising the marchers after he had conferred with their leaders for an hour and fifteen minutes in his White House office.

"We have witnessed today in Washington tens of thousands of Americans—both Negro and white—exercising their right to assemble peaceably and direct the widest possible attention to a great national issue," the President said.

Discuss Legislation

Mr. Kennedy and the biracial committee held a friendly meeting, discussing the possibilities of the passage of civil rights legislation this year. But all was not business, for during a part of the period there was considerable banter among the participants as they munched sandwiches and sipped tea and coffee.

The President followed the demonstration via the television set in his office, in between official appointments and conferences with his staff. He was greatly relieved at the orderliness of the march and congratulated the ten leaders on its outcome and significance.

While posing for pictures with the march organizers, Mr. Kennedy remarked that he had heard some of the speeches.

A. Philip Randolph, president of the Brotherhood of Sleeping Car Porters and march chairman, asked him if he had heard the speech of Walter Reuther, head of the United Auto Workers.

"No, I did not hear Walter—but

(Continued, Page 11, Column 6)

D.C. March

By PHILIP POTTER
[Washington Bureau of The Sun]

Washington, Aug. 28 — A huge crowd of Negroes and whites—one of the biggest ever to come to the national capital -- today mingled good-humoredly at the Washington Monument and Lincoln Memorial and pledged itself to a continuing struggle for jobs and freedom for all Americans.

Marching on Washington by train, bus, plane, private automobile and on foot, they assembled about 200,000 strong on the great capital mall to hear Negro leaders, heads of the Catholic, Protestant and Jewish faiths and Negro and white entertainers express the need for "togetherness" of black man and white.

They sang, clapped hands to the music as ballad and folk singers canted of Negro troubles, they munched on box lunches; some fainted with exhaustion and heat; many, after all-night rides on buses and trains, simply laid down on the dry sod under the trees along Constitution and Independence avenues and slept.

"Pass the Bill"

They applauded celebrities from Hollywood and Broadway, greeted senators and House members with chants of "Pass the Bill, Pass the Bill."

They were moved by impassioned appeals from such Negro leaders as the Rev. Martin Luther King, the Rev. Fred Shuttlesworth, and A. Philip Randolph, president of the Brotherhood of Sleeping Car Porters, for "Freedom now."

But they were a peaceful, orderly crowd of Americans.

They had come to witness for integration and to cry an end to "second-class citizenship" for the Negro race, but the only bitterness that found voice today was that of a few white men on the periphery, a cluster of American Nazis around the person of George Lincoln Rockwell, who smoked a corncob pipe as he held a day-long news conference for any reporter who would listen to his views.

Observes Rules

The little group of twenty or so—Rockwell had hoped for 10,000, but said the white "cowards" of Virginia and Maryland had not responded—malevolently eyed the gigantic jubilee across Fourteenth street, but held rigidly to the conduct Police Chief Robert Murray had laid down for them.

They were out of their khaki uniforms with Swastika armbands, carried no placards, as is their wont, and except for the loquacious chief they were silent and morose.

When Carl Allen, deputy commander, tired of this pattern and sought to break it with a speech, the police promptly arrested him.

This was a day of white and black "togetherness" and they were no part of it.

It was also a day, according to Senator Humphrey (D., Minn.), assistant Democratic leader of the Senate and a march participant, "of good manners, good humor, yet solid purpose — good for Washington, good for the country and good for the world."

Noting that it was a fully integrated audience of whom a substantial part were white, and that a goodly number of priests, min

(Continued, Page 11, Column 1)

The Weather
Windy with occassional rain today. Rain ending tonight. High today in the 60's. Colder tonight. Yesterday's high, 60; low, 48.
(Details and Map, Page 24)

THE SUN

Kennedy Death Mourned By City, State: Back Page

Vol. 254—No. 6—E | PAID CIRCULATION SIX MONTHS ENDED 3/31/63 MORNING, 186,944 EVENING, 215,427 402,371 || SUNDAY 329,670 | BALTIMORE, SATURDAY, NOVEMBER 23, 1963 | Published daily except Sunday by The A. S. Abell Co. Calvert & Centre Sts., Baltimore, Md. Second class postage paid at Baltimore, Md. | 32 Pages | 7 Cents

Kennedy Murdered By Dallas Sniper; Johnson Sworn In As 36th President; Congressmen Stunned; World Mourns

Doctors Unable To Help

President Kennedy was shot to death yesterday by a sniper as his motorcade rolled down a Dallas street. Minutes later, Lyndon B. Johnson took the oath as thirty-sixth President. A self-proclaimed Marxist is being held in connection with the assassination. The martyred President's body will lie in state in the Capitol Rotunda tomorrow and Monday morning. Funeral services will be held Monday in St. Matthew's Cathedral, Washington.

PRESIDENT DESCRIBED AS 'MARTYR,' HIS FATE COMPARED TO LINCOLN'S

Warren Blames 'Bigots'; Britain Laments Kennedy's Death As If He Were One Of Its Own Leaders

Independence, Mo., Nov. 22 (AP) — Former President Harry Truman issued this statement today in the assassination of President Kennedy:

"I am shocked beyond words at the tragedy that has happened to our country and to President Kennedy's family today.

"The President's death is a great personal loss to the country and to me.

"He was an able President, one the people loved and trusted.

"Mrs. Truman and I send our deepest sympathy to Mrs. Kennedy and the family."

In The U.S.

By PETER J. KUMPA
[Washington Bureau of The Sun]

Washington, Nov. 22—The shooting of President Kennedy stunned and shocked the Congress today; his death brought tears and expressions of grief and sorrow as the nation's capital went into mourning.

Flags from the Capitol to the White House dropped to half-staff in tribute to the slain Chief Executive. So did the national flags of scores of foreign embassies, including the Red Banner of the Soviet Union, slip to the traditional position of tribute to the dead.

In Silence And Sorrow

All Government workers were let out of work an hour early and went home in silence and sorrow.

On this warm and sunny fall day, the capital went through an hour of torment and anxiety from the first news of the shooting to the official announcement that he had died in the Texas hospital. Work in most private and Government offices slowed to a halt during the long anxious minutes. Telephone circuits were overstrained as friends called each other to pass along the news.

"They Shall Not Prevail"

On Capitol Hill, many angry and bitter voices were raised against those responsible for the President's death.

Representative Boggs (D., La.), the House whip, compared his "martyrdom"to that of Abraham Lincoln and then blamed the "radicals and haters in politics" for causing his death.

"They are the ones who really pulled the trigger and killed a great American," said Boggs. "But they shall not prevail."

Said Chief Justice Earl Warren: "A great and good President has suffered martyrdom as a result of the hatred and bitterness that has been injected into the life of the nation by bigots, but his memory will always be an

(Continued, Page 6, Column 5)

And Britain

By DAVID M. CULHANE
[London Bureau of The Sun]

London, Nov. 22—Britain mourned the assassinated John Fitzgerald Kennedy tonight with a personal grief, as if at the death of one of its own leaders.

Prime Minister Sir Alec Douglas-Home, in a television tribute, said:

"There are times in the life when minds and hearts stand still and one such is now . . . everything in one cried out in protest at the news. . . ."

Obviously Deeply Moved

Sir Alec, obviously deeply moved, spoke of "this young gay and brave statesman, killed in the full vigor of his manhood, when he bore on his shoulders all the cares and hopes of the world." The entire nation paused in shock as the news came from the United States just after 7 P.M. British time.

Churches held immediate services, radio and television schedules were canceled and little crowds gathered on the streets of central London to hear the truth and register their bereavement.

Churchill Issues Statement

Former Prime Minister Sir Winston Churchill, 88, made an honorary citizen of the United States during President Kennedy's last year in office, issued this statement from his London home tonight:

"This monstrous act has taken from us a great statesman and a wise and valiant man.

"The loss to the United States

(Continued, Page 6, Column 6)

On Other Pages

Fabian Bachrach

John Fitzgerald Kennedy, Thirty-Fifth President

Major Challenges Marked Term

By JOSEPH R. L. STERNE
[Washington Bureau of The Sun]

Washington, Nov. 22 — John Fitzgerald Kennedy attached the label of the New Frontier to a career of daring and vision that culminated in the Presidency of the United States.

He was the first Catholic to hold the nation's highest office, the youngest man ever elected President, a Chief Executive who confronted the threat of nuclear catastrophe in a countdown atmosphere and a man faced with the most serious domestic issue—the race problem—since the Civil War.

Famous Inaugural Phrase

When he was killed today in Dallas he had served 34 months and 3 days as the thirty-fifth American President.

During this short span in office, Mr. Kennedy enriched the nation's political lore with his inaugural phrase—"Ask not what your country can do for you; ask what you can do for your country."

His rocking chair, his Boston-Harvard brogue, his shock of brown hair, his zest for political combat, his instinctive humor, his quest for peace through strength in a "world of diversity" all left their mark on an era of American history.

Scant months before his death, he had the satisfaction of concluding a treaty with the Soviet Union that banned nuclear tests that had poisoned the world's atmosphere for eighteen years.

In his characteristic caution, the late President greeted the Soviet acceptance of what was essentially an American formula for the test-ban with a warning that only a "first step" had been taken and that many trials lay ahead.

The existence in Cuba of Fidel Castro's Communist regime produced the greatest defeat and the greatest victory for Mr. Kennedy in the cold war struggle.

It was in April, 1961, less than three months after he took office, that the Bay of Pigs fiasco occurred. Anti-Castro exiles, lacking direct United States military support, were massacred or imprisoned in an abortive invasion that lowered American prestige and led to recriminations in Washington.

Khrushchev Warned

Mr. Kennedy took full blame upon himself. But he also seized the occasion to issue this warning to Soviet Premier Khrushchev:

"Let the record show that our patience is not inexhaustible . . . I want it clearly understood that this government will not hesitate in meeting its primary obligations which are the security of our nation."

Until the Cuban crisis in October, 1962, when Mr. Kennedy faced down Khrushchev and forced the removal of Soviet missiles from Cuba. Khrushchev apparently doubted the mettle of the young American President.

1961 Meeting In Vienna

At the Kennedy-Khrushchev meeting in Vienna in June, 1961, the Soviet leader was unyielding in his demands for the still-frustrated Communist "solution" to the Berlin problem.

Later that summer, Khrushchev announced a Soviet arms build-up—a provocation that Mr. Kennedy countered by stepping up the United States defense effort by $6,000,000,000.

And a year later, when the Soviet built the Berlin wall, Mr. Kennedy sent Vice President Johnson to Berlin and dispatched an armored column of 1,500 men through the autobahn to the beleaguered German city.

This show of United States strength etched deeper in the

(Continued, Page 5, Column 1)

ALL PROCEEDINGS STOPPED AT U.N.

Stevenson Says 'We Can Only Turn To Prayer'

By PAUL W. WARD
[Sun Staff Correspondent]

New York, Nov. 22—Word of President Kennedy's death swept through United Nations headquarters here this afternoon with something like hurricane force.

It put an abrupt end to all United Nations Assembly proceedings and an equally abrupt, if only temporary, end to Afro-Asian and Soviet bloc attacks on the United States Government as an "accomplice" of South African and Portuguese"racists" that had continued until 1.15 P.M.

Tributes Paid

It also produced a spate of tributes to the late Chief of State, including one by Adlai E. Stevenson, chief United States delegate, that said:

"The tragedy of this day is beyond instant comprehension. All of us who knew him will bear the grief of his death to the day of ours. And all men everywhere who love peace and justice and freedom will bow their heads.

"At such a moment we can only turn to prayer—prayer to comfort our grief, to sustain Mrs. Kennedy and his family, to strengthen President Johnson and to guide us in time to come. May God help us."

The first bulletins from Texas, reporting only that President Kennedy had been shot, sent delegates of 111 governments scurry-

(Continued, Page 8, Column 1)

Close Parallels Are Noted In Kennedy, Lincoln Deaths

By GERALD GRIFFIN
[Washington Bureau of The Sun]

Washington, Nov. 22—President Kennedy's sudden death today in Dallas ended a brief but brilliant chapter in American history.

In the flash of an assassin's gun the nation was sent plunging into grief for the young, popular President, who already had seemed well on the way to a triumphant re-election next year.

Was Close To President

At the same time the country was abruptly faced with the immediate change in command to a new President, Lyndon B. Johnson, and a new Administration which, while still Democratic in politics, will inevitably be different in tone and emphasis.

President Johnson has been close to President Kennedy, personally and officially, throughout the past three years. He has taken part in the formation and execution of high policy, and hence is thoroughly equipped, in knowledge of foreign and domestic policy matters, for his new responsibilities.

It was not lost upon Washington, which has been thinking much of President Lincoln during these centennial years of the Civil War, that President Kennedy's assassination today was an awesome parallel to Lincoln's death at the hands of an assassin in 1865.

Subjected To Abuse

Lincoln's death came at the end of the Civil War fought over the issue of slavery. Kennedy, in the Presidency during the nation's most violent argument over civil rights since the Civil War, was still in the midst of the controversy over passage of a new civil rights bill.

In the South, and even in some other sections of the country, Mr. Kennedy—even while enjoying

(Continued, Page 8, Column 1)

Oath Of Office Given Aboard Plane As 27 Watch

By WILLIAM KNIGHTON, JR.
[Washington Bureau of The Sun]

Washington, Nov. 22—Lyndon Baines Johnson became the thirty-sixth President of the United States today, succeeding John Fitzgerald Kennedy, whose meteoric career was cut short by an assassin's bullet.

Two hours after shots rang out in Dallas, Vice President Johnson took the oath of office. The ceremony was held in the Presidential quarters of Air Force One—the Presidential jet plane—in Dallas.

First Statement

On landing at Andrews Air Force Base in nearby Prince Georges county tonight, Mr. Johnson made his first statement as Chief Executive. He said.

"This is a sad time for all people.

"We have suffered a loss that cannot be weighed. For me, it is a deep personal tragedy.

"I know that the world shares the sorrow that Mrs. Kennedy and her family bear.

"I will do my best. That is all I can do.

"I ask for your help—and God's."

The Presidential oath was read to Mr. Johnson by Judge Sarah T. Hughes of the Dallas Federal District Court, an old personal and political friend.

27 Witness Ceremony

Twenty-seven persons—all the plane compartment could hold—heard Mr. Johnson take the oath Jacqueline Kennedy was one of the 27. Dark splotches on her suit and stockings showed where her husband's blood had flowed upon her.

At that time, the President's body was aboard the plane in which Mr. Kennedy had so often ridden—in the United States, Latin America, Europe and Canada. The body was in a bronze casket with black cloth top.

Mrs. Kennedy sat with it in silent vigil in the Presidential lounge at the rear of the plane. Several closest members of his personal staff, long personal friends, sat with her for much of

(Continued, Page 6, Column 1)

PRESIDENT JOHNSON

SAD TRIBUTES BEGIN TODAY

Kennedy Family To Gather At The White House

By MURIEL DOBBIN
[Washington Bureau of The Sun]

Washington, Nov. 22—The Kennedy family will gather once again at the White House tomorrow, this time it will be to pay their last respects to their brother, President John Fitzgerald Kennedy, who was assassinated today and whose body will lie "in repose" in the East Room.

The body, flown from Dallas, Texas, to Andrews Air Force Base today, was taken from there to Bethesda Naval Hospital.

It was believed Mrs. Kennedy, who returned to Wáshington on the Presidential jet carrying her husband's body, would remain at the naval hospital tonight.

Johnson To Follow Family

Tomorrow at 10 A.M. the family will be the first to see his body in the White House. During the day, their visit will be followed by that of President Johnson, who was sworn in just before the return flight from Dallas to Washington.

Others who will make the sad visit to the East Room will include former President Dwight Eisenhower, the Speaker of the House of Representatives, John W. McCormack, members of the

(Continued, Page 8, Column 8)

Shots At Motorcade Wound Kennedy In Neck, Head

By PHILIP POTTER
[(Sun Staff Correspondent]

Dallas, Nov. 22—President Kennedy died today at 2 P.M. here from an assassin's bullet.

An hour and 39 minutes later, Lyndon B. Johnston was sworn in as the nation's thirty-sixth President aboard Air Force One, the Presidential plane, a few minutes before it took off for Washington carrying the body of Mr. Kennedy.

President Kennedy and Gov. John Connally were both shot as they neared the end of a triumphal motorcade that brought them from Love Field through downtown Dallas. The Governor remains in serious condition at Parkland Hospital, to which both men were taken.

Rifle Believed Used

The bullets that took the President's life and struck Connally down apparently were fired by a rileman from an upper-floor window of a book warehouse on the parade route.

In the car with the two were both men's wives and two Secret Service agents. Only the President and Governor were hit.

Mrs. Kennedy and Mrs. Connally both grabbed their husbands as they slumped and sought shelter with them on the floor of the open Presidential Lincoln Continental.

"Oh, no," Mrs. Kennedy moaned.

The motorcade slowed and a Secret Service man lifted a submachine gun toward the window from which the shots—three or four of them—apparently came.

Radio Telephone Used

Then. Mrs. Connally said, an agent in the front seat of the car picked up a radio telephone and ordered a full-speed dash to Parkland Hospital.

The President had wounds on both the front of the neck and back of the head, the first possibly an entry wound and the second an exit wound.

Mrs. Connally said she did not believe he said anything after he was shot.

Dr. Malcolm Perry, attending surgeon at Parkland and first to attend the President in the emergency room, said Mr. Kennedy never regained consciousness as eight or nine physicians attempted to save him, even using external heart massage.

Dr. Kemp Clark, chief of neuro-surgery, said the attending physicians elected 2 P.M. as the time of death, about 30 minutes after the Presidential limousine drew up at the hospital.

Johnson In Third Car

Vice President Johnson, his wife and Senator Yarborough (D., Texas) were two cars back—a Secret Service car between theirs and the President's—when the shooting occurred about 1:30 P.M.

The Presidential car and those carrying the Secret Service men and the Johnsons, after the mo-

(Continued, Page 5, Column 7)

Texan Who Lived In Russia Quizzed In Assassination

Dallas, Texas, Nov. 22 (AP)—A 24-year-old man who said four years ago he wanted Russian citizenship was questioned today to see whether he had any connection with the assassination of President Kennedy.

He was identified as Lee Harvey Oswald, of Fort Worth, Texas. He was pulled screaming and yelling from the Texas theater in the Oak Cliff section of Dallas shortly after a Dallas policeman was shot to death.

Four Miles Away

Murder charges were filed against him in the death of the patrolman. Capt. Will Fritz, of the Dallas police homicide department, said it had been established the man had been in the building from which the shots that felled the President came—at the time they were fired.

The theater where Oswald was arrested is some 4 miles from the triple underpass where Mr. Kennedy was shot.

Just before 7 P.M., Fritz said Oswald had been identified from a police line-up as the man who shot Patrolman J. D. Tippett. He said an eyewitness made the identification.

As Oswald was returned from the line-up, a reporter shouted, "Did you kill the President?"

Oswald replied in a loud voice, "No, I did not kill the President. I did not kill anyone."

Married A Russian

Police said Oswald, who worked at the book depository building from which the fatal shots came had lived in Russia and married a Russian woman. On November 1, 1959, he had said he was applying for Russian citizenship.

Oswald told the United States Embassy in Moscow that he had been a tourist in Russia since October 13 that year.

The Fort Worth *Star-Telegram* confirmed that the man held in Dallas was the same Oswald and said his mother was being taken

(Continued, Page 8, Column 5)

Other News Of Tragedy

The Weather
Quite warm and humid today and tomorrow with scattered thundershowers. Highs in low 90's. Yesterday's high, 94; low, 76.
(Details and Map, Page 24.)

THE SUN FINAL

(Registered United States Patent Office)

Vol. 255—No. 41— F | PAID CIRCULATION SIX MONTHS ENDED 3/31/64 MORNING. 187,058 EVENING. 215,564 402,622 || SUNDAY 333,759 | BALTIMORE, FRIDAY, JULY 3, 1964 | Published daily except Sunday by The A. S. Abell Co. Calvert & Centre Sts., Baltimore, Md. Second class postage paid at Baltimore, Md. | 36 Pages | 7 Cents

Johnson Signs Broad Civil Rights Bill Into Law; Many Southern Business Men Pledge Compliance

U.S. EXPECTED TO ACT FAST IF REDS INCREASE SOUTHEAST ASIA WAR

Confidence Now Growing In Washington That Greater Use Of American Arms Will Be Made Wherever Situation Warrants It

Copter guns save ambushed convoy in Vietnam..........Page 2
General Taylor quits Army for duty at Saigon .... Page 2

By MARK S. WATSON
[Sun Military Correspondent]

Washington, July 2—There is greatly increased confidence in Washington that any sharp increase in Communist insurgency either in South Vietnam or Laos will trigger a swift and vigorous response for American arms in Southeast Asia.

The ability to provide that response, whether by United States land, sea or air forces has always existed. The will to provide it now is apparent.

It is coincidence that this confidence rises at the very time when Gen. Maxwell D. Taylor, late chairman of the Joint Chiefs of Staff, is going out to Saigon, this time as United States Ambassador to South Vietnam.

Lodge Suggests Change

This new and stronger policy, however, was plainly suggested yesterday by Henry Cabot Lodge, the retiring Ambassador, when he acknowledged that, beyond today's United States activities, there are things which can be done to hurt the Communist aggressors. But Lodge stated meticulously that these matters are "classified" and hence not free for his public discussion.

Today those "things" become much plainer. They can be described as follows:

1. Aerial attack in much more determined fashion on Pathet Lao targets in Laos. This must be conditioned on a request from Souvanna Phouma, Laos's neutralist Premier, for punitive action by his American allies against invaders who continue violating their 1962 pledge of support for a peaceful, neutral Laos.

Targets Small

2. The targets referred to are for the most part small and not nearly as lucrative as were the big installations of conventional warfare in World War II which our bombers destroyed. But they include roads, ammunition dumps, supply points, anti-aircraft batteries and troop encampments—enough to "annoy" the Pathet Lao command and warn that still more will follow if necessary.

3. A conceivable second step would be against targets in North Vietnam, the source of most of the Red insurgent supplies pouring down through Laos and into the guerrilla strongholds in South Vietnam.

4. A "tit-for-tat" operation so plainly carried out as to impress the Red command at higher levels. That is, if the Viet Cong guerrillas should blow up a bridge, a bridge in North Vietnam would be taken out; a road for a road; a very strong reprisal for an assassination, etc. The aim would be to follow precisely what the Red guerrilla does with a like performance against the higher Red command—only more of it.

5. This would undeniably be "escalation" of the present insurgency war, but escalation under very tight control. Most significantly, one hears from responsible sources no suggestion whatever of the sort of escalation which is universally most

(Continued, Page 2, Column 2)

LODGE CHIDED BY DIRKSEN

Vietnam Will Be Campaign Issue, Senator Says

By PHILIP POTTER
[Washington Bureau of The Sun]

Washington, July 2 — Republican congressional leaders chastized former Ambassador Henry Cabot Lodge today for doubting that Administration policy in South Vietnam can be made an effective campaign issue.

It will be, said Senator Dirksen (R., Ill.), Senate GOP leader, and Representative Halleck (R., Ind.), House leader. They asserted that the Administration's promotion of "coexistence" and expanded trade with the Soviet bloc also will be a good target for Republican attack.

Dirksen also got back at Lodge today for saying in effect yesterday that Dirksen did little good for Senator Robert Taft of Ohio in 1952 by nominating him for President at the GOP convention. Lodge thus implied that Senator Goldwater will derive no more advantage when Dirksen gets up to nominate him at this year's convention.

Lodge Aiding Scranton

Lodge, who helped mastermind Dwight Eisenhower's nomination in 1952, this year is working for Gov. William Scranton of Pennsylvania.

At a news conference today, Dirksen recalled that he had contributed money and energy to the losing Republican campaign in 1960 when Lodge had second place on the ticket.

"Perhaps if he hadn't kept banker's hours, we would have fared a little better," Dirksen said. "You can put that in capitals and emphasize it."

Rubbing it in, Dirksen continued that if Goldwater is the nominee he will put on a "rugged, vigorous and robust" campaign.

(Continued, Page 5, Column 5)

BULLETIN

Washington, July 2 (AP)—The State Department said tonight it has received a report that Honduran authorities have taken into custody several shrimp boats off Honduras' Caribbean coast.

A spokesman said it is believed that some or possibly all of the eight or nine vessels held today are American owned.

He said the report came from Charles R. Burroughs, United States Ambassador to Honduras.

Burroughs also reported, the spokesman said, that Honduran authorities examined the ships for papers and found them without proper documentation. Four other boats also were examined and released after proper documentation was established, Burroughs's report said.

U.S., RUSSIA CLASH OVER NATO A-FORCE

Hope For Pact To Bar Nuclear-Arms Spread Receives Setback

Geneva, July 2 (AP)—Hope for an international agreement to prevent the spread of nuclear weapons received a severe setback here today as the United States and Russia clashed head-on over the proposed multilateral force for the Atlantic alliance.

In a strongly worded speech to the seventeen-nation disarmament conference, the Soviet Deputy Foreign Minister, Valerian Zorin, demanded that the West cancel plans for the multilateral nuclear force.

Otherwise, he said, the West must face the consequences if nuclear weapons get into the hands of other nations.

Sharply Worded Reply

The chief United States delegate, William C. Foster, in a sharply worded reply, accused the Soviet Union of using "groundless political arguments against the multilateral force in the pursuit of its long-standing aim to disrupt NATO defensive arrangements."

Foster said the Russian allegations against the mixed-manned force were based on "false reasoning and ungrounded fears."

Zorin repeated Soviet charges that the proposed force — ships armed with nuclear weapons and manned by men of different nationalities—is just an excuse to give West Germany access to nuclear weapons.

Claim Challenged

Challenging the American claim that the force is the best way of preventing other nations from getting their hands on the nuclear trigger, Zorin said:

"If they really mean this, it can only signify one thing: The Government of the United States itself considers the creation of the NATO multilateral force to be at least as effective a means of quenching the nuclear thirst of West German revenge-seekers as the creation of their own nuclear weapons."

Foster said the multilateral force is designed to protect Western Europe against the Soviet nuclear threat and is the only alternative to the spread of nuclear weapons in Europe and throughout the world.

The United States delegate called for an international agreement to prevent the spread of nuclear weapons and warned of the dangers of these weapons falling into the hands of powers which at present have no nuclear armaments.

Refers To Proposals

He referred to series of United States proposals to achieve this aim, including international control of all transfers of fissionable material for peaceful purposes and arrangements for such bodies as the International Atomic Energy to control the nuclear activities of the atomic powers.

Defending West Germany

(Continued, Page 2, Column 5)

Erhard To Ask Paris-Bonn Action On European Unity

[Bonn Bureau of The Sun]

Bonn, July 2—Chancellor Ludwig Erhard will propose bilateral French-German action for European political unity when General Charles de Gaulle is here for talks tomorrow and Saturday.

Erhard's decision, revealed by authoritative sources today, has been reached under the impression of yet another failure to get the six nations of the European Common Market to move for political unity.

3 Nations Reject Plan

A proposal by Erhard, made secretly to the other Common Market five last week, for setting up a joint experts commission to "screen possibilities" for political cooperation acceptable to all of the six, has been turned down by Holland, Italy and Belgium.

Only tiny Luxembourg had agreed to cooperate in the commission.

Now Erhard, under growing pressure from his Christian Democratic party, is reportedly ready to go ahead with France alone

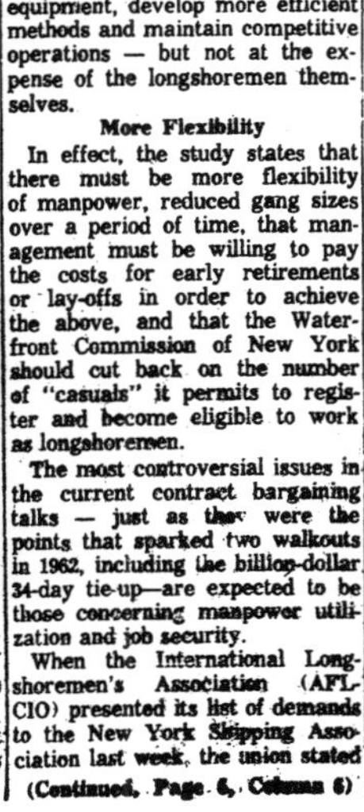

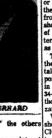

CHANCELLOR ERHARD

in order to "nudge" the others into following.

Reliable sources here point out that the Erhard offer, which hints

(Continued, Page 2, Column 8)

THE PRESIDENT SIGNS—President Johnson signs the civil rights bill into law yesterday. Looking on, from left, are Senators Dirksen and Humphrey and Representative Halleck.

Goldwater Concerned About Rights Issue

By GERALD GRIFFIN
[Washington Bureau of The Sun]

Washington, July 2 — Senator Barry Goldwater, looking ahead to the campaign he will conduct if he wins the Republican Presidential nomination, is seriously concerned about the explosive civil rights issue.

His own position is that, while he voted against the bill in the Senate, he would uphold the civil rights law if he were elected President, and would have an Attorney General who would enforce it.

Won't Seek Repeal

He would not seek its repeal, as he said to the Illinois delegates on Monday. His hope, as he also said in Illinois, is that civil rights will not be an issue in the autumn election campaign.

It can be said, further, that he does not intend to exploit the so-called white backlash, which many politicians think will operate in his favor in northern cities and suburbs.

The white backlash refers to the resentment and fears of white persons who are disturbed by Negro demonstrations for equal rights and who are concerned, in particular, about the effects Negroes may have on their own jobs or on the value of their properties.

Goldwater Uncertain

Yet the Arizona Senator is fully aware that such feelings exist, and could explode into violence when, for example, anti-Goldwater Negro demonstrators may

(Continued, Page 6, Column 2)

STUDY ASKS DOCK CHANGES AT N.Y.

Use Of Men, Job Security Involved In U.S. Report

By HELEN DELICH BENTLEY
[Maritime Editor of The Sun]

New York, July 2 — Sweeping changes in the use of longshoremen and their job security on the New York waterfront are called for in the Department of Labor's report which was presented to both management and labor this week.

Many changes that might be effected here in contract bargaining as a result of the 54-page study — released publicly late today—would naturally spread to other East and Gulf Coast ports, including Baltimore.

Both sides are told that they should take concrete steps toward implementing technological changes which would enable the shipping industry to improve equipment, develop more efficient methods and maintain competitive operations — but not at the expense of the longshoremen themselves.

More Flexibility

In effect, the study states that there must be more flexibility of manpower, reduced gang sizes over a period of time, that management must be willing to pay the costs for early retirements or lay-offs in order to achieve the above, and that the Waterfront Commission of New York should cut back on the number of "casuals" it permits to register and become eligible to work as longshoremen.

The most controversial issues in the current contract bargaining talks — just as they were the points that sparked two walkouts in 1962, including the billion-dollar 34-day tie-up—are expected to be those concerning manpower utilization and job security.

When the International Longshoremen's Association (AFL-CIO) presented its list of demands to the New York Shipping Association last week, the union stated

(Continued, Page 6, Column 6)

SCRANTON POSES ISSUE TO PANEL

Wants GOP Unit To Declare Rights Law Valid

By ERNEST B. FURGURSON
[Sun Staff Correspondent]

Sioux Falls, S.D., July 2—Gov. William W. Scranton today said he would ask the GOP Platform Committee to take direct issue with Senator Barry Goldwater by specifically stating that the new civil rights law is constitutional.

Scranton, moving out of the Northwest area and back into the Dakotas in search of delegate backing for his Presidential nomination drive, is scheduled to address the Platform Committee next Thursday.

Opposed 2 Major Parts

Goldwater, who said when he voted against the civil rights measure that he considered two of its major parts to be unconstitutional, will appear before the body Friday.

The Pennsylvania Governor told a Eugene (Ore.) press conference he had not asked anyone to place his name in nomination at the Republican convention, nor had he asked anyone else to enlist a third person for the task.

Decisions on this and other points of convention strategy will be made this weekend when he returns to Harrisburg, Scranton said.

Will Return To Illinois

After these final preconvention strategy sessions, Scranton will fly back to Illinois, where at least 48 of the State's 58 delegates have been captured by Goldwater, to make another effort to arouse public pressure on the delegation.

He will spend all day Monday and Tuesday there, probably meeting with Henry Cabot Lodge, who has resigned his ambassadorship to South Vietnam to help Scranton's nomination drive. Scranton plans to arrive at San Francisco late Wednesday.

Although Goldwater has said that if elected President he would

(Continued, Page 6, Column 1)

289-126 Vote In House Passes Senate Version

'Some Real Trouble' Is Predicted In Mississippi

Atlanta, July 2 (AP)—Passage of the civil rights bill by Congress today brought varied reactions in the South ranging from ready compliance to outright defiance.

Lester Maddox, operator of a segregated restaurant in Atlanta, said he would go to jail before he would serve Negro customers. Charles Lebedin, who said demonstrators had ruined his restaurant business, displayed a huge sign in a window offering to sell out at a reasonable price.

Directors of the Georgia Restaurant Association urged members to abide by the civil rights act. The association vigorously opposed the bill but said with its passage "we have no alternative but to comply."

Compliance Urged

The Atlanta grand jury urged compliance with the new law "in fact and in spirit, for where law ends tyranny begins."

A number of Atlanta hotels, motels and restaurants voluntarily dropped racial bars even before passage of the civil rights bill became certain.

Gov. Paul Johnson of Mississippi said he expected "some real trouble" when Negroes seek to desegregate public accommodations in his State.

He told a news conference at Jackson, Miss., that he did not know of any measures that could be taken at this time to avert trouble.

Asked if he felt hotel owners should comply with the law, Johnson said, "I don't think they should. I think it should be tested in the courts. A great many people feel it is unconstitutional."

The Governor said some owners of public accommodations will go out of business rather than comply with provisions of the law.

In South Carolina, hotel, motel and restaurant owners indicated they would abide by the law. But one who declined to be quoted said he had no intention of serving Negroes.

Hugh Smith, manager of a hotel in Columbia, S.C., said he believed there would be so little business for major hotels from Negro customers "that it won't be noticed."

Tests Expected

Another South Carolina hotel manager who declined use of his name said he expected hotels, motels and restaurants to be tested by Negroes for compliance "but when the tests have died down, things won't be much different from the way they have been."

Wesley Graves, manager of a hotel in Charleston, S.C., where Negroes made integration attempts a year ago, said "the liberal left hasn't given us much choice . . . with great reluctance we must give it [the new law] consideration as the law."

In New Orleans, where the Hotel Roosevelt has held out against the integration movement among

(Continued, Page 4, Column 5)

C.O.R.E. Tests Rights Bill Swiftly

Kansas City, July 2 (AP)—The Congress of Racial Equality tested the civil rights bill a minute after its signing today with a sit-in at a barbershop in the hotel where C.O.R.E. is holding its convention.

Gene Young, a 13-year-old Negro from Jackson, Miss., walked into the Muehlebach Hotel's basement barbershop and asked for a haircut.

Gus Imbeau, head barber, said he told the boy, "If you can find anyone here to cut your hair, O.K." The shop has eleven chairs with nine barbers on duty.

Imbeau said Young then asked for an appointment tomorrow and Imbeau replied that he was booked up.

Young then left the shop and returned with about 25 demonstrators, some of whom took seats on the waiting benches.

UNION FOUND GUILTY OF BIAS

Metal Workers Local Loses NLRB Certification

Unemployment rate rises to 5.3% in June............Page 5

Washington, July 2 (AP) — The National Labor Relations Board today ruled a labor union guilty of racial discrimination and a civil rights spokesman hailed the decision as a more effective weapon for Negro employment rights than the new civil rights bill.

The NLRB ruling stripped the Independent Metal Workers Union of its Government certification at the Hughes Tool Company, in Houston, Texas, opening the door for another union to displace it.

"Almost Revolutionary"

"This decision, I think, is of almost revolutionary proportions," said Robert L. Carter, general counsel for the National Association for the Advancement of Colored People.

Union discrimination, particularly in the building trades, has long been a focus for demonstrations on the part of civil rights groups.

Carter said the ruling would have more immediate practical effect than the fair employment section of the civil rights bill and would pave the way for acceptance of the new law.

"I would certainly encourage any Negro employee who feels he is being discriminated against to try this procedure" rather than seek relief under the civil rights act, Carter said.

He gave a number of reasons, including the delayed effectiveness of the fair employment provision of the civil rights bill and the position of the NLRB as a

(Continued, Page 5, Column 1)

President Promises To Enforce Law Without Delay

Text of President's statement on signing rights bill........Page 4

By JOSEPH R. L. STERNE
[Washington Bureau of The Sun]

Washington, July 2—The strongest, broadest, most controversial civil rights bill in the nation's history became the law of the land tonight.

President Johnson, in a White House ceremony attended by the legislators and Negro leaders who pushed the measure to enactment, signed the bill five hours after it was given final approval by Congress.

Urging Americans to "close the springs of racial poison," the President announced that he had directed Government agencies to enforce the law "without delay."

Vengeance Decried

But he cautioned against any spirit of vengeance against the South, emphasized the national coverage of the law and said the Federal Government would step in only when state and local organizations fail.

In what may have been a gesture to show his desire for voluntary and harmonious compliance, Mr. Johnson appointed Leroy Collins, a former Florida governor, as the first director of the Community Relations Service.

This is an agency established by the new law to help communities settle disputes arising from discriminatory practices.

Broad Authority

Other sections of the eleven-title measure give the Federal Government far-reaching authority to combat bias in voting, in public accommodations, in publicly operated facilities, in schools, in the use of Federal funds locally and in the operation of labor unions and private employment.

With the exception of the fair employment practices provisions, all parts of the law go into effect immediately.

Industry will have one year to prepare before the law is applied first to businesses with 100 employees or more and then, on a sliding scale, to businesses with 25 or more employees in five years.

Kennedy Pressed Bill

National attention will focus almost immediately on the ban against discrimination in restaurants, hotels, theaters and other privately owned accommodations catering to the public.

The barring of Negroes from such facilities in many parts of the South set off demonstrations in Birmingham, Ala., last year which, in turn, impelled the late President Kennedy to ask vast new Federal powers against discrimination.

Today—one year and two weeks after Mr. Kennedy sent his civil rights bill to Capitol Hill—Congress approved a measure even stronger than the late President proposed.

No Changes Made

Final passage came when the House, by a vote of 289 to 126, accepted without change the Senate-passed version of the measure, which was first passed by the House February 10.

Today's passage of the bill without change, a product of the bipartisan leadership, avoided a Senate-House conference on the

(Continued, Page 4, Column 2)

Senators Vote Pay Raises For Themselves And Others

By RODNEY CROWTHER
[Washington Bureau of The Sun]

Washington, July 2—After two days of debate, devoted mainly to warding off amendments, the Senate late today by a 58 to 21 roll-call vote passed a $564,000,000 pay raise bill.

The lawmakers voted to give themselves a $7,500 salary boost to $30,000 and to raise salaries throughout the rest of the Federal Government in response to President Johnson's urgent plea that such a pay boost is desperately needed.

Lausche Rejects Raise

The breakdown of the vote on passage showed 43 Democrats and 15 Republicans in support of the measure, and 12 Democrats and 9 Republicans against it. Both Maryland senators voted for the bill.

One Democrat, Senator Lausche (Ohio), who bitterly opposed the measure throughout, announced that he will "not accept" his salary increase. He charged it is reckless for Congress to vote itself a pay raise while the Federal budget is still operating in the "red."

Before moving to a final vote on the measure the senators decided that they were giving members of the Supreme Court too big a pay boost and lopped $5,000 off what they had planned.

Supreme Court Cut

On a proposal by Senator Allott (R., Col.) they decided that a $2,500 increase for each of the nine justices is enough. They voted 46 to 40 to give the Chief Justice $38,000 a year, instead of the $43,000 in the bill, and associate justices $37,500 instead of the $42,500 in the bill.

The measure as approved must now go to a conference with the House to adjust a number of differences the senators made in the original House-passed bill, which

(Continued, Page 6, Column 4)

On Other Pages

The Weather
Rain or drizzle this morning and cloudy this afternoon. High temperature near 64. Yesterday's high, 55; low, 42.
(Details and Map, Page 27.)

THE SUN FINAL

(Registered United States Patent Office)

Vol. 256—No. 71—F | PAID CIRCULATION SIX MONTHS ENDED 9/30/64 MORNING, 190,628 EVENING, 213,008 403,636 | SUNDAY 339,420 | BALTIMORE, MONDAY, FEBRUARY 8, 1965 | Published daily except Sunday by The A. S. Abell Co. Calvert & Centre Sts., Baltimore, Md. 21203 Second class postage paid at Baltimore, Md. | 36 Pages | 10 Cents

49 U.S. Planes Raid North Vietnam Military Base In Retaliation For Red Attacks On GI Compounds; Johnson Sends Missile Battalion To South Vietnam

President Also Orders Dependents Flown Out

'We Seek No Wider War,' Administration Insists

Washington, Feb. 7 (AP) — McGeorge Bundy, Presidential adviser, returned home tonight from a special mission to Vietnam and promptly sped to the White House for a direct report to the President.

By ERNEST B. FURGURSON
[*Washington Bureau of The Sun*]

Washington, Feb. 7—President Johnson ordered American forces to "clear the decks" for possible further action today after authorizing air strikes against North Vietnamese targets.

He began by directing the orderly withdrawal of some 1,800 United States dependents from South Vietnam. Military and commercial aircraft will be made available to Ambassador Maxwell D. Taylor to carry out the evacuation.

Marines Ordered In

Mr. Johnson also ordered a Marine battalion of Hawk anti-aircraft missiles rushed into South Vietnam.

The White House and top officials of the State and Defense departments all insisted that "we seek no wider war" in the area.

They emphasized that the action was a carefully considered reprisal to surprise attacks on United States troops in South Vietnam.

Word "Crisis" Avoided

All the public statements made here today avoided using the word "crisis." Robert S. McNamara, Secretary of Defense, said he did not consider the new developments to be a "turning point" in the Vietnamese war.

The American air raid had no connection with the presence of Soviet Premier Alexei N. Kosygin in Hanoi or that of McGeorge Bundy, special presidential assistant, in Saigon, according to George W. Ball, acting Secretary of State.

Trying To "Test Will'

Ball said there was no question but that Viet Cong attacks on American bases were a deliberate attempt to "test the will" of the Saigon government and the United States.

American forces could not fail to respond without giving a "misleading signal" to the regime in Hanoi, he declared.

He said he hoped the raid would convince the Communists that the United States was firm in its commitment to help South Vietnam in its struggle.

This was in the same spirit as the original White House announcement of the raids, which followed the second urgent National Security Council meeting called by the President within twelve hours.

Mr. Johnson was notified of the Viet Cong attacks against American installations yesterday afternoon, as soon as word was received in Washington.

He conferred immediately with Defense and State Departments and Central Intelligence Agency officials, then called a National

(Continued, Page 4, Column 3)

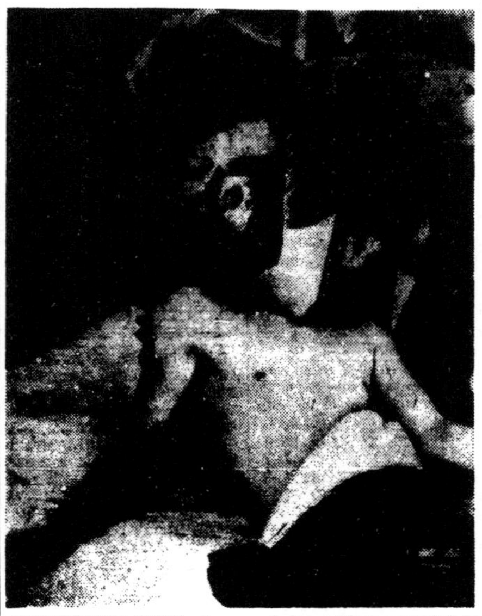

COMFORTING HAND—A nurse helps soldier wounded in Viet attack at Pleiku at 8th Army Hospital at Nha Trang.

U.S. Denies Raid Is Linked To Kosygin's Hanoi Visit

By JOSEPH R. L. STERNE
[*Washington Bureau of The Sun*]

Washington, Feb. 7—The United States promptly informed the Russians today that the American retaliatory attack on North Vietnamese bases had nothing to do with the presence in Hanoi of Soviet Premier Alexei N. Kosygin.

Through diplomatic channels, the Soviet Union was given to understand that the United States considered the Communist Viet Cong raids on installations in South Vietnam an obvious provocation that absolutely demanded a response.

Far From Hanoi

In striking back, the Russians were told, the United States hit targets far from Hanoi which could not possibly subject Kosygin and his visiting Russian delegation to personal danger.

Also emphasized was the White House statement that the United States seeks "no wider war" and that any further escalation will be due to North Vietnamese aggression.

These reported American assurances were based, in part, on a hunch Kosygin may not have been informed beforehand of the Communist raids and may have found himself somewhat on the spot diplomatically.

If so, the United States apparently wanted him to know that the future of the tenuous detente between Washington and Moscow will depend to some extent on his method of handling the current crisis.

Informed sources surmised that the North Vietnamese carefully timed their attack to coincide with the visit to Hanoi of the high-level Soviet delegation and the concurrent inspection tour of South Vietnam by President Johnson's personal representative, McGeorge Bundy.

"Paper Tiger" Theme

If this country had not retaliated, the North Vietnamese probably would have triumphantly informed their Soviet visitors that Uncle Sam is a "paper tiger" who can be taunted even with a Presidential representative on the ground.

Since the North Vietnamese were sure to have considered the other alternative—the American counterattack that did occur—it was expected here that the Hanoi regime would try to use the crisis

(Continued, Page 5, Column 2)

MADDOX TO SELL HIS RESTAURANT

Closes Door, Puts Up Sign As Negro Seeks Service

Atlanta, Feb. 7 (AP)—Lester A. Maddox, avowed segregationist who only yesterday said he would integrate his restaurant after a Federal judge found him in contempt, said today his cafeteria is up for sale.

The weary but smiling Maddox told a news conference, called shortly after a lone Negro tried to eat at the cafeteria, "The life I have lived and the torment that has been mine since yesterday, would make death itself seem sweet."

Loses Court Fight

Maddox lost a lengthy court fight Friday when United States District Judge Frank A. Hooper ruled that he was in civil contempt, the first such ruling under the Civil Rights Act.

Maddox was under Federal injunction to cease discriminating against Negroes. When that court order was handed down last August he closed the Pickrick Restaurant. But he opened again September 26 under a new name, Lester Maddox Cafeteria. He again refused to serve Negroes and the contempt citation followed.

Hooper ruled that Maddox would

(Continued, Page 9, Column 1)

PIER PACT NEARS IN PHILADELPHIA

Agreement Reached On Key Point Blocking Peace

By HELEN DELICH BENTLEY
[*Maritime Editor of The Sun*]

Washington, Feb. 7 — Negotiators late tonight finally hurdled the obstacle holding up longshore bargaining in the port of Philadelphia and reached an agreement on an annual wage guarantee and flexibility for Local 1291.

However, this does not mean the end of the country's costliest waterfront strike—in its twenty-eighth day today—because contracts must be settled for four other crafts in Philadelphia, for all longshoremen in Texas and the South Atlantic ports.

No Meetings Scheduled

As a matter of fact, the general consensus tonight was that it will be at least Thursday night or Friday before any longshoremen are back at work—and then only if the Philadelphia contracts are all closed out tomorrow and ratified by the membership, and settlements are achieved immediately in Galveston and Miami.

No meetings are scheduled yet at either one of the two latter sites.

But the Philadelphia break-

(Continued, Page 11, Column 1)

On Other Pages

U.S. INFORMS U.N. OF ACTION IN VIETNAM

Tells Security Council Its Attack Was In Self-Defense

By PAUL W. WARD
[*Sun Staff Correspondent*]

New York, Feb. 7—The United States formally advised the United Nations' Security Council here tonight of the retaliatory action its air forces took early today against a Communist troop concentration point in North Vietnam as "a justified matter of self-defense."

In the process, it also differentiated — by the manner in which it addressed the council —between that action and a bombing raid against North Vietnamese torpedo-boat bases carried out at President Johnson's order last August 4.

Then, it asked for an "urgent" meeting of the Security Council on "the serious situation created by deliberate attacks of the Hanoi regime on United States naval vessels."

Written Notice

This time, instead of asking for action by the council, it merely gave the eleven-nation body written notice of Washington's latest reprisal action in accordance with a provision in the United Nations' charter that Adlai Stevenson, chief United States delegate, had cited while pressing for a council meeting that both North Vietnam and the Soviet Union resisted last August.

In its report tonight, however, the United States reserved "the right to bring this matter to the Security Council if the situation warrants it" and added:

"In a statement issued this morning on behalf of President Johnson, the United States Government once again emphasized that 'We seek no wider war; (but) whether or not this course can be maintained lies with the North Vietnamese aggressors.' "

What Provision Says

The provision in the world organization's constitution to which Stevenson had referred last August says: "Nothing in the present charter shall impair the inherent right of individual or collective self-defense if an armed attack occurs against a member of the United Nations."

But that self-defense action shall be exercised only "until the Security Council has taken measures necessary to maintain international peace and security," the charter provision (Article 51) also stipulates before adding:

"Measures taken by members in the exercise of this right of self-defense shall be immediately reported to the Security Council and shall not in any way affect the authority and responsibility of the Security Council . . . to take at any time such action as it deems necessary in order to maintain or restore international peace and security."

Johnson's Approval

Employing phraseology carefully worked out in exchanges between the White House and United States delegation headquarters here that began at mid-day and lasted until after 6 P.M., Stevenson's report, bearing President Johnson's personal approval, was

(Continued, Page 5, Column 5)

KOSYGIN BARS HANOI'S PLEA FOR RED UNITY

Tass Says 80,000 Hear Ideological Attack On Peking

By ADAM CLYMER
[*Moscow Bureau of The Sun*]

Moscow, Feb. 7—Soviet Premier Alexei N. Kosygin today in effect spurned a Vietnamese bid for Sino-Soviet unity by charging that Chinese ideology hindered the revolutionary forces of the world.

Speaking before a reported crowd of 80,000 people in Hanoi, Kosygin was quoted by the Soviet agency Tass as saying:

"The Communist party of the Soviet Union firmly and unswervingly opposes all attempts to weaken the unity of actions of the revolutionary forces of the world. We fight both against revisionism and against dogmatism, which distort our revolutionary teaching."

Dogmatism is the Soviet epithet used to describe the Peking approach to Communist theory. Revisionism in turn has been hurled at the Kremlin by Peking, and has been used by both to criticize Yugoslavia.

But his remarks came in a particular Sino-Soviet context, since last night Premier Pham Van Dong of North Vietnam repeatedly urged Moscow and Peking to get together. The Vietnam leader's remarks were published here in *Pravda* this morning. He said then:

"The unity of the whole Socialist camp, the unity of the Soviet Union and China—the two biggest Socialist powers—are the most important tasks."

Failure Predicted

Kosygin charged also that imperialist countries were seeking to split the Communist bloc, but he predicted ultimate failure for such attempts.

He said that through a strengthening of ties, Socialist countries would "eventually triumph by overcoming great difficulties."

Kosygin also lauded the Soviet Union's version of the "Leninist policy of peace and peaceful coexistence," which the Chinese scorn, at least in the terms used by Moscow.

Economy Stressed

He also said the construction of Communism in the Soviet Union and the building of its economy were vital to all the Socialist countries. China in the past has accused the U.S.S.R. of adopting a bourgeois attitude and forgetting to aid its allies.

Soviet sources in Peking reportedly told correspondents today that Kosygin still planned to stop once more in Peking, on his way home after his four-day visit to North Vietnam. He was expected to travel through Peking coming home, although he had a chilly reception when he stopped there Friday.

There were also reports that Kosygin had again asked Premier Chou En-lai of China to be represented at Moscow's March meeting to prepare documents for a world Communist conference on the Sino-Soviet split. It was reported that Chou again refused.

Pravda today published a smiling picture of Kosygin and Chou greeting each other at the Peking airport.

A.M.A. Backs 'Eldercare,' Rival Plan For The Aged

Chicago, Feb. 7 (AP)—The American Medical Association's House of Delegates today rejected the Johnson Administration' program for health care of the aged. It voted to "indorse and enthusiastically support" a rival plan it calls "eldercare."

The 234-member governing body of the nation's biggest organization of physicians thus reaffirmed its opposition to a Social Security-financed program which would be administered by a Federal Government agency.

It broadened its earlier stand in favor of state programs financed with general Federal tax funds and administered by the states through private health agencies.

Specifically, the A.M.A. delegates accepted the bill (H.R.-3727) now before Congress which was introduced by Representative Herlong (D., Fla.) and Curtis (R., Mo.) and adopted the A.M.A. board of trustees' promotion program for the Herlong-Curtis measure.

The promotion expense will come from the A.M.A.'s $14,000,000 reserve fund. No special tax or assessment on individual doctors will be made, the delegates said.

Expressing concern for the health of needy persons "regard-

(Continued, Page 12, Column 5)

Air Strike Launched From Two Carriers

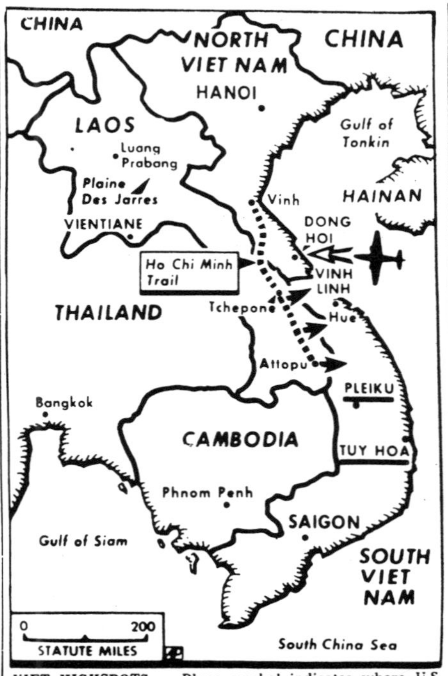

VIET HIGHSPOTS — Plane symbol indicates where U.S. planes made air strikes, in retaliation for Red attacks at underlined Pleiku and Tuy Hoa. Broken line and arrows mark Ho Chi Minh Trail, Communist supply route from the north.

Weather Balks Other Missions From 3d Ship And Field

By ALBERT SEHLSTEDT, JR.
[*Washington Bureau of The Sun*]

Washington, Feb. 7 — Forty-nine United States carrier planes today attacked a North Vietnamese military base following Communist guerrilla raids in South Vietnam that killed eight Americans and wounded 109 others.

The air strike, with high-explosive bombs and rockets, was launched from the carriers Hancock and Coral Sea, steaming in the South China Sea, 100 miles off the coast of the Southeast Asia peninsula.

Weather Balks Others

Land-based planes of the South Vietnamese Air Force and another group of planes from the American carrier Ranger, were turned back from their assigned missions because of bad weather over targets they had been ordered to hit.

The Defense Department said one American plane, from the carrier Coral Sea, was lost, but the pilot was seen to eject himself from the cockpit of his craft.

Tonight, the department identified the missing man as Lt. Edward A. Dickson, son of Mr. and Mrs. Edward F. Dickson, of Wyoming, Pa.

Details of the carrier-plane attack were described this afternoon by Robert S. McNamara, Secretary of Defense, in a press conference at the Pentagon.

Necessary Response

McNamara, who has just recovered from pneumonia, characterized the American attack as a "clear and necessary response to a test . . . of will and purpose and policy" of the United States and the South Vietnamese Government.

He said the raid was "a test that was clearly intended as a test by the North Vietnamese, and a test directed both against the South Vietnamese Government and the United States Government."

The base struck by the carrier planes was Dong Hoi, approximately 45 miles north of the Seventeenth Parallel, which divides the two Vietnamese nations.

Skyhawks And Crusaders

Returning combat crews reported extensive fires and smoke rising from the area of Dong Hoi, which is a barracks and staging area for Communist soldiers who eventually move down into South Vietnam to carry on the guerrilla war there.

Today's attack, which occurred about 2 A.M. Washington time, was the first large-scale retaliatory air raid by American carrier planes since two United States destroyers had been attacked in the Gulf of Tonkin last summer. The gulf is immediately east of North Vietnam.

The planes taking part in today's raid were 33 A-4 Skyhawks and 16 F-8 Crusaders.

The single-seat Skyhawk can carry about 6,000 pounds of bombs and 3 Bullpup air-to-ground missiles. The Crusader can also carry a heavy bomb load. Both planes are armed with 20-mm. cannon.

Among the sixteen Crusaders

(Continued, Page 2, Column 2)

Analysis

U.S. Reprisal In Vietnam Called Big Satisfaction

By MARK S. WATSON
[*Sun Military Correspondent*]

Washington, Feb. 7—To a great many observers, both military and civilian, the United States' prompt counterattack on positions in North Vietnam itself brings great satisfaction.

It is comparable to that of 1964 when Communist attacks on our naval patrol in the Gulf of Tonkin resulted in immediate American ships' fire on the attacking Red vessels, followed by severe punitive air assaults on the Red bases from which the raiders had come.

That was unmistakably a "tit-for-tat" response, such as had been announced as United States policy when Gen. Maxwell D. Taylor first went out to South Vietnam as United States Ambassador.

Today's heavy United States air raids on North Vietnam, following swiftly the Red guerrillas' three raids on our positions, seem exactly comparable, despite the reluctance of Robert S. McNamara, Secretary of Defense, to use the "tit-for-tat" term this time.

On only these two occasions, it should be noted, has American reprisal gone into North Vietnam itself. Otherwise it has been directed against Viet Cong forces after they had emerged from that country, or against the bridges and trails through Laos which the Viet Cong used, and the camps, fueling points and ammunition dumps they had set up. The American attacks had stopped short of the North Vietnam border.

This may easily have led the

(Continued, Page 4, Column 7)

RED AID PLEDGES AT RECORD HIGH

1.3 Billion Committed In '64 Triple Amount In '63

By JOSEPH R. L. STERNE
[*Washington Bureau of The Sun*]

Washington, Feb. 7 — Communist aid commitments to developing countries hit a record high of $1,300,000,000 in 1964, the Agency for International Development reported today.

It said this amount was triple the aid promised last year and higher than the previous peak of $1,100,000,000 pledged in 1961.

Actual expenditures by the Communists continued a steady rise that has gone on without a break for five years, the agency stated in a resume soon to be submitted to Congress.

Viewed As "Lever"

It published a graph indicating that Communist expenditures totaled about $500,000,000. This was only slightly higher than a year ago and represented a temporary leveling out probably caused by the 1962 and 1963 drop in commitments.

The rise in expenditures plus the new burst of aid commitments caused the agency to conclude that the Communist world

(Continued, Page 7, Column 1)

HANOI REPORTS 4 JETS DOWNED

'Many Others' Damaged, Red Radio Says

Tokyo, Feb. 7 (AP)—Radio Hanoi claimed today four United States jets were shot down and "many others" damaged in the strike against North Vietnam today.

In Washington, Robert S. McNamara, Secretary of Defense, said one Navy plane was lost and that its pilot bailed out.

The Communist broadcast said bombing and strafing runs were carried out against the Gulf of Tonkin towns of Dong Hoi and Vinh Linh. It charged the planes hit at civilian homes, a hospital and the office of the International Control Commission in Dong Hoi.

"Extremely Serious"

The broadcast said the Communist Government in Hanoi considers the attacks an "extremely serious act of aggression" and warned that the United States and South Vietnam would have to bear the responsibility.

Referring to its claim that four United States planes were brought down, the Hanoi Radio said:

"Once again, the United States pirates were duly punished."

The radio also noted that the

(Continued, Page 5, Column 4)

New Viet Red Attack Fails

Saigon, *Monday*, Feb. 8 (AP)—Viet Cong guerrillas slammed 15 heavy mortar shells into Soc Trang airbase last night less than 24 hours after a similar but much larger attack on Pleiku air base.

There were no casualties and no damage in the Soc Trang barrage. The shells all landed away from the runway and building area.

The attack on Pleiku brought on a retaliatory United States air strike against North Vietnamese installations.

Soc Trang, a town in the Mekong River delta 100 miles southwest of Saigon, is one of the most important United States Army helicopter installations in the southernmost part of the country.

The Weather
Sunny, windy and cold today with the high in the 30's. Clear and cold tonight. Yesterday's high, 54; low, 32.
(Details and Map, Page 24.)

THE SUN FINAL

Vol. 256—No. 83—F | PAID CIRCULATION SIX MONTHS ENDED 9/30/64 MORNING, 190,628 EVENING, 213,008 403,636 ‖ SUNDAY 339,420 | BALTIMORE, MONDAY, FEBRUARY 22, 1965 | Published daily except Sunday by The A. S. Abell Co Calvert & Centre Sts., Baltimore, Md. 21203 Second class postage paid at Baltimore Md | 34 Pages | 10 Cents

Suspect Held In Malcolm X Murder

Khanh Quits As Vietnam's Military Commander

REJECTION OF JOHNSON BIDS URGED

C. Of C. Group Opposes School Aid, Highway, Health Proposals

By RODNEY CROWTHER
[*Washington Bureau of The Sun*]

Washington, Feb. 21—The Council of State Chambers of Commerce wants six of President Johnson's key programs rejected by Congress.

With the aim of putting a leash on budget expenditures the business organization urged rejection of new spending programs involving $2,000,000,000 in proposed 1966 appropriations and $805,000,000 in anticipated 1966 expenditures as follows:

1. Appropriations of $1,255,000,000 and budged expenditures of $500,000,000 to help finance public school operating costs in "poverty impacted areas," school library resources, instructional materials, and educational research.

2. Appropriation requests of $260,000,000 and estimated first-year expenditures of $100,000,000 for grants for higher education, including students assistance beyond the loan and work-study assistance already provided under existing programs.

Opposes Omnibus Health Plan

3. The $1,100,000,000 proposal of highway construction and other resources development in the Appalachian area. The budget proposes a supplemental appropriation of $365,000,000 for 1965 of which $3,000,000 would be spent in this fiscal year and $107,000,000 in 1966.

4. An omnibus health proposal calling for $106,000,000 in appropriations and $58,000,000 expenditures in 1966 to provide increased Federal support for health facilities, services and education.

5. A new program of grants to help finance local water pollution control activities with $60,000,000 appropriations and $12,000,000 expenditures budgeted for 1966. This program would be a supplement to an existing $100,000,000-a-year program for construction of waste treatment facilities.

6. A $25,000,000 annual grant program to finance school health care programs.

Oppose Expansions

The council also urged that certain proposed expansions of existing programs be rejected by Congress which, it said, would reduce 1966 appropriations by $1,454,000,000 and expenditures by $446,000,000 as follows:

1. A proposed increase in the authorization and appropriation for the War on Poverty to $1,500,000,000 from the 1965 appropriation level of $800,000,000. This could save $700,000,000 in appropriations, the council argued.

2. An additional authorization and appropriation of $40,000,000 in the area redevelopment program of which $40,000,000 would actually be spent in 1966.

3. Expansion of manpower development and training programs and an increase in the Federal matching percentage, with a 1966 appropriation request of $140,000,000 and $92,000,000 in spending.

4. Extension and liberalization of existing public assistance programs covering aged persons and dependent children, with a first-year cost of $214,000,000 in appropriations and expenditures. The estimated public assistance cost under existing legislation for 1966 was $3,242,000,000.

On Other Pages

105,000 Killed In Accidents In U.S. In '64

Chicago, Feb. 21 (AP)—The National Safety Council said today that 105,000 persons in the United States were killed in accidents in 1964, with motor vehicle deaths contributing 46 per cent of the total.

The council said deaths due to falls were next with 18 per cent, followed by fires, burns and deaths associated with fire, 7 per cent, and drowning, 6 per cent.

All other types accounted for about 23 per cent.

Three catastrophes in 1964 caused more than 50 deaths in each: an airplane crash near Lake Tahoe, Cal., took 85 lives; the Alaskan earhtquake took more than 100 lives and 58 died in a plane crash into Lake Pontchartrain, La.

Last year's 105,000 death toll was 4 per cent more than the 100,669 fatalities in 1963, and it pushed the death rate to 54.9 fatalities per 100,000 population, compared to 53.3 in 1963.

TEXAS PORTS EYE GANG SIZE

Key Issue, Long Avoided, Could Break Impasse

Local issues gain importance in labor dealings ....Page 6

By HELEN DELICH BENTLEY
[*Maritime Editor of The Sun*]

Bal Harbour, Fla., Feb. 21—The first sign of a breakthrough in the 42-day longshore strike of the Texas ports was in a report from there today that the West Gulf Maritime Association is talking about a seventeen-man general-cargo gang (plus a foreman).

If that issue should be resolved in the top-echelon, secretive talks today at a hideaway on Galveston Island, it would break the impasse still tying up all of the South Atlantic and Gulf Coast ports.

Minimum Gang Size Argued

The eighteen-man gang was brought up in the first round of the talks that ran over a span of about seven hours yesterday in Houston.

And it is the first time in the nogotiations under way since last August that the Texas management group has even agreed to talk about a minimum gang size.

Today's talks at Galveston broke up at 8 P.M. and will resume tomorrow afternoon.

Labor leaders here attending the Executive Council of the AFL-CIO are concerned about the longshore strike because of the adverse effects its continuation could have on the entire labor movement.

Effect In Congress

Continuation of the tie-up of the South Atlantic and West Gulf ports, plus the threat of a resumption of the strike in the North Atlantic by the International Longshoremen's Association (AFL-CIO) if a settlement is not achieved soon in the Southern areas, could prevent the Johnson Administration from carrying out its promise that Section 14B, the right-to-work clause, of the Taft-Hartley Act would be repealed by this Congress.

It is not that there is any direct tie-in between the right-to-work

(Continued, Page 6, Column 5)

NEGRO VOTERS PLEDGED AID BY HUMPHREY

Administration To Ask For New Laws To Ease Registration

Washington, Feb. 21 (AP) — Vice President Humphrey said today that the Johnson Administration has concluded that additional legislation will be necessary to guarantee Negro voting rights.

Humphrey did not say on a television program taped with Senator Clark (D., Pa.), just what recommendations may be made by the President. But he did say:

"What we are trying to do . . . is to simplify the procedure of registration to see to it that every person of voting age is permitted to vote without these impediments and without all of these gimmicks that seem to deny the opportunity to register."

Selma Pattern Cited

He said roadblocks such as those encountered by Negroes attempting to register in Selma, Ala., "bring us to the conclusion that additional remedies will be necessary.

"I cannot imagine anyone defending the proposition that you ought to exclude people from the right to vote, particularly when they are of voting age and have met other qualifications that may be established," Humphrey said.

"The President feels strongly about this, as do members of the Congress, and I'm sure that we'll be able to design legislation which is both effective and constitutional. . . ."

Problems Admitted

The Vice President said that there are "constitutional problems" to be faced in any effort to abolish state literacy tests in Federal elections.

"That is one of the areas where we are seeking advice and counsel," he said.

Humphrey noted that he has been designated by Mr. Johnson to head the Equal Opportunities Council with the assignment of coordinating government activities in the field of civil rights.

Meanwhile, John M. Bailey announced that the Democratic National Commitee has asked the Justice Department, the Civil Rights Commission, and all 50 state Democratic chairmen to help in a drive against discrimination in registration and voting laws.

Lawrence Heads Panel

Bailey, the party chairman, said the request was made by former Gov. David L. Lawrence of Pennsylvania, who is head of a special committee set up by the 1964 national convention to deal with the problem.

Bailey said Lawrence has asked each state chairman for his party rules governing voter participation. They also have been asked for copies of any statutes controlling the degree of party participation by any particular segment of the population.

Lawrence also has asked Nicholas Katzenbach, Attorney General, and William L. Taylor, general counsel of the Civil Rights Commission, to provide the Democratic committee with advice in the anti-discrimination program voted by last year's party convention.

Police Blame Slaying On Black Muslim Feud

Lawyer Says Victim Was About To Give Names of Men Trying To Kill Him

New York, Feb. 21 (AP). Police tonight charged a 22-year-old Negro, Thomas Hagan, with the murder of Malcolm X.

Hagan, shot in the leg in the melee that followed the assassination, was held in the prison ward of Bellevue hospital. Police Capt. Paul Glaser said Hagan killed Malcolm with a sawed-off shotgun, and was himself wounded by one of Malcolm's followers.

MALCOLM X

New York, Feb. 21 (AP)—Malcolm X, fiery renegade of the Negro radical movement, was assassinated today as he rose to address a rally in an upper Manhattan ballroom. At least 5 men were believed to have sprung the fatal ambush, after lurking amid the ranks of 500 of his disciples.

His lawyer claimed the slim, goateed Malcolm had known he was marked for murder and was preparing in his speech to disclose "the names of those who were trying to kill him.

Police blamed the slaying on a feud between Malcolm, 39, and the Black Muslim movement, with which he broke in 1963. The Muslims, however, denied any complicity.

A diversion in the rear of the ballroom drew attention from the stage long enough for the assassins to race down an aisle and pump bullets into Malcolm's chest from three weapons. He had just begun to address his followers, starting, "Brothers and sisters. . ."

Malcolm's wife, Betty, 37, was nearby. She screamed, "They're killing him — they're killing him."

The killers turned around and raced from the second-floor ballroom with a mob shouting at their heels, "Kill them—don't let them get away."

Outside the hall, quickly converging police grabbed three

(Continued, Page 5, Column 2)

SOVIET DECLARES NEW ARTS ACCORD

Pravda Assails Khrushchev Policy On Intellectuals

Moscow, Feb. 21 (AP)—The new Soviet regime proclaimed today a new deal for intellectuals.

The Kremlin also criticized former Premier Nikita Khrushchev's attitude toward Soviet intellectuals in terms reserved in the past for criticism of Josef Stalin.

The policy statement was delivered by Alexei M. Rumyantsev, editor-in-chief of *Pravda*, the Soviet Communist party newspaper.

Policy Spokesman

Rumyantsev, who took over *Pravda's* editorship after Khrushchev's ouster, has become one of the Kremlin's most important policy spokesmen.

Without mentioning Khrushchev by name, he referred to him as an "autocratic *vozhd* (leader)" who "decided for all."

Stalin was usually referred to as the *vozhd* during his lifetime. The term is rarely used now except in a derogatory sense because it is so closely identified with Stalin.

Rumyantsev announced that Soviet intellectuals, who were alienated by Khrushchev's treatment, will get a new deal under the Soviet leadership.

"Clash" Is Supported

In the key passage of his article, he said scientific and cultural creativity is "possible only under conditions of search and experiment, free expression and the clash of opinions.

"The fruitful development of science, literature and art calls for different schools and trends, different styles and genres, competing with each other and united at the same time by their common dialectical-materialistic outlook and unity of the principles of Socialist realism," he wrote.

His statement was strikingly similar to Mao Tze-tung's call to "let a hundred flowers bloom, let a hundred schools contend," which unleashed a flood of public criticism of the Peking regime in the summer of 1957. This was followed by harsh repressions.

The Soviet policy statement was heavily qualified with a reaffirmation of the party's commitment to its basic ideological positions.

"The party cannot tolerate attempts to drag idealistic and metaphysical concepts into science and push art into the swamp of absence of ideological value, decadence and naked formalism," Rumyantsev wrote.

POPE TO ELEVATE CARDINALS TODAY

Archbishop Shehan Among 27; Pontiff Will Speak

By WELDON WALLACE
[*Rome Bureau of The Sun*]

Rome, Feb. 21 —Preparations were completed today for the creation of 27 new cardinals of the Catholic Church, including the Archbishop of Baltimore, the Most Rev. Lawrence J. Shehan.

Two ceremonies are scheduled. One is a secret consistory tomorrow morning and the other a mass to be celebrated by Pope Paul VI and all the new cardinals in St. Peter's Basilica Thursday.

One Remains In Spain

Reportedly 26 of the cardinals-designate are in Rome. The twenty-seventh, the Most Rev. Angel Herrera y Oria, Bishop of Malaga, Spain, is to remain in his own country and, following long custom, will receive the badges of his rank from his government.

Delegations of visitors from all parts of the world have crowded Rome's major hotels to be present here for the first creation of cardinals since March, 1962, during the reign of Pope John XXIII.

Tomorrow morning Pope Paul and all the present cardinals in Rome are to gather at 9.30 o'clock in the Consistorial Hall of the Apostolic Palace. There the Pontiff will announce the names of the new members he has chosen for the Sacred College, and the present members will give their assent, after which the Pope says the words that mark the formal elevation of the 27.

May Discuss World Situation

It is said that the Pope also is to give an address in Latin on this occasion. It could be that he will take opportunity to discuss some acute world problem, though there has been no indication of the subject.

From the consistory, notification is to go out to the new cardinals, who are to be divided into groups at four different locations. In former times each selected his own place for the receipt of the news, but this time Pope Paul directed that the new cardinals gather at four places only, as specified by himself.

Cardinal-designate Shehan and six others will be waiting at the Pontifical North American College on the Janiculum Hill.

Seven Thrones Erected

Today seven gilded thrones upholstered in red, were placed in the great refectory on the second floor of the college, which is the seminary in Rome to train Americans for the priesthood

The windows of this immense

(Continued, Page 2, Column 6)

Man, Buried In Avalanche For 79 Hours, Is Rescued

Ketchikan, Alaska, Feb. 21 (AP)—A Finnish construction worker survived for 79 hours under tons of snow and ice that avalanched onto a mining camp east of here.

Einar Myllyla, about 30, was pulled from the smashed remains of a bunkhouse at the Granduc Mining Camp this afternoon. He was nearly frozen but conscious and coherent.

"Very Serious"

Dr. James Wilson, head of a medical team treating Myllyla at Ketchikan, described his condition as "very serious." He said more than half of the man's arms and legs were frozen solid and parts probably would have to be removed later.

Myllyla, a bachelor from Winnipeg, Man., was pulled from the snowy graveyard where at least twelve other men perished. Rescuers, carefully probing the glacial debris, stumbled across the man and a Canadian helicopter flew Myllyla to Ketchikan.

Dr. Wilson said Myllyla told him he slept most of the time while buried. Myllyla said he thought he was in a coma, but he wasn't sure.

Had "Wonderful" Thoughts

"I thought the most wonderful things," Myllyla said. He did not elaborate.

He was one of 130 men in the Granduc camp when the avalanche squashed the area Thursday a few minutes before 10 A.M.

So far, rescuers have uncovered a dozen bodies. Fourteen others are missing and feared dead.

Myllyla arrived at the hospital with his arms swathed in bandages. He held them up as he was wheeled into emergency on a stretcher.

Dr. Wilson tapped the man's

(Continued, Page 10, Column 5)

SHIP BOARDED BY ULBRICHT ON U.A.R. TRIP

East Germans' Leader First Takes Plane To Slav Port

Dubrovnik, Yugoslavia, Feb. 21 (AP)—President Walter Ulbricht of Communist East Germany set out today for Egypt on a trip that is sorely straining West Germany's ties in the Middle East.

The West Germans fear that an elaborate reception for Ulbricht by President Gamal Abdel Nasser of the United Arab Republic will mean recognition of the East German regime. Ulbricht himself has said he does not think so.

Nasser has ignored West German warnings about a cut in economic aid or a possible break in relations.

Special Plane Lands

Ulbricht's special airliner landed at this Yugoslav coastal resort to permit his official party to board the East German ship Voelkarfreundschaft. The vessel is due in Alexandria Wednesday and Ulbricht will go by train to Cairo for an official welcome from Nasser.

Ulbricht is accompanied by his wife Lotte and high officials.

The Yugoslav press supported Nasser in his clash with West Germany over Ulbricht's visit, his first to a non-Communist nation.

The newspapers said West Germany was guilty of applying "pressure on a sovereign country" in trying to persuade Nasser to call off the visit.

West Germany Bows

Nasser maintained his invitation to Ulbricht even though the West Germans met his long-time demand to cut off arms aid to Israel.

The arms cut by Chancellor Ludwig Erhard's Government in Bonn led the Israelis to accuse the West Germans of giving in to blackmail.

The Israeli Prime Minister, Levi Eshkol, angrily rejected Bonn's offer of money in place of the $15,000,000 worth of arms left to be delivered to Israel.

Bonn had hoped that its cutting arms aid to Israel would make Nasser drop his invitation to Ulbricht. Nasser refused.

Relations Hurt Twice

Thus Bonn's relations with both Israel and the United Arab Republic sank sharply.

Erhard spent four hours yesterday, usually a day of rest in Bonn, talking with his ministers about the Middle East.

Erhard's government has been having trouble lately in the fight to maintain its claim as the only representative of the German people. The East German Communist state has been making gains.

To Erhard, his actions are logical enough, but his position is uncomfortable.

Erhard's announcement that Egypt would get no new aid from West Germany was not an effective gesture since Ulbricht is planning to sign an aid agreement with Egypt.

Humphrey Calls Viet Goal Peace; Javits Asks Parleys

Washington, Feb. 21 (AP)—Vice President Humphrey said today the Johnson Administration's objective in Vietnam is peace. But Senator Javits (R., N.Y.,), called on the President to signal United States willingness to negotiate a settlement.

Mr. Humphrey said on a television program taped with Senator Clark (D., Pa.), that the Vietnamese situation "doesn't lend itself much to talk of peace."

Calls For Arms Cuts

"But what is our objective there?" he said. "Our objective is peace. Our objective is the territorial integrity, the protection of the sovereignty and the integrity of South Vietnam, and the way to bring peace there is simply for people to leave each other alone. Our Government's position is just that."

Despite the political problems in Vietnam, Mr. Humphrey said he thinks the United States should continue to seek a meaningful agreement for reduction in world armaments.

Javits said, on a separate taped TV program, he thinks the President should announce that this country is in Vietnam because the majority of the South Vietnamese want the United States to help preserve their freedom.

He said the President ought to say that "so long as we are convinced that that is so, we will stay there and help them fight that battle."

Supports Retaliation

"If and when we are convinced that this is not so, we will not stay there," he said.

Javits, who said he supports Mr. Johnson's policy of trading strike for strike with the North Vietnamese, said that United States allies are not doing enough to support the American position in South Vietnam. In the end, the New York Senator said the conflict is going to have to be settled by negotiation and the United

(Continued, Page 2, Column 2)

JUNTA SENDS 3 MEN TO PRESS EXILE ON GENERAL AT RETREAT

Apparent Capitulation Ends Present Threat Of Military Uprising; Saigon's Envoy In Washington Delighted

Saigon, Vietnam, *Monday*, Feb. 22 (AP)—Lt. Gen. Nguyen Khanh resigned today as South Vietnam's military chief, the Armed Forces Council announced. It sent three men to his mountain hideaway to persuade him to go into exile.

Khanh's apparent capitulation to the junta of generals and colonels ended for the moment the threat of an uprising by troops loyal to Khanh to return him to power.

Envoy Jubilant

In Washington, South Vietnam's Ambassador, Lt. Gen. Tran Thien Khiem, jubilantly hailed word of Khanh's downfall and urged him to leave the country. "With Khanh we did not have stability and without him we will have the stability we need," Khiem said.

The Armed Forces Council stripped Khanh of his title as commander-in-chief and voted to send him into exile yesterday. But the little general, survivor of previous comeback attempts, flew to Dalat, 200 miles northeast of Saigon, to drum up support for another return.

Stay At Airport

Apparently unsuccessful, Khanh sent word to his fellow generals he had agreed to resign but wanted to talk things over, a spokesman for the Armed Forces Council said. "We are sending three emissaries to Dalat," he added.

A group of rebellious officers decided to ditch Khanh after they had put down an attempted military coup Friday.

Barricading themselves through the night inside Saigon airport, the generals feverishly debated the country's fate among themselves and their American advisers. By radio they negotiated with Khanh in Dalat.

Tank Column Report

The tension heightened when a column of tanks led by men loyal to Khanh was reported moving on the airport. Artillery fire was heard near the field and fighter-bombers dropped flares on the countryside in an apparent search for the tanks, but they never appeared.

Maj. Gen. Tran Van Minh was designated "temporary acting chairman" of the Armed Forces Council—or armed forces chief.

Speaking for the generals was Brig. Gen. Nguyen Chanh Thi, powerful 1st Corps commander.

Bomb-Dropping Bar

Among the anti-Khanh leaders was Air Force commander Brig. Gen. Nguyen Cao Ky, whose planes had saved Khanh on previous occasions. This time he showed no inclination to come to the rescue of his former chief.

"Personally I am not worried that Khanh will try to enter the airport by force," Ky said. "Any forces that may still be loyal to him are insignificant."

United States Air Force Brig. Gen. Robert Rowland, a peacemaker during previous coups, again used his influence to prevent the Air Force commander from dropping bombs.

Expectant Vigil

As dawn came to Saigon, the city resumed its languid pace, apparently oblivious to the intensive talks at the airport. Planes circled the city but caused no concern.

The anti-Khanh forces began their vigil at the airport in expectation of an attack by Khanh's men. Ky ordered his planes into the air to search out Khanh's forces, and the other generals set up a joint command post at the field.

Advised To Quit Country

But nothing developed. The generals kept in radio contact with Khanh through most of the night and the United States advisers stayed with them to urge no further shooting.

By dawn the crisis seemed over.

General Khanh had been Vietnam's Government maker and breaker almost continuously for thirteen months.

But Ky said the Armed Forces Council had advised Khanh to leave the country in his own best

(Continued, Page 2, Column 3)

LAOS BUILDUP IS REPORTED

Army Expected To Try To Retake Strongpoints

Vientiane, Laos, Feb. 21 (AP)—The Laotian Army was reported being reinforcing today in northeastern Laos to retake the key strongpoint of Hua Muong, lost to Communist forces one week ago.

The Pathet Lao captured the village, 170 miles northeast of Vientiane and 30 miles southwest of Sam Neua, the provincial capital, in an offensive that began in mid-December.

2 Battalions Were Taken

It had been the headquarters of two battalions of the Laotian Army although the Communists have controlled most of Sam Neua province for years.

Reports that a Communist mop-up drive against pockets of Government resistance had tapered off coincided with renewed Pathet Lao charges today that United States aircraft bombed and strafed Sam Neua village.

A Peking Radio broadcast claimed earlier that the Communists shot down four United States F-101 jet fighters in northeastern Laos Friday, but a United States Defense Department spokesman said there was no information to substantiate the charge.

One Pilot Missing

The United States has acknowledged that one United States Air Force pilot was missing after his plane was shot down Friday in Laos. He was identified as Maj. Robert F. Ronca, 41, of Norristown, Pa.

United States propeller-driven T-28 fighter-bombers have been flying missions against the Pathet Lao since last May at the request of Premier Prince Souvanna Phouma. United States aircraft have also been conducting air strikes against Communist supply routes in southern Laos leading into South Vietnam.

A special White House assistant, Michael V. Forrestal, is conferring in Vientiane with Laotian officials and Army leaders. He arrived yesterday for an unofficial three-day visit.

Military sources say the Com-

(Continued, Page 2, Column 5)

The Weather
Cloudy with showers today, high 72. Clearing tonight, lows in 40's. Yesterday's high 79; low, 58.
(Details and Map, Page C 13.)

THE SUN

FINAL

Vol. 259—No. 126—F BALTIMORE, MONDAY, OCTOBER 10, 1966 18 Pages 10 Cents

WOULD YOU BELIEVE IT? FOUR STRAIGHT!

Sunpaper photo—Hutchins

JUMP FOR JOY—Brooks Robinson (5), Oriole 3d baseman, almost literally flies in to commend winning pitcher Dave McNally (19) as catcher Andy Etchebarren also rushes up.

PRESIDENT, GROMYKO TO MEET TODAY

Talks Linked To Drive For Better Relations With Soviet Union

By ERNEST B. FURGURSON
[Sun Staff Correspondent]

Stonewall, Texas, Oct. 9—President Johnson flies back to Washington tomorrow to confer with Andrei A. Gromyko, Soviet Foreign Minister, during an all-out American effort to improve relations with Moscow.

So far, there have been stated indications that the Russians are responsive to Washington's blandishments, especially the attempt to enlist Soviet aid in getting North Vietnam to negotiate an end to the Southeast Asian war.

Hanoi To Get Aid

Only last week Moscow signed an agreement to increase aid to Hanoi, and only this weekend Gromyko turned down a proposal from George Brown, British Foreign Secretary, that peace talks be arranged by reconvening the 1954 Geneva conference in Indochina.

But by a gesture here and a civil attitude there, Soviet officials have contributed to an atmosphere in which some bilateral Soviet-American agreements are foreseen despite the continuing war.

Contrast Noted

One of the contributors to this feeling is Gromyko himself, who made a typically hostile attack on Western policy in his speech at the opening of the United Nations General Assembly session, but in private conversations with Dean Rusk, Secretary of State, was said to be more restrained and less propagandistic than usual.

Another mild hint of Moscow's interest in, at least, not worsening relations was the release last week of Thomas Dawson, the Annapolis Peace Corpsman who had been held prisoner after accidentally crossing the Soviet-Iranian border.

On the American side, Mr. Johnson set the stage for the talk with Gromyko when he announced a series of steps toward reconciliation in a major speech in New York Friday.

Cooperation Sought

The address recounted American moves in the fields of trade and credit, travel and space co-operation, and let Russia and the Eastern European nations know "that we and our allies shall go step by step with them as far as they are willing to advance."

Mr. Johnson also said that reduction of Soviet forces in Central Europe could help lead to "a gradual and balanced revision in force levels on both sides" possibly resulting in a "new political environment."

Although Washington had said many times that any cut in American troop strength in Europe could only accompany a reduction of Soviet forces, this was the first time in recent years that the idea has been put forward as a positive suggestion by an American President.

Purchases Fall Short

Western conversation about reduction of forces has increased with Bonn's insistence that it can no longer completely offset the cost of keeping American troops in West Germany by purchases of arms in this country.
already are planned to seek means of adjusting the current financial problem—possibly by European troop cuts.

The New York speech followed one in the same conciliatory tone.

(Continued, Page A2, Column 5)

On Other Pages

PRISONER-OF-WAR CONTACT PLANNED

U.S. Hopes To Work It Via Canadian Quakers

Washington, Oct. 9 (AP)—The Government hopes it can gain indirect contact with United States war prisoners by letting an American religious group help send medical supplies to the North Vietnamese.

The strategy unfolded over the weekend as the Treasury Department confirmed it has given a Yale University group permission to send $300 worth of medical goods to North Vietnam and Viet Cong-held areas of South Vietnam via a Canadian Quaker organization.

A Treasury official said in an interview that the Canadian Friends Service Committee has told the United States Government it is negotiating with Hanoi and the Viet Cong for permission to dispatch observers to North Vietnam.

Red Cross Was Refused

The observers want to check distribution of the supplies and make contact with United States prisoners of war.

North Vietnam so far has refused to discuss an exchange of war prisoners and has not let International Red Cross representatives talk with the prisoners.

There are believed to be more than 100 captured Americans in North Vietnamese hands.

The official said the State Department and Commerce Department were consulted "at adequately high levels" before the Treasury issued its license to the group of Yale religious leaders.

Partly As Experiements

The Yale group plans to send money to the Canadian Friends group, which will purchase the supplies and put them aboard the Russian freighter Alexander Pushkin, which sails from Toronto Wednesday.

The official said the limited license would remain under constant review, and that no decision had been made about issuing further licenses.

He acknowledged that the

(Continued, Page A2, Column 1)

Reds Using Populous Areas To Guard Viet Missile Sites

Saigon, Oct. 9 (AP)—Reconnaissance photographs show the North Vietnamese to have established launching places for some of their surface-to-air missiles within populated places, a United States intelligence officer said today.

American policy is to avoid bombing in areas cities or hamlets where North Vietnamese civilians might be killed or wounded in any numbers.

The Hanoi high command apparently is trying to use this policy to advantage in protecting its Soviet-built missiles.

Duplicates Oil Drum System

The same thing happened after the United States began a large scale campaign in June to knock out North Vietnam's oil storage depots. The North Vietnamese placed much of their oil in drums and dispersed many of these drums in villages.

According to the latest count, there are about 130 missile sites. Only about 20 per cent are reported occupied at any one time.

The North Vietnamese move their mobile launchers and radar vans about to shift defenses where necessary and to make it more difficult for United States planes to knock them out.

Officers say the shooting score of these sites remains poor. Only about 20 American planes have been downed in more than 500 firings of such missiles.

Tactics Changed Constantly

Contrary to recent reports, high-ranking air officers told a reporter there is no evidence the Russians have sent North Vietnam any improved antiaircraft missiles.

These officers said, however, the North Vietnamese missilemen, trained by Russians, are learning from experience how to use their weapons and are showing evidences of more coordination.

But the air officers said United States pilots have not been sticking to the same tactics. This would be suicidal.

In general the enemy has strengthened air defenses, particularly in antiaircraft gun batteries.

And American jets are giving the defenses plenty do. They are flying more than 400 sorties daily against targets in the north.

An objective now in reach with increased United States air resources is to maintain what one officer called a "constant presence over critical areas" such as choke points through which southbound infiltration traffic passes.

A major choke point is the Mu Gia Pass, a target of occasional B52 raids and constant harassment by fighter-bombers.

MCNAMARA PAYS VISIT TO VIETNAM

He Says At Airport U.S. Will Not Invade Buffer Zone

Saigon, Monday, Oct. 10 (AP)—Robert S. McNamara, Secretary of Defense, arrived today for a four-day inspection of the war zone to assess American needs in men, money and materiel.

In a brief airport statement McNamara said he thought the visit was appropriate because nearly twelve months had passed since his last trip and United States strength had more than doubled in the interval.

Asked if the United States would ever occupy the Demilitarized Zone—the area dividing North and South Vietnam—with ground forces, McNamara said. "No, our objectives remain as they always have been."These, he said, are to enable the South Vietnamese Government to act without fear of pressure from the North.

Destruction Not Intended

"We do not intend to destroy the Communist regime in North Vietnam," he said.

McNamara's arrival was marked by a new American victory in the air and another success in the week-old allied ground action on South Vietnam's central coast.

Navy pilots shot down two MIG-21 jets south of Hanoi

(Continued, Page A 2, Column 8)

2D PERSON FLOWN ABROAD BY ERROR

Man Leaves Chicago For Boston, Goes To London

New York, Oct. 9 (AP) — A young Californian flew the Atlantic twice today to get from Los Angeles to Boston. It was the second time in a week that a passenger boarded the wrong Trans World Airlines plane at Chicago's O'Hare Airport and flew to London rather than a United States destination.

Neither one had to pay for the extra trip, but Fred Hildreth, 26, complained today that during a stopover at Shannon Airport, Ireland, "T.W.A. did not even buy me breakfast."

Hildreth, who made a connection for Boston here, said he was tired from the long plane rides, but took the whole incident in stride.

"After all," he told reporters, "I've got some Irish in me, and I've never been to Ireland before."

Flight Made Regular Stop

Hildreth, manager of a safety equipment manufacturing firm in Glendale, Cal., boarded a T.W.A. jet in Los Angeles yesterday to spend a vacation with his parents in Chelmsford, Mass.

His flight, T.W.A. 770 bound for London via Chicago, made its regular stop in the Great Lakes city. Hildreth got off the plane and went in search of T.W.A. 120 flight for Boston.

An Airline official, after asking Hildreth to show his routing envelope, directed him back to the plane he had just left. When an hour out of Chicago, Hildreth, who had listened to various announcements on the loudspeakers, suddenly became aware his plane was flying to London.

2½ Hours In London

Hildreth called for the purser and asked if the plane was stopping in Boston. He was told it didn't.

He finally arrived in London, several hours late. His plane had to make an intermediate diversionary landing at Shannon, Ireland, due to fog over London.

T.W.A. officials immediately

(Continued, Page A 4, Column 8)

Analysis

Capitol Hill Data Contradict Johnson's Legislative Math

By JOSEPH R. L. STERNE
[Washington Bureau of The Sun]

Washngton, Oct. 9—President Johnson has raised some eyebrows higher than the Capitol dome with his assertion that 85 of his 90 requests might be enacted at this "very outstanding" session of Congress.

Scorekeepers in both parties, and those professionally neutral, have trouble following the President's arithmetic.

As they figure it, considerably more than five Johnson proposals already are dead, and execution may be the fate of several others in the closing days of Congress.

Mr. Johnson has indeed some major legislation to which he can point wth pride, although his 1966 record cannot compare with the "fabulous" achievements of 1965.

This year's Congress has raised and broadened minimum-wage coverage, funded $200,000,000 for the Asian Development Bank, authorized Federal automobile and tire standards, speeded emergency food aid to India and imposed Government controls on the handling of animals used in research.

Money to finance Mr. Johnson's pioneering Teachers Corps and rent supplement plans has been wrested from reluctant lawmakers.

Bills May Pass

With a vigorous end-of-session drive, Administration forces may yet salvage bills to create a new department of transportation, strengthen air and water pollution abatement, bolster aid to health services and establish a much-desired "demonstration cities" program.

But even a strong finish will not eradicate the losses Mr. Johnson has suffered on Capitol Hill. Following are examples of presidential proposals which never made it to the lawbooks:

1. Civil rights. This landmark request to ban discrimination in housing and jury selection arrived tardily from the White House, was watered down in the House and killed in the Senate.

2. Taft-Hartley revision. This request to repeal Section 14b of the Taft-Hartley Act, which permits states to ban union shop contracts, was blocked by a Senate filibuster.

3. East-West trade. This

(Continued, Page A 4, Columns 6)

FUNDS FOR SPACE MAY BE BIG ISSUE

Debate Forecast As Costs Cut Into Other Goals

By ALBERT SEHLSTEDT, JR.
[Washington Bureau of The Sun]

Washington, Oct. 9—Amid the challenges and problems associated with Vietnam, civil rights and inflation, there is emerging another issue which may soon achieve the status of a national debate.

The issue is how much effort and money do the people of the United States want to spend on space exploration? This question is not new in Washington but it has not been debated long enough or loudly enough within the Government to receive national attention.

On May 25, 1961, President Kennedy called for an American goal, "before this decade is out of landing man on the moon and returning him safely to earth."

First Earth Orbit

This objective was a rousing commitment for a nation looking for a latter-day Lindbergh in space while still smarting from the maghnificent success of the Soviet Union.

Six weeks before Mr. Kennedy's announcement, the Russian cosmonaut Maj. Yuri A. Gagarin had become the first man to orbit the earth.

But in the autumn of 1966, the

(Continued, Page A 4, Column 3)

BIRDS MAKE WINNING IT SEEM EASY

Shutout By McNally, Robinson's Homer Sew It Up

The Orioles won baseball's world championship yesterday, and they made it look easy.

Their fourth straight World Series victory was a brilliant 1-0 shutout of the Los Angeles Dodgers by Dave McNally, who gave up only four Dodger hits. Frank Robinson sewed it up for the Orioles with a home run into the left field stands.

Baltimore went wild over the Orioles' first World Series triumph. Teen-aged girls danced in the street, drivers leaned on their horns and a city-wide celebration to top all New Year's Eve parties was in progress.

Few Dared To Believe

"Would you believe four straight?" read the billboard planted across the center strip of Thirty-third street outside Memorial Stadium.

Few people had dared to believe it, but it happened yesterday, and Hank Bauer's Orioles became the first American League team to win the series in four straight games since 1950.

The Dodgers themselves beat the New York Yankees in four games in 1963, but at Memorial Stadium yesterday they set the sort of record they will not care to remember.

The Orioles kept them from scoring for 33 successive innings, breaking a 61-year-old World Series record 28, set by the New York Giants in the 1905 series with the Philadelphia Athletics.

McNally Mobbed

At the Stadium yesterday, a crowd of 54,458 fans stood and roared as Oriole centerfielder Paul Blair placed himself under the last fly ball of the game, hit by Lou Johnson with two out in the ninth inning.

Blair, who had won Saturday's game with a home run, caught the ball easily and jumped for joy.

At the pitcher's mound, the Orioles mobbed McNally. They grabbed him around the shoulders, pounded him on the back and nearly ripped his uniform off before they reached the dugout.

Robinson Is Hero

In the Orioles dressing room a bit later, Frank Robinson who during the regular season was the first player in a decade to lead the league in batting, home runs and runs batted in— was the center of attention as the series hero.

"I've been playing this season since December 9," he said. That was the day he learned the Cincinnati Reds management, thinking him too old at 31, had traded him to the Orioles.

"I wanted to have a good year it was the first thought in my mind at the time," he said.

In the Dodgers' dressing room, the losing pitcher Don Drysdale, looked at the floor and spoke in a whisper.

"Just One Of Those Things"

"I got the ball up, maybe a little too high," he said, describing the pitch that Robinson hit 410 feet into the left field stands in the fourth inning. "It was just one of those things."

Vice President Humphrey visited both dressing rooms. He congratulated Robinson and consoled Drysdale, he also lost the first game of the series.

The championship was Baltimore's first in the major leagues since the days of Ned Hanlon's old Orioles in 1894, 1895 and 1896.

(Details on Pages C 1 and C 24)

WEATHER
Fair tonight. Lows 65 to 75. Tomorrow mostly sunny and hot. Highs 90 to 95.
Detailed Report on A 2

THE EVENING SUN

7 STAR ★★★★★★★ 2:30 STOCKS

Vol. 115—No. 49 BALTIMORE, TUESDAY, JUNE 13, 1967 54 Pages 10 Cent

Convention Vote Called 'Lowest In Memory'

MARSHALL NAMED TO HIGH COURT

U.N. Assembly Session Asked By Russia

United Nations, N.Y. (AP)—The Soviet Union requested today an emergency special session of the General Assembly to press its demands that Israel withdraw from occupied territory in Egypt, Jordan and yria.

The Soviet request came in advance of a meeting of the United Nations Security Council, also asked by the Russians.

Soviet Ambassador Nikolai T. Fedorenko presented the request for the emergency session to Secretary General U Thant.

Thant said he would notify all members of the 122-nation assembly by telephone immediately of the Soviet request. In the event that 62 affirmative replies are received he will summon the special session "within 24 hours," a United Nations spokesman said.

High-Level Delegation

In Moscow, diplomatic sources said the Soviet Union is expected to send a high-level delegation, possibly headed by Foreign Minister Andrei A. Gromyko, to a special session.

The Assembly was meeting this morning to wind up its special session on South-West Africa, peacekeeping and outer space that has been in progress intermittently since April 21.

It could go into special session on the Middle East crisis within two days, if the members so desire.

The Soviet Union obviously hopes to push through a resolution critical of Israel and calling for a withdrawal to positions held before the outbreak of hostilities.

But the Assembly does not have the enforcement powers of the Security Council and its resolutions are mainly in the form of recommendations.

Assembly Chances Better

The Soviet Union has a resolution pending before the Security Council that demands that Israel "remove all its troops on the territory of those (the Arab) states and withdraw them behind the armistice line" fixed after the 1948 Arab-Israeli war.

But Council delegates figure that the resolution can get only four of the nine votes necessary for adoption in the 15-nation Council—those of Mali, India, Bulgaria and the Soviet Union.

They say a similar resolution would have a much better chance of adoption in the Assembly, where it could count on the votes of most of the 12 Communist countries, many of the 61 African and Asian countries and maybe even some of the Latin American-Caribbean countries and five of the Nordic countries.

The approval of two thirds of those voting would be necessary for adoption, with abstentions reducing the essential minimum.

[Continued, Page A 3, Col. 3]

Israel Eying Atom Bomb, Report Says

Toronto, Canada (AP)—A Canadian Press reporter said in a dispatch from Nicosia, Cyprus, today that authoritative military sources in Tel Aviv say Israel's next major military move will be to make the atom bomb.

The dispatch added that when a Canadian Press reporter tried to report this from Tel Aviv the dispatch was killed by the censor.

Sources in Tel Aviv, the Nicosia dispatch added, say it is likely the Israeli Government will make a formal decision to join the nuclear club as soon as a Middle East peace agreement is worked out because it is said to feel it can no longer accept any guarantees for its security from any of the major powers.

Arab Chiefs Ask Economic War

Beirut, Lebanon (AP) — Arab leaders called today for the struggle against Israel, the United States and Britain to be waged on the economic front. A Saudi Arabian proposed the nationalization of all Arab oil fields where there are heavy United States and British investments.

In Cairo, the semi-official Egyptian Middle East ANew Agency reported Arab oil-producing countries are ready to accept offers from France and Spain to replace the British and Americal oil companies that have developed most of the Middle East's petroleum industry.

In New York, a spokesman for Arabian-American Oil Company which operates in Saudi Arabia, said the company's operations had "returned to normal."

"Back To Work"

He said the refineries were operating and "all employees are back to wirk." Loading of oil tankers began Monday, he said, and shipments were on their way out, although an embargo against sending oil to the United States and the United Kingdom remained in effect. The consortium produces an average of 2,900,000 barrels of oil daily.

A spokesman for Caltex said that firm's refinery operations in Bahrain were functioning normally as were production operations in Libya.

"Our Sharpest Weapon"

Sheik Abdulla Tariki, former Saudi Arabian oil minister, writing in Beirut's newspaper Al Anwar, called oil "our sharpest weopon." He proposed nationalization of the oil industry under one authority to coordinate pro-

[Continued, Page A 2, Col. 1]

Vote Turnout 'Lowest In Memory'

Election judges sitting through dull day..........[Page B 32]

By Jerome Kelly

Only a trickle of voters showed up at the polls today to elect 142 delegates to Maryland's historic Constitutional Convention.

Scattered complaints cropped up in the city due to changes in voting locations. But few voting machine failures were reported.

Election judges in Baltimore and the surrounding counties were calling the turnout "the lowest in memory."

Little Electioneering

The abnormally small turnout was met by an equally small number of volunteers electioneering for their favorite candidates.

However, a Fifth district candidate, E. Clinton Bamberger, charged two volunteers with accepting illegal election day pay for promoting candidates backed by James H. (Jack) Pollack, Northwest Baltimore political leader.

Mr. Bamberger lodged official charges with the State's attorney's office, which sent two policemen to polling places cited by Mr. Bamberger to take statements.

Room For Criticism

Today's light vote could be used as an argument by those opposed to changing Maryland's present 100-year-old constitution.

Peter Parker, president of the Election Board, said after completing a tour of city polling places that "things are running very smoothly.

"As far as we know all polling places are open and no one has to stand in line," he commented in all seriousness.

These were the 10 A.M. figures at a sampling of city polling places, compared with the vote in last November's gubernatorial election at the same hour.

4TH PRECINCT, 12TH WARD, 3000 Huntingdon avenue — 18 votes compared to 78, described as "very light."

38TH PRECINCT, 27th WARD, Ailsa avenue and Morello road —35 votes compared with 156 in November; "very light."

5TH PRECINCT, 12th WARD, 2659 Miles avenue—6 votes compared with 67; "very, very light."

61ST PRECINCT, 27TH WARD, Govane avenue and Campbell lane—35 votes compared with 190; "very light."

88TH PRECINCT, 27TH WARD, Cross Country boulevard at Glen avenue—313 votes out of 2,861 registered; "light."

26TH PRECINCT, 9TH WARD, 35th street and Hillen road—100

[Continued, Page A 3, Col. 1]

ANYONE FOR BRIDGE?—Baltimore city election supervisors at Eastern High School chat and read while waiting for voters today to cast their ballots for convention delegates. Left to right are: Mrs. Margaret Collins and Mrs. Virginia Wright, at desk; Walter Froyd and Mrs. Doris E. Lamdin. The predicted light vote held true early.

LBJ Reaffirms Mideast Stand

Washington (AP) — President Johnson reaffirmed today his May 23 statement on United States support of the territorial integrity of ntaions in the Middle East.

How it can be effectuated will be determined by events in the days ahead, Mr. Johnson said.

It depends a great deal on the nations themselves, their views and proposals, he said.

Mr. Johnson discussed the Middle East, Vietnam, domestic policies and civil rights troubles at a new conference announced only a few minutes before reporters were summoned into his office.

Russian Cooperation

On a question of working with Russia to secure peace in the Middle East, Mr. Johnson said this country "likes for all nations to do everything they can to promote an honorable and acceptable peace."

He added that he hoped that peace can be achieved and that it would require the best efforts "of all of us."

Switching to Vietnam, Mr. Johnson was asked if an apparent lull there meant a change in the situation. He replied he would not say that, that "the fighting goes up and down depending on a good many factors."

Racial Violence

As to racial violence in American cities, Mr. Johnson said that "We are trying to do everything we can" in cooperation with

[Continued, Page A 3, Col. 4]

1,000 Lawmen In Tampa Gird For New Rioting

Tampa, Fla. (AP)—A thousand police and National Guardsmen battled rioting Negroes through a second nightmarish night in Tampa's sprawling slums, then pulled back today to rest up for renewed violence expected when night falls again.

As a hot sun rose over the smoking ruins of more than a dozen burned-out buildings, only a token force remained on duty in the littered streets of a city torn for the first time by major civil riots.

11 Hours Of Rioting

But Col. K. C. Bullard, commander of the Tampa National Guard post, said the Guard's manpower would be fully deployed again long before darkness.

Chanting, "Get whitey, Get whitey"—the Negro term for the white man—mobs burned and looted for eleven hours Monday night, starting their rampage in the bright light of midafternoon and continuing until after 2 A.M.

Roving bands tossed Molotov cocktails into buildings and at passing autos and snipers took pot shots at police cruisers.

The outbreaks were numerous and widespread as opposed to Sunday's trouble which was confined mainly to the Central Village area, a huge, festering ghetto only blocks from the heart of the city.

Slum Sealed Off

Gov. Claude Kirk supervised 500 National Guardsmen, 350 police and 150 armed deputies. They sealed off the main slum area but were generally unable to keep up with the guerrilla-like squads of rioters who spread to outlying slum areas, burning and pillaging as they went.

Firemen had extinguished at least eighteen fires. And for the second consecutive night they were shot at by the rioters as they fought the blazes.

One Negro was stabbed in the hand by a guardsman and another was shot in the wrist. A third, reportedly a boy of about 15, caught a buckshot blast from a policeman's riot gun.

In all, five Negroes were hospitalized and many other per-

[Continued, Page A 2, Col. 4]

On Other Pages

Stennis Urges Dodd Censure

Washington (AP)—Senator John Stennis, chairman of the Senate Ethics Committee, said today Senator Thomas J. Dodd had used political funds indiscriminately for his personal benefit and the Senate could not afford to condone or ignore it.

Dodd, a Connecticut Democrat whose censure has been recommended by the bipartisan ethics panel, denied any deliberate misuse of funds and appealed to his colleagues to listen to him with open minds.

"I do not ask for mercy. I ask for justice," he said in a prepared speech that he released in advance of its delivery in the Senate.

The conversion of campaign funds to personal use was one of two counts on which the committee recommended censure. The other was double billing for travel expenses.

Dodd Airs Plea

Dodd said that if the Senate should conclude that he was guilty of a deliberate attempt to defraud the Government for travel expenses, he would urge that he be expelled from the Senate rather than censured.

Dodd said that stealing money from the Government is "a crime as mean and wicked and contemptible as any that a public servant could commit."

Stennis, a Mississippi Democrat, led off the debate in a crowded chamber as Dodd's

[Continued, Page A 2, Col. 6]

L.B.J. Appoints First Negro To Seat

Washington (AP) — President Johnson announced today he is nominating the first Negro ever chosen to serve on the Supreme Court, Solicitor General Thurgood Marshall.

Marshall, 58, a native of Baltimore and one-time chief legal officer of the National Association for the Advancement of Colored People, would succeed Associate Justice Tom C. Clark who resigned Monday at the conclusion of the high court's 1966-1967 session.

Cark stepped down because his son, Ramsey Clark, had been selected by Mr. Johnson earlier in the year to be Attorney General.

Accompanied by Marshall, Mr. Johnson went before newsmen and photographers in the White House Rose Garden to announce his choice for Clark's successor.

The Chief Executive said Marshall has earned and deserves a place on the Supreme Court and is the man best qualified for the job by training and experience."

"Place In History"

"I believe he has already earned his place in history," Johnson said.

But he predicted Marshall's stature will be greatly enhanced by service on the Supreme Court.

Immediate reaction to the Marshall appointment was mixed among senators who will be called on to confirm the nomination.

Senator Allen J. Ellender (D., La.) said he was "neither surprised nor disappointed" at the action.

Senator Sam J. Ervin, Jr. (D., N.C.), who has led opposition to civil rights legislation in the puast, sai dhe was reserving judgment until he studies the record Marshall made as a Federal official and as chief legal officer of the N.A.A.C.P.

Confirmation Predicted

Senator George A. Smathers (D., Fla.) said he does not expect there will be "much trouble" about getting Marshall confirmed for his new post since the Senate acted favorably on his appointment as solicitor general.

Ramsey Clark said he had strongly recommended to Mr. Johnson the selection of Marshall.

"I have no doubt that his future contributions will add even more prominence to his already well established place in American history," the Attorney General said in a statement.

Mr. Johnson, at a news conference shortly after he made the announcement of his Supreme Court selection, said he had not chosen a successor to Marshall as solicitor general.

Marshall has been the nation's solicitor general—No. 3 official of the Justice Department—

[Continued, Page A 2, Col. 6]

THURGOOD MARSHALL
Nominated for Supreme Co

REMNANTS OF EGYPTIAN ARMY

Desert Panorama Of Death, Devastation Testifies To Swiftness Of Israeli Advance

By Hugh A. Mulligan

With Israeli Troops on the Suez Canal (AP)—The drifting hot sands of the Sinai desert are slowly obliterating the blackened remnants of a major part of the Egyptian Army.

Arab military leaders can only look on the scene and despair, as for the third time in recent history their dreams of driving the Jews from Palestine have come to grief in the sands of Sinai.

All the way from the Gaza Strip to the banks of the Suez Canal, the scorching desert is littered with the black hulks of hundreds of burned-out tanks, broken vehicles and anti-aircraft guns and command cars, thousands of pieces of mobile equipment, long lines of scorched trucks, still in convoy formation, hit so fast from the air that they had no time and no place to scatter to.

Overturned Rail Cars

Rail cars — overturned, stacked up, strewn about in chaotic confusion like a toy train swept off the tracks by a child in a tantrum—line the tracks snaking across the arid desert.

In two days of jolting through the Sinai peninsula in an Israeli Army truck, I saw an endless panorama of death and devastation testifying to the swiftness of the Israeli sweep to the Suez Canal and the savage fury of fighting in the scorching desert.

Everywhere the seering desert winds brought the fetid pitiless sun Even though the Israeli Army hurried in bulldozer crews to help bury the dead and head off epidemics, the victims were scattered all along the road from Gaza to the canal, hands and legs stretched out almost suppliantly in the death rigor.

Here and there the carcass of a camel lay next to the blackened body of its Bedouin master. Caravan dogs stood lonely vigil over the remains of slain owners. Desert flies swarmed over the decaying bodies and made life even more miserable for the Israeli troops stationed in the Sinai.

Arabs Surrender

In the drab, destroyed Arab villages, the people — mostly women, children and old men—hurried through the streets with their hands stretched in surrender over their heads, always preceded by one or two elders waving a white flag.

On the road from El Arish to stench of bodies rotting in the the Suez Canal, a dozen or so Egyptian soldiers in uniform, a few carrying rifles, were seen hurrying across the sand dunes, trying to get to the blue green ribbon of the canal stretching across the horizon like a turquoise mirage.

Let Them Swim

"They will be caught sooner or later," said an Israeli colonel, "or else they will lay down their arms and try to swim to the west bank of the canal. In which case we will not bother them."

A little farther along the road, an Egyptian soldier knelt in the sand, pleading for water with a tongue already turning black and lips hardening like baked clay. He babbled hysterically, then fell forward on his face.

Our trucks rolled on as the sun reached its meridan and the burning sands gave off shimmering heat waves.

Halted At Roadblock

Farther along the road from El Arish, we were halted at a roadblock. A squad of Israeli

[Continued, Page A 3, Col. 4]

. . . RUSSIA REARMING ARABS?

U.S.S.R. Reported Delivering New Arms To Nasser, Including MIG's

Washington (AP)—Russia is reported delivering new shipments of arms to Egypt following last week's Israeli-Arab war. Jet MIG fighters are said to be among the supplies unloaded at Alexandria.

United States officials said today they are aware of the reports but believe the deliveries represent previously scheduled shipments rather than a crash effort by Russia to rebuild Egypt's shattered military power.

The United States was said to be receiving contradictory reports about Soviet intentions toward rearming the Arab states in the aftermath of the fighting.

Soviet Threats

On the one hand, informants said, the Soviets have been threatening to deliver massive new supplies of weapons to the Arab nations unless Israel yields to Arab demands to pull back its forces to the positions they occupied before the week-long war.

On the other hand, informants said, in some foreign capitals where Western and Soviet officials are in contact, Soviet diplomats have said privately they were disgusted with the Arab defeat in the war and had no intention of pouring more weapons into the Middle East.

The judgment in Washington for the moment is that these contradictory comments, apart from the Soviet effort to pressure Israel into pulling back its forces from conquered territory, probably do represent a division of view in Moscow over what military assistance Russia should supply to Egyptian President Gamal Abdel Nasser and his allies in the future.

Estimate Of Supplies

State and Defense Department authorities have estimated that in the ten years preceding the latest Israeli-Arab war the Soviets supplied about $1,000,000,000 worth of arms to Egypt and more than $1,000,000,000 total to other Arab countries.

United States officials said that if the deliveries to the Egyptians in the past few days had been designed as quick replacement for war-lost equipment, much of it would certainly have arrived by air rather than by ship.

But they reported the evidence is that the new arms were unloaded at Alexandria in crates and the identification of MIGs was said to be based on the size and shape of crates.

During last week's fighting various Arab countries sent men with arms to reinforce Egypt and Jordan. According to reports to the United States Government, Algeria sent 20 MIG fighter planes and would have sent a total of 36 except for some confusion with the Egyptians over arrival arrangements.

The Weather
Partial clearing, turning cooler today. Fair, colder tonight and tomorrow. Yesterday's high, 75; low, 54.
Details and Map, Page C 16)

THE SUN

FINAL

Vol. 262—No. 121—F | BALTIMORE, FRIDAY, APRIL 5, 1968 | 48 Pages | 10 Cents

Dr. King Killed By Sniper In Memphis

JOHNSON VISITS THANT, DISCUSSES VIET PEACE PROSPECTS WITH HIM

'It Was A Good Meeting,' President Says Following Surprise Call Made During Trip To Bishop's Installation

By PHILIP POTTER
[Sun Staff Correspondent]

New York, April 4—President Johnson paid a surprise call on U Thant, Secretary General, at the United Nations building today after attending the two-hour investiture of New York's Archbishop Terence J. Cooke at St. Patrick's Cathedral.

After an hour and ten minutes with Thant in the 38-story, glass-walled building on the East River, President Johnson climbed back into his limousine for a motorcade ride through downtown New York, where rush-hour crowds lined the streets, to waiting helicopters at Sheep Meadow in Central Park.

Vietnam Discussed

He told an accompanying pool of newsmen that he, Thant, Arthur J. Goldberg, Ambassador to the United Nations, and Ralph Bunche, United Nations Under Secretary for special political affairs, had discussed prospects for peace in Vietnam and Southeast Asia.

"It was a good meeting," the President said. "I thought it was very constructive. I am going to ask the Secretary General to visit with us in Washington later when it can be arranged. . . .

"He gave me his assessment of the situation since my Sunday night's speech. He was encouraged."

Mr. Johnson said Ambassador Goldberg had briefed Thant before Mr. Johnson's speech on Sunday, coupling an appeal for peace negotiations with the announcement of a partial American bombing halt in North Vietnam.

The President added that Thant had explained attitudes of various United Nations missions as well as his own and quoted the Secretary General as saying, "Sunday was quite a day—one he had been waiting for."

A joint White House-United Nations Secretariat statement on the meeting said only "the President and the Secretary General met to discuss peace in Vietnam and Southeast Asia. Under Secretary General Ralph Bunche and United States Ambassador Arthur Goldberg took part in the discussions."

Also present were Thomas Johnson, assistant White House press secretary, and James Jones, a deputy special assistant on the White House staff.

Greeted on Sidewalk

The President was greeted warmly on the sidewalk outside the United Nations building by Thant, Goldberg and Bunche. They came out after the conversations to give the President a warm send-off, Thant waving as the Chief Executive drove off.

Thant later described his talk with Mr. Johnson as "cordial" and said it was "highly privileged."

The meeting had been arranged in a whispered conversation between Goldberg and the President during the cathedral ceremonies and details were worked out by telephone as the President's motorcade progressed to Sheep Meadow and the waiting helicopters. Newsmen had already boarded their helicopter and were awaiting take-off for John F. Kennedy International Airport when they were told to get back in their bus for the trip to the United Nations building.

The President returned to Washington after the meeting, taking a helicopter from Central Park to Kennedy Airport to board Air Force One for the trip home.

In contrast to Mr. Johnson's trip here last December for the funeral of Francis Cardinal Spellman, there were no hostile pickets along his motorcade route in downtown New York.

At the cathedral he got the second standing ovation in the history of the huge Catholic edifice. The first was for Pope Paul VI, who made his first visit to the United States October 4, 1965.

After his investiture, Archbishop Cooke praised the Presi-

(Continued, Page A 2, Col. 1)

NEW BOMBING CURB HINTED

No Viet Attacks Reported Near Parallel For Day

Saigon, *Friday*, April 5 (AP)—American sources said today no United States air strikes had been reported near the Twentieth Parallel in North Vietnam for more than 24 hours, prompting speculation that President Johnson may be further curtailing the bombing of the North.

On the ground, the relief of the Marine combat base at Khe Sanh, in South Vietnam's northwest corner, appeared imminent. Lead elements were reported within half a mile of the beleaguered base's perimeter last night.

Conflicting Reports

The United States command said 17 Americans had been killed and 159 wounded in the first four days of the Khe Sanh relief drive, which began Monday. A North Vietnamese broadcast monitored in Tokyo claimed 400 of the Americans were killed in fighting yesterday.

The United States command declined comment on missions flown today over North Vietnam, leaving unconfirmed the speculation about new bombing curbs near the Twentieth Parallel, set by President Johnson as the northern limit for United States raids under his order announced Sunday to de-escalate the air war.

Earlier Report

In this morning's communique, United States headquarters mentioned a strike 225 miles north of the border zone between North and South Vietnam and less than 1 mile south of the Twentieth Parallel during the early morning hours yesterday.

Operation Pegasus, the drive to open Khe Sanh, reported meeting only light opposition from artillery and mortar fire since jumping off from Ca Lu, 12 miles away. Soviet reports in London said yesterday that the North Vietnamese were beginning to withdraw as a

(Continued, Page A 2, Col. 2)

UPI Telephoto

AT THE U.N.—U Thant talks to President Johnson at U.N. headquarters in New York.

HOUSE PASSES TAX ON PLANE TRIPS ABROAD

Action Taken In Hopes Of Cutting Back U.S. Deficit

By RODNEY CROWTHER
[Washington Bureau of The Sun]

Washington, April 4—A bill to impose a 5 per cent tax on airplane tickets to foreign countries was approved by the House today by a 279-to-102 vote with the hope of making a modest dent in the nation's multi-billion-dollar deficit in its balance of payments.

The measure also whittles down drastically the amount of goods a traveling citizen may bring in duty-free from abroad. It now goes to the Senate for action.

Originally the Administration, as a part of its program to reduce the payments deficit, asked for a stiff tax on citizens' expenditures abroad as well as a ticket tax. The House Ways and Means Committee deferred action on the expenditures part of the President's request after hearing extensive testimony from travel organizations, teachers, spokesmen for aviation concerns and others.

Exemptions Reduced

The tax on airline tickets for foreign travel and the changes in duty-free exemptions were expected to reduce the balance-of-payments deficit by $140,000,000.

Changes in the customs regulations for tourists would be:

1. The personal exemption for returning residents would be reduced from $100 to $50 on a permanent basis, and for the period up to October 16, 1969, the allowance would be cut to $10.

2. For residents arriving from the Virgin Islands and other United States insular possessions during the period to October 16, 1969, the exemption would be cut to $100, after which it would go back to $200.

10 Per Cent Duty

3. The rate of duty on articles accompanying a person arriving in the United States is to be 10 per cent of the fair retail value where the aggregate value does not exceed $500 wholesale.

4. The exemption on gifts mailed by a resident traveling abroad has been cut from $10 to $1. The duty per package on shipments valued between $1 and $10 is to be a flat $1.

5. On dutiable noncommercial importations the rate is to be a flat 10 per cent of the fair retail value where the wholesale value of the shipment does not exceed $250.

The Administration had hoped to reduce the payments deficit by $500,000,000 as a result of the ticket tax plus a levy on amounts persons traveling out of the Western Hemisphere spend abroad.

In offering the bill Representative Mills (D., Ark.), Ways and Means chairman, said, "We are not presenting this bill as a monumental proposition—we al-

(Continued, Page A 5, Col. 1)

Brother Reports Rockefeller Is Still A Candidate

Little Rock, Ark., April 4 (AP)—Gov. Winthrop Rockefeller of Arkansas said today his brother, New York Gov. Nelson A. Rockefeller, had told him he was still a candidate for the Republican presidential nomination.

Although the New York Governor said after the New Hampshire primary that he would enter no primaries to actively seek delegate votes, "He told me he thought he made it clear that he is a candidate," Winthrop Rockefeller told newsmen.

The Arkansas Governor said there was confusion over his brother's status because of his post-New Hampshire announcement, but he indicated the New Yorker would clarify his position within three days.

HINTS GIVEN BY HUMPHREY

He Tantalizes Labor Group With Prospect Of Running

By JOSEPH R. L. STERNE
[Sun Staff Correspondent]

Pittsburgh, April 4 — Vice President Humphrey tantalized an enthusiastic labor audience today with broad hints he will soon decide to run for the presidency.

He made it clear, however, that he will coordinate his political plans with President Johnson's attempts to move toward a Vietnam peace settlement and "will do nothing that might hinder the delicate work of diplomacy that lies ahead."

Speaking before the Pennsylvania AFL-CIO Convention, Mr. Humphrey allowed he could "not think of anything more enjoyable than a good campaign against that fellow with the new image," an obvious reference to Richard M. Nixon, front-running Republican presidential contender.

"Getting Interested"

When the 2,500 union members roared their approval, Mr. Humphrey remarked: "You know, I'm getting interested."

But then, lest his audience think he was responding to their shouted pleas to announce immediately, the Vice President added: "After all, its a normal operation of most of us to reassess our position. Let's back up just a little bit."

He assured the convention he was determined to carry the Johnson Administration program "to every part of this country."

"A decision will come," Mr. Humphrey said, "in due time."

Upon his arrival in Pittsburgh, the Vice President received the indorsement of I. W. Abel, president of the United Steelworkers Union, and received word that Williard Wirtz, Secretary of Labor, also had come out for him.

Abel not only urged but pleaded with Mr. Humphrey to make his decision "to be our candidate" the minute President

(Continued, Page A 4, Col. 2)

SATURN RIDES TO ORBIT WITH 3 ENGINES OUT

Misfirings In Key Test May Delay Manned Moon Landing

By ALBERT SEHLSTEDT, JR.
[Sun Staff Correspondent]

Cape Kennedy, April 4—The Saturn 5 rocket was successfully launched here today but failed to achieve proper firing of its two upper stages, which may slow the pace of the nation's program to land men on the moon in this decade.

It was the first serious setback in a Saturn flight record that began with the launching of the comparatively small Saturn 1 rocket October 27, 1961, and reached its high point last November 9 with the initial flight of the enormous Saturn 5. The November flight was virtually flawless.

Dr. George E. Mueller, head of the manned space flight program for the National Aeronautics and Space Administration, tonight described this second Saturn 5 flight as "on balance, a most successful mission."

Mueller said later, however, that NASA would list the flight as a failure in its annual report to Congress. He explained that anything less than 100 per cent success is reported as a failure to Congress.

Today's launching, sixteenth in the Saturn series, was to have qualified the 281-foot rocket for manned flight, possibly as early as this October.

2 Engines Shut Down

However, about eight minutes after the 7 A.M. launching, two of the five engines in the second stage of the rocket shut down. The cause of the problem was not immediately determined.

Despite the loss of this power the Saturn 5 was able to carry its payload, a pilotless Apollo spacecraft, to orbit, with a final boost from the third stage.

The third stage then shut down, as planned, but was to restart again in orbit, flying along a translunar trajectory that reached 320,000 miles into space.

It is this type of firing of the Saturn 5's third stage that would rocket astronauts to the moon on a real lunar mission.

The restart of the third stage was to have occurred at 10.13 A.M. at the end of the second orbit over the United States.

But nothing happened.

As an alternative to the third stage firing, flight controllers at the mission control center in Houston used an on-board rocket of the Apollo spacecraft to achieve a desired orbit from that vehicle.

The on-board engine is in the second section, or module, of the Apollo spacecraft. The Apollo is made up of a command module, to house the astronauts on most of the lunar journey; a service module which carries support equipment in addition to the engine, and the lunar module, the vehicle designed to actually touch down on the moon's surface.

13,800-Mile High Point

Firing of the on-board engine which produces 21,500 pounds of thrust, occurred at 10.16 P.M., lasted for seven minutes and placed the Apollo craft in an elliptical orbit with a high point of 13,800 miles.

The low point of the orbit was 20 miles, meaning that the spacecraft, at the completion of its long loop into space, would come back into the atmosphere for a landing in the Pacific Ocean.

After this morning's lift-off, the Apollo had gone into an initial orbit with a high point of 216 miles and a low point of 112 miles.

Pacific Splash-Down

Apollo's flight ended shortly before 5 P.M. when the command module splashed down in the Pacific, northwest of the Hawaiian Islands.

The command module, lowered to earth on parachutes, had separated from the service module at 4.35 P.M., and from the lunar module much earlier in the flight.

The command module's entry into the atmosphere was a test of its heat shield. Heat builds up around the spacecraft because of friction with small particles in the atmosphere.

With the landing of the Apol-

(Continued, Page A 3, Col. 4)

Civil Rights Leader Shot While On Motel Balcony

DR. MARTIN LUTHER KING, JR. AP

Hit In Neck, He Dies Within Hour; Police Hold 2 Suspects

Memphis, April 4 (AP) — The Rev. Dr. Martin Luther King, Jr., the apostle of non-violence in the American civil rights movement, was killed by a sniper's bullet here tonight.

Dr. King, 39, was shot in the neck as he stood on the balcony of a motel. He died less than an hour later in St. Joseph Hospital.

Gov. Buford Ellington immediately ordered 4,000 National Guard troops back into the city. A curfew, which was clamped on Memphis after a King-led march turned into a riot a week ago, was reimposed.

Police said incidents of violence, including several fire bombings, were reported following Dr. King's death.

Dr. King, the 1964 Nobel Peace winner, had come to lead protests in behalf of the city's 1,300 striking garbage workers, most of them Negroes, when he was shot.

Assassin "In Flophouse"

Police said early investigation indicated the assassin was a white male, who was "50 to 100 yards away in a flophouse." They said they had no definite leads, but that two men were arrested several blocks from the motel.

Police also said they found a .30-06 rifle on Main street about one block from the motel, but it was not confirmed whether this was the weapon that killed Dr. King.

An aide who was standing nearby said the shot hit Dr. King in the neck and lower right part of his face.

"Martin Luther King is dead," said Henry Lux, assistant police chief, delivering the first word of the death.

Hospital Confirmation

Paul Hess, assistant hospital administrator, confirmed later that Dr. King died at 7 P.M. of a bullet wound in the neck.

The Rev. Jesse Jackson said he and others in the King party were getting ready to go to dinner when the shooting occurred.

"King was on the second-floor balcony of the motel," Jackson said. "He had just bent over. If he had been standing up, he wouldn't have been hit in the face."

Dr. King had just told Ben Branch, another member of his party, "My man, be sure to sing 'Blessed Lord' tonight and sing it well."

A shot then rang out, Jackson said.

Jackson said the only sound Dr. King uttered after that was: "Oh!"

"Knocked Him Down"

"It knocked him down," he said. "When I turned around, I saw police coming from everywhere. They said, 'Where did it come from?' and I said, 'Behind you.' The police were coming from where the shot came."

Branch said, "The bullet exploded in his face. It knocked him off his feet."

Solomon Jones, Dr. King's chauffeur, said he saw a "man in white clothes" running from the scene.

Dr. King had returned to Memphis yesterday to lead another massive protest march next Monday in support of the garbage strikers. Sympathizers from other parts of the country had announced they would join, and as many as 10,000 or more were expected for the march.

Dr. King's Memphis involvement was a wayside stop before his big demonstration in Washington scheduled in a few weeks.

The Washington effort—a huge camp-in to demand jobs or income—had taken most of his time since January.

Dr. King's first Memphis march March 28 of about 6,000 erupted into the first violence here since the beginning of the civil rights movement. Police and march leaders, alike, blamed the outburst on Negro youths on the fringe of the march.

Violence erupted again shortly after Dr. King was shot. Police reported snipers firing on police and National Guard units

(Continued, Page A 6, Col. 2)

Shocked Johnson Bids U.S. Reject Acts That Killed King

[Washington Bureau of The Sun]

Washington, April 4—President Johnson paid shocked tribute tonight to the Rev. Martin Luther King, Jr., and postponed his trip to a Vietnam strategy conference in Hawaii. Mr. Johnson, stern-faced and somber, spoke in the doorway of the White House offices over all radio and television networks. He urged prayers for peace and asked the nation to "reject the blind violence that has struck Dr. King, who lived by non-violence."

Official Washington reacted with shocked dismay to the slaying in Memphis, while civil rights leaders, anguished and in disarray, expressed both grief and bitterness.

Paradox Noted

Officials and private citizens alike seemed to look apprehensively to the future. The paradox that the "apostle of non-violence" died by violence was remarked on repeatedly, as the nation's political leaders groped to make their feelings known.

Vice President Humphrey interrupted a gala Democratic fund-raising dinner at a hotel here with word of the "heavy tragedy" that struck in Memphis.

"Martin Luther King has been shot and he is dead," Mr. Humphrey said.

There was a hushed murmur in the crowd, many of whom had already been told of the assassination.

"The criminal act that took his life brings shame to our country," Mr. Humphrey said. "He now stands with other

(Continued, Page A 6, Col. 2)

MINOR VIOLENCE HITS NEW YORK

Looting, Arson Break Out In Negro Neighborhoods

New York, April 4 (AP)—Sporadic arson, looting, rock-throwing and other minor violence broke out in most of the city's Negro neighborhoods tonight following the assassination of Dr. Martin Luther King, Jr.

Mayor John V. Lindsay and top police officials set up a command post on Harlem's 125th street, where the first disturbances broke out shortly after the Memphis killing.

Looting then began in Brooklyn's Bedford-Stuyvesant section and spread to nearby Crown Point and the Fulton street area.

In East New York, police said a large, disorderly crowd stopped automobiles and another group stoned buses.

Washington Negroes Loot

Washington, April 4 (AP)—Crowds of Negroes gathered in a predominantly Negro shop-

(Continued, Page A 6, Col. 1)

Senators Move Crime Bill, But Gun Controls Are Weak

By OSWALD JOHNSTON
[Washington Bureau of The Sun]

Washington, April 4—The Senate Judiciary Committee voted approval today of the Administration's anti-crime bill, but, in an unusual move, suspended action on three key amendments that could seriously modify it.

The committee action definitely approved President Johnson's $100,000,000 safe streets measure, which the committee originally approved Tuesday, and it included also a watered-down version of the Administration's gun-control bill, now pertaining only to handguns.

It also includes a section, approved last week, that would legalize bugging and wiretapping under strict court supervision.

Still suspended on a possibly inconclusive 8-to-7 vote were three amendments that proved to be the main controversy of the afternoon-long closed session. All three are aimed at undercutting recent Supreme Court decisions in criminal law.

While the crime package has been officially ordered reported to the full Senate, the question of whether the court-hobbling amendments will be reported also depended for much of the afternoon on the votes of three absent senators.

As the meeting broke up, liberals and conservatives were reported deadlocked 6 to 6 on the amendments.

Telephone Votes

Two absentees, Senators Burdick (D., N.D.) and Long (D., Mo.) voted later by telephone to strike the amendments, which were written into the bill by Senators McClellan (D., Ark.) and Ervin (D., N.C.).

Senator Scott (R., Pa.) on a train bound for Philadelphia during much of this deliberation, telephoned a tally for the

(Continued, Page A 5, Col. 1)

The Weather
Cloudy and warmer today, high in the lower 70's. Lows tonight around 50. Yesterday's high, 59; low, 40.
(Details and Map, Page B 7.)

THE SUN

LIGHT FOR ALL
(Registered United States Patent Office)

FINAL

Vol. 262—No. 123– F | BALTIMORE, MONDAY, APRIL 8, 1968 | 32 Pages | 10 Cents

1,900 U.S. Troops Patrolling City; Officials Plan Curfew Again Today; 4 Dead, 300 Hurt, 1,350 Arrested

BOMB CURB EXTENSION REPORTED

Johnson Said To Have Limited Air Strikes To 19th Parallel

Saigon, *Monday*, April 8 (AP)—President Johnson has **taken another step** to restrict the bombing of North Vietnam, United States sources said today.

The President, without announcing it, has limited American air strikes over the North from the buffer zone to the Nineteenth Parallel, a stretch of about 170 miles, the United States informants said.

American bombers confined their raids over the North for the fourth straight day yesterday within the 145 miles from the buffer zone to Vinh city, a sector entirely below the Nineteenth Parallel.

Orders Delivered

Publicly, Mr. Johnson's order announced March 31 stands. This curtailed United States air strikes over North Vietnam to an area of about 225 miles between the buffer zone and the Twentieth Parallel.

The sources said orders have gone out to air wings to limit their attacks to the Nineteenth Parallel. They said this was not being publicized because the President wanted to leave open the option of bombing up to the Twentieth parallel.

The Pentagon has said 90 per cent of the United States air strikes are being carried out within 60 miles of the buffer one.

Missions Doubled

While the geographical limits of the raids have been curtailed, United States warplanes have more than doubled the number of strike missions being flown in North Vietnam's southern panhandle. Most of the raids are against military supply facilities.

The President has said the limited bombing of the North could be ended if North Vietnam showed similar restraint.

The North Vietnamese Vietnam News Agency quoted the central committee of the North Vietnam Fatherland **Front today as saying Hanoi's** peace terms include an end to all bombing attacks on the North.

Sunpapers Photo—Rotz

CONFLAGRATION — Fed by dry-cleaning plant fluids, an early Sunday morning fire rages out of control at Federal street and Harford avenue.

AGNEW WIRES JOHNSON; 'INSURRECTION' SPILLS TO SLUMS ON WEST SIDE

First Federal Soldiers Called Into City Since 19th Century Swell Riot Force To 9,000; Gas And Alcohol Sales Curbed

President Johnson ordered 1,900 regular Army soldiers into riot-torn Baltimore last night after Governor Agnew **declared** that an "insurrection" was under way.

The troops, from 18th Corps Airborne Artillery, were bused to Druid Hill Park from Andrews Air Force Base in Prince Georges county.

The Governor sent a telegram to the President declaring': "Under existing circumstances, the law enforcement resources of the State of Maryland are unable to suppress the serious domestic violence in and near the city of Baltimore."

The President's action at 6.14 P.M. meant that 5,500 Maryland National Guard troops in the city since Saturday night are now under Federal command.

First Since Just After Civil War

The decision to call in Federal troops—the first to be brought into the city since a railroad strike at the 1870's—came as burning and looting in slums near the center city went into the second full day.

As the civil turmoil went into its second night, at least four persons had died in riot-related violence.

More than 300 had been injured.

More than 420 fires had broken out.

More than 550 cases of looting had been reported, and more than 1,350 slum-area Negroes had been arrested.

Governor Agnew invoked regulations approaching martial law Saturday night, five hours after rioting broke out in the Gay street area at 5.30 P.M. By then, city officials declared the rioting out of control and the Governor ordered in the National Guard and 400 State Police to reinforce the more than 1,200 city police on duty. An 11 P.M.-to-6 A.M. curfew was invoked.

As the rioting continued unabated yesterday, the Governor, after consulting with Maj. Gen. George M. Gelston, the adjutant general and city and State police officials, ordered the curfew hour advanced to 4 P.M., banned the sales of gasoline and other inflammables except when pumped into automobile gas tanks in no more than 5-gallon lots, banned the sale of firearms and prohibited the sale or dispensing of alcoholic beverages in the city and in Baltmore, Anne Arundel and Howard counties.

The Governor said that after consultation with military and police officials, he will reset curfew hours today.

Police manning the battered east side Negro district seemed confident by 10 P.M. that they had the rioting there under control, but it was reported after mid-night that west-side looting was "heavy."

The military command reported the city "relatively quiet" at 1.45 A.M., saying: "Sporadic reports of minor fires and looting continue but there has been a significant decrease in such activity."

At that moment, police reported a sniper firing on cruisers at the intersection of North Fulton and Lafayette avenues.

Fred M. Vinson, an assistant attorney general, was the presidential representative on the scene in Baltimore as the Federal troops moved into the riot area.

Early in the day it was the east side, already pitted with burned buildings and shattered businesses from Saturday night, that again bore the brunt of the rioting.

The mood of the crowds seemed uglier than the night before, when much of the looting was done openly and almost cheerfully.

Then a large fire broke out on West North avenue, surrounding stores were looted and later in the evening, the first reported exchanges of gunfire between police and rioters was reported in the west side of the city.

By late yesterday aternoon, the fist victims killed during the outburst of racial trouble in the city had been identified.

NAPOLEON K. SLAY, 37, of the 2100 block Koko lane, who was pronounced dead on arrival at 9.30 P.M. Saturday at the Johns Hoopkins Hospital. Police said he was shot once in the head at a tavern at Harford and Lafayette avenues during looting in the area.

JOSEPH ROMANS, a white man whose age and address were not yet known. He was found Saturday with a Negro man in a burned building at Federal and Chester streets. Officials said Mr. Romans died of smoke inhalation and the Negro, not yet identified, had been badly burned.

LOIS T. MAJETTE, 20 of the 1200 block Linworth avenue, who was killed when a car driven by her husband, Arthur L. Majette, east bound on North avenue smashed into a police car driving north on Barclay street amid unruly crowds at 12.50 A.M. Police said the radio car skidded 100 feet into a fire hydrant after the accident. Two of the three policemen in the car received minor injuries.

Police also said Alphonso Boyd, 17, of the 3800 block Derby Manor road, was shot

(Continued, Page A7, Col. 1)

NEUTRAL COUNTRY ASKED FOR TALKS

Saigon Wants Peace Parley In Geneva, Tokyo Or Delhi

Saigon, April 7 (AP)—South Vietnam prefers a neutral country as the site for any talks to end the war. Tran Van Do, Foreign Minister, said today.

He ruled out Paris as well as capitals of Communist countries such as the Soviet Union or Poland. Present thinking in Saigon, he added, is that talks should be held in Geneva. Tokyo or New Delhi.

U Thant, United Nations Secretary General, said Geneva is "quite a good possibility" for preliminary talks which he asserted would begin very soon "and result in the unconditional cessation of the bombing of North Vietnam."

A sudden return to Moscow

(Continued, Page A 2, Col. 5)

Capital Maps Riot Repairs While Troops Enforce Calm

By RALPH H. KENNAN
[Washington Bureau of The Sun]

Washington, April 7—The nation's capital enjoyed a troop-enforced calm Palm Sunday today as officials began to map ways of repairing ghetto burning and looting that broke out Thursday night.

While 11,600 troops patrolled the city, Cyrus R. Vance, presidential troubleshooter, said it was still too early to say for sure "if we've passed the crest" of violence.

Human Problems

Washington's Mayor said early tonight he thought "matters are settling down. I think it's well in hand." Now facing the city, he said, were human problems like food, shelter, clothing and jobs.

Officials blamed the violence for 6 deaths and 929 injuries, estimating that 80 to 90 per cent of those hurt required only minor medical treatment.

A 4 P.M. curfew was clamped on the city as officials sought ways to try to return the capital to something like normal tomorrow. Their biggest headache this afternoon came from sightseers

(Continued, Page A 6, Col. 7)

HOSTAGES FREED AT TUSKEGEE U.

Some Held 13 Hours Until Guard Was Moved In

Tuskegee, Ala., May 7 (AP) — Angry Negro students at Tuskegee Institute locked twelve prominent trustees in a campus guest house and held them hostage for several hours until the National Guard moved in early today.

The students finally backed down after a confrontation with Alabama's only Negro sheriff, Lucius Amerson, who told them:

"I've got the National Guard and the State troopers less than 2 miles away."

Captives Released

Then the students released their prestigious captives, which had included retired Gen. Lucius Clay, Representative Bolton (R., Ohio) and Basil O'Connor, of the National Foundation.

About 300 National Guardsmen and 7 State troopers, assembled in town, rolled onto the campus—and found it quiet. They stayed two hours and left.

Clay, contacted at his home in New York today, said he was freed by three or four friendly students after seven hours, when he told them he had to catch a plane.

Most of the other trustees

(Continued, Page A 6, Col. 3)

ATLANTA HONORS MEMORY OF KING

Friends, Visitors File Past Negro Leader's Casket

Atlanta, April 7 (AP)—The Rev. Martin Luther King's closest friends poured out their sorrow in special Palm Sunday services today while his widow, in seclusion, took personal charge of funeral arrangements.

The streets of Dr. King's home town, untroubled by the major violence that has ravaged other cities, remained quit and uncrowded under a gray sky as Atlanta observed the national day of mourning requested by the President.

Long Line

Visitors continued to file past the body of Dr. King, resting on an unadorned bier in a campus chapel. By mid afternoon the line was backed up a quarter of a mile.

The body was placed on view in a glass-covered bronze coffin yesterday afternoon. It will be taken tomorrow to Ebenezer Baptist Church, where Dr. King was co-pastor with his father. The funeral will be at the Ebenezer church Tuesday.

City officials, hotel keepers, airport authorities and others were preparing to accommodate as many as 100,000 visitors for the funeral.

Interaith Service

Churches of all faiths held special memorial services and others planned memorials tomorrow. An interdenominational service was held at the Episcopal Cathedral of St. Philip.

Dr. King's brother, the Rev. A. D. King, conducted the service today for Dr. King's own flock at the Ebenezer Baptist Church.

He said Dr. King had told him a half hour before he was shot Thursday that he planned to preach a sermon entitlted "Why America may go to hell." Mr. King adopted that topic in his sermon today.

He said America, like the prodigal son of the Bible sto-

(Continued, Page A6, Col. 6)

MAYOR SPURNED AT KING'S RITES

6,000 Gather In Stadium To Show 'Memphis Cares'

By ERNEST B. FURGURSON
[Sun Staff Correspondent]

Memphis, April 7—More than 6,000 persons gathered in Crump Stadium this after**noon to testify that "Memphis** Cares" enough to right its wrongs in the wake of the death of the Rev. Martin Luther King, Jr.

Presence Objected To

But the first citizen of Memphis, Mayor Henry Loeb, was not welcome.

A member of the committee that organized the "Memphis Cares" rally said the Mayor was invited and had accepted but others had then vowed they would not attend in his

(Continued, Page A6, Col 1)

Westmoreland Voices Optimism On Vietnam

By PHILLIP POTTER
[Washington Bureau of The Sun]

Washington, April 7—Gen. William C. Westmoreland **said today that the "spirit of** the offensive" prevails among allied troops in Vietnam against a "weakened" enemy and "militarily, we have never been in better relative position."

The American commander in Vietnam reviewed his two days of talks here with Presi**dent Johnson and the Chief Executive's senior advisers while facing television cameras in front of the White House before returning to Saigon.**

Debate Over Site

His evaluation of the situation came as the United States and North Vietnam were jockeying over the site for preliminary talks to get Vietnam peace negotiations going.

Westmoreland said topics during the two days of White House talks included the military situation, the status of enemy forces, the performance of South Vietnamese military forces and plans for their increase and modernization and current and future military operations and plans.

The general said he had reported that despite the initial

(Continued, Page A 2, Col. 2)

South Viet Regime Is Wary Of Decreasing U.S. Concern

By JOHN S. CARROLL
[Sun Staff Correspondent]

Saigon, April 7—As the United States turns its attention to its own domestic ills, the Government of South Vietnam is growing more apprehensive about the latest prospects for talks between North Vietnamese and American diplomats.

Over the past several days, nearly every high officeholder in Saigon, in one way or another, has expressed concern that the United States will abandon South Vietnam at the conference table.

Principles Listed

The magnitude of the turmoil after the death of the Rev. Martin Luther King, Jr., has reinforced the belief here that the United States will soon concentrate its resources on problems closer to home than South Vietnam.

Almost uniformly, the Saigon politicians in power have reacted by stating several principles which, they say, cannot be compromised. Among the principles are the following:

1. That any peace negotiations will be led by the South Vietnamese Government, with the United States playing a subordinate role.

2. That the partial halt of the bombing of North Vietnam is a "last warning," after which no further concessions will be made.

3. That a "coalition government" or a "neutralized" Vietnam are completely unacceptable in any form.

All Aired By Thieu

All of these principles have been stated by President Nguyen Van Thieu, and have been amplified by senators, representatives and members of the Cabinet.

Tran Van Do, South Vietnam's Foreign Minister and a veteran diplomat, says that

(Continued, Page A 2, Col. 1)

Efficient, Weary Guardsmen Unable To Prevent Looting

By EDWARD G. PICKETT

Maryland's National Guard moved into action yesterday with a speed and efficiency which surprised many people, but was unable to break the pattern of looting.

From late Saturday night through yesterday, Room 12B on the third floor of the Fifth Regiment Armory was the command post for those seeking to secure a city from anarchy.

Across the city, 5,500 Maryland Guard troops patrolled the streets, carrying live ammunition. But despite a night of violence and a day of continued disturbances, there was not a shot fired by the Guardsmen.

It was not until darkness came last night that it became clear that the weary Maryland soldiers, stretched thin across a smoldering city, needed more help, and Federal troops were called for.

Army troops of the 18th Airborne Corps began arriving in Baltimore before 9 P.M. and by 11 P.M. had occupied an area of several acres in Druid Hill Park, north of the lake and south of the Mansion House.

Jeeps And Tents

Scores of jeeps, with bales of barbed wire on their hoods, flanked acres on which had been pitched the traditional pup tents.

Some of the troops were moved out rapidly to West Baltimore, but military authorities refused to say how many or where specifically they were going.

Large cooking and supply tents were being erected, and the regular Army forces appeared to be prepared for a stay of at least several days.

Three times before the Guard has been called up for racial disturbances in Maryland, in Cambridge—in 1963, 1964 and again last July.

This time, the operation

(Continued, Page A9, Col. 1)

The Weather
Sunny, warmer today; high, upper 80's.
Fair, mild tonight. Fair, warm tomorrow.
Yesterday's high, 86; low, 64.
(Details and Map, Page C 9)

THE SUN

FINAL

(Registered United States Patent Office)

Vol. 263—No. 18—F | BALTIMORE, THURSDAY, JUNE 6, 1968 | 52 Pages | 10 Cents

Kennedy Condition Remains Critical

MAYOR ASKS RENEWAL OF BUS SERVICE

Full Restoration Urged At 4.30 A.M. Today: Cash Remains Issue

By JANE L. KEIDEL

Mayor D'Alesandro issued an appeal yesterday for full restoration of bus service, beginning at 4.30 A.M. today.

Last night union leaders said they felt many of the men would respond to the Mayor's appeal and return to work.

Frank P. Baummer, president of Local 1300 of the Amalgamated Transit Union (AFL-CIO), said that after "checking around" he felt that the majority of the drivers would be on the job.

Some May Hold Out

There are "a hard core who plan to hold out," he added.

It was unclear how many might be in this hard core.

Union officials said that regardless of whether daytime service is restored, they will insist that drivers not carry any cash for change on night runs.

And Mr. Baummer said he doubts there will be any bus service tonight because a mass meeting of union members is scheduled for 8 P.M.

MTA Calls Meeting

The Mayor's plea to the drivers yesterday came after a meeting called by the Metropolitan Transit Authority with officials of the Baltimore Transit Company, union representatives, police and city officials.

Mr. D'Alesandro said the same group of people will meet again at 9.30 A.M. today "after the union men have shown their responsibility" by returning to work at 4.30 A.M.

Putting the onus squarely on union leaders, Mr. D'Alesandro said: "It's up to labor to deliver their membership tomorrow morning."

Normally Carry $65

He said he was asking restoration of "full service" with the drivers carrying their "regular cash load." Drivers normally carry $65 for making change for customers.

But after a rash of holdups and the murder Saturday night of one driver, the drivers have refused to carry any cash on night runs.

When the company ordered drivers to carry cash, night bus service stopped here Monday night.

Yesterday morning, day service also stopped, when drivers, in a wildcat strike unsanctioned by the union leadership, refused to take their buses out.

Walter Bierwagen, an international vice president of the transit union, said after yesterday's meeting that a solution to the drivers' complaints about carrying money at night could have been worked out yesterday afternoon if drivers had not taken "this more or less irresponsible step . . . this morning."

Although the drivers' grievances seemed to be the major cause of the wildcat walkout, union politics also appeared to have played a role.

Mr. Baummer reluctantly

(Continued, Page A 12, Col. 1)

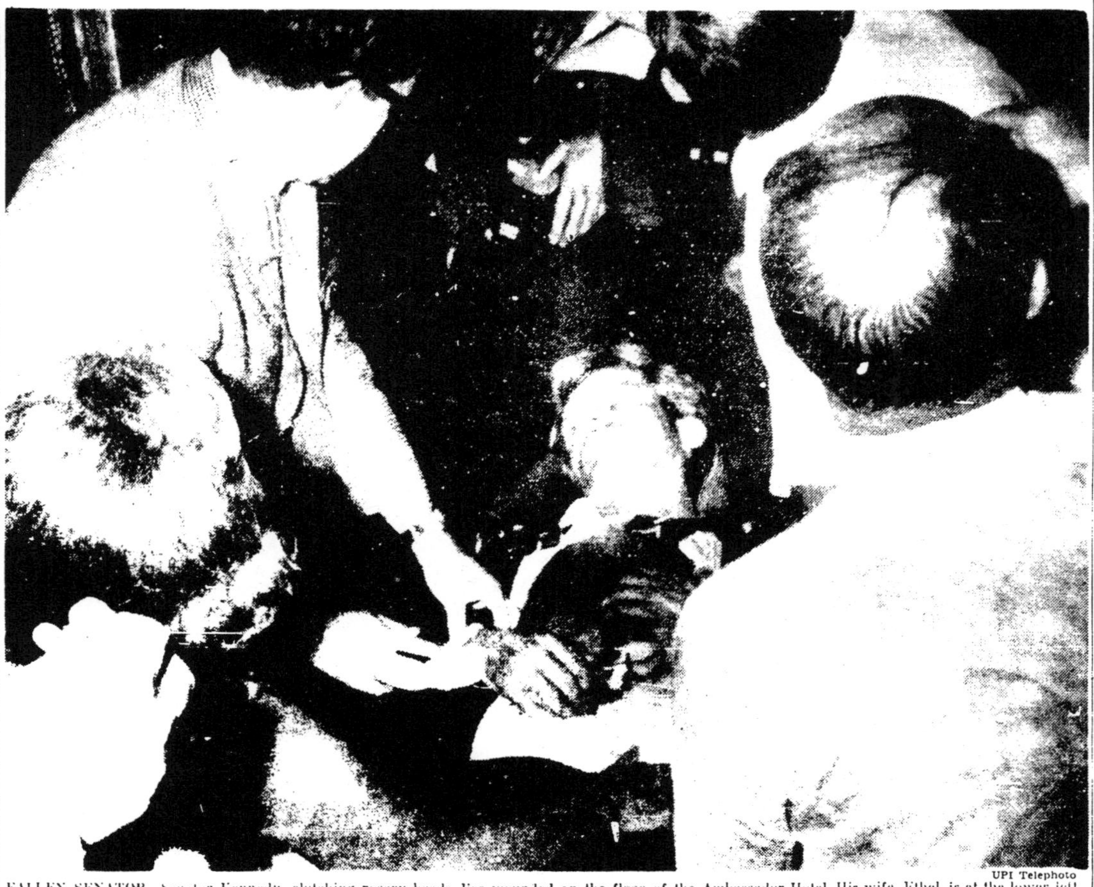

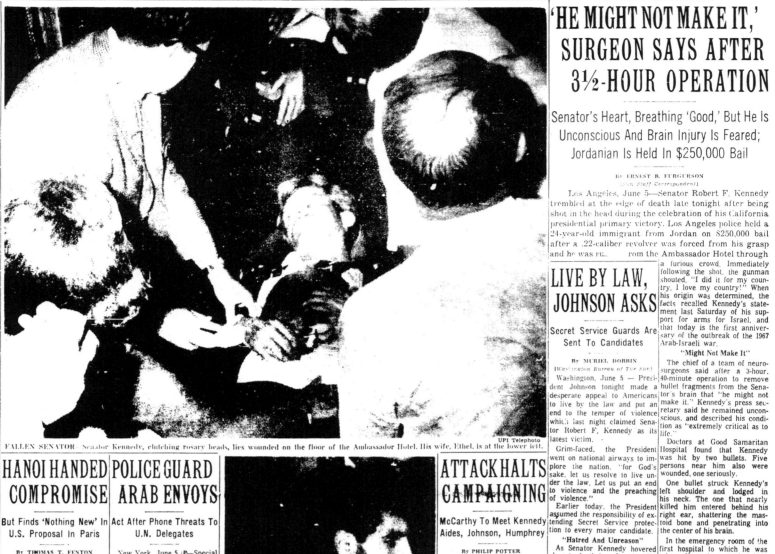

FALLEN SENATOR—Senator Kennedy, clutching rosary beads, lies wounded on the floor of the Ambassador Hotel. His wife, Ethel, is at the lower left. UPI Telephoto

'HE MIGHT NOT MAKE IT,' SURGEON SAYS AFTER 3½-HOUR OPERATION

Senator's Heart, Breathing 'Good,' But He Is Unconscious And Brain Injury Is Feared; Jordanian Is Held In $250,000 Bail

By ERNEST B. FURGURSON
(Sun Staff Correspondent)

Los Angeles, June 5—Senator Robert F. Kennedy trembled at the edge of death late tonight after being shot in the head during the celebration of his California presidential primary victory. Los Angeles police held a 24-year-old immigrant from Jordan on $250,000 bail after a .22-caliber revolver was forced from his grasp and he was ru... rom the Ambassador Hotel through a furious crowd. Immediately following the shot, the gunman shouted, "I did it for my country, I love my country!" When his origin was determined, the facts recalled Kennedy's statement last Saturday of his support for arms for Israel, and that today is the first anniversary of the outbreak of the 1967 Arab-Israeli war.

"Might Not Make It"

The chief of a team of neurosurgeons said after a 3-hour, 40-minute operation to remove bullet fragments from the Senator's brain that "he might not make it." Kennedy's press secretary said he remained unconscious, and described his condition as "extremely critical as to life."

Doctors at Good Samaritan Hospital found that Kennedy was hit by two bullets. Five persons near him also were wounded, one seriously.

One bullet struck Kennedy's left shoulder and lodged in his neck. The one that nearly killed him entered behind his right ear, shattering the mastoid bone and penetrating into the center of his brain.

In the emergency room of the first hospital to which he was taken, Kennedy was found to be "breathless and pulseless" and adrenaline, a resuscitator and heart massage were used, in effect to bring him back to life.

The operation removed all but one of the fragments of bullet and bone but major arteries in the brain were severed, and that vital organ suffered from loss of blood and oxygen. There also was possible injury to the spine.

Damage To Brain

A physician's report said there was damage to the Senators cerebellum, right cerebral hemisphere and mid-brain. The mid-brain controls motion, sensation, sight and such life functions as breathing and heartbeat.

Frank Mankiewicz, the Senator's press secretary, said almost eight hours after the operation ended that new X-ray and electroencephalograph examina-

(Continued, Page A 6, Col. 2)

LIVE BY LAW, JOHNSON ASKS

Secret Service Guards Are Sent To Candidates

By MURIEL DOBBIN
(Washington Bureau of The Sun)

Washington, June 5 — President Johnson tonight made a desperate appeal to Americans to live by the law and put an end to the temper of violence which last night claimed Senator Robert F. Kennedy as its latest victim.

Grim-faced, the President went on national airways to implore the nation, "for God's sake, let us resolve to live under the law. Let us put an end to violence and the preaching of violence."

Earlier today, the President assumed the responsibility of extending Secret Service protection to every major candidate.

"Hatred And Unreason"

As Senator Kennedy hovered close to death in a Los Angeles hospital, the President delivered a nine-minute speech in which he bluntly told the nation that once again it faces "the consequences of lawlessness, hatred and unreason in its midst."

Mr. Johnson, speaking in the Fish Room of the White House, declared "these awful events give us ample warning that in a climate of extremism, of disrespect for law, of contempt for the rights of others, violence may bring down the very best among us."

The President exhorted Congress to "pass laws to bring the insane traffic in guns to a halt."

Mr. Johnson admitted that the gun-control bill which he has urgently advocated and which has so far been bogged down by a reluctant Congress, will not end violence—"but reason and experience tell us that it will slow it down: that it will spare many innocent lives."

"Never Any Justification"

In an obvious reference to those who preach violence on racial or moral grounds, the President emphasized: "There is never—and I say never—any justification for the violence that tears at the fabric of our national life; that inspires such fear in peaceful citizens that they arm themselves with deadly weapons: that sets citizen against citizen or group against group."

Speaking in what he termed

(Continued, Page A 7, Col. 6)

HANOI HANDED COMPROMISE

But Finds 'Nothing New' In U.S. Proposal In Paris

By THOMAS T. FENTON
(Paris Bureau of The Sun)

Paris, June 5 — American negotiators proposed a compromise today in an effort to break the deadlock that has blocked any progress since the Vietnam peace talks began here over three weeks ago.

The immediate reaction of Hanoi's negotiators appeared to be a rejection of the United States suggestion.

A spokesman for the North Vietnamese delegation told correspondents after the 3-hour 45-minute session that he had found "nothing new" in the presentation by the American side.

The compromise suggested by Ambassador W. Averell Harriman, chief American negotiator, was a last-minute addition to the statement he had already prepared for today's session, the seventh since the talks started.

Harriman proposed that the United States acknowledge it has a "responsibility" to stop the bombing of North Vietnam. In turn, the North Vietnamese would agree to take up other aspects of a Vietnamese peace settlement at the same time as conditions for the bombing halt were being discussed.

"You have asked that we acknowledge or determine our responsibility for the cessation of all bombing and acts of war," Harriman told Nguyen

(Continued, Page A 2, Col. 2)

POLICE GUARD ARAB ENVOYS

Act After Phone Threats To U.N. Delegates

New York, June 5 (AP)—Special New York city police and United Nations security forces were posted tonight to protect Arab ambassadors against possible harm following the Kennedy assassination attempt in Los Angeles. Police acted after telephoned threats against Arab envoys were reported in the afternoon.

The man identified as the assassin, Sirhan Bishara Sirhan, 24, is of Jordanian origon but an Arab source here pointed out he has lived in the United States since he was 13, and added: "He's not a Jordanian. He's an American."

Special Precautions

Nevertheless, special precautions were taken to protect three Arab ambassadors at a Security Council meeting called urgently for this evening at the request of both Jordan and Israel on armed attacks and counterattacks across their borders yesterday.

The urgencies of that conflict were quickly sidetracked and the fifteen-nation Council adjourned at Arab request after unanimously agreeing to send a message of sympathy to Mrs. Robert F. Kennedy, wife of the Senator shot earlier in the day.

No date was set for the next Council session.

The special guard was arranged—city police outside and United Nation forces inside this world diplomatic headquarters

(Continued, Page A 2, Col. 5)

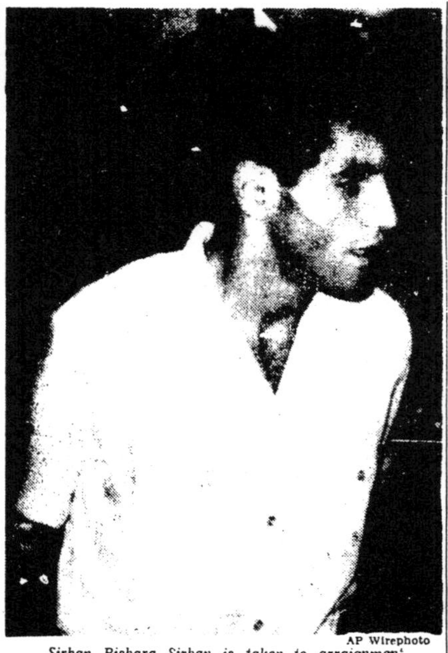

Sirhan Bishara Sirhan is taken to arraignment. AP Wirephoto

ATTACK HALTS CAMPAIGNING

McCarthy To Meet Kennedy Aides, Johnson, Humphrey

By PHILIP POTTER
(Washington Bureau of The Sun)

Washington, June 5—The would-be assassin's bullets that cut down Senator Robert F. Kennedy as he registered triumphs in the California and South Dakota primaries brought new uncertainty into this year's campaign to elect a new President.

Only one thing seemed certain. The grave brain injuries inflicted on the man whose brother was slain 4½ years ago as he neared the end of three years in the presidency undoubtedly have taken the New York Senator out of contention for the Democratic nomination.

His survival is in question.

His shocked rivals, Vice President Humphrey and Senator Eugene J. McCarthy, canceling all political activity indefinitely, are back in Washington.

McCarthy said as he sorrowfully prepared to leave Los Angeles, scene of this morning's fateful shooting of yesterday's primary victor, that he intended while here to confer with Kennedy's spokesmen and with President Johnson and the Vice President "before resuming any political activity."

He did not indicate what was on his mind.

McCarthy said last night that despite his trailing Kennedy by 4 percentage points in California and 30 percentage points in

(Continued, Page A 7, Col. 2)

RAFFERTY OUSTS SENATOR KUCHEL

GOP Picks Conservative; Kennedy's Margin Is 4%

By STEPHEN E. NORDLINGER
(Sun Staff Correspondent)

Los Angeles, June 5—Thomas H. Kuchel, the liberal Republican assistant floor leader of the Senate since 1959, was ousted by Dr. Max Rafferty, the conservative State superintendent of public instruction, in a close race in yesterday's California primary election.

In the Democratic presidential primary, eclipsed by the shooting of Robert F. Kennedy, the New York Senator won 46 per cent of the vote compared to 42 per cent for Senator Eugene J. McCarthy and 12 per cent for the uncommitted slate headed by Thomas C. Lynch, the California attorney general, most of the members of which favored Vice President Humphrey.

Rafferty, who won support of right-wingers throughout the country, attributed his victory to two factors:

1. "The people are sick and tired of disorder and anarchy in the country, and they are voting a protest against the establishment and anybody connected

(Continued, Page A 7, Col. 3)

TIGHT SECURITY SET FOR SIRHAN

Suspect Hospitalized With Ankle, Finger Injuries

Los Angeles, June 5 (AP)—Sirhan Bishara Sirhan was kept under maximum security guard today in a hospital ward at the Los Angeles County Central Jail. Police said he is the only suspect in the shooting of Senator Robert F. Kennedy.

He has been booked on six counts of suspicion of assault with intent to commit murder. Bail was set at $250,000.

Hospitalization was required, an official jail source said, because Sirhan suffered a broken index finger and a sprained left ankle in the melee surrounding his capture.

Bulletin Reported

(Other sources revealed that, according to a bulletin sent by the Los Angeles police to the FBI, Sirhan is "believed to have been in jail," at Pasadena, Cal., December 18, 1963, in connection with an attempted murder.

(There was no indication whether Sirhan was ever formally charged or brought to trial.

(The bulletin also revealed that Los Angeles police are

(Continued, Page A 6, Col. 1)

House Speeds Anti-Crime Bill

By OSWALD JOHNSTON
(Washington Bureau of The Sun)

Washington, June 5 — The House, responding today with shocked emotion to the shooting of Senator Robert F. Kennedy, overwhelmingly rejected a move to change or delay passage of the Senate-passed omnibus anti-crime bill.

By a 317-to-60 vote, the congressmen made final passage of the bill tomorrow a virtual certainty.

The vote was a rarely used parliamentary maneuver to bypass the customary House-Senate conference in which the wide differences between the modest House bill and the far-reaching Senate version would be ironed out.

Gun-Control Measure

The same maneuver was employed two months ago to assure passage of the Senate's civil rights bill in the aftermath of the assassination of the Rev. Martin Luther King, Jr.

Among the Senate additions to the basic House crime bill, a $400,000,000 program of Federal grants to improve local law enforcement, is a moderate gun-control measure, banning the

(Continued, Page A 7, Col. 8)

Orioles Rout Angels, 7 To 1

June 5, 1968.

Dave Johnson slugged a grand-slammer and Curt Motton a solo home run to back Jim Hardin's five-hitter and propel the Orioles to a 7-to-1 victory over California at the Stadium.

[Details on Page C 1]

Wheels Turn Again In Paris As Transport Men Go Back

(Paris Bureau of The Sun)

Paris, June 5—Reports tonight that strikes were ending in the critical areas of transportation, communications and mail were a major breakthrough in the nation-wide strike movement that has paralyzed the French economy and government for almost three weeks.

The news was a boost for the harassed regime of President Charles de Gaulle, which has been struggling to return the nation to normalcy before national elections later this month.

There was little possibility that elections could be held or full government control reestablished in the wake of France's bloodless student and worker revolt until communications and transportation were restored.

As results of workers' votes on strike settlements became known, union officials said tonight railroad workers appeared to be voting strongly in favor of a general return to work tomorrow.

Unions representing bus and subway workers in Paris, which has been without public transportation for nineteen days, announced the systems would be running tomorrow.

A majority of postal, telephone and telegraph workers

(Continued, Page A 2, Col. 4)

A Scattered Kennedy Clan Hears Another Son Is Shot

New York, June 5 (AP)—In the big white house on Cape Cod, a sick father was allowed to sleep through the night. He could be told in the morning, when there was more definite news.

In London, it was 8.30 in the morning, and a princess and her prince were just getting up when a telephone call from America told them the news.

Reached The Embassy

They at once called a young widow in New York. She was asleep and when they asked her for news, she thought they were talking about the election returns.

In Paris, a new ambassador was on his way to his office and only learned the news when he reached the embassy. He immediately telephoned his wife, and they began trying to get a call through to the United States.

Thus, the numerous and widely scattered Kennedy clan began to learn of the horrible and shocking few minutes in Los Angeles during which a victorious Robert F. Kennedy was shot and critically wounded by an assassin.

The first to know, because they were there, were Kennedy's wife Ethel, his sister Jean and her husband Stephen Smith and another sister, Patricia Lawford.

Ethel had become separated

(Continued, Page A 6, Col. 6)

The Weather

Hot and humid today and tonight; high, mid 90's. Cloudy, not so hot tomorrow. Yesterday's high, 96; low 73.

(Details and Map, Page C 11)

THE SUN

Registered United States Patent Office

FINAL

Vol. 263—No. 83—F BALTIMORE, WEDNESDAY, AUGUST 21, 1968 44 Pages 10 Cents

Bloc Troops Seize Czechoslovakia, Man Frontiers; Prague Radio Bitter

EISENHOWER CONDITION IS UNCHANGED

Nixon Visits Family At The Hospital, Extols General's Spirit

By JAMES MACNEES

[Washington Bureau of The Sun]

Washington, Aug. 20—Former President Eisenhower remained comfortable but in critical condition late tonight, doctors at the Walter Reed Army Medical Center reported.

A late bulletin issued at the hospital read:

"General Eisenhower's condition remains essentially unchanged. He continues to have brief episodes of irregular heart action from time to time. He is resting comfortably and enjoys brief visits from members of the immediate family."

Nixon Visits Family

Richard M. Nixon, Republican presidential nominee, visited the Army hospital today, although he did not see the General. Mr. Nixon spent 54 minutes with Mrs. Eisenhower, the ex-President's son, Col. John Eisenhower, and medical specialists.

Mr. Nixon told reporters on emerging from the Pershing Suite of the hospital that "what is more encouraging in addition to today's medical report is the General's outstanding spirit.

"All the medical specialists said the General is giving them a lesson in courage. He has the will to live . . . [and] . . . that is seeing him through.

"Tremendous Factor"

"We are all praying for his recovery," Mr. Nixon said. "His tremendous spirit makes his chances for recovery certainly not to be underestimated. A tremendous factor is his wonderful will to live."

The GOP nominee did not see the General in person. Only members of the close family see him and medical specialists attached to his case.

It was the judgment of the cardiologists treating the former President that he must be guarded against any experience which might cause him excitement.

Mr. Nixon said it was the decision of the General's physicians "that I should not see him."

Eisenhower Was Informed

Before microphones outside the east wing of the hospital Mr. Nixon said "the General was informed a couple of days ago that I hoped to come and see him, but I don't think he expected to see me."

"Anything in the political field would excite him" said Mr. Nixon, who came here from Harrisburg and left immediately afterward for New York to continue his political activities.

Before Mr. Nixon's arrival, his daughter, Julie, and her fiance, General Eisenhower's grandson, David, had been visiting with Mrs. Eisenhower. They were leaving Walter Reed as Mr. Nixon arrived. The GOP nominee sat somber-faced in his limousine in the courtyard of the main hospital building until a Secret Service man gave him a signal to get out of the car.

Groups of aides, Secret Service, medical center military police, patients, nurses and doctors watched as Colonel Eisenhower greeted Mr. Nixon on the steps of the portico. The two men entered the building together.

The candidate had high praise for Mrs. Eisenhower. "She is taking it remarkably. This has been a difficult period for her. She has spent two weeks in a room next to the General. As she put it, 'When you see the General's spirit, its contagious.' All of those in attendance have picked up his will to live," Mr. Nixon said.

He left the hospital accompanied by Brig. Gen. Frederic Hughes, commanding general of Walter Reed Army Medical Center. Mr. Nixon had nothing to report on Mr. Eisenhower's medical condition.

Crisis Forces Rusk To Leave Party Hearings

AP Wirephoto

Dean Rusk confers with Hale Boggs, Platform Committee chairman, before leaving upon word of the Czechoslovak crisis

By JOSEPH R. L. STERNE

[Washington Bureau of The Sun]

Washington, Aug. 20—Dean Rusk, Secretary of State, cut short his appearance before the Democratic Platform Committee tonight after receiving the first bulletin on the new Czech crisis.

Moments earlier, a dozen critics of the Administration's policy in Vietnam had been on their feet clamoring for recognition in order to cross-examine the Secretary.

They and a capacity audience in the Hotel Statler's Presidential Ballroom suddenly became silent, sensing something was wrong, when Mr. Rusk left the podium to speak to the committee chairman, Representative Boggs (D., La.).

Reads Dispatch

Mr. Boggs then read the first lines of the Associated Press dispatch: "Prague Radio announced Wednesday that troops of the Soviet Union, Poland and East Germany started to cross the Czechoslovak border at 11 P.M. Tuesday. . . ."

There were gasps and a few low whistles from the audience as Mr. Boggs said questioning would have to be ruled out. "The Secretary does have a problem," he remarked.

"I didn't expect that report when I came in," Mr. Rusk commented, "but I think I will go and see what it is all about."

Then, flanked by aides, the Secretary excused himself from the hearing, walked swiftly to his limousine and began another night of crisis-watching.

Tonight's dramatic development was expected to bolster the position of those on the hotly divided Platform Committee who are opposed to the kind of Vietnam peace plank demanded by supporters of Senators Eugene McCarthy and George McGovern.

Former Senator William Benton of Connecticut, a backer of Vice President Humphrey for the Democratic nomination, said the reported Soviet invasion showed how "infinitely more complex" the world situation is than Vietnam critics make out.

Theodore Sorensen of New

(Continued, Page A 6, Col. 2)

PRESIDENT SUMMONS TOP COUNCIL

Security Group Called After Soviet Envoy Delivers Message

By NATHAN MILLER

[Washington Bureau of The Sun]

Washington, Aug. 20 — President Johnson summoned the National Security Council into an emergency session tonight to discuss the unfolding Czech crisis.

George Christian, White House press secretary, said the President called the meeting, attended by eleven ranking Government officials, on the basis of a message he had been given earlier by Anatoly Dobrynin, the Soviet Ambassador in Washington.

Mr. Christian declined to reveal the contents of the message, but said that after the President reviewed it and other information that was available he called the Security Council into session to consider the situation in Czechoslovakia.

55-Minute Meeting

During the 55-minute meeting, Mr. Christian said, the President asked Dean Rusk, Secretary of State, to call on Mr. Dobrynin tonight "to discuss the matter further."

Mr. Rusk and the envoy met at the State Department from about 11.30 P.M. to 11.45 P.M. The department declined to comment on the meeting.

But one United States official said, "We certainly didn't have any information on this move."

Sitting in on the meeting were George Ball, Ambassador to the United Nations, and John Leddy, Assistant Secretary of State for European affairs.

Mr. Christian declined to give any details of the Security Council meeting or to say whether United States troops in western Europe or at home had been alerted.

"Hot Line" Not Used

He did say that the "hot line" between the White House and the Kremlin had not been put into use.

Mr. Christian was unable to give the exact time when the Soviet Ambassador arrived at the White House, but said it occurred while Mr. Rusk was testifying on the Administration's Vietnam policy before the Democratic Platform Committee.

He refused to say whether Ambassador Dobrynin had contacted the White House before the situation," said Brig. Gen. R. the Prague radio had broadcast reports that Soviet and other Warsaw Pact troops had crossed its frontiers.

"The meeting was ordered on

(Continued, Page A 4, Col. 1)

STATION ASKS CALM; CROWDS FIRED UPON; TASS DEFENDS MOVE

By STUART S. SMITH

Bonn, Wednesday, Aug. 21 — Radio Prague resumed broadcasting this morning and announced that Soviet troops had occupied Karlovy Vary, a spa in western Bohemia, and had assumed responsibility for the defense of Czechoslovakia's frontiers.

The station implored the populace to "go to your places of work. Trust us . . . Do not acknowledge the invaders . . . we do not want to wait another twenty years Do not let them into your homes . . . We begs you to remain calm."

Radio Prague promised to continue broadcasting, vowing to "back the legal Government of the country for as long as possible."

Radio Prague reported that airplanes flew over Prague this morning dropping leaflets declaring that Antonin Novotny, the state and party chief replaced last winter by Alexander Dubcek, remained the country's legal leader.

About 7.25 A.M. Soviet troops began firing on demonstrators around the Radio Prague building. At about the same time the transmitter went off the air.

Justification

By BRUCE WINTERS

[Moscow Bureau of The Sun]

Moscow, Wednesday, Aug. 21 —The Soviet Government today justified the invasion of Czechoslovakia in the name of socialism and peace in Eastern Europe.

Tass, the official news agency, declared in a formal statement that "the further aggravation of the situation in Czechoslovakia affects the vital interests of the Soviet Union and other Socialist states."

It said the troops would immediately be withdrawn as soon as the "threat to the gains of socialism" was crushed.

Infringement Denied

"The actions which are being taken today are not directed against any state and in no measure infringe state interests of anybody," the Tass statement added. "They serve the purpose of peace and have been prompted by concern for its consolidation.

"Tass is authorized to state that party and government leaders of the Czechoslovak Socialist Republic have asked the Soviet Union and other allied states to render the fraternal Czechoslovak people urgent assistance, including assistance with armed forces.

"This request was brought about by the threat which has arisen to the Socialist system, existing in Czechoslovakia, and to the statehood established by the constitution, the threat emanating from the counter-revolutionary forces which have entered into a collusion with foreign forces hostile to socialism."

Further Justification

The entire operation was further justified as merely an extension of what has been called the "spirit of Bratislava."

"This decision is fully in accord with the rights of states to individual and collective self defense envisaged in treaties of alliance concluded between the fraternal socialist countries," Tass said.

The 1,000-word Tass statement was read in its entirety over Radio Moscow as this city was preparing for another routine work day.

"This decision is fully in accord with the right of states to individual and collective self-defense envisaged in treaties of alliance concluded between the fraternal Socialist countries," Tass said.

Czechoslovakia occupies a linch-pin position in the Communist military organization, the Warsaw Pact.

"This decision is also in line with vital interests of our countries in safeguarding European peace against forces of militarism, aggression and revenue, which have more than once plunged the peoples of Europe

(Continued, Page A 4, Col. 6)

Invasion

By STUART S. SMITH

[Bonn Bureau of The Sun]

Bonn, Wednesday, Aug. 21—Soviet, Polish, Hungarian, Bulgarian and East German troops have invaded Czechoslovakia, Radio Prague announced early this morning.

The Warsaw Pact soldiers entered the country "without the knowledge of the President of the Republic, National Assembly chairman, the Premier or the first secretary of the Czechoslovak Communist party," Radio Prague declared.

Shortly after 5 A.M. (Central European Time) Vincent Buist, a Reuters correspondent in Prague, reported that all taxis and automobiles in the Czechoslovak capital began racing through the city at about dawn this morning blaring their horns to alert the population.

Carrying Machine Guns

At about the same time, Russian troops wearing red berets and carrying machine guns took up positions outside the Radio Prague headquarters building.

Soviet tanks guarded the Vltava River bridges in the center of the city. A constant stream of Soviet bombers flew low over the city.

Thousands of young Czechoslovaks grabbed blue, white and red national colors and marched on the party Central Committee building in the city chanting "Liberty-Liberty" and "Where is Dubcek?" The whereabouts of Alexander Dubcek, the Czechoslovak Communist party leader, is unknown.

As the sun came up, Soviet tanks and armored cars surrounded the Central Committee building.

Shortly after dawn, the Soviet

(Continued, Page A 4, Col. 5)

Angels Whip Orioles, 7-2

August 20, 1968

Rick Clark and Clyde Wright collaborated on a one-hitter and the California Angels rode a five-run fourth-inning rally to a 7-to-2 victory over the Orioles in Anaheim, Cal., tonight.

[Details on Page C 11

JOHNSON BACKS U.S. JOB CUTBACK

Move To Limit Rehiring To Only 70% Approved

By OSWALD JOHNSTON

[Washington Bureau of The Sun]

Washington, Aug. 20—President Johnson approved today a tough employment rollback policy designed to meet stringent congressional demands for economy in Federal agencies.

At the same time, the policy is tailored to allow for the special manpower demands of such top priority programs as the "safe streets" anti-crime program in the Justice Department and the special needs of the main Federal regulatory agencies.

The new formula was announced today in the form of a memorandum prepared by Charles Zwick, director of the budget.

In question is the manpower cutback demanded by Congress

(Continued, Page A 7, Col. 3)

Democratic Credentials Unit Ousts Mississippi Delegation

By CHARLES WHITEFORD

[Convention Bureau of The Sun]

Chicago, Aug. 20—The Democratic National Convention's Credentials Committee voted 84 to 10 late tonight to oust the racially tinged regular Mississippi delegation to the conclave.

Then, the 110-member group voted overwhelmingly to seat in the place of the Deep South delegation a rival one from Mississippi composed almost equally of Negroes and whites.

Joseph L. Rauh, Jr., a Washington lawyer long active in civil rights causes, said with a broad grin as he confirmed the word:

"The Democratic party has gained its integrity tonight. This was a crippling defeat for the racists of the party.

"Symbolic" Of Problem

"Mississippi was symbolic of what has been wrong with our great party."

The Mississippi regular delegates, representatives of a long line of "lily white" politicians who have controlled affairs in that State since the Civil War, prepared to make a last-ditch battle for places in the convention opening next Monday on the convention floor.

It is probably that floor fights will develop over the seating of three other Southern delegations.

(Continued, Page A 6, Col. 4)

TROOPS TO SERVE CONVENTION DUTY

5,469 In Illinois Guard Called At Daley's Request

Springfield, Ill., Aug. 20 (AP)—Gov. Samuel H. Shapiro authorized 5,469 Illinois National Guardsmen to active duty today during the Democratic National Convention in Chicago.

The guard troops were requested by Mayor Richard J. Daley of Chicago.

The tour of duty will start by 8 A.M. Friday.

Brig. Gen. Richard T. Dunn was designated commander of the troops.

In an executive order, Governor Shapiro said it is apparent that demonstrations by dissident organizations "may result in a tumult, riot or mob disorder" and "it is deemed that a time of public disorder and danger exists."

Units Called Up

The Governor said Mayor Daley had advised that "this threatened situation in Chicago may become beyond the control of the civil authorities."

Units ordered to duty are from Chicago, Joliet, Elgin, Kankakee, Waukegan and Woodstock.

More than 5,000 regular Army soldiers at Fort Hood, Texas, underwent three days of civil disturbance exercises last week—drills that could prepare them also for possible duty during next week's Democratic convention in Chicago.

A Fort Hood spokesman said the exercises, completed Fri-

(Continued, Page A 6, Col. 3)

Index

7 INMATES SHOT AT OHIO PRISON

2 Seriously Hurt As Guards Quell Lebanon Riot

Lebanon Ohio, Aug. 20 (AP)—A State prison official said seven prisoners were shot tonight before guards put down a riot at the Lebanon Correctional Institution.

No one was killed. Two prisoners were reported in serious condition.

The State adjutant general's office at Columbus said two units of the Ohio National Guard, totaling about 300 men, were ordered to duty at the Lebanon Armory.

250 Inmates Participated

"We'll decide what to do when we have assessed that situation," said Brig. Gen. R. H. Canterbury, deputy adjutant general.

Maury Koblentz, State correction chief, said about 250 inmates who participated in the

(Continued, Page A 8, Col. 4)

Shriver, 3 Others Are Listed As Humphrey Running Mate

By ERNEST B. FURGURSON

[Convention Bureau of The Sun]

Chicago, Aug. 20—There is an excellent chance that Vice President Humphrey, like Richard M. Nixon, will turn to a native Marylander as a running mate if he is nominated for President next week.

R. Sargent Shriver, the Ambassador to France, who was born in Owings Mills, Md., is high on the list of Democrats considered most likely choices for Mr. Humphrey. The others are Senator Fred R. Harris of Oklahoma, Senator Edmund Muskie of Maine and Gov. Richard J. Hughes of New Jersey.

Top Four

Delegates and newsmen arriving here for next week's convention have been encouraged by the Humphrey staff to consider these the top four possible vice presidential selections.

Among them, Senator Harris is a very slight favorite today, mainly because he has worked hard as co-chairman of the Humphrey campaign.

The list of others whose names have been floated before the delegates includes former Gov. Terry Sanford of North Carolina, Gov. John B. Connally, Jr., of Texas, Mayor Joseph

UPI

R. SARGENT SHRIVER

Alioto of San Francisco, John W. Gardner, former Secretary of Health, Education and Welfare, Senator Joseph D. Tydings of Maryland, Senator Philip A. Hart of Michigan, and Senators Eugene J. McCarthy and George

(Continued, Page A 7, Col. 4)

Dissenting Theologians Air Their Views On Birth Control

By WELDON WALLACE

[Religion Editor of The Sun]

Washington, Aug. 20—Patrick Cardinal O'Boyle met with theologians of Catholic University today and agreed to take "under advisement" the dissent which a number of them have expressed to Pope Paul's birth-control encyclical.

He made known this decision after a meeting lasting more than two hours.

At his request, the theologians freely aired their views on the right to take issue with the encyclical or, by implication, any other non-infallible statement of a Pope.

600 Sign Dissent

Those who defended this right included two theologians who had not signed a statement of dissent which originated at Catholic University and which now bears the signatures of 600 theologians across the nation.

Cardinal O'Boyle said he would probably submit the matter of the theologians' position to the university's board of trustees at a special meeting.

In answer to a question, however, he was vague about when this meeting could be held. He said it was difficult to find a time agreeable to all board members. Normally the board meets in November.

Clerical observers here regarded Cardinal O'Boyle's position as a major step toward eventual recognition by bishops of the right to dissent.

Position Strengthened

"Time is on our side," said one theologian who opposes the encyclical. "Every minute that we gain strengthens our position."

Dissenters found further cause for gratification in a confidential "summit meeting" of theologians and bishops held in New York Sunday and yesterday. There, the question of the right to dissent was explored with what one participant described as "candor of a type never before experienced in the American Catholic Church between theologians and bishops."

Participants included seven theologians who had signed the statement of dissent, and seven theologians and bishops who had not.

Each side presented its views

(Continued, Page A 2, Col. 6)

The Weather
Variable cloudiness and warm with a chance of showers today. Highs in the upper 80's. Yesterday's high, 87; low, 74
(Details and Map, Page C8)

THE SUN

FINAL

(Registered United States Patent Office)

Vol. 265—No. 56—F | BALTIMORE, MONDAY, JULY 21, 1969 | 38 Pages | 10 Cents

Astronauts Walk On The Moon After A 'Very Smooth' Landing

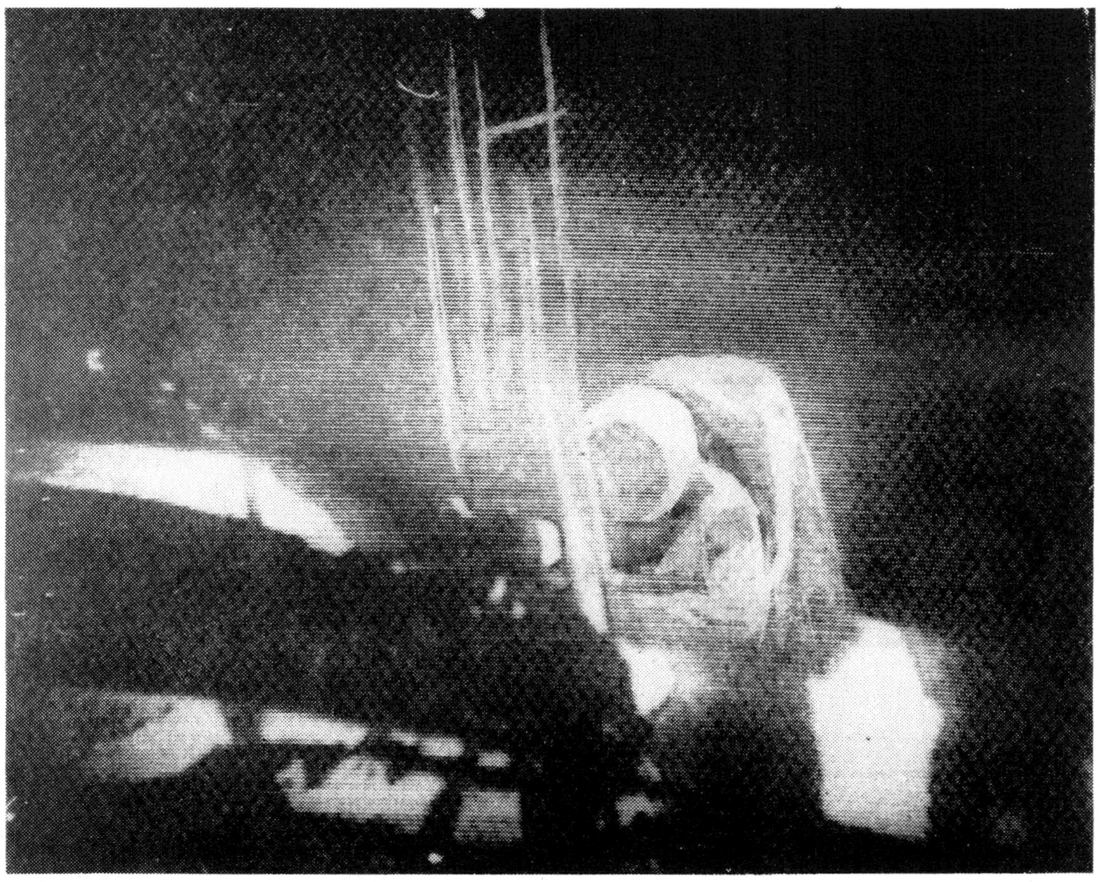

Helmeted Neil Armstrong climbs down the ladder attached to one of the legs

Armstrong Calls Step 'One Giant Leap For Mankind'

By ALBERT SEHLSTEDT, JR.
Sun Staff Correspondent

Houston, July 20—Men from earth stepped onto the surface of the moon tonight.

Two American astronauts realized a dream of centuries by treading on the powdery lunar surface nearly seven hours after making a "very smooth" landing in the moon's Sea of Tranquillity.

Neil A. Armstrong, 38, of Wapakonela, Ohio, made the first historic step at 10.56 P.M., descending a ladder of nine rungs on one of the four legs of the lunar landing craft. He was followed by Col. Edwin E. Aldrin, Jr., 39 USAF, of Montclair, N.J., at 11.14 P.M. As Mr. Armstrong put his first foot on the surface, he said: "That's one small step for man; one giant leap for mankind."

The step was televised to earth by a small TV camera on the side of the lunar module, named Eagle.

"I only go in a small fraction of an inch," Mr. Armstrong said of his foot impressions. He said the moon's surface near the landing craft was "very fine-grained—almost like a powder."

No Trouble Moving Around

"There seems to be no difficulty in moving around," Mr. Armstrong said, adding that it was easier to walk on the moon than in simulations of lunar walking on earth.

"Actually, no trouble to walk round,"he added.

The Mission Control Center reminded the astronaut to collect a contingency sample of lunar soil—a small amount of lunar material the two explorers could take back to earth with them if they had to leave quickly.

"I'll try to get a rock here—just a couple," Mr. Armstrong said.

At times, he seemed a little breathless as if it were something of an effort to move in the bulky pressure suit. He commented on the lunar scenery.

"Stark Beauty"

"It has a stark beauty all its own," he said.

After Colonel Aldrin came out of the lunar module, the astronauts set up the camera some distance from the ladder and transmitted pictures of Eagle and nearby scenes of the surface.

Mr. Armstrong called attention to "a large angular rock in the foreground" and a larger one "very rounded" at another point.

The astronauts moved about the surface with orange packs on their backs which contained portable oxygen supplies and communications equipment. Television pictures of the two men in their flight suits standing in front of the landing vehicle had an almost ghostlike quality.

In their movements, they seemed to almost float over the surface.

The moon's gravitational pull is one-sixth that of earth's.

At 11.40 P.M., Mr. Armstrong and Colonel Aldrin erected an American flag on a small staff near the Eagle.

They stepped back away from the flag and stood still for a few moments.

Earlier, Mr. Armstrong called attention to a plaque on the side of the landing craft which stated "We came in peace for all mankind.

Kangaroo Hop

The plaque bore their signatures and those of President Nixon and Lt. Col. Michael Collins, orbiting the moon in the command module.

Colonel Aldrin then demonstrated hopping about on the moon, moving like a football player snaking his way through the line. Then he did a kangaroo hop.

At 11.47 P.M., President Nixon called the astronauts from the White House, saying "for every American, this has to be the proudest day of our lives." Mr. Nixon said "the heavens have become a part of man's world."

Mr. Armstrong replied by saying it was an honor and privilege for him and Colonel Aldrin to be there.

The distance from the moon to earth today was approximately 242,000 miles.

The astronauts had landed their craft in the southwestern part of the Sea of Tranquillity.

Continued Their Inspection

The astronauts continued their inspection of the surface as the evening wore on.

Mr. Armstrong walked back to check the lunar module and said he saw no abnormalities on the craft.

Colonel Aldrin said he was surprised by the lack of penetration of the footpads into the moon's surface.

The penetration was 3 inches at the most.

The two men then prepared to deploy several scientific experiments on the moon which would be left behind.

Passive Seismometer

One was a passive seismometer to record moon quakes. Another was a laser ranging reflector designed to reflect laser beams back to earth and thereby measure precisely the distance between the two bodies.

Colonel Aldrin reported he was having a little

(Continued, Page A 4, Col. 1)

MOON LANDING STIRS ELATION

Astronauts Feat Greeted By Worldwide Goodwill

London, July 20 (AP)—Crowds screamed joyously in Trafalgar Square, people danced in Chile, a Russian yelled "Hooray." Almost everyone on earth was somehow touched by man's arrival on the moon.

Pope Paul VI praised America's three astronauts as "conquerers of the moon" minutes after the Eagle spacecraft touched down on the lunar surface. He said man faces "the expanse of endless space and a new destiny."

Soviet news media did not dramatize the landing. Reports of the touchdown were buried in Soviet television and radio newscasts behind other news of the day. But individual Muscovites cheered and expressed congratulations to Americans in the Soviet capital. "Hooray," one yelled. "It's a great day," shouted another.

Bulletins Interrupted

In the war-torn Middle East, Arab radio stations interrupted their bulletins on a major air battle over the Suez Canal to acclaim the event and praise Edwin Aldrin and Neil Armstrong for "making history."

The streets of some of the world's largest cities—Mexico City, Oslo, Belgrade, Rome—were nearly deserted as millions stayed home glued to their television screens.

One Yugoslav teen-ager said "They have stolen the romance out of the moon and it will never be the same again. Now the moon is real, and lovers won't have it for themselves alone any more."

In the middle of a war broadcast from Beirut the announcer said: "Ladies and gentlemen, The moon is now within man's

(Continued, Page A 6, Col. 7)

Israeli, Egyptian Jets Stage Raids, Battle

By ADAM CLYMER
[Sun Staff Correspondent]

Jerusalem, July 20—Israeli and Egyptian planes bombed each other's territory today for the first time since the 1967 war, Army spokesmen announced.

Israel said its pilots downed 5 Egyptian planes, but also conceded that for the first time it lost 2 of its own in dogfights. Egypt said 17 Israeli planes were shot down.

The Israeli air attacks, accompanied by shelling, were aimed at artillery and anti-aircraft installations. Two surface-to-air missile sites were hit, an Israeli Army spokesman said.

The clashes ranged along the entire canal area but penetrated most deeply in the northern sector, from Port Said on the Egyptian side to Romani on the Israeli side.

Follow Pre-Dawn Assault

Cairo has previously accused Israel of launching air attacks. Never before has Israel admitted it.

This afternoon's five-hour battle followed a pre-dawn Israeli assault on an Egyptian island fortress guarding the southern entrance to the canal. Israeli authorities said they destroyed or heavily damaged four 85-mm. anti-aircraft guns, killed at least 25 Egyptians, and escaped from the concrete island with 6 killed and 9 wounded.

But Egypt said the assault on man-made Green Island was beaten off, with 30 Israelis killed when two fully loaded assault boats were sunk.

A senior Israeli staff officer, denying that charge, said there were "no boats in the area." He declined to say whether helicopters had been used, but described the method of reaching the island, about 2½ miles off Port Taufiq, as "quite an ingenious way."

Egypt also claimed to have shot down an Israeli Mirage jet fighter in the clash. Israel denied it.

(The Associated Press report-

(Continued, Page A 2, Col 6)

LUNA MISSION STILL ENIGMA

Unmanned Russian Satellite May Be Observing Apollo

Jodrell Bank, England, July 20 (AP)—Luna 15 darted dramatically nearer the moon today in a maneuver that Jodrell Bank scientists said could mean only that the Soviet unmanned probe was bent on reconnaissance during the Apollo 11 mission or was preparing to land.

The observatory's director, Sir Bernard Lovell, said that, after Luna 15 had carried out two course corrections, its mean altitude was 40 miles above the lunar surface.

In Moscow, the Soviet news agency Tass said that Luna 15 was within 10 miles of the moon at its lowest point. It added that the probe was functioning normally in its scientific exploration of lunar space.

Semi-official leaks in Moscow before last Sunday's launching

(Continued, Page A 5, Col. 6)

'Tranquillity Base Here—The Eagle Has Landed'

Houston, July 20 (AP) — "Houston, Tranquillity Base here. The Eagle has landed."

Thus Neil Armstrong, seated in a landing craft named Eagle beside his crewmate, Col. Edwin Aldrin, began the first conversation between earth and the moon.

Here are excerpts:

Mission Control—Roger, Tranquillity. We copy you on the ground. You got a bunch of guys about to turn blue. We're breathing again. Thanks a lot."

Eagle — Armstrong: Thank you. . . . That may have seemed like a very long final phase. The auto targeting was taking us right into a football field-size, uh, football field-size crater. There's a large number of big boulders and rocks for about one or two crater diameters around it. And it required us to plunk down in P66 (nonautomatic flight) and fly in manually over the rock field to find a reasonably good area.

We'll get to the details of what's around here, but it looks like a collection of just about every variety of shape, angularity, granularity—every variety of rock you could find.

The colors, well, it varies pretty much depending on how you're looking relative to the . . . There doesn't appear to be

(Continued, Page A 6, Col. 4)

NEW ERA BEGUN, SAYS NASA HEAD

Paine Sees Man Setting Up Extra-Earthly Abodes

By FREDERICK P. McGEHAN
[Sun Staff Correspondent]

Houston, July 20—"We have entered a new era," the administrator of the National Aeronautics and Space Administration said here today following the historic landing of men on the moon.

Speaking to reporters about an hour and a half after the touchdown—and after talking with President Nixon—Dr. Thomas O. Paine, the NASA administrator, said: "The significance of the trip is that mankind is going to establish places of abode outside of his planet earth."

Dr. Paine said he talked with Mr. Nixon by telephone a few moments after Neil A. Armstrong and Col. Edwin E. Aldrin, Jr., had landed safely.

Great Tensions Relieved

He told the President: "It is my honor on behalf of the entire NASA team to report to you that the Eagle has landed on the Sea of Tranquillity and our astronauts are safe and looking forward to starting the exploration of the moon."

Dr. Paine said Mr. Nixon, who listened in the White House to the landing with Col. Frank Borman, a former astronaut and now a NASA field director, offered his congratulations on the success of the landing and hoped

(Continued, Page A 5, Col. 3)

Index

Kennedy Will Face Charge In Leaving Accident Scene

Edgartown, Mass., July 20 (AP)—A complaint charging Senator Edward M. Kennedy with leaving the scene of an accident will be sought as the result of an auto wreck in which a woman died, police said today.

The victim, Miss Mary Jo Kopechne, 28, of Washington, former secretary to the late Senator Robert F. Kennedy, was riding in a car that skidded off a narrow bridge and into a pond on Chappaquiddick Island. Senator Edward Kennedy was driving. He reportedly escaped with what apparently was only a mild concussion.

The accident happened between 11 P.M. Friday and 1 A.M. yesterday, but went unreported until 10 A.M. yesterday.

"I am firmly convinced there was no negligence involved," the Edgartown Chief of Police, Dominic J. Arena, said today. "But the matter of the time period after the accident—there is, in my opinion, a violation concerning going from the scene, leaving the scene.

Chief Arena said that he would seek a formal complaint tomorrow in Edgartown District Court. He said Senator Kennedy would have 24 hours in which to request a hearing. If no such request is forthcoming, Mr. Arena said, a summons will be issued automatically.

Under Massachusetts law, persons convicted of leaving the scene of an accident in which personal injury has been sustained may be imprisoned for from two months to two years.

In Seclusion

Senator Kennedy remained in seclusion today at the family compound in Hyannis Port, on Cape Cod, and issued no statement. His wife Joan was believed to be with him.

The New York *Times* quoted a physician as saying the 37-year-old Massachusetts Democrat had sustained a mild concussion in the accident, but had been given a sedative and was resting comfortably.

The physician, Dr. Robert D. Watt, of Hyannis Port, was quot-

(Continued, Page A 3, Col. 1)

City Has Space-Happy Day As Astronauts Land On TV

By JANELEE KEIDEL

From Ellicott City, to Dundalk, yesterday was a space-happy, astronaut-watching, glued-to-the-TV kind of day for most Baltimore-area residents.

Business was off at golf clubs, restaurants, bars and even The Block, according to employees who left their own television sets to answer the telephone.

Those who were old enough to remember Charles A. Lindbergh recalled the first flight across the Atlantic as they watched the first landing on the moon. Children too young to understand the importance of Apollo 11 asked to stay up to watch the astronauts walk on the moon.

In Essex, Mrs. Thomas G. Page, Jr., said her sons, aged 5 and 7, were "talking about" staying up for the moon walk. "If they can stay awake," she aid. "I'm going to let them."

Even the Baltimore city Police Department succumbed to the astronautical-atmosphere affecting the city.

About 5 P.M., the following bulletin was put out on the police wire: "Assault by touching down. Wanted in the district for the above offense, which occurred at 09.54 degrees of the Sea of Tranquillity, three white men wearing white suits."

State Police reported that traffic yesterday afternoon was slightly down at the Harbor Tunnel, very light on the Baltimore Beltway but heavy on the roads leading out of Ocean City.

Heavy In Bay Bridge

By late afternoon, traffic on the Bay Bridge had been ordered westbound only three times, indicating that not even a moon shot can stem the tide of motorists bent on beating other motorists on the race from a weekend at the beach.

In Baltimore, even the Orioles took second place for the day to the astronauts.

A spokesman for WJZ-TV estimated that about 40 persons had telephoned the station by 3.3

(Continued, Page A 6, Col. 7)

Red Sox Down Orioles, 6-5

Boston reserve Syd O'Brien stroked a single, triple and home run as the Red Sox nipped the Orioles, 6 to 5, today at Fenway Park for a sweep of the three-game series. *(Details on Page C1)*

The Weather

Variable cloudiness, high near 73. Mostly sunny weather tomorrow. Yesterday's high, 60; low, 56.

(Details and Map, Page C 11)

THE SUN

FINAL

(Registered United States Patent Office)

Vol. 266—No. 82—F

BALTIMORE, TUESDAY, MAY 5, 1970

50 Pages 10 Cents

Guardsmen Kill 4 Kent State Students

HE'S SHOT—A coed screams over the body of a classmate killed in confrontation at Kent State University. AP

Sniper Is Blamed For Provoking Soldiers To Fire Into Crowd Of Protesters

Kent, Ohio, May 4 (AP)—Four students—two boys and two girls—were shot to death and 11 other persons were wounded, four seriously, in a confrontation today with Ohio National Guardsmen and police at Kent State University. A state official said the shooting started when a sniper opened fire on the guardsmen from a rooftop.

The university, with an enrollment of 19,000, was closed and the town was sealed off by police and guardsmen.

Gov. James A. Rhodes called on the FBI for help in probing the disorders.

Nixon Statement

President Nixon issued a statement which said the killing of four students should remind everyone that "when dissent turns to violence it invites tragedy."

"It is my hope that this tragic and unfortunate incident will strengthen the determination of all the nation's campuses, administrators, faculty and students alike, to stand firmly for the right which exists in this country of peaceful dissent and just as strongly against the resort to violence as a means of such expression."

Speaking in Washington tonight, Vice President Agnew said the deaths at Kent State showed that his statements against violent dissent were correct.

"In several recent speeches, I have called attention to the grave dangers which accompany the new politics of violence and confrontation and which have found so much favor on our college campuses," Mr. Agnew said.

"Those dangers were not imaginary," he told the American Retail Federation, "and today at a state college in Ohio the powder keg exploded, resulting in tragedy that was predictable and avoidable."

The gunfire broke out as guardsmen dispersed an anti-war rally on the campus.

Adj. Gen. S. T. Del Corso said guardsmen were forced to open fire on their attackers.

"Regretiably but unadvoidably several individuals were killed and a number of others were wounded," he said in a statement.

The shooting came after guardsmen moved in with tear gas to disperse a rock-throwing crowd of 400 to 500 students in the Commons area near the football practice field.

"A lot of people felt their lives were in danger," said Brig. Gen. Robert Canterbury, who was on the scene, "which in fact was the case and the military man always has the option to fire if he feels his life is in danger."

"He has the right to protect himself."

General Del Corso said tear

(Continued, Page A 8, Col. 1)

SOVIET ASKS U.S. OUSTER FROM ASIA

Kosygin's Bitter Attack Hints At Strain On Arms Talks

Moscow, May 4 (Reuters)—Premier Alexei N. Kosygin bitterly denounced President Nixon today for his decision to send troops into Cambodia, saying it would make the Vienna strategic arms limitations talks more difficult and complicate the entire international situation.

Speaking at his first news conference in more than five years as Premier, Mr. Kosygin also bluntly rejected the idea of a new Geneva-type conference on Indo-China and called for a program of "energetic measures" to drive the U.S. out of the area.

But he gave no clue what these measures might be and said his government has not yet decided whether to step up military aid to the North Vietnamese Communists.

Televised Live

Observers said Mr. Kosygin's personal denunciation of Mr. Nixon was the most bitter statement issued by a top Kremlin leader on an American President for many years, and boded ill for Soviet-U.S. relations in the foreseeable future.

The crowded conference was called only a few hours before it was held. Andrei Gromyko, foreign minister, presided over the meeting which was televised and broadcast live—a first in the Soviet Union.

During a question-and-answer session after he read a government statement on Indo-China, the Premier sidestepped a question asking for confirmation of Israeli allegations last week that Russian pilots are flying operational missions over Egypt.

Rumors Spiked

And he poured cold water on a recent spate of rumors about changes in the Kremlin leadership and scrapping of the country's economic reform policies.

But his main stress throughout was Indo-China and the U.S. military move into Cambodia, which he said could result in further general complications of the international situation.

Accusing the United States of violating the 1954 and 1962 Geneva agreements, he asked, "What is the value of international agreements in which the United States takes part or intends to take part if it violates commitments it has undertaken so unceremoniously?"

Asked About Arms Talks

"It is impossible not to give serious thought to the fact that President Nixon's practical steps in the field of foreign policy are fundamentally at variance with those declarations and assurances that he repeatedly made both before assuming the presidency and when he was already in the White House," the Premier said.

Asked later whether Russia intended to break off the strategic arms talks in Vienna, Mr. Kosygin did not reply directly.

But he said that when the Soviet delegation went to Vienna last month to resume the talks

(Continued, Page A 7, Col. 2)

INDO-CHINA MOVE SCORED IN SENATE

Panel Terms Cambodian Action Unauthorized

By GENE OISHI
(Washington Bureau of The Sun)

Washington, May 4—The Senate Foreign Relations Committee sought to move a step further in reasserting Congress's foreign policy role today, declaring that the administration is "conducting a constitutionally unauthorized, presidential war in Indo-China."

Committee members also indicated they will continue to press for a private meeting with the President to fulfill what they said was their constitutional advise-and-consent responsibility in connection with the American attack into Cambodia.

Further indication of an impending foreign policy showdown between the Senate and the administration came in a report issued today by the Foreign Relations Committee, which asserted that the President had no constitutional authority for waging the war in Indo-China.

Written By Mansfield

The report, written by Senator Mike Mansfield (D., Mont.), a senior member of the committee, was on the joint resolution to repeal the 1957 Middle East resolution and the 1964 Gulf of Tonkin document. The committee approved the repealer last week and it is scheduled to reach the Senate floor Wednesday.

But the report goes far beyond an explanation of the resolution involved. It deals more with Congress's historic and constitutional role in formulating foreign policy—a role which Con-

(Continued, Page A 2, Col. 3)

Guardsmen, Police Occupy UM

College Park Declared Emergency Area As New Disorders Erupt

(By a Sun Staff Correspondent)

College Park, Md., May 4—More than 1,000 National Guardsmen and law enforcement officers occupied the University of Maryland campus tonight, using tear gas and mass arrests to put down the fourth day of student anti-war demonstrations.

Scores of students were treated for minor injuries. The arrest total moved past the 200 mark within a few hours after Governor Mandel declared a "state of emergency" at 8.30 P.M. and slapped on an overnight curfew that included the entire campus and the area adjacent to it.

One junior member of the faculty was peppered in the back and legs by a shotgun blast. A student was hurt in an automobile accident on U.S. 1 near the campus, which was blocked for almost six hours by 1,500 demonstrators.

The wounded junior faculty member, identified as Lawrence J. Babbett, 26, of College Park, was treated at Prince Georges County Hospital, Cheverly, then released. The student, Robert E. Wilson, 23, was treated in the same hospital.

Several policemen were hurt by flying objects.

The fumes from almost-continuous tear-gas barrages on the highway and the campus permeated buildings to the point where several dormitories were made temporarily uninhabitable.

At 10.30 P.M., the main campus was deserted except for the guardsmen, with bayonets but no ammunition in the rifles they carried, and police in riot gear.

Authorities said the situation was under control—for the time being, at least.

Some 200 Baltimore city policemen who were sent to College Park this morning by the Governor were released from duty at that time

Before tonight's big blow-up, university officials had conceded the dissenters a point. It was agreed that there would be no formal classes tomorrow so that all students and faculty members could participate in a one-day protest on the Southeast Asia war.

That news, transmitted at 3.30 P.M. via bullhorn to the students milling around on U.S. 1 (the old Washington boulevard) failed to halt the demonstration that had effectively blockaded the road.

Crowd Grows

Instead, the crowd blocking the highway grew. A rock band blared as collegians danced with co-eds.

But things became ugly again as suppertime approached.

A group painted a big motto in the middle of the highway: "Today, U.S. 1—tomorrow the world."

Police, who had cleared dozens of onlookers from the roofs of a College Park shopping center, finally started moving in on the demonstrators from two sides.

Maj. Donald E. Shanahan, who led the contingent of Baltimore city police ordered to the scene by Governor Mandel on the theory that they had special riot-control training, and could better cope with the situation, ordered the demonstrators from the roadway.

"Now I'm telling you to move," Major Shanahan shouted.

The major then offered to take into custody "anybody who

(Continued, Page A 8, Col. 2)

JUSTICES UPHOLD CHURCH-TAX BAN

High Court, 7-To-1, Keeps Current Exemptions

By STUART S. SMITH
(Washington Bureau of The Sun)

Washington, May 4—The Supreme Court today affirmed the ancient right of religious institutions to receive tax exemptions in common with other charitable organizations.

The 7 to-1 decision dismissed a suit brought by a recluse from New York city who charged that the nation's churches are improperly escaping taxation on more than $100 billion worth of real estate.

Writing his first major high court opinion, Chief Justice Warren E. Burger declared that "the grant of a tax exemption is not sponsorship since the government does not transfer part of its revenue to churches but simply abstains from demanding that the church support the state."

"Few concepts are more deeply embedded in the fabric of our national life, beginning with pre-revolutionary colonial times, than for the government to exercise at the very least this kind of benevolent neutrality toward churches and religious exercise generally so long as none was favored over others and none suffered interference," he noted.

The case involved a New York state exemption granted all charitable, welfare, patriotic, religious literary and similar organizations.

Frederick Walz, a lawyer who lives in the Bronx and who owns a 22-by-29-foot piece of Staten Island property taxed at $5.24 a year, challenged the inclusion of

(Continued, Page A 12, Col. 5)

Index

U.S., Viet Troops Launch New Drive In Cambodia

Saigon, Tuesday, May 5 (AP)—Thousands of American and South Vietnamese troops launched a new offensive into northeast Cambodia today, seeking to smash more North Vietnamese base camps and sanctuaries, the United States command announced.

The American command said the operation kicked off early this afternoon in the Se San base area, about 50 miles west of Pleiku, in the Central Highlands.

North Of Fishhook

A spokesman said troops of the U.S. 4th Infantry Division and the South Vietnamese 22d Infantry Division are participating in the operation.

The new operation is taking place in rugged, mountainous jungle 160 miles north-northeast of the Fishhook area where another task force of more than 8,000 Americans launched the first U.S. offensive into Cambodia last Friday. The new theater of operations is 210 miles northeast of Saigon.

The ground drive was preceded by heavy raids by about 40 B-52 bombers that dropped more than 1,000 tons of bombs along 40 miles of the border.

Cambodian military maps show a total of 6,000 North Vietnamese and Viet Cong troops in the area stretching from tri-border region of South Vietnam, Laos and Cambodia to the vicinity of the Ia Drang valley southwest of Pleiku. The area includes part of Cambodia's Ratanakiri and Mondulkiri provinces.

The first big battle of the war between American and North Vietnamese troops was fought in 1965 just across the border in the Ia Drang valley.

Meanwhile, U.S. and South Vietnamese forces in the Fishhook region were making their

(Continued, Page A 4, Col. 3)

City Police Ignore Requests For Aid In 'Sensitive Areas'

Top Officials Cite Danger Of Ambush, Racial Confrontations, But Refuse To Specify Where 'Screening' Process Is Appiied

Police Commissioner Pomerleau denies the Black Panther arrests last week caused a rise in tensions. ......Back Page

By DAVID M. ETTLIN

High-ranking police department officials said yesterday that patrol cars are not responding to distress calls from certain "sensitive areas" of the city.

The officials cited the dangers of possible ambushes and the possibility of racial "confrontations" as reasons behind the decision. Ralph G. Murdy, the department's deputy commissioner, refused to identify the areas because, he said, public knowledge of them would be "harmful to the general public, to good reporting and to this police department."

The deputy commissioner said a method of "screening out" calls for police assistance has been established, and that the calls would be answered through "special internal machinery for dealing with them."

The screening system, which Mr. Murdy refused to explain, will "add some self-restraint and a little bit of cool to the situation," he said, so that police will not be "accused of precipitating a disorder" and will not enter "a situation in which they are ambushed."

Governor Mandel, who appoints the city police commissioner, said in Annapolis that he was "unaware of the new policy, but will certainly look into it." He declined to comment further until he discussed the situation with Donald D. Pomerleau, the city police commissioner.

Mayor D'Alesandro, who was in New York signing bonds, could not be reached for comment.

The admission that specific areas of the city were receiving special handling of calls came after *The Sun* was informed of a complaint that police refused to respond to a call Saturday night from a church in the 4100 block of Old York road.

Help Sought

The Rev. Richard T. Lawrence, of the Church of the Blessed Sacrament, said a middle-aged man knocked on the rectory door about 8.30 P.M. Saturday for help because he was being "terrorized by a group of teen-agers."

The Rev. A. Thomas Baumgartner called the police emergency phone number at 8.40 P.M., and waited more than an hour without result. Father Baumgartner contacted Father Lawrence shortly before 10 o'clock to tell him the story.

Father Lawrence, who has had experience in police-community relations, phoned the emergency number at 10 P.M., and said he was informed that the communications officer did not know what happened to the patrol car and that he would take care of the situation.

The priest called the chief of patrol's office at 10.30, where an officer on duty informed him, he said, that the department "would not send a car into that area" because it was a "gray area" with a "racial problem" and were "afraid that the car would be hit with rocks or bottles or overturned."

Father Lawrence said he asked to talk with the highest-ranking officer on duty, and the patrolman in the chief of patrol's office said he would call Col. Maj. George C. Schnabel, the deputy chief of Area I, who was in charge that night.

By 11.30 P.M., when Father Lawrence had not heard from Major Schnabel, he said he called the patrol office again and was informed by the same officer that the major flatly refused to send a car into the area.

Father Lawrence said he followed the officer's suggestion to use his own car to drive the man to Northern district station, several miles away to make the report personally.

When informed of the complaint yesterday, Lt. Col. Frank J. Battaglia, the Police Department's chief of patrol, asked if the church on Old York road was "near the area of the 600 block Cator avenue."

"We're not responding to certain areas on a selective basis," Colonel Battaglia explained, "in areas where we may have a confrontation."

Colonel Battaglia described

(Continued, Page A 14, Col. 6)

BROWN FAILS TO SHOW UP

U.S., State Warrants Issued For Black Leader's Arrest

By GEORGE J. HILTNER

A bench warrant for the arrest of H. Rap Brown was issued yesterday in the Howard County Circuit Court after the militant civil-rights leader failed to show up for his trial on arson and riot charges.

A hearing that lasted only 17 minutes brought to an end nearly three years of pretrial litigation in both state and federal courts, which up until yesterday had delayed the formal calling of Mr. Brown to answer to the charges.

When the defendant failed to reply to the court clerk's calling of the case, prosecutors immediately asked for the issuance of a bench warrant and also urged Judge James Macgill in the Ellicott City court to find the accused in contempt of court for being absent.

Late in the day, Judge R. Dorsey Watkins signed a warrant in Federal Court for the arrest of Mr. Brown on charges that he fled Maryland to avoid prosecution for inciting to arson.

Mr. Brown, former head of the Student Non-Violent Coordinating Committee, the name of which has since been changed by substituting the word "National" for Non-Violent, is charged with inciting a riot in Cambridge in July, 1967.

In the early morning hours after Mr. Brown had spoken there, vandalism and fires ravaged a portion of the city and a school was set afire.

At yesterday's abortive hearing, Judge Macgill also ordered forfeited $10,000 bail which had been put up in Cambridge by the Eastern Shore Bail Bond Service.

Judge Macgill declined to find Mr. Brown in contempt of court "at this time" and also refused the request of defense attorneys to place certain restrictions on police in executing the bench

(Continued, Page A 14, Col. 1)

PUSHED BACK—State Police use tear gas to disperse demonstrators on the University of Maryland campus. AP

The Weather

Cloudy, warm and humid with scattered thunderstorms today, tonight and tomorrow. The high today will be near 90.
(Details and Map, Page C 10)

THE SUN

LIGHT FOR ALL
[Registered United States Patent Office]

FINAL

Vol. 266—No. 90—F | BALTIMORE, THURSDAY, MAY 14, 1970 | 54 Pages | 10 Cents

U.S. TO LIMIT ITS ARMS AID TO CAMBODIA

But Rogers Says Air, Naval Patrols May Remain Awhile

By PAUL W. WARD
[Washington Bureau of The Sun]

Washington, May 13—The United States, except for supplying limited amounts of rifles and like equipment, will deny direct military support to "any Cambodian government," William P. Rogers, Secretary of State, asserted today.

Contesting suggestions that the administration's plan for turning all combat responsibilities over to South Vietnamese forces is getting "bogged down" because President Nixon sent American troops into Cambodia two weeks ago, he also asserted:

1. That American air operations over Cambodia, begun long ago, probably will continue after those troops have been withdrawn and so will the Navy patrol recently established in the Gulf of Siam to block any North Vietnamese or Viet Cong attempt to run supplies to their forces in Cambodia.

"Understands Concern"

2. That the Thieu government at Saigon has been told about and "understands" the Nixon administration's "concern" that continuance of South Vietnamese military operations in Cambodia after those of U.S. forces there have ceased might make "more difficult" the scheduled withdrawal of American forces from South Vietnam.

3. That there will be combat units among the 284,000 American troops to be left in South Vietnam a year from now, but all will be "out of combat" by mid-1971.

4. That President Nixon has "a plan" for getting all American forces out of Southeast Asia after 1971 but has no "intention" to announce a "target date" at this time.

Insistent Demands

Mr. Rogers spoke at a State Department press conference that he convened without prior notice and in response, he said, to "insistent" demands by newsmen for a chance to question him about his role in the consultations leading up to President Nixon's decision, announced April 30, to send American troops into Cambodia.

That was "the only decision the President could make under the circumstances and the right one," Mr. Rogers said.

Questioned about the Middle East situation, he blamed the "great deal of guerrilla activity in the area" for Israel's thrust into Lebanon yesterday. "We, of

(Continued, Page A 2, Col. 4)

SECRETARY, ROGERS AP

REDS ATTACK U.S. FIRE BASE

Viet Cong Lose 50 Men In 1st Raid Inside Cambodia

Saigon, Thursday, May 14 (Reuters)—Viet Cong guerrillas mounted their first attack on an American base inside Cambodia and wounded four United States troops while losing 50 men themselves, a U.S. spokesman said today.

An estimated 120 guerrillas yesterday stormed the perimeter of a U.S. fire support base two miles inside Cambodia to the northeast of the Fishhook area.

Copters Called In

The spokesman said the attackers were driven off after the defenders, an infantry unit of the 1st Air Cavalry Division, called in helicopters, air strikes and artillery support.

Meanwhile, a South Vietnamese spokesman announced a major battle in the Parrot's Beak salient of Cambodia in which 199 guerrillas were killed for the loss of 18 government troops. Another 63 South Vietnamese were wounded, he reported.

Red Unit Thrashed In Cambodian Clash

Saigon, May 13 (AP)—Heavy firepower almost wiped out a North Vietnamese company that stumbled into an American base camp 3 miles inside Cambodia today. But South Vietnamese troops driving toward the capital of Phnom Penh ran into heavy resistance from an estimated 500 enemy soldiers.

These were the major ground actions reported in the war, in which another American gener-

(Continued, Page A 2, Col. 7)

NIXON UPHELD ON RESHUFFLE OF EXECUTIVE

House Rejects Veto Of Reorganization Plan, In Effect Saturday

By GENE OISHI
[Washington Bureau of The Sun]

Washington, May 13—What appeared to be a coalition of Republicans and Southern Democrats defeated today an attempt in the House to veto President Nixon's program for reorganizing the executive branch of government and creating a cabinet-level domestic council.

The plan would create a domestic counterpart to the National Security Council, and would reorganize the Budget Bureau and place it more firmly under the control of the executive branch.

Despite protests that the reorganization plan would farther erode congressional prerogatives, the House sustained the President's plan, 193 to 164.

Committee Is Overridden

In doing so, it overrode the recommendation of the Government Operations Committee, which had submitted a resolution of disapproval.

According to the 1949 Reorganization Act, an executive reorganization plan goes into effect automatically unless it is vetoed by either House of Congress within 60 days after its submission.

The statutory time limit expires at midnight Friday, and the reorganization plan will become law unless the Senate rejects it by that time. Senate sources knew, however, of no move to veto the plan.

While there have been some grumblings of disapproval among Senate liberals, it is acknowledged generally that there is not sufficient time to mount a campaign to block the plan.

The domestic council would be headed by the President and would include the Vice President and all members of the Cabinet except the secretaries of State and Defense and the Postmaster General.

It would have broad functions, including defining national goals, coordinating the establishment of national goals and priorities, reviewing ongoing domestic programs and generally advising the President on domestic policy.

Staff Of 75

The council would have its own staff of about 75 persons headed by an executive director, who also would have the title of assistant to the President. The executive director would be the domestic counterpart of Dr. Henry A. Kissinger, who is the President's chief adviser on foreign and national security affairs.

One of the chief objections to the plan was that of the excutive director would be appointed by the President without the advice and consent of the Senate.

Opponents of the plan argued that the plan would create "a super bureaucracy" that would not be responsive to Congress and would further isolate the President from outside advice.

The other key element of the plan is that it would merge the Budget Bureau into a new Office of Management and Budget. The functions currently vested by law in the bureau, or in its

(Continued, Page A 8, Col. 1)

Fist fight breaks out in Mount Vernon place's West Square before police move in during yesterday's Flower Mart disturbances

Sunpapers photo—Carl D. Harris

ROAD SAFETY BILL DEFINED

Tight U.S. Standards Asked For Licenses, Inspections

Washington, May 13 (AP)—An auto insurance bill providing among other things for beefed-up federal drivers' license standards and compulsory auto inspection will be introduced soon by Senator Philip A. Hart (D., Mich.).

Senator Hart said tonight that the measure stems from a three-year investigation into skyrocketing insurance premiums and repair costs. He said it will include compulsory rating of cars as to relative vulnerability to crash damage of both vehicle and passengers.

"I am convinced that industry by itself cannot produce a system with both adequate compensation for victims and a reasonable price tag," Mr. Hart said.

Tentative Outline

Senator Hart, chairman of the Antitrust and Monopoly Subcommittee, unveiled a tentative outline of his bill in remarks prepared for the Washington Metropolitan Auto Body Association.

He said the measure may include some combination of the "fault" and "no fault" insurance systems.

Under the current "fault" system, whoever is assessed the blame bears some or all of the cost in an accident.

Under the "no fault" system, insurance companies would pay off damages suffered by their own customers without regard to who caused an accident.

The "no fault" system in most cases also would end the costly and time-consuming court litigation that some blame for the high cost of insurance.

Mr. Hart said a recent study by the Department of Transpor-

(Continued, Page A 8, Col. 1)

Disturbances Mar Annual Flower Mart; At Least 50 Arrested, 16 Hospitalized

Police, Bands Of Youths Skirmish In Square Off Mt. Vernon Place

By LOUIS P. PEDDICORD

The annual Flower Mart, Baltimore's traditional springtime festival, was briefly rocked by violence yesterday as bands of youths attacked other youths, then skirmished with helmeted squads of city policemen in the West square of Mount Vernon place.

Scores of persons were injured during the hour-long noontime melee, including at least 16 who required hospitalization. Police said they arrested 27 persons then many of them apparently high school youths.

Later in the day, police again moved in against a small part of the Flower Mart crowd, arresting about two dozen more young people from a group that allegedly throwing rocks and bottles at police.

Police Stations

About 45 of the arrested persons were take to Southeastern District police station and 9 others were booked at Central District.

Scores of parents relatives and friends gathered at Southeastern station to post bail for or talk with the arrested persons.

Suspects were crowded four to a one- or two-man cell for several hours as desk police worked frantically to locate arresting officers and determine exact charges.

By 10.45 P.M., some 20 accused were still in custody, either because they were unable to post bond or because their relatives could not be located. Because of the confusion, desk officers were instructed to release any suspect on payment of $110, the standard bond for disorderly conduct.

They face hearings at 9 A.M. today in Southeastern Municipal Court. Several teen-agers arrested in the melee with be subject to juvenile court action.

The disturbances, though extremely violent at times, apparently went largely unnoticed by much of the curb-to-curb crowd that jammed Mount Vernon place for the 58th annual Mart.

Even as the youths, largely black students squared off against white, fought in the West square, and later, as police cleared the square with clubs and chemical Mace, the festival continued unabated in the rest of the Mart area.

"Beautiful Success"

Said Mrs. Theodore R. Klemm, Jr., chairman of the Mart's central committee, "I think the Mart has been a beautiful success and I know that a lot of people thoroughly enjoyed themselves."

The question of whether the annual event will be continued after yesterday's violence was "up to next year's chairman," Mrs. Klemm said. "But when it isn't in Mount Vernon place, it isn't the Flower Mart," she added, noting that she was "confident" the festival would continue.

Mayor D'Alesandro expressed a similar hope in a statement on the Mart disorders issued later in the day.

"Every effort must be made to continue the Flower Mart in the future under conditions of peace and order," he said.

The Women's Civic League, organizers of the event, estimated that 100,000 people moved through the Mart's two-block square in downtown Baltimore during the course of the day. Other observers, including those long familiar with the festival, said yesterday's crowd was one of the largest ever to besiege Mount Vernon place.

The violence, which broke out shortly before noon in the West square, was apparently sparked by the arrests of several black youths at Park avenue and Monument street minutes before.

Lt. Col. Frank J. Battaglia, the police department's chief of patrol, intimated later that the violence had been "planned," and was part of an attempt to shut down the Mart. "I think that's what they were trying to do—to shut the whole thing down," he said.

Band Surrounded Police

Witnesses reported that a small band of about 40 young people surrounded the police who were making the arrests. Police then apparently called for reinforcements and as extra men began arriving on the scene, the youths marched quickly into the West Square, two blocks away.

Once there, the youths started scattered fist fights among the young students jammed into the area.

By 12.10 P.M., the fights had escalated into a general violence that involved bystanders and workers at the Mart.

An earlier arrest, at 11.40, in the 100 block West Monument street, also apparently fueled the disturbances that moved into the Flower Mart area.

Patrolman Punched In Mouth

According to police, a crowd of youths surrounded Stanley L. Harrison, 18, of the 1700 block East 31st street as he was being arrested for fighting in the area. During the ensuing struggle, police said, Patrolman Samuel Venturella, 25, of the Tactical Section, was punched in the mouth by a youth.

The fighting in the West square, which, according to police, was carried on largely by bands of black youths attacking white youths, including several girls, continued unchecked by police for about 15 minutes.

Reporters on the scene, some of whom were cursed and chased by the youths, said that a number of these beaten by the unruly crowd were young girls. One was reportedly chased into a tree in the West square.

Another girl, who was sitting in a car with three other youths on Cathedral street, was reportedly attacked by a band of youths, who tore her blouse off.

At 12.15 P.M., Major George C. Schnabel, a deputy chief of patrol led a squad of about 35

(Continued, Page A 14, Col. 4)

Malik Blames U.S., Britain For Delay In Mideast Peace

New York, May 13 (AP)—The Soviet chief delegate at the United Nations brought into the open today a deadlock in Big Four talks on the Middle East. He said the boundaries of Israel as they stood before the war in June, 1967, should become permanent.

Jacob A. Malik, the Soviet ambassador, speaking in the Security Council on Israel's incursion into Lebanon yesterday, blamed the United States and Britain for the failure of the four chief delegates to achieve a settlement of the third Arab-Israeli war.

In that war, Israel seized Egypt's Sinai Peninsula, including the Gaza Strip; Syria's Golan Heights; the west bank of the Jordan, and Arab Old Jerusalem, and has refused to return any Arab territories.

Mr. Malik traced that failure to "the stubborn reluctance" of the U.S. and Britain to agree to the withdrawal of all Israeli troops from all Arab territories, behind the lines which existed on June 5, 1967," and to their "stubborn refusal to accept this line as the border between Israel and the Arab states."

The idea that the prewar line should become the permanent boundary clashed with the U.S. position that there should be "insubstantial alterations" in that line for mutual security, as William P. Rogers, Secretary of State, suggested in a Washington speech December 9.

Malik Rebuts Rogers

Specifically rejecting Mr. Rogers's formulation, Mr. Malik accusingly told Lord Caradon, the chief British delegate: "You actively support the American formula of alteration of boundaries . . . in favor of the aggressor."

"Not an inch of the territory of the victims of aggression

(Continued, Page A 5, Col. 1)

Dow Stocks Dip To 7-Year Low

Stock market prices dropped sharply yesterday, the decline sending the Dow Jones industrial average below the 700 level for the first time in nearly seven years. The Dow closed at 693.84, its lowest since July 29, 1963.

The number of stocks that declined in price outnumbered those that gained by about 5 to 1.

Analysts said the market continues to be depressed by high interest rates, inflation, lower corporate earnings and the war in Southeast Asia.

One analyst said many investors tend to regard numbers on the Dow scale, especially at the 100 levels, as milestones and that when the 30 industrials fell below 700, this triggered a further decline.

(Details on Page C7, C8)

MISSION'S END—Israeli troops dismount from tanks on the Israeli-Lebanese frontier on return from raid. AP

Denied Platform In Illinois, Gardner Assails War On TV

By ARNOLD R. ISAACS
[Washington Bureau of The Sun]

Washington, May 13—John W. Gardner, who was invited several months ago to address the Illinois Constitutional Convention today, suddenly was disinvited when the Republican convention chairman learned that he planned to criticize President Nixon's national leadership.

Mr. Gardner, the chairman of the Urban Coalition and former Secretary of Health, Education and Welfare, then flew back to Washington where he read parts of his spech for the television cameras.

"Ill-Considered Statements"

He condemned "provocative and ill-considered statements from those in high places" and "leaders who exploit our fear and anger and prejudice." Calling the Vietnam war "the most divisive element in our national life," he urged an immediate withdrawal of all American troops from Cambodia, a commitment against any form of further escalation, and a one-year timetable for the "termination of our presence in Vietnam."

An advance copy of his speech was available to Constitutional Convention officials yesterday, and last night, Samuel Witwer, the convention chairman and a long-time Illinois Republican leader, called one of Mr. Gardner's aides to ask that the speech be scrapped.

Mr. Witwer spoke several times with Lowell Beck, director of the Urban Coalition Action Council—the coalition's lobbying arm.

According to Mr. Beck, Mr. Witwer said he "preferred not to have the President criticized" at the convention. He also warned that some pro-war Democratic

(Continued, Page A 10, Col. 1)

Index

Twins Edge Orioles, 5-4

May 13, 1970.

After winning eight straight games, the Orioles dropped their bid for No. 9 tonight in Minnesota, 5 to 4, on Rich Reese's two-out single in the tenth inning.

(Details on Page C 1)

The Weather
Cloudy and cool today, highs in the mid 60's. Fair and cool tonight, lows in the 40's. Yesterday's high, 71; low, 65.
(Details and Map, Page C 14)

THE SUN

FINAL

(Registered United States Patent Office)

Vol. 267—No. 131—F BALTIMORE, FRIDAY, OCTOBER 16, 1970 48 Pages 10 Cents

Orioles Soar To World Series Victory

OUTPUT UP SLIGHTLY IN 3D QUARTER

Gross National Product Pleases Officials, But Inflation Continues

By ART PINE
Washington Bureau Of The Sun

Washington, Oct. 15—The nation's total output of goods and services rose slightly during the third quarter, the Commerce Department reported today, but inflation continued unabated at the same pace as that of last spring.

Preliminary estimates pointed to another small increase in the gross national product, but this figure's "deflator" — the broadest measure of inflation—showed prices still rising at their second-quarter rate.

At the same time, the Federal Reserve Board's index of industrial production dipped slightly in September for the second month in a row, indicating continuing sluggishness despite the current upturn.

Auto Strike Hurts

Administration economists, however, attributed the bulk of the apparent gloominess in the industrial-production statistics to the effects of the strike at General Motors, now in its fourth week.

Had production remained normal, they said, total output would have risen more substantially, inflation would have slackened somewhat and the Federal Reserve index would have remained relatively stable.

"All in all, we think it's just great," a White House economist said ebulliently. "We've been saying all along there would be a moderate upturn, and essentially this proves it's here."

Harold C. Passer, assistant secretary of commerce, said in a statement that the gross-national-product figure — which rose at double the previous quarter's jump—"show that the economy has been growing at a moderate pace."

Without adjustment for inflation, the gross national product rose $14 billion over the past three months to a third-quarter level of $985.2 billion—a jump of

(Continued, Page A 8, Col. 2)

Stewardess Killed In Soviet Hijacking

Jewish Father, Son Also Wound 3 Crewmen In Forcing Flight To Turkey; Asylum Sought

Trabzon, Turkey, Oct. 15 (AP) — A Jewish father and his son carrying shotguns, pistols and grenades hijacked a Soviet airliner today and forced it across the border into Turkey. The plane landed at this coastal town with the stewardess fatally shot and three crewmen wounded.

It was the first known successful hijacking of a Soviet passenger plane, although there have been at least four other attempts. Moscow promptly asked Turkey to extradite the hijackers and return the plane.

Sought Asylum

Officials identified the hijackers as Brazinskas Koroyero, 46, and his son, Algedas, 18. They surrendered to police and asked for political asylum.

Turkish newspapers said the Koroyeros were Jewish and that the father was a native of Lithuania.

No motive was given immediately for the hijacking, but the Soviet Union has refused thousands of Jews permits to leave Russia and many Lithuanians still are bitter over the Soviet absorption of their country in 1940.

Police surrounded the twin-engined Aeroflot airliner as soon as it touched down at this Black Sea port. It had been hijacked about 100 miles north of here while on a domestic flight inside the Soviet Union. Aeroflot is the Soviet Union's government-run airline.

The two hijackers were the first to emerge and handed over two shotguns, five pistols and three hand grenades.

The chief pilot was taken to a hospital, where he was reported to be in critical condition with a chest wound. The plane had a crew of five.

Turkish authorities quoted Mr. Koroyero as saying he and his son opened fire when the crew refused to change course and break radio communications with Soviet air controllers.

The hostess, Natasha Kurcinerko, 18, was slain as she tried to block the door to the pilots' compartment. Then the chief pilot, a copilot and the radio operator were wounded.

Officials said the copilot took over the controls and brought the plane in for a normal landing.

"More Complicated"

A Turkish Foreign Ministry spokesman said it would be Turkey's duty to return the plane and personnel but that the extradition question "is a more complicated matter."

Tass, the Soviet news agency, called the hijackers "criminal murderers" in its published account of the incident. Ordinarily, the Soviet press does not report internal crimes and accidents, and previous hijack attempts have not been reported for several days or weeks after they happened.

The plane, a Tupelev F-27, was seized 10 minutes after it took off from the Georgian town of Batumi, on the eastern edge of the Black Sea, for Sukhumi, 100 miles to the north.

Nixon Signs Bill Sharpening U.S. Tools Against Bombers

Washington, Oct. 15 (AP)—Pledging to win the war against organized crime and anarchist terrorism, President Nixon signed legislation today giving federal authorities strong tools against mobsters and bombers.

Court Challenge

Flanked by John N. Mitchell, the Attorney General, and J. Edgar Hoover, director of the Federal Bureau of Investigation, Mr. Nixon deplored the recent wave of bombings and said those responsible must be brought to justice.

Even before the signing, opponents of certain provisions in the measure said they would challenge the bill in court.

Lawrence Speiser, national legislative director of the American Civil Liberties Union, said his group feared the bill's provisions would be used not against organized crime but "against militant groups, Black Panthers and others the administration considers as dissident."

The bill makes participation in a fatal bombing a capital offense, gives the FBI immediate jurisdiction in campus bombings and allows agents to use electronic surveillance in bombing

(Continued, Page A 8, Col. 4)

Sunpapers photo—William Hotz

EGYPT IS SEEKING NEW PEACE PATH

Move Imperils U.S. Plan On Mideast Crisis

By PETER J. KUMPA
Sun Staff Correspondent

New York, Oct. 15—Hopeful Mideast negotiations were severely set back here tonight when the Egyptian foreign minister, Mahmoud Riad, told the Secretary of State, William P. Rogers, that his country would seek "new ways" to implement the 1967 Security Council resolution for the region.

He said Egypt would be seeking a new course in the special General Assembly debate on the Middle East, requested by Cairo yesterday, and tentatively set to begin October 26.

If such "new ways" were found, they would kill the carefully prepared American peace plan that led to a 90-day standstill cease-fire August 7 that is due to expire November 5.

Warning By Israel

Israel has already warned that if the American initiative is dropped its agreement to negotiate with the Arab states would lapse.

Leaving an hour-and-50-minute session with Mr. Rogers at the Secretary's suite in the Waldorf

(Continued, Page A 4, Col. 2)

WHAT BIG RED MACHINE? — Happy teammates race around Mike Cuellar as Orioles clinch their World Series title (above). But the first man to reach the winning pitcher as he dashed, arms outstretched, from the mound, was the third baseman, Brooks Robinson, who was voted the outstanding player of Series.

BIRDS BEAT REDS, 9 TO 3 IN 5TH GAME

Cuellar Allows 6 Hits; Brooks Robinson Is Named Standout

By JIM ELLIOT

The Orioles saved their biggest comeback of 1970 until yesterday, allowing the Cincinnati Reds 3 runs in the first inning and then annihilating the Big Red Machine, 9 to 3, with 15 hits to capture their second World Series within 5 years, 4 games to 1.

Mike Cuellar, who won 24 games for the Orioles during the season, was a bleak figure on a rainy day when he gave up 4 hits including 3 doubles in the first inning nearly breaking the hearts of 45,341 fans who ignored the weather.

Within one more hit of being removed from the mound, Cuellar halted the Reds's initial surge and was near-perfect the rest of the way. He gave up only two seventh-inning singles and one walk after his shaky start.

Meanwhile, the Orioles hammered six Cincinnati pitchers for the most hits gathered by either team in any of the five contests. They included home runs by Frank Robinson and Merv Rettenmund, and doubles by Boog Powell and Dave Johnson.

Every regular Oriole player participated in the tremendous offense which brought the world's baseball title back to Baltimore after four years.

The Orioles swept the Los Angeles Dodgers in four games in 1966, and bowed last year to the New York Mets in five games.

Paul Blair and Dave Johnson each collected three hits, including a double for Johnson, while Frank Robinson, Powell and Rettenmund each got two hits.

Brooks Robinson was limited to only a single in five trips. But that base hit helped him to a World Series record of 17 total bases in a 5-game Series and enabled Brooks to tie the record for most hits—9—in a 5 game series.

He shares the last record with seven others, including Blair, whose three hits yesterday gave him a total of nine for the series.

Take those accomplishments, plus his record-tying four extra-base hits, add the greatest glove by far in the Series and you have the ingredients which made Brooks Robinson the choice—everyone's choice—as the fall classic's outstanding player.

If the Orioles were as dismayed as their thousands of followers during that first-inning bulldozing by the Big Red Machine, they did not show it on the field.

They came back with two runs in their half of the first on Frank Robinson's home run. Then they grabbed the lead with two more in the second on singles by Mark Belanger and Blair.

Those two hits chased the Cincinnati starting pitcher, left-handed Jim Merritt, from the mound. He was later charged with the loss when the relief pitchers, Wayne Granger, Milt Wilcox, Tony Cloninger, Ray

(Continued, Page C 5, Col. 3)

NIXON VIET PLAN GIVEN 'FIRM' NO

Red Envoys In Paris Now Stress Word 'Rejection'

By SCOTT SULLIVAN
[Paris Bureau of The Sun]

Paris, Oct. 15 — President Nixon's five-point peace plan was rejected "firmly, radically and categorically" today by the North Vietnamese and Viet Cong delegations to the Paris peace talks.

Spokesmen for the Communist delegations, who last week carefully skirted the word "rejection," took pains today to emphasize the term.

"Perfidious Maneuver"

"The American State Department is trying to make people believe that we have not rejected the so-called peace initiative of Mr. Nixon," said Duong Dinh Thao, the Hanoi delegation's spokesman. "That is a perfidious maneuver that we intend to unmask."

Despite the vehemence of today's rejection, David K. E. Bruce, America's chief negotiator here, said he did not believe "that all has been foreclosed."

After still another barrage of derision from the North Vietnamese, Stephen Ledogar, a United States spokesman, expanded on Ambassador Bruce's statement: "Mr. Bruce feels there is a difference between a hope and an expectation. We always hope," Mr. Ledogar said.

The negotiating session today

(Continued, Page A 2, Col. 4)

Viet Cong Offensive Threat Is Finished, Thieu Declares

Saigon, Oct. 15 (AP)—President Nguyen Van Thieu said today the Viet Cong no longer were able to launch a military offensive. He also reassured his countrymen that the United States was not running out on them.

"American forces will not withdraw until we have become strong enough to defend ourselves," President Thieu told village and hamlet officials in the Mekong Delta, the original Viet Cong stronghold.

4th Phase Ended

As he spoke, the United States formally ended the fourth phase of its troop cutback. This phase reduced American manpower in Vietnam by 50,000, leaving 384,000 troops there. This is the lowest total since the end of 1966, when there were 376,000 Americans in the country.

The figure of 384,000 was reached by not replacing men who have completed their tours in Vietnam. The last unit to be withdrawn was the 375-man Marine 5th Communications Battalion, which left October 3.

President Thieu said he does not believe the Viet Cong would accept a political settlement of the war.

"A coalition government is the minimum they could accept," Mr. Thieu declared. "No other type of settlement would do them any good and, of course,

(Continued, Page A 2, Col. 4)

Zoning Moves Aid 6 In Politics

2 On Council Included Among Those Who Would Benefit

On October 19, the Baltimore City Council will hold public hearings on its proposed new zoning code for the city. Following is the fifth in a series of articles on this proposed legislation.

By JOHN B. O'DONNELL, JR.

The City Council on September 21 adopted amendments to the proposed zoning code which favor at least six political figures, including two of its own members.

City Councilman Robert L. Douglass (D., 2d) and Councilwoman Catherine O'Dea Duffy (D., 1st) each has an interest in a piece of land which was the subject of a favorable Council amendment.

Other political figures who received similar treatment were James H. (Jack) Pollack, the Northwest Baltimore political boss; State Senator Harry McGuirk (D., 6th, Baltimore); Delegate James J Silk (D, 1st, Baltimore), and Leroy Frederick, a south Baltimore political figure who recently took a leave of absence from his job with the city Department of Housing and Community Development to work for the city elections board.

The list is based on an extensive, but incomplete, check of the interests in properties affected by the hundreds of amendments the City Council made to the proposed zoning maps.

Knowledgeable sources have indicated that other political interests may also have benefited by councilmanic map changes, but they refuse to disclose those interests.

In the cases which did come to light during a check of the amendments, arguments can be made that the changes were reasonable, and that, in some cases, the changes were made simply to give the political figure the zoning he now has.

On the other hand, it can also be argued that the change has the effect of increasing the value of the land over what it would have been had the zoning designation proposed by the Zoning Commission—the supposed experts in the matter—been adopted.

Introduced 2½ Years Ago

It also can further be argued that a change to benefit a councilman or politician can more easily be made—and is open to less public scrutiny—if it is made on the proposed new zoning maps rather than through regular channels.

In drawing the zoning maps

(Continued, Page A 11, Col. 1)

Students and associates at the National Institutes of Health drink champagne toast to Dr. Axelrod for his Nobel Prize AP

Maryland Biochemist Wins Nobel Prize

By FREDERICK P. McGEHAN
Sun Staff Correspondent

Rockville, Oct. 15—Julius Axelrod was seated in the dentist's chair having a tooth filled here this morning when he got the word—he was a winner of the 1970 Nobel Prize for Medicine-Physiology.

Dr. Axelrod chief of the pharmacology section at the National Institute of Mental Health, shared the $80,000 award with Sir Bernard Katz of London, and Ulf Von Euler, of Stockholm.

The three men received the coveted award for independent research on nerve cells which could open up new avenues for treating mental illness.

For Dr. Axelrod, a 58-year-old biochemist, today was anything but normal.

Following the abrupt news in the dentist's chair (conveyed by a call from a local television station), the New York native was roundly cheered by his co-workers when he showed up at his small laboratory in the sprawling National Institutes of Health complex.

Later he faced television cameras and reporters in an hour-long press conference and, in the afternoon, was toasted by colleagues in a nearby restaurant.

Still later, the slight, greying research scientist sat in the living room of his Rock-

(Continued, Page A 6, Col. 1)

The Weather
Variable cloudiness and cold today and tomorrow. Highs about 28 degrees today. Yesterday's high, 30; low, 22.
(Details and Map, Page C 11)

THE SUN

FINAL

(Registered United States Patent Office)

Vol. 268—No. 53—F | BALTIMORE, MONDAY, JANUARY 18, 1971 | 40 Pages | 10 Cents

Colts Top Cowboys, 16-13, In Super Bowl

U.S. STEPS UP WAR ROLE IN CAMBODIA

7th Fleet Copter Ship, U.S. Liaison Officers Back Allied Units

Saigon, Jan. 17 (AP)—The United States has increased its direct involvement in the fighting in Cambodia with Navy support ships, Army helicopters and liaison personnel, according to authoritative sources and field dispatches.

On the Vietnam war front, U.S. fighter-bombers attacked two surface-to-air missile sites in North Vietnam today in the third straight day of "protective reaction" strikes inside the enemy's borders.

The U.S. command said two U.S. helicopters were shot down today in South Vietnam. A chopper on a medical evacuation mission went down in Chau Doc province 120 miles west of Saigon and about 5 miles from the Cambodian border, killing one American and wounding three. One crewman was wounded in the downing of an OH6 light observation craft in the northern quarter of the country.

The Cambodian moves, which included the stationing of a U.S. 7th Fleet helicopter carrier off Cambodia in the Gulf of Siam, were made without official announcement.

The reason for the expanded involvement apparently is to provide U.S. support for the joint South Vietnamese-Cambodian offensive now under way to break the Communist command's blockade of Highway 4, Phnom Penh's life-line to the sea.

Pass Taken

[Reuter quoted the Cambodian high command late tonight as saying government troops had reached and retaken the enemy-held pass of Pich Nil, on Highway 4.

["The most difficult section on Highway 4 had been retaken and our troops are pushing down toward Stung Chhay on the other side of the pass," a spokesman said.

[South Vietnamese troops continued to push up toward Phnom Penh from Kompong Som.

[The Viet Cong were reported to have mortared and fired small arms into Kompong Speu, where the headquarters of the joint Cambodian-South Vietnamese operation is situated.]

American Photographed

The operations became known today from military sources, eyewitness accounts and photographs taken on the scene.

A photograph taken yesterday near Ta New, south of the Stung Chhay Pass along Highway 4, showed an American in a camouflaged jungle suit on the

(Continued, Page A 5, Col. 4)

Moorer Praises Saigon Troops

Washington, Jan. 17 (AP)—Adm. Thomas H. Moorer, returning from Southeast Asia, said today that South Vietnamese military forces have come of age and have shown in Cambodia that they are capable of "planning and executing joint operations to perfection."

The chairman of the Joint Chiefs of Staff coupled this with an optimistic forecast that the Cambodians will be able to stand up to the North Vietnamese. "Just give them time," he said.

Admiral Moorer gave no hint of any significant step-up in United States help to Cambodian and South Vietnamese forces fighting in Cambodia.

But the admiral indicated more clearly in public than have other U.S. officials that American policy permits use of American air power for direct support of friendly forces in Cambodia.

Asked about U.S. armed helicopters in Cambodia, Admiral Moorer said that "if helicopter gunships are required, they will be used."

The official U.S. stance is that American airpower is used in Cambodia to interdict—that is, prevent movements of or destroy—enemy supplies and

(Continued, Page A 4, Col. 4)

Guerrilla Radicals Warned By Al Fatah

Arafat Aide Threatens Force, Says Ambushers Of Jordanian Army Patrol Will Be Tried

Beirut, Lebanon, Jan. 17 (AP)—Yasser Arafat's Al Fatah guerrillas threatened today to use armed force against leftist Palestinian groups calling for the overthrow of King Hussein's regime in Jordan.

Al Fatah's chief spokesman, Kamal Adwan, said guerrillas of the Popular Front for the Liberation of Palestine responsible for the recent ambush of a Jordanian Army patrol will be brought to trial before a special guerrilla tribunal.

In his first public statement since the Jordanian civil war last September, the front's leader, Dr. George Habash, said yesterday that the guerrillas had no alternative but to topple King Hussein and replace him with a leftist regime.

Habash Called Adventurer

Mr. Adwan denounced Dr. Habash as an adventurer who had double-crossed the Palestinian resistance movement.

He claimed Dr. Habash approved and signed a new peace and co-operation agreement with the Jordanian government January 13, but secretly sent word to his guerrillas to ignore it.

The tenor of Mr. Adwan's remarks suggested that Al Fatah may attempt to bring Dr. Habash himself to trial.

"We shall prevent any attempt to divert the Palestinian revolution from its essential goal of fighting Israel, even if we have to use armed force," Mr. Adwan said in a statement here.

He accused the Liberation Front of having caused all previous clashes between the guerrillas and the Jordanian Army.

The new split of the two main Palestinian guerrilla groups came into the open when the front refused to disarm its militia in Amman in accordance with the January 13 agreement.

Militia Key Element

The militia—part-time guerrillas living for the most part in refugee camps—constitute the principal strength of the front, the group responsible for last year's spectacular plane hijackings, which also was denounced by Al Fatah.

Guerrilla sources report that several front men who are believed to have taken part in Friday's ambush of the Jordanian Army patrol in northern Jordan already have been arrested by Al Fatah. They say Al Fatah appears determined to eliminate all rival guerrilla groups to create a united resistance movement against Israel.

"The march of the Palestinian revolution should be united from now on and no individuality will be permitted any more," Mr. Adwan declared.

Al Fatah is prepared to fight a guerrilla war against King Hussein only if his government violates the new peace agreement, he added.

"The policy of appeasement is over forever," he warned.

Viet Cong Eschew Ideology For United Anti-U.S. Appeal

By JOHN E. WOODRUFF
Sun Staff Correspondent

Saigon, Jan. 17—South Vietnam's Communists have launched a massive political reconstruction plan, aimed both at repairing war damage and at filling long-standing gaps in the Viet Cong structure in South Vietnam.

The reconstruction plan seems to have the dual intention of increasing pressure on the Saigon government as the American forces withdraw and laying the groundwork for a broader Viet Cong political base after the Americans are gone.

Ouster Of Americans

The heart of the reconstruction program is a new application of the "united front" approach that Communist movements often have used to broaden their appeal.

The tactic now being adopted is to de-emphasize the Communist social revolution, which won the Viet Cong millions of adherents in the countryside by giving land to debt-ridden peasants, and instead to put still greater stress on the patriotic goal of driving out the "American imperialists."

The extent to which the Communists now are willing to compromise to gain adherents and allies has been made clear by a series of broadcasts in which various components of the National Liberation Front—political arm of the Viet Cong—have been urged to find means of recruiting even bourgeois groups into the common anti-American struggle.

"Regardless Of Views"

A typical broadcast related the gist of a circular issued by the central executive committees of the South Vietnam Liberation Youth Union and the Vietnamese People's Revolutionary Youth Group.

That broadcast urged that the two organizations' local chapters "broadly unite all strata of youths — regardless of political views, occupations, religion and nationality — in the anti-U.S. struggle in order to insure that they become reliable members of the NLF and that they support the provisional revolutionary government."

The new theme of seeking all possible allies, "regardless of political views, occupations, religion and nationality," is consistent with a new emphasis the Vietnamese Communists have put on urban struggle in recent months.

The Communists quickly seized upon and encouraged student outbursts last month after a young central Vietnamese school boy was shot by an American soldier, an incident that the Communists used to test the depth of feeling in the cities after several months of Viet Cong efforts to exploit the growing discontent of students, slum-dwellers and disabled veterans.

All of these groups had been visibly disaffected long before the Communists began to increase their attention some time last fall.

"This fact makes it difficult, as one Western analyst put it, "to know which is cause and which is effect" that is, to know to what extent the Communists actually may succeed in instiga-

(Continued, Page A 5, Col. 2)

VICTORY—Colts' Jim O'Brien leaps for joy after kicking the winning field goal. At right are tackle Bob Vogel (72), quarterback Earl Morrall (15), who held the ball for the kick, and guard Glenn Ressler (62). AP

POLISH WORKERS STAY SKEPTICAL

Despite Pay-Boost, Gdansk Shipyard Halt Is Staged

By JOSEPH R. L. STERNE
Sun Staff Correspondent

Gdansk, Poland, Jan. 17—Many Polish shipyard workers remain restive and discontented despite government efforts to placate them with pay raises larger than those being granted nationally.

This was stated here today by Polish sources after a National Broadcasting Company report of a protest demonstration yesterday in the Lenin shipyard, where the "December events" began that led to a government upheaval in Warsaw.

Location Of Graves

According to the NBC report, several thousand workers walked off their jobs for two hours demanding to know the whereabouts of the graves of Gdansk residents killed in December disturbances.

The Associated Press reported today that shipyard workers plan a sit-in strike tomorrow to protest new production targets.

[One worker said a non-union

(Continued, Page A 2, Col. 3)

U.N. Urges Natural Power Use

New York, Jan. 17 (AP)—A United Nations report just released suggests that the way to give the world enough pollution-free power is to take it from harnessed tides, dammed rivers and underground heat—and spread it around with an intercontinental electrical grid.

The Secretary General, U Thant, released the 19-page report, on "Environmental Problems of Energy Production," for the first session here February 22 to March 5 of a new committee on natural resources created by the Economic and Social Council.

Energy industries, it says, now "probably form one of the largest sources of pollution."

Foul Smells And Sights

Coal mining spoils the earth, oil extraction and shipping blacken the coasts, oil refining creates foul smells, and the generation of electricity by coal-fueled steam plants pollutes the air with grit and sulfur, carbon and nitrogen compounds and the rivers with waste hot water, it says.

The report suggests that the owners of electrical plants build very high chimneys to diffuse air pollutants and cooling towers to lower the waste-water temperature. It calls for internationally coordinated research to develop pre-treated, low-pollution fuels and a cheap way of removing pollutants from the flue gases.

But it hints that the cost of adopting such preventive methods may make electricity generated by steam plants more expensive than tidal power, hydroelectric power and so-called geo-thermal—or earth heat—energy.

Pollution Disregarded

Past comparisons of these non-polluting energy sources with so-called thermal—or steam electric generating—stations, the report remarks, "have been based on conventional economic analysis which has disregarded the question of environmental pollution."

The growing cost of keeping thermal-power stations within legally established pollution limits will harm their competitive position compared with the non-polluting power sources, it adds, and "there will be a re-examination of many schemes which have hitherto been considered uneconomic."

The report speculates that the usable world resources of geo-thermal energy may, in the past, have been considerably underestimated."

It says 20 to 25 countries "have a known potential for the development of geo-thermal resources" and recent estimates are that the Soviet Union's geo-thermal waters are comparable to its combined coal, peat, oil and gas resources, and that those under California's Imperial Valley could produce 20,000 megawatts of electricity.

Power Sites Listed

The report lists tidal-power sites in Canada, the United States, Britain, India, Australia, the Soviet Union and Argentina, and says France's 240-megawatt tidal-power station at St. Malo "has demonstrated that the technical problems associated with tidal power have been solved." It notes that cheaper construction methods have been developed since that plant was built.

It remarks that there are many excellent hydro-power sites in South America and Africa, remote from the power markets in the industrialized countries.

The report proposes:

1. An international estimate of

(Continued, Page A 5, Col. 1)

Poverty Found To Be Growing Among Elderly

Washington, Jan. 17 (AP)—One out of every four Americans aged 65 and over now is forced to live on a poverty-level income, the Senate special committee on aging reported today.

"A most distressing fact—a disgrace in a nation pledged to an all-out war on poverty—is that there was an increase in both the number and the proportion of aged poor between 1968 and 1969," the panel said in a report on the "Economics of Aging."

4.8 Million Aged Poor

"In 1969, there were approximately 4.8 million people aged 65 and older who were living in poverty, almost 200,000 more than in 1968."

In this same period, the report said, those in poverty declined by 1.2 million for all other age groups.

Senator Harrison A. Williams, Jr. (D., N.J.), the committee chairman, said in a preface that, to meet "this unnoticed income crisis," Congress should vote a 10 per cent Social Security increase for 1971 and 20 per cent for 1972.

Last year, the Senate voted a 10 per cent increase effective January 1, 1971, and the House approved the 5 per cent increase asked by President Nixon. But the two branches never got together and the proposal died.

General Revenues

The committee's report said serious consideration must now be given to using Treasury general revenues to finance a part of Social Security so that more adequate payments can be made.

The system now is financed wholly through payroll taxes on employers, employees and the self-employed.

Older persons are suffering heavily in the current economy, the report said.

Health Cost

It asserted that they were hard hit by unemployment in the economic slump and that soaring property taxes have jeopardized their efforts to hold onto their homes.

Rapidly rising health costs also are a serious problem for

(Continued, Page A 6, Col. 5)

Senator Edmund S. Muskie (left) talks with West German Chancellor Willy Brandt AP

Muskie Hails Bonn's Moves Toward East

By BRIGITTE FALBE
Bonn Bureau of The Sun

Bonn, Jan. 17—Senator Edmund S. Muskie today lauded West Germany's Eastern European policy as healthy, both in substance and pace.

The Maine Democrat told reporters at the Bonn airport before his departure for Washington that his 45-minute talks today with Chancellor Willy Brandt, Walter Scheel, the foreign minister, and Egon Bahr, state secretary, made his support for Bonn's Ostpoliti "if anything, stronger than before."

"I think that the Eastern policy is sound and constructive and is being conducted in a very healthy way," the senator said, adding later that he considered it "healthy, both in substance and pace."

Mr. Muskie said he believed that West Germany's real interest also coincided with the best long-range interests of the United States. A quarter of a century after World War II, he said, it was about time to erase the

(Continued, Page A 6, Col. 2)

O'BRIEN KICK DECISIVE IN LAST MINUTE

Loss To Jets Redeemed As Morrall Steps In For Injured Unitas

The Baltimore Colts captured pro football's biggest prize—the Super Bowl—in Miami yesterday when rookie Jim O'Brien kicked a 32-yard field goal with 5 seconds remaining to defeat the Dallas Cowboys, 16 to 13.

Until the 22-year-old O'Brien's boot settled the issue, the contest appeared to be heading for the first sudden-death finish in Super Bowl history.

But the Colts salvaged the victory in regulation time to redeem themselves for their 16-to-7 upset by the New York Jets in the third Super Bowl two years ago.

Morrall At Helm

Backup quarterback Earl Morrall was at the controls in place of the injured John Unitas as Baltimore fought back from a 13-to-6 deficit to earn the $15,000 pay-off that goes to each member of the world-championship team. Unitas was sitting on the bench with a rib injury suffered in the first half, but was ready to play if needed.

The Colts, who lost the ball 7 times on turnovers, rallied for 10 points in the fourth quarter with Tom Nowatzke's 2-yard touchdown run and O'Brien's conversion tying the score at 13-13.

Just over a minute remained when Colts' middle linebacker Mike Curtis intercepted Craig Morton's pass at the Dallas 40 and ran to the 28-yard line. [illegible] yards in two carries as Morrall positioned the Colts for O'Brien's winning field goal.

2 Cowboy Field Goals

The Cowboys had used field goals of 14 and 30 yards by Mike Clark and Morton's 7-yard touchdown pass to Duane Thomas to establish a 13-to-6 halftime advantage.

Baltimore's only score in the first half was produced by Unitas's 75-yard touchdown pass to John Mackey, but O'Brien's extra-point attempt was blocked.

Unitas completed three of nine passes, had two intercepted and fumbled once before giving way to Morrall. The Colts' relief quarterback found the target on 7 of 15 passes for 147 yards with one interception.

Thomas Stifled

The Baltimore defense limited Thomas, the Cowboys' rookie star, to 37 yards in 18 carries while Morton was limited to 12 completions in 26 attempts for 113 yards.

Nowatzke was the Colts' top ground gainer with 33 yards in 10 tries. Bulaich contributed 28 yards in 18 carries. Both trailed the Cowboys' Walt Garrison, most productive ground gainer of the day, who gained 65 yards in 12 attempts.

(Details on Page C 1)

3-Family Abduction Foiled By Ex-Legislator's Gunfire

Bennettsville, S.C., Jan. 17 (AP)—An apparent attempt by two men to kidnap members of three families was foiled last night when a former state legislator exchanged gunfire with the pair as they tried to take him from his home.

One of the alleged kidnapers was wounded during the shoot-out and was captured almost immediately. The second turned himself in through his attorney tonight in Columbia.

Also wounded during the exchange of gunfire was the wife of state Senator John C. Lindsay. She was injured critically.

The man who gave himself up tonight was identified as Grover Bennett, 23, of Charlotte, N.C. Chief J. P. Strom of the State Law Enforcement Division said the man was taken to the state penitentiary in Columbia.

The other suspect, identified as Charles Leonard Scales, 22, of Bennettsville, was arrested after being wounded in the shooting with the former state representative, James F. Lee.

Mr. Scales and Mr. Bennett were charged with kidnaping, robbery, burglary and assault and battery with intent to kill.

The police chief, Marion Driggers, offered no motive for the plot. He said only that "Scales was against the establishment." Chief Driggers said the two men, both Negroes, were carrying black militant literature.

Mrs. Lindsay reportedly offered the abductors jewels and cash if they would leave her alone, but one said, "We don't want diamonds or money."

The shooting occurred at Mr. Lee's home after the men already had abducted Mrs. Lee and her sons, and Mr. and Mrs. Wayne Chavis and three of their four children, authorities said.

Mr. Lindsay quoted Chief Driggers and Chief J. P. Strom of the State Law Enforcement Division who said the abductors had forced their way into Mr. Lee's home holding Mrs. Lindsay at gunpoint. She was shot in the throat, arm and leg by one of the men after Mr. Lee broke

(Continued, Page A 7, Col. 3)

The Weather
Mostly sunny today, with highs in the upper 30's. Partly cloudy tonight. Yesterday's high, 30; low, 19.
(Details and Map, Page C9)

THE SUN

FINAL

Vol. 270—No. 81— F | BALTIMORE, MONDAY, FEBRUARY 21, 1972 | 36 Pages | 10 Cents

President begins historic visit to China

UPI
Soldiers of the Chinese People's Liberation Army watch as American newsmen arrive at Peking's airport.

Chou greets Nixon in Peking

By PHILIP POTTER
Sun Staff Correspondent

Peking—President Nixon got a polite but low-key welcome when his official party of 15 arrived today for talks with leaders of the Chinese People's Republic.

His visit has been little heralded here.

Besides American correspondents and the resident press with their interpreters, the President and Mrs. Nixon were met at the capital's airport by only a handful of Chinese officials, led by Premier Chou En-lai, a 500-man honor guard and 200-man military band.

As the President and Mrs. Nixon left their plane, Premier Chou advanced for the first handshake, marking a new direction in relations between the United States and chairman Mao Tse-tung's government.

At the Geneva conference on Indochina in 1954, Mr. Chou was refused a handshake by the then American Secretary of State, John Foster Dulles, and has frequently commented about the slight in interviews with American journalists.

The Nixons arrived here at 11.30 A.M. (10.30 last night, Baltimore time) after a brief stopover in Shanghai.

The American flag flew beside the Chinese flag, a red banner with five gold stars, on the terminal building here while across the airstrip huge signs carried such slogans as "The Proletariat and the Oppressed Peoples of Oppressed Nations Unite" and "Struggle, Fail Again, Struggle Again Up to Victory."

President Nixon and Premier Chou reviewed the honor guard.

Mrs. Nixon followed behind as the band played the national anthems.

There were no speeches.

Neither were there crowds of any great size along the route the President's motorcade took to the guest house where he is staying for the first five days of his eight-day visit.

Correspondents who had often traveled abroad
See NIXON, A2, Col. 3

AP
Premier Chou En-lai greets President Nixon with a handshake at the ramp of the President's plane in Peking.

3 U.S. air bases hit in Vietnam

By the Associated Press

Communist-led forces shelled three United States air bases, shot down two helicopters and damaged four others in a surge of action yesterday and today. Two Americans were killed and 10 wounded, the U.S. command announced.

The two dead Americans were involved in a helicopter action 25 miles northwest of Saigon.

The command said two 107-mm. rockets hit the Phu Loi airfield, 10 miles north of Saigon, wounding five Americans and causing light damage to one helicopter.

6 rockets fired

Six 122-mm. rockets were fired at the Bien Hoa air base, 15 miles northeast of the capital but only three hit. Two Americans were wounded and some buildings and vehicles suffered light damage.

The U.S. air base at Phan Rang on the central coast received two 122-mm. rockets, but they caused no American casualties or damage, the command said.

In a swirling air action 25 miles northwest of Saigon, enemy gunners shot down a U.S. Army OH-6 light observation helicopter on a reconnaissance mission.

Three other light observation helicopters and a Cobra helicopter gunship flying in support of the downed aircraft also were hit and one had to make a forced landing. The command said two Americans were killed and one was wounded. One helicopter was destroyed and three others sustained major damage.

In the Mekong Delta, about 90 miles south of Saigon, Viet Cong troops shot down another Army helicopter on a reconnaissance mission. The crewmen escaped uninjured, the command said.

A Sheridan tank triggered a mine 25 miles northeast of Saigon. Two Americans were wounded and the tank suffered moderate damage, the command said.

There had been intelligence reports that Saigon and the surrounding 3d Military Region would be targets for a surge of rocket, mortar and sapper attacks. The reports said the attacks, coinciding with President Nixon's arrival in China, would represent a Viet Cong and North Vietnamese effort to grab headlines and embarrass the President.

However, there were fewer incidents than expected.

Changed plans

"We had a good reason to expect something overnight," said one American officer in Saigon. "The enemy apparently changed his plans. Either he didn't have the capability, he found out we knew and were on the alert, or he was ordered by higher headquarters to cancel."

Enemy forces launched 67 attacks over the weekend. Heavy losses were dealt to several
See WAR, A4, Col. 3

300 troops battle rioters, return fire in Londonderry

Londonderry, Northern Ireland (AP)—Three hundred British troops battled rioters and exchanged fire with guerrilla gunmen last night. It was the worst violence in Londonderry since "Bloody Sunday" three weeks ago, but no casualties were reported.

An Army search for terrorist arms in Belfast turned up a Soviet-made Kalashnikov machine gun in a large haul of ammunition and firearms. It was only the second time in hundreds of swoops that a Russian weapon has been found in Northern Ireland, officials said.

Soldiers also clashed twice with civilians from Ireland who crossed into Northern Ireland. The civilians came to fill craters blasted in cross-border roads by the British as a means of reducing guerrilla infiltration.

The trouble erupted as this Protestant-dominated British province embarked on a critical round of the struggle to end three years of strife, and the Catholic republic moved to crack down on outlaw bands. The British government was re-
See ULSTER, A5, Col. 1

China's welcome is gracious, although austere, reporters find

By PHILIP POTTER

Peking—For newsmen who arrived in Peking yesterday hours before President Nixon, the China of Chairman Mao Tse-tung seems a gracious and cordial, if austere, host to "American imperialists."

We were greeted at the Shanghai airport by members of the information department of the Foreign Ministry and city representatives, including women interpreters. We were handed our credentials and were given an excellent luncheon of Chinese delicacies, interrupted often by toasts in beer, wine or the fiery mao tai, a vodka-like drink.

A typical toast was, "I wish you a pleasant stay, the best of health and every success in your work. Through your visit we hope the relations between us will become better."

"Eat a little more"

But substantive news was hard to come by. When a correspondent at one table asked an official about the fate of Lin Piao, who apparently has been removed as defense minister, he was told, "Why don't you eat a little more?"

At the airport in Peking each pair of newsmen was taken in tow by courteous and cordial interpreters, and I was lucky enough to draw Wu Chien-ta, borrowed by the Foreign Ministry from the All-China Journalists Association.

Mr. Wu had just returned to his wife and daughter in Peking after three years in a May 7 camp, where during the now quiet cultural revolution bureaucrats and intellectuals have been learning through labor with farmers and others how better to serve the people. During his stay at the May 7 camp, Mr. Wu was allowed to see his family once a year on leave.

It was clear as we rode by bus into the city along tree-lined streets as clean as a Dutch matron's floor—as were the courtyards of block after block of apartment houses—that Mr. Wu is proud of the accom-
See PEKING, A2, Col. 7

AP
United States newsmen were invited to an elaborate Chinese luncheon by the Shanghai Revolutionary Council after their welcome during a stopover in that city. From left are Theodore White, Walter Cronkite and William F. Buckley, Jr.

Walter Winchell dead at 74

Los Angeles (AP)—Walter Winchell, the fast-talking song-and-dance man who became the best-read newspaper columnist and the most-heard newscaster on radio, died yesterday at 74.

Mr. Winchell died of prostate cancer, relatives reported.

Death came at the UCLA Medical Center, where the columnist had been confined since November 19. A hospital spokesman said Mr. Winchell had been in the hospital several times in the past few years. He underwent surgery for a growth two years ago, but said he had recovered.

For 30 years, most Americans were familiar with his radio opening, a shouted: "Good evening, Mr. and Mrs.
See WINCHELL, A6, Col. 1

Soviet promise of arms for Egypt coupled with warning against war

By OSWALD JOHNSTON
Sun Staff Correspondent

Cairo—The Soviet Union has promised to send Egypt more weapons and has agreed to give the Egyptian military establishment a greater voice in selecting the equipment Egypt receives.

At the same time, like a grudging governess, the Russians again have told President Anwar Sadat that he would lose a war with Israel now.

According to informed sources here, they also warned the Egyptian president that the Soviet Union would move to end any such war within 24 hours—in co-operation with the United States, if necessary.

Brezhnev's warning

The promise and the warning were delivered to Mr. Sadat during his meeting early this month with the top Soviet leadership, according to an account of the Moscow visit told by well-informed sources here.

The warning is said to have been delivered by Leonid I. Brezhnev, the Communist party chairman, in retort to a claim by Mr. Sadat that the Egyptians alone would decide whether to make war and that the Russians could not restrain them.

The main business of the Soviet delegation here on a four-day visit, and headed by Marshal Andrei Grechko, the defense minister, reportedly is to work out the method of selecting future arms supplies.

The Egyptians have been pressing, mostly unsuccessfully, for sophisticated, modern offensive and defensive weaponry to match the flow of American equipment into Israel. Mr. Sadat is reported to have complained in Moscow that much of the armament Egypt receives is old—and in many cases second hand.

The Russians are known to be skeptical of the ability of Egyptian pilots and ground soldiers to handle the equipment they receive now—old or new—and this, too, is understood to have been a bone of contention in the Moscow talks.

Well-placed observers here estimate that the Egyptian Air Force loses between 15 and 20 per cent of its men and jet fighters a year in training acci-
See EGYPT, A4, Col. 1

UPI
President Anwar Sadat of Egypt (right) exchanges greetings with the Soviet defense minister, Marshal Andrei A. Grechko, during Cairo arms-aid talks.

Logic, politics explain Peking's media attacks

By EDWARD K. WU
Hong Kong Bureau of The Sun

Hong Kong—Attacks on United States policies continued in Chinese government statements and in media commentaries while President Nixon was en route to China for his historic visit.

Such rhetoric, especially on Indochina, may even continue during the President's stay in China.

Only yesterday, on the eve of Mr. Nixon's arrival in Peking, the Chinese Foreign Ministry issued a formal statement strongly condemning the stepped-up U.S. air strikes in North Vietnam, Laos and Cambodia. The official newspaper *People's Daily* called them "new war provocations."

"If the eight-point proposal recently dished up by the U.S. government was camouflaged with the cloak of ending the war, then these acts on the battlefields have completely shed the disguise of sham peace and laid bare the aggressive features of the U.S. aggressors in procrastinating and intensifying the war," the Foreign Ministry statement said.

Repeating the standard pledges, the statement and the *People's Daily* reaffirmed China's support for the Indochinese Communists vows to fight the Americans to the end.

With or without the Nixon visit, these statements and editorial comments would have been published.

For example, yesterday's pronouncements came in response to the North Vietnamese government statement of February 17. It would have been strange, indeed, if Peking had not followed past practice and had remained mute just because Mr. Nixon was coming.

The same logic holds for the Chinese utterances in the recent weeks over the eight-point U.S. Indochina peace proposal, the President's State-of-the-Union and foreign policy messages to Congress, and the Taiwan question.

As Mr. Nixon and the Chinese leaders have conceded, there
See CHINA, A2, Col. 8

Wilbur Mills campaign

'The Chairman' gets a hearing

By SANDRA BANISKY
Sun Staff Correspondent

Washington—No one is really sure what Wilbur Mills is up to.

The chairman of the House Ways and Means Committee has announced he is an active candidate for the Democratic nomination.

But even his aides say they are uncertain if Mr. Mills really wants to be President. He may be hoping to be noticed as a vice presidential possibility or want to help choose the Democratic nominee. He simply may be enjoying the glamour of a national campaign.

Few observers believe the Arkansas Democrat actually wants to occupy the White House.

The popular view is that Mr. Mills, the strong leader of a committee that handles tax legislation, Social Security laws, health-care proposals and foreign-trade agreements, holds far more control over Congress now than he could from the executive mansion.

Even his colleague on Ways and Means, Representative Sam M. Gibbons (D., Fla.), has asked, "Wilbur, why in the world would you want to be President and give up all this power?"

The Mills candidacy began coyly last spring when "The Chairman"—as his staff calls him—began adding national speaking dates to his crowded schedule.

All the while, Mr. Mills denied he had even the slightest interest in the nomination. The "Mills For President" bumper stickers and other candidate-like trappings were the result of a draft movement over which he had no control, he said.

But some in Washington
See MILLS, A5, Col. 1

Index

The Weather
Chance of thundershowers today, high 74. Partly cloudy tonight, low 51 to 57.
(Details and Map, Page C6)

THE SUN

FINAL

Vol. 270—No. 154—F | BALTIMORE, TUESDAY, MAY 16, 1972 | 46 Pages | 10 Cents

Wallace shot and critically wounded in Laurel; suspect arraigned here; two guards, woman spectator also hit

Saigon retakes base in effort to protect Hue

AP

By The Associated Press

South Vietnamese infantrymen using helicopter assault tactics recaptured Fire Base Bastogne, a key site southwest of Hue, yesterday in the second phase of an effort to preempt North Vietnamese plans to attack the former imperial capital.

The surprise conquest of the base, which had been abandoned under enemy attack 18 days ago, came as renewed fighting was reported in the Central Highlands.

Foe cuts two roads

Communist command troops also cut two key highways by destroying culverts.

The 6½-week siege of An Loc continued as enemy forces hurled another 2,500 rounds of artillery, rocket and mortar fire into the town, 60 miles north of Saigon.

The United States command disclosed the loss of three more planes in raids over North Vietnam with all six crewmen listed as missing. This raised to 142 the number of Americans reported killed or missing in air action since Hanoi's general offensive began March 30.

At Bastogne, field reports said, a platoon of volunteers riding six South Vietnamese helicopters assaulted the base in mid-afternoon. They quickly secured it for ground forces that drove westward along Route 547 behind a shield of U.S. air strikes.

Enemy possibly surprised

The attackers encountered only light resistance, the reports said, indicating North Vietnamese forces around Bastogne possibly were surprised by the bold attack.

At nightfall the South Vietnamese 1st Division was reported to have full control of the base. But some troops still were reported trying to recapture a nearby mountaintop outpost called Checkmate, which also fell to the enemy April 28.

Like the Vietnamese Marine raid over the weekend into enemy-held territory just northwest of Hue, the Bastogne operation indicated a determination by South Vietnamese commanders to seize the initiative from enemy forces threatening Hue.

Military sources said more such forays can be expected by forces under Lt. Gen. Ngo Cong

See WAR, A2, Col. 3

Brandt foes find treaties acceptable

By GENE OISHI
Bonn Bureau of the Sun

Bonn—The leadership of the opposition Christian Democratic Union issued a statement yesterday saying that its previous objections to the Brandt government's treaties with the Soviet Union and Poland have been removed.

The statement was passed by a 27-to-1 vote of the Christian Democratic National Executive Committee, indicating that the opposition leadership, at least, will push for ratification of the detente treaties when they come up for a vote in the West German parliament tomorrow. Issued after a four-hour meeting, the statement amounted to a vote of confidence for Rainer Barzel, the opposition leader, who has been negotiating with Chancellor Willy Brandt and other government leaders over a Bundestag resolution giving the West German interpretation of the treaties.

Party caucus

Mr. Barzel, however, is expected to encounter a sterner test of his leadership when members of his party, including its more conservative Bavarian affiliate, the Christian Social Union, caucus today in an effort to find a common position.

The opposition faction includes a number of hard-liners—estimated at roughly 20 per

See TREATY, A5, Col. 2

CBS Newsphoto via AP

A man wearing dark glasses (right center) fires a pistol at Gov. George C. Wallace of Alabama (not shown) in the middle of a crowd of about 1,000 during a campaign rally in the Laurel Shopping Center.

'George, take my hand'...then shots

By FRED BARBASH

"George, come here. George, take my hand."

Those were the last words witnesses heard before shots rang out at the Laurel Shopping Center.

"He fell back. I thought he might be dead or dying," said Lauren Pierce, a CBS cameraman, in a WTOP-TV interview.

"But then he opened his eyes after a long while and his wife came running to his side, embraced him briefly, then turned and came back. It was total confusion."

Then there was a momentary silence, a crowd "in shock," as Capt. E. G. Husk of the Prince Georges County Police described it.

Then "everyone rushed forward, and everyone came running back, then everyone rushed forward again," recalled Gary Miller, 16, one of dozens of Laurel High School students who had come to hear Governor Wallace.

He said, "I thought it was irecrackers, then I realized . . ."

"I thought there was a firecracker," said Charles Naltz, 28, an assistant professor at the University of Maryland. "Then somebody yelled 'he's shot.' I thought immediately of Kennedy," he said.

"Kill him, get him," members of the crowd yelled, referring to the assassin.

"God help you," cried the rally's master of ceremonies, who earlier had said a prayer for a man like George Wallace to "save the country."

"The crowd froze," said Captain Husk. "They wouldn't move for two to three minutes."

Then, from the fringes, a few people began to run in panic, looking for cover.

"A woman knocked me down to get under a car," said Phillip Epling, of Laurel. "Then I ducked under the car, too," he recalled.

Another small segment of the crowd moved in toward the area of the shooting. Security guards and civilians swarmed around Governor Wallace and his assailant.

"There was a mass of bodies just massed on top of him," said Mr. Pierce. "One arm came out still firing . . . looked like a cheap .38 special firing at point-blank range."

Witnesses said they saw people punching the assailant. "He had blood coming out of his nose and a cut on the back of his neck," said Fred Knapp, 16, a newspaper delivery boy who had stopped to hear Governor Wallace.

Then 15 or 20 uniformed policemen joined security personnel in civilian clothes to move the crowd back.

There were a few reports—unconfirmed by police—of members of the crowd chasing

See CROWD, A8, Col. 3

Accused assailant called 'quiet,' kept Wallace sticker on his door

Milwaukee, Wis. (AP)—Arthur H. Bremer, a 21-year-old one-time photography student accused of shooting George C. Wallace, was described yesterday as a lonely, quiet person who was something of a puzzle even to his family.

"Nobody could talk to him," said Mr. Bremer's teen-age brother, Roger. "We never knew much about him."

A former neighbor said Mr. Bremer kept a Wallace sticker across the door of his apartment. Officials said he was a below average student in high school.

Moved to apartment

In Mr. Bremer's apartment, newsmen, who arrived after it had been visted by FBI agents, found a Confederate flag, a gun catalog, a box of firearm cartridges, a comic book, hotel advertisements and several newspaper clippings, one of them relating the frustrations of newsmen trying to get past security guards to reach presidential candidates.

Mr. Bremer left the family's wood-frame south side home last year and moved to an apartment, working as a custodian in public schools and at a private club.

Mr. Bremer's father, William, 58, a truck driver, said the family "had no idea he was in Maryland. He never mentioned anything about Wallace, never mentiond anything political."

"God knows that we hope he isn't connected with this," the father said. "If he is accused of this, he must have got really sick. We can't believe it."

"He never had a gun to my knowledge," the father said. "He never went hunting."

Another brother, Theodore, related: "He was against the radical part of the system of American life. He just stayed away from it."

The Bremer family includes four sons: Theodore, 34; William, 32; Arthur, 21, and Roger 18.

Government agents investigated Mr. Bremer's small apartment, and talked for several hours with a teen-age girl

See BREMER, A8, Col. 3

Bullets fell candidate in midst of crowd

By STEPHEN J. LYNTON
Sun Staff Correspondent

Laurel—Gov. George C. Wallace was shot and seriously wounded yesterday as he campaigned on a hot, muggy afternoon at a shopping center here.

Mr. Wallace was struck in the chest and abdomen and was paralyzed, at least temporarily, in the lower part of his body. Two other men and one woman also were wounded, none of them seriously.

Police immediately arrested a white man, who later was identified by the FBI as Arthur H. Bremer, 21, of Milwaukee. He was arraigned last night in Baltimore on charges of assaulting a Secret Service agent and a presidential candidate, both federal crimes.

Shaking hands with crowd

The other persons wounded were identified as an Alabama state policeman, Capt. E. C. Dothard, who is one of the Governor's bodyguards; a federal Secret Service agent, and a woman spectator.

The 52-year-old Alabama Governor, who is seeking the Democratic nomination for President, was in the midst of a final day of campaigning before Maryland's primary election today. He was shaking hands with an enthusiastic crowd at 3.58 P.M. when at least four pistol shots rang out.

Mr. Wallace fell to the pavement, where he lay on his back, his eyes open.

The motive for the attempted assassination was not immediately known. The suspect was reported by witnesses to have been wearing pro-Wallace emblems. The FBI said it was seeking an accomplice in the shooting.

The Associated Press quoted a source close to the investigation last night as saying that FBI agents searching Mr. Bremer's Milwaukee apartment had found scraps of paper linking him with "left-wing causes," but the report could not immediately be confirmed.

"He looked rational"

Arthur A. Marshall, Jr., the Prince Georges county prosecutor, observed Mr. Bremer during a medical examination and later said: "He looked rational, quiet, obviously unhappy, but coherent."

At Holy Cross Hospital in Silver Spring, Mr. Wallace underwent surgery from about 5.50 to 10.35 P.M. One bullet was reported to have been removed from his chest, but another remained in his abdomen and was lodged near his spine, leaving the danger of permanent paralysis.

Dr. Joseph Schannon, a vascular surgeon who was part of the medical team that operated on Mr. Wallace, said that "four or five bullet wounds of varying degrees" were found in his right arm, chest and abdomen. At least two of them were superficial wounds, he added.

The sun had just broken through a dreary, over-

See WALLACE, A8, Col. 1

Maryland voters to choose presidential candidates today

By BENTLEY ORRICK

Maryland voters, stunned at the attempted assassination of Gov. George C. Wallace as he was campaigning in Laurel, will get their first chance in eight years today to vote their party choice for President.

For the first time in Maryland, the voters will also decide who will represent them at their party conventions.

The polls are open from 7 A.M. to 8 P.M. around the state. The weather bureau predicts a better-than-even chance of rain throughout most of Maryland.

The shooting of Mr. Wallace brought campaigning in Maryland to a halt.

Senator Hubert H. Humphrey (D., Minn.) was campaigning at a day care center in Baltimore when an aide whispered the news of the shooting to him. He quickly canceled the remainder of his schedule.

A confusing ballot and a generally lackluster campaign in the state had resulted in predictions of light voter turnout. However, the shooting of Mr. Wallace is bound to awaken interest.

There are 11 names on the Democratic presidential ballot and 3 on the Republican. All the names were put there by

See PRIMARY, A9, Col. 6

Senators McGovern and Humphrey cancel TV spots in Michigan primary A7

Palmer shines in Oriole win

Jim Palmer allowed Detroit just four hits—two of them solo home runs—and scored the winning run after tripling in the seventh inning as the Orioles defeated the Tigers, 3 to 2, in Detroit last night.

(*Details on Page C1*)

Index

Supreme Court exempts Amish from school laws

By WALTER R. GORDON
Washington Bureau of The Sun

Washington—The Supreme Court ruled yesterday that the Amish cannot be required to attend school beyond the eighth grade.

The justices also agreed to hear a Silver Spring case posing the issue of whether racial discrimination by community recreation associations violates the 1964 Civil Rights Act.

And with only Justice William O. Douglas dissenting, the court upheld a 1968 law that allows federal agents to search gun shops for illegal weapons without obtaining a warrant.

The Amish case marked the first time the justices had restricted the power of the states to require school attendance, although it had been decided long since that private and religious schools were an acceptable alternative to public education.

The decision rested on the

See COURT, A6, Col. 1

Swagger

Arthur H. Bremer (left), the accused assailant of Gov. George C. Wallace of Alabama, tries to duck behind an unidenti federal officer following arraignment proceedings in Federal Court.

The Weather
Sunny today and fair tonight. High today, 73. Lows tonight near 45. Yesterday's high, 68; low, 46.
(Details and Map, Page B11)

THE SUN

FINAL

Vol. 271—No. 10—F | BALTIMORE, SATURDAY, MAY 27, 1972 | 38 Pages | 10 C[illegible]

Nixon, Brezhnev sign arms-limit treaty

UPI
South Vietnamese troops wait behind their tank as an explosion from a U.S. air strike sends clouds of smoke into the air near Kontum.

Reds hit Kontum a 3d time

Saigon troops report 7 tanks knocked out

By The Associated Press

Saigon—A column of North Vietnamese tanks swept down on Kontum from the north today in a third day of assaults on the Central Highlands provincial capital.

South Vietnamese spokesmen at Pleiku said seven enemy tanks were destroyed during the night.

Allies claim 19 tanks

It raised to 19 the number of tanks claimed knocked out by allied air and ground forces during the past two days.

South Vietnamese spokesmen said the seven tanks were knocked out by an armed United States C-119, light anti-tank weapons and artillery fired by South Vietnamese defenders.

Casualties in the Kontum fighting continued to mount. South Vietnamese spokesmen said 370 North Vietnamese troops were killed in dawn-to-dusk fighting yesterday while government losses were 42 men killed and 126 wounded.

Attack reported stopped

The tank attack was reported stopped.

U.S. B-52's carried out more than 30 strikes in support of the defenders of Kontum, unleashing 800 tons of explosives on North Vietnamese troop positions on both the northern and southern sides of the city. Some of the strikes were as close as 2 miles to the city.

One American was killed and another wounded yesterday during an enemy ground attack against a South Vietnamese position, and five more Americans were wounded when accidentally hit by their own rocket fire, the U.S. command announced today.

Both actions were in the Saigon area.

The command also reported that two jets were lost in the northern quarter of South Vietnam but all four crewmen were rescued by helicoptes. None of the crewmen was reported injured.

Heavy fighting also was reported on the southern front at

See WAR, A7, Col. 1

UPI
Leonid I. Brezhnev offers a toast to President Nixon after signing the strategic arms treaty

ABM sites and weapons output curbed

By PETER J. KUMPA
Sun Staff Correspondent

Moscow—The United States and the Soviet Union took the important first step in controlling their strategic arms late last night, concluding a treaty limiting anti-ballistic missile systems and agreeing to a partial freeze on the build-up of offensive weapons.

Signing 46 minutes before midnight in the dazzling white, gold and green Vladimir Hall of the Great Kremlin palace was President Nixon and the general party secretary, Leonid I. Brezhnev.

It took but 11 minutes for the two leaders to finish the treaties that had taken negotiators for both sides about 30 months to complete in secret sessions at both Vienna and Helsinki.

Ambassador Gerard C. Smith, the chief American negotiator during the strategic arms limitation talks, was still putting finishing technical touches on

Text of the arms treaty A8

the treaty aboard a plane bound here from Helsinki short hours before the signing.

Praised immediately by both sides, the ABM treaty limits each side to one ABM site for defense of their national capitals, Moscow and Washington, as well as one site each for the defense of an intercontinental ballistic missile field.

The Russians now protect Moscow and the Americans defend an ICBM field.

ICBM's limited

The offensive freeze—to last at least five years while a fuller treaty is negotiated—limits the number of ICBM's to those now under construction or deployed. This would mean 1,618 ICBM's for the Soviet Union and 1.054 for the U.S.

It also freezes the construction of submarine-launched ballistic missiles beyond those started. Any further construction of additional nuclear submarines would require the dismantling of an equal number of older, land-based ICBM's or older submarine launchers.

On behalf of President Nixon, Henry A. Kissinger, the White House national security adviser, congratulated the negotiating team under Ambassador Smith.

See SALT, A8, Col. 1

Congress generally favors pact

Washington (AP)—The United States-Soviet arms limitation agreement evoked both delight and derision among congressional leaders, but the initial tide appeared to run heavily in favor of the pact signed yesterday in Moscow.

The House Republican leader, Gerald R. Ford (Mich.), proclaimed the move as "the most momentous such international agreement reached by two major powers in modern history."

"Decade of danger"

But a GOP presidential contender, Representative John M. Ashbrook of Ohio, declared in California that it will "doom the United States to a decade of danger."

Senators Strom Thurmond (R., S.C.); Henry M. Jackson (D., Wash.), and James L. Buckley (C.-R., N.Y.) also quickly expressed discontent.

The Senate Democratic whip, Robert C. Byrd of West Virginia, potentially a key figure in guiding parts of the agreement to ratification, was somewhat cautious in his enthusiasm but said, "The world could be a step closer to a lasting peace."

"What we have gained," said Mr. Byrd, "is to break the Soviets' momentum, apparently without endangering our own security."

Another important figure, Senator John C. Stennis (D., Miss.), chairman of the Armed Services committee, declined to commit himself pending his panel's examination of the pact.

But he said: "I trust that this

See REACTION, A8, Col. 6

Snags limit trade accord

By PETER J. KUMPA

Moscow — The failure of the United States and Russia to reach a lend-lease settlement, plus possible political complications, resulted yesterday in a disappointing trade agreement between the two countries.

The agreement only calls for the establishment of a joint U.S.-Soviet-commercial commission that will be charged with negotiating a broad trade agreement. Talks will begin here in July.

At the same time, the two sides agreed to hold parallel talks on the lend-lease negotiations that long preparation and the summit conference here failed to solve.

The two matters are obviously connected. So are maritime negotiations that also failed to produce an agreement here. It would have opened up American ports to Russian shipping while giving a share of the two-way trade to ships of both countries.

Peter Flanigan, a White House assistant on international economic affairs, denied flatly here yesterday that trade was in any way connected to the Vietnam question.

"There was no attempt," he said, "to link the expansion of trade with the state of affairs in Vietnam."

The roadblock to a broader arrangement was apparently the difficulty in working out reciprocal arrangements, as well as the lend-lease question.

A permanent commission

The joint commission is to be a permanent one, charged with expanding economic relations in a number of fields.

It's tasks are:

1. To negotiate a trade agreement to deal, among other things, with most-favored-nation treatment. Talks can be expected to last many months.

2. To make reciprocal government credits available. This largely means the opening of Export-Import Bank credits for American sales to the Soviet Union so as to put U.S. merchandise on a competitive basis with Japan and Western Europe.

3. To establish reciprocal business facilities.

4. To develop possible joint

See TRADE, A8, Col. 7

U.S. trade deficit exceeds $2 billion

Washington (AP)—The nation's 1972 trade deficit surpassed the $2 billion mark last month, as the value of imports exceeded exports by the second highest amount on record, the Commerce Department said yesterday.

In only four months, the nation managed to exceed last year's trade deficit of $2 billion. For January through April the deficit was $2.2 billion.

First since 1888

For April alone, the department said, the value of imports exceeded exports by $699.4 million, a figure topped only by last October's $821.4 million.

In 12 of the last 13 months the nation has had a deficit in its merchandise trade balance, and last year's deficit was the first since 1888.

A trade deficit puts additional pressure on the strength of the dollar overseas since it means that more United States money is flowing out of the country. It also reflects on the ability of American industry, to compete with foreign imports.

But, as far as consumers are concerned, a trade deficit is not necessarily bad, since it means a wider choice of goods to choose from.

In April, exports actually declined from the March level by 3.4 per cent, largely because not so many jumbo jets were shipped out as in March.

Small decline in imports

The drop in exports, however, was combined with only a 0.3 per cent decline in imports.

A Commerce Department official said the main reason for the continued deficit is that the American economy is expanding fast, making it a good market for imports, while the economies of other countries are still sluggish, making them relatively poor markets for American goods.

"Until foreign economies

See DEFICIT, A5, Col. 5

Explosion in Belfast kills 1, ends 2-day lull

Belfast, Northern Ireland (Reuter) — A bomb devastated a crowded marketplace in downtown Belfast yesterday, killing a woman and leaving 41 injured.

A police spokesman said the death toll could go higher. "Many of the injured have undergone emergency operations. . . . Some of them received the most terrible wounds," he said.

48-hour lull ended

The explosion, together with four other bombings throughout Northern Ireland, shattered a 48-hour lull in guerrilla violence by the Irish Republican Army and offset hopes of peace.

The explosions came just as Northern Ireland's Social Democratic and Labor party, the main opposition party, urged its Catholic supporters to co-operate with the British administrators of the province.

Two of the bombings occurred in Belfast, two in Londonderry and one in a small town near Londonderry. There were no reports of death outside Belfast.

The big explosion in the capital—estimated by the British Army to be a bomb containing 150 pounds of gelignite—went off in a parked car.

Flying glass landed in surrounding streets, jammed for market day.

Police cars carry victims

There were so many casualties that police cars were called in to help ambulances rush the injured to hospitals.

The blast damaged buildings a quarter of a mile away and shook nearby Queens Bridge over the River Lagan, which bisects Belfast.

The new outbreak of violence appeared aimed at the opposition party's plea for co-operation and an appeal it made for Catholics to open talks with Protestant leaders of the province.

The call, coming after mounting Catholic anger this week at the IRA's guerrilla tactics and shootings, was viewed as one of the most important political peace gestures since Britain assumed direct rule of Northern Ireland two months ago.

"We ask our Protestant fellow citizens to agree that it is now time to show real faith in one another," the party's statement said.

The party said it was convinced the strife-torn province's problems could be resolved without another shot being fired and without life being lost.

The party welcomed the peace movements started by Catholic women in Londonderry and Belfast and asked the IRA "what possible justification can there be for any further loss of life when we can achieve the objectives that the people desire by peaceful means?"

"We feel it is now time to demonstrate our determination to create community reconciliation. It is time for a positive response to be made by us to

See ULSTER, A6, Col. 1

Baltimore bus improvements win $4.9 million U.S. grant for state

By GILBERT LEWTHWAITE
Washington Bureau of The Sun

Washington—Improvements in Baltimore's public bus service have qualified the Maryland Mass Transit Authority for a federal grant of $4.9 million, the Department of Transportation announced yesterday.

The new money will be added to the $14.8 million given in 1970 to help the state buy the privately owned and ailing Baltimore Transit Company.

It brings federal aid for modernization of the Baltimore bus system up to the maximum two-thirds share.

Announcing the grant, John A. Volpe, the Secretary of Transportation, praised the Baltimore service and said the state takeover had averted "a near-certain transportation crisis in Baltimore."

The state's intervention turned a decline in the number of passengers on metropolitan area buses into a 2 per cent gain over the last two years. The introduction of 370 new buses reduced the average age of vehicles from 15 years to 6 years.

"This has been accomplished at no increase in fares," Mr. Volpe said. "Moreover, the recent introduction of reduced fares for senior citizens should further increase ridership and provide the mobility we are seeking for all Americans."

"A prime example"

The $4.9 million grant was acknowledgment that plans for the Baltimore bus system were finally in line with the requirements of the Urban Mass Transportation Act of 1964, which sets the standards for two-thirds federal financing.

"Baltimore is a prime example of President Nixon's $3.1 billion, five-year program of assistance to preserve and improve the nation's public transportation services," said Carlos C. Villareal, the administrator of the Urban Mass Transportation Administration, the federal agency that made the award.

Another agency official said, "The Baltimore system really has been quite successful. The top priority that we are trying to do with the $3.1 billion is to save existing systems.

"The Baltimore system was in pretty bad shape and was on the verge of not having any services until it was taken over publicly. What the President wants to do is keep transportation going for the public," he said.

The $4.9 million award leaves one massive Maryland financial application outstanding with the urban transportation agency.

This is a request for $437

See BUS, A13, Col. 1

Birds blank Indians, 2-0

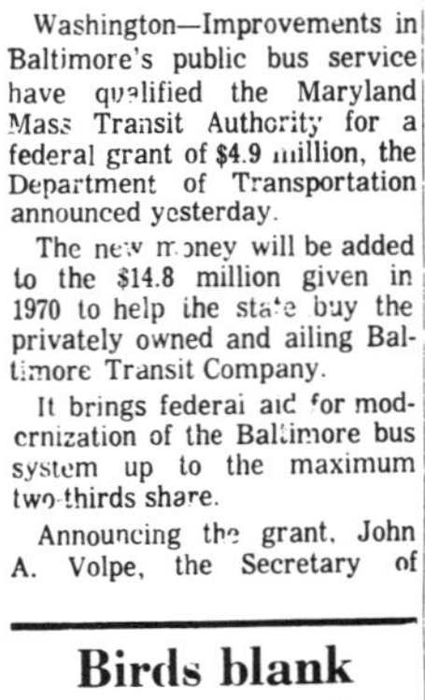

Paul Blair drove in one run and scored another after hitting a triple as the Orioles defeated the first-place Cleveland Indians, 2 to 0, behind Mike Cuellar's 4-hit pitching.

(Details on Page B1)

Von Braun quits NASA to take corporate post

By ALBERT SEHLSTEDT, JR.
Washington Bureau of The Sun

Washington — Wernher von Braun, who directed development of the giant Saturn moon rockets for the National Aeronautics and Space Administration, is resigning from the agency as of July 1.

Dr. von Braun, 60, will become corporate vice president for engineering and development of Fairchild Industries, Inc., the space agency said yesterday. Fairchild is an aerospace company with corporate headquarters at Germantown, Maryland.

Principal contractor

The rocket expert said he regretted leaving the space agency, but wanted to "devote my time to help implement some space projects I feel are of particular importance.

"I think I can do this best in private industry where the tools of progress are being made," he added.

Fairchild, whose stock jumped 1 and ⅜ points on the New York Stock Exchange with the announcement of Dr. von Braun's move, is the principal government contractor for the applications-technology satellite, a new spacecraft designed to improve television and radio

See VON BRAUN, A2, Col. 3

WERNHER VON BRAUN

Index

AP
Egon Bahr, West Germany's state secretary (left), exchanges documents in East Berlin with Michael Kohl, East Germany's state secretary, after the two countries signed their first treaty ever—a traffic-transport accord.

Bonn, East Germany sign pact on transport, traffic matters

By BRIGITTE FALBE
Bonn Bureau of the Sun

Bonn—In a short, solemn ceremony in East Berlin yesterday, East and West German negotiators signed the transport and traffic treaty, the first between the two Germanys in their 23-year history.

The two nations announced they will continue efforts to normalize relations by working toward a fundamental political agreement after the four-power accord on Berlin is signed June 3.

Negotiations between the two Germanys in one of several agreements that will define their political status in the world and to each other are expected to begin June 15. Their entry into the United Nations will be one of the issues.

However, in response to questions after the ceremony, Egon Bahr, the West German negotiator, said that an exchange of ambassadors between the two countries will "certainly" not be the result.

The transport and traffic treaty deals with highly technical details that will facilitate vehicle, railway and ship traffic across the fortified East-West German border and across the territories of the two states. It mentions co-operation on train schedules, traffic information and construction, among other things.

Michael Kohl, the East German negotiator, confirmed after the signing that East Germany intends to combine the implementation of the treaty with moves that will make visits between the two states easier.

The Weather
Partial cloudiness today and tonight. Chance of thundershowers. High, 92; low, 72 to 77. Yesterday's high 92, low 76.
(Details and Map, Page C7)

THE SUN

FINAL

Vol. 271—No. 53—F | BALTIMORE, MONDAY, JULY 17, 1972 | 34 Pages | 10 Cents

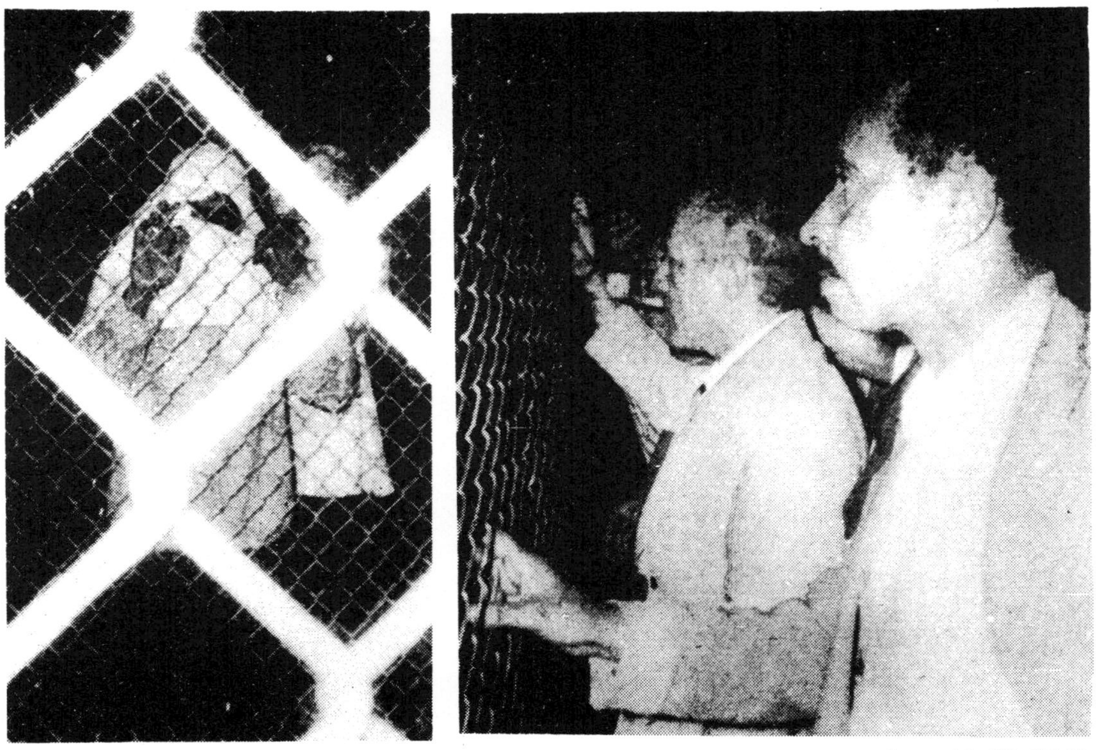

Sunpapers photos—Walter McCardell

Governor Mandel and Representative Parren J. Mitchell (right) talk to prisoners. Two convicts hide their faces with towels

Jessup riot ends as Mandel, Mitchell meet with inmates

By JIM FLANERY
Sun Staff Correspondent

Jessup—A Maryland House of Correction riot, which officials said caused at least $1.5 million damage, was quelled early yesterday after Governor Mandel and Representative Parren J. Mitchell (D., 7th) met with a contingent of rioters inside prison walls.

The meeting —demanded by the rioters to air their grievances—was held on the condition that 300 to 400 other inmates, who had controlled a recreation yard, agree to return to their cells.

They did so by 5.15 A.M., moving in groups of 12 and supervised by about 150 State Police troopers called from all portions of the state. The return to cells ended a tense, 10-hour disturbance resulting in injuries to 4 inmates and 3 guards.

Four of the convicts and one of the guards were shot, prison officials reported. The guard was hit by a ricocheting bullet fired by another guard, officials said. Two other guards suffered minor injuries during a melee in the prison recreation yard. All were taken to University Hospital.

Ralph L. Williams, the warden, said that, contrary to earlier reports, no shots were fired by inmates and that no guns were found in their possession.

Governor's promise

At 6.30 A.M., a weary Governor Mandel emerged from the meeting with the inmates to tell newsmen waiting in front of the prison that he would "look into" five grievances he said had been the inmates' explanation for the rioting.

A key grievance, the Governor said, was the inmates' belief that a prisoner involved in an escape attempt Saturday night just before the riot had been shot by a guard unnecessarily. Mr. Williams, the prison warden, said, however, that the guard had acted "within the rules and regulations" in shooting the inmate.

Governor Mandel called the riot the worst he had seen in a Maryland prison. His assessment was echoed by Col. Thomas S. Smith, the superintendent of the State Police, who led his forces at Jessup.

The riot damage was "conservatively estimated" at $1.5 million, according to Elmanus Herndon, the head of custody for the prison system.

Switchboard destroyed

Rioters' firebombs destroyed a switchboard said to be worth $200,000 and heavily damaged an ammunition and firearms room. Lesser fires demolished the interior of a captain's office, mattresses and furniture.

Fourteen pieces of fire equipment from the Anne Arundel County Fire Department were used to quell the fires, which flared off and on for more than five hours in what prison officials said were all three major wings of the prison.

Convicts also bent or broke levers that control the locking mechanisms in a large number of cells, prison officials said. Last night, most of the institution's 1,500 prisoners were 4 to a cell, instead of the normal 2, officials said.

Half the population

One senior prison officer said the disturbance involved more than half the prison's population—the largest of any prison in the 5,000-inmate Maryland system. Other officials said perhaps a third of the convicts participated.

Telephone communication within the prison and to outside phones was cut off completely at about 9 P.M. Saturday when the switchboard was engulfed in flames, officials said.

The Chesapeake and Potomac Telephone Company planned to send crews to the prison last night or early today to install temporary telephone lines, restoring service partially. A company official said, however, that a new switch-

See RIOT, A6, Col. 1

'We're ready to die'

Attica's spectre haunts Jessup

By JEROME W. MONDESIRE
Sun Staff Correspondent

Jessup—For more than eight hours late Saturday and yesterday more than 400 rebellious stick-wielding convicts at the Maryland House of Correction here faced 150 shotgun-armed guards and state troopers.

With the spectre of the Attica prison rebellion still fresh in many minds, each group waited tensely for the other to act. Separated only by two wire fences, voices on both sides clearly could be heard admitting they didn't want to repeat the carnage at Attica, where 43 persons died.

"Want to negotiate"

"We ain't fools," shouted an inmate during the early hours of the riot. "We want to negotiate. Help us, man. We're human beings, too."

Armed state troopers and prison guards stood anxiously watching the milling crowd in the recreation yard. Their brows glistened with perspiration as the temperature held at a muggy 84 degrees.

Early reports from the prison staff were extremely sketchy.

Rumors of sniping

Rumors of convicts sniping at guards and firefighters were broadcast over the police radio in the early stages and other rumors circulated that Saturday night's riot had been planned several months ago.

But when the riot was finally quelled at dawn yesterday, prison officials said no firearms were found among the inmates and that they believed the uprising was "spontaneous" and "unplanned."

In the early hours of the riot, key correctional personnel, including the pistol wearing warden, Ralph L. Williams, stayed in the west wing of the prison, which contained the most violent riot activity. Numerous fires had been set on several floors of the wing and property destruction was wholesale.

Telephone service with the outside had been knocked out at the outset when inmates fire bombed the switchboard and the nearby ammunition storage room.

Anne Arundel county firefighters hastily yanked their hoses across the grounds in an attempt to combat the blazes. But whenever they had squelched one fire, orange flames and spirals of smoke would spring from some other window.

Floodlights were trained on the major trouble spots. And a helicopter was audible overhead as its searchlights illuminated the crowded recreation yard.

Force moves in

Shortly after midnight about 150 state troopers and guards moved to retake the south and west wings of the prison.

They entered in three phases: First, 20 unarmed men wearing tear gas masks, helmets and flack jackets led large German shepherds; then, about 50 men armed with shotguns and tear gas launchers; and finally a group of 80 men carrying shotguns.

"We didn't encounter any serious resistance as we moved through both wings, but a few missiles were hurled at the outset," said Col. Thomas S. Smith, the State Police superintendent.

The west wing was cleared by 1 A.M. And within 2½ hours state troopers had also secured the larger south wing.

Screaming and yelling

The routed inmates ran into the recreation yard, many of them screaming and yelling, state troopers said. Many covered their faces with towels to avoid being identified. Some

See DISORDER, A6, Col. 1

2,000 flee homes in Belfast protest

Belfast, Northern Ireland (AP)—A Catholic priest led 2,000 people from their homes in West Belfast in protest against British troop concentrations yesterday as five more persons lost their lives, making this the bloodiest year since Northern Ireland's partition 50 years ago.

The Rev. Jack Fitzsimmons led his flock from the Lenadoon avenue district where the Irish Republican Army and British troops have been locked in a suburban battle since Thursday.

The procession, mainly of women and children, headed by an accordion band, carrying blankets and pushing baby carriages, streamed from the district and set up camp on a soccer ground about a mile away. Most of the men remained guarding their homes.

"Army must leave"

Father Fitzsimmons said the British Army had refused pressing requests to evacuate the area. Its presence, he said, was endangering the lives of the inhabitants—"our people have endured enough hardship already. The Army must leave."

Earlier, two British soldiers were killed and one was seriously injured by a land mine at Crossmaglen, near the border with the Irish Republic. An 18-year-old youth was killed in a riot at Strabane, another border town.

In Belfast, a young policeman was shot dead, and a 43-year-old civilian, shot in the head Saturday, died in the hospital.

Their deaths raised the known death toll since August, 1969, to 444.

So far this year, 236-persons have been killed, surpassing in less than seven months the 232 who died in all of 1922, Northern Ireland's worst previous year of sectarian strife.

Lenadoon avenue is in the Suffolk area of the provincial capital's western outskirts. The British moved heavy concentrations of armored cars into the district, where nights of heavy shooting have brought a confrontation crisis that threatens to erupt into full-scale battle.

It was not clear whether the walkout of the Catholic population was a token protest against the Army or an IRA preparation to clear the area for battle.

There was a holiday atmosphere about the procession. According to the IRA, 70 per cent of the Catholic families had left. Some of the children carried placards: "Give Us Back Our Houses."

Tents set up

After reaching the soccer ground, mothers spread out blankets and picnic suppers began. A number of tents had been set up. Yesterday's exodus follows the pattern of a steady walkout of Catholic families as the violence intensified. A steady stream of families left all last week by train and car for the Republic of Ireland. More than 5,000 persons, mainly women and chil-

See ULSTER, A2, Col. 4

The gate to the yard stands open, and the prisoners' path is strewn with shoes, garbage, bedding and other debris after the riot.

Fischer leads in 3d game

From Wire Services

Reykjavik, Iceland — After threatening again to fly home, Bobby Fischer returned to the chess board yesterday in a game that was adjourned with the American challenger apparently holding the edge over the Russian world champion, Boris Spassky.

If Mr. Fischer wins when the game resumes today—and there are few chess experts here who doubt that he will—it will put him back in the running for the championship. Mr. Spassky now leads, 2-0.

Mr. Spassky had five pawns at adjournment, Mr. Fischer six. Each retained a queen and a bishop in addition to his king, but Mr. Fischer was reported in a strong position for mate.

The game was played in an upstairs room with no spectators present. Mr. Fischer had threatened to fly back to the United States unless he and Mr. Spassky had privacy for the contest.

The American challenger never has beaten Mr. Spassky. Before this match he had lost three games to the Russian playing black and had drawn two when he played white and had the first move.

He lost the opening game of the championship playing black, and forfeited the second game by failing to appear.

Sealed envelope

The chief referee, Lothar Schmid, of West Germany, stopped play after Mr. Spassky had made his 41st move and Mr. Fischer had handed in his reply move in a sealed envelope.

The decision to hold the game in a private upstairs room instead of in the vast auditorium was apparently a condition set by Mr. Fischer for continuing the match on a day in which he seemed on the point of leaving Iceland.

The 29-year-old challenger had seats booked on three flights to New York but apparently changed his mind about leaving around midday.

Informed sources said that up to that time he had been against going ahead with the tournament, angered at the decision that he forfeit the second game and by the refusal of match officials to have backstage cameras removed.

Fred Cramer, Mr. Fischer's chief administrative adviser, was asked what changed the American's mind about continuing the match.

"I think it was the hundreds of thousands of telegrams he received from the United States. They just flooded in asking him to play on," he replied.

Mr. Fischer, playing the black pieces and thus moving second, played aggressively and seized the initiative on the 11th move with an unexpected counterattack down the king-side. Mr. Spassky seemed a little shaken by the thrust and when mid-game was reached Mr. Fischer had the upper hand.

He forced the Russian to give up one of his bishops for a knight and then proceeded to exert pressure on the world champion's center pawn.

Some skirmishing

After some skirmishing on both sides, apparently aimed chiefly at gaining time on the clock, Mr. Spassky lost a pawn and when play was adjourned, Mr. Fischer clearly had a winning advantage.

Mr. Spassky's two closest aides, grandmasters Efrim Geller and Nickolai Krogius, both confirmed that their man was losing the game.

When the game was adjourned, Mr. Spassky emerged

See CHESS, A2, Col. 4

Index

THOMAS EBOLI
. . . slain Mafia leader

B-52's hit Red troops moving south

By The Associated Press

More than a score of B-52 bombers flew across the border demarcation zone yesterday to attack North Vietnamese military bases and reinforcements which were reported to be moving southward toward Quang Tri.

United States military sources said the targets included elements of two North

See WAR, A2, Col. 7

Mafia leader murdered

New York (AP)—Thomas Eboli, top Mafia figure and underboss for the late Vito Genovese, was found dead early yesterday in what police indicated was a gangland slaying. He had been shot five times in the face.

Police said Mr. Eboli, 61, also known as Tommy Ryan, apparently had been taken "for a ride" by other mobsters and was cut down in a burst of gunfire as he struggled to get out of the car.

His body, clad in a blue jumpsuit, was found sprawled on a sidewalk in the quiet Crown Heights section of Brooklyn, surrounded by broken, blood-stained glass from a car window. Police said he had more than $2,000, mostly in $100 bills, on him.

Tried to get out

They theorized that when Mr. Eboli realized what was about to happen, he tried to force his way from the car. They said at least two shots from a small caliber gun hit him while he still was in the vehicle.

They said the shooting occurred about 1 A.M.

A witness told authorities that at about that time, he saw flashes near a truck in the area and heard a man say, "Let's get out of here."

The truck, apparently stolen, was found abandoned with its engine running about a block from Mr. Eboli's body.

Police said they also found a .45-caliber, M-3 machine gun with a silencer in a car registered to a Newark (N.J.) owner and parked near the murder scene. They said the weapon was of a type used by paratroopers during World War II.

They were unable to determine immediately whether either the truck or machine gun was connected to the shooting.

Police said Mr. Eboli might have been shot while riding in his own car, a blue, late-model Cadillac with New Jersey license plates.

"Alien neighborhood"

They said they did not know what Mr. Eboli, who lived in Fort Lee, N.J., was doing in Crown Heights. They called it an "alien neighborhood" for Mr. Eboli, who usually frequented social clubs in Manhattan's Little Italy section.

The murder of Mr. Eboli was the latest in a series of shootings involving reputed underworld figures which began over a year ago with the wounding of Joseph A. Colombo, Sr., identified by authorities as head of the Cosa Nostra family in Brooklyn once headed by Joseph Profaci.

Six alleged underworld figures, including Joseph (Crazy Joe) Gallo, were slain within 12 days here this spring. Gallo was said to have been behind the shooting of Mr. Colombo at an Italian-American Unity Day rally in Columbus Circle in June, 1971.

"Boss of bosses"

Federal authorities have identified Mr. Eboli as an underboss in the Genovese family while Genovese himself, who was known as the "boss of bosses," was in prison for bankrolling a narcotics smuggling operation.

State Investigation Commission sources said Mr. Eboli's poor health prevented him from gaining the top spot in the mob after Genovese's death in prison in 1969.

Mr. Eboli had been arrested in 1963 on a charge of assaulting a referee in Madison Square Garden after a boxer he managed lost a fight on a TKO decision.

He also was taken into custody in a police raid four years later after the so-called "little Apalachin" meeting of organized crime leaders.

He was a subject of a 1969 New York State Crime Commission probe of incursions by organized crime into legitimate

See EBOLI, A6, Col. 5

Orioles trim Chicago, 6-1

Boog Powell and Brooks Robinson drove in two runs apiece, Powell with his third home run in four games, as the Orioles whipped Chicago, 6 to 1, in the rain-shortened opener of a scheduled doubleheader at Memorial Stadium yesterday. Play was halted with the Orioles batting in the seventh inning of the opener. The second game was rained out.

(Details on Page C1)

The Weather
Mostly sunny. High, 77; low, 58 to 62. Yesterday's high, 74; low, 60.
(Details and Map, Page C11)

THE SUN FINAL

Vol. 271—No. 97—F BALTIMORE, WEDNESDAY, SEPTEMBER 6, 1972 46 Pages 10 Cents

9 members of Israel's Olympic team killed by Arab terrorists near Munich

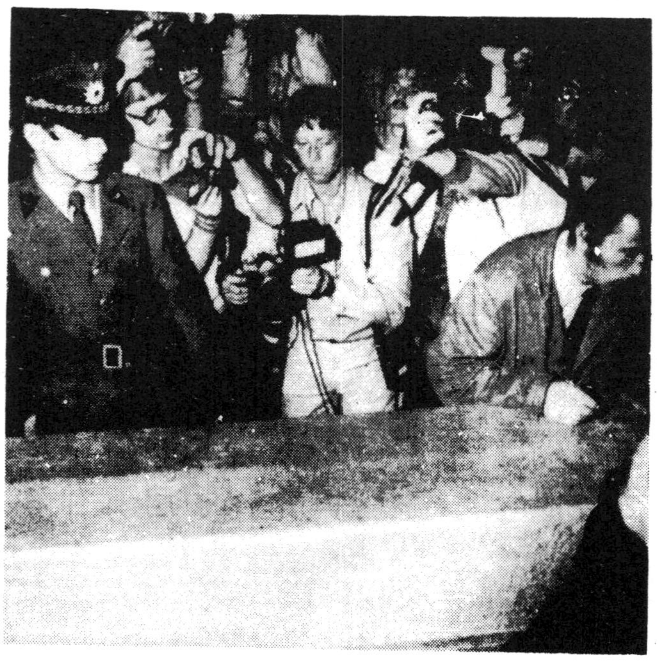

AP

A coffin with the body of one of the two Israelis murdered by Arab guerrillas in the Olympic Village is carried out into a waiting ambulance outside the village.

4 gunmen slain in battle

By GENE OISHI
Bonn Bureau of The Sun

Munich—At least nine members of the Israeli Olympic team were killed yesterday by Arab terrorists, who first staged an attack on Olympic Village and later tried to flee Germany with hostages.

Two members of the Israeli team were killed during the early-morning attack on the building in which the Israeli team was housed.

Some 18 hours later, during a shoot-out with police at a nearby military airfield, at least seven of the nine Israeli hostages were killed.

Hope persists

German authorities said there was a faint hope that one and possibly two of the hostages escaped. But their fate would not be known until the wreckage of one of the helicopters—in which the terrorists and the hostages were ferried to the airfield—is examined.

One of the helicopters was blown up during the gun battle.

Four of the terrorists were killed during the battle and three others were arrested. One policeman also was killed and one of the helicopter pilots was seriously wounded.

Because of yesterday's events, the Olympic Games were suspended for the first time in their history.

"A death sentence"

(Willi Daume, the president of the West German Olympic Organizing Committee, announced early today that he would ask the International Olympic Committee to meet tomorrow to decide whether the current games should continue, Reuter reported.)

Otto Merk, the Bavarian state interior minister, said, in his account to the press, that when police opened fire on the terrorists, the guerrilas turned their weapons on the hostages as they had threatened to do.

All the hostages, including the
See MUNICH, A2, Col. 3

UPI

Otto Merk, the Bavarian minister of the Interior, tells newsmen of the death of the Israeli hostages.

Body of Laurel girl found at Bowie; autopsy due today

By a Sun Staff Correspondent

Bowie—The massive 3-day search for Amy Morrison, the 7-year-old Laurel girl who was reported missing Sunday morning, ended at 12.45 P.M. yesterday with the recovery of her body near the Bowie race track, some 15 miles from her home.

When found, lying in short grass just off Race Track road, the brown-eyed girl with long blond hair and pony tail was fully clad and had not been shot or stabbed, according to Dr. John Kehoe, medical examiner for Prince Georges county.

Dr. Kehoe refused to comment on the possibility, however, that the girl might have been strangled or molested. Such questions, he said, could not be determined until after an autopsy, which is scheduled to be performed in Baltimore today.

Detectives working on the case appeared to be under the impression yesterday that the victim had not walked from her home in the 600 block Main street, in Laurel, to Bowie during the time she was missing.

They said that her clothes—an orange blouse and lilac shorts—were so visible that they almost certainly would have been spotted from a State Police helicopter that has been participating in the massive search.

For the same reason they discounted the possibility that she could have been long at the spot where she was found, since her body was clearly visible from the nearby road.

Detectives said the body was found by a passer-by, whom they refused to identify, shortly before 12.45 P.M.

The passer-by, police said, stopped a line truck for the Maryland Electrical Testing Company, which was driving on Race Track road, and called the Greenbelt barracks of the Maryland State Police on the truck's radio.

Soon afterward the State Police discontinued the massive search for the missing girl, which yesterday involved over 500 persons.

Detectives at the scene said they had no suspects in the apparent abduction. Crime laboratory personnel were seen making plaster casts of tire marks in the vicinity of the body, however, but investigators described that as a standard procedure.

Dr. Kehoe and a member of
See GIRL, A9, Col. 1

Where Laurel child was found

President voices 'outrage' in leading swift U.S. reaction to Olympic murder

By RICHARD O'MARA
Washington Bureau of The Sun

Washington—Reaction in the United States to the murder of the Israeli athletes by Arab guerrillas at Munich's Olympic Village yesterday was swift and angry.

From San Clemente, Calif., President Nixon expressed through a spokesman his "sense of deep outrage" at the attack.

"International outlaws"

The President later called the Israeli Premier, Golda Meir, from San Francisco and offered her the total co-operation of the U.S. in obtaining the release of those Israelis still being held by the guerrillas.

"We are dealing with international outlaws of the worst sort who will stoop to anything to accomplish their goals and who are totally unpredictable," the President said.

Mr. Nixon also spoke of his "concern for the families of the victims" and described the incident as a "great tragedy."

At United Nations headquarters in New York, Secretary General Kurt Waldheim said the attack was "more shocking for having taken place at the Olympic Games, which represent one of man's oldest and noblest efforts to foster friendship."

In Washington, the Secretary of State, William P. Rogers, issued a statement expressing his "sense of sorrow at the callous, outrageous attack this morning on the Israeli athletes."

"This assault on the Israeli Olympic team is offensive to men and women of good will everywhere for whom the Olympic Games are a symbol of man's striving for reconciliation and peace," the statement said.

Senator George S. McGovern, the Democratic presidential nominee, issued a statement saying, "I am sickened by the outrage that has occurred at the Olympic Games."

The statement added that "the dead and those held hostage are the most recent victims of an unremitting and unrelenting refusal by a few nations to accept the statehood of Israel."

Senator McGovern scrapped a slashing attack on President Nixon he had planned to deliver at a rally in Los Angeles and said that the incident had made this "a night for quiet contemplation."

He said that the athletes had gone to Munich in a "celebration of common humanity." said they were "struck down by an act which is ultimate denial of humanity."

He told a crowd of 5,000 ... have no careful solution ... offer."

He added, "What does n...
See REACTION, A2, Col.

Nun draws year and a day

Berrigan gets 2 years

By WELDON WALLACE
Sun Staff Correspondent

Harrisburg—Judge R. Dixon Herman yesterday sentenced the Rev. Philip F. Berrigan, S.S.J., to a total of two years' imprisonment and Sister Elizabeth McAlister, R.S.H.M., to one year and a day, for smuggling letters in and out of the Lewisburg (Pa.) Federal Penitentiary.

Then Judge Herman, acting on a request by the prosecution, dismissed all government conspiracy charges against the priest, the nun and six other defendants.

Seven of them had been tried in federal court here early this year.

Maximum sentences

Father Berrigan and Sister Elizabeth were found guilty of the smuggling charges last April by a jury, but it failed to convict the seven defendants on government charges that they had conspired to raid draft boards, kidnap Henry A. Kissinger, President Nixon's national security adviser, and destroy the heating tunnels of Washington buildings.

On the smuggling charges, the priest was liable to a maximum sentence of 40 years, and the nun 30 years.

An immediate appeal of the sentences was filed in the District Court by J. Thomas Menaker, a Harrisburg attorney who is representing the seven defendants. The appeal will go to the 3d Circuit Court of Appeal in Philadelphia.

Bail of $10,000 was continued for Sister Elizabeth, and shortly after the sentencing Father Berrigan was returned to the Danbury (Conn.) Federal Prison, where he is serving sentences for the destruction of draft board files in Baltimore and Catonsville.

Judge Herman imposed a sentence of two years on Father Berrigan for each of four charges of smuggling.

He ruled that they would run concurrently and that they would be concurrent also with the sentences the priest is now serving.

The judge sentenced Sister Elizabeth to one year and a day on one charge and gave her suspended sentences, with probation for three years, on each of two other charges.

The statute under which the two were sentenced provides that they may be paroled immediately at the discretion of the Parole Board.

Defendants who were cleared through the dismissal of conspiracy charges included the Reverend Joseph R. Wenderoth of Baltimore; the Reverend Neil R. McLaughlin of Baltimore; Anthony and Mary Cain Scoblick of Baltimore; Eqbal Ahmad, a Pakistani who lives in Washington, and John Theodore Glick of Lancaster, Pa.

Mr. Glick was not tried with
See BERRIGAN, A6, Col. 1

$4.7 billion compromise poverty bill sent to Nixon

Washington (AP)—Congress passed a $4.7 billion compromise anti-poverty bill and sent it to President Nixon.

The action marked the end for this year of efforts to give independent status to the legal services program for the poor.

The measure cleared the Senate by voice vote and then the House passed it by a vote of 223 to 97.

The result was that an almost two-year effort to give permanent independent status to the legal services program went down the drain.

However, Senator Gaylord Nelson, (D., Wis.) and Senator Jacob K. Javits, (R., N.Y.), the Senate managers of the bill, announced they would renew the fight in the next Congress.

Mr. Javits said it was "most regrettable and unfortunate" that the corporation had to be dropped.

The bill as it finally passed authorizes $2.3 billion for anti-poverty and manpower-training programs in the current fiscal year, and $2.4 billion in 1974.

Conferees cut these back a total of $1.4 billion in an attempt to meet the President's objections that their original figures were too high.

Elimination of the separate corporation for legal services means that the program will continue to be run by the Office of Economic Opportunity, and will be subject to governors' vetoes.

UPI

Mark Spitz (right) addresses a news conference in Munich. At left is the head coach of the United States swimming team at the Olympic games, Peter Daland.

Spitz flies back to U.S. prematurely as attacks arouse fears for his safety

Munich (AP)—Mark Spitz flew home to California ahead of schedule yesterday in the wake of the terrorist attacks on Israeli team members.

"As a human being and as a Jew," said the swimmer who won a record seven gold medals, "I am shocked and saddened by the outrageous act in Olympic Village."

Mr. Spitz left Olympic Village a few hours after the Arabs stormed the nearby Israeli dormitory. He was under guard because of his prominence and because he is a Jew.

Mr. Spitz held a 40-minute news conference at the Olympic press center and then was escorted by German Army bodyguards to a television studio, to a downtown hotel and then to the airport.

"Mark left a little ahead of schedule," said Sherm Chavoor, the millionaire owner of Arden Hills Swim Club in Carmichael, Calif. "He just felt it was the best thing in view of what was going on."

Mr. Chavoor is Mr. Spitz's personal coach and is acting as the Olympic hero's business adviser now that the w... cleared for the swimmer to turn professional.

As the German soldiers escorted Mr. Spitz from the press center, a spokesman for the Olympic Organizing Committee said: "He is much too popular to take chances. Spitz is being guarded for his own well-being."

Yankees nip Orioles, 7-6

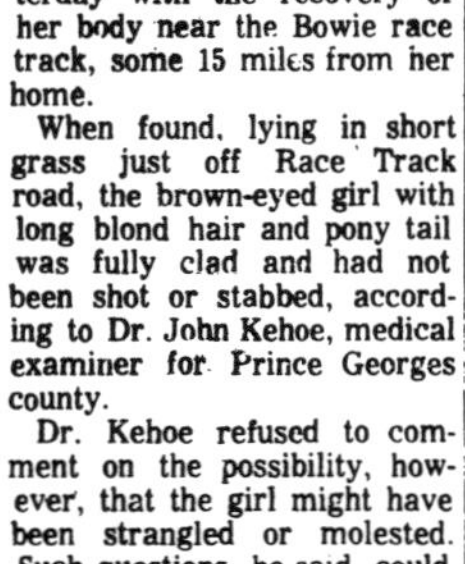

The New York Yankees chased old Baltimore nemesis Dave McNally during a five-run first inning at the Stadium last night, scored a 7-to-6 victory and knocked the Orioles from a first-place tie in the tight American League East race.

(Details on page C1)

Kissinger to meet with Brezhnev

By PHILIP POTTER
Sun Staff Correspondent

San Francisco—Henry A. Kissinger, President Nixon's adviser for national security, will leave Washington Friday for meetings in Moscow with Leonid I. Brezhnev, Soviet party chairman, and other leaders on matters of mutual interest, including the Vietnam war, the White House announced yesterday.

Dr. Kissinger will stop in Munich on his way to the Soviet Union for meetings with West German leaders.

Mr. Nixon, winding up his western trip that began the day after his renomination for President, stopped briefly here en route to Washington for a 15-minute meeting with his 15-member Advisory Board on Environmental Quality.

The President issued a statement blasting the Democratic Congress for alleged inaction on environmental problems. He also made a helicopter and boat inspection of the San Francisco Bay area to look at the prospective site of the Golden Gate National Recreation Area for which legislation is pending in Congress.

Cruising the area on both ends of the Golden Gate
See KISSINGER, A4 Col. 1

Index

The Weather
Increasing cloudiness today, high 40. Occasional rain likely tonight, low 36. Yesterday's high, 50; low, 36.
(Details and Map, Page C9)

THE SUN

FINAL

Vol. 272—No. 40—F | BALTIMORE, WEDNESDAY, JANUARY 3, 1973 | 40 Pages | 10 Cents

Friendship hijacker surrenders to FBI

Shehan, psychiatrist spoke to suspect

A 37-year-old man who held two stewardesses at gunpoint during a takeover of a Piedmont Airlines jet at Friendship Airport surrendered peacefully at 8.30 last night.

The stewardesses, held hostage for two hours, were released—crying but unharmed—at 8 P.M., after an FBI agent, a psychiatrist and Cardinal Shehan spoke with the would-be hijacker.

And at 8.30, with assurances of safety from Cardinal Shehan, the gunman left the airplane and surrendered. FBI agents identified him as Charles August Wenige, 37, formerly of Baltimore.

The attempted hijacking was the first at Friendship Airport and, according to an airline spokesman, the first involving Piedmont.

The hijacking attempt began about 5.30 P.M. after Piedmont Flight 928 arrived at Friendship and the passengers and pilots had disembarked.

Officials said a man who had hidden in a washroom walked out and took the two stewardesses remaining aboard hostage at gunpoint. They were identified as Teri Ann Meadows and Jackie Wisecup.

Initally, airport officials did not know where the man wanted to go, or what other demands he might have. They learned through radio contact with the plane that the gunman was aboard, and alerted the FBI.

The FBI arrived at 6 P.M. and took control of the situation.

Vehicle traffic was permitted access to the airport throughout the incident, and other planes continued to land and take off.

About 250 curiosity seekers gathered in the terminal building after hearing reports of the hijacking attempt on the radio. But they saw little more than the scores of federal agents and police who crowded into the terminal.

All windows and vantage points overlooking the darkened 60-passenger turboprop plane were blocked off by officials. Above the terminal, at rooftop level, FBI sharpshooters were stationed, and waited

See HIJACK, A7, Col. 4

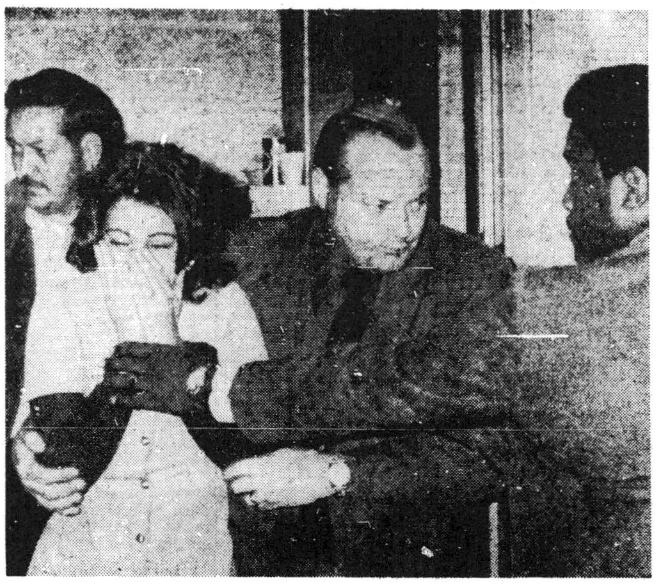

Sunpapers photo—Irving Phillips

Sunpapers photo—Walter McCardell

Piedmont stewardess is helped into the Friendship Airport terminal following release. (left) Hijacking suspect is later led into Federal Court building

Sunpapers photos—George H. Cook

The Piedmont Airlines twin-engine turboprop plane that the hijacker attempted to commandeer sits on a Friendship runway

U.S. jets resume bombing

Strikes above 20th Parallel remain banned

By the Associated Press

American bombers attacked the southern panhandle of North Vietnam yesterday, ending a 36-hour pause in the air strikes for the New Year holiday.

The United States command announced that the bombing halt above the 20th Parallel remained in effect, thus sparing Hanoi and Haiphong.

Bombing above the 20th Parallel was ordered stopped Saturday by President Nixon, a move obviously tied to the resumption of the Paris peace talks next Monday. Preliminary sessions got under way yesterday between technical experts from both sides.

No details

In a brief communique, the U.S. command said, "U.S. air crews resumed operations over North Vietnam at 1300 hours today after a 36-hour cease-fire." For reasons of security, the command said no other details of the strikes would be made available.

Other U.S. officials said, however, the U.S. bombers were hitting supply routes in the panhandle to stop North Vietnam's annual dry-season drive to bring men and materiel into South Vietnam across the border demarcation zone and through Laos.

The command also announced that bombing strikes were resumed in South Vietnam at dusk Monday at the conclusion of a 24-hour holiday cease-fire. The bulk of the strikes, the command said, were concentrated in the northernmost part of the country below the DMZ.

Air strikes elsewhere

During the holiday bombing halt in Vietnam, U.S. air strikes moved against enemy targets in Laos and Cambodia, including the Ho Chi Minh supply route and base camps. American bombers also flew missions in support of Royal Laotian forces battling North Vietnamese troops in the Plain of Jars in northern Laos, the command said.

Ground fighting generally was light and scattered in South Vietnam, although a battle was reported in an area along Highway 1, about 40 miles northeast of Saigon.

Lt. Col. Le Trung Hien, Saigon command spokesman, said the fight raged throughout most of the day, but gave few details.

Colonel Hien said it was not known whether the enemy troops were North Vietnamese regulars or Viet Cong.

In North Vietnam the official newspaper *Nhan Dan*, said in an editorial: "The U.S. imperialists' plot in applying military pressure to subdue us has once again failed with shame.

"We have rendered them heavy punishment. We are determined to be well prepared

See WAR, A2, Col. 7

NGUYEN CO THACH
. . . Hanoi negotiator

U.S., Hanoi split called unchanged

By SCOTT SULLIVAN
Paris Bureau of The Sun

Paris—Highly placed French officials, who apparently played a key role in getting the Vietnam peace talks resumed, said yesterday that neither the United States nor North Vietnam has changed its basic position on a cease-fire.

The pessimistic French assessments came as second-level negotiators from the two sides met for the first time since December 23 to go over the fine print of the treaty and its technical protocols.

The "technical experts" meetings, which the North Vietnamese suspended 10 days ago in protest against American bombing north of the 20th Parallel, were set up by Henry A. Kissinger and Le Duc Tho, the two top negotiators, to deal with very detailed aspects of the treaty—including the identification of Communist-held and loyalist-held areas in the event of a stand-still cease-fire.

Substantive negotiations are due to resume next Monday,

See TALKS, A2, Col. 3

Caucus votes to end war

Democrats in House make POW proviso

By JAMES S. KEAT
Washington Bureau of The Sun

Washington — Democratic members of the House of Representatives voted overwhelmingly yesterday to end United States participation in the Vietnam war promptly, if American prisoners of war are returned.

Ignoring White House efforts to postpone action, the Democratic caucus adopted a resolution demanding an immediate cut-off of funds for U.S. combat operations in Indochina, once arrangements are made for the safe withdrawal of U.S. troops there and the prisoners are returned.

At about the same time, the Senate Foreign Relations Committee was informally agreeing to launch legislation to end the war if there is no cease-fire by Inauguration Day, January 20.

Senator J. William Fulbright (D., Ark.), the committee's chairman, said this was the "consensus" of the committee at a two-hour closed meeting attended by 12 of its 16 members. Senate Democrats will caucus this morning and may take action similar to that of their party colleagues in the House.

In the 154-to-75 vote, the House Democrats went significantly beyond their previous stand. Last spring the party caucus called for legislation to set a deadline for a U.S. withdrawal, again subject to the return of the U.S. prisoners.

A bill to end the war by last October 1 was narrowly approved by the House Foreign Affairs Committee in July, but the full House rejected it 228-to-178 the following month.

Anti-war congressmen were elated at the vote in the caucus, which overrode efforts by administration allies to soften the party stand. Some House hawks claimed, however, that the resolution as finally adopted by the caucus said

See CONGRESS, A2, Col. 3

Albert to get 2d term as speaker of the House

By ALBERT SEHLSTEDT, JR.
Washington Bureau of The Sun

Washington—Representative Carl B. Albert (D., Okla.) was nominated yesterday for a second term as speaker of the House and called upon Congress to reassert its role as an equal branch of the government.

Congress, which many critics contend has dribbled away some of its constitutional prerogatives to the executive branch in recent years, convenes today for the 93d time with the Democrats still firmly in control.

Mr. Albert, whose election as speaker of the House on a party line vote this afternoon is assured, spoke of congressional responsibility and also issued a call for party unity in an extemporaneous speech lasting three or four minutes to a Democratic caucus in the House chamber.

The caucus was closed to the public but, according to one report from the assembly, Mr. Albert gave a "tough talk" to his colleagues on the need for recapturing congressional power and influence.

The 64-year-old speaker was not regarded as a strong leader in the 92d Congress, but one congressional source observed last week that Mr. Albert has been a "rookie

See DEMOCRATS, A6, Col. 1

Nixon seeing leadership of Congress

By ADAM CLYMER
Washington Bureau of The Sun

Washington—As contacts with the North Vietnamese resumed in Paris, President Nixon started another round of delicate negotiations yesterday, beginning a series of meetings with congressional leaders.

Although no open warfare yet exists between the Presi-

See NIXON, A2, Col. 3

Pentagon says Hanoi hospital may have been hit

Washington (AP)—Backtracking from a previous denial, the Pentagon acknowledged yesterday that United States bombers may have inflicted "some limited accidental damage" on a North Vietnamese hospital.

Jerry W. Friedheim, a Pentagon spokesman, did not go so far as to admit that U.S. bombs caused the damage to the Bac Mai hospital and the Gia Lam field which normally is used by civilian airliners. He said the cause still is uncertain and suggested that the destruction could have resulted from North Vietnamese anti-aircraft explosives.

But Mr. Friedheim's new statement, volunteered at a press briefing, was a partial turnabout from his flat denials last week that U.S. bombs had struck a North Vietnamese hospital at Bac Mai, 7 miles southwest of Hanoi.

It was the second time in more than two months that the Pentagon has conceded accidental damage to nonmilitary facilities during U.S. bombings of military targets in the Hanoi area. Last October, the Defense Department admitted that a U.S. Navy bomb "inadvertently struck" the French diplomatic mission.

In his formal statement yesterday, Mr. Friedheim said:

"It appears that some limited accidental damage has occurred to some facilities at Gia Lam Airport and at a hospital the enemy calls Bac Mai.

"The exact extent of this damage is uncertain, as is its cause.

"Our information does not square with Hanoi's propaganda claims of massive destruction at these sites."

At roughly the time that Mr. Friedheim was meeting with newsmen, an anti-war activist who was in Hanoi during nearly two weeks of non-stop U.S. bombing gave a different picture to another group of reporters elsewhere in Washington.

The Rev. Michael Allen of the Yale Divinity School said he was shown a civilian hospital and that "by all standards I know the hosptial was destroyed.' He said he was certain that he had been shown the Bac Mai hospital.

He quoted North Vietnamese officials as saying that 25 staff members were killed at the 955-bed facility.

Mr. Friedheim stressed, as he has repeatedly, that "our strikes have been targeted only at military targets."

But he said: "We know . . . that from time to time accidental damage to other than military targets occurs, sometimes involving United States ordnance or aircraft and some-

See PENTAGON, A2, Col. 4

Girl, 17, is found frozen to death in arms of 2d mountain-climber

Flagstaff, Ariz. (AP)—A 17-year-old girl was found dead yesterday in the arms of a fellow mountain-climber on the slopes of Arizona's highest mountain, where a sudden storm broke New Year's Eve.

The dead girl, Allison Clay, of Scottsdale, and her frostbitten companion, Clint Miller, 24, of Phoenix, were airlifted from 1,000 feet below the summit of 13,000-foot Humphreys Peak, part of the San Francisco Peaks considered sacred by the Navajo Indians.

"She was in a sleeping bag in his arms," said Norm Johnson, of Flagstaff, a member of the search party. "She was dead, and I don't know how he was alive—it was so cold."

Four others from their climbing party were hospitalized here Monday.

Mr. Miller was in satisfactory condition. "He is a robust outdoorsman," his mother said; "I think that saved him."

"We all contemplated whether we would die," said Rick Hufnagel, 19, of Scottsdale, telling how the six members of the Arizona Mountaineering Club felt when pleasant weather conditions changed abruptly Sunday afternoon.

"It became windy and cold," he said. "Two of our three tents collapsed. The wind and snow caved in the tents.

"All six of us got in one tent. It rolled downhill and ripped

See RESCUE, A6, Col. 4

Index

Bodies of 39 crash victims finally identified in Miami

Miami (AP)—The bodies of 39 victims of an Eastern Airlines jumbo jet crash, which went unclaimed for nearly four days, were identified yesterday, the Dade county medical examiner, Joe Davis, said.

An airline spokesman, Bill Wooten, said a final count showed 99 persons died as a result of the crash and 77 survived. The Lockheed 1011 plunged into the Everglades swamp Friday night.

More than 200 relatives of the 176 persons aboard the jet have been flown to Miami by the airline to claim the bodies of the victims, the Eastern Airlines official said.

An Eastern spokesman in

See CRASH, A6, Col. 4

UPI

Carl Albert, who is to be re-elected House speaker, meets with POW's wives and mothers at the Capitol.

The Weather
Sunny today, high 43. Fair tonight, low 30. Yesterday's high, 55; low, 48.
(Details and Map, Page C11)

THE SUN

FINAL

Vol. 272—No. 58— F
BALTIMORE, WEDNESDAY, JANUARY 24, 1973
43 Pages 10 Cents

VIET WAR SETTLED

Cease-fire set Saturday

UPI

Le Duc Tho and Henry A. Kissinger wave to newsmen in Paris after initialing the Vietnam accord

Kissinger, Tho initial agreement

By JAMES S. KEAT
Washington Bureau of The Sun

Washington — A cease-fire will take effect in Vietnam Saturday night, President Nixon announced last night.

Speaking briefly on television and radio, Mr. Nixon said a peace agreement had been initialed earlier yesterday in Paris by Henry A. Kissinger and Le Duc Tho.

Later, Ronald L. Ziegler, the White House Press Secretary, said the documents would be made public this morning. Dr. Kissinger will hold a press conference to discuss the terms in late morning, Mr. Ziegler said.

The agreement will be formally signed in Paris Saturday and will take effect that night, 7 P.M. Baltimore time—8 A.M. Sunday in Vietnam.

In his 9-minute address, the President disclosed no details of the agreement, the product of 3½ years of secret talks in Paris between the two high-level emissaries.

He said the pact would fulfill his long-standing goal of "peace with honor," including the return of all United States prisoners in Indochina, a total withdrawal of American troops from South Vietnam and self-determination for the South Vietnamese.

Thieu's full support

The text of the agreement, plus the protocols that spell out details of implementing the pact, will be made public today, Mr. Nixon said.

The agreement so painstakingly worked out by Dr. Kissinger, Mr. Nixon's national security adviser, and Mr. Tho, a member of the North Vietnamese Politburo, has the full support of President Nguyen Van Thieu of South Vietnam, Mr. Nixon said.

As Mr. Nixon spoke from his office in the White House, Mr. Thieu was speaking to his people in an address prepared in advance. It was believed here to contain substantially the same message as Mr. Nixon's.

Although Mr. Nixon did not say so, the pact to be signed Saturday will deal simply with the military disengagement by the four forces engaged in

See NIXON, A7, Col. 1

PRESIDENT NIXON
. . . announcing Vietnam settlement

Analysis

Has peace vindicated air power?

By CHARLES W. [illegible]
Washington Bureau of The Sun

Washington—The Vietnam settlement leaves an endless wake of unanswered questions, and one of the most disturbing is whether a different politico-military strategy could have brought Hanoi to negotiations years sooner.

Many military men think so. They see the settlement as vindicating the war strategy that President Nixon adopted after North Vietnam's massive onslaught in the South last spring.

And the point is that this was a strategy that President Lyndon B. Johnson rejected in 1965, when it was recommended by the joint chiefs of staff before the large-scale American buildup on the ground in South Vietnam.

The twin instruments of this strategy were the swift, systematic and sustained bombing campaign over North Vietnam, with greatly intensified pressure in December, and the closing of its ports by naval mining.

The objective was to cut off North Vietnam to the maximum possible extent from its Soviet and Chinese support and

See AIR, A6, Col. 1

Truce ends a war, begins another

By SCOTT SULLIVAN
Paris Bureau of The Sun

Paris—The second war of Indochina ended, for all practical purposes, yesterday morning in the old grand ballroom of the Hotel Majestic on Paris's Avenue Kleber.

The very clever, and very weary, men who set their initials to the cease-fire agreement harbored no delusions about the document they had forged.

It will mean the end of American involvement in South Vietnam.

It will signal the opening of the third Indochina war in half a century.

The very hall where Henry A. Kissinger and Le Duc Tho "completed" their long and slow and bloody forced march to compromise reflected the awful ambiguities of the war, the fearsome ambiguities of the peace.

The property of French collaborationists in World War II, the Majestic served as headquarters to the Paris Gestapo contingent.

For the last four years, it had served as the setting for the farcial propaganda forum that described itself as a "peace conference."

Even the weather yesterday contributed to the tentative, unsatisfactory atmosphere that surrounded the consummation of a peace that hardly pretends to be a peace for the persons directly involved.

A grim, chill rain spilled down on Dr. Kissinger and Le Duc Tho as they arrived to reread and initial a document on which agreement had already been reached.

That the agreement had, in fact, already been approved, if grudgingly, by all four parties to the Vietnam conflict was common knowledge among the scores of newsmen who waited shivering in the rain on Avenue Kleber.

Still, neither side would ac-

See TALKS, A7, Col. 6

For Hanoi the fight continues

By JOHN E. WOODRUFF
Sun Staff Correspondent

Saigon—For Hanoi, the signing of a Vietnam cease-fire will mean not the end of the struggle for South Vietnam but the beginning of a new phase.

The agreement stops well short of giving North Vietnam certain advantages it demanded during four years of negotiating and fighting—among them an end to the administration of President Nguyen Van Thieu and the dismantling of the South Vietnamese police apparatus.

But it also gives the Vietnamese Communists two solid steps forward as the progress

See STRUGGLE, A5, Col. 6

Hanoi doubles pre-truce attacks

By the Associated Press

Communist forces nearly doubled their attacks across South Vietnam in a high point of activity before a cease-fire, the Saigon command announced today.

Military headquarters reported 95 Communist attacks during the 24-hour period ending at 6 A.M. today, compared with 52 in the previous 24 hours. About two-thirds were rocket and mortar assaults.

American warplanes pounded Communist positions throughout South Vietnam yesterday and South Vietnamese infantrymen mounted spoiling operations on the ground.

Military sources said the air raids—the heaviest in one day in five months—and the ground thrusts were designed to prevent a Communist land-grab before a cease-fire.

President Nguyen Van Thieu, in a special Tet lunar new year letter read by an announcer over government television last night, warned his nation not to trust the Communists during a cease-fire.

"If the Communists have to agree to sign a cease-fire agreement it is only because their war of invasion has been defeated," the president said. "We should not believe that the Communists will respect the agreement. We should not rely on their signature, and should not believe that they have renounced their intensification of efforts to take control of South Vietnam."

The United States command reported that fighter-bombers

See WAR, A6, Col. 8

Thieu terms truce only a first step

By ARNOLD R. ISAACS
Sun Staff Correspondent

Saigon—President Nguyen Van Thieu announced his acceptance of a Vietnam cease-fire today, but declared it is "only a first step toward peace, not a real peace."

In a radio speech broadcast as President Nixon was announcing the agreement in Washington, Mr. Thieu also insisted that South Vietnam has not given up its demand for the withdrawal of North Vietnamese troops and he hinted

See THIEU, A7, Col. 5

Price rise is slight, but surge is forecast

By ART PINE
Washington Bureau of The Sun

Washington—A sudden halt in the food-price spiral held consumer prices to a moderate pace last month, the government reported yesterday, but analysts predicted immediately that the respite probably would be short-lived.

After adjustment to account for seasonal patterns, the overall consumer price index rose by only 0.2 per cent in December—a tenth of a percentage point below the previous month's pace. Before adjustment, the rise was 0.3 per cent.

However, the figures were compiled too early to reflect either the staggering increase in wholesale prices last month, or the loosening of wage-price controls in January. December's wholesale index surged at its fastest pace in 21 years.

Herbert Stein, chairman of the President's Council of Economic Advisers, warned in a statement that "rising retail food prices are to be expected in the months ahead." A general price spurt also is expected in the wake of Phase 3.

The 0.2 per cent increase in December brought the pace of inflation at year-end to an annual rate of 2.4 per cent—technically within President Nixon's goal of trimming price increases to "between 2 and 3 per cent" by this time.

However, on a longer-term basis, the index missed the administration's goal. Over the full fourth quarter, consumer prices rose at an annual rate of 3.2 per cent. In the two previous quarters, the rises were 4.6 and 2.2 per cent.

For 1972 as a whole, consumer prices essentially held their own, despite the imposi-

See PRICES, A8, Col. 1

Index

AP

Lady Bird Johnson stands with her older daughter, Lynda Bird Johnson Robb, and son-in-law, Charles Robb, as a minister delivers a short eulogy over the flag-draped casket of former President Johnson. The body of the former President was to lie in state at the LBJ Library in Austin, Texas, until today.

Johnson lies in state at library

Austin, Texas (AP)—The body of former President Lyndon B. Johnson lay in state yesterday in the library he created as his own memorial and as a school for better government.

The closed and flag-draped casket was placed on a raised platform in the Great Hall of the eight-story LBJ Library on the University of Texas campus.

Mr. Johnson, the nation's 36th president, died Monday of what doctors described as "severe coronary artery disease." He was 64 and had been wracked by heart problems since the 1950's.

Mrs. Johnson, accompanied by her daughters, Lynda and Luci, and their husbands, stood together as the casket was carried by eight servicemen to the bier in the hall.

Mrs. Johnson wiped a tear from her eye as she embraced a family friend who had joined the line of mourners.

As the body was transferred from the hearse, a military

See JOHNSON, A9, Col. 1

Nixon orders office closings

President Nixon has ordered all departments, agencies and other establishments of the federal government closed tomorrow in respect for former President Lyndon B. Johnson.

The postal service will suspend regular mail deliveries.

The New York and American stock exchanges will be closed all day.

In Maryland, state offices and departments will remain open and banks will do business as usual.

The war: its chronology, repercussions, closing

The Weather
Sunny and warmer today, high 84. Fair tonight, low 67. Yesterday's high, 78; low, 63.
(Details and Map, Page C13)

THE SUN

FINAL

Vol. 273—No. 50—F | BALTIMORE, FRIDAY, JULY 13, 1973 | 60 Pages | 10 Cents

Delegate Scott slain

Dope suspect killed

Legislator, 48, found dead in Sutton Place

By JEROME W. MONDESIRE

Delegate James A. (Turk) Scott (D., 2d Baltimore) was found shot to death early this morning in the basement garage of his Bolton Hill apartment building.

The 48-year-old delegate had been awaiting trial in Federal Court on charges of conspiring to transport about 40 pounds of heroin from New York to Baltimore.

Police said his body was discovered about 1.45 A.M. in the basement garage of Sutton Place Apartments by another tenant. His body had several bullet wounds, police said.

The body was surrounded by several pieces of paper which police refused to identify, pending further investigation.

Arrested April 2

Delegate Scott was arrested the night of April 2 near the State House in Annapolis after the federal grand jury returned an eight-count indictment against him. He had been free on $30,000 bail.

Charges against Mr. Scott and another defendant allege they conspired to bring raw heroin from New York in multi-kilogram amounts.

Other counts alleged that about 40 pounds of heroin—worth about $10 million in street sales was handled by the operation in 1971 and 1972. The delegate had pleaded innocent to all the charges.

Delegate Scott had been appointed last December to the Legislature by Governor Mandel to fill the vacancy caused by the death of Delegate Floyd B. Adams.

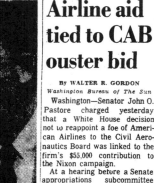

Sunpapers photo—Lloyd Pearson

Firemen fight 8-alarm blaze

Baltimore firefighters trained hoses on the E-Zee Supermarket in the 3600 block Elm avenue early yesterday as smoke billowed from the roof. More than 300 firemen responded to the eight-alarm blaze which was brought under control in slightly under three hours. Three firemen were treated for injuries received while fighting the fire. (Dispatch on Page C7)

Violent crimes reported off 6% in city for first half of 1973

By ROGER TWIGG

Violent crimes reported in the city decreased 6 per cent during the first six months of 1973, the Police Department reported yesterday.

In six of the seven major categories, crime in the city showed decreases ranging from 3.3 per cent for rape to 22.9 per cent for burglary, according to department statistics.

Only aggravated assaults showed an increase. They rose by 362 cases, or 12 per cent. The Police Department pointed out that most aggravated assaults take place among family members, neighbors or acquaintances.

Like murder, which occurs usually under similar circumstances, aggravated assault is regarded as a largely unpreventable crime, according to the Police Department.

Major crimes are considered to be murder, rape, robbery, aggravated assault, burglary, larceny and automobile theft.

Police reported a total of 30,275 crimes in the seven categories, a decrease of 5,617 or 5.6 per cent fewer than occurred in the same period last year.

19 fewer murder cases

Property crimes declined 18.4 per cent during the first six months of this year compared with the same period last year. Police in the auto-theft section attributed the decline in car thefts to the addition of steering-wheel locks on newer model cars.

There were 19 fewer cases of murder and 8 fewer cases of rape in the 6-month period this year, decreases of 13 per cent and 3.3 per cent respectively.

The number of robberies went down by 815 cases from 4,558, a decrease of 17.9 per cent.

Donald D. Pomerleau, the police commissioner, attributed the decrease in crime to "a variety of efforts—the Mayor's Co-ordinating Council on Criminal Justice, street lighting programs, community efforts and the police."

In the Central district, encompassing the downtown area, crimes in the seven categories

See CRIME, A12, Col. 1

GI records burn

A fire in a storage warehouse near St. Louis yesterday destroyed or damaged hundreds of thousands of United States military personnel records.

Dispatch on Page A3

Ervin to meet Nixon

Mitchell ends testimony to Senate panel

By MURIEL DOBBIN and GILBERT A. LEWTHWAITE
Washington Bureau of The Sun

Washington—President Nixon yesterday agreed to an urgent request from Capitol Hill that he discuss the Watergate scandal at a private meeting with Senator Sam J. Ervin, Jr. (D., N.C.), the chairman of the Senate committee investigating the illegal political activities of the GOP in 1972.

In a special message to the President, the Senate Watergate committee emphasized that there was "a very grave possibility of fundamental confrontation" between the Congress and the presidency unless differences could be reconciled over congressional access to White House documents relating to the Watergate affair.

However, the official White House reaction to the proposed meeting was that it would relate only to "procedural matters" and would "in no way" change the President's mind about committee access to White House documents.

2½ days of testimony

The announcement of a forthcoming "Watergate summit" was made after the conclusion of 2½ days of testimony by John N. Mitchell, former attorney general and Mr. Nixon's former campaign director.

Both Mr. Mitchell's credibility and his sense of responsibility as a presidential adviser were criticized harshly during his 10 hours on the witness stand.

The President last week hardened his position on permitting access to Watergate-related documents in White House files, refusing a committee request to study them and terming it "constitutionally inappropriate." Mr. Nixon has flatly turned down suggestions that he appear before the Senate committee.

The Watergate committee was said to have postponed an imminent decision on subpoenaing the White House papers

See WATERGATE, A6, Col. 1

AP

President Nixon is shown earlier yesterday during his meeting with West Germany's foreign minister, Walter Scheel.

Haldeman said to deny role

Washington (NYT)—H. R. Haldeman, President Nixon's former chief of staff, has told Senate investigators that he took no part in planning the Watergate burglary and did not know of efforts to block the investigation and cover up the facts until March.

Mr. Haldeman's statements, in an interview with the staff of the Senate Watergate committee May 4, contradict the sworn testimony of other witnesses, including John W. Dean 3d, the former White House counsel; Jeb Stuart Magruder, once the deputy campaign director, and John N. Mitchell, the former attorney general.

A 20-page report of the Haldeman interview that was prepared afterward by the committee's staff has been obtained by the New York *Times*.

Mr. Haldeman has also denied any involvement in the overall Watergate affair in public statements, in a civil deposition and in testimony given privately to a Senate subcommittee.

None the less, federal prosecutors are known to believe

See HALDEMAN, A8, Col. 1

Nixon goes to hospital

Decision taken after reports of pains, fever

By PETER J. KUMPA
Washington Bureau of The Sun

Washington—President Nixon unexpectedly entered Bethesda Naval Hospital last night suffering from what White House doctors diagnosed as viral pneumonia.

Dr. Walter Tkach, the President's personal physician, said he expected Mr. Nixon to remain in the hospital for "not over a week."

The doctor said that overwork or anxiety could lead to the condition that struck Mr. Nixon.

Discomfort in the chest

The President called his personal physician at 5.30 yesterday morning complaining of discomfort in his right chest. He was able to continue a full schedule throughout the day despite discomfort and moderately high fever.

When the President left the White House shortly before 9 P.M. last night, he was described by Ronald L. Ziegler, the White House press secretary, as being in "excellent spirits, but in a weakened condition." He was suffering, however, from fever that was ranging between 101 and 102 degrees.

He entered the hospital at 9.15 P.M.

Medical tests, including X-rays of the President's chest and electrocardiograms were normal. Doctor Tkach said there were no complications to the case.

Agnew notified

It was the first time Mr. Nixon has been hospitalized for any ailment since 1960, when he had a knee problem.

Vice President Agnew was notified about the President's entry into the hospital at his Washington home.

Dr. Tkach said he doubted that antibiotic medication would be necessary. He added that such treatment was required in only 10 per cent of cases of viral pneumonia. The

See NIXON, A5, Col. 3

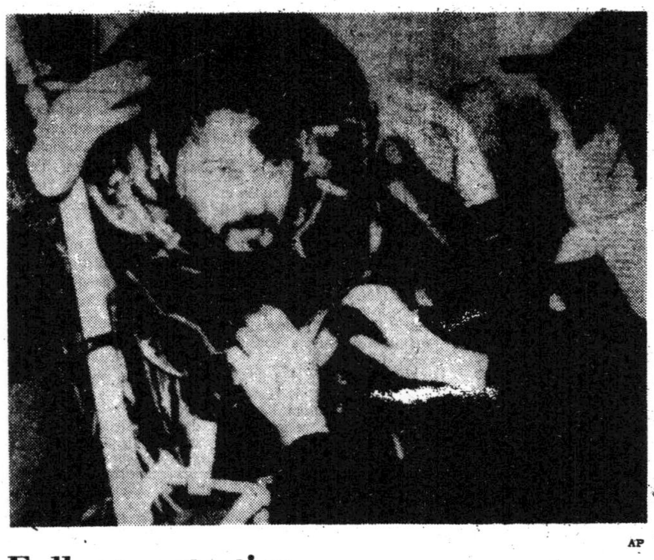

AP

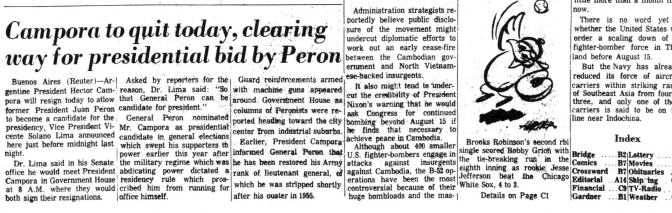

Fallout protection

Petty Officer John S[illegible], a marine engineer aboard the New Zealand frigate Otago cruising in the French nuclear test zone in the Pacific to protest an upcoming series of nuclear tests, had a helmet fitted to his ventilation suit yesterday during a fallout exercise. (Dispatch on Page A2)

U.S. said to start pulling out B-52's from war on weekend

Washington (AP)—The United States will start pulling B-52 bombers out of the Southeast Asia war this weekend, Nixon administration sources reported yesterday.

Departure of 13 B-52's from Guam apparently will mark the beginning of a gradual withdrawal of at least half of the 200 heavy bombers committed to the war before the August 15 cut-off of all U.S. military operations in Indochina.

There may be no announcement of the first B-52 pullback to the United States.

Cambodia truce

Administration strategists reportedly believe public disclosure of the movement might undercut diplomatic efforts to work out an early cease-fire between the Cambodian government and North Vietnamese-backed insurgents.

It also might tend to undercut the credibility of President Nixon's warning that he would ask Congress for continued bombing beyond August 15 if he finds that necessary to achieve peace in Cambodia.

Although about 400 smaller U.S. fighter-bombers engage in attacks against insurgents against Cambodia, the B-52 operations have been the most controversial because of their huge bombloads and the massive destruction they can cause.

B-52 sorties, costing up to $30,000 each, are much more expensive than flights of tactical fighter-bombers, which run to about $6,600 each.

Because of a tight budget problem, the Pentagon cut back B-52 flights over Cambodia in late May from an average of about 60 a day.

At his first news conference last Friday, James R. Schlesinger, the Secretary of Defense, said the level of tactical bombing flights would fluctuate until August 15 but that B-52 sorties would be "at a level no higher than at the present time."

That left room for a reduction in B-52 operations.

Sorties increased

Fighter-bomber sorties over Cambodia recently were increased from about 160 to more than 200 a day in what congressional critics claim is an effort to apply military pressure before the cut-off a little more than a month from now.

There is no word yet on whether the United States will order a scaling down of its fighter-bomber force in Thailand before August 15.

But the Navy has already reduced its force of aircraft carriers within striking range of Southeast Asia from four to three, and only one of these carriers is said to be on the line near Indochina.

Orioles edge Chisox, 4 to 3

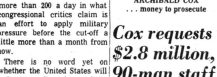

Brooks Robinson's second rbi single scored Bobby Grich with the tie-breaking run in the eighth inning as rookie Jesse Jefferson beat the Chicago White Sox, 4 to 3.

Details on Page C1

Index

UPI

ARCHIBALD COX
... money to prosecute

Cox requests $2.8 million, 90-man staff

Washington Bureau of the Sun

Washington — Archibald Cox, the special prosecutor, told a friendly Senate appropriations subcommittee yesterday he will need $2.8 million and a 90-man staff to investigate, during the next year, Watergate and political espionage and corruption.

Senator John O. Pastore (D., R.I.), the subcommittee chairman, made it clear Mr. Cox will have little difficulty getting what he wants.

Mr. Cox said $1.8 million of

See COX, A7, Col. 1

Airline aid tied to CAB ouster bid

By WALTER R. GORDON
Washington Bureau of The Sun

Washington—Senator John O. Pastore charged yesterday that a White House decision not to reappoint a foe of American Airlines to the Civil Aeronautics Board was linked to the firm's $55,000 contribution to the Nixon campaign.

At a hearing before a Senate appropriations subcommittee over which he presides, the Rhode Island Democrat asked Archibald Cox, the special Watergate prosecutor, to investigate the allegation. Mr. Cox agreed to do so.

Oklahoman chosen

Senator Henry Bellmon (D., Okla.), who sponsored the man chosen to replace Robert T. Murphy, said in an interview that an executive of American Airlines approached him and asked if there was anything he could do to help with the Murphy replacement.

Mr. Bellmon also said the appointment was arranged through Peter M. Flanigan, a top White House aide who has been dubbed "Mr. Fix It" because of his frequently controversial role in assisting big business.

The man chosen to replace Mr. Murphy was Lee R. West, a special justice of the Oklahoma Supreme Court.

Senator Norris Cotton (R.,)

See AIRLINES, A5, Col. 1

Campora to quit today, clearing way for presidential bid by Peron

Buenos Aires (Reuter)—Argentine President Hector Campora will resign today to allow former President Juan Peron to become a candidate for the presidency, Vice President Vicente Solano Lima announced here just before midnight last night.

Dr. Lima said in his Senate office he would meet President Campora in Government House at 8 A.M. where they would both sign their resignations.

Asked by reporters for the reason, Dr. Lima said: "So that General Peron can be candidate for president."

General Peron nominated Mr. Campora as presidential candidate in general elections which swept his supporters to power earlier this year after the military regime which was abdicating power dictated a residency rule which proscribed him from running for office himself.

Guard reinforcements armed with machine guns appeared around Government House as columns of Peronists were reported heading toward the city center from industrial suburbs.

Earlier, President Campora informed General Peron that he has been restored his Army rank of lieutenant general, of which he was stripped shortly after his ouster in 1955.

The Weather
Partly cloudy. High, 85; low, 66. Yesterday's high, 81, low, 73
(Details and Map, Page C11)

THE SUN FINAL

Vol. 273—No. 54—F BALTIMORE, WEDNESDAY, JULY 18, 1973 46 Pages 10 Cents

Man found shot dead on Pimlico lawn after 'Black October' call to newsman

Pipeline foes blocked

Near-tie vote in Senate bars court review

By STEPHEN E. NORDLINGER
Washington Bureau of The Sun

Washington—After listening to an attack on "environmental extremists," the Senate by a vote of 49 to 48 approved an amendment designed to exempt the proposed trans-Alaska oil pipeline from further review by the federal courts on environmental grounds.

Vice President Agnew cast the decisive vote against reconsidering the close vote on the exemption measure, which was strongly backed by the oil industry and opposed by environmental groups. The move to reconsider lost, 49 to 50.

Control removed

It was the first time that either house of Congress had voted to remove a public works project from the control of the National Environmental Policy Act of 1969, which requires that every federal agency submit to the President and Council on Environmental Quality a statement detailing what impact any project would have on the environment.

The measure, sponsored by Senator Mike Gravel (D., Alaska), states that an already issued government impact statement on the pipeline complies with the law and cannot be further reviewed by the courts.

Reflects frustration

In addition, the Secretary of the Interior would be permitted to approve any step he deems necessary to build and operate the pipeline system, a State of Alaska highway and three Alaska airports without the need for environmental impact statements.

Senate observers said the vote reflected the frustration felt by many legislators over the years of delay in construction of the pipeline stemming from court challenges brought by environmental groups. This frustration was said to be es-

See PIPELINE, A5, Col. 1

Leaflets strewn next to victim

By JEROME W. MONDESIRE

An unidentified man claiming to be from "Black October" called a *Sun* reporter early this morning within minutes after a Pimlico-area man was found slain.

Police said George L. Evans, 33, of the 4900 block Chalgrove avenue, was shot dead shortly before 12.24 A.M., when they were called to the scene.

The Sun reporter received a call from a man claiming to represent Black October at 12.27 A.M. Crudely lettered leaflets with "Black October" printed on them were scattered near the body lying on a row house lawn.

The same leaflets

The leaflets, identical to the ones found near the body of Delegate James A. (Turk) Scott (D., 2d, Baltimore), under indictment for narcotics trafficking said the victim had been slain for selling drugs. The anonymous caller made the same claim.

Moments after Mr. Scott's death, the *Sun* reporter got an anonymous call telling him of the delegate's murder and claiming Black October was responsible.

A source close to the federal Drug Enforcement Administration said Mr. Evan's name "meant absolutely nothing" to the agency.

Milton B. Allen, the Baltimore state's attorney, said "we have absolutely nothing on this man."

Police records showed that Mr. Evans had been arrested and charged with a narcotics violation in 1971, but had been found innocent.

Slogans on walls

Black October has made itself known in predominantly black areas of the city mainly through crudely lettered slogans on walls threatening death to narcotics pushers in the community.

The graffiti began appearing about five months ago, and their appearance was quickly accompanied by rumors that the group had sworn to kill known drug dealers.

Mr. Evans was found lying on a lawn next to his house in the 4900 block Chalgrove avenue. Police said he apparently had just parked his car, a 1972 black Cadillac with a vinyl sun roof, and was going to his house when he was shot.

A neighbor several doors away, who asked not to be identified, said she heard two loud reports at 12.30 A.M., as she was watching television went to her front door, and saw two men, dressed in black hats, black shirts and black pants, run down the street. They dodged between parked cars, and ran into an alley

See MURDER, A8, Col. 1

A phone call in the night

Following is the 12.27 A.M. phone conversation in which a *Sun* reporter learned of the death of George L. Evans, 33, in the 4900 block Chalgrove avenue:

Caller—I want you to check the 4900 block of Chalgrove avenue.

Question—Why?

Caller—There's been another one.

Q.—What's his name?

A.—That's not important.

Q.—How was he killed?

A.—He was shot.

Q.—How was he shot?

A.—He was shot with a .38 in the chest and in the back.

Q.—Is this Black October?

A.—Yes.

Q.—Was he killed for selling drugs?

A.—Yes.

The conversation ended when the caller hung up. The voice appeared to be identical to the voice of last Friday's caller telling the reporter Delegate James A. (Turk) Scott had been shot.

Nixon silences guards

Privilege claimed on them, tapes

By MURIEL DOBBIN
Washington Bureau of The Sun

Washington — The White House yesterday indicated that its refusal to permit a Senate committee to examine presidential documents could extend to tapes of conversations that may contain vital evidence regarding President Nixon's knowledge of the Watergate scandal.

Ronald L. Ziegler, White House press secretary, told newsmen that the tapes and recordings made of presidential conversations for more than two years would "certainly" be considered presidential documents.

Testimony forbidden

In a related Watergate development, the President forbade Secret Service agents to testify before the Senate committee on the grounds that their testimony would violate executive privilege.

Mr. Ziegler qualified his statement about the status of the presidential tapes only by saying that the White House would be "prepared to discuss this subject in perspective at some point in the near future." That seems to mean that now the tapes are covered by the blanket of executive confidentiality flung over all presidential papers by Mr. Nixon earlier this month.

The latest of the series of roadblocks placed by the White House in the path of the Senate Watergate committee led to a deadlock between the executive branch and Capitol Hill, where there is contemplation of subpoenaing the controversial documents.

Senator Sam J. Ervin, Jr. (D., N.C.), chairman of the Watergate committee, announced at yesterday's hearings that the committee had voted in executive session to ask for access to the tapes and recordings, the existence of which was disclosed for the

See TAPES, A7, Col. 1

AP

Herbert W. Kalmbach, formerly President Nixon's lawyer, testifies that his suspicions about funds for Watergate burglars did not prompt him to warn Mr. Nixon.

Ex-Nixon officials on a tape

Probe hears Ehrlichman, Kalmbach call

By GILBERT A. LEWTHWAITE and DEAN MILLS
Washington Bureau of The Sun

Washington — John D. Ehrlichman, former domestic chief in the White House, secretly taped a conversation with Herbert W. Kalmbach on the eve of a grand jury appearance by Mr. Kalmbach, then the President's personal attorney, it was revealed yesterday.

A transcript of the tape, produced at the Watergate hearings, appeared to indicate that Mr. Ehrlichman suggested Mr. Kalmbach should commit perjury.

Senator Sam J. Ervin, Jr. (D., N.C.) implied that the conversation was also an effort by Mr. Ehrlichman to make John W. Dean 3d., former White House counsel, the "scapegoat" for the Watergate coverup.

"Self-serving"

Mr. Kalmbach yesterday described the conversation as "self-serving" on Mr. Ehrlichman's part, and said he personally felt he had been "kicked in the stomach" when he learned it had been taped.

The tape was produced by Mr. Ehrlichman in response to a committee subpoena for all personal documents and information relevant to the Watergate case.

In the conversation Mr. Ehrlichman told Mr. Kalmbach that he had made no personal judgment over the propriety of collecting money for the original seven defendants.

According to Mr. Kalmbach, Mr. Ehrlichman gave explicit approval to the payment of $220,000 to the defendants' lawyers and families at a July 26, 1972, meeting in the White House.

Mr. Kalmbach said he approached Mr. Ehrlichman for his assurance on the propriety of the fund-raising mission after he became concerned about the clandestine transfer of the funds.

But in the taped phone conversation of April 19, 1973, the day before Mr. Kalmbach was to appear before a grand jury investigating Mr. Ehrlichman's activities, Mr. Ehrlichman had this exchange with Mr. Kalmbach:

Mr. Ehrlichman: "As far as propriety is concerned I think

See KALMBACH, A6, Col. 1

Ehrlichman-Kalmbach tape

Washington Bureau of The Sun

Washington—Following is the text of the tape recording of a telephone conversation between Herbert W. Kalmbach and John D. Ehrlichman released yesterday by the Senate Watergate committee:

Ehrlichman: Hi, how are you?

Kalmbach: I'm pretty good. I'm scheduled for 2 tomorrow afternoon.

E: Where, at the jury or the U.S. attorney?

K: At the jury, and I'm scheduled at 5.30 this afternoon with [Earl J.] Silbert, [assistant United States attorney, then a Watergate prosecutor.]

E: Oh, are you?

K: Yeah. I just wanted to run through quickly several things, John, in line with our conversation. I got in here last night and there was a telephone call from [Paul] O'Brien [Nixon re-election committee attorney]. I returned it, went over there today, and he said the reason for the call is [Frederick] LaRue has told him to ask him to call me to say that he had to identify me in connection with this and he wanted me to know that and so on.

E: Did he tell you about [John] Dean?

K: Nope.

E: Well, Dean has totally co-operated with the U.S. attorney in the hopes of getting immunity. Now what he says or how he says nobody seems to be able to define. But he . . .

K: The whole enchilada?

E: He's throwing off on Bob [Haldeman] and me heavily.

See TRANSCRIPT, A6, Col. 2

Kalmbach held funds, let GOP pay

Washington (KNI)—Herbert W. Kalmbach, the President's former personal attorney, secretly sat on $1.6 million in leftover 1968 Nixon campaign funds, while the Nixon administration forced the financially strapped Republican party to swallow $1.3 million in unpaid bills from that campaign.

This little-understood fact has come to light through recent disclosures in the Watergate hearings and related investigations.

It is likely to do little to improve the mood of national and local GOP officials already angered by what they call the administration's downgrading of the party and its candidates in the 1972 campaign.

In his testimony before the Senate Watergate committee yesterday, Mr. Kalmbach, con-

See FUNDS, A6, Col. 1

UPI

Two of President Nixon's advisers, Bryce Harlow (left) and Melvin R. Laird (center), chat with George P. Shultz, the Secretary of the Treasury, after visiting the President at the National Naval Medical Center in Bethesda.

Phase 4 to be revealed today

Washington (AP)—The Nixon administration said it will announce today the fourth phase of its wage and price control program.

Government economists clearly hope that the Phase 4 program will be the last government venture at wage and price controls, although they warn that Americans should not expect it will stop all price increases.

A congressional source said yesterday that Phase 4 is expected to contain relatively stringent provisions on prices but would leave the current guidelines on wages essentially unchanged.

"The two Georges"

"I believe the two Georges, Shultz and Meany, have gotten together on that," said the source. George P. Shultz is Secretary of the Treasury and George Meany is president of the AFL-CIO.

Phase 4 will mean an end to the current across-the-board price freeze, which was imposed to slow the rapid price increases under Phase 3, a largely self-administered program which was widely regarded as a failure.

Under Phase 3, during the first five months of this year prices soared at an 8.7 per cent annual rate, led by food costs which increased at a 22.4 per cent annual rate. Wholesale prices went up 24.4 per cent.

Mr. Shultz, after meeting with President Nixon yesterday, told reporters at the National Naval Medical Center in Bethesda that the new program would be announced today. Mr.

See ECONOMY, A8, Col. 1

Index

Republic set up after Afghan coup

New Delhi (AP)—Afghanistan was proclaimed a republic yesterday in a palace coup that apparently ended the monarchy and the 40-year reign of King Mohammed Zahir Shah.

Lt. Gen. Sardar Mohammed Daud Khan, the leader of the coup and husband of the king's sister, pledged to give the landlocked central Asian nation genuine democracy in place of what he described as the "pseudodemocracy" of King Zahir Shah.

The King, 59, was taking mud-bath health treatments on the Italian island of Ischia near Naples, when news of the coup was broadcast from Kabul, the capital.

General Daud pledged to continue Afghanistan's foreign policy of nonalignment. Under King Zahir Shah, Afghanistan had friendly relations with, and received substantial economic aid from, the United States, Russia and China.

General Daud was prime minister from 1953 to 1963 while the King, barred by his relatives from exerting any powers, was a figurehead ruler of Afghanistan's more than 13 million people.

But the King struck back 10 years ago, deposing General Daud, taking all powers for himself and promising Afghanistan a limited parliamentary democracy.

General Daud, in a statement read over Radio Kabul in Pushtu, the local language, bitterly attacked the King's form of democracy, saying its foun-

See COUP, A4, Col. 1

Oakland trips Orioles, 3-1

Vida Blue hurled a four-hitter as Oakland handed the Orioles a 3-to-1 loss last night in Oakland.

Details on Page C-1

Secret sorties put at 4,000

By CHARLES W. CORDDRY
Washington Bureau of The Sun

Washington—Close to 4,000 B-52 bombing flights were launched against North Vietnamese base areas in Cambodia during the secret 14-month campaign in 1969 and early 1970, informed sources reported yesterday.

Hinting at the magnitude of the bomber strikes, now under inquiry in the Senate Armed Services Committee, the Defense Department spokesman said officially that they "probably ran in the hundreds of B-52 sosorties [individual flights] per month. The clandestine bombing lasted from March, 1969, to May, 1970, after which air operations over Cambodia no longer were secret.

"Major campaign"

"It was a very major campaign in the [North Vietnamese] sanctuary areas," and it occurred at a time when America was preparing to withdraw its military forces from South Vietnam, according to Jerry W. Friedheim, the defense spokesman.

Later inquiry established that the actual number of B-52 sorties more nearly approximated 4,000, not the more than 1,400 inferred from Mr. Friedheim's statement.

The Pentagon spokesman indicated that the massive bombing campaign had its origins in the March, 1969, visit to South Vietnam of Melvin R. Laird, then defense secretary. Gen. Creighton W. Abrams, then American commander there, reportedly had warned about the threat from the North Vietnamese base areas to the forthcoming American withdrawals.

"Reasonable request"

Striking at the bases was determined to be a "reasonable request" on General Abrams's part, Mr. Friedheim said.

Defense Department comments on the Cambodian bombing followed Monday's testimony of a former Air Force major, Hal M. Knight, who told the Senate Armed Services Committee that there had been deliberate falsification of reports to indicate that

See BOMBING, A4, Col. 1

WEATHER

Cloudy, highs in 70's today and tomorrow. Lows in 50's tonight.

THE EVENING SUN

7 STAR ★★★★★★★ **2 30 STOCKS**

Vol. 127—No. 149 Second-class postage paid at Baltimore, Md. BALTIMORE, WEDNESDAY, OCTOBER 10, 1973 122 Pages 10 Cents

AGNEW RESIGNS

Syria, Egypt Hit; U.S. Reports Big Soviet Airlift

Airlift

Washington (AP)—The Soviet Union has begun a big airlift to resupply Syria and Egypt, United States officials said today.

The officials said the Russians, using their biggest and best transport planes, are delivering "very large tonnages" of military supplies to airports in both Egypt and Syria.

The officials spoke only in vague terms, declining to say in what amounts or types of equipment the supplies were being delivered.

They said, however, that so far there has been no evidence that the Soviets are replacing Syrian or Egyptian fighter planes knocked down by the Israeli air force.

Mum About U.S. Aid

Meanwhile, Jerry W. Friedheim, Pentagon spokesman, would say only no comment when asked if the United States was engaged in any extraordinary resupply measures for Israel, which regularly receives millions of dollars of U.S. aid.

Of the Soviet resupply, the U.S. officials said transport planes are flying directly from Russia across the Mediterranean Sea to various airports in Egypt and Syria.

So far, there have been no reported attacks by Israeli planes on the Russian transport aircraft, though there have been some Israeli attacks at airports where the Russian transports are continuing to land.

Missiles Are A Factor

U.S. military analysts said, meanwhile, that the heavy use by both Egypt and Syria of surface-to-air missiles is keeping Israel from gaining the easy mastery of the air that it had in the 1967 war.

Knowledge sources said Israel obviously would request Washington to speed up delivery of Phantom jets and other equipment for which Israel holds contracts through this year and next. These sources said the Israelis had suffered great losses of equipment.

Most of the Israeli warplanes that have been lost since the war began Saturday have fallen to these Soviet-built missiles, United States intelligence sources say.

Unless the Israelis can neutralize these weapons, they'll be able to push Egyptian and Syrian forces out of the Sinai Peninsula and the Golan Heights only at very considerable costs, the analysts say.

Arabs Doing Better

"The Arabs are doing better this time than they have in the past," one official said.

Defense Department and other United States govern-

[Continued, Page A 3, Col. 5]

Fighting

By The Associated Press

Israel claimed its warplanes blasted Damascus airport and other strategic targets in the Syrian and Egyptian heartlands today.

Iraq announced its air and ground forces have joined the war, and Jordan called up its reserves in wht could herald another escalation of the five-day-old struggle.

Syria reported its air defenses drove the Israeli airport raiders away from Damascus before they could get close enough to damage the four-year-old airport.

But as reports of ground fighting slackened off, Damascus charged other Israeli jets were hitting civilian targets at the central industrial city of Homs and Syria's major ports on the Medterranean.

The Israeli command described the target's as "strategic and military."

Tel Aviv and Damascus reported major aerial engagements also swirled over the Golan Heights battleground, and each side claimed downing large numbers of the other's planes.

"No Longer Civilian Airport"

The Israeli military command said its raiding jets inflicted "considerable damage" on the Damascus airport. A spokesman said the facility "is no longer a civilian airport but a base for military strikes into Israel."

It was the second reported raid on the Syrian capital. Israeli jets bombed the Defense Ministry and government radio station on the eastern fringes of the city Tuesday. Civilian casualties were reported heavy.

The heavy air battles coincided with indications the ground fighting had tapered off in the Golan Heights and the Sinai peninsula, where the Israelis have admitted backing off from their main Suez Canal defense lines against Egyptian forces trying to retake the desert lost to Israel in the 1967 war.

Iraq Enters War

Iraq's announcement that its air and ground forces were playing an active role in the fighting on both fronts formally brought in the Iraqis as the fourth Arab country ranged against Israel in the fourth Arab-Israeli struggle since 1948.

The Beirut newspaper An Nahar reported the Iraqis had committed 18,000 troops and 100 tanks btsides air power to support Egyptians in the Sinai and Syrians in the Golan Heights.

These reports were seen as

[Continued, Page A 3, Col. 4]

Court Upholds Curbs On Retail Gas Prices

Washington —The Temporary Emergency Court of Appeals today upheld the government's Phase 4 controls on retail gasoline prices.

The court overturned a preliminary injunction issued by a lower court in a suit brought by the National Congress of Petroleum Retailers.

The dealers have protested a Cost of Living Council prohibition against automatically increasing their prices to reflect higher wholesale costs of gasoline.

The council maintained that the rigid controls are necessary because gasoline prices have risen sharply this year because of the gasoline shortage and have made a "disproportionate" contribution to the country's inflation problems.

The appeals court was created especially to consider

[Continued, Page A 2, Col. 8]

Index

The Evening Sun today is printed in nine sections.

ON THE ATTACK—Israeli infantryman, protected by armored personnel carriers, run up a sand dune in the Sinai as the bloody Israeli-Arab conflict continues.

U.S. Jews Spur Fund Appeals, Seek Volunteers To Aid Israel

Sudan backs Arabs, editor says; Pikesville rally draws 6,000 .... D 24.

By The Associated Press

American Jewish leaders are urging stepped-up emergency fund-raising efforts to help Israel in its fight with the Egyptians and Syrians. Some Jewish groups also are recruiting American volunteers to replace Israeli civilians summoned to battle.

A gathering of hundreds of Jewish leaders in Washington was told Tuesday that the latest war has already cost Israel some $1 billion.

"Israel has lost huge quantities of critical defense material, aircraft, radar and missile installations, tanks and transport," said Jacob Stein, chairman of the Conference of Presidents of Major Jewish Organizations. Stein said he had been advised of the battle cost estimate by Pinhas Sapir, Israeli finance minister.

The State of Israel Bond Organization said Tuesday it had raised about $120 million since the outbreak of the fighting Saturday.

Sam Rothberg, general chairman of the organization, said Jews of the New York metropolitan area pledged $19.4 million for Israel bonds at a fund-raising dinner Tuesday night.

According to Rothberg, the sum was the biggest ever pledged in a single community event since the U.S. campaign began 22 years ago.

The United Jewish Appeal, meanwhile, reported it was "absolutely swamped" with contributions. "Things are happening so fast that we have not

[Continued, Page A 3, Col. 5]

U.S. Trying Its Best To Mediate In Middle East, President Says

Washington (AP) — President Nixon said today the United States was "trying its best" to mediate the "very dangerous situation" in the Middle East.

But the President gave no indication of headway in the administration's peace-seeking efforts, which won the unanimous endorsement of congressional leaders after a White House meeting earlier in the day.

Without giving details, Mr. Nixon said the United States was playing "a responsible role, very fair to both sides."

Senator Mike Mansfield (Mont.), Democratic leader, said following the 90-minute White House meeting that he doesn't anticipate "any U.S. involvement" in the Middle East war.

The 19 Democratic and Republican leaders who attended the session with President Nixon and Henry Kissinger, Secretary of State, endorsed unanimously the administration's efforts to end the renewed Arab-Israeli fighting, Mansfield said.

Mr. Nixon's comments on the Mideast war came as he bade farewell to the visiting president of Zaire and as he presented awards a short time later to 11 top scientists.

He said at the awards presentation that "the flare-up in the Middle East reminds us again of how dependent" the

[Continued, Page A 3, Col. 1]

UPI Telephoto

MEET WITH PRESIDENT—Congressional leaders leave the White House after a bipartisan meeting with I resident Nixon in regard to the Middle East crisis and how the conflict can be contained. From left, Senator Hugh Scott (R., Pa.), Senate minority leader; Representative Carl Albert (D., Okla.), House speaker, and Senator Mike Mansfield (D., Mont.), Senate majority leader.

Spy Worked Into Staff Of McGovern

Washington (AP)—A former Nixon campaign spy testified today that he worked his way through the cmapaigns of three 1972 Democratic presidential contenders and right into Senator George McGovern's penthouse suite at the party's Miami convention.

Michael W. McMinoway, 26, a private detective from Louisville told the Senate Watergate committee that he rose from volunteer ranks to McGovern's convention security staff.

He was present with McGovern when the candidate watched on television as his delegates regained crucial, contested votes from the California delegation, McMinoway said.

McMinoway was code-named Sedan Chair 2 by onficials of President Nixon's re-election committee and the White House.

"Immoral Activity"

He testified that while working for McGovern in Miami he provided transportation for a delegate and two women who "engaged in immoral activity" with the delegate in the back seat of a car. He said he drove them from McGovern's Doral Hotel headquarters to the Playboy Plaza Hotel not far away.

Questioned about the incident, McMinoway said he wasn't certain whether the women were protstitutes or where they came from.

He testified he was acting on orders of an upper-echelo McGovern staff member whose name he could not recall. He did not identify the delegate.

McMinoway said he first saw the delegate when the man appeared on the Doral Hotel's 17th floor, where McGovern and his top aides stayed. He said that the man asked to see campaign manager Gary Hart, that Hart asked to have the man ushered in and that Hart later said, "Send him on back."

Drove Staff Car

When the delegate emerged from Hart's quarters later, a McGovern staffer told McMonoway to bring a staff car around to the front of the hotel and wait for the delegate, McMinoway said.

He said when he pulled up with the car, he found the delegate with two women.

McMinoway testified that he was certain the two women were of "low moral standards."

Republican committee counsel Fred Thompson questioned McMinoway in some detail about the incident.

"Did anything happen to make you believe they were not 'ladies,' but 'women?' "

"Yes sir," McMinoway said. "I'm not going to go into

[Continued, Page A 2, Col. 4]

Israelis Load Bombs In Va., Paper Says

Virginia Beach, Va. (AP)—A Boeing 707 with Israeli markings on its tail section was loaded with mssilies and bombs at Oceana Naval Air Station today, the Norfolk Ledger-Star reported.

While the arms—Sparrow and Sidewinder air-to-air missiles—were being put aboard, sailors covered the Israeli marks with paper and masking tape, then painted the covering, the newspaper quoted wt-inesses as saying.

Earlier today, a C-141 aircraft from the U.S. Military Airlift Command landed at Oceana and taxied to a point near the Israeli plane. The U.S. plane pulled alongside the aircraft and began loading bombs directly into it, the Ledger-Star said.

Capt. Robert C. Mandeville, commanding officer at Oceana, would not comment on the loading.

Ervin Ordered To Give Evidence In Vesco Trial

Washington (AP)—The chairman of the Senate Watergate committee said today he has been served with subpoenas to give evidence in the Vesco case trial of two former Cabinet members, and that he will attempt to comply.

"I just don't believe in suppressing evidence," said Senator Sam J. Ervin, Jr. (D., N.C.), the chairman.

Resolution Planned

He said subpoenas were issued to him at the request of lawyers for John N. Mitchell, former attorney general, and Maurice H. Stans, former commerce secretary.

They are accused of perjury, conspiracy and obstruction of justice in connection with a secret $200,000 cash contribution of President Nixon's re-election campaign from fugitive financier Robert L. Vesco.

Ervin said he would introduce a resolution in the Senate seeking its approval for him to comply with the three subpoenas.

He said the subpoenas seek any documents the Watergate committee has relating to Vesco, all information on the matter given to the committee by former Nixon campaign treasurer Hugh W. Sloan, Jr., by ousted White House counsel John W. Dean 3d and by the Securities and Exchage Commission, and all names and addresses of persons the committee knows to have given $1,000 or more to any presidential candidate last year.

Bulletin

Washington (AP)—Vice President Spiro T. Agnew resigned today, his secretary said.

The word came from a secretary who said Agnew's staff had been informed of the decision at a midday meeting.

The Vice President himself was here at the federal courthouse, the purpose of his visit was unannounced.

Agnew has been under federal investigation in connection with alleged kickbacks in Maryland, where he served as governor before becoming Vice President.

Mrs. Lisa Brown, the Agnew secretary, told the Associated Press of the resignation. She said she was speaking on behalf of J. Marsh Thomson, press secretary to Agnew.

She was in tears.

Agnew Pleads 'Nolo Contendere'

Vice President Spiro T. Agnew pleaded "nolo contendere" here today to one count of evading federal income taxes for the year 1967 in court here.

By James P. Day

Vice President Spiro T. Agnew abruptly appeared in a courtroom in the old Post Office building here today, moments before a hearing concerning the federal investigation into government corruption was scheduled to begin.

Also in the court room were Elliot L. Richardson, United States Attorney General, Henry E. Peterson, head of the Justice Department's criminal division, George Beall, U. S. attorney for Maryland and his three assistants.

The Vice President's surprise appearance at the hearing was scheduled for 2 P.M. before Judge Walter E. Hoffman. The exact nature of the hearing would not be determined immediately.

A half hour before it began, United States marshals opened tne courtroom on the fifth floor of the building and allowed newsmen and court employes to enter.

Earlier today, attorneys for nine newsmen and two publications today filed motions to quash subpoenas from the Vice President's attorneys which demand that they reveal their news sources.

Some of the individuals and publications requested a hearing from Judge Hoffman on the motions, which generally claim

[Continued, Page A 2, Col. 3]

Grand Jury Is Meeting To Hear Agnew Data

By Nick Yengich

The special grand jury investigating political corruption in Maryland was meeting today to hear for the fourth time allegations against Vice President Spiro T. Agnew.

It was not known who would appear before the 22-member panel, but prosecutors, nearing a statute-of-limitations deadline, are known to have met last week with one long-time Agnew associate and with the attorney of another.

Security measures at the old Post Office building where the jury meets were tighter than they have been in recent weeks. United States marshals ushered persons from elevators into the prosecutor's office without letting newsmen learn their identity while the number of General Service Administration guards and marshals deployed around and in the building was increased.

Beall In D.C.

Meanwhile, George Beall, United States attorney, and Barnet D. Skolknik, one of the three assistant prosecutors in the Agnew case, were in Washington yesterday. The reason for the trip was not made public.

In a related development, Samuel A. Green, Jr., Baltimore county state's attorney, today said he is exploring the possibility of seeking indictments against persons who have been granted immunity in the federal investigation.

Mr. Green intimated that

[Continued, Page A 2, Col. 4]

Cambodian Premier Resigns

Phnom Penh, Cambodia (Reuter) — Cambodian Prime Minister In Tam announced today that he had tendered his resignation to President Lon Nol. He gave no reason for his decision.

In Tam made the resignation announcement at the end of the five-minute television speech in which he reassured the people of Phnom Penh that there was no crisis in the capital. In Tam, who was appointed prime minister May 15, gave no indication in his speech whether Lon Nol had accepted the resignation.

Government sources said the prime minister's decision to resign from office and the ruling four-member poiltical council stemmed from his dissatisfaction over the appointment of a cabinet.

The Weather
Rainy and cloudy. High, 43; low, 34.
Yesterday's high, 31; low, 25.
(Details and Map, Page C11)

THE SUN

FINAL

Vol. 274—No. 70—F | BALTIMORE, THURSDAY, FEBRUARY 7, 1974 | 10 Cents

Alternate-day gas sales start Monday

Jury convicts Green on all 16 counts

Most controls on economy to end April 30

By ART PINE
Washington Bureau of The Sun

Washington—The Nixon administration proposed to Congress yesterday phasing out virtually all mandatory wage and price controls by April 30 and replacing them with a small-scale monitoring agency designed to deal mostly with long-term inflation problems.

The new agency, a pared-down version of the Cost of Living Council, would have no real power to roll back wage or price boosts, but could call companies or unions to public hearings in order to "spotlight" any increases it considers excessive.

Under the plan, mandatory controls would be retained after April 30 on only two sectors of the economy—health care and petroleum—with the rest exempted gradually over the next 83 days in return for pledges to keep price increases moderate.

However, officials raised the possibility that they might later recommend maintaining mandatory controls after April 30 on other industries or sectors where companies refuse to make long-term commitments on pricing and production capacity.

The council has made such long-term commitments from companies a virtual precondition to exemption during its policy of gradual decontrol over the past six months. Since July 26, such trade-offs have been made with 24 specific industries.

The administration's proposals, about in line with general expectations, were unveiled before a Senate banking subcommittee by George P. Shultz, the Secretary of the Treasury, and John T. Dunlop, director of the Cost of Living Council.

The package constitutes the first formal step in negotiations over what to do about the controls when authority for the present programs expires, next April 30. Congress may extend or amend the legislation, or allow the authority to lapse.

Congressional reaction to the proposal appeared to be one of skepticism, with subcommittee members seemingly unenthusiastic both about continuing the controls program or dropping it on April 30, as the administration was suggesting.

However, administration spokesmen took pains to invite the legislators to "work to-

See CONTROLS, A5, Col. 1

Congress gets Nixon health plan

By ADAM CLYMER
Washington Bureau of The Sun

Washington—President Nixon yesterday sent Congress a national health insurance plan designed to reimburse every American for three-fourths of his annual medical expenses after the first $150—which the patient would pay himself.

The individual would pay 35 per cent of the health insurance premium (costing each family an estimated $185), and employers, or the government in the case of the poor, would pay the rest. And no one would have to pay more than $1,500 in medical expenses in a year.

Mr. Nixon said his program would cost the Treasury only $5.9 billion (and the states another $1 billion) and would require no new taxes. It would "build upon the strengths of the medical system we now have, not destroy it," he said.

The health bill is the administration's major legislative initiative of the year, and if Congress considers it seriously, it will be placed in opposition to a plan urged by Senator Edward M. Kennedy (D., Mass.) with wide labor support. That scheme would have the government pay all medical and hospital costs, and finance that spending through new payroll taxes and general revenues.

Mr. Nixon did not directly refer to the Kennedy plan in his message, but he said his plan was preferable "to an extreme program that would place the entire health care system under the dominion of social planners in Washington."

His plan, the President said, would "assure all Americans financial access to high quality medical care and preserve basic freedoms for both the patient and doctor. The patient would continue to have a freedom of choice between doctors. The doctors would continue to work for their patients, not the federal government."

Senator Kennedy assailed the administration proposal, saying: "It may cost the government very little, but it will cost American families far

See NIXON, A7, Col. 1

Sunpapers photo—Clarence B. Garrett

Sixth-grader Mark A. Larichiuta carries a picket sign outside Hazelwood Elementary School in support of striking teachers. He is student council vice president.

School attendance 16%; talks break off again

By MIKE BOWLER

Operations in the city school system ground to a standstill yesterday, as attendance dropped to 16 per cent and the three-day-old teachers strike appeared to lose little of its strength.

As negotiations between the school board and Public School Teachers Association broke off at 10.30 P.M. last night—after 14 hours of nonstop bargaining—the positions of the two sides appeared virtually unchanged and no progress was reported.

More than 2,000 teachers rallied a third day at the War Memorial building, this time receiving the support of the city's major public employees unions.

The same group of labor leaders met at 5 P.M. with Mayor Schaefer, and there were threats that the teachers strike could be a prelude to a general labor stoppage in the city.

Ernest B. Crofoot, director of Council 67 of the American Federation of State County and Municipal Employees (AFL-CIO), said, "We're going to start negotiations as soon as possible—and I'm talking about a matter of days—and if he [the Mayor] gives us the same type of offer, there might well be a general strike."

Mr. Crofoot said that if teachers are jailed as a result of a Circuit Court injunction against the strike obtained Monday, "We will hold an emergency meeting, probably resulting in a work stoppage."

Similar threats came from

See SCHOOLS, A8, Col. 5

Nixon bars tapes

President Nixon refused to turn over five tapes of conversation with John W. Dean 3d, his former legal counsel, to the Senate Watergate Committee.

Dispatch on Page A6

Impeachment probe powers voted 410-4 for House panel

By WALTER R. GORDON
Washington Bureau of The Sun

Washington—The House gave overwhelming approval yesterday to a resolution formally authorizing the Nixon impeachment investigation and granting the House Judiciary Committee sweeping subpoena powers.

The House first beat back, 342 to 70, a Republican-sponsored effort to open the way for a series of restrictive amendments. Then it approved the resolution without change by a margin of 410 to 4.

The resolution marked the first time the House had expressly granted the Judiciary Committee authority to conduct the impeachment probe. Representative John J. Rhodes (R., Ariz.), the minority leader, said it was only the second time in American history the House had voted on such a resolution.

The resolution said the committee "is authorized and directed to investigate fully and completely whether sufficient grounds exist for the House of Representatives to exercise its constitutional power to impeach Richard M. Nixon, President of the United States."

Subpoenas may be issued for any documents or witnesses, including the President himself. A subpoena can be authorized by majority vote of the full committee or by the chairman and ranking Republican acting jointly — a kind of

See IMPEACH, A6, Col. 5

Catholic confession is revised

New York (AP) — The Catholic Church issued a revised ritual for penance yesterday which loosens up the format and allows for either retaining or eliminating the age-old, darkened confessional booth.

"The 'box' as we have known it may be done away with," the Rev. Thomas Krosnicki, associate director of the United States bishops' liturgy committee, said of the revamped, variable procedures. "The more likely setting will be the confessional room."

Except in unusual circumstances, however, the new provisions do not alter the requirement for individual confession for forgiveness in case of grave or "mortal" sin, nor do they deal with the theology on this point.

The new rites, issued by the

See CONFESS, A6, Col. 1

$1 tax checkoffs rising for '76 presidential race

Washington Bureau of The Sun

Washington — Public financing of the 1976 presidential election may become a reality even if Congress takes no further steps toward reformation of the electoral process.

Federal income tax dollars earmarked for the presidential race have been pouring in at a rate that would yield about $50 million for the candidates to divide two years from now, according to a statement by Senator Hugh Scott (R., Pa.), Senate minority leader, and Senator Edward M. Kennedy (D., Mass.).

The contribution mechanism already in place is the $1 checkoff box printed on the face of the forms used for paying individual income taxes.

First proposed in 1966 by Senator Russell B. Long (D., La.), chairman of the Senate

See CAMPAIGN, A7, Col. 3

Index

State's attorney 'stunned'

County office status unclear; appeal likely

By STUART S. TAYLOR, JR.
Towson Bureau of The Sun

Samuel A. Green, Jr., the Baltimore county state's attorney, was convicted last night on all 16 criminal counts against him.

The county Circuit Court jury of eight men and four women brought in the unanimous verdict at 10.25 P.M., after more than eight hours of deliberation.

Green, obviously shaken, would say only that he was "stunned."

James R. White, the county prosecutor's lawyer, asked Judge David Ross to give him time to prepare a motion for a new trial before taking further action.

Status unclear

Green could be sentenced to a substantial jail term if the guilty verdict on charges of obstruction of justice, conspiracy to obstruct justice, misconduct in office and attempted subornation of perjury stands up through the expected appeal process.

Green's status as the chief elected prosecutor of crime in the county was unclear last night. The state Constitution provides for removal of state's attorneys from office "for incompetency, willful neglect of duty, or misdemeanor in office, on conviction in a court of law, or by a vote of two-thirds of the Senate, on the recommendation of the attorney general."

Francis B. Burch, the Maryland attorney general, said late last night that it would be at least another week before his office's study on the possibility of impeaching Green could be completed.

Mr. Burch, who is vacationing in Florida, said Maryland had never before in its history faced a similar situation and that "there is no law on the subject as such."

Officials of the state attorney general's office, which prosecuted Green, said last night that they knew of no other case in recent history in which a state's attorney has been convicted of a crime.

The charges against Green all stem from a conspiracy he masterminded to cover up a $750 payment illegally collected by Louis W. Irvin, his aide, from a man who wanted his arrest records expunged, according to testimony.

Green orchestrated the conspiracy to deceive State Police investigators at a series of meetings with Irvin and Stuart E. Hirsch, then his deputy,

See GREEN, A7, Col. 3

Mandel seeks oil-depletion benefit's end

By ANTHONY BARBIERI, JR.
Annapolis Bureau of The Sun

Annapolis—Governor Mandel signed an executive order last night to implement an emergency fuel distributon plan midnight Sunday allowing motorists to buy gasoline only on alternate days.

Under the plan, motorists with even-numbered license tags and "vanity" plates will be allowed to buy gasoline only on even-numbered dates; motorists with odd-numbered plates and ham radio tags will be able to purchase gas only on odd-numbered dates.

Thus, when the plan begins Monday, February 11, only motorists whose license tag digits end in 1,3,5,7 and 9 will be able to buy gas. On the next day, the 12th, only motorists whose tag digits end in 0, 2, 4, 6 or 8 will be able to go to the pumps.

The Governor also introduced a bill that could make Maryland the first state to try to strip the oil companies of their income-tax exemptions for the oil depletion allowance.

Mr. Mandel's bill, which is expected to touch off a furious legislative fight and the largest lobbying effort since the auto insurance battle of 1972, may well set a precedent for otner states and pose a serious problem for the major oil companies.

Hard to stop states

"If the federal government doesn't act on this, it's going to be difficult for the oil companies to keep the other states from getting involved in the same type of legislation," Alan M. Wilner, chief legal aide to the Governor, said.

Mr. Wilner said that forcing the oil companies to add the depletion amount onto their state taxable income will double the income tax paid by oil companies to Maryland. Over the past three years, oil companies have paid the state an average of about $1.2 million in income tax each year.

Mr. Mandel said last night he will submit the odd-even order to the Joint Committee on Administrative, Executive and Legislative Review, which must approve all executive orders issued under the emer-

See GAS, A8, Col. 1

Shutdown hurts area business

By JOSEPH J. CHALLMES and ROGER TWIGG

Major industries in the metropolitan area yesterday began to feel the pinch of the nationwide independent truckers' shutdown, and angry drivers, protesting rising costs of diesel fuel, picketed the state's largest marine terminal yesterday.

Meanwhile, Governor Mandel ordered the National Guard to transport gasoline into the extreme western counties of the state, which have been virtually paralyzed by the six-day-old strike.

Governor Shapp of Pennsylvania walks out of trucker talks A8

However, the National Guard trucks were unable to go last night because they were not equipped with interior heating. Instead three commercial trucks were supposed to go, but had not left by late last night, officials said.

Across the nation, stepped-up violence forced lawmen in several areas to escort truck convoys of food, fuel and other needed items. At the same time, mounting layoffs and food shortages, mostly at the distribution level, were reported.

In Maryland, where food supplies are considered adequate through the end of the weekend, the economic impact of the shutdown by truckers, who are protesting high fuel prices, low speed limits and other fuel-related problems, continued to be felt.

Some breweries, paper companies, bottling plants and poultry producers said their production was being curtailed because of the shutdown.

A spokesman for the state Office of Economic Research said it was impossible to put a dollar-and-cents figure on the

See TRUCKERS, A8, Col. 7

Bill approved giving Nixon ration power

From Wire Services

Washington — A House-Senate conference committee last night approved a controversial bill giving President Nixon emergency authority to ration gasoline and also ordering price reductions for domestic crude oil.

The bill now must win final approval from both the Senate and the House of Representatives.

Senator Henry M. Jackson (D., Wash.), floor manager of the bill, said the Senate would take up the measure this morning. However, it appeared unlikely that Congress would enact the legislation before the Lincoln Day recess, which begins Friday.

"I'm anticipating trouble," Mr. Jackson said. Jackson aides said they had received reports of a threatened Republican filibuster, and a White House lobbyist said the administration would support efforts to delay the bill's passage.

On the House side, the Rules Committee raised a procedural roadblock which forces the bill to gain a two-thirds majority in order to pass before the recess.

Opposition to the bill, which would give President Nixon authority to order gasoline rationing and other mandatory energy-conservation measures,

See ENERGY, A8, Col. 1

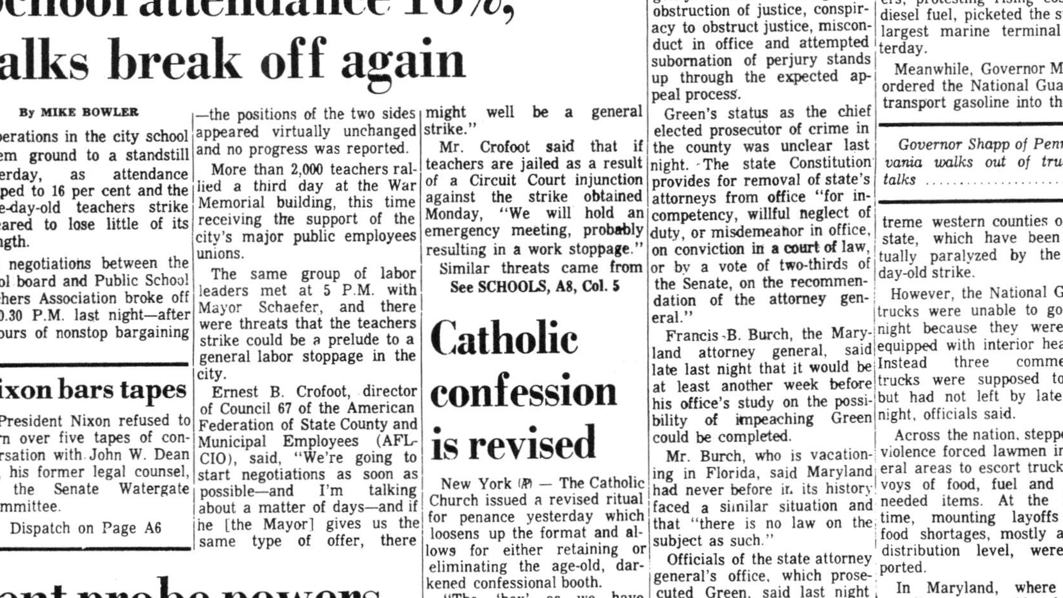

Sunpapers photo—Richard W. Childress

The Mandel administration hopes its gasoline-sales plan will shorten lines like this 40-car string, at Cold Spring lane and Falls road.

The Weather
Rain ending and windy today, high 48 to 53; partly cloudy tonight, low 30 to 35. Yesterday's high, 58; low, 52.
(Details and Map, Page C2)

THE SUN FINAL

Vol. 274—No. 122—F BALTIMORE, TUESDAY, APRIL 9, 1974 10 Cents

Aaron hits 715th homer, passes Ruth

Connects on his 1st swing

Al Downing, of Dodgers, yields blow

By KEN NIGRO
Sun Staff Correspondent

Atlanta—Henry Aaron hit a high fast ball from Los Angeles pitcher Al Downing 400 feet into baseball history last night and became the sport's all time home run king.

The 715th home run of Aaron's career came in the bottom of the fourth inning on his second trip to the plate but was struck with the first swing of his bat during the game.

Aaron had tied the legendary Babe Ruth's total of 714 home runs last Thursday with his first swing of the 1974 season,

Aaron record is a feat of consistency .... Page C7

and walked on five pitches when he first faced Downing in the second inning last night.

Then in the fourth inning, with Darrell Evans on first base through an error, Aaron took one pitch and hit the next one over the 385-foot sign in left-center field, touching off an 11-minute ovation from the standing-room-only crowd of 52,870.

"I was trying to get it down and didn't," Downing said. "He hit it like good hitters do."

"Just thank God it's all over," Aaron told the crowd as plaques and tributes were presented him while the game was interrupted. Aaron had followed the flight of the ball closely as he ran toward first base, saw it clear the fence as he rounded the base and broke his stride into his familiar home run jog.

Ironically, the record-breaking home run soared in a long, majestic arc that resembled the towering drives for which Ruth is remembered more than the low flat trajectory most of Aaron's home runs have taken.

"Hope this thing gets over with tonight," he told the huge crowd as he was honored in pre-game ceremonies.

At 9.07 P.M., as the ball bounced into the Braves' bullpen behind the left-center field fence, it was.

Aaron was called immediately by President Nixon, but he was in the outfield when the telephone message from the White House was put through into the Braves' dugout, and it was not until the bottom of the sixth inning that Aaron received congratulations from Mr. Nixon and an invitation to visit him.

Although Aaron had dealt with the mounting pressure with remarkable composure, he made it plain before last night's game that he was weary of chasing the ghost of Ruth.

AP

Swatting second pitch from Dodger lefthander Al Downing in only his second at bat in Atlanta this year, Hank Aaron ends his 20-year pursuit of the most coveted of all records, the 714 home runs that made George Herman Ruth, of Baltimore, "The Babe" of baseball.

Legislature ends; passes city aid bill

Annapolis Bureau of The Sun

Annapolis—The Maryland General Assembly adjourned its 90-day session early this morning after pushing through hundreds of last-minute bills, including five measures to funnel $15 million in new state aid to Baltimore in order to relieve city taxpayers of nearly half their expected property tax rise.

The Assembly bowed to the tradition of local courtesy and ignored warnings of fiscal irresponsibility by enacting a bill to give the Baltimore County Council the power to substitute a local income tax for the current property tax.

Through subtle parliamentary maneuvering, Senate leaders managed to avoid tying up the last crucial hours in endless debate and possible filibuster over two controversial issues: abortions and the reinstitution of the death penalty.

Among the measures that did gain enactment in the session's last day were:

- A $9.7 million state aid program for private and parochial schools—already threatened by a referendum drive.
- A bill to raise the state's ceiling on home mortgage-loan interest-rates from 8 per cent to 10 per cent.
- A one-year extension of the Maryland rent-control law, holding increases to 5 per cent of the July 1, 1974, rental but allowing landlords to pass on rises in taxes and heating fuel costs.
- A bill to require price competition in award of scandal-plagued state architectural and engineering contracts and completely revamp contract award procedures.
- Two horse racing bills that transfer 36 lucrative racing dates to the politically well-connected Bowie track and put the state's thoroughbred tracks on a year-round racing schedule.
- A stripped-down version of the land-use bill that does little to extend the state's powers to control development in Maryland.
- A constitutional amendment to be presented to the voters in November raising the Governor's salary from $25,000 to $45,000.

And, by refusing to take steps to reject a constitutional commission's salary recommendations, the legislators ended up with a $1,500 salary increase for the next four years, from the current $11,000 to $12,500 starting next year. The commission report, which now takes effect automatically, also sets up a dual salary scale for publicly employed

See SESSION, A9, Col. 1

Right split as 4 vie in French vote

By GILBERT A. LEWTHWAITE
Paris Bureau of The Sun

Paris—Two new major contestants entered the French presidential race yesterday, with three candidates from the government ranks lined up against one from a united left in the real fight for power May 5.

The split in the right-wing camp carries with it the threat of an end to the Gaullists' 10-year-old grip on France's Fifth Republic, and the possibility of Communists in the Cabinet here as members of a victorious left-wing coalition.

Rejecting Gaullist pleas to forgo his candidacy, Valery Giscard d'Estaing, 48, the finance minister, joined the right-wing rush, announcing he would challenge the two other government-aligned front-runners—Jacques Chaban-Delmas and Edgar Faure, both former premiers.

As expected, Francois Mitterrand, 57, the leader of the Socialist party, formally presented himself as the sole candidate for the left, including Communists and radicals.

He pledged himself to a campaign involving five key points—freer men, a more just society, a stronger franc, a more brotherly people and a more active France.

In an effort to allay fears raised by his alliance with the Communists, he said: "We do not condemn profit, but we do not want it to decide everything."

Mr. Giscard d'Estaing, leader of the Independent Republicans who are the Gaullists major partners in the present coalition government, appealed for support from "a new, enlarged majority" from across the political spectrum.

The Gaullist endorsement went last weekend to Mr. Chaban-Delmas, 59, the mayor of Bordeaux, a handsome and charming figure whose major personal drawback is a rather reedy voice.

As if to take advantage of this, Mr. Giscard d'Estaing announced his candidacy in unusually stentorian tones, and projected himself from the TV screens as very much a man of power.

In a deliberately slighting aside aimed at Mr. Chaban-Delmas and Mr. Faure, who both announced their candidacies on the day of President Georges Pompidou's funeral, Mr. Giscard d'Estaing said that those who wished to honor the president's memory should have observed the national mourning before worrying about succession.

He claimed for himself the legitimacy of having enjoyed the confidence of President Pompidou until his death last week.

To underline this connection with President Pompidou—political "legitimacy" is all-important in certain circles here—he chose to make his formal announcement in Chamalieres, the town of which he is mayor, and which lies in the late

See FRANCE, A2, Col. 4

Judiciary panel fights over rules

By THOMAS PEPPER
Washington Bureau of The Sun

Washington — Members of the House Judiciary Committee, who as individuals are still on the sidelines of the impeachment inquiry, broke into another partisan wrangle yesterday over the rules to be adopted in that inquiry.

Although tempers flared at times, the seriousness of the dispute remains to be seen.

With the White House scheduled to reply today to a six-week-old request for records of 41 or 42 conversations between President Nixon and Watergate-implicated aides, the committee's attention is expected to shift immediately to a discussion of this reply.

White House aides have not said yet whether the requested material will be turned over, but they have indicated that some of the conversations in question were not recorded and some may require sifting to eliminate material not related to Watergate.

John M. Doar, chief majority counsel of the special impeachment staff, told committee members that he already had initiated procedures to look into President Nixon's tax activities. He said that the staff was seeking an Internal Revenue Service report on Mr. Nixon's taxes, and that the question of possible tax fraud on Mr. Nixon's part would be included in this probe.

The long partisan wrangle

See IMPEACH, A6, Col. 1

Sawhill to become energy chief

By STEPHEN E. NORDLINGER
Washington Bureau of The Sun

Washington — John C. Sawhill, the deputy director of the Federal Energy Office, is to become the administration's chief energy official, informed sources said yesterday. An announcement is expected this week.

Mr. Sawhill, a 37-year-old former Baltimore businessman, will take over the $42,500-a-year post from William E. Simon, who is scheduled to be named secretary of the treasury, succeeding George P. Shultz.

In his new post, Mr. Sawhill will be immediately in charge of a transformation of the energy agency from one established by executive order of President Nixon in the midst of the energy crisis last December to one given statutory authority by Congress. A bill to create a federal energy administration is expected to clear the Senate and House and be sent to the President in the next few days.

The agency will embrace six divisions responsible for collecting energy information, determining policies for dealing with shortages, administering fuel allocation programs, assessing the national security implications of the nation's energy programs, reducing demand for energy through conservation measures and expanding production of energy.

Some of these functions were carried out by the Federal Energy Office headed by Mr. Simon but the law will provide Mr. Sawhill with the statutory authority to implement the program.

The agency over which Mr. Sawhill is to preside will employ this year about 2,400 persons here and in a dozen regional offices and operate with a budget of $48.4 million.

Before becoming deputy director in early December, Mr. Sawhill served as an associate director of the Natural Resources and Energy Division of the Office of Management and Budget.

Until recently there had been some doubt whether Mr. Sawhill would be named to head the energy program. The White House took umbrage last January when Mr. Sawhill, at a news conference, declined to go along fully with President Nixon's comment in his State of the Union message that the back of the energy crisis had been broken.

Apparently this annoyance has disappeared, although some observers here doubt that Mr. Sawhill, at least ini-

See SAWHILL, A9, Col. 1

White House will not say if IRS has assessed Nixon for negligence

By ADAM CLYMER
Washington Bureau of The Sun

Washington—President Nixon's spokesman refused to say yesterday if the Internal Revenue Service had assessed Mr. Nixon for negligence, announcing instead that the President's taxes were now "a closed book."

Gerald L. Warren, Mr. Nixon's deputy press secretary, said he would not answer because "some element of privacy" should be maintained about Mr. Nixon's tax situation. The important thing, he said, was that Mr. Nixon would pay the $432,787.13, plus interest, levied against him by the IRS.

Mr. Warren also cited as a reason for his silence his opinion that "there has been very little benefit of the doubt, if any, given by those who studied the President's tax returns and by those who commented on them."

The Internal Revenue Service has said it found no fraud, either civil or criminal, on Mr. Nixon's part, but asked the Watergate special prosecutor to look into fraud by his tax attorney, Frank DeMarco, Jr.

The House Judiciary Committee announced yesterday that it would investigate the returns for fraud.

Mr. Warren answered almost none of the questions put to him at the White House news briefing about Mr. Nixon's tax problems—not only about the negligence matter but also questions on whether he would try to claim a charitable contribution for some of his payments and where he would borrow the money, or whether that would be announced later.

That question produced this response:

"... He will pay it, and

See TAXES, A7, Col. 1

Israeli pilots captured in Lebanon

By The Associated Press

An Israeli fighter-bomber went down in flames over the embattled Golan Heights front yesterday, and the two pilots bailed out and were captured in Lebanon. It was the first Israeli warplane lost over the front since the October war.

Tank and artillery duels raged from dawn to dusk along the length of the 40-mile Golan cease-fire line for the 28th consecutive day. No casualties were reported.

Syria said the Israeli F-4 Phantom was brought down over Mount Hermon by its air defense system, apparently meaning a missile. But Israel denied this, saying the plane burst into flames because of "a technical hitch."

Lebanon said the plane crashed in the Arkoub region near the village of Chebba, only 6 miles north of the Israeli border and about 40 miles south of Beirut.

A Lebanese spokesman said the two pilots were safe and said they were picked up about 3 miles west of Chebba. He did not say where they were being held.

Israel admitted Saturday

See MIDEAST, A4, Col. 1

Weicker says IRS spies filed data on thousands

By MURIEL DOBBIN
Washington Bureau of The Sun

Washington—A Republican senator yesterday offered evidence to a congressional committee that the domestic-intelligence network set up by the Nixon administration probed into everything from movie stars' tax returns to allegations linking the President's nephew with "lovemaking groups."

Senator Lowell P. Weicker, Jr. (R., Conn.) produced a pile of secret White House memoranda before the Senate Judiciary Subcommittee on Administrative Practice to bolster his charges that the administration had abused its power by permitting government agencies to engage in political snooping.

Senator Weicker cited the establishment of a secret intelligence committee in the Internal Revenue Service a few months after President Nixon took office, asserting that this turned the IRS into "a public lending library on American citizens."

When the IRS intelligence unit was disbanded last summer—in the wake of domestic-surveillance revelations made at the Senate Watergate hearings—it had amassed secret files containing 12,000 classified documents on about 10,000 Americans, the senator declared.

For more than two hours, the senator, who was drawing upon his own staff investigation as well as material collected through the Watergate committee's inquiries, read from documents illustrating the lengths to which the White House had gone to harass

See WEICKER, A7, Col. 2

AP

President Nixon signs the $2.30 minimum-wage bill as Peter J. Brennan, the Secretary of Labor, looks on

Nixon signs $2.30 pay floor he opposed earlier

Washington (AP) — Legislation raising the federal minimum wage in stages from $1.60 to $2.30 an hour was signed into law yesterday by President Nixon.

Mr. Nixon had vetoed similar legislation last year, and voiced reservations about the measure sent him by Congress. But he said he was signing it because "raising the minimum wage is now a matter of justice that can no longer be fairly delayed."

The measure raises the minimum wage for 36 million workers covered under the 1966 minimum-wage law from $1.60 to $2.00 on May 1, with other increases boosting it to $2.30 by January 1, 1976. The $2.30 rate will be effective for all affected workers by 1978.

In addition, the legislation extends federal minimum wage and overtime requirements to an additional 7.4 million workers. When fully effective, the new law will cover 56 million workers.

Mr. Nixon signed the bill in his Oval Office, telling Peter J. Brennan, the Secretary of Labor seated alongside, that "we

See WAGE, A6, Col. 2

Index

The Weather
Considerable cloudiness today and to-night with chance of showers tonight. High today, 80; low tonight, 60 to 65. Yesterday's high, 78; low, 66.
(Details and Map, Page C2)

THE SUN

FINAL

Vol. 275—No. 73—F | BALTIMORE, FRIDAY, AUGUST 9, 1974 | 10 Cents

NIXON RESIGNS

Ford will become president at noon

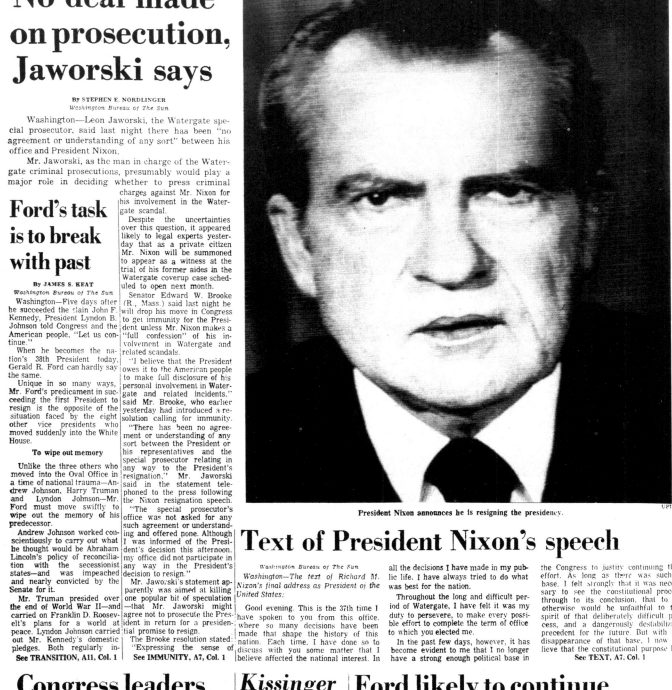

President Nixon announces he is resigning the presidency. UPI

No deal made on prosecution, Jaworski says

By STEPHEN E. NORDLINGER
Washington Bureau of The Sun

Washington—Leon Jaworski, the Watergate special prosecutor, said last night there has been "no agreement or understanding of any sort" between his office and President Nixon.

Mr. Jaworski, as the man in charge of the Watergate criminal prosecutions, presumably would play a major role in deciding whether to press criminal charges against Mr. Nixon for his involvement in the Watergate scandal.

Despite the uncertainties over this question, it appeared likely to legal experts yesterday that as a private citizen Mr. Nixon will be summoned to appear as a witness at the trial of his former aides in the Watergate coverup case scheduled to open next month.

Senator Edward W. Brooke (R., Mass.) said last night he will drop his move in Congress to get immunity for the President unless Mr. Nixon makes a "full confession" of his involvement in Watergate and related scandals.

"I believe that the President owes it to the American people to make full disclosure of his personal involvement in Watergate and related incidents," said Mr. Brooke, who earlier yesterday had introduced a resolution calling for immunity.

"There has been no agreement or understanding of any sort between the President or his representatives and the special prosecutor relating in any way to the President's resignation," Mr. Jaworski said in the statement telephoned to the press following the Nixon resignation speech.

"The special prosecutor's office was not asked for any such agreement or understanding and offered none. Although I was informed of the President's decision this afternoon, my office did not participate in any way in the President's decision to resign."

Mr. Jaworski's statement apparently was aimed at killing one popular bit of speculation—that Mr. Jaworski might agree not to prosecute the President in return for a presidential promise to resign.

The Brooke resolution stated: "Expressing the sense of

See IMMUNITY, A7, Col. 1

Ford's task is to break with past

By JAMES S. KEAT
Washington Bureau of The Sun

Washington—Five days after he succeeded the slain John F. Kennedy, President Lyndon B. Johnson told Congress and the American people, "Let us continue."

When he becomes the nation's 38th President today, Gerald R. Ford can hardly say the same.

Unique in so many ways, Mr. Ford's predicament in succeeding the first President to resign is the opposite of the situation faced by the eight other vice presidents who moved suddenly into the White House.

To wipe out memory

Unlike the three others who moved into the Oval Office in a time of national trauma—Andrew Johnson, Harry Truman and Lyndon Johnson—Mr. Ford must move swiftly to wipe out the memory of his predecessor.

Andrew Johnson worked conscientiously to carry out what he thought would be Abraham Lincoln's policy of reconciliation with the secessionist states—and was impeached and nearly convicted by the Senate for it.

Mr. Truman presided over the end of World War II—and carried on Franklin D. Roosevelt's plans for a world at peace. Lyndon Johnson carried out Mr. Kennedy's domestic pledges. Both regularly in-

See TRANSITION, A11, Col. 1

Decision is laid to weakness of political base

By ADAM CLYMER
Washington Bureau of The Sun

Washington—President Nixon, neither admitting guilt nor proclaiming innocence, abandoned his fight against impeachment and announced last night that he was resigning at noon today.

Vice President Ford will be sworn in as the nation's 38th president then, and Mr. Nixon, who chose him in the wake of Spiro T. Agnew's scandal-forced resignation, asked the country to "put the bitterness and divisions of the recent past behind us" and rally behind Mr. Ford.

Mr. Ford then made a brief statement, praising Mr. Nixon's sacrifice, promising to keep Henry A. Kissinger on as Secretary of State in the pursuit of peace and pledging to work with Democrats and Republicans in Congress, where, he said, "I don't think I have a single enemy."

After saying farewell to the Cabinet and the White House staff, Mr. Nixon and his family will leave the White House at 10 A.M. and fly to California on Air Force One. He will leave Washington as President, but his formal letter of resignation will be delivered to Dr. Kissinger's office before noon and he will arrive at San Clemente as a former president.

Mr. Nixon, in his speech from the Oval Office, said he was resigning because his support in Congress had disappeared. He insisted, "I have never been a quitter" and said that resignation was personally "abhorrent" to him. Moreover, his family "unanimously" opposed the step, he said.

"Interests of America first"

But, "as President, I must put the interests of America first," he said, and therefore he would resign.

In one remark that recalled past complaints that the nation was too preoccupied with Watergate and ignoring its other problems, he said, "America needs a full-time President and a full-time Congress." Earlier, in a meeting with congressional leaders, he had sounded a similar note, saying, according to Carl Albert (D., Okla.), speaker of the House, that he "couldn't be President and worry about Watergate, too."

The President scarcely spoke directly of what he called "the Watergate matter"—the break-in and bugging at Democratic national headquarters on June 17, 1972, and the subsequent coverup—which had made impeachmeant and conviction a virtual certainty.

"If some of my judgments were wrong—and some were wrong," he said, "they were made in what I believed at the time to be based in the best interests of the nation."

But after saying he would be "eternally grateful" to those who had stood behind him, he offered a unique conciliation "to those who have not felt able to give me your support," saying:

"I leave with no bitterness toward those who have opposed me—because all of us in the final analysis have been concerned with the good of the country, however our judgments might differ."

The President recounted many of the foreign policy accomplishments of his administration, from the ending of American involvement in the Vietnam war to more recent successes in the Middle East, where, he said, many who "considered us their enemies for nearly 20 years now look on us as their friends."

Some voices critical

And he spoke of the challenges which faced Mr. Ford and the country, emphasizing foreign policy and the importance of peace.

It struck many observers as a singularly graceful exit, but there were voices from Capitol Hill critical of the absence of any admission of guilt rather than just mistakes in the Watergate area that compelled the first resignation of a president in American history.

And there was indeed no tracing of the recent events in that critical area.

Nor were there many of the typical figures of speech Mr. Nixon employs, although he did note, as the 37th President, that this was the 37th speech he had made as President on national television.

No previous president ever resigned, but for a President who once exulted in "historic firsts"—varying from his trip to China or the U.S landing on the moon to an address to a state legislature never previously graced by a presidential visit— it appeared preferable to another historic alternative—impeachment and removal from office.

That result, which seemed very likely after the

See NIXON, A6, Col. 1

Text of President Nixon's speech

Washington Bureau of The Sun

Washington—The text of Richard M. Nixon's final address as President of the United States:

Good evening. This is the 37th time I have spoken to you from this office, where so many decisions have been made that shape the history of this nation. Each time, I have done so to discuss with you some matter that I believe affected the national interest. In all the decisions I have made in my public life, I have always tried to do what was best for the nation.

Throughout the long and difficult period of Watergate, I have felt it was my duty to persevere, to make every possible effort to complete the term of office to which you elected me.

In the past few days, however, it has become evident to me that I no longer have a strong enough political base in the Congress to justify continuing that effort. As long as there was such a base, I felt strongly that it was necessary to see the constitutional process through to its conclusion, that to do otherwise would be unfaithful to the spirit of that deliberately difficult process, and a dangerously destabilizing precedent for the future. But with the disappearance of that base, I now believe that the constitutional purpose has

See TEXT, A7, Col. 1

Congress leaders sad but optimistic

By THOMAS PEPPER
Washington Bureau of The Sun

Washington—Congress, in the midst of impeaching President Nixon, expressed relief yesterday that it would be spared the task of carrying out the process to a full conclusion.

Representative John J. Rhodes (R., Ariz.), the House Republican leader, caught the mood of the Capitol when he said, "I feel relief, sorrow, gratitude, but also optimism."

Senator Hugh Scott (R., Pa.), the Senate Republican leader, said Mr. Nixon's decision to resign "is in the national interest and now opens the way to a healing and mending process under President Ford."

"The country has been on the verge of a nervous breakdown long enough," Mr. Scott said, adding that he had "the greatest sympathy for the President and his family, but no sympathy at all for the dreadful conduct of those asso-

See CONGRESS, A11, Col. 6

Nixon move protects pension

Washington Bureau of The Sun

Washington—By resigning rather than facing apparently certain conviction by the Senate, President Nixon loses his $200,000 annual salary but manages to keep a $60,000-a-year presidential pension.

Mr. Nixon, had he been convicted, would have forfeited the pension, which equals the salary of a Cabinet member but is likely to increase in the future with inflation.

The law that provided for this pension also allows for additional emoluments for former presidents, reflecting a desire by Congress not to force former presidents in their old age to live near poverty.

Among these additional bene-

See MONEY, A7, Col. 6

Index

Kissinger staying on for Ford

By DEAN MILLS
Washington Bureau of The Sun

Washington—Henry A. Kissinger will stay on as Secretary of State under the administration of Gerald R. Ford, Mr Ford announced last night.

The President-designate underlined the importance he attaches to the presence of Dr. Kissinger in his Cabinet by making the announcement almost immediately after President Nixon had announced his resignation.

"Let me say without any hesitation or reservation," Mr. Ford said, "that the policy

See STATE, A9, Col. 6

Ford likely to continue present economic policies

By ART PINE
Washington Bureau of The Sun

Washington—Gerald R. Ford is expected to continue the same basic economic policies already set in place by the Nixon administration—but with a decidedly more "activist" stance—his key advisers and associates indicated yesterday.

Although final plans are still undecided, Ford strategists assert there will be no major change in the administration's previously announced plans for a prolonged period of austerity, with sharp budget cuts and continued tight money.

The main difference, associates say, will be a concerted effort by the new President to rally business, labor and consumers into a "nationwide consensus" to combat inflation, and to attempt to restore "credibility" to economic policymaking.

Mr. Ford also is considered likely to explore more ways to relieve economic hardship in specific sectors of the economy, through a public-service jobs program, added subsidies for housing and relief for low-income groups.

However, advisers say the basic thrust of the Nixon administration policy will continue unchanged. Mr. Ford is said to be vigorously opposed to changes in the tax rate or to reimposition of wage and price

See ECONOMY, A11, Col. 1

Price explosion

A sharp resurgence in farm prices sent wholesale prices exploding last month, the government reported yesterday. The rise was the second largest recorded since 1946.

Details on Page A3

'Death watch': The denouement

By MURIEL DOBBIN
Washington Bureau of The Sun

Washington — They stood all day in a gray drizzle, gazing, through black iron railings at the White House.

Theirs was a death watch, yet what they mourned was the presidency, not the man who held the office.

Those who watched and waited were a mixture of conservative middle-class Americans — the silent majority the Nixon administration had wooed — and those who would have qualified for its lists of political enemies.

There were middle-aged couples, tourists in paper hats who had come to tour the White House no matter who was its tenant, young girls in long cotton dresses, carrying babies and Bibles, and bearded young men in ragged jeans.

They had perhaps nothing in common except that they were standing on Pennsylvania avenue outside the White House on an August day when history was being made. The President of the United States was about to resign, and who he was had been transcended by what he was about to do.

"It's never happened before and I hope it never happens again. It's a burden on all of us," said a large woman in bulging blue shorts.

"I voted for him. I believed he was a good man. Now I think he betrayed us all and what's worse, he betrayed the job we put him there to do," said a white-haired woman in a neat navy blue dress. She had tears in her eyes.

"Yeah," said a college student who had been staring so

See SCENE, A11, Col. 1

The Weather
Cloudy and fair today and tonight. High today near 80; low tonight, 60 to 65. Yesterday's high, 75; low, 64.
(Details and Map, Page C2)

THE SUN

FINAL

Vol. 275—No. 99— F

BALTIMORE, MONDAY, SEPTEMBER 9, 1974

40 Pages

10 Cents

FORD PARDONS NIXON

Former chief regrets causing 'anguish'

AP

President Ford signs the document granting former President Nixon, a "full, free and absolute par[illegible]

Courts assured tape access

Evidence

Washington Bureau of The Sun

Washington—A complex plan that confirmed former President Nixon's ownership of his tapes and documents, but safeguarded them for court action, emerged yesterday as a key to his pardon by President Ford.

Philip W. Buchen, the White House counsel, denied that the pardon was contingent upon any action by Mr. Nixon. But the White House announced the pardon and the arrangements for disposition of Mr. Nixon's explosive presidential records at the same time.

Mr. Buchen acknowleged, moreover, that the two announcements had moved forward together in the final stages. A near final draft of an agreement on the records was discussed at San Clemente, Calif., Friday by the two sides, he said. Meanwhile, a White House lawyer informed Mr. Nixon's counsel a pardon was all but certain.

Under the agreement on the tapes only Mr. Nixon, under supervision, will have access to them for five years except for other persons under court order. Then ownership will revert to the federal government, though the material will be destroyed during the following five years.

As for other materials, Mr. Nixon again will determine access, except in the case of court orders, but this time for only three years. After that he can do what he wishes with the records.

RICHARD M. NIXON
. . . in farewell address

Events surrounding the pardon announcement began yesterday with the release of a ruling by William B. Saxbe, the Attorney General, on the rights of former presidents to their official records. He held that precedent and the skimpy law on the subject support their ownership of those documents under debate—subject to disclosure under court order.

Mr. Nixon's records and tapes have been held in the White House since his resignation August 9. It was the contents of some tapes already

See TAPES, A8, Col. 4

President cites 'mercy'

By ADAM CLYMER
Washington Bureau of The Sun

Washington—President Ford pardoned former President Nixon yesterday—a step he once said the American people would not "stand for"—because he said such an act of "mercy" was necessary to preclude further national anguish.

He said Mr. Nixon already had "suffered enough" and the accusations against him were "threatening his health."

The pardon covers any "offenses" Mr. Nixon "committed or may have committed" while he was President.

The federal prosecutions, which the very rare advance pardon short-circuited, would not afford Mr. Nixon equal justice, President Ford said, but would penalize him unfairly because of the "many months" that would have to pass before an unprejudiced jury could be empaneled to try him.

The decision led to the swift resignation of Jerald F. terHorst, Mr. Ford's press secretary and the first appointment of his administration.

While general reaction from public figures was mixed, the White House telephone switchboard was immobilized with angry calls from ordinary citizens, in a flood that recalled the storm at the times of the firing of Archibald Cox and immediately preceding Mr. Nixon's resignation. Telegrams also ran very heavily against the decision, one White House aide reported.

A spokesman for Leon Jaworski, the Watergate special prosecutor, said no deal had been made with him before the pardon was issued. And Philip W. Buchen, counsel to Mr. Ford, said Mr. Jaworski had been given 45 minutes advance notice but had neither been asked nor volunteered his views.

Mr. Nixon, who was told of the likelihood of a pardon on Thursday by a White House emissary, issued a statement in San Clemente, Calif., apologizing for the pain caused to the nation by "my mistakes over Watergate." And he said he could see how his mistakes "seemed" to support the idea that his actions were "intentionally self-serving and illegal."

"Statement of contrition"

Mr. Buchen, who characterized Mr. Nixon's press release as a "statement of contrition," said the pardon was announced on a Sunday because it was a "very solemn moment" and "Sunday is a good time to think about" the subject of mercy. Mr. Ford took communion at St. John's Episcopal Church before announcing the pardon. Afterward he played golf.

He and Melvin R. Laird, former secretary of defense, finished third in a best-ball tournament at Burning Tree Club, in Bethesda, Md., each of them winning a pair of slacks.

Mr. Nixon also agreed to guarantee that the papers and tapes of his administration—which the Ford administration agreed yesterday were his property—would be secured and kept available for use in any trials for which they are subpoenaed.

But Mr. Buchen, though conceding that Mr. Ford knew of this agreement before he decided finally on the pardon yesterday and conceding that the pardon, the Nixon statement and the papers-tapes agreement were discussed jointly between the White House and the former President, insisted that the pardon was not a result of those actions by Mr. Nixon.

The pardon covers "all offenses against the

See FORD, A8, Col. 1

Citizen Nixon still has legal vulnerabilities

By MURIEL DOBBIN
Washington Bureau of The Sun

Washington—The President's announcement yesterday of a full pardon for former President Nixon, who was forced from the White House by the Watergate scandal, did not mean an end to the troubles of Richard M. Nixon, private citizen.

Mr. Nixon no longer has to live in fear of prosecution for any federal offenses, which, as the President put it, he may have committed during his term in office—offenses that might have led to the indictment of the former chief executive for obstruction of justice, misuse of campaign funds and income tax evasion.

But the former President has been subpoenaed to testify as a defense witness at the forthcoming trial of six of his former aides, who have been charged with obstructing justice by concealing White House involvement in the Watergate political scandal—a case in which the grand jury also named Mr. Nixon as an unindicted co-conspirator.

According to sources in the Watergate defense team and in the office of Leon Jaworski, Watergate special prosecutor, President Ford's action may make it difficult and even dangerous for Mr. Nixon to avoid testifying in open court.

There has been speculation that Mr. Nixon might seek the protection of the Fifth Amendment when he takes the witness stand at United States District Court, as he has been ordered to do in a subpoena served on him recently. The subpoena was sought by attorneys for John D. Ehrlichman, former chief White House domestic adviser who is one of the Watergate defendants.

However, legal authorities pointed out that although the presidential pardon in effect grants Mr. Nixon immunity from prosecution on federal offenses such as obstruction of justice, which is the main charge in the Watergate trial, such immunity does not apply to offenses within state jurisdiction.

Consequently, if the former President contends in court that he wishes to remain silent because of the possibility of self-incrimination, his attorneys must explain to the court what, under the circumstances, is the rationale for such a plea.

This could resurrect the theory that the effort to cover up the Watergate burglary of June 17, 1972, was part of an overall bid to conceal what the White House viewed as a "national security" break-in committed at the office of Dr. Lewis J. Fielding, a Los Angeles psychiatrist, in September, 1971. That burglary, committed by a secret presidential intelligence unit known as the "plumbers," already has led to the conviction of Ehrlichman and three other men on conspiracy charges.

However, it has been contended so far by Mr. Nixon that, although he set up the plumbers unit, he never ordered it to commit burglary as a way of obtaining more information about Daniel Ellsberg, the man who released the Pentagon papers.

If Mr. Nixon chooses to take the Fifth Amendment at the Watergate trial, and his plea is linked to the Fielding break-in, the court could reject such an argument on the grounds that

See NIXON, A8, Col. 8

Portugal troops patrol colony

By The Associated Press

Portugal ordered its forces yesterday to "restore peace and tranquility" in the Mozambican capital, Lourenco Marques, where armed white rebels have taken over key points in a bid to stop the imminent transfer of power to a black, guerrilla-dominated regime.

A communique from Premier Vasco dos Santos Goncalves reported that two whites were killed and a black was wounded in an incident "somewhere in Mozambique."

Mr. Goncalves said a high-ranking Army officer flew to Lourenco Marques from Army headquarters at Nampula, 1,000 miles north of the capital, to negotiate with the rebels.

In an earlier communique the premier said the armed forces have avoided using arms thus far because the rebels were "using women and children as hostages.

He described the rebels as "a small, desperate minority with no understanding of the

See FRELIMO, A4, Col. 6

Indians halt Bird streak, 7-4

Home runs by George Hendrick, Tom McCraw and Charlie Spikes helped Cleveland to a 7-to-4 victory yesterday at Municipal Stadium in Cleveland to end the Orioles' 10-game winning streak.

Details on Page C3

Index

Western finance chiefs call inflation top enemy

By GILBERT A. LEWTHWAITE
Paris Bureau of The Sun

Paris — The finance ministers of six of the leading industrial nations in the West yesterday followed President Ford's lead, naming inflation as "Public Enemy No. 1."

The current inflation rate — around an average of 14 per cent for industrial nations — and the prospect of a further increase due to another boost in oil prices was at the center of their weekend talks here.

Jean-Pierre Fourcade, the French Foreign Minister, said yesterday that William E. Simon, the United States Treasury Secretary, and the ministers from Britain, West Germany, Japan and Italy all agreed that the fight against inflation must take priority.

At the same time, he said, the ministers recognized the need for individual countries to protect the level of domestic industrial activity and employment and also to co-operate to insure healthy world commerce.

The ministers, accompanied by the governors of the six nations' central banks, also agreed to take action to increase stability in the banking sector.

To avoid further banking collapses, due to temporary liquidity difficulties arising out of foreign exchange dealings under the present system of floating parties, the ministers endorsed the need for a greater exchange of information and improved surveillance of the exterior money operations of banks.

They also passed on unspecified control measures and other ideas for consideration at the international meeting of central bankers in Basle, Switzerland, today.

The finance ministers of the "Big Five" — Italy was a special guest at this session because of the particular

See MONEY, A2, Col. 7

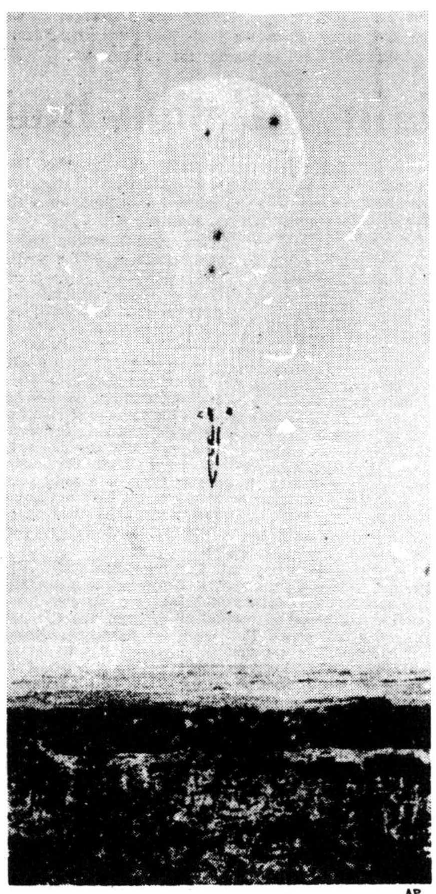

AP

Downward goes Evel Knievel into Snake River Canyon.

Knievel lives but stunt fails

By MICHAEL K. BURNS
Sun Staff Correspondent

Twin Falls, Idaho—The gaping jaws of the Snake River Canyon swallowed Evel Knievel yesterday afternoon when his steam rocket's parachute fired prematurely, but the Montana daredevil escaped unscathed and told a colleague he wants to try it again.

The aluminum-skinned craft fell short of the projected landing site on the far north rim of the 1,700-foot-wide canyon, spinning twice in the air before floating down, bouncing off one ledge and lodging about 20 feet from the water's edge.

Perils of river

The 34-year-old motorcycle stuntman, making his first flight in the 1,000-pound missile, was immediately plucked from the wrecked machine. He rode to the rescue helicopter aboard a red motor raft

Mr. Knievel emerged with cuts under his right eye and the bridge of his nose and cuts on his knees. But he waved jauntily to the crowd and talked with David Frost, the closed-circuit television interviewer, as he lighted on ground and walked to the trailer where his wife and three children were watching the ballyhooed launch.

"If I had gone into the river, I never would have made it. Never," he told the audience. But the rescue team of two

See KNIEVEL, A6, Col. 1

TerHorst, protesting pardon, quits Ford staff

Washington Bureau of The Sun

Washington —Jerald F. terHorst, President Ford's press secretary, quit yesterday in protest against the pardon to former President Nixon.

In a brief statement read to a reporter by his wife, he said he was not critical of President Ford's motives. "The President acted in good conscience, and I also found it necessary to resign in good conscience," he said in the statement.

President Ford, in a statement issued late last night, said he "deeply" regretted his aide's resignation. "I understand his position. I appreciate the fact that good people will differ with me on this very difficult decision," the President said.

Mr. Ford continued, "However, it is my judgment that it is in the best interests of our country."

A member of his press office staff said Mr. terHorst had

See terHORST, A7, Col. 1

Reaction, analysis, texts

The Weather
Mostly sunny today, high near 70. Partly cloudy tonight, lows 52 to 57. Yesterday's high, 68; low, 50.
(Details and Map, Page C2)

THE SUN

FINAL

Vol. 277—No. 104—F BALTIMORE, MONDAY, SEPTEMBER 15, 1975 32 Pages •• 15 Cents

Pope canonizes Mother Seton as first American-born saint

By GILBERT A. LEWTHWAITE
Sun Staff Correspondent

Rome—Elizabeth Ann Bayley Seton was declared a saint yesterday by Pope Paul VI, who hailed her as "the first daughter of the United States of America to be glorified with this incomparable attribute."

More than 100,000 Catholics—about 20,000 from the U.S.—attended the open-air canonization in St. Peters Square of the New York-born former Protestant who founded the nation's first Catholic women's religious order and its parochial school system in Baltimore and Emmitsburg, Md., in the last century.

The Pope called her "a true daughter of the New World." Pope Paul was applauded repeatedly as he said:

"Saint Elizabeth Ann Seton is an American. All of us say this with spiritual joy, with the intention of honoring the land and the nation from which she marvelously sprang forth as the first flower in the calendar of the saints.

"Rejoice we say to the great nation of the United States of America. Rejoice for your glorious daughter . . . . This most beautiful figure of a holy woman presents to the world and to history the affirmation of new and authentic riches that are yours: that religious spirituality which your temporal prosperity seemed to obscure . . . . May you always be able to cultivate the genuine fruitfulness of evangelical holiness, and ever experience how—far from stunting the flourishing development of your economic, cultural and civic vitality—it will be in its own way the unfailing safeguard of that vitality."

For the thousands of Americans, including about 500 from the Baltimore Archdiocese, in the square it was a moment of pride and emotion, the end of a 93-year effort to have Mother Seton's sanctity recognized. Her feast day will be January 4.

From the early morning they had assembled in the famed square, patiently watching the gray first light turn into the full-color spectrum of the midmorning sun.

Even before the solemn two-hour ceremony started at 9.30 A.M. Rome time (3.30 A.M. Baltimore time) the heat was shimmering over their heads. The altar in front of the basilica was still being garlanded with pink and white dahlias, matching the floral frame round the tapestry-edged painting of the new saint floating above the globe, which hung over the main door and dominated the scene.

The light walls of the great church formed classic background for the splash of cardinal red and the flood of bishop purple which spilled onto the gray-tiled terrace as the clergy assembled. The diplomatic corps to the Vatican, all courteous bows, practiced hands and flashing teeth, weaved their own color pattern into the pageant. The men, mostly were in black-and-white morning attire, sparkling with silk sashes and silver and golden medals, the women in monotone black veils and dresses like so many morning Spaniards.

The U.S. was represented by its ambassadors to the Vatican, Italy and Hungary.

Around the altar, assistants scurried to prepare for the grand ceremony, placing books, candles and incense burners, so that the complex ritual of homage, offerings, prayers, infallible declaration and mass would proceed without a hitch.

Swiss Guards, traditional protectors of the popes, took up their positions, white-gloved hands grasping the staves of their burnished pikes, their medieval maroon, gold and blue-banded uniforms postively kaleidoscopic compared to the somber suits of the more effective security guards lurking around.

Onto the scene came the 125 priests who were to serve the thousands in the square below with Holy Communion, and in the meantime formed a black and white frieze around the altar area.

Next, the entry of the four U.S. admirals and other officers, whose presence with J. William Middendorf, the secretary of the Navy, testified to the naval service of St. Elizabeth Ann's two sons.

And, suddenly, the music. The sounds of organ and choirs boomed out of amplifiers, bounced off the marble floor up to the flat blue sky and back again to linger, loud and long, echoing through the tall galleries edging the square. A broadcast invitation to join in the singing of "All People Who on Earth" brought a hurried rustle, quickly drowned by the forceful singing of the choir which in turn drew a hesitant response from the crowd.

A trumpet fanfare heralded the arrival of Pope Paul behind a procession of the eight cardinals and bishops assisting him in the ceremony. The concelebrants included Lawrence Cardinal She-

See SETON, A5, Col. 1

UPI
Pope Paul VI is flanked by two priests during canonization ceremony for Mother Seton

Lisbon moderates unite on program

From Wire Services

Lisbon — Portugal's moderate political parties and soldiers yesterday seemed to have succeeded in drafting a political program that appeared aimed at reversing the trend toward Communist domination of the country.

The program, outlined in a speech to the nation Saturday night by the premier-designate, Adm. Jose Pinheiro de Azevedo, calls for law and order, cementing ties with Western Europe and restoring the nation's economy.

The speech contained little to satisfy the Communists, who will participate in the sixth provisional government since last year's revolution along with Socialists, center-left Popular Democrats and officers representing diverse political currents in the Armed Forces Movement.

The new government, to be announced in the next few days, is counting on strong military backing. Admiral Azevedo said in the speech that he had obtained the "total support" of the Supreme Council of the Revolution, the 30-member ruling group of the Armed Forces Movement.

The Socialists and Popular Democrats are expected to dominate the Cabinet. The Communists are assuming the ambiguous position of allowing party members to participate without officially representing the party.

A further indication of military support came with the confirmation of the appointment of Maj. Ernesto Melo Antunes as foreign minister, a post he held before the government crisis occurred in July. The confirmation meant that a group of nine officers whom he had led against the ousted premier, Vasco Goncalves, and his Communist backers were with the new government and had obtained guarantees that would assure their predominance over the pro-Communist forces in the military.

The guarantees were understood to have been made final Saturday at a meeting of high officers including Gen. Carlos Fabiao, the Army chief of staff, and Gen. Otelo Saraiva de Carvalho, chief of military security forces, who will be mainly responsible for public order and for executing government decisions requiring force.

The ouster of Brig. Gen. Eurico Corvacho, a Goncalves backer, from the Northern Military Command in Porto was be-

See PORTUGAL, A2, Col. 3

Ethiopians seek raider hide-out

Addis Ababa, Ethiopia (AP)—Government security forces searched Eritrea province yesterday for two Americans and six Ethiopians abducted by raiders who attacked a United States Navy satellite tracking station of the Kagnew communications facility near Asmara.

The military government said 9 civilians were killed and 23 injured in Saturday's raid, believed to have been carried out by rebels seeking independence for the northern province.

The missing Americans were identified by the Pentagon in Washington as Navy Electronics Tech. 3 Thomas C. Bowidowicz, of Jersey City, N.J., and Army Spec. 5 David Strickland, of Orlando, Fla.

The statement by the Ethiopian information ministry did not further identify those who had been killed, but informed sources said the term civilians could be taken to include rebels.

Brig. Gen. Teferi Bante, chairman of the provisional military government in Addis Ababa, told reporters that security forces were trying to locate the area where the eight were being held. He said the situation required "utmost caution" and that U.S. officials were being kept informed.

Two American civilians were kidnaped from Kagnew in

See ETHIOPIA, A2, Col.7

First class plan

Washington (AP)—The Postal Service announced yesterday that its plan to upgrade first-class mail service, eliminating the need to buy domestic airmail stamps, will go into effect October 11.

The cost of mailing a first-class letter weighing less than an ounce now is 10 cents, with each additional ounce costing 9 cents. Airmail stamps are 13 cents.

The Postal Service is expected to begin action this week that will increase the cost of mailing a first-class letter to 13 cents after Christmas.

Under changes in operating and dispatch procedures, the Postal Service said it will be able to program more than 90 per cent of all first-class mail for either next-day or second-day delivery.

27,000 crowd into Emmitsburg to pay tribute to St. Elizabeth Ann

By ANTERO PIETILA
Sun Staff Correspondent

Emmitsburg—They expected crowds in this Western Maryland town where Elizabeth Ann Seton did much of her religious work and died, but nothing like the estimated 27,000 people who trekked here yesterday to celebrate her elevation to the sainthood.

By 8.20 A.M.—40 minutes before the starting time of the first of six masses honoring her—the 800-seat Seton Shrine was filled and those in the overflow crowd who were clothed warmly enough attended a field mass in the chilly morning air. The field masses continued throughout the day.

After the 11 A.M. mass, it became evident that the 15,000 hosts the Sisters of Charity had reserved for the day's eucharistic celebrations would be running out.

Sister Anna Mae Schaben said she called about 15 parishes from Washington and Baltimore to nearby Taneytown and Hanover, Pa., to secure additional wafers because "people are coming from such distances counting on receiving the Eucharist."

And from distances they came: There were pilgrims from as far away in the United States as the state of Washington.

And when Jose Isada, who is on a two-week visit to the United States from the Philippines, heard about the canonization, he, too, wanted to come.

He drove up from the Virginia suburbs of Washington with his host, Alfredo Manuel, a young civil engineer.

A group of Vietnamese refugees also came, as did many many Spanish- and Italian-speaking pilgrims, who heard homilists pray, "Mother Seton, Saint of God, help us!"

Between 3,500 and 7,000 persons have been elevated into sainthood in the history of the Catholic church—nobody even in the Vatican seems to be sure—but only 199 are in the official Vatican Calendar.

When the canonization of Mother Seton was initially announced last year after a 93-year process that cost $1 million, according to one estimate, many liberal Catholics tended to belittle it as an unnecessary anachronism.

But if there were nonbelievers yesterday in Emmitsburg, they kept their doubts to themselves as they waited up to two hours to be admitted to a mass inside the shrine or 50 minutes even to the gift shop, where commemorative gold-on-sterling coins could be bought at $30, silver at $17 and bronze at $5.

There were varieties of medals and bumper stickers with Saint Elizabeth Ann's picture also available.

Each of yesterday's six masses was a "carillon" mass by Robert Grogan, of the Washington's National Shrine of the Immaculate Conception. The music for the high masses was based on bell-figurations and motifs.

The main celebrants were the Most Rev. Joseph H. Hodges, bishop of Wheeling and Charleston, W. Va.; the Most Rev. Michael J. Begley, bishop of Charlotte, N.C.; the Most

See MASS, A5, Col. 4

3 Sect.

Moscow cancels Egyptians' training

By CHARLES W. CORDDRY
Washington Bureau of The Sun

Washington — Moscow has canceled military training courses for Egyptian students in the Soviet Union, and Cairo apparently intends to oust both Russian and Czechoslovakian instructors from Egypt's technical military academy, intelligence sources said here.

These developments were cited as some of the latest examples of the deterioration in Soviet-Egyptian relations, which accelerated in the wake of the new Sinai disengagement accord between Egypt and Israel. Moscow has kept up a steady drumfire of attack on the agreement, receiving vitriolic responses from President Anwar Sadat of Egypt.

There has even been some suggestion in the war of nerves with Mr. Sadat, the sources here said, that Moscow might encourage reconstitution of the Egyptian Communist party, which was disbanded 10 years ago. Cairo was reported unconcerned on this score.

The Russians have been especially irritated, it was said, by Cairo's requesting the United States Navy to clear mines from the Port Said area—an operation now in progress—claiming this violated an agreement not to let Soviet-supplied equipment fall into another country's hands.

Only small numbers are involved in both the cancellation of training in the Soviet Union and the expected ouster of instructors from Egypt, the intelligence sources said. The significance is almost wholly political, attesting to the worsening Egyptian-Soviet relations.

There were said to be 25 Soviet and Czechoslovakian instructors at the Egyptian academy—about half the number there a year ago—and they were expected to be gone by the

See EGYPT, A2, Col. 3

New strife in Lebanon kills six

Beirut, Lebanon (AP) - Sectarian warfare betwee Muslims and Christians sprea to the streets of the Beirut sul urbs yesterday, and police re ported 6 persons killed an more than 25 wounded in fierc mortar and machine-gun ba tles.

Residents said six corpse were found in alleys after figh ing in the eastern suburbs (Sinnel Fil, Nabaa and Bo Hammoud. Witnesses said Pa estinian guerrillas were shoo ing against Christian militi men of the Lebanese Phalang party.

Reports from northern L banon said Tripoli and neart Akkar were quiet but still e plosive after two weeks of wa between private militias th has killed at least 130 persons.

Most of the sectarian figh ing has been between left-wir Lebanese Muslems and righ wing Lebanese Christians ove longtime political and econon ic differences, fueled by th presence in Lebanon of 250,0(Palestinian refugees. Th Christians generally oppose th activities of the 12,000 guerri las among the Palestinians.

Security forces tried to i tervene in yesterday's fightin but it raged on unabated in th three suburbs. Sporadic gunfir and explosions also rocked fou other suburbs.

The Dowreh road, Beirut sole link with the mountain re sort area, was blocked by gu men. Vacationers were trappe in the area, and private ca were turned back to Beirut b security men.

Informed sources said th Phalangists abducted five gue rillas and the Palestinians re acted by kidnaping five Phal angists.

Police reported that the pa pal nuncio in Lebanon, Alfred Bruneira, escaped injury Satur day night after his car came un der heavy machine-gun fire a it passed through the suburb o Hazmiyeh.

Other scattered incidents in cluded the blowing up of a sho in the Christian suburb of Ash rafiyeh, the shelling of cars a Hadath, the kidnaping of 1 persons at Karantina and Mas lakh, and the setting up of road blocks along the seaside road.

Security and Palestinian of-

See LEBANON, A2, Col. 5

Lebanon fighting based on class, not religion

By MICHAEL PARKS
Sun Staff Correspondent

Beirut, Lebanon—Recurrent fighting in Lebanon, where more than 2,600 persons have been killed this year, has called the country's political structure and future into serious question.

Each bloody clash brings the country closer to another civil war, most Lebanese believe, and this in turn increases the possibility of an even larger conflict involving Israel, the Palestinian commandos and other Arabs.

"The next Middle East war could start in southern Lebanon more easily than in the Sinai Desert or even on the Golan Heights," a senior official said. "And it would start over a traffic accident or a fight over a girl."

Most clashes this year have been sparked by such minor incidents—an auto accident in the northern port city of Tripoli, a brawl over a pinball machine, the molestation of a girl—but fighting has spread quickly and widely as Lebanese factions vented political and economic frustrations.

The pessimism here reflects the realization that basic problems, themselves disputed, are not being dealt with. The gap between rich and poor is widening, the presence of 300,000 Palestinian refugees here is a growing burden and the political structure remains frozen as it was in 1943.

"There is no consensus on what the problems are, how they should be resolved nor on a new political system that would make compromises easier," a Chamber of Deputies member, a leading Muslim moderate, commented last week.

"And now it takes less and less to set off the fighting and more and more to stop it. We are rapidly losing our political equilibrium with no solution—just temporary reprieves, cease-fires—in sight."

Leftists here, in fact, see the past political equilibrium as the principal problem and they are

See BEIRUT, A2, Col. 4

Priceless Rembrandt slashed

Amsterdam (AP)—Rembrandt's priceless Seventeenth Century masterpiece "The Night Watch" was slashed and disfigured yesterday by a man with a serrated bread knife, who fought off a museum guard and told bystanders that he "did it for the Lord."

Officials said the man arrived just after the afternoon opening of the Rijksmuseum, went directly to the spacious chamber where "The Night Watch" hangs, and began slashing at the lower center section of the 14-by-11-foot painting. It was the second knife attack on the painting in this century.

A guard grabbed the man's arm, but the heavily built attacker held him off and moved across the masterpiece to the right, slashing with the knife. He hit in more than a dozen places, leaving a section some 7 feet wide severely defaced. Knife marks were more than 2 feet long. In the center section, a piece of canvas measuring about 12 inches by 2½ inches was ripped off.

Dr. P. J. Van Thiel, the museum's acting director, said the damage was not irreparable but would take four months or longer to repair.

The attacker, who eventual-

See PAINTING, A6 Col. 1

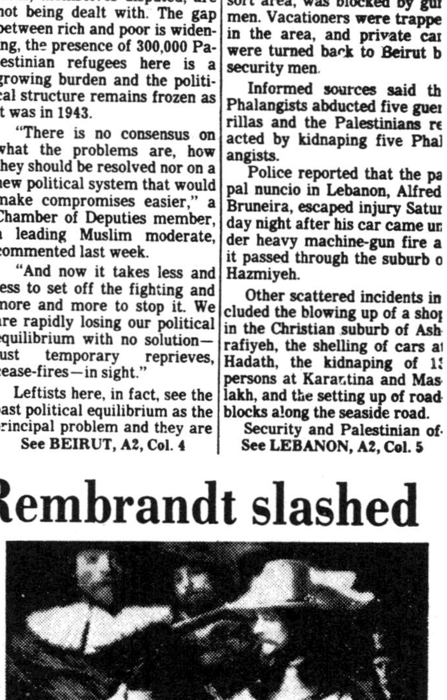

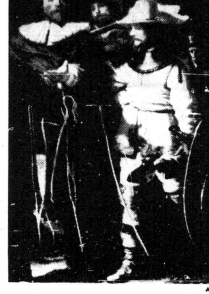

AP
Slashes and a 12-inch triangular strip cut from the canvas disfigure lower part of Rembrandt's "The Night Watch."

Birds top Tigers to stay within 4

Don Baylor drove in 3 runs with a single and a homer and Elrod Hendricks hit a 2-run homer as the Orioles powered their way past the Tigers, 9 to 3, in Detroit yesterday. The win kept Baltimore four games behind Boston as the Red Sox overcame an early 5-1 deficit to defeat visiting Milwaukee, 8 to 6.

Details on Page C3

Critical week for Mrs. Gandhi

By ADAM CLYMER
Sun Staff Correspondent

New Delhi — Sometime this week the Supreme Court of India will have heard all it wants to hear about whether Prime Minister Indira Gandhi can hold onto office with a constitutional amendment taking her election case out of the courts.

Two years ago, the court decided it had the power to declare constitutional amendments unconstitutional if they change the "basic structure or framework of the constitution."

For the last three weeks, the court has been listening to lawyers argue about an amendment Mrs. Gandhi rushed through Parliament in August—excluding the courts from applying the ordinary election laws to prime ministers and three other officeholders, and voiding pending court challenges against her.

One side contends that the amendment offends the constitution's "basic structure." The other maintains it is a relatively minor bit of tinkering with the constitution, though necessary.

If Mrs. Gandhi wins, the last immediate threat to her continuance in office will be removed. Her sentence of having to give up office for six years, along with the June 12 corrupt practice conviction that led to the sentence, will be erased.

There is widespread expectation that the state of emergency declared when her foes sought to capitalize on that ruling and drive her from office—a decree that has imprisoned or silenced all significant opposition—will be relaxed if she wins.

But if she loses, she will have lost only one round, although the Supreme Court will be in the difficult tactical position of having moved against her, if only tentatively.

The court would still have to consider the legitimacy of an election law change, another August measure, that retroactively declared legal the kinds of government aid the judge had convicted her of using illegally. And if she were to lose on that score, too, the court would consider her appeal against the conviction on its merits (along with a cross-appeal complaining that she had been wrongly acquitted on other counts).

But for now, the Supreme Court is concerned only with the constitutional amendment, the 39th in India's 25-year constitutional history.

When is a constitutional amendment unconstitutional in

See COURT, A2, Col.3

The Weather
Mostly cloudy today, high 48. Partly cloudy tonight, lows 29 to 35. Yesterday's high, 46, low, 37.
(Details and Map, Page C2)

THE SUN

FINAL

Vol. 278—No. 8—F BALTIMORE, TUESDAY, NOVEMBER 25, 1975 • 15 Cents

Governor Mandel indicted

Hess, Kovens, 2 Rodgerses, Cory cited

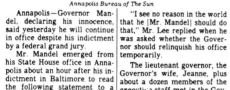

Governor says he is innocent, will not resign

By ANTHONY BARBIERI, JR.
Annapolis Bureau of The Sun

Annapolis—Governor Mandel, declaring his innocence, said yesterday he will continue in office despite his indictment by a federal grand jury.

Mr. Mandel emerged from his State House office in Annapolis about an hour after his indictment in Baltimore to read the following statement to a horde of reporters and cameramen:

"I regret, of course, that the United States attorney has brought charges against me.

"The culmination of the lengthy investigation with a formal indictment does, however, have a positive effect. I now have the opportunity to prove my innocence in a court of law, which I intend to pursue with every resource I have and to the fullest extent allowed. I will ask my attorney to request a prompt trial.

"The months ahead will be difficult for my family and me, as well as for the citizens of Maryland. Let me assure those who elected me that I shall continue to serve them to the best of my ability and always in their best interest, just as I have for the past 2½ years.

"Now more than ever I need your wisdom and understanding of the fundamental American precept that a person is innocent unless proven guilty—and that will not happen."

Under Maryland law, Mr. Mandel is under no legal obligation either to resign, step aside, or in any way curtail his activities.

He can under the Constitution, however, voluntarily declare that he is "temporarily unable to perform the duties of his office" and appoint Lt. Gov. Blair Lee 3d acting governor in his place.

But both the Governor, Mr. Lee and Mr. Mandel's closest aides and advisers said yesterday that this would not be done, although it is expected that Mr. Lee will assume more of the burden of government as Mr. Mandel prepares his defense.

"I see no reason in the world that he [Mr. Mandel] should do that," Mr. Lee replied when he was asked whether the Governor should relinquish his office temporarily.

The lieutenant governor, the Governor's wife, Jeanne, plus about a dozen members of the executive staff met in the Governor's office for about an hour before they came out, en masse, to watch Mr. Mandel read his statement.

"My God, there won't be room enough for me to read my statement," Mr. Mandel quipped when he saw approximately 50 reporters waiting in the ornate reception room to his office.

The Governor, dressed in a conservative gray plaid suit, blue shirt and striped tie, appeared calm and composed.

After reading his statement, he and his aides returned to his inner office to await further details of the indictment.

"The prevailing mood in there was one of relief," said Mr. Lee. "Everyone was afraid there would be things in the indictment no one knew about."

Another source who spoke with the Governor soon after the indictment was handed down said Mr. Mandel "certainly wasn't cowed or intimidated by the indictment; he said he was confident and ready to take 'em on."

Mr. Mandel's lawyer, Arnold M. Weiner, called Mr. Mandel shortly after he himself was notified that his client had been indicted.

Before receiving his call from Mr. Weiner, the Governor strolled to a restaurant near the State House—Auberge de France—for a leisurely lunch with his wife. Though he was pursued by a pack of photographers and reporters both to and from the restaurant, he made no comment.

Mrs. Mandel said, "You

See MANDEL, A13, Col. 6

AP

Governor Mandel makes a brief statement after being indicted on 22 counts of a "corrupt relationship" with five others who also were indicted. Frank A. DeFilippo (right), the top Mandel aide, listens to his remarks.

Legislators back his decision

Colleagues say Mandel should stay

Save a few lonely Republicans and Democratic mavericks, leaders of the General Assembly and other top state officials appeared yesterday to support Governor Mandel in his decision to stay in office while he fights the charges against him.

"Assuming he continues to perform his duties effectively, I think he should remain in office," Steny H. Hoyer (D., Prince Georges), the president of the Senate, said.

"No, certainly not. There's no reason for him to [temporarily step aside]," said Lt. Gov. Blair Lee 3d, who would become acting governor should Mr. Mandel decide to take a leave.

One of the Governor's most vocal Democratic critics took the opposite view, however. Senator Julian L. Lapides (D., 39th, Baltimore) said, "I do not see how he can continue to govern. I hope he would at least take a leave of absence until this is over."

The maverick Bolton Hill Democrat continued, "Regardless of what the Governor says, he's going to be preoccupied with the trial and the pre-trial activity and I just don't see how he'll be able to address the serious problems of the state, particularly with a legislative session coming up in January."

But another of Mr. Mandel's most bitter critics, Senator John J. Bishop, Jr. (R., 11th, Baltimore county), passed up the opportunity to call on Mr. Mandel to step aside.

"I don't want to tell him what to do," Mr. Bishop said. He did, however, say that he thought the Governor should to "some very serious thinking" to determine if he will be able to devote the necessary time to his duties while he is under indictment.

The leader of the Republicans' tiny eight-member minority in the state Senate did call on Mr. Mandel to step down temporarily, however.

"He should not resign yet—a resignation is not in order," said Senator Edward J. Mason (R., Western Maryland). "But he should step aside and let the lieutenant governor take over until this matter is cleared up."

The indictment had been long expected by almost everyone in Annapolis, including the Governor and members of his staff. Only Mr. Mandel's closest ally in the Legislature, the Senate majority leader, Roy N. Staten (D., 8th, Baltimore county) said he was "suprised" by the charges.

Nevertheless, Mr. Mandel's indictment comes at a critical time for both the Legislature and the state Democratic party.

Most legislators interviewed said they felt Mr. Mandel would be unlikely to strike out in any bold new governmental initiative until the charges against him were cleared up.

"He'll probably stick to the motherhood issues," said Delegate John S. Arnick (D., 8th, Baltimore county), the majority leader of the House of Delegates.

"I doubt he's going to do anything very controversial or exciting," Delegate Benjamin L. Cardin (D., 42d, Baltimore),

See REACTION, A13, Col. 7

6 are charged with 'corrupt relationship'

By ROBERT A. ERLANDSON and THEODORE W. HENDRICKS

A special federal grand jury yesterday indicted Governor Mandel and five of his close associates on 24 mail-fraud and racketeering counts, charging a "corrupt relationship" in which the Governor used his official position to fraudulently and secretly participate in and enhance his friends' business interests.

Mr. Mandel, 55, was charged with engaging in a "pattern of racketeering activity"—mail fraud and bribery. The indictment includes 20 counts of mail fraud and 2 counts of prohibited activities under anti-racketeering laws.

Those indicted with Governor Mandel in the latest 18-month phase of a nearly 3-year investigation of Maryland political corruption, were:

• Harry W. Rodgers 3d, 48, a founder of Tidewater Insurance Associates, Inc., an insurance firm that has expanded and diversified its activities since Mr. Mandel became Governor in January, 1969. He was charged with 20 counts of mail fraud and 2 counts of illegal activity under the anti-racketeering statute.

• William A. Rodgers, 49, also a Tidewater executive, who, like his brother, Harry, faces 20 counts of mail fraud and 2 counts of prohibited activity.

• W. Dale Hess, 45, a former Harford county legislator, real-estate developer and Tidewater executive, who faces 20 mail-fraud charges and 2 counts of prohibited activities. Mr. Hess and the Rodgers brothers have been among Governor Mandel's leading political fund-raisers and personal friends.

• Irvin Kovens, 57, the millionaire Baltimore businessman who is considered the Governor's political mentor. He was charged with 20 counts of mail fraud and a single count of prohibited activity. Mr. Kovens was formerly the owner of the Charles Town (W. Va.) Race Track, and is accused of having a secret interest in the Marlboro Race Track in Maryland after selling Charles Town and agreeing not to participate in a competing track for five years.

• Ernest N. Cory, Jr., 61, a Laurel lawyer, who was charged with 20 mail-fraud counts and 1 charge of prohibited activity under the anti-racketeering laws. Mr. Cory was involved in the Marlboro Race Track and according to this year's state racetrack audit, said he purchased the interests of Mr. Hess and the Rodgers brothers in 1973.

There was almost dead silence in the vast courtroom as Judge Alexander Harvey 2d accepted the indictments from the grand jury at 3.33 P.M. After announcing there were 24 counts, he read the six defendants' names, but set no date to arraign the men.

On conviction, the racketeering counts each carry a maximum penalty of 20 years in prison and $25,000 fine, while each mail-fraud count carries a maximum of 5 years in prison and $1,000 fine.

According to the Library of Congress, Mr. Mandel is the third sitting governor known to have been indicted. In 1924, Indiana Gov. Warren T. McCray resigned the day after his conviction on federal mail-fraud charges and then began a 10-year sentence. In 1934, Gov. William Langer of North Dakota was convicted of extorting political contributions. He remained in office after conviction, but was defeated for re-election that year.

The Justice Department said yesterday that Governor Mandel is the 20th present or former elected official to be indicted in federal courts this year, including David Hall, who had just stepped down as governor of Oklahoma, and who was charged with bribery, extortion and conspiracy.

According to the prosecutors, the central allegation of yesterday's indictment is that from the time Mr. Mandel became Governor, January 7, 1969, he and his associates:

"Devised and executed a scheme to defraud the executive agencies, legislators and citizens of Maryland through Mr. Mandel's efforts on behalf of legislation and other governmental actions favorable to the secret ownership interests held by the other defendants in a Maryland racetrack [Marlboro], in return for valuable secret financial interests in two Maryland enterprises which were transferred to Mr. Mandel by the others."

One of those enterprises, the prosecutors said, was a company that owns part of the complex of buildings leased to the federal Social Security Administration, in Woodlawn.

The other enterprise involves an Eastern Shore land deal at Ray's Point, in Talbot county, in which the Governor received a 15 per cent interest through his friends. The government alleged in the indictment that it was in exchange for the Governor's help in obtaining

See INDICT, A13, Col. 1

Beirut fighting intensifies

Beirut, Lebanon (AP)—Muslim-Christian warfare intensified yesterday, leaving at least 91 persons killed and 188 wounded in the past 72 hours. Snipers again took up positions in the Mour Tower, Beirut's tallest building, putting all the luxury hotels in their gun sights.

Angry politicians walked out of a meeting of Lebanon's National Reconciliation Committee when President Suleiman Franjieh and the interior minister, Camille Chamoun, failed to show up. Mortars thudded nearby.

A weary Premier Rashid Karami said he had done what he could but "one hand cannot clap alone." He hinted he might resign unless the private armies of Christians and Muslims end their eight-month-old civil war.

Muslims aided by Palestinian guerrillas are demanding reform of the political system that concentrates power in the hands of the 40 per cent Christian minority. Christians insist reforms can only come when state authority is imposed over the Palestinian refugee camps.

A small strike force of Lebanese security men and Army troops has given up attempts to

See LEBANON, A2, Col. 4

Index

UPI

New Yorkers gather in Times Square to support aid to city. Rally attracted 10,000 people.

Carey, legislators in accord on new taxes to aid New York

Albany (AP)—Gov. Hugh L. Carey and legislative leaders reached what the Governor called a "broad understanding" last night on new taxes for New York city to stave off default.

The agreement, which was understood to have centered on minor technical changes in revenue legislation, came as Mr. Carey sought to pressure legislators into quick action on the proposed $200 million in tax increases.

"We're aboard," Warren Anderson, the Republican majority leader in the state Senate, yelled to Mr. Carey after attending the lengthy meeting with the Democratic Governor.

Mr. Carey said the leaders would explain the new agreement to their party members this morning.

Mr. Carey would not provide details about the changes in the tax package but indicated they were not significant. He said a demand for minority representation on the state's Emergency Financial Control Board had

See NEW YORK, A7, Col. 1

Complete text of indictments

The following is the text of the federal indictments handed up by the special grand jury yesterday against Governor Mandel, Harry W. Rodgers 3d, William A. Rodgers, Irvin Kovens, W. Dale Hess and Ernest N. Cory, Jr.:

The Special Grand Jury (June 1974 Term) for the District of Maryland charges:

1. Beginning on January 7, 1969, and at all times material herein MARVIN MANDEL, a defendant herein, was the Governor of the State of Maryland.

2. At all times material herein W. DALE HESS, a defendant herein, was a resident of the State of Maryland engaged in various business enterprises in the State of Maryland and elsewhere.

3. At all times material herein HARRY W. RODGERS 3d, a defendant herein, was a resident of the State of Maryland engaged in various business enterprises in the State of Maryland and elsewhere.

4. At all times material herein WILLIAM A. RODGERS, a defendant herein, was a resident of the State of Maryland engaged in various business enterprises in the State of Maryland and elsewhere.

5. At all times material herein IRVIN KOVENS, a defendant herein, was a resident of the State of Maryland engaged in various business enterprises in the State of Maryland and elsewhere.

6. At all times material herein ERNEST N. CORY, JR., a defendant herein, was a resident of the State of Maryland engaged in the practice of law in the State of Maryland and elsewhere with his principal law office located in Laurel, Maryland.

7. At all times material herein, Marlboro Associates was a partnership created and used for the purpose of holding financial interests in the Marlboro Race Track and, later, the Bowie Race Track. The partners of Marlboro Associates at various times included among others the defendants W. DALE HESS, HARRY RODGERS 3d, WILLIAM A. RODGERS, and ERNEST N. CORY, JR. The defendant IRVIN KOVENS held through a nominee a substantial undisclosed financial interest in Marlboro Associates.

8. At times material herein the Marlboro Race Track was a half-mile race track located in Prince Georges County, Maryland and was engaged in the business of conducting thoroughbred horse racing.

9. At all times material herein the Bowie Race Track was a one-mile race track located in Prince Georges County, Maryland and was engaged in the business of conducting thoroughbred horse racing.

10. At all times material herein Security Investment Company was a partnership doing business in the State of Maryland and elsewhere. Its principal assets were of substantial value and consisted of

See TEXT, A11, Col. 1

Other probe articles

The Weather
Sunny and warmer today, fair tonight. High, 72; low, 46. Yesterday's high, 67; low, 40.
(Details and Map, Page C2)

THE SUN

FINAL

Vol. 278—No. 128— F

BALTIMORE, WEDNESDAY, APRIL 14, 1976

15 Cents

Councilman Leone shot to death, 4 wounded when gunman demands to see Mayor, holds City Hall in terror; Schaefer escapes harm

U.S. swears jury to probe city contract awards

By THEODORE W. HENDRICKS

A special United States grand jury was sworn in yesterday to probe Baltimore city contract awards in a continuation of the investigation into Maryland political corruption that has resulted in the downfall of former Vice President Spiro T. Agnew, the conviction of two county executives and the indictment of Governor Mandel and five associates. Federal prosecutors have subpoenaed Hyman A. Pressman, the city comptroller and secretary to the Board of Estimates, to appear before the next meeting of the 23-member grand jury Monday.

Mr. Pressman was ordered to bring with him the minutes of Board of Estimates meetings for 1972 to 1976.

The minutes will show the names of firms and amounts of contracts awarded to them during the administration of Mayor Schaefer, who controls the five-man board.

Although city contract awards top $100 million in a single year, most of them are clearly documented awards based on competitive bidding, Richard A. Lidinsky, the deputy city comptroller, said yesterday.

Mr. Lidinsky and other city personnel were interviewed on the sidewalk yesterday after police cleared the temporary City Hall to search for a suspected accomplice in the shootings there.

Mr. Lidinsky said that so far no specific contracts awarded by the Board of Estimates have been sought by federal prosecutors. He added that the minutes are readily available in city reference rooms.

According to Mr. Pressman, the minutes "are the place to start" if a major investigation is under way into suspected political corruption.

Mr. Pressman spent more than an hour before the city grand jury last month to enlarge on his remarks made at a Board of Estimates meeting about the award of architectural and consulting contracts.

Consulting contract awards vary in amount from year to year, but have gone as high as $28 million in one year. Although they are non-bid contracts, Mayor Schaefer has maintained that he has strict procedures to insure the best firm is chosen.

Yesterday, Jervis S. Finney, the United States attorney, refused to comment on the areas of the investigation.

"We just cannot comment on

See JURY, A7, Col.1

Agreement on election law sealed

By STEPHEN E. NORDLINGER
Washington Bureau of The Sun

Washington—Senate and House conferees approved yesterday a compromise bill to reconstitute the Federal Election Commission and to make numerous changes in the controversial election law.

After almost two weeks of debate, the conference agreed on the final half-dozen major issues. But the action came too late to allow a resumption of federal subsidies for the financially hard-pressed presidential candidates and the national party conventions for several weeks.

The conferees scheduled a meeting April 27 after the Easter recess to clear the bill for floor action in the Senate and House.

Under the most optimistic timetable, this meant that the commission will not be restructured to be able to authorize the payments from a six-week backlog of campaign subsidies until early May after the major primaries in Pennsylvania and Texas.

A backlog of subsidies totaling $1.5 million has accumulated since the commission last approved payments March 22 before its authority was suspended.

The matching funds could be delayed longer if President Ford decides to veto the bill, which goes far beyond his request for a simple measure to reconstitute the commission to meet the Supreme Court ruling.

After the conference, Senator Hugh Scott (R., Pa.), the Senate minority leader and a conferee, said that the bill "is still subject to a considerable risk of a veto." But Representative Charles E. Wiggins (R.,

See ELECTION, A5, Col.1

IRS fines milk co-op $7.8 million in fraud

Washington (AP)—The Internal Revenue Service has revoked the tax-exempt status of the nation's largest milk producer co-operative and billed it for $7.8 million in taxes and fraud penalties, apparently primarily because of political campaign contributions.

The IRS action surfaced in documents filed in United States Tax Court last month by Associated Milk Producers, Inc., which came to light yesterday. The co-operative, based in San Antonio, Texas, has obtained a Tax Court hearing of its protests that the IRS action is unwarranted.

The action represents the latest in a series of legal problems for the milk producers group growing out of charges of antitrust violations and illegal campaign contributions.

The co-op's former top officials, Harold S. Nelson and David L. Paar, have received fines and prison sentences on illegal-contribution charges.

Jack L. Chestnut, a former campaign manager for Senator Hubert H. Humphrey (D., Minn.), has also received a fine and prison sentence on charges of accepting a $12,000 contribution for Mr. Humphrey in 1970.

The co-op has also been accused by the Justice Department of antitrust violations and has been fined in Texas for violation of state antitrust laws.

Although agricultural co-operatives are normally exempt from federal income taxes, the IRS reserves the right to revoke that exemption if a co-op engages in improper activities.

The tax agency did not spell out why the action was taken in notifying the milk group in February of the determination. But

See MILK, A7, Col.1

Article on Page C7

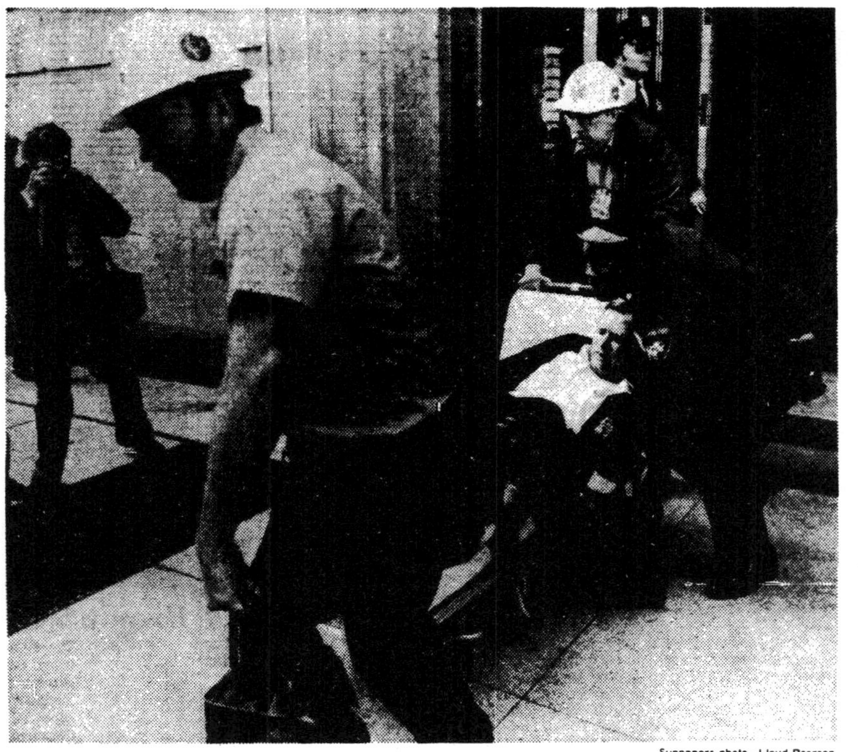

Sunpapers photo—Lloyd Pearson

Officer Thomas G. Gaither is wheeled away from the City Hall incident with a bullet wound in the lower left leg.

Vetoed public jobs voted anew

Washington (AP)—Ignoring warnings of a probable new veto, the Senate yesterday approved a $5.3 billion public works jobs bill to replace the one that President Ford rejected earlier this year.

The Senate approved the measure 54 to 28 and sent it to the House.

The action came after Senate Democrats succeeded, on a 48-to-32 vote, in boosting the price tag of the bill from the $2.5 billion scaled-down version sent to the floor.

This came despite warnings by Republican leaders that the bill is almost certain to be vetoed again.

President Ford vetoed the earlier, $6.1 billion measure February 13, calling it "little more than an election-year pork barrel."

The House voted 319 to 98 to override the veto, but the Senate failed to do so by 3 votes.

The Senate Public Works Committee sent to the floor the trimmed-down measure which its chairman, Jennings Randolph (D., W.Va.), said was designed to meet with Mr. Ford's approval.

But Senator Edmund S. Muskie (D., Maine) led the fight to add to the measure two expensive programs which had been in the vetoed bill but were deleted by the committee.

These included a $1.4 billion revenue-sharing program to assist state and local governments whose budgets have been badly eroded because of the recession and another $1.4 billion in new federal grants for waste treatment plants.

Mr. Muskie called it a "comprehensive package" which "represents the best opportunity we have to ease the pain of this recession."

Backers said the full $5.3 billion would only be spent if unemployment reached 9 per cent. At the current jobless level of about 7.5 per cent, they said, the amount actually to be spent would be about $3.9 billion.

This includes about $1 billion for new jobs on public

See JOBS, A8, Col.1

Index

Suspect's family tells of his anger, failures

By TRACIE ROZHON

The family of Charles A. Hopkins was huddled around the dining room table, trying to watch a television soap opera. There were brothers and sisters, nieces, nephews and cousins.

Some were polite to a reporter, but others were not.

"You come here asking all these questions," said a sister, "but you don't give us any answers."

"He was right," said another young woman. "It takes something like this to make white people move." She stormed out of the room and did not come back.

Charles Hopkins's mother sat quietly in the corner of the room, on a small hard wooden chair. A rotund woman, she wore her hair in a few tiny braids.

"Everywhere he went, they threw him away," she said slowly, sadly, almost in a daze. "He rented the restaurant, he invested a lot of money and then the landlord didn't do what he said, he didn't fix it up.

"Then he went downtown and took the flag down," she said.

On March 12, Mr. Hopkins, 34, was arrested when Stephen R. Tully, an assistant state's attorney for the city, saw him ripping the American flag from beside the Battle Monument. The lawyer rushed down and grabbed Mr. Hopkins, but not before he had crumpled the flag into a ball and set a match to it. Several holes were burnt in the flag.

Before he went to trial, Mr. Hopkins reportedly told court officers he had been frustrated because no one would listen to him at City Hall about a problem he was having with his restaurant's lease.

On April 1, he was fined $220 by Judge Robert R. Gerstung, who ordered him to fly an American flag in front of his restaurant, Flat's Carry-Out, in the 1800 block Rutland avenue.

According to Mr. Hopkins's mother, Judge Gerstung's order about the flag bothered him more than the money.

"They fined him . . . and they said he had to buy a flag," she said. "He said he definitely wasn't going to do it. It seemed like it was unfair, punishing him that way.

See HOPKINS, A6, Col.2

DOMINIC M. LEONE
. . . murdered councilman

CARROLL J. FITZGERALD
. . . wounded by gunman

Fitzgerald, Mayor's aide, policeman hit

By DONALD KIMELMAN

City Councilman Dominic M. Leone was shot to death and four other persons were wounded—three seriously—yesterday when a lone gunman invaded temporary City Hall with the stated intention of finding the Mayor.

For a terrifying 10 minutes the gunman took control of the sixth and seventh floors of the city's rented offices on South Calvert street, leaving a bloody trail behind him as he searched vainly for Mayor Schaefer, who was locked in his office eating lunch and was not harmed.

Councilman Carroll J. Fitzgerald, a Third district councilman; Kathleen E. Nolan, an aide to the Mayor; Officer Thomas G. Gaither, a city policeman, and the suspected gunman himself, Charles A. Hopkins, all lay wounded when the rampage ended in a shoot-out just outside the City Council president's office.

The drama was already over when thousands of curious onlookers and city workers began thronging outside the office buildings to watch the wounded being rushed into ambulances. Mounted police blocked off the intersection of Calvert and Redwood streets for several hours, and the crowd lingered on throughout the afternoon.

Mr. Hopkins, 34, of the 1700 block Chapel street, was identified as the owner of an East Baltimore carry-out restaurant. He was arrested March 12 for hauling down the American flag from the Battle Monument and setting it afire. He was listed in critical condition at University Hospital last night.

Mr. Fitzgerald, 41, was listed in "stable but serious condition" at Mercy Hospital following surgery for a bullet wound in the abdomen. Miss Nolan, 38, of the 6000 block Clearspring road, was also in "serious but stable condition" at Mercy after surgery for a chest wound. They were both described as "improving."

Officer Gaither, 27, a member of the Police Department's Tactical Section, was in fair condition at University Hospital with a leg wound.

Mr. Leone was pronounced dead at Mercy Hospital with a bullet wound in the chest at 1.38 P.M., less than an hour after he was shot.

Yesterday evening, Councilman J. Joseph Curran, Sr. (D., 3d), visiting the Fitzgerald family at Mercy Hospital, complained of chest pains and was admitted to the coronary intensive care unit, where he was listed in "serious but stable" condition, according to the night nursing supervisor.

Mr. Curran, 71, was in the Council offices when Mr. Leone was shot. He escaped harm when a shot was fired in his direction.

When Mr. Hopkins was tried April 1 for the flag-burning incident, court officials said that he told them he had been protesting the lack of a sympathetic ear at City Hall about problems with his restaurant lease.

At the District Court trial, Judge Robert L. Gerstung fined him $220 for malicious destruction and desecrating the flag—to be paid by July 4—and ordered him to fly the Stars and Stripes in front of his Rutland avenue carry-out for the next six months.

Dennis S. Hill, the Police Department spokesman, said suspects wounded in a crime generally are not charged until after they leave the hospital.

Hyman A. Pressman, the city comptroller, said yesterday that on Monday Mr. Hopkins "burst into" a budget meeting of the city Board of Estimates and City Council, shouting: "I've got a problem. I've got a problem. They're

See SHOOTING, A6, Col.1

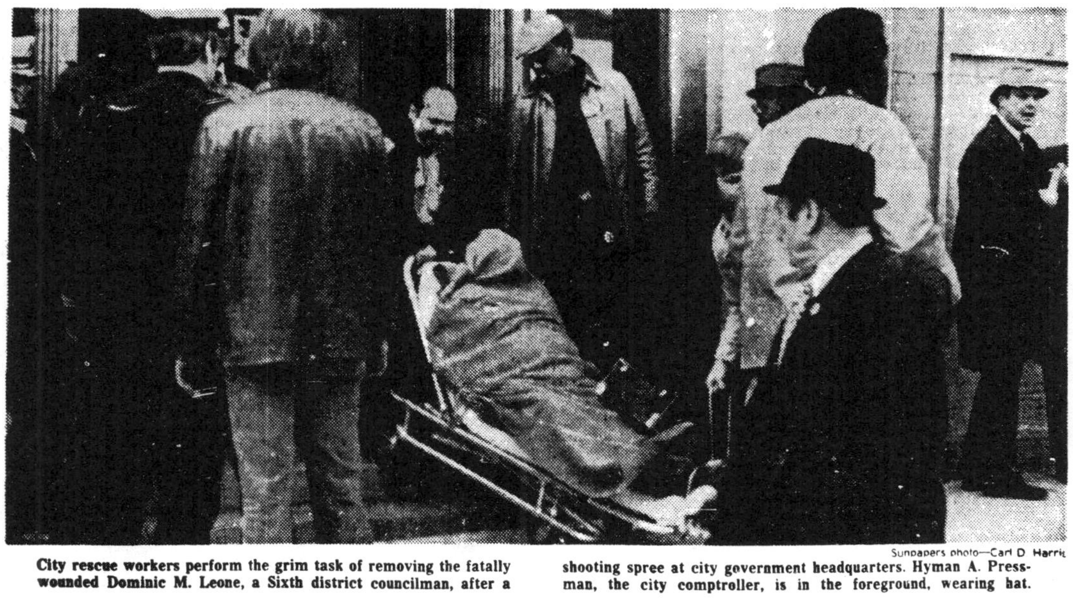

Sunpapers photo—Carl D. Harris

City rescue workers perform the grim task of removing the fatally wounded Dominic M. Leone, a Sixth district councilman, after a shooting spree at city government headquarters. Hyman A. Pressman, the city comptroller, is in the foreground, wearing hat.

The Weather
Sunny and hot today, fair and mild tonight. High, 90; low, 58. Yesterday's high, 90; low, 54
(Details and Map, Page B2)

THE SUN

FINAL

Vol. 278—No. 131— F

BALTIMORE, SATURDAY, APRIL 17, 1976

•• 15 Cents

City sniper kills officer, wounds 5 others

DR. KARAN SINGH
. . . explains India's stand

Birth curbs get India's priority

New Delhi (NYT)—The Indian government yesterday outlined a new birth control policy designed to give "top national priority" to slowing the rapid growth of India's population.

The long-awaited program, which included raising the minimum marriage age and paying more money to people who voluntarily have themselves sterilized, stopped short of nationwide compulsory sterilization, which has been intensely debated by Indians in recent months.

But the government made it clear that it had no objection to laws pending in several Indian states to compel the sterilization of people who already have two or three children.

"We are of the view that where a state legislature, in the exercise of its own powers, decides that the time is ripe and it is necessary to pass legislation for compulsory sterilization, it may do so," said Dr. Karan Singh, the minister for health and family planning.

Outlining the government's position in a major policy statement marked by an unusual sense of urgency, Dr. Karan Singh declared:

"We are facing a population explosion of crisis dimensions which has largely diluted the fruits of the remarkable eco-

See INDIA, A2, Col.7

Lebanon gets new proposal

Syria, Arafat hint of action if war goes on

From Wire Services

Beirut, Lebanon—Syria and the Palestinian guerrilla movement announced agreement yesterday on moves to end the Lebanese civil war and said they would take "a unified stand against any party that resumes military operations."

After a six-hour meeting in Damascus that ended early yesterday, the government of President Hafez el Assad and the Palestinian Liberation Organization, headed by Yasser Arafat, proclaimed a seven-point program that was also apparently aimed at ending their own differences.

Meanwhile, intense fighting in Lebanon claimed the highest daily death toll in the last three months of the Muslim-Christian civil war.

Police said 208 persons were killed and hundreds wounded.

"It is a mad day of killing," a security official who gave the death toll said. "People are falling, and doctors are unable to approach them because of heavy gunfire."

Yesterday's Syrian-Palestinian communique, which was in only the most general terms, made no mention of an estimated 2,000 to 4,000 Syrian and Syrian-controlled Palestinian troops that have recently entered Lebanon. Western diplomatic sources predicted that these forces would remain to guarantee against a major resumption of hostilities.

The communique left a number of questions unanswered, such as when a new cease-fire would officially go into effect. But it underlined the extent to which Lebanon's political destiny was in the hands of Syria and the Palestinians.

President Assad's govern-

See LEBANON, A2, Col.3

Sunpapers photo—Richard Childress

Police stand in the third-floor bedroom from which a sniper shot 7 persons, one officer fatally, on West Lombard street.

Youth seized after battle; civilian hurt

One policeman was killed and five other officers and a passer-by wounded last night during a fierce hour-long gun battle with a sniper who barricaded himself in a house in the 1300 block West Lombard street. A seventh officer was also injured, but not shot.

The fight in which dozens of shots were fired in sporadic bursts ended dramatically when an 18-year-old youth leaped through the front door, landing on his feet amid a shower of glass in front of the bullet-pocked brick row house. The youth tried to run, collapsed and was grabbed by his legs by police, then dragged face down across the broken glass with several policeman striking him with the butts of their rifles as they placed him in a paddy wagon.

OFFICER JAMES HALCOMB
. . . slain in shootout

The arrested youth was identified as John Earl Williams, Col. Simon Avera said. The suspect was taken to University Hospital and treated for lacerations.

The motive for the shooting was still being pieced together last night, but police sources said it possibly stemmed from a domestic argument earlier in the day.

Neighbors identified the arrested youth as a former mental patient and one said he had had an argument with his stepmother.

Police said they recovered a small arsenal—possibly as many as 10 firearms and some with telescopic sights—from the house.

A tentative partial list of guns recovered from the residence included a .357 magnum handgun, a 30-30 rifle, a .22 automatic handgun, a 12-gauge shotgun, a .308 rifle, a 20-gauge shotgun and a .22-caliber rifle.

A University Hospital spokesman said eight persons were brought in by ambulance and police cars, only one of whom was not a policeman.

One officer was only grazed by a bullet. The dead officer was identified as James Halcomb, 31, of the Western district plainclothes operation unit.

A police spokesman said Officer Halcomb was the father of two children and that his wife is pregnant. He had been on the force since 1969.

In serious condition was Officer James Brennan, 25, Officer Halcomb's partner, who was shot in the left side and left elbow. He also had a broken left arm.

One of the Western district officers, it could not be determined which one, was dramatically pulled from the line of fire where he had fallen when a citizen drove his Volkswagen van out onto the street and a homicide detective and another

See SHOOT, A7, Col.1

Hearst said to accuse Yoshimura

San Francisco (AP)—Patricia C. Hearst has told investigators that Wendy Yoshimura, the fugitive artist arrested with her, drove a get-away car in a fatal bank robbery last year, it was reported yesterday.

Quoting sources close to the probe, the San Francisco *Examiner* said the Hearst woman told investigators that terrorist robbers fled the Crocker National Bank in a car April 21, 1975, then switched to a second car blocks away with Miss Yoshimura behind the wheel.

Witnesses have told authorities that four robbers took $15,000 from the Carmichael (Calif.) bank at gunpoint, and one robber killed a woman customer with a shotgun blast.

Steven Soliah, who shared an apartment here with the Hearst woman and Miss Yoshimura, is being tried in the robbery, but no one else has been charged.

The *Examiner* also reported that Miss Yoshimura's palm print was found in a Sacramento bungalow used as a base camp for the Symbionese Liberation Army from February until June, 1975.

The broadcast reports stated also that the Hearst woman had admitted that she joined Miss

See HEARST, A6, Col.1

Syrians held deep in Lebanon despite Israeli hints of action

By CHARLES W. CORDDRY
Washington Bureau of The Sun

Washington — Intelligence sources reported evidence yesterday that Syria has moved a battalion of troops into southern Lebanon where Israel has indicated Syrian involvement would risk Israeli military reaction.

The unit, it was reported, is stationed in the port city of Tyre, south of the Litani River, which Israel—through informed sources in Tel Aviv rather than through specific official declarations—has indicated is the "red line" beyond which it would not tolerate Syrian invasion.

The intelligence sources also reported that Syrian President Hafez el Assad has alerted the equivalent of two Army divisions for possible intervention in Lebanon if there is continued failure of mediation efforts and he decides to impose a political solution.

These reports reached here before the escalation of fighting in Lebanon yesterday, followed by reports of a new Syrian peace proposal for ending the year-old civil war.

Mr. Assad was represented as seeking to avoid total intervention at this time, but keeping open his options by making necessary military preparations. Syrian regulars and Syrian-controlled Palestinians control key positions, which appears to insure that large forces could be moved into Lebanon on short notice.

An intelligence calculation here holds that there are 3,200 to 3,950 Syrian regulars now in Lebanon, the main movements having occurred last weekend, and more than 8,000 Palestinian guerrillas of the Syrian-

See SYRIA, A2, Col.3

U.S. says appraisers foster bias

Washington (AP)—The Justice Department yesterday charged a major segment of the real estate industry with illegally discriminating against blacks by forcing property values down in racially integrated neighborhoods.

Four national trade associations representing thousands of real estate appraisers and home mortgage lenders were named defendants in the civil suit filed in U.S. District Court in Chicago.

The defendants, all based in Chicago, are the American Institute of Real Estate Appraisers, the Society of Real Estate Appraisers, the United States League of Savings Associations and the Mortgage Bankers Association of America.

The lawsuit attacks standards allegedly established by the appraisers, and followed by the lenders, in assessing property values.

The assistant attorney general, J. Stanley Pottinger, head of the department's civil rights division, called the lawsuit "groundbreaking litigation."

He said the standards established by the appraisers' associations affect virtually all homes sold with conventional mortgage loans. The standards do not apply to home mortgages obtained through the Veterans Administration or the Federal Housing Administration.

The department accused the defendants of using a homeowner's race as a factor in determining the value of his property.

The appraisers' associations require appraisers automatically to reduce property values in neighborhoods that have become integrated, the department charged.

Mr. Pottinger said at a news conference that appraisers and others in the industry have perpetuated a myth that property values decline when black families move into a white neighborhood.

"This automatic presump-

See SUIT, A4, Col.2

Carter would phase in national health care

By ART PINE
Washington Bureau of The Sun

Washington—Jimmy Carter unveiled yesterday the broad outlines of a mandatory national health insurance program similar in scope to the $76 billion plan advocated by Senator Edward M. Kennedy (D., Mass.).

Although the proposal would provide comprehensive health-care benefits for every American, it would be phased in gradually over four years, to ease its budgetary impact. Coverage would go first "to those who need it most."

Mr. Carter declined to commit himself on two key details crucial to any health-care plan —whether the program should be administered by the government or through private insurance companies, and specifically how the plan would be financed.

The former Georgia governor said only that he favored using both general tax revenue and increased payroll taxes to pay for the program. Beyond that, he insisted, "I want to keep the option" open until after he would take office.

The proposal came as, separately, Mr. Carter complained that supporters of his Democratic presidential rivals were "locking together in a very tight-knit effort" to head off his nomination by deadlocking the convention in July.

In remarks at a private fund-raising breakfast, the candidate charged that "some . . . labor organizations" are continuing to back Henry M. Jackson even though "they know" he "doesn't have a chance," simply as a stop-Carter ploy.

Mr. Carter, however, did not support his charge with specific examples, involving Mr. Jackson or any of the other Democratic candidates. Mr. Carter has alluded to his competitors' strategy before, although not in quite those terms.

Mr. Carter's rush to unveil his health-insurance proposal, even before he had worked out many of the key details, apparently stemmed from pressure by Leonard A. Woodcock, president of the United Auto Workers union, who is pressing for the plan.

Mr. Carter said yesterday he had "consulted directly with

See CARTER, A7, Col.5

Index

Raid victim told to pay 8 raiders

Alton, Ill. (AP)—John Meiners was arrested in a drug raid three years ago by agents who had no warrants for the raid or his arrest. He was held for 77 hours without charge. Now he has been ordered to pay $15,000 to each of eight of the raiding officers who claimed he libeled them.

The order came Thursday from a three-man, three-woman federal court jury which heard a $2.8 million civil suit filed by Mr. Meiners and a $5 million counter-claim made by the agents.

Mr. Meiners, 30, now a resident of Dallas, was arrested in his rural Edwardsville home early April 19, 1973. Officers took him to the St. Louis City Jail where he was held for 77 hours without charge. The agents did not have warrants for his arrest or for the raid, court testimony showed.

Mr. Meiners charged that the entry, arrest and incarceration deprived him of his constitutional rights. Also, he said, the officers had stolen and damaged personal property.

Eight of the nine officers named by Mr. Meiners in the suit charged him, in turn, with libeling them in statements made at a news conference at which he discussed the raid.

See RAID, A6, Col.1

13 die as oil rig sinks, rescue fails in Gulf

Corpus Christi, Texas (AP) —A capsule-lifeboat packed with workers who escaped a sinking oil rig capsized in the stormy Gulf of Mexico, and 13 men died as rescuers battled waves two stories high and gale force winds in an attempt to right the craft.

Officials said yesterday that a rapidly developing storm trapped the $20 million Ocean Express oil rig and 35 crewmen in high seas Thursday night. It sank in 187 feet of water as it was being towed to a new location.

The crew tried to escape in two saucer-shaped capsules similar in appearance to the spacecraft used by the Apollo astronauts.

One of the capsule-lifeboats turned over and the hatch opened, allowing 6 of the occupants to escape, but drowning 13 others as the water rushed in. A tugboat tried in vain to pluck it from heavy seas.

A second capsule with 15 aboard was hoisted to safety by a tug.

The captain, Peter van der Graff, was the last man to leave the rig. He was pulled off when it was more than half-submerged by a Coast Guard helicopter that lowered a basket.

All the survivors were taken to hospitals in nearby Port O'Connor and Port Aransas, and some were held for held for observation.

"Everyone got off the rig safely. The casualties occurred while they were trying to rescue them from one of the survival capsules," said Cmdr. John DeCarteret, in charge of marine inspection for the Coast Guard in Corpus Christi.

Nobody could say exactly what happened, although officials said rigs are most vulnerable to storms during a move because their 250-foot legs are pulled from the water and are sticking up into the air.

An official of Ocean Drilling & Exploration Co. of New Orleans, owners of the rig, was asked what happened. "It was apparently overturned by the waves." He said the rig was new and had gone into operation in December.

Earlier, another company official said, "It's just a freak accident. We don't know exactly what happened. These capsules are supposed to float head up."

A Coast Guard spokesman said the first distress call was received Thursday night about

See RIG, A4, Col.2

Analysis

Polarized tactics crack veneer of Sarbanes, Tydings alikeness

By THOMAS B. EDSALL

This is the last of three articles on the campaigns of the chief contenders for the Democratic nomination for the U.S. Senate seat held for six years by a Republican, J. Glenn Beall, Jr. Results of the second Sun Poll on the Senate race will appear tomorrow in the Sunday Sun.

The senatorial campaigns of Paul S. Sarbanes and Joseph D. Tydings, although superficially similar—both are politicians whose roots are in the reform wing outside the Democratic party establishment—are almost diametrically opposed in strategy and tactics.

These strategic differences, which grow out of the way the candidates approach the winning of elective office, are critical to the outcome of the May 18 Maryland primary and demonstrate the strengths and weaknesses of the two campaigns.

The dominant characteristic of the Sarbanes campaign has been a heavy emphasis on organization: the creation of a centrally controlled campaign structure, the obtaining of endorsements from politicians and clubs, the use of labor backing and expertise and a media blitz in the closing weeks of the campaign.

The Sarbanes approach is viewed by many politicians as a successful tack in running for lower office, such as the U.S. House of Representatives, and the state Senate and House of Delegates, but it is coming under increasing criticism from within and without the campaign by those who contend that it is inadequate in a statewide contest where a broader, more diffuse appeal must be made.

Mr. Tydings, in contrast, is conducting a more widespread, media-directed campaign in which a far higher proportion of his funds are going to radio and television advertising and a calculated effort is being made to receive news coverage in weekly and daily papers and on radio and television.

Mr. Tydings is, however, weak in organizational support in Baltimore city, which is Mr. Sarbanes's base of strength and an area that produced 27 per cent (152,000) of the total votes cast in the state in the 1972 Democratic presidential primary.

Mr. Sarbanes began campaigning long before Mr. Tydings, and his early effort paid off in two ways: He locked up the backing of a majority of elected officials in the state, and he constructed an image as a probable winner.

In more recent months, however, Mr. Tydings has been able to make some inroads into organizational backing; groups that were holding off have, in some cases, either split their leadership between the candidates, or gone to Mr. Tydings. In addition, very few politicians would now grant Mr. Sarbanes the stature of the sure winner in the race.

This change in tone results from a number of factors, one of which has been Mr. Sarbanes's restriction of decision and policy-making matters to a small group of Baltimore-based supporters. This has had serious consequences in at least one important political subdivision, Prince Georges county.

Mr. Sarbanes is a cautious politician, cautious not only in the taking of publicized controversial positions, but in his willingness to delegate au-

See SENATE, A8, Col.1

The Weather
Partly cloudy today and tonight, chance of afternoon showers. High, 80; low, 66. Yesterday's high, 86; low, 67.
(Details and Map, Page C2)

THE SUN

FINAL

Vol. 279—No. 43—F

BALTIMORE, MONDAY, JULY 5, 1976

32 Pages 15 Cents

Area celebrates a joyous bicentennial as proud nation lights up night skies

Bells ring in unison

Ships of sail stream forth in tribute

By The Associated Press

Americans, 215 million strong, lit up the night skies, filled their waters with ships and sail, marched up their streets with streaming colors, trembled the air with pride and song and cheered their 200th Fourth of July.

Strangers on the streets of the nation smiled and greeted one another with "happy birthday."

At 2 P.M. New York time, 1 P.M. Chicago time, noon Denver time, 11 A.M. Los Angeles time, 9 A.M. Anchorage (Alaska) time, 8 A.M. Honolulu time, the President rang a ceremonial bell on the deck of the USS Forrestal in New York harbor, setting off a nationwide chorus of chimes, carillons and church bells.

People were up before dawn—to see the rocket's red glare above Fort McHenry, to pray at the Lincoln Memorial, to keep vigil at Independence Hall and touch the Liberty Bell, to crowd the banks of New York harbor for a spectacle of maritime splendor past and present.

Americans all over the world celebrated in their own way. In Peking, in an area near the Ming Tomb, Americans on the United States mission staff picnicked on hotdogs. And in Hiroshima, Japan, an American scientist studying radiation effects served hamburgers and hot dogs to 18 Japanese friends who wore red, white and blue neckties.

Westward the celebration moved with the sun in a massive salute perhaps no nation had known before.

President Ford punctuated the initial events. He was at Valley Forge, Pa., early to receive the 200 wagons of five wagon trains that traversed the nation to memorialize those Revolutionary soldiers who, said Mr. Ford, "came here in the snows of winter over a trail marked with the blood of their rag-bound feet."

Then he flew to Independence Hall where, under a brilliant sun, the square was jammed with a hundred thousand Americans who ringed the red brick, white steepled shrine and filled the block-long mall to the pavilion where hangs the

See NATION, A4, Col.3

Sunpapers photo—Pauline Lubens

Fireworks light the July 4 sky over Fort McHenry, reminiscent of the shelling that inspired Francis Scott Key to write The Star-Spangle Banner.

Marylanders rejoice on nation's day

By ROBERT A. ERLANDSON and TOM HORTON

Marylanders joined the rest of the nation yesterday in a jubilant salute to America's 200th birthday.

Fireworks, parades, church services, "good old-fashioned picnics" and backyard barbecues highlighted festivities from the state's Western mountains to the Atlantic shore at Ocean City.

The impressive climax of Baltimore's Fourth of July came last night at Fort McHenry when Judge Edward S. Northrop, Maryland's chief federal judge, welcomed 33 men and women to "full partnership" in the United States.

As the newly naturalized citizens, from 17 countries, turned to face the fort to pledge allegiance, the 42-by 30-foot Star-Spangled Banner rose majestically to the peak of the staff, to the strains of the national anthem, and with brilliant fireworks streaking the night sky behind it.

Judge Northrop told the new citizens, "For each of you, of course, this evening will always have a very special meaning—to be remembered by you as the day when, after a long period of waiting, you became full and complete partners in the American Republic.

"Equal partners with each of us who has been privileged to spend all of our lives here—equal partners with all of those great names in American history who dreamed the dream which became America, and who, in the immortal words of the Declaration of Independence, 'with a firm reliance on the protection of divine providence pledges their lives, their fortunes and their sacred honor' so that this nation could come into being."

Among the new citizens were Sergiu Comissiona, director of the Baltimore Symphony Orchestra, and his wife, Robinne, who surrendered their Israeli citizenship to become Americans.

There was heavy security at the fort by city and federal authorities, but no untoward incidents occurred. Several of the extra teams of National Park Service rangers who had been brought to Baltimore for the weekend were transferred by helicopter during the evening to Philadelphia to aid the hard-pressed rangers there.

Following the oath-taking, Gen. Leonard F. Chapman, Jr., the retired commandant of the U.S. Marine Corps who now is commissioner of the Immigration and Naturalization Service, presented the new Americans with their certificates of citizenship.

He told them of the contributions immigrants had made to the growth and greatness of the United States during the past two centuries and that half a million immigrants still resettle yearly in this country.

"No other country comes close to matching this record of welcome which the United States has set," General Chapman said.

The Fort McHenry crowd, which was estimated to be about 3,000 persons during the two-hour program of music and speeches that preceded the naturalization, swelled by several thousand late in the evening for the 45-minute display of fireworks that burst, rocket after rocket, over the fort.

Houses throughout the city and surrounding suburbs were decorated with flags of all sizes, many representing flags from revolutionary days, and at 2 P.M. many house-

See CITY, A7, Col.1

Flags massed

Couple weds, many parade in Arundel

By ROBERT P. WADE
Annapolis Bureau of The Sun

Annapolis—A Severn River regatta, a Glen Burnie wedding, a Severna Park parade and the spectacle of 150 flags massed in Annapolis marked the bicentennial Fourth in Anne Arundel county.

Thousands marched in parades and picnicked, shot firecrackers and watched fireworks, enjoyed backyard barbecues or tramped down to the Naval Academy to watch an unusual boat parade.

In the northern end of the county, Deborah Franklin and Calvin Peterson, Jr., took advantage of the holiday to get their families together and get married. And their neighbors took advantage of the wedding to close off the 1000 block of Louise road in Glen Burnie and throw a bicentennial bash in honor of the day and the bride and bridegroom.

As the new Mr. and Mrs. Peterson, resplendent in white, drove up, they were greeted by cheers, firecrackers and appropriate wisecracks about nuptial fireworks.

"Who'd want to get married on a day like this?" one young man asked. "At least they'll remember when they did it," answered a neighbor, Jay Williams.

"The celebration is nice, but what's important is our commitment to each other," the bridegroom said of the day.

A few miles down Ritchie highway, hundreds of families gathered along Severna Park roads to watch hundreds more

See ARUNDEL, A7, Col.1

Orioles, 7; Tigers, 4.
Article on Page C3

County rejoices

Proud memories, hoopla, mark 4th

By KAREN E. WARMKESSEL
Towson Bureau of The Sun

Baltimore county's bicentennial Fourth of July was marked by community gatherings, proud remembrances of the past, pledges for the future and some old-fashioned, star-spangled hoopla.

Celebrations ranged from a sunrise service on a hillside in Cockeysville to a brassy bicentennial parade in Catonsville, dedication of a 200-year partially restored mansion in Essex to a traditional "old-fashioned family picnic" in Lansdowne.

And, of course, it would not have been the Fourth of July without the colorful fireworks that burst upon the dark evening skies throughout the county.

A crowd estimated at 10,000 witnessed the fireworks during the Baltimore Symphony Orchestra's concert at Goucher College, where Representative Paul S. Sarbanes (D., 3d) narrated Aaron Copland's "Lincoln Portrait."

At 2 P.M., church bells, from the rural north to the industrial south county, had rung out to proclaim the nation's 200th birthday.

But, underlying the flag-

See COUNTY, A6, Col.6

AP

A member of the commando team that rescued the hijack hostages is welcomed at Tel Aviv's airport. His face is blacked out for security reasons.

Israeli raiders rescue all but 3 hijack hostages

Tel Aviv (AP)—Israeli commandos who made a 4,800-mile round-trip stab into the heart of Africa early yesterday rescued all but 3 of the more than 100 hostages held in Uganda by pro-Palestinian air hijackers.

Israeli officials said 102 hostages, the majority Israelis, had come back to a joyous and triumphant welcome here. They said three hostages, one Israeli commando, seven terrorists and some Ugandan soldiers had been killed in an hour-long battle at Entebbe Airport, 20 miles from the Ugandan capital of Kampala.

Uganda's president, Idi Amin, said in a broadcast statement that 20 Ugandan troops had been killed and 32 injured.

The dead Israeli commando, Col. Yehonatan Netanyahu, 30, immigrated with his family from the United States in 1948, the military command said.

Lt. Gen. Mordechai Gur, the Israeli chief of staff, said the Israelis had had to fight both hijackers and Ugandan troops to get the hostages out. Shimon Peres, the Israeli defense minister, accused President Amin of co-operating with the hijackers.

At least 11 hostages were hospitalized in Tel Aviv and 3 injured hostages were left behind in Africa, 2 in Nairobi, Kenya, and 1 in Uganda.

"When I heard the shots I knew God had come to take us out," said a weeping Israeli hostage, her eyes ringed with fatigue. "It was a miracle. We were so far from Israel and they came for us."

In Madison, Wis., yesterday, Mrs. Harvey Robey, the mother of one freed hostage, said she had spoken by telephone with her daughter, Janet Almog, after Mrs. Almog and her Israeli husband, Ezra, had arrived safely in Tel Aviv.

"It never occurred to them that they would not get out," said Mrs. Robey, recounting her conversation with her daughter. "But they never dreamed they would get out the way they did."

The early morning airborne raid on Entebbe, more than five hours' flying time from Tel Aviv, came a week after the hijackers seized an Air France jet over Athens, and only 10 hours

See RESCUE, A2, Col.4

7,000 survive all-night party to see Fort McHenry rockets

About 7,000 die-hards, rumpled from 10 hours of partying, cheered and toasted yesterday as Fort McHenry survived its second American re-enactment of its first bombardment by the British.

The bombardment, accompanied by Ethel Ennis singing The Star-Spangled Banner, marked the climax of a 12-hour nationally televised bicentennial birthday party for America.

At its height, near midnight, when the world's largest birthday cake was towed through the bay waters off Locust Point, the city's bicentennial committee was host to about 30,000 visitors.

Hundreds of additional spectators viewed the bombardment from cabin cruisers and sailboats anchored off the fort and the Clinton street piers.

And millions more watched on a nationwide hookup of 103 television stations that broadcast 12 hours of entertainment from the fort, the Iwo Jima monument in Washington, the carrier USS Constellation off the coast of Southern California, King's Park in Ohio, Wolf Trap in Virginia and the deck of the frigate Constellation near Fort McHenry.

From 7 P.M. Saturday until well after dawn, the party-goers at the fort stomped and clapped for a succession of performers on stage. Among the crowd, there were some virtuoso soloists on instruments such as the beer keg, the marijuana pipe, the frisbee and the sleeping bag.

The size of the crowd did not meet the expectations of the party's organizers, led by Walter S. Orlinsky, the City Council president.

Mr. Orlinsky and the National Park Service, which administers Fort McHenry, vowed to "cut off" the fort to all additional visitors after 60,000 persons had arrived. No more than half that number ever tried the entrance.

"You can tell this wasn't a really big crowd," said Michelle LeFavre, of the 2500 block Madison street. "Nobody was born during the night."

Some members of the crowd said the well-publicized worries about overcrowding may have kept the numbers down. The threat of rain late Saturday afternoon also discouraged some people who had planned to visit the fort.

Robert M. Thompson, of the 5600 block McClean boulevard, said the imposition of a 25-cent fare for shuttle buses this year kept some people away and angered others.

"It's only 25 cents, but it's the principle of the thing," said Mr. Thompson, better known to the 15 persons he

See FORT, A6, Col.6

Index

The birthday of 1876

One hundred years ago today *The Sun's* front page reported on the nation's 100th birthday celebration.

In every neighborhood of Baltimore and every city and town across Maryland residents gathered to mark the occasion with speeches and fireworks.

Few of the 25,000 picnicking in Druid Hill Park turned out for the official celebration just east of the Mansion House where three hours of speeches produced "very little enthusiasm or applause." Smaller local celebrations were more lively, as Hampden, Harlem Park, East, South and West Baltimore, as well as Annapolis, Towsontown and the more distant Maryland communities did their part.

This account of how mid-Victorian America celebrated a milestone Fourth is on Page A5.

Tomorrow Lexington Market burns

The Weather
Mild today with rain likely, high 54. Windy and cooler tonight, low in 20's. Yesterday's high, 53; low, 33.
(Details and Map, Page C2)
Vol. 280—No. 29—F

THE SUN

FINAL

BALTIMORE, MONDAY, DECEMBER 20, 1976

••• 15 Cents

Plane slams into Stadium after Colts loss

Fireman sprays foam on a small plane that crashed into the upper deck of Memorial Stadium after Colts-Steelers play-off game. The Colts lost 40 to 14. (More on game, Page C3) AP

4 injured; most of fans were exiting

A light plane crashed into the stands of the upper deck of Memorial Stadium minutes after the Colts-Steelers National Football League play-off game ended yesterday.

Most of the sellout crowd of more than 60,000 had dispersed when the blue-and-white Piper Cherokee plummeted into the last three rows of chair-back seats at the south end of the Stadium, in a section just above the baseball press box behind home plate.

Most seats were filled until the game ended at 4.59 P.M. The plane crashed into the seats about 5.05 P.M.

The aircraft landed nose down, its tail sticking into the air.

"I'm sure if the Colts had won, they [the crowd] would still have been there," said Daniel Karczeski, 20, a Pinkerton guard. Since the Steelers won, 40-14, the hometown fans had no reason to linger.

The pilot of the low-wing monoplane apparently escaped serious injury but was held overnight at Union Memorial Hospital. He was identified as Donald Kroner, 33, an MTA bus driver, of the 7500 block Twincrest road, Rosedale.

Police who helped Mr. Kroner from the wrecked plane said he was able to walk. Seemingly dazed, he was given oxygen by a Fire Department ambulance crew.

Hospital officials said Mr. Kroner received cuts and bruises of the head and chest.

Three city policemen also were injured. Two of them were taken to Union Memorial, and one was admitted.

Baltimore county police said last night that a man named Donald Kroner of Rosedale, a former Air Force flyer, was arrested last Tuesday on a warrant charging him with reckless flying, littering and making a bomb threat against Bill Pellington, a former Colt, and the restaurant Mr. Pellington operates in the York Ridge shopping center north of Towson.

Rolls of toilet paper and a bottle had been dropped on the Pellington restaurant December 7, according to detectives. The defendant was released on $2,100 bail for later trial, county police said.

At least 20,000 fans still were in the Stadium when the plane crashed, but almost all of them were in runways and tunnels or on their way through exits, officials said.

There were only 3,000 or so widely scattered fans still in their seats, the officials added, and Section 41, where the plane fell, was empty.

Governor Mandel, who had attended the game, was getting into an elevator when he heard that the plane had crashed. He went back and stayed at the Stadium for more than an hour and a half.

"Thank God it happened when it did," he said. "It could have been a terrible tragedy."

Police reported three other crashes of light planes in Maryland yesterday. Two persons were killed in one of them and, in another, two men were injured, one critically.

At the Stadium, police feared fire or explosion, because fuel was leaking from the wrecked plane, and rushed remaining members of the crowd to the nearest exits. The crowd was cautioned not to smoke.

Witnesses said the plane swooped in from the open north end with its landing lights on.

Ben Roth, assistant Stadium manager, said he was supervising the ground crew, which was putting a tarp over the field.

He said he shouted to the crew, "Hey, get out of the way. This guy's coming in."

Another Stadium employee said the plane flew in only 15 or 20 feet above the north goal posts. The pilot "looked as if he was going to land," he said.

But 40 or 50 persons were on the field, the witness said, and the pilot banked upward in the direction of the west stands. "It looked as if he put on power, but the engine faltered and he crashed," he said.

Stoney Smith, another Pinkerton guard,

See CRASH, A11, Col, 1

Majority loss brings Rabin crisis

Jerusalem (AP) — Prime Minister Yitzhak Rabin lost his majority in parliament yesterday by dismissing three cabinet ministers and immediately faced a motion of no confidence that threatened to topple his government.

The three ministers ousted were members of the National Religious party, the chief coalition partner of Mr. Rabin's Labor party.

The right-wing Likud opposition presented the no-confidence motion, and the National Religious party said it would support it in parliament when it comes up for debate tomorrow. Mr. Rabin's coalition could lose a vote on the issue, requiring early elections.

Political analysts said this may have been Mr. Rabin's intention. They noted that general elections were scheduled for October, and said the fall of the government would merely advance the election date by a few months.

Politicians on the right and left praised the move as good political tactics by the prime minister, calling it a pre-emptive attack aimed at hitting Mr. Rabin's foes before they were ready to go to the polls.

Mr. Rabin made no immediate comment on elections. He dismissed the three National Religious party cabinet ministers after two of them joined the party's faction in parliament in abstaining on a vote of confidence last week.

The Torah Front, a splinter faction of ultra-orthodox rabbis, had presented the no-confidence motion over a welcoming ceremony for three F-15 fighter planes from the United States that continued past the beginning of the Jewish sabbath at sundown Friday, December 10.

Zevulun Hammer, the welfare minister who was ousted, said it was "inconceivable" Mr. Rabin would continue to govern with a minority and promised the National Religious party would "do everything to advance the election date."

The other dismissed ministers were Yosef Burg, the interior minister, and Yitzhak Raphael, the religion minister.

Diplomatic analysts thought early elections might speed up Middle East peace moves. The United States-sponsored peace efforts have developed slowly, partly because of the weakness of Mr. Rabin's cabinet and his disagreement with the National Religious party about how much captured Arab territory Israel should give up.

Mr. Rabin's move took the nation by surprise. As the prime minister was announcing his decision to the ministers, Israeli newspapers were reporting that he had decided to overlook the affair.

The ministers' resignations, which were to be presented to parliament today, in effect broke up Mr. Rabin's coalition.

See ISRAEL, A4, Col. 1

Index

Carter reported ready to name Bell

By STEPHEN E. NORDLINGER
Sun Staff Correspondent

Americus, Ga.—President-elect Carter was reported yesterday to have decided to name Griffin B. Bell, a former federal judge from Atlanta, to be attorney general.

Mr. Carter scheduled another news conference this morning to announce three additional appointments to the Cabinet. Mr. Bell may be among those to be nominated then.

Some of the lawyers in the South familiar with Mr. Bell's career as a federal appellate judge, described him as a judicial moderate.

He played an instrumental role in the school desegregation cases in Mississippi in the Sixties. He is a law partner of Charles Kirbo, one of Mr. Carter's leading advisers.

The president-elect, as he completed his Cabinet selections, was said to have decided to name a black as secretary of housing and urban development, with Mayor Kenneth A. Gibson of Newark, N.J., the most likely nominee. Robert C. Embry, Jr., the housing commissioner in Baltimore, is expected to be appointed under secretary in the department.

Mr. Carter also was reported to have decided to name Joan Manley, a vice president of Time, Inc., in charge of its book division, as secretary of commerce. She would be the first woman to hold that post. Mrs. Manley met with Mr. Carter at his home in nearby Plains three days ago.

John T. Dunlop was reported to be the likely nominee for secretary of labor. Mr. Carter has been strongly urged by the AFL-CIO to name Mr. Dunlop, who resigned a year ago from the post after President Ford vetoed a construction bargaining bill that Mr. Dunlop had been instrumental in developing. Womens and black groups had opposed this appointment on grounds that Mr. Dunlop was antagonistic to federal anti-discrimination programs.

Mr. Carter was expected to name Dr. Juanita Kreps, vice president of Duke University and a labor economist, as under secretary in the Labor Deparetment. She also met with Mr. Carter at Plains three days ago.

The appointments to these four Cabinet posts were decided recently as Mr. Carter tried to end his search in time to finish announcing his selections by Christmas. Earlier, Mr. Carter reportedly had made the following choices for his Cabinet, although they have not been announced as yet:

- Harold Brown, president of the California Institute of Technology and a former secretary of the Air Force in the Johnson administration, as secretary of defense.
- Representative Bob S. Bergland (D., Minn.), a member of the House Agriculture Committee and a friend of Vice President-elect Mondale, as secretary of agriculture.
- Joseph A. Califano, a well-known Washington lawyer and a former top aide to President Johnson, as secretary of health, education and welfare with a women to be named as under secretary.

The announcements of the selections for those seconds-in-command in the departments are expected after Mr. Carter completes his Cabinet, which is to meet with him early next week at St. Simons Island off the Georgia coast.

Mr. Carter was also reported to be considering naming Charles D. Ferris, counsel of the Senate Democratic Policy Committee, as the deputy attorney general under Mr. Bell.

Mr. Bell, 58, Mr. Carter's selection as attorney general, was a judge in the United States Court of Appeals for the Fifth Circuit from 1961 until last March when he resigned to resume law practice in the Atlanta firm of King and Spaulding. Mr.

See CARTER, A5, Col. 2

New foreign policy takes shape

Carter team to focus on allies

By HENRY L. TREWHITT
Washington Bureau of The Sun

Washington—As President-elect Carter neared completion of his foreign policy team, an outgoing official summed up the prospect for change: "In style, enormous. In substance, limited."

Only one critical assignment is yet to be filled on that team, the office of secretary of defense. It already includes Zbigniew Brzezinski as national security adviser in the White House, Cyrus R. Vance as secretary of state and W. Michael Blumenthal as secretary of the treasury.

From the known views of those men and Mr. Carter, Washington's foreign policy establishment already is producing a rough consensus about what will continue and what will change in America's relations with the rest of the world after January 20, the day of Mr. Carter's inaugural. With allowance for Mr. Carter's campaign language, it includes the following:

- Greater emphasis on relations with the other capitalist democracies—Japan and those of Western Europe. All of the team so far, including Mr. Carter, are right out of an influential organization called the Trilateral Commission, which regards the health of those countries, with the United States, as the key to world order.
- A more demanding attitude toward the Soviet Union, at least initially, as the price of detente in such areas as arms control and human rights. Mr. Brzezinski, more than the others the theoretician of the group, acknowledges the awesome power of the Soviet Union. But he also feels that Moscow lacks the economic and political capability to assume leadership.
- Continued increases in the defense budget, as Mr. Carter's advisers agree on the growing power of the Soviet Union. Those who interpreted campaign language as promises of defense cuts, an outgoing official says, "had better forget it."
- Tougher criteria for arms sales to other countries and greater emphasis on human rights. Whether Mr. Carter's serious concerns in these areas can be translated into concrete results is a matter of skepticism, however. among those in the outgoing administration.

On the matter of style, there is little disagreement about differences within the incoming and outgoing administrations. Henry A. Kissinger, the outgoing Secretary of State and former national security adviser, is regarded as the ultimate intellectual pragmatist, given to secret diplo-

See POLICY, A5, Col. 2

Bukovsky calls Soviet jail worse after Helsinki pact

Zurich, Switzerland (AP)—Vladimir K. Bukovsky, a Soviet human rights activist freed in an international exchange of political prisoners, said yesterday prison life got much rougher after the Helsinki accord on East-West co-operation was signed.

Denouncing the Soviet system, the 33-year-old dissident assailed the 1975 Helsinki agreement as a Soviet maneuver to disarm the West and curb the fight for human rights in the Soviet Union.

The pale and haggard Mr. Bukovsky told his first news conferenee in the West he intends to dedicate all his energy to the cause of political prisoners in the Soviet Union and throughout the world.

Mr. Bukovsky said conditions at Vladimir Prison, 120 miles east of Moscow, "worsened considerably as soon as the Helsinki accord was signed." He said this included new restrictions on reading matter for prisoners, who even were barred from reading Western Communist publications and an official United Nations review.

"The Soviet Union still sees the West as an enemy with which it is in a state of belligerency," he declared.

Mr. Bukovsky, his mother, sister and ailing nephew, were flown to Switzerland by the Kremlin Saturday in exchange for the Chilean Communist party leader, Luis Corvalan, who had been in prison since the Chilean military overthrew the late President Salvador Allende in 1973.

The exchange was "an extraordinary event because it is the first time that the Soviet Union officially recognized it has political prisoners," Mr. Bukovsky said. ". . . It is a victory for everybody. This exchange brings forward the problem of political prisoners as a universal problem."

Mr. Corvalan, who was freed Friday by the military regime in Santiago. flew on to Moscow with his wife Saturday night in the exchange, which was assisted by the United States.

Chile's president, Gen. Augusto Pinochet, said in Santiago yesterday that his government had taken the initiative in asking the United States to mediate. Moscow, he said, "responded in evasive and distant terms" to the early Chilean approaches but later came around.

A Swiss physician said Mr. Bukovsky

See BUKOVSKY, A2, Col. 4

UPI

Soviet wishes Brezhnev happy birthday

Nikolai V. Podgorny (left), the Soviet chief of state, awarded two new medals to Leonid I. Brezhnev, the Soviet Communist party leader, on his 70th birthday yesterday. Mr. Brezhnev was wished "many, many" more years of leadership during festivities at the Kremlin. (Article on Page A2)

The Weather
Sunny and cool today, high near 50. Fair and cold tonight, lows 23 to 31. Yesterday's high, 57; low, 44.
(Details and Map, Page B2)

Vol. 284—No. 8—F

THE SUN

FINAL

BALTIMORE, SATURDAY, NOVEMBER 25, 1978

• • • 15 Cents

U.S. okays freight, steel boosts

Rails trim request; major banks raise prime rate to 11½%

By The Associated Press

The nation's largest steel company raised its prices and major banks pushed their prime lending rates to a four-year high of 11½ per cent yesterday as inflationary pressures continued.

In its first major actions under President Carter's new inflation guidelines, the Council on Wage and Price Stability approved an increase in rail freight rates and the average 3.2 per cent price increase announced by United States Steel Corporation.

The railroads got the approval after trimming their request for a general increase in freight rates from 8.1 per cent to 7 per cent. The railroads said the cut will cost them more than $200 million a year.

Brock Adams, the Secretary of Transportation, hailed the railroads' action as a "breakthrough in the administration's efforts to hold down prices" and said that if the financially troubled railroads could comply with the guidelines, "then other industries ought to be able to do the same thing, and I think they should."

U.S. Steel cited increased costs as it raised prices on a wide range of steel products. Steel-price increases have a major effect on the economy because steel is a key ingredient in such products as automobiles and appliances.

Railroad freight charges directly affect only shippers and railroads, but they usually are passed on to consumers in the form of higher prices.

The prime rate, the interest rate banks charge their best corporate borrowers, has been increased 14 times since the beginning of the year, when it stood at 7¾ per cent. The rate is not directly linked to rates on consumer loans or home mortgages, but increases do signal the upward trend in the cost of borrowing.

The raise from 11 to 11½ per cent was initiated by Citibank of New York, the nation's second largest, and was quickly followed by most major banks, including the largest, San Francisco-based Bank of America.

The Federal Reserve Board has been pushing up interest rates in an effort to slow the economy, fight inflation and to bolster the U.S. dollar overseas. But demand for loans has remained strong despite the higher rates and some analysts think the prime will rise above the record 12 per cent rate set during the 1974 recession.

The Carter administration's voluntary wage standards allow companies to raise prices by one-half per cent less than the average of all increases posted by the company in the last two years.

A spokesman for the Council on Wage and Price Stability said the guidelines al-

See STEEL, A11, Col. 3

UPI

A United States body recovery unit removes the corpses of more victims from a helicopter at the Georgetown airport in Guyana.

Family, promised 'paradise' in Guyana, found nightmare in cult's death camp

Georgetown, Guyana (KNI)—This is the story of an American family that lived for 7½ months in a concentration camp called Jonestown.

The Parks family, of Springfield, Ohio, came to this jungle settlement in search of a tropical paradise. Five of the six family members left with a tale of horror.

They left behind the body of Patricia Parks, 44, a wife and mother of three, who was shot to death at the airstrip near Jonestown in the ambush last Saturday.

The family's nightmare began as a dream of working for social equality 20 years ago, when they first became acquainted with the Rev. Jim Jones, who until his death last week was the head of the Peoples Temple church and the Jonestown commune.

They grew to respect Mr. Jones and 12 years ago moved from Ohio to California, where Mr. Jones set up his church, Jerry Parks, 42, said. Over those 12 years, they gave Mr. Jones 23 per cent of their income and savings, Mr. Parks recounted.

Then last year Mr. Jones convinced them to sell their house and turn all their money and possessions over to him. In return he promised them an idyllic life in his "agrarian paradise" in Guyana. They would be able to eat the fruit off the trees, would have their own home and would get "excellent medical treatment," Mr. Jones promised.

More importantly, they would be able to live out their dream of social equality as members of Mr. Jones's "special and select" family.

But from the moment the Parks family arrived at the camp, they knew they had bought a share in a nightmare.

Guards immediately opened their suitcases and confiscated everything except those items Mr. Jones determined they needed.

The adults were assigned to one-room cottages, 12 feet by 20 feet, housing 14 people. All—even the married couples—were assigned bunk beds.

Soon Patricia Parks became ill on the diet of rice and gravy. She went from 137 pounds to 111 pounds and developed severe pains in her legs and hips. It was then that they discovered that the "excellent" medical care they had been promised was nothing more than a young doctor who had not completed his internship.

Life at the camp meant being roused for work at 6 A.M. and ordered to bed at 9.30 P.M. A speaker system blared out instructions all day. Residents were plagued by lice. And if they could not remember their lessons they were forced to the back

See FAMILY, A2, Col. 5

Mass-death toll rises near 800 in Jonestown

Georgetown, Guyana (AP)—United States soldiers removing bodies from Jonestown's field of death uncovered "more and more and more" corpses of American cultists and their children yesterday.

The count rose to 775, and about 180 victims of the suicide-murder ritual last Saturday were under the age of 15, U.S. officials said.

That was nearly double the 409 reported earlier from the settlement of the California-based Peoples Temple hacked out of the jungle in this former British colony on the northeastern shoulder of South America.

Many bodies found yesterday were of children covered by the corpses of their parents, U.S. Embassy officials said, and the toll is expected to increase as the layers of bodies are removed.

Investigators had been baffled since the mass suicides first came to light Sunday in trying to account for about 500 of the commune's residents. Before the discovery, it had been thought that hundreds must have fled into the surrounding forest rather than take poison with the rest of the Rev. Jim Jones's followers.

Ptolemy Reid, the deputy prime minister of Guyana, told Parliament yesterday that the count of 775 bodies left 103 sect members unaccounted for. He said the government believed that 950 members of the U.S. cult were in Guyana, and 72 are known to be alive here—32 from Jonestown and the others from the cult's Georgetown center.

Guyanese soldiers and police, with "valuable assistance from the United States," are continuing "a diligent search" for settlers who may have fled into the jungle, Mr. Reid said.

Among the survivors are three Americans arrested as suspects in the Saturday attack on an investigative party led by Representative Leo J. Ryan (D., Calif.) that preceded the Jonestown suicides and killings. Mr. Ryan, three American newsmen accompanying him and a woman cultist wanting to leave the settlement were murdered in the attack at the Port Kaituma airstrip shortly after they left Jonestown.

A U.S. Embassy source said it was not until yesterday morning, after three days of working at the camp, that American military teams removing bodies found that corpses in one area were stacked in "several layers."

The soldiers began clearing out what they thought would be the final group of bodies, said Air Force Capt. John Moscatelli. "We got into an area on a different side of the temple [the camp's central pavilion] and found more and more bodies . . . and we found more and more and more."

Patricia Moser, a spokesman for the embassy, said: "Many children were found under the bodies of their parents and were not counted originally."

Captain Moscatelli said that, as far as could be determined, the newly found victims, like nearly all of those counted earlier, died by swallowing poison doled out by Mr. Jones's medical team.

How could about 360 bodies have been overlooked?

"When we were out there originally, there were bodies under bodies as we were working, but we were working on a total estimated count," Captain Moscatelli said. "That count had been approximately

See GUYANA, A2, Col. 2

Arriving bodies strain mortuary

By ROBERT RUBY

A total of 421 bodies of American victims of the mass murder-suicide at Jonestown, Guyana, filled five refrigerated trucks last night outside the giant government mortuary at Dover Air Force Base in Delaware, where facilities were beginning to be strained.

Army Maj. Brigham Shuler said the sixth C-141 cargo plane to land since early Thursday arrived at 8.50 P.M. with 70 more bodies in temporary aluminum caskets. Only one body, that of the Rev. Jim Jones, the leader of the Peoples Temple cult, had been positively identified. The body of Mr. Jones arrived Thursday night on the second flight from Georgetown, Guyana's capital.

Major Shuler said earlier plans had been abandoned to begin the embalming process. He said the bodies will not be fully processed until they are identified and are being preserved in the green refrigerated trucks backed up to the one-story, cinder block morgue.

"We are beginning to feel the pinch," the major said, but he added that more trucks were available. Each vehicle holds 100 bodies, which have been removed from their aluminum caskets and are being stored in green plastic bags.

A State Department spokesman said at least 775 bodies had been found in Jonestown as of last night, but that "the number is expected to continue to creep up."

"We have found that bodies were stacked," said Fred L. Henneke, the spokesman. "Something that looked like one adult body sometimes turned out to be on top of a smaller adult, and there would be a child underneath that."

All of them will be flown the 3,200 miles to Dover, which State Departmen and Pentagon officials say is the only mortuary large enough to handle that number of bodies. Each cargo plane can

See BODIES, A2, Col. 1

Street rallies in Peking call for purge of officials who backed radical leaders

By MICHAEL PARKS
Hong Kong Bureau of The Sun

Hong Kong—The tempo of political activity quickened again in China yesterday as street rallies in Peking called for a purge of officials who had supported radical leaders in the past and for the rehabilitation of their moderate opponents.

New wall posters in the Chinese capital continued the anti-radical campaign, again attacking political figures close to Chairman Hua Kuo-feng and openly supporting Teng Hsiao-ping, the senior vice premier.

The late Chairman Mao Tse-tung came under the most sweeping and harsh criticism yet yesterday. A sprawling, 66-page poster directly across from his mausoleum in central Peking said Chairman Mao was "about 70 per cent good, but 30 per cent bad," asserting that he had continued China's history of dictatorship.

The time has come to press the people's struggle for human rights and democracy, to re-evaluate the whole cultural revolution and other Maoist policies and to force from their posts officials who had oppressed the people, the poster declared. "We have had enough of dictatorship," it said.

"Chinese, arise. The time has come to oppose all dictators, whoever they may be," the poster declared. "We must judge them and settle scores with them right along the line."

The 20,000-word poster drew crowds of hundreds late into the night, according to reports from Peking. Signed by a group of youths who said they were struggling against "the old thoughts of the cultural revolution," the poster has thrust the issues of democracy and human rights into the center of the political debate now under way in China.

Their assault on Maoist polices went further than any attack on the late Chinese leader so far, comparing him with Chin Shih Huang, the emperor of the Third Century B.C. with whom Chairman Mao identified as the unifier of the country but who, the poster said, "oppressed the people and burned books." As detailed as it was sweeping, the critique, in fact, called into question the nature of the Communist regime in China.

The Communist party's policy-making Central Committee is thought to be meeting, or preparing to do so, in an effort to resolve the apparent dispute between Chairman Hua and Mr. Teng and to deal with the now widespread popular demand that supporters of the radicals be punished and to assess the overall impact of the growing political debate in the country.

Chinese authorities have yet to confirm a Central Committee meeting, but activity has increased around the Great Hall of the People in central Peking. Party workers appear to be receiving briefings on the discussions and most of the country's top political leaders, from the provinces as well as the capital, have made no public appearances for almost a week.

The Central Committee is likely to be

See CHINA, A4, Col. 1

China to get U.S. reactor via France

Washington (NYT)—The Carter administration has approved a request by France to sell an American-designed nuclear power plant to China, government officials said yesterday, with a condition that France obtain assurances from Peking that the facility be used for peaceful purposes.

The officials said that, after considerable internal debate, the administration informed the French government early this week that it could go ahead with the sale of one, and possibly two, Westinghouse power reactors built under license in France. However, they said that the administration has attached some strings to its approval, including requirement of a pledge by Paris that it obtain Peking's approval to some form of inspection system to insure that the reactors are not used for military purposes.

If Peking is willing to supply the assurances, the officials said, the proposed deal would represent the first-ever sale of Western nuclear technology to Peking. They added that the deal would also go far beyond the level of Chinese-Soviet nuclear co-operation that existed in the 1950's.

The proposed sale has generated unusual interest within the government because it is viewed as signifying the extent to which China in recent months has opened up to Western trade and technology. James R. Schlesinger, the Secretary of Energy, visited China last month and aides report that Peking exhibited an intense interest in modernizing its nuclear establishment. The Westinghouse reactors are viewed as only a forerunner to a variety of advanced technology nuclear deals with Western nations.

The debate within the government over the sale, however, is also indicative of the dilemmas that Peking's new policies have posed for the administration. The White

See PLANT, A4, Col. 6

Index

2 sections

Coup topples Bolivian leadership

La Paz, Bolivia (AP)—The Bolivian Army toppled the 4-month-old government of Air Force Gen. Juan Pereda in a bloodless coup yesterday and promised to hold prompt elections "to return the people their rights and liberties."

Gen. David Padilla Arancibia, the Army commander, emerged as the strongman in the new three-man junta. He announced in a speech to the nation that elections would be held July 1 and power turned over to the elected president August 6, Bolivia's National Day.

General Padilla swore in a Cabinet that included military men considered to be of moderate or progressive views.

General Pereda, a 47-year-old Air Force general who seized power in a nonviolent coup in July, had promised recently to hold free elections in May, 1980.

But the 16-month time lapse infuriated his civilian opponents and apparently set the stage for the coup, the fifth in this Latin American country in 14 years. Historians say nearly 200 have been carried out or attempted since Bolivia became independent in 1825.

The Democratic and Popular Unity Coalition of former President Hernan Siles Zuazo had planned a "March for Democracy" yesterday afternoon.

The armed forces said late Thursday, however, that it would not allow the march or any "disorder and anarchy," and shortly after midnight the coup was under way.

Three Army trucks first surrounded the Interior Ministry and troops took command. The interior minister, Lt. Col. Faustino Rico Toro, was detained. An hour later, troops with automatic weapons filled the narrow streets leading into the Plaza Murillo, site of the presidential palace.

General Pereda was in his private home, and the coup apparently caught him by surprise. Callers were told he had rushed out. At 4 A.M., the palace issued a statement saying General Pereda had resigned "to avoid hours of pain and bloodshed for the country and the armed forces."

General Padilla said the armed forces had taken power "to return the people to their rights and liberties, including electing their leaders by universal democratic vote."

Mr. Siles Zuazo, president from 1956 to 1960 under the banner of the old National Revolutionary Movement, gave his immediate support to General Padilla. But he said the members of his center-left coalition would be vigilant to see to it that the promised elections are held and the transfer of power carried out.

General Pereda took control of this country of 6.1 million persons July 21 after a one-day rebellion in Santa Cruz that forced the resignation of President Hugo Banzer, an Army general who had ruled for seven years and who, like General Pereda, came to power in a coup.

After the July coup, General Pereda appointed Mr. Banzer ambassador to Argentina.

The July coup came two weeks after inconclusive presidential elections called by Mr. Banzer. General Pereda, the candidate hand-pick d by Mr. Banzer to succeed him, had been leading in the vote when the counting was halted by the Electoral Court and the election declared void because of fraud.

General Pereda, 47, had claimed he won the election, which was Bolivia's first in 12 years. Mr. Siles Zuazo was running a distant second in a field of seven candi-

See BOLIVIA, A2, Col. 4

AP

An Air Force worker steam-cleans a metal casket to be sent back to Guyana for reuse after recovery teams found hundreds more bodies at the Jonestown mass suicide site

The Weather
Sunny and pleasant today, high 63; fair tonight, low 38 to 44. Yesterday's high, 64; low, 41.
(Details and Map, Page C2)

THE SUN

FINAL

Vol. 281—No. 106—F

BALTIMORE, WEDNESDAY, MARCH 21, 1979

15 Cents

Mistrial declared for Robaczynski

PAUL CURRAN
. . . to head Carter family probe

Republican set to head Carter probe

By CARL P. LEUBSDORF
Washington Bureau of The Sun

Washington—Paul J. Curran, a New York Republican and former federal prosecutor, was named yesterday to supervise the politically touchy investigation into bank loans to President Carter's family peanut warehouse business by the National Bank of Georgia.

Mr. Curran, 45, was named "special counsel" by Griffin B. Bell, the Attorney General, who cited "the unique combination of circumstances" in the case that could lead to criminal charges against the President, his brother Billy and Bert Lance, the bank's former president and later Mr. Carter's first budget director.

However, the designation of Mr. Curran, and the granting to him of virtually complete authority over the complex probe, failed to satisfy Republican demands for appointment of a special prosecutor with total control.

Senator Howard H. Baker, Jr. (R., Tenn.), the Senate GOP leader, said the Carter administration is guilty of a "double standard" for refusing to name a special prosecutor with total independence. "The parallel with Watergate is inescapable," Mr. Baker said, citing the Nixon administration's efforts to deal with that scandal with an in-house investigation.

Later in the day, all seven Republicans on the Senate Judiciary Committee agreed to sign a letter asking Mr. Bell to name an independent prosecutor. Under a law passed last year, if the attorney general refuses, he has to send a written explanation of his reasons.

In announcing the appointment, Mr. Bell said that Mr. Curran, who was U.S. attorney in New York from 1973 to 1975, "will have full authority over the warehouse inquiry, and will supervise that investigation on a day-to-day basis." He will have authority to draw on existing Justice Department personnel, files and records, and to conduct a grand jury investigation.

However, final authority on such mat-

See CARTER, A6, Col. 1

Tax rate would stay in city

But budget offered would reduce services, employees

By JOHN SCHIDLOVSKY
and STEVEN M. LUXENBERG

City residents will continue to pay property taxes at a rate of $5.97 but will get reduced services from fewer city workers under a $1.95 billion budget that will be recommended today to the Board of Estimates.

The proposed fiscal 1980 budget, prepared by the Department of Finance, falls short of Mayor Schaefer's publicly stated goal in this election year—to cut the tax rate by 10 cents.

"I don't think that you could call this the Mayor's budget," said George A. Piendak, head of the city's budget office. "He didn't like our failure to cut the rate."

Mayor Schaefer could still manage a tax cut, however, if the General Assembly approves additional money for Baltimore. But budget officials expressed concern that the state legislature will not approve enough money to pay for growing deficits in some city agencies.

Budget officials said that this was "the first time in memory" that the Finance Department had recommended a decrease in the operating budget. Usually, the city is forced to spend more money just to meet rising costs and promised salary increases.

Budget officials admitted last night that the city currently is running as much as $12 million in the red, and that the revenues contained in the proposed budget will not cover all of that deficit or deficits that will probably occur again in the next budget year.

A balanced budget is required under the City Charter. Asked how he would describe a budget that appears to anticipate further deficits, Mr. Piendak called it a "precariously balanced budget."

In the past two years, the budget had been balanced through the help of certain one-time windfalls, but Mr. Piendak said there was no such help on the horizon and that "one-time gimmicks don't solve problems."

The proposed budget would reduce the amount of money spent on operating the city's government to $1.09 billion—$25.8 million less than the current operating budget.

Money budgeted for construction (known as the capital budget) would rise by $723.7 million for the fiscal year beginning July 1. This huge increase is due almost entirely to $695 million in federal funds for highway construction.

By holding to the current tax rate, the Finance Department rejected the requests from various city agencies, which asked for a total of $80 million in increases.

The Finance Department chose the same stance last year, telling department heads to cut back on the number of their employees by not filling positions that become vacant through retirements and resignations.

Mr. Piendak said he realized that some

See BUDGET, A10, Col. 1

AP
Yigael Yadin (background), Israel's deputy prime minister, and Moshe Dayan, foreign minister, listen to Israeli Prime Minister Menachem Begin's speech to the Knesset during yesterday's debate on the peace treaty between Israel and Egypt. During the debate, hecklers interrupted Mr. Begin with shouts.

Israel, Egypt disagree on where pact will lead

By DOUGLAS WATSON
Sun Staff Correspondent

Jerusalem—Israeli Prime Minister Menachem Begin yesterday opened the Knesset's debate on the pending peace treaty by bluntly taking issue with Egyptian Prime Minister Mustafa Khalil over what will result from the proposed autonomy for the occupied West Bank and Gaza Strip.

King Hussein of Jordan warns of the peace treaty's effect on U.S. ties with the Arab states..........A2

White House prepares for a Monday afternoon signing ceremony for the Mideast peace treaty..........A2

"I want to tell Dr. Khalil, never will Israel withdraw to the 1967 line," the Israeli prime minister declared.

He was reacting to a speech last week in which the Egyptian prime minister claimed that the peace treaty eventually will mean a return to Arab control of all areas occupied by Israel in the 1967 war, including East Jerusalem, and the creation of a Palestinian state.

Prime Minister Begin continued yesterday: "I say to Dr. Khalil, Jerusalem

See ISRAEL, A2, Col. 1

Jury votes acquittal in mercy-killing case of nurse, 10-2

By THEODORE W. HENDRICKS

Judge Robert L. Karwacki declared a mistrial in the mercy-killing case against Mary Rose Robaczynski at 11.30 last night after 20 hours of deliberation failed to produce a verdict.

Jurors interviewed later said that the final vote was 10 to 2 for acquittal.

The jury deadlocked after spending two days trying to reach a verdict on the charge of murdering Harry Gessner, 48, a terminally ill patient at Maryland General Hospital.

Judge Karwacki called in the jury after sending them a note inquiring about their progress. He said their answer showed that they were apparently deadlocked. The judge asked the jury forewoman, Beverly A. Skotarski, to step aside and he declared a mistrial in the case.

"We will review these charges very carefully in looking toward a decision on the retrial," Howard B. Gersh, an assistant state's attorney, said. Mr. Gersh added that he would set no time limit on the decision whether the case should be retried.

Joseph F Murphy Jr., who with George J. Helinski, was defense counsel, said "I was very much impressed with the attention the jury gave to this case. Of course, I am disappointed that we did not get an innocent verdict."

As soon as the judge announced that he was declaring a mistrial, Mrs. Robaczynski leaned her head on Mr. Helinski's shoulders and wept bitterly.

Later, the 24-year-old defendant was surrounded by her family, who have attended every session of the protracted trial, and was led from the courtroom leaning on their arms.

Outside the courthouse, Mrs. Robaczynski did not speak as she was ushered through a crowd of reporters and television cameramen by members of her family and taken to a waiting car.

Mr. Gersh said one member of the jury told him it was "just unfair to ask a jury to decide" whether Mr. Gessner was alive or dead at the time his respirator was disconnected.

The prosecutor also said the case was "tried in uncharted [legal] waters. The jury had a very difficult issue to deal with."

During the trial, the state attempted to show that Mrs. Robaczynski unhooked the respirator on which Mr. Gessner depended while he was still alive, causing his death. Witnesses called by the prosecution said that Mrs. Robaczynski had expressed agreement with euthanasia, or mercy killing, in casual conversations with them at the time some respirator disconnections were found.

At a dramatic moment in the trial, Mrs. Robaczynski took the witness stand to weep bitterly about the actions of coworkers which caused her to lose her nursing job, "which I loved." She testified that she thought Mr. Gessner was dead when she disconnected the respirator.

She admitted that she had no authority to interrupt his oxygen supply but pleaded that his sudden death caused her to become confused.

"I wouldn't hurt anyone," Mrs. Robaczynski asserted in describing her nursing care which started when she became interested in helping handicapped children while in her Catholic high school.

Mrs. Robaczynski also admitted that she disconnected the respirators of two other patients who were in her care in the Maryland General special care unit. How-

See NURSE, A9, Col. 1

Jurors find 'too many loose ends'

Uncertainty whether Harry Gessner was dead or alive when Mary Rose Robaczynski unplugged his respirator led to the deadlock that caused a mistrial in the mercy-killing case.

"I don't know how I can honestly convict this woman," said Alfred R. Beacher, 47, one of the 10 jurors who voted in favor of acquittal on the final ballot.

Two male jurors favored a guilty verdict, according to other jurors.

"There were too many loose ends and questions even the so-called experts couldn't agree on," he said early this morning after the jury was dismissed.

For Mr. Beacher and his fellow jurors, the key issues were how did Mr. Gessner die and when did his death occur—issues that Mrs. Robaczynski's lawyers raised from the day of indictment and pressed continually during the trial.

"The decision we had to make was: What constitutes brain damage?" Mr. Beacher recalled. "Perhaps there was some brain function left" when the nurse decided to unplug the respirator that was hooked up to Mr. Gessner during his stay as a patient at Maryland General Hospital.

Interviews with six jurors after the trial ended shortly before midnight revealed that the jurors took at least six ballots plus informal "straw votes" to see if any one had changed his or her mind during discussions.

In the beginning, five jurors voted a guilty verdict, four voted for acquittal and three were undecided, according to juror Juan Domenech, 32. The next balloting resulted in a split, 6 to 6, nearing the end of Monday night's deliberations.

The final votes that night and in resumed deliberations early yesterday morning brought the vote to 10 to 2, where it remained to the end, Mr. Domenech said.

"Ten of us were not convinced beyond a reasonable doubt that he [Mr. Gessner] was alive," Mr. Domenech, who started out as one of the undecided jurors, said. "Two felt without any doubt he was alive" and that Mrs. Robaczynski therefore was guilty, Mr. Domenech recounted.

"We all agreed she shouldn't have done what she did," he said. "But then we start-

See JURY, A9, Col. 1

Ethics unit says violations by Brooke were not serious

Washington (AP)—Former Senator Edward W. Brooke testified falsely and violated Senate rules on financial disclosure, but his misdeeds were not serious enough to warrant punishment, the Senate ethics committee concluded yesterday.

Release of the report concluded the committee's investigation of Mr. Brooke, a Massachusetts Republican who lost his Senate seat in the November elections.

The committee found that Mr. Brooke testified falsely during an acrimonious divorce settlement about the amount of a loan made to him. It also found that on four occasions he violated Senate financial-disclosure rules, adding that the violations could have resulted from poor bookkeeping.

But, "the committee does not believe the violations . . . are sufficiently serious to justify the severe disciplinary actions" specified by Senate rules, it added.

In any event, the committee could have taken no action against Mr. Brooke since he is no longer a senator. The only sanctions it can recommend involve a member's standing in the Senate, and the most severe sanction is expulsion.

Mr. Brooke said in a statement that, "With the single exception of the original misstatement [about the loan], which I acknowledged and apologized for nearly 10 months ago, the committee has searched in vain for anything more serious than poor record-keeping. . . .

"A Senate seat has been lost, a career jeopardized and family, friends and associates been wrung through an emotional ordeal almost beyond imagining, all in order that the ethics committee could repeat what I myself told the public and press last May 26," he added.

As for the infractions of Senate financial-disclosure rules, Senator Robert Morgan (D., N.C.), a committee member, said, "We found some infractions which we concluded were due to the careless manner in which the reports were made."

Senator Adlai E. Stevenson (D., Ill.), the committee's chairman, said the investigation would have gone no further even if Mr. Brooke still were a senator, because the violations found were not serious enough to recommend punishment.

Both Mr. Brooke and Mr. Morgan criticized allegations made against Mr. Brooke just before the election by Richard Wertheimer, the former special counsel to the committee.

Mr. Wertheimer alleged on October 24 that Mr. Brooke's attorneys were delaying the proceedings and that documents relating to the probe had been altered. The committee found no evidence to support the allegations.

Mr. Brooke said in a telephone interview that Mr. Wertheimer's statements were "very, very harmful in my Senate race."

Mr. Morgan said the statements were "uncalled for and unwarranted" and that they did undue harm to Mr. Brooke.

Mr. Brooke testified under oath May 12, 1977, during his divorce settlement that he owed A. Raymond Tye the sum of $49,000. On May 15, 1978, in his public finance-disclosure statement filed with the Senate, Mr. Brooke said the loan was $2,000.

Index

The Afro-Baltimoreans—IV

New generation reaps fruits of Sixties

By ANTERO PIETILA

In an era when fewer and fewer blacks can claim "firsts," Richard N. Dixon, at 40, has been the first black to:

• Work as an investment broker in the Baltimore office of Merrill Lynch, Pierce, Fenner and Smith.

• Serve on the Carroll county school board, and to be elevated to its presidency.

• Win a legislative primary race in the 97 per cent white county.

Though there was some racist talk among some candidates for other local offices about his campaign and both he and his white Democratic running mate lost to the Republican incumbents in last year's general election, Mr. Dixon thinks he is on the way to proving that "the system works."

"Politics and economics go hand in hand," the broker, who manages the portfolios of many wealthy Baltimore blacks, said recently after the close of the market in his office near the Inner Harbor. "But you have to be a candidate for all the people rather than for a certain segment of the people."

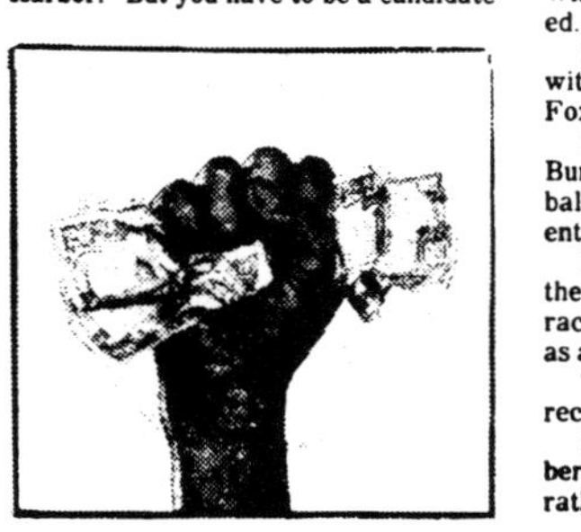

Mr. Dixon is a Carroll county native who lives in New Windsor, teaches at Morgan State University part-time and is visible in the university's alumni activities.

He is an example of a new generation of black professionals who are coming closer to racial equality than any previous generation of blacks.

His is a generation galvanized by the civil rights struggle of the 1960's and now reaping the benefits—not necessarily because of tokenism or affirmative action programs but also because of experience and expertise that any institution or business needs.

Because of those performance-based qualities, this new generation can build capital and move up society's ladders like its counterparts in white America—without having to resort to the kind of illegal activity that got William L. (Little Willie) Adams and several others started.

Contrast Mr. Dixon's experiences with the memories of Charles T. (The Fox) Burns.

Like the investment broker, Mr. Burns went to Morgan. He played football there in the late 1930's, and his parents wanted him to go on to law school.

But his first cousin had graduated at the top of his law class and, because of racial segregation, could find work only as a waiter.

"To hell with law school," Mr. Burns recalls deciding.

Instead, he went into backing numbers, though his mother told him, "I'd rather see you as a janitor, or dead."

HENRY EDWARDS
. . . Super Pride executive

RICHARD N. DIXON
. . . "firsts" in several fields

After leaving the rackets, Mr. Burns did well. He now is the principal owner of Super Pride Markets, a chain of inner-city supermarkets that expects to exceed $20 million in sales in its current fiscal year, which ends in September.

The first cousin who did go to law school eventually also did well: Thurgood Marshall now is a Supreme Court justice.

At 65, Mr. Burns recognizes that, "I can't plan a decade ahead, I can't plan five years ahead, I can't plan a year ahead."

That's why he brought Henry Edwards to Super Pride, hiring the 32-year-old holder of a Harvard master's degree in business administration away from a district manager's job at the Chicago-based Jewel Foodstores, Inc., one of the nation's largest supermarket chains.

Explains Mr. Burns, who bought Super Pride when it was more than $800,000 in the hole, "I'd call myself an entrepreneur par excellence. But when the entrepreneur's work is done, one needs professional management. I don't have the talent to turn this into a $100 million company, but there is a lot of talent out there that can do it. Brains are the cheapest thing I can buy."

Mr. Adams, too, has chosen the holder of a Harvard M.B.A. as his business heir.

He is Theo C. Rodgers, 37, who is president of the A. & R. Development Corporation. Although Mr Adams still is

See POWER, A10, Col. 1

The Weather
Sunny today, high 48; clear tonight, low 30 to 35. Yesterday's high 46, low 38 (Details and Map, Page C2)

THE SUN

FINAL

Vol. 284—No. 111—F

BALTIMORE, TUESDAY, MARCH 27, 1979

15 Cents

Egypt, Israel sign peace treaty

AP

'Nation shall not lift up sword against nation, neither shall they learn war anymore'

Carter praised as 2 nations end 30 years of war

By GILBERT A. LEWTHWAITE
Washington Bureau of The Sun

Washington—Quoting the Old Testament prophets and praising the New World President, the leaders of Egypt and Israel yesterday put a formal end to their 30-year state of war.

President Carter, architect of the tenuous treaty, witnessed their signatures on the dotted line of peace at an open-air ceremony on the White House's front lawn.

Signed were the English, Hebrew and Arabic versions of the treaty, mandating Israeli withdrawal from the Sinai within three years, an end to Egypt's economic embargo against Israel, an eventual establishment of full Egyptian-Israeli diplomatic relations, and a letter of intent on future negotiations covering the status of the Israeli-occupied West Bank of the Jordan River and the Gaza Strip.

Late agreement was reached between the United States and Israel on a treaty-support package. The United States agreed, according to Israeli sources, "to take care of" any future sea blockade of Israel, and to guarantee Israeli oil supplies for 15 years.

Last night, in a bright orange and yellow circus tent, for which $6,000 was paid for the occasion, Mr. Carter entertained the two old foes, President Anwar el Sadat of Egypt and Prime Minister Menachem Begin of Israel, and 1,300 other VIP guests at a salmon and roast beef state dinner in his backyard.

For the first time in his White House tenure President Carter opened a state dinner by saying grace. Asking for Divine blessing, he said: "We have come through difficult times. We face those same times in the future . . . let us, the leaders of our nations, represent the hopes of our people."

Later, in his toast, President Carter said: "We pray that the season of weeping is past, that now will come a time to heal, a time to plant, a time to build up, a time to laugh, a time to dance, a time to embrace, a time to love. We pray that at last the children of Abraham have come to a time for peace."

Both Mr. Begin and Mr. Sadat later proposed that President Carter receive the 1979 Nobel Peace Prize for his efforts.

Mr. Begin, who shared the 1978 prize with Mr. Sadat, said he was certain both he and the Egyptian leader would be in Oslo next December to see President Carter accept the award.

It was the first peace agreement between Arab and Jew since the state of Israel was founded in 1948, but it represented only the start of the search for an even more elusive settlement throughout the Middle East.

Even as Washington's church bells tolled joyously and President Sadat and Mr. Begin smilingly penned their names to the historic documents, the chants of 2,000 Arab demonstrators opposed to the peace package could be heard on the chill northerly wind that blew across Lafayette Square.

But the immediate celebration was of two ancient belligerents who had buried the sword, a peaceful initiative which prompted President Carter to join both the Egyptian and Israeli statesmen in quoting the prophet Isaiah: "Nations shall beat their swords into plowshares and their spears into pruninghooks; nation shall not lift up sword against nation, neither shall they learn war anymore."

If Isaiah was unquestionable the most popular prophet of the day, President Carter was obviously the most admired man of the moment.

Said President Sadat: "Hundreds of dedicated individuals on both sides have given generously of their thought and effort to translate a cherished dream into

See TREATY, A4, Col. 2

Beyond treaty lie bleak times

By HENRY L. TREWHITT
Washington Bureau of The Sun

Washington—"We have no illusions," President Carter said, looking beyond the triumph of the Israeli-Egyptian peace treaty to the certain bleak times ahead.

Even furious Arab opponents acknowledge the treaty as a historic turning point. At least it raises a great new barrier against another Arab-Israeli war. For Egypt, hostile American Arabs said yesterday, presents the only "credible military threat" to Israel.

But even at best, painful negotiations lie ahead. The political schedule in documents accompanying the treaty begins with an exchange of ratified treaties in about two weeks. If all goes easily, which hardly anyone expects, it would be completed in six years with a permanent solution to the Palestinian issue and regional stability.

As the dogged patron of the negotiations, Mr. Carter now has accepted for the United States a more formal role in whatever happens next. It is a measure of his

Analysis

commitment, and of U.S. interests, that the precise nature of that role still was being negotiated after the treaty and a handful of other documents were signed yesterday.

American interests have dictated a cumbersome sequence of political juggling. Ever since the Mideast war and oil embargo of 1973-1974, the U.S. has attempted to reconcile its historic support for Israel with its critical need for Arab—especially Saudi Arabian—oil.

In that process, peace between Egypt, as the foremost Arab military power, and Israel is seen as an essential step. The daring initiative of President Anwar el Sadat of Egypt, reinforced by American pressure on Israel, led finally to the ceremony yesterday on the White House lawn.

The next phase has dual specific objectives: to fulfill the complex terms of the treaty package while making participation attractive to other hostile or reluctant Arabs. For the U.S., the abstract strategic goals are even broader.

Apart from retaining oil supplies,

See MIDEAST, A5, Col. 1

Begin pays tribute to mother of war dead

By LYNNE OLSON
Washington Bureau of The Sun

Washington—In acknowledging all the "distinguished guests" at the signing of the Israeli-Egyptian peace treaty yesterday, Prime Minister Menachem Begin of Israel paid special tribute to "Mrs. Gover, the mother of the sons."

Many guests turned to each other with puzzled looks; no one knew to whom Mr. Begin was referring.

Later, it was discovered the woman in question is 77-year-old Rivka Gover, who lost her two sons in the 1948 Israeli war of independence.

She was a member of the official Israeli delegation at the ceremonies, representing all Israeli mothers whose children have been killed in battle.

—o—

About 5,000 tourists and curious Washingtonians gathered in Lafayette Park, across Pennsylvania avenue from the White House to witness the historic treaty signing. But they heard a lot more than they saw.

Blocking their vision were dozens of park policemen on horseback, hundreds of police officers on foot and 1,600 invited guests who witnessed the event on the White House front lawn.

But thanks to loudspeakers set up near them, onlookers in the park could hear the speeches of the three leaders, as well as the hoarse shouts from the back of the park of 2,000 Arab demonstrators who were Palestinian supporters.

Wearing Arab headdresses and waving posters reading, "Sadat is U.S. Property" and "Down with Carter, Begin, Sadat," the demonstrators chanted such slogans as "Long Live the PLO" and "Carter, Carter, Got to Go. We Support the PLO."

AP

Demonstrators march toward rally.

But the demonstration was peaceful, and the crowds tried to ignore it and concentrate on the event across the street. Many of the tourists applauded loudly during the speeches, along with the guests on the White House grounds.

One young man however, was not satisfied with his vantage point and climbed into a tree in the park for a better view.

A policeman climbed up and wrestled him down to the ground to the cheers of the crowd. Police said they could not permit anyone in the trees for security reasons.

—o—

Among Marylanders invited to the treaty-signing, in addition to the state's congressional delegation, were Governor Hughes, Mayor Schaefer; state Senator Rosalie S. Abrams (D., 42d, Baltimore), the Senate majority leader and Democratic state party chairperson; Jerold C. Hoffberger, the Baltimore Orioles owner; and A. Dwight Pettit, the Baltimore lawyer and a Carter backer in the 1976 state primary.

Missing from the guest list was state Senator James Clark, Jr. (D., Howard), president of the Senate and one of the earliest Maryland supporters of Mr. Carter three years ago.

—o—

The entertainment for last night's gala state dinner on the White House South Lawn was personally chosen by the leaders of the three countries signing the peace treaty.

President Anwar el Sadat selected three Egyptian musicians playing a guitar, table drum and electric organ. Prime Minister Begin chose Itzhak Perlman and Pinchas Zukerman, the noted violinists. And President Carter picked Leontyne Price, the opera singer.

More than 1,300 guests, one of the largest guest lists in the history of White House social events, attended the event, held in a huge orange-and-yellow striped tent on the South Lawn.

Businessmen who contributed $5,000 or more to defray the costs of the dinner were invited to come, but the White House turned down unsolicited offers of financial contributions.

Mary Hoyt, press secretary to Rosalynn Carter, said her office had received several dozen calls from some persons who offered small amounts of money and expressed no desire to attend the dinner, and others who made it clear they wanted to buy a seat.

The calls started after news reports that the White House was soliciting money from corporations to pay for the dinner.

Seated at 130 round tables decorated with forsythia branches and hurricane lamps, the guests dined on Columbia River salmon in aspic, roast sirloin of beef with spring vegetables, hazelnut guanduja mousse and petit fours for dessert and demitasse.

The wines were all from California: Louis Martini Pinot Chardonay, Paul Mas-

See SIGNING, A5, Col. 1

OPEC may raise oil prices 20% higher than planned

By DOUGLAS WATSON
Sun Staff Correspondent

Geneva—There are strong indications that the Organization of Petroleum Exporting Countries (OPEC), which yesterday began a special meeting here, will agree on an immediate and substantial oil price increase of 10 to 20 per cent beyond the petroleum price rises already planned for this year. No decisions were announced yesterday.

But reports coming out of OPEC's closed-door sessions were of broad support within the 13-nation cartel that supplies half the world's oil for an abrupt and major boost of prices capitalizing on the present petroleum shortage.

Cyrus Ebrahimzadeh, a member of the Iranian delegation, told reporters that considerable backing was voiced in yesterday's morning meeting for now lifting the base price of a barrel of light crude oil to over $17.

This would amount to about a 20 per cent increase over the $14.54 a barrel price that has been scheduled to go into effect at the end of this year. Iraq's oil minister, Tayeh Abdul Karim, said before the opening session that he favored OPEC raising its basic price to $16.50 a barrel.

Even this would be more than $3 a barrel [illegible] the present OPEC base price of $1[illegible] a barrel, an increase that would have [illegible] negative impact on the world and United States economies and on the price that American motorists would have to pay for gasoline. None of the OPEC countries reportedly argued against an oil price increase.

There also is strong support within OPEC for some cuts in oil production to offset the expected gradual increase in Iranian production in the next two months to about twice its present production level of about two million barrels a day.

Offsetting cutbacks by countries such as Saudi Arabia, which had raised their oil output when the Iranian revolution halted all exports from what had been the world's second largest oil exporter, would be aimed at maintaining a tight market of scarcity that would sustain the planned price rises.

Ali Ardalan, Iran's new minister of economic affairs and finance, told the OPEC representatives yesterday, "The victorious revolutionary government of Iran, having achieved its freedom and joining the petroleum exporting countries once more, expects all countries which have increased productions in order to supplement Iranian oil, will return to their previous levels of productions, enabling us to attain our righteous export level and obtain the necessary funds needed for our development. No doubt, Iran will adjust its export level of production with the market situation."

Mr. Ardalan continued, "It seems appropriate that OPEC should also reduce its total exports from the previous year's

See OPEC, A2, Col. 2

Trudeau sets new Canadian vote May 22

Ottawa (Special)—Prime Minister Pierre Elliott Trudeau of Canada dissolved Parliament last night and announced federal elections for May 22.

Moments after he had seen Gov. Gen. Edward Richard Schreyer to dissolve Parliament, Mr. Trudeau held a press conference to outline his campaign strategy.

Sources report that Prime Minister Trudeau actually had wanted to call for a new election last Friday or Saturday, but government strategy in Parliament had misfired on getting two vital pieces of legislation passed, so he had to wait until 9 P.M. last night.

One of the bills, which finally passed earlier yesterday, gives the government emergency energy rationing powers; the other extends the existing Bank Act, because the government has been unable to get new legislation drafted.

Both the Conservatives and the minority left-wing New Democratic party were delighted that Mr. Trudeau has ended

See CANADA, A2, Col. 1

Index

3 sections

UPI

President Carter shakes hands with Menachem Begin after the treaty-signing as President Anwar el Sadat (left) looks on.

The Weather
Partly cloudy and warm today, thunderstorms tonight. High, 80; low, 58. Yesterday's high, 82; low, 62.
(Details and Map, Page B2)

THE SUN

FINAL

Vol. 284—No. 115—F

BALTIMORE, SATURDAY, MARCH 31, 1979

••• 15 Cents

Possibility of reactor meltdown debated; pregnant, young leave

Stricter rules predicted

Ex-NRC official alleges defects at 8 other facilities

By PETER BEHR
and CARL P. LEUBSDORF
Washington Bureau of The Sun

Washington—President Carter said yesterday that "more stringent" standards for nuclear power plants will almost certainly be adopted in the aftermath of the accident at the Three Mile Island power plant near Harrisburg.

In a meeting with newspaper editors, Mr. Carter said the incident "will make all of us reassess our present safety regulations and precautions."

Meanwhile, a former safety engineer with the Nuclear Regulatory Commission charged yesterday that eight other nuclear power plants in six states may have mechanical defects similiar to the problems that apparently caused the Three Mile Island plant accident.

Robert D. Pollard, now with the Union of Concerned Scientists, said NRC documents show repeated problems involving reactor cooling systems, not only with the two units at the Harrisburg plant, but with others at plants in Crystal River, Fla.; Russellville, Ark.; Clay Station, Calif.; Oak Harbor, Ohio, and three near Greenville, S.C. All have cooling systems designed by Babcock & Wilcox, a leading New York-based nuclear engineering firm.

"At the Three Mile Island plant itself, the basic cooling system began to experience failures shortly after the plant was licensed in February, 1978," Mr. Pollard said.

NRC documents that he released also described serious problems at the Rancho Seco nuclear power plant in Clay Station, Calif., and the Davis-Besse power plant in Oak Harbor, Ohio, according to Mr. Pollard. His organization has been a vocal critic of the NRC's safety regulations and procedures.

The documents include letters from NRC files by a Babcock & Wilcox operations manager to the plant superintendent at the Davis-Besse plant last year, relating problems with the electronic controls at several B. & W. plants.

In a March 20, 1978, incident at the Rancho Seco plant, a short circuit in a control panel caused a warning instrument in the control room to malfunction, giving incorrect signals to the technicians.

The plant's computerized reaction system then responded—incorrectly—to the false signals, causing the nuclear reactor to shut down under high pressure.

"The erroneous signals" to the control system "contributed to the rapid cooldown" of the reactor. "Plant operators had extreme difficulty in determining the true status of some of the plant parameters and in controlling the plant because of the erroneous indications in the control room," said a B. & W. official, Ivan D. Green, in an August 9, 1978, letter to T. D. Murray, the Davis-Besse station superintendent.

Attempts to contact the B. & W. officials were not successful.

According to Mr. Pollard, the NRC records give reason to suspect a possible mechanical failure of the plant cooling system, or an electrical failure which then

See CARTER, A4, Col. 1

Map (below) shows proximity of damaged and leaking nuclear power plant on Three Mile Island in the Susquehanna River to south central Pennsylvania towns and number of persons living within 5 and 10 miles of the plant. Four surrounding counties (detail)—Dauphin, Cumberland, York and Lancaster—have personnel preparing to evacuate residents, should the health risk be deemed great enough. So far, only high-risk persons—the pregnant and the very young—have been advised to leave the area.

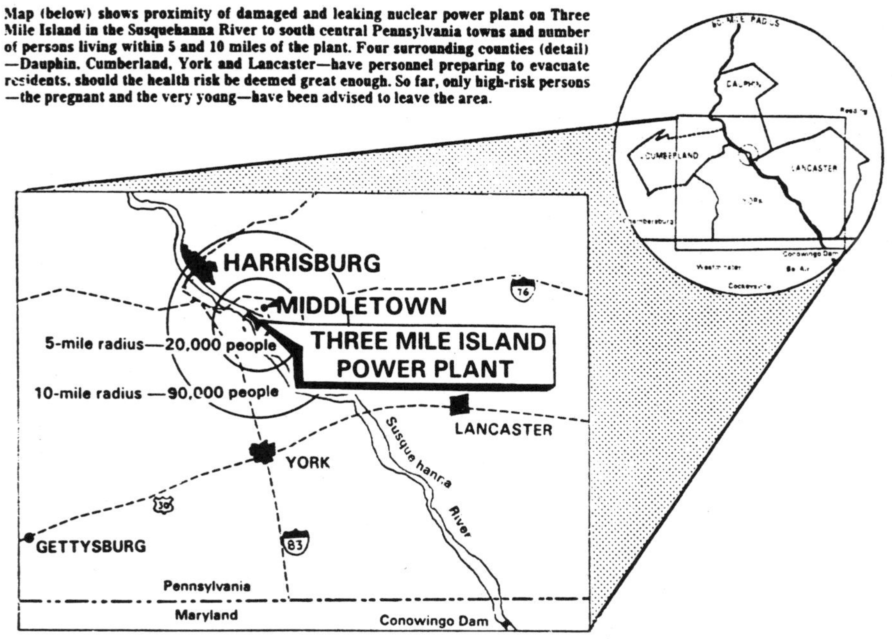

Distrust, frustration pervade area near A-plant as some prepare to leave

Sun photo—Richard Childress

Mary Louise Taleff, who lives across the road from the Three Mile Island nuclear plant, packs her car as she prepares to leave the area of the radiation leak and stay with relatives in Harrisburg.

By ANTERO PIETILA
Sun Staff Correspondent

Middletown, Pa.—"I think they are a big bunch of liars," George Taleff, a 63-year-old retired grocery salesman muttered as he packed family belongings to leave his house just across from the Three Mile Island nuclear plant.

"Those jerks don't know what they are doing," he continued. "Everybody has a conflicting statement—Metropolitan Edison, the Governor, the Civil Defense. They kept telling everybody it was safe and we took the government's word."

Trust was the biggest casualty yesterday as hundreds of people within a 5-mile radius of the power plant on the Susquehanna River near Harrisburg decided to leave their homes for safer areas, on their own or heeding the advice of Gov. Richard L. Thornburgh that pregnant women and preschool-age children voluntarily evacuate.

"I don't really trust them. I did, but I'll never trust them again," Suzanne Machita, 38, a clerk at New Cumberland Army Depot said, preparing to leave her house for that of relatives in Pennsylvania's coal country.

"I don't think it was one thing that happened," she continued. Referring to yesterday's "uncontrolled release of radiation" at the crippled plant less than a mile away, "I think it was a lot of things. They covered it up. But what can you do? If you are in a car accident, at least you can be mad at the guy who hit you."

But at a house next door, Kathleen Krodel, the mother of three teen-agers, said "We are just going to stay here. I figure that when you are going to go, you are going to go."

When most residents of the Harrisburg area went to bed Thursday night, they were being reassured that the danger was past. When they awoke the next morning and went off to work, they switched on their radios to hear Kevin J. Molloy, a Civ-

See COMMUNITY, A6, Col. 1

Pa. won't evacuate en masse; efforts to cool core hampered

By TOM HORTON and ROBERT RUBY

Pregnant women and young children evacuated a 5-mile radius around a damaged nuclear power plant near Harrisburg yesterday, as authorities began debating openly the possibility of a meltdown of the reactor core, the ultimate disaster at a nuclear installation.

"We face the ultimate risk of a meltdown," said Dudley Thompson, a senior inspector for the Nuclear Regulatory Commission, but added that for the time being, the situation at the plant is considered stable and the reactor is being cooled normally.

Last night Gov. Richard L. Thornburgh of Pennsylvania announced that he had decided against a general evacuation following a 90-minute meeting with Harold Denton, President Carter's personal representative on the scene. Mr. Denton, a high Nuclear Regulatory Commission official, had spent all day touring the Three Mile Island plant.

The Governor also said the advisory to pregnant women and children would remain in effect until sometime today. He lifted at midnight a request that persons stay indoors if they lived within 10 miles of the plant, located on an island in the Susquehanna River, 10 miles south of Harrisburg and 60 miles north of Baltimore.

Mr. Denton said relatively low levels of radiation were still being vented continuously from a part of the plant outside the reactor building, the result of contaminated coolant that was spilled Wednesday when the accident began.

The major problem—the reactor and its potential for meltdown—is not of an immediate nature, a source in the Nuclear Regulatory Commission explained. But steps must be taken within days to deal with a growing gas bubble formed within the reactor that threatens to shut off the flow of cooling water to it. The bubble is the result of hydrolysis: Some of the water is being broken down into its elements, hydrogen and oxygen.

Steps to deal with the gas almost certainly will involve great risks, the NRC acknowledged.

"The decisions to be made in the next few days are unprecedented," Mr Thompson said yesterday afternoon.

His characterization of a potential for meltdown was disputed as "not in the proper perspective" by a statement from Mr Denton issued through the Governor's office.

What was the proper perspective" the Governor's spokesman was asked.

"We don't have any more to say," he replied.

Later last night Mr. Denton said, "My first concern was the reactor core—could it be cooled?" He answered his own question vaguely, saying there are plenty of backup systems which could be used in emergencies.

He said he considered the possibility of a meltdown "remote."

But at the rate the reactor is being cooled off now, he admitted, it could be months before it is safe. He said a decision would have to be made in the next three or four days on how to cool the core down faster.

Documents in Harrisburg show that the Nuclear Regulatory Commission last year raised serious questions about the reactor's water injection system, a part of the emergency core cooling backups to which Mr. Denton referred.

The NRC told the utility the injection system would not be able to cool the reactor in an emergency without quick work by control room engineers

On November 28, 1978, the commission and the utility agreed on design changes in the injection system according to the utility's engineers, but they were scheduled for April, 1980, and had not been done at the time of the accident.

Twenty-three schools were closed yesterday within a 5-mile radius of the plant. Emergency management officials in the surrounding York, Cumberland, Lancaster

See NUCLEAR, A6, Col 5

Tests find no radiation in state air, water, milk

State and county health officials in Maryland said their samples of the air, water and milk from dairy cows yesterday continued to show no traces of the radioactivity being released from the damaged Three Mile Island nuclear plant in Harrisburg.

A State Police helicopter, using instruments that measure radiation directly from the air without having to take samples back to a lab, flew a course from Aberdeen north to Rising Sun, then west along the Maryland-Pennsylvania border to Interstate 83, and south along I-83.

"They picked up no radiation at all above normal background levels," said Jon Crosby, a spokesman for the state health department.

Water samples taken yesterday morning in the Susquehanna river, where 120,000 gallons of radioactive water were dumped Thursday from the Three Mile Island plant, likewise turned up clean.

The water was mostly ordinary industrial waste that had become slightly contaminated with small quantities of xenon, a relatively mild radioactive element.

Mr. Crosby said the state had not been notified of plans to dump any more contaminated water into the river.

Samples taken at several dairy farms near the Pennsylvania line yesterday also turned out negative when tested for radioactivity, Mr. Crosby said. He said the state would continue all its sampling activities today.

In Baltimore county, four health officials and two civil defense workers re-

See MARYLAND, A6, Col. 4

Ulster spokesman, key Thatcher adviser, killed by bomb; IRA group takes credit

By PETER J. KUMPA
London Bureau of The Sun

London—The Conservative spokesman for Northern Ireland, Airey Neave, was killed yesterday when a bomb exploded in his car as he was driving out of the underground parking lot of the House of Commons.

The closest adviser to the leader of the opposition, Margaret Thatcher, and head of her personal office, Mr. Neave was pronounced dead eight minutes after reaching nearby Westminster Hospital. Both of his legs had been blown off and his face pulverized by the blast of a half-pound bomb that had been placed under the hood of his car.

A splinter group of the Provisional Irish Republican Army took credit for the murder A spokesman for the Irish National Liberation Army telephoned a Dublin newspaper to warn that the bombing was "the first attack in a new campaign against the British political and military establishment." Its message to the British was to get out of Ireland.

The killing stunned London.

Mrs. Thatcher canceled a television broadcast she had planned as a reply to Prime Minister James Callaghan's opening statement on the elections.

Mr. Callaghan led a long line of political leaders expressing their shock and horror at the "cowardly" murder of the 63-year-old member of Parliament and wartime hero. "No effort will be spared to bring his murderers to justice," the prime minister said.

Queen Elizabeth II sent her condolences to Mr. Neave's wife.

It was the Irish of all political persuasions who issued the toughest denunciations of the murder. Premier Jack Lynch in Dublin called it "a particularly heinous crime for which no condemnation can be too strong."

"The IRA has again demonstrated its contempt for human life and values, and for the reputation of the Irish people," he said. Speaking for his government and people, Mr. Lynch offered all possible cooperation to catch the killers, or "the common enemy," to use his words.

Meanwhile, London braced for another round of IRA bomb attacks. The last had been in the fall of 1975 and the winter of 1976.

Mr. Neave was best known to the public for his wartime exploits. In 1942, he was the first British officer to escape from Colditz Castle, where the Germans locked up prominent prisoners and persistent escapers. He then commanded an operation that rescued thousands of allied pilots from behind enemy lines. He was part of the prosecution team at the Nuremburg trials, where he personally served indictments on Air Marshal Hermann Goering and other Nazi war criminals.

He wrote books on his own escapades ("They Have Their Exits") and on wartime intelligence. His Colditz vanishing act inspired a popular television series.

If the Tories had won the coming election, Mr. Neave would have been appointed minister to Northern Ireland. As shadow spokesman, he visited Ulster many times and offered some tough suggestions. He wanted the death penalty for terrorist murderers. He warned against withdrawing British troops to prevent a "massive" civil war.

Gerry Fitt, the lone Social Democratic Labor party member from Belfast in

See BOMBING, A2, Col. 1

Index

2 sections

Tanzanians shell capital of Uganda

Nairobi, Kenya (AP)—Artillery shells from encircling Tanzanian units blasted the Ugandan capital of Kampala yesterday and one well-informed observer said: "We think it could all be over in a day or a few days."

President Idi Amin's troops, besieged by the Tanzanians and Ugandan exiles, still held Kampala, but their discipline reportedly was breaking down. One resident, reached by telephone, said "drunken deserters" were wandering through the streets, firing into the air. Marshal Amin's whereabouts were not known.

"There are explosions everywhere," a Kampala man said. "We are trapped in our home. We pray for tomorrow. The town is being turned into smoke."

He said Marshal Amin's command post on Kololo Hill was destroyed by a hit and other artillery rounds exploded near the Mulago Hospital and French Embassy.

Tanzania charged that a Soviet-made Libyan warplane bombed the Tanzanian town of Mwanza on the shore of Lake Victoria Thursday and said one person was wounded.

The State Department issued a state-

See UGANDA, A2, Col. 3

United halts 1,600 flights as Machinists call strike

By JEFF KOSNETT

United Air Lines mechanics, baggage handlers and food service personnel notified the nation's largest airline yesterday that they would strike at 12.01 A.M. today

Late last night, the company announced that it had canceled its 1,600 daily flights through April 9 to give travelers a chance to make other plans.

Unless an 11th-hour settlement occurs, much of the east-west service from Baltimore-Washington International Airport would be suspended.

Donald C. Merton, a special assistant to United's president, said from his Cleveland office that the airline received word from the union early yesterday morning of the impending strike action.

The dispute involves 18,611 members of the International Association of Machinists (AFL-CIO), including 210 United employees at BWI. The union turned down a company offer in early February and another offer 12 days ago.

United, with 19 daily departures, is the third-busiest carrier at BWI, after Allegheny Airlines and Eastern Airlines. Nationally, United carried 24 per cent of U.S. domestic passenger traffic in 1978

Its routes from Baltimore extend to Chicago, Cleveland, Denver, Kansas City, Los Angeles, Richmond and Norfolk, with connections to many of the major cities in the Midwest and West. United is also the primary carrier between Baltimore and the Pacific Northwest

While other airlines serve many of these points either by connections or directly from BWI, United operates six of the seven daily departures to and from Chicago, with one such flight provided by Trans World Airlines.

A TWA spokesman, John J. Corris, said yesterday that he doubted TWA would be able to add many flights if United is shut down for any long period. TWA and American Airlines also serve Chicago from Washington.

When U.S. airlines have been struck in the past, other airlines have provided extra flights and made cash payments to the struck company under a mutual-aid agreement. Both of these ways to cope with strikes have been materially changed because of 1978 industry developments.

Last summer mutual-aid agreements were weakened to make it impossible for an airline to turn a profit while shut down by a strike. This did happen in 1978 in the case of Northwest Airlines

Deregulation and changes in schedules that allow for the operation of planes for

See UNITED, A13, Col 5

The Weather
Sunny and fair today, fair tonight. High, 83; low, 58. Yesterday's high, 78; low, 58.
(Details and Map, Page C2)

THE SUN

FINAL

Vol. 285—No. 24—F

BALTIMORE, WEDNESDAY, JUNE 13, 1979

••• 15 Cents

250-truck convoy closes tunnel

Sun photo—J. Pat Carter

The truck convoy stops on the Harbor Tunnel throughway near Moravia road, where truckers left their rigs to discuss whether to pay the toll at the tunnel or detour to the Baltimore Beltway. Police were determined to force them into the tunnel.

'We have done it,' a protesting trucker exults on a jam-packed tunnel thruway

By ROBERT RUBY

Nancy Moore was relaxing in the living room of her home last night, in the southbound lane of the Harbor Tunnel thruway, when she turned with a serious question.

"Tell me," she said. "Who supports the country most, these trucks or the cars?"

Mrs. Moore and her husband, John, sat in the cab of their $65,000 truck—comfortably outfitted as both home and office—and watched as the thruway was transformed for nearly two hours yesterday into the state's largest parking lot.

Both of the tunnel's southbound lanes were filled with dozens of tractor-trailers, parked to protest what the owners contended was the scandalously high cost of diesel fuel.

"We've done something today I never thought we would do," John Moore broke in, the grin of a satisfied person on his face. "We have done it."

What had they done?

They had stopped traffic, brought the State Police out of their patrol cars to talk and drawn considerable attention to themselves, hoping that people might consider their point of view.

Tractor-trailers are home, office and probably vacation for people like the Moores, who had come from the state of Washington. They drive upwards of 200,000 miles a year, and they are outraged at paying just under $1 a gallon for fuel that cost less than 70 cents only six months ago.

There is a lot of dark talk. The drivers say President Carter has been duped, that Congress has been fooled, that the oil companies are calling the shots, and that is why some of the drivers said they carrying, or driving, their protest to Washington.

"We're going broke," said a blue-eyed driver named John, who said he hailed from Millersville.

In May, he said, "I ran all month, and I

See TUNNEL, A8, Col. 1

Caravan crawls to D.C.

Drivers protest high fuel costs, cargo weight limits

By RICHARD H. P. SIA and CATHERINE A. STROTT

A convoy of about 250 trucks and tractor trailers crept southward through Maryland on Interstate 95 yesterday afternoon, snarling rush-hour traffic in the Baltimore area and briefly closing down the Harbor Tunnel thruway.

Maryland State Police made a futile attempt to keep the truck traffic moving in an orderly fashion as it approached the Harbor Tunnel, trying to limit trucks to the middle and slow lanes of the three-lane southbound route outside the Baltimore Beltway.

But the trucks, moving no faster than 10 miles an hour and as slowly as 1 mile an hour, often clogged all three lanes and both southbound lanes of the tunnel thruway, forcing commuting motorists to back up the John F. Kennedy Memorial Highway and the tunnel for 4 to 5 miles, according to troopers.

Many of the trucks dispersed after leaving the tunnel about 9 P.M. and police said about 100 headed west to Frederick county on Interstate 70 while many splintered into groups of a dozen or more, tying up traffic on the Capital Beltway outside Washington late last night.

There were no reports of violence, and 30 arrests were made along I-95, 21 of them in Cecil county, 6 at the tunnel and 3 on I-70. William Clark, a State Police spokesman, said late last night. Those truck drivers were cited for impeding traffic, or in the case of the I-70 arrests, failing to stay in the slow lanes as ordered by police.

Elsewhere along the interstate, traffic

See TRUCKERS, A8, Col. 1

LT. GEN. EDWARD L. ROWNY

Negotiator to quit over arms treaty

Announcement set for eve of Carter's SALT signing trip

By CHARLES W. CORDDRY
Washington Bureau of The Sun

Washington—Lt. Gen. Edward L. Rowny, unable to support the SALT II treaty as it now stands, will quit his post on the United States arms negotiating team and retire from military service June 30.

An announcement that General Rowny, a native Baltimorean, will leave the

President Carter is doing extensive homework for weekend summit meeting in Vienna....... A2

American delegation is scheduled to be made today, on the eve of President Carter's departure for the Vienna summit conference.

Mr. Carter and Soviet President Leonid I. Brezhnev are to cap their four-day meeting with a ceremony signing the new strategic arms limitation treaty (SALT II) Monday.

General Rowny's departure will be a setback for the administration's SALT prospects in the Senate, where the general is highly respected for his long service on the U.S. SALT team and his intimate knowledge of arms control issues.

His known distress over the outcome of negotiations leading to SALT II will not be noted in the announcement scheduled for today. But it forms a further part of the backdrop of foreign policy challenges for Mr. Carter as he leaves Thursday.

These challenges, in the Senate, cover policies on arms control, Zimbabwe Rhodesia and Taiwan. In the House, legislation for implementation of the Panama Canal treaty is threatened and a vote is expected to be delayed until after Mr. Carter comes home from Vienna.

Acquaintances described General Rowny yesterday as a "very torn man" who has invested more than six years in SALT negotiations, disagrees with major provisions accepted by the administration, but will reserve his criticisms until called before Senate committees.

Some treaty supporters, recognizing the consequences General Rowny's opposition could have, said they hoped he would weigh the arguments and, however reluctantly, back the pact as better than none.

General Rowny was said to have outlined his objections in a letter to Gen. David C. Jones, the chairman, and other members of the Joint Chiefs of Staff.

Essentially, he does not believe the treaty has emerged as equitable from the

See GENERAL, A2, Col. 1

Somoza girds for showdown

By GILBERT A. LEWTHWAITE
Sun Staff Correspondent

Managua, Nicaragua — Sixty-one American citizens were flown to safety from war-torn Nicaragua yesterday, as President Anastasio Somoza Debayle girded for a showdown with his guerrilla opponents.

As the Americans, mostly wives and children of United States Embassy employees here, fled the fighting, General Somoza ordered convoys of his national guardsmen into this capital city.

Senior uniformed Sandinista guerrilla commandos were reported to have slipped into the explosive slum areas, suggesting a new initiative.

At the same time, the first serious breach appeared in General Somoza's grip on his armed forces with the desertion of a fighter pilot who attacked the airport as he flew his rocket-launching propeller plane to Costa Rica.

U.S. citizens were taken out in a C-130 transport flown here from the American Air Force base in the Panama Canal Zone. A second airlift is being considered for more than 80 other Americans who have told the embassy they would like to leave.

Yesterday's airlift took off from an undisclosed coastal airstrip under special arrangement with the National Guard.

A National Guard patrol escorted the convoy of embassy cars 40 miles from Managua to the secret airstrip among banana plantations. The remote airfield was chosen after guerrillas kept the road to the main airport here blocked for the second day.

The deserting pilot, Capt. Armengal

See NICARAGUA, A2, Col. 2

A movie legend

John Wayne, America's top film hero and the star of more than 200 movies, died Monday of cancer. The star was as indomitable in real life as he was on the screen. (Articles on Page A14)

Mrs. Talmadge describes $30,000 cache

By THOMAS B. EDSALL
Washington Bureau of The Sun

Washington—Testifying under protest and breaking into tears at one point, Senator Herman E. Talmadge's ex-wife yesterday described a cache of $100 bills totaling well over $30,000 kept in an overcoat pocket in the Georgia Democrat's apartment.

Betty Talmadge told the Senate Select Committee on Ethics that both she and Mr. Talmadge took money from the supply of cash. At one point in 1974, she said, she took $12,000 to $15,000 from the overcoat stash, about one third of the total.

"For years, it was a way of life," she said.

Mrs. Talmadge testified the practice began when Mr. Talmadge first ran for Georgia governor in 1948, although at the start, the money was in small denominations, while in recent years "almost all of it was $100 bills."

Mrs. Talmadge, who was married to Mr. Talmadge for 36 years and who turned a small family ham business into a million dollar sales operation, initially attempted to assert the right of a wife not to testify against her husband. "Senator Talmadge and I are still the parents of our son, Gene, and the grandparents of five grandchildren," she told the committee.

Describing the bitter divorce proceedings, she broke into tears while reading from a prepared statement discussing the fight she and Senator Talmadge had over "the homeplace [in Georgia] where our late son, Bobby, is buried."

The committee denied her request to avoid testifying, but she was allowed not to discuss private conversations she had held with Mr. Talmadge.

The restriction resulted in convoluted testimony because she could never be asked about anything Mr. Talmadge may have said about the cache of money in the overcoat pocket. She did testify that she did not know the source of the money, which was periodically replenished.

Her comment about the supply of cash appeared to buttress the case of the ethics committee against Mr. Talmadge. He has been accused of five counts of financial impropriety in violation of Senate rules.

On a separate issue, however, Mrs. Talmadge flatly contradicted the testimony of Daniel Minchew, the key witness in the case whose charges are critical to proving the most serious of the allegations.

Mr. Minchew, who was Mr. Talmadge's administrative assistant from 1971 to 1974, has claimed that he and the senator set up a secret account in the Riggs National Bank to siphon off Senate expense claims for nonexistent expenses and campaign contributions.

He testified that he gave money from the fund not only to the senator, but also to Mrs. Talmadge and to their late son, Robert, who died in 1975 in a drowning accident.

Mrs. Talmadge said yesterday she never received money from Mr. Minchew, and she seriously questioned whether her

See TALMADGE, A9, Col. 3

UPI

Bryan Allen, of Bakersfield, Calif., sets out on his man-powered flight across the English Channel.

U.S. flier pedals across English Channel

Cap Gris Nez, France (AP)—Bryan Allen, 26, a lanky, bespectacled Californian, joined the ranks of aviation's pioneers yesterday by pedaling the fragile "Gossamer Albatross" on the first man-powered flight across the English Channel.

His daring and stamina won a $200,000 prize for him and the designer.

The Gossamer Albatross, named for its delicate body and outsize wings, crossed the channel in 2 hours and 49 minutes, powered only by the legs of Mr. Allen.

He pushed on pedals, rotating a bicycle-like chain that in turn twirled a propeller on the craft's rear.

Once in France, he emerged drenched in sweat from the stifling cockpit, and quoted the operation's motto: "If the wind don't blow and the chain don't break . . . we'll make it across."

Exultant, he added: "Although the wind did blow a bit, the chain driving the propeller didn't break and we made it."

"I feel tired, but . . . whooeeee!" he shouted as he accepted a bouquet of flowers and French and American flags from the nearby town of Wissant's sole American resident.

A pretty red-haired French girl, coaxed by photographers, gave Mr. Allen a kiss of welcome.

His was the second major aerial feat by Americans to end in success on French soil within a year. On August 17, three Americans completed the first successful Atlantic balloon crossing and landed in a wheat field in Normandy, about 250 miles southwest of Cap Gris Nez.

Never more than 15 feet above the rising waves, and sometimes only inches from the gray waters, Mr. Allen fought air

See FLIER, A4, Col. 5

Carter dealt Senate blow on Zimbabwe

Washington (NYT)—President Carter lost the first round of a showdown that he deliberately sought with Congress as the Senate in effect voted 52 to 41 yesterday to force the ending of sanctions against Zimbabwe Rhodesia.

By this margin, the Senate defeated an amendment by Senator Jacob K. Javits (R., N.Y.) that would have allowed the President to maintain sanctions until December 1 and even after that date if he certified to Congress that it would be in the national interest to do so.

The vote left in the $40 billion defense authorization bill for 1980 an amendment by Senator Harry F. Byrd (Ind., Va.) to mandate the lifting of the sanctions.

Mr. Javits wrote his amendment after Mr. Carter had rejected an earlier version that would have given him another six months to consider the sanctions question but would have empowered Congress to overturn his decision at the end of that period.

Senator Frank Church (D., Idaho), chairman of the Foreign Relations Committee, had asked Cyrus R. Vance, Secretary of State, to consult the President on this version, which he acknowledged would leave the final decision on sanctions up to Congress.

The White House reacted quickly, indicating it would prefer an up-and-down vote on the repeal of sanctions to any amendment that it regarded as raising a constitutional question about the President's right to conduct the nation's foreign policy.

It was Mr. Vance who warned the Foreign Relations Committee that the President was "quite likely" to veto any bill

See ZIMBABWE, A4, Col. 1

Diplomatic juggler

Schmidt seeks balance, stresses need for SALT

By HENRY L. TREWHITT
Sun Staff Correspondent

Mr. Trewhitt, diplomatic correspondent of The Sun, has interviewed European officials on the SALT II treaty recently concluded between the United States and the Soviet Union. This is the fourth of several articles examining the impact of the treaty on U.S.-European and intra-European relations.

Bonn—Because he guides Germany or the democratic part of it, Chancellor Helmut Schmidt has more diplomatic juggling to do than any other European leader.

He must court President Valery Giscard d'Estaing of France without overirritating President Carter, and vice versa. He must pursue relations with the Russians without giving his allies nightmares about Germany's past.

None of the conditions that could make Germany a threat to peace exists currently, except its continued division between East and West. Every objective indicator points the other way.

Yet sooner or later every discussion of long-term geopolitics touches the subject. There are pessimists. The blackest speculation envisions political and economic erosion of the West, with the federal republic going nuclear and cutting a deal with Moscow in exchange for German reunification.

"Balderdash," says a State Department official. Neither the Soviet Union nor West Germany's allies, he insists, would tolerate such a course.

Such discussion appears irrelevant to a vital democracy committed to European development. Mr. Schmidt, 60, self-confident and abrasive, is firmly in command of his Social Democratic party, happily watching the opposition Christian Democrats and Christian Socialists brawl among themselves.

Yet Mr. Schmidt recognizes that Germany's past influences present attitudes. He told Parliament not long ago that overcoming the Nazi past was not finished. But he added that the federal republic, 30 years old, "now has a history of its own, that is the best and most dignified part of German history."

It is precisely to extend that history that Mr. Schmidt, like all European leaders, has a strong commitment to the Strategic Arms Limitation Treaty package that President Carter and President Leonid I. Brezhnev of the Soviet Union will sign in Vienna next Monday. Like some of his European colleagues, Mr. Schmidt is not enamored of the SALT II terms, at least until he has seen the actual text.

But, also like most other European leaders, he believes its failure could leave President Carter impotent and many power centers unstable. Some of the very trends the pessimists fear could appear.

Of all major figures in Europe, Mr. Schmidt is most aware of his need for the United States. He apparently has ceased his former semi-private criticism of American leadership—or the lack of it—that included obvious doubts about President Carter's capability. Last

See GERMANY, A2, Col. 4

The Weather
Clearing and warmer today, high 47. Fair tonight, low 30. Yesterday's high, 39; low, 27.
(Details and Map, page C2)

THE SUN

FINAL

Vol. 286—No. 101—F
BALTIMORE, FRIDAY, MARCH 14, 1980
15 Cents

A crane, a cage and two men bring trucker Ronnie Creason (without hat) to safety on the westbound span of the Bay Bridge. His vehicle's cab hangs over the icy bay.

Trucker takes short, dry dive off Bay Bridge

By JOEL McCORD
Anne Arundel County Bureau of The Sun

Annapolis—Trapped in the cab of his tractor-trailer, Ronnie Creason dangled over the icy waters of the Chesapeake Bay for more than an hour yesterday before rescuers could reach him.

The 31-year-old truck driver from Siler City, N.C., could see boats circling in the gray, choppy waters beneath him but could not tell what crews on the bridge were doing to get him out of his predicament.

"It might sound ridiculous," he said later from a bed in the emergency room of Anne Arundel General Hospital, "but I wasn't worried. I knew they'd get me out of there."

Mr. Creason lost control of his truck and empty livestock trailer at about 11 a.m. on the rain- and ice-slicked surface near the eastern end of the westbound span, skidded against one guardrail and smashed through another, 6-foot-high

Winter storms pose numerous problems for Maryland drivers..................C1

rail. The cab flipped on its side and hung precariously over the edge of the bridge about 5 feet below the road surface, while the trailer remained on the span.

Rescuers shouted to Mr. Creason to tell him help was on the way and warn him not to try to get out of the cab as they tied it to the bridge with chains. After Bay Bridge and State police steadied the cab, a mobile construction crane was used to lower a cage to the cab and delicately remove Mr. Creason, who received only minor injuries.

"I thought about everything, just everything, while I was there," he recounted. "Yeah, I thought about my wife and kids. I was hoping they don't hear about this before I can tell them."

Mr. Creason, who drives for Horney Livestock in North Carolina, said he had unloaded livestock in Port Chester, N.Y., about 2.30 a.m. and was heading home when the accident occurred.

"I stopped and slept in Delaware and then headed on," he said. "I called my wife just before I left there."

He said he did not know what caused the skid on the bridge, about ¼ mile from the eastern end. "When I came up on the bridge, it just went sideways on me. I don't know what happened. Whether it was ice or wind or what. I just lost it."

As he dangled there, Mr. Creason said, he could see only the water, 40 feet below, and occasionally feel what he thought was the rumble of trucks going by on the eastbound span.

Officer Paul Jones of the Bay Bridge police said rescuers at first considered using a large tow truck to pull the cab, which had come loose from the tractor engine and chassis, back onto the

See BRIDGE, A7, Col. 4

Stadium grant breezes past test in House

By KAREN HOSLER
Annapolis Bureau of The Sun

Annapolis—The $22 million state grant for improvements to Memorial Stadium, once expected to encounter major opposition because the Orioles refused to sign a lease beyond this season, breezed past an early test in the House yesterday and now seems assured of final approval there.

The bond bill, which won preliminary approval on a voice vote yesterday, is threatened only by a last-minute bargaining maneuver by Prince Georges county delegates—which House leaders say they can easily overcome—and the vagaries of the always unpredictable state Senate.

A rough count on the issue by House leaders yesterday revealed there are already 64 votes in favor of the bill before any pressure is applied. Only seven more votes are needed for final approval.

That preliminary count does not include any of the 24 Prince Georges county delegates, who say they have not yet taken a position on the issue.

"I don't think our county delegation wants to make a commitment to vote for it until we are convinced it is a fiscally responsible course of action," explained Delegate Timothy F. Maloney (D, Prince Georges), a leading advocate of the stall maneuver.

"We were told last fall that both teams [the Orioles and the Colts] would sign lease agreements, but the Orioles will not," he said. "We also don't like the amendment that says if the Orioles move to a new stadium built in another Maryland subdivision, which might be our county, that subdivision would have to give some of its admission-tax revenue to Baltimore.

The amendment actually provides that the subdivision in which a new baseball stadium is built would pay half of the $800,000 a year the bond bill would require Baltimore to contribute to the cost of the stadium improvements over the next 15 years.

"They're just playing games," Delegate Gerard F. Devlin, (D, Prince Georges), who as vice chairman of the Ways and Means Committee is also part of the House leadership, said of his county delegation.

"They want to get something" for voting for the stadium bill, Mr. Devlin continued.

"I asked them, 'What do you want to get?' We've already got everything we came down here for—the metro funding

See STADIUM, A12, Col. 1

Inflation package said to set oil-import fee

Washington (NYT)—The White House announced yesterday that President Carter would disclose his new anti-inflation package today. Congressional and administration sources said that it would include a fee on imported oil intended to raise gasoline prices by up to 10 cents a gallon.

The announcement will come at 4:30 p.m. in the East Room of the White House before network television cameras and an audience consisting of members of Congress, Cabinet members, economic policy officials and staff members, Jody Powell, the White House press secretary, said. A televised news conference was scheduled for 9 p.m.

[All three major commercial networks said they planned live television and radio coverage of Mr. Carter's speech on the economy, starting at 4.30 p.m. EST.]

[The NBC and CBS networks said yesterday that they planned to provide live television and radio coverage of President Carter's news conference at 9 o'clock tonight, while ABC said that it would telecast it at 11.45 P.M. EST.]

The White House announcement came as the Chase Manhattan Bank, the nation's third largest bank, raised its prime lending rate to a record 18¾ percent from the previous record of 17¾ percent, established just last week.

The prime rate increase sent the stock market down by 9.98 points and a huge demand for dollars pushed the value of the currency to a six-month high, while the price of gold bullion sank to its low for 1980.

The administration also formally announced yesterday what it leaked earlier this week—that it had accepted a guideline for restraining wage increases in the range of 7½ to 9½ percent a year, up from 7 percent.

The oil import fee, which would produce up to $11 billion a year in revenues, became essential, White House aides said, after two weeks of looking for budget cuts.

They added that administration and congressional leaders remained several billion dollars short of the $21 billion in

See CARTER, A12, Col. 1

Navy studies new carriers for launching 'jump jets'

By CHARLES W. CORDDRY
Washington Bureau of The Sun

Washington—The Navy, in a major air power study, has concluded it may need several new types of smaller aircraft carriers with "jump jet" planes to complement its 12 giant nuclear- and oil-powered flattops over the rest of this century.

The study of sea-based air power needs was begun a year and a half ago—well before the Iranian and Afghanistan crises led President Carter to declare America's intention to defend the Persian Gulf region and its oil.

But those crises and the new policy, requiring the Navy to operate permanently in the Indian Ocean as well as in the Atlantic and Pacific, are seen by the admirals as validating the air power conclusions reached in the exhaustive study.

Moreover, a most powerful ally is rallying to the Navy's side in the person of Senator John C. Stennis (D, Miss.), chairman of the Senate Armed Services Committee. He has started calling for a new class of carriers, in the 40,000-ton range, and experimentation with "jump jet" planes.

Jump jets, as the British forces have named them, take off and land vertically or with a short roll and thus need much less runway or deck space than the conventional takeoff and landing (CTOL) plane types.

The only jump jet available today is the British-designed AV-8B Harrier, but the Navy is looking to several American manufacturers for new designs, including one that could fly at supersonic speed by the late 1990s.

The Navy analysts concluded, *The Sun* was told, that a nominal 30,000-ton ship, costing just under $1 billion and carrying

See NAVY, A7, Col. 5

Ford found innocent in Pinto deaths

Winamac, Ind. (AP)—A jury from the nation's heartland yesterday acquitted the Ford Motor Company of reckless homicide in the first criminal prosecution of a corporation in a product-defect case—a verdict the prosecutor said "vindicates" the giant automaker.

Defense attorney James F. Neal said the verdict on charges stemming from the fiery highway deaths of three teenagers showed even a giant corporation can win if it has "a fair and reasonable story."

In Dearborn, Mich., yesterday Henry Ford II retired as chairman of the company and hinted he might have done so last fall when he gave up the job of chief executive officer had the trial not been pending. His departure from the chairman's job, which had been expected, was delayed, he said, because of "a lot of things facing the company then." Asked what they were, he replied, "Such as lawsuits."

The three teenagers were burned to death when their 1973 Pinto exploded in flames after being hit from behind by a van on an Indiana highway in August, 1978. The state contended defects in the subcompact's fuel system made it likely to leak fuel in rear-end crashes at low to moderate speeds. Ford attorneys said the force of the impact, rather than any alleged defect, caused the gasoline tank to explode.

The verdict came in the fourth day of the jury's deliberations, including a marathon session that went into the early morning hours yesterday.

Some of the jurors said yesterday they did not think the Pinto was a safe car but that they voted for acquittal because the

See PINTO, A8, Col. 4

House OKs $227.7 billion windfall tax after 1,000-barrel exemption move fails

By THOMAS B. EDSALL
Washington Bureau of The Sun

Washington—The House, after a year of bitter fighting between energy producers and energy consumers, yesterday gave final approval to a $227.7 billion windfall profits tax.

The measure passed easily, 302 to 107, but the key vote was on a motion to send the legislation back to conference committee with instructions to exempt the first 1,000 barrels of oil produced daily by independent oilmen. The motion was rejected 227 to 185.

One of the largest tax measures in the nation's history, the bill is expected to be taken up by the Senate next week for a final vote. Senator Henry Bellmon (R, Okla.), who represents a major oil-producing state, has threatened to filibuster, but most participants in the legislative fight expect the bill to be enacted.

Independent producers, hardhats cradled in their laps, watched the debate and vote from the galleries as their last-minute lobbying campaign faltered. They claimed that exempting the first 1,000 barrels they produce daily would, in the long run, free up enough venture capital to result in 42,000 additional exploratory wells and increased daily production of just under 1 million barrels a day.

However, calculations by the Congressional Budget Office suggest that the profits to be made by the oil companies from decontrol are so large that the entire windfall profit tax will reduce oil production by a total of 500,000 barrels a day by 1990.

The windfall profits tax, the financial basis of President Carter's energy program, was proposed by the administration at the same time Mr. Carter announced the gradual decontrol of domestically produced crude oil.

An excise tax, it will transfer to the federal treasury $227.7 billion of the $1 trillion in additional gross revenues oil companies are expected to make by 1990 as a result of decontrol. Without the tax, the oil companies would have made a net profit of $529.8 billion, according to congressional figures. The net profit is minus

See WINDFALL, A12, Col. 3

Austria breaks with West by recognizing PLO envoy

Vienna (Reuter)—Neutral Austria broke ranks with the West yesterday by granting official status to a Palestinian diplomat in a move described as "a new form of diplomatic recognition."

The Austrian government said it was ready to talk with a Palestine Liberation Organization (PLO) envoy based in Austria "when there are questions concerning the Palestinian people or the PLO."

While it was unclear whether this meant full diplomatic recognition for the PLO, the Austrian action astonished Western and Israeli diplomats. Israel demanded an immediate explanation.

Diplomats said the Austrian formula appeared to be an ingenious step just short of formal recognition of the PLO. The move provides further impetus for a West Europoean policy shift in favor of the PLO.

Socialist Chancellor Bruno Kreisky, in a radio interview, said the status granted to PLO diplomat Ghasi Hussain represented a "new form of diplomatic recognition," which was unprecedented since it involved a people without their own state or territory.

Dr. Hussain, a Palestine-born lawyer who has been a PLO observer accredited to Vienna-based U.N. agencies for the last three years, would now be regarded also as PLO representative by the Austrian government, the chancellor said.

Western diplomats said the Austrian decision apparently gives the PLO a greater degree of recognition than other West European countries, which have allowed the organization to open offices in their capitals.

The basic Western view, previously shared by Austria, is that the presence of PLO offices does not imply political recognition.

The U.S. and other Western embassies said they were seeking clarification of the decision from Austrian officials.

The action was made known in a newspaper interview with Foreign Minister Willibald Pahr and later confirmed by a ministry spokesman. Dr. Pahr said Dr.

See AUSTRIA, A7, Col. 6

Index

Tests at Three Mile Island

A physics technician came out of No. 2 airlock at the Three Mile Island nuclear plant yesterday to tell engineers they could enter the lock. The engineers are conducting tests essential to decontaminating the plant near Harrisburg crippled by an accident last March 28. Operators purged a trace of radioactive krypton gas from the airlock for three days to let workmen enter. Yesterday's steps were a preliminary to letting workmen enter the containment building, which houses the reactor.

The Weather
Partly cloudy today, becoming cloudy tonight. High, 72; low, 53. Yesterday's high, 72; low, 56.
(Details and Map, Page D2)

Vol. 286—No. 137—F

THE SUN

FINAL

BALTIMORE, FRIDAY, APRIL 25, 1980

• • • 15 Cents

U.S. aborts bid to free hostages; planes collide in Iran; eight die

Growing flotilla heads for Cuba

From Wire Services

Key West, Fla.—Hundreds of Cuban refugees poured into Key West yesterday, and up to 1,000 boats were reported on their way to Cuba to pick up others, many of whom had taken refuge in the Peruvian Embassy in Havana.

Key West Mayor Sonny McCoy said 700 to 1,000 boats already had embarked and about 500 more had been brought to this island community off Florida's southern tip yesterday to make the 90-mile trip across the Straits of Florida.

Immigration officials said more than 500 refugees arrived here yesterday and estimated that about 1,000 have landed since the sealift began last weekend.

Sun diplomatic correspondent Henry L. Trewhitt reports from Washington that the growing wave of unregulated Cuban immigrants apparently left the State Department helpless in the face of a humanitarian dilemma.

If it seized and deported the immigrants and arrested their rescuers, it would appear callous. If it did nothing to stop the movement, the United States would again appear helpless to enforce its immigration laws.

As matters stood last night, department spokesmen declared the laws would be enforced while enforcement agencies did little to enforce them. But officials said they still had hope of establishing international control of the problem.

Increasingly U.S. officials acknowledged that President Fidel Castro, confronted with mass unemployment and growing resentment, was allowing everyone to leave who could find transportation. In the process, he had managed to seriously embarrass his critics in the United States.

Supplies of boat fuel quickly became strained in Key West. "The fuel situation is critical," said Jabe Sherertz, dockmas-

See CUBA, A5, Col. 3

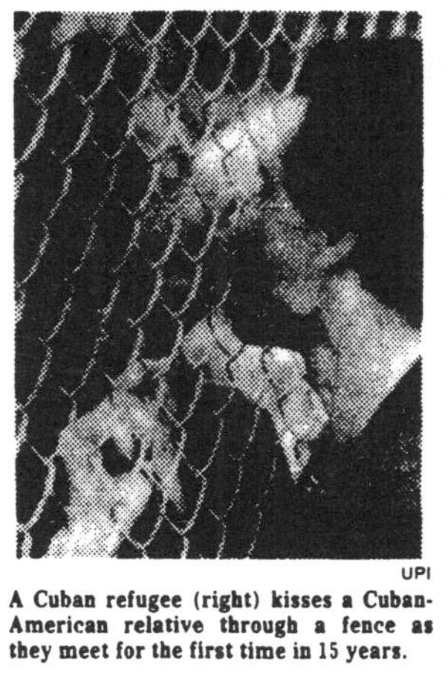

UPI

A Cuban refugee (right) kisses a Cuban-American relative through a fence as they meet for the first time in 15 years.

Rescuers airlifted out

By HENRY L. TREWHITT
Washington Bureau of The Sun

Washington—An effort to rescue the American hostages in Iran collapsed early this morning when two planes collided on the ground at a remote airstrip in Iran, killing eight Americans.

A White House spokesman said President Carter ordered the mission canceled immediately after the accident. As the spokesman put it: "The mission was terminated because of equipment failure."

There was no contact between the would-be rescuers and Iranians, American officials said. Besides the eight dead, all crew members of the two aircraft and an unspecified number of other Americans were injured.

"The Americans involved in the operation have now been airlifted from Iran," a White House statement said, "and those who were injured are being given medical treatment and are expected to recover."

The White House refused to issue further details, such as the time of the accident, the number of military personnel involved and how they expected to reach the hostages in the U.S. Embassy in Iran. Jody Powell, the White House press secretary, said he expected to make a further announcement about 7 o'clock this morning.

Pentagon officials were called to a midnight meeting in the office of Defense Secretary Harold Brown. Key congressional leaders and the families of the hostages were also notified of the aborted rescue attempt.

There has been frequent speculation, with the failure of diplomatic efforts to free the 50 hostages, that the adminstration might attempt a rescue. By all accounts that would be difficult because of Tehran's great distance from the sea and from any country which might provide a base for an American military effort.

The militants holding the American hostages since the U.S. Embassy was seized November 4 have threatened repeatedly to kill the hostages if there was any military attempt to rescue them.

On November 27, barely three weeks after the takeover, the militants said they had planted mines throughout the embassy compound and would set them off if American agents tried to storm the embassy and free the hostages.

The few details made public early this morning suggested that the rescue attempt was being staged from inside Iran. The White House said the operation was not motivated by hostility toward Iran or the Iranian people and there were no Iranian casualties. Whether any Iranians were aware of the effort, perhaps among friendly Iranian military personnel, was not revealed.

With the failure of the mission, President Carter repeated the now familiar position toward Iran: He still holds its revolutionary government responsible for the safety of the 50 Americans in the embassy and the three who remain prisoners in all but name in the Iranian Foreign ministry.

The White House statement said Mr. Carter accepted full responsibility for the rescue attempt. He ordered the attempt, the statement continued, for humanitarian

See HOSTAGES, A5, Col. 1

City accepts 8.41% bid in bond sale

By ANTERO PIETILA

Overriding the city's finance director's recommendation to wait for a more opportune market, Baltimore yesterday accepted a lone bid of 8.4112 percent on its unprecedented $85.25 million bond issue.

"We never speculated. I don't think this is the time to start," R. Austin Tydings, a member of the Board of Finance Commissioners, said in opposing the recommendation of Charles L. Benton, Jr., the finance director, that the city reject the bid and wait for three months.

Mayor Schaefer and Lawrence B. Daley, chief of the city's treasury management, supported Mr. Tydings's view.

"I don't think we should outguess the market," Mr. Daley said.

Mayor Schaefer, saying that a decision to delay floating the issue should have been made earlier, contended that by waiting now, "We'd do more damage than good."

"From what I gather from our experts in finance, this is not a bad rate," he added.

Last year, the city sold $30 million in bonds at a 5.8443 percent rate. But given the current market, this year's 8.41 average interest rate over the 30-year life of the bonds was regarded as good by both outside experts and the city's financial managers.

"I guess it's a good rate, considering the market," noted Mr. Daley. "It's more than a full percentage point below the high of the year."

The high for the year was 9.47 percent.

A difference of one percentage point—that is, the difference between 8.4 percent and 9.4 percent—would amount to a $10 million difference in interest payments over the 30-year term of the bonds.

In recent weeks, the interest index rates have been coming down somewhat—to 9.07 percent for the week of April 10 and to 7.89 percent for the week of April 17.

But leading experts expect that interest rates will continue on a seesaw course for the rest of a year, making it impossible for municipalities like Baltimore, which are tied to preannounced bond selling dates, to take full advantage of those fluctuations.

That was one of the reasons the Board of Finance Commissioners decided not to accept Mr. Benton's recommendations for a delay.

"We have never had as volatile a mar-

See BONDS, A14, Col. 1

Iran threatens to close gulf to Western supertankers

From Wire Services

Tehran—Iran threatened yesterday to cut off the West's Persian Gulf oil if the United States mines Iranian ports.

"We shall close the Persian Gulf at any price," Foreign Minister Sadegh Ghotbzadeh said in an interview with Iranian radio and television.

Mr. Ghotbzadeh did not say how the Iranians might try to halt supertanker

In Europe, hostages' wives call for mass letter campaign..........A2

traffic out of the gulf, which accounts for some 60 percent of all world oil exports. But if they succeeded, the United States would lose 10 percent of its oil supply, and Western Europe and Japan an ever greater percentage.

The threat came as Iran sought greater help from the Soviet Union as the West increased its pressure to win the freedom of the 50 American hostages held at the U.S. Embassy in Tehran.

The Soviets confirmed they would open their highways to increased Iranian traffic if President Carter blockaded Iranian ports, and announced renewed negotiations for Iranian natural gas.

In rebellious Kurdistan, the war raged on. A Turkish newspaper told yesterday of hundreds killed in Iranian air attacks, and a Kurdish group appealed to world organizations for help.

In Tehran, the hostages spent their 173d day in captivity.

President Carter said last week that military action would be the next U.S. option unless economic and diplomatic pressure by America and its allies led to the hostages' release. The principal tactic under consideration is a naval blockade, probably by mining Iranian ports.

Referring specifically to this threat, Mr. Ghotbzadeh was quoted by Tehran radio as saying, "If the decision is made by these gentlemen to mine . . . then there is no reason why we should allow any more oil to be exported to the rest of the world from the Persian Gulf. In such a case, we shall close the Persian Gulf at any price."

SADEGH GHOTBZADEH
". . . we shall never surrender"

In an earlier briefing for foreign broadcasters, the foreign minister said: "If economic sanctions or anything else keep[s] Iranian oil from leaving the gulf, no other

See TEHRAN, A2, Col. 3

Senators seek consultation before Carter uses force

By HENRY L. TREWHITT
Washington Bureau of The Sun

Washington—Citing President Carter's threats to use force in the Persian Gulf area, leaders of the Senate Foreign Relations Committee called yesterday for formal consultation with the administration about its plans for that region.

It was the first such application of the so-called war powers resolution, enacted in 1973.

Hours later, the aborted attempt to rescue the American hostages in Tehran was announced. The committee's move clearly could become a complicating element in policies that shift untidily with events in Iran and the gulf region generally.

Senators Frank Church (D, Idaho), the committee chairman, and Jacob K. Javits (R, N.Y.), said their purpose was to make any decision to use force a joint undertaking of the president and Congress. In a letter to Cyrus R. Vance, the Secretary of State, they asked for consultations "at an early date."

Acknowledging receipt of the letter, a State Department spokesman said merely that Mr. Vance will consult President Carter before he replies. The first question for the White House is whether the circumstances justify application of the resolution.

Mr. Church and Mr. Javits, a primary author of the joint resolution, based their request on Mr. Carter's responses to the seizure of American hostages in Iran and to what they called "the brutal military occupation of Afghanistan by the Soviet Union."

Mr. Carter had spoken of "not ruling out the use of military force" if the hostages are not freed, they pointed out. Moreover, they recalled, he had threatened directly the use of force against any nation that tried to gain control of the Persian Gulf and its oil.

In that light, they said, "we believe that the time has come to commence the consultation procedures" of the war powers resolution. Whatever the outcome, it appeared likely that the exchanges to follow

See IRAN, A2, Col. 1

Seniors offered retesting out of concern that writing scores depend on grader

By M. WILLIAM SALGANIK

Does a student's score on the city's writing proficiency test—a requirement for high school graduation—depend on writing ability, or on who marks the test paper?

Some teachers and principals are complaining that it is the grader.

City school officials are concerned enough about the complaints to offer seniors an extra chance to pass the test, but have rejected suggestions the test not be used as a graduation requirement this year.

Those who are concerned about the fairness of the marking cite incidents such as these:

- At Douglass High School, seven English teachers were asked to grade the same student's writing proficiency exam. The teachers came up with seven different scores, ranging from 43 to 77. (Passing score is 70.)
- At Baltimore Polytechnic Institute, three seniors received failing grades on their first try at the test, and asked for their exams to be regraded. The second gradings gave them scores that raised their marks above the passing level.
- At Patterson High School, English teachers comparing notes found they had marked the exam different ways.

Of course, different teachers marking an essay exam are liable to give different grades, but—particularly with a diploma at stake—educators want to make the grading as consistent as possible.

While only one teacher marks each paper in Baltimore, such exams elsewhere are generally read by two different graders and, if they assign significantly different grades, a third marker is called in.

Within the past few weeks, the English departments at Douglass and Patterson wrote to the coordinator of English for the city public schools, suggesting the test not be used as a graduation standard this year.

"I don't object to a standard, but the students are not all being judged by the same standard," said Carolyn Tyson, head of Douglass's English department.

Although scores from the last writing test—given in January—have been compiled, Dr. John L. Crew, the school superintendent, said yesterday the results have not been made public because he has not reviewed them.

Informal figures from several high schools indicate, however, that perhaps a quarter to a third of the city's 7,000 seniors have not yet passed the writing test.

The writing test—along with the multiple-choice reading and math exams that have also been required for graduation since last year—will be given again next week. That was to have been the last chance for seniors, but because of the complaints there will be another retesting May 17.

The Douglass teachers made no attempt to organize support for their position, although copies of their letter were sent to other schools.

The Patterson teachers, however, called a meeting earlier this month, which was attended by some teachers

See TESTS, A14, Col. 1

Anderson quits GOP race to run as an independent

By ERNEST B. FURGURSON
Washington Bureau of The Sun

Washington—Representative John B. Anderson withdrew from the Republican presidential race yesterday to run as an independent because, he said, "too many people in our nation are disillusioned with the prospective choices our party structures are offering."

The silver-haired, 58-year-old Illinoisan set his campaign theme by maintaining, "There is a new willingness to accept sacrifice, to accept discipline, to accept unpleasant truths" in America.

The most unpleasant truth for the other presidential contenders is that Mr. Anderson's candidacy will draw votes from both major parties, and the Democrats particularly fear that it will decisively damage their nominee.

His move was a concession that he is too liberal to be nominated within the GOP. Now he hopes to put together a winning coalition of liberal Republicans, independents and dissatisfied Democrats, although U.S. history says no such independent effort has ever elected a president.

But Mr. Anderson denied strongly that he was running independently as a "spoiler." He said he hoped to bring millions of new voters into the political process. He insisted that he was not making an assault on the two-party system or risking fragmentation of the country.

The congressman, who has run in six Republican state primaries this year without winning one, acknowledged that he will have financial problems as well as difficulty getting his name on the November ballot in every state.

He predicted that although he is returning the unspent federal matching funds he obtained as a Republican, he will be able to raise the $10 million to $12 million he estimated he will need for his independent run. He also vowed to challenge state laws that "restrict access to the ballot."

That may include Maryland's, which would have required him to raise a total of 55,517 voter signatures, a third of them submitted by last March 3.

An early deadline also has passed in four other states, and in others an independent is required to list his vice presidential running mate. Even if these requirements could be overcome, Mr. Anderson still will face a huge signature-gathering project to petition himself onto enough ballots to win an electoral majority.

AP

JOHN B. ANDERSON

Nevertheless, he insisted that was his aim. "If I thought for one minute that I were simply a divisive voice in this country rather than offering an honest alternative to the American people, I would not be on this platform today," he said in a news conference at the National Press Club.

"I cannot accept the idea that inevitably this election is going to the House of Representatives" (because no candidate receives an electoral college majority), he continued. "I know that charge is going to be made. It's going to be one, frankly, of the scare tactics that are going to be employed. . . ."

Asked whether he had invited Senator Daniel P. Moynihan (D, N.Y.) to be his running mate, Mr. Anderson said no—it would be premature to make such a deci-

See ANDERSON, A8, Col. 1

Christians split over fears of 'right-wing' rally

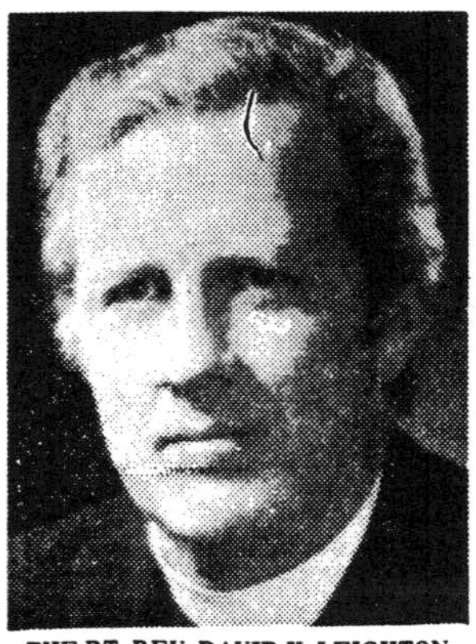

THE RT. REV. DAVID K. LEIGHTON
. . . Episcopal bishop of Maryland

By FRANK P. L. SOMERVILLE
Religion Editor of The Sun

A well-organized religious rally intended to draw a million Christians of all denominations and political persuasions to the Mall in Washington Tuesday for a simple demonstration of faith has split Catholics from Catholics and Protestants from Protestants.

Opponents say that, given the principal sponsorship of the long-heralded "Washington for Jesus" event, it cannot help but turn into a "right-wing" political rally.

Supporters acknowledge that they are concerned about such volatile issues as abortion and "removal of voluntary prayer from public schools" but say they are determined to keep the rally itself "totally nonpolitical."

A Catonsville dentist who is one of two local volunteer coordinators of the million-dollar interfaith project said yesterday that, despite the controversy, 300 buses will be transporting Christians to the rally from Maryland alone.

Early last month, more than 100,000 pastors and parishioners from every part of the United States had already registered to attend Washington events scheduled Monday and Tuesday in connection with the rally, its sponsors say.

Typical of the confusion engendered by the widely varying positions on the rally taken by prominent church leaders nationally and locally is the flip-flop by the Right Rev David K. Leighton, Episcopal bishop of Maryland.

In a newsletter sent to the Episcopal clergy of the Maryland diocese last month, Bishop Leighton mentioned the upcoming "Washington for Jesus" event—described as a day of prayer and fasting for concerned Christians of all types—and said he supported it.

But in a letter to the same clergy dated April 10, Bishop Leighton said he was withdrawing his endorsement. " 'Washington for Jesus' claims to represent Christians at large, but it represents only a segment . . . [it] claims to be nonpolitical but espouses . . . the New Right," the bishop said.

One of the people who originally persuaded Bishop Leighton to take a stand for the rally was the Right Rev. William J. Cox, the suffragan bishop of the Episcopal diocese here who recently resigned to be assistant bishop of Oklahoma.

Although the two bishops are friends, they have not always seen eye to eye on religious questions. Bishop Cox could not be reached last night for comment on the Washington rally.

In his recent letter, Bishop Leighton said that "it was purported to be a religious gathering in our nation's capital where 1 million would gather to pray. . . . Instead, I have discovered, it is a political rally organized by voting precincts and congressional districts with massive effort toward lobbying the Congress."

The event is "supported by persons whose philosophies and convictions are quite different from those of the Episcopal

See SPLIT, A13, Col. 2

Index

The Weather
Partly cloudy with a chance of showers or thunderstorms this afternoon and tonight. High today, 80; low tonight, 63. Yesterday's high, 70; low, 59.
(Details and Map, page C2)
Vol. 287—No. 2—F

THE SUN

FINAL

BALTIMORE, MONDAY, MAY 19, 1980

••• 15 Cents

A Miami police car lay overturned and afire Saturday night during racial violence that spread through several sections of the city. AP

18 die in racial violence in Miami; weekend riots prompt federal action

By Wire Services

Miami—Bullets and firebombs ignited a Sunday of deadly racial violence in Dade county that left 18 dead and sent a spasm of terror through merchants, motorists and community leaders—black and white.

At least 264 persons have been injured since violence erupted Saturday night after the acquittal of four white ex-policemen charged in the beating death of Arthur McDuffie, a black insurance executive.

The U.S. attorney's office announced yesterday that a federal grand jury will begin investigating the McDuffie incident this week for civil rights violations, but the announcement appeared not to calm the rioters. Widespread looting, rock-throwing and firebombing continued most of the day.

Most of yesterday's dead were gunshot victims, reflecting a grim trend away from the rock-and-bottle episodes that opened Miami's worst outbreak of racial violence Saturday night.

Shouting a one-word battle cry—"McDuffie"—crowds of blacks surged into Miami streets Saturday night. What began about 6 p.m. as isolated instances of rock- and bottle-throwing, mainly in the northwest part of the city, quickly developed into a major disturbance that eventually included widespread looting, dozens of fires, beatings and shootings.

Yesterday's dead included two suspected looters shot by police, a police lieutenant who suffered a heart attack, a motorist shot by police when he allegedly tried to run down officers, and a black teenager shot in the head on his way to the store.

Dozens of fires erupted last night at intersections, stores and businesses—many of them in areas where firemen could not go because of violence. "It's absolutely unreal. They're burning down the . . . north end of town," said Miami Fire Inspector George Bilberry.

At least two persons, both black, died in Jackson Memorial Hospital's emergency room of bullet wounds to the head and neck yesterday.

Andre Dawson, 14, was hit twice by gunfire from a passing truck or van as he walked near his home.

"Somebody just ran down the street and shot him in the head. Blew my baby's brains out. Oh, no. Why my baby?" sobbed Augustus Dawson, the boy's father. Andre's body lay in the street for more than an hour while an ambulance crew waited for a police escort before answering the call.

Police began searching for a blue van with four Latin males who were reportedly firing at people on the street.

At about the same time, three Miami policemen were slightly wounded by gunfire yesterday afternoon as they patrolled

See MIAMI, A3, Col. 1

D.C. bank in turmoil under union leaders' growing influence

By HELEN WINTERNITZ
and TIMOTHY M. PHELPS

Behind the stately, columned facade of the National Bank of Washington—the capital's oldest and third-largest bank—there is a financial institution in turmoil.

There is a story of questionable loans made in recent years by a board of directors increasingly influenced by the leadership of the nation's coal miners union.

It is a story of the NBW's willingness to bail out customers in trouble at other banks—including one loan arranged by a former key aide to Marvin Mandel—and of an extraordinary turnover among its high-level officials.

The growth of the union's interference with the bank's affairs has paralleled the rise of the new president of the United Mine Workers of America, Sam Church. The union exerts its influence through its ownership of the bulk of the bank's stock.

The problems of the bank, while they

First of two articles

do not threaten its overall stability, are significant.

A three-month investigation by *The Sun*, involving a score of interviews with bank and union sources as well as an examination of internal bank documents, shows that in the last two years:

• A report by federal bank regulators who examined the bank's books last year criticized $9 million in recent loans. Almost $5.7 million of these loans went to men with ties to the bank's board and the union.

• Despite the objections of loan officers, the bank lent $4.5 million to Joseph Shamy, then owner of the financially troubled Laurel Raceway in Howard county. At the time, Mr. Shamy had defaulted on a loan from another bank, and the FBI was investigating his use of the raceway's funds. That investigation led to his indictment and conviction on charges of fraud and racketeering.

• The Laurel deal, which was among those criticized by federal regulators, was engineered by Maurice Wyatt, an aide to former Governor Marvin Mandel, and forced on the bank with the help of two directors, one of them Willie Runyon, owner of several ambulance companies in Baltimore.

• Dozens of professional banking officers and several directors have left the bank, many because union influence on the NBW's operations had become too much to bear.

• The bank's 21-member board has been packed with an unlikely assemblage of individuals, such as Mr. Runyon, who have connections to the United Mine Workers' leadership but do not have the kind of qualifications that banks normally look for.

• While citing "record" earnings in 1979, the bank's annual report showed sharp increases in defaulted and problem loans. The report did not show when these loans were made.

The mine workers' union has controlled the National Bank of Washington for more than 30 years. It currently holds three-quarters of the bank's stock, on which it earns about $2 million annually.

The stock is a major asset of an organization that represents about 270,000 miners, both retirees and those still laboring in one of the nation's most dangerous jobs.

During the decades that the mine workers have owned the NBW, union leaders on occasion have used the NBW for their own purposes. Never before, however, has the union leadership exercised such pervasive control.

When a reform movement swept through the hierarchy of the union in the 1970s, union leaders made a conscious effort to separate the two institutions—and to leave the union's multi-million-dollar investment in the hands of professional bankers.

But in 1977, when Sam Church became the union's vice president, he began expanding his power in the union and at the bank. Last year, he took over the presidency from an ailing Arnold Miller, his running mate in 1977, who had resigned.

"The atmosphere was unhealthy, paranoid," said one person who resigned from the bank. "Bank officers got in a habit of looking over their shoulders. They would be handed a loan request and never really knew who was behind it."

"You'd start out as a banker, and then if they dropped a name on you, suddenly alarm bells would go off in your head and you realized you had an unusu-

See BANK, A8, Col. 1

At least 8 die as volcano erupts, spewing ash and smoke 9 miles up

Vancouver, Wash. (AP)—Mount St. Helens blew its top yesterday with a blast felt 200 miles away, belching ash which blotted out the sun for more than 100 miles and killing at least eight people. Mudflows and floods destroyed bridges and forced the evacuation of about 2,000 people.

At least three people were missing.

Late yesterday, a mile-wide wall of mud was seen oozing down the north fork of the Toutle River, snapping concrete and steel bridges like toothpicks and sweeping cars and houses in its wake.

The eruption at 8:39 a.m. shot smoke and ash 9 miles into the sky, and a spectacular lightning storm in the rising plume started numerous forest fires. By evening, the fires covered 3,000 acres on the mountain.

There were no immediate reports of lava.

In Walla Walla, 160 miles to the east, drifting ash made the sky so dark that automatic street lights went on. By evening, more than a foot of ash had accumulated at Camp Baker, 15 miles west of the volcano.

Ash was also reported falling in parts of Idaho, more than 200 miles downwind, and even in western Montana. Montana police said roads were closed due to near-zero visibility west and south of Missoula, about 500 miles downwind from the volcano. Ash was said to be a half-inch deep on the ground there.

The eruption was visible in Vancouver, Wash., more than 50 miles to the southwest, and the explosion was felt in Vancouver, British Columbia, more than 200 miles to the north.

By yesterday evening, the once snow-covered 9,677-foot peak was reduced to about 9,100 feet, a U.S. Geological Survey

AP
Mount St. Helens spews smoke and ash 9 miles into the air in its biggest eruption.

spokesman, Worner Gerhard, said. The crater was one-half mile across.

A reporter flew over the mudflow heading down the Toutle River and said it was moving at 50 mph, carrying cars, trees, logging trucks and houses.

A helicopter pilot on a rescue mission watched three persons in a pickup truck perish in flooding near the town of Toutle, said Phil Cogan, a spokesman for the state Department of Emergency Services. State officials had said earlier that five deaths were known, although details were available only on four.

The bodies of two people found at a Weyerhaeuser Company logging camp near the mountain were flown to Kelso, Wash., by an Air Force Reserve helicopter, Air Force Lt. D. E. Schroeder said. They were killed by heat, Lieutenant Schroeder said, but no details were immediately available.

Two bodies were found in a car about 1.5 miles east of Camp Baker, about 15 miles west of the volcano, Air Force Reserve Capt. Robert J. Wead said.

"These people were fried with the heat," Captain Wead said. "Trees and all the vegetation was laid out flat—singed, burned, steaming, sizzling—a terrible-looking thing."

"The devastation on the mountainside is incredible," Lieutenant Schroeder said. "Trees are knocked down, animals are standing around in shock, covered with ash."

In addition to the eight deaths, two loggers were seriously burned by hot gas and cinders, officials of the Emanuel Hpspital Burn Center, in Portland, Ore., said.

Mr. Gerhard said that "pryoclastic flows" of debris made fluid by hot gas were going down the mountain's sides. He and a Forest Service spokesman said the debris was reaching Spirit Lake at the north base of the mountain, making the lake boil.

Before the large mudflow was reported late yesterday, mudflows had entered both forks of the Toutle River on the north flank of the mountain in Washington's southwestern corner, swelling the river to three times its normal width, aerial ob-

See VOLCANO, A6, Col. 1

Sun photo—Weyman Swagger
A young Cuban refugee girl, clutching a Mickey Mouse doll, waves as a bus arrives at Fort Indiantown Gap, Pa.

Alaskans getting prepared as gold fever strikes again

By MURIEL DOBBIN
Sun Staff Correspondent

Fairbanks, Alaska—"You might buy out some of my gold operation for about a million dollars," said the weather-beaten little man who sat shirt-sleeved in a modest clapboard house behind a white picket fence.

Carl Heflinger found the gold he sought in Alaska, but it took him almost a life-

Thinking of grubbing for gold? Do your homework first..........B1

time of setbacks and economic struggles before he "got well," as he describes it. And he chuckles when he reflects on the prospects of the thousands of would-be prospectors who are expected to pour into Alaska this summer with visions of gold nuggets—at $500 an ounce—dancing in their heads.

State mining officials said inquiries in April were coming in at the rate of 600 a week, compared with 150 a week during the winter.

Gold fever was what brought Mr. Heflinger's father through the miseries of the Chilkoot Pass in the stampede of 1897, when more than 100,000 prospectors set out for the treasure territory of the Klondike. But of the few thousand who found gold, only a few hundred kept it and became rich. The elder Mr. Heflinger stampeded to Nome and Fairbanks and amassed perhaps $50,000, none of which he kept long enough to bequeath to his son. What he left Carl was a passion for mining.

"I would say 50 to 70 percent of gold

See GOLD, A4, Col. 1

Tigers, 6; Orioles, 4
Details on Page C3

Index

326 Cuban refugees arrive at Pa. fort seeking 'a little liberty, a loaf of bread'

By SANDY BANISKY
Sun Staff Correspondent

Fort Indiantown Gap, Pa.—A small, smiling girl clutched a Mickey Mouse doll with one arm and waved with the other. An old man in a rust-colored suit bounded down the airplane steps and bowed jauntily to the Army men standing on the ground. A teenager in jeans kneeled and kissed the ground.

Three hundred twenty-six Cuban refugees arrived in Pennsylvania from Key West, Fla., yesterday as Fort Indiantown Gap became the third center for their processing and housing in the country.

Most of the 50 women, 12 children and 264 men had no luggage. Many wore only sleeveless shirts and shorts as they stepped off a chartered DC-10 at Harrisburg International Airport into a rainy morning with temperatures in the 50s.

But the Cubans smiled and waved to reporters and Army personnel who led them onto yellow school buses for the 20-mile trip to this Army National Guard and Reserve Center, which will be their home for from 10 days to 6 months.

Some of the new arrivals seemed dazed, but manage to smile quietly when asked how they felt.

"It feels very good," said Andres Casanova, a stocky man who looks older than his 41 years. "I want to have a little bit of liberty, a loaf of bread and to be able to work and make a life for myself," he told his interpreter.

"I had to turn in the key to my house and leave everything," Rafael Soler Prado, 52, said. "And I did it with pleasure just to get out of there."

The Cubans who arrived at Indiantown Gap yesterday were part of a trial run for the Army and the Federal Emergency Management Agency as they opened the newest refugee center.

An Army staff of 1,100, including 274 from Fort Meade have been moved here to help settle the refugees in this Army camp of green and white buildings set neatly on the central Pennsylvania hills.

Beginning today, Cuban refugees are expected to arrive in Pennsylvania from Florida at the rate of about 2,000 a day, Robert J. Adamcik, the deputy regional director of the emergency agency, said.

Since President Fidel Castro began allowing Cubans to leave the island in a flotilla of small boats almost a month ago, about 56,000 refugees have landed in Florida, federal officials say.

The refugee center at Eglin Air Force

See REFUGEES, A2, Col. 3

The Weather
Partly cloudy and pleasant today and tonight. High, 80; low, 65. Yesterday's high, 83; low, 60.
(Details and Map, Page C2)

Vol. 287—No. 11—F

THE SUN

FINAL

BALTIMORE, THURSDAY, MAY 29, 1980

••• 15 Cents

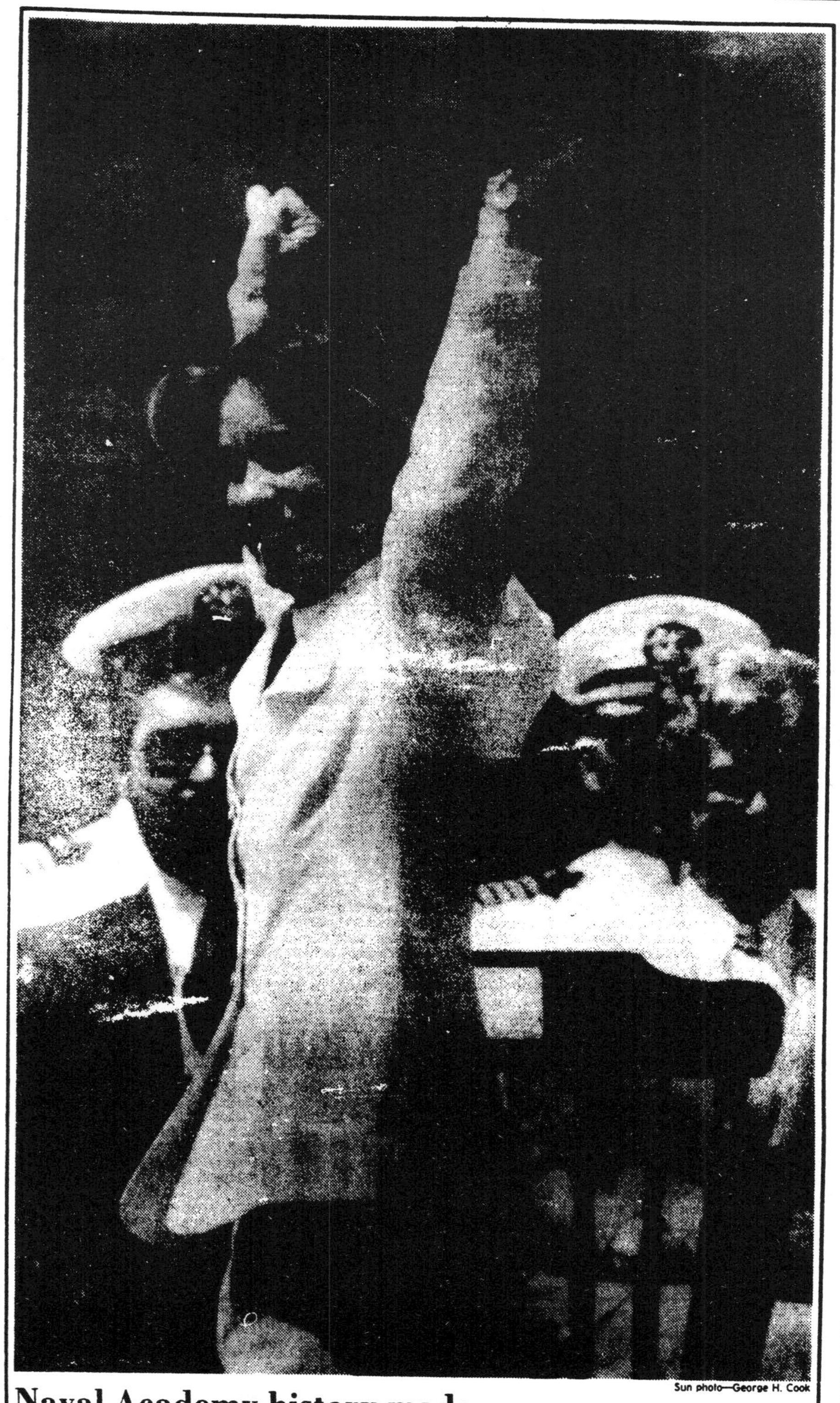

Sun photo—George H. Cook

Naval Academy history made

Elizabeth Belzer of Westminster raised her arms in triumph yesterday after becoming one of the first women to graduate from the Naval Academy. Ms. Belzer, a physics major, was the highest ranking of 55 women in the 938-member class and the first woman Trident Scholar. After the ceremony, the male and female officers tossed their caps with traditional graduation glee. (Article on C1.)

U.S. court upsets block to Hart-Miller dike; opponents plan appeal

By DAVID RESS

A federal appeals court yesterday removed a major legal roadblock to a controversial disposal site for Baltimore harbor dredge spoil proposed by the state.

The action by the 4th Circuit Court of Appeals in Richmond reversed an October, 1978, ruling by Judge Herbert F. Murray, of the U.S. District Court in Baltimore, invalidating a 1976 Army Corps of Engineers permit for the proposed Hart and Miller islands disposal site, located just off the Baltimore county shore.

That decision stopped all construction and engineering design work on the $38 million Hart-Miller project, which the state and local port businesses believe is essential to meet long-range Baltimore harbor dredging needs, including a $225 million proposal to deepen Chesapeake Bay and Baltimore harbor shipping channels from 42 to 50 feet.

But the appeals court ruling, the latest development in the long and hard-fought legal battles over the dredge site, does not mean the state will proceed immediately to build the 52 million-cubic-yard capacity spoil disposal facility, W. Gregory Halpin, Maryland port administrator, said yesterday.

"The appeals court ruling is an important victory, but we still have other legal battles to fight," Mr. Halpin said.

One hangup would be an appeal of the Richmond court's ruling by opponents of the Hart-Miller project, Mr. Halpin said.

A second is the still-uncertain status of 10 other legal challenges still pending before the district court, Mr. Halpin said.

"Once we have absolutely no more legal challenges to Hart-Miller, it will be three years before we're ready to take the first drop of dredge spoil," Mr. Halpin said. The 50-foot channel project will take eight years to complete, according to the Corps of Engineers.

Joseph Bormel, president of the Hart and Miller islands Area Environmental Group, the plaintiffs in the lawsuit, said, "We will appeal this to the Supreme Court if necessary. . . . There are many other avenues we can pursue, and we will."

Mr. Bormel's group has been fighting the Hart-Miller project since the state first sought state and federal permits for the facility in 1972.

Mr. Bormel said it was too early to say what course of action his group would take, because it hadn't seen the appeals court ruling yet.

None of the parties involved, who were notified of the court's ruling by phone yesterday afternoon, actually read the court's decision, which was mailed from Richmond late yesterday afternoon. The court would not release copies of the decision to the press until lawyers for both sides received their copies.

Representative Clarence D. Long (D., Md., 2d), who also opposes the Hart-Miller project, said through a spokesman the appeals court ruling "is in any case an intermediate action on one of the 11 counts now before the courts."

The appeals court judges based their ruling on their understanding that an 18-foot-high dike around the islands did not

See HART, A6, Col. 5

In calls to police, Welzant twice warned he'd 'take a gun' to youths

By RUSS ROBINSON
Baltimore County Bureau of The Sun

Roman George Welzant told police at least twice the night of January 4 that he would "take a gun" to teenagers throwing snowballs at his house before he finally shot one youth fatally and wounded another, according to police tape recordings and testimony introduced as evidence yesterday in Mr. Welzant's murder trial.

"Christ. They're busting the hell out of my house," Mr. Welzant said when he called police at 9:26 p.m. "Get a car over here, will you? I'll take a gun to these people."

About an hour later, Mr. Welzant did take a gun outside his home, witnesses in the 68-year-old retiree's murder trial have testified. When it was all over, Albert R. Kahl, Jr., 18, lay dead in the street, and James K. Willey, 16, was wounded in the stomach.

Mr. Welzant is charged with second-degree murder, assault with intent to murder and two counts of misuse of a handgun.

As the trial entered its third day of testimony in Towson yesterday, jurors listened to tape recordings of Mr. Welzant's calls to county police, and they heard from the police officer who went to Mr. Welzant's home before the two teenagers were shot.

They also heard a medical examiner's testimony that Mr. Kahl had .22 percent alcohol in his blood at the time of his death, making him legally drunk. That blood alcohol level was the equivalent of consuming 10 ounces of whiskey, the examiner said.

Mr. Welzant first called police at 9:26 p.m., after a group of seven teenaged boys began throwing snowballs at his Eastwood home.

"I got a gang of people over across the street here bombarding my house with snowballs, trying to break my windows," Mr. Welzant told the police dispatcher.

After giving his address and threatening to take a gun to the youths, Mr. Welzant said, "Hurry it up, please."

Officer David Humes, 26, of the Baltimore County Police Department, said he first went to Mr. Welzant's home about 9:30.

"He wanted me to go out and arrest a

See WELZANT, A9, Col. 1

County Council OKs fiscal 1981 budget; pay boosts deferred, tax rate unchanged

By KATHERINE WHITE
Baltimore County Bureau of The Sun

The Baltimore County Council yesterday unanimously adopted a $534.7 million budget, retaining the current $2.93 tax rate in fiscal 1981 and overriding the county solicitor's objections that a Council deferral of some employee salary increases is illegal.

The Council, in rejecting County Executive Donald P. Hutchinson's proposed 6-cent increase in the tax rate, trimmed the executive's $541.2 million budget by broad cuts in a few areas, such as salaries and hiring, rather than numerous small cuts throughout the budget.

The executive had called for an 11.3 percent increase in expenditures of local funds; the Council limited that rise to 9.6 percent. The budget adopted yesterday calls for expenditure of $407.9 million in local funds, with the rest of the budget derived from state and federal aid and revenues from certain user fees.

One of the largest cuts by the Council—$1.471 million—was derived by postponing until September a 7 percent cost-of-living salary increase for county employees who earn $21,000 or more as of July 1. About 4,500 county employees are affected by the delay, as are union contracts that call for the increase to become effective July 1.

Yesterday, Mr. Hutchinson said he may veto the employee classification and compensation law, adopted by the Council as companion legislation to the new budget, because "there is a serious question as to whether or not the Council can determine salary packages."

He based his view on a legal analysis by Leonard S. Jacobson, the county solicitor, which concluded that the Council action in deferring the raises was "an unlawful invasion of executive authority. . . ."

Mr. Jacobson's opinion limits its discussion to restrictions in the County Char-

See BUDGET, A13, Col. 1

Trucking deregulation now appears likely

By STEPHEN E. NORDLINGER
Washington Bureau of The Sun

Washington—Landmark legislation designed to bring competition to the trucking industry appears assured of passage next month because the trucking industry withdrew its opposition yesterday and agreed to support it.

The American Trucking Association, apparently fearful that defeat of the bill would bring even more sweeping decontrol measures by the Interstate Commerce Commission, decided to go along with the bill cleared last week by the House Public Works and Transportation Committee.

The compromise measure was worked out by the House panel, the Carter administration and key members of the Senate, where a tougher deregulatory measure was passed last month. The Senate is expected to accept the House version quickly and send the bill to the White House within two or three weeks.

Passage would be a major victory for President Carter, who has made deregulation a major part of his anti-inflation drive. The House estimates that injecting competition into the heavily protected trucking industry would save consumers $5 billion a year.

The executive committee of the American Trucking Association, at a meeting yesterday, approved a resolution stating it accepts the House bill "with reservations." An association spokesman said no attempt will be made to have the measure amended when the House votes.

Consumer and other groups met yesterday afternoon to map final strategy in case of a last-minute hitch, but backers of the measure expect quick passage in view of the ATA support.

"We think it is a pretty good bill," said Ann McBride, legislative director of Common Cause, the citizens lobbying group that helped lead the fight for passage. "It may not go as far as the Senate bill but it will result in lower rates and a more competitive industry."

The legislation would ease the way for new trucking companies to enter the busi-

See TRUCKING, A8, Col. 3

Indians 10, Orioles 6
Details on Page C9

Grand jury clears Jordan in drug case

By GILBERT A. LEWTHWAITE
Washington Bureau of The Sun

Washington—Presidential assistant Hamilton Jordan was cleared of allegations of cocaine use by a New York grand jury, the special prosecutor in the case announced yesterday.

Mr. Jordan, the White House chief of staff, immediately issued a statement saying: "I have always respected the law and our system of justice. The outcome today has vindicated my faith.

"I wish to thank my family and friends who have stood by me through this process," he said.

President Carter was one of those who consistently supported his aide while Mr. Jordan was under investigation for allegedly using cocaine June 27, 1978, at the Studio 54 disco in New York.

Mr. Carter said yesterday in a statement issued by the White House press office: "My confidence in Hamilton Jordan's integrity has never wavered."

Mr. Carter said he was "gratified" the special prosecutor and the grand jury had agreed with an earlier conclusion by the attorney general that the charges against Mr. Jordan were unsubstantiated.

In a 53-page report on his five-month investigation, special prosecutor Arthur H. Christy said he and the grand jury found insufficient evidence to prosecute Mr. Jordan on narcotics charges.

Earlier this week, *The New York Times* reported that three of Mr. Jordan's accusers, including the co-owners of the disco where he allegedly used the cocaine, were unable to pass lie detector tests.

Mr. Christy's report said a grand jury sitting May 21, in the last of its 19 sessions, agreed with his own finding that

See JORDAN, A8, Col. 1

In search of modernization, China rediscovers Marx

By MICHAEL PARKS
Peking Bureau of The Sun

Peking—Searching for a political and economic strategy to speed its modernization, China is rediscovering classic Marxism, which had been forgotten in the decades of Maoism here but which now could help shape the country's future.

Chinese theoreticians are beginning to conclude that Chairman Mao Tse-tung, the late Chinese leader, was a great revolutionary, but perhaps not a true Marxist. Some believe this is one reason China fell into such destructive radicalism.

In rereading Karl Marx, China's current leaders are finding a realism that matches their own, and increasingly they speak of Marxism, not "Mao Tse-tung thought," as the philosophy of China's "socialist modernization."

This retreat from Maoism, clear to all but never discussed as such, began nearly two years ago, and it has brought a sweeping reorientation of national policy that is felt everywhere.

Economic development, not class struggle, is to provide the country's momentum in the future. Revolution is not an end in itself, but a means to realize China's centuries-old dream of becoming a rich and powerful nation. As a goal, socialism depends in this new context on concrete economic progress, not on political fervor.

Gone are most of the romantic notions of man's "revolutionary consciousness," favored by Chairman Mao over an emphasis on the material forces of production, as in Marxist theory.

This shift goes well beyond ideology and political theory to affect the daily lives of every worker and peasant in the country.

Production-related bonuses for workers are in; equal pay for all is out. To encourage peasants' initiative, they are getting back control of their land, and if some become richer than others through various sidelines, so much the better.

In industry, managers are receiving more authority to run their enterprises. Central planning dictates are not so inflexible as they once were, and most basic industries are being permitted to respond to market forces.

For the consumer, this already has brought more and better products into the stores—and last year, a 5 percent rate of inflation.

To many Chinese, accustomed to thinking in Maoist slogans, this all sounds like a

See MARX, A2, Col. 1

MARXISM
THE IDEAL
THE REALITY

Last of a series

Budget bill's chances dim as O'Neill joins opponents

By THOMAS B. EDSALL
Washington Bureau of The Sun

Washington—Prospects for passing the balanced budget in the House were dealt a severe—if not fatal—blow last night as Speaker Thomas P. (Tip) O'Neill declared that he is opposed to the measure, scheduled for a House vote today.

Abandoning his prior support, Mr. O'Neill said the bill went too far in cutting domestic programs and "goes against the basic Democratic philosophy" of providing for those in need, particularly with the likelihood of a worsening recession.

His last-minute decision represents a significant blow toward prospects for passage of the defense-heavy bill. On Tuesday, President Carter announced his opposition to the controversial bill.

Mr. O'Neill would not say in an interview whether he intends to take the floor to speak against the budget, but he noted, "Everybody out there knows what my position is."

Although historically a supporter of military spending, Mr. O'Neill said, "There is too much money for defense in this budget."

Before Mr. O'Neill's announcement, everyone involved in the controversy considered the House vote today to be very close, if not leaning slightly toward the likelihood of defeat.

Until yesterday, Mr. O'Neill had given begrudging support to the budget on the grounds that he did not want to disrupt the 6-year-old congressional budget-making process. The president's opposition, however, apparently cleared the way for him to join the opponents while still remaining loyal to a Democratic administration.

The president's decision to oppose the $613.3 billion budget heavily weighted to

See O'NEILL, A8, Col. 1

Index

THE SUN

VOL. 287—NO. 41—F | BALTIMORE, THURSDAY, JULY 3, 1980 | •••15 CENTS | FINAL

Sun photo—J. Pat Carter

The Pride of Baltimore arrives in the Inner Harbor to take part in the festivities at the opening of Harborplace as thousands line the shore and jam the pavilions.

100,000 flock to the opening of Harborplace

By John Schidlovsky

Harborplace, the Rouse Company's $18 million "festival marketplace" at the Inner Harbor, opened its doors yesterday and received a passionate, daylong embrace from more than 100,000 persons.

In an exuberant setting of fireworks, flowers, patriotic songs, balloons, mayoral tears of joy, cannon fire and the resonant sound of hundreds of cash registers operating, the long-awaited mall was jammed with visitors all day after its noontime opening.

Merchants scramble all night to meet opening-day deadline D1

A parking nightmare at the Inner Harbor never materialized..................D1

"Harborplace is of, by and for the people of Baltimore," said Mayor Schaefer, moments after stepping off the clipper ship Pride of Baltimore to dedicate the project that has become, for him and others, a symbol of the city's revitalization efforts.

Mr. Schaefer, wearing a brown Baltimore Is Best tie and a yellow rose in his lapel, spoke to a noontime crowd of thousands at the foot of the Inner Harbor. Next to him stood James W. Rouse, the founder of the company that built the mall in the heart of the city's downtown.

"This is a day of celebration, of new life in this great old city," said Mr. Rouse, clad in his usual madras sportsjacket and a straw hat that shielded his head from the 90-degree heat.

Last night, a crowd estimated by police at more than 200,000 people, clapped their hands rhythmically to the Baltimore Symphony Orchestra's rendition of the "1812 Overture" and "Stars and Stripes Forever" accompanied by a booming barrage of fireworks that capped Harborplace's debut day.

The pyrotechnics came 11 hours after Mr. Schaefer and Mr. Rouse had cruised into the harbor aboard the Pride, which had led a parade of some 50 vessels.

Also aboard the pennant-festooned Pride was Mathias J. DeVito, the president of the Rouse firm, who described the retail-dining complex as "a symbol of the new Baltimore."

After delivering their speeches, the three men embarked on a wild, headlong ribbon-cutting dash through a crowd of thousands of early visitors to the two 40-foot-high pavilions. The trio was chased by a galloping contingent of Rouse officials, security men, reporters and dignitaries.

As they entered the Light street pavilion—the larger of the two glassed-in, green-roofed buildings—the officials were greeted by applause from eager mer-

See HARBORPLACE, A6, Col. 1

TMI utility assailed in Senate study

By Frederic B. Hill
Washington Bureau of The Sun

Washington—Conditions were so serious and risks so great after the accident at Three Mile Island last year that utility, federal and state officials should have considered immediate evacuation of the area, a Senate committee concluded in a report released yesterday.

The Senate Subcommittee on Nuclear Regulation said officials of Metropolitan Edison Company were aware of major problems in the first hours after the accident but failed to inform appropriate federal and state authorities of their doubts.

"The utility was remiss in not clearly communicating its uncertainty on the morning of the first day to the Nuclear Regulatory Commission and the state [of Pennsylvania]," the committee report said. While finding no indication of an intentional cover-up, the committee also faulted the NRC and the state for not pinning down utility officials on the severity of plant conditions.

The 423-page, yearlong study also concludes that delays in the cleanup of the damaged facility may be increasing the possibility of additional releases of radioactive material or another accident. "Deliberate procedures" are needed, it said, but "further deterioration can be assumed" as the plant remains unrepaired.

With the exception of these two points, the findings of the study are similar to those of the presidential commission on the accident at Three Mile Island, the nation's worst nuclear accident.

In addition to calling for restructuring of national regulatory procedures and tougher safety measures, the studies attributed the accident to a combination of design problems, lack of preventive steps and human error.

While insisting it is wrong to blame the people involved in the plant's operation, Senator Gary Hart (D, Colo.) compared

See TMI, A8, Col. 5

UPI

Senators Gary Hart (right) and Alan K. Simpson yesterday released a Senate study of the accident at the Three Mile Island nuclear plant.

High court defends press's access to trials

Right to gather news established

By Curt Matthews
Washington Bureau of The Sun

Washington—In a sweeping decision that for the first time establishes the right of the press to gather news as well as publish it, the Supreme Court ruled yesterday that reporters may not be barred from criminal trials.

By a vote of 7-1, the high court held that the right of the press and the public to attend criminal trials is guaranteed under First Amendment provisions that assure freedom of press, freedom of speech and freedom of individual citizens to gather in public places.

The court's majority said there may be some unusual circumstances in which a criminal trial may be closed to the public and the press, but the reasons for doing so must be clearly established and the limits on access "reasonable."

Although the ruling yesterday opens criminal trials to press coverage, it leaves largely undisturbed the court's ruling last year permitting a judge to bar the press and the public from pretrial proceedings.

Referring to the First Amendment freedoms of press, speech and assembly, the Supreme Court said: "These expressly guaranteed freedoms share a common core purpose of assuring freedom of communication on matters relating to the functioning of government."

Chief Justice Warren E. Burger, often the brunt of criticism from press commentators, expressed the view of the

See COURT, A11, Col. 1

OSHA dealt setback on benzene

Washington Bureau of The Sun

Washington—The Department of Labor lost a three-year legal fight to reduce worker exposure to benzene when the Supreme Court ruled yesterday that the department's standards for exposure to the cancer-causing chemical were based on assumptions rather than facts.

Officials for the Occupational Safety and Health Administration said, however, the ruling does not severely threaten its current policies for regulating cancer-causing substances in the workplace.

The decision, which pertained only to benzene, was actually a relief to agency officials who feared it could have damaged the agency's new policy of automatically regulating substances proved to cause cancer in animals.

It has been estimated by the Department of Labor that as many as 30,000 workers in the United States are regularly exposed to some level of benzene and that the exposure levels imposed by the 1977 regulations affect the work practices of about 600,000 workers.

The court, in its 5-4 decision, took care to note that it had made no finding of fact regarding the appropriate level of exposure to benzene but had only concluded that in the absence of further evidence the standards imposed by OSHA were not justified by what is known about benzene.

Although a number of studies, dating back to 1928 and as recent as 1976, have indicated that there is "a distinct possibil-

See BENZENE, A10, Col. 1

Court upholds contract quotas for minorities

Washington (NYT)—The Supreme Court, in a broad endorsement of the power of Congress to remedy racial discrimination, yesterday upheld the constitutionality of a federal public works program that reserved 10 percent of the money for minority contractors.

The 6-3 ruling was an important legal victory for the concept of affirmative action. For the first time, the Supreme Court explicitly endorsed the awarding of federal benefits based on the race of the recipients.

Two opinions, each signed by three justices, made up the majority ruling, with no one rationale commanding a majority of the high court. One opinion, written by Chief Justice Warren E. Burger and signed by Associate Justices Byron R. White and Lewis F. Powell, Jr., was based primarily on the special powers of Congress to enforce the equal protection guarantees of the Constitution.

Yesterday's ruling therefore neither addresses nor resolves the extent to which other branches or institutions of government can implement race-based preferences.

Those questions will be addressed in the Supreme Court's next term in two cases the justices accepted for review yesterday. One case, Minnick vs. California Department of Corrections, is a constitutional challenge by two white, male corrections officers to an affirmative action plan designed to increase the number of women and minorities among California prison guards.

The other, Johnson vs. Board of Education, is a suit by several black students against the Chicago School Board, which imposed a ceiling on the number of blacks admitted to two public high schools in an effort to "stabilize" the racial composition in transitional neighborhoods.

Yesterday's case, Fullilove vs. Klutznick, was one of three major cases the justices decided on the final day of their 1979-80 term. In none of the three cases was there an opinion for the Supreme Court that commanded the votes of five justices. Rather, the decisions included 17 separate opinions comprising 277 pages.

The genesis of yesterday's decision was the enactment by Congress of a $4 billion

See QUOTAS, A11, Col. 1

Inside

Orioles 6, Blue Jays 2

Lee May drove in 4 runs to help Mike Flanagan record his eighth win B1

Fee plans suspended

Two banks have suspended plans to charge credit card membership fees....A15

Strike settlement

A tentative agreement to end a two-day-old strike of maintenance workers at city public housing projects was reached......D1

Muggy

Hot and humid today, high near 93. Fair tonight, lows in the 70s D2

Index

Bridge	C2	Lotteries	B5
Business	A15	Movies	C6
Comics	C11	Obituaries	A13
Crossword	C11	Shipping	A14
Editorials	A20	Sports	B1
Gardner	C6	TV-Radio	C3

4 Sections

Turkish political factions wage deadly ideological war

By Michael K. Burns
Sun Staff Correspondent

Ankara, Turkey—Across the office from a picture of a gray wolf howling at the moon, the photo of Gun Sazak, deputy leader of the Nationalist Action Party, hung over his empty desk.

"His death was not unexpected," said Sadi Somuncuoglu, a former cabinet minister and an official of the ultra-rightist party, as if discussing a man with a terminal disease.

But Mr. Sazak was gunned down outside his home a month ago, several weeks after asking police for protection. He was the most senior politician to die in a wave of violence that has claimed some 3,000 victims over the last two years of ideological warfare in Turkey.

His death signaled that political leaders would no longer be immune from terrorism and set off fears of rightist reprisals. Rightist groups attacked offices and meeting places of the left-wing Republican People's Party and labor unions in provincial Turkey, defying martial law authorities.

Alparsan Turkes, the 63-year-old retired colonel who heads the Nationalist Action Party, blamed the RPP leader, Bulent Ecevit, for inciting the left to violence against Mr. Sazak, but urged restraint on the NAP followers. The question was which half of his speech would be listened to.

The NAP's Gray Wolves, youth groups trained for combat with leftist radicals at Turkish universities, have been blamed for escalating the right-left armed confrontation, pushing it beyond the campus into broader public involvement.

Predictably, the left hit back with violent vigor. It is generally agreed that the Nationalist Action Party and its right-wing extremist admirers have suffered the majority of casualties over the last several years.

The sad but stoic acceptance of Mr. Sazak's death as "a continuation of long-standing tactics of the Communists and the left," as Mr Somuncuoglu puts it, underlines the party's belief that the clashes will continue until a strong government takes power in Turkey.

Critics say the party would welcome the ultimate apocalyptic solution of the polarization of Turkish society—an authoritarian regime that would mercilessly uproot the leftist infidel.

But Mr. Somuncuoglu stressed that a military government, such as Turkey has experienced twice since 1960, would simply exacerbate tensions and lead to success for anarchists and Communists in

See TURKEY, A2, Col. 3

Notice

The Sun will be published as usual tomorrow, Independence Day. *The Evening Sun* will not be published.

The business office will be closed Friday through Sunday. Classified ads will be accepted by telephone (539-7700) tomorrow from 8:30 a.m. until 6 p.m. On Saturday and Sunday classified ads will be accepted from 8:30 a.m. until 9:30 p.m.

UPI

Greetings for the pope

Flag-waving residents of Vidigal, a hillside shantytown overlooking the wealth and splendor of the Rio de Janeiro shoreline, greeted Pope John Paul II from their porches during his 75-minute tour of their village. The pope blessed a chapel built by residents and, pledging that "the church wants to be the church of the poor," gave the parish his personal gold ring. (Article on Page A4)

THE SUN

VOL. 288—NO. 20—F BALTIMORE, TUESDAY, DECEMBER 9, 1980 •••15 CENTS FINAL

John Lennon slain outside home

Wife saw ex-Beatle shot down; man held

From Wire Services

New York—Former Beatle John Lennon, who with the long-haired British rock group was catapulted to stardom in the 1960s, was shot to death last night outside his luxury apartment building on Manhattan's Upper West Side, police said.

Authorities said Mr. Lennon, 40, was rushed in a police car to Roosevelt Hospital, where he was pronounced dead shortly after arriving.

Doctors said he received seven severe wounds in his chest, back and left arm, but they did not know how many bullets had hit Mr. Lennon. Dr. Stephen Lynn said, "I am sure he was dead [very shortly after] when he was shot."

Police said the shooting occurred outside the Dakota, the century-old apartment house across the street from Central Park where Mr. Lennon lived in virtual seclusion with his wife, Yoko Ono, and son Sean, 5.

Sgt. Robert Barnes of the 20th Precinct said Mr. Lemmon was shot in the back twice after getting out of a taxicab and walking into the Dakota.

"Obviously the man was waiting for him," said Sergeant Barnes, referring to an unidentified man who has been taken into custody. The suspect was called a "screwball." There was no apparent motive to the shooting.

The suspect was described by one witness as a man about 30 to 40 dressed in a white shirt and brown pants.

Lt. John Schick said he expected the man, who the officer said was in his mid-20s, to be held through the night. He said police were being careful with the case.

About 300 people gathered outside the entrance to Dakota, many of them weeping.

AP

JOHN LENNON

Jack Douglas, Mr. Lennon's producer, said he and the Lennons had been at a studio called the Record Plant in midtown earlier in the evening and that Mr. Lennon left at 10:30 p.m. Mr. Lennon said he was going to get a bite to eat and go home, Mr. Douglas said.

Neighbors said the musician was emerging from the Dakota with Yoko Ono at about 11 p.m. when a gunman dashed out from 72d street and fired several shots at Mr. Lennon through the front gate.

AP

Yoko Ono is aided by police as she leaves Roosevelt Hospital in New York after the death of her husband, John Lennon.

A neighbor identified only as "Nina" said she heard Yoko Ono scream "Help me," and saw Mr. Lennon lying on the ground.

"He looked pretty bad. He was unconscious," the woman said.

A bystander, Sean Strub, said he was walking south near 72d street when he heard four shots. He said he came around the corner to Central Park West and saw Mr. Lennon being put into the back of a police car.

"Some people they heard six shots and

See LENNON, A4, Col. 1

Soviet issues ominous attack on Polish union

By Anthony Barbieri, Jr.
Moscow Bureau of The Sun

Moscow—The Soviet Union yesterday issued one of its most ominous statements on the crisis in Poland, charging that the Solidarity free trade union movement was being used as a front in a counter revolutionary struggle against public order in Poland.

The statement, by the official Tass news agency, came only days after the Kremlin and its Warsaw Pact allies seemed to have reassured Polish leaders that they had more time to restore Communist Party authority.

Thus the Soviet Union seems to be trying to keep Poland's restive workers, the Polish government and the Western powers off balance.

Yesterday's Tass statement adds another, more serious, charge to the required bill of particulars against Poland should one be needed to justify an invasion.

Tass quoted only "reports coming from various regions of Poland" as saying: "Counter revolutionary groups operating under the cover of local Solidarity sections turn to open confrontation with the local organizations of the Polish [Communist] Party and with the administration of some enterprises and institutions."

It said that at one industrial plant in the Polish city of Kielce, "so-called protectors of the workers' interest" disarmed plant guards and evicted management from the factory.

[In Poland, a spokesman for the official Polish agency Interpress denied that anything unusual had happened in Kielce.]

The Kremlin news agency even hinted at foul play, saying opponents of strong-arm tactics "were missing" after voicing their opposition publicly.

"It is indicative that a campaign has been started in a number of Solidarity committees in recent days of replacing trade union workers with persons who openly adhere to anti-government positions," Tass said.

"These and other facts show that counter revolution is leading the situation in the country towards further destabiliza-

See SOVIET, A2, Col. 5

Officials try to hurt free union

By Hal Piper
Sun Staff Correspondent

Warsaw—Polish authorities are trying to shift public attention from the social and political issues raised in last summer's wave of strikes to the alleged counterrevolutionary threats posed from within the workers' movement.

Although the last strike ended nearly two weeks ago, the tenor of a series

Analysis

of recent official statements has been that the labor movement has been infiltrated by "extremists," "adventurers" and "counter revolutionary elements."

At the same time, while nearly every public statement continues to emphasize the need for social reform, serious discussion of reform has almost stopped. And a documentary film about the stirring events of last summer, which might reawaken public discussion of the issues it raises, is being suppressed.

Meanwhile, private farmers in Poland yesterday demanded a meeting with Prime Minister Jozef Pinkowski and said they would consider strike action if the government refused to legalize their independent trade union.

A spokesman said all action was being closely coordinated with the Solidarity leadership, which had called for a moratorium on strikes in view of the country's tense political and economic situation.

Polish authorities have said that farmers who own their own farms are

See POLAND, A2, Col. 3

Couple connected to city got $55,000 loan

By John Schidlovsky
and Pamela Constable

The city's Board of Estimates approved last month an apparently unprecedented $55,000 home-purchase loan by the city's trustees to a city couple—one of whom works for a consultant to the trustees and the other for the city's Finance Department.

One city official familiar with the special loan called it "irregular," noting that it was not made through any existing loan programs of the city's Department of Housing and Community Development.

The official added that the initial approval of the loan might "be reversed" at this week's Board of Estimates meeting.

"There's a whole lot of people who are concerned about this," said the official, who asked not to be named.

The recipients of the loan, which was approved by the board November 19, were Cynthia L. Fryer, who works as an assistant to Arthur McHugh—a consultant who runs the trustees' loan portfolio—and Norman Fryer, who works in the Finance Department under Charles L. Benton, Jr., the city's finance director and currently its sole trustee.

The Fryers sought the loan in order to buy a property at 3464 Seneca avenue, a three-unit apartment building in Woodberry that the couple intends to "develop" as their residence.

Neither of the Fryers could be reached last night for comment.

According to one high-ranking city official, the loan was approved by M. Jay Brodie, the city's housing commissioner, "even though it is not a city loan."

Mr. Brodie could not be reached last night for comment, either.

The Board of Estimates approved the loan after it had been informed in a letter from Mr. Brodie that the transaction was part of a specific city program to encourage neighborhood redevelopment.

"There is no such program," City Council President Walter S. Orlinsky said last night when informed about the loan, and about the city housing department's stated justification for the transaction.

Mr. Orlinsky, who is the president of the five-member Board of Estimates, said he did not recall the transaction at the meeting three weeks agc.

City Comptroller Hyman A. Pressman, who is also a member of the board, said he did remember the transaction and felt it was "not an unuusal one."

Mr. Benton said last night he had not been aware of the details of the loan when

See LOAN, A13, Col. 3

Chrysler asks $350 million in new U.S. loan guarantee

Washington (NYT)—The Chrysler Corporation told the government yesterday that it must have an additional $350 million of federal loan guarantees within the next 30 days if it is to keep operating.

The three-member Chrysler Loan Guarantee Board reacted cooly during a two-hour meeting with Chrysler executives, indicating reservations about enlarging the government's risk—$800 million of guarantees have been issued so far—but not refusing outright, according to government sources.

G. William Miller, chairman of the loan board and Secretary of the Treasury, suggested that the company had to raise additional capital funds to sustain itself for the next two years or so.

"That's absolutely essential," a federal official said after the meeting.

Two methods of raising additional capital were discussed, informants said. One way would be for Chrysler to join forces with another company, either through a joint venture or by sale of a fractional interest, like the American Motors Corporation's agreement to sell a 46 percent interest to Renault of France.

Some officials speculated that Chrysler might be able to raise money from Mitsubishi, a Japanese automaker, or Peugeot, the French auto company. Chrysler owns a minority interest in both.

A second way would be to persuade holders of Chrysler debt to exercise their option to convert the debt to equity—shares of ownership—for an additional cash payment. That, if done, would dilute the value of outstanding Chrysler common stock.

Lee A. Iacocca, Chrysler's chairman,

See CHRYSLER, A21, Col. 4

Inside

Harford official shot
Mervyn G. Thompson, Sr., a Harford county zoning official, was wounded by two shotgun blasts near his home C1

Optimism on hostages
The speaker of the Iranian parliament said the United States is closer to meeting demands for release of the hostages A8

Cloudy, chance of showers
Cloudy with a chance of showers this afternoon, high 63. Rain likely tonight, low 45. Yesterday's high 72; low 50 .... C2

Index

Bridge	B5	Lotteries	C11
Business	A17	Movies	B6
Comics	B7	Obituaries	A21
Crossword	B7	Sports	C7
Editorials	A22	TV-Radio	B4

3 Sections

Election set tomorrow

In urban Uganda, the black market is the only real post-Amin economy

By Antero Pietila
Sun Staff Correspondent

Kampala, Uganda—Twenty months after the fall of Idi Amin Dada, gunfire still frequently heralds the curfew hour in this capital; each day brings a new test of the survival skills of its half million people.

How Kampala's residents keep themselves surprisingly well clothed and adequately fed is a miracle of the magendo.

The magendo—the local word for black market—is the only real economy of this Oregon-sized country of 12 million people.

Particularly in Kampala and some of the other big cities you have to participate in the magendo or you simply will not survive.

Many Ugandans—such as one veteran journalist—simply have given up Kampala and moved to the countryside where food is easier to get and life often more orderly—and safer.

Without the magendo, living would be impossible in Uganda's ramshackle economy.

A hotel maid here earns the equivalent of $86 a month, a truck driver $214. Yet the asking price for a loaf of bread is about $11, while a live chicken costs as much as $25 and a carton of 30 eggs $48.

Consequently, many Kampala residents who may have an office job during the week return to till plots in their native villages during the weekend.

The few restaurants that serve meals here are no bargain, either.

A lunch, consisting of a glass of water, a deep plate filled with robust beef stew and a saucerette of grainy salt, costs $17. No soft drinks are available and beer is usually sold out.

"It's not easy, but we make do," one Ugandan said of life here.

When Idi Amin's tyranny collapsed under the combined attack of Tanzanian armed forces and Ugandan exiles April 10, 1979, it was officially estimated that 200,000 people had been murdered by the Amin regime in its eight years of rule.

Uganda's foreign debt, according to an official statement at the time, stood at $396 million, with debt-service payments some $72 million in arrears.

A Commonwealth team of economic

See UGANDA, A2, Col. 1

Argentine Jews, uneasy, try to keep a low profile

By James Neilson

Buenos Aires (Special)—Behind the repeated denials that anything is amiss, it is easy to detect a deep uneasiness among many of Argentina's Jews. Though well-integrated on the surface,

Soviet Jewish emigrant says repression creates dissenters B1

many fear that the day could come when the rest of the society could decide they do not really belong.

A few Jewish activists here think the vast majority of their Jewish compatriots are living in a fool's paradise and should get out as soon as possible. The picture they paint of the status of Argentina's Jews differs radically from the one held by most Jews and the bulk of non-Jews.

Most Jews yearn to believe that Argentine anti-Semitism is grossly exaggerated abroad and that the periodical spasms of anti-Semitism that occur presage no''ing of importance.

After the United States, Argentina is believed to be home for the largest concentration of Jews in the Western hemisphere. Estimates of the size of the community range up to half a million, out of a population of about 26 million. But Rabbi Marshal Meyer, the American founder of the Latin American Rabbinical Seminary, doubts that the number far exceeds 300,000.

ANTI-SEMITISM

Is there a worldwide upsurge in anti-Semitism today? In a series of four articles, The Sun looks at the status of Jews in four of the countries in which they are found in the largest numbers.

Anti-Semitism, at times, has been virulent, and a number of attacks on synagogues and individual Jews have

See ARGENTINA, A7, Col. 1

Jacobo Timerman, a prominent Jewish editor, emigrated to Israel with his wife, Rishe, after his expulsion from Argentina.

Zimbabwean official freed in slaying of white farmer

From Wire Services

Salisbury, Zimbabwe—The High Court freed cabinet minister Edgar Tekere and seven bodyguards yesterday in the death of a white farmer, saying they were responsible but were protected from prosecution by a white-passed law allowing such action if done "in good faith" to suppress terrorism.

The court said Mr. Tekere, 43, who ranks third in the hierarchy of Prime Minister Robert Mugabe's black-majority regime, took part in the August 4 shooting of Gerald Adams, 68, at a farm outside Salisbury, and that bodyguard Joseph Chakanetsa fired the fatal shots.

Cheering broke out in the court when the judge read the decision, and Mr. Tekere was carried from the courtroom on the shoulders of supporters.

Whites, who had taken to calling the case a test of the eight-month-old government's readiness to uphold legal standards, were generally stunned by the outcome even though it came without any suggestion of political interference.

"It's amazing," said a bitter police reservist who had been assigned to sit in the public galleries in plain clothes to reduce the number of seats available for Mr. Tekere's supporters. "Come to Rhodesia and commit murder."

Judge John Pittman, the South African-born white jurist, was overruled by his two nonwhite assessors from convicting the men of murder, for which the penalty is hanging.

Under Roman Dutch law, introduced in the past century, assessors sit with the High Court judge to assist in determining issues of fact and can overrule his decisions. The assessors are also judges, but from lower courts. There are no juries in Roman Dutch law.

A grim-faced Judge Pittman announced that his wish to convict Mr. Tekere and his bodyguards "regrettably" had been overturned by the assessors, Chris Greenland, who is of mixed race, and Peter Nemapare, who is black.

The judge and his assessors did not disagree about whether Mr. Tekere and bodyguards took part in the killing, which was

See ZIMBABWE, A2, Col. 2

THE SUN

VOL. 288—NO. 46—F | BALTIMORE, FRIDAY, JANUARY 9, 1981 | •••15 CENTS | FINAL

Sun photo—Richard Childress

Reagan hints he might alter hostage stand

From Wire Services

Washington—President-elect Ronald Reagan said yesterday he would feel free to review all hostage negotiations with Iran and possibly take a different stand than the Carter administration if the American captives are not released before he takes office.

He also refused to declare flatly that he would go along with the terms of a hostage agreement completed before he moves into the White House on January 20.

"I'm quite sure that any agreement would be one that, yes, I could carry out," Mr. Reagan declared. "On the other hand I don't think anyone should be asked to sign a blank check, and so I can't give you an unequivocal yes."

"I can tell you I am confident that the president is working toward an agreement that does preserve the honor of our country and is aimed at trying to get those people home which we all hope he'll be successful in doing."

In a statement issued September 13, during the presidential campaign, Mr. Reagan said of efforts to free the hostages: "I will not make those negotiations a partisan issue in the campaign. I also pledge that if elected, I will observe the terms of an agreement" reached by the Carter administration.

Mr. Reagan spoke with reporters briefly yesterday as he concluded his final preinaugural visit to Washington and headed back to California. He will return to the capital Wednesday, six days before he is inaugurated as the nation's 40th president.

Standing before a bank of microphones and cameras in the lobby of the State Department, where he held his first business meeting with his designated cabinet secretaries, Mr. Reagan said he and his staff are not receiving day-to-day briefings on negotiations for the hostages' release.

He said they have not sought the information because "I worry about the possibility of anything that could possibly throw a monkey wrench in there or reveal something that shouldn't be revealed."

Asked if he would feel free to review the negotiations and take some different stand if the hostage stalemate remains unresolved when he takes office January 20, Mr. Reagan replied, "That's right, yes."

Meanwhile, as Warren M. Christopher, the U.S. deputy secretary of state, met for three hours with the Algerian foreign minister, Mohamed Benyahia, to discuss the status of negotiations with Iran on the American hostages, Tehran Radio heaped scorn on what it called Mr. Reagan's tough policies.

An Iranian radio commentary said Mr. Reagan's "slogan of militarism" meant he was doomed to meet the same ignominious fate as Presidents Nixon and Carter.

This would happen because U.S. imperialism, faced with growing liberation movements, was in the throes of decline, said the state-owned radio, which does not necessarily reflect government views.

After initially saying they did not care whether Mr. Reagan or Mr. Carter won last November's presidential election, Iranian politicians and commentators have become increasingly hostile toward the

See HOSTAGES, A5, Col. 1

Sun photo—Lloyd Pearson

Fire strikes Howard st. in rush hour

The first block North Howard street was the site of a four-alarm fire yesterday that sent thick smoke billowing east across the city. The blaze destroyed Henry's Drapery & Shade Company, a family firm founded in 1929 by Henry and Anne Grodnitzky.

By the time the fire was under control, 36 pieces of equipment and 119 fire fighters had been dispatched to the blaze, which broke out at 3:08 p.m. and caused severe congestion for rush-hour traffic for several hours. Some fire fighters were expected to stay at the scene until early this morning to deal with any "hot spots," and the building will be examined today for structural weakness.

No one was injured in the blaze, which authorities believe was accidental.

Photos show the Henry's facade (left), a fire fighter on a ladder with the old Bromo Seltzer-Baltimore Arts Tower in the background (right) and the view looking southeast from the Hecht Company's parking garage. (Article, Page C1)

Sun photo—April Saul

DAVID HENRY BARNETT
. . . sentenced to 18 years

Ex-CIA man gets 18 years for espionage

By Allegra Bennett

David Henry Barnett, a former CIA operative who admitted selling U.S. intelligence secrets to the Soviet Union in the most serious security breach in recent years, was sentenced in federal court yesterday to 18 years in prison.

Barnett, who had been free on personal recognizance while cooperating with the FBI and intelligence authorities since pleading guilty to espionage last October, was placed immediately in the custody of the U.S. marshal to await a prison assignment.

The former Central Intelligence Agency operative showed little emotion throughout the proceeding and declined comment after hearing the sentence imposed by U.S. District Judge Frank A. Kaufman.

The length of the sentence came as a surprise, however, to Barnett's attorney, Dennis C. Kolenda, who said after the sentencing that he thought his client's cooperation with authorities—which spanned nine months of debriefing, since last March—should have resulted in a more lenient prison term.

"What was the point of cooperating?" he asked, explaining that if Barnett had been sentenced to the maximum term of life imprisonment after a trial and a guilty verdict, he would be eligible for parole within 10 years.

With the 18-year sentence, he is eligible for parole after serving one-third of the sentence, or 6 years. "There doesn't seem to be much of a difference," Mr. Kolenda said.

As a CIA agent, Barnett had top-secret security clearance and was privy to sensitive classified information—information authorities say he sold for $92,600.

Last March, Barnett confessed that he had provided the KGB, the Soviet Union's intelligence agency, with a description of HABRINK, a covert U.S. operation that procured technical information on Soviet weaponry. He pleaded guilty to one count of espionage seven months later.

According to government accounts of his activities, he also revealed the true identities of seven CIA undercover operatives, exposing them and their operations to danger.

As part of his dealings with the KGB, Barnett was to secure reemployment in the U.S. intelligence sector by applying for positions on both the House and Senate intelligence committees, government prose-

See SPY, A2, Col. 6

Brock in line for trade post in cabinet

By Carl P. Leubsdorf
Washington Bureau of The Sun

Washington—William E. Brock III, the Republican national chairman whose party-building efforts brought some conservative condemnation despite last November's GOP successes, has been tapped as special trade representative, one of the last remaining major posts in the Reagan administration, transition sources said yesterday.

Mr. Brock, a former Tennessee senator and businessman, had hoped for a cabinet job but was apparently happy to settle for the trade job with the assurance that it will retain the cabinet rank it has enjoyed under the Carter administration.

Interestingly, the same post went four years ago to Robert S. Strauss, who was chairman of the Democratic National Committee when Mr. Carter was elected.

A formal announcement of the selection of Mr. Brock is expected next week, as are several others, including the new chairman of the Council of Economic Advisers and many of the No. 2 people for cabinet departments.

Mr. Reagan met for 30 minutes yesterday with most of his cabinet appointees—some were on Capitol Hill at their Senate confirmation hearings—before flying back to California for a final, six-day visit that will end next Wednesday when he comes back to Washington for his inauguration.

Mr. Reagan's press secretary, James S. Brady, said the president-elect had some advice for his cabinet-to-be.

"The one no-no . . . is I don't want anyone ever to bring up the political ramifications of an act," Mr. Reagan was quoted as saying.

"We should operate as if there is no next election."

Mr. Brady said Mr. Reagan also told his cabinet he wants "free, open discussion" because "only through that way will I find out what I need to know to make the decision."

In a comment reminiscent of the early days of the Carter administration, Mr. Brady said: "I think you'll probably see some reductions in the White House staff," but declined to deal in any specifics.

In addition to the president-elect, the

See BROCK, A6, Col. 6

AP

WILLIAM E. BROCK III
. . . Republican national chairman

Budget chief-designate hints he will seek cuts in aid to both urban and farm areas

By James A. Rousmaniere, Jr.
Washington Bureau of The Sun

Washington — David A. Stockman, President-elect Reagan's nominee for budget chief, yesterday hinted at a broad sweep in spending cuts that would affect both urban and farm areas.

Specifically, the Republican representative from Michigan suggested he would press for spending restraints in both urban construction grants, which have been used extensively by Baltimore, and farm price supports for such commodities as milk and tobacco.

Meanwhile, Mr. Reagan told reporters that he was beginning to draft plans to cut federal spending "across the board" in order to pare the projected $60 billion deficit in the current fiscal year.

Neither Mr. Reagan nor his prospective director of the Office of Management and Budget provided specific figures. Both indicated, however, that the range of spending cuts would be wide.

Their formal budget plans will not be known in full until the beginning of next month at the earliest, after the new administration assumes office January 20.

Mr. Stockman, appearing at a five-hour-long confirmation hearing, indicated that many of his planned spending reductions may be similar to budget-cutting strategies advanced by Mr. Carter.

In particular, Mr. Stockman told a Senate panel that he will attempt to reduce federal loan and loan guarantee programs and will propose that savings be made in social assistance programs by targeting aid to smaller population groups.

The Reagan administration's cutback proposals are expected to be more severe than those advanced by Mr. Carter, who had notably little success in winning con-

See STOCKMAN, A9, Col. 1

Inside

Singleton signs with O's
Oriole outfielder Ken Singleton signs a contract that keeps him in an Oriole uniform for four, perhaps five, more years. C5

Cloudy, flurries possible
Mostly cloudy with a chance of flurries through tonight. High, 27; low, 17. Yesterday's high, 26; low, 17. C2

Index

For Begin's government, torn by crisis, the crunch could come this weekend

By Douglas Watson
Jerusalem Bureau of The Sun

Jerusalem—Torn by conflicting and apparently unresolvable demands, Israel's government is moving rapidly toward a crisis that seems likely to force its resignation or ouster and the holding of parliamentary elections in the spring.

The crunch could come at Sunday's weekly cabinet meeting, when Finance Minister Yigael Hurvitz and Education Minister Zevulun Hammer are expected to acknowledge they have been unable to reach agreement on a demand by Israeli teachers for a 30 percent pay raise.

One or both cabinet members are likely to carry out their threats to resign, with a strong possibility that enough Knesset colleagues will join in the walkout from the government to deprive it of its majority.

It is also possible that Prime Minister Menachem Begin, realizing that his government faces defeat in a no-confidence vote, will decide to ask President Yitzhak Navon to dissolve the government and arrange for a caretaker government until elections are held.

Mr. Begin was reported last night as saying there was no point in continuing his government if the crisis could not been resolved and if Mr. Hurvitz resigned. If that happened, he said, he would "go to the president."

Israel's 3½-year-old government is beset by an accumulation of crises and scandals that have cut sharply into its credibility, its cohesion and its capacity to act decisively.

The major issue over which the government is divided is the salary, status and responsibilities of Israel's public school teachers. Two years ago the cabinet obligated itself to accept the findings of an independent arbitration body known as the Etzioni Commission, which has called for the 30 percent pay raises and increased duties for the teachers. Mr. Hammer, a rising power in the National Religious

See ISRAEL, A5, Col. 5

Weather
Cloudy tonight, tomorrow. Lows 30 to 35, highs 38 to 43.

The Evening Sun

Final EDITION

Vol. 142—No. 79 BALTIMORE, MARYLAND TUESDAY, JANUARY 20, 1981 15 Cents

HOSTAGES FREE

All 52 flying to Algiers, Germany

From wire services

The 52 American hostages flew to freedom today after 444 days of captivity in Iran.

Their departure coincided with the inauguration of President Reagan, and touched off celebrations and a cacophony of sirens and bells across the United States.

Departure of the hostages was marked by the same confusion and uncertainty that characterized the entire hostage crisis. There was also uncertainty as to whether the hostages were aboard more than one plane

Pars, the official Iranian news agency, said the hostages boarded aircraft in Tehran to shouts by Iranians of "down with America, down with Reagan."

Mr. Reagan confirmed in Washington that the aircraft had taken off from Tehran.

And Edmund S. Muskie, secretary of state under former President Carter, said Mr. Carter who flew home to Plains, Ga., this afternoon, would return to Washington tonight and leave for West Germany at about 8 o'clock.

The 3,000-mile flight of the hostages from Iran to Algiers could up to 10 hours, depending on refueling stops, and it was anticipated that the hostages would go on to a U.S. Air Force hospital in Wiesbaden, West Germany.

Behzad Nabavi, Iran's chief hostage negotiator, had said today the last hurdle to the hostages' freedom was removed when frozen Iranian assets were in place and the American hostages were "ready to fly."

There were reports from Western sources monitoring the hostage situation in Ankara that flight plans filed by the Algerian aircraft included a refueling stop in Rome, Athens, Ankara, Turkey, or Damascus, Syria.

The report on the hostages' departure came in the final hour of President Carter's term of office. He had tried to complete an agreement with Iran yesterday, but as the hours slipped away, Mr. Carter was deprived of a chance to greet the hostages before he left office.

Thus, the reported freedom for the Americans —50 men and two women—coincided with the end of the Carter presidency as power was transferred to Ronald Reagan at inauguration ceremonies in Washington

Nabavi arrived at the airport with two Swiss diplomats who have been representing U.S. interests in Iran, officials said.

In Washington, where Mr. Carter was trying to end the hostage ordeal in the final hours of his presidency, White House press secretary Jody Powell said earlier today Algerian intermediaries had officially notified Iran that its frozen assets had been transfered

[Continued, Page A 4, Col. 6]

Reagan sworn in, pledges 'national renewal'

AP photo

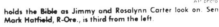

Chief Justice Warren Burger administers the presidential oath of office to Ronald Reagan. The new President's wife, Nancy, holds the Bible as Jimmy and Rosalynn Carter look on. Sen. Mark Hatfield, R-Ore., is third from the left.

Hostages' state kin rejoice

By Nick Yengich

Allen Howland threw his hand, then his feet, into the air and asked the question on everyone's mind: "Can we let ourselves believe it yet?"

He did.

Yes, the hostages were out

Allen, twin brother of hostage Michael Howland, stopped watching television, left the couch in his Laurel home, hugged his wife Sharon and broke down crying

"I'm sorry, I just need a moment," the 34-year-old Defense Department engineer said to a suddenly quiet room of reporters and television crewmen.

"I want to be happy. I think we ought to open that bottle of champagne now," he said. But then, looking at the bottle of bubbly from Wiesbaden, West Germany, where the hostages were headed and obviously thinking of other disappointments,. he said, "No, we'll open it when the call from the State Department comes."

When that official call came about 30 minutes later, Allen grabbed the phone in the bedroom. His face lit up, his thumbs went up in the air, and he yelled, "Hey, that's fantastic!"

Walking from the room, he said, "Now I'll get the champagne for sure."

As he poured it with shaky hands, he quietly said, "I want to say thank you to the world. Man, what a relief; it's like you just gave birth to 52."

Allen Howland's brother Michael,

[Continued, Page A 2, Col. 3]

Upstaged by hostage drama

By Robert Timberg and Norman Wilson

Evening Sun Washington bureau

WASHINGTON—Ronald Reagan, his inauguration upstaged by events in Iran, called on the American people today to join him in beginning "an era of national renewal."

"Let us renew our determination, our courage and our strength," he said. "Let us renew our faith and hope. We have every right to dream historic dreams."

In his first major act as President, Mr. Reagan signed an executive order putting an immediate freeeze on the hiring on non-military government workers.

Moments before, Mr. Reagan had been invested with the awesome power of the American presidency, transformed by the simple words of the oath of office into the single most powerful figure in the non-Communist world.

Mr Reagan's 20-minute inaugural address played strongly on the themes of his successful presidential candidacy —the need for a sharp reduction in the size of government, reduced taxes and a stronger national defense.

The new President made no direct reference to the hostage situation but he did seem to be sending a message to the Iranians when he spoke of "will and moral courage" as the strongest weapons in any nation's arsenal.

"It is a weapon our adversaries in today's world do not have," he said. "It is a weapon we as Americans do have. Let that be understood by those who practice terrorism and prey upon their neighbors."

In repeating the themes of his successful presidential campaign, Mr. Reagan pledged to direct his administration to the concerns of "We the people."

He termed the country's citizens a special interest group too long neglected.

Mr Reagan spoke of the nation's eco-

[Continued, Page A 6, Col. 1]

A handshake, a prayer, then a new President

By Carl Schoettler
Evening Sun Correspondent

Ronald Wilson Reagan, the actor-president, was waiting in the wings today when the news came from Iran that the hostages had been freed.

Vice President-elect George Bush and his wife, Barbara, had just been ushered to the inaugural stand when the report that the hostages had taken off from Iran flashed through the crowd massed on the West Front grounds of the Capitol.

That odd, anticipatory silence that precedes the appearance of the new President had stilled the crowd noises.

"The hostages are free!" a dozen people with transistor radios said at once. Transistor radios were a whole lot more common at today's Inauguration than the mandated formal attire.

"That's the most uncanny timing," said William F. Buckley, Jr., the proprietor of the *National Review*, who was in formal clothes. (His wife, Pat wore a sable-trimmed suede suit with a brocaded back.)

"Why do they make us wait so long?" said another preferred spectator in the A-1 section under the inaugural stand. It was hard to tell if she was speaking of

[Continued, Page A 2, Col 1]

Index

Conservatives' tactics scare up the votes

This is the second in a series of articles on the New Right. The series will run through Saturday

By Robert Timberg
Evening Sun Washington bureau

Washington—"THESE POLITICIANS ARE RUNNING FOR RE-ELECTION IN 1980," screamed the boldface type above the picture of George McGovern and three other senators. "WHILE THIS LITTLE ONE IS RUNNING FOR HIS LIFE RIGHT NOW!"

The "little one" was a 16-week-old fetus, encased in its placenta and prominently displayed on a 1980 fundraising solicitation from the National Pro-Life Political Action Committee

"Abortion means killing a living baby, a tiny human being with a beating heart and little fingers ... killing a baby boy or baby girl with burning deadly chemicals or a powerful machine that sucks and tears the little infant from its mother's womb."

That description was from STOP THE BABY KILLERS, the political action arm of an organization called Americans for Life, another anti-abortion group after Mr. McGovern.

"LAPAC is supporting Larry Schumaker who is a Democrat and is running against McGovern in the Democrat Primary," said a letter to South Dakota pastors from a third anti-abortion group, Life Amendment Political Action Committee.

"Larry has visited our office in Washington D.C. and has met with representatives of Dr. Jerry Falwell's Moral Majority as well as other Christian and conservative committees, and we are convinced that he, by far, best represents the Christian pro-family position on these issues."

Anti-abortionists were not the only single issue or conservative group, many affiliated with the New Right, out to get McGovern last year

Even before the June primary, in which McGovern was bloodied for the general election battle he would

[Continued, Page A 8, Col. 1]

Evening Sun collage—Jef Dauter

Literature from the right.

New Right linked for effective impact

By Robert Timberg
Evening Sun Washington bureau

Washington—The hard-hitting organizations of the New Right are linked in a network of formal and informal relationships through which seemingly independent groups coordinate their activities.

This coordination permits the New Right to maximize its impact on public policy and political campaigns.

As a result, senators backing the Panama Canal treaties were likely to face heavy anti-treaty lobbying by New Right groups in Washington and grass-roots pressure from movement activists back home

In addition, when those same senators became candidates for re-election, many found a different batch of New Right crusaders promoting their opponents and still others waging negative campaigns against them

The network has been expanded in the last year or so as fundamentalist preachers have teamed up with the political operatives of the New Right

The organizations themselves, when ideological considerations are ignored, bear a distinct resemblance to institutions on the opposite side of the political spectrum

"I've jokingly said, but there's some truth to it, that I'm sort of a Japanese mechanic of the New Right, copying—and hopefully making a little better—the operations of the left."

The speaker, Paul M. Weyrich, is a 38-year-old political operative who has had a big hand in founding a number of organizations that form the cornerstone of the New Right.

Weyrich maintained that he and his allies have merely put in place a number of right wing groups that constitute a mirror image of the left.

Thus, according to Weyrich, the Brookings Institution, a liberal Washington think tank, finds itself competing for influence on Capitol Hill with the Heritage Foundation, which is associated with the New Right.

Similarly, the AFL-CIO's Committee on Political Education, which tries to elect organized labor's friends and

[Continued, Page A 8, Col. 1]

THE SUN

VOL. 288—NO. 115—F BALTIMORE, TUESDAY, MARCH 31, 1981 •••20 CENTS FINAL

Reagan shot; prognosis excellent; police hold 25-year-old suspect; press aide Brady badly injured

Three men lie wounded after assassination attempt on President Reagan outside the Washington Hilton hotel. In the background, Secret Service agents subdue the suspect in the shooting, John W. Hinckley, Jr. AP

Shots fired outside D.C. hotel

Secret Service man, capital policeman are also wounded

By Ernest B. Furgurson
Washington Bureau of The Sun

Washington — A gunman pushed through newsmen to shoot President Reagan in the left chest and wound three other persons yesterday as the president left a Washington hotel after speaking to a labor group.

Last night, after surgery that lasted about two hours, Mr. Reagan's prognosis was described as "excellent." A physician said the president had "sailed through" the operation.

Mr. Reagan was able to walk into the hospital after being rushed away from the scene, and joked cheerfully as he was wheeled into the operating room for

Related stories on Pages A6, A7, A8, A9 and A10.

removal of a bullet that passed near his heart and partly collapsed his left lung.

James S. Brady, the president's press secretary, was critically wounded by a bullet in the head. A Washington policeman, hit in the shoulder, also was in serious condition, and a Secret Service man was hit in the chest.

Secret Service agents and police, suddenly bristling with pistols and submachine guns, wrestled the assailant to the sidewalk. They later identified and charged John Warnock Hinckley, Jr., 25, of Evergreen, Colo., an affluent mountain suburb 20 miles west of Denver.

Early today, the subdued, puffy-faced defendant was brought to a tightly guarded courtroom where a U.S. magistrate ordered him held without bond for a hearing Thursday at 10 a.m.

Authorities in Nashville reported that Mr. Hinckley was arrested there carrying three handguns when President Jimmy Carter was in town last October for a campaign meeting. Federal agents said records show he bought two more .22-caliber handguns—the kind used yesterday—at a pawnshop in Dallas four days later.

Mr. Hinckley's father is president of Vanderbilt Energy Corporation, an oil and

See SHOOTING, A6, Col. 1

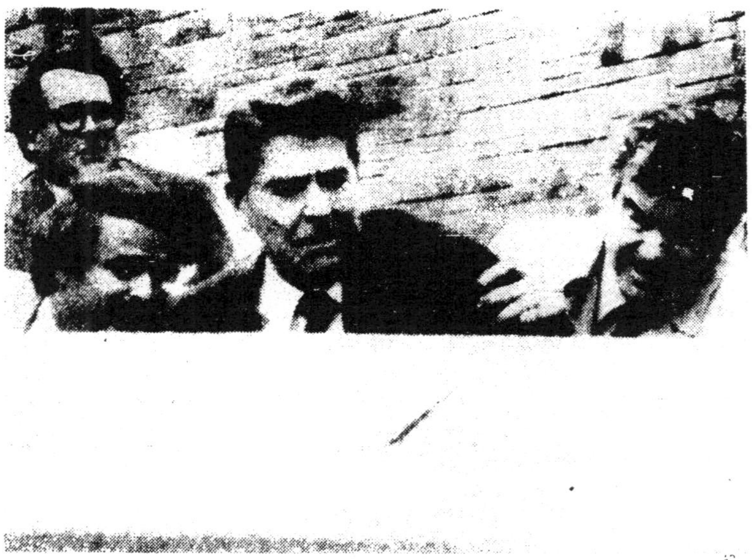

Two Secret Service agents push President Reagan into his limousine after he is shot.

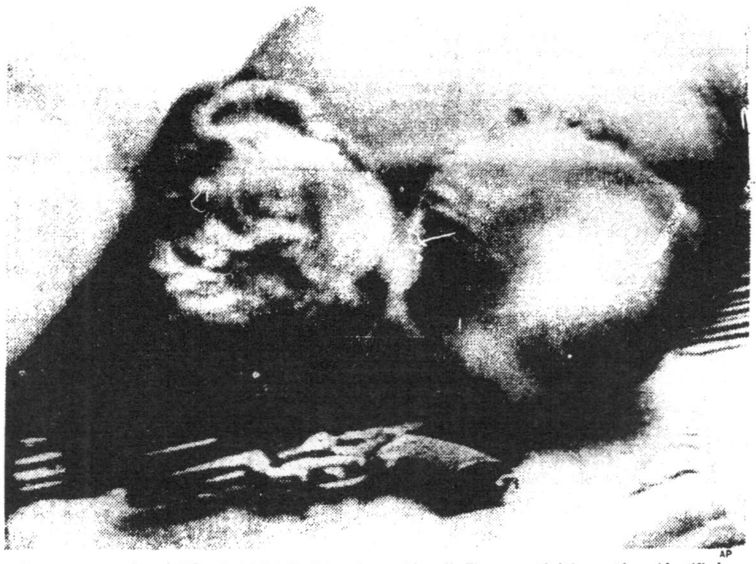

Press secretary James S. Brady (right) lies injured on a sidewalk. The man at left has not been identified. AP

Secret Service Agent Timothy J. McCarthy reacts as a bullet strikes him.

Suspect Hinckley said to have received psychiatric care, faced Tenn. gun charge

By Sandy Banisky

John Warnock Hinckley, Jr., accused of shooting President Reagan yesterday in Washington, has "recently" been under psychiatric care and reportedly was arrested last year on a gun charge in Tennessee.

The son of a wealthy oil man who is a Republican, Mr. Hinckley grew up in the most exclusive area of Dallas.

The family moved to Denver after their son's 1973 graduation from Dallas's Highland Park Senior High School. The Hinckleys now live in a luxury development in Evergreen, about 20 miles from Denver.

Yesterday, in a statement from a neighbor's home, the Hinckleys said they were heartbroken by the news from Washington.

"John has been recently under psychiatric care, but the evaluation did not alert us to the seriousness of his condition," the statement said.

It was unclear last night how long Mr. Hinckley, 25, had been receiving treatment and what he was being treated for.

Mr. Hinckley's movements over the last few months also were unclear. He attended Texas Tech University, in Lubbock, during the 1980 summer semester.

But two members of a self-described Nazi organization said last night that Mr. Hinckley had corresponded with the group —later severing his relationship with the Nazis because he felt they were not militant enough.

Meanwhile, the FBI in Nashville confirmed that a man named John Hinckley was arrested October 9 as he tried to carry three handguns aboard a Nashville-to-New York flight.

President Carter had been campaigning that day in Nashville.

Four days later, Mr. Hinckley reportedly bought a pair of .22-caliber revolvers

See HINCKLEY, A8, Col. 3

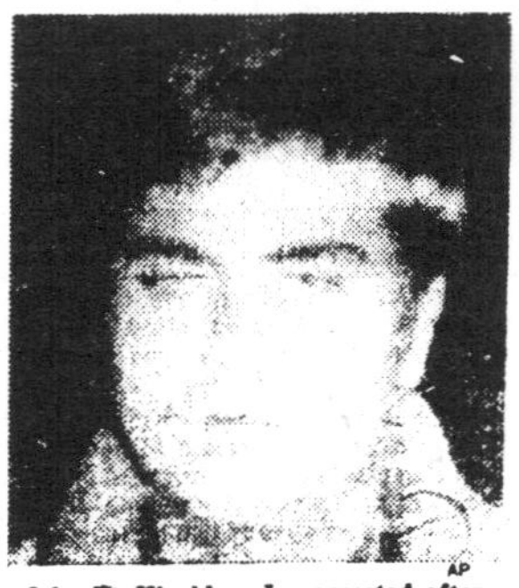

AP

John W. Hinckley, Jr., arrested after yesterday's assassination attempt, appears here in Colorado Highway Department driver's license photo.

A reporter who witnessed the attack recalls the 'bloody seconds,' the chaos

By Gilbert A. Lewthwaite
Washington Bureau of The Sun

Washington—Already it is a frozen moment of sharp sound, soft smoke and sudden chaos.

A sidewalk dripping a friend's blood and possibly life into a rusty grating, a gaping wound in his temple.

Two other victims motionless on the rain-soaked pavement, their clothing becoming as limp as their bodies in the endless rain. Dark figures bending solicitously over them all.

A knot of men so entwined and locked in intense life-and-death struggle for a deadly weapon that it is impossible to attach arms to shoulders and legs to hips. The protectors and the alleged assailant are one grunting, steaming, pulsating tangle at the foot of a 15-foot-high stone wall above which bloom the first flowers of spring.

A president, welcomed so properly and so warmly just moments earlier, now pushed gracelessly into his limousine and whisked away with textbook speed as immediate assurances are given that he is not hit. All too quickly we learn the truth.

And now—everywhere—screams, shouts, panic.

This is what that ceaseless vigil reporters keep on a president is all about: the awful climax of that most morbid of journalistic chores—"the body watch."

Why here on T street? It is a nondescript service road between the main arteries of Connecticut and Florida avenues —the most discreet point of entry, for whatever purpose, into the white immensity of the Washington Hilton, be it for presidents or paying guests.

Why, just after Mr. Reagan had warned that the price of expecting government to run our lives instead of "protecting" them was a 10 percent increase in violent crime?

Why should that young man with short, straight fair hair, the tan raincoat, the light blue shirt, the dark blue trousers, his hands now cuffed behind him, be bundled —no, almost thrown—into the police car?

Why should someone here have murder in mind?

Why? Why? Why?

There are no answers here as the cameras and microphones are poked into the faces of anyone who saw anything, recording their bewilderment, their shock, their

See WITNESS, A9, Col. 1

Inside

Kamka resigns

Gordon C. Kamka, state public safety secretary, and Edwin R. Goodlander, commissioner of correction, resign C1

Poland settlement

Poland's Communist Party and Solidarity, the independent labor union, reach a last-minute pact averting a strike A2

Sunny and warm

Sunny and warm today, high 75. Chance of showers late tonight, low 50. Yesterday's high, 68; low, 58 ....C2

Index

3 Sections

THE SUN

VOL. 288—NO. 126—F | BALTIMORE, MONDAY, APRIL 13, 1981 | •••20 CENTS | FINAL

Rising faultlessly into the clear skies above the Kennedy Space Center, the shuttle Columbia begins its maiden flight into space. AP

Winged space shuttle blasts off into orbit

By Albert Sehlstedt
Sun Staff Correspondent

Kennedy Space Center, Fla.—The space shuttle Columbia flew into Earth orbit yesterday after one of the most spectacular launches ever seen here.

Seeming to rise on a frozen pillar of white smoke against a background of blue sky, Columbia arched out over the Atlantic Ocean, dropping its two solid rocket boosters en route, and climbed to an orbit of 132 nautical miles for a 54-hour mission around the globe.

The spacecraft, with John W. Young and Robert L. Crippen at the controls, is expected to land at Edwards Air Force Base in Southern California tomorrow if no serious problems develop during this first test flight of the winged shuttle vehicle.

Columbia lost about a dozen small thermal protection tiles from its surface while it was on its way into orbit, but space officials said the loss would not jeopardize the progress of the flight or the craft's safe return to Earth.

After three hours aloft, Mr. Young, a veteran of four previous space flights, gave Columbia a perfect rating.

"This thing is just performing outstanding," the astronaut radioed to the shuttle control center at Houston.

Mr. Crippen, making his first space flight, was impressed with the lift-off.

"I tell you, John's been telling me about it for three years, but there ain't no way you can describe it," he said.

Soon after 8 p.m., on their ninth orbit of Earth, the astronauts went to bed, ending a day that had begun at 2:05 a.m.

"Get a good night's rest," the astronauts were told. "See you manana," Mr. Crippen replied.

The launching was a triumph for the National Aeronautics and Space Administration, which has been feeling the heat of criticism because the shuttle development program is three years behind schedule and has cost more than $8 billion—$1 billion more than originally estimated.

NASA officials were elated.

"We're thrilled," said George F. Page, the launch director. "We're proud today. It's a proud day for America."

In Houston, flight director Neil Hutchinson said: "I just kept waiting for something to go wrong, and nothing did."

"I am just ecstatic at where we are," he added.

The shuttle is more than just another spacecraft and rocket system. It is the prototype of a space transportation system that will make it possible to carry satellites into orbit and repair them up there or bring them back to Earth for extensive refurbishment.

The concept should save money over conventional space shots and should open up new avenues of scientific exploration.

A space telescope, which will be used by astronomers working at a special institute at the Johns Hopkins University in Baltimore, is one of the major payloads scheduled for a shuttle flight in 1985.

AP
Astronauts John Young (front) and Robert Crippen make their way to the spacecraft Columbia to prepare for takeoff.

The shuttle, about the size of a DC-9 jetliner, has an enormous cargo bay, enclosed by two 60-foot-long doors hinged to the midsection of the vehicle just aft of the cabin.

The astronauts opened the doors to test the hinge mechanisms on their second orbit of the Earth.

They worked.

However, not everything was perfect on this maiden voyage of the delta-winged space plane.

Less than two hours after the 7 a.m. lift-off, the astronauts turned a television camera to the tail section of their craft and discovered the loss of a few of its 37,000 protective tiles.

Mr. Hutchinson insisted, in response to many questions at a press conference, that the missing tiles were not a serious problem and represented no hazard to the mission.

"I am just not concerned about it," he said.

He said the tiles were in a "non-critical area" of the

See SHUTTLE, A6, Col. 1

Ex-champion Joe Louis dies of heart failure at 66

New York Times News Service

Joe Louis, who held the heavyweight boxing championship of the world for almost 12 years and the affection of the American public for most of his adult life, died yesterday of cardiac arrest in Las Vegas at the age of 66.

Mr. Louis, champion from 1937 until 1949, collapsed in the bathroom of his home about 12:30 p.m. (EST). Efforts to revive him were unsuccessful. He was de-

Sports figures react to death of 'Brown Bomber' C3

clared dead at Desert Springs Hospital at 1:05 p.m. His wife, Martha, was with him at the hospital.

Mr. Louis's death came only a few hours after he had attended the heavyweight championship fight Saturday night between Larry Holmes and Trevor Berbick at Caesars Palace where for many years he was employed as a "greeter."

Since 1977, Mr. Louis had been confined to a wheelchair following surgery to correct an aortic aneurysm. His health over the last decade had been poor, beset with heart problems, emotional disorders and strokes. An electronic pacemaker was implanted near his heart last December 23.

A spokesman for the Louis family said that the former champion's body will lie in state on Thursday at Caesars Palace in Las Vegas. Burial will be on Friday morning at a site yet to be determined.

Slow of foot but fast with his hands, Mr. Louis dominated heavyweight boxing from 1937 to 1949. As world champion he defended his title 25 times, facing all challengers and fighting the best that the world could offer.

In the opinion of many boxing experts, the plain, simple, unobtrusive Brown Bomber—as he was known—with his crushing left jab and hook, was probably the best heavyweight fighter of all time.

The 6-foot-1½-inch, 197-pound Louis won his title June 22, 1937, in Chicago by knocking out James J. Braddock in eight rounds, thus becoming the first black heavyweight champion since Jack Johnson, who had reigned earlier in the century. Before Mr. Louis retired undefeated as champion March 1, 1949, his last title defense had been against Jersey Joe Walcott. Mr. Louis knocked him out June 25, 1948 in New York.

While he was titleholder, his fights had grossed more than $4.6 million, of which he received about $800,000.

Since he was a fighter who wasted little time in dispatching his opponents, Mr. Louis's earnings per round were extraordinarily high. Of the 25 title defenses, only three went the full 15 rounds. Tony Galento, for example, survived four rounds in

See LOUIS, A4, Col. 1

AP
Joe Louis, shown on June 22, 1937, upon winning the heavyweight championship from James J. Braddock after an eighth-round knockout in Chicago.

Lessons of the past directed action after Reagan was shot

By Curt Matthews
Washington Bureau of The Sun

Washington—From the moment Secret Service agents guarding President Reagan heard the first shot March 30, they began playing out a dreaded scene with each man around the president in a familiar role.

Six shots were fired in less than four seconds. Before the echo of the fusillade had faded in the streets outside the Washington Hilton Hotel, the well-rehearsed duties had been fulfilled:

Shield the president; get him—throw him, if necessary—into his limousine or other protective cover; neutralize the assailant; assess the situation (are others involved?), and protect the assailant from attack by vengeful onlookers or possible accomplices.

For millions of Americans, the most recent attack on a president will be forever remembered as a single chaotic scene in which a Secret Service agent in a three-piece gray suit suddenly produces a menacing Uzi submachine gun, crouches like an athlete ready for action, and barks orders, taking charge of the melee around him.

As history, that scene will take its place with those of other traumatic days: An open limousine speeding down a Dallas boulevard with the fatally wounded John F. Kennedy, the floor of a Los Angeles hotel where Robert F. Kennedy lay dying, and the balcony of a Memphis motel where Martin Luther King lay prone as those around him pointed toward the lair of an assassin.

There is, however, a difference. The scene outside the Hilton will be remembered with a natural patina of authority and cool professionalism that boosted some of those involved to the threshold of heroism. That scene reflects what has become more clear in the days that followed: The sad experiences of the past have wrought important and positive changes in official and unofficial reactions to assassination attempts.

"Certain functions have always been done by certain agents in those situations," says Richard Hartwig, the public affairs officer for the Secret Service, regarding attacks on the president. "We've always had procedures, but in recent years they've been expanded."

One crucial responsibility that law enforcement officers have been particularly sensitive about since the assassination of President Kennedy is protecting the life of the suspected assailant—the "key witness" in any subsequent trial or investigation arising from an assassination attempt.

When Lee Harvey Oswald was shot the day after he was arrested as a suspect in the Kennedy assassination, it put the nation on a twisting path of doubt regarding motives for the assassination and the pos-

See CHANGES, A4, Col. 4

Beneath calm surface, Poles' anxiety mounts

By Anthony Barbieri, Jr.
Sun Staff Correspondent

Warsaw—On a vast concrete lot on the outskirts of Warsaw, where on most Sunday afternoons communism and capitalism are given an opportunity to coexist nicely, a group of men huddled over a small portable scale as an animated conversation swirled around them.

The matter at hand was cucumbers.

Prices were mentioned, voices raised in disbelief, shoulders shrugged, and—finally—fistfuls of Polish currency exchanged for large wooden crates of produce.

It was another deal on another business day at the officially sanctioned wholesale produce market for local private farmers.

A few miles away in downtown Warsaw, the weekly military parade wound its way through Victory Square and before the Tomb of the Unknown Soldier. As the colors passed by, old men pressed their cloth caps against their hearts, while young children out with their parents tried to keep step with the oom-pah of the brass band.

In short, a scene of absolute normality on a warm and sunny spring afternoon in Warsaw—a scene of calm and order that, according to Poles and Western observers living here, is becoming less and less reflective of the tensions that have grown in past weeks about the ultimate fate of the most audacious experiment ever tried in 35 years of Communist rule in Eastern Europe.

With the possible exception of some of the leading actors in the drama—leaders of the independent trade union Solidarity—the prospect that the experiment may end in civil strife, violence, or a potentially catastrophic invasion by the Soviet Union no longer is being dismissed automatically as unthinkable here, or as simply the product of the imaginations of Western governments.

This is in sharp contrast to the way it was last August, when Polish officials indignantly refused to even acknowledge the possibility of such a disastrous failure, and when most ordinary Poles laughed it off as just another excuse by government leaders for dragging their feet on reform.

At that time, it was generally assumed that the Polish army would "never" be called out against Polish workers, and that the Russians would never come because there would be nothing for them to do when they got here.

The nine intervening months of conflict—and particularly the menacing maneuvers recently completed by Warsaw Pact forces on Poland's borders—seem to a visitor who was last here in August to have changed all that noticeably.

There is, to be sure, no invasion mania here, nor are there obvious signs that "the future of the nation is at stake," as Poland's harried leaders tend to put it when they are asking for concessions, but there is a pessimism that was not here before, a feeling that it all may not be destined to end happily, and that the government's cries of wolf may not have been phony.

"There may be a light at the end of the tunnel," a Warsaw resident said recently, "but a lot of people think it's on a train coming at them."

While unofficial inquiries to Polish officials about the prospect of a Soviet

See POLAND, A2, Col. 1

Inside

Annapolis mayor critical
Acting Mayor Gustav J. Akerland, of Annapolis, remains in "critical" condition from a gunshot wound to the head..........C1

Reagan to the airwaves
President Reagan may promote his economic program with a radio address this week and a televised speech later..........A5

Cloudy and cool
Cloudy and cool with a chance of drizzle today, high 56. Showers likely tonight, low 46. Yesterday's high, 69; low, 45..............C2

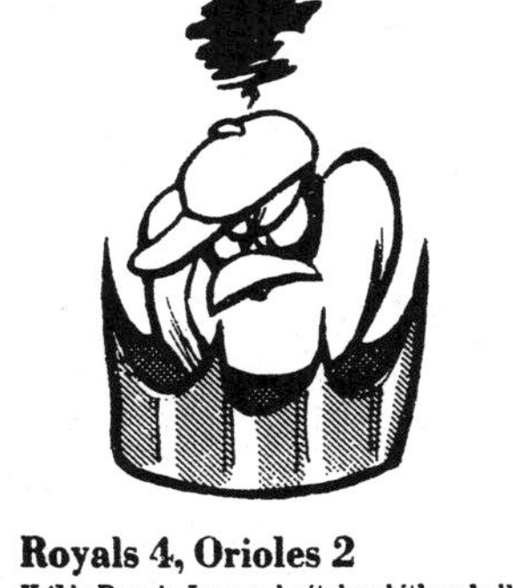

Royals 4, Orioles 2
K.C.'s Dennis Leonard pitches hitless ball for six innings on a soggy day..................C3

Index

THE SUN

VOL. 288—NO. 153–F | BALTIMORE, THURSDAY, MAY 14, 1981 | •••20 CENTS | FINAL

POPE SHOT AT VATICAN

AP photos

Pope John Paul II is helped by aides after being wounded during an audience in St. Peter's Square.

Surgery called successful; gunman held

By Kay Withers

Rome (Special)—Pope John Paul II was shot in the abdomen yesterday in St. Peter's Square by a gunman police identified as a right-wing Turkish terrorist who had vowed to kill the pontiff.

His doctors said early today that the 60-year-old pope had come through 5½ hours of successful surgery at Rome's Vatican-sponsored Gemelli Hospital in "good and stable" condition.

They said the prognosis remained "guarded," largely because of the risk of infection, but added that the pontiff was conscious and breathing on his own.

A member of the operating team, Dr. Carlo Castiglione, said there was "good hope for his recovery" despite vast abdominal damage.

The pope was hit, probably by three bullets, at 5:19 p.m. (11:19 a.m. EDT) as he circled St. Peter's Square in a white jeep to begin his regular Wednesday general audience. About 18,000 people were in the square.

He was reaching out to pat small children and had just given a small blond boy back to his mother when the shooting occurred.

"The pope had gone round the square once," said a priest who was there. "He was just starting the turn to bring him up to his throne when the shots sounded."

The pope turned his head and slumped in the jeep. Bystanders saw blood staining his cassock. His personal waiter and his Polish private secretary, Msgr. Stanislaw Dziwisz, grabbed him as the jeep, surrounded by racing security men, sped out of the square to the Arch of the Bell, where an ambulance is always on duty during audiences.

The pope, who had collapsed into a half-prone position

See POPE, A6, Col. 1

The pope's assailant (second from right), identified as Mehmet Ali Agca, a Turkish prison escapee, is escorted by Italian policemen following the shooting.

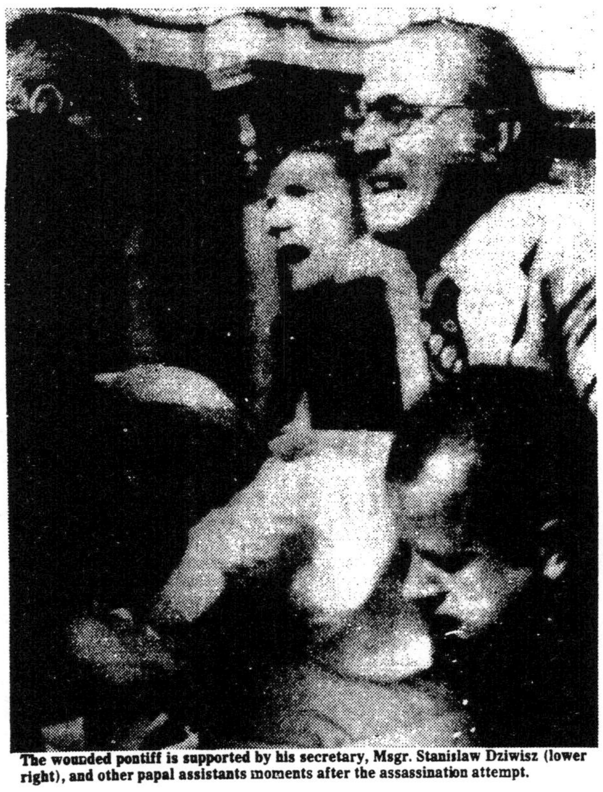

The wounded pontiff is supported by his secretary, Msgr. Stanislaw Dziwisz (lower right), and other papal assistants moments after the assassination attempt.

Attacker identified as Turkish terrorist, killer

Rome (NYT)—The first reports said only that he spoke no Italian, that he was young and that he had dark hair.

But within a matter of minutes, a picture of the man accused of shooting Pope John Paul II in St. Peter's Square yesterday afternoon, began to emerge—a picture of a militant Turkish terrorist, already convicted of one murder, who escaped from a maximum-security prison in 1979 and then threatened in a letter to assassinate the pope.

The Turkish ambassador in Washington, Sukru Elekdag, said after the news of the shooting had flashed around the world: "The Turkish police have been under instruction to shoot him on sight."

Moments after he was wrestled to the ground by pilgrims who had been standing near him, the alleged assailant told Italian police his name was Mehmet Ali Agca. He gave his age as 24 and said he was Turkish. He said also that he was a student at the University for Foreigners in Perugia in central Italy, but the records of the university showed no such registration.

Agca was described by the police and by bystanders as a dark-haired young man, clean-shaven, with an angular face. He was wearing an open-neck white shirt under a lightweight jacket.

According to sources in Rome, Washington, New York and Turkey, Agca was convicted in February, 1979, of having murdered Abdi Ipekci, the editor of the independent Turkish daily newspaper *Milliyet*. He was jailed. But in late November that year, he escaped from the military prison where he was being held—with the help of prison officers who sympathized with his right-wing views, according to Turkish authorities. He had apparently been in hiding ever since.

When he fled from the prison, he left behind a letter, addressed to *Milliyet*, threatening the life of the pope. Agca is said to have written that if the pontiff did not cancel his visit to Turkey, which was then imminent, he would shoot him in revenge for the attack by Muslim extremists on the Grand Mosque in Mecca earlier that year.

Muslims considered the attack a desecration of the Islamic holy place, and Agca charged that the incident was of American or Israeli origin. His letter denounced the pontiff as "the masked leader of the Crusades."

A partial text of the letter, made available by the Turkish police, reads as follows:

"Western imperialists who are afraid of Turkey's unity of political, military and economic power with the brotherly Islamic countries are sending Crusader Commander John Paul under the mask of a religious leader. If this ill-timed and meaningless visit is not called off, I will definitely shoot the pope. This is the only reason I escaped from prison."

His threats were taken seriously

See GUNMAN, A6, Col. 1

Shocked Americans pray for pope's recovery

By Frank P. L. Somerville
Religion Editor of The Sun

Americans, from President Reagan to a Baltimore widow who hurried to the downtown Basilica to pray, reacted with horror and concern yesterday to the news of the shooting of Pope John Paul II.

Catholics and non-Catholics joined in prayers for the pope's recovery and in appeals for a lessening of violence in the world.

"Shock" was the word most often heard in a nation now used to such events.

A common reaction, echoed in a meeting of the National Council of Churches in Philadelphia and by Chicago's Mayor Jane Byrne, was renewal of calls for gun control. In the Connecticut legislature knowledge of the attempt on the pope's life led to immediate passage of a handgun control law that had failed earlier in the week.

President Reagan, who survived a shooting himself just six weeks ago, said, "I'll pray for him."

Mr. Reagan called Terence Cardinal Cooke, the Catholic archbishop of New York, to express "the sorrow of the American people" and the president's personal concern, a message that the cardinal said he would relay to the Vatican.

Archbishop Borders of Baltimore, like leading figures of many religious denominations, referred to the pontiff as a man of peace and said it was "hard to understand how an act of violence can be committed against such a person."

"I am sure," the Baltimore archbishop said, "that with his concern for the welfare of all people, he is even now praying for those who are involved in the attempted assassination."

Sister Jane Desmond, a nun who led eight persons in a noon prayer service in the chapel of Bolton Hill's Corpus Christi rectory, said she appealed for the healing not just of the pope "but the whole world we live in." One of the penitential prayers she offered "reflected on the seeds of violence in each of us."

Both within the pope's own church and outside it, theological disagreements with some of his strong stands were pushed to the background, while expressions of admiration for him as a courageous and forthright moral leader came forth.

Meeting in Philadelphia, the National Council of Churches passed a resolution offering "a prayer of thanksgiving that the pope's life was spared."

The statement of the delegates, who represent a broad spectrum of Protestant and Orthodox churches, added: "In unity with Christians and believers of all faiths we pray that despite instances of evil, terror and violence, the goodness and peace to which the pope has dedicated his life will triumph in the world, through the victory won by Jesus Christ."

The Rev. Jerry Falwell, of Lynchburg, Va., a Baptist who heads the conservative and controversial Moral Majority organization, called the pope a "brave and decent man" and said that "my prayers and

See REACT, A7, Col. 3

U.S. said to consider three-month delay on Social Security raises to save money

Washington (AP)—The Reagan administration is considering postponing an 11.2 percent cost-of-living increase due in July for 36 million Social Security recipients as a cost-saving move, sources disclosed yesterday.

A three-month delay in paying the increase—to October 1—would cost the average Social Security recipient roughly

The Social Security Administration is planning to hire 1,000 new employees in the Baltimore area....................C1

$100 and move nearly $4 billion in federal spending from the 1981 budget to the 1982 budget, which starts October 1.

One knowledgeable administration source, asking that he not be identified, said postponing the upcoming 1981 increase is one of several items Budget Director David A. Stockman is considering as a way to offset an unanticipated increase in the projected budget deficit for the current fiscal year, which ends September 30.

The source emphasized that a final decision has not been made by President Reagan, who would have to submit the proposal to Congress for its approval.

Disclosure of the administration's consideration of postponing the 1981 cost-of-living increase came just one day after the administration called for an unprecedented 10 percent cut in Social Security benefits by 1986 to save an estimated $53 billion.

Part of that plan calls for pushing back annual cost-of-living adjustments until October 1, starting in 1982.

A spokesman for Social Security Commissioner John A. Svahn, asked about whether delaying the 1981 cost-of-living increase is under consideration, would say only, "We have no idea where that rumor could have come from."

Health and Human Services Secretary Richard S. Schweiker, in unveiling the Reagan administration's proposal to cut nearly $53 billion in Social Security benefits by 1986, emphasized the only cut affecting "36 million beneficiaries now on the rolls would be a three-month delay" in the July, 1982, cost-of-living raise.

Mr. Svahn, on ABC-TV's "Good Morning America" show yesterday, denied the 1982 delay would cost retirees money. "It's a little bit overblown to say you are going to lose money. . . . They will get it over the long run."

However, his agency's own estimates show that the three-month delay in 1982 would wind up costing Social Security beneficiaries $6.3 billion in foregone benefits by 1986.

The Senate has already voted to recommend postponing the scheduled July 1, 1982, increase to October 1—pushing the payments back to the 1983 fiscal year. Under the Senate suggestion, subsequent cost-of-living boosts would go into effect each October 1.

The House budget resolution contains no such recommendation, however, and the difference will have to be worked out by a conference committee.

Mr. Stockman now estimates that the anticipated deficit for fiscal 1981 appears likely to top $60 billion, more than $5 billion above his estimate of three months ago.

Rising interest rates in recent weeks, which drive up government payments on the national debt, are partly responsible for the growing deficit. Administration officials have vowed to seek further cuts beyond those already proposed as a way to minimize the size of the deficit.

The cost-of-living raise due Social Security retirees, disabled workers, their families and survivors is based on a rise in the consumer price index and is estimated to cost the Treasury $15.4 billion over the course of a full year.

Postponing the increase until October would take it out of the current budget and add the cost to the 1982 budget.

A final decision by the president is expected shortly, perhaps before the end of this week.

Inside

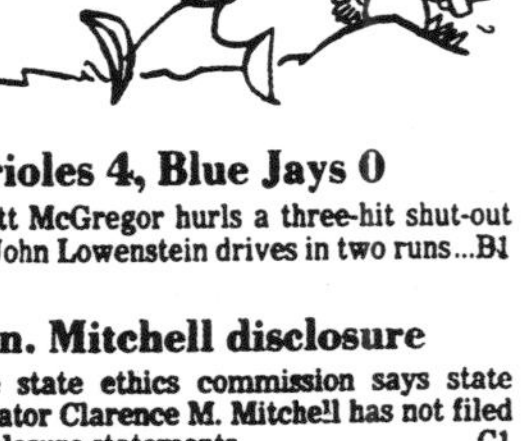

Orioles 4, Blue Jays 0

Sen. Mitchell disclosure

Partly cloudy

Index

City teacher is charged with assaulting student

By Robert Benjamin

A Baltimore schoolteacher was arrested and taken from Garrison Junior High by police yesterday afternoon, after the mother of a student charged the teacher with assaulting her 14-year-old son.

Viola Garner, described as a 50-year-old veteran with more than 20 years' teaching experience, was escorted to a police patrol wagon at the rear of the Northwest Baltimore junior high about 2 p.m. She was in police custody until shortly before midnight, when she was released by a court commissioner on her own recognizance.

She then went with a friend to the Northwestern District station, where she was giving a report to officers early this morning and could not be reached for comment.

The incident involving Mrs. Garner, a special education teacher, and one of her students, Alfonso R. Jacobs, a seventh-grader, began in a school bathroom as Mrs. Garner attempted to get Alfonso to come to her class, which had already begun. After the confrontation, the assault charge was filed by Alfonso's mother, Gloria Copes.

Key details of what happened remained in dispute last night.

For instance, Mrs. Garner said she grabbed the student, according to a police report and Garrison Junior High's principal.

But Mrs. Copes, of the 2400 block Chelsea terrace, alleged in an interview that Mrs. Garner repeatedly hit her son, who attends special classes for students with learning disabilities, with a "long, round stick that had black tape around the handle."

Police, who examined the child for bruises or other signs of a beating, found no marks.

And Garrison's principal, Elzee Gladden, who did not witness the incident, said that he can't find anyone at the school who admits to seeing what happened firsthand.

Whatever the case, both city school and teachers' union officials said last night that the arrest of a teacher on such a charge is extremely uncommon.

However, Irene Dandridge, president of the Baltimore City Teachers Union, added that parents' leveling informal charges of teachers physically abusing students is "becoming more and more common."

"We've had about 10 cases so far this school year in which we've had to defend teachers, many of them involving special-education teachers," Mrs. Dandridge said. "But this is the only one I've heard of in

See TEACHER, A9, Col. 1

THE SUN

VOL. 289—NO. 64—F BALTIMORE, THURSDAY, JULY 30, 1981 •••20 CENTS FINAL

Prince Charles and Princess Diana walk down the steps of St. Paul's Cathedral after their wedding yesterday. AP

Prince Charles, Lady Diana wed

600,000 gather along streets to cheer royal pair

By Robert A. Erlandson
London Bureau of The Sun

London—When Lady Diana Spencer said, "I will," to Prince Charles yesterday to become Princess of Wales, there was a solemn hush inside St. Paul's Cathedral among the 2,500 guests invited for the first royal wedding ever to take place in Christopher Wren's masterpiece.

But in the streets outside arose tumultuous cheers that echoed block by block as loudspeakers broadcast the exchange of vows—which included two minor fluffs by the couple—to the estimated 600,000 spectators along the route.

The newlyweds—the bride looking radiant in an ivory-colored silk gown with 25-foot train and an heirloom dia-

Lady Diana wears one of the most fairy-tale gowns ever seen on a royal bride..........B1

mond tiara holding her veil, and the prince proud in his naval uniform—emerged from St. Paul's into brilliant sunshine as the central figures of the royal spectacular.

As they walked down the red carpet to the open state landau—drawn by four matched greys with silver mane decorations—for the return to Buckingham Palace, the mass outpouring of affection, according to veteran commentators, was like nothing seen here in living memory.

After the royal family and the wedding party reached the palace, police removed the barriers that had held back the crowd. Soon a sea of people, waving thousands of Union Jacks, extended from the palace gates down the Mall to Trafalgar Square, and overflowed into St. James Park.

They sang "You'll Never Walk Alone" and "Rule, Britannia," and chanted, "We want Charlie, we want the queen."

When Prince Charles and Princess Diana appeared on the balcony—and treated the people to the sight of their first married kiss in public—the throng went wild.

Then, in a series of virtual curtain calls, the royal family, the bridesmaids and pages, and Earl Spencer and Lady Fermoy (Princess Diana's father and grandmother) appeared again and again—four times in all—on the balcony overlooking the palace forecourt.

Princess Diana is the first English bride of an heir to the British throne in more than 300 years, and her family's roots are deep in British history.

As he left home yesterday, Earl Spencer put in perspective his view of his youngest daughter's new role in the family's— and the nation's—life:

"The Spencer family has throughout the centuries fought for king and country. Diana will be vowing to help

See WEDDING, A6, Col. 1

Reagan tax bills win in House and Senate

By Stephen E. Nordlinger
Washington Bureau of The Sun

Washington—By a surprisingly wide margin of 43 votes, the Democrat-controlled House of Representatives passed President Reagan's tax-relief bill yesterday.

Moderate and conservative Democrats rejected the appeals of their leadership and backed the president, who won by a vote of 238 to 195.

The Republican-controlled Senate also approved the president's program, by a vote of 89 to 11.

The twin votes assured that the president has achieved his hard-fought battle

Members of Maryland's congressional delegation explain their votes on President Reagan's tax-cut bill..A10

for a three-year, across-the-board cut of 25 percent in individual tax rates, a central part of his economic-recovery program.

A 5 percent tax cut will take effect October 1 as the first part of personal tax relief. Overall, the record business and individual tax cuts will amount to about $35 billion in the 1982 fiscal year, rising to $251 billion in 1986.

A triumphant President Reagan hailed his landslide tax-cut victory yesterday as "a new beginning."

"Now we can face the future with confidence and courage because we know we are united," said Mr. Reagan, emphasizing the bipartisan nature of his support.

The vote in the House of Representatives, he said, "removed one of the most important remaining challenges to our agenda for prosperity."

Asked when the promised prosperity would arrive, Mr. Reagan said he hoped there would be "some signs" by year's end, but added that the economic blueprint was a three-year program.

The presidential victory also will bring about a major change in the nation's tax system by adjusting personal taxes to offset inflation. This "indexing" system will take effect in January, 1985, in both the House and Senate measures.

After a four-year Republican campaign, the votes of the Senate and House put into place the "supply side" theory of economics, in which long-range tax cuts for top earners as well as others are designed to stimulate savings and investment. This turnaround by Congress replaces past policy of targeting tax relief to low- and moderate-income taxpayers.

At a news conference after the vote, Representative Dan Rostenkowski (D, Ill.), chairman of the House Ways and Means Committee, attributed his startlingly large defeat to President Reagan's televised speech Monday night and the avalanche of phone calls and telegrams to Capitol Hill offices in the two days following the speech.

"We were holding out very well until yesterday," he said.

Even before the debate began at 9.34 a.m., House Speaker Thomas P. O'Neill, Jr. (D, Mass.) virtually conceded defeat as he told newsmen a "blitz" by the White House had had "a devastating effect."

The dispirited Democrats slouched in their seats, resting their heads on their hands as the day progressed. Republicans, sensing victory, even gave a standing ovation to Mr. Rostenkowski.

In the final voting, 48 Democrats joined 190 Republicans in voting for the president's bill. A total of 194 Democrats and one Republican, Representative James M. Jeffords (Vt.), voted against.

The Democratic bill for a two-year, 15 percent tax cut with a third year reduction tied to economic conditions, never came to a vote.

Maryland Representatives Roy P. Dyson (D, 1st), Marjorie S. Holt (R, 4th) and Beverly B. Byron (D, 6th) voted for the president's tax cut and the other five

See TAXES, A8, Col. 3

Conferees OK $36 billion in cuts

By Robert Timberg
Washington Bureau of The Sun

Washington—A House-Senate conference committee yesterday placed its seal of approval on a $36 billion package of spending cuts, despite storm warnings that the measure might get blown away over Social Security.

Even as key conference leaders were signing the completed bill, a move to reopen the bill to restore the minimum So-

The Social Security system appears to be in better shape than previously reported, study says..........A4

cial Security benefit was gaining momentum in the Democratic House.

The vehicle, a resolution directing House conferees to push for elimination of the language in the conference report dropping the benefit, had picked up 126 cosponsors by late yesterday afternoon.

The largely Democratic group included Majority Leader James C. Wright, Jr. A few Republicans, including Marjorie S. Holt (R, Md.), also signed the resolution.

It could not immediately be determined if this latest snag would disrupt the harmony that has characterized action on the conference committee report and delay final action in both houses, currently scheduled for tomorrow.

Representative Bruce F. Vento (D, Minn.) the resolution's chief sponsor, said "elimination of the minimum benefit is surely one of the unkindest of all the Reagan administration's Social Security cuts."

Until this latest development, the legislative skids seemed greased for final budget action Friday.

The 225 conferees, 72 senators and 183 congressmen, completed in an astonishing two weeks their seemingly mammoth task of ironing out differences in separate budget measures previously passed by both houses.

The bill approved by key conference committee members yesterday resolves hundreds of disputed items and touches virtually every important federal programs.

For all those differences, however, the final vote, when it comes, will do little more than ratify the final form of President Reagan's earlier budget victories, which mandated unprecedented cuts in spending, primarily for domestic social programs.

Representative James R. Jones (D, Okla.), chairman of the Democrat-controlled House Budget Committee, called the conference report "clearly the most monumental and historic turnaround in fiscal policy that has ever occurred."

Senator Pete V. Domenici (R, N.M.), Mr. Jones's counterpart in the Republi-

See BUDGET, A4, Col. 5

Casey wins support of Senate panel

By Curt Matthews
Washington Bureau of The Sun

Washington—The Senate Intelligence Committee agreed unanimously yesterday that it has found no basis to press for the removal of William J. Casey as director of the Central Intelligence Agency.

At the same time, Senator Barry Goldwater (R, Ariz.), chairman of the committee, said the committee staff inquiry would continue. Mr. Goldwater and Senator Daniel P. Moynihan (D, N.Y.), a ranking Democrat on the committee, said the committee staff still had "loose ends" to investigate.

"Based upon the staff review to date, and Mr. Casey's lengthy testimony today, it is the unanimous judgment of the committee that no basis has been found for concluding Mr. Casey is unfit to serve as director of central intelligence," Mr. Goldwater said after Mr. Casey gave his side of the controversy focusing on his fitness to run the CIA,

Though the Intelligence Committee members appeared to give Mr. Casey a clean bill of health, it did not call for President Reagan's former campaign chairman to stay on his job.

"The staff will follow up on points that need clarification." Mr. Goldwater said. "There will be, in a timely fashion, a final report treating the issues concerning Mr. Casey's past activities and also the appointment of Mr. Hugel."

[The Associated Press reported last night that Democratic committee sources said investigators were still pursuing substantive questions that could alter the panel's preliminary judgment of Mr. Casey.

[Mr. Moynihan announced that Democrats on the committee will appoint a counsel to assist Fred Thompson, who was hired as special counsel to the committee by Mr. Goldwater Monday, the AP said.

["There is a range of questions for which full answers haven't been got yet—work that hasn't been done, records that haven't been fully read and such like," Mr. Moynihan said in describing the nature of the continuing inquiry.]

Only last Thursday, Mr. Goldwater led the opposition to Mr. Casey.

Mr. Goldwater said then that Mr. Casey should "retire" because he was involved in questionable stock transactions before joining the CIA and because he placed a potential security risk, Max Hugel, in charge of clandestine operations at the agency.

Allegations of irregular stock market dealings—supported by tape-recorded evidence—forced Mr. Hugel to resign abruptly July 14. Mr. Casey's critics have charged that he should have been more careful than to place Mr. Hugel, who critics charge was vulnerable to blackmail, in one of the nation's most sensitive national

See CASEY, A12, Col. 3

Inside

Bishop Walsh dies
James E. Walsh, a Western Marylander who became the first Maryknoll bishop and last Christian missionary in China, dies at 90..........C1

New York builder dead
Robert Moses, powerful builder who had a major influence on New York City, is dead at [illegible]..........C4

Sunny today
Mostly sunny today, clear tonight. High, [illegible]; low, [illegible]. Yesterday's high, 84; low, 68.C2

Index

Bridge	B7	Lotteries	D8
Business	D11	Movies	B6
Comics	B11	Obituaries	C4
Crossword	B11	Sports	D1
Editorials	A14	TV-Radio	B8

4 Sections

Bani-Sadr escapes to France in pirated jet, gains asylum

From Wire Services

Paris—Former President Abolhassan Bani-Sadr shaved off his telltale moustache and escaped Iran in a pirated Boeing 707 early yesterday to join the exile opposition to the Islamic regime of Ayatollah Ruhollah Khomeini.

Mr. Bani-Sadr, impeached in June and a casualty of the Iranian revolution he once tried to guide, was accompanied by Massoud Radjavi, leader of the Marxist group Mujahedeen Khalq, and Col. Behzad Moezi, the pilot, who Tehran Radio said was the personal pilot of the late shah.

Mr. Bani-Sadr, 47, whose extradition was immediately demanded by the Iranian government, will be permitted to stay in France as long as he refrains from political activity. He signed an agreement to that effect before leaving the military airfield at Evreux, 60 miles west of Paris, where his plane landed at 4:30 a.m. local time yesterday.

After four hours of talks with French officials, Mr. Bani-Sadr left the air base and, accompanied by several carloads of gendarmes, was driven to the apartment in Cachan, a suburb just south of Paris, in which he lived while in exile from the government of the late shah. The apartment has been occupied by Mr. Bani-Sadr's two teenage daughters and his sister in recent years.

In granting him asylum, France warned Mr. Bani-Sadr not to make political statements. On arrival, he said the

See BANI-SADR, A2, Col. 5

Area faces a test world needs to pass

Brazil, Argentina A-options open on continent free of nuclear arms

By Robert Ruby
Sun Staff Correspondent

Vienna—The admiral from Argentina justified his country's nuclear program in a single sentence: "We feel any country has the right to develop the technologies she needs."

Adm. Castro Madero, director of Argentina's Atomic Energy Commission, managed at the same time to touch the sore spot between nuclear-haves and nuclear-have-nots, a difference exploited by two South American countries, Argentina and Brazil, to keep their doors to nuclear bombs propped ever so slightly open.

South America faces a test the world needs to pass, the test of whether a continent free of nuclear weapons can be kept in the same pristine state. It is one of the last proving grounds for the safeguards system of the International Atomic Energy Agency, and for the nonproliferation policies of the countries exporting nuclear goods. It is the rare place where nations can't excuse a weapons program by saying it is needed to match that of a neighbor.

It also is where Argentina and Brazil, traditional rivals for influence and prestige, keep their nuclear options open by obtaining advanced technology—and jointly argue about having the right like the major powers to buy whatever know-how they want.

Argentina and Brazil have purchased, or are building from scratch, the types of nuclear plants that nuclear-exporting countries no longer sell. Together, Argentina and Brazil will have the complete nuclear fuel cycle—from uranium mining to the reprocessing of plutonium—by the end of the decade. And they thus will have the expertise and materials for both reactors and weapons.

In shopping for the technology, Argentina has adeptly used safeguards as a bargaining tool, beating the IAEA at its own game of encouraging nations to make the strongest possible safeguards a condition of any sale.

"The point is, safeguards are the coin of interchange," said Admiral Madero, speaking of his reservations about safeguards while at the IAEA headquarters. "We use [them] to obtain the exchange of sensitive technology."

You use them by agreeing, after great haggling, to pay a certain price for a new plant only if the seller does not require you to obtain safeguards on all your other plants.

If you design a plant yourself, you

See ARGENTINA, A7, Col. 1

This is the fifth of a series of articles about the world's nuclear reckoning—about the growing imbalance between the number of nations with the ability to make a nuclear bomb and the systems by which those nations are monitored—and why those systems fail.

THE SUN

VOL. 289—NO. 123—F | BALTIMORE, WEDNESDAY, OCTOBER 7, 1981 | ••20 CENTS | FINAL

SADAT ASSASSINATED

Egypt's president slain by 6 soldiers

AP photos

Egyptian security forces crowd around the doorway of a building in Cairo where President Anwar el Sadat was taken after he was fatally wounded while reviewing a military parade yesterday. Mr. Sadat was flown from the parade ground in the helicopter at left. The body of a slain security man lies on the ground at right.

Attack at parade kills 7 others

By Douglas Watson
Sun Staff Correspondent

Cairo—Egyptian President Anwar el Sadat, a leader admired by most of the world for making peace with Israel, was assassinated yesterday by six Egyptian soldiers during a military parade.

Military sources in Cairo reported that the assassins were Muslim fundamentalists. Their identities and political affiliations were still being withheld yesterday.

The assault on the Egyptian president left 7 others dead and 27 wounded. Most of the victims were seated near President Sadat in the reviewing stand during the annual parade marking the October 6 anniversary of the Egyptian army's successful crossing of the Suez Canal eight years ago in its last war with Israel.

President Sadat, 62, was wearing the black military uniform of the commander in chief of the Egyptian armed forces, with the Star of Sinai medal around his neck, when he was struck down by a hail of bullets fired by the six soldiers wearing blue berets who rushed from a passing artillery truck toward the reviewing stand.

The fallen leader was rushed to the Maadi military hospital by helicopter.

A medical bulletin said he arrived in the hospital unconscious with "two holes in the left side of the chest, a bullet in the neck, just above the right collarbone, a wound above the right knee and a huge gash at the back of the thigh, with a complicated fracture of the thigh."

He never revived.

Moussa Sabry, the editor of the Cairo daily *Al Akhbar*, said that Mr. Sadat was hit both by bullets and by fragments from grenades.

Egyptian authorities have yet to report on the fate of the assassins, but all of those directly involved in the attack are believed to have been apprehended or killed on the spot.

One unconfirmed report said that one of the fleeing attackers was stopped when he was run through with a loyal soldier's lance.

The government has released no information about the assassins' identities, ages or religious or political leanings.

Three separate opposition groups claimed responsibility for the assassination in phone calls in Beirut. It was not known if any of the groups actually was involved.

For hours, the world waited for news of the fate of the Nobel Peace Prize winner, whose death could diminish the chances of a lasting Middle East peace.

Last evening, Egyptian Vice President Hosni Mubarak, the man expected to succeed President Sadat, went on the air to say, "The tongue becomes paralyzed, my feelings choke as I mourn the hero of war and peace."

Vice President Mubarak reassured Mr. Sadat's admirers and supporters that he intends to follow the same peaceful course.

He said, "The Egyptian people all over the country, although gripped with pain and chagrin, declare we will follow his path, we will not deviate from the path of peace because we believe it is the path of righteousness, justice and freedom."

He went on to say, "Our leader has been martyred on the anniversary of the day when he restored dignity and glory to the Arab nation," referring to the initially successful surprise attack against Israel in the 1973 war.

He also said that Sofi Abu Taleb, the speaker of the Peoples' Assembly, the Egyptian parliament, had assumed the presidency until a new election could be held within two months. The speaker also

See SADAT, A9, Col. 1

Egyptian President Anwar el Sadat smiles at the start of the Cairo military parade where he was fatally shot.

Grieving Reagan lauds Sadat

By Gilbert A. Lewthwaite and Walter Taylor
Washington Bureau of The Sun

Washington—A grieved President Reagan yesterday lauded Egyptian President Anwar el Sadat as "a man of hope" and denounced his assassins' "cowardly infamy" as top administration officials urgently analyzed the implications of the murder.

U.S. forces in the Middle East area were ordered to take "necessary and prudent precautions."

At the Pentagon, it was announced that "ships in the area as well as some elements of the rapid deployment . . . force have been placed on increased readiness." That did not include, the statement said, any "unusual troop movements in the United States."

Mr. Reagan met yesterday for 45 minutes in the White House Situation Room with his top national security advisers to assess the diplomatic and strategic fallout of the assassination, and to weigh the wisdom and safety of a presidential presence at the funeral. An announcement on the funeral is expected today.

Officials refused to discuss reports that President Reagan had passed onto Egyptian Vice President Hosni Mubarak at a White House meeting last Friday U.S. intelligence reports that Libyan extremists had infiltrated the Egyptian army and were planning an assassination attempt.

Asked about the plot reports, David R. Gergen, the chief White House spokesman, said: "It may be our government will have more to say about this in the future."

Out of confusion at day's end in Washington came an eloquent epitaph to a "humanitarian unafraid to make peace," openly expressed relief at a traumatized Egypt's perceived dedication to continuing the Camp David "peace process" and the public hope that the latest episode of bloody instability in the world's most ex-

See REACTION, A8, Col. 5

Sadat was laughing—then the carnage began

By Steven K. Hindy
Associated Press

Cairo—Just before it happened, President Anwar el Sadat was laughing heartily with his top advisers.

Thousands of Egypt's finest soldiers and its best tanks and armor had flowed past the reviewing stand in the first 90 minutes of the parade.

At one point, paratroopers marched to within a few yards of the reviewing stand to salute the 62-year-old president.

Then, about 1:05 p.m. (7:05 a.m. EDT), six Egyptian air force jet fighters thundered over the reviewing stand, trailing red, blue, white and yellow smoke. Most of us in the grandstands behind Mr. Sadat were watching the jets.

Then we heard the "pop, pop, pop" of automatic-weapons fire.

Lowering my eyes, I saw two young, bareheaded men in military uniforms on the back of a moving truck firing at the reviewing stand. The thought flashed through my mind, "It's part of the show!"

Then I saw the young men leap to the ground and charge the president. They wore olive-drab fatigues and fired their weapons from their shoulders as they raced toward the reviewing stand.

An Egyptian television cameraman, sitting near the presidential platform, said later that he saw six assassins in all and heard them shout: "Glory to Egypt! Attack! You are agents! You are intruders!"

Others said the attackers threw hand grenades. I heard two muffled explosions, but it was difficult to hear anything distinctly. The jets were still looping overhead.

From my vantage point about 100 yards behind and to the left of President Sadat, I saw military police wearing red berets rushing toward the assassins and toward those on the reviewing stand—generals, Muslim and Christian clergymen and diplomats, all sitting around the president.

The wounded diplomats and soldiers were scattered among the overturned chairs on the platform.

The crowd of military men and government officials around me stampeded, screaming and falling over each other. I

See CAIRO, A8, Col. 4

An unidentified man, shown by Egyptian television with an arm shattered by gunfire, lies on the reviewing stand floor after the attack that killed President Sadat.

Mideast policy depends on keeping Sadat plan

By Henry Trewhitt
Washington Bureau of The Sun

Washington—With the assassination of Anwar el Sadat, critical policies of at least three countries, possibly more, were exposed to the unpredictable buffeting of the world's most volatile region.

The Egyptian leader was the pivotal figure in the fragile peace between Israel and Egypt. America's whole Mideast policy rests on continuation of his policies. Other countries, even some publicly estranged from Mr. Sadat, could be affected to an only slightly lesser degree.

At worst, of course, the whole fragile balance of Israel-Arab power created by Mr. Sadat's peacemaking could collapse. That is the earnest hope of his enemies. But paradoxically, some U.S. analysts see a faint hope that, with time, momentum might be not only preserved but even accelerated if moderates support his successors.

For four years the world has reckoned that sudden death, from assassination or natural causes, could strike either Mr.

Analysis

Sadat or Israeli Prime Minister Menachem Begin. Both had had heart attacks. Mr. Sadat, especially, was judged vulnerable to assassination.

But when the moment came yesterday, no one was fully prepared. It is "the sort of thing," a State Department official said, "that you can never really be prepared for."

From the U.S. standpoint, three things are vital in the next weeks or months:

- Keeping Egypt on the course set by Mr. Sadat.
- Reciprocal understanding by Israel.
- Belief throughout the region in the power and policies of the United States.

It is not surprising that U.S. officials, citing that last point, treat the plan to strengthen the Saudi Arabian air force as an essential ingredient.

For a few hours after the attack on Mr. Sadat, Washington worried that it might signal a military revolt. With time, officials settled on the judgment that it was the action of a small group of military dissidents, probably inspired by Libyan leader Muammar el Kadafi.

American officials know well and trust Hosni Mubarak, the vice president, who is most likely to succeed Mr. Sadat as Egypt's political process runs its course. They have dealt with him during and since the tortuous negotiations that led to the Egypt-Israel peace treaty of 1979.

But Mr. Mubarak lacks the daring and magnetism of Mr. Sadat. U.S. officials expect that he will continue, as he has promised, the exchanges with Israel aimed at Palestinian autonomy. They also expect, however, that he will be more vulnerable to opposing pressure both inside

See MIDEAST, A9, Col. 4

Massive deposit of copper, other ores found in ocean

Washington (AP)—U.S. scientists have discovered an immense undersea ore deposit worth billions of dollars 350 miles off the coast of Ecuador. They say the rich lodes of copper, silver and other minerals can be mined easily.

Scientists of the National Oceanic and Atmospheric Administration (NOAA) said yesterday the deposit they discovered in deep dives last month are on the surface of the seabed and ready to be scooped up.

The deposit is about 10 percent copper, estimated to be worth $2 billion by itself, and 10 percent iron. Other minerals in rich supply include molybdenum, vanadium, zinc, cadmium, tin and lead.

The deposit, almost three-quarters of a mile long, is dotted with dead volcanic vents up to 60 feet tall. The ore body, about 650 feet wide and 130 feet deep, has an estimated mass "exceeding 25 million tons, the scientists said.

"The ores are incredibly rich and they are on the surface around old volcanic vents," said Dr. Alexander Malahoff, chief scientist on the dives. "You don't have to dig out millions of pounds of rock to get to them."

Even though the minerals are 8,500 feet below the ocean surface, Dr. Malahoff said, most of the technology to get to them already exists. Currently no international treaties restrict recovery of the minerals, NOAA officials said.

"It's up to industry to start looking at it

See ORE, A5, Col. 1

Inside

Hearing-less divorce
The state Court of Appeals adopts rules, effective January 1, permitting uncontested divorces without a court hearing.......D1

House OKs budget buster
The House approves an $87 billion social services appropriation that exceeds congressional budget guidelines..................A2

Sunny and breezy
Sunny and breezy today, fair and cool tonight. High, 69; low, 48. Yesterday's high, 73; low, 52..................D2

Index

Israelis mourn loss of a genuine friend while most Arabs celebrate Sadat death

Israel

By Ruth Cale

Jerusalem (Special)—The news of President Anwar el Sadat's murder struck most Israelis like a bolt from the blue.

Although ever since the Egyptian-Israeli peace treaty was signed in 1979 there had been speculation over whether it would hold "after Sadat," there was only sorrow and a wave of anger that "the enemies of peace" assassinated one of the world's great statesmen.

The overwhelming majority of Israelis—barring the right-wing fringe of militant activists—mourned the loss of a genuine friend.

After President Sadat launched his peace initiative

See ISRAEL, A9, Col. 1

Arabs

From Wire Services

Beirut, Lebanon—The news of the assassination of Egyptian President Anwar el Sadat was met with joy throughout most of the Arab world.

A Palestinian leader congratulated the assassins, and gunmen in Beirut, Lebanon, fired their rifles into the air to celebrate the death of the man who became an outcast among most of his fellow Arab leaders because of his peace overtures to Israel.

Motorists in the Muslim sector of the divided Lebanese capital honked their horns. Palestinians on the Israeli-occupied West Bank and in East Jerusalem said there were

See ARABS, A9, Col. 6

Maryland and Navy lose heartbreakers: B1

THE SUNDAY SUN

LIGHT FOR ALL

VOL. 82—NO. 45—D* BALTIMORE, SUNDAY, NOVEMBER 14, 1982 ONE DOLLAR

Reagan lifts sanctions on Soviet gas pipeline

By Henry Trewhitt
Washington Bureau of The Sun

Washington—President Reagan lifted sanctions against the Soviet natural gas pipeline yesterday after America's allies agreed, as he put it, to tighten credit and restrain the sale of strategic goods to the Soviet bloc.

The president's action was a retreat from a policy that had angered allied governments, Soviet leaders and businessmen in the United States and Western Europe. In exchange, the president got what officials described as a promise of greater Western restraint and a detailed study of long-term practices.

Most unofficial analysts in Washington interpreted the agreement as a cosmetic device that enabled Mr. Reagan to reverse an unsuccessful policy. Whether the move would produce stiffer conditions for East-West economic relations was not clear.

The French government apparently was refusing to concede anything to appearances. Administration spokesmen had just finished a background explanation of the deal when the French Foreign Ministry issued a statement saying that France "was not a party to the agreement announced this afternoon in Washington by Ronald Reagan on East-West trade conditions."

The Foreign Ministry's communique took note "of the American decision to lift the embargo." Although it excluded France from the agreement, it observed that France "took part in the negotiations which led to the agreement being reached."

That, one official here remarked furiously, amounted to "a total case of having it both ways." For the record, an administration spokesman reported "our understanding [was] that during the extensive discussions . . . the French were in substantive agreement."

There had always been differences of perception about the relationship between the sanctions and overall East-West trade policy, he said. Sources added that there had been agreement on the presentation of the arrangement as recently as two days ago.

Mr. Reagan is expected to receive more sympathetic treatment tomorrow from West German Chancellor Helmut Kohl, who arrived in Washington yesterday and is scheduled to visit Mr. Reagan at the White House tomorrow.

Despite the dissonant tone from France, the administration stood by its position that "something stronger" had been substituted for the sanctions. American firms now are free to try to regain $600 million in suspended contracts with the Soviet Union. They also may revive $1.6 billion in contracts with European suppliers of the 3,200-mile pipeline project.

For their part, Mr. Reagan said, the European allies and Japan agreed not to sign new contracts for Soviet natural gas while a long-range study is under way. They also pledged to strengthen controls over the transfer of strategic goods to the Soviet Union, to closely monitor financial relations with the Soviet bloc and to cooperate in export credit policies. But for the most part their immediate commitments required nothing beyond existing plans.

"The understanding we've reached demonstrates that the Western alliance is fundamentally united and intends to give consideration to strategic issues when making decisions on trade with the U.S.S.R.," the president said in his noon radio broadcast. He called it "a victory for all the allies."

Most economic and political analysts privately treated the weeks of negotiations that

See SANCTIONS, A4, Col. 4

Poles say they freed Walesa

But union leader fails to appear; speculation grows

From Wire Services

Warsaw—Lech Walesa, chief of Poland's outlawed union Solidarity, failed to surface yesterday after the martial law government said it had freed him, and speculation grew that he remained in custody or had been spirited to a secret place by the Catholic Church.

The state-run news agency PAP yesterday claimed Mr. Walesa had rejoined his family at their home in the northern port of Gdansk, but it later withdrew the report without explanation. Mr. Walesa's wife, Danuta, told the Associated Press she had not seen him.

At the same time, PAP announced that the Sejm, or parliament, would meet in special session December 13, the first anniversary of military rule. Some speculated that martial law might be lifted at the session. Others were skeptical.

In an interview taped for government television, Mr. Walesa said he wanted an agreement with the martial law authorities, but not "on my knees."

A transcript of the interview was obtained by some Western reporters yesterday, but it is not scheduled to be broadcast on Polish television until tonight. The transcript did not reveal when or where the interview was made.

In the interview, Mr. Walesa said he felt there was a chance for agreement but "there is something wrong because we are not being able to understand each other.

"We are talking about the same thing but not in the same way," he said. "I want to talk about the same thing, but in a different way.

"I define the situation as greatly in need of agreement, agreement not with me on my knees, but a fair, proper agreement because we are all talking about agreement—the government and myself, but there is something wrong," Mr. Walesa said in the interview.

There was speculation that Mr. Walesa's comments would disappoint some of his militant follow-

See WALESA, A5, Col. 4

The Sun/Jed Kirschbaum

Rick Seiver, of Mount Airy, holds an American flag in his mechanical hand along the parade route in Washington. Vietnam veteran Joe Rebstock of Lindenwold, N.J., consoles his wife, Anna Marie, whose brother, Joseph Sweeney, died in Vietnam.

150,000 dedicate Vietnam memorial

By C. Fraser Smith
Washington Bureau of The Sun

Washington—About 150,000 people triumphantly dedicated a national memorial to the men and women who fought in Vietnam yesterday, consecrating it to the nearly 58,000 who died there and to the goals of national unity and peace.

A spirited parade down Constitution avenue, with about 2,000 Marylanders in the informal ranks, preceded the dedication. Spectators lined the parade route and then joined the veterans at the memorial.

It was a day to affirm the virtues of patriotism and the gallant service of men and women who served their country in a time of national divisiveness unparalleled in the nation's history.

But now, said Jan C. Scruggs, the Columbia resident who conceived and doggedly pursued completion of the memorial, "Americans can agree that Vietnam Veterans deserve recognition and appreciation for their sacrifices. . . ."

Many of the day's official and unofficial speakers hailed the veterans and those who joined them yesterday as "a

See PARADE, A14, Col. 1

Panel seeks compromise on Security

Reagan, O'Neill must be involved, commissioners say

By Stephen E. Nordlinger
Washington Bureau of The Sun

Washington—The National Commission on Social Security Reform, deferring a final vote on recommendations until next month, agreed yesterday that President Reagan and House Speaker Thomas P. O'Neill, Jr. (D, Mass.) would need to be involved in working out a compromise to shore up the finances of the retirement system.

After three days of meetings in Alexandria, Va., the 15-member commission postponed voting until a December 10 meeting in hopes that there will be an agreement on at least a set of options that can be submitted to Congress in January.

Propsects for reaching a compromise were considered about 50-50 by the commission members, but there appeared to be little chance that they would fulfill their chief mission of developing a single bipartisan solution for covering the huge deficit the system is projected to have.

That was the chief purpose of the commission when it was created by President Reagan early this year. But the 10 Republicans, who generally want reductions in the growth of future benefits, and the 5 Democrats, who want tax increases, have not been able to reconcile their basic differences, although the sides moved closer to each other last week.

"We have accomplished less than I had hoped but certainly far in excess of what I realistically expected," said Alan Greenspan, the commission chairman and an outside economic adviser to the president.

Mr. Greenspan said he wants to develop a "finite list" of options for the commission to review at its December meeting. He is expected to play the critical role in trying to forge an agreement that might defuse the crisis.

The commission's five Democrats, after conferring with Mr. O'Neill during a midmorning caucus, said they supported a three-part plan that would:

See SECURITY, A19, Col. 1

Associated Press

Soviet Ambassador Anatoly Dobrynin salutes President Reagan at signing of condolence book.

Andropov must break with Brezhnev era

By Anthony Barbieri, Jr.
Moscow Bureau of The Sun

Moscow—While paying lip service to the continuation of Leonid I. Brezhnev's policies, Yuri V. Andropov's first task as new head of the Soviet Communist Party probably will be to find ways of changing them.

Both Western and Soviet analysts predict that the policy changes expected to occur over the next year to 18 months will not be accompanied by a significant public downgrading of Mr. Brezhnev, who in his 18 years of power had honor after honor heaped upon himself and is now being given a hero's sendoff by his Kremlin colleagues.

Rather, the changes will come in response to what has become the Soviet Union's most urgent problem—getting the country moving again after the long stagnation of the later Brezhnev years.

The critical areas are almost all in the domestic sphere: repeated failures in agriculture, lagging economic growth caused by low productivity, and a growing technological gap with the West.

Analysis

Solutions to all these problems either had been held in abeyance or had been unable to win approval from a deadlocked Kremlin leadership grown accustomed to the comfort of Mr. Brezhnev's consensus politics.

"This is the kind of period when a lot of things that have been waiting to be resolved will suddenly be brought up for a solution," a senior Western diplomat said yesterday.

If some of the solutions, as expected, require rather sharp departures from Mr. Brezhnev's policies, they may encounter resistance.

Konstantin U. Chernenko, the man Mr. Andropov defeated in the struggle to succeed Mr. Brezhnev as head of the party, was Mr. Brezhnev's closest associate and clearly considers himself the executor of the Brezhnev legacy.

In a significant speech to the party leaders after the election of Mr. Andropov Friday morning, Mr. Chernenko let it be known that the new party boss would be expected to do "everything that [Mr. Brezhnev] had no time to do," and that it was now "twice, thrice more important" to adhere to the often-violated principle of collective leadership.

To be sure, Mr. Andropov promised to do it all, but he could have hardly done otherwise with Mr. Brezhnev lying in state only a few blocks away.

The funeral ceremonies will all be over tomorrow, however, and already Soviet sources have let it be known that on Tuesday morning they will be ready to get down to business.

"I think we're going to see a new team taking a new look at a whole range of issues, and I think we're going to get a look at some of the inside debate we knew has been going on all along," a Western envoy said.

It is no secret what the issues are.

First is agriculture, Mr. Brezhnev's most glaring failure. Not only has the Soviet Union's inability to feed itself caused internal political

See ANDROPOV, A5, Col. 1

Associated Press

President Reagan announces the end of U.S. sanctions against the Soviet natural gas pipeline.

Begin's wife dies; U.S. trip is cut short

By G. Jefferson Price III
Sun Staff Correspondent

Los Angeles—Prime Minisiter Menachem Begin cut short his 10-day trip to the United States yesterday and returned to Israel immediately after learning of the death of his wife, Aliza.

The Israeli prime minister was informed of the death of his 62-year-old wife less than an hour before he was to address the Council of Jewish Federations in his first appearance before a major Jewish group in America since the Lebanon invasion last June.

The Secret Service contingent accompanying the prime minister said he went immediately to the Israeli Air Force jet transporting him around the country in a visit that was to conclude with a meeting between President Reagan and Mr. Begin next Friday.

In Washington, White House spokesman Mark Weinberg said, "The president and Mrs. Reagan have been informed and are deeply saddened" over Mrs. Begin's death. Mr. Weinberg said Mr. Reagan would convey his condolences to Mr. Begin directly later.

The two leaders were to come together Friday at a time of considerable strain in relations between Jerusalem and Washington over their policies in the Middle East.

There was no immediate word on when Mr. Begin and the president, or ranking Israeli and American officials, might get together to discuss these differences.

Not much progress was expected, however, in breaking the impasse that has grown between the United States and Israel, paticularly since President Reagan announced his Middle East policy last September. The policy included a call for a freeze on Jewish settlements in the Israeli-occupied West Bank and Gaza Strip.

The president announced last week that Philip C. Habib would return to the Middle East as his special representative to get negotiations going on the withdrawal of foreign forces, in-

See BEGIN, A2, Col. 1

Inside

Space walk postponed
Today's space walk was delayed a day because one of the astronauts became nauseous A3

Teller assailed
A Nobel prize-winning physicist has charged that faulty calculations by Edward Teller and other technical problems hindered development of the hydrogen bomb A3

Longer sentences
Sentences are getting tougher, according to data used in four Maryland jurisdictions C1

Sunny skies
Sunny today, chance of rain or sleet tonight. High, 50; low, 35. Yesterday's high, 63; low, 40 .... C2

Index

3 Section

Sports Final

THE SUN

VOL. 293—NO. 131—F BALTIMORE, MONDAY, OCTOBER 17, 1983 • • 25 CENTS

WORLD CHAMPIONS

Mob greets conquerors at stadium

Joyous fans wait hours for return of 'the best of '83'

By Patrick A. McGuire and Rafael Alvarez

The bus carrying the Baltimore Orioles, the best baseball team on the planet as a result of their World Series-clinching win over the Philadelphia Phillies yesterday, rolled triumphantly into the Memorial Stadium parking lot just after midnight this morning to be greeted by a delirious crowd of 40,000.

"We are the best of '83," slugger Eddie Murray exhorted the fans, some of whom had waited four hours for a glimpse of their heroes.

The Orioles' general manager, Hank Peters, eschewed a boast for a thank you. "We brought you the only thing we could to pay you back for what you've done for us," he said, referring to the two million attendance mark broken this year for the first time.

Giddy fans had been pouring steadily into the stadium lots since shortly after the game ended at about 7:40 p.m. By 11:30, one police officer surveyed the crowd that ringed the stadium lot on all sides and said: "We're surrounded. There must be 35,000 to 40,000 people here."

Fans literally hung from the rafters as the Orioles descended from their bus and worked their way through the crowd to a special stage that had been erected for them.

Many of the fans had climbed to the roof of the Orioles ticket window portico for a better view of the stage, and many had cheered themselves hoarse by the time the team arrived.

See STADIUM, A8, Col. 1

In city's streets, bars, fans cheer their champions

By Patrick A. McGuire

The kid with the earphones and the portable radio, doodling his way down a deserted Frederick avenue a few minutes before 6:00 last night, stopped suddenly as if someone had sneaked up behind him and jacked up his volume knob.

His hands went to both ears, and his hat actually leapt from his head. A look of utter shock contorted his face.

One hundred miles to the north, a baseball struck by Eddie Murray was finding its way into orbit over the city of Philadelphia.

So, too, the kid with the radio in Catonsville seemed to rise from the sidewalk in tandem with that mighty home run, his feet clicking together, his fist duking out the air of a golden autumn afternoon.

At precisely the same moment, with the fifth

See CELEBRATION, A8, Col. 4

The Sun/J. Pat Carter

Rick Dempsey (No. 24), Orioles catcher, embraces battery mate Scott McGregor moments after the final out of the World Series in Philadelphia. McGregor pitched the entire game, while Dempsey hit a home run and was selected most valuable player of the Series. Third baseman Todd Cruz was running to join in. It was the first world championship ring for each of the three men.

Orioles win Series in 5 games

Birds' 5-0 victory over Phillies brings 1st title in 13 years

After four years of second-best, of near-misses, of watching other teams celebrate on *their* turf, the Baltimore Orioles sit atop the baseball world today, conquerors of the Philadelphia Phillies in five games.

Forget about the three consecutive second-place finishes. Forget about the loss to the Milwaukee Brewers on the last day of the 1982 season. Say good-bye to the memory of the 1979 World Series loss to the Pittsburgh Pirates.

Remember, instead, a remarkable year — a year of adversity, a year of mission and, finally, a year of redemption.

Remember Scott McGregor, the loser in the seventh game of the 1979 World Series and the loser of the first game this year, coming back to win yesterday's game, 5-0, in classic McGregor style — not by overpowering the Phillies but by wearing them down.

Remember the way they won the Series in five games — not by the effort of one or two players but by Rick Dempsey's extra-base hits (a record), Sammy Stewart's scoreless relief pitching, Benny Ayala's pinch-hitting, rookie Mike Boddicker's pitching.

It was a victory of many sorts: a victory for the Orioles' farm system, which provided key replacements early in the season when they lost three key pitchers; a victory for Joe Altobelli, who had to prove that his predecessor, Earl Weaver, was not the only reason for the team's success, and a victory for the 15 members who remained from the 1979 team, who had to prove they could win it all.

It also was a victory for the fans. For the first time in the club's history more than two million people went through the turnstiles at Memorial Stadium, something that didn't happen in 1966 or 1970, the years the Orioles brought home their other world championships.

And when it was all over yesterday — as Baltimore danced late into the night on 33d street and at the Inner Harbor — it was clear to all that the Orioles had won and won convincingly. The Phillies never really came close.

For complete coverage of the Series, see Page C1.

Oriole pride to go on parade

A parade to honor the World Champion Orioles will take place downtown today at noon.

The "We Love The Orioles" parade will start at the Washington Monument and go south on Charles street to Baltimore street, east on Baltimore to Holliday and then north to City Hall.

McFarlane called choice for security adviser post

From Staff and Wire Reports

Washington — President Reagan has decided to appoint Robert C. McFarlane, his special Mideast envoy, to succeed William P. Clark as national security adviser, White House officials said yesterday.

The national security post will be vacated upon Mr. Clark's confirmation as secretary of the interior, replacing James G. Watt, who resigned a week ago.

Mr. Reagan was not expected to announce the appointment of Mr. McFarlane until today at the earliest.

One official, speaking on the condition that he not be identified by name, said the president's key foreign policy and national security advisers had been notified of the president's decision, which was reached during the weekend.

"All that remains is the president making it formal," said another official.

The officials said that Mr. Reagan had not taken the final step of offering the job to Mr. McFarlane, who, in addition to the Middle East job, is the deputy national security adviser.

See MCFARLANE, A2, Col. 3

Associated Press

ROBERT C. McFARLANE

EPA ends slowdown in testing

By Vernon A. Guidry, Jr.
Washington Bureau of The Sun

Washington — After a halt of nearly two years, the Environmental Protection Agency is again starting new examinations of a backlog of as many as 75 pesticides and chemicals that may present a risk to public health despite their usefulness.

The formal reviews being initiated this fiscal year include 15 chemicals whose potential health effects warrant "serious concern," say agency officials.

The remedies available to the government range from specifying safety precautions to be observed when the chemicals are used to declaring an outright ban.

One of the 15 chemicals is daminozide, a growth-regulating product sold under the name Alar by Uniroyal Chemical Company. Studies show that Alar produces cancer in some laboratory animals.

Sources close to the issue say that EPA staff members have been trying to initiate a special review of Alar for two years but that former agency officials took no action.

Another 45 to 60 chemicals will be given a preliminary examination for potential health risks to determine if a more rigorous, formal review is necessary.

One EPA expert predicts that per-

See PESTICIDES, A5, Col. 1

Marine killed, 3 hurt in Lebanon fighting

From Wire Services

Beirut, Lebanon — One U.S. marine was killed and three were wounded yesterday in seven hours of sniping and rocket-propelled grenade attacks on Marine positions at Beirut's airport, a U.S. military spokesman said.

It was the third consecutive day of attacks on the marines and raised the toll of Marine combat deaths to six since the U.S. peacekeeping contingent arrived here 13 months ago. A seventh marine died when a mine he was attempting to defuse exploded.

Maj. Robert Jordan, the spokesman, said the marines serving with Alpha Company at the southernmost end of Beirut's airport first came under fire at about 4:20 p.m. (10:20 a.m. EDT) and that firing from small arms and rocket-propelled grenades continued for more than six hours.

Major Jordan said the marines fired back with anti-tank rockets and small arms.

He said the dead marine had been wounded in the head. One marine had

See MIDEAST, A2, Col. 2

Mass. citizens took own action

By Judy Foreman
The Boston Globe/Independent Press

AMERICA'S TOXIC TOWNS
PART 2 OF A SERIES

Acton, Mass., a cross between old New England village and high-tech bedroom suburb, is as toxic as the next town on the Environmental Protection Agency's list of poisoned places.

But Acton, 25 miles west of Boston, has had two things going for it that many communities don't: abundant homegrown expertise and virtually no economic dependency on its major polluter.

Most of Acton's 18,000 residents are well-paid, well-educated professionals who drive along woodsy roads to the computerized corridors of nearby Digital Equipment Corporation, Wang Laboratories, Inc., and Polaroid Corporation. Fewer than 20 Acton residents work at the W. R. Grace chemical plant off in the woods near the Concord city line.

Five years ago Acton residents discovered that Grace was pouring 75,000 gallons a day of toxic waste into the aquifer that supplied 40 percent of the town's drinking water. The discharge included 13 known pollutants, among them the suspected carcinogen vinilidine chloride, or VDC.

Their response was swift and savvy, even though, as far as anybody could tell, nobody had died or become sick because of the pollutants.

A local birdwatcher began snapping pictures of drums of chemicals leaking in Grace's isolated landfill.

A railroad commuter, after jotting down the names of chemicals in labeled tank cars near the Grace site, called in the press to document the presence of the chemical at the plant.

Other residents formed technical advisory committees, the most important of which was ACES — Acton Citizens for Environmental Safety.

See ACTON, A9, Col. 1

Inside

Orioles 5, Phillies 0

Canada pact

Buses for handicapped

Partly cloudy

Index

Sports Final

Colts bow to Miami in rain, 21-7: D1

THE SUN

VOL. 293—NO. 137—F | BALTIMORE, MONDAY, OCTOBER 24, 1983 | 25 CENTS

147 U.S. marines killed as bomb destroys barracks in Lebanon

Associated Press

Two U.S. marines search the rubble of their barracks after an explosion at Beirut International Airport leveled the building. The early morning blast ripped through the structure as more than 300 marines were asleep. The explosion left 147 marines dead and scores wounded.

Suicide truck rams through gates of base

By G. Jefferson Price III
Sun Staff Correspondent

Beirut, Lebanon — At least 147 U.S. marines and an undisclosed number of French soliders attached to the multinational peacekeeping force were killed in two separate suicide bombings yesterday, authorities reported as the flood-lit search for more bodies — and possibly some survivors — continued late into last night.

American sources here said that as many as 300 marines may have been in the building at Beirut International Airport yesterday morning when a truck packed with 2,000 pounds of explosives crashed into the lobby, where they were detonated by the driver.

The sources put the number of marines wounded at 70. The explosion completely destroyed the four-story building, where most of the soldiers were sleeping at the time. However, marine rescuers, assisted by some Italian members of the multinational force, were still pulling bodies from the wreckage late last night and the death toll was expected to climb much higher.

French casualties were estimated at 25 dead and 12 wounded, according to Lebanese civil defense personnel working through the night in the rubble of a nine-story building struck in an identical suicide-bombing mission within minutes of the attack on the American Marine headquarters.

The French Defense Ministry gave more conservative figures, listing 9 dead, 11 wounded and 53 unaccounted for in the wreckage of the building, where the moans and cries of some trapped survivors encouraged the hope that they might be rescued.

[A revolutionary Islamic group claimed responsibility for both blasts.

[According to Associated Press, the U.S. State Department said an anonymous caller told the Beirut office of the French news agency Agence France Presse that the Islamic Revolutionary Movement mounted the attacks.

[The caller said two of the movement's fighters, Abu Mazin, 26, and Abu Sija'n, 24, perished in the bombings.

[The group had not been heard of before in Beirut, and some officials expressed doubt about the claim.]

The devastation at both places created a ghastly scene as night fell and floodlights were set up to illuminate the work of the rescuers.

At the U.S. Marine building, a former PLO headquarters damaged in the 1982 Israeli bombardment of Beirut, bulldozers grotesquely pushed aside the debris, trying clumsily to avoid doing more damage to the bodies underneath, and trying to avoid killing survivors, even though by nightfall little hope remained that any would be found.

"This is not combat," said Maj. Robert Jordan, spokesman for the 1,600-man Marine force in Beirut.

"It's murder," he said, lowering his eyes as another dead marine was pulled awkwardly from beneath the jagged blocks of collapsed concrete.

Warrant Officer George Allen, a 45-year-old marine veteran, wept as he commented bitterly, "This is just as much our country now as it is Lebanese. Our blood is still here."

Around him, the noisy work of front-end loaders and cranes and bulldozers and pneumatic drills rattled on in the frantic search for casualties. The marines themselves, who by nightfall had been working without stop for 12 hours, looked dazed and bewildered.

At the French-occupied building about a mile from the Marine base at

See BLAST, A4, Col. 1

The Beirut bombings

■ Marine reinforcements are dispatched as White House officials react with horror to the attacks and some congressmen voice doubts about the U.S. role in Lebanon..........A4
■ Leaders around the world denounce the bombings, but France, like the U.S. administration, resolves to remain part of the peacekeeping force..........A6
■ A chronology of the U.S. Marine presence in Lebanon..........A4
■ Defense Secretary Caspar W. Weinberger says evidence points to Iranian involvement in the tragedy..........A6
■ U.S. officials have little hope of devising an ironclad defense to prevent terrorist attacks like yesterday's from succeeding again..........A7
■ Families and friends of the members of the Marine unit involved in the bombing wait anxiously to learn who survived and who did not..........A7
■ Baltimoreans react to the events and ponder their consequences..........A7
■ A photographic record of the tragedy..........A5

Choice facing Reagan on Lebanon not easy

By Henry Trewhitt
Washington Bureau of The Sun

Analysis

Washington — In the flash of one massive bomb yesterday, President Reagan came face to face with the politics of death in the Middle East.

Death has been the currency of political movement in that region in recent years, apart from the Camp David accords of 1978. The civil war in Lebanon has taken tens of thousands of lives, producing the present fragmentation. Hundreds were reported to have died in the Israeli bombing of Beirut two years ago.

During the Israeli occupation last year, 600 to 800 Palestinians died, apparently at Christian hands. Israel had to withdraw to its current Lebanese positions, yielding territory to the enemy, because of domestic unrest over growing casualties.

By these standards, the American losses yesterday were small. But they are not small for America, and they are unlikely to be perceived as small in their political effect on the administration's ravaged Middle East policy. With time, they may have a tidal impact on the U.S. role in the region.

For the moment, nothing the administration does will be free of traumatic consequences. To withdraw the Marines could have political results far beyond the Middle East. To add to their numbers and expand their mission might be politically unacceptable, apart from the longer-term military risks. It is impossible to do nothing. The attackers will not permit it.

How will Mr. Reagan respond? The first answer seemed to call simply for giving the survivors and replacements greater protection. But U.S. policy, the administration seemed to say, would be unchanged. It is by no means clear, however, that the first answer will be the more considered one.

Congress and the public doubtless will have something to say about the adequacy of that response. The policy for which the Marines and French troops died has produced little positive movement. It is not certain, though it is arguable, that U.S. interests have been advanced at all since the Marines landed in Lebanon 14 months ago.

What is certain is that the U.S. commitment increased as the promise of the Camp David accords eroded. It used to be an article of faith in Washington that American troops would not intervene in the region, short of a direct threat to U.S. strategic interests, such as oil. That assumption was reversed with the commitment, carried out 18 months ago, of troops to stand between Israel and Egypt in the Sinai peninsula.

There always is a question, of course, whether a great power with its own clear interests can serve credibly between powerful competing forces. The U.S. role in Korea under United Nations sponsorship is a partial answer. It is not a precise one, since the good and the bad are clearly perceived in Korea, and not in the Middle East.

See POLICY, A6, Col. 1

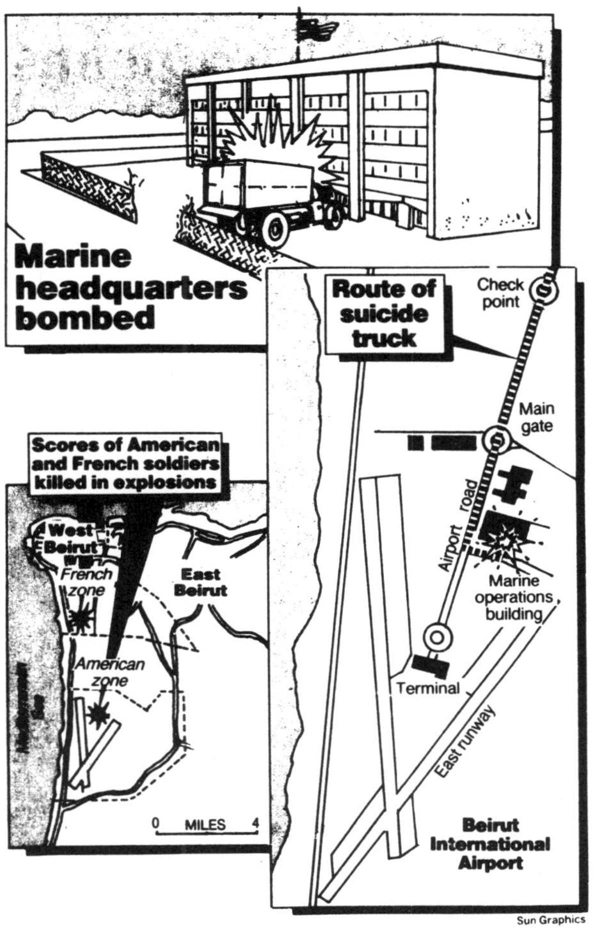

Sun Graphics

De Lorean tape shown on TV with court OK

Los Angeles (AP) — An FBI videotape showing automaker John Z. De Lorean examining contents of a suitcase purportedly containing cocaine was broadcast nationally last night by CBS-TV, which earlier in the day had won a court battle allowing it to show the tape.

The tape is thought to be a key piece of evidence against Mr. De Lorean, who is facing a trial on federal drug trafficking charges. An attorney for Mr. De Lorean had warned that showing the tape would "unleash a circus unprecedented in court history."

The tape, broadcast on the evening news, showed Mr. De Lorean lounging on a couch in a hotel room with a glass in his hand and talking to a man sitting across from him, who is barely visible.

Another man, identified by CBS as an undercover agent, entered carrying a suitcase, which he placed on a coffee table and opened.

"This is the other batch that's going out of here," the man is heard to say, and he added, "It'll generate about four and a half, not less than four-and-a-half mil."

Mr. De Lorean responded "[unintelligible] good as gold. Gold weighs more than this, for God's sake."

Then the suitcase is put out of sight, a champagne cork is popped and Mr. De Lorean raises his glass in a toast.

"Here's to . . . lot of success," said the man identified as an agent.

Then another man entered, identified himself as an FBI agent and arrested Mr. De Lorean, who put his arms behind his back to be handcuffed.

"Hi, John. We're the FBI," the agent said. "We're here to arrest you on narcotics law violation. Would you stand up, please?"

Mr. De Lorean responded, "I don't understand," but stood. He was handcuffed and sat back down again, where he was read his rights.

Earlier yesterday, at a hastily called hearing that drew attorneys to court in blue jeans and sweatshirts, three justices of the 9th U.S. Circuit Court of Appeals indicated they had no authority to impose prior restraint on the media to prevent them from publishing or broadcasting material.

Mr. De Lorean's attorney Howard Weitzman and co-counsel Donald Re told the appeals court judges that broadcast of the surveillance tapes would make it virtually impossible to find an impartial jury anywhere in the country to judge Mr. De Lorean on cocaine conspiracy charges.

They indicated that the broadcast might create prejucial pretrial publicity that could cause a motion to dismiss all charges and abort Mr. De Lorean's scheduled November 1 trial.

Federal prosecutor James Walsh argued emotionally against the re-

See DE LOREAN, A10, Col. 5

Inside

Federal raises curbed
New rules will end automatic raises for 1.4 million government workers unless Congress intervenes shortly .B1

Colts in muddy defeat
The Colts lost a soggy battle to the Miami Dolphins, 21-7, at the Stadium yesterday afternoon..........D1

Hostage taker no loner
Man suspected of taking presidential aides hostage is described as having "a certain amount of popularity" at the paper mill where he worked......A3

Edwards wins in La.
Edwin Edwards wins Louisiana governor's race with a landslide that surprises even him..........A11

Fashion show finale
Tired workers breathe sigh of relief as Paris fashion show ends..........C1

Argentina to vote
Argentines go to polls next week with a mixture of hope and wariness A2

Rain today
Rain turning to drizzle today, high 60
Occasional drizzle tonight, low 50
Yesterday's high, 60; low, 50..........D2

Index

Bridge	C2	Lottery	D2
Business	D12	Movies	C5
Classified	B4	Obituaries	B3
Comics	C7	Sports	D1
Crossword	C7	Television	C6
Editorials	A14	Weather	B2

4 Sections

FRIDAY
MARCH 30 1984

THE SUN

SPORTS FINAL

VOL. 294 NUMBER 115—F | BALTIMORE, MARYLAND | 25 CENTS

Baltimore's Colts are gone

The Sun/George H. Cook

Mayor Schaefer wipes his eye at a City Hall press conference dealing with the Colts' move to Indianapolis.

Eminent domain bill signed; city may sue

By J. S. Bainbridge, Jr.

Legislation that would permit an extraordinary legal effort to block the Colts' move from Baltimore sped to enactment by the General Assembly yesterday, and city officials appeared ready to go to court today.

The emergency law allows the city government to buy or condemn the National Football League franchise under the principle of eminent domain. Eminent domain is used by governments to acquire privately owned property for public use.

While Mayor Schaefer dodged questions yesterday about possible legal action, he assured reporters, "We certainly aren't going to just sit and watch the world go by. You can bet on that."

Maneuverings in Annapolis and Baltimore strongly suggest that the city will file a legal challenge to the Colts' move before the close of court business today, perhaps immediately after an emergency City Council session at 1:30 p.m.

Judge Robert L. Karwacki, the administrative judge of the city Circuit Court, said last night that the city solicitor's office has asked to meet with him at 1:30 p.m. today. He said he "assumed" the meeting had to do with the eminent domain question but said he did not know for sure.

Benjamin L. Brown, the city solicitor, refused to comment when asked about the meeting.

"I don't know what else we can do," City Council President Clarence H. (Du) Burns said of the likely litigation. "It looks like it's leading in that direction."

Yesterday, according to state officials knowledgeable about the effort to keep the Colts, the city wired a $40 million offer to Robert Irsay, the team's owner. Such an offer of purchase is normally a prelude to an eminent domain action.

But the first shots in the legal war over the Colts were fired last night by lawyers from a Baltimore financial institution.

Equitable Bank's lawyers persuaded Judge Thomas Ward to put under

See LEGAL, A14, Col. 1

The Sun/Robert K. Hamilton

Governor Hughes has a press conference at the State House after signing the eminent domain bill.

Irsay ends the 31-year 'marriage'

By Vito Stellino

Under the cover of darkness and downpour, the Baltimore Colts galloped to Indianapolis early yesterday in a caravan of Mayflower trucks to end the city's 31-year era in the National Football League.

Reneging on a promise, the team's controversial owner, Robert Irsay, did not even call the mayor to say good-bye.

While Indiana's governor prepared to send troopers to the Ohio border to escort the moving vans to the team's new home in the Hoosier Dome, Maryland's governor and Baltimore's mayor set in motion a legal battle to bring the Colts back through condemnation proceedings.

Mayor Schaefer, who stepped out his front door yesterday morning to face reporters and photographers camped on his lawn, called the team's midnight move "the final humiliation."

"I'm trying to retain what little dignity I have left in this matter. If the Colts had to sneak out of town at night, it degrades a great city," the mayor said, then shrugged and abruptly ended his remarks by adding, "I hate to see a man cry."

The team's departure ended a saga of triumph and tragedy spanning three decades.

The Colts were credited with fueling the modern-day pro football boom with their 1958 overtime championship victory over the New York Giants — the first of three championships, including Super Bowl V — before their first owner, the late Carroll Rosenbloom, traded his franchise to Mr. Irsay for the Los Angeles Rams.

A descent into ignominy gradually ensued — years in which beloved

See COLTS, A14, Col. 1

Loyalty is nothing, money all

MICHAEL
OLESKER

"What'll we do with ourselves this afternoon?" cried Daisy, "and the day after that, and the next 30 years?"

"Don't be morbid," Jordan said. "Life starts all over again when it gets crisp in the fall."

— F. Scott Fitzgerald, in "The Great Gatsby"

—o—

Not anymore, it doesn't.

There are to be no more late autumn Sunday afternoons at Memorial Stadium. Game called on account of darkness. Robert Irsay is taking his football team to Indianapolis.

Do we listen to our hearts or our heads?

Our heads say: The community is better off without Irsay. Indianapolis can have him. Getting Irsay in your town is like getting food poisoning.

But our hearts say: Something precious and irreplaceable has died. Not just a football team, but a symbiotic relationship between a team and a town that transcended athletics and even, once, transcended money.

When the moving vans appeared in the dark of night at the Colt complex, it was a message to every city in America that has a team owned by somebody from out of town: Nothing is forever. Loyalty means nothing. Money is all.

Are you listening, Oriole fans?

Before the body is entirely cold, the mind does back flips through a 31-year history.

Once there was Unitas throwing heart-stopping passes to Raymond Berry in the overtime dusk at Yankee Stadium. Once there was Matte and the wrist band on the frozen turf at Green Bay. Once there were Marchetti and Donovan and Lenny Moore and Big Daddy Lipscomb, people whose names symbolized not only a football team but a way of life in this town.

Once there was a kid named Joe Ehrmann. In the twilight at Memorial Stadium, in sudden death overtime, a little guy named Toni Linhart had kicked the Colts into the 1975 championship playoffs.

Moments later, in the steamy Colt locker room there was Ehrmann, blubbering, "Those people out there, they're unbelievable. I'd like to hug 'em all, one by one, honest to God I would."

Now there is no hugging, except by mourners at the grave site. Memorial Stadium on autumn days becomes a kind of sacred burial ground for memories of the Baltimore Colts.

Is Bob Irsay aware of any of this?

He can take his team to the brand new Hoosier Dome in Indianapolis, and for a few moments he will feel the new town's love on him like velvet, and he will feel very briefly as though he is beginning his life again.

See OLESKER, A14, Col. 6

12 years of Irsay denials

The Sun/Gene Sweeney, Jr.

On January 20, Robert Irsay (left) said angrily that Colts weren't leaving.

By Eric Siegel

From his inaugural press conference at the Chesapeake Restaurant after becoming owner of the Baltimore Colts July 13, 1972, to his infamous exchange with the media at Baltimore-Washington International Airport January 20, Robert Irsay repeatedly swore he'd never do what he has done.

He said he'd never move the team from Baltimore.

Even as he shamelessly shopped the Colts from town to town, he repeatedly assured the press and the public that the team was here to stay.

At that first press conference in July, 1972, for example, he said:

"I bought the Colts to play in Baltimore. I have no thought of taking

See QUOTES, A14, Col. 3

The Colts leave

☐ The Colts played the game that changed the face of pro football and John Unitas became king in Baltimore. **C1**

☐ Baltimoreans offer differing reactions to the move. **A15**

☐ For players past and present, the emotions are mixed. **C2**

Complete report on Pages A14, A15, C1, C2, C3 and C4

Tornado toll reaches 60; 10 die in blizzard

From Wire Services

A ferocious spring storm that left at least 60 dead from tornadoes in the Carolinas attacked the Northeast yesterday with a blizzard, blowing hurricane-force winds, dumping more than a foot of snow in some areas and forcing thousands of evacuations in coastal areas.

At least 10 deaths were blamed on the snowstorm. Along with the dead in North and South Carolina, almost 700 were injured there.

"This storm is going to go into the books as having spawned more problems than maybe we have seen in a century on the East Coast," said David Lesher, a meteorologist in Maryland's Frederick county.

The unusual storm ravaged most of the East, including Maryland *A10, A11, A12*

Part of Atlantic City's famed boardwalk fell into the churning sea, and the gambling town built on islands was cut off from the mainland by high

See TEMPEST, A12, Col. 1

Associated Press

Teresa Milliken removes belongings from the wreckage of her sister's house in Greenville, N.C. Greenville, in the east-central part of the state, was along the route of Wednesday's tornadoes.

National Guard helps evacuate in Shore floods

By Joel McCord and Ann LoLordo

Crisfield — National Guard trucks sloshed through the flooded streets of Crisfield yesterday evacuating dozens of residents and ferrying schoolchildren home as Marylanders recovered from a fierce storm that left high tides, sleet and snow.

The storm initially moved into Maryland Tuesday under a cloud of steady rain. But by late yesterday it had dumped 6 inches of snow in Western Maryland, forced school closings throughout the Baltimore area and left parts of the Eastern Shore under several feet of water.

There were no deaths reported in the state because of the storm.

Tidal flooding, driven by winds gusting at 50 mph, struck the lower Shore, principally the Crisfield area, and covered the roads with 3 feet to 4 feet of water, officials said.

On the orders of Governor Hughes, 21 national

See WEATHER, A12, Col. 5

Senate gives initial nod to Salvador military aid

By Nancy J. Schwerzler
Washington Bureau of The Sun

Washington — The Senate last night gave preliminary approval to $61 million in emergency military aid to El Salvador, where U.S. military advisers have come under guerrilla gunfire three times since last November, according to a Pentagon document released in the Senate yesterday.

Under an agreement reached last night, the Senate is expected to vote on final passage of the aid bill next week, following further debate of Central America policy Monday. A handful of senators agreed on a voice vote last night to give preliminary approval to the aid funds, thus ending a filibuster by critics of the military assistance.

From the outset of more than 12 hours of debate yesterday, it was clear that Senate leaders had sufficient votes to win approval of the military aid funds, but critics sought to use the aid bill to air a host of objections to the conduct of American policy in Central America. But supporters of the aid, led by Senator Daniel K. Inouye (D, Hawaii), said that to deny the aid now or cut it drastically could "fan the flames of discontent" in El Salvador when it faces crucial runoff elections.

During debate yesterday, Senator James R. Sasser (D, Tenn.) disclosed a report that U.S. military advisers in El Salvador had been fired upon by anti-government guerrillas. No Americans were injured in the attacks but Senator Sasser said the disclosures, which had not previously been reported to Congress publicly, indicated that the 1973 war powers law and other statutes may have been violated by the Reagan administration.

The war powers law requires the

See LATIN, A2, Col. 1

Inside

New USW president

Lynn Williams says he's been elected United Steelworkers president C12

Medals shower

The Army bestowed 8,612 medals for individual performance in the Grenada invasion, though it never had more than 7,000 troops there A4

Windy

Windy and cool today, fair and cold tonight. High, 44; low, 30. Yesterday's high, 41; low, 35 ....D16

Index

Heart transplant patient

Grace Jacques, Johns Hopkins Hospital's first woman heart transplant recipient, demonstrates recovery.......D1

WEDNESDAY
JANUARY 29 1986

THE SUN

LIGHT · FOR · ALL

SPORTS FINAL

VOL. 298 NO. 63 BALTIMORE, MARYLAND 25 CENTS

ALL OF US WERE UP THERE WITH CHALLENGER

By Ernest B. Furgurson
Chief of The Sun's Washington Bureau

CHRISTA McAULIFFE was a gutsy schoolteacher, a sunny character with whom millions of Americans could identify. Understandably, she got most of the public attention yesterday when the Challenger spacecraft went up, and after its explosion.

The way the world focused on her testified to the success of NASA's outreach program, which is frankly a public relations project in which the agency has sent up a senator and a representative, and planned to orbit a teacher and a reporter.

But there were six others on board yesterday, too. They got less publicity because they were professionals, doing their jobs, trained to do over and over what the non-professionals gamble but once. Better than the rest of the world, they understood that however ho-hum the shuttle excursions might look by now, they still involve shooting into space atop a huge, barely controlled explosion.

Few of us, even now, can name those who were in the Challenger crew with Christa McAuliffe. But a look at them and their backgrounds shows that this mission spanned the nation geographically and ethnically, touching families and groups far beyond the innocent, squeaky-clean children at Mrs. McAuliffe's school in Concord, N.H.

A quarter-century ago, when the first Mercury as-

See USA, 9A, Col. 6

NASA PHOTO

The crew of ill-fated mission: in front row, pilot Michael J. Smith, commander Francis R. "Dick" Scobee, and mission specialist Ronald E. McNair; in rear, specialist Ellison S. Onizuka, teacher Christa McAuliffe, Hughes engineer Gregory B. Jarvis, and specialist Judith A. Resnik.

Shuttle explodes after liftoff, killing 7

Halt is expected to manned flights during inquiry

By Charles W. Corddry and Nancy J. Schwerzler
Washington Bureau of The Sun

WASHINGTON — The Challenger explosion could halt U.S. manned space operations for many months and could force a decision on whether the nation should now build a fifth shuttle to carry out a crowded exploration schedule running into the 1990s, government and independent authorities said yesterday.

As the White House and members of Congress said the country was determined to go on with space exploration, officials at the National Aeronautics and Space Administration and the Defense Department said the structural parts of a new shuttle were already built and could be assembled on relatively short notice.

But NASA associate administrator Jesse Moore announced a suspension of operations for now, while investigation of yesterday's tragedy proceeds, and the outcome could determine whether radical redesign or simpler changes are needed in the shuttle.

That, in turn, would affect the speed with which another of the $1.2 billion spacecraft could be put into operation and the time it would take to get back on a regular schedule of civilian and military operations.

Immediately cast in doubt was the schedule for the first shuttle to be fired from Vandenberg Air Force Base, Calif. Until yesterday, the shuttle Discovery was slated to be launched from Vandenberg into a polar orbit in mid-July, carrying significant experiments related to the "star wars" missile defense program.

While congressmen expected the space effort to go on, some questioned the merits of continuing to

See FUTURE, 4A, Col. 1

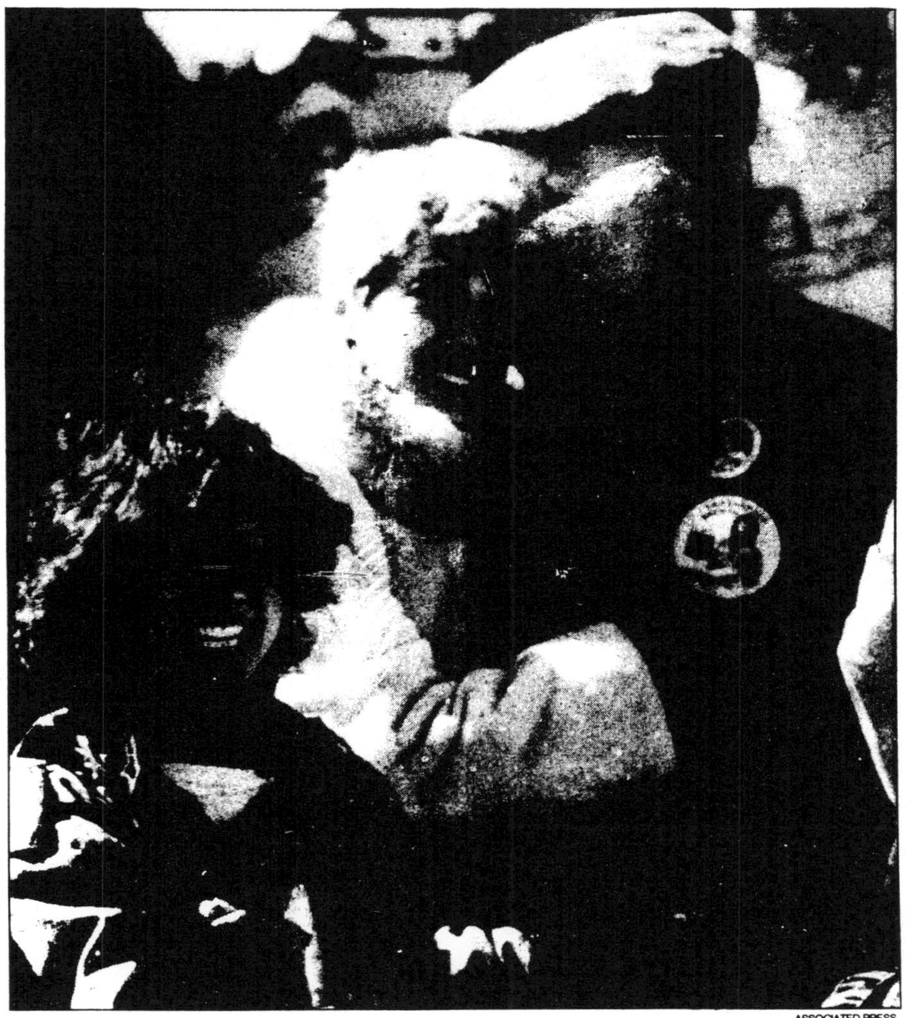

ASSOCIATED PRESS

Christa McAuliffe's sister, Betsy, and parents, Grace and Ed Corrigan, console one another after Challenger's explosion off Florida that killed the New Hampshire teacher and her six fellow astronauts.

Teacher's family, thousands see fire engulf Challenger

By Albert Sehlstedt Jr.
Sun Staff Correspondent

CAPE CANAVERAL, Fla. — The space shuttle Challenger exploded 74 seconds after liftoff yesterday, killing all seven astronauts, including New Hampshire high school teacher Christa McAuliffe.

Two orange balls of fire shot from either side of the shuttle's normal white trail of engine smoke before the entire craft disappeared into an enormous fireball eight miles east of the launching site as Challenger climbed toward orbit in an often delayed 25th shuttle mission. One of the balls appeared to be the flaming exhaust from one of the two solid rocket boosters — each 149 feet long — that help lift the shuttle into orbit and then normally separate from the ascending craft a full two minutes after the launching.

The disaster was seen by uncounted thousands of people at Kennedy Space Center here and at dozens of other Florida viewing sites along the Atlantic Coast.

"Oh, my God," one spectator cried out.

"What happened?" yelled another.

Rescue helicopters from Patrick Air Force Base about 20 miles south of Cape Canaveral and a cutter and a hydrofoil from the Coast Guard sped toward the scene after the 11:39 a.m. explosion, but officials stopped them to protect them from debris falling into the ocean.

Three miles from the launching pad at the press site, journalists ran in different directions — one frantically calling to another to speed to the 15,000-foot runway four miles west of pad 39-B in the belief that the shuttle might have survived the explosion and be able to land there.

Other people searched the bright blue sky for some sign of Challenger above the trail of smoke that had shielded their view of how the explosion might have occurred.

There was nothing intact to be seen — only arcing smoke trails from pieces of debris that seemed to be falling earthward in slow motion, like the remnants of a Fourth of July rocket.

It took tens of seconds for the reality of the horror to sink in: It was the worst disaster in 25 years of manned spaceflight that has seen 55 missions launched to Earth orbit and the moon with astronauts aboard.

Then the tears began to flow — everywhere.

Two women hugged each other in an embrace of utter grief.

Some people stood as rigid as statues, apparently unable to comprehend fully the enormity of the catastrophe.

The National Aeronautics and Space Administration's Mission Control Center in Houston, which takes command of every manned

See SHUTTLE, 12A, Col. 4

The Shuttle Inside

THE SUN INSIDE

Across country, students' celebrations change to numb disbelief

McAuliffe's town reels from shock

By Gilbert A. Lewthwaite
Sun Staff Correspondent

CONCORD, N.H. — It was a day that started with cheers, broke into weeping, and ended with prayers for the friends of Christa McAuliffe. And everyone here in her hometown was a friend of Christa.

This small community lost more than a heroine it shared with the nation yesterday. It lost a neighbor, a teacher, a parishioner, a citizen.

That a living, breathing, laughing 20th century spacewoman could emerge from this quiet corner of America, so steeped in the quiet ways of yesteryear, only made the pride that much brighter, and the pain that much sharper.

"A great lady," said Katharyn Hok, one of Mrs. McAuliffe's students, who was in the full spirit of

See CONCORD, 8A, Col. 2

THE SUN/GENE SWEENEY JR

Concord High School students mourn at service for Christa McAuliffe, who taught at their school.

Teachers wonder what to tell pupils

By Alice Steinbach and Will Englund

All of Thomas Johnson Middle School was geared up yesterday. Lessons shut down as televisions were turned on. The Snoopy poster in the lobby said it all: Printed across a large rocket were the words, "Good luck, Christa."

It was at this Prince George's County school that Christa McAuliffe, picked to be America's first teacher in space, had taught from 1971 to 1978.

And by 11:20 yesterday most of the 550 students were gathered around television sets in classrooms or in the school's large media center.

When the explosion came 74 seconds after liftoff, "the students were very quiet," said Darlene Musitano, a guidance counselor who had worked

See SCHOOLS, 8A, Col. 1

O's McGregor throttles Chicago, 8-1: 1G

TAMPA BAY MAKES BO JACKSON NO. 1 DRAFTEE: CHIEFS TAKE JOZWIAK: 1G

WEDNESDAY
APRIL 30, 1986

THE SUN
LIGHT · FOR · ALL

SPORTS FINAL

VOL. 298 NO. 141 BALTIMORE, MARYLAND 25 CENTS

Thousands of Soviets evacuated

Region of Ukraine contaminated by nuclear accident

Bethlehem Steel loses $91 million

Trautlein retires; units to be sold

By Ellen L. James
Sun Staff Correspondent

WILMINGTON, Del. — Donald H. Trautlein, Bethlehem Steel Corp.'s chairman for six years, announced his retirement yesterday as shareholders at the company's annual meeting here were told the company posted a first quarter loss of $91.8 million on sales of $1.17 billion.

As part of its struggle to stay liquid and stem the series of "devastating losses" that have bled the company in 15 of the last 17 quarters, Bethlehem said it would soon sell off more than $300 million worth of non-steel assets, including Kusan Inc., its nationwide plastics and building products subsidiary, which is worth $163 million.

Bethlehem's marine construction division, which includes the Sparrows Point shipyard in Baltimore, is one of the properties under "study" for possible sale as part of a survival strategy to focus all the company's limited resources on core steel operations, according to Walter F. Williams, Bethlehem's president and chief executive officer.

Beside Kusan, two Bethlehem divisions based in Baltimore are certain to be sold. One is the Buffalo Tank Division, which produces underground gas holding tanks. It employs 233 workers, including 94 at its main plant located in the Fairfield section of Baltimore. The other is the Fabricating Reinforcing Bar Division, a producer of steel bars for construction materials. It is located in South Baltimore and employs 50.

In an interview with reporters, Mr. Williams acknowledged yesterday there is a "slim chance" that Bethlehem's financial problems could compel it to try to reorganize under Chapter 11 of the federal bankruptcy code. In fact, he said, several steel companies could be headed for trouble if steel prices fail as much this year as they did in 1985.

Mr. Williams also confirmed that Bethlehem is negotiating with competitors, including U.S. Steel Corp., the nation's largest steel maker, for the sale of semifinished steel pro-

See BETHLEHEM, 12A, Col. 6

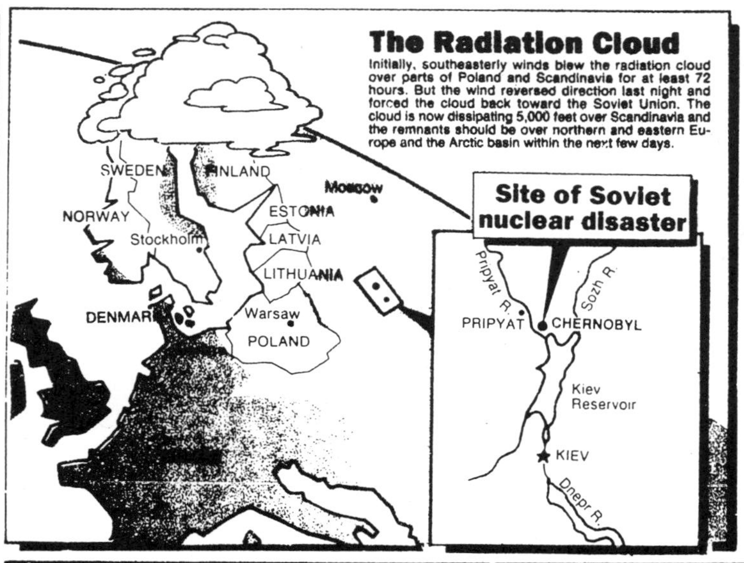

Chernobyl plant technicians, shown in February issue of *Soviet Life* magazine, work on top of reactor core.

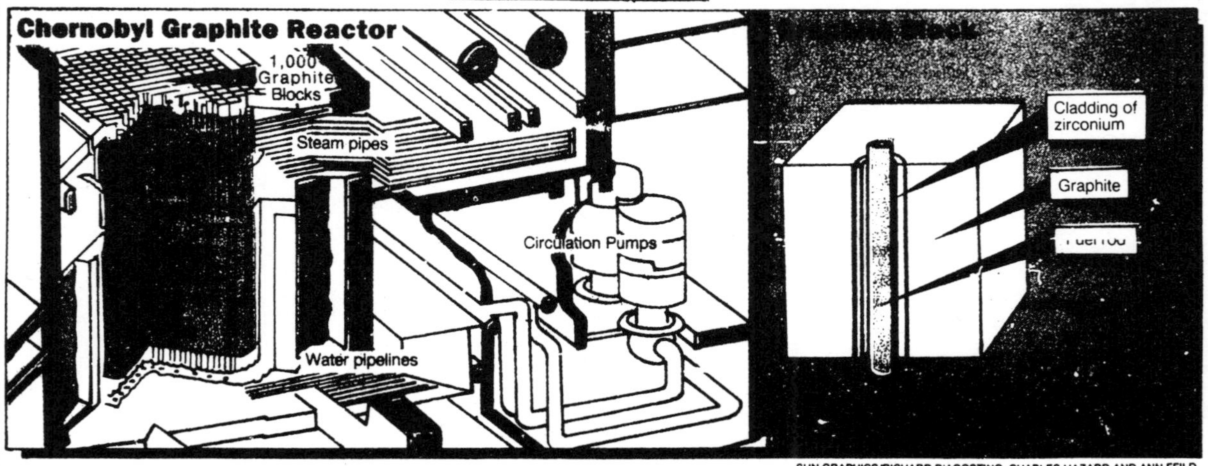

SUN GRAPHICS/RICHARD D'AGOSTINO, CHARLES HAZARD AND ANN FEILD

Help sought to contain graphite fire

By Antero Pietila
Moscow Bureau of The Sun

MOSCOW — Tens of thousands of residents have been evacuated from contaminated areas around a leaking Ukrainian nuclear power plant after a weekend accident there killed at least two people, Soviet authorities said last night.

But as Swedish experts were speculating that one of the Chernobyl nuclear power station's four reactors had melted down and as Soviet authorities themselves approached Sweden and West Germany for help in extinguishing burning graphite, a government statement offered little solid information about the accident.

The statement said that "two persons were killed during the accident" but did not disclose how many may have perished after the mishap or how many may have been affected by leaking radiation.

The 23-line statement disclosed that the inhabitants of the nuclear power station settlement and three nearby localities had been evacuated but gave no figures. It is believed that the town of Chernobyl alone has as many as 100,000 residents.

Because of general travel restrictions in the Soviet Union and a special security zone around the Chernobyl nuclear power station, visiting the area was impossible.

As Soviet authorities thus controlled the flow of information about the world's worst recorded nuclear power plant accident, they used their powers to reassure the population about the situation.

"Priority measures have been taken to deal with the effects of the

See NUCLEAR, 5A, Col. 5

Worst nuclear accident, scientists in West say

By Robert Ruby
Paris Bureau of The Sun

PARIS — Traces of radioactivity detected in Scandinavia from the Soviet Union's Chernobyl nuclear reactor suggest that the accident there was the most serious in the history of nuclear power, according to Western scientists.

There is strong evidence that the radiation in the plant and in the surrounding area reached lethal levels and that the severity of the accident was caused in part by the Soviet Union's using a reactor design lacking safety features considered standard in the West, specialists say.

Based on the radioactive contamination measured in the West and traced to the plant, West German scientists calculated yesterday that radiation in the immediate vicinity of the plant could have reached 1,000 rems an hour. Five hundred rems, if received over a short period of time, are generally fatal; a typical chest X-ray results in a small fraction of one rem.

"We cannot yet say that exactly this or that happened, but we know we have not had an accident like this in the West," said Werner Gries, a spokesman for West Germany's Research Ministry, where Soviet officials yesterday asked for assistance in getting the reactor under control. "We've calculated that lethal doses to workers and maybe to the public have been present."

See REACTORS, 4A, Col. 2

Chernobyl disaster

- ☐ After a CIA briefing, senators say that damage is extensive and that the disaster is far worse than any nuclear accident imagined. **7A**
- ☐ U.S. utility stock prices fall sharply, and stocks of firms with incomplete or unlicensed reactors are hurt most. **1E**
- ☐ Polish TV warns of a radioactive cloud. **3A**
- ☐ Soviet media carry almost nothing on Chernobyl, forcing residents to turn to Western broadcasts. **5A**
- ☐ A former Soviet scientist who defected says the Kremlin bureaucracy would be unable to cope with the crisis. **6A**
- ☐ For residents of Middletown, Pa., Chernobyl brings back memories of the Three Mile Island accident in 1979. **1C**

U.S. health risk is slight, EPA, local experts agree

By Vernon A. Guidry Jr. and Tom Horton
Sun Staff Correspondents

WASHINGTON — The Environmental Protection Agency yesterday ordered increased atmospheric radiation monitoring in the United States, but federal officials said it was unlikely that the Soviet nuclear disaster would prove a health threat in this country.

"If airborne contamination does reach this continent, it is unlikely to pose a significant risk to people because of the dilution that would occur during transport," said EPA spokesman Chris Rice.

Other administration officials said the accident at the reactor complex at Chernobyl near Kiev occurred Saturday.

These officials, relying on intelligence data, said the "fire was still clearly going" yesterday morning and smoke was coming from the reactor whose roof and walls had caved in.

The accident occurred at the southernmost of the four reactors in the complex. These administration sources said the adjoining reactor was apparently not out of danger, at least as of yesterday morning.

According to the EPA, it was not even certain contamination would reach North America based on sketchy information about the apparent reactor meltdown available yesterday afternoon.

See CLOUD, 4A, Col. 1

THE SUN
INSIDE

Scott McGregor hurls a four-hitter and Cal Ripken and Floyd Rayford homer as the Orioles beat the White Sox, 8-1. **1G**

Prosecutors reportedly will seek indictment of a former city parks official today on charges of masterminding a fraud scheme that netted him $90,000. **1B**

The government's main economic forecasting gauge rose 0.5 percent last month, signaling a rebound in economic growth. **1E**

Sunny today, fair tonight. High, 80; low, 60. Yesterday's high, 83; low, 60. **6B**

Index

Bridge	2C	Lottery	11G
Classified	1F	Movies	6C
Comics	7C	Obituaries	1F
Editorials	14A	Television	4C
Horoscope	8C	Weather	6B

8 SECTIONS

Shuttle seal was due to fail, test shows

New York Times News Service

WASHINGTON — New and unpublished test results show that a failure of a safety seal on the space shuttle Challenger was virtually inevitable because of a combination of cold temperatures on the morning of the launching and serious design flaws.

The test results, conducted for the presidential panel studying the accident and summarized for *The New York Times*, also determined that the joint would sometimes begin to fail at temperatures as high as 50 degrees Fahrenheit. In the past, officials of the National Aeronautics and Space Administration testified that they felt confident the shuttle could be launched at far lower temperatures without any undue risk to the crew.

The Challenger was launched Jan. 28 in 36-degree weather, but investigators estimate that the tem-

See SHUTTLE, 12A, Col. 1

THE SUN/BO RADER

Salutes for an astronaut

The remains of Christa McAuliffe, the schoolteacher-astronaut who died aboard the shuttle Challenger, were carried past an honor guard yesterday at Dover Air Force Base, Del. Her remains and those of the six other astronauts who died were flown to Dover yesterday. (Article on Page 12A)

Review urged of safety rules at U.S. plants

By Lynda Robinson
Special to The Sun

WASHINGTON — Noting that five U.S. nuclear reactors operate without accident-containment structures, lawmakers and anti-nuclear activists yesterday called for a reassessment of U.S. safety standards in the wake of the Soviet nuclear disaster.

"The fact is that we are currently witnessing an attack on nuclear safety in this country," declared Representative Edward J. Markey, D-Mass., chairman of the House Subcommittee on Energy Conservation and Power.

Mr. Markey cited the Nuclear Regulatory Commission's recent decision to issue new regulations limiting the federal government's ability to order safety improvements at operating reactors and its proposal for legislation that would curtail public participation in the licensing of new

See IMPACT, 5A, Col. 1

FINAL

The Evening Sun

Vol. 153—No. 22 BALTIMORE, MONDAY, MAY 19, 1986 25 CENTS

PRIDE OF BALTIMORE SINKS

8 rescued; 4 missing; 2 dead reportedly sighted

The Pride of Baltimore cruises in the outer harbor before the clipper ship started out last year on what proved to be a fatal voyage.

2 survivors follow lure of the wind

By Mike Adams
Evening Sun Staff

Two surviving crew members were drawn to the Pride of Baltimore by their love for adventure and wind-powered sailing vessels.

The veteran seamen, Joe McGeady, 26, of Severna Park, and Robert Foster, 23, of Alexandria, Va., were listed among the eight crew members who were rescued from a raft after the Pride sank during a violent storm in the Atlantic. Four other crew members are missing, two of them presumed dead.

Foster graduated in June from the Merchant Marine Academy in Kings Point, N.Y. As part of his training at the academy, he had voyaged to distant ports of the world aboard tankers and freighters.

McGeady comes from a sailing family. His parents own a 30-foot sailboat and he began taking sailing courses when he was in the sixth grade. His parents, Joseph and Emily McGeady, live in the 500 block of Bayberry Drive in Severna Park.

Emily McGeady said her son called about 4:30 a.m. today and told her the Pride had sunk. He said he and the other survivors had spent 4½ days in a raft before they were plucked from the sea by a tanker.

Mrs. McGeady said her son didn't give details about the sinking or the lost crew members. She said he gave her the map coordinates where the Pride sank and where the survivors were picked up. She said she used a map in her home to plot the coordinates and see where the incidents occurred.

Mrs. McGeady said her son made his first voyage on the Pride several years ago. She described him as an experienced seaman who knew the ship well.

"They had a good crew and they had good equipment," she said. "I

See SURVIVOR, A4, Col. 1

City symbol capsizes in a storm

By Frank D. Roylance
Evening Sun Staff

Baltimore's goodwill ship, the Pride of Baltimore, has sunk in the Atlantic after it was blown over in a storm somewhere east of the Bahamas.

Eight of the 12 crew members were rescued in good condition early today by a Norwegian tanker after drifting for 4½ days in a rubber life raft, said Christopher C. Hartman, secretary of the Pride's board of directors.

The other four crew members, including the captain, Armin Elsaesser 3rd, were missing at sea. Two of them are now presumed dead after survivors reported seeing two bodies floating face down in the sea after the sinking.

The U.S. Coast Guard and the Air Force have sent a total of five C-130 aircraft into the area to search for the missing crew members.

Hartman said the first word of the sinking was received at 5 a.m. today when one of the surviving crew members cabled the news from the Norwegian tanker Toro, which had plucked them from the Atlantic.

The cable indicated the sinking occurred about noon last Wednesday, May 14. The last contact from the crew was on Friday, May 9, when they telephoned Baltimore from St. Thomas, in the U.S. Virgin Islands.

"We had an experienced crew," Hartman said. "The captain had sailed it many times, and knew the ship as well as anybody."

Gail Shawe, executive director of the Pride of Baltimore Inc., the non-profit corporation that operates the ship, said, "We talked to [the survivors] this morning. . . . They are in pretty good shape."

See PRIDE, A5, Col. 1

Today

RELIEF FROM HEAT: Showers and thunderstorms likely tonight and tomorrow. Low tonight in the 60s. High tomorrow in the 70s.
DETAILS, A2

FELLS POINT FIRE: A spectacular, six-alarm blaze at the 100-year-old Terminal Warehouse in the 1600 block of Thames St. sends a dark cloud of smoke through Fells Point and the Inner Harbor.
METRO, D1

THE QUIET MAN: Eddie Murray goes on a tear—with the Orioles beating the A's, 13-4—and now, as usual, he is among league leaders in everything but interviews.
SPORTS EXTRA, C1

GETTING SEA LEGS: Naval Academy "youngsters," in their second year, are in a sleepy limbo: no longer lowly plebes but still not ready for leadership roles.
METRO, D1

Index

Tomorrow

Memorial Day ushers in the vacation season and teens want colorful, cool clothes for summer fun. See the best play clothes for juniors in Tuesday's Fashion Accent.

Racial bias turns subtle on Shore

First of two articles.
By Derek Reveron
Evening Sun Staff

ON THE STREETS OF downtown Centreville, blacks and whites move easily between banks, government buildings, restaurants and stores.

The view from the front lawn of the Queen Anne's County Courthouse yields no evidence that local blacks are excluded, unwelcome or shunted aside. But it's a different story inside the buildings.

Few blacks work downtown, and they are virtually absent from managerial positions. For example, one of 14 postal employees is black, and he is a janitor. One of 30 workers at a bank is black, and he also is a janitor.

A tour of 20 other business establishments in Centreville, the county seat, turns up three black employees: a young male clerk in a pharmacy, an elderly man working in a hardware store and a waitress.

Leaders in the black community say that, a quarter-century after the demise of legalized segregation, blacks in Queen Anne's still must travel the back roads of opportunity.

"Prejudice remains and it will always remain, but today this thing is subtle," says Leon Taylor, a retired teacher who has held high positions on county boards and commissions.

"There aren't too many blacks with prestigious jobs," Taylor says.

Sylvanus Brown, president of the county chapter of the National Association for the Advancement of Colored People, makes the same point more sharply. There are "very few" jobs of any kind for blacks in Queen Anne's, he says.

See BLACKS, A4, Col. 1

LEON TAYLOR
"Prejudice remains"

Photos by Jed Kirschbaum—Evening Sun Staff

Lawn-jockey statuettes are painful reminders for many blacks.

Rep. Parren Mitchell, down off the fence, decides not to run

By Michael A. Fletcher
Evening Sun Staff

Rep. Parren J. Mitchell, tears welling in his eyes, said today he would not run for re-election.

"I cannot seek another term," Mitchell told a packed press conference at his West Baltimore 7th Congressional District office.

"In my heart of hearts, as of now, I do not believe I can sustain the level of service that I have tried to maintain during my years of public service. This has been a wrenching, soul-searching decision, made all the more difficult because of the faith and confidence in me so many people have shown."

In 1984, when Mitchell contemplated retirement, supporters responded with the now familiar pleas of "Run, Parren, Run."

Mitchell, a Democrat, heard the same cries again this year.

Mitchell, who originally announced his retirement last October, decided to reconsider his decision this month at the request of an influential group of Baptist ministers.

The clergymen, members of the Baptist Ministers Conference, said Mitchell's experience was needed to lead the city's black community over the next two years, a time when a new mayor and governor are likely.

The ministers also reportedly were unimpressed with the candidates who had announced their intentions to seek the congressional seat Mitchell has held since 1971.

Mitchell met with the ministers today to inform them of his decision.

Democrats Augustus A. Adair, a Morgan State University professor; City Councilman Kweisi Mfume; Del. Wendell H. Phillips; A. Dwight Pettit, an attorney; and Hazel Judd, a follower of extremist Lyndon LaRouche, have filed for the race.

Sandra B. Stewart, a consultant; the Rev. Daki Napata, of the American Friends Service Committee, and the Rev. St. George Crosse 3rd, a Republican, say they will run.

State Sen. Clarence M. Mitchell 3rd, a nephew of the congressman, also was expected to enter the contest, but his plans now are unclear.

The younger Mitchell is under federal investigation on suspicion of influence-peddling, according to published reports.

Clarence Mitchell, who attended the press conference with four of the candidates who have officially entered the race, refused to comment.

"I'm here as a part of his family," he said. "I will make my plans known at the appropriate time."

When Parren Mitchell announced his decision to reconsider retirement, several political observers said Parren Mitchell was being asked to run to prevent the Mitchells—one of the great families of civil rights—from being embarrassed by any revelations arising from his nephew's investigation.

Parren Mitchell called such speculation an attack on his "personal integrity."

"This has been very, very hard on me," Mitchell said of the past two weeks. "It was almost a living hell . . . It hurts when people ascribe ulterior motives" to his decisions.

But Mitchell's decision to reconsider retirement put political plans of several of the candidates—most close allies—in jeopardy.

For that, Mitchell apologized. "If the delay in arriving at this final, binding decision has caused anyone anguish, I am truly, sincerely sorry that it did," Mitchell said.

His decision to retire came as good news to candidates vying to

See MITCHELL, A2, Col. 4

The 150th Anniversary Issue

SUNDAY
MAY 17, 1987

THE SUN

LIGHT FOR ALL

SUNNY
AND SUMMERY
SEE PAGE 24B

VOL. 87 NO. 19 BALTIMORE, MARYLAND $1.25

Immunity is given to Secord aide

Dutton reportedly links contra aid to Bush's staff

New York Times News Service

WASHINGTON — The special prosecutor in the Iran-contra case has granted immunity to a key figure in the operation, Robert C. Dutton, and has questioned him before a grand jury, according to a federal investigator and others with knowledge of the inquiry.

The investigator said Mr. Dutton was a "potential gold mine" for the special prosecutor, Lawrence E. Walsh. He is thought to be the most valuable witness to whom Mr. Walsh has granted immunity.

A retired Air Force colonel, Mr. Dutton helped run the private supply network for the Nicaraguan contras and was also linked to the shipment of American arms to Iran last year.

He worked with Richard V. Secord, the retired Air Force major general who is a leading suspect in Mr. Walsh's investigation.

An associate said Mr. Dutton was able to provide new information that indicates links between the contra supply effort and officials on the staff of Vice President George Bush.

Mr. Dutton, the associate said, has verified accounts provided by Mr. Secord of a meeting in the vice president's office last August with Felix Rodriguez, another leader of the contra supply effort. It remains unclear exactly who took part in the meeting.

According to a federal investigator, Mr. Dutton appeared before the grand jury within the last three weeks and has spent several hours in interviews with investigators working for Mr. Walsh.

Under a grant of immunity, Mr. Dutton cannot be prosecuted for crimes he discusses before the grand

See DUTTON, 14A, Col. 1

THE SUN/PERRY E. THORSVIK

Two down, one more to go

Jockey Chris McCarron held a trophy aloft as he stood in the Pimlico winner's circle with trainer Jack Van Berg (right) after winning the Preakness aboard Alysheba, who also won the Kentucky Derby. The McCarron-Van Berg team could get a sweep of the Triple Crown races in three weeks at the Belmont Stakes in New York. (Stories in Preakness Section C).

Soviets test huge rocket successfully

Launcher Energia a 'breakthrough'

From Wire Reports

MOSCOW — The Soviet Union yesterday announced the successful test launch of the world's most powerful rocket, capable of putting a 100 ton space shuttle into orbit.

The Energia, launched from the Baikonur space center in Kazakhstan on Friday at 7:30 p.m. Moscow time (11:30 a.m. EDT), was propelled by "the most powerful engines in the world today," a Soviet television reporter said on the evening news program last night.

The Energia can lift five times more weight than the next-largest Soviet launch vehicle, according to U.S. experts on the Soviet space program.

Eight liquid hydrogen engines, four of which hugged the rocket body in a configuration called "strap-on" by U.S. space experts, sent the 197-foot, two-stage rocket hurtling into the night sky atop a huge red column of flame.

"This is a major breakthrough for them," said James Oberg, an author and expert on the Soviet space program. Mr. Oberg said that three previous Soviet attempts to send up a heavyweight launch vehicle ended in failure in the late 1960s and early 1970s.

The total weight of the rocket and its dummy payload was more than 2,000 tons, the Soviet news agency Tass reported.

Tass said that the automated control system worked normally, and "the aims and objectives of the first launching have been fully met."

The news agency added that the on-board systems on a mock-up satellite that the rocket attempted to deploy failed and that the payload splashed into the Pacific Ocean instead of reaching orbit.

Soviet leader Mikhail S. Gorbachev, who visited Baikonur for three days last week, was reported to have told the Soviet technicians there not to "hurry" the launch of the Energia. "Check and weigh everything," Mr. Gorbachev said, according to Soviet television.

Tass said that the engines of the rocket's

See ROCKET, 13A, Col. 1

Army air defense a total departure from failed York

By Vernon A. Guidry Jr.
Sun Staff Correspondent

HUNTSVILLE, Ala. — The loss of the Sergeant York, the Army's junked air-defense gun, "was a very painful, very traumatic thing," recalls Brig. Gen. William J. Fiorentino, the man in charge of providing the hardware to solve the service's resulting air-defense crisis.

"We really wanted that program. We put a lot of our treasure into it . . . money, emotion, careers and all

First of two parts

the rest of it. When we lost it, I think it is fair to say the Army was shaken," he said.

But since Defense Secretary Caspar W. Weinberger canceled it in August 1985, the Army has completely abandoned the thinking that drove the once-cherished program, chiefly that a rapid-fire cannon could adequately protect tanks and infantry fighting vehicles from air attack at the front in a European war. In fact, it has abandoned the notion that a single weapon of any description could do it.

Those changes were the product of a basic re-examination of what the Soviet Union and its allies could do from the air, which was a great deal, and how it could be countered.

See FAADS, 13A, Col. 1

After 150 years of chronicling events, The Sun gives itself a party

By Phillip Davis
and Deborah I. Greene

The first copy of this newspaper was set by hand, covered four pages, had no photographs and cost a penny. The copy you are reading today — the 150th anniversary edition, and *The Sun*'s largest ever — was printed on computerized presses, weighs 6.1 pounds, runs 1,090 pages, comprises 24 sections, will have a circulation of at least 555,000, includes color photographs and costs $1.25.

No fireworks or civic celebrations accompanied the publication of Volume 1, No. 1 on Wednesday, May 17, 1837. But fireworks burst spectacularly over Baltimore's Inner Harbor last night as Maryland's largest newspaper threw a party for itself and its readers.

A crowd estimated at several hundred thousand — police last night said 500,000 — gathered at the water's edge, along Federal Hill and at the windows of the office, shopping and hotel buildings that symbolize Baltimore's renaissance. The fireworks followed free concerts, including performances by the Preservation Hall Jazz Band and Chuck Mangione.

The bursts were synchronized to pop and rock tunes — including "Here Comes the Sun" — broadcast on speakers and an FM radio station.

"We loved it, it was just like 3-D," said Jane Hildebrand of Westview, who was watching the thunderous finale with her husband, daughter and granddaughter. "They were just gorgeous."

"It's better than the Fourth of July," said her husband, Harry Hildebrand.

"At the end of 150 years of success, you need to put something back into the community — a communitywide celebration," Reg Murphy, president and publisher of *The Baltimore Sun*, commented earlier on the

See NEWSPAPER, 15A, Col. 3

Biotechnology is speeding up change

Altering life forms a Md. growth industry

BIOTECH
THE NEXT REVOLUTION
First of four parts

By Mary Knudson

Across from the National Aquarium in downtown Baltimore, University of Maryland scientists are trying to break a genetic code in search of a way to prevent bacteria and barnacles from destroying the submerged surfaces of ships.

In College Park, researchers will begin this summer trying to find a gene that makes a certain variety of plant resist disease, in hopes of transferring the gene to Maryland crops.

Johns Hopkins University and Health Service broke ground Friday on a $500 million park in East Baltimore to house scientists working on new drugs and other projects, following the University of Maryland's start late last year on a $7.6 million research center.

All of this activity is part of a technological revolution some experts believe will eclipse the computer age. This new biotechnology, as it is called, has emerged swiftly from a half-dozen key discoveries during the last three decades.

"Biotechnology is going to have a very forceful impact on society in the next century. It will transform the chemical industry, the energy industry, and most importantly, it will change the medical and health-care industries," said Michael K. Hooker, chancellor of the University of Maryland Baltimore County and a national authority on commercial biotechnology. "I think life is going to be radically changed, because of medical discoveries."

With tools such as gene splicing and switching, the new technology

See BIOTECH, 12A, Col. 1

THE SUN/WILLIAM G. HOTZ SR

Toxin gene glows under laboratory's fluorescent light.

5 yards put S. Africans on wrong side of law

By Peter Honey
Special to The Sun

JOHANNESBURG, South Africa — Nassim and Isa Pahad live five yards outside the law.

That's the distance from their front door to the middle of the road that marks the dividing line between the Indian and white sections of Johannesburg's Mayfair suburb.

The Pahads are Indian South Africans and live across the road from another Indian family. But the narrow stretch of tar is not all that separates them, for the Pahads are living officially — and illegally — in white Johannesburg.

It makes them, and not their neighbors, liable for prosecution under the Group Areas Act, the law that has ordained, in one form or another for 37 years, that South Africans of different races cannot live in the same neighborhood.

The Pahads knew what they were doing when they bought the property through a white nominee and built their house two years ago. They knew it could mean prosecution and the possible confiscation of their home.

But they were sick of a law that relegated them to the crowded Indian suburb of Lenasia, 20 miles away, while their import-export business depended on mainly white clients in the city center.

"I believe it is my God-given right to own a home of my choice, even though I am not granted that choice by the government," Mr. Pahad says.

Not long after they moved into their new home, the Pahads were visited by two policemen from the so-called Group Areas unit, who demanded a bribe to overlook their presence in the area. Mr. Pahad says he sent them packing.

"It doesn't help. It might buy a

See S. AFRICA, 4A, Col. 1

Inside The 150th Anniversary Issue

TUESDAY
OCTOBER 20, 1987

THE SUN

SPORTS FINAL

VOL. 301 NO. 134 | BALTIMORE, MARYLAND | 25 CENTS

Panic selling slashes Dow index by 508

U.S. attacks Iranian oil site, warning against retaliation

The U.S. operation

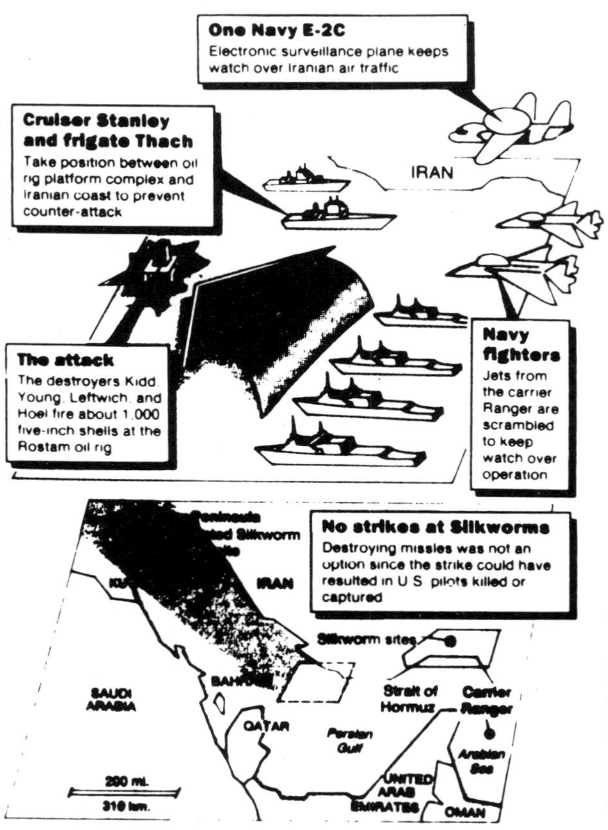
One Navy E-2C
Electronic surveillance plane keeps watch over Iranian air traffic
Cruiser Stanley and frigate Thach
Take position between oil rig platform complex and Iranian coast to prevent counter-attack
IRAN
The attack
The destroyers Kidd, Young, Leftwich, and Hoel fire about 1,000 five-inch shells at the Rostam oil rig
Navy fighters
Jets from the carrier Ranger are scrambled to keep watch over operation
No strikes at Silkworms
Destroying missiles was not an option since the strike could have resulted in U.S. pilots killed or captured
IRAN
Silkworm sites
SAUDI ARABIA
BAHRAIN
QATAR
Strait of Hormuz
Carrier Ranger
Persian Gulf
Arabian Sea
UNITED ARAB EMIRATES
OMAN
200 mi.
319 km.

SUN GRAPHICS/TONY DEFERIA

By Robert Ruby
Sun Staff Correspondent

DUBAI, United Arab Emirates — U.S. Navy warships destroyed an Iranian oil platform complex yesterday in the Persian Gulf in an attack accompanied by a warning from the United States of still stronger actions if Iran made a military response.

U.S. Defense Secretary Caspar W. Weinberger said in Washington that four destroyers fired on a platform in the central gulf about 75 miles south of Iran in retaliation for a missile attack Friday on a U.S.-flagged tanker, an attack the United States blamed on Iran.

A Pentagon spokesman said the destroyers began their bombardment at 2 p.m. (7 a.m. EDT) and fired 1,000 5-inch shells, without encountering return fire. The Pentagon said there were no American casualties.

Twenty to 30 Iranians were on the platform before the attack began and were given 20 minutes' warning to leave, Mr. Weinberger said. It remained unclear last night whether any of the Iranians, who tried to escape in at least one small boat, had been injured.

Both President Reagan and Mr. Weinberger said the attack was designed to reply in kind to Iranian actions rather than to mark an escalation.

Although U.S. officials portrayed the action as the closing of a chapter, Iran, in its first public comments on the attack, warned that it would inexorably lead to more serious conflict.

Iran's official Islamic Republic News Agency initially reported that U.S. forces had attacked two platforms about 30 miles apart, and it

See GULF, 5A, Col. 3

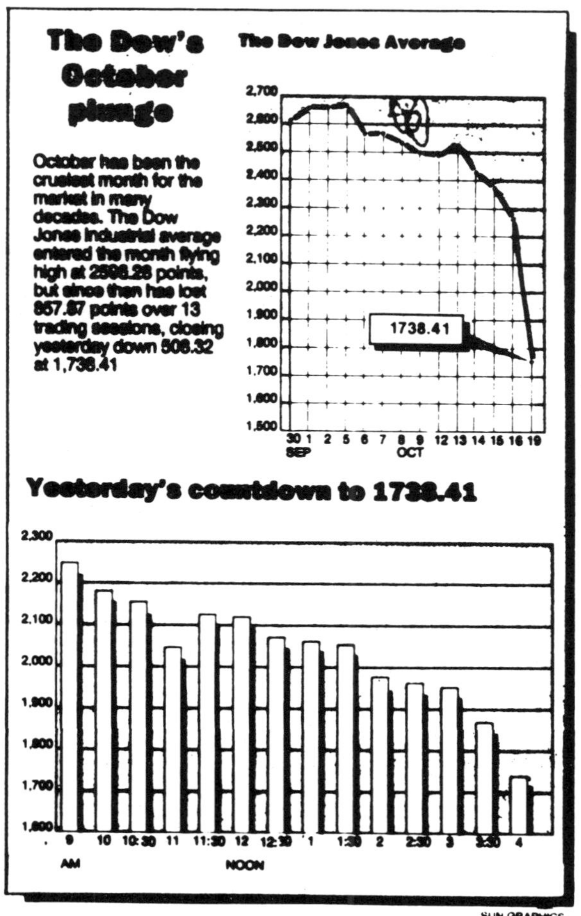
The Dow's October plunge
The Dow Jones Average
October has been the cruelest month for the market in many decades. The Dow Jones industrial average entered the month flying high at 2596.28 points, but since then has lost 857.87 points over 13 trading sessions, closing yesterday down 508.32 at 1,738.41
2,700
2,600
2,500
2,400
2,300
2,200
2,100
2,000
1,900
1,800
1,700
1,600
1738.41
30 1 2 5 6 7 8 9 12 13 14 15 16 19
SEP
OCT
Yesterday's countdown to 1738.41
2,300
2,200
2,100
2,000
1,900
1,800
1,700
1,600
9 10 10:30 11 11:30 12 12:30 1 1:30 2 2:30 3 3:30 4
AM
NOON

SUN GRAPHICS

Collapse exceeds percentage loss before Depression

By Thomas Easton
New York Bureau of the Sun

NEW YORK — The bull market of 1987 disappeared yesterday, butchered by unprecedented waves of trading that sent the Dow Jones industrial average crashing 508.32 points to 1,738.41 in a collapse that exceeded even the one immediately preceding the Great Depression.

The financial markets lost $636 billion in value yesterday alone, and $1.173 trillion since the Dow peaked at 2,722 Aug. 25, estimated Hugh Johnson, an analyst at First Albany Corp. "This is a financial panic," Mr. Johnson said. "It's a game of confidence, and the confidence has been shattered."

The reverberations appeared throughout the world with market after market reporting serious declines.

In percentage terms, the market dropped 22.6 percent yesterday, as opposed to a mere 12.8 percent on the commencement of the 1929 debacle. Indeed, not since the 24 percent decline of 1914 has a decline of greater magnitude been recorded.

The implications of the most recent slide are far from certain but potentially devastating. Some pensions, once considered overfunded because of huge stock gains in their portfolios, now may have too little to meet expected obligations.

Firms recently refinanced with junk debt have seen rapid deterioration in their balance sheets at the same time as the interest on their loans is rising. They could face insolvency. And brokerage houses themselves are at risk, with one firm publicly denying rumors that it had been badly, if not fatally, damaged by recent trading losses.

Volume of 604.4 million shares on the New York Stock Exchange was beyond anything seen, planned

See MARKET, 6A, Col. 2

Reagan says strike in gulf was 'restrained'

By Robert Timberg and Stephens Broening
Washington Bureau of The Sun

WASHINGTON — President Reagan called the U.S. attack on an Iranian oil platform complex in the Persian Gulf yesterday a "prudent yet restrained response" to Iran's previous belligerent actions and warned that the United States was determined to protect its interests in the region.

"The United States has no desire for a military confrontation with Iran, but the government of Iran should be under no illusion about our determination and ability to protect our ships and our interests against unprovoked attack," the president said in a written statement.

Late yesterday, the United States was preparing a diplomatic note for Iran warning of further military action should the Iranians continue their attacks on U.S.-flagged ships, senior administration officials said.

Officials said the note would emphasize that yesterday's attack was

See REAGAN, 4A, Col. 4

Choosing response began hours after tanker attack

By Robert Timberg
Washington Bureau of The Sun

WASHINGTON — President Reagan put aside temporarily Friday morning his concern for his wife, who was to enter a hospital for an operation for possible cancer later that day, and set in motion a chain of events that culminated in yesterday's U.S. action in the Persian Gulf.

The president learned early Friday morning that a U.S.-flagged tanker, the Sea Isle City, had been struck by a suspected Iranian Silkworm missile and that several crewmen, including the ship's American captain, had been wounded.

At about 10 a.m., two hours before presidential spokesman Marlin Fitzwater would announce that Mrs. Reagan would be undergoing surgery for possible breast cancer, Mr. Reagan headed for the Situation Room in the basement of the White House to discuss the gulf situation.

The president presided over a meeting of the National Security Planning Group, which includes top officials from the executive departments and agencies that make up the nation's national security apparatus.

The president held a strategy session the day his wife was to have surgery for possible breast cancer.

A number of retaliatory options, maybe a dozen in all, were presented to Mr. Reagan at the meeting, but no decisions were made. "They were all over the board at that time," said a senior White House official of the alternative proposals.

The official, who spoke on the condition he not be named, said Mr. Reagan laid down at the meeting broad criteria that would guide the administration's deliberations over the next day or so and ultimately result in yesterday's naval bombardment.

Mr. Reagan, the official said, told his lieutenants that the U.S. re-

See DECISION, 5A, Col. 3

Markets around world continue record tailspin

From Staff and Wire Reports

TOKYO — Stock prices fell record levels in early trading today on the Tokyo Stock Exchange as the market, reflecting a massive plunge on Wall Street, was gripped by an onslaught of sell orders.

At the end of the morning session, the first section of the Nikkei Stock average had fallen 7.45 percent in value, while the second-section index had fallen 5.16 percent.

The morning declines in Tokyo, as on Wall Street yesterday, far surpassed the largest previous one-day decline.

In Hong Kong, where the main index fell 10 percent yesterday, officials of the stock exchange held a special meeting and then announced they were suspending trading until Monday.

Australia's all-ordinaries index dropped 20.2 percent of its value in its first hour.

Sources in the Tokyo exchange, the largest in the world in terms of total value of shares traded, said the market was almost completely flooded with sell orders. Trading in the market's first section totaled a relatively small 10 million shares during the morning session.

"As I speak, about 80 percent of the stocks on the board are untraded because of a deluge of sell orders," one Japanese trader said.

See GLOBAL, 6A, Col. 6

Stocks recede

- President Reagan says he remains convinced that the economy is sound. [illegible]
- Mutual fund and foreign investors apparently had a key role in sending the market into a tailspin. 9A
- Many mutual fund shareholders who joined the frantic sell-off switched to bond and money-market funds. [illegible]
- Bond prices rebound as investors flee the plunging stock market. [illegible]

On Wall St. or in Pikesville, it was grim

By Ted Shelsby

It was a tough day for the "regulars" at the Legg Mason office in Pikesville.

These are the half-dozen investors — most of them retirees with more than a casual interest in the stock market — who gather daily in the board room of the investment office to monitor the ticker tape, brag about the wisdom of past moves that turned out right, and bemoan the great opportunities that could have been.

While they occasionally laughed and tried to project an upbeat attitude toward yesterday's stock-market plunge, which rivaled the Great Crash of 1929, there were expressions of concern showing on their faces.

"My God," groaned Peter Soltman do at around 1:30 p.m., when the Dow Jones industrial average was down 193 points after having rebounded slightly from its earlier low. "My God."

"I think we are seeing a panic market," said Philip Vaio. "Things are going to stabilize in a day or two, and then there will be a tremendous comeback. For myself, I'm looking for some buys. It looks like an opportunity to pick up some bargains.

"If I'm wrong, I jump off the step," he added with a laugh.

He was referring to the two steps leading into the Legg Mason office from the curb.

See INVESTORS, 6A, Col. 1

Arundel starts new sentencing program tied to home by phone

By Tom Bowman
Anne Arundel Bureau of The Sun

ANNAPOLIS — A man's home might be his castle, but it could turn into a prison for some Anne Arundel County offenders.

County Executive O. James Lighthizer yesterday unveiled a new sentencing program allowing those convicted of drunken driving or other minor crimes to remain at home but verify their presence to corrections officials through the use of a visual telephone.

"It's not an alternative to prison, it's an alternative to freedom," said Mr. Lighthizer.

It will provide judges a sentencing option that stops short of incarceration but is more stringent than probation.

Known as the House Arrest Alternate Sentencing Program (HAASP), the program will begin the first week of November with the leasing of 30 "Telecoms," which allow correction officials to see offenders they are calling through a camera system.

The offenders are to bear the $24,000 cost of the system, based on their ability to pay.

Anne Arundel County will be the first jurisdiction in Maryland to use the Telecom system, which has been used in several other states, including Virginia, to keep track of parolees.

It has never been used as a sentencing alternative, county officials said.

The Telecom system works over standard phone lines and requires the installation of camera and monitor equipment in the offender's home. It provides officials at the county detention center with a television picture, as well as a hard copy photograph of the offender, along with a time stamp. It also has a breathalyzer attached that flashes the offender's results on the screen.

The system has a privacy feature

See PHONES, [illegible]

Goetz receives 6 months on handgun charge

NEW YORK (AP) — Subway gunman Bernhard Goetz was sentenced yesterday to six months in jail, ordered to see a psychiatrist and fined $5,000 by a judge who rejected a probation report that recommended Goetz go free.

Goetz, whose shooting of four youths nearly three years ago touched off a nationwide debate over vigilantism, stood impassively as acting state Supreme Court Justice Stephen G. Crane sentenced him on the single gun possession count of which he was convicted.

The crime carries a maximum penalty of seven years in prison, although first-time offenders like Goetz rarely go to jail.

Goetz, who was acquitted of more serious charges in the shootings, [illegible] was sentenced to five years probation and 280 hours of community service at New York University Medical Center.

A [illegible] jail sentence for Mr. Goetz

See GOETZ, [illegible]

THE SUN
INSIDE

A Curtis Bay chemical firm is charged with water pollution. 1C

Noboru Takeshita picked as Japan's next prime minister. 2A

Billy Martin is named manager of the New York Yankees for the fifth time. 1D

Home health kits are a big and growing business. Tabloid

Cloudy, chance of afternoon and evening showers. High 68, low 50. Yesterday's high 68, low 50. 12C

Index

Dogged pursuit was presidential threat

Mating dogs killed; Kan. runway safe

TOPEKA, Kan. (AP) — Security guards killed two dogs mating near an airport runway last month out of fear they posed a danger to a plane carrying President Reagan.

The incident has prompted letters of complaint to the White House and threats on the life of the man who ordered the shooting.

"We did what we had to do," said Marvin Hancock, deputy director of the Metropolitan Topeka Airport Authority. "We were told anything that moves has to be removed."

Mr. Hancock said Forbes Field security officers were combing the grounds Sept. 6 just before Mr. Reagan's scheduled arrival on Air Force One. Mr. Reagan was traveling to Topeka for a 100th birthday celebration for former Gov. Alf Landon, who died last week.

Douglas W. Buchholz, special agent in charge of the Secret Service's Kansas City office, said airport security had been ordered to "take care of the problem" of the dogs, but he said he did not know shooting the animals was going to be the solution.

Security officers first beat the dogs with heavy welding gloves in order to separate them. When that failed, they shot the dogs, Mr. Hancock said. The bodies were carted off in plastic bags and burned.

Mr. Hancock said the dogs might have entered the runway and interfered with the Boeing 707 jet carrying the president. He said there

See DOGS, [illegible]

THURSDAY

THE SUN

SPORTS FINAL

VOL. 304 NO. 31 — BALTIMORE, MARYLAND — 25 CENTS

747 bound for N.Y. crashes in Scotland

ASSOCIATED PRESS

Buildings burn in Lockerbie, Scotland, after a Pan Am 747 crashed in the village. Wreckage of the plane can be seen in the foreground.

Of 258 aboard, no survivors are expected

By Gilbert A. Lewthwaite
London Bureau of The Sun

LONDON — A Pan Am jumbo jet carrying 258 passengers and crew, including a number of Americans heading home for Christmas, plunged 31,000 feet to crash in a fireball in a Scottish village yesterday.

No survivors were expected from the wreckage of Frankfurt-London-New York-Detroit Pan American World Airways Flight 103. The Boeing 747 Clipper Maid of the Seas carried 243 passengers, including three children, and 15 crew members.

A Maryland man, Army 1st Lt. George W. Williams of Joppatowne, 24, who was returning home for Christmas, was among those aboard the plane.

["The aircraft clearly experienced some form of explosion," said Scottish Secretary Malcolm Rifkind, the Associated Press reported. But Mr. Rifkind, who arrived early at the scene early today, refused to speculate on the cause.

[Some 40 homes in the village of Lockerbie were destroyed as a result of the crash, killing an unknown number of people, the AP said. The Royal Air Force said the plane "demolished two rows of houses. There are no survivors from those houses."]

Houses and cars in Lockerbie, a community of 3,000 people 10 miles from the English-Scottish border, were ablaze around a 40-foot-deep crater left by the impact of the crash, which centered on a gas station.

Choking smoke and fumes billowed throughout the village, and police said wreckage and victims were spread over a wide area. Nine or 10 bodies were found miles from the main crash. The forward section of the plane was found three miles east of Lockerbie, near the village of Tundergarth.

Jim Ferguson, an aviation expert with *Flight International* magazine, said: "We are looking at something catastrophic. It could be structural failure. It could be sabotage. They have ruled out midair collision."

See **PLANE**, 8A, Col. 4

Monitoring ordered for BG&E plant

Safety violations upset commission

By Liz Bowie

The Nuclear Regulatory Commission put Calvert Cliffs nuclear power plant on its list of plants in need of special monitoring yesterday, signaling its dismay over repeated safety violations.

Short of closing the plant, the NRC could have taken no stronger regulatory action to tell the Baltimore Gas & Electric Co. that it needs to improve its performance at the plant, which generates half of central Maryland's power. Only 10 of 108 nuclear reactors generating electricity in the nation are on the NRC list.

"We are not arguing with the NRC action," said Edward A. Crooke, BG&E's president and chief operating officer. "Our focus now is on what can be done to correct the problem."

The action will increase the number of NRC inspectors based at the plant to determine why problems have occurred. Currently, two inspectors are assigned to the plant, which is 50 miles southeast of Baltimore on the Chesapeake Bay.

The NRC move was based on the plant's poor safety performance in the past year, which resulted in $450,000 in NRC fines since mid-April.

But three incidents this summer in particular led the NRC to list the plant as one that needed special attention.

In each incident, BG&E workers didn't follow the proper procedures

See **BG&E**, 4A, Col. 5

Delayed by traffic jam, Md. man took Flight 103

By Phillip Davis

First Lt. George W. Williams of Joppatowne didn't want to be on Pan Am Flight 103 — but because of a traffic jam, he was on the Boeing 747 that crashed in Scotland yesterday.

"I just talked to him this morning," his father, George Williams, said last night from his home in the 300 block of Garnett Road. "Because he missed his flight from Frankfurt ... he had to make new connections. He told me there was a big backup on the Autobahn," he said, referring to West Germany's high-speed highway.

Mr. Williams and his wife, Judy, spent last night waiting by the phone until Pan Am officials called about 11 p.m. to tell them their son had been aboard Flight 103.

Although only 24, Lieutenant Williams seemed content with making the Army his life, his father said. He won an ROTC scholarship after graduating from Joppatowne High School in 1982 and attended Tulane University before graduating from Western Maryland College in 1986.

He was stationed at Bad Kreuznach, an Army base near Frankfurt, where he was a helicopter crewman. Because of his extensive training in helicopter operations, Lieutenant Williams, who was single, was serving a three-year tour in West Germany and had been there a year and a half.

"He enjoyed being in the army. He enjoyed his time in Germany. He was doing well — he was up for the captain's list next month," his father said.

Mr. Williams, known as Harvey to his friends, called Pan Am as soon as he heard the news of the crash. "They checked everything out and told us there was a G. Williams aboard the flight, and that he didn't make the connecting flight from New York . . ." he said.

A longtime friend of the lieutenant, Steven K. Downing of the first block of Rambling Oaks Way in Catonsville, remembered the young man last night as "a real good guy."

"He'd do anything for you," Mr. Downing said. "He was just a great

See **WILLIAMS**, 8A, Col. 6

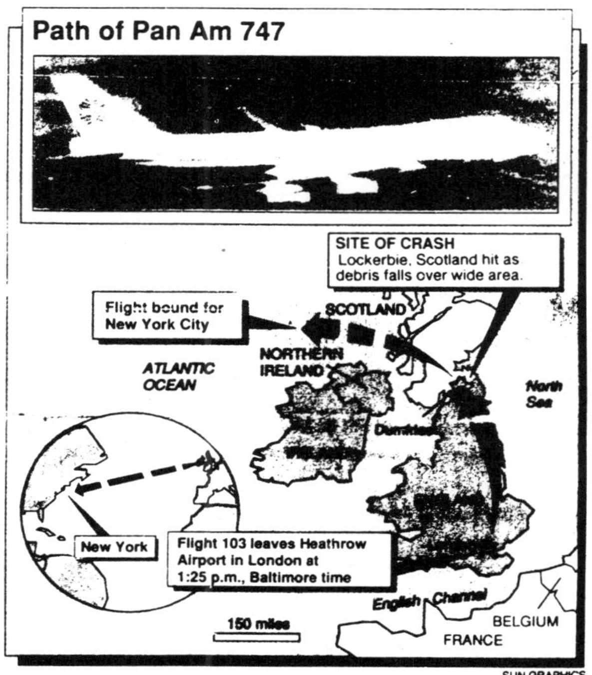

SUN GRAPHICS

Army specialist is arrested as spy suspect

Los Angeles Times

WASHINGTON — Moving to shut off what one official called "a massive hemorrhage" of U.S. defense secrets to East Germany and the Soviet Union, federal agents yesterday arrested an Army specialist in electronic eavesdropping equipment and a Turkish citizen accused of serving as his courier in a six-year espionage operation.

Warrant Officer James W. Hall III, 30, whose "high-living style" first alerted U.S. authorities, was arrested by Army intelligence agents at Fort Stewart, Ga., after detailing his espionage activities in the United States and West Germany to an undercover FBI agent posing as a Soviet intelligence officer. No charges have yet been filed against Warrant Officer Hall.

Huseyin Yildirim, 60, a Turkish national living in Florida who is also known as "Meister," was arrested in Tampa, Fla., by FBI agents on charges of conspiring with Warrant Officer Hall and "others" to turn over defense secrets to foreign agents.

Federal law enforcement sources said Warrant Officer Hall had been paid at least $100,000 for selling Army secrets to the East Germans and

See **SPY**, 9A, Col. 1

Drexel to pay $650 million fraud fine

Few details released in record settlement

By Thomas Easton
New York Bureau of The Sun

NEW YORK — The largest investigation ever aimed at a participant in the U.S. financial markets culminated yesterday in an "agreement in principle" under which the investment bank Drexel Burnham Lambert Inc. will pay at least $650 million in penalties and plead guilty to six felony counts.

The sketchy surrender by Drexel follows a two-year investigation and months of intermittent negotiations with federal prosecutors and remains contingent upon approval by the Securities and Exchange Commission as well as by the U.S. Department of Justice.

In response to a cacophony of rumors that had steadily swelled during recent weeks, an announcement, devoid of all but the slimmest details, was broadcast over Drexel's intercom system by Chief Executive Frederick Joseph at about 5 p.m.

The settlement was confirmed shortly thereafter by the government in a packed news conference hastily arranged in Manhattan.

U.S. Attorney Rudolph W. Giuliani called the terms of the agreement "more than sufficient" to satisfy the government.

"We are dealing with a corporate entity, not an individual," he said.

The prior record for a monetary settlement was the $100 million paid by jailed financier Ivan F. Boesky, who was an informant for the government in its case against Drexel. Drexel will pay $500 million immediately and $50 million annually for each of the next three years, according to sources.

Moreover, Drexel will have to hire an accounting firm to provide more information to the government. That suggests the investigation into Drex-

See **DREXEL**, 4A, Col. 3

City hires special counsel for probe of public works

By Brian Sullam

The city Board of Estimates approved yesterday the hiring of a special counsel to investigate the propriety of Public Works Department officials soliciting contributions from contractors and consultants to pay for a department Christmas party.

Mayor Kurt L. Schmoke said the Board of Ethics, which has been asked to investigate the fund raising by public works chief George G. Balog and other department officials, indicated that "from an appearance standpoint" it would be best for an outside attorney to conduct its investigation.

The Board of Estimates approved the hiring of Andrew J. Graham for a fee of $22,000 with little fanfare. Mr. Balog, one of the five members on the board, did not attend the meeting, and his deputy, George Winfield, abstained from voting.

Mr. Schmoke said that the Ethics Board chairman, Alan Yuspeh, took the unusual step of asking for outside counsel because he felt that lawyers from the city solicitor's office might not appear totally impartial.

See **COUNSEL**, 4A, Col. 1

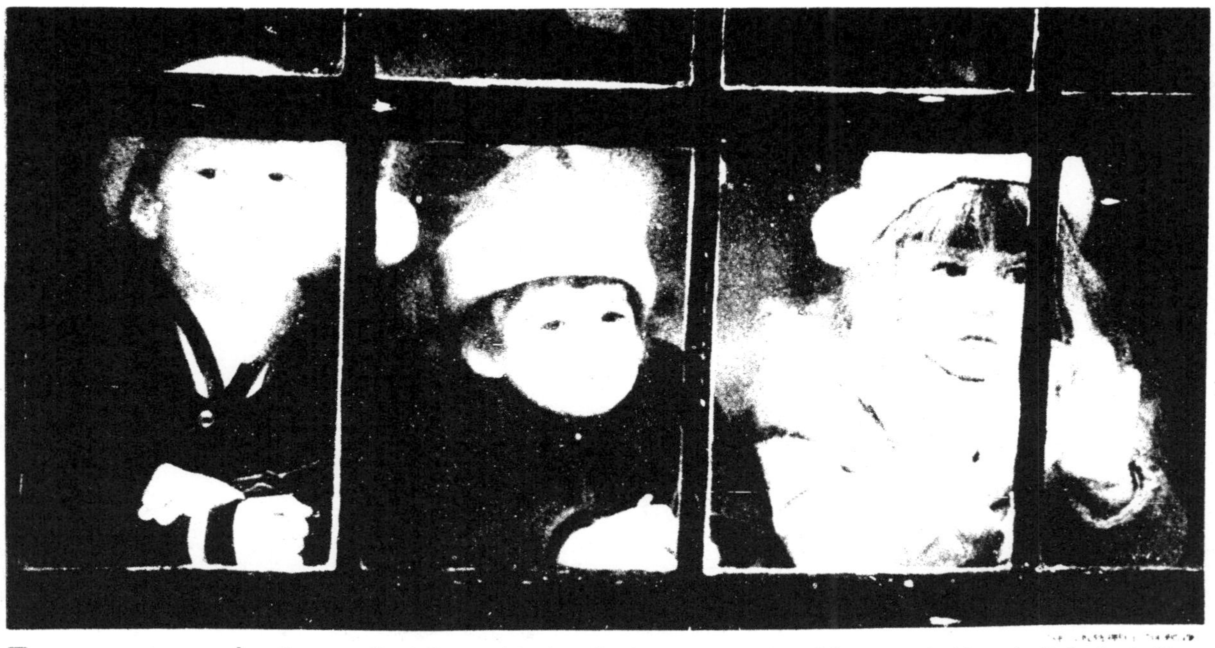

Faces at a window Kurtis Hargett (left), Amy Brocious (center) and April Parsons waited impatiently for Santa Claus to arrive by horse drawn buggy yesterday at St. John's Cooperative Nursery School in Linthicum.

8 arms makers probed in alleged buying of secrets

Knight-Ridder News Service

WASHINGTON — Eight major defense contractors, including Bethesda-based Martin Marietta, are under criminal investigation for illegally buying top-secret Pentagon documents to give them an edge in competing for contracts, a top Pentagon official said yesterday.

John F. Donnelly, director of the Pentagon's Defense Investigative Service, identified the firms as Boeing, General Dynamics, Litton, Martin Marietta, McDonnell Douglas, Northrop, Sanders Associates and TRW.

The eight defense firms have been "involved in what appeared to be systemic company-approved activities," Mr. Donnelly said. The cases have been referred to Pentagon criminal investigators for further investigation and possible prosecution, he said.

This investigation is separate from a similar probe, code-named Operation Ill Wind, that was made

See **DEFENSE**, 9A, Col.

THE SUN

INSIDE

FRIDAY
MAY 5, 1989

THE SUN
LIGHT · FOR · ALL

SPORTS FINAL

VOL. 304 NO. 146 — BALTIMORE, MARYLAND — 25 CENT

North convicted on three counts

'Victory' is declared by students

Chinese protesters to return to classes

By John Schidlovsky
Beijing Bureau of The Sun

BEIJING — China's student protesters declared "victory" yesterday and promised to return to classes today following a concession by Communist Party boss Zhao Ziyang, who announced plans for "extensive consultations and dialogues" with "students, workers, intellectuals, non-communist parties and leading personages from all walks of life."

The students ended their 18-day siege of the government with a huge march for democracy yesterday on the anniversary of China's most famous campaign for democracy 70 years ago.

For the second time in eight days, more than 100,000 students and supporters — including Chinese journalists protesting censorship — paralyzed the capital of the world's most populous nation, winning cheers from onlookers as they marched for greater freedom in defiance of a government move to block the demonstration.

Surging through rows of helpless police, the student protesters arrived triumphantly in central Tiananmen Square, where they unfurled banners demanding democracy and where they sang the communist anthem, the Internationale, in an apparent climax to the largest protest demonstrations in Communist China's 40-year history.

"It is magnificent, isn't it?" said a 22-year-old graduate student from Nanjing as he stood in the square yesterday afternoon and surveyed

See **CHINA**, 6A, Col. 3

ASSOCIATED PRESS
The space shuttle Atlantis lifts off launch pad at Cape Canaveral.

Honduran deal to help contras denied by Bush

By Sheila Dresser
Washington Bureau of The Sun

WASHINGTON — President Bush adamantly denied yesterday that while vice president he had promised the president of Honduras increased aid in retui ı for helping the Nicaraguan contras at a time when Congress had barred the administration from assisting the rebels.

"The allegation that's been made on me was that I went to Honduras and talked to President Suazo about some quid pro quo," Mr. Bush said yesterday at a news conference. "I can now state declaratively, without any fear of contradiction, that there wasn't."

There had been speculation that Mr. Bush could have made the plan clear to President Roberto Suazo Cordova without stating it in blunt terms. But Mr. Bush ruled that out yesterday also.

"The word of the president of the United States, George Bush, is: There was no quid pro quo," he said firmly. "The records of the meeting demonstrate that there was no quid pro quo . . . no implication, no quid pro quo, direct or indirect" during the visit to Honduras in March 1985.

"Everybody that attended the meeting says there was no quid pro quo. And for those who suggest there was, the onus is on them" to prove it, the president said.

Mr. Bush went even further later in the press conference, when he said that aside from the question of his own meeting with Mr. Suazo, "as far as I know" there was also no government-to-government arrangement at the time.

Disclosure of the meeting with President Suazo came during Oliver L. North's criminal trial. Several documents released during the trial suggested that the Reagan administration planned to use U.S. aid as a lever to get help for the contras from Honduras, where many rebel base camps were located.

One document used the words "quid pro quo" in discussing aid to Honduras, and another outlined a plan to use a "special emissary" to President Suazo to explain the U.S. linkage. When Mr. Bush met with the Honduran president, he told Mr. Suazo that President Reagan had or-

See **BUSH**, 13A, Col. 1

ASSOCIATED PRESS
Oliver North arrives at his lawyer's office after the verdict.

Backers foresee political future for ex-Marine

By Mark Matthews
Washington Bureau of The Sun

WASHINGTON — In the words of F. Andy Messing Jr., one of his most devoted supporters, he's now "a flawed American hero."

Oliver L. North, jobless and suddenly stripped of his U.S. Marine Corps pension, now faces what he says is "many months and perhaps years" of fighting his conviction on three federal felony counts.

But among a core of prominent conservative activists, "Olliemania" survives. With it comes pressure for an eventual pardon.

"George Bush will be in big trouble with conservatives if this man goes to jail," says Paul Weyrich, president of the Free Congress Research and Education Foundation.

With it also comes the potential organizational and fund-raising basis for a future in public life if he wants one, various movement officials say.

"Overnight," says L. Brent Bozell,

See **FUTURE**, 9A, Col. 2

Jurors find for acquittal on nine charges

By Lyle Denniston and Mary Beth Marklein
Washington Bureau of The Sun

WASHINGTON — Oliver L. North, a once-obscure Marine who rose to a dominant role in managing a secret war against Nicaragua from his office in the White House complex, was found guilty of three crimes yesterday.

A jury, breaking a deadlock with a "strong prayer," decided early in the afternoon to convict him on two counts of attempting to hide key facts about the Iran-contra scandal and one count of accepting an illegal gift in return for some of his official help for the contras.

It found him not guilty on nine other charges.

On one of the cover-up counts, the jury concluded that he was not the principal figure in a cover-up attempt but only "aided and abetted" someone else.

On the other, it found him guilty of destroying official government records — a conviction that means that, in addition to facing a criminal sentence, he loses his status as a retired Marine lieutenant colonel and his $1,900-a-month pension.

The pension would be reimbursed if he wins a planned appeal.

At the same time, the jury found North innocent of a variety of other cover-up crimes, including allegedly lying repeatedly to Congress and to a presidential fact-finding inquiry set up by then-President Ronald Reagan after the scandal broke.

In the most important criminal case yet to emerge from the complex plan to sell U.S. arms secretly to Iran and use some of the profits to buy weapons for the Nicaraguan contras, the jury picked and chose its way through a 12-count indictment and came up with a verdict in the 64th hour of deliberations on the 12th day.

If he receives maximum sentences on all three counts on which he was found guilty, North could be sentenced to 10 years in prison and fined $750,000.

U.S. District Judge Gerhard A.

See **NORTH**, 8A, Col. 3

Congress OKs $1.2 trillion budget accord

WASHINGTON (AP) — The House and Senate voted yesterday to approve $1.2 trillion budgets that uphold a much-criticized agreement with President Bush to reduce the deficit without cutting spending or significantly raising taxes.

Both chambers rejected several attempts to overhaul their blueprints for tax and spending policy in fiscal 1990 and then ratified the packages strongly in their final votes.

The House approved its plan, 263-157, after the budget committee chairman, Leon E. Panetta, D-Calif., called it "the only choice for us to fulfill our budget responsibilities and avoid crisis."

The Senate then passed its version, 68-31, after some minor tinkering and much grumbling that the deficit reduction in it was inadequate.

"It's clearly an attempt for this administration to be able to muddle its way through its first year," said Sen. Lloyd Bentsen, D-Texas, who was the Democrats' vice-presidential candidate last year.

Both chambers overwhelmingly rejected more ambitious proposals to "freeze" government spending and cut further into the deficit. The House also soundly defeated a pro-

See **BUDGET**, 13A, Col. 6

Atlantis roars into orbit, slings probe toward Venus

CAPE CANAVERAL, Fla. (AP) — The shuttle Atlantis found a hole in the clouds and thundered into orbit yesterday, sailing 184 miles above Earth, where five astronauts later propelled NASA's $550 million Magellan probe on a mapmaking journey to Venus.

The Magellan spacecraft, reviving a U.S. planetary-science program that has been dormant for a decade, slipped from the shuttle's cargo bay at 9:01 p.m. EDT and drifted into space.

"Magellan is deployed," reported shuttle Commander David Walker.

An hour later, after Atlantis moved a safe distance away, both stages of the spacecraft motor fired to start Magellan on a 456-day journey to Venus, 158 million miles away. It will travel 806 million miles, looping 1½ times around the sun, before reaching and orbiting its target in August 1990.

"While it's too early to tell about the major portion of Magellan's mission, we're pleased it's gone so well so far," Commander Walker said when told that both stages had fired.

Earlier yesterday, in a spectacular start, the space shuttle vaulted

> *"It was another cliffhanger. I'm glad you stuck with it."*
>
> **NASA OFFICIAL**
> **Commenting to launch team**

from its seaside launch pad at 2:47 p.m. EDT, after being delayed 59 minutes by shifting clouds and winds that had threatened to postpone the launch for the second time in six days.

Atlantis departed just five minutes before its 64-minute "launch window" for the day would have closed — a window dictated by a requirement to have the shuttle in the proper position in orbit to dispatch Magellan to Venus.

The launch team had advanced the countdown to the 5-minute mark and held there, waiting for a break in the clouds that obscured a runway near the launch pad where Atlantis would land in an emergen-

See **SHUTTLE**, 13A, Col. 4

California insurance revolt is upheld

Court backs voters on rate rollbacks

By Ellen Uzelac
West Coast Bureau of The Sun

SAN FRANCISCO — In a stinging defeat for the insurance industry, the California Supreme Court upheld yesterday a controversial voters initiative that will mean dramatic cuts in insurance rates worth billions of dollars to consumers.

The eagerly awaited ruling on the sweeping insurance reforms approved by voters last November is expected to have a profound effect on consumers nationwide if the "voter's revolt" that started in California spreads to other states.

"Clearly, it's a new day for insurance regulation in California," said Richard Wiebe, a spokesman for the Alliance of American Insurers.

The justices, in a 7-0 ruling, upheld the major portions of Proposition 103, which requires insurance companies to roll back automobile and property insurance rates to a level 20 percent below those in effect Nov. 8, 1987. Drivers with good records will get an additional 20 percent off. The initiative also covers many forms of business insurance.

California residents stand to save billions of dollars in annual premiums as a result of the ruling, which also upheld tighter regulations on the insurance industry.

In addition, consumers will receive rebates — estimated by the insurance industry at $4 billion — as insurers adjust premiums to comply with the proposition.

See **INSURANCE**, 15A, Col. 6

THE SUN INSIDE

The Allegany Central Railroad, run by Jack and Sally Showalter, begins operations in Cumberland this weekend. **1E**

Repairs to the battleship Iowa's damaged gun turret will be $15 million to $20 million. **3A**

Negotiations that could lead to Terps basketball coach Bob Wade's resignation reportedly began two weeks ago. **1D**

NSA's control over sophisticated computer security technologies in the U.S. is criticized. **1C**

House Speaker Jim Wright allegedly got favorable treatment on a 1983 investment. **13A**

Rain, possibly a thunderstorm, today. High, 70; low, 55. Yesterday's high, 70; low, 51. **13E**

Index

5 SECTIONS

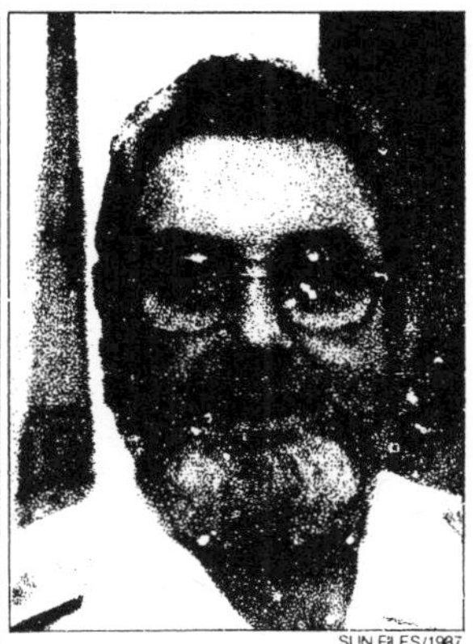

SUN FILES/1987

Stepping down

Dr. C. Everett Koop said yesterday he would resign after seven years as surgeon general in mid-July. (See article on Page 3A)

U.S. agents descend on N.Y. futures traders

New York Daily News

NEW YORK — Federal authorities descended on Wall Street commodity exchanges yesterday, pulling traders off the floor in a wide-ranging criminal investigation into futures trading in New York.

At least 27 traders from four of New York's five commodity exchanges were subpoenaed for information at 4 World Trade Center.

Government officials refused to say what they are looking for. However, Bruce Baird, chief of the Manhattan U.S. attorney's Securities and Commodities Fraud Unit, confirmed "search warrants were executed by U.S. Postal Service inspectors in conjunction with a federal Commodity Futures Trading Commission investigation connected with an ongoing criminal investigation conducted by this office."

What appeared to be the beginning of a massive inquiry into trading practices began early yesterday when about 16 Postal Service inspectors walked into exchange and commodity firm offices on the eighth and ninth floors of the World Trade Center tower in lower Manhattan.

See **PROBE**, 13A, Col. 3

Board of Regents panel votes for UM divestiture

By Patricia Meisol

Joining millions of people worldwide who have voted with their pocketbooks against legal racism in South Africa, a committee of the University of Maryland Board of Regents voted yesterday to sell off its stock in companies that do business in that segregated country.

Not only that, the regents' finance committee said university divestiture, which student demonstrators have advocated for the past three months, does not go far enough as a statement against government policies that inherently contradict those of educational institutions.

They asked the students to think up more creative ways in which the university can protest the policies of a "government of evil," as Ann R. Hull, finance committee chairwoman, called South Africa.

Yesterday's unanimous action is expected to be approved by the full board in June. It came three years after the arrest of 12 College Park students for building a shanty on campus as a symbol of suffering by poor blacks in South Africa, and the refusal by the old board of regents to

See **DIVESTITURE**, 14A, Col. 1

THE SUN/IRVING H. PHILLIPS JR
Students listen to proceedings held at Towson State University.

Orioles slam past Yankees, 16-3: 1B

ORIOLES MAKE McDONALD NO. 1 PICK IN DRAFT; NBA FINALS PREVIEW: 1B

TUESDAY
JUNE 6, 1989

THE SUN
LIGHT · FOR · ALL

SPORTS FINAL

VOL. 305 NO. 18 | BALTIMORE, MARYLAND | 25 CENTS

Civil war fears grow in China amid gunfire

Troops in Beijing apparently girding for assault by rebel soldiers

ASSOCIATED PRESS

Protester stands in front of column of tanks heading down main Beijing thoroughfare in an attempt to halt their advance after they pulled out of Tiananmen Square . . .

ABC NEWS VIA ASSOCIATED PRESS

. . . but finally is rushed to safety by fellow protesters.

Job bias proof is toughened

Ruling increases burden on plaintiff

By Lyle Denniston
Washington Bureau of The Sun

WASHINGTON — The Supreme Court, stirring protests from three justices that it may have forgotten that race bias is a problem, made it much harder yesterday for minorities to prove complaints that job practices hit them hardest and thus are illegal.

In another part of the ruling, the court made it much easier for businesses to fight off complaints that their job policies have a discriminatory — and therefore illegal — impact on minorities.

The decision, which appeared to mark a retreat from a series of job bias rulings dating to 1971, dealt a major blow to non-white workers as they pursue a 15-year-old complaint against two companies that operate salmon canneries in Alaska.

Those workers complained that the majority of non-white workers were concentrated in the unskilled jobs on the cannery production lines, having been hired from the local population near the canneries. The higher-skilled jobs, with better pay, are most often filled with whites recruited with a union's help in the cannery companies' offices in the states of Washington and Oregon.

Although the new ruling dealt specifically with how federal courts are to handle cases on race bias in employment, the legal interpretations appear to apply also to cases on sex bias in the workplace.

The decision split the court 5-4. The fifth vote for the majority was

See COURT, 3A, Col. 3

Ruling favors free-lance artists. 1C
Court to rule on price wars. 1E
Appeal from Maryland on police 'protective sweeps' to be taken up. 3D

Bush suspends arms shipments, rejects sanctions

By Stephens Broening and Karen Hosler
Washington Bureau of The Sun

WASHINGTON — President Bush imposed a temporary U.S. arms embargo on China yesterday in reaction to the bloody repression of the Chinese democratic movement.

"I think it's important that the Chinese leaders know it's not going to be business as usual, and I think it's important that the army know we want to see restraint," the president said.

Mr. Bush said the suspension of U.S. military sales and deliveries was aimed at deterring the People's Liberation Army from further assaults on civilians involved in promoting political reforms.

The embargo — curbing transfers of an estimated $540 million worth of military hardware — was one of several steps the president came to the White House press room to announce after a weekend of intense high-level deliberations.

He said the United States also had decided to suspend visits by U.S. and Chinese military leaders, to give a "sympathetic" hearing to requests by any of the 20,000 Chinese students in this country to lengthen their stays and to offer aid through the Red Cross to the army's victims in Beijing.

Mr. Bush said "other aspects" of relations with China will be reviewed "as events . . . continue to unfold."

The president revealed that he had been under pressure to order economic sanctions against China,

See BUSH, 11A, Col. 1

Thousands on campuses brace for expected attack

By John Schidlovsky
Beijing Bureau of The Sun

BEIJING — Fears of a civil war gripped this city yesterday as scores of tanks lined up at key intersections as if to prepare for a heavy assault by rebel troops who are rumored to be opposed to the savage killings of thousands of Beijing civilians.

The capital degenerated into general warfare as troops fired randomly at crowds of unarmed citizens, killing many Beijing residents who defiantly manned barricades in the face of tanks and soldiers wielding machine guns.

[Gunfire spread around the capital this morning, the Associated Press reported. Soldiers were fighting other soldiers around Tiananmen Square and in southwestern Beijing, sources told the AP on condition of anonymity.]

Thousands of students braced yesterday for an expected invasion of their campuses by troops who have spent the last two days killing pro-democracy demonstrators and hundreds of Chinese citizens outraged by the army's action.

"They are not human beings," a female student at Beijing University said of China's leaders, Deng Xiaoping and President Yang Shangkun, who are widely held responsible for the crackdown. "They are animals."

Mr. Deng, 84, who reportedly is ill, has not been seen in public in nearly three weeks. But internal government memos circulated by Chinese sources have made it plain that he ordered the bloody attacks on students.

The army's actions have alienated the vast majority of Beijing's 10 million residents, many of whom stayed home — partly out of fear and partly in response to calls by students for a general strike yesterday. Shops, banks and government offices were closed, and there were no public buses on the largely deserted streets.

As gunfire crackled throughout the city, foreigners began fleeing. Officials of the U.S. Embassy sent vans to evacuate U.S. students from the city's campuses; other embassies provided planes to take their citizens out of China.

"A lot of the students have already left the schools," said a U.S. spokeswoman. She said only 14 of the estimated hundreds of American

See CHINA, 10A, Col. 1

Battle for Beijing

- World leaders express grief and outrage over China's violent crackdown, and some cancel planned contacts with Beijing. 9A
- Western analysts focus on army factionalism and on a faction believed to be headed by China's president and linked by family ties. 11A
- President Bush's halt to military sales chills a relationship between the Chinese and U.S. armed forces that has been warming for six years. 11A
- Thousands of Chinese students rally on the Capitol steps and march to the White House to urge cutoff of U.S. ties to China. 11A

Protests spread rapidly; strike snarls Shanghai

By John Woodruff
Sun Staff Correspondent

HONG KONG — Factories halted or cut back operations in Shanghai yesterday as about 60 percent of the city's workers stayed home for a general strike protesting the government-ordered massacres in Beijing.

Foreign residents reported that the capital of Anhui province in eastern China was "basically in the hands of the demonstrators."

Protests continued to spread rapidly but spottily across China throughout the day yesterday as word of the central government's continuing action against demonstrators in Beijing began to filter through the official news blackout.

Protesters in Shanghai, always one of the country's most volatile cities, seemed the best organized.

They maintained barricades of trucks, buses and utility poles throughout the day, giving workers an excuse to stay home and support the general strike.

Foreign residents estimated that about 60 percent of the city's work-

See CITIES, 10A, Col. 5

Major banks cut prime rate by half a point

Los Angeles Times

NEW YORK — Several of the nation's leading banks dropped their prime lending rate — the benchmark for many consumer and small-business loans — to 11 percent from 11.5 percent yesterday, convinced that the weakness in the economy is bringing a general easing of credit.

Several banks in Maryland followed suit later in the day, citing the New York banks as the impetus for their actions.

The move, which reversed a year-long upward drift in the prime, was kicked off by Citibank in New York, followed by Morgan Guaranty Bank, Chase Manhattan Bank, Bank of America, Wells Fargo Bank

See RATES, 6A, Col. 1

THE SUN
INSIDE

The Orioles get a gift from New York, a 16-3 win, to run their winning streak to 8. **1B**

Embattled House Democrats eagerly await the election of Thomas S. Foley as speaker. **3A**

Cloudy today with periods of rain. High, 80; low, 70. Yesterday's high, 83; low, 67. **18D**

Index

Bridge	4C	Editorials	16A
Business	1E	Horoscope	5C
Classified	10D	Lottery	4B
Comics	4C	Movies	3C
Deaths	10D	Television	6C

6 SECTIONS

Solidarity rolls to victory in historic Polish election

By Kay Withers
Special to The Sun

WARSAW, Poland — As unofficial returns in the Polish parliamentary elections indicated a landslide victory for the Solidarity labor union and a humiliating defeat for the Communist authorities, the government conceded defeat and pledged to keep on with its program of economic reform.

But the emotional protest vote against Communist rule could pose a threat to party reformers throughout Eastern Europe.

Sunday's elections, the freest ever staged in the Soviet bloc, fielded 2,318 candidates of different political persuasions in an unprecedented Western-style competition for 100 senatorial seats and 460 places in the Sejm, or lower house of parliament.

It was the first time ever that a one-party Communist state had allowed organized electoral opposition.

Official returns are not due for several days, due to complicated ballots and prolonged counting, but Solidarity issued unofficial partial figures as union representatives on electoral commissions telephoned results.

See POLAND, 4A, Col. 1

State tightens inmate-release program

Murder conviction would bar eligibility

By Dennis O'Brien

State corrections officials tightened restrictions yesterday on the release of certain prison inmates so those like Booker T. Jones — slain by police after he is believed to have killed two children — would be kept off the streets longer.

Jones, 25, was shot 11 times May 18 as he rushed with a butcher knife at police trying to apprehend him as a suspect in the murders of two youngsters in Glen Burnie five days earlier.

He was released from prison April 30, 1987, after entering a special rehabilitation program that meant he served a little more than five years of a 25-year sentence on a second-degree murder conviction.

Maryland Department of Public Safety and Correctional Services Secretary Bishop L. Robinson said yesterday that, effective June 15, no one convicted of first- or second-degree murder would be accepted into the program.

State officials yesterday also released a series of reports that detail some of Jones' behavior while on parole.

The records, requested by *The Sun* through its attorneys, show that Jones was trained to work in the prison system as a meat cutter, was to undergo substance abuse therapy while on parole, had a "sporadic" employment record after his release, and spent at least one night in the Baltimore City Jail for driving with a suspended license.

Assistant Attorney General Emory A. Plitt Jr. said the records suggest that Jones was given probation before judgment on the driving violation.

The Sun had requested records, including Jones' medical file, his parole commission file, any notes by his parole agents and his inmate base file, which documents all information concerning the inmate while in prison, including psychological evaluations, family background, work information and progress re-

See JONES, 8A, Col. 1

Bullets triumph, go to 4-1: 1B

SATURDAY
NOVEMBER 11, 1989

THE SUN

LIGHT · FOR · ALL

SPORTS FINAL

VOL. 305 NO. 154 | BALTIMORE, MARYLAND | 25 CENTS

Berlin Wall begins to come down

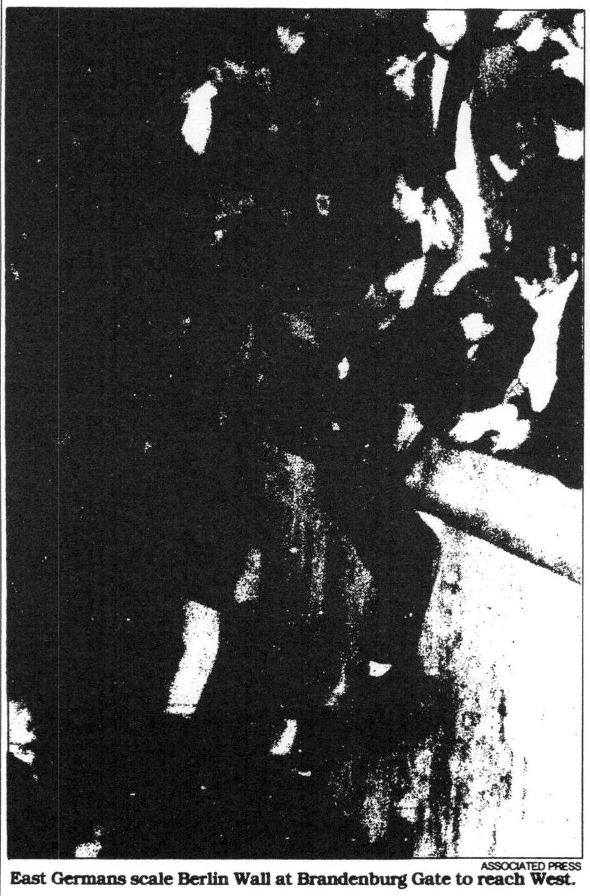

ASSOCIATED PRESS
East Germans scale Berlin Wall at Brandenburg Gate to reach West.

ASSOCIATED PRESS
Berlin women embrace on Western side of a border crossing point.

ASSOCIATED PRESS
As East German guards watch, crane's jaws open up a new crossing.

Krenz sets 'action' plan for reforms

By Diana Jean Schemo
Sun Staff Correspondent

EAST BERLIN — East Germany began tearing down a part of the Berlin Wall last night, in the first steps effectively reconnecting this city and people divided by it for 28 years through Cold War confrontation.

In yet another night of unexpected and breathtaking change here, East German army bulldozers arrived at the wall by Eberswalderstrasse, bringing howls of joy from crowds of Germans on both sides as they began ramming away a section of the wall that would become a border crossing by 8 a.m. today.

"It's a miracle, in the last place miracles were supposed to happen," said one awe-struck East Berliner.

Meanwhile, East German leader Egon Krenz submitted a "program of action" that he said yesterday was designed to win confidence in the Communist Party. While lacking in details, the program as released calls for free and secret balloting, a separation between the party and the state apparatus, freedom of association and travel, and relaxed press laws.

The program apparently did little to win Mr. Krenz support among the grass-roots party membership. The conflict became even more open and Mr. Krenz's future less certain on the streets of East Berlin last night.

At a mass rally at Alexanderplatz, Communist Party members complained that the Central Committee had opted to call a party conference next month instead of a party congress that could make broad changes to the Central Committee. The conference may make only limited changes in the membership of the powerful Central Committee, two-thirds of whose 163 members are resistant to reforms.

Though the party members ap-

See **GERMANS,** 6A, Col. 5

Poland seeks security guarantees. **6A**
Willy Brandt back in limelight. **7A**
Bush vows to promote democracy. **7A**

Germans in Md. transmit joy to overseas relatives

By Jean Marbella

Though separated from their ancestral homeland by years and miles, some of the 1 million-plus Marylanders of German descent have heated up the trans-Atlantic phone lines in recent days to join in a celebration that knows no boundaries.

"I spoke to my sister [in West Berlin], and her two sons of course had gone to the Wall to celebrate," says Brigitta Puthawala, a native Berliner who has lived in Hagerstown for about 25 years. "They picked up two young East Germans and took them on a tour of the sights of West Berlin. I talked to her . . . about 6 a.m. [Friday] her time, and they had just returned home. She said — maybe she was joking, she's like that — some restaurants in Berlin ran out of beer."

"My cousin said they were dancing on the Wall," says Edith Hagen, 62, a retired secretary in Baltimore, who, after finding the phone lines jammed to East Germany, called relatives in West Germany Thursday evening.

"It was in total uproar. My cousins said, 'Now we're not confined.' No matter where they would go in West Berlin, they hit the Wall."

In Maryland — where an estimated one-fourth of the population is partially or fully of German ancestry — there's special reason to cheer East Germany's opening of the Berlin Wall Thursday night because many residents have relatives living there.

"This to me gives rise to real hope that we'll pull that stupid wall down," said Dorothy Galway ("I married an Irishman," she says, in ex-

See **RELATIVES,** 7A, Col. 1

Bush plans $6.8 billion for housing

Ownership central to HUD proposal

By Nancy J. Schwerzler
Washington Bureau of The Sun

WASHINGTON — President Bush proposed yesterday a three-year, $6.8 billion housing program to aid the poor, the homeless, the elderly and first-time homebuyers with the first major federal housing initiative in more than eight years.

Mr. Bush, appearing with Secretary of Housing and Urban Development Jack F. Kemp in Dallas before a convention of the National Association of Realtors, dubbed the program "HOPE" — an acronym for "homeownership and opportunity for people everywhere" — and said that the initiative would help the needy and also "recapture the American dream for home ownership for those who have been left behind."

The administration proposals — including $4.2 billion in spending spread out over three years and an estimated $2.6 billion in tax incentives during the same period — amount to about the same total dollars that federal auditors now believe HUD has lost in recent years because of fraud and mismanagement, as well as massive mortgage foreclosures in the Southwest.

Mr. Kemp has already proposed wide-ranging reforms of HUD to clean up what he has called the "swamp" of abuses that occurred during the administration of his predecessor, HUD Secretary Samuel R. Pierce Jr.

The Bush administration's initiative, although modest in its proposed spending levels, addresses a broad range of housing problems and advances some of Mr. Kemp's pet proposals for urban enterprise zones and steps to establish resident-owned cooperative housing. The administration did not specify how the new programs would be paid for, or whether the money would be allocated from existing programs.

The administration proposals will no doubt be welcome on Capitol Hill as a sign of a renewed White House interest in housing, but there are already several other comprehensive housing proposals pending in Congress.

The main component of the new plan is a $2.1 billion program of "HOPE grants" to promote tenant takeovers of local public housing projects, HUD-owned apartment projects and properties acquired by the federal government as part of the bailout of failed savings and loan associations.

The grant program would require state or local governments, or non-profit groups participating in a project, to match federal aid at the rate of $1 for every $2 in federal funds.

For first-time homebuyers, the

See **HUD,** 8A, Col. 4

THE SUN
INSIDE

Baltimore agrees to take back the unwanted sludge train that has become known as the "poo-poo choo-choo." **10A**

The Kremlin orders four Soviet republics to drop new laws that it says violate the constitution. **2A**

A judge freezes the personal assets of Baltimore talk-show hosts Alan Christian and Lester Kinsolving. **10A**

A group of Canadians plans to develop downtown Leningrad into the Soviet Union's first international free-trade zone. **15B**

Despite progress in talks, an accord between Nicaragua and the contras remains far away, according to diplomats. **2A**

Timonium-based Kirschner Medical Corp. has fallen on hard times. **15B**

Mostly sunny today, fair tonight. High, 52; low, 42. Yesterday's high, 60; low, 45. **18C**

Index

Bridge	3D	Editorials	14A
Business	15B	Horoscope	6D
Classified	5C	Lottery	4B
Comics	4D	Movies	2D
Deaths	12A	Television	8D

3 4 SECTIONS F

Bulgaria's leader of 35 years quits; reforms vowed

SOFIA, Bulgaria (Reuters) — Bulgarian President Todor Zhivkov, Eastern Europe's longest-serving leader, resigned yesterday amid mounting pressure for reforms in the East Bloc, and his successor said there was no alternative to restructuring.

Mr. Zhivkov, 78, bowed out after 35 years in power. He was replaced as Communist Party chief by Foreign Minister Petar Mladenov, 53.

In his first speech as party leader, Mr. Mladenov said there was no alternative to reforms, although he stressed they must take place within the framework of a Communist system.

"Restructuring has no alternative," he told a meeting of the party's Central Committee, "[but] only within the framework of socialism, in the name of socialism and along the road to socialism."

Mr. Mladenov, foreign minister since 1971, pledged complete openness of information and active dialogue with the people — "both in the process of discussion of socially significant issues as well as in the taking of important decisions."

Although the changeover followed by less than a month the fall of East Germany's hard-line Communist Party chief Erich Honecker and came amid reforms sweeping most of the Eastern Bloc, Western diplomats said it did not appear to herald major changes in the Balkan Communist state's direction.

The diplomats said Mr. Mladenov's words were similar to promises Mr. Zhivkov himself has made in the past but not put into practice.

"It doesn't represent a radical change by any means," one Western diplomat said. "He's still fundamentally a traditionalist who very much believes in the old Eastern European ways."

Another said of Mr. Mladenov, "He's a hard-liner, but he has been a bit of a moderating influence on

See **BULGARIA,** 4A, Col. 4

Pratt staffer's bequest starts to promote reading today

By Will Englund

Margaret Alexander Edwards had no use for the unobtrusive librarian.

To her, putting the book on the shelf wasn't what mattered. Getting the ideas out of the book and into the minds of readers — particularly teen-agers, at that pivotal moment when they might become lifelong readers — was what the job was all about.

She believed in "brokering" books and people, as one of her disciples, Anna Curry, now director of the Enoch Pratt Free Library, put it yesterday.

She also believed — somewhat seditiously — that libraries exist to promote reading, not to provide "informational services." She even went so far as to spell that out in her will.

To counteract the "neglect of the promotion of reading" in today's libraries, she directed that a trust be established to be used to inspire and encourage reading among young adults.

Mrs. Edwards, a 30-year veteran of the Pratt, died in April 1988. Her trust, which will be making its first awards tonight, is valued at about $675,000, according to her lawyer, state Sen. Julian L. Lapides. It is perhaps the largest amount bequeathed to the promotion of reading since Enoch Pratt himself left the money for Baltimore's public library.

THE SUN/1974
Margaret Edwards left a trust that will make its first awards tonight.

Mrs. Edwards was a plain-spoken and direct woman, with her own way of charging through life. She left Waxahachie, Texas, in 1927 to study Latin at Columbia University, although she had never taken Latin before. She met a young man with a Stutz Bearcat and a liking for Broadway, nearly flunked out, disposed of the young man, came to Towson to teach and got fired.

In 1932, she was hired at the Pratt and put in charge of the young adult collection. "They wanted someone who would keep the high school kids off everyone's necks for about two hours in the afternoon," she said later.

But for the next 30 years she did everything she could to put teen-agers and books together. During World War II, she hired a street arab's horse and cart and trundled books through South and East Baltimore. She sent her staff out to the city's schools to give book talks. One of her trainees said she was like "one of those people who could be found walking up and down a Roman slave galley."

"It was hard, tough training," said Sara L. Siebert, a retired librarian

See **READING,** 9A, Col. 1

El Salvador reportedly arms Guatemalan rightists

By John M. McClintock
Sun Staff Correspondent

GUATEMALA CITY — Guatemalan intelligence agents have concluded that high officials of El Salvador's ruling party sent hand grenades and other explosives to ultra-rightists here to foment a "violent, lawless atmosphere leading to the election of a strongman" in next year's presidential elections, President Vinicio Cerezo said in an interview.

Government sources linked the arms shipments to a series of hand grenade attacks in August, including those against the offices of two human rights groups. At least one person died in the six attacks, and several were injured.

Mr. Cerezo said that "of course" among those involved was former Maj. Roberto D'Aubuisson, founder of the Nationalist Republican Alliance (ARENA), the party that controls El Salvador's presidency, legislature and judiciary.

Mr. Cerezo's disclosure comes at a time when Salvadoran President Alfredo Cristiani is seeking to blunt charges of renewed death squad activity by extremist elements within his party.

Mr. Cerezo said that the evidence in the about-to-be-completed investigation in no way implicates Mr. Cristiani. Calls to Mr. D'Aubuisson and other party leaders in El Salvador were not returned.

Guatemalan intelligence agents obtained the evidence through wiretaps of telephone conversations between ARENA officials and unidentified right-wing groups here, according to Deputy Edmond Mulet, who was present at a Cerezo briefing on the matter to congressional leaders in September. Mr. Cerezo declined to say on the record how the evidence was obtained, but government sources confirmed that wiretaps were involved.

Mr. Mulet said Mr. Cerezo reported that one conversation involved a discussion of hand grenades by Mr. D'Aubuisson and an unidentified Guatemalan ultra-rightist.

In interviews Thursday, Mr. Cerezo and Defense Minister Hector Alejandro Gramajo Morales said an undetermined amount of explosives were sent to Guatemala in August when the country was torn by a serious of strikes by government workers.

"The idea was to create a climate of instability

See **GUATEMALA,** 4A, Col. 5

Celtics roll past Bullets, 120-101: 1D

THURSDAY
JANUARY 4, 1990

THE SUN
LIGHT · FOR · ALL

SPORTS FINAL

VOL. 306 NO. 42 BALTIMORE, MARYLAND 25 CENTS

Noriega gives himself up to U.S.

Baltimore due All-Star Game in '93

Orioles last served as host team in '58

By Mark Hyman

Major-league baseball's midsummer jewel, the All-Star Game, is coming back to Baltimore.

According to sources close to the selection process, the city has been chosen as host for the 1993 game at the Camden Yards stadium in the Inner Harbor, which should then be a year old. A formal announcement is expected today at Memorial Stadium.

The 1993 game will be the second All-Star Game to be played in Baltimore and the first since 1958. Except for the Orioles, Texas Rangers and Toronto Blue Jays, every major-league team has been host to the game at least once since then.

In Baltimore's only All-Star Game, the American League topped the National League, 4-3, at Memorial Stadium. It was the first All-Star Game without an extra-base hit.

Baltimore has been a candidate to be host of the game since September, when Orioles officials formally expressed their interest in a meeting with American League President Bobby Brown in Milwaukee. The Kansas City Royals and Cleveland Indians also were candidates.

Larry Lucchino, president of the Orioles, declined to discuss whether a decision had been made but said, "We are expecting a formal announcement from the league. . . . Hope springs eternal."

Dr. Brown could not be reached for comment last night.

The Orioles had set their sights on the 1993 game because it is the next one available. This year's game will be at Wrigley Field, the elderly home of the Chicago Cubs. In 1991, the Toronto Blue Jays will be hosts at the SkyDome, and the 1992 game will be played at Jack Murphy Stadium in San Diego. The game alternates between American League and National League parks.

As host of the 1993 All-Star Game, Baltimore will get a healthy dose of national publicity and a sub-

See ALL STAR, 7A, Col. 1

AGENCE FRANCE-PRESSE

Jubilant Panamanians pour into the streets to celebrate Gen. Manuel Antonio Noriega's departure to the United States.

Panamanian dictator is flown to Florida to face drug charges

By Mark Matthews and Karen Hosler
Washington Bureau of The Sun

WASHINGTON — Ousted Panamanian dictator Manuel Antonio Noriega left his sanctuary in the Vatican's embassy in Panama City and surrendered to U.S. authorities last night for trial on drug charges in Miami.

President Bush, announcing that General Noriega had surrendered — with "the full knowledge" of the new Panamanian government — declared that all of his objectives for the U.S. invasion of Panama on Dec. 20 had been met.

Mr. Bush, in remarks televised from the White House press room, said that General Noriega had turned himself in at 8:50 p.m. and been taken to Howard Air Force Base, where he was arrested by agents of the Drug Enforcement Administration.

He was then placed on an aircraft bound for Homestead Air Force Base in Florida for arraignment on charges contained in his indictment in February 1988 on cocaine smuggling and other charges.

After arriving in the United States, he was to spend last night at Homestead Air Force Base.

The former strongman's surrender ended a diplomatic standoff between the United States and the Vatican, which had vowed not to hand him over to an occupying power against his will.

Administration officials said last night that during the negotiations about his fate, General Noriega dealt solely with Vatican officials.

"The Vatican was basically telling Noriega his only viable option was to give himself up," one official said.

A turning point in General Noriega's talks with the papal nuncio apparently came Saturday when the Vatican indicated it considered

See NORIEGA, 4A, Col. 5

Military menaces stability of Endara government

Noriega holdovers remain in several key positions

By John M. McClintock
Sun Staff Correspondent

PANAMA CITY, Panama — By failing to fully reform Panama's armed forces, the U.S.-backed Endara government may face a military coup within six months to a year, say Western diplomats and military experts here.

Instead of training new top leaders, the Endara government has appointed 23 U.S.-screened officers from the old Panamanian Defense Forces, many of them of questionable loyalty to the new regime.

Two officers belonged to a special committee created by Gen. Manuel Antonio Noriega to thwart coups. Another appointee was wounded defending General Noriega on Oct. 3 during the last coup attempt against him.

Four others were promoted just eight days before the U.S. invasion on Dec. 20, in which 23 U.S. servicemen were killed and more than 300 wounded.

The anxiety about the new force seemed to be reflected in the abrupt resignation yesterday of Col. Roberto Armijo, the most senior Noriega holdover, who was placed in command of the armed forces immediately after the invasion.

See ARMY, 6A, Col. 1

New commander of security force resigns under investigation of corruption. 6A

FDA OKs tests of contraceptive vaccine for men

Boston Globe

For the first time in this country, a contraceptive vaccine to block sperm production in men has received U.S. Food and Drug Administration approval for preliminary investigation in humans.

The Population Council received written permission a month ago to study the safety and effectiveness of the vaccine in four male patients with prostate cancer and got a verbal OK for 20 such patients, according to Rosemarie Thau, director of contraceptive development at the international, non-profit organization.

[In the meantime, researchers at the University of Washington have been studying about four dozen couples in the Seattle area since April 1987 as part of a global research project sponsored in part by the World Health Organization, the *Los Angeles Times* reported.

[The goal is to find out whether men who receive weekly injections of testosterone enanthate, a synthetic hormone, become infertile.]

The vaccine works by producing antibodies to block a brain hormone, LHRH, that sets off the chain of hormonal events leading to sperm production.

"The vaccine, I would say, is many years off, from the time one gets the permit for the initial investigation," said Ms. Thau. She estimated it would be at least 10 years before a vaccine could be marketed.

Ms. Thau said the Population Council would go to clinical trials

See BIRTH CONTROL, 3A, Col. 1

Soviets reinforce troops on Azerbaijan-Iran border

By Scott Shane
Moscow Bureau of The Sun

MOSCOW — The Soviet Union reinforced its troops on the Iranian border yesterday, saying Azerbaijani nationalists planned further attacks on border installations following three days of vandalism and arson in which one man was killed and millions of rubles' worth of property was destroyed.

But Soviet Azerbaijani activists, accusing Moscow of distorting the events, said frustrated crowds had acted only because officials had long ignored demands that they be permitted to visit relatives in Iran.

"It's exactly like East and West Germany," said Mehdi Mamedov, a historian and activist in the Azerbaijani People's Front. "The northern part of Azerbaijan is under Soviet occupation, and the southern part of Azerbaijan is under Iranian occupation. We're a divided people."

Officials of the KGB border guard, local Azerbaijani officials and Azerbaijani activists all gave conflicting accounts of the disorders, which began Dec. 31.

But it was clear that the volatile 500-mile border between Soviet Azerbaijan and Iran joins the long list of nationalist challenges to Soviet President Mikhail S. Gorbachev, who is struggling to hold the empire together while preserving political and economic reform.

As KGB troops tried to regain control of the southern border, the leader of Lithuania's breakaway Communist Party flew to Moscow last night for talks in the Kremlin today.

An aide to Algirdas Brazauskas said he would not give in to pressure

See AZERBAIJAN, 8A, Col. 1

THE SUN
INSIDE

Spring fashions, while exposing skin, are not as daring as the clothes designers exhibited. **1F**

The New Kids on the Block come to Baltimore, and teeny-boppers go wild. **1E**

MNC will begin notifying employees who will lose jobs as result of merger with Equitable. **1C**

Equitable Bank raises its credit card rates. **1C**

Rain likely today, partial clearing tonight. High, 55; low, 40. Yesterday's high, 53; low, 33. **8B**

PHOTO BY DAVID EVANS

Marina fireball Fire swept through a 43-foot powerboat yesterday morning at a fuel dock at the Baltimore Yacht Basin, near the Hanover Street Bridge. The fire caused more than $70,000 worth of damage to the boat.

In rural Romania, peasants were often down-and-out on the farm

But new leaders promise to curtail cooperatives

By Robert Ruby
Sun Staff Correspondent

PERIS, Romania — When the people of Peris finish their regular jobs for the day, their habit for the last 41 years has been to travel to a second job in the fields of a state cooperative farm.

They have volunteered their labor or have gone hungry, and in recent years they have often done both.

Of all the whirlwind changes in Romania, it is probably safe to say that the most welcomed in this and every other village is the government's pledge to reduce the role of state farms. For people living in rural areas, a breakup of cooperative farms would mean an end to virtual servitude to the state.

Peris, a community of about 2,000, is not a center of political dissent. But in 24 years of authoritarian rule, deposed Communist leader Nicolae Ceausescu managed to change Romania's large peasant population from largely passive to hostile and fearful.

There is, for example, the man who can be

See RURAL, 2A, Col. 2

For some, it is too late to reclaim lost villages

By Robert Ruby
Sun Staff Correspondent

GHERMANESTI, Romania — Marion Enache, his wife and their young daughter live in a new apartment, in a new building, in a new neighborhood created by their government to break people's hold on the land.

The Enaches are among Romania's newly dispossessed. Of all the victims of the regime of Nicolae Ceausescu, they are among those with the least hope of recovering what they lost. They are among hundreds of thousands of one-time villagers within the last five years to have their homes and villages destroyed and then to be forcibly moved into state-owned apartments.

Probably none of Mr. Ceausescu's iron-fisted policies was crueler, or more idiosyncratic, than was the willful destruction of villages. Mr. Ceausescu had advertised the program as the capstone of his government. He demanded that more than 8,000 villages be destroyed as part of a plan to make the peasantry more dependent on the state.

See VILLAGE, 2A, Col. 1

Tyson knocked out by Douglas: 1E

AS APRIL 15 NEARS, TAXPAYERS NEED A HELPING HAND--AND HERE IT IS: TAX GUIDE

SUNDAY
FEBRUARY 11, 1990

THE SUN

LIGHT · FOR · ALL

SUNNY
BUT COOLER
SEE PAGE 14B

VOL. 90 NO. 6 BALTIMORE, MARYLAND **$1.25**

"He is a friendly man. He is an elderly, dignified man, and he is an interesting man."

SOUTH AFRICAN PRESIDENT F. W. De KLERK, speaking of NELSON MANDELA

Mandela's 27-year ordeal to end today

Headway reported in arms talks

Chemical weapons will be destroyed

By Scott Shane
Moscow Bureau of The Sun

MOSCOW — The United States and the Soviet Union have agreed to destroy most chemical weapons and have made substantial progress toward completing a treaty to cut strategic nuclear weapons by 50 percent at next June's Washington summit, officials said as talks here concluded yesterday.

Secretary of State James A. Baker III topped off three days of negotiations with Foreign Minister Eduard A. Shevardnadze with an unprecedented appearance before the Supreme Soviet Committee on Foreign Affairs yesterday morning.

Mr. Baker parried sharp criticism of the U.S. invasion of Panama and replied by expressing incomprehension over continuing massive Soviet aid to Cuba.

But his major note, following marathon negotiating sessions described by both sides as unusually productive, was positive.

"Now is the time to put the legacy of struggle behind us," Mr. Baker said. "Now is the time to move beyond the Cold War."

The Soviet side agreed to a U.S. plan, proposed last year by President Bush at the United Nations, under which the two superpowers will phase out chemical weapon stocks over a 10-year period. The agreement will be signed at the June summit, officials said.

The destruction of stocks will begin when a convention on chemical weapons now being negotiated by 40 nations in Geneva is completed, according to a joint U.S.-Soviet statement issued yesterday. Production of chemical weapons would be halted immediately by countries signing the convention.

See **BAKER**, 10A, Col. 1

Kohl and Gorbachev discuss German reunification. **6A**

AGENCE FRANCE-PRESSE

South African President F. W. de Klerk (left) stands with Nelson Mandela during a secret meeting at the presidential residence in Cape Town.

De Klerk declares release ends doubt of leaders' sincerity

By Peter Honey
Sun Staff Correspondent

CAPE TOWN, South Africa — Jailed black leader Nelson R. Mandela will be released from his prison grounds at 3 p.m. (8 a.m. EST) today, President Frederik W. de Klerk said yesterday.

The release "will bring us to the end of a long chapter," Mr. de Klerk told reporters at a crowded news conference here.

"There can no longer be any doubt about the government's sincerity to create a just dispensation based on negotiations."

Anti-apartheid activists, church leaders and businessmen hailed the long-awaited announcement as one of the most momentous events in South African history.

Thousands of jubilant Mandela supporters celebrated in the streets of cities and townships as news of the impending release spread across the country.

But right-wing whites furiously denounced the move and vowed to mount nationwide protests. The militant neo-fascist Afrikaner Resistance Movement threatened violent reprisals at what it called "de Klerk's treachery."

The Mandela Reception Committee said the 71-year-old African National Congress leader would address a news conference and a mass rally in Cape Town shortly after his release. It would be his first public appearance since his imprisonment almost 28 years ago.

He was expected to return to his home in the black township of Soweto near Johannesburg tomorrow, the

See **RELEASE**, 4A, Col. 1

Bush, lawmakers praise move. **3A**
De Klerk faces daunting hurdles **3A**
Baltimoreans cheer the news but fear that apartheid may linger. **3A**

Mandela emerges as statesman, symbol of struggle

By Peter Honey
Johannesburg Bureau of The Sun

JOHANNESBURG, South Africa — Most South Africans were not born when Nelson Mandela went to prison 27 years ago. Only a select few have actually seen or heard him since.

The world knows him from a few speeches and writings, mostly from a bygone age, and from the accounts of family, friends and admirers. His writings are eloquent, sensitive and perceptive. Personal accounts of him glow with unbridled admiration: "Charismatic, courteous, down-to-earth, disciplined."

"There was definitely something special about Nelson. But I think it's true to say that his fame was spread mostly by government propaganda."

GODFREY PITJI

Laudable qualities, but hardly enough to explain the appearance in London of a Mandela Street or in Grenoble of the Place Mandela. Or why Rome, Glasgow, Olympia and Aberdeen accorded him honorary citizenship. Or why universities as far afield as New York and Lesotho conferred upon him honorary doctorates.

Books, poems and popular songs have been written about him. India has given him the Jawarlal Nehru Award for International Understanding, East Germany the Star of International Fellowship. He received Austria's Bruno Kreisky Human Rights Prize and the Playa Giron Prize from Cuba. He shared with King Juan Carlos of Spain Vene-

See **MANDELA**, 4A, Col. 1

Fight over furs has begun to get under Aspen's skin

ASSOCIATED PRESS

Gail Baumrin brought along her fur when she moved to Aspen.

By Ellen Uzelac
Sun Staff Correspondent

ASPEN, Colo. — The fur hasn't flown this fast and furious in the glitter capital of the Rockies since Dwight D. Eisenhower was president.

A proposal to ban the sale of fur in star-studded Aspen has put the community on edge — some say over the edge. Voters will decide the fate of the fur ban on Tuesday.

Furriers are calling for "fur-eedom" of choice while animal rights activists, led by Mayor Bill Stirling, decry the cruelty to animals that they say goes into the making of a fur garment.

The *Aspen Daily News* noted in its Friday editions that the fur ban vote appears to be "the biggest single event in Aspen since developer Walter Paepcke squinted up at Aspen Mountain in 1945 and said, 'Yeah, we could sell lift tickets here.' "

The controversy has triggered boycotts, angry debate, character assassination and even death threats — by fax machine. It has also led to a March referendum to recall the outspoken four-term mayor, who dressed up as a wolf and pounded people over the head at a Fourth of July parade in this city of 6,000 year-round residents.

People are talking about the fur ban over croissants in the morning and over cognac in the evening —

See **FUR**, 13A, Col. 1

SUN GRAPHICS

Tax proposal rewards homeownership

Balto. Co. plan seen as more progressive

By James Bock and Deborah I. Greene

When anyone proposes to fiddle with Thurman M. Roberts' taxes, the 77-year-old Dundalk man reaches for a yellow legal pad, a freshly sharpened pencil and the neat ledger where he has recorded his finances since he retired in 1974.

So when Baltimore County Executive Dennis F. Rasmussen made an election-year proposal last week to cut the county's property tax rate over seven years if the General Assembly allows him to raise the local income tax, Mr. Roberts was primed to see how the plan would affect him.

To his surprise, Mr. Roberts came out a winner: He would pay $109.42 less in taxes if the Rasmussen plan were fully deployed — with a 55-cent cut in the current property tax rate of $2.895 for each $100 of assessed value and a local income tax raised from 50 percent to 65 percent of what a person pays in state income tax.

But Thurman Roberts still doesn't buy it.

"I think it's a smoke screen," he said. "People are up in arms about

See **TAXES**, 15A, Col. 1

THE SUN

INSIDE

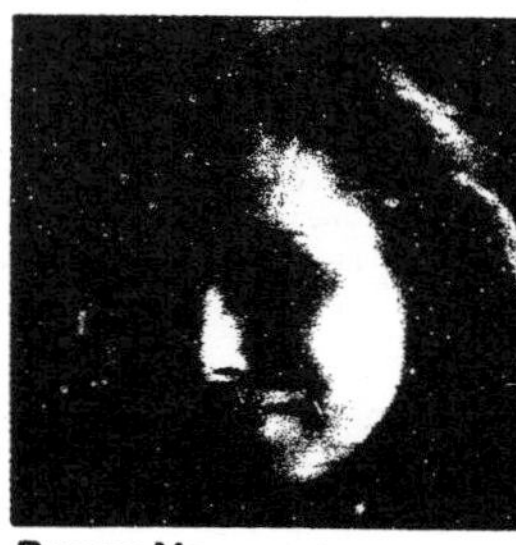

Peggy Noonan has written speeches for Presidents Reagan and Bush, but her background says theirs should have been a philosophical mismatch. **1F**

Texas Instruments employees at the firm's Hunt Valley office are now subject to random drug testing. **1C**

State reviewers find much at fault in the operation of the Juvenile Services Dept. **1B**

Partly sunny and cooler. Today's high, 48; low, 32. Yesterday's high, 64; low, 46. **14B**

Index

Facing a leaner defense budget, lobbyists try a different sell

By Dan Fesperman
Washington Bureau of The Sun

WASHINGTON — In the kill-or-be-killed lobbying wars of big defense contracts, combat strategy used to be as blunt and simple as a bombing run.

You took your expensive project and spread the work around in as many states and congressional districts as possible, building an alliance of lawmakers eager to win jobs for their voting public. For good measure, you took some committee chairmen on a duck hunt and lavished practically every member with generous campaign donations.

If all else failed, you sent in the Marines. When they decide they like a new weapon, they're reputed to be the most effective lobbying force of all the armed services.

That's what makes the V-22 Osprey so interesting. This fancy hybrid of helicopter and turbo-prop plane has all the traditional ingredients for success — jobs spread across 47 states, crack lobbyists and a support system of political action committees among seven of its largest contractors that contributed $2.02 million to 1988 congressional campaigns. It even has the gung-ho backing of the Marines.

But the lobbying landscape of old has been blown to smithereens by an outbreak of peaceable behavior and by the crumbling of the Communist threat in Eastern Europe. Budget cutting is the order of the day, and Defense Secretary Dick Cheney has decided for the second year in a row that he doesn't want to build any Ospreys. Just build more helicopters, he says. They're slower, yes, but cheaper.

That has forced the Osprey's backers to

See **OSPREY**, 11A, Col. 1

A's beat Orioles in 12th, 4-3: 1D

CAPS STOP RANGERS IN OT, 4-3; SKIPJACKS LOSE TO AMERICANS IN OT, 5-4: 1D

THURSDAY
APRIL 26, 1990

THE SUN

LIGHT · FOR · ALL

SPORTS FINAL

VOL. 306 NO. 138 | BALTIMORE, MARYLAND | 25 CENTS

NASA TELEVISION via ASSOCIATED PRESS

The Hubble telescope, with the Earth in background, is still attached to the shuttle's robot arm in this TV picture before its release into orbit.

Hubble telescope released into 380-mile-high orbit

By Luther Young
Sun Staff Correspondent

GREENBELT — The $1.5 billion Hubble Space Telescope was released safe and sound into orbit yesterday, after a tense series of deployment problems that had shuttle astronauts ready in the wings for a dramatic rescue.

An hour and a half later than originally planned, at 3:38 p.m., the observatory was finally set free from Discovery's robot arm into the far-seeing orbit from which it will probe the universe for the next 15 years.

"Hubble really is in its element now," Adm. Richard H. Truly, NASA administrator, said at Goddard Space Flight Center here. "It's a great and historic day for the space program."

Adding to the day's excitement were spectacular live television views of the brilliant, foil-wrapped observatory as it floated against the blue-green Earth below.

The 380-mile-high orbit — the highest of any of the 35 shuttle flights since 1981 — provided the best camera perspective of Earth since the Apollo moon missions in the 1960s and 1970s.

"It's still a little too early for the party, but I think you can get ready," said NASA's deputy administrator, J. R. Thompson, referring to the one critical remaining milestone: the opening around noon tomorrow of the telescope mirror's lens cap, or aperture door.

The jubilation for NASA officials, project managers and astronomers — some of whom had waited two decades for the sweet moment — was almost scuttled yesterday by one of the telescope's two 40-foot-long

See **HUBBLE**, 13A, Col. 1

Md. schools chief seeks major reforms

Plan aims to ensure student readiness for job or college

By Kathy Lally

THE SUN/1988

JOSEPH L. SHILLING
State schools superintendent

The state superintendent of schools, seeking dramatic changes in the way Maryland's 700,000 public schoolchildren are educated, proposed a set of sweeping reforms yesterday aimed at making sure that almost every student in the state leaves high school prepared for either college or a job.

Joseph L. Shilling, the superintendent, told members of the state Board of Education that he wants to extend the school year by four weeks; require all students to stay in school until they reach age 18; offer high school classes in the evenings and on Saturdays to accommodate working youngsters; double the number of computers in Maryland schools; and improve the teaching force, among other ideas.

The changes, if carried out, would result in one of the most comprehensive revisions ever undertaken in public education in Maryland.

"This is going to make us start thinking differently," Dr. Shilling said. "This is going to put us out front in education."

Though Dr. Shilling did not consult with Gov. William Donald Schaefer in advance — he said he sent him a copy of his plan Tuesday — one of the governor's most trusted advisers predicted that Mr. Schaefer would love it.

"This is an enormous development," said Walter J. Sondheim, who headed the Governor's Commission on School Performance, which influenced some of Dr. Shilling's recommendations. "He could really put the state on the map. You can be damned sure the governor will like it."

Much of what Dr. Shilling wants to do would require more money and legislative approval, but his proposal also included a clear strategy: to tie money to specific proposals, such as buying computers, so that the legislature could clearly see where money was going and could judge whether programs were successful.

The proposals created evident excitement among members of the state school board, which Governor Schaefer expanded last year in order to create a board that would take more initiative in reforming education in the state.

"This is a fine piece of work," said

See **SCHOOLS**, 9A, Col. 1

College Park dropouts include many achievers

By Patricia Meisol
Sun Staff Correspondent

COLLEGE PARK — More good students than bad have dropped out of the University of Maryland at College Park in recent years, apparently to enroll at other universities.

Although the overall dropout rate has improved, fewer students are being dismissed on academic grounds, and the majority of those who do leave are in good standing, according to a study not yet released by the university.

The data suggest that as better students are admitted, as they have been at College Park in recent years, the university will have to make more improvements in the academic environment to keep them. The trend holds true for black and white students alike, and calls into question traditional assumptions about dropouts and dropout prevention.

In the study, believed to be the first to look at the academic records of students who leave, College Park found that 71 percent of the students who dropped out in 1988 after two years of college were in good standing. Among black students who left, 55 percent were in good standing.

In tracking over five years the

See **REPORT**, 13A, Col. 1

NCAA rejects UM on May hearing **1D**

ASSOCIATED PRESS

Violeta Chamorro (wearing presidential sash) is applauded by outgoing President Daniel Ortega (right).

Chamorro inaugurated in Nicaragua

Army appointment provokes criticism

By John M. McClintock
Sun Staff Correspondent

MANAGUA, Nicaragua — Violeta Chamorro assumed the presidency of Nicaragua yesterday, ending 10 years of Sandinista rule and declaring, "We will sell the guns to buy productive machinery."

In her inaugural address, the 60-year-old widow abolished the draft and told the draftees they could go home as "soon as possible." Draftees make up about a third to a half of the army's strength.

Naming herself defense minister, she said she would "personally direct the demobilization and demilitarization process to bring an end to the war."

But the appointment of Gen. Humberto Ortega, the Sandinista defense minister and brother of outgoing President Daniel Ortega Saavedra, as army chief of staff provoked a round of boos from her supporters. Two members of her Cabinet resigned in protest.

Mrs. Chamorro declared an amnesty for "all political crimes," promised an economy based on free-market principles and vowed to investigate Sandinista land confiscations to see if they should be reversed.

Mrs. Chamorro asked the contras to live up to their agreement to disarm by June 10, but it was not clear how the rebels would react to General Ortega's staying on.

Yesterday was the date set for the 10,000 rebels to start laying down

See **NICARAGUA**, 8A, Col. 5

Official says U.S. won't cite Japan for trade actions

By Stephen E. Nordlinger
Washington Bureau of The Sun

WASHINGTON — U.S. Trade Representative Carla A. Hills ruled out yesterday citing Japan in the next few days for any unfair trade practices, despite sharp criticism from some members of the Senate Finance Committee.

During a tense hearing on trade policy, the panel's chairman, Sen. Lloyd Bentsen, D-Texas, warned Mrs. Hills that failing to name Japan could "poison the well" for congressional approval of trade agreements, including the one being drafted with the Soviet Union.

But she stood her ground, praising Japan for "moving further" than other countries over the past year in lowering barriers to U.S. products.

At a dramatic moment in the hearing, Mrs. Hills announced that Japan had agreed at an all-night session in Tokyo Tuesday to further open its markets to U.S. wood products.

That agreement removed the last of the three Japanese trade barriers targeted by the administration last year under the threat of possible retaliation if Tokyo did not remove the obstacles. During the last month, agreements were reached in the other two areas, space satellites and U.S.-made supercomputers.

In addition, Japan agreed earlier this month to end some of its deeply entrenched business practices that the United States contends impede imports and foreign investment.

The Cabinet-level Economic Poli-

See **TRADE**, 7A, Col. 1

THE SUN

INSIDE

West German political leader stabbed at rally

BONN, West Germany (AP) — Opposition leader Oskar Lafontaine was attacked at a campaign rally yesterday by a woman who stabbed him in the neck. Officials said he was in serious condition at a Cologne clinic.

Mr. Lafontaine, 46, the Social Democratic governor of Saarland state and Chancellor Helmut Kohl's leading challenger in December elections, was stabbed with a knife as he was about to sign his autograph for his attacker, police said.

Hospital authorities said that he was in serious condition because of blood loss but that his life was no longer in danger.

A neck artery was severed in the attack, ministry officials said.

Police late yesterday identified the assailant as Adelheid Streidel, 42, from Bad Neuenahr southwest of Bonn. The television network ZDF quoted relatives as saying the woman had a history of mental illness.

Hans-Juergen Foerster, a spokesman for the Federal Prosecutor's Office, said there was no evidence the woman has a "terrorist background."

Authorities said there was no known motive for the 9 p.m. attack.

See **GERMANY**, 5A, Col. 3

Survey finds women more sensitive--to flaws in men

Associated Press

NEW YORK — American women increasingly believe most men are mean, manipulative, oversexed, self-centered and lazy, according to a survey released yesterday. And the women are getting annoyed.

The Roper Organization poll found growing numbers of women expressing sensitivity to sexism and unhappiness with men on many issues. It compared data from identical questions asked 20 years ago. Some of the changes were sizable. In 1970, for example, two-thirds of women agreed that "most men are basically kind, gentle and thoughtful." In the new poll, only half of the 3,000 women who were surveyed agreed.

The reason? "Women's growing dissatisfaction with men is undoubtedly derived from their own rising expectations," the survey's authors said. "The more independent women of today expect more from men."

Those expectations apparently are going unfulfilled. Most women rated men negatively on their egos, libidos and domesticity. Sizable minorities went further: 42 percent, for instance, called men "basically selfish and self-centered."

Prudence took a particular pounding. Fifty-four percent of the women who were surveyed agreed that "most men look at a woman and immediately think how it would be to go to bed with her." In 1970, 41 percent had agreed.

The survey, financed by Philip Morris USA in the name of its Virginia Slims cigarettes, was conducted July 22 through Aug. 12 by in-person in-

See **MEN**, 12A, Col. 5

THURSDAY
JANUARY 17, 1991

THE SUN

LIGHT • FOR • ALL

SPORTS FINAL

VOL. 308 NO. 53 | BALTIMORE, MARYLAND | 35 CENTS

WAR IN GULF

Missiles, planes of four nations hit key targets in Iraq, Kuwait

WAR NEWS SUMMARY

'BATTLE HAS BEEN JOINED'

Cruise missiles and aircraft launched heavy bombing raids at targets in Kuwait and Iraq, aimed at destroying Iraq's offensive capabilities — including nuclear and chemical weaponry.

Accounts of the pre-dawn attack by the United States and its allies, dubbed Operation Desert Storm, were broadcast live by television correspondents in Baghdad, with vivid descriptions of anti-aircraft fire and explosions lighting the sky.

"Tonight, the battle has been joined," President Bush told the world. **Page 1A**

'WAIT NO LONGER'

President Bush told the nation he had ordered the United States into war because "the world could wait no longer," and he sought to put all the blame on Iraq's president, Saddam Hussein.

Mr. Bush sought to reassure the Iraqi people that the U.S. aim was not total conquest. He said he was praying for the safety of "the innocents [in Iraq] caught in this conflict," and spoke hopefully of the day when "Iraq itself" could "rejoin the family of peace-loving nations." **Page 1A**

'IT STARTED'

Across Maryland, word of war overrode all concerns: at a Naval Academy basketball game, where it was announced at Halsey Fieldhouse; at homes where families gathered around television sets; in a telephone call from a friend with the abrupt message: "It started." **Page 1A**

FOLLOWING SCRIPT

The massive air assault appeared to have followed almost precisely the script that military experts had for months been expecting the U.S.-led coalition to follow. Warplanes of four allied forces took aim at targets including the communications system that allows Saddam Hussein to command troops in the field. **Page 4A**

HOPE AT DAWN IN ISRAEL

Dawn today found Israelis huddled in their closed homes, anxiously watching for missiles from Iraq or violence from Palestinians. They felt cautious hope because the initial attack was not answered by a salvo of missiles launched at Israel, as Saddam Hussein had vowed. **Page 6A**

PROTEST AND PRAYER

Demonstrators across the street from the White House dusted off a chant used against President Lyndon B. Johnson during the Vietnam War and gathered in prayer. **Page 6A**

LIVE FROM BAGHDAD

ABC and CNN were in a league by themselves, delivering the first dramatic eyewitness accounts of Operation Desert Storm. **Page 8A**

OIL PRICES FROZEN

Major oil companies said they would freeze gasoline prices at current levels, minutes after U.S. officials confirmed bombing in Iraq and Kuwait. President Bush authorized the tapping of the Strategic Petroleum Reserve late last night, after oil prices soared to $40 a barrel in cash trading. **Page 1C**

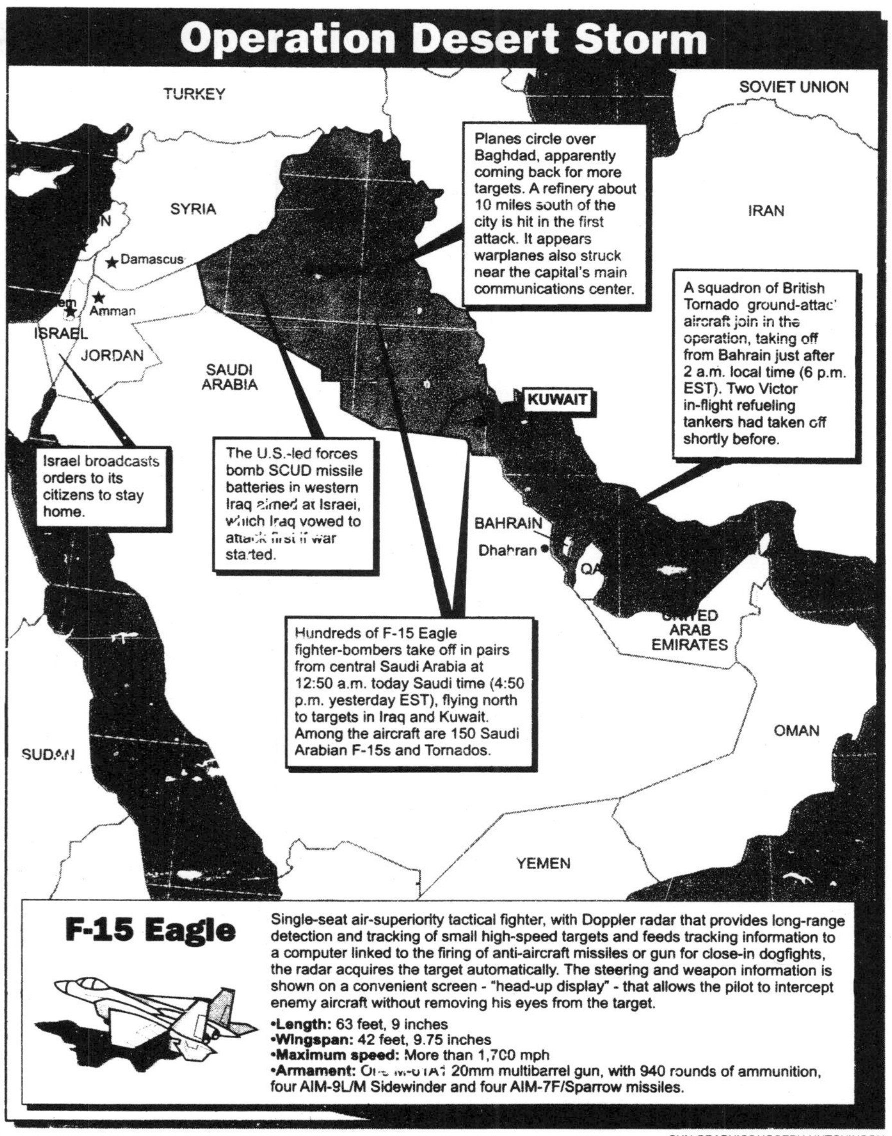
Operation Desert Storm
TURKEY
SOVIET UNION
SYRIA
IRAN
Damascus
Amman
ISRAEL
JORDAN
SAUDI ARABIA
KUWAIT
BAHRAIN
Dhahran
UNITED ARAB EMIRATES
OMAN
YEMEN
SUDAN
Planes circle over Baghdad, apparently coming back for more targets. A refinery about 10 miles south of the city is hit in the first attack. It appears warplanes also struck near the capital's main communications center.
A squadron of British Tornado ground-attack aircraft join in the operation, taking off from Bahrain just after 2 a.m. local time (6 p.m. EST). Two Victor in-flight refueling tankers had taken off shortly before.
Israel broadcasts orders to its citizens to stay home.
The U.S.-led forces bomb SCUD missile batteries in western Iraq aimed at Israel, which Iraq vowed to attack first if war started.
Hundreds of F-15 Eagle fighter-bombers take off in pairs from central Saudi Arabia at 12:50 a.m. today Saudi time (4:50 p.m. yesterday EST), flying north to targets in Iraq and Kuwait. Among the aircraft are 150 Saudi Arabian F-15s and Tornados.
F-15 Eagle
Single-seat air-superiority tactical fighter, with Doppler radar that provides long-range detection and tracking of small high-speed targets and feeds tracking information to a computer linked to the firing of anti-aircraft missiles or gun for close-in dogfights, the radar acquires the target automatically. The steering and weapon information is shown on a convenient screen - "head-up display" - that allows the pilot to intercept enemy aircraft without removing his eyes from the target.
•Length: 63 feet, 9 inches
•Wingspan: 42 feet, 9.75 inches
•Maximum speed: More than 1,700 mph
•Armament: 20mm multibarrel gun, with 940 rounds of ammunition, four AIM-9L/M Sidewinder and four AIM-7F/Sparrow missiles.

SUN GRAPHICS/JOSEPH HUTCHINSON

Battle is now joined, Bush tells U.S. public

By Mark Matthews
Washington Bureau of The Sun

WASHINGTON — The United States and its allies opened war against Iraq last night in a massive rush of air power, raining bombs and missiles on Baghdad and targets elsewhere with the aim of forcing Saddam Hussein's troops quickly from occupied Kuwait.

"The liberation of Kuwait has begun," President Bush said, in a statement read to reporters by White House spokesman Marlin Fitzwater as news correspondents in Baghdad reported wave after wave of pre-dawn attacks on the Iraqi capital.

Begun with Tomahawk missiles launched from ships, the battle, called Operation Desert Storm, proceeded with hundreds of U.S., British, Saudi and Kuwaiti planes, but no ground forces initially.

Several hours later, a confident chairman of the Joint Chiefs of Staff, Gen. Colin L. Powell, said that the offensive had met "no air resistance" and appeared so far "to have gone very, very well."

There were no official accounts of casualties, although eyewitnesses cited extensive damage to structures in Baghdad.

At the United Nations this morning, the United

See **WAR,** 5A, Col. 1

With news of gulf fighting come prayers in Maryland

It was just before the second half of last night's basketball game in Annapolis that one of the Navy players left the court, ran up into the stands and wrapped his arms around the neck of a woman seated in the fourth row.

"He's going to be all right, don't worry," Midshipman Mel Davis said softly to the woman, Barbara Rees. "He's going to be all right. I love you."

The moment came just a few minutes after it was announced to the Halsey Fieldhouse crowd, gathered to watch Navy play the University of Richmond, that the United States had begun military action against Iraq.

And with that announcement, Barbara Rees leaned on the shoulder of her husband, Tom, and cried. Their son Cliff, Navy's 11th all-time leading scorer and now a Marine pilot, was somewhere in the Persian Gulf.

"I just had this funny sensation all day — it was just in the pit of my stomach that this would happen tonight," said Mrs. Rees, an Ellicott City resident.

"I thought all day that they would announce it at the ballgame, and when they did, that shocked me as much as anything," she said.

The last time the Rees family heard from their son was just before

See **MARYLAND,** 7A, Col. 1

Bush blames Hussein for gulf war, says world 'could wait no longer'

By Karen Hosler and Lyle Denniston
Washington Bureau of The Sun

WASHINGTON — President Bush told the nation last night that he had ordered America into war because "the world could wait no longer."

Managing a small smile now and then, with his face showing no sign of strain, the commander in chief sought to put all of the blame for war on Iraq's president, Saddam Hussein.

It was "the dictator of Iraq" who actually had started the conflict — by invading Kuwait Aug. 2, Mr. Bush said.

The president spoke at 9 p.m., two hours after the moment Mr. Bush himself had fixed for the bombs to begin falling on Iraq's capital and on key military installations in that country.

As the fighting started, Mr. Bush was watching television news reports. In shirt sleeves and surrounded by aides, the president was "very matter-of-fact and calm," press secretary Marlin Fitzwater said.

The first smashing blows at Iraq came only from the skies, the president informed the country. "Ground forces are not engaged," he said as he began the 12-minute, sober but not gloomy speech from the Oval Office.

Bombs were continuing to fall as he spoke, Mr. Bush

See **BUSH,** 5A, Col. 4

President Bush, in 12-minute speech from Oval Office, says ground forces "are not engaged."

THE SUN
INSIDE

USF&G eliminates 900 jobs, including 360 in Baltimore, in an initial round of layoffs aimed at saving $42 million this year. **1C**

Index

Weather
Partly cloudy and windy. High, 50, low, 30. Yesterday's high, 53, low 39. **4B**

Gov. Schaefer begins his second term saying he will be undaunted by tough times. **1B**

A dentist suspected of infecting three patients with AIDS is faulted on sanitation practices. **13A**

Milligan's hit in 9th defeats Twins, 5-4: 1C

PENGUINS TOP CAPS, 6-4, FORCE GAME 7; EX-COLTS GM ACCORSI QUITS AS BROWNS VICE PRESIDENT: 1C

THURSDAY
APRIL 30, 1992

THE SUN

LIGHT · FOR · ALL

SPORTS FINAL

VOL. 310 NO. 300 BALTIMORE, MARYLAND HOME DELIVERY: 25 CENTS (in most areas) · NEWSSTAND: 50 CENTS

L.A. ERUPTS AFTER VERDICT

Rampage, scores of fires follow acquittal

'System failed,' Mayor Bradley says of outcome

By Linda Deutsch
Associated Press

SIMI VALLEY, Calif. — Four white Los Angeles police officers were acquitted of all but one assault charge yesterday in the videotaped beating of black motorist Rodney King. A mistrial was declared on one count.

The acquittals stunned and angered many in Los Angeles, where people had come to regard the videotape of the incident as incontrovertible evidence of brutality, racism and a police force out of control.

Violence, including looting and fires, broke out on Los Angeles' largely black south side a few hours after the verdict. As the violence spread across the residential and business area, Mayor Tom Bradley declared a local state of emergency and asked Gov. Pete Wilson to send in the National Guard.

President Bush, at a state dinner in Washington, appealed for calm.

"The court system has worked, and what's needed now is calm and respect for the law until the appeals process takes place," he said.

The verdicts, in the seventh day of deliberations, came after a year of political uproar sparked by the graphic videotape of a black man being beaten by white officers, denounced in many quarters as brutality. The backlash brought down the Los Angeles police chief.

"My client and I are just outraged," said Mr King's lawyer, Steve Lerman. "It sends a bad message. It says it's OK to go ahead and beat somebody when they're down and kick the crap out of them."

Mr. Bradley also blasted the jury's decision.

"Today, the system failed us," he said. "Today, this jury told the world what we all saw with our own eyes wasn't a crime. Today, that jury asked us to accept the senseless and brutal beating of a helpless man."

The Rev. Cecil L. Murray, sur-

See **KING**, 12A, Col. 5

REUTERS

A fire engulfs businesses on Vermont and Manchester streets in Los Angeles during rioting after the verdict.

1 killed, 72 hurt in riots; state of emergency called

From Wire Reports

LOS ANGELES — Angry rioters rampaged through the streets of the Los Angeles last night, smashing and looting stores, beating passing motorists and setting scores of fires.

At least one person was killed and at least 72 were injured.

California Gov. Pete Wilson ordered the National Guard to report for duty as scattered violence evolved into the city's largest riot since Watts erupted in flames in 1965.

The violence was ignited by the acquittals of four white Los Angeles police officers who were shown on videotape beating black motorist Rodney G. King in what has become a symbol here of the antagonisms between the city's minority groups and its peacekeepers.

In a drama that unfolded on live television, violence erupted first at the intersection of Florence Boulevard and Normandie Avenue in South Central Los Angeles and radiated to areas throughout the city.

Before the night's end, more than 100 fires raged in the city and sporadic gunfire flared in the streets. Fire companies were called in from other cities. Police with shotguns guarded firefighters.

"The fires in many cases have been very difficult for us to get to because of the hostility in the area. We're apparently getting police assistance in every case now." We're maxed out now," said Fire Chief Donald Manning. "It's a very, very tense situation for us."

Downtown, rioters massed outside Parker Center, hurling rocks and setting fire to a small kiosk. Then they moved onto City Hall and the *Los Angeles Times*, smashing windows along the way. Others set fires to palm trees lining U.S. Highway 101 near downtown.

Gunshots were heard in Lake View Terrace , where Mr. King was beaten 14 months ago. Demonstrators there marched on the Foothill

See **VIOLENCE**, 12A, Col. 1

Geography, prejudice swung verdict, experts say

By Henry Weinstein and Paul Lieberman
Los Angeles Times

LOS ANGELES — The acquittal of four white Los Angeles police officers accused of beating a black motorist was determined not so much by intricate courtroom strategy or any piece of evidence, but by geography and preconceived notions, legal experts said yesterday.

The case may have been decided the day Superior Court Judge Stanley Weisberg ordered the trial moved from Los Angeles to Simi Valley, an overwhelmingly white, conservative community 40 miles northwest of downtown that is long known as a popular home for law enforcement officers.

In another locale, jurors might have understood "the implications of being a black man in a car being chased by police," said a former Manhattan prosecutor, Ruth Jones.

But in Simi Valley, "the thought that these guys were just doing their job was not a leap of faith for them," said Ms. Jones, who monitored the trial for the Courtroom Television Network.

Several experts similarly said that the verdicts clearly reflected pre-existing attitudes — support of police, fear of street crime, perhaps

> *"This was a jury of people who ran away from Los Angeles to get away from Rodney King."*
>
> **BURT NEUBORNE**
> **New York University law professor**

See **JURY**, 12A, Col. 5

Operation Rescue to halt abortion clinics blockade

But group says it may resume efforts

By Arthur Hirsch
Staff Writer

BUFFALO, N.Y.— The anti-abortion forces of Operation Rescue, facing strong opposition from pro-choice activists and poor local support in this heavily Roman Catholic city, yesterday suspended their efforts to blockade abortion clinics.

The unexpected decision brought a halt to 11 days of sometimes violent protests marked by more than 400 arrests. But spokesmen for the organization said they might resume their street action by this morning.

Operation Rescue spokeswoman Karen Swallow Prior said sessions of prayer and discussion would continue "indefinitely," but added that more direct action was likely before the operation, dubbed "Spring of Life," ends Saturday.

"We are motivated by God," Ms. Prior said, facing reporters yesterday afternoon outside the St. John Maron Parish Center in the Buffalo suburb of Williamsville, where 200 Operation Rescue activists met behind closed doors. "We'll take this time and see what He wants us to do."

Group spokesman Gary McCullough said he considered it "rather unlikely" that Operation Rescue forces would remain cloistered inside the parish hall for another day.

Ms. Prior rejected published assessments that the campaign had failed to live up to its billing as an encore to the massive Operation Rescue abortion clinic blockade in Wichita, Kan. last summer. In July and August, 2,657 arrests were made there in six weeks and one abortion clinic chose to close for a week.

The suspension of street action buoyed pro-choice advocates, who

See **PROTEST**, 16A, Col. 1

ASSOCIATED PRESS

Death, injury on rails

Firefighters and rescue workers help injured passengers from Amtrak's northbound Colonial, which derailed when it collided with a truck in Newport News, Va. The truck's driver was killed and 53 people on the train were injured. (Article on 3A)

House votes 347-64 to give bank records to Justice Department

Democratic members buck leadership on key votes

By Larry Margasak
Associated Press

WASHINGTON — The Democratic-controlled House buckled under Republican pressure yesterday and voted 347-64 to comply with a Justice Department subpoena for voluminous records from the now defunct House bank.

The department's special counsel, Malcolm R. Wilkey, said he wants the microfilm records for his criminal investigation of the bank, where House members wrote thousands of overdrafts.

"By turning over these records, we answer that final, that lingering, ultimately that very painful question: whether anybody here broke the law," said Rep. Scott L. Klug, R-Wis.

Several Democrats argued that the Republican resolution to comply with the subpoena was political and would come back to haunt lawmakers if

See **BANK**, 7A, Col. 1

THE SUN

INDEX

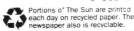

Weather,
Chance of showers.
High, 72; low, 48.
Yesterday's high,
70; low, 49. **10B**

0 83455 1

Portions of The Sun are printed each day on recycled paper. The newspaper also is recyclable.

3 6 SECTIONS F

Israelis allow Palestinians' 'Berkeley' to reopen after 4 years

By Doug Struck
Jerusalem Bureau

BIR ZEIT, Israeli-Occupied Territories — He smuggled the grade of his last student for the year out from behind the walls of prison: a B-plus in English communications.

By then, 1989, Professor Izzat Ghazzawi's classes had been closed down for a year. He was in prison, starting a 27-month term for political activities. And Bir Zeit University was taking its instruction underground.

The Palestinian university 15 miles north of Jerusalem reopened yesterday morning for the first time since it was closed by Israeli military authorities Jan. 8, 1988.

It was the last to reopen of six universities closed down during the Palestinian "intifada," or uprising. It was the last because authorities described it as a center for the plotters of revolt.

This was true, Mr. Ghazzawi says, remembering the 1980s, when the students were infused with the zeal of political indignation, and each week brought clashes with the Israeli army.

"Bir Zeit was a great place then. Although everything was done under the feeling of harassment, students were proud of expressing their political views, of writing their own opinions of saying their own speeches," recalls the 42-year-old English instructor.

Bir Zeit was the Berkeley of Palestine: a place of free speech, free love (at least, by the strict moral standards of Palestinian society), and political idealism.

"Bir Zeit students and faculty came from all over the country," Mr. Ghazzawi said. "They thought they were responsible for ending the occupation and responsible for getting freedom for their people."

When there was an incident elsewhere in the West Bank and Gaza, the first reaction was often at Bir Zeit. Students poured off the campus to demonstrate. They often made roadblocks of rocks and burning tires in the village of Bir Zeit or nearby Ramallah, and waited for the army to arrive.

The resulting conflicts were often violent. Many students were arrested; at least three students were killed. The students often retreated to the dormitories and conducted negotiations with the surrounding army. The authorities closed the university more than 15 times in the 1980s.

But after a traffic accident in Gaza Dec. 8, 1987, sparked the violence and mass demonstrations that became the intifada authorities put locks on the university's gates. At all the Palestinian universities, 14,500 students were shut out.

"It never came to my mind that this clo-

See **BIR ZEIT**, 6A, Col. 1

ANNE ARUNDEL

North County High

Pulling together gets cheerleaders a regional championship

Page 3B

Crofton

Association broke own rules governing bonuses for employees

Page 4B

A heavy favorite

Towson's Devin Boyd slims down and leads way to top of Big South

Sports, 1C

THE SUN

LIGHT • FOR • ALL

MONDAY, JANUARY 25, 1993 • VOLUME 312, NUMBER 60 BALTIMORE, MARYLAND HOME DELIVERY: 25¢ (in most areas) • NEWSSTAND: 50¢

Justice Thurgood Marshall dies

Nation mourns Baltimore native, rights leader, 84

By Albert Sehlstedt Jr.
Staff Writer

Thurgood Marshall, the indefatigable legal champion of America's mid-century civil rights movement, who became the first black person to serve on the Supreme Court, died yesterday of heart failure.

Justice Marshall, who had been in poor health for the past several years, died at 2 p.m. at Bethesda Naval Medical Center, according to Toni House, Supreme Court spokeswoman.

He was 84.

"He was a giant in the quest for human rights and equal opportunity in the whole history of our country," President Clinton said of the Baltimore native. "Every American should be grateful for the contributions he made as an advocate and as a justice of the United States Supreme Court."

Justice Marshall was to have appeared at the Clinton inaugural ceremony Wednesday to swear in Al Gore as vice president. But Justice Marshall was hospitalized, and the duty went instead to Justice Byron White.

Yesterday, Justice Marshall was characterized as a towering figure in the nation's history, not simply for his 24 years on the Supreme Court, but for the period before when he effected the legal strategies that ended discrimination in the country.

"The question looms in my mind," said Parren J. Mitchell, a civil rights leader and former congressman, "where would we be as a race today if there had been no Thurgood Marshall?"

Rep. Kweisi Mfume, Mr. Mitchell's successor representing the Baltimore area's 7th District, said that Justice Marshall "rewrote the dreams of young black people everywhere."

But Justice Marshall's contributions transcended race, said A. Leon Higginbotham, chief judge emeritus of the Third Circuit U.S. Court of Appeals: "For if he had not won the Brown case [in which the Supreme Court ruled that "separate but equal" school systems were unconstitutional], the door of equal opportunity would have been more tightly closed also to women, other minorities and the poor."

Lawrence Tribe, constitutional scholar and professor at Harvard Law School, called Justice Marshall simply "the greatest lawyer in the 20th century."

Civil rights leader Jesse L. Jackson said, "For most of us who grew up under segregation, we have never known a day without Thurgood Marshall hovering over us to protect us."

Justice Clarence Thomas, who replaced Marshall on the bench in 1991, said: "He was a great lawyer, a great jurist and a great man, and the country is better for his having lived."

Despite his failing health, Justice Marshall remained active in judicial matters until a few months ago.

In October, due to a viral infection, he canceled a trip to Baltimore, where he had volunteered to serve on a three-judge appellate panel hearing some 20 cases.

The Rev. Benjamin L. Hooks, executive director of the NAACP, called Justice Marshall, an "indispensable linchpin" in the civil rights movement.

"Baltimore has a particular reason to be proud," Mr. Hooks said, "that two of the giants of the movement were from here, Clarence Mitchell [Parren Mitchell's deceased older brother and for many years the NAACP's influential Washington lobbyist] in the legislative field and Thurgood Marshall in the legal field. Whatever else we say, without the work they did, we would be living in a segregated world."

Gov. William Donald Schaefer echoed the thought. "As Marylanders, we can be proud to call Thurgood Marshall as one of our own," the governor said. "We will miss his wisdom, determination and courage."

Mayor Kurt L. Schmoke called Justice Marshall "an inspiration to me since I first entered school."

Enolia McMillan, a Marshall contemporary who was the longtime president of the local chapter of the NAACP as well as the national president for six years, paid homage to Thurgood Marshall's intellect and his courage.

Despite his achievements, she

See **MARSHALL**, 6A, Col. 1

Justice Marshall, shown here on his first day on the Supreme Court, became a frequent dissenter as it shifted to the right.

A man who, sometimes alone, toppled color barriers

By Lyle Denniston
Washington Bureau

NEWS ANALYSIS

Thurgood Marshall used simple brilliance, raw courage and rasping humor to force America to think and act differently about race.

A son of Baltimore who never stopped resenting the city's racist past revolutionized the law by using a Constitution that he believed had been born out of racial bigotry.

Mr. Marshall found enough promise and flexibility within the Constitution to turn it into an instrument of sweeping reform that destroyed Jim Crowism in the United States.

Saddened in his later years as the Supreme Court's first black justice by the passing of liberalism, both from the court and from U.S. public policy, Justice Marshall died yesterday an ailing man of 84.

His last disappointment had come just last week, when he was not well enough to fulfill a promise to give the oath of office to Vice President Al Gore.

But Justice Marshall had already passed into history on the strength of a whole nation's remembrance that it was he, sometimes almost alone, who had broken down most of his country's color barriers.

He was as much a man of the past as of the future in recent years, unable to adjust to the fads of political correctness and constitutional compromise.

He never quite understood why he, of all people, would have been thought of as being wrong when he continued to refer to black people as "Negroes," even after it became politically obligatory to refer to them as "African-Americans."

Given to back-slapping, barracks room jokes and unrelieved stubbornness about his own views, Justice Marshall was never successful at "massing" the court to follow his lead.

See **LEGAL**, 7A, Col. 1

Bentsen hints at broad increase in energy taxes

Goal is to slash federal deficit

By Robert A. Rankin
Knight-Ridder News Service

WASHINGTON — Treasury Secretary Lloyd Bentsen hinted strongly yesterday that President Clinton will propose raising taxes on all forms of energy — including gasoline, oil, coal, natural gas and electricity — as part of his economic program.

Mr. Bentsen also all but buried any lingering hope that Mr. Clinton will cut taxes for the middle class, and he also played down expectations for expanded tax breaks for Individual Retirement Accounts, a cause he championed as a senator.

Speaking on NBC's "Meet the Press," Mr. Bentsen left no doubt that Mr. Clinton's most important economic goal is to reduce the mammoth federal budget deficit and stressed that an important element of that effort will be raising taxes on consumption.

President George Bush, in his final budget, projected that the shortfall will hit a record $327 billion in fiscal 1993, which ends Sept. 30.

The treasury secretary dismissed the idea of a national sales tax but said proposals to increase taxes on Social Security and Medicare benefits remain "on the table," as do proposals to raise excise taxes on sales of tobacco and alcohol.

In addition, he reaffirmed that the income tax rate on families making

See **TAXES**, 7A, Col. 3

ASSOCIATED PRESS

Treasury Secretary Lloyd Bentsen says final decisions to come.

State budget cuts wound drug treatment efforts

Many seeking help put on waiting lists

By Mike Klingaman
Staff Writer

In sub-freezing cold, Doris, a 45-year-old heroin addict, waits in line for hours outside a drug-counseling center in Baltimore.

No luck. Not enough openings. She's told to go home and come back in a week. Doris weeps in frustration. "I've hit bottom and I'm tired. Tired of the streets. Tired of myself. And I can't get help," she says.

Like stabs from a blunt needle, state budget cuts caused by the recession have left serious wounds in Maryland's drug treatment efforts.

Since 1991, the substance-abuse budget, including federal funds, has decreased from $55.5 million to $50.8 million, closing some clinics and paring many others to the bone. And cuts in the state medical-insurance program for the poor also have hurt drug treatment.

At least 16 state-funded or hospital-based centers have closed, including:

☐ Three detoxification units in Baltimore, at Bon Secours Hospital, Liberty Medical Center and at Church Hospital.

☐ Seven long-term care clinics, totaling 292 beds, in the city and four counties: Anne Arundel, Carroll, Somerset and Worcester.

☐ Three halfway houses, a residential treatment center in Southern Maryland, and an adolescent group home in Montgomery County.

In addition, the state Division of Correction's drug-counseling program has been shut down.

Overall, the number of Marylanders getting help is expected to drop about 11 percent, from 55,000 in fiscal 1992 — which ended last June 30 — to an estimated 49,000 this fiscal year. State health officials be-

See **DRUGS**, 5A, Col. 1

In weighty Japanese ruling, American to gain sumo crown

By John E. Woodruff
Tokyo Bureau

Akebono's last step to promotion came with a blaze of thrusts to the throat.

TOKYO — No choice this time. The next Yokozuna — grand champion of sumo wrestling, the most Japanese of all sports — will have to be an American despite years of official and semiofficial resistance.

Akebono, or Chad Rowan to his friends back home in Hawaii, unceremoniously drove Japan's great nativist hope out of the ring in a matter of seconds yesterday to win his second tournament championship in a row.

Two championships in a row is traditionally the one sure way to get the nod from the sober-faced men of the Yokozuna Promotion Council. Winning the fall tournament 14-1 and the New Year's one 13-2, as the huge Akebono did, only makes it harder to deny the promotion.

The council has long been reluctant to promote a foreigner, but Japanese sports newspapers published full-color extra editions last night to say the taboo will die at a meeting today. Television sportscasters said Akebono's promotion was already decided in telephone calls among the 12 council members.

Akebono thus broke through where fellow-Hawaiian Konishiki, or Salevaa Atisanoe, spent much of the past decade at the verge.

A year ago, Konishiki won two tournaments out of three and placed second in the one between, but he was denied promotion.

Akebono seemed painfully aware yesterday that personal demeanor was one of the arguments used against his fellow Hawaiian a year ago. He kept a tight grip on his emotions as he accepted the truckloads of trophies, foodstuffs, kitsch and other booty that are heaped upon a tournament champion.

He let loose none of the tears that became Konishiki's post-tournament trademark. At his post-victory press conference, he ignored sweat trickling down the sides of his face and kept his countenance grim and his lips tightly together, parting them only for a few syllables in response to each question.

"Maa, shiremasen" — meaning, "Well, I can't say" — he said over and over, especially when asked whether he was ready for promotion to his sport's highest rank.

Just once, he went this far: "When I came to Japan. Yokozuna was my dream."

Taciturnity can only stand him in good stead with the stewards of a sport whose roots run deep in the

See **SUMO**, 5A, Col. 3

ASSOCIATED PRESS

United States' Akebono (left) out-duels Japan's Takahanada, earns right to become the first non-Japanese sumo grand champion.

On her own

Winnie Mandela, estranged from both the African National Congress and her famous husband, says she has found new causes and new freedom.

Article on Page 3A

THE SUN

INDEX

Weather

Partly cloudy, windy. High, 40; low, 20. Yesterday's high, 60; low, 40. 14B

Portions of The Sun are printed each day on recycled paper. The newspaper also is recyclable.

1 SP 4 SECTIONS

INSIDE

Newest columnist

Susan Reimer shares life as parent, wife and daughter

Today, 1D

Snooze blues

Sleep patterns often get worse with aging

Today, 1D

Orioles weather storm

Orioles outlast two rain delays, beat Royals, 6-5

Sports, 1C

THE SUN

LIGHT • FOR • ALL

SPORTS FINAL

TUESDAY, JULY 20, 1993 • VOLUME 313, NUMBER 56 — BALTIMORE, MARYLAND — HOME DELIVERY: 25¢ (in most areas) • NEWSSTAND: 50¢

Rostenkowski alleged to embezzle $21,300

Ex-official links him to House postal scam

New York Times News Service

WASHINGTON — The former postmaster of the House of Representatives has told prosecutors that he helped Rep. Dan Rostenkowski, the powerful Illinois Democrat, embezzle $21,300, according to prosecutors, defense lawyers and public records that describe some of the transactions.

The postmaster, Robert V. Rota, pleaded guilty in federal District Court in Washington yesterday to one count of conspiracy and two counts of embezzlement and said he had helped an undisclosed number of lawmakers embezzle tens of thousands of dollars since his appointment in 1972 until 1991, when he resigned.

Government and defense lawyers said that the guilty plea was a significant step toward indicting Mr. Rostenkowski but that it could be weeks before the government would move against the Chicago Democrat. Still, the plea by Rota, who has agreed to testify against Mr. Rostenkowski, came at a delicate moment, when the House and Senate have just begun negotiations on President Clinton's economic program.

As chairman of the House Ways and Means Committee, Mr. Rostenkowski will be one of the central figures in those talks, and Mr. Clinton will also need him badly in months to come as Congress considers health care, welfare, trade and other issues.

In court yesterday, Rota did not identify Mr. Rostenkowski, referring instead to "Congressman A" and to "Congressman B," who, the former official said, had stolen $9,300. The government also did not identify either lawmaker, but documents supporting Rota's plea arrangement clearly showed that Mr. Rostenkowski was Congressman A and that Joe Kolter, a Democrat who lost his Pennsylvania seat last year, was Congressman B.

Mr. Rostenkowski's aides said the lawmaker was in Chicago and could not be reached for comment. A reporter was unable to find the lawmaker at his home in Chicago, and the aides in Washington declined to discuss Rota's guilty plea. The lawmaker's Washington lawyer, Stanley Brand, did not return telephone calls.

"Over the course of two decades,

See **POST**, 4A, Col. 4

Clinton issues gay policy

REUTERS

President Clinton salutes at the National Defense University at Fort McNair, applauded by (from left) Gen. Colin L. Powell, Adm. Frank Kelso II and Gen. Merrill McPeak.

Military chiefs back directive; gay leaders angry

By Carl M. Cannon
Washington Bureau

WASHINGTON — President Clinton, clearly indicating that he wanted to go further, chipped away at the military ban on homosexuals yesterday in announcing a policy he called "an honorable compromise," but which gay leaders termed a near-complete retreat.

In a speech to senior military officers assembled at Fort McNair here, the president conceded that the new policy dubbed "don't ask, don't tell, don't pursue" is hardly "a perfect solution," adding that it is "not identical with some of my own goals."

Under the new policy, homosexuals will be allowed to serve in the military as long as they stay in the closet, remain celibate and, under most circumstances, deny their homosexuality.

But the president said the policy was a step forward for gays — and for the military — and called on the brass to help him implement it.

"As your commander in chief, I charge all of you to carry out this policy with fairness, with balance and with due regard for the privacy of individuals," the president said. "We must and will protect unit cohesion and troop morale. We must and will continue to have the best fighting force in the world."

The president's plan, which came not in an executive order but in a directive from Defense Secretary Les Aspin to the service chiefs, faces two immediately hurdles. The first is in Congress, where Sen. Sam Nunn, a fierce opponent of lifting the ban against gays, will hold hearings today. The Georgia Democrat has said that if he is not satisfied, he will move to codify the ban in legislation, which would make it harder to change in the future.

House leaders, including openly gay Rep. Barney Frank, a Massachusetts Democrat, were predicting that Mr. Clinton's policy would satisfy House members, meaning that they might not go along with the Senate.

The second challenge is in the courts. Gay rights lawyers, denouncing the new policy as flatly

See **GAYS**, 8A, Col. 1

Gays in military fear careers will end

Many went public to help fight ban

By Ann LoLordo
Staff Writer

It was soon after the president put to rest yesterday any hope that Lt. Zoe Dunning might remain in the Navy Reserve that the telephone call came.

The naval officer, whom she didn't even know, was calling to say he was sorry for the way the military has treated the 29-year-old Naval Academy graduate and lesbian.

It was the lone bright spot in a day of disappointment for the lieutenant.

Like several other service members whose futures in the military rested on the policy announced yesterday, Lieutenant Dunning said Pentagon directive would do little to change the lives of homosexual service members. Earlier this year, buoyed by the commander in chief's pledge to rescind the ban on gays in the military, she announced to the world she was a homosexual.

> *"The people who came out [have] been left to slide through the cracks."*
>
> LT. ZOE DUNNING

The new policy — dubbed "don't ask, don't tell, don't pursue" — offers them no protection to live openly as a homosexual and seems to assure that she and others will be discharged, they say.

"The people who came out [have] been left to slide through the cracks," said Lieutenant Dunning, who after serving six years of active duty transferred into the reserves to attend graduate school at Stanford University in 1991. "I'm disappointed he didn't stand his ground and do the right thing."

Lieutenant Dunning, who began her annual reserve training yesterday just hours before the new policy was announced, stood in her fatigues listening to Mr. Clinton on the radio yesterday at the Alameda, Calif., Naval Air Station.

"A lot of people say we have taken a small step forward. We have not," says Lt. Tracy W. J. Thorne, a Naval aviator who publicly announced that he was gay last year and is being processed for dis-

See **CAREERS**, 8A, Col. 1

After first quarter, city No. 2 in NFL sales race

Trails Charlotte in premium seat effort

By Jon Morgan
Staff Writer

Two weeks into a two-month effort to sell pricey NFL tickets, Baltimore is ahead of flood-battered St. Louis but behind Charlotte, N.C., in the race to prove fan support.

"The response has been overwhelming. The response has been beyond our projections," said Herbert J. Belgrad, chairman of the Maryland Stadium Authority and coordinator of the city's effort to land an NFL expansion franchise. "We could not be more pleased."

Cities competing for an NFL team were asked to file updates with a league-appointed accounting firm based on sales through last Friday. The next update is due July 30.

League officials say they are not concerned about the speed of sales, but merely want to see if the cities can support the projections in their applications. Five cities are competing for two franchises, but only three — Charlotte, N.C., Baltimore and St. Louis — are engaged in the market-testing sales effort.

Of the 100 sky boxes being marketed for Baltimore's downtown stadium, 70 were officially leased as of Friday, most for the longest, seven-year term. About half, or 3,800, of the 7,500 "club seats" have been leased. Club seats are roomier than regular seats and have access to the luxury lounges.

Charlotte reported all of its 8,314 club seats and 82 of its 102 sky boxes leased. St. Louis, where resi-

See **TICKET**, 7A, Col. 2

PLAYGROUNDS AS KILLING FIELDS

America's young ending disputes, lives of potential with violence

ByFrank Langfitt
Staff Writer

ASSOCIATED PRESS

Jason Smith, 15, is escorted from a hearing in Pennsylvania on murder, voluntary manslaughter and other charges last month.

After a year of bullying by a classmate, a high school freshman in rural Pennsylvania shot him in the head last May during biology class.

On the stoop of a Brooklyn brownstone two weeks later, police say, a 10-year-old boy ended an argument by driving a steak knife into the chest of his 12-year-old friend.

This month in a central Florida subdivision, a 14-year-old was accused of shooting and killing his younger step-sister.

Snapshots of human tragedy, these stories of youth homicide flash across the front pages of newspapers and television screens every week in America. Behind the words and images lie an increasing number of lost lives and potential.

They point to a change in human relations that concerns authorities: young people are killing more often in America, and often they are killing each other.

Between 1965 and 1990, the murder arrest rate for juveniles age 10 to 17 grew by 332 percent, according to a recent FBI study. And, while that part of the youth population declined by more than 2 million, the number of arrests mushroomed from 822 to 3,284.

There has been a "tremendous change in attitude," says James Alan Fox, dean of the College of Criminal Justice at Northeastern University in Boston. "It reflects a desensitization to violence."

Researchers lay blame for the increase on the usual suspects of social science: dysfunctional families, substance abuse, television violence, child abuse and poverty. The declining influence of churches and schools have left children with fewer guidelines.

But the most obvious and fatal factor, they say, is guns.

See **MURDERS**, 9A, Col. 1

59% of students claim access to gun, poll says

Third say guns will cut their lives short

By Sandy Banisky
Staff Writer

Guns have become so commonplace in the lives of U.S. children, a new survey says, that 59 percent of students from sixth grade through high school say they could get a handgun if they wanted one — and a third of those say they could get one "within an hour."

The survey, released yesterday by the Chicago-based Joyce Foundation, also found that 15 percent of the students said they had carried a handgun in the past 30 days.

Nine percent said they had shot a gun at someone.

"The poll shows that yesteryear's adolescent fistfight has become today's adolescent shootout," said Jay Winsten, director of Center for Health Communication at the Harvard School of Public Health. "Yesteryear's black eye and injured pride is today's gaping, 2-inch exit wound."

Guns and violence, the survey concludes, have helped create a deep pessimism among youth.

About 35 percent said they believed "my chances of living to a ripe old age will be cut short because of the threat of my being wiped out from guns."

> *"Yesteryear's adolescent fistfight has become today's adolescent shootout."*
>
> JAY WINSTEN
> Harvard School of Public Health

The poll of 2,508 students in sixth through 12th grade was conducted by Louis Harris of LH Research for the Harvard School of Public Health with a grant from the Joyce Foundation. It has a margin of error of 3 percentage points.

The students came from 96 elementary, middle and senior high schools — public, private and Catholic — in urban, suburban and rural areas across the country.

Among the poll's findings:

□ Four percent of the students say they have taken a handgun to school in the past year.

□ Eleven percent say they have

See **GUNS**, 9A, Col. 6

INDEX

President Clinton is expected today to name Louis J. Freeh, an ex-FBI agent who is now a federal judge, as director of the FBI. The president fired William S. Sessions (above) as director yesterday. **Page 7A**

Miyazawa hangs on

Leaders of Japan's ruling party turned on Prime Minister Kiichi Miyazawa, above, demanding that he resign. **Page 3A**

Bridge	8D	Editorials	10A
Business	10C	Horoscope	9D
Classified	6B	Lottery	12B
Comics	9D	Movies	3D
Deaths	5B	Television	7D

Weather

Sunny and hot. High 95; low, 70. Yesterday's high, 84; low, 76. **12B**

0 083455 1

Portions of The Sun are printed each day on recycled paper. The newspaper also is recyclable.

SP 2 4 SECTIONS F

INSIDE

Pet cures

Dogs and cats are good for what ails you

Today, 1D

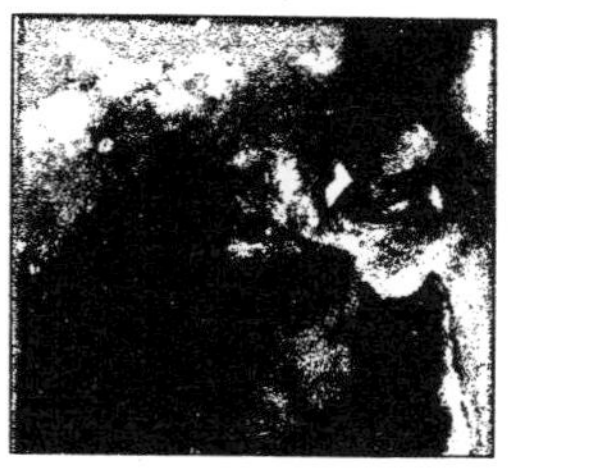

Purple reign

Prince's newest all-hits release keeps him on top

Today, 1D

O's bullpen falters

Orioles lose 4-run lead, fall, 6-4, in Boston, drop to 2 games back

Sports, 1C

THE SUN

LIGHT • FOR • ALL

SPORTS FINAL

TUESDAY, SEPTEMBER 14, 1993 • VOLUME 313, NUMBER 104 BALTIMORE, MARYLAND HOME DELIVERY: 25¢ (in most areas) • NEWSSTAND: 50¢

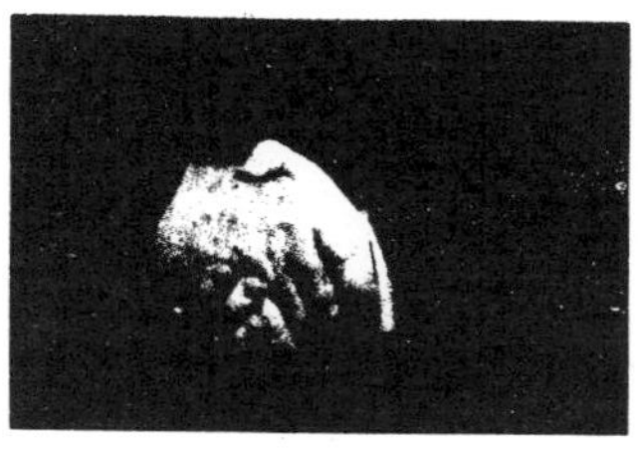

YITZHAK RABIN

"We who have fought against you, the Palestinians, we say to you today in a loud and a clear voice, enough of blood and tears. Enough!"

PRESIDENT CLINTON

"A peace of the brave is within our reach. Throughout the Middle East, there is a great yearning for the quiet miracle of a normal life."

YASSER ARAFAT

"My people are hoping that this agreement . . . marks the beginning of the end of a chapter of pain and suffering . . ."

A day of 'history and hope'

Israel, PLO sign peace agreement in Washington

ASSOCIATED PRESS

Israeli Prime Minister Yitzhak Rabin and PLO Chairman Yasser Arafat clasp hands in a sign of peace as President Clinton looks on.

Gaza Palestinians celebrate signing of interim pact

By Doug Struck
Jerusalem Bureau

GAZA, Israeli-Occupied Gaza Strip — The celebration in the Gaza Strip over yesterday's peace agreement between the PLO and Israel erupted like a shaken soda, spraying thousands of Palestinians into the street in a froth of joy.

They waved palm fronds, scattered sweets on the street, ~~applauded and~~ cheered with an enthusiasm unseen in the grim warrens of Gaza, where the rigors of poverty and the rule of a military occupation force had long ago jelled into a permanent gloom.

One old man with weak and watery eyes watched the celebration honk its way down the street, trucks overflowing with men waving the Palestinian flag, women trilling welcome to the new promise of peace.

He said he had waited for this day since 1937, the year the British Lord Peel Commission recommended giving Jews a state.

But his wait was not important, he had concluded. He waved his cane at several small boys.

"Look at the children. Look at how happy they are," he mused, contemplating them with curiosity. "This is the first day they have really felt this."

For a change, the crowd in the street was not an angry mob. For a change there were no stones launched by young boys in frustration, answered by young soldiers with bullets.

Gazans said there had not been such large and festive crowds on the streets for decades, certainly not since the start of the Palestinian uprising in 1987.

In Jericho, there were similar scenes, as Palestinians celebrated the Israeli-PLO agreement. In Jerusalem, the Palestinian flag was hoisted above Orient House, the gracious old mansion that houses the Palestinian negotiating delegation.

The flag symbolized the suddenness of change. Two weeks ago, Is-

See **GAZA**, 11A, Col. 1

Accord may lead to comprehensive peace in Mideast

By Mark Matthews
Washington Bureau

WASHINGTON — Israeli and Palestinian leaders overcame a century of hatred and bloodshed yesterday to unite behind a vision of peace on land sacred to both.

Two old warriors, Israeli Prime Minister Yitzhak Rabin and Yasser Arafat, chairman of the Palestine Liberation Organization, used the White House signing of an interim accord between their peoples to say it was time, finally, to "give peace a chance."

"Enough of blood and tears. Enough," Mr. Rabin exclaimed in a raspy voice that evoked decades of suffering.

Mr. Arafat, who had led an armed campaign to replace Israel with a Palestinian state, said "the land of peace yearns for a just and comprehensive peace."

With symbolic handshakes and muted nationalist rhetoric, the simple, graceful South Lawn ceremony, televised worldwide, marked a clear turning point in the bloody history of Israelis and Palestinians and a major step toward a comprehensive settlement of the conflict between the Jewish state and its neighbors.

President Clinton called it an occasion of "history and hope." Among the psychological breakthroughs toward reconciliation was a line of Arab ambassadors shaking hands with Israel's prime minister and foreign minister.

"That is a first in the history of the Middle East conflict," a senior Clinton aide said.

With Mr. Clinton between them, the leaders looked on as Israeli Foreign Minister Shimon Peres and Mahmoud Abbas of the PLO signed a declaration of principles on interim Palestinian self-government. It calls for withdrawal of Israeli occupation forces from much of the Gaza Strip and from Jericho on the West Bank and for the establishment of Palestinian authority there.

The pact also calls for a phased Israeli withdrawal from elsewhere in the West Bank, although Israel

See **PEACE**, 10A, Col. 1

INSIDE

Pain of past yields to promise of future

By Gilbert A. Lewthwaite
Washington Bureau

WASHINGTON — To be a witness to history yesterday was to share a moment of tremendous emotion and hope, a moment that brought a hush like no other to the South Lawn of the White House, a hush so still that you could almost hear the signatures being penned to the new Middle East peace agreement.

It was, said President Clinton, "one of history's defining dramas."

That drama, at its simplest, was a handshake between two foes grown old in the blood and bitterness of war. Hands that once took up arms against each other were now clasped in a sign of peace between Yasser Arafat, chairman of the Palestine Liberation Organization and Israeli Prime Minister Yitzhak Rabin, a sign of reconciliation between Arab and Jew that all the world was waiting to see.

Sharing the experience at the White House were two former presidents, eight former secretaries of state and an assembled cast of international and national dignitaries, some reduced to tears by the poignancy and promise of it all.

At its loftiest, it was a day of vision, an occasion for turning to the Bible, the Torah, the Koran for

See **CEREMONY**, 10A, Col. 1

Clarke reveals intention to run for mayor in 1995

Bid by Schmoke would not deter her

By Eric Siegel and Michael A. Fletcher
Staff Writers

Baltimore City Council President Mary Pat Clarke, whose political skirmishes with Mayor Kurt L. Schmoke have grown more frequent and bitter, says she intends to run for mayor in 1995 even if Mr. Schmoke is in the race.

The second-term City Council president said "it's a very sure shot" that she will seek the mayor's office in 1995, even if it means running against Mr. Schmoke, who for the past several months has been contemplating a bid for governor next year.

"My plans are as sure as plans can be that people make," said Ms. Clarke, adding that she could not foresee any circumstances in which she would run for council president again instead of running for mayor.

"I have to just move forward as best I can and let everyone else do what they will and see what happens."

Ms. Clarke's statements about her political plans for 1995, made in interviews with *The Sun*, mark the first time she has said publicly that she would consider challenging Mr. Schmoke for the city's highest office.

See **CLARKE**, 8A, Col. 4

INDEX

Portions of The Sun are printed each day on recycled paper. The newspaper also is recyclable.

SP 4 4 SECTIONS F

125 mids now suspected as exam scandal grows

6 already convicted of cheating

By Tom Bowman and JoAnna Daemmrich
Staff Writers

The Navy's inspector general is building cases against a growing number of midshipmen who escaped charges earlier this year in what is becoming the largest cheating scandal in memory at the Naval Academy.

Investigators now suspect at least 125 midshipmen had some knowledge of the final exam for Electrical Engineering 311, ranging from receiving a computer message urging them to study a particular question to actually getting a copy of the test.

While some bought copies of the test for one of the school's toughest courses, others may have been unaware that they saw the actual exam, believing it was "good gouge," academy slang for old tests, sources familiar with the investigation said.

Initially, 28 juniors were accused of cheating from copies of the fall-semester final.

Eleven were convicted by honor boards made up of midshipmen, but senior academy officials later cleared five of them.

But investigators now believe that a far larger group saw at least some

See **ACADEMY**, 6A, Col. 1

FINAL EDITION

OQUIST HELPS O'S RALLY TO BEAT TORONTO, 6-3, 1D

THE SUN

LIGHT • FOR • ALL

LATEST NEWS & SPORTS

WEDNESDAY, MAY 11, 1994 | HOME DELIVERY: 25¢ (in most areas) • NEWSSTAND: 50¢ | BALTIMORE, MARYLAND

STREISAND SHINES

GENE SWEENEY JR./SUN STAFF PHOTO

Barbra Streisand demonstrated her star power in a performance that thrilled fans at the USAir Arena in Landover last night. Ms. Streisand, touring for the first time in 28 years, offered more of a one-woman revue than a traditional concert for the 18,000 fans who paid up to $350 apiece to see the show.

Review, Page 1C

South Africa enters new era

Inauguration climaxes Mandela's turbulent journey

By Michael Hill
Johannesburg Bureau of The Sun

PRETORIA, South Africa — Nelson Mandela was inaugurated as president of South Africa yesterday, culminating one of the most remarkable journeys in the history of modern nations.

For Mr. Mandela, the journey began in a rural village of the Transkei, went through the turbulence of black township politics, persevered during imprisonment and, finally, reached triumph at the ballot box.

And in his triumph, the 75-year-old president pleaded for reconciliation among a people torn by decades of hatred and rivalry.

"The time for the healing of the wounds has come," he said. "The moment to bridge the chasms that divide us has come.

"Never, never, and never again shall it be that this beautiful land will again experience the oppression of one by another," he vowed, drawing the loudest applause. "Let freedom reign. God bless Africa!"

The gala day was full of symbolism and irony.

Mr. Mandela took the oath of his new office during a 45-minute ceremony in an amphitheater at the Union Buildings, the impressive administrative capital built of sandstone in 1912 to mark the unity of the previously warring white-run states that joined to make up the Union of South Africa.

That building was not pockmarked by the shells of revolution, the toll that history usually exacts in transformations as stunning as South Africa's. Instead, it was handed over

See **SOUTH AFRICA**, *12A*

REUTERS

President Nelson Mandela (right) and Deputy President F. W. de Klerk join in celebration of a new South Africa.

Clinton set to send U.S. troops to Haiti

Officials confirm president's plans

By Kenneth Freed
Los Angeles Times

PORT-AU-PRINCE, Haiti — The United States plans to send at least 600 heavily armed and protected troops to purge this nation's military, even if a broader, tougher program of international sanctions forces the army regime to give up power, diplomats and Haitian sources say.

The only question is the timing and ultimate size of the force, sources say.

"When [the U.S. forces] come is under discussion in Washington right now," a U.S. official in Haiti said yesterday.

He said the choices are to send the troops in before or after the local military leaders leave. The Americans "prefer that they leave first," said one source, "but if they don't, the troops will go in anyway."

A United Nations Security Council resolution has given three Haitian military leaders until May 21 to resign and leave the country. The leaders are Lt. Gen. Raoul Cedras, the army commander-in-chief; Maj. Gen. Philippe Biambi, the deputy army chief, and Lt. Col. Joseph Michel Francois, the national police commander.

If they do not resign, an international economic embargo will take effect, banning all trade and commercial dealings with the tiny nation except for certain essentials.

President Clinton has said if General Cedras and the others resist, the United States will consider using military force.

But he has maintained that he has not made a decision and wants to let the sanctions strategy play out.

But U.S. officials in Washington, as well as diplomats and experts in Haiti, say that the president is only employing semantics in a political ploy to ease U.S. congressional objections to a major American military action.

"It is not a question of whether there will be an American military intervention here," said a diplomat from another country, "but its size and when it gets here. I think by the time it is all done, we will see several thousand U.S. troops here, even if Cedras leaves tomorrow and [ousted President Jean-Bertrand] Aristide arrives the day after."

"What Clinton will want to do is say [that his course of action] is a reconstituted 'Harlan County' and that it doesn't represent any change from what was agreed to at Governors Island," he said. "I can tell you this will be a far different situation."

He was referring to an agreement signed in July on Governors Island in New York Harbor that provided for

See **HAITI**, *16A*

LLOYD FOX/SUN STAFF PHOTO

At Harborplace, Marci Russian (left), Melissa O'Hara and Melanie Riedel of Edgewood, N.J., use filtered viewers.

Sun eerily subdued by interloping moon

Marylanders view eclipse in Texas

By Frank D. Roylance
Sun Staff Writer

SIERRA BLANCA, Texas — The quiet rangeland four miles north of this lonely truck stop grew even quieter yesterday.

As the moon's shadow crossed into Texas from Mexico and dimmed the morning sunshine, the temperature fell from 83 degrees to 71, and the desert birds settled into the sagebrush.

"They think it's evening coming," said astronomer David W. Dunham, 51, of Greenbelt, who had traveled from Maryland to Texas seeking the best view of yesterday's solar eclipse.

The subdued sunlight was eerie, a dimness similar to the sensation a person gets at the onset of a faint. And the sun was like a winter sun, offering little warmth to the skin.

At 10:10 a.m. MDT, the two cusps or "horns" of the crescent sun looked like jet contrails on a collision course in the viewfinder of

See **ECLIPSE**, *14A*

Jordan a major attraction in minors

Like teammates, ex-NBA superstar still learning game

By Peter Schmuck
Sun Staff Writer

BIRMINGHAM, Ala. — It is playoff time in the NBA, where Michael Jordan once ruled both earth and sky, but that seems a world away as he lopes across the outfield at Hoover Metropolitan Stadium.

Is this a second chance or a second childhood? The Birmingham Barons don't really care. Air Jordan has inflated home attendance and pumped up interest in the Double-A Southern League as he pursues his unlikely quest to reach the major leagues.

Everybody likes Mike, though it is unclear whether they have come for a sideshow or a serious assault on the seemingly impossible. He is certainly a curiosity — a 31-year-old rookie who could buy the team with his pocket change — but there no longer seems to be any doubt that he is in earnest.

Not when he is the first to arrive at the ballpark, five hours before game time for a one-on-one coaching session. Not when he is willing to spend 12 hours on a bus with his youthful teammates. This has become as much a test of character as of his long-dormant baseball skills.

"There are different ways to look at it," Jordan said. "This is the game I started out to play, and this is the game I'm going to end my career with. I started out in a humbling situation, and this is a humbling situation. I'm not afraid to show that humble side. I'm not afraid to fail. Maybe people can learn something from that."

Maybe Jordan can learn the nuances of a complex game before he is too old to play it in the major leagues. Opinions vary, but he has made remarkable progress during the four weeks he has spent with the Barons. It is only Double-A, but he recently ran off a 13-game hitting streak and is tied for second in the league with 10 stolen bases.

There is a downside, too. Jordan has made more than his share of mental and physical errors, and he has yet to hit a ball out of the ballpark — which would appear to be a prerequisite for a 6-foot-6 outfield prospect. He remains a long shot to develop into a quality major-league player, but there is no indication that he'll be going home any time soon.

"There has been so much written about Michael trying to do this," Barons manager Terry Francona said. "He's handled it as well as anyone

See **JORDAN**, *16A*

ASSOCIATED PRESS

Michael Jordan's presence could help draw 1.2 million fans to Birmingham Barons games.

INDEX

Palestinian police delayed
A Palestinian police force of 150 crosses into the Gaza Strip from Egypt, but their expected arrival is delayed. **Page 3A**

Finalists for court
As President Clinton inches toward naming his second appointment to the U.S. Supreme Court, his aides say he's added a fifth finalist to the list. **Page 3A**

Weather
Mostly sunny. High 75; low 55. Yesterday's high, 71; low, 58. **16B**

0 83455 1

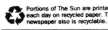

Portions of The Sun are printed each day on recycled paper. The newspaper also is recyclable.

6 SECTIONS

Physicians mobilize to run for Congress

47 doctors, dentists launch campaigns

By John Fairhall
Washington Bureau of The Sun

WASHINGTON — Believing that they can cure what ails America, an extraordinary number of doctors are pinning campaign buttons on their white jackets and running for Congress in states from Maryland to California.

Forty physicians and seven dentists launched races for the House or Senate this year, the most in recent memory, campaign analysts say.

Although a few have dropped out already, the next Congress could have more doctors than Capitol Hill has seen in decades. There have been no more than seven in any Congress in the past 40 years, according to *Congressional Quarterly*; only four hold office today.

"This is an amazing number of candidates," observes Paul Starr, a Princeton sociologist who has written a history of American medicine and is a White House health adviser. "I take it to be a mobilization in response to health care reform."

> *"This is an amazing number of candidates. I take it to be a mobilization in response to health care reform."*
>
> **PAUL STARR**
> **White House health adviser**

No other legislation would affect the medical profession as much as the health reforms proposed by President Clinton. And doctors like David Doman of Rockville have decided that Congress needs some help.

"I personally believe the nation's need for a physician-legislator will be there for many years to come," says the 43-year-old gastroenterologist, a Democrat who began running last year for the seat held by Republican

See **CANDIDATES**, *16A*

FINAL EDITION

NBA MAY CLOSE DOOR ON BIG PAYDAYS FOR ROOKIES, 1C

THE SUN
LIGHT • FOR • ALL
LATEST NEWS & SPORTS

THURSDAY, APRIL 20, 1995 | HOME DELIVERY: 25¢ (in most areas) • NEWSSTAND: 50¢ | BALTIMORE, MARYLAND

TERROR STRIKES THE HEARTLAND

'We didn't hear anything, just death'

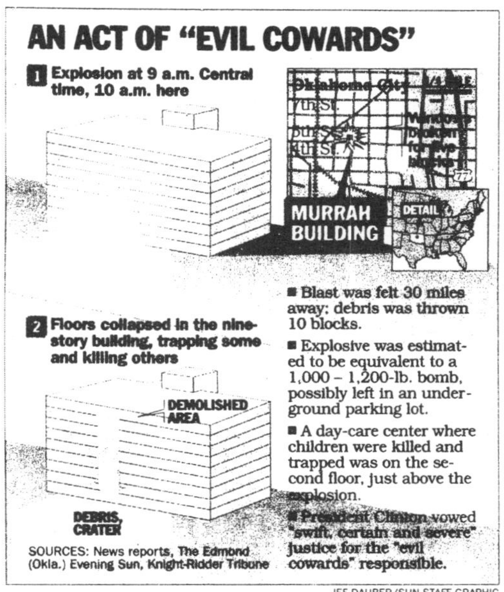
AN ACT OF "EVIL COWARDS"
1 Explosion at 9 a.m. Central time, 10 a.m. here
MURRAH BUILDING
DETAIL
2 Floors collapsed in the nine-story building, trapping some and killing others
DEMOLISHED AREA
DEBRIS, CRATER
■ Blast was felt 30 miles away; debris was thrown 10 blocks.
■ Explosive was estimated to be equivalent to a 1,000 – 1,200-lb. bomb, possibly left in an underground parking lot.
■ A day-care center where children were killed and trapped was on the second floor, just above the explosion.
■ President Clinton vowed "swift, certain and severe" justice for the "evil cowards" responsible.
SOURCES: News reports, The Edmond (Okla.) Evening Sun, Knight-Ridder Tribune

JEF DAUBER/SUN STAFF GRAPHIC

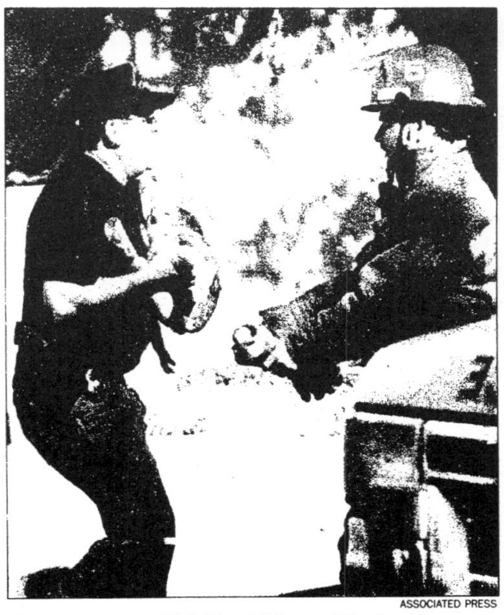

ASSOCIATED PRESS

Rescuers carry a child. The child's condition is unknown.

ASSOCIATED PRESS

The explosion tore the front off the Alfred P. Murrah Federal Building, and nine floors collapsed into rubble.

Car bomb kills dozens in Okla. City

By Judy Gibbs
Associated Press

OKLAHOMA CITY — A car bomb ripped deep into America's heartland yesterday, killing dozens and leaving 300 missing in a blast that gouged a nine-story hole in a federal office building. Some of the dead were children whose parents had just dropped them off at a day care center.

There was no immediate claim of responsibility for the attack, the deadliest U.S. bombing in 75 years.

By midnight, authorities said that at least 31 people had been killed, 12 of them children, and at least 200 injured, nearly 60 of them critically. Scores still were feared trapped in the pancaked rubble of the Alfred P. Murrah Federal Building.

Two people were pulled from the rubble last night but soon died, said Assistant Fire Chief Jon Hansen. He said rescuers were talking to a woman trapped in the basement, who said there were two others there. She didn't know if they were dead or alive.

The death toll was certain to rise.

"Our firefighters are having to crawl over corpses in areas to get to people that are still alive," Chief Hansen said.

Attorney General Janet Reno would not comment on who might have been behind the attack. President Clinton called the bombers "evil cowards," and Ms. Reno said the government would seek the death penalty against them.

A police source, who requested anonymity, said FBI agents were trying to piece together a van or a truck that was believed to have carried the explosives. An axle of the vehicle was found about two blocks from the scene, the source said.

Their clothes torn off, victims covered in glass and plaster emerged bloodied and crying from the building, which looked as if a giant bite had been taken out of it, exposing its floors like a dollhouse.

"I dove under that table," said Brian Espe, a state veterinarian who was giving a slide presentation on the fifth floor. "When I came out, I could see daylight if I looked north

See BOMB, 14A

People react with disbelief, sorrow

Relief workers awed by damage

By Scott Higham
Sun Staff Correspondent

OKLAHOMA CITY — There is nothing but sorrow on Northwest Fifth Street.

"I think we have a live one," a rescue worker yelled in the night, her voice competing with the drone of generators supplying power to search lights.

But minutes later the worst is confirmed. Another body is bundled in green burlap, placed on a gurney and wheeled through a crowd of beleaguered rescue workers to an ambulance.

"Out of the way," a medic commands.

Terror has come to middle America.

Surrounded by wheat and oil fields and cattle farms, Oklahoma City is home to the college football Sooners, the National Cowboy Hall of Fame and an airport named after humorist Will Rogers.

Now the state capital is the site of the deadliest car bombing on U.S. soil.

"I've never seen anything as devastating as this," said James Lee Witt, director of the Federal Emergency Management Agency, as he stood in awe in front of the rubble.

Mr. Witt and a team of FEMA supervisors surveyed the damage shortly before midnight and planned to report back to President Clinton this morning.

What they saw was startling. The Alfred P. Murrah Federal Building looked like it had suffered a sustained mortar attack. The north side of the building had been sheared away, exposing nine floors of offices and hallways that were once filled with people.

Slabs of concrete hang over the edges of the floors, clinging to twisted bars of steel.

Below, rescue workers and trained search-and-rescue dogs

See SCENE, 14A

MORE INSIDE

Day-care center took the brunt of the blast

Parents search hospitals, morgue

By Julia Prodis
Associated Press

OKLAHOMA CITY — The blast occurred at the start of the work day, as parents were dropping off their youngsters at the day-care center in the federal building. Before the smoke had cleared, Heather Taylor, an emergency worker, had tagged the feet of 17 children at the morgue.

Two were burned beyond recognition. The bodies of the rest, up to 7 years old, were mangled.

Ten to 20 other children were unaccounted for late in the day. Ms. Taylor knew of only two who had survived. One was in surgery, the other in intensive care.

"The day-care center is totally gone," said Dr. Carl Spengler, who helped Ms. Taylor with the victims.

It was on the second floor of the Murrah federal building, just above the spot where the car bomb exploded.

TV stations broadcast a descrip-

See CARE, 15A

INDEX

Weather
Increasing cloudiness. High 75, low 55. Yesterday's airport high, 90; low, 57 **12B**

Portions of The Sun are printed each day on recycled paper. The newspaper also is recyclable.

4 SECTIONS

Gas incident in Tokyo

In Tokyo, about 400 people are hospitalized after phosgene gas spreads through a commuter train and several stations on the heavily traveled 20-mile route to Yokohama. **Page 3A**

Lugar in race

Sen. Richard G. Lugar, an Indiana Republican, joins the presidential race with a pledge to abolish the federal income tax and provide steady leadership in world affairs. **Page 3A**

Glowing tributes seek to keep Bereano out of prison

High and mighty lobby now for lobbyist

By Marcia Myers
Sun Staff Writer

For a convicted felon, Bruce C. Bereano's credentials appear impeccable.

Police officers, lawyers, state senators, members of Congress, even judges and former Gov. William Donald Schaefer are willing to vouch for his character.

Honest. Compassionate. Hard-working. He even remembers birthdays, they wrote.

Altogether, 383 effusive letters of praise for Bereano have been sent to U.S. District Judge William M. Nickerson. That weighs in at more than 6 pounds of testimonials for the man who until recently was the most powerful lobbyist in Maryland.

Judge Nickerson is busy — with a little help from Bereano's friends — deciding just what price the lobbyist should pay for defrauding clients of more than $16,000 to make illegal campaign contributions.

Convicted last November of eight counts of mail fraud, Bereano is scheduled to be sentenced tomorrow. Prosecutors are recommending 2½ years in prison and a $60,000 fine. Defense lawyers are pushing for community service.

Former state Sen. Julian L. Lapides, a stalwart supporter of tougher ethics laws, says he is uneasy about the mass of letters. "Just because they think Bruce may have been a nice guy or done them favors, I question the propriety of letters supporting someone who a jury found was guilty of subverting the system."

Said Deborah Povich, executive director of Common Cause Maryland: "It is my hope that judges are above lobbying and will not be swayed by this effort."

But many of Maryland's public figures say Bruce Bereano is a very fine fellow who shouldn't go to jail.

There's Anne Arundel County Executive John G. Gary, a former state delegate. He distrusted lobbyists when he arrived at the State House 13 years ago, he wrote, but Bereano was different.

"If anything, I find the behavior of some of my colleagues to be questionable, and often Mr. Bereano was forced to remind them of the boundaries of the law."

American Joe Miedusiewski, the former Baltimore senator and gubernatorial candidate, also wrote. "When Bruce traveled with our exchange group to Germany several

See BEREANO, 12A

A partial list of those who wrote in support of Bruce C. Bereano **12A**

FINAL EDITION

THE SUN

LIGHT • FOR • ALL

LATEST NEWS & SPORTS

THURSDAY, SEPTEMBER 7, 1995 | HOME DELIVERY: 25¢ (in most areas) • NEWSSTAND: 50¢ | BALTIMORE, MARYLAND

★SPECIAL **2,131** COVERAGE★

Immortal Cal

He touches home with victory lap

By Ken Rosenthal
Sun Columnist

It was a victory lap for the ages. Rafael Palmeiro and Bobby Bonilla pushed Cal Ripken out of the Orioles' dugout, and off the game's all-time Iron Man went.

Down the right-field line, shaking hands with fans in the front row. Into the outfield, greeting the grounds crew and police officers. Above the center-field wall, where fans tumbled out of the bleachers as he leaped to slap them five.

Ripken's mother, Vi, leaned against his father, Cal Sr. Earlier, Senior had clapped and waved from his luxury box. Now he stood in his suit, hands behind his back, this incredibly tough man, biting his lower lip to fight back tears.

Junior had done it. One more time, the banner had dropped from the warehouse, revealing the number so many thought unattainable. The number 2,131. Never have four digits produced so many tears.

Grown men cried at Lou Gehrig's retirement ceremony 56 years ago, but those tears were born out of tragedy, the knowledge that Gehrig was seriously ill. These tears were born out of joy. And hometown pride. And love.

The game was delayed 22 minutes, 15 seconds. For a while, it seemed like play would never resume. For a while, it seemed Camden Yards would crumble from emotion.

He's just always there, you know? That's what was so celebrated, that's what this was all about. He's there when his team needs him. There now that his sport needs him. And there for a city that lost its football team and baseball glory long ago.

It's a simple virtue, perhaps, but in this harried age, simple can be remarkable. Such is the magic surrounding 2,131. A dozen years ago, Ripken was a local boy making good. Now, thanks to the streak, he's a national hero.

President Clinton shook both fists in exultation shortly after the celebration began. Vice President Albert Gore stood next to him, cheering.

See **ROSENTHAL**, *7A*

More Inside

More Cal coverage can be found in a 24-page special section inside today's newspaper. More stories on the historic game are on six pages in the Sports section, starting on **Page 1C.**

KARL MERTON FERRON/SUN STAFF PHOTO

The emotion of the moment shows on Cal Ripken's face during a 22-minute, 15-second standing ovation in the fifth inning.

Ripken now baseball's top iron man

By Peter Schmuck
Sun Staff Writer

Cal Ripken has had the baseball world on a string for more than 13 years, but that didn't do anything to lessen the impact when he played in his 2,131st consecutive game last night to pass Lou Gehrig and become the most durable player in the history of the sport.

The old record, which stood for 56 years and was considered untouchable until the Ripken streak got serious, officially fell at 9:20 p.m., when the Orioles left the field in the middle of the fifth inning and touched off another long and heartfelt celebration. No. 2,131 was unfurled on the wall of the B&O warehouse in a shower of rooftop fireworks and a standing ovation that didn't want to end.

Ripken, bathed in both sweat and adulation, acknowledged the crowd several times and struck a poignant pose with his two young children. Then, as the cheers rose to a crescendo, he broke into a celebratory lap around Oriole Park, shaking hands and high-fiving with the crowd, the grounds crew, the Orioles bullpen and even the California Angels, who have played the perfect foil for two nights of Ripkenmania. The ovation lasted 22 minutes, 15 seconds. Joe DiMaggio cried. The Orioles won again, 4-2. It was that kind of night.

In the more than 13 years since Ripken settled into the Orioles starting lineup for good, he has received a Rookie of the Year award, two Most Valuable Player trophies, a World Series championship and countless standing ovations, but last night's game clearly was the crowning achievement of a Hall of Fame career. He even hit his third home run in as many games to punctuate the occasion.

"Tonight I stand here, overwhelmed, as my name is linked with the great and courageous Lou Gehrig," Ripken said in a postgame address. "I'm truly humbled to have our names spoken in the same breath. Some may think our strongest connection is because we both played many consecutive games. Yet I believe in my heart that our true link is a common motivation — a love of the game of baseball, a passion for our team and a desire to compete at the very highest level."

The record-breaking game was played before a sellout crowd of 46,272, many of whom went to great lengths and considerable expense to view one of the defining moments in the sports history. That included President Clinton and Vice President Al Gore, who apparently became the first chief executive and vice presi-

See **STREAK**, *6A*

Senate ethics panel backs expulsion of Packwood

By Karen Hosler
Washington Bureau of The Sun

WASHINGTON — In a stunning development, the Senate Ethics Committee recommended unanimously yesterday that Bob Packwood be expelled from the Senate for a long pattern of groping and kissing women against their will and for obstructing an investigation of his actions.

Last night, Mr. Packwood angrily denounced the committee's actions and said he had no plans to resign. "I want to think about this for a minute, and I want to talk to some people and I am not going to make instantaneous decisions," he said at a news conference.

The 6-0 decision by the committee, which is evenly split between Republicans and Democrats, was an unexpectedly sharp repudiation of the Oregon Republican.

Expulsion is the most severe penalty the Senate can exact. No senator has been recommended for expulsion since 1982, when Harrison Williams, a New Jersey Democrat, was caught in the Abscam bribery scandal. Mr. Williams resigned just before the Senate vote.

Two-thirds of the Senate must approve an expulsion, but it appeared likely that the committee's decision had the blessing of Senate Majority Leader Bob Dole. Committee

See **PACKWOOD**, *12A*

INDEX

USAir chief to retire

USAir Chairman Seth Schofield retires a day after the company projected its first profit since 1988. **Page 13C**

Weather

Mostly sunny. High, 90; low, 65. Yesterday's high, 92; low, 70 **12B**

5 SECTIONS

Fuhrman returns to stand, takes Fifth

By Linda Deutsch
Associated Press

Simpson defense asks whether he planted evidence

LOS ANGELES — Former Detective Mark Fuhrman was called back to the witness stand yesterday and was asked point-blank whether he planted evidence against O. J. Simpson. He refused to answer, invoking his Fifth Amendment right against self-incrimination.

Climaxing months of defense claims that Mr. Simpson was framed by a racist detective, Mr. Fuhrman refused to answer any question. Jurors weren't in the courtroom to see the brief confrontation between defense attorney Gerald Uelmen and the subdued former detective who, five months earlier, told the panel that he found a bloody glove on Mr. Simpson's property.

"Detective Fuhrman, did you plant or manufacture any evidence in this case?" Mr. Uelmen asked.

"I assert my Fifth Amendment privilege," Mr. Fuhrman replied, his attorney standing at his side.

Mr. Fuhrman gave a similar answer to three other questions including, "Have you ever falsified a police report?"

As Mr. Fuhrman was led out of court, Mr. Simpson appeared upset. His eyes reddened, he rubbed his face and he mouthed words to his attorneys.

Later, his attorneys addressed reporters about the extraordinary courtroom development.

"We are not gloating. What we are saying is it's a very, very serious day for justice, not only in this county but in this country," Johnnie L. Cochran Jr. said. "We're going to move forward on this case and get what we believe we richly deserve — an acquittal."

Mr. Fuhrman's appearance was preceded by his attorney's announcement that he had advised his client not to answer any questions. Mr. Uelmen said he wanted to hear that from Mr. Fuhrman's own lips.

The courtroom was hushed as the tall, solemn-faced detective, who retired this summer from the Los Angeles force, walked to the witness stand. He had last been on the stand in March, when he testified about

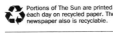

See **SIMPSON**, *10A*

FINAL EDITION COMMEMORATIVE PAGES INSIDE, 22A-29A

THE LATEST NEWS & SPORTS

The Evening Sun

FRIDAY, SEPTEMBER 15, 1995 HOME DELIVERY: 25¢ (in most areas) • NEWSSTAND: 50¢ BALTIMORE, MARYLAND

GOOD NIGHT, HON

Thanks for a great 85 years; will you love us in the morning?

Inside, one last time...

■ Born as the "Front Page" era began, *The Evening Sun* showed audacity, high spirits and keen writing, Carl Schoettler says. H.L. Mencken played a big part in setting the paper's personality. **Page 24A-25A.**

■ Fred Rasmussen recalls, in a series of briefs, the milestones, oddities and turning points in the 85-year-old history of *The Evening Sun* since 1910. **Page 22A-23A.**

Columnists reminisce

■ Jacques Kelly discusses evening newspapers here. **Page 28A.**

■ Wiley Hall looks at race relations in Maryland. **Page 2A.**

■ Kevin Cowherd finds humor in odd places. **Page 1D.**

■ Elise Chisolm tells of columns since the 1960s. **Page 1D.**

■ Bill Tanton, Phil Jackman and John Steadman recall good, bad, sad and funny times as sports columnists. **Page 1C.**

■ Some *Evening Sun* alumni are listed **Page 29A.**

Paper tales never die

■ On the editorial, Other Voices pages, William Manchester, Margaret McManus, Bradford Jacobs offer newspaper memories from other days. An editorial says goodbye. **Pages 30-31A.**

JED KIRSCHBAUM/EVENING SUN STAFF PHOTO

Frank Novotny, a Sun pressman since 1951, checks one of the last Evening Suns running off the presses at Sun Park. Mr. Novotny picked today to retire. "I wanted to put the paper to rest. It's a sad day. I liked the paper very much," he said. Two other pressmen, Bob Noppenberger and Alan Krakovitz, are also retiring today.

Evening Sun memories will glow forever within us

"I hate to see the evenin' sun go down."
— W.C. Handy

By Dan Rodricks
Sun Columnist

My first deadline assignment for *The Evening Sun* took me to the old federal courthouse on Calvert Street. It was September 1976. A couple of older, wiser and bearded reporters — they called me "Snookie" — needed help taking notes and filing copy for the late editions. They were covering a big trial. Whose trial? The governor's trial. Right then, right there, I knew Baltimore could not be the sleepy backwater snobby friends in New York and Boston had warned it would be.

We covered breaking news at *The Evening Sun*, and there was plenty of it. We wrote stories at 6 a.m. that were in print by 10, wrote stories at 10 that were in print by noon, wrote stories at 3 that were in print by evening rush. A reader could pick up the 7-Star or Final as *The Sun* set on the city and know, pretty much, what had happened that day in the trial of former Maryland Gov. Marvin Mandel.

Or what had happened in Dundalk overnight.

Or what had happened in Arbutus that morning.

Or which horses had won the first couple of races at Pimlico.

Or what the pope had said in Rome.

Often, I went home, turned on the TV news at 6, and heard anchormen (and, once upon a time, an anchorwoman named Oprah) recite, almost word-for-word, local news stories *Evening Sun* reporters had dictated to the city desk from pay phones that afternoon. And across the open newsroom of *The Sunpapers* — that's what native Baltimoreans called us — morning *Sun* editors and reporters examined our paper (sometimes with sneers) to see what they had missed.

They scooped us. We scooped them. Some days, *The News American* scooped both of us.

For the first 10 years that I worked in Baltimore, there was a delicious newspaper rivalry, and the town was better for it. *The News American* folded in 1986. *The Evening Sun* sets today. This paper — my paper, our paper — lost its identity when the morning and evening news staffs were merged in 1992. But for most of the years, *The Evening Sun* was as distinct from *The Sun* as Haussner's from Hampton's.

I loved working for *The Evening Sun*. It was hard, with lots of deadline mania, and too much cigarette smoke. But it was fun — something different every day — and the news was offered to readers with our own spin, sometimes an irreverent or folksy one.

We took our work seriously, but not

See **RODRICKS**, *27A*

Circulation faltered, but heart never did

By Frank D. Roylance
Sun Staff Writer

Today, *The Evening Sun* writes its own obituary.

Baltimore's last evening newspaper, which publishes its final editions today, is 85 and a victim of failing circulation.

It was both a child and a casualty of changing times. Born in 1910, the new evening paper was a morning *Sun* gambit to snatch readers, advertising and profits from its afternoon rivals, the *News* and the *Star*.

This "paper of the future" took breaking stories flashed across the nation or the ocean by the new telegraph news associations, set them in type and raced fresh editions all day long to Baltimore's eager readers.

It succeeded, and for most of its years gave the city a colorful, irreverent report from a remarkable roster of talented writers and editors, including Henry L. Mencken. It outlived all its afternoon competitors, and even outsold the morning *Sun* for 41 years — from 1936 to 1976.

The evening paper dies today a victim, in part, of a faster and flashier technology — television. But more lethal were the nation's changing lifestyles, which have left fewer readers with the time or inclination to spend their evenings with words on newsprint.

Nationwide, there are 470 fewer evening newspapers today than in 1946. They still outnumber morning papers 3 to 2, but 26 million more readers now take a morning paper

The Evening Sun's once-robust paid circulation — which peaked at 220,000 in 1960 — had been slipping for nearly three decades. It fell below the morning *Sun's* rising sales at 174,000 in 1977. After a 1992 newsroom merger made the two papers' local pages almost indistinguishable, it plunged below 100,000.

See **GOOD NIGHT**, *26A*

INDEX

NOTICE TO OUR READERS

This is the last issue of *The Evening Sun*. It is a souvenir edition with articles, photographs and columns on the paper's 85-year history.

Home delivery subscribers of *The Evening Sun* will automatically begin receiving *The Sun* on Monday, Sept. 18.

The Sun has been redesigned and expanded to better serve both our morning and evening readers. We have incorporated the most popular features of the two papers into the morning paper. A special six-page section to be delivered with Monday morning's paper will explain the new look and the added features.

If you have any questions, please call 539-1280 or 1-800-829-8000.

Weather
Fair tonight, low 55. Sunny tomorrow but showers Sunday, high 75, low 65 both days. **14B**

5 SECTIONS

Raging blaze hits church on Gay Street

By Richard Irwin
Sun Staff Writer

An East Baltimore landmark was extensively damaged early today when a five-alarm fire swept through the Emmanuel Apostolic Faith Church in the 1300 block of N. Gay St., sending flames more than 30 feet into the air and heavy smoke over areas as far away as Fells Point.

The cause and origin were unknown. The two-story brick building was empty at the time.

Three firefighters suffered smoke inhalation and minor injuries and were released after being treated at

See **FIRE**, *14A*

KARL MERTON FERRON/SUN STAFF PHOTO

Brett Bond of Timonium watches firefighters battle the five-alarm blaze in East Baltimore.

SIMPSON VERDICT EXTRA

THE SUN

October 3, 1995 | Baltimore, Maryland | 50 cents

TUESDAY

Loss of a stable threatens way of life of Sandtown a-rabs

Urban renewal will eliminate a popular a-rab stable. But supermarkets and vendors in pick-up trucks are also pushing out the horse-drawn carts. [*Page 1B*]

Nation and World

Angkor Wat is being restored amid skepticism. [*Page 2A*]

Terrorist convictions prompt tighter security measures. [*Page 3A*]

Supreme Court opens term. [*Page 3A*]

Rabin says U.S. Jews have no right to interfere in Israel's peace process. [*Page 7A*]

Maryland

Nationally sought suspect caught through work of a Baltimore agent. [*Page 1B*]

Jury exonerates officer in the 1993 shooting death of a fleeing prisoner. [*Page 1B*]

Clipper Industrial Park fire may have been intentionally set. [*Page 1B*]

Hopkins Laboratory develops system that calls for help after accident. [*Page 1B*]

Dripping Pond Run has a self-appointed protector in Howdie Burns. [*Page 1B*]

Opinion

The power of justice has scored a victory against terrorism. [*Page 10A*]

Colin Powell, military man and prospective politician, is a lot like Ike. [*Page 11A*]

Three types of Democrats can be found in Washington. [*Page 11A*]

Sports

The Seattle Mariners beat the California Angels, 9-1, for the AL West title. [*Page 1D*]

The San Antonio Spurs trade Dennis Rodman to the Chicago Bulls. [*Page 1D*]

Business

Chesapeake Power Co. may be new name for merged utilities. [*Page 1C*]

Communications company establishes Maryland base. [*Page 1C*]

$4.25 billion settlement on silicone breast implants falls through. [*Page 1C*]

Baltimore pathologist plans $10 million complex in Canton. [*Page 1C*]

Today

Breast reconstruction isn't anti-feminist, some former patients say. [*Page 1E*]

Boy George is back, with a harder edge to his music and an autobiography to sell. [*Page 1E*]

Randallstown author writes book about self-discovery for black women. [*Page 1E*]

Weather

Partly cloudy. High 78, low 61. Yesterday's Baltimore high, 87; low, 61. [*Page 12B*]

Bridge	11B	Editorials	10A
Classified	5B	Horoscope	8E
Comics	6-7E	Lottery	2B
Xword	11B,7E	Movies	3E
Deaths	5B	Television	8E

NOT GUILTY

Simpson hugs lawyer, mouths thanks to jurors

FOX TELEVISION

"Thank you": *O. J. Simpson looks toward the jury to express a "thank you." Counsel Johnnie L. Cochran Jr. is at right.*

Judge Ito orders former football hero to be released

Prosecution stunned

Victims' kin react with disbelief; crowd outside cheers

ASSOCIATED PRESS

LOS ANGELES — O.J. Simpson was acquitted today of murdering his ex-wife and her friend, a suspense-filled climax to the courtroom saga that obsessed the nation.

With two words, "not guilty," the jury freed Mr. Simpson to try to rebuild a life thrown into disgrace.

Sobs could be heard in the courtroom as the verdicts, acquitting Mr. Simpson of first- and second-degree murder, were read. Mr. Simpson hugged his attorney Johnnie Cochran Jr. and looked toward the jury and mouthed, "Thank you," after the panel was dismissed.

Mr. Simpson's relatives smiled and wiped away tears. His son Jason sat in his seat, his face in his hands, shaking and sobbing. Prosecutor Marcia Clark and Christopher Darden sat stone-faced.

Prosecution lawyers looked stunned.

Outside the court house, the thousands gathered erupted into cheers.

The families of the victims reacted with disbelief. Mr. Goldman's father, Fred, sat with a look shock on his face, his mouth agape. Goldman's sister, Kim, sobbed.

Nicole Brown Simpson's parents and sisters sat quietly and plaintively.

Judge Lance A. Ito ordered Mr. Simpson released from custody "forthwith." He thanked the jurors for their service and released them as well. The jury members indicated they had no desire to speak to either attorneys or the media.

Ms. Simpson, 35,, Mr. Simpson's former wife, and her friend Mr. Goldman, 25, were slain June 12, 1994.

The curious throngs and an army of media came to the courthouse today to await the verdict, while police went on tactical alert to brace for possible trouble in the streets.

News helicopters roared outside. Barricades blocked the street. In the courthouse lobby, hundreds of people vied for the few precious public seats in the courtroom. As their lottery numbers were pulled, the lucky few cheered.

The verdict came yesterday without warning. As the judge brought in the jury, two-thirds of the hottest seats in town were empty, two of the leading attorneys in the case weren't even present, and most of the media — not expecting such a swift verdict — were upstairs in the press room.

Judge Ito suggested jurors use their time before the verdict's announcement to pack and bid farewell to nearly nine months of sequestration.

"Ladies and gentlemen, have your last pleasant evening," he told them.

The verdict capped a legal journey as surreal — and at times as slow — as Mr. Simpson's bizarre Bronco flight from justice.

The case wasn't just about murder. It was about fame and wealth, love and hate, fragile egos and misdirected power. It was about the judicial system, the media, domestic violence, racism, sexism and crass opportunism.

At the center, of course, was Orenthal James Simpson, who made it from the housing projects of San Francisco to the mansions of Brentwood with charm, good looks and a pair of feet that could run like the wind.

His public life was the object of envy.

His private life, was something else. Prosecutors said Mr. Simpson was a man whose outward strength of body and personality hid psychological weakness. He was, they said, racked by jealousy and bent on control.

LA police brace for any disturbances

'We are confident LAPD will respond vigorously to unrest'

LOS ANGELES DAILY NEWS

LOS ANGELES — Law enforcement officials swiftly put in motion plans to handle disturbances if any develop in the wake of today's O.J. Simpson verdict.

Los Angeles Police Department spokesman Eduardo Funes said the police would be prepared — this time — to handle any disturbances.

"The process failed in 1992 in the riots, and measures will be taken to make sure it doesn't happen again," Mr. Funes said.

"We are confident the LAPD will respond vigorously to any unrest, any unusual occurrences," he said. "However, we don't foresee or know about any planned disturbances, rallies or protests."

Police and fire officials praised Judge Lance Ito's decision to wait to announce the verdict today.

"This gives us additional time to put our plan into motion, the jury's action was so quick, came so unexpectedly," Mr. Funes said.

Mayor Richard Riordan cut short a trade mission to Asia to return to Los Angeles. "In important times, it's my responsibility to be with my fellow Angelenos," he said. He was expected to arrive this morning Pacific time, Deputy Mayor Robin Kramer said.

With Mr. Riordan and Council President John Ferraro out of town yesterday, Councilman Joel Wachs was the acting mayor. "I am very, very certain our city is prepared for anything," Mr. Wachs said yesterday. "I also feel the people of Los Angeles will act responsibly. Los Angeles is more than just the Simpson trial. I believe the people of our city very much wants fairness and the people will act responsibly."

The number of Los Angeles Police Department patrol officers was doubled this morning [*See Security, 5A*]

Keeping tabs on tab for the papal visit

Archdiocese seeks in-kind donations; many answer the call

By MICHAEL OLLOVE
SUN STAFF

The pope is an expensive guest. The Baltimore Archdiocese is trying to make sure he is an affordable one.

Toward that end, church officials have made a determined effort to solicit donations of goods and services to keep the archdiocese's cash outlay to a minimum. Dozens of businesses and institutions have answered Cardinal William H. Keeler's call, making contributions of everything from funeral home limousines to the altar at Oriole Park at Camden Yards.

The donations are intended to help the archdiocese keep its cash expenses under $250,000, the amount raised from parishes in a special collection last year. If necessary, the archdiocese also has a cash reserve of $250,000 more in case costs are higher than anticipated.

"The cardinal recognized early on that [$250,000] probably would not be enough," said Bill Blaul, a spokesman for the archdiocese. "Knowing that, he emphasized from the start the idea of working with individuals and businesses and corporations to secure donations in time and in kind."

Many were [*See Cost, 6A*]

AMY DAVIS : SUN STAFF

Banner days: *Banners heralding the visit Sunday of Pope John Paul II line Pratt Street downtown. "It's a once-in-a-lifetime event," said archdiocesan spokesman Bill Mitchell.*

United weighs buying USAir

American Airlines is also involved in negotiations

By SUZANNE WOOTON
SUN STAFF

United Airlines said yesterday that it is considering buying USAir, a move that would give the nation's largest airline access to valuable East Coast routes but one that raises concerns for BWI, whose future has long been linked to USAir.

The Arlington, Va.-based carrier, by far the largest airline at Baltimore-Washington International Airport, confirmed that it was negotiating with United and said it also has held preliminary discussions with American Airlines, the nation's second-largest airline.

"We've had discussions with both American and United regarding strategic relations up to and including possible acquisition of USAir," Richard Weintraub, a spokesman for USAir, said yesterday.

USAir, the nation's sixth-largest airline, has lost $3 billion since 1988 but recently has seen a turnaround, posting a $112.9 million profit in the second quarter and predicting its first profitable year since 1988. But USAir's costs remain the highest in the industry. And this summer, the carrier abandoned its efforts to secure $2.5 billion in cost-cutting agreements from its unions.

On the horizon is more competition from Southwest Airlines, the low-cost carrier that is launching service into USAir's lucrative territory this winter with low-cost flights to Florida.

A deal with either American or United could spell trouble for BWI, where USAir operates the smallest of its four hubs but handles more than half the airport's 31,000 daily passengers.

"It would give United the opportunity to strip out operations they didn't want," said Alex C. Hart, airline analyst for Ferris Baker, Watts Inc. in Baltimore.

"They'd get access to USAir's extensive route structure with feeds into Florida and the whole Boston-Philadelphia-Washington corridor. Then United could pick and choose what hubs they want," Mr. Hart said. "Those may be choices USAir just hasn't been able to make."

But after yesterday's announce- [*See Airlines, 6A*]

FINAL ★★★★★

THE SUN

October 9, 1995 — Baltimore, Maryland — 50 cents

SPECIAL PAPAL COVERAGE

MONDAY

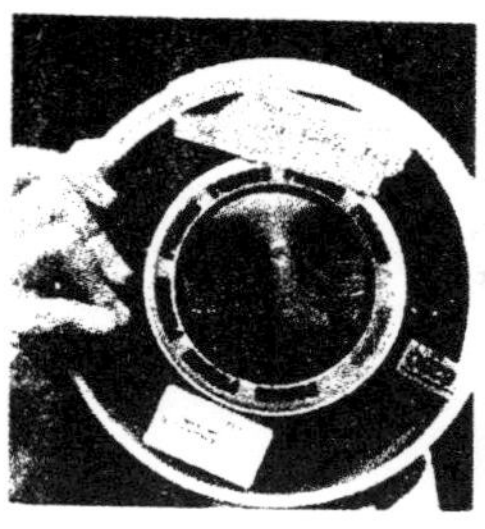

Computer museum is a welcoming home to vintage models

The owner of a Hunt Valley company has created a museum dedicated to the personal computer. He joins a growing number of computer collectors nationwide. *[Page 1B]*

Nation and World

Maryland

Sports

Business

Opinion

Today

Weather

Mostly sunny. High, 71; low 46. Yesterday's high, 73; low, 62. *[Page 12B]*

A day of prayer and joy

CHIAKI KAWAJIRI : SUN STAFF

Quiet moment: *Pope John Paul II prays with Cardinal William H. Keeler (center) and Cardinal Angelo Sodano at the Basilica of the Assumption.*

Pope John Paul II welcomed to city with ritual and exuberance

'Always be guided by truth'

After outdoor Mass, pontiff visits with the high, the hungry

By JOHN RIVERA
SUN STAFF

Pope John Paul II, the most traveled pope in history, came yesterday to Baltimore, the birthplace of American Catholicism, and presided over a day of celebration, pageantry and prayer.

His 10-hour tour of Catholic Baltimore showed the pontiff the many facets, both grand and humble, of the city: from celebrating Mass at Camden Yards to a jubilant welcome along downtown streets by people of many faiths; from lunch with the poor and afflicted at a soup kitchen to a tour of the city's grand cathedrals; and ending the day with a meeting with some of the men who will one day be priests.

The pope's visit, the first ever to Maryland by a pontiff, capped more than a year of anticipation. A trip scheduled for last year was canceled because of his health.

At Camden Yards, he called on the congregation to live a life of faith, service and witness to the Gospel:

"Catholics of America! Always be guided by the truth — by the truth about God who created and redeemed us, and by the truth about the human person, made in the image and likeness of God and destined for a glorious fulfillment in the Kingdom to come."

Although he appeared haggard on this final day of a five-day U.S. visit, the 75-year-old pope displayed some of the personality and warmth that have charmed millions, even many who disagree with his views on the church's moral teachings.

Whenever he encountered children, at the airport, at the Mass and at lunch, he embraced and kissed them.

And when he realized his microphone was not turned on as he started to lead the congregation in the sign of the cross to begin the Mass, he stopped in mid-sentence and tapped on it loudly several times. The pope kept a deadpan face, but the crowd let out a collective chuckle.

Cardinal William H. Keeler greeted the pope on behalf of the *[See Pope, 19A]*

Expanded coverage

Today's editions of *The Sun* provide 12 additional pages of coverage of Pope John Paul II's historic visit to Baltimore, including:

On Pages 8 and 9, an account of the Mass at Camden Yards.

On Pages 10 and 11, color photographs of the pontiff's arrival at BWI, pre-Mass ceremonies and the Mass itself.

On Pages 12 and 13, the parade, the protesters and the ceremony at the Cathedral of Mary Our Queen.

On Pages 14 and 15, the worshipers who rode buses and the impact of Pope John Paul's visit on Baltimore's tourism.

On Pages 16 and 17, an account of the pope's visit to Our Daily Bread, and a look at the entire five days of the U.S. trip, and more.

'Such charisma, so much emotion'

JED KIRSCHBAUM : SUN STAFF

Lifted voices: *Members of the Baltimore Archdiocese Urban Mass Choir, under the direction of Fernando Allen, sing at the Mass.*

Smiles, tears, awe greet appearance by pope in the downtown

By MICHAEL OLLOVE AND DAVID SIMON
SUN STAFF

At times, the only sound to be heard in the heart of downtown Baltimore was the flutter of gold-and-white papal flags in the autumnal breeze.

It was a rare quietude, an air of gentle contemplation that settled over the tens of thousands who gathered around the Inner Harbor yesterday, lining the streets to mark the presence nearby of Pope John Paul II. The city has seen such crowds before, but no other moment — not a World Series victory or a Preakness festivity or a New Year's party — has produced such a contented silence.

Beneath the flags in McKeldin Square — renamed Celebration Square for this one day — the crowd sat or stood, encircled by three huge screens televising the Sunday Mass being celebrated four blocks away at Camden Yards. Some held hands, others closed their eyes in prayer; a few murmured familiar portions of the liturgy.

Baltimore's harbor has had many incarnations — bustling waterfront, rotting skid row, glittering showpiece — but this transformation was perhaps the most unlikely. This was an open-air cathedral.

"Never in our wildest dream did we picture ourselves sitting in the middle of Light Street watching a Mass on a big screen, waiting for the popemobile," said Ida Sarsitis.

Ms. Sarsitis, who grew up in nearby Little Italy, was among scores who sat in the crosswalk at Pratt and Light streets, watching the stadium ceremony and waiting for their chance to glimpse the pontiff. Others sat in the center lanes of Pratt, or rested themselves in the ivy-covered berns that border the square.

The Catholic devout turned out in large numbers, but the spirit of the papal visit resonated with others as well. Theo Schamerhorn, a blond, 50-year-old woman wearing a University of Nebraska sweat shirt, was raised in the faith but had not been inside a Catholic church in 15 *[See Spirit, 18A]*

AMY DAVIS : SUN STAFF

Communion rite: *Rachel Watkins (foreground) prays during papal Mass, as husband, Matt (behind her), also joins in Camden Yards service.*

Wounded family gets healing hand

■ **Touch of peace:** *The pope takes the hands of, and murmurs words of comfort, to a Baltimore-area couple who lost a 13-year-old son in a traffic accident.*

By DAN RODRICKS
SUN COLUMNIST

On a day when he extolled the power of faith and family, Pope John Paul II held the hands of a man and woman who had their faith and family shattered.

Patricia and Jim McDonnell were given the high privilege of holding the hand of the pope during the handshake of peace at yesterday's Mass. They were the only Baltimoreans so chosen.

"God bless you ... " the pope said as he held Patricia McDonnell's hand.

" ... on the loss of your son," he added, holding Jim's.

The pope knew. He had been told. The McDonnells had lived every parent's nightmare — the death of a child.

Now, 18 months later, they were among those of us at the altar in the warm sun, soft breezes and incense-laced air of Oriole Park.

They ascended the steps and reached for the hand of the man in the billowing green *[See Rodricks, 8A]*

FINAL ★★★★★

THE SUN

LIGHT FOR ALL

November 5, 1995 — Baltimore, Maryland — $1.66

Sunday

In special epiphany, he discovers a new kind of music

Faith began tugging at concert pianist Paul Maillet. [Page 1M]

Stallions defeat Blue Bombers in CFL playoffs

Mike Pringle scores two TDs in Baltimore's 36-21 victory. [Page 1D]

Israeli leader Rabin slain

Clinton mourns a friend and ally

Peace will be Rabin's 'lasting legacy,' president pledges

By MARK MATTHEWS
SUN NATIONAL STAFF

WASHINGTON — A visibly shaken President Clinton, leading the nation in mourning Israeli Prime Minister Yitzhak Rabin, last night committed the United States to preventing a violent reversal of the Middle East peace process.

"Peace must be and peace will be Prime Minister Rabin's lasting legacy," Mr. Clinton said in a brief statement from the White House Rose Garden. Minutes later, aides announced that the president would leave Washington today to attend Mr. Rabin's funeral tomorrow in Jerusalem.

Of the fallen Israeli leader, Mr. Clinton said, "The world has lost one of its greatest men — a warrior for his nation's freedom, and now a martyr for his nation's peace."

In a more personal tribute, the president — his voice choked with emotion — said, "Yitzhak Rabin was my partner and my friend. I admired him, and I loved him very much. Because words cannot express my true feelings, let me just say, shalom, haver — goodbye, friend."

Mr. Clinton spoke not far from where he had stood with Mr. Rabin and Palestinian leader Yasser Arafat in September 1993, when the former enemies signed a historic peace agreement and sealed it with a handshake.

Echoing Mr. Clinton's tribute, former President George Bush declared: "He was a true peacemaker whose efforts and sacrifice will be remembered through the ages." Former President Jimmy Carter, who brokered the first Arab-Israeli peace in 1978, called Mr. Rabin "a great hero in peace."

In an extraordinary salute by key Arab leaders to Mr. Rabin's legacy of forging peace with Israel's former enemies, Mr. Clinton's statement was followed minutes later by a CNN television interview with Jordan's King Hussein, who nearly matched the U.S. president in his warm words of praise and friendship for the slain prime [See Reaction, 25A]

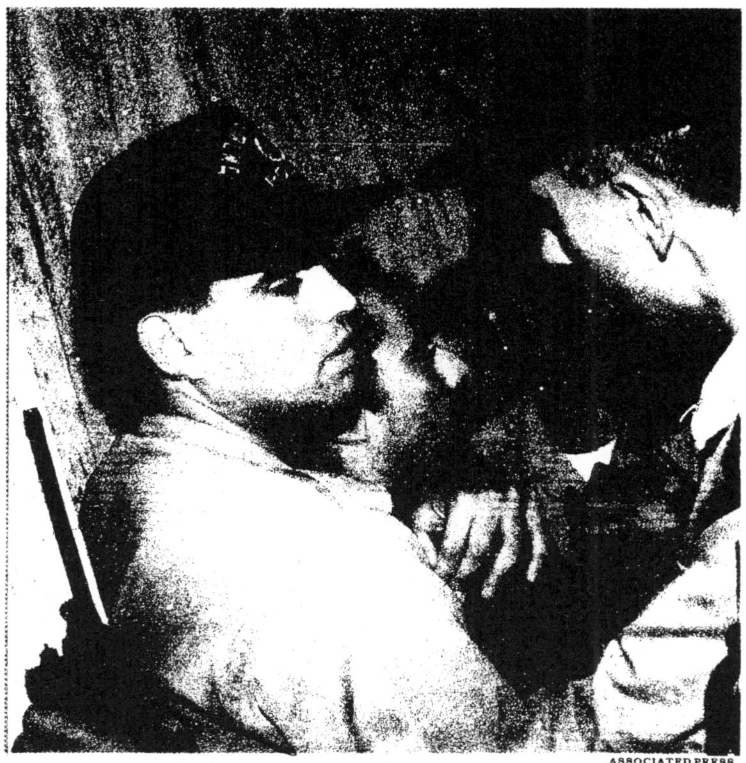

ASSOCIATED PRESS

Suspect captured: *Israeli police surround Yigal Amir, 27, the suspected assassin of Prime Minister Yitzhak Rabin, who was was shot three times as he left a peace rally in Tel Aviv.*

AGENCE FRANCE-PRESSE

Peace rally: *Yitzhak Rabin (right) and Foreign Minister Shimon Peres greet Tel Aviv crowd before assassination.*

Prime minister cut down by gunfire at peace rally

Jewish law student held

Shimon Peres appointed interim head of government

By DOUG STRUCK
SUN FOREIGN STAFF

JERUSALEM — A gunman shot and killed Yitzhak Rabin last night in Tel Aviv as the prime minister left a joyful rally supporting his peace plans.

The Israeli Cabinet met and named Foreign Minister Shimon Peres as interim prime minister. After a mourning period, Mr. Peres will likely be asked by Israel's president to form a new government.

Mr. Rabin, 73, was shot three times as he walked toward his car at the end of the huge public rally in the Tel Aviv municipal square. He had spoken glowingly of peace, and with his wife had watched in clear enjoyment at the turnout, estimated at 80,000, in favor of his government's peacemaking with the Palestinians.

A man identified as Yigal Amir, 27, a law student at Tel Aviv's Bar-Ilan University, was arrested and charged with the assassination. Israel radio said he had lived temporarily in a Jewish settlement on the West Bank.

"I acted alone, on God's orders, and I have no regrets," Israeli police quoted Mr. Amir as telling them.

Authorities said Mr. Amir told them he had tried three times before to attack the prime minister.

Mr. Rabin, bleeding from the chest, was taken to a Tel Aviv hospital. Government officials said he had no heartbeat or blood pressure on arrival, and the bullets had pierced major arteries and his spine. [See Israel, 24A]

Inside

Fear follows the shock in Israel

In candlelight vigils, mourners are wary of verbal violence

By DOUG STRUCK
SUN FOREIGN STAFF

JERUSALEM — At the hospital where the dying Yitzhak Rabin was taken, a small candlelight vigil began. One marcher carried a handwritten sign: "This hatred will kill us."

That fear quickly followed in the steps of Israel's shock, and the lament sprang immediately from many mouths here.

The political debate over Mr. Rabin's peace with the Palestinians has been carried out in the terms of rage, often with the language of violence. Some worried that Israel's own anger could tear the nation apart.

"Death to Arabs. Death to Rabin," became a standard slogan at the right-wing demonstrations.

The speakers at the rallies, even mainstream opposition politicians, described the prime minister as a traitor who was endangering the country by negotiating with Palestinians.

"There is no doubt the verbal violence of the last year and a half added to this," Israel's president, Ezer Weizman, said last night. "I hope this is an end to the way that has developed, the way of verbal violence."

The prime minister's security guard in recent months had worried that someone would be moved by the emotional rhetoric to try to carry out an assassination against a top government minister, according to frequent reports.

Mr. Rabin's advisers discussed the danger openly, and it became grist for editorials. But few really expected it to happen. Loud shouting was just a part of the culture, they said. Extreme language was only words; in the Israeli communi- [See Mideast, 25A]

City schools plot moves to erase budget shortfall

Plans set for layoffs, seeking $10 million cut in EAI contract

By JEAN THOMPSON
SUN STAFF

The financially troubled Baltimore school system will start the week by taking steps on two fronts to resolve its multimillion dollar budget shortfall.

School and city officials will prepare to lay off 100 administrative employees in January to help reduce anticipated expenses for the school year by an estimated $32 million to the approved budget level of $647 million.

They also will continue talks that began late Friday with Education Alternatives Inc. with the goal of cutting by $10 million the private, for-profit company's $44 million contract for managing nine city public schools.

The EAI negotiations, which are to resume Tuesday, have produced an "agreement in principle" for the Minneapolis company to continue managing the schools through June.

Neither Mayor Kurt L. Schmoke nor EAI chairman and founder John T. Golle wants to disrupt programs affecting students at midyear, said participants in Friday's negotiations. After two grueling hours, contract talks led by Mr. Schmoke adjourned about 10 p.m. with no agree- [See Schools, 10A]

"The Browns are ours, and keep your hands off them."

Cleveland fighting for its Browns

Mayor plans offer of financial package, but it may fall short

By MICHAEL JAMES
SUN STAFF

CLEVELAND — While this city was pelted by sleet, snow and the virtual certainty that the Browns were moving to Baltimore, Mayor Michael R. White angrily declared yesterday that a "cruel hoax" was unfolding in Maryland, and he vowed that the football team won't leave without a battle.

"The message is clear: The Cleveland Browns are ours, and keep your hands off them, any other city in America," Mr. White said at a news conference in which he outlined plans — which include possible legal action — to keep the Browns.

LLOYD FOX : SUN STAFF

Trying to stop a Brown-out: *Mayor Michael R. White tells Clevelanders to get "fighting mad" about their team.*

On Wednesday, Mr. White said, he will submit a financial package to Browns owner Art Modell. The package is dependent on approval of a "sin tax" in a Tuesday referendum.

However, Cleveland apparently can't match Baltimore's offer, which could bring the [See Browns, 21A]

Inside

INSIDE

Mechanical arms provide blessing for thalidomide victim

Beatriz Lopez-Perez was born without arms because her mother used the drug thalidomide. Now 21, the Canary Islands native has received mechanical arms after rigorous therapy at Johns Hopkins Hospital. The artificial limbs, she says, are a testament to faith. [Page 1C]

Weather

Sunny to partly cloudy. High, 49; low 29. Yesterday's high, 52; low 39. [Page 8C]

FINAL ★★★★★

THE SUN

September 2, 1996 | Baltimore, Maryland | 50 cents

Monday

Bat confiscated, Rodriguez retaliates with HR to beat O's, 5-1

Nine pitches after Orioles manager Davey Johnson has Alex Rodriguez's bat confiscated to be checked for cork, the Seattle shortstop hits a three-run home run to lead the Mariners to a 5-1 win. The Orioles remain four games back in the American League East and dropped to one game back in the wild-card race. [Page 1c]

Nation/World

Business

Maryland

The Maryland summer of '96 has yielded unseasonably cool weather, an Olympic star and bountiful crops for gardeners such as Manchester Mayor Elmer C. Lippy (above). [Page 1B]

Sports

Opinion

Today

Weather

Partly cloudy. High, 87; low, 64. Yesterday's airport high, 86; low, 65. [Page 16B]

0 08345 00005
1 L F

'It was just a great day'

KENNETH K. LAM : SUN STAFF

Saving grab: *The Ravens' Ray Lewis (52), along with teammate Stevon Moore, celebrates his interception in the end zone during the second quarter.*

Ravens kick off regular season with 19-14 victory

64,124 see NFL's return

Link is formed between old Colts and city's new club

By PETER SCHMUCK
SUN STAFF

The first day of the rest of Baltimore's football history couldn't have been more perfect.

The sun shone brightly on sold-out Memorial Stadium, and the transplanted Baltimore Ravens glistened in the first regular-season NFL game here since 1983, coming from behind to score a 19-14 victory over the Oakland Raiders before a raucous crowd of 64,124.

It was the largest number of fans to see a professional football game in Baltimore, and why not? They had waited long enough ... waited through an NFL ice age and an unsuccessful expansion effort and even a couple of Canadian Football League seasons. Waited patiently when there seemed to be little chance that their patience ever would be rewarded.

That's why the parking lots were filling up nearly three hours before game time yester- [See Ravens, 5A]

More inside

A Colts family dons its wings

■ **Fans:** *3 generations of Baltimore football followers eagerly embrace the new team.*

By MIKE KLINGAMAN
SUN STAFF

The gray-haired man in the Ravens shirt leaned back in his end-zone seat, closed his eyes and wept. Not because of where he sat. Because of where he was.

Maynard "Butch" Ergott thought he'd never watch another NFL game in Baltimore, let alone in Memorial Stadium, bygone home of his beloved Colts.

"I've waited 13 years for this," said Ergott, 50, of Reisterstown.

Never mind the poor view or that his Ravens tickets cost twice what he used to shell out to watch the Colts from midfield.

"Doesn't matter," said Ergott. "What's important is being here today. This is Christmas for me."

And like any holiday, the whole family was there — three generations of Ergotts, raised on the Colts but now loyal to the Ravens.

They included:

■ Ergott's wife, Christina. More vocal than her husband, she settled into her seat, cleared her throat and began drag- [See Fans, 5A]

JOHN MAKELY : SUN STAFF

Congratulations: *Earnest Byner shares the jubilation with fans behind the end zone after scoring what turned out to be the winning touchdown.*

U.S. vows to punish Iraq for incursion

Administration keeps all options open; U.N. delays oil-for-food deal

NEW YORK TIMES NEWS SERVICE

WASHINGTON — The Clinton administration vowed yesterday to punish Saddam Hussein for Iraq's military thrust into the Kurdish enclave in northern Iraq, and U.N. Secretary-General Boutros Boutros-Ghali suspended the recent agreement to allow Iraq to sell oil to raise cash for food and medicine.

On a day full of diplomatic contacts in which the Clinton administration kept all of its options open, there were indications last night that the United States had stepped up military activity even further in the region.

Among other things, one official said, the aircraft carrier USS Carl Vinson and accompanying warships moved north in the Persian Gulf. The ships are capable of striking deep into Iraq with aircraft or missiles.

The suspension of the oil sales agreement was the first international response to Iraq's incursion north against the Kurds, whose enclave has been protected by the United [See Iraq, 12A]

Presidential rivals hurl holiday pitches

Clinton, Dole, Perot vie for attention

By KAREN HOSLER, CARL CANNON AND FRANK LANGFITT

The day before the traditional Labor Day kickoff to the presidential campaign, the three candidates vied for attention yesterday — Bob Dole and Ross Perot during competing national television appearances and President Clinton in his home state of Arkansas.

In an interview on CBS' "60 Minutes" last night, Dole made a broad declaration that he would not raise taxes as president. Aides said the statement referred to tax rates, but did not preclude closing loopholes and getting rid of some tax breaks, many of which are already in his economic plan.

In earlier appearances in Washington, the Republican presidential nominee described the Clinton administration's cautious response to the latest Iraqi provocations as an example of what he called "a failure of American leadership," and he pledged to use the National Guard to fight drugs.

Clinton came back to a bittersweet homecoming in Little Rock yesterday, lately the site of Whitewater-related trials. The city served as a resting stop for Clinton, and his wife, Hillary Rodham Clinton, and daughter, Chelsea, too — a welcome respite after his eight-day planes, trains and automobiles trip through Middle America.

Returning to his strategy of four years ago, Perot took to the airwaves last night in a half-hour commercial on ABC in which he criticized the two major parties for failing to address the nation's impending "financial meltdown" and, in a departure, asked viewers to contribute to his campaign.

Dole used an address to thousands of members of the National Guard Association to charge that Iraqi President [See Campaign, 6A]

REUTERS

Bob Dole *shows off a game given to him during his appearance before the National Guard Association.*

The $151 million convention wager

■ **Risk:** *The expansion of the Baltimore Convention Center is the opening move in a high-stakes gamble: Bonanza or boondoggle?*

Second of three articles

By GARY GATELY
SUN STAFF

A few steps from Bruce H. Hoffman's office in the brick warehouse at Camden Yards, a panoramic view of Oriole Park unfolds outside the windows, the green seats and manicured field glistening in the summer sun. Just beyond the ballpark lies the site of a planned new football stadium, the $200 million future home of the Baltimore Ravens.

But Hoffman, executive director of the Maryland Stadium Authority, fixes his gaze away from stadiums present and future and instead on the modern glass, concrete and steel structure his office overlooks: the Baltimore Convention Center expansion.

For all the civic pride and bragging rights associated with the stadiums, Hoffman says, neither will come close to the expected economic windfall from the convention center. "People don't realize that this building should bring more money into the city than baseball and football combined," he said.

Projections used to make the case for the $151 million expansion and renovation of the convention center suggest that it will [See Risk, 8A]

FINAL ★★★★★

THE SUN

June 3, 1997 Baltimore, Maryland 50 cents

TUESDAY

Chapter 3: "I may not live through this," says Wayne Shipley, director of the spring musical at North County High School. His cast is on an emotional roller coaster. [*Page 1E*]

High court to decide if police can be sued over chase damage

The Supreme Court agreed yesterday to spell out the duty of the police to avoid injuring or killing someone during high-speed chases, an issue that has arisen repeatedly in recent years. [*Page 3A*]

0 08345 00002 0

Count 1
■ Conspiracy to use a weapon of mass destruction.

Count 2
■ Use of a weapon of mass destruction.

Count 3
■ Destruction by explosive of government property.

Counts 4-11
■ First-degree murder for the deaths of eight law officers.

McVeigh guilty

Jury convicts gulf vet in Okla. blast

ASSOCIATED PRESS

A hero's welcome: *Blast survivors and victims' family members cheer as lead prosecutor Joseph Hartzler leaves the U.S. Courthouse in Denver after the guilty verdict was announced.*

Bombing killed 168 in deadliest act of domestic terrorism

'We got the right verdict'

Survivors elated, emotional after 4 days of waiting anxiously

By SANDY BANISKY
SUN NATIONAL STAFF

DENVER — In a courtroom filled with tension and tears, Timothy J. McVeigh stared stonily yesterday as a federal jury found him guilty on all counts in the bombing of the Oklahoma City federal building — the nation's deadliest act of domestic terrorism.

Outside the federal courthouse, there were whoops and cheers from a crowd that had assembled as news of an imminent verdict spread. Some federal workers stood at the windows of the U.S. Customs House, across the street, to applaud as word came just after 1:30 p.m.

In court, survivors of the attack and relatives of the 168 who died clutched hands and wept silently as the verdict was read — mindful of Judge Richard P. Matsch's warning against any disruptions in the courtroom. Some people lowered their heads and trembled with sobs.

At least one juror appeared to have tears in her eyes.

McVeigh, 29, a decorated Persian Gulf war veteran, looked neither surprised nor concerned as the judge read the 11-count verdict. Three federal marshals had positioned themselves behind him, but McVeigh, in a button-down shirt and khaki slacks, sat calmly. He did not change his expression.

After 23½ hours of deliberations, the jury had found him guilty of conspiracy, use of a weapon of mass destruction and first-degree murder in the April 19, 1995, bombing of the Alfred P. Murrah Federal Building.

Prosecutors said McVeigh hoped the [*See McVeigh, 6A*]

Life or death decision is next

Jurors will decide on McVeigh's punishment

'Defense has a hard job'

Vote must be unanimous for him to be executed

By SANDY BANISKY
SUN NATIONAL STAFF

DENVER — Now the jurors have another decision: Should Timothy J. McVeigh die?

Tomorrow, the same jury that found McVeigh guilty of bombing the Oklahoma City federal building will return to the federal courtroom for the sentencing phase of the trial.

In sessions that could last a week or more, jurors will hear prosecutors argue that McVeigh should be executed. And they will listen as McVeigh's lawyers plead for his life.

Survivors of the bombing and relatives of the dead will take the witness stand to tell the jury about some of the lives McVeigh ruined. The defense may call friends and relatives of McVeigh to ask that he be spared. Just as in a trial, the witnesses will be questioned and cross-examined.

The crime for which McVeigh stands convicted was monstrous: 168 dead, more than 500 injured. In a case so emotional, "the defense has a hard job," says Richard Dieter, director of the Death Penalty Information Center in Washington.

Federal death sentences are rare. Of about 3,150 people on [*See Penalty, 7A*]

Aberdeen Army chief announces retirement

Admission of adultery follows tip, inquiry, Pentagon officials say

'Where does this end?'

Officer was separated when affair occurred

NEW YORK TIMES NEWS SERVICE

WASHINGTON — The commanding general of the Army's Aberdeen Proving Ground has decided to retire after admitting that he committed adultery while separated from his wife more than five years ago, Pentagon officials said yesterday.

The officials said the commander, Maj. Gen. John Longhouser, became the subject of an inquiry after an anonymous tip about the affair was received over a telephone hot line established because of a flurry of sex abuse cases at Aberdeen, where male drill sergeants had preyed on young female recruits.

Pentagon officials noted that while adultery is a crime in the military, Longhouser's case involved an affair with a civilian that occurred long before he arrived at Aberdeen, and that his offenses were not in any way equivalent to those committed by the drill sergeants, in cases that have included rape.

Longhouser, a West Point graduate and Vietnam War veteran with a long list of awards and decorations, is a two-star, or major, general. But because he has not completed the required three years at that rank, he will retire at the rank of one-star, or brigadier, general, which means a reduction in retirement benefits.

"Where does this end?" one senior Pentagon official said. "It's terrible that it's come to the point where a distinguished soldier like General Longhouser has his career ended by something like this. This is a good man. Does this make any sense?"

Longhouser will retire June 30, but he will be relieved of his post command today. His temporary replacement will be Maj. Gen. George E. Friel, commander of the U.S. Army Chemical and Biological Defense Command in [*See Aberdeen, 10A*]

Best and brightest are fiercely recruited

■ **Education:** *Laptop computers, free parking and travel abroad are among the inducements colleges are offering top high school students.*

By MIKE BOWLER
SUN STAFF

Joy Pansini went shopping for colleges this year and found the colleges shopping for her.

The 18-year-old senior at the Institute of Notre Dame applied to 11 schools, visited 10, gained admission to nine. All nine offered her scholarships and other inducements if she'd sign up:

From Virginia Tech, a laptop computer if she'd choose the Blacksburg, Va., school. An offer of free instrumental music lessons came from the University of Delaware. From the University of Maryland Baltimore County, the prospect of overseas study trips with like-minded honors students.

Pansini, who graduated from IND on Sunday, chose UMBC because the Catonsville university offered her the ultimate inducement: a full scholarship for four years, small honors classes taught by senior faculty and the opportunity to do serious research as an undergraduate.

She [*See Colleges, 9A*]

KIM HAIRSTON : SUN STAFF

Sought after: *Joy Pansini (left, next to Jodie DeSantis) rehearsed last week for graduation, which was Sunday.*

Gambling interests lobbied expensively

Annapolis spending topped $900,000

By THOMAS W. WALDRON AND WILLIAM F. ZORZI JR.
SUN STAFF

In their unsuccessful push to bring casino-style gambling to Maryland, a host of companies and special-interest groups spent nearly a million dollars to lobby the General Assembly during this year's legislative session.

In all, casino companies, horse racing interests and others involved in gambling paid more than $928,000 to lobby the 188-member General Assembly, according to financial disclosure reports filed with the state.

The reports, which had to be filed with the State Ethics Commission yesterday, offer an insightful financial summary of the immense efforts undertaken to influence the legislative process.

While the spending reports cover the six-month period ending April 30, the bulk of the expenditures came during the annual 90-day legislative session, which ended April 7.

A record number of people are now registered to lobby in the state — 1,618 as of last month, compared with 1,514 in May 1996.

"Lobbying continues to be a growth industry in Maryland," said Deborah A. Povich, executive director of Common Cause of Maryland, which itself lobbies for stricter laws [*See Lobbyists, 10A*]

FINAL ★★★★★

THE SUN

August 31, 1997 | Baltimore, Maryland | $1.66

Sunday

Kathleen Kennedy Townsend: She's an elected official, but she's still a big sister

As her generation's elder, she has special responsibilities. [*Page 1H*]

'Homicide' cast talks about the show as it opens 6th season

Low ratings and bumps aside, series has a lot going for it. [*Page 1E*]

INSIDE

Mets pound Orioles for 19 base hits in 13-6 victory

Orioles starter Rick Krivda and the bullpen can't hold a three-run lead, as the New York Mets roll to a 13-6 victory. Home runs by Brady Anderson (above, arguing with umpire Larry Barnett over a called third strike) and Chris Hoiles aren't nearly enough. [*Page 1C*]

Pennant watch

AL East standings:

	W	L	Pct.	GB
Orioles	85	47	.644	—
Yankees	78	55	.586	7½

Yesterday: Expos 7, Yankees 2

Nation/World

Journal: Wash. Monument under wraps. [*Page 2A*]

Race debate takes place in shadow of Clinton. [*Page 4A*]

Tiger taken from Phila. rowhouse rests at zoo. [*Page 6A*]

Rushdie marries secretly on Long Island. [*Page 7A*]

Mideast posturing precedes Albright visit. [*Page 17A*]

Illegal Mexican labor said to be miscounted. [*Page 20A*]

Maryland

State expects $60 million budget surplus. [*Page 1B*]

Building a dream into a home. [*Page 1B*]

Tiny creek threatens Aigburth Vale sale. [*Page 1B*]

Sports

Ravens won't forget '96 losses to Jags. [*Page 1C*]

Champion Packers dream of perfect season. [*Page 1C*]

Rosenthal: Debt, depth define '97 Ravens. [*Page 1C*]

Business

Sudden millionaires advised to plan far ahead. [*Page 1D*]

Back-to-school buying season grows longer. [*Page 1D*]

Books

Labor movement: Is it thriving or dying? [*Page 1H*]

Travel

Miami rejuvenated into home for the hip. [*Page 1K*]

Weather

Mostly sunny. High, 85; low, 61. Yesterday's city high, 87; low, 66. [*Page 6B*]

SunSpot

The Sun on the Internet: http://www.sunspot.net

0 108345 00008 2 3

Princess Diana dies in crash

Accident in Paris occurs as her car is chased by paparazzi

Companion, driver killed

Five photographers taken into custody for questioning

By BILL GLAUBER
SUN FOREIGN STAFF

LONDON — Britain's Princess Diana was killed early today in a Paris car crash that also killed her companion, Dodi Al Fayed, after their car was chased by photographers on motorcycles, French and British officials said.

Diana, 36, died at 4 a.m. (10 p.m. EDT) after suffering heavy internal bleeding and going into cardiac arrest, doctors at Salpetriere hospital said.

The death was announced two hours later by a hospital anesthesiologist.

"The queen and the Prince of Wales and the prime minister have been informed of the death of the Princess of Wales," said British Ambassador Sir Michael Jay, who was at the hospital. "The death of the Princess of Wales fills us all with shock and deep grief."

The royal family was informed by the French ambassador to Great Britain, who telephoned Queen Elizabeth's private secretary at Balmoral, Scotland, where the queen, Prince Charles and Diana's two sons, Prince William, 15, and Prince Harry, 12, were spending the summer holidays.

Diana and Fayed died after the dark blue Mercedes-Benz in which they were riding crashed about 12:35 a.m. in a four-lane tunnel skirting the right bank of the Seine river at the Pont de l'Alma, not far from the Eiffel Tower.

The crash demolished the front of the car, pushed the car's radiator into the front seats and crushed most of the roof down to the level of the door handles.

The accident also killed the driver of the car and seriously injured a security guard riding with them. It came as paparazzi — the commercial photographers who constantly tailed Diana — followed the Mercedes at high speed.

Several people were trapped in the tunnel, and police cars and vans with flashing lights quickly filled the streets outside and kept spectators away.

Five photographers were taken into custody for questioning after the crash, police said.

France Info radio said at least some of the photographers took pictures before help arrived.

Buckingham Palace released a brief statement, saying, "The prince and the queen are deeply shocked by this terrible news."

ASSOCIATED PRESS : 1995

Fatal injuries: *Princess Diana died at 4 a.m. (10 p.m. EDT) after suffering cardiac arrest after internal bleeding.*

Charles, who was divorced from Diana last August after 15 years of marriage, told William and Harry of their mother's death.

Prime Minister Tony Blair called the crash a "quite appalling tragedy."

"I am utterly devastated," Blair said. "The whole of our country, all of us, will be in a state of shock and mourning. Diana was a wonderful, warm and compassionate person who people not just in Britain but throughout the world loved and will be mourned as a friend."

"Our thoughts and prayers are with her family, particularly her two sons and with all the families bereaved in this quite appalling tragedy."

Diana had been due to return to London today to meet her sons. Thursday marked the first anniversary of her divorce from Charles, heir to the British throne.

Diana and Fayed had arrived in Paris yesterday afternoon after vacationing in Saint Tropez, their third holiday in five weeks. They had taken a cruise on a yacht owned by Fayed's father, Mohamed Al Fayed, owner of Harrods department store.

They had dined at the Ritz Hotel, owned by the elder Fayed. They left through a back entrance to avoid the photographers waiting for them in front, and the driver of their car was said to be a hotel employee.

An American witness, Tom Richardson, told CNN that the car "looked like it hit the wall."

Witnesses say they heard the crashed car's horn sounding for about two minutes after the crash.

French Interior Minister Jean-Pierre Chevenement, Paris Police Chief Philippe Massoni and British Ambassador Michael Jay went to see Diana at the hospital.

"In the name of the French government, I express my great sorrow and pain," Chevenement said in confirming her [*See Diana, 18A*]

More inside

Princess: A look back at Princess Diana's life. [*PAGE 19A*]

Dodi Al Fayed: The heir to the Harrods fortune lived a fast and stylish life. [*PAGE 19A*]

Photo essay: A review of Diana's years in the public eye. [*PAGE 19A*]

REUTERS

Dodi Al Fayed: had been vacationing with the princess in Saint Tropez.

With O's, Ravens home today, fans choose nest

■ **Sports:** *Baltimore's two major teams have regular-season home games on the same day, a rarity that underscores the competition for attendance, advertisers and TV ratings.*

By JON MORGAN
SUN STAFF

Today's rare double bill of Orioles and Ravens home games represents a quandary for the city's sporting faithful: Which game to attend?

Although Baltimore has had major-league baseball and football on and off for the better part of 40 years, the two sports have maintained a polite distance. For most of those years, the teams shared a stadium and couldn't play on the same day. And beginning next year, they will share a parking lot, making same-day games a practical impossibility.

But today, for perhaps the first and last time, they will go head-to-head with regular-season games, a vivid illustration of the newfound competition for the attention, affection and allegiance of Baltimore's fans.

Up for grabs are millions of dollars worth of television ratings, attendance and sponsorships.

"They can be both competitive and complementary," Jim Bailey, the Ravens' executive [*See Teams, 8A*]

KARL MERTON FERRON : SUN STAFF

Split loyalties: *Frank Fillmore holds Orioles and Ravens season tickets, but today he'll be watching football at Memorial Stadium — while listening to the baseball game.*

State fails to stem loss of wetlands, study says

Bay foundation finds monitoring flawed

By TIMOTHY B. WHEELER
SUN STAFF

Maryland is failing to stem the loss of freshwater wetlands to development because of serious flaws in the government's efforts to replace the ecologically important areas, according to a study by the Chesapeake Bay Foundation.

Challenging assertions by the Glendening administration that it has reversed the state's decline in wetlands, the Annapolis-based environmental group contends that overburdened state regulators are unable to ensure that the wet areas being bulldozed for houses and highways are properly replaced.

Regulators are "swamped," said Thomas V. Grasso, director of the foundation's Maryland office. He said the group found that the state lacks the staff to keep up with the workload and that many man-made wetlands built under state supervision do not measure up to the naturally damp areas they were meant to supplant.

Efforts last week to reach Gov. Parris N. Glendening for comment on the bay foundation's review were unsuccessful, but officials of the state Department of the Environment, which regulates wetlands, vow to correct problems in constructing replacements.

"It's not there yet, but we're [*See Wetlands, 13A*]

Memory loss led to human toxin link

Pfiesteria affects brain, scientists say

By JONATHAN BOR
AND CAITLIN FRANCKE
SUN STAFF

A distinctive pattern of memory loss was the thread that enabled a medical team to establish for the first time a probable connection between human illnesses and the microorganism that has been killing fish by the thousands.

Doctors who investigated reports of ailments among people who worked on the Pocomoke River said yesterday that they had been skeptical of finding a link between the complaints and Pfiesteria piscicida.

But after subjecting 13 people to hours of physical and psychological testing, doctors were startled to find that most had trouble remembering simple details of everyday life: errands, groceries, phone numbers, tasks just completed.

"What all these people had in common was the Pfiesteria exposure, and all of them had this common [*See Illness, 8A*]

Smoke, smoking guns draw Bossie

Aide probes abuses in Washington, fights fires in Maryland

By SUSAN BAER
SUN NATIONAL STAFF

WASHINGTON — Home for David N. Bossie is a painfully claustrophobic cinder-block dorm room, with two twin beds and a ceiling fan, at the Burtonsville Volunteer Fire Station. A high-powered Capitol Hill aide as well as a volunteer firefighter, Bossie sacks out there every night so he can pull on his boots and hop onto the truck whenever the alarm sounds.

Bossie loves the excitement of fighting fires, his friends say.

He also relishes starting them. To his job as chief investigator for the House committee that's exploring campaign fund-raising abuses, the 31-year-old Marylander brings a take-no-prisoners style and a reputation as a ferocious conservative activist — some would say zealot — intent on seeing the Clinton administration go up in smoke.

Though he can be personable and engaging, Bossie is such a hot wire that last month the committee's chief counsel, John P. Rowley III, and other top Republican staffers quit the House investigation, complaining of Bossie's unprofessionalism and "self-promotion." The walkout was a major setback for the House Government Reform and Oversight Committee, which hopes to begin hearings next month.

"I'm not surprised Dave rubs some people raw," says state Del. Michael W. Burns, a conservative Republican from Anne Arundel County who worked with Bossie in Maryland politics. "He's a very aggressive guy. Dave not only loves to find the smoking gun; Dave loves to wave it around."

With Bossie in such a key position, [*See Bossie, 8A*]

FINAL ★★★★★

THE SUN

September 6, 1997 | Baltimore, Maryland | 50 cents

SATURDAY

Orioles knock around Yankees, 13-9, boost East lead to 8½ games

The Orioles punish the Yankees — including pitcher Andy Pettitte (above), who had to leave after being hit in face by a Cal Ripken line drive — and roll to a 13-9 win in the longest nine-inning game ever played, 4 hours and 22 minutes. Their 8½-game lead is their largest since July 4. [Page 1c]

Pennant watch

AL East standings

	W	L	Pct.	GB
Orioles	87	51	.630	—
Yankees	79	60	.568	8½

Nation/World

Journal: Martha's Vineyard, land of islanders. [Page 2A]
Thalidomide recommended for U.S. sale. [Page 3A]
Budget surplus of $63 million seen by 2003. [Page 3A]
Vice President Gore has unflattering week. [Page 4A]
Lugar defies Helms on Weld nomination. [Page 4A]
Cosmetics regulation issue in FDA changes. [Page 5A]
Mir crew makes spacewalk to check damage. [Page 6A]
Bosnian Serbs fail to comply on TV deal. [Page 6A]

Opinion

Ocean City can't afford to stand still. [Page 10A]
Letter writers express feelings on Diana. [Page 10A]
Moscow's 850th-birthday extravaganza. [Page 10A]

Maryland

Judge overturns jury award to minister. [Page 1B]
Living on the outside at Towson High. [Page 1B]
Glendening criticizes tobacco settlement. [Page 1B]
S&L swindler loses bid for prison release. [Page 1B]
Federal agency asks states' help on pfiesteria. [Page 1B]
Kane: Tabloid readers' role in Diana's death. [Page 1B]

Sports

Williams, Hingis advance to U.S. Open final. [Page 1C]
Olympic Games returning to Athens in 2004. [Page 1C]
San Diego State holds off Navy, 45-31. [Page 1C]
Ravens' secondary braces for Bengals. [Page 1C]

Business

Davco chief leads group buyout offer. [Page 11C]
U.S. unemployment rate up to 4.9%. [Page 11C]
UPS struggles to regroup from strike. [Page 11C]
Howard hospital considers sale offers. [Page 11C]

Weather

Partly cloudy. High, 81; low, 57. Yesterday's city high, 86; low, 62. [Page 16B]

Bridge	15B	Editorials	10A
Classified	5B	Horoscope	5D
Comics	6D	Lottery	2B
Xword	15B, 7D	Movies	4D
Deaths	4B	Television	5D

SunSpot

The Sun on the Internet: http://www.sunspot.net

Gibson defects to new camp

Top state organizer rejects Glendening for '98, assists Rehrmann

By C. Fraser Smith and JoAnna Daemmrich
SUN STAFF

Larry S. Gibson, the premier political organizer in Maryland and Mayor Kurt L. Schmoke's closest adviser, said yesterday that he will back Harford County Executive Eileen M. Rehrmann in the 1998 race for governor.

Schmoke said Gibson was acting on his own, but the high-level defection will be seen as a blow to the re-election prospects of Gov. Parris N. Glendening.

"I think Glendening has almost no chance of winning the general election," Gibson said in an interview in which he was highly critical of the Democratic governor's performance and integrity.

"A vote for Glendening in the primary is a vote for Ellen Sauerbrey," Gibson said, referring to the likely Republican nominee. He said it is fear of a Republican takeover in the General Assembly and State House that has turned him away from his party's incumbent governor.

The Rehrmann campaign eagerly acknowledged that Gibson is serving as a strategist and adviser for her.

"Larry's definitely on our team, and we're glad to have his help. He's a smart man," said George Harrison, one of the managers of the Rehrmann campaign. "He has extensive knowledge of grass-roots politics, how to get out the vote."

Demo- [See Gibson, 5A]

Israel freezes peace accords

More transfers of land to Palestinians halted

By Ann LoLordo
SUN FOREIGN STAFF

JERUSALEM — In the wake of the latest terrorist bombing in Jerusalem, Israeli Prime Minister Benjamin Netanyahu declared yesterday that he is no longer bound by peace accords and said he will withhold returning land to the Palestinians until he feels that Yasser Arafat has cracked down on terrorism.

"We decided that the process in which Israel, time after time, hands land to the Palestinian authority, and then murderers use these territories as their launching ground, shall not continue," he told Israel TV.

"We declare here today that if the other side does not meet its obligations, we of course are exempt from meeting our obligations."

Netanyahu's comments came on a day in which Israel buried school girls and soldiers.

The two teen-agers died on the stone [See Israel, 7A]

A 'contemporary saint' dies

KENNETH K. LAM : SUN STAFF

Inspiration: *Mother Teresa, shown in Baltimore in 1996, said her chief task was to provide "free service to the poor and the unwanted, irrespective of caste, creed, nationality or race."*

Destitute of the world lose voice, comfort with passing of Mother Teresa at 87

FROM WIRE REPORTS

CALCUTTA, India — Mother Teresa, the Albanian-born nun and Nobel laureate who followed a call to serve the dying in the squalor of Calcutta almost 50 years ago, and eventually became an inspiration for people of all faiths throughout the world, died yesterday.

The 87-year-old nun died of cardiac arrest at 9:30 p.m. (1:30 p.m. EDT) in the heart of the order she founded there.

Indian authorities said she would be buried Wednesday in Calcutta, in the headquarters of the Missionaries of Charity, the religious order she founded in 1950.

Mother Teresa was hospitalized several times last year with heart, lung, kidney and other problems, and also suffered ill health in earlier years. Her physician in Rome, Vincenzo Bilotta, said her heart had failed during the evening at her convent in Calcutta.

As her health deteriorated over the past year, Mother Teresa stepped aside and the Missionaries of Charity chose a new leader, Sister Nirmala, in March.

Mother Teresa, an ethnic Albanian born in what is now Macedonia, was revered in India, where she lived and worked for 68 years and became a citizen.

She also came to be honored around the world for the compassionate, effective way she set up and oversaw projects to provide care and comfort to the very poor and the very sick. [See Teresa, 9A]

More inside

Influence: Five Marylanders reflect on how Mother Teresa touched their lives. [Page 9A]

JED KIRSCHBAUM : SUN STAFF

Recalls: *The Rev. John McLoughlin of St. Wenceslaus Roman Catholic Church in East Baltimore.*

Visit touched E. Side area

■ **Meeting:** *She brought a message of hope for residents of the Hopkins-Middle East neighborhood and perhaps had a hand in a healing.*

By John Rivera and Christian Ewell
SUN STAFF

An East Baltimore neighborhood where drugs are rampant and violence commonplace remembered yesterday a visit by a small, stooped woman who offered a ray of hope and, perhaps, a miracle.

It was at the intersection of Collington and Ashland avenues, near where a group of men were shooting a game of craps yesterday afternoon, that Mother Teresa came in May 1996 to visit her Missionaries of Charity at the Gift of Hope Convent. The Hopkins-Middle East neighborhood turned out in force to see what the fuss was all about.

"People just came out and there was a sense of 'there is a holy person among us,'" said the Rev. John McLoughlin, a Redemptorist priest who is associate pastor of the adjacent St. Wenceslaus Roman Catholic Church.

Mother Teresa's ministry was to the poorest of the poor, and there are plenty of poor people in East Baltimore. Many who waited in the rain to see her on that rainy day last year may not have known exactly who she was, but they were nevertheless drawn to her.

"Living in East Baltimore, I've seen people die on the street," McLoughlin said. "When she came, everyone was in awe, and there was a sense of peace, a sense of joy, a sense of unity. Because people felt the presence of God here on the street."

Constance Pierce, 31, a barmaid who lives at St. Wenceslaus Apartments, said she really didn't know much about Mother Teresa before she visited that day, but she came to see her out of curiosity. A lot of people stood in line to shake Mother Teresa's hand, and Pierce was one of them.

"Something went through me, like a warm chill, as she shook my hand. It was as if I had touched God," Pierce said. [See Church, 9A]

Royal family ends public silence

In unusual speech, queen calls Diana 'exceptional,' 'gifted'

Charles and two sons greet, thank mourners

By Bill Glauber
SUN FOREIGN STAFF

ASSOCIATED PRESS

Flowers: *Queen Elizabeth, breaking with tradition by approaching and speaking to a crowd outside Buckingham Palace in London, accepts flowers from a well-wisher.*

LONDON — With a brief speech and tearful walks among throngs of their grieving subjects, Britain's royal family rallied itself and its country on the eve of this morning's funeral for Diana, Princess of Wales.

Queen Elizabeth II praised her former daughter-in-law yesterday as "an exceptional and gifted human being," adding that "no one who knew Diana will ever forget her."

Meanwhile, Diana's sons, Princes William, 15, and Harry, 12, accompanied by her former husband, Prince Charles, made an emotional pilgrimage to her former London palace as Britons by the score bowed and wept.

But it was Queen Elizabeth, normally above the fray, who galvanized Britain with an uncharacteristically touching salute to Diana.

"In good times and bad, she never lost her capacity to smile and laugh, nor to inspire others with her warmth and kindness," Elizabeth said during an unusual live address from Buckingham Palace. It was the first time a member of the royal family had spoken directly since Diana's death Sunday after a car accident in Paris.

The long royal silence had triggered simmering public fury with the monarchy.

True or not, there was a sense among many that the royal family continued to harbor resentment against Diana.

For days, while the rest of Britain was convulsed in grief, the royal family remained silent, behind closed doors at Balmoral Castle in Scotland, where they were vacationing when word of the princess' death reached them.

But yesterday the royals reappeared in full force in London.

It was Elizabeth, the 71-year-old monarch, who led the royal family's emotional display, giving [See Diana, 12A]

More inside

Speech: Text of Queen Elizabeth II's televised address to her British subjects. [Page 12A]

Dissent: Some Britons have begun to criticize the life of Princess Diana. [Page 12A]

★ EXTRA ★

THE SUN

LIGHT FOR ALL

December 19, 1998 Baltimore, Maryland 50 cents

Impeached

ASSOCIATED PRESS

Facing Senate trial: *President Clinton, shown last week in the Rose Garden, stayed out of sight this morning.*

House party-line vote charges Clinton on perjury, obstruction

Two articles defeated; censure fails

Historic vote, 228-206, opens way for trial in the Senate

By Jonathan Weisman and David Folkenflik
SUN NATIONAL STAFF

WASHINGTON — William Jefferson Clinton, the 42nd president of the United States, was impeached today for perjury and obstruction of justice, setting in motion a constitutional crisis the nation has not seen this century.

Virtually along party lines, 228-206, the House voted at 1:24 p.m. to charge President Clinton with lying under oath when called to testify before independent counsel Kenneth W. Starr's federal grand jury.

Only five Democrats voted to impeach, offset by five Republicans who voted against impeachment.

The Republicans barely managed to push through a second impeachment article, charging that Clinton obstructed justice to hide his affair with Monica Lewinsky, a former White House intern. The vote was 221-212, with 12 Republicans voting against the third article of impeachment.

As the voting began, Democrats streamed out of the House chamber in protest, only to return hurriedly minutes later to cast their votes in dissent.

When the first impeachment article reached the critical 218 votes needed for passage, a muffled, perhaps rueful cheer rose from the House floor, with scattered clapping in the otherwise silent public galleries.

On a parliamentary maneuver, the House also beat back a Democratic effort to introduce [See Impeach, 9A]

Clinton reiterates resolve

Spokesman decries the 'politics of personal destruction'

President won't resign

He asks Livingston to reconsider plan to stand down

By Susan Baer
SUN NATIONAL STAFF

WASHINGTON — In the climactic hours before William Jefferson Clinton was voted into history today as the second president to be impeached, the White House fiercely denounced the "politics of personal destruction" and said the president would not give in to calls for his resignation.

Clinton's spokesman, Joe Lockhart, said the president was "very disappointed" by this morning's announcement by Speaker-elect Robert L. Livingston that he would resign from Congress next year because of revelations that he had had extramarital affairs. He said Clinton was calling on Livingston to reconsider his decision.

"The president firmly believes that the politics of personal destruction in this town and this country has to come to an end, and it has to stop soon," Lockhart said.

Rejecting Livingston's challenge to Clinton to resign, Lockhart said: "The president is going to do what's in the best interest of this country. He's going to keep on pushing his agenda forward, and I think it would be wrong to give in to this insidious politics of personal destruction that seems so pervasive now."

The president's comments, delivered through his spokesman outside the White House this morning, came shortly before the House voted to impeach him, and shortly after Hillary Rodham Clinton made a rare trip to Capitol Hill to rally House Democrats privately to continue to support her husband.

Greeted with wild applause from Democratic lawmakers, she assured them that the president would not resign and said she believed he had been treated unfairly by the Republican-led House.

She said the impeachment process "should be done right, and that up to now it has not been," said House Democratic leader Richard A. Gephardt, [See Clinton, 9A]

ASSOCIATED PRESS

Not germane: *Speaker Pro Tempore Ray LaHood of Illinois rules against the Democrats' proposal for censure.*

More inside

News: Business of government continues, but the public is focused elsewhere. [Page 8A]

Notebook: No solemnity, no best sellers in evidence, but Starr report toilet paper in demand. [Page 8A]

Delegation: Rep. Constance A. Morella's indecision comes to an end. [Page 10A]

Livingston quits, stuns House

Presumptive speaker will also resign his seat in Congress

By Fred Monyak
SUN NATIONAL STAFF

WASHINGTON — In a stunning announcement, Rep. Robert L. Livingston told a hushed House of Representatives today that had gathered to impeach President Clinton that he will not accept the speakership and will quit Congress next year because of his disclosure of adulterous affairs.

Livingston dropped his news on the House just a few hours before it voted to impeach Clinton for misdeeds stemming from an improper sexual relationship of his own. The Louisiana Republican said he was resigning to set an example, and he called on Clinton to follow suit and resign as well.

"I was prepared to lead our narrow majority as speaker, and I believe I had it in me to do a fine job," Livingston said. "But I cannot do that job or be the kind of leader that I would like to be under current circumstances."

His announcement drew gasps in the House chamber.

On Thursday night, Livingston, [See Livingston, 9A]

ASSOCIATED PRESS

"I must set the example that I hope President Clinton will follow ..."

Rep. Robert L. Livingston

Analysis

Fight becomes mortal combat

What looked unlikely became inevitable; can Clinton survive?

By Paul West
SUN NATIONAL STAFF

WASHINGTON — Bill Clinton was consigned to an unwanted place in American history today as the first elected president ever to be impeached.

A Senate trial of the president — an extraordinary spectacle no living person has witnessed — will be gaveled to order in coming weeks.

While the entire nation tries to grasp the staggering significance of events that seemed impossible a month ago, official Washington has moved on to the next question: Will Clinton's presidency survive?

The answer is not nearly so clear as it once appeared to be. Today's breathtaking announcement by House Speaker-designate Robert L. Livingston — that he is resigning in the wake of disclosures of marital infidelity — will only increase the pressure on Clinton to do so as well.

Today's largely party-line vote of impeachment deepens the corrosive partisanship that pervades this shell-shocked capital. Clinton and conservative Republicans in Congress remain locked in mortal political combat. And everyone else — including the American public — is caught in between.

"A reckless president and a Republican Congress driven by a blind animus for him have brought us to this moment in history," retiring Rep. Vic Fazio said on the House [See Analysis, 8A]

Saturday

Telecommunications company in Columbia plans major expansion

Corvis Corp., a Columbia telecommunications equipment firm that was founded by one of the state's most successful high-technology entrepreneurs, is planning to expand from 96 to 1,500 employees in Howard County by 2001. [Page 3C]

Juan Dixon, who lost his parents to AIDS while at Calvert Hall, returns home to Baltimore tonight as a redshirt freshman for the No. 5 Maryland men's basketball team. [Page 1C]

Weather

Mostly cloudy. High, 51; low, 40. Yesterday's city high, 45; low, 36. [Page 10B]

SunSpot

The Sun on the Internet: http://www.sunspot.net

The Sun's 162nd Year: Number 353

FINAL

THE SUN

SUNDAY

July 18, 1999 | Baltimore, Maryland : $1.66

JFK Jr., wife feared dead

Tragedy follows America's Kennedys

On a day meant for joy, the family once again draws together in pain

By Ellen Gamerman
SUN NATIONAL STAFF

The Kennedys were gathered in Hyannis Port yesterday for what was to be a joyous occasion — the wedding of Rory, the daughter Robert F. Kennedy never lived to see. Instead, they found themselves uniting in the all-too-familiar rituals of grief in what seems likely to become the latest in the unending series of tragedies that has struck this family.

"It's like a novel with one bad chapter after another, and there's no end to the ... book," said John Seigenthaler, a friend of the Kennedy family, shortly after learning of the disappearance of John F. Kennedy Jr. off Martha's Vineyard. "You cry until the tears won't come. I just don't understand, I cannot understand why this family has to suffer this way."

Kennedy; his wife, Carolyn Bessette Kennedy; and her sister, Lauren Bessette, were feared dead after remnants of the plane John Jr. was believed to have piloted washed ashore not far from the former Martha's Vineyard estate of his mother, the late Jacqueline Kennedy Onassis. John Jr. and his sister, Caroline, were the only members of their immediate family left.

Members of the extended family at the Kennedy compound in Hyannis reportedly attended a Mass with two priests who had arrived there for Rory's wedding. They were the same two priests who had presided at the funeral for her brother, Michael, who died at 39 in a skiing accident two years ago in Aspen, Colo. [*See Tragedy, 20A*]

AGENCE FRANCE-PRESSE

The couple: John F. Kennedy Jr. and Carolyn Bessette Kennedy at a wedding in Italy in August.

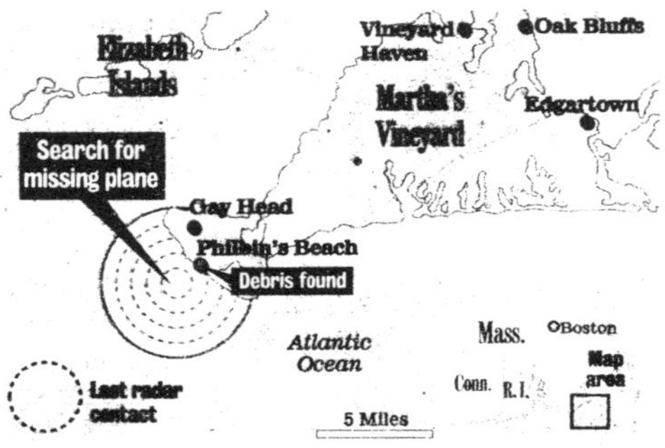

SOURCE: wire reports — JENNIFER IMES : SUN STAFF

More inside, Pages 17A-22A

Sorrow: For a generation of Americans, the tragedies of the Kennedy family have become a grim but familiar national ritual. [*Page 21A*]

Scene: Outside the Kennedy compound, the crowd grew as hopes for survival dwindled. [*Page 22A*]

Wife: With her grace and elegance, Carolyn Bessette Kennedy drew comparisons to Jacqueline Onassis and became a tabloid favorite after her wedding. [*Page 17A*]

Images: The life of John F. Kennedy Jr. in pictures. [*Page 18A*]

Aircraft also carrying her sister vanishes off Massachusetts coast

They were en route to wedding

Luggage from airplane found by sunbathers off Martha's Vineyard

By Todd Richissin and Tom Bowman
SUN NATIONAL STAFF

GAY HEAD, Mass. — Helicopters swirled above the westernmost coast of Martha's Vineyard yesterday as rescue boats bobbed below, looking for the plane carrying John F. Kennedy Jr. and the relatives who apparently crashed into the ocean with him in the latest tragedy to befall the country's most charmed and cursed family.

Police closed miles of beach here, where earlier in the day several vacationers and investigators reported finding debris — including three pieces of luggage belonging to the family, the nose wheel of a plane of the same design as Kennedy's single-engine, six-seat Piper Saratoga, and a prescription drug bottle bearing the name of Carolyn Bessette Kennedy.

Kennedy, 38; his wife, Carolyn, 33; and his sister-in-law, Lauren Bessette, 34, left Essex County Airport in Fairfield, N.J., at 8:38 p.m. Friday, bound for the wedding of his cousin Rory Kennedy and Mark Bailey at the family compound in Hyannis Port, Mass. Kennedy was believed to be piloting the plane.

It was expected on Martha's Vineyard, an island off Cape Cod, about 10 p.m. The Kennedy family alerted authorities about 2:15 a.m. that the plane was overdue.

Yesterday, people gathered on bluffs above the rocky beach where rescuers are focusing their search. Few of the onlookers had much hope for a miracle and instead prayed for the lost travelers and the family enduring yet more grief.

"If you lived through that day when President Kennedy was shot, it's really even more of a tragedy," said Louise Grant, 52, of Newton, Mass., who was vacationing. "It really sickens you."

President Clinton, who is spending the weekend at Camp David in Western Maryland, was told about the disappearance of the Kennedy plane by his chief of staff, John [*See Search, 19A*]

ASSOCIATED PRESS : 1963

John-John: Salute at JFK funeral is enduring image.

A life lived in celebrity

Fame: John F. Kennedy Jr. endured the spotlight with rare grace and humor.

By Scott Shane
SUN STAFF

In his 38 years, John Fitzgerald Kennedy Jr. has been an actor, a prosecutor, a philanthropist and a magazine publisher. But first and forever, from the moment of his birth as the son of a just-elected president to a plane crash Friday night, he was that quintessential American phenomenon, the celebrity. He was famous chiefly for being famous.

Yet JFK Jr., in the face of overwhelming evidence to the contrary, insisted repeatedly in interviews that his was a "normal" life. And grieving friends recalled him yesterday not as a brilliant mind or stunning talent but as a man who embraced life and bore the weight of fame with good humor.

"He was the most graceful human being I ever met," said longtime friend John Perry Barlow, a Wyoming cattle [*See Life, 17A*]

Today Inside

44 years later, a journalist thanks a gentle reading teacher

It was 1955, in a small elementary school at Turner's Station. For one second-grader, the tales of Dick and Jane were a struggle. But Florence Herbert, with her warm support, made sure the child succeeded. [*Page 1D*]

SunSpot

The Sun on Internet: http://www sunspot.net

The Sun's 163rd Year: Number 199

Weather

Partly cloudy, hot and humid. High, 97; low, 72. Yesterday's downtown high, 94, low, 74. [*Page 12B*]

0 08345 00008 2

Index

GOLD-PLATED DREAM

Red-hot fighter, trail of deception

By Greg Schneider : SUN STAFF

Procurement: Planning the F-22, the Pentagon took the pledge: no more costly excess. Now, taxpayers are getting a plane designed for the Cold War, which is over. And the price tag is a shocker.

Albert C. Piccirillo felt trapped. He was trying to create the world's greatest fighter jet, and his bosses at the Pentagon promised Congress the plane could be built for the bargain price of $35 million apiece.

"Everybody knew it wasn't going to be $35 million," the now-retired Air Force colonel said recently.

But the military had to make the plane seem affordable to win funding from Congress. So the F-22 fighter program was born in the mid-1980s with a false promise, and deception has become routine over the past 16 years as the Air Force tries to protect its top-priority new weapon system.

Today, the last great superplane of the Cold War is set to enter service in 2004 with an average sticker price of $97.7 million each. Research and other expenses bring the total public investment to at least $184 million per plane, making the F-22 Raptor the most expensive fighter ever built. It is a decade behind the original schedule, and the number of planes on order has been slashed to 339 from 750.

That might sound like a typical case of Pentagon excess, except for one thing: The military planned the F-22 as the weapon that would break the cycle of waste, dubbing it "the showpiece for Air Force [*See F-22, 14A*]

More inside

The House of Representatives will consider this week whether to cut $1.8 billion that was to purchase six F-22s. [*Page 13A*]

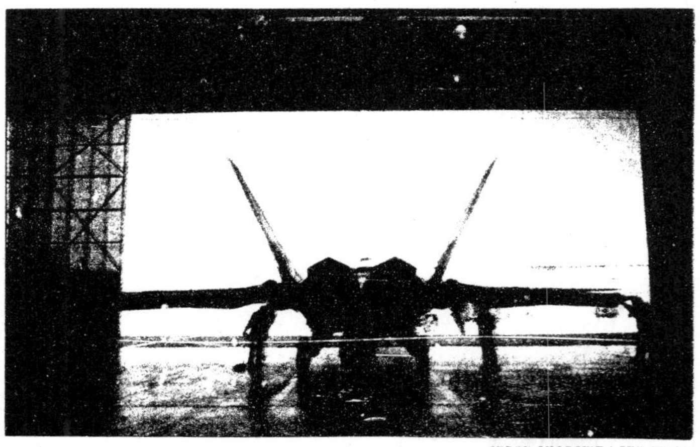

PERRY THORSVIK : SUN STAFF

At Edwards Air Force Base, Calif.: The F-22 Raptor is scheduled to enter the service in 2004 at a likely cost of about $97.7 million per plane.